One of the splendid waterfalls on the north shore of the Geirangerfjord, in western Norway. The fjords, steep-sided narrow inlets, characterize the long Norwegian coastline.

Anne Simon–Photo Researchers, Inc.

Funk & Wagnalls New Encyclopedia

VOLUME 17

MARINO to MONADNOCK

LEON L. BRAM
Vice-President and Editorial Director

Funk & Wagnalls Corporation

Publishers since 1876

Funk & Wagnalls
New Encyclopedia
Copyright © MCMXCVI, MCMXCIII
by Funk & Wagnalls Corporation
A K-III COMMUNICATIONS COMPANY
MCMXC by Funk & Wagnalls L.P.
MCMLXXXVI,
MCMLXXXIII, MCMLXXIX,
MCMLXXV, MCMLXXI,
by Funk & Wagnalls, Inc.

Volumes are published subsequent
to copyright dates to contain
the latest updated information

Copyright Under the Articles of the Copyright Convention
of the Pan-American Republics and the United States

FUNK & WAGNALLS and F&W are registered
trademarks of Funk & Wagnalls Corporation

TimeScope™ is a registered trademark of
Funk & Wagnalls Corporation

CompuMap™ is a registered
trademark of Funk & Wagnalls Corporation

MapScope™ is a registered trademark
of Funk & Wagnalls Corporation

ISBN 0-8343-0103-2
Library of Congress Catalog
Card Number 72–170933

MANUFACTURED IN THE UNITED STATES OF AMERICA
PRINTED AND BOUND BY R.R. DONNELLEY & SONS COMPANY
ALL RIGHTS RESERVED

iie 10 9 8 7 6 5 4 3 2 1

Funk & Wagnalls New Encyclopedia is liberally provided with **finding devices** that aid in the search for information. The brief descriptions and suggestions that follow are intended to encourage the proper use of these devices so that full use is made of the information resources within these pages.

The **index** in volume 29 should be the starting point in a search for information. If a search is made *without* the use of the index, the following suggestions should be kept in mind:

- If the search is *unsuccessful*, the index should be used to search again. The topic may be discussed in an article that was overlooked. Only after use of the index can a search be considered thorough or completed.

- If the search is initially *successful*, the index should be used to find additional information. A topic may be discussed in several articles; the index can locate the less-obvious ones.

The use and structure of the index is explained in the Guide to the Index, volume 29, pages 6–8.

Cross-references of several types are used frequently within most articles in Funk & Wagnalls New Encyclopedia. Each cross-reference directs the search for information to other articles that contain additional or related information. The types of cross-references and their specific uses are explained in the Guide to Funk & Wagnalls New Encyclopedia, volume 1, pages 60–63, under the subhead, Cross-references.

Bibliography cross-references follow all the major articles in Funk & Wagnalls New Encyclopedia. They direct the search for further information from the articles to appropriate **reading lists** of books and periodicals in the **bibliography** in volume 28. The reading lists may also be used for independent study. A full description of bibliography cross-references and reading lists is found in the Preface and Guide to the Bibliography, volume 28, pages 186–87.

SELECTED ABBREVIATIONS USED IN TEXT*

AC	alternating current	F	Fahrenheit	Nor.	Norwegian
AD	anno Domini (Lat., "in the year of the Lord")	Finn.	Finnish	O.E.	Old English
		fl.	flourished	O.Fr.	Old French
		FM	frequency modulation	O.H.G.	Old High German
alt.	altitude			O.N.	Old Norse
AM	ante meridiem (Lat., "before noon")	Fr.	French	Op.	Opus (Lat., "work")
		ft	foot, feet	oz	ounce(s)
		g	gram(s)	Pers.	Persian
AM	amplitude modulation	gal	gallon(s)	PM	post meridiem (Lat., "after noon")
		Ger.	German		
amu	atomic mass unit(s)	GeV	billion electron volts	Pol.	Polish
Arab.	Arabic			pop.	population
Arm.	Armenian	Gr.	Greek	Port.	Portuguese
A.S.	Anglo-Saxon	ha	hectare(s)	q.v.	quod vide (Lat., "which see")
ASSR	Autonomous Soviet Socialist Republic	Heb.	Hebrew		
		hp	horsepower	r.	reigned
atm.	atmosphere	hr	hour	R.	River
at.no.	atomic number	Hung.	Hungarian	repr.	reprinted
at.wt.	atomic weight	Hz	hertz or cycle(s) per second	rev.	revised
b.	born			Rom.	Romanian
BC	before Christ	Icel.	Icelandic	Rus.	Russian
b.p.	boiling point	i.e.	id est (Lat., "that is")	S	south; southern
Btu	British Thermal Unit			sec.	second(s); secant
		in	inch(es)	SFSR	Soviet Federated Socialist Republic
bu	bushel(s)	inc.	incorporated		
Bulg.	Bulgarian	Ital.	Italian	Skt.	Sanskrit
C	Celsius	Jap.	Japanese	Span.	Spanish
c.	circa (Lat., "about")	K	Kelvin	sp.gr.	specific gravity
cent.	century	kg	kilogram(s)	sq	square
Chin.	Chinese	km	kilometer(s)	sq km	square kilometer(s)
cm	centimeter(s)	kw	kilowatt(s)	sq mi	square mile(s)
Co.	Company, County	kwh	kilowatt hour(s)	SSR	Soviet Socialist Republic
cu	cubic	Lat.	Latin		
d.	died	lat	latitude	St.	Saint, Street
Dan.	Danish	lb	pound(s)	Sum.	Sumerian
DC	direct current	long	longitude	Swed.	Swedish
Du.	Dutch	m	meter(s)	trans.	translated, translation, translator(s)
E	east; eastern	mass no.	mass number		
ed.	edited, edition, editors	MeV	million electron volts		
				Turk.	Turkish
e.g.	exempli gratia (Lat., "for example")	mg	milligram(s)	Ukr.	Ukrainian
		mi	mile(s)	UN	United Nations
Egypt.	Egyptian	min	minute(s)	U.S.	United States
Eng.	English	ml	milliliter(s)	USSR	Union of Soviet Socialist Republics
est.	established; estimated	mm	millimeter(s)		
		m.p.	melting point	v.	versus; verse
et al.	et alii (Lat., "and others")	mph	miles per hour	Ved.	Vedic
		Mt(s).	Mount, Mountain(s)	vol.	Volume(s)
EV	electron volt(s)	N	north; northern	W	west; western
				yd	yard(s)

*For a more extensive listing, see ABBREVIATIONS AND ACRONYMS. Charts of pertinent abbreviations also accompany the articles DEGREE, ACADEMIC; ELEMENTS, CHEMICAL; MATHEMATICAL SYMBOLS; and WEIGHTS AND MEASURES.

FUNK & WAGNALLS NEW ENCYCLOPEDIA

MARINO, Giambattista (1569–1625), Italian poet, born in Naples. Included among his patrons was Marie de Médicis, queen consort of France. Marino (or Marini) is known chiefly as the author of *Adone* (1623), a poem of more than 40,000 lines, recounting the story of Venus and Adonis. His florid, grandiose style inspired a literary fashion called *marinismo*. Other poems of Marino's are contained in the collection *La lira* (1608–14).

MARION, city, seat of Grant Co., central Indiana, on the Mississinewa R., in a rich grain-producing area; inc. as a city 1889. Motor-vehicle parts, electronic equipment, plastic goods, processed food, wire, paper, and machinery are manufactured here. Indiana Wesleyan University (1920) is in the city. The community was founded in the 1820s in a region inhabited by Miami Indians, whose descendants still live here. Much natural gas and petroleum were produced in the area in the late 19th century. The city is named for Francis Marion, a hero of the American Revolution. Pop. (1980) 35,874; (1990) 32,618.

MARION, city, seat of Marion Co., central Ohio; inc. as a city 1890. It is an agricultural and manufacturing center; local products include power shovels, road-building equipment, corrugated containers, motor-vehicle parts, household appliances, and processed food. The Marion branch of Ohio State University (1957) and a junior college are here. Marion was the home of President Warren G. Harding; the Harding Memorial, where he and his wife are buried, and the restored Harding home and museum are points of interest. The community, settled in 1820, is named for the American Revolution hero Francis Marion. Pop. (1980) 37,040; (1990) 34,075.

MARION, Francis (c. 1732–95), American general, born near Georgetown, S.C. In 1775 he represented Saint John's Parish, Berkeley Co., in the provincial congress of South Carolina. At the beginning of the American Revolution, he was commissioned a captain and took part in the occupation of Fort Johnson. After his promotion to major in 1776, he was stationed at the unfinished Fort Sullivan (later called Fort Moultrie), in Charleston Harbor. In June 1776 he was made lieutenant colonel in the regular service. When the British captured Charleston in 1780 and began to overrun the state, Marion organized the major colonial force in South Carolina. With a group of irregulars who were poorly equipped and who suffered from a shortage of provisions, Marion demonstrated himself to be a great guerrilla leader; after a daring attack he would withdraw to swamp country unfamiliar to the British, earning him the epithet the Swamp Fox. Near the end of the war, Marion and Gen. Nathanael Greene joined forces. Marion was elected to the South Carolina Senate in 1781, 1782, and 1784.

MARIONETTE. *See* PUPPETS AND MARIONETTES.

MARIS, Roger Eugene (1934–85), American baseball player, born in Hibbing, Minn. A sturdy, left-handed batter and an excellent outfielder, Maris began his major league career in 1957 with the Cleveland Indians, and later played with the Kansas City Athletics, the New York Yankees, and the Saint Louis Cardinals. During the 1961 season with the Yankees he hit 61 home runs, thereby breaking the most famous record in baseball, the 60 home runs hit by Babe Ruth in 1927. Maris's record was achieved in a season of 162 games and that of Ruth in 154 games. After the 1966 season the Yankees traded Maris to the Cardinals; he retired in 1968. Maris was named most valuable player in the American League in 1960 and 1961.

MARITAIN, Jacques (1882–1973), French philosopher, known for his application of the teachings of the medieval Scholastic philosopher St. Thomas Aquinas to the problems of modern life.

Born in Paris, Nov. 18, 1882, Maritain was educated at the Sorbonne, where he came under the influence of the philosopher Henri Bergson, and at the University of Heidelberg. Reared as a Protestant, Maritain converted to Roman Catholicism in 1906. He did a study of the philosophy of St. Thomas Aquinas, applying it to modern culture. Maritain lectured at the Institut Catholique in Paris (1914–33), the Institute for Medieval Studies in Toronto (1933–45), and Princeton University (1948–52). From 1945 to 1948 he was ambassador of France to the Vatican. Later he lived in retirement in Toulouse, France, where he died April 28, 1973.

Maritain's approach to philosophical problems took into account data from anthropology, sociology, and psychology. His deepest and most lasting achievements were in epistemology, in which he studied the different degrees of knowledge and their interrelationships, and in political philosophy. His writings stress that reality can be known in many different ways—through, for instance, science, philosophy, art, or mysticism—each of which contributes something distinctive to human knowledge. Maritain maintained that to exist is to act; cooperation is always possible when humanity pursues a common good. He also wrote much in the area of aesthetics. His more than 60 books include *Art and Scholasticism* (1920; trans. 1930), *Degrees of Knowledge* (1932; trans. 1937), *Art and Poetry* (1935; trans. 1943), *Existence and the Existent* (1947; trans. 1948), and *Moral Philosophy* (1960; trans. 1964). The Jacques Maritain Center, established in 1958 at the University of Notre Dame, promotes research and study of Maritain's thought.

MARITIME ADMINISTRATION, agency of the U.S. Department of Transportation, established in 1950. Prior to 1981, the agency was part of the Department of Commerce. The agency is charged with encouraging the development and maintenance of a merchant marine sufficient to meet peacetime commercial needs of the U.S. and capable of serving as a naval and military auxiliary in time of war or national emergency.

The agency administers operating- and construction-differential subsidies, to make up the difference between U.S. costs of building and operating ships and the estimated costs of foreign competitors, and determines the service of U.S. operators in return for government aid. It pays the cost of national defense equipment, exceeding commercial requirements, that is incorporated in U.S. ships. Decisions on subsidy grants are made by the Maritime Subsidy Board.

As part of planning for possible national emergencies, the administration maintains a National Defense Reserve Fleet. In emergencies it can also charter ships to U.S. operators and requisition ships owned by U.S. citizens for defense needs.

The administration also promotes the use of American ships to carry U.S. trade, grants approval of transfers of U.S. ships to foreign flags, authorizes government guarantees for privately granted ship-construction loans, designs vessels, engages in research to improve ship transportation systems, participates in international programs and meetings on maritime problems, provides a War Risk Insurance program to insure both seamen and operators against losses from hostile action; operates the U.S. Merchant Marine Academy at Kings Point, N.Y., and supervises government grants and student aid to the six state maritime academies in California, Maine, Massachusetts, Michigan, New York, and Texas.

MARITIME LAW, branch of law relating to commerce and navigation on the high seas and on other navigable waters. Specifically, the term refers to the body of customs, legislation, international treaties, and court decisions pertaining to ownership and operation of vessels, transportation of passengers and cargo on them, and rights and obligations of their crews while in transit.

History. The origins of maritime law go back to antiquity. Because no country has jurisdiction over the seas, it has been necessary for nations to reach agreements regarding ways of dealing with ships, crews, and cargoes when disputes arise. The earliest agreements were probably based on a body of ancient customs that had developed as practical solutions to common problems. Many of these customs became part of Roman civil law. After the fall of the Roman Empire, maritime commerce was disrupted for about 500 years.

After maritime activity was resumed in the Middle Ages, various disputes arose and laws were formulated to deal with them. Gradually the laws of the sea were compiled; among the best-known collections of early maritime law are the *Laws of Oleron* and the *Black Book of the Admiralty,* an English compilation prepared during the 14th and 15th centuries. Special courts to administer sea laws were set up in some countries. In Great Britain today, maritime law is administered by courts of the admiralty.

The U.S. According to provisions in the U.S. Constitution, U.S. maritime law is administered by federal courts that have jurisdiction over all maritime contracts, injuries, offenses, and torts. Maritime causes are deemed to be those directly affecting commerce on navigable waters that form a continuous highway to foreign countries. In any dispute the fact that commerce is practiced only on waters within a single state does not necessarily affect the jurisdiction of the federal courts. Many aspects of maritime law are now governed by federal statutes and thus are no longer dependent upon the constitutional power of Congress to regulate commerce.

The Scope of Maritime Law. Liability for common-law wrongs is enforced by the maritime law of the U.S. and Great Britain (see COMMON LAW; TORT). Maritime torts include all illegal acts or direct injuries arising in connection with commerce and navigation occurring on navigable waters, including negligence and the wrongful taking of property. The law permits recovery only for actual damages. Maritime law also recognizes and enforces contracts and awards damages for failure to fulfill them.

The adjustment of the rights of the parties to a maritime venture in accordance with the principles of general average, which pertain to the apportioning of loss of cargo, is also an important function of maritime courts, and the doctrines pertaining to general average are among the most important of the maritime law. The British admiralty courts have acquired jurisdiction by statute over crimes committed on the high seas outside the territorial waters of Great Britain. Similar jurisdiction has been conferred by Congress on the U.S. federal district courts. International agreements have been made to handle the problems of safety at sea, pollution control, salvage, rules for preventing collisions, and coordination of shipping regulations.

International Ocean Law. Some aspects of ocean law affect relationships among nations. Issues of neutrality and belligerency that occur in wartime are dealt with in international law. The UN Convention on the Law of the Sea, adopted in 1982 but not yet in force, addresses ocean law issues, including rights of navigation and overflight, fishing, marine scientific research, seabed minerals development, and marine environmental protection. It allows each coastal nation to exercise sovereignty over a territorial sea up to 12 nautical mi (22.224 km) wide and jurisdiction over resources, scientific research, and environmental protection in an exclusive economic zone up to 200 nautical mi (370.4 km) offshore; beyond this zone, seabed minerals development will be regulated by an international body. The U.S. has not signed the accord because it objects to the system for minerals development in the international seabed, but it has generally endorsed all other provisions of the convention.

See also INTER-GOVERNMENTAL MARITIME CONSULTATIVE ORGANIZATION; SEAS, FREEDOM OF THE.

For further information on this topic, see the Bibliography in volume 28, section 248.

MARITIME PROVINCES, collective name for the E Canadian provinces of New Brunswick, Nova Scotia, and Prince Edward Island. A meeting in 1864 to discuss the unification of the Maritimes was a forerunner to the formation, in 1867, of the Dominion of Canada. Atlantic Provinces refers to the Maritime Provinces plus Newfoundland.

MARITIME TERRITORY (Rus. *Primorskiy Kray*), administrative division, extreme SE Russia, bounded by the Sea of Japan on the E and by China on the W. In the coastal region coal, lead, zinc, and tin are mined. Other industries in the territory include agriculture, fishing, and lumbering. The capital, Vladivostok, and the cities of Nakhodka and Spaask-Dalniy are noted for manufacturing. The Maritime Territory lies within the former Far Eastern Territory; it was formed in 1938 of the former Primorskaya and Ussuri oblasts. Area, about 165,760 sq km (about 64,000 sq mi); pop. (1979 est.) 1,978,000.

MARITSA (Turk. *Meriç*; Gr. *Évros*; Eng. *Marica*), river, SE Europe, in the Balkan Peninsula. About 485 km (about 300 mi) long, it rises in the Rila Mts. of W Bulgaria and flows SE across a fertile valley before forming a short section of the Bulgaria-Greece border and then a longer part of the Greece-Turkey boundary. The river subsequently turns S at Edirne, Turkey, and then SW before entering the Aegean Sea, near Enez, Turkey.

MARIUPOL (Ukr. *Mariupil*). See ZHDANOV.

MARIUS, Gaius (c. 157–86 BC), Roman general and statesman, who led the Populares during the civil war of 88–86 BC.

Marius was born at Arpinum (now Arpino). As a young man he served in Spain under the Roman general Scipio Africanus the Younger. In 119 BC he was elected tribune of the people. His marriage to Julia, the aunt of Julius Caesar, improved his social status, but as leader of the popular party he retained his sympathy with the lower classes. After serving as praetor in 115 BC, he returned to Spain, where he waged a successful campaign against the brigands and cutthroats who had been terrorizing the country. He accompanied the Roman general Quintus Caecilius Metellus to Africa in 109 BC. He was elected consul two years later and was vested with the conduct of the war against Jugurtha, king of Numidia. Assisted by his chief aide, Lucius Cornelius Sulla, Marius captured Jugurtha and brought the war to a successful conclusion in 106 BC. The enemies of Marius gave the credit for the victory to Sulla, thereby laying the foundation of the later hatred between the two leaders.

After spending two years in subjugating Numidia, Marius again became (104 BC) consul and advanced northward to oppose the invading Germanic tribes of the Cimbri and the Teutons. He annihilated the Teutons at Aquae Sextiae (now Aix-en-Provence, France) in 102 BC and defeated the Cimbri the following year near Vercellae (now Vercelli, Italy). Marius was considered the savior of his country and in 100 BC was made consul for the sixth time.

When Sulla, as consul, was entrusted with the conduct of the war against the powerful Asian king Mithradates VI in 88 BC, Marius, who had developed a jealous hatred for his patrician rival, attempted to deprive him of his command. Civil war broke out between the partisans of the two leaders. Marius was forced to flee, and Sulla proceeded to Asia Minor to take up his command. Marius then hurried back to Italy, where an uprising of his friends had taken place under Lucius Cornelius Cinna, a bitter opponent of Sulla. Marius and Cinna marched against Rome, which was forced to capitulate. Marius then took his revenge on the aristocracy in a veritable orgy of indiscriminate murder. He had himself and Cinna named to the consulship in 86 BC. By then an old man, Marius died in Rome on January 13 of that year after holding the office for only a few days.

MARIVAUX, Pierre Carlet de Chamblain de (1688–1763), French dramatist and novelist, born in Paris. He wrote a number of comedies about self-discovery, which his characters attain emotionally rather than intellectually. The French word *marivaudage* ("mild, witty flirting") is derived from his manner of writing. Among his comedies are *Love in Livery* (1730; trans. 1730) and *The Legacy* (1736; trans. 1915). In his several unfinished novels he pungently portrayed 18th-century middle-class French life. In 1742 he was elected a member of the French Academy.

MARJORAM, common name for perennial herbs of the genus *Origanum*, of the mint (q.v.) family, Lamiaceae. The herbs, native to Eurasia, are cultivated in the U.S. for the highly aromatic young leaves, which are used either fresh or dried as a seasoning. The flowers, which are borne in spikes, have a five-toothed calyx (outer floral envelope) and a two-lipped corolla (inner floral envelope). Either two or four stamens (male flower part) and a solitary pistil (female flower part) are present. The fruit is an achene (dry and one-seeded). The wild marjoram, more commonly called oregano, *O. vulgare*, is a perennial; sweet-marjoram, *O. majorana*, is an annual, or frost-free, perennial.

MARK, monetary unit of Germany, from a Norse term for a unit of measure that probably dates as far back as the 3d century AD. It was employed as a monetary unit by the Goths and then the Germans. It was given a uniform value (0.35842 metric grains of fine gold) throughout the German Empire in 1873. After a period of inflation it was again stabilized as the reichsmark in 1924. It was reestablished (1948) as the deutsche mark in West Germany and the ostmark in East Germany. When Germany unified in 1990, the deutsche mark, divided into 100 pfennigs, became the national monetary unit. It remains one of the world's strongest currencies.

MARK, Saint, full name JOHN MARK (fl. 1st cent. AD), the reputed author of the second Gospel. His life can be reconstructed from incidental facts in the New Testament. He was the son of Mary, a householder of Jerusalem, at whose home the early Christians held meetings in the days of persecution (see Acts 12:12). That he was a Hellenist is confirmed by his Roman surname (Marcus) and his relationship to St. Barnabas, a Cyprian (see Col. 4:10). St. Peter called him "son" (see 1 Pet. 5:13), an appellation indicating the strong personal bond between them.

Mark was probably converted to Christianity under Peter's ministry in Jerusalem and thereafter acted as Peter's interpreter because the apostle had little knowledge of Greek. He went with his cousin Barnabas and St. Paul to Antioch in Pisidia from Jerusalem but left them at Perga in southern Asia Minor and returned to Jerusalem (see Acts 12:25, 13:5). He accompanied Barnabas to Cyprus in about AD 50, but Paul was unwilling to take him on another journey. Nothing is known about Mark's activities during the next ten years, but during Paul's first Roman captivity, about AD 60, Mark was in Rome preparing to leave for Asia Minor. They became reconciled, so that five years later Paul wrote to St. Timothy, who was probably then at Ephesus, asking that he bring Mark to him (see 2 Tim. 4:11).

According to tradition, Mark wrote his Gospel in Rome, basing it on Peter's teachings. It is supposed that he last worked at Alexandria; he may have been organizer and first bishop of the Alexandrian church. Mark is a patron saint of notaries. His feast day is April 25.

MARK, GOSPEL ACCORDING TO, second book of the New Testament.

Authorship. The earliest evidence pertinent to the authorship of Mark comes from the 3d-century church historian Eusebius of Caesarea, who quotes an earlier writer named Papias (60?–125?). Papias himself quotes a statement concerning Mark's Gospel by a still earlier figure whom he calls the "presbyter" (elder): "And the presbyter used to say this: 'Mark, being Peter's interpreter, wrote down accurately, but not in order, that which he remembered of what was said and done by the Lord.'!" It is virtually certain that, in Papias's opinion, this Mark was the John Mark, cousin of Barnabas, mentioned in Acts (see, for instance, Acts 15:37–39), in several letters of Paul (see Col. 4:10; 2 Tim. 4:11; Philem.

24), and in 1 Pet. 5:13. Critical research has been able neither to prove nor to disprove this opinion, but there are reasons to doubt it.

Early Christians tended to link the gospels with one of the 12 apostles. If the text was firmly attributed by early tradition to a man named Mark, Papias's presbyter probably did the best he could with this tradition by identifying this Mark with John Mark in order to link him to the apostle Peter. Hence, many scholars believe that the Gospel was written by an otherwise unknown early Christian named Mark who drew on a large number of traditions in order to compose a tightly organized and compelling narrative.

Date and Place of Composition. In chapter 13, Mark refers to the destruction of Jerusalem either as an event that may shortly happen or as one that has recently happened. Consequently, although scholars do not know whether to date the Gospel shortly before or shortly after AD 70, it is virtually certain that it is not far removed from that date.

A tradition as early as the 2d-century Greek theologian Clement of Alexandria gives Rome as the place of composition, but that view is probably dependent on the assumption that the author wrote down things said by Peter. Clues in the Gospel itself have suggested to numerous scholars that it may have been written in Galilee or Syria.

Contents. The Gospel tells the story of the adult Jesus from the time of his baptism by John the Baptist to his crucifixion and the angel's report of his resurrection. The opening scenes, set in Judea, portray the activity of John the Baptist, Jesus' baptism, and his temptation by Satan in the wilderness. The scene then shifts (1:14) to Galilee, and for the bulk of the Gospel the reader is taken to various locales in the north, notably in the vicinity of the Lake of Galilee, where Jesus teaches about the kingdom of God and heals the sick. Jesus then travels south (10:1) to the region of Judea, and from Mark 11:11 through the end of the Gospel the scenes are set in and around Jerusalem, where Jesus is arrested, crucified, and buried. When some women from among his followers go to the tomb to care for the body, they discover that the tomb is empty. An angel commands them to tell the disciples, but they speak to no one because they are afraid.

Thus, the Gospel begins and ends in Judea, but a large segment of the intervening activity is located in Galilee. The importance of Galilee is further indicated by a twice-spoken prophecy that after his resurrection Jesus will go to Galilee, and that Galilee will be the locale in which the disciples will see him (14:28, 16:7).

Literary Structure. It is reasonable to assume that the earliest church would have had, as an oral tradition, a rudimentary account of Jesus' Passion, presented as a sequence of developments in Judea, notably in Jerusalem. The church would also have had collections of Jesus' teachings (for example, the parables now in Mark 4) and stories of his deeds, tied—at least in some cases— to locales in Galilee (for example, the miracle stories now in Mark 4, 5, and 6). Mark's most obvious literary achievement lies in his having drawn together many of these Galilean sayings and stories to form an extended introduction to the Jerusalem tradition of Jesus' Passion. Furthermore, the narrative has remarkable dramatic vitality. A note of tension is struck at the very beginning by the brief picture of Jesus' conflict with the cosmic force of evil, Satan, and by the prophetic shadow that the arrest of John the Baptist casts over the inauguration of Jesus' preaching. The tension mounts (see, for instance, 2:6-7; 3:2, 6, 22), until it culminates in open confrontation over Jesus' audacious activity in the Temple (11:18) and his verbal attacks on the Jewish authorities (12:1-12, 38-40). The confrontation then leads to a plan for disposing of Jesus (14:1-2) and finally to his arrest, trial, and crucifixion. In the Passion narrative Jesus' antagonists are human beings, but even here one senses dramatic notes of cosmic conflict in the reference to worldwide darkness at the crucifixion and in the corresponding reference to the rising sun on Easter morning.

Thus, Mark may have drawn his major clues for organizing and presenting the Galilean traditions from the tense, dramatic structure inherent in the Jerusalem tradition of Jesus' Passion. That is to say, he may have threaded the theme of dramatic conflict back through the Galilean materials, consequently presenting the vignettes of Jesus' deeds and teachings as points of confrontation anticipating the climactic events in Jerusalem. The resulting drama is fundamentally apocalyptic, in that it presents Jesus' story as a dualistic cosmic struggle between the kingdom of God and the kingdom of Satan. It is inaugurated when Jesus, as God's son, invades the territory of Satan, in order to free human beings from Satan's grasp (3:27). The ultimate outcome of the struggle is assured with the resurrection of Jesus, the event after which his true identity, initially kept secret (1:34, 44; 3:12; 5:43; 7:36; 8:26, 30; 9:9), can be clearly revealed (9:9).

The Conclusion of the Gospel. There are two textual traditions for the ending of the gospel. The majority of Greek manuscripts have the "long ending," closing with 16:20, but a smaller number extend only through 16:8. The dominant scholarly opinion is that the shorter version is the earlier one—that Mark came to his intended closure with 16:8, and that a 2d-century scribe, finding that an abrupt and unsatisfying ending, drew on the Gospel of Luke in order to compose what seemed to him a more satisfying conclusion.

J.L.Ma.

MARKA, also Merka or Merca, town, SE Somalia, in Banaadir Region, on the Indian Ocean, near Mogadisho. The town has oilseed-processing and fishing industries, and textiles, boats, and paper products are manufactured here. Bananas are exported, shipped to the coast from the rich irrigated area around nearby Janhale on the Webi Shebelle R., 13 km (8 mi) to the NW. An agricultural college is situated in Janhale, which also trades in corn, sorghum, peanuts, sugarcane, tobacco, and cotton. Under Italian rule the name of the town was spelled Merca. Pop. (1985 est.) 70,000.

MARK ANTONY. See Antony, Mark.

MARKET, any established operating means or exchange for business dealings between buyers and sellers. As opposed to simple selling, a market implies trade that is transacted with some regularity and regulation, and in which a certain amount of competition is involved. The earliest markets in history conducted bartering. After the introduction of money, commercial codes were developed that ultimately led to modern national and international enterprise. As production expanded and became less practical, communications and so-called middlemen came to play an ever growing role in markets. Types of markets include retail, wholesale or distributors', producers', raw material, and stock.

The term *market* is also used to denote a place where goods are bought and sold, and to refer to potential or estimated consumer demand.

MARKETING, activities involved in getting goods from the producer to the consumer. The producer is responsible for the design and manufacture of goods. Early marketing techniques followed production and were responsible only for moving goods from the manufacturer to the point of final sale. Now, however, marketing is much more pervasive. In large corporations the marketing functions precede the manufacture of a product. They involve market research and product development, design, and testing.

Marketing concentrates primarily on the buyers, or consumers, determining their needs and desires, educating them with regard to the availability of products and to important product features, developing strategies to persuade them to buy, and, finally, enhancing their satisfaction with a purchase. Marketing management includes planning, organizing, directing, and controlling decision making regarding product lines, pricing, promotion, and servicing. In most of these areas marketing has complete control; in others, as in product-line development, its function is primarily advisory. In addition, the marketing department of a business firm is responsible for the physical distribution of the products, determining the channels of distribution that will be used and supervising the profitable flow of goods from the factory or warehouse.

Tailoring the Product. Merchandise generally similar in appearance, that is, in style or design, but varying in such elements as size, price, and quality is collectively known as a product line. Product lines must be intimately correlated with consumer needs and wants.

In order to develop a line effectively, marketing research is conducted to study consumer behavior. Changing attitudes and modes of living directly affect the salability of products. For example, the trend to informal dress has changed clothing styles dramatically. Also, a high-income economy triggers a demand for products very different from those selected in a declining business cycle. The availability or lack of disposable income, meaning income over and above that spent for basic necessities such as food, shelter, and clothing, affects the buying pattern for so-called luxury products. Similarly, the purchase of durable or long-lived goods, such as refrigerators, automobiles, and houses, may be deferred when the economy is declining and may increase rapidly in periods of prosperity. Staple products, such as food and clothing, tend not to be seriously affected by the business cycle.

The life cycles of products require careful study. Virtually all product ideas lose in time the novelty that initially attracted purchasers of the merchandise. Manufacturers may also accelerate the obsolescence of a product by introducing new, more desirable features. Consumers today are conditioned to expect product innovations and tend to react favorably to new features. This has an important bearing on the usable life deliberately designed into a product, which in turn has a significant effect on the costs to the manufacturer and ultimately on the price to the consumer. Competition between manufacturers of similar products naturally accelerates the speed of changes made in those products.

Pricing the Product. The two basic components that affect product pricing are costs of manufacture and competition in selling. It is unprofitable to sell a product below the manufacturer's production costs and unfeasible to sell it at a price

MARKETING

higher than that at which comparable merchandise is being offered. Other variables also affect pricing. Company policy may require a minimum profit on new product lines or a specified return on investments, or discounts may be offered on purchases in quantity.

Attempts to maintain resale prices were facilitated for many years under federal and state fair-trade laws. These have now been nullified, thereby prohibiting manufacturers from controlling the prices set by wholesalers and retailers. Such control can still be maintained if the manufacturers wish to market directly through their own outlets, but this is seldom feasible except for the largest manufacturers.

Attempts have also been made, generally at government insistence, to maintain product-price competition in order to minimize the danger of injuring small businesses. Therefore, pricing decisions are reviewed by the legal department of the marketing organization.

Promoting the Product. Advertising, personal (face-to-face) selling, and sales promotion are the methods for inducing people to buy.

The primary objective of advertising is to presell the product, that is, to convince consumers to purchase an item before they actually see and inspect it. Most companies consider this function so important that they have allotted extensive budgets and engaged special advertising agencies to develop their program of advertising. By repeatedly exposing the consumer to a brand name or trademark, to the appearance or package of a product, and to special features of an item, advertisers hope to incline consumers toward a particular product. Advertising is most frequently done on television, radio, and billboards; in newspapers, magazines, and catalogs; and through direct mail to the consumers. In recent years, advertising agencies have been joining forces to become giant agencies, making it possible for them to offer their clients a comprehensive range of worldwide promotion services. *See* ADVERTISING.

As the costs of personal selling have risen, the utilization of salespeople has changed. Simple transactions are completed by clerks. Salespeople are now used primarily where the products are complex and require careful explanation or customized application. For example, in the typical automobile sale, the salesperson's activities generally center on negotiating price and arranging terms of payment; the actual product has usually already been presold through advertising. *See* SALES PROMOTION.

The purpose of sales promotion is to supplement and coordinate advertising and personal selling; this has become increasingly important in marketing. Often it is necessary to work closely with the dealers who handle a manufacturer's products if the products are to move satisfactorily. Displays must be supplied and set up, and cooperative advertising programs may be worked out. Store clerks should be trained in a

New department-store marketing strategy resulted in the great consumer appeal of The Cellar at Macy's in New York City. This row of boutiques selling household wares and foods re-creates the intimacy of old-time Main Street shopping. Macy's

MARKETING

knowledge of the manufacturer's products. Often the manufacturer must provide services such as installation and maintenance for a specified time. On the consumer level, sales promotion may involve special inducements such as discount coupons, contests, a premium with the purchase of a product, or a lower price on the purchase of a second item. See MERCHANDISING.

Distributing the Product. Some products are marketed most effectively by direct sale from manufacturer to consumer. Among these are durable equipment—for example, computers, office equipment, industrial machinery and supplies, and consumer specialties such as vacuum cleaners and life insurance. The direct marketing of products such as cosmetics and household needs is very important. Formerly common "door-to-door" products, these are now usually sold by the more sophisticated "house party" technique.

Direct marketing by mail has been expanded to virtually all types of products and services. Working people find it easy to shop in their leisure hours by catalog, and comparison shopping is made easier because catalogs generally contain extensive product information. For retailers, the use of catalogs makes it possible to do business considerably beyond their usual trading area and with a minimum of overhead. Also important are credit cards, which have made it relatively easy to purchase by mail or telephone even such high-priced items as appliances, electronic equipment, and cameras. At least half the nation's 50 leading corporations have mail-order divisions.

Television is a potent tool in direct marketing because it facilitates the demonstration of products in use. Direct sale of all kinds of goods to the public via home-shopping clubs broadcasting on cable television channels is gaining in popularity. Also carving its own niche is telephone marketing, called telemarketing, a technique used in selling to businesses as well as to consumers. Most consumer products, however, move from the manufacturer through agents to wholesalers and then to retailers, ultimately reaching the consumer. Determining how products should move through wholesale and retail organizations is another major marketing decision.

Wholesalers distribute goods in large quantities, usually to retailers, for resale. Some retail businesses have grown so large, however, that they have found it more profitable to bypass the wholesaler and deal directly with the manufacturers or their agents. Wholesalers first responded to this trend by adapting their operations so that they moved faster and called for a lower margin of profit. Small retailers fought back through cooperative wholesaling, the voluntary banding together of independent retailers to market a product. The result has been a trend toward a much closer, interlocking relationship between wholesaler and independent retailer.

Retailing has undergone even more change. Intensive preselling by manufacturers and the development of minimum-service operations, for example, self-service in department stores, have drastically changed the retailer's way of doing business. Supermarkets and discount stores have become commonplace not only for groceries but for products as diversified as medicines and gardening equipment. More recently, warehouse retailing has become a major means of retailing higher-priced consumer goods such as furniture, appliances, and electronic equipment. The emphasis is on generating store traffic, speeding up the transaction, and rapidly expanding the sales volume. Chain stores—groups of stores with one ownership—and cooperative groups have also proliferated. Special types of retailing, for example, vending machines and convenience stores, have also developed to fill multiple needs. See RETAILING.

Transporting and warehousing merchandise are also technically within the purview of marketing. Products are often moved several times as they go from producer to consumer. Products are carried by rail, truck, ship, airplane, and pipeline. Efficient traffic management determines the best method and timetable of shipment for any particular product.

Services and Marketing. Services, unlike products, are intangible commodities. A service is the provision of work, accommodations, or ministrations desired by a consumer. Consumers pay for a service as they would for a product. Already more people are employed in the provision of services than in the manufacture of products, and this area shows every indication of expanding even further. Services familiar to most consumers are in the fields of maintenance and repair, transportation, travel, entertainment, education, and medical care. Business-oriented services include computer applications, management consulting, banking, accounting and legal services, stock brokerage, and advertising.

Services, like products, require marketing. Usually, service marketing parallels product marketing with the exception of physical handling. Services must be planned and developed carefully to meet consumer demand. For example, in the field of temporary personnel, a service that continues to increase in monetary value, studies are made to determine the types of employee skills needed in various geographical locations and fields of business. Because intangibles are more difficult to sell than physical products, promotional campaigns for services must be even more aggressive than those for physical commodities. Through extensive promotion, temporary-personnel agencies have convinced many companies that hiring on a temporary basis only in times of need is more economical than hiring permanent, full-time personnel.

Marketing Research. Marketing research involves the use of surveys, tests, and statistical studies to analyze consumer trends and to forecast the quantity and locale of a market favorable to the profitable sale of products or services. The social sciences are increasingly utilized in customer research. Psychology and sociology, for example, by providing clues to people's activities, circumstances, wants, desires, and general motivation, are keys to understanding the various behavioral patterns of consumers.

Coupled with applications from the social sciences has been the introduction of modern measuring methods when surveys are made to determine the extent of markets for a particular product. These methods include the use of statistics and the utilization of computers to determine trends in consumers' desires for various products. Scientific analysis is being used in such areas as product development, particularly in evaluating the sales potential of new product ideas. For example, use is made of mathematical models, that is, theory-based projections of social behavior in a particular social relationship. Sales projections become the basis for many important marketing decisions, including those relating to the type and extent of advertising, the allocation of salespeople, and the number and location of warehouses.

Forces Affecting Modern Marketing. An important influence in marketing theory is the continuous and rapid change in consumer interests and desires. Consumers today are more sophisticated than those of past generations. They attend school for much longer; they are exposed to newspapers, magazines, movies, radio, television, and travel; and they have much greater interaction with other people. Their demands are more exacting, and their taste changes more volatile. Markets tend to be segmented as each group calls for products suited to its particular tastes. "Positioning" the product—that is, determining the exact segment of the population that is likely to buy a product, and then developing a marketing campaign to enhance the product's image to fit that particular segment—requires great care and planning.

Competition also has sharply intensified, as the number of firms engaged in producing similar products has increased. Each firm tries to differentiate its products from those of its competitors. Profit margins, meaning the profit percentages made by a business per dollar of sales, are constantly being lessened. While costs continue to rise, competition tends to keep prices down. The result is a narrowing spread between costs and selling prices, and an increase in a business' sales volume is necessary to maintain or increase profit.

The consumer movement, that is, the insistence on reputable products and services by consumer groups, gives every indication of becoming a permanent influence on marketing techniques. Both consumer groups and government agencies have intensified their scrutiny of products, challenging such diverse elements as product design, length and legitimacy of warranty, and promotional tactics. Warranty and guarantee practices, in particular, have been closely examined. New legislation has generally defined and extended the manufacturer's responsibility for product performance.

Ecological concerns have also affected product design and marketing, especially as the expense of product modification has increased the retail cost. Such forces, which have added to the friction between producer and consumer, must be understood by the marketer and integrated into a sound marketing program.

Even the way a firm handles itself in public life, that is, how it reacts to social and political issues, has become significant. No longer may a corporation cloak its internal decisions as private affairs. The public's dissatisfaction with the actions and attitudes of a firm has sometimes led to a reduction in sales; conversely, consumer enthusiasm, generated by a firm's intentional establishment of a good public image or public relations, has led to increased sales.

Specialized Marketing Developments. The success of specialized marketing developments has caused many older organizations to revise their operating methods. In recent years, for example, franchise distribution has become an important force in retailing. Under this plan, the retailer is given the right to sell, within a certain area, without competition from another retailer dealing in the same product.

Many consumers now find it more desirable to rent products than to purchase them outright. For example, a homeowner may find it preferable to rent an electric floor polisher when needed, rather than purchase the appliance at the list price, use it only infrequently, and then have to provide storage space within the home. Another

Automobile rental has become a common practice. Here at a southeastern airport, visitors arrange for car rentals with representatives of the Hertz rental service.
Hertz Corporation

item consumers have found easier and less expensive to rent is the automobile. The renting of equipment also figures in large industry. Corporations are finding it to their economic advantage to rent computers and office and industrial machinery, thereby assuring themselves of product servicing and repair and allowing a changeover, without great expense, to newer equipment models as they become available.

The use of credit has had a great impact on marketing. Customers with credit cards can make purchases without the normal immediate presentation of cash, and sales are thus stimulated. Stores often further stimulate sales by the use of premium promotions whereby customers making purchases receive free goods or the opportunity to buy special merchandise at very low prices.

Businesses must strive daily to outdo competitors. The methods available to businesses for distinguishing their commodity from others in the market are subject only to their ingenuity. Such methods may include product improvement, a unique promotional campaign, a new twist in servicing, a change in distribution channels, or an enticing price adjustment.

The Marketing Profession. Perhaps nothing is more conducive to the success of a firm than the image that it conveys of itself to the public. The marketing activities of a company, because they act directly on the consumer, do most to shape this image and thus must be developed with great care. As marketing has become increasingly more complex, a need has arisen for executives trained in the social sciences who also possess statistical, mathematical, and computer backgrounds. Many colleges and universities now have programs designed to train marketing executives. Courses are offered at the undergraduate and the graduate level in such specialized fields as advertising, administrative practices, financial management, production, human relations, retailing, and personnel administration.

In recent years, as many U.S. manufacturing industries such as steel and automobiles have been weakened because of foreign competition, marketing departments have become increasingly responsible for generating profitable sales volume. Thus, their stature in top-level business decision making has been enhanced. This trend gives every indication of continuing in the foreseeable future. As competition continues to increase and businesses become even more diversified, the marketing profession is likely to provide more personnel in the ranks of top management. A.Gr.

For further information on this topic, see the Bibliography in volume 28, sections 327, 620–21.
MARKET RESEARCH. *See* MARKETING.

MARKHAM, town, Regional Municipality of York, SE Ontario, on the Rouge R. It is a suburb of Toronto in an area of diversified agriculture. Major products include processed food and wood items. The community, settled in 1794, is named for William Markham (1720–1806), an archbishop of York. The township of Markham was annexed by the town of Markham in 1971. Pop. (1986) 114,597; (1991) 153,811.

MARKHAM, (Charles) Edwin Ansan (1852–1940), American poet, born in Oregon City, Oreg. In 1899 his poem "The Man with the Hoe," based on a 19th-century French painting by J. F. Millet, was published in the San Francisco Examiner and brought Markham national fame. He then moved to New York City and devoted himself to writing and lecturing. His books of poetry include *The Man with the Hoe* (1899), *Lincoln* (1901), *Gates of Paradise* (1920), *Eighty Songs at Eighty* (1932), and *The Star of Araby* (1937).

MARKOVA, Dame Alicia, professional name of LILLIAN ALICIA MARKS (1910–), British ballerina, who was an important figure in modern British ballet. Born in London, she danced with the ballet company of the Russian impresario Sergey Diaghilev in 1925–29 and with the Vic-Wells Ballet (now the Royal Ballet) in 1931–35. With the British dancer Anton Dolin (1904–83) she directed the Markova-Dolin Ballet in 1935–38; together they founded the London Festival Ballet in 1950. In 1963–69 she was director of the Metropolitan Opera Ballet in New York City. Known for her lightness, delicacy, and humor, Markova excelled in classical roles such as Giselle and in roles by modern British choreographers such as Antony Tudor.

MARK TWAIN. See TWAIN, MARK.

MARL, town, W central Germany, in North Rhine-Westphalia, on the N fringe of the great Ruhr industrial district. Major industries are coal mining and the manufacture of chemicals. The town was first mentioned in the 9th century but did not develop as an industrial center until the late 19th century. Pop. (1989 est.) 89,700.

MARL, deposit of amorphous calcium carbonate, clay, and sand, in various proportions, characterized usually by the more prominent ingredient, for example, clay marl, sand marl, or shell marl. Shell marl, found in freshwater lakes, is formed from mollusk shells and fine mud. The lake marls of Indiana and Michigan are used in the manufacture of portland cement. Shale and chalky marls are valuable fertilizers.

MARLBOROUGH, also Marlboro, city, Middlesex Co., E Massachusetts, near Boston; inc. as a city 1890. Major manufactures include computers, electronic and electrical equipment, footwear and footwear-making machinery, and paper and metal products. The community, settled in the 1650s, is named for Marlborough, England. In the early 19th century footwear manufacturing began here, and at one time Marlborough ranked fifth in the U.S. in shoe production. Pop. (1980) 30,617; (1990) 31,813.

MARLBOROUGH, John Churchill, 1st Duke of (1650–1722), English general, considered one of the greatest military commanders in history.

Churchill was born in Musbury on May 26, 1650. From 1672 to 1673 he served with distinction under his patron, the duke of York, later James II, king of England, who commanded the English troops sent to assist France in a war against the Netherlands. In 1682 Churchill, then a colonel, was raised to the peerage. During the rebellion of 1685, which was led by James Scott, duke of Monmouth, Churchill was second in command of the forces of James II and was made a major general. Later, fearing that James intended to make Roman Catholicism the state religion of England, Churchill joined the conspiracy to replace James with the Dutch prince William of Orange. When William landed in England in 1688, Churchill was promoted to lieutenant general by James and sent to fight William, but instead he deserted to the latter. William was crowned king as William III, and in 1689 he made Churchill a privy councillor and earl of Marlborough.

In 1692 and again in 1696 Marlborough was charged with treason because he corresponded with James, who was then living in exile in France; Marlborough was not imprisoned, but he lost favor at the royal court. When James's daughter, Anne, succeeded as queen of England in 1702, Marlborough regained his position at court. That same year, during the War of the Spanish Succession (see SPANISH SUCCESSION, WAR OF THE), he was commander in chief of the armies of England and the Netherlands, and he was created 1st duke of Marlborough as a reward for his brilliant victories over the French. Marlborough's greatest triumphs were in the battles of Blenheim (1704), Ramillies (1706), and Audenarde (1708).

In 1711 Marlborough was falsely accused of embezzling public funds, removed as commander in chief, and stripped of the public offices that he had been given in gratitude for his military exploits. He lived abroad in self-imposed exile from 1712 to 1714. After the accession of George I as king of Great Britain, Marlborough returned to England in 1714, and his military rank was restored to him. He died June 16, 1722, at Windsor.

MARLIN, common name for several large, edible game fishes of the genera *Tetrapturus* and *Makaira* of the family Istiophoridae, which also contains the sailfish and the spearfish (qq.v.). Marlins, which are rapid swimmers found in most warm seas, closely resemble the sailfish, differing chiefly in having smaller dorsal fins. As in the sailfish, the nasal bones of the upper jaw are elongated into a long, rounded spear. Marlins attain a maximum weight of about 630 kg (about 1400 lb). The black marlin, *M. indica,* and the striped marlin, *T. audax,* are common Pacific species. The white marlin, *M. albidus,* is a popular Atlantic Ocean sports fish. The name is sometimes applied to the spearfish.

For further information on this topic, see the Bibliography in volume 28, sections 468, 813.

MARLOWE, Christopher (1564–93), English playwright and poet, considered the first great English dramatist and the most important Elizabethan dramatist before William Shakespeare, although his entire activity as a playwright lasted only six years. Earlier playwrights had concentrated on comedy; Marlowe worked on tragedy and advanced it as a dramatic medium. His masterpiece is *The Tragical History of Doctor Faustus.*

Born in Canterbury on Feb. 6, 1564, the son of a well-to-do merchant, Marlowe was educated at the University of Cambridge. Going to London, he associated himself with the Admiral's Men, a company of actors for which he wrote most of his plays. He was reputedly a secret agent for the government and numbered some prominent men, including Sir Walter Raleigh, among his friends, but he led an adventurous and dissolute life and held unorthodox religious views. In 1593 he was denounced as a heretic; before any action could be taken against him, in May of that year he was stabbed to death in a tavern brawl at Deptford over payment of a dinner bill.

Marlowe was the first English playwright to write in blank verse, and by revealing the possibilities for strength and variety of expression in this verse form, he helped to establish it as the predominant form in English drama. He wrote four principal plays, three of which were published posthumously: the heroic dramatic epic *Tamburlaine the Great* (1590), about the 14th-century Mongol conqueror; *Edward II* (1594), which was one of the earliest successful English historical dramas and a model for Shakespeare's *Richard II* and *Richard III; The Tragical History of Doctor Faustus* (c. 1604), one of the earliest dramatizations of the Faust legend; and the melodrama *The Jew of Malta* (1633). He was also the author of two lesser plays: *Tragedy of Dido, Queen of Carthage,* completed by the English dramatist Thomas Nashe (1594); and *Massacre at Paris* (1600). Some authorities believe he also wrote parts of several of Shakespeare's plays. Each of Marlowe's important plays has as a central character a passionate man doomed to destruction by an inordinate desire for power. The plays are further characterized by a sonorous beauty of language and by a vitality of emotion, which is, at times, unrestrained to the point of bombast.

As a poet Marlowe is best known for "The Passionate Shepherd" (1599), which contains the lyric "Come Live with Me and Be My Love." He also translated from the works of the ancient Latin poets Lucan and Ovid.

MARMARA, SEA OF *or* **SEA OF MARMORA** (anc. *Propontis*), inland sea, NW Turkey, connected to the Black Sea by the Bosporus Strait and to the Aegean Sea by the Dardanelles Strait. It separates the European part of Turkey from the Asian part. The sea contains several islands on which are located famous quarries of white marble; the largest island is Marmara (129 sq km/50 sq mi). The sea is 277 km (172 mi) long and has an area of about 11,140 sq km (about 4300 sq mi).

MARMOSET, common name for any of the small, long-tailed, tropical American monkeys of the family Callitrichidae. They differ from other monkeys in having two instead of three molars on each side of the upper jaw and in having long,

Golden marmoset of the genus Leontopithecus.
Arthur W. Ambler–National Audubon Society

curved claws (rather than nails) on all the toes except the great toe. Marmosets also have non-opposable thumbs. The animals all have soft, silky fur and are gentle in disposition. They are arboreal and feed on fruits and insects. Litters contain one to three young.

The family consists of five genera: *Callithrix*, containing the true marmosets; *Saguinus*, containing the tamarins; *Cebuella*, containing the pygmy marmosets; *Leontopithecus*, containing the golden lion marmoset; and *Callimico*, containing Goldi's marmoset, *C. goldii*, which retains the third molar and is sometimes placed in its own family, Callimiconidae.

The true marmosets are larger than the tamarins, and they also differ in having long fringes of hair on the ears. The best known of the true marmosets is the common marmoset, or wistiti, *Callithrix jacchus*. The wistiti, so called from the sound of its chirping, birdlike cry, is about 30 cm (about 12 in) in body length; it has a round head with a flattened black face, thick white tufts on its ears, and long black and white fur. The tail, which is almost twice as long as the body, is white, ringed with black. Most marmosets are endangered through loss of habitat.

MARMOT, common name for any of the large, robust rodents constituting the genus *Marmota* of the family Sciuridae (see SQUIRREL), found in North America, Europe, and Asia. Marmots have blunt snouts, short ears, short, bushy tails, and short legs. The fur is coarse. The animals live in burrows and hibernate during the winter; the length of hibernation varies with the severity of the climate. Marmots feed on vegetation and are sometimes destructive to cultivated crops. The cry of the marmot is a shrill whistle.

The common European marmot is *M. marmota*, found high in the Alps and Pyrenees mountains. The bobac, *M. bobak*, is the marmot of eastern Europe and Asia. The common marmot of eastern North America is the woodchuck, or groundhog, *M. monax*. This animal is gray, streaked with black or brown above and paler below. It attains a length up to 0.6 m (2 ft) and has a bushy tail up to 0.3 m (1 ft) long. The whistler, or hoary marmot, *M. caligata*, is a larger, white and gray species found in northwestern North America. The yellow-bellied marmot, *M. flaviventris*, is found from southwestern Canada to New Mexico.

MARNE, river, NE France, rising S of Langres on the Langres Plateau, and flowing generally W until, after a course of 523 km (325 mi), it joins the Seine R. near Paris. Château-Thierry, Épernay, Châlons-sur-Marne, and Meaux are situated on its banks. During World War I two famous battles were fought near the Marne.

MARNE, BATTLE OF THE, name of two battles of World War I, which took place near the Marne River in northeastern France.
First Battle of the Marne. (Sept. 6-9, 1914), a decisive battle that halted the German advance near the Marne River, less than 48 km (30 mi) from Paris. The German forces had been encountering little resistance in their march on Paris. Then, supposedly because of an error in decoding an order, they wheeled to the southeast. Joseph Simon Gallieni, the military governor of Paris, persuaded the French commander in chief, Joseph Jacques Césaire Joffre, to attack the flank thus exposed. Joffre ordered troops rushed to the front by all available means, including taxicabs, and the Allied attack was begun on September 6. By September 9 the German armies had retreated, and the threat to Paris was ended.
Second Battle of the Marne. (July 15-Aug. 4, 1918), the action that marked the turning point of the war. The Germans, according to Gen. Erich Ludendorff's plan, attacked to the east and west of Reims. West of Reims they crossed the Marne but made little subsequent progress. On July 18 the Allied commander general Ferdinand Foch counterattacked with forces that included several American divisions. One of the centers of fiercest combat was at Château-Thierry, where the American troops won their first decisive victory. The German armies were forced back across the Marne. This counterattack destroyed Ludendorff's plan for a massive attack in Flanders and gave the Allies the initiative thereafter.

MARONITES, Christian community of Arabs, centered in Lebanon and in communion with the pope. Smaller Maronite groups also exist in Cyprus, Palestine, Syria, and the U.S.; their total number worldwide is about 1.3 million. In the 7th century Maronites adhered to the heresy of Monothelitism (q.v.); in the 12th century they reestablished communion with the Western church. Ruled autonomously by the patriarch of Antioch, in Lebanon, Maronites use a liturgy, the Antiochene rite recited in the Syriac language, with elements from the Latin rite. In 1966 the Holy See erected an exarchate (province) for the Maronites in the U.S. The exarch, or delegate of the patriarch of Antioch, resides in Detroit, Mich. Maronites in the U.S. number about 150,000. According to the Oriental Code of Canon Law (1957), celibacy is not a general law for the Maronite clergy but is regulated in accordance with the particular law of the region or country.

MAROT, Clément (c. 1496-1544), French poet, born in Cahors. Writing lilting *rondeaux, ballades,* and epigrams earned Marot a good reputation and the patronage of Francis I and his sister,

Margaret of Navarre. His best poems include *L'adolescence Clémentine* (1532) and *Enfer* (1542), which he wrote while exiled for heresy. He is also noted for a French translation (1541–43) of the Psalms.

MARPRELATE CONTROVERSY, religious controversy of the late 16th century that developed in England. It rose from an attack on the authoritarianism of the Church of England, in the form of satirical pamphlets issued in 1588 and 1589 by a Puritan writer, or group of writers, under the pen name Martin Marprelate. Much literature was published both defending and attacking Martin Marprelate. The Puritan author John Penry (1559–93) is believed to have been the major contributor to the Marprelate tracts; the writers John Lyly and Thomas Nashe were among those who responded in defense of the church.

MARQUESAS ISLANDS, island group, French Polynesia (an overseas territory of France), in the S Pacific Ocean. The 10 volcanic islands of the group are mountainous and fertile; breadfruit, coconut, and tobacco are grown here. Hivaoa, the largest island of the group, is the site of the grave of the French painter Paul Gauguin. Nukuhiva, the second largest, contains the administrative seat, Hakapehi. The islands were annexed by France in 1842. Total area, 1274 sq km (492 sq mi); pop. (1988) 7538.

MARQUETRY. *See* VENEER.

MARQUETTE, city, seat of Marquette Co., N Michigan, in the Upper Peninsula, on Lake Superior; inc. as a city 1871. It is the port for iron ore produced nearby and the commercial, cultural, and administrative center of a tourist and dairying region. Mining equipment and chemicals are manufactured here. Marquette is the home of Northern Michigan University (1899) and a large wooden-domed sports training complex. Nearby are Hiawatha National Forest and Pictured Rocks National Lakeshore. Founded in 1849, when the first iron forge was erected, the community was named in 1850 for the 17th-century French missionary and explorer Jacques Marquette. Pop. (1980) 23,288; (1990) 21,977.

MARQUETTE, Jacques, known as Père Marquette (1637–75), French missionary and explorer in America, born in Laon, in northern France. He landed at Québec in the New World in 1666 and passed the next 18 months studying Indian languages. He founded a mission at Sault Sainte Marie (now in Michigan) in 1668 and served at La Pointe (now in Wisconsin) from 1669 to 1671. The Sioux Indians forced him to flee to Mackinac (now in Michigan), where he founded a mission at Point Saint Ignace (now Saint Ignace). He was visited there by the French explorer Louis Jolliet, who invited him to take part in an expedition to chart the Mississippi River. Joined by five others, they set sail in May 1673. They entered the Mississippi on June 17 and were the first Europeans to travel on the river. Marquette later worked as a missionary among the Illinois Indians. His account of the Mississippi journey was posthumously published in 1681.

MARQUETTE UNIVERSITY, independent institution of higher learning in Milwaukee, Wis., under sponsorship of members of the Society of Jesus. It grew out of Saint Aloysius Academy (1857), was chartered as Marquette College in 1864, and held its first college classes in 1881. The present name was adopted and the charter amended in 1907. Divisions include continuing education and summer sessions; colleges of arts and sciences, business administration, engineering, nursing, communication, journalism, and performing arts; schools of dentistry, education, graduate studies, and law; and curricula in dental hygiene, medical technology, and physical therapy. The degrees of bachelor, master, and doctor are conferred in the arts, sciences, and professions.

MARQUIS, Don, full name DONALD ROBERT PERRY MARQUIS (1878–1937), American writer and columnist, born in Walnut, Ill. He first became successful with his column "The Sun Dial," which he began writing in 1912 for the *New York Sun*. He is best remembered for his satirical prose and poetry and for his creation of the character "archy the cockroach." His major books include *Hermione* (1916), *The Old Soak* (1921), *archy and mehitabel* (1927), *archy's life of mehitabel* (1933), and *archy does his part* (1935).

MARRAKECH, also Marrakesh, city, W Morocco, capital of Marrakech Province, on the fertile Haouz Plain, at the foot of the High Atlas Mts. The traditional S capital of the sultans and a major trade center, Marrakech is a rail terminus and a road and caravan center, connected with the Atlantic port of Safi. Industries include the processing of fruit, vegetables, and palms; tanning; and the manufacture of wool, flour, building materials, and handicrafts, notably leather goods and carpets. Lead, zinc, copper, molybdenum, and graphite mines are nearby, and the area is studded with date-palm oases. Of interest in the city are the ruined walls, twisting streets, and markets; the casino; the sultan's palace and gardens; the 12th-century Koutoubia mosque; the royal tombs; and Aguedal Park. Founded in 1062, Marrakech was capital of the Almoravides and, in the 12th century, capital of the Almohades. The city prospered under the later Saadis and was an important Saharan trade center. After the French occupation, the modern part of the city was built in 1913. The city was also called Morocco. Pop. (1982 prelim., greater city) 482,605.

MARRIAGE, social institution uniting men and women in special forms of mutual dependence for the purpose of founding and maintaining families. In view of the necessity for human offspring to undergo a long period of protracted development before attaining full maturity, the care of the young during their years of relative incapacity appears to have been the chief incentive for the evolution of the family structure. Marriage as a contract between a man and a woman has existed since ancient times, and as a social practice, entered into through a public act, it reflects the purposes, character, and customs of the society in which it is found.

Customs. Although marriage customs vary greatly from one culture to another, the importance of the institution is universally acknowledged. In some societies, community interest in the children, in the bonds between families, and in the property connections established by a marriage are such that special devices and customs are invoked to arrange for or protect these values. Infant betrothal or marriage, prevalent in places such as India and Melanesia, is a result of concern for family, caste, and property alliances. Levirate, according to which a man might marry the wife of his deceased brother, was a custom, practiced chiefly by the ancient Hebrews, that was designed to continue a connection already established. Sororate, a custom still practiced in remote parts of the world, permits a man whose wife is barren to marry one or more of her sisters. Monogamy, the union of one man and one woman, is the prototype of human marriage and its most widely accepted form, predominating also in societies in which other forms of marriage are accepted. All other forms of marriage are generally classed under polygamy, which includes both polygyny, in which one man has several wives, and polyandry, in which one woman has several husbands.

Under Islamic laws, one man may legally have as many as four wives, all of whom are entitled to equal treatment. Polygyny was practiced briefly in the U.S. during the 19th century by the Mormons in Utah. The incidence of polyandry is

A heavily veiled young bride of the Stara Zagora District of Bulgaria wears the elaborate wedding costume of her people. UPI

limited to Central Asia, southern India, and Sri Lanka in communities where, usually, the traditional practice of female infanticide resulted in a shortage of women. Frequently polygyny or polyandry involves a man or woman marrying two or more siblings. Polygyny sometimes results in the maintenance of separate households for each wife, although more frequently the shared-household system is employed, as with Muslims and among many North American Indian tribes before the colonization of North America.

Ritual. In most societies, marriage is entered into through a contractual procedure, generally with some sort of religious sanction. In Western societies the contract of marriage is regarded as a religious sacrament, and it is indissoluble only in the Roman Catholic and Eastern Orthodox churches. Most marriages are preceded by a betrothal period, during which various ritual acts, such as exchanges of gifts and visits, lead to the final wedding ceremony and give publicity to the claims of the partners on one another. In societies where arranged marriages still predominate, the families concerned must negotiate dowries, future living arrangements, and other important matters before marriage can be arranged. Most wedding ceremonies involve rituals and symbolism that are concerned with the desire for fertility, such as the sprinkling of the bridal couple with rice, the bride's adornment with orange blossoms, and the circling of the sacred fire, which is part of the marriage ritual in Hinduism. Because marriage arouses apprehension as well as joy, Hindus, Buddhists, and many other communities consult astrologers before and after marriages are arranged to avoid unlucky times and places. In some societies fear of hostile spirits leads bridal couples to wear disguises at their weddings or sometimes even to send substitutes to the ceremony. In some countries, including Ethiopia, it was long customary to place an armed guard by the bridal couple during the wedding ceremony to protect them from demons.

The breaking of family or community ties implicit in most marriages is often expressed through gifts made to the family of the bride, as among many American Indian, African, and Melanesian tribes. The new bonds between the married couple are frequently represented, as in the U.S. and many other countries, by an exchange of rings or the joining of hands. Finally, the interest of the community is expressed in many ways, through feasting and dancing, and, in Christian communities, through the publishing of banns, the presence of witnesses, and the official sealing of marriage documents.

Social Regulation. The taboos and restrictions imposed on marriage throughout history have been many and complex. Endogamy, for example, limits marriage to partners who are members of the same tribe or the same section of a tribe, to adherents of the same religion, or to members of the same social class. Fear of incest is a universal restriction to the freedom of marriage, although definitions of incest have varied greatly throughout history. In most cases, the prohibition extends to mother and son, father and daughter, and all offspring of the same parents. Among certain groups, such as ancient Egyptian royalty, marriages between brothers and sisters were decreed by the prevailing religion. In many societies, taboos are broadened to include marriages between uncles and nieces, aunts and nephews, first cousins, and, occasionally, second cousins. Exogamy, or marriage outside a specific group, usually involves the separation of a tribe into two groups, within which intermarriage is not allowed. Practiced by American Indians and some other groups, it is believed to be an extension of taboos against incest to include much larger groups of people who may be related to one another.

The traditional importance of marriage can be observed in the customs surrounding widows and widowers, such as the times of waiting prescribed before remarriage, the wearing of mourning, and the performance of ceremonial duties owed to the dead. The most extreme custom, abolished by law in India in 1829, was that of suttee, in which Hinduism required that a widow immolate herself on her husband's funeral pyre.

Termination of Contract. Most societies have allowed for some form of divorce, except those dominated by religions such as Hinduism and Roman Catholicism that regard marriage as indissoluble. The most frequently accepted grounds for divorce have been infertility, infidelity, criminality, and insanity. Among some Hindus, an unsatisfactory wife can be replaced by another but cannot be divorced. In primitive societies divorce is uncommon, mainly because it generally requires the repayment of dowries, purchase prices, and other monetary and material exchanges dating from the time of the wedding.

Modern Marriage. Because the family unit provides the framework for most human social activity, and since it is the foundation on which social organization is based in most cultures, marriage is closely tied to economics, law, and religion. The sociocultural implications of marriage, sexuality, family, and parent-progeny relations today form an important branch of behavioral science, generally known as social hy-

In the 1980s there was a distinct trend toward more formal church weddings and elaborate receptions.
Tom Kelly

giene. This field of empirical research attempts a correlation and analysis of these phenomena in all their aspects in an effort to preserve and improve the family as a social institution.

The institution of marriage has altered fundamentally in Western societies as a result of social changes brought about by the Reformation and the Industrial Revolution. The rise of a strong middle class and the growth of democracy gradually brought tolerance for romantic marriages based on the free choice of the partners involved. Arranged marriages, which had been the accepted form of marriage almost everywhere throughout history, eventually ceased to predominate in Western societies, although they continued to persist as the norm in aristocratic society to the mid-20th century. The most extreme application of the custom of arranged marriages was in prerevolutionary China, where a bride and groom often met for the first time only on their wedding day. Among the social changes that have affected marriage in modern times are the increase in premarital sexual intercourse occasioned by the relaxation of sexual taboos and the gradual rise in the average marriage age; the increase in the number of wives pursuing careers outside the home, which has led to the changed economic status of women; and the liberalization of divorce laws, including the legalization of divorce for the first time in Italy in 1970. Also significant have been the legalization of abortion, the improvement and increased accessibility of contraceptives, the removal of legal and social handicaps for illegitimate children, and rapid changes in the accepted concepts of male and female roles in society.

Common-law marriages usually are those that have acquired legal status through a certain number of years of continuous cohabitation. Such marriages are recognized in some states of the U.S. Requirements for marriage vary from state to state. The legal age for marriage with parental consent ranges from 12 for women and 14 for men in some states to 16 for women and 18 for men in others. The required age for marriage without parental consent varies from 16 to 21 for women to 18 to 21 for men. A blood test for syphilis is now required by most states, and many states require a waiting period of from one to five days between the issuing of the marriage license and the wedding ceremony. Bigamy and polygamy are prohibited in all states, and many states prohibit marriage between first cousins. In most states it is required that the marriage be formalized before a minister of religion, or before a qualified public official in a ceremony usually referred to as a civil marriage, and in all states a marriage certificate must be registered with the civil authorities.

For further information on this topic, see the Bibliography in volume 28, sections 152–54.

MARRIAGE, ANNULMENT OF. See ANNULMENT OF MARRIAGE.

MARROW. See BONE.

MARRYAT, Frederick, known as Captain Marryat (1792–1848), English novelist and seaman, born in London. He joined the British navy in 1806 and retired as a captain in 1830. He then began to write about adventures at sea. His books include *Frank Mildmay* (1829), *Peter Simple* (1834), *Mr. Midshipman Easy* (1836), *Snarleyyow* (1837), and *Diary in America* (1839).

MARS, in Roman mythology, god of war, the son of Jupiter, king of the gods, and of his wife, Juno. One of the most important Roman deities, Mars was regarded as the father of the Roman people, because he was the father of Romulus, the legendary founder of Rome. Originally a god of the year, especially of the spring, Mars was identified by the Romans with the Greek god of war, Ares. The month of March was named for him.

MARS, planet in the solar system (q.v.), named for the Roman god of war. It is the fourth planet from the sun and the third in order of increasing mass. Mars has two small, heavily cratered moons, Phobos and Deimos, which some astronomers consider asteroidlike objects captured by the planet very early in its history. Phobos is about 21 km (about 13 mi) across; Deimos, only about 12 km (about 7.5 mi).

Appearance from Earth. When viewed without a telescope, Mars is a reddish object of considerably varying brightness. At its closest approach to earth (55 million km/34 million mi), Mars is, after Venus, the brightest object in the night sky. Mars is best observed when it is at opposition (directly opposite the sun in earth's sky) and also at its closest distance from earth. Such favorable circumstances repeat about every 15 years when the planet comes to perihelion (its closest approach to the sun) almost exactly at opposition. The last perihelic opposition occurred in 1971.

Through a telescope Mars can be seen to have bright orange regions and darker, less red areas, the outlines and tones of which change with Martian seasons. (Because of the tilt of its axis and the eccentricity of its orbit, Mars has short, relatively warm southern summers and long, relatively cold southern winters.) The reddish color of the planet results from its heavily oxidized, or rusted, surface. The dark areas are thought to consist of rocks similar to terrestrial basalts, the surfaces of which have been weathered and oxidized. The brighter areas seem to consist of similar but even more weathered and oxidized material that apparently contains more fine, dust-sized particles than do the dark regions. The mineral scapolite, relatively rare on earth, seems widespread; it may serve as a store for carbon dioxide (CO_2) in the atmosphere.

Conspicuous bright caps, apparently made of frost or ice, mark the planet's polar regions. Their seasonal cycle has been followed for almost two centuries. Each Martian autumn, bright clouds form over the appropriate pole. Below this so-called polar hood, a thin cap of carbon dioxide frost is deposited during autumn and winter. By late winter, the cap may extend down to latitudes of 45°. By spring, and the end of the long polar night, the polar hood dissipates, revealing the winter frost cap; the cap's boundary then gradually recedes poleward as sunlight evaporates the accumulated frost. By midsummer the steady recession of the annual cap stops, and a bright deposit of frost and ice survives until the following autumn. These remnant polar caps are believed to consist mostly of frozen water. They are 300 km (185 mi) wide at the south pole and 1000 km (620 mi) wide in the north. Although their true thickness is not known, they must contain frozen gases and water vapor to a thickness of possibly 2 km (1.3 mi).

In addition to the polar hoods—presumed to

COMPARISON OF MARS AND EARTH

	Mars	Earth
Distance from sun		
Perihelion	1.38 AU	0.98 AU
Mean	1.52 AU	1.00 AU
Aphelion	1.66 AU	1.02 AU
(1 AU, or astronomical unit = 149,600,000 km, or 92,956,000 mi)		
Orbital period (earth days)	687	365.3
Eccentricity of orbit	0.093	0.017
Spin period (length of day)	24 hr 37 min	23 hr 56 min
Tilt of axis	23°27'	23°59'
Radius	3390 km (2100 mi)	6371 km (3960 mi)
Mean density	3.9 gm/cu cm (2.3 oz/cu in)	5.5 gm/cu cm (3.2 oz/cu in)
Surface gravity	0.38	1.00
Atmospheric pressure at surface	4.6 torrs	760 torrs
Mean surface temperature	−23° C (−9° F)	22° C (72° F)
Natural satellites	2	1

consist of clouds of frozen carbon dioxide—other clouds are common on the planet. High-altitude hazes and localized water ice clouds are observed. The latter result from the cooling associated with lifting air masses over elevated obstacles. Extensive yellow clouds, consisting of dust lifted by Martian winds, are especially prominent during southern summers.

Observation by Spacecraft. The most detailed knowledge of Mars has come from six missions carried out by unmanned U.S. spacecraft between 1964 and 1976. The first views of Mars were obtained by *Mariner 4* in 1964, and further information was gained by the flyby missions of *Mariners 6* and *7* in 1969. The first Mars orbiter—*Mariner 9*, launched in 1971—studied the planet for almost a year, giving planetary scientists their first comprehensive global view of the planet and the first detailed images of its two moons. In 1976 two Viking lander craft touched down successfully on the surface and carried out the first direct investigations of the atmosphere and surface. The second Viking lander ceased operating in April 1980; the first lander worked until November 1982. The Viking mission also included two orbiters that studied the planet for almost two full Martian years. The Soviet Union in 1988 sent two probes to land on the moon Phobos; both missions failed, although one relayed back some data and photographs before being lost to radio contact.

Atmosphere. The Martian atmosphere consists of carbon dioxide (95 percent), nitrogen (2.7 percent), argon (1.6 percent), oxygen (0.2 percent), and trace amounts of water vapor, carbon monoxide, and noble gases (q.v.) other than argon. The average pressure at the surface is near 4.6 torrs, which is 0.6 percent that on earth and equal

MARS

to the pressure at a height of 35 km (22 mi) in earth's atmosphere. Surface temperatures vary greatly with time of day, season, and latitude. Maximum summer temperatures may reach 290 K (63° F), but average daily temperatures at the surface do not exceed 240 K (−27° F). Due to the thinness of the atmosphere, daily temperature variations of 100° C (180° F) are common. Poleward of about 50° lat, temperatures remain cold enough (less than 150 K/−189° F) throughout winter for the atmosphere's major constituent, carbon dioxide, to freeze into the white deposits that make up the polar caps. The total atmospheric pressure on the surface fluctuates by about 30 percent due to the seasonal cycle of the polar caps.

The amount of water vapor present in the atmosphere is extremely slight and variable. The concentration of atmospheric water vapor is highest near the edges of the receding polar caps in spring. Mars is like a very cold, high-altitude desert. Surface temperatures are too cold and surface pressures too low for water to exist in the liquid state in most places on the planet. It has been suggested, however, that liquid water may exist just below the surface in a few localities.

At certain seasons, some areas on Mars are subject to winds strong enough to move sand on the surface and to suspend dust in the atmosphere. A major weather event occurs in the southern hemisphere between late spring and early summer when Mars is near perihelion and the heating of southern equatorial latitudes is most intense. Dust storms begin to form, and some reach global proportions, obscuring the planet's surface for weeks or even months. The dust entrained in these clouds is very fine and takes a long time to settle.

Surface and Interior. The Martian surface can be divided into two approximately hemispherical provinces by a great circle inclined at about 30° to the equator. The southern half consists of ancient cratered terrain dating from the planet's earliest history, when Mars and the other planets were subjected to a much more intense meteoroidal bombardment than is the case today. Considerable erosion and filling of even the largest craters have occurred since then.

The northern half of Mars has a much less cratered, and hence younger, surface, believed to consist of volcanic flows. Two major centers of past volcanic activity have been identified: the Elysium Plateau and the Tharsis bulge. Some of the solar system's largest volcanoes occur in Tharsis. Olympus Mons, a structure showing all the characteristics of a basaltic volcano, reaches an elevation of more than 25 km (15.5 mi) and measures more than 600 km (370 mi) across its base. No definite evidence exists of current volcanic activity anywhere on the planet.

Faults and other features suggestive of crustal fracture due to local bulging and expansion are

The large, bright area at the lower left of this Viking 1 *orbiter photograph is near the south pole and probably results from frost cover. The bright area at the top of the disk is caused by cloud activity near the Tharsis bulge.* NASA

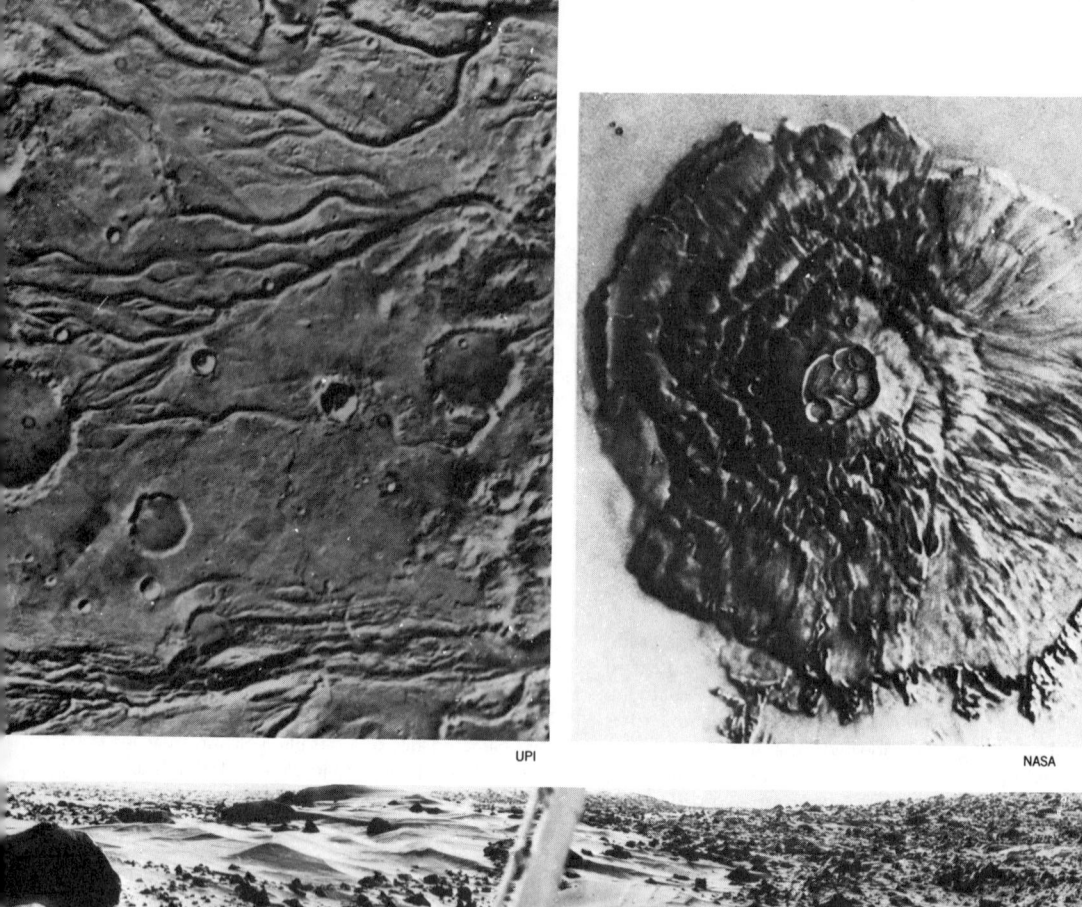

Photographs of Martian features, relayed by spacecraft. Top, left: Channels across the cratered terrain of Lunae Planum, near the equator, were carved by a massive flood, the source of which is not known. Sharp young ridges on some Martian channels raise the possibility of periodic flash flooding from melted subsurface permafrost. Top, right: View from above of Olympus Mons, largest volcano on Mars, measuring more than 25 km (15.5 mi) high and more than 600 km (370 mi) across. The gigantic size of Martian volcanoes may be due to the absence of crustal plates; on earth plate movements shift volcanoes away from hot spots in the mantle and end their growth. Bottom: Panoramic view from Viking 1 lander of dune field on Chryse Planita. The features are remarkably similar to many deserts on earth. Large boulder at left is about 1 by 3 m (about 3 by 10 ft).

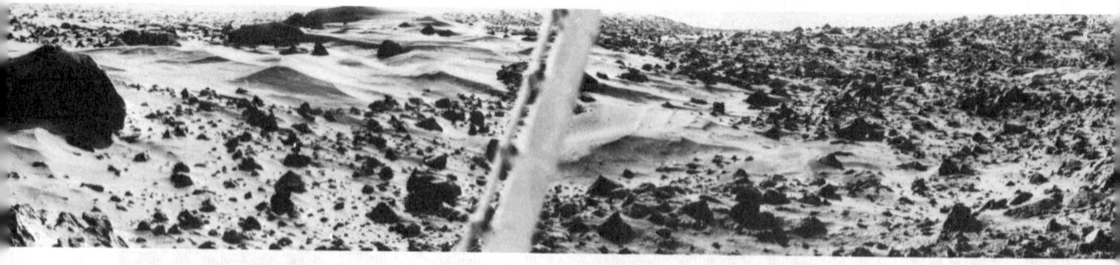

widespread on Mars. On the other hand, no features due to large-scale compression have been found. Specifically, folded mountain belts, so common on earth, are lacking, indicating an absence of plate tectonics. This suggests, in turn, that Mars may have a thicker crust and a cooler thermal history than earth. An escarpment near the Martian equator that was studied in 1988, however, may prove to be a strike-slip fault, which would indicate some plate-tectonic activity, after all.

Evidence of subsurface ice prevails, especially in the form of petal-shaped ejecta blankets around some craters, vast areas of collapsed chaotic terrain, and so-called patterned ground at high northern latitudes. By far the most spectacular geologic discovery has been the channels that superficially resemble the valleys of dried-up rivers. Two major types are known. Large outflow channels may have been formed by the sudden catastrophic release of vast amounts of liquid water from areas of collapsed chaotic terrain. Most of these channels drain from the higher southern hemisphere to the generally lower northern hemisphere. The cause of the localized melting of the ground ice in the source areas remains uncertain, but these features probably date from the first third of the planet's 4.6-billion-year history. In addition to the large outflow channels, there are numerous small channellike features for which evidence of erosion by liquid water is less compelling, but possible. Because liquid water cannot exist on the surface of the planet today, the channels have been singled out as proof that Mars had higher pressures and warmer temperatures in the past.

Today, however, Mars is a windblown desert. Vast expanses of sand dunes and other wind-formed erosional features abound, all attesting to the efficacy of both depositional and erosional wind processes in the current Mars environment.

Little is known about the interior of Mars. The planet's relatively low mean density indicates that Mars cannot have an extensive metallic core. Furthermore, any core that may be present is probably not fluid, because Mars does not have a measurable magnetic field. Judging from its ability to support such massive topological features as Tharsis, the crust of Mars may be as thick as 200 km (125 mi)—five or six times as thick as earth's crust. A seismometer on board *Viking 2* lander failed to detect any definite "Marsquakes."

The Search for Life. The idea that life can or even does exist on Mars has a long history. In 1877 the Italian astronomer Giovanni Schiaparelli claimed to have seen a planetwide system of channels. The American astronomer Percival Lowell then popularized these faint lines as canals and held them out as proof of a vast attempt by intelligent beings to irrigate an arid planet. Subsequent spacecraft observations have shown that there are no canals on the planet, and various other alleged proofs of life on Mars have turned out to be equally illusory. Not only are there no canals, but dark areas once thought to be oases are not green, and their spectra contain no evidence of organic materials. The seasonal changes in the appearance of these areas are not due to any vegetative cycle, but to seasonal Martian winds blowing sterile sand and dust. Water probably occurs only as ice on or below the surface or as trace amounts of vapor or ice crystals in the atmosphere. The strongest evidence against the presence of life, however, is the thinness of the atmosphere and the fact that the surface of the planet is exposed not only to lethal doses of ultraviolet radiation (q.v.) but also to the effects of highly oxidizing substances (such as hydrogen peroxide) produced by photochemistry.

Perhaps the most fundamental and far-reaching information obtained by the Viking landers is that the soil contains no organic material (there is no reason to assume that the two landing sites are not representative of Mars). Although small amounts of organic molecules are continually being supplied to the surface of Mars by carbonaceous meteorites, apparently this material is destroyed before it has a chance to accumulate. The results of the soil analysis for organic molecules carried out by the Viking landers provide no evidence for the existence of life.

A more difficult question is whether life ever existed on Mars, given the strong evidence of climatic change and the indications of a previously warmer, thicker atmosphere. Answering this question will probably involve collecting carefully selected subsurface samples and returning them to earth for detailed analysis. The U.S. National Aeronautics and Space Administration has proposed a manned voyage to Mars early in the 21st century. J.F.V.

For further information on this topic, see the Bibliography in volume 28, sections 382, 384.

MARSALA (anc. *Lilybaeum*), city and seaport of Italy, at the W tip of Sicily, on the Mediterranean Sea. Marsala trades in grain and salt, and is well known for its sweet Marsala wine. Here, in 1860, the Italian nationalist Giuseppe Garibaldi began his conquest of the kingdom of the Two Sicilies. Pop. (1990 est.) 80,900.

MARSEILLAISE, LA, French national anthem, the words and tune of which were written in 1792, by the French army engineer Claude Joseph Rouget de Lisle (1760–1836), in Strasbourg. It got its name *La marseillaise* after it was adopted by the troops from Marseille who took part in the storming of the Tuileries in Paris in the French Revolution. Designated the national anthem on July 14, 1792, it was banned twice in the 19th century for its revolutionary associations.

MARSEILLE or **MARSEILLES**(Gr. *Massalia;* Lat. *Massilia*), city, S France, capital of Bouches-du-Rhône Department, on the Gulf of Lions (an arm of the Mediterranean Sea). The second largest city of France, it is a major seaport and an important commercial and industrial center. The city is linked by canal with the Rhône R. and is served by extensive rail and air transport facilities; the large petroleum port of Fos, chiefly developed in the 1970s, is nearby. Manufactures include iron and steel, chemicals, plastic and metal products, ships, refined petroleum, construction materials, soap, and processed food.

In the bay fronting Marseille are several islands, including the islet of If, site of the 16th-century Château d'If, mentioned in *The Count of Monte Cristo,* by the French novelist Alexandre Dumas *père*. Several forts protect the harbor, and on a high strip of land projecting W into the bay is the 19th-century Church of Notre Dame de la Garde. The main thoroughfare, Canebière, is one of the great avenues of the world. Marseille has few ancient relics, although it is the oldest city in France. In the late 1960s archaeologists uncovered parts of the Hellenistic ramparts, and a section of the medieval Cathedral of La Major still stands. In the 11th-century crypts, over which the Church of Saint Victor was built in the 13th century, is an image of the Virgin Mary supposed to have been done by St. Luke. Educational and cultural facilities in the city include the universities of Aix-Marseille I and II (1970) and museums of archaeology, shipping, and fine arts.

About 600 BC the site of the city was colonized by Greeks from Asia Minor and called Massalia. The settlement flourished, and in the Punic Wars it sided with Rome against Carthage. In 49 BC, after supporting Pompey the Great in the civil war against Julius Caesar, the city was annexed by Rome. The inhabitants were converted to Christianity during the 3d century AD, and in 304 St. Vincent was martyred here. In the 10th century it became a dominion of the counts of Provence, and in the 13th century it was made a republic. The city was incorporated into the kingdom of France in 1481.

Commerce at the port increased in the 18th century, before suffering a severe setback during the French Revolution and the Napoleonic Wars. After 1850 port facilities were greatly expanded, and many industries were established at Marseille. The city was occupied and badly damaged by the Germans in World War II. Subsequently, major construction programs transformed Marseille into a modern community with many high-rise buildings. Pop. (1990) 807,726.

MARSH, Othniel Charles (1831–99), American paleontologist, who discovered numerous dinosaur fossils in the western U.S. Born in Lockport, N.Y., he was educated at Yale University and in Germany. He then became a professor (1866–99) at Yale, where his finds are now housed in the Peabody Museum of Natural History. Besides dinosaurs, his discoveries included fossils of the primitive bird *Hesperornis*, the flying reptiles called pterodactyls, and early ancestors of the horse. Marsh was a strong early proponent of Charles Darwin's evolutionary theory.

MARSH, Reginald (1898–1954), American painter, whose pictures of the raffish aspects of New York City life have a Hogarthian liveliness. His works, for all their slapdash exuberance and piled-on detail, are skillfully composed and carefully drawn. After working as a magazine illustrator in the 1920s, he went on to paint his most characteristic work—street scenes, crowds, and honky-tonks. In the 1930s, Marsh also executed a series of large murals in the rotunda of the U.S. Custom House in New York City.

MARSHALL, Alfred (1842–1924), British economist, born in Wandsworth, England, and educated at Saint John's College, University of Cambridge. His interest in philosophy led him to the study of ethics. After his appointment to a special lectureship in moral science at St. John's in 1868, Marshall turned to the study of political economy, to which he later gave the name *economics*. In 1875 he went to the U.S. to observe the effects of tariff protection. He returned to England and became the first principal of University College at Bristol, then taught at the University of Oxford and the University of Cambridge. Marshall, the foremost British economist of his time, exerted a strong influence on the following generation of economists; his principal contribution to economics lay in systematizing classical economic theories and in developing a concept of marginal utility. He emphasized the importance of detailed analysis and adjustment of theory to emerging facts. Marshall's writings include *Principles of Economics* (1890) and *Industry and Trade* (1919).

MARSHALL, George Catlett (1880–1959), American military commander, army chief of staff during World War II; as secretary of state (1947–49) he played an important role in aiding the postwar economic recovery of Western Europe.

Marshall was born on Dec. 31, 1880, in Uniontown, Pa., and was educated at Virginia Military Institute. He was commissioned a second lieutenant in the infantry in 1901 and served in the Philippine Islands from 1902 to 1903. During World War I he served as chief of operations with the U.S. First Army in France and received wide recognition for his handling of troops and equipment during the Saint Mihiel and Meuse-Argonne operations. From 1919 to 1924 he was aide to the U.S. commander in chief, Gen. John Pershing, and during the next three years he saw service in China. Marshall taught in various army schools and organizations from 1927 to 1936.

In 1939 Marshall was appointed U.S. army chief of staff with the rank of general. He directed U.S. preparations for war over the next two years, and after the nation's entry into World War II in December 1941 he was chiefly responsible for the training, organization, and deployment of U.S. troops in all sectors of the fighting, and for the appointment of commanders in all major operations. As one of President Franklin D. Roosevelt's principal advisers on strategy, Marshall participated in the Allied conferences at Casablanca, Québec, Tehran, Yalta, and Potsdam. In

1944 he was promoted to the rank of General of the Army. When he retired in 1945, President Harry S. Truman appointed him special representative, with the rank of ambassador, to China. He spent two years in China attempting to mediate the differences between the Chinese Communist and Nationalist leaders, but was unsuccessful. In 1947 Marshall succeeded James Francis Byrnes as U.S. secretary of state and initiated the so-called Marshall Plan (see EUROPEAN RECOVERY PROGRAM), by which the U.S. provided economic assistance to strengthen anti-Communist elements in the war-torn countries of Western Europe. Marshall was secretary of defense in 1950–51. He won the 1953 Nobel Peace Prize for his contribution to European recovery. Marshall died in Washington, D.C., on Oct. 16, 1959.

MARSHALL, John (1755–1835), American jurist and statesman, who as the fourth chief justice of the U.S. was principally responsible for developing the power of the U.S. Supreme Court and formulating constitutional law in the nation.

Marshall was born in Germantown, Va., on Sept. 24, 1755, the eldest of 15 children. His childhood was spent under pioneer conditions in Fauquier Co., Va., and his parents provided his early education. Marshall served in the American Revolution, first as a lieutenant and then as a captain. He received his only formal education in 1779, when he briefly studied law at the College of William and Mary. Admitted to the bar in 1780, he began practice in the West. Two years later he moved to Richmond, Va., and was soon a leader among Virginia lawyers.

Early Career. As a member of the Virginia Assembly (1782–91), Marshall worked for ratification of the U.S. Constitution and became a prominent member of the Federalist party. In 1795 he turned down George Washington's appointment of U.S. attorney general; he later declined appointment as a minister to France. After Marshall's second term in the Virginia Assembly (1795–97), however, Washington prevailed upon him to serve as a member of a commission to arbitrate diplomatic affairs with France (see XYZ AFFAIR). Although the mission failed, Marshall's activities in this dispute made him a popular figure and earned him a monetary reward from Congress. He was elected to the U.S. House of Representatives in 1799, where he acted as spokesman for the Federalist party. In 1800 he became secretary of state in the cabinet of President John Adams, and a year later Adams appointed him chief justice of the U.S. Marshall held this office for 34 years until his death.

The Chief Justice. The most important judicial figure in U.S. history, Marshall is justly famed as the "great chief justice." Before his appointment to the bench, the Supreme Court was regarded as ineffectual. By the force of his personality and the wisdom of his decisions, Marshall raised the Court to a position of great power in the federal government. He succeeded in making it the ultimate authority in constitutional matters.

The first and perhaps most important of Marshall's great cases was *Marbury* v. *Madison* (1803), which established once and for all the right of judicial review. The decision upheld the Court's power to review legislation and to overrule acts of Congress and of state legislatures that it considered unconstitutional. The power of judicial review was fundamental to Marshall's interpretation of constitutional doctrine.

Marshall and the Court followed this with decisions that made sure federal law would be exercised under a unified judicial system. In *Fletcher* v. *Peck* (1810) the Court ruled that a state could not arbitrarily interfere with an individual's property rights. *Dartmouth College* v. *Woodward* (1819) reaffirmed the inviolability of a state's contract (see DARTMOUTH COLLEGE CASE).

One of the most famous cases to come before the Court during Marshall's tenure was *McCulloch* v. *Maryland* (1819), which established the principle that the Constitution granted certain implied powers to Congress—in this case, the power to create a U.S. bank. The importance of this decision was in its affirmation of a broad interpretation of the Constitution, thus making it a flexible instrument to support the federal government.

In *Cohens* v. *Virginia* (1821) the Supreme Court again upheld its right to overrule state action that violated the Constitution. *Gibbons* v. *Ogden* (1824) confirmed congressional control over foreign and interstate commerce. These cases and others during Marshall's tenure made up a body of judicial rulings that generally favored federal power as opposed to states' rights.

Marshall's judicial activities brought him into conflict with several presidents. His quarrels with Thomas Jefferson peaked in 1807 when Marshall presided at the treason trial of the former vice-president Aaron Burr. President Jefferson, who had publicly condemned Burr before the trial, was hoping for a speedy conviction. According to Marshall's interpretation of the Constitution, however, conviction for treason required proof of an overt treasonous act, rather than only proof of engaging in a conspiracy (see TREASON). Burr was acquitted in a generally unpopular decision.

Although Marshall's decisions were controversial, his personal integrity, wit, and charm made him much admired even among his enemies. His legal opinions were characterized by a precise and lucid style, literary skill, and thorough, logi-

MARSHALL

cal analysis. He was the author of *Life of George Washington* (5 vol., 1804–7). Marshall died in Philadelphia on July 6, 1835. According to tradition, the Liberty Bell cracked while being tolled in mourning for him.

See also SUPREME COURT OF THE UNITED STATES.

For further information on this person, see the section Biographies in the Bibliography in volume 28.

MARSHALL, Thomas Riley (1854–1925), 28th vice-president of the U.S., born in North Manchester, Ind., and educated at Wabash College. He practiced law in Columbia City, Ind. From 1909 to 1913 he was governor of Indiana, and from 1913 to 1921 he was vice-president under President Woodrow Wilson. Marshall is perhaps most famous for his remark made during a Senate debate: "What this country needs is a good five-cent cigar."

MARSHALL, Thurgood (1908–93), American jurist, civil rights leader, and associate justice of the U.S. Supreme Court (1967–91).

Marshall was born in Baltimore, Md., July 2, 1908, and educated at Lincoln University, Pennsylvania, and at Howard University Law School. Marshall first practiced law in Baltimore, specializing in civil rights cases. He moved to New York City, serving the National Association for the Advancement of Colored People (NAACP) as special counsel (1938–50) and as director and counsel of the NAACP Legal Defense and Education Fund (1938–61).

He was admitted to practice before the U.S. Supreme Court in 1939. He won 29 of the 32 cases he pleaded before the Court, most in the field of civil rights. Perhaps his major victory was the 1954 Court decision banning racial segregation in public schools (see EDUCATION IN THE UNITED STATES). He

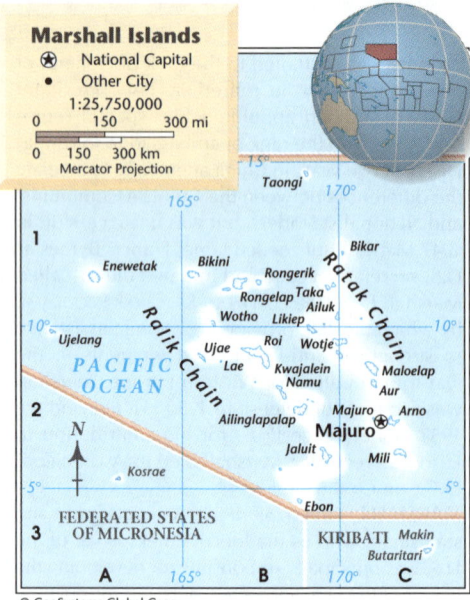

Thurgood Marshall — UPI

Marshall Islands: Map Index

Cities and Towns

Majuro, *capital* C2

Other Features

Ailinglapalap, *island* .. B2
Ailuk, *island* B1
Arno, *island* C2
Aur, *island* C2
Bikar, *island* C1
Bikini, *island* B1
Ebon, *island* B3
Enewetak, *island* A1
Jaluit, *island* B2
Kwajalein, *island* B2
Lae, *island* B2
Likiep, *island* B1
Majuro, *island* C2
Maloelap, *island* C2
Mili, *island* C2
Namu, *island* B2
Ralik, *island chain* A1
Ratak, *island chain* B1
Roi, *island* B2
Rongelap, *island* B1
Rongerik, *island* B1
Taka, *island* B1
Taongi, *island* B1
Ujae, *island* B2
Ujelang, *island* A2
Wotho, *island* B1
Wotje, *island* B2

served in the U.S. Second Circuit Court of Appeals from 1961 to 1965 and as U.S. solicitor general from 1965 to 1967. In October 1967, appointed by President Lyndon B. Johnson, he was sworn in as the first black member of the Supreme Court. He remained a stalwart defender of civil rights and individual liberties until his retirement in 1991.

MARSHALL ISLANDS, republic, central North Pacific Ocean. It is an archipelago comprising 34 islands in two groups: the SE Ratak Chain and the NW Ralik Chain. The chief industries are agriculture and fishing; the major exports are shells, copra, and fish. The islands are atolls and coral reefs, and the inhabitants are Marshallese, a Micronesian people. Kwajalein is the largest atoll; Majuro (pop., 1988, 19,664) is the capital island. The U.S. dollar is the legal currency.

The islands were sighted by the Spanish in 1526 but remained essentially uncolonized until the late 19th century. They were a German protectorate from 1885 to 1914, when they fell to Japan. In 1920 the archipelago was mandated to Japan. In February 1944 American forces took Majuro, the first Japanese possession captured in World War II. Other islands were subsequently occupied. The archipelago remained under American military control for the duration of the war. In 1946 an American task force used Bikini (q.v.) atoll as a nuclear testing ground. The Marshalls became a trusteeship of the U.S. in 1947 and self-governing in 1979, with a locally drafted constitution, a popularly elected legislature, and a president. A compact of free association, delegating to the U.S. the responsibility for defense and approved by plebiscite in 1983, came into effect in 1986. The trusteeship was formally dissolved by the UN Security Council in 1990, and the country was admitted to the UN in 1991. Area, 181 sq km (70 sq mi); pop. (1993 est.) 50,000.

MARSHALL PLAN. See EUROPEAN RECOVERY PROGRAM.

MARSHALLTOWN, city, seat of Marshall Co., central Iowa, on the Iowa R.; inc. 1863. It is a commercial, transportation, and manufacturing center. Industrial control valves and measuring instruments, furnaces, air-conditioning equipment, corrugated containers, furniture, and pork products are manufactured. A community college is located here. The city was founded in 1853 and is named for Marshall, Mich. Pop. (1980) 26,938; (1990) 25,178.

MARSHALS SERVICE, law enforcement agency under the U.S. Department of Justice, responsible to the deputy attorney general, and made up of executive officers of the federal courts. Established in 1789, the service has at present one marshal in each federal judicial district, and numerous deputy marshals. The service cooperates with state and local law enforcement forces.

Duties of marshals and deputy marshals include enforcing federal and district court orders; custody and transportation of federal prisoners; providing security for court witnesses, federal judges, jurors, and attorneys; preserving order on federal property; and disbursing certain appropriated funds. A marshal has the authority, with or without a warrant, to arrest violators of federal law. The service also supports activities of the Department of Justice during civil disturbances.

MARSH GAS. See METHANE.

MARSHLAND

MARSHLAND, treeless land in which the water table is at, above, or just below the surface of the ground; marshlands are dominated by grasses, reeds, sedges, and cattails. These plants typify emergent vegetation, which has its roots in soil covered or saturated with water and its leaves held above water.

Types of Marshes. Marshes may be freshwater or salt. Freshwater marshes develop along the shallow margins of lakes and slow-moving rivers, forming when ponds and lakes become filled with sediment. Salt marshes occur on coastal tidal flats. Inland salt marshes occupy the edges of saline lakes. The nature of a marsh—its plant composition, species richness, and productivity—is strongly influenced by its relationship to surrounding ecosystems. They affect the supply of nutrients, the movement of water, and the type and deposition of sediment.

In the prairie pothole country of glaciated central North America, freshwater marshes undergo a cyclic renewal that is induced by periodic drought and dependent on the feeding habits of muskrats. The cycle begins with a nearly dry marsh in which seeds of aquatic plants germinate in the mud. When the marsh fills, the aquatic plants grow densely. Muskrats eat large areas of the emergent vegetation, creating patches of open water. This causes the shallow-water emergent species to decline, but the submerged and floating species persist. When the next drought

The great egret, Casmerodius albus, *pictured in the Louisiana wetlands, nests from southern Canada south through Central and South America and the West Indies. With its long legs it is well adapted to living in marshland.*
© 1981 Dan Guravich–Photo Researchers, Inc.

MARSHMALLOW

comes, the cycle begins again.

Salt marshes are best developed on the Atlantic coasts of North America and Europe. In eastern North America the low marsh is dominated by a single species, salt-marsh cordgrass. The high marsh consists of a short cordgrass called hay, spike grass, and glasswort. Glasswort is the dominant plant of Pacific Coast salt marshes.

Water and Vegetation Patterns. In some marshes, such as the saw-grass wetlands of the Everglades (q.v.) or in salt marshes that are swept twice daily by tidal floods, water flows like a sheet across the surface, and the terrain is typically dominated by one or two species of emergent vegetation. In other marshes the water flows in channels rather than in sheets, flooding only at times of snowmelt and heavy precipitation and bringing in nutrients and sediment. Such irregular deposition of sediments provides variations in water depth, thus creating conditions favorable for a variety of wetland species. Deep marsh water is colonized by aquatic submerged plants (pond weeds) and floating plants (pond lilies). Shallower water supports reeds and wild rice. Very shallow water supports sedges, bulrushes, and cattails.

As sediments and organic deposits raise the bottom of a marsh above the water table, aquatic vegetation is gradually replaced by shrubs and eventually by a terrestrial ecosystem of upland grasses or forest trees.

Importance. Freshwater marshes provide nesting and wintering habitats for waterfowl and shorebirds, muskrats, frogs, and many aquatic insects (see FRESHWATER LIFE). Salt marshes are wintering grounds for snow geese and ducks, a nesting habitat for herons and rails, and a source of nutrients for estuarine waters (see ESTUARY). Marshes are important in flood control, in sustaining high-water tables, and as settling basins to reduce pollution downstream. Despite their great environmental value, marshes are continually being destroyed by drainage and filling.

See also PEATLAND. R.L.S.

For further information on this topic, see the Bibliography in volume 28, section 445.

MARSHMALLOW, common name for a tall, leafy, perennial plant, *Althaea officinalis,* of the family Malvaceae (see MALLOW), native to eastern Europe. It has toothed, heart-shaped, or three-lobed leaves and clusters of showy, pinkish flowers about 2.5 cm (1 in) across; it reaches a height of up to 1.2 m (4 ft). In the U.S. the marshmallow grows wild in marshy areas as far west as Michigan and Arkansas. The roots of the marshmallow were once used to make a creamy confection, a pufflike imitation of which is popular in the U.S. today.

MARSH MARIGOLD, common name for a perennial herb, *Caltha palustris,* of the family Ranunculaceae (see BUTTERCUP). Marsh marigolds, which are often erroneously called cowslips, are native to marshes and wet places of the eastern U.S. and eastern Canada; they are also widely distributed in Eurasia. They are stocky plants, about 20 to 60 cm (about 8 to 24 in) high, which bear round, heart-shaped, or kidney-shaped leaves and bright, golden-yellow flowers.

The Brigantine National Wildlife Refuge, an extensive marshland in New Jersey, is visited by many migratory birds, including the snow geese shown here.

Dr. E. R. Degginger

Marsh marigold, Caltha palustris
© 1987 Gregory K. Scott–Photo Researchers, Inc.

The flowers have five to nine petallike sepals, no petals, many stamens, and five to ten pistils. The fruit is a many-seeded follicle. Slender and creeping kinds of marsh marigold are native to the colder parts of eastern North America.

MARSTON, John (c. 1575–1634), English dramatist, born in Coventry, and educated at the University of Oxford. His first works, under the pseudonym of W. Kinsayder, were the erotic poem *The Metamorphosis of Pigmalion's Image* and the collection of 12 bitter satires on the vice of the times, *The Scourge of Villanie;* both books were published in 1598. Among his other works are the melodrama *Antonio's Revenge* (1602) and the comedies *Dutch Courtezan* (1605) and *What You Will* (1607). Marston's exaggerated situations and bombastic diction were satirized by the playwright Ben Jonson; the literary quarrel was soon resolved and Marston dedicated his comedy *The Malcontent* (1604) to Jonson. In the comedy *Eastward Ho* (1605) Marston collaborated with Jonson and George Chapman. About 1609 he became an Anglican clergyman and from 1616 to 1631 was rector of Christchurch, Hampshire.

MARSTON MOOR, moor, N England, near York. On July 2, 1644, during the Civil War, it was the scene of a great victory of the Parliamentarians, led by Oliver Cromwell, over the Royalists.

MARSUPIAL, common name for any mammal of the large subclass Marsupialia, sometimes called Metatheria, most of which carry their young in an abdominal pouch after birth. All are native to Australia, Tasmania, and New Guinea except the opossums *(see* OPOSSUM); the shrew opossums of South America, family Caenolestidae; and the monito del monte of Chile, family Microbiotheriidae. Marsupials range from shrew size to the size of an adult human. Some smaller marsupials are the dunnarts, genus *Sminthopsis,* with about 12 species; the marsupial "mice" and "cats" and Tasmanian devil (q.v.) of the family Dasyuridae; the marsupial mole of the family Notoryctidae; the tree-inhabiting cuscus (*see* PHALANGER); the wallabies (*see* KANGAROO); the bandicoot (q.v.); the tiny, nocturnal, flying squirrellike gliders of the genus *Petaurus;* and the diurnal numbat, or banded anteater, genus *Myrmecobius.* Larger marsupials include the kangaroo, the koala, and the wombat (qq.v.).

Female marsupials have two vaginas, which share a common opening but do not fuse. The placenta is not well developed, as it is in all other except monotreme (q.v.) mammals. The birth canal forms from an opening that develops in the connective tissue between the two vaginas. The young are born in an incomplete state of development some two to five weeks after conception. Immediately after birth they enter the mother's abdominal pouch, in species that have pouches, or else simply anchor themselves to a teat, which expands to hold the young in place. They remain attached to a teat, inside a pouch or not, until old enough to forage for their own food. The penis of the male marsupial is forked, and the testes generally lie in front of the penis.

The oldest known marsupials lived in the Cretaceous period (q.v.). They spread widely, but were later reduced in numbers or eliminated by competing placental mammals that had filled many ecological niches. Only the opossums, caenolestids, and monito del monte persisted in territory inhabited by placental mammals in the New World, and the opossums were highly adaptable. Australia and the surrounding islands had fewer placental mammals than the larger continents; marsupials there underwent amazing evolutionary radiation.

See also MAMMAL.

For further information on this topic, see the Bibliography in volume 28, sections 460–61.

MARSYAS, in Greek mythology, one of the satyrs. He found the flute that Athena, the goddess of wisdom, had invented and later discarded because playing on it puffed out her cheeks and distorted her features. Marsyas became so accomplished a musician that he challenged Apollo, god of music, to a contest, the winner of which would have the right to punish the loser. The Muses awarded the victory to Apollo, who played the lyre. The god thereupon flayed Marsyas, from whose blood a river sprang.

MARTEL, Charles. *See* CHARLES MARTEL.

MARTEN, common name for several musteline carnivorous animals in the genus *Martes* and allied genera, of the family Mustelidae, which also contains weasels, skunks, and badgers. Martens are widely distributed throughout the northern hemisphere; they are valued for their thick fur. Martens are long and graceful ani-

The pine marten, Martes martes, *lives in the forests of Europe.* Bruce Coleman, Inc.

mals, with short legs, and toes armed with sharp claws. Martens live in hollows of trees when they are not in search of the rodents, birds, and birds' eggs that constitute their food. The common American species is the American sable, or American pine marten, *M. americana,* which is about 60 to 90 cm (about 12 to 36 in) in total length, with a tail about 20 cm (about 8 in) long. The animal is yellowish-chestnut in general body color, with darker feet, and orange or white on the throat and chest.

The American sable is extensively hunted and today survives in abundance only in areas where it is protected. About five young are produced in each litter. The baum marten (or pine marten), *M. martes,* with a yellow throat, and the stone marten (or beech marten), *M. foina,* with a white throat, are found in Europe and Asia. Other martens include the sable (q.v.) and the fisher, *M. pennanti,* which is dark brown and about 90 cm (36 in) long with a 46-cm (18-in) bushy tail.

For further information on this topic, see the Bibliography in volume 28, sections 461, 475, 633.

MARTHA'S VINEYARD, island, Dukes Co., SE Massachusetts, separated from Cape Cod by Vineyard Sound. It measures 32 km (20 mi) from W to E and 16 km (10 mi) from N to S. It is noted as a summer resort. Edgartown, the chief town, was a whaling center. The island, which still shows traces of colonial life, was settled in 1642. Pop. of Dukes Co. (1980) 8942; (1990) 11,639.

MARTÍ, José Julian (1853–95), Cuban writer and patriot, whose death in battle made him the martyred symbol of Cuban aspirations to independence.

Martí was born on Jan. 28, 1853, in Havana, where he received his primary education. At the age of 16 he was imprisoned in Cuba as a revolutionary and then banished to Spain. There he published the first of many pamphlets advocating Cuban independence from Spain and at the same time finished his education at the University of Saragossa; he earned a law degree in 1874. He subsequently went to France, Mexico, and Guatemala, where he taught for a while at the University of Guatemala. He returned to Cuba in 1878 but was banished again in 1879 for his continued revolutionary activities. While living in the U.S. from 1881 to 1895, Martí was active in the Cuban Revolutionary Party and founded its journal, *Patria* (1892). Planning an invasion of the island, he set out for Cuba with a group of armed revolutionaries in 1894, only to be intercepted in Florida and turned back. The following year, however, he reached Cuba, along with the independence hero Gen. Máximo Gómez y Báez (1826–1905). Martí was killed a month later (May 19, 1895) during a skirmish with Spanish troops at Dos Ríos.

As a writer Martí was a precursor of modernismo in Spanish letters; he was noted for his simple, fluent style and his personal, vivid imagery. His writings include numerous poems, essays, and a novel. His *Obras completas* (Complete Works), consisting of 73 volumes, was published from 1936 to 1953.

MARTIAL, full name MARCUS VALERIUS MARTIALIS (c. 40–c. 104), Spanish-Roman poet, one of the most noted writers of satiric epigrams in antiquity. His verses evoke a remarkably vivid and often unflattering picture of imperial Rome during the last half of the 1st century.

Martial was born in Bilbilis, Spain, and in about 64 went to Rome to seek his fortune. In Rome he led the life of an itinerant man of letters, encountering frequent financial difficulties. Among his friends he numbered many individuals prominent in letters or the legal profession, including Pliny the Younger, Juvenal, and Quintilian. Eventually, he won the patronage of the Roman emperors Titus and Domitian and became a member of the equestrian order.

Martial's *Liber Spectaculorum* (Book of Spectacles), his earliest surviving work, celebrates the performances presented by Titus at the opening of the Colosseum in 80. His later *Epigrams* (86–102), in 12 books, are the works on which his reputation rests. Short poems written in varied meters and stanzas, the epigrams are concerned with universal foibles and are marked by a cynical view of human nature and a clever, biting turn of phrase. After some 35 years in Rome, Martial went home in 98 to Spain, where he died.

MARTIAL ARTS

MARTIAL ARTS, various methods of unarmed combat, originally used in warfare in the Far East and shaped by Oriental philosophical concepts, notably Zen Buddhism (*see* ZEN).

In the early 6th century AD, Bodhidharma, an Indian priest and knight, brought Zen Buddhism to China along with a system of 18 self-defense exercises. The exercises evolved into a form of boxing, which spread, with Zen, throughout China and in the 12th century reached Japan.

The martial arts are popular in many parts of the world today as means of self-defense, law enforcement tactics, competitive sports, and exercises for physical fitness. Among them are karate (q.v.), kung fu, jujitsu, judo, aikido, tai chi chuan, sumo wrestling, and kendo.

Types and Techniques. In some forms of the martial arts practitioners customarily wear colored belts to denote rank. A white belt indicates a novice; a black belt signifies proficiency at various levels. The levels of black belt are designated by *dan* (Jap., "degree"). For example, first *dan*, or first degree black belt signifies beginning black belt; fifth *dan*, or fifth degree black belt, usually signifies a master.

Tactics basic to the martial arts include hand, arm, and foot blows; knee kicks; throws and trips; gripping or immobilizing; and blocks or parries using wrist, forearm, or elbow.

Kung fu (Chinese boxing) is, with karate, the most popularly known of all the martial arts. It employs kicks, strikes, throws, body turns, dodges, holds, crouches and starts, leaps and falls, handsprings and somersaults. These movements include more techniques involving the open hand, such as claws and rips, than those used in karate.

Jujitsu, or jiujitsu (from Jap. *Jū*, "gentle"), uses holds, chokes, throws, trips, joint locks, kicks, and *atemi* (strikes to vital body areas). The techniques are gentle only in the sense that they are directed toward deflecting or controlling an attack; they can maim or kill.

Judo is a popular wrestling form developed from jujitsu by Jigorō Kanō (1860–1938), a Japanese educator. Like jujitsu, it attempts to turn an attacker's force to one's own advantage. Techniques include throwing and grappling. Judo was first included in Olympic Games in 1964.

Aikido was, like judo, derived from jujitsu within the last century. In aikido, an attack is avoided with flowing, circular movements. The opponent can then be brought to the ground with painful, immobilizing joint locks. Aikido is, with tai chi chuan, the gentlest martial art and is not practiced as a competitive sport.

Tai chi chuan, more popularly referred to as tai chi, is an ancient Chinese exercise and fighting system, still practiced in China and elsewhere in the world, mainly for its health benefits. It employs slow, graceful movements that are stylized renditions of original arm and foot blows.

Sumo wrestling, a popular Japanese sport, prohibits kicking, gouging, hair pulling, and the like,

Martial arts experts demonstrate karate kicks. Karate, one of the best-known forms of unarmed self-defense, employs a variety of sharp blows of the feet and hands to subdue an opponent.
Mitchell B. Reibel–Sports Photo File

MARTIAL LAW

but allows such actions as pushing, pulling, slapping, throwing, and grappling.

Kendo, or Japanese fencing, is a sport derived from ancient sword fighting, now using bamboo swords.

Recent Popularity. Worldwide contemporary interest in the martial arts often focuses on their spiritual aspects, as means of increasing self-confidence, assertiveness, and concentration. Personal defense is also increasingly an important issue, particularly for women and the elderly. Special programs in many of the martial arts have been designed to train a smaller or more fragile person to handle a larger, stronger assailant. The martial arts have also recently become popular not only as competitive sports and as ways of maintaining physical fitness but as forms of self-expression, similar to dance or gymnastics. This is, in fact, the main purpose of *wu shu* (martial arts) as practiced today in China.

For further information on this topic, see the Bibliography in volume 28, section 801.

MARTIAL LAW, in the U.S., conduct in part or in whole of government in domestic territory by military agencies, with the consequent supersession of some or all civil agencies.

Martial law derives its justification from the need, when civil authority is inadequate, to use military force to suppress insurrection, riot, or disorder, or to deal with public calamity. Inasmuch as martial law is called forth by necessity, the extent and degree to which it may be employed and may supersede civil authority also are measured by necessity. In the U.S., the military force that is used may be furnished by either the federal or state government. Martial law in the U.S. is not a statutory body of law as is military law, which is the system of rules governing military personnel at all times. Although the U.S. Constitution and statutes set forth certain situations in which federal military force may be used to quell disorder, martial law is essentially a branch of the common law.

Martial Law and the Courts. The civil courts have the ultimate responsibility for determining the limits of martial law and whether or not those limits have been overstepped in particular cases. Yet for many years it was believed that the acts of the military were not subject to review by the civil courts, and that, once martial law was proclaimed, civil law was superseded and civilians became triable by military commissions. In part this belief was based on a statement by the U.S. Supreme Court in the case *Moyer* v. *Peabody,* which was decided in 1909. The court stated, "... the Governor's proclamation that a state of insurrection existed is conclusive of the fact."

Numerous state courts adopted this view and refused to hear cases involving martial law. In 1932, however, the Supreme Court in *Sterling* v. *Constantin* held as follows: "What are the allowable limits of military discretion, and whether or not they have been overstepped in a particular case, are judicial questions." Following that decision both state and federal courts have enjoined the use of military force where no justification was shown to exist.

Martial law in the U.S. may or may not involve the suspension of the privilege of the writ of habeas corpus. In many instances, the privilege of the writ has not been suspended, and judicial inquiry into the cause of a detention by the military has been held pursuant to a writ. In most such instances, however, the petitioner has been remanded to military custody by the court on a showing that the facts warranted detention. Inasmuch as martial law depends for its validity on necessity, a proclamation of martial law is not a prerequisite.

History. Martial law in the U.S. has been imposed mostly by state governments. The federal government expressly declared a state of martial law only during the American Civil War and in Hawaii during World War II; however, federal forces have been used in other instances to enforce law or suppress disorder without an express declaration of martial law having been made. The phrase *martial law* is not used in the U.S. Constitution; however, authority for the federal government to impose martial law has been found inferentially in the four following constitutional provisions: Article I, Section 9, which reads, "The privilege of the writ of habeas corpus shall not be suspended, unless when in cases of rebellion or invasion the public safety may require it"; Article IV, Section 4, which provides, in part, that "The United States ... shall protect each ... [state] on application of the Legislature, or of the Executive (when the Legislature cannot be convened) against domestic violence"; Article II, Section 3, which requires, in part, that the president "... take care that the laws be faithfully executed"; and Article I, Section 8, which provides Congress with the power "To provide for calling forth the militia to execute the laws of the Union, suppress insurrections, and repel invasions."

In the Civil War Abraham Lincoln suspended the privilege of the writ of habeas corpus by executive action before receiving authorization by a statute enacted early in 1863. By the consensus of present-day authority, federal suspension of the privilege of the writ requires congressional authorization. Because the military may detain suspects when necessary to the public safety, however, formal suspension of the privilege of the writ of habeas corpus is of little importance.

Trials of civilians by federal military commissions during the Civil War were held invalid by the Supreme Court in the celebrated case of *Ex parte Milligan*, decided in 1866. The case involved the arrest and trial in 1864 of the American civilian-pacifist Lambdin Milligan (1812–99) by a military commission in Indiana, which was not a theater of military operations and in which the courts were open and functioning. The court held that ". . . martial law cannot arise from a threatened invasion. The necessity must be actual and present; the invasion must be real, such as effectively closes the courts and deposes the civil administration . . . . Martial rule can never exist when the courts are open and in the proper and unobstructed exercise of their jurisdiction . . . ." The Court also held that the president may not institute trial by military commission, even in times of rebellion and civil war, in the absence of congressional legislation. Some trials of civilians in state military courts were sustained on the authority of *Moyer v. Peabody*, but the Hawaiian Organic Act, under which a valid state of federal martial law was declared in Hawaii during World War II, was held by the Supreme Court not to include the power to try civilians by military courts. Accordingly, the Court set aside such wartime trials in Hawaii.

In several instances the president has intervened in states to execute federal laws despite the objections of the governor of the state. Thus, President Grover Cleveland sent troops to Illinois over the objection of Gov. John Altgeld to keep the mails moving in the Pullman and railroad strike in 1895. In 1957 President Dwight D. Eisenhower, despite the protest of Gov. Orval Faubus (1910–94), sent federal troops to Little Rock, Ark., to enforce the order of a federal court that blacks be admitted to a high school formerly reserved for white students. Federal troops have been utilized to restore order in several instances when requested by a state, for example, in Colorado during the 1954 mine strikes.

International Aspects. In wartime, a nation may invoke martial law over its own territory as part of the war effort; such action is distinct from military occupation by an invading power. Martial law may also be invoked in cases of severe internal dissension or disorder, either by an incumbent government seeking to retain power or by a new government after a coup d'état. Often in the case of a military coup, military authorities take over the state administrative and judicial apparatus, and civil and political liberties are suspended. Nations experiencing significant periods of martial law during the 1970s and '80s included Chile, the Philippines, Poland, and Turkey.

MARTIN, common name for several birds of the family Hirundinidae (see SWALLOW). In British usage, members of the family with forked tails are called "swallows," and those that lack such tails are called "martins," hence the two British short-tailed species are called house martin (*Delichon urbica*) and sand martin (*Riparia riparia*); the latter is called bank swallow in America. This distinction is not used in the New World, where the term martin applies only to swallows of the genus *Progne*. There are several tropical species, but the only North American species is the purple martin, *P. subis*, which is about 20 cm (about 8 in) long. Adult males are entirely bluish black; females and young males have the forehead and underparts gray. They are highly colonial and readily accept apartment-style birdhouses.

MARTIN, Saint (c. 316–97), bishop of Tours and patron saint of France, who established monasticism in Gaul. Born the son of a Roman soldier in what is now Szombathely, Hungary, Martin became a Christian at the age of ten. Upon his discharge from the Roman army he went to Poitiers, France, and became a disciple of St. Hilary, bishop of Poitiers and a leading opponent of Arianism (q.v.). After a period in Italy, Martin rejoined Hilary and founded the first monastery in Gaul at Ligugé. In 371 Martin, against his will, was named bishop of Tours. As bishop, he established a monastery at Marmoutier that became an important religious center and continued his missionary work in Touraine and throughout Gaul. Many miracles are attributed to him. According to tradition, he offered half of his cloak to a beggar at Amiens and afterward experienced a vision of Christ relating the charitable act to the angels. His feast day is November 11 (Martinmas).

MARTIN I, Saint (d. 655), pope (649–55), who convoked the synod that condemned the heresy of Monothelitism (q.v.). Born in Todi, in Tuscany, Italy, he was elected to succeed Pope Theodore I (580?–649). The chief concern of Martin's papacy was the promulgation in the Eastern church of Monothelitism, the doctrine that Christ has only one will. The Eastern emperor Constans II (630–68), attempting to keep the church united at a time when the empire was under attack by Muslims, had issued (648) the Typos, an order forbidding any further discussion of Christ's will. When Martin presided over the Lateran Synod (649) in Rome, which condemned the Typos and Monothelitism, the emperor ordered his arrest (653). Martin was taken to Constantinople in 654, where he was insulted by the populace, charged with treason, and sent to exile in the Crimea (now in Ukraine), where he died. He is considered a martyr, and his feast day is November 12.

MARTIN IV (c. 1210–85), pope (1281–85). Born Simon de Brie in Brie, France, Martin was a supporter of French influence in Europe. In 1260 King Louis IX named him chancellor of France, and the following year he was created cardinal. On Feb. 22, 1281, he was elected pope. Martin supported Charles of Anjou, brother of Louis IX and founder of the Angevin dynasty of southern Italy, in his attempt to secure the crown of Sicily. Acceding to Charles's wishes, he excommunicated Emperor Michael VIII Palaeologus in 1281. As a result, the ties between the Latin and Greek churches established in 1274 at the Council of Lyons were broken. He remained loyal to Charles in the latter's conflict with Pedro III of Aragón (1239–85). His allegiance to the French made him unpopular among the Romans, and he was later expelled to Perugia, where he died.

MARTIN V (1368–1431), pope (1417–31), whose election ended the Great Schism (see SCHISM, GREAT). He was born Ottone or Oddone Colonna in 1368 at Genazzano, Italy, into an influential Roman family. While a cardinal subdeacon, he helped organize the Council of Pisa, which met to settle differences between rival popes at Rome and at Avignon. Martin's election as pope during the Council of Constance (see CONSTANCE, COUNCIL OF) settled the question of papal succession and ended the schism in the Western Church.

Martin recognized the need to reestablish the primacy of the Holy See in order to facilitate the reunification of the Western church and the Papal States (q.v.). He thus condemned the popular "conciliar theory," which held that the pope was subordinate to church councils. Also, he reached agreements with rulers of five European nations on the regulation of ecclesiastical matters.

In 1420, after declining an invitation from the French to live at Avignon, Martin settled in Rome, which was then in ruins. He rebuilt some of Rome's churches and other public buildings and attempted to restore order in the Papal States with the help of his politically powerful Italian relatives. His gifts of offices and honors to his family anticipated the practice of nepotism during the Renaissance. Martin instituted reforms concerning the treatment of Jews and sought to organize a crusade against the followers of John Huss (Jan Hus).

MARTIN, Frank (1890–1974), Swiss composer, the most eminent of his generation. He taught briefly at the Jaques-Dalcroze Institute in Geneva, and its approach to rhythm influenced his music. His early works show the influence of the Belgian-French composer César Franck and the French composer Gabriel Fauré; later he experimented with varied rhythmic techniques and a free, lyrical adaptation of the twelve-tone technique. His inventive style may be seen in *Rhythmes* (1926), for orchestra. His subtle use of tone color and harmony characterize his dramatic oratorio *Le vin herbé* (The Love Potion, 1942).

MARTIN, Glenn Luther (1886–1955), American airplane manufacturer, known for the design of many transoceanic aircraft. He was born in Macksburg, Iowa, and taught himself to fly an airplane in 1908. In the following decade he became one of the world's outstanding pilots. Between 1929 and 1945 he designed and built the famous China Clipper, Hawaiian Clipper, and Philippine Clipper, used in transpacific airmail and passenger service, as well as bombers that were used by the army and navy during World War II.

MARTIN DE PORRES, Saint (1579–1639), Peruvian Dominican friar, born in Lima of an unknown father and a black mother. When he was eight years old, Martin was adopted by a Spanish nobleman, who provided for the boy's education. Although trained as a *cirujano*—a barber, pharmacist, doctor, and surgeon in one—Martin devoted himself to the poor. Admitted as a lay helper in the Dominican monastery of the Most Holy Rosary, he entered the Dominican order nine years later. Martin's principal claim to sainthood was the great purity of his life and his love of all people. He was canonized in 1962 by Pope John XXIII; his feast day is November 3.

MARTINEAU, Harriet (1802–76), English writer, born in Norwich, and privately educated. She first gained public attention with a number of books on economics, including *Illustrations of Political Economy* (1832–34), *Poor Laws and Paupers* (1833), and *Illustrations of Taxation* (1834). After 1832 she was a literary celebrity, and her friends included the economist Thomas Malthus and the writers George Eliot and Thomas Carlyle. A visit (1834–36) to the U.S. made her a fervent abolitionist; British interest in this subject was first aroused by an article of hers in the *Westminster Review*. Her writings, characterized by advanced views on social, economic, and religious questions, caused considerable controversy. They include *Society in America* (1837), *Eastern Life, Present and Past* (1848), *Letters on the Laws of Man's Nature and Development* (1851), and a condensed translation (1853) of *Philosophie positive* by the French philosopher Auguste Comte. She also wrote novels, tales for children, a history of England, and an autobiography.

MARTÍNEZ RUIZ, José (1873–1967), Spanish essayist, novelist, and critic known as Azorín, born in Monóvar, Alicante. He was active in politics during the early part of his career. The dominant theme of his writings is timelessness and continuity as symbolized by the changeless ways of the peasant. He won critical acclaim for his essays, collections of which include *El alma castellana* (The Castilian Soul, 1900), *Los pueblos* (The Villages, 1904), and *Castilla* (1912). Most widely read are his autobiographical novels, *La Voluntad* (The Choice, 1902), *Antonio Azorín* (1903), and *Las confesiones de un pequeño filósofo* (Confessions of a Humble Philosopher, 1904). He brought a new, invigorating style to Spanish prose. He also is noted the perceptive literary criticism contained in such works as *Los valores literarios* (Literary Values, 1913) and *Al margen de los clásicos* (Marginal Notes to the Classics, 1915).

MARTINI, Simone. See SIMONE MARTINI.

MARTINIQUE, island, overseas department of France, French West Indies, in the E Caribbean Sea, off the NW coast of South America. One of the Windward Islands, Martinique is largely of volcanic origin and essentially mountainous. The area of the island is 1102 sq km (425 sq mi).

Martinique had a population (1990) of 363,031. Fort-de-France, the most populous city (101,540), is the capital and chief seaport. Other important towns are Sainte Marie (19,760), and Le Lamentin (30,596). Although the official language of the department is French, a majority of the inhabitants use a Creole dialect in conversation.

Martinique's economy is based largely on agriculture, and about 19% of the island is cultivable. Bananas, sugarcane, and pineapples are the island's principal agricultural products. Refined petroleum products, rum, sugar, cement, and processed food are major manufactures. Tourism and fishing are also important to the economy. In the early 1990s Martinique's budget included revenue and expenditure balanced at about $310 million. The island's imports cost about $1.7 billion, and its exports earned approximately $216 million. Principal trading partners were France and Guadeloupe. The French franc is the legal currency (5.6567 francs equal U.S.$1; 1994).

Martinique is administered by an appointed prefect and an elected general council of 45 members and a regional council of 41 members. The department is represented in the French National Assembly by two senators and four deputies.

Martinique was visited, probably in 1502, by Christopher Columbus. From 1635 to 1674 it was owned by a private French concern established for the purpose of colonizing America. In 1674 the island was purchased by the French government. During the colonial wars between France and Great Britain in the 17th and 18th centuries, Martinique was occupied by the British on several occasions. The island was the birthplace of Joséphine, wife of Napoleon. Mont Pelée, about 1463 m (about 4800 ft) above sea level, erupted in 1902, destroying Saint-Pierre, which was once the largest city on the island. In 1946 Martinique became an overseas department of France.

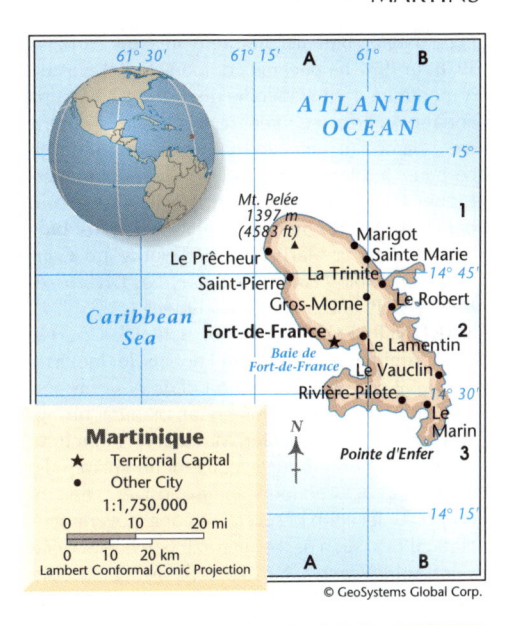

MARTINS, Peter (1946–), Danish ballet dancer and choreographer, born in Copenhagen, Denmark. Martins began his career with the Royal Danish Ballet in 1964 and was elevated to principal dancer in 1967. That year he first appeared with the New York City Ballet under the direction of George Balanchine and in 1970 joined the company as principal dancer. Balanchine subsequently choreographed many of his late works for Martins and encouraged Martins to become a choreographer. Martins's first piece, *Calcium*

MARTINSBURG

Light Night, had its premiere in New York in 1978. In 1981 he became company ballet master. A month before Balanchine died in 1983, Martins and the American choreographer Jerome Robbins were named to succeed him, each with the title co-ballet master-in-chief. Martins retired as a performer the following season. He has been sole ballet master-in-chief since 1989, when Robbins retired. Among Martins's other works are *Concerto for 2 Solo Pianos* (1982), *Delibes Divertissement* (1983), and *Shubertiad* (1984).

MARTINSBURG, city, seat of Berkeley Co., NE West Virginia, in the Eastern Panhandle; inc. as a city 1859. Situated in a region of dairy farms and fruit orchards, it is a commercial, manufacturing, and transportation center. Manufactures include glass and wood products, construction materials, clothing, processed food, and explosives. The city is also the location of several regional governmental facilities, such as the Internal Revenue Service Computing Center. Nearby is the Morgan Cabin of Torytown (built 1731–34, restored 1977), the home of West Virginia's first permanent non-Indian settler. Martinsburg, settled by the 1750s, was laid out in 1778 by Adam Stephen (1718–91), an American Revolution military leader whose home here is now a museum. It is named for Thomas Bryan Martin (1731–98), a nephew of Thomas Lord Fairfax (1693–1781), a proprietor of Virginia. Martinsburg enjoyed a boom during the construction (1837–43) of the Baltimore and Ohio Railroad and changed hands several times during the American Civil War. A violent strike by railroad employees took place here in 1877. Pop. (1980) 13,063; (1990) 14,073.

MARTINSON, Harry Edmund (1904–78), Swedish author and Nobel laureate. He was born May 6, 1904, in Jämshög, Blekinge Province. The son of a sea captain, he ran away to sea himself; many of his literary themes stem from his lonely childhood and from his six years at sea. Martinson wrote about 20 novels and numerous collections of essays, poems, and short stories. Best known outside Sweden is his lyrical epic *Aniara* (1956; trans. 1963), a cycle of 103 poems about the voyage of a spaceship carrying 8000 humans away from a radiation-destroyed earth. Among his other notable writings are the travel book *Cape Farewell* (1933; trans. 1936), the autobiographical *Flowering Nettles* (1935; trans. 1936), and the novel *The Road* (1948; trans. 1955). In 1949 he was elected to the Swedish Academy. He shared the 1974 Nobel Prize for literature with his countryman Eyvind Johnson, being cited for "writings that catch the dewdrop and reflect the cosmos."

MARTINŮ, Bohuslav (1890–1959), Czech composer, most esteemed in the 20th century after Leoš Janáček. Born in Polička, he studied under the Czech violinist-composer Josef Suk (1874–1935) and in 1923 in Paris with the French composer Albert Roussel. Martinů lived in the U.S. from 1940 to 1946. During this time, he was known as a romantic symphonist. The composer's music is neoclassical and often reflects sensitivity to Czech folk music. His *Memorial to Lidice* (1943), for orchestra, his Sixth Symphony (1953), and his opera *The Greek Passion-Play* (1958) are highly regarded.

MARVELL, Andrew (1621–78), English poet and satirist, who belongs to the metaphysical school. He was born in Winestead, Yorkshire, and educated at the University of Cambridge. While tutor to the daughter of Lord Thomas Fairfax (1612–71), he wrote the well-known lyric works "The Garden," "To His Coy Mistress," "The Definition of Love," and "Bermudas." These works generally weigh conflicting values. As assistant to John Milton from 1657 to 1659, he wrote many poems in praise of the Lord Protector of England, Oliver Cromwell, notably "Horatian Ode upon Cromwell's Return from Ireland." From 1659 until his death, Marvell served in Parliament; his letters to constituents reveal much about his times.

Marvell's prose satire, little read today, was once considered wittier than his verse. His bitter verses against the corruption of the monarchy include "Last Instructions to a Painter" (1667), "Britannia and Raleigh," and "Poem on the Statue in the Stocks Market" (1672).

MARWAR. See JODHPUR.

MARX, Karl (1818–83), German political philosopher and revolutionist, cofounder with Friedrich Engels of scientific socialism (modern communism), and, as such, one of the most influential thinkers of all times.

Marx was born in Trier on May 5, 1818, and educated at the universities of Bonn, Berlin, and Jena. In 1842, shortly after contributing his first article to the Cologne newspaper *Rheinische Zeitung,* Marx became editor of the paper. Although his political views were radical he was not yet a communist. His writings in the *Rheinische Zeitung* criticizing contemporary political and social conditions embroiled him in controversy with the authorities, and in 1843 Marx was compelled to resign his editorial post, and soon afterward the *Rheinische Zeitung* was forced to discontinue publication. Marx then went to Paris. There, as a result of his further studies in philosophy, history, and political science, he adopted communist beliefs. In 1844, when Engels visited him in Paris, the two men found that they had independently arrived at identical views on the nature of revolutionary problems. They undertook to collaborate in a systematic elucidation of the theoretical principles of communism and in

Karl Marx with his daughter, Jenny. UPI

the organization of an international working-class movement dedicated to those principles. For information on their collaboration, which continued until Marx's death, *see* ENGELS, FRIEDRICH.

The Communist Manifesto. In 1845 Marx was ordered to leave Paris because of his revolutionary activities. He settled in Brussels and began the work of organizing and directing a network of revolutionary groups, called Communist Correspondence Committees, in a number of European cities. In connection with the consolidation of these committees in 1847 to form the Communist League, Marx and Engels were commissioned to formulate a statement of principles. The program they submitted, known throughout the world as the *Communist Manifesto* (q.v.), was the first systematic statement of modern socialist doctrine and was written by Marx, partly on the basis of a draft prepared by Engels. The central propositions of the *Manifesto*, contributed by Marx, embody the theory, later explicitly formulated in his *Critique of Political Economy* (1859), called the materialist conception of history, or historical materialism. These propositions are that in every historical epoch the prevailing economic system by which the necessities of life are produced determines the form of societal organization and the political and intellectual history of the epoch; and that the history of society is a history of struggles between exploiting and exploited, that is, between ruling and oppressed, social classes. From these premises, Marx drew the conclusion in the *Manifesto* that the capitalist class would be overthrown and that it would be eliminated by a worldwide working-class revolution and replaced by a classless society. The *Manifesto* influenced all subsequent communist literature and revolutionary thought generally; it has been translated into many languages and published in hundreds of millions of copies.

Political Exile. After the *Manifesto* appeared, revolutions occurred in France and Germany, and the Belgian government, fearful that the revolutionary tide would engulf Belgium, banished Marx. He thereupon went first to Paris and then to the Rhineland. In Cologne he established and edited a communist periodical, the *Neue Rheinische Zeitung,* and engaged in organizing activities. In 1849 Marx was arrested and tried in Cologne on a charge of incitement to armed insurrection; he was acquitted but was expelled from Germany, and the *Neue Rheinische Zeitung* was suppressed. Later in the same year he was again banished from France; he spent the remainder of his life in London.

In England Marx devoted himself to study and writing and to efforts to build an international communist movement. During this period he wrote a number of works that are regarded as classics of communist theory. These include his greatest work, *Das Kapital* (vol. 1, 1867; vol. 2 and 3, edited by Engels and pub. posthumously in 1885 and 1894, respectively; trans. 1907-09), a systematic and historical analysis of the economy of the capitalist system of society, in which he developed the theory of the exploitation of the working class by the capitalist class through the appropriation by the latter of the "surplus value" produced by the former. *See* CAPITAL.

Marx's next work, *The Civil War in France* (1871), analyzed the experience of the short-lived revolutionary government established in Paris during the Franco-German War (*see* COMMUNE OF PARIS, 1871). In this work Marx interpreted the formation and existence of the Commune as a historical confirmation of his theory of the necessity for workers to seize political power by armed insurrection and then to destroy the capitalist state; he hailed the Commune as "the finally discovered political form under which the economic emancipation of labor could take place." This theory was explicitly projected in *The Gotha Program* (1875; trans. 1922): "Between the capitalist and communist systems of society lies the period of the revolutionary transformation of the one into the other. This corresponds to a political transition period, whose state can be nothing else but the revolutionary dictatorship of the proletariat." During his residence in England Marx also contributed articles on contemporary political and social events to newspapers in Europe and the U.S. He was a correspondent of the *New York Tribune,* edited by Horace Greeley, from 1852 to 1861, and in 1857 and 1858 he wrote a number of articles for the *New American Cyclopedia,* edited jointly by the American writer and editor Charles Anderson Dana (1819–97) and George Ripley (1802–80).

Later Years. When the Communist League dissolved in 1852, Marx maintained contact and corresponded with hundreds of revolutionists with the aim of forming another revolutionary organization. These efforts and those of his many collaborators culminated in 1864 in the establishment in London of the First International. Marx made the inaugural address, wrote the statutes of the International, and subsequently directed the work of its general council or governing body. After the suppression of the Commune, in which members of the First International participated, the International declined, and Marx recommended the removal of its headquarters to the U.S. The last eight years of his life were marked by an incessant struggle with physical ailments that impeded his political and literary labors. Manuscripts and notes found after his death in London on March 14, 1883, revealed that he had projected a fourth volume of *Das Kapital* to comprise a history of economic doctrines; these fragments were edited by the German socialist Karl Johann Kautsky and published under the title *Theories of Surplus Value* (4 vol., 1905–10; trans. 1952). Other works planned and not executed by Marx included mathematical studies, studies embodying applications of mathematics to economic problems, and studies on the historical aspects of various technological developments.

Influence. Marx's influence during his life was not great. After his death it increased with the growth of the labor movement. Marx's ideas and theories came to be known as Marxism, or scientific socialism, which constitutes one of the principal currents of contemporary political thought. His analysis of capitalist economy and his theories of historical materialism, the class struggle, and surplus value have become the basis of modern socialist doctrine. Of decisive importance with respect to revolutionary action are his theories on the nature of the capitalist state, the road to power, and the dictatorship of the proletariat. These doctrines, revised by most socialists after his death, were revived in the 20th century by Lenin and, as developed and applied by him, constituted the core of the theory and practice of bolshevism and the Third International.

For further information on this person, see the section Biographies in the Bibliography in volume 28.

MARX BROTHERS, four 20th-century American comedians, born in New York City. They were known by their professional names: **Chico Marx** (Leonard, 1891–1961), **Harpo Marx** (Arthur, 1893–1964), **Groucho Marx** (Julius, 1895–1977), and **Zeppo Marx** (Herbert, 1901–79).

Trained as musicians, they began their careers in vaudeville with their mother and aunt as the Six Musical Mascots. Later they appeared as the Four Nightingales, and finally billed themselves as the Marx Brothers. The brothers appeared in a number of film comedies noted chiefly for their zany sight gags. Such films include *Animal Crackers* (1930), *Horse Feathers* (1932), and *Duck Soup* (1933). After Zeppo retired in 1935, Harpo, Chico, and Groucho appeared with great success in *A Night at the Opera* (1935), *A Day at the Races* (1937), and *Room Service* (1938). Their last film as a team was *Love Happy* (1948).

Each brother had readily identifiable characteristics. Groucho had a caustic wit and appeared with a cigar and moustache; Chico spoke in an Italian accent and played the piano; Harpo communicated in pantomime and played the harp. After the brothers ceased making films, Groucho continued his entertainment career as master of ceremonies of the television series "You Bet Your Life." He wrote the autobiographical *Groucho and Me* (1959) and *Memoirs of a Mangy Lover* (1964). Harpo published his autobiography, *Harpo Speaks,* in 1961. The brothers inspired the musical *Minnie's Boys* (1970), which was coauthored by Groucho's son Arthur (1921–   ).

MARY, also the Virgin Mary, the mother of Jesus Christ, venerated by Christians since apostolic times. The Gospels give a brief account of Mary, mentioning her in connection with the annunciation, and the beginning and the end of Jesus' life. Matthew speaks of Mary as Joseph's wife, who is "with child of the Holy Spirit" before they "came together" as husband and wife (see Matt. 1:18). After the birth of Jesus, she is present at the visit of the Magi (see Matt. 2:11), flees with

MARY

Joseph in Egypt (see Matt. 2:14), and returns to Nazareth (see Matt. 2:23). Mark simply refers to Jesus as the son of Mary (see Mark 6:3). Luke's narrative of the nativity includes the angel Gabriel announcing to Mary the coming birth of Jesus (see Luke 1:27-38); her visit to her kinswoman Elizabeth, mother of John the Baptist, and Mary's hymn, the Magnificat (see Luke 1:39-56); and the shepherds' visit to the manger (see Luke 2:1-20). Luke also tells of Mary's perplexity at finding Jesus in the Temple questioning the teachers when he was 12 years old. The Gospel of John contains no infancy narrative, nor does it mention Mary's name; she is referred to as "the mother of Jesus" (see John 2, 19). She is present at the first of Jesus' miracles at the wedding feast of Cana (2:1,3,5) and at his death (19:25-27). Mary is also mentioned as being present in the upper room at Olivet with the apostles and with Jesus' brothers before Pentecost (see Acts 1:14).

The Early Church. As early as the 2d century Christians venerated Mary by calling her Mother of God, a title that primarily stresses the divinity of Jesus. During the 4th-century controversies concerning the divine and human natures of Jesus, the Greek title *Theotokos* ("Mother of God") came to be used for Mary in devotional and theological writing. The Syrian monk Nestorius (d. about 451) contested this usage, insisting that Mary was mother of Christ, not of God. The Council of Ephesus (431; see EPHESUS, COUNCIL OF) condemned Nestorius's teaching and solemnly affirmed that Mary is to be called *Theotokos*, a title that has been used since that time in the Orthodox and Roman Catholic churches.

Closely allied with the title Mother of God is the title Virgin Mary, affirming the virginal conception of Jesus (see Luke 1:35). Initially, this title stressed the belief that God, not Joseph, was the true Father of Jesus. In the Marian devotion that developed in the East in the 4th century Mary was venerated not only in the conception, but also in the birth of Jesus. This conviction was expressed clearly in the 4th century baptismal creeds of Cyprus, Syria, Palestine, and Armenia (373-74). The title used was *Aieiparthenos* ("ever-virgin"), and by the middle of the 7th century the understanding of the title came to include the conviction that Mary remained a virgin for the whole of her life. The passages in the New Testament referring to the brothers of Jesus (for instance, Mark 6:3, which also mentions sisters; see 1 Cor. 9:5; Gal. 1:19) have been accordingly explained as references to relatives of Jesus or to children of Joseph by a previous marriage, although no textual evidence supports these interpretations.

Beginning in the 2d and 3d centuries Mary was called Holy or Blessed Virgin to express the belief that, because of her intimate union with God through the Holy Spirit in the conception of Jesus (see Luke 1:35), Mary was completely free from any taint of sin. A Roman Council in 680 spoke of her as the "blessed, immaculate ever-virgin."

In both the Eastern and Western churches, feast days in honor of the events of Mary's life came into existence between the 4th and 7th centuries. They celebrate her miraculous conception and her birth, narrated in the apocryphal protogospel of James (September 8), the Annunciation (q.v.; March 25), her purification in the Temple (February 2), and her death (called the Dormition in the Eastern church) and bodily assumption into heaven (August 15; see ASSUMPTION OF THE VIRGIN).

The Middle Ages. During the late Middle Ages (13th-15th cent.) devotion to Mary grew vigorously. One of the principal reasons was the image of Christ that developed in the missionary efforts of the early Middle Ages. To the extent that the Gothic and other tribes of central and northern Europe were Christian, they remained strongly influenced by Arianism (q.v.), a teaching that denied the divinity of Christ. In response, preaching and the arts of this period particularly stressed Christ's divinity, as in the Byzantine depictions of Christ as *Pantokrator* ("universal and all-powerful ruler") and in the western images of Christ as the supreme and universal judge. As Christ became an awe-inspiring, judgmental figure, Mary came to be depicted as the one who interceded for sinners. As the fear of death and the Last Judgment intensified following the Black Plague in the 14th century, Mary was increasingly venerated in popular piety as mediator of the mercy of Christ. Her prayers and pleas were seen as the agency that tempered the stern justice of Christ. Among the popular devotions that came into being at this time were the rosary (q.v.; a chaplet originally consisting of 150 Hail Marys in imitation of the 150 Psalms in the psalter, later augmented by 15 interspersed Our Fathers as penance for daily sins); the angelus (q.v.) recited at sunrise, noon, and sunset; and litanies, invocations of Mary using such biblical titles as Mystical Rose, Tower of David, and Refuge of Sinners (see LITANY). Hymns, psalms, and prayers were incorporated into the Little Office of the Blessed Virgin, in imitation of the longer divine office (q.v.) recited or chanted by monks and priests.

Doctrine of Immaculate Conception. The principal theological development concerning Mary in the Middle Ages was the doctrine of the Im-

MARY I

maculate Conception (q.v.). This doctrine, defended and preached by the Franciscan friars under the inspiration of the 13th century Scottish theologian John Duns Scotus, maintains that Mary was conceived without original sin (q.v.). Dominican teachers and preachers vigorously opposed the doctrine, maintaining that it detracted from Christ's role as universal savior. Pope Sixtus IV, however, defended it, establishing (1477) a feast of the Immaculate Conception with a proper mass and office to be celebrated on December 8. This feast was extended to the whole Western church by Pope Clement XI in 1708. In 1854 Pope Pius IX issued a solemn decree defining the Immaculate Conception for all Roman Catholics, but the doctrine has not been accepted by Protestants or by the Orthodox churches. In 1950, Pope Pius XII solemnly defined as an article of faith for all Roman Catholics the doctrine of the bodily assumption of Mary into heaven.

Shrines. Marian shrines and places of pilgrimage are found throughout the world. At Monserrat in Spain the Black Virgin has been venerated since the 12th century. The icon of Our Lady of Częstochowa has been venerated in Poland since the early 14th century. The picture of Our Lady of Guadalupe commemorates an alleged apparition of Mary to the Indian Juan Diego (1476?–1548) in Mexico in 1531. In the 19th century a number of apparitions were reported that inspired the development of shrines, devotions, and pilgrimages—for instance, in Paris (1830, Our Lady of the Miraculous Medal), Lourdes (1858, Our Lady of Lourdes), and Knock, in Ireland (1879, Our Lady of Knock). The most well known in the 20th century was that in Fatima, Portugal (1917, Our Lady of Fatima); and apparitions of Mary were reported in Medjugorge, Bosnia, in the 1980s.

Mary has also been the subject of innumerable artistic representations.

For further information on this person, see the Bibliography in volume 28, section 68.

MARY I, called Mary Tudor (1516–58), queen of England (1553–58).

Mary was born in London on Feb. 18, 1516, the daughter of Henry VIII of England, by his first wife, Catherine of Aragón. On the death of her half brother, Edward VI, on July 6, 1553, she became the legal heir to the throne. Lord High Chamberlain John Dudley, duke of Northumberland, however, favored the succession of his daughter-in-law, Lady Jane Grey. He proclaimed her queen on July 10, but the country supported Mary.

Mary began her reign by sweeping away the religious innovations of her father. Mass was restored without opposition and the authority of the pope reestablished, but Parliament refused to restore the

Queen Mary I of England — Superstock

church lands seized under Henry VIII. Mary, however, restored the property that the Crown still possessed. Even more disastrous was her marriage in 1554 to Philip II, king of Spain. The engagement was greeted in England by a formidable rebellion under the leadership of Sir Thomas Wyatt (1521–54) to depose Mary and put her half sister, Elizabeth, later Elizabeth I, on the throne. Philip was an uncompromising Roman Catholic and unpopular in England. At his order, Mary joined in a war against France, with the result that Calais, the last remnant of the English conquests of the Hundred Years' War with France, was lost in 1558.

The ferocity with which Mary's personal character has been assailed by certain writers must be ascribed to religious zeal. She was called Bloody Mary because of a large number of religious persecutions that took place during her reign; almost 300 people were condemned to death as a result of trials for heresy. Mary died in London on Nov. 17, 1558, and was succeeded by Elizabeth I.

For further information on this person, see the section Biographies in the Bibliography in volume 28.

MARY II (1662–94), queen of England, Scotland, and Ireland (1689–94), born in London. She was the daughter of James, duke of York—who in 1685 became king of England as James II—and his first wife, Anne Hyde (1637–71). Although her father was a convert to Roman Catholicism, Mary was brought up as a Protestant and was married at the age of 15 to the Dutch Protestant prince

44

William of Orange. In 1688, English opponents of James, unhappy with his autocratic rule and favoritism toward Roman Catholics, initiated the Glorious Revolution, forcing James into exile and giving the throne to Mary and William (who became king as William III). They were crowned as joint rulers in April 1689. Mary governed as regent while William was campaigning in Ireland (1690–91) and on the Continent (1692–94), but for the most part she simply carried out policies formulated by her husband. William continued to rule alone after her death.

MARY (1867–1953), queen consort of Great Britain (1911–36), the wife of King George V, and daughter of the German nobleman Francis Alexander, duke of Teck (1830?–1900), and the granddaughter of King George III. She was born in Kensington Palace, London, and her given name was Victoria Mary Augusta. In 1893 she married George, then duke of York, and in 1911 was crowned with him in Westminster Abbey. During World War II she won international acclaim for her work for charities and hospitals. Two of her sons became kings of Great Britain as Edward VIII and George VI.

MARY, QUEEN OF SCOTS, also Mary Stuart (1542–87), daughter of James V, king of Scotland, by his second wife, Mary of Guise.

Born in Linlithgow in December 1542, Mary became queen before she was a week old. Raised in France, in 1558 she was married to the Dauphin, who succeeded to the French throne as Francis II in 1559 but died the next year. Mary returned to Scotland in 1561. Although Roman Catholic, at first she accepted the Protestant-led government that she found in place. Her chief minister was her half brother James Stuart (1531?–70), whom she soon afterward created earl of Moray.

Mary's marriage in 1565 to her cousin, the Catholic Scottish nobleman Henry Stewart, Lord Darnley, was performed with Roman Catholic rites. The marriage aroused Protestant feelings and was the signal for an insurrection by Moray and a Scottish noble family who hoped to be joined by the whole Protestant party. Their hope was disappointed, however, and the queen, taking the field in person, at once quelled the revolt. Her triumph was scarcely over when misunderstandings began to arise between her and Darnley. She had given him the title of king, but he now demanded that the crown be secured to him for life and that, if the queen died without children, it should descend to his heirs.

Before Moray's rebellion Mary's secretary and adviser had been David Rizzio (1533?–66), a court favorite and a Roman Catholic. The king was now persuaded that Rizzio was the obstacle to his designs upon the crown. Acting on this belief, he entered into a formal compact with Moray; Lord Patrick Ruthven (1520?–66); James Douglas, 4th earl of Morton (1525–81); and other leaders of the Protestant party. The result of this conspiracy was the murder of Rizzio in 1566. Early in 1567 the house in which Darnley lay sick was blown up by gunpowder, probably at the instigation of the Scottish nobleman James Hepburn, 4th earl of Bothwell, who, since Moray's revolt and still more since Rizzio's murder, had been favored by the queen. Darnley was discovered strangled close by the scene of the explosion. It was suspected that Mary herself was not wholly ignorant of the plot. Evidence substantiating this theory is reflected in incriminating letters and sonnets, allegedly written by Mary to Bothwell and found later that year in a silver casket. Bothwell was brought to a mock trial and acquitted; soon afterward he divorced his wife and married Mary in a Protestant ceremony.

This step at once turned the Scottish nobles against Mary. She was able to lead an army against them, and although it was equal in number to the confederate army, it was visibly inferior in discipline. On June 15, 1567, Mary's forces were defeated at Carberry Hill, and she was forced to abandon Bothwell and surrender herself to the confederate lords. On July 24, at Lochleven, she was prevailed upon to sign an act of abdication in favor of her son, who was crowned as James VI five days afterward at Stirling. Escaping from her island-prison at Lochleven on May 2, 1568, she was able within a few days to assemble an army of 6000 men. On May 12 her army was defeated by the regent Moray at Langside, near Glasgow. Four days afterward, in spite of the entreaties of her best friends, Mary crossed Solway Firth and sought refuge at the court of Elizabeth I, queen of England, only to find herself a prisoner of Elizabeth for life.

Of the ensuing intrigues to effect her deliverance and to place her on the throne of Elizabeth, the most famous was that of Mary's page, Anthony Babington, who plotted to assassinate Elizabeth. The conspiracy was discovered, and Mary was brought to trial in October 1586. She was sentenced to death on October 25, but not until Feb. 1, 1587, did Elizabeth sign the warrant of execution, which was carried out a week later.

For further information on this person, see the section Biographies in the Bibliography in volume 28.

MARY OF GUISE (1515–60), queen consort (1538–42) of James V of Scotland and regent of Scotland (1554–60); also known as Mary of Lorraine. The widowed daughter of the French soldier Claude

MARYLAND

de Lorraine, 1st duc de Guise (1496–1550), Mary married King James in 1538. After his death in 1542, she engaged in a power struggle with James Hamilton, 3d earl of Arran (c. 1517–75), who had been appointed regent for his infant daughter, Mary, queen of Scots. In 1548 she arranged her daughter's betrothal to the French Dauphin. Mary secured Arran's resignation and succeeded him as regent in 1554. When she began persecuting the Scottish Protestants in 1559, they rebelled against her. Both France and England intervened in the struggle, which ended with Mary's death.

MARYLAND, one of the South Atlantic states of the U.S., bordered on the N by Pennsylvania, on the E by Delaware and the Atlantic Ocean, on the S by Virginia, and on the SW and W by West Virginia. The District of Columbia, site of the U.S. capital, is an enclave in the W part of the state. The Potomac R. forms most of Maryland's W boundary, and Chesapeake Bay deeply indents the E section of the state.

Maryland entered the Union on April 28, 1788, as the seventh of the 13 original states. The economy of the state, known for the production of tobacco in colonial times, became dominated by manufacturing in the late 19th century and depends primarily on the service and government sectors today. Baltimore, Maryland's largest city, is a major seaport, and the SE region of the state produces large quantities of broiler chickens. The state is named for Henrietta Maria, the wife of Charles I of England. Maryland is called the Old Line State and the Free State.

LAND AND RESOURCES

Maryland, with an area of 32,135 sq km (12,407 sq mi), is the 42d largest state of the U.S.; 3.1% of the land area is owned by the federal government. Maryland has an irregular shape, and its extreme dimensions are about 320 km (about 200 mi) from E to W and about 200 km (about 125 mi) from N to S. Elevations range from sea level, in various places, to 1024 m (3360 ft), atop Backbone Mt., in the NW. The approximate mean elevation is 107 m (350 ft). Maryland's coastline along the Atlantic Ocean is only 50 km (31 mi) long, but the state's tidal shoreline, which includes Chesapeake Bay and its many arms, has a length of 5134 km (3190 mi). The Atlantic coast is formed here by a narrow barrier island, which in part sets off Chincoteague, Assawoman, and Isle of Wight bays.

Physical Geography. Maryland can be divided into five major geographical regions, all of which extend into neighboring states. About one-half of Maryland is part of the Atlantic Coastal Plain, which is divided into two sections in the state by Chesapeake Bay: The Eastern Shore, part of the Delmarva Peninsula, is a flat plain nowhere more than 30 m (100 ft) high; the Western Shore is more rolling, with summits as much as 61 m (200 ft) above sea level. The soil of the Coastal Plain has much sand, clay, and silt and is relatively low in fertility. Chesapeake Bay contains many is-

The Inner Harbor at Baltimore, Md., featuring the U.S.S. Constellation (foreground) and the National Aquarium with its colorful mural wall (background). John Scowen/FPG

MARYLAND

lands. Roughly one-fourth of Maryland is part of the Piedmont Plateau region. The E two-thirds of this region, underlain by igneous and metamorphic rock, is an area of rolling hills rising to about 365 m (about 1200 ft) at Dug Hill Ridge in the N; soils are more fertile than those in the Coastal Plain. The W third of the Piedmont Plateau, underlain by limestone and sandstone, is much flatter.

The Blue Ridge region is underlain by quartzite and metamorphosed volcanic rock. Most of the area is situated at least 305 m (1000 ft) above sea level. Catoctin Mt. is a major component of the Blue Ridge in Maryland. The Valley and Ridge Region is an area of folded sedimentary rock, in which valleys underlain by limestone and shale are separated by narrow, sharp-crested ridges attaining heights of up to about 610 m (about 2000 ft). The state's fifth region, the Allegheny Mts., in the NW, also is an area of folded sedimentary rock. It is about 610 to 1024 m (about 2000 to 3360 ft) high and has broader, more rounded ridges and wider valleys than the Valley and Ridge Region. Both regions have shallow soils that are relatively infertile except where they have developed on limestone.

Rivers and Lakes. Maryland has two large rivers. The Potomac R. forms most of the W boundary of the state, and its tributaries drain the W half of Maryland except for a small area of the NW, which is drained toward the Ohio R. The other major river, the Susquehanna, enters Maryland from Pennsylvania and flows into Chesapeake Bay after a short course. Most of the E half of the state is drained toward Chesapeake Bay, which is Maryland's biggest body of water, with an area in the state of some 4470 sq km (some 1725 sq mi). Rivers on the Eastern Shore include the Chester, Choptank, Nanticoke, and Pocomoke, and rivers of the Western Shore include the Gunpowder, Patapsco, and Patuxent. Maryland has no large natural lakes; its artificial lakes are relatively small, the biggest being Deep Creek Lake, in the NW.

Climate. Except for the Allegheny Mts. region, Maryland has a humid subtropical climate. Average monthly temperatures in winter generally are above freezing, and snow remains on the ground usually for only a few days. Minimum daily temperatures do fall below freezing, however, typically more than 80 times a year. Summer temperatures average about 24° C (about 75° F), with maximum daily readings above 32° C (90° F) on 20 to 40 days a year. Baltimore has an average January temperature of about 0.8° C (about 33.5° F) and an average July temperature of about 24.7° C (about 76.5° F). The normal annual precipitation is about 1016 mm (about 40 in), distributed evenly throughout the year.

The Allegheny Mts. region in the NW has a humid temperate climate, which differs from that of the rest of the state in that average monthly temperatures in winter are below freezing, average annual snowfall is more than 1520 mm (more than 60 in), snow stays on the ground for long periods, and average monthly temperatures in summer typically are less than 20° C (68° F). The recorded temperature in Maryland has ranged from a low of –40° C (–40° F), in 1912 at Oakland in the NW, to a high of 42.8° C (109° F), in 1898 at Boetcherville and in 1936 at Cumberland and Frederick.

Plants and Animals. Forests cover 43% of Maryland, with oak and pine forests prevailing on the Atlantic Coastal Plain; beech, tulip tree, maple, and basswood forests dominating in the Allegheny Mts.; and oak and tulip tree forests being most common elsewhere. Widespread tree species include red, white, chestnut, and willow oak; Virginia, loblolly, and pitch pine; hickory; ash; walnut; tulip tree; sweetgum; and red maple. Among the numerous wild flowers are columbine, Indian pipe, black-eyed Susan, fringed milkwort, violet, turtlehead, azalea, and rhododendron.

White-tailed deer, red and gray fox, raccoon, skunk, opossum, cottontail rabbit, groundhog, gray squirrel, and muskrat are found throughout the state. The Chesapeake Bay region is a major wintering area for waterfowl. The dominant fish of the bay is the striped bass; large numbers of oysters, blue crabs, clams, alewives, menhaden, bluefish, Norfolk spot, and perch also live in its waters.

Mineral Resources. The principal mineral resources of Maryland are construction materials and coal. Sand and gravel deposits are most extensive on the Western Shore but also occur on the Eastern Shore and along river valleys outside the Atlantic Coastal Plain region. Limestone, serpentine, granite, gneiss, gabbro, quartzite, sandstone, and slate, found both on the Piedmont Plateau and in the Valley and Ridge Region, are used as crushed stone and building stone. Important coal beds are located in the Allegheny Mts., and the state also has deposits of clay, natural gas, and talc.   C.A.R.

POPULATION

According to the 1990 census, Maryland had 4,781,468 inhabitants, an increase of 13.4% over 1980. The average population density in 1990 was 149 persons per sq km (385 per sq mi); considerably higher population concentrations were in the central part of the state. Whites made up 71% of the population and blacks 24.9%; addi-

MARYLAND

tional population groups included 30,868 persons of Chinese ancestry, 30,320 persons of Korean origin, 28,330 Asian Indians, 19,376 persons of Filipino background, 12,601 American Indians, 8862 persons of Vietnamese descent, and 6617 persons of Japanese extraction. Approximately 125,100 Maryland residents claimed Hispanic ancestry. Maryland's largest single religious group consisted of Roman Catholics (24.9%); other religious groups included Baptists (17.4%), Methodists (13.8%), Lutherans (6%), Presbyterians (3%), and Jews (2.8%). In 1990 about 81% of all Marylanders lived in areas defined as urban, and the rest lived in rural areas. The state's largest cities were Baltimore, one of the largest cities in the U.S.; Rockville; Frederick; Gaithersburg; and Bowie. Annapolis is the state capital.

EDUCATIONAL AND CULTURAL ACTIVITY
Maryland has a number of well-known educational and cultural institutions and is noted as a center for horse racing and the game of lacrosse.

Education. The first free school in Maryland, King William's School, was established in Annapolis in 1696, and a statewide system of public schools was set up in 1826. In the late 1980s, Maryland had 1217 public elementary and secondary schools, with a total annual enrollment of about 507,000 elementary pupils and about 191,800 secondary students. Approximately 99,300 children attended private schools.

In the same period, Maryland had 57 institutions of higher learning, with an aggregate yearly enrollment of about 255,300 students. Among the colleges and universities are those of the University System of Maryland, including the five former campuses of the University of Maryland as well as six other Maryland institutions; Johns Hopkins University and Morgan State University (1867), both located in Baltimore; the U.S. Naval Academy and Saint John's College, in Annapolis; Goucher College (1885), in Towson; Hood College (1893), in Frederick; and Washington College (1782), in Chestertown.

Cultural Institutions. Baltimore is Maryland's principal cultural center. In the city are some of the state's leading museums, such as the Peale Museum (1814), with historical exhibits relating to the area; the Baltimore Museum of Art, with collections of European and American art; the Walters Art Gallery, with diverse exhibits of art from antiquity to the 19th century; the Baltimore Maritime Museum; the Maryland Academy of

A drill ceremony at the U.S. Naval Academy, located in Annapolis, the capital of Maryland. Maryland Division of Tourist Development–Department of Economic & Community Development

MARYLAND

Maryland: Map Index

Counties

Allegany D6
Anne Arundel H4
Baltimore..................H1
Calvert H5
Caroline L4
Carroll G2
Cecil..........................L1
Charles G6
Dorchester K6
Frederick E1
Garrett......................B6
Harford......................J1
Howard G2
Kent L2
Montgomery C3, F3
Prince Georges C5, G5
Queen Annes............K3
St. Marys H6
Somerset M7
Talbot K4
Washington..............C1
Wicomico M6
Worcester N7

Cities and Towns

Aberdeen..................K2
Accident A6
Accokeek..................F5
Adelphi C4
Annapolis, *capital* J4
Antietam D2
Arden-on-the-Severn H3
Arnold J3
Aspen Hill............B3, F3
Avenue G7
Baltimore..................H2
Barclay L3
Barnesville E3
Barton......................C7
Bel Air......................J1
Bel Alton..................G6
Beltsville C3, G3
Benedict H5
Berlin........................P6
Berwyn Heights C4
Bethesda............B4, F4
Betterton K2
Bladensburg C4
Bond Mill Park..........D3
Boonsboro D1
Bowie G4
Bowleys Quarters J2
Braddock Heights D2
Brandywine G5
Brentwood C4
Bridgeport................D1
Brookeville F3
Brookmont B4
Brookview L5
Broomes Island H6
Brunswick D2
Bryans Road F5
Bucktown K6
Burkittsville D2
Burtonsville C3
Cabin John A4
California J6
Calvert Beach J6
Calverton C3
Cambridge K5
Cape St. Claire J3
Camp Springs C5
Capitol Heights C5
Cardiff J1
Carney......................H2
Cascade D1
Catonsville................H2
Cecilton L2
Centreville................K3
Charlestown..............L1
Charlotte Hall G6
Chesapeake Beach......H5
Chesapeake City L1
Chesapeake Ranch
  Estates J6
Chester J4
Chestertown K3
Cheverly....................C4
Chevy Chase B4, F4
Chevy Chase View B3
Chillum C4, G4
Church Creek K5
Church Hill................L3
Clear Spring C1
Clinton......................G4
Clover Hill E2
Cloverly C3
Cobb Island..............G6
Cockeysville..............H2
Colesville C3
College Park C4, G4
Columbia..................G3
Contee D3
Copenhaver..............A3
Coral Hills C5
Cresaptown C6
Crisfield L7
Crofton H3
Crownsville H3
Cumberland D6
Damascus F2
Darlington K1
Deale........................H4
Deal Island L7
Deer Park..................A7
Delmar M6
Denton L4
Derwood A3
District Heights D5
Dufief A3
Dundalk H2
Eagle Harbor H5
East New Market L5
Easton K4
Edgemere J3
Edgewood J2
Eldersburg G2
Eldorado L5
Elkridge G3
Elkton L1
Ellicott City G2
Emmitsburg E1
Essex J2
Ewell K7
Fair Hill......................L1
Fairland C3
Fairmount Heights....C4
Fallston J1
Federalsburg L5
Ferndale H3
Fishing Creek K6
Flintstone D6
Forest Heights....B5, G4
Forestville G4
Fountain Head D1
Frederick E2
Friendly G4
Friendsville A6
Frostburg..................C6
Fruitland M6
Funkstown D1
Gaithersburg F3
Galena L2
Galestown M5
Garrett Park B3
Garrison G2
Germantown E3
Glen A3
Glenarden D4
Glen Burnie H3
Glen Echo A4
Glen Echo Heights B4
Glen Hills A3
Glenmont B3
Golden Beach H6
Goldsboro L3
Grantsville B6
Grasonville................K4
Green Haven H3
Greenbelt D4, G3
Greensboro L4
Hagerstown..............D1
Halethorpe H3
Halfway C1
Hampstead G1
Hampton H2
Hancock B1
Havre de Grace K1
Hebron M6
Henderson L3
Herald Harbor H3
Hereford H1
High Ridge D3
Highland Beach J4
Hillandale C3
Hillcrest Heights C5
Hillsboro L4
Hillsmere Shores J4
Hollywood................H6
Hudson J5
Hughesville G5
Hunting Hill A3
Huntingtown............H5
Hurlock L5
Hyattstown E2
Hyattsville C4, G4
Indian Head..............F5
Jarrettsville J1
Jessup G3
Joppatowne J2
Keedysville D2
Kemptown E2
Kensington..........B3, F3
Kentland D4, G4
Kettering G4
Keysers Ridge............B6
Kingstown K3
Kingsville J2
Kitzmiller B7
Knollwood C3
Lake Shore................J3
Landover C4, G4
Langley Park C4
Lanham D4

49

A
B
C
D
E
F
G
1
2
3
4
5
6
7
BUCHANAN STATE FOREST
Gettysburg
GETTYSBURG NATL. MIL. PARK
Hanover
Waynesboro
PENNSYLVANIA
MARYLAND
Cascade
Fountain Head
Emmitsburg
Hancock
WASHINGTON
ALLEGANY
GREEN RIDGE S.F.
Clear Spring
Hagerstown
Smithsburg
Taneytown
Manchester
Prettyboy Res.
Hampstead
Halfway
Bridgeport
Funkstown
Williamsport
Thurmont
Berkeley Springs
Potomac R.
Mt. Aetna
CATOCTIN MT. PARK
Union Bridge
Westminster
Appalachian N.S.T.
Woodsboro
New Windsor
Boonsboro
Myersville
FREDERICK
CARROLL
Walkersville
ANTIETAM N.B.
Keedysville
Middletown
Reisterstown
Martinsburg
Sharpsburg
Clover Hill
Liberty Res.
Owings Mills
Braddock Heights
Frederick
Oakland
W. VIRGINIA
VIRGINIA
Antietam
New Market
Eldersburg
Burkittsville
Sykesville
CHESAPEAKE AND OHIO CANAL N.H.P.
MONOCACY N.B.
Mount Airy
Kemptown
Randallstown
HARPERS FERRY N.H.P.
Rosemont
Milford
Brunswick
Woodlawn
Hyattstown
Damascus
HOWARD
BLUE RIDGE
Point of Rocks
Ellicott City
Laytonsville
Columbia
Elkridge
Barnesville
Montgomery Village
Brookeville
Germantown
Poolesville
MONTGOMERY
Olney
Jessup
Leesburg
Gaithersburg
Redland
MD.
VA.
Aspen Hill
Laurel
Rockville
White Oak
Wheaton
Beltsville
Kensington
Sterling
Potomac
Greenbelt
Chevy Chase
Silver Spring
Bowie
Reston
Bethesda
Chillum
College Park
Hyattsville
Landover
Vienna
Washington
Arlington
Kentland
Largo
Kettering
Centerville
Fairfax
Annandale
Suitland
Forestville
Alexandria
MANASSAS N.B.P.
Temple Hills
Manassas Park
Forest Heights
Clinton
Woodyard
Manassas
Friendly
Marlton
FORT BELVOIR MIL. RES.
Piscataway
PRINCE GEORGES
Lorton
Accokeek
Brandywine
Dale City
Woodbridge
Bryans Road
Potomac Heights
Pomonkey
Waldorf
QUANTICO U.S.M.C. RES.
Indian Head
White Plains
St. Charles
Marbury
Pisgah
LaPlata
Hughesville
Port Tobacco
CHARLES
Charlotte Hall
Bel Alton
Mechanicsville
Popes Creek
Wicomico R.
Cobb Island
FORT A.P. HILL MIL. RES.
GEORGE WASHINGTON BIRTHPLACE N.M.
Avenue
Derwood
Norbeck
Spencerville
High Ridge
Rossmoor Leisure World
Cloverly
Maydale
Burtonsville
Hunting Hill
Layhill
Bond Mill Park
Oak Crest
Glen Hills
Copenhaver
Colesville
Glenmont
Fairland
Contee
Randolph Hills
WHEATON REG. PARK
Calverton
Montpelier
Glen
Luxmanor
Garrett Park
Muirkirk
Hillandale
Knollwood
NATIONAL AGRICULTURAL RESEARCH CENTER
Wildwood Hills
Chase View
Oakview
C & O CANAL N.H.P.
N. Chevy Chase
Cabin John
Adelphi
Takoma Park
Langley Park
Berwyn Heights
Glen Echo
Glen Echo Heights
Somerset
Lewisdale
Seabrook
Riverdale
D.C.
Brookmont
Tysons Corner
McLean
New Carrollton
Lanham
Bladensburg
Brentwood
Mount Rainier
Cheverly
Glenarden
Pimmit Hills
Palmer Park
Falls Church
Fairmount Heights
Seat Pleasant
ARLINGTON NATL. CEMETERY
Capitol Heights
Coral Hills
Ritchie
Walker Mill
District Heights
Hillcrest Heights
Silver Hill
Morningside
Temple Hills
ANDREWS A.F.B.
Oxon Hill
Camp Springs
0 2 4 6 mi
0 2 4 6 8 km
FORBES S.F.
PA.
Keysers Ridge
Grantsville
Friendsville
Flintstone
Frostburg
Cumberland
LaVale
Accident
SAVAGE RIVER STATE FOREST
Cresaptown
Midland
Lonaconing
GARRETT
Deep Creek L.
Nikep
Barton
Westernport
Luke
Youghiogheny R.
N. Br. Potomac R.
ALLEGHENY FRONT
W. VA.
Oakland
Deer Park
Keyser
Mountain Lake Park
Loch Lynn Heights
Kitzmiller
Oldtown
Romney
Redhouse
Backbone Mt. 1024 m (3360 ft)
Mt. Storm L.
same scale as main map

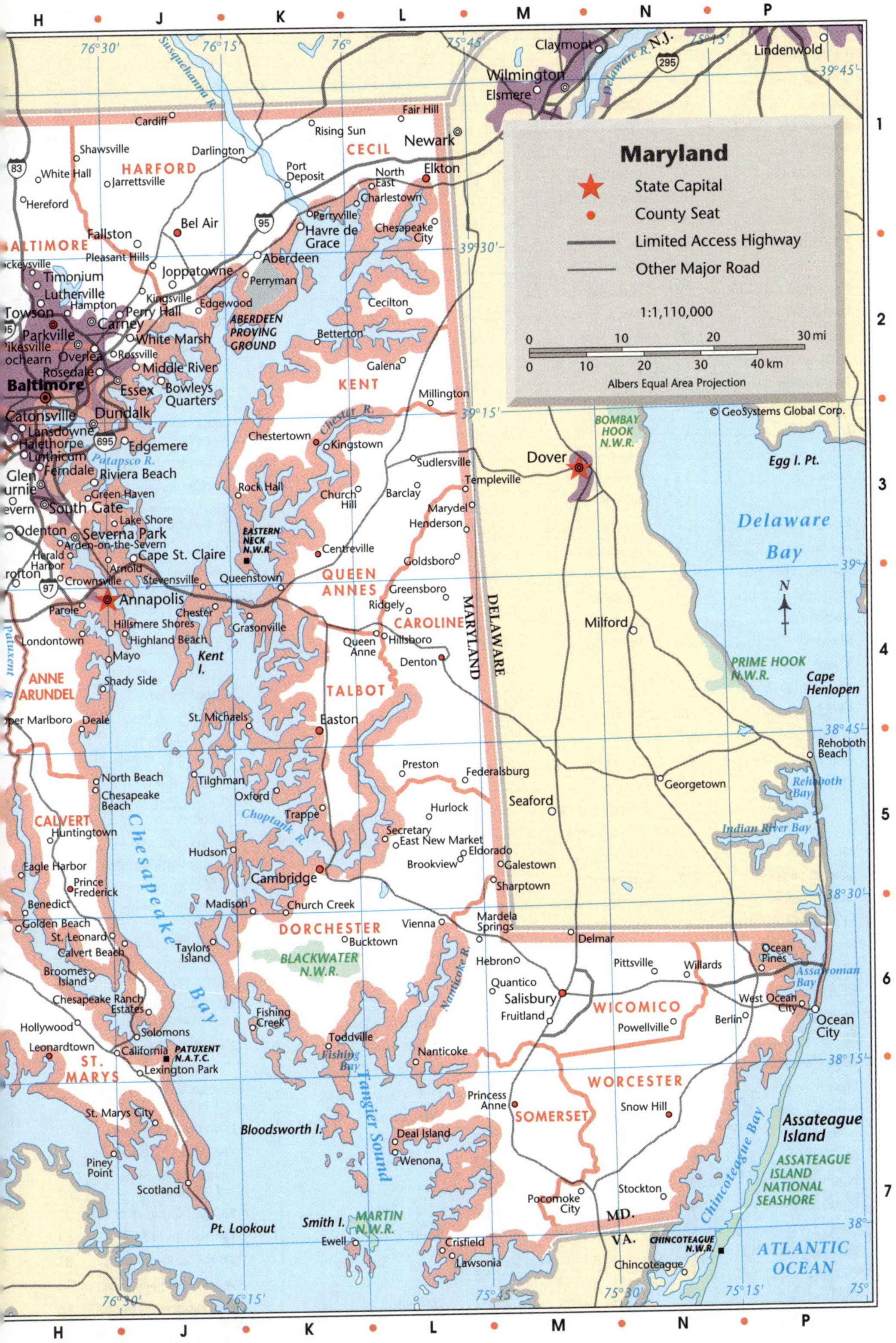
Maryland
State Capital
County Seat
Limited Access Highway
Other Major Road
1:1,110,000
0 10 20 30 mi
0 10 20 30 40 km
Albers Equal Area Projection
© GeoSystems Global Corp.
H J K L M N P
1 2 3 4 5 6 7
76°30'
76°15'
76°
75°45'
75°15'
75°30'
75°
39°45'
39°30'
39°15'
39°
38°45'
38°30'
38°15'
38°
N.J.
Claymont
Wilmington
Elsmere
Lindenwold
Delaware R.
Susquehanna R.
Cardiff
Fair Hill
Rising Sun
CECIL
Newark
Shawsville
Darlington
HARFORD
White Hall
Jarrettsville
Hereford
Port Deposit
North East
Elkton
Charlestown
Perryville
Havre de Grace
Chesapeake City
Bel Air
Fallston
BALTIMORE
Pleasant Hills
Cockeysville
Timonium
Lutherville
Joppatowne
Aberdeen
Perryman
Towson
Hampton
Kingsville
Edgewood
Perry Hall
Carney
Parkville
White Marsh
ABERDEEN PROVING GROUND
Cecilton
Betterton
Pikesville
Overlea
Rossville
Rosedale
Middle River
Galena
Baltimore
Essex
Bowleys Quarters
KENT
Millington
Catonsville
Dundalk
Lansdowne
Halethorpe
Linthicum
Edgemere
Chestertown
Chester R.
Kingstown
Patapsco R.
Glen Burnie
Ferndale
Riviera Beach
Sudlersville
Templeville
Dover
Green Haven
Rock Hall
Church Hill
Barclay
South Gate
Lake Shore
Marydel
Henderson
Odenton
Severna Park
Arden-on-the-Severn
EASTERN NECK N.W.R.
Centreville
Herald Harbor
Cape St. Claire
Goldsboro
Crofton
Arnold
Crownsville
Stevensville
Queenstown
QUEEN ANNES
Greensboro
Ridgely
Annapolis
Parole
Chester
Grasonville
CAROLINE
MARYLAND
DELAWARE
Milford
Hillsmere Shores
Highland Beach
Londontown
Queen Anne
Hillsboro
Mayo
Kent I.
Denton
ANNE ARUNDEL
Shady Side
TALBOT
Patuxent R.
Upper Marlboro
Deale
St. Michaels
Easton
BOMBAY HOOK N.W.R.
Egg I. Pt.
Delaware Bay
PRIME HOOK N.W.R.
Cape Henlopen
Rehoboth Beach
Preston
Federalsburg
Georgetown
Rehoboth Bay
North Beach
Chesapeake Beach
Tilghman
Oxford
Seaford
Hurlock
CALVERT
Huntingtown
Choptank R.
Trappe
Secretary
East New Market
Indian River Bay
Eldorado
Hudson
Brookview
Galestown
Eagle Harbor
Prince Frederick
Cambridge
Sharptown
Chesapeake Bay
Benedict
Madison
Church Creek
Golden Beach
DORCHESTER
Vienna
Mardela Springs
Delmar
St. Leonard
Bucktown
Calvert Beach
Taylors Island
BLACKWATER N.W.R.
Nanticoke R.
Hebron
Pittsville
Willards
Ocean Pines
Broomes Island
Quantico
Assawoman Bay
Salisbury
West Ocean City
Chesapeake Ranch Estates
Fishing Creek
WICOMICO
Fruitland
Berlin
Ocean City
Hollywood
Solomons
Powellville
Toddville
Leonardtown
California
PATUXENT N.A.T.C.
Fishing Bay
Nanticoke
ST. MARYS
Lexington Park
WORCESTER
Tangier Sound
Princess Anne
Snow Hill
St. Marys City
SOMERSET
Bloodsworth I.
Deal Island
Chincoteague Bay
Assateague Island
Wenona
ASSATEAGUE ISLAND NATIONAL SEASHORE
Piney Point
Scotland
Stockton
Pocomoke City
MD.
Pt. Lookout
Smith I.
MARTIN N.W.R.
VA.
Ewell
Crisfield
CHINCOTEAGUE N.W.R.
ATLANTIC OCEAN
Lawsonia
Chincoteague
83
95
695
97
295

MARYLAND

Maryland: Map Index

Lansdowne	H3
LaPlata	G5
Largo	G4
Laurel	D3, G3
LaVale	C6
Lawsonia	L7
Layhill	B3
Laytonsville	F3
Leonardtown	H6
Lewisdale	C4
Lexington Park	J6
Linthicum	H3
Lochearn	H2
Loch Lynn Heights	A7
Lonaconing	C6
Londontown	H4
Luke	B7
Lutherville	H2
Luxmanor	B3
Madison	K5
Manchester	G1
Marbury	F5
Mardela Springs	L6
Marlton	G4
Marydel	L3
Maydale	C3
Mayo	J4
Mechanicsville	G6
Middle River	J2
Middletown	D2
Midland	C6
Milford	G2
Millington	L2
Montgomery Village	F3
Montpelier	D3
Morningside	D5
Mount Aetna	D1
Mountain Lake Park	A7
Mount Airy	F2
Mount Rainier	C4
Muirkirk	D3
Myersville	D1
Nanticoke	L6
New Carrollton	D4
New Market	E2
New Windsor	F1
Nikep	C6
Norbeck	B3
North Beach	H5
North Chevy Chase	B4
North East	L1
Oak Crest	D3
Oakland	A7
Oakland	G2
Oakview	C3
Ocean City	P6
Ocean Pines	P6
Odenton	H3
Oldtown	D6
Olney	F3
Overlea	H2
Owings Mills	G2
Oxford	K5
Oxon Hill	C5
Palmer Park	D4
Parkville	H2
Parole	H4
Perry Hall	J2
Perryman	K2
Perryville	K1
Pikesville	H2
Piney Point	H7
Piscataway	G5
Pisgah	F5
Pittsville	N6
Pleasant Hills	J2
Pocomoke City	M7
Point of Rocks	D2
Pomonkey	F5
Poolesville	E3
Popes Creek	G6
Port Deposit	K1
Port Tobacco	F5
Potomac	A3, F3
Potomac Heights	F5
Powellville	N6
Preston	L5
Prince Frederick	H5
Princess Anne	M7
Quantico	M6
Queen Anne	L4
Queenstown	K4
Randallstown	G2
Randolph Hills	B3
Redhouse	A7
Redland	F3
Reisterstown	G2
Ridgely	L4
Rising Sun	K1
Ritchie	D5
Riverdale	C4
Riviera Beach	H3
Rock Hall	K3
Rockville	A3, F3
Rosedale	H2
Rosemont	D2
Rossmoor Leisure World	B3
Rossville	J2
St. Charles	G5
St. Leonard	H6
St. Marys City	J7
St. Michaels	K4
Salisbury	M6
Scotland	J7
Seabrook	D4
Seat Pleasant	D5
Secretary	L5
Severn	H3
Severna Park	H3
Shady Side	H4
Sharpsburg	C2
Sharptown	M5
Shawsville	H1
Silver Hill	C5
Silver Spring	B4, F4
Smithsburg	D1
Snow Hill	N7
Solomons	J6
Somerset	B4
South Gate	H3
Spencerville	C3
Stevensville	J3
Stockton	N7
Sudlersville	L3
Suitland	C5, G4
Sykesville	G2
Takoma Park	C4
Taneytown	F1
Taylors Island	J6
Temple Hills	C5, G4
Templeville	L3
Thurmont	E1
Tilghman	J5
Timonium	H2
Toddville	K6
Towson	H2
Trappe	K5
Union Bridge	F1
Upper Marlboro	H4
Vienna	L6
Waldorf	G5
Walker Mill	D5
Walkersville	E2
Wenona	L7
West Ocean City	P6
Westernport	B7
Westminster	F1
Wheaton	B3, F3
White Hall	H1
White Marsh	J2
White Oak	C3, G3
White Plains	G5
Wildwood Hills	A3
Willards	N6
Williamsport	C1
Woodlawn	G2
Woodsboro	E1
Woodyard	G4

Other Features

Aberdeen Proving Ground	K2
Allegheny Front, mt. ridge	C7
Andrews Air Force Base	D5
Antietam Natl. Battlefield	D2
Appalachian Natl. Scenic Trail	D2
Assateague Island Natl. Seashore	P7
Assawoman, bay	P6
Backbone, mt.	A7
Blackwater Natl. Wildlife Refuge	K6
Catoctin Mt. Park	E1
Chesapeake, bay	J5
Chesapeake and Ohio Canal Natl. Hist. Park	A4, D2
Chester, river	K3
Chincoteague, bay	N7
Choptank, river	K5
Deep Creek, lake	A6
Eastern Neck Natl. Wildlife Refuge	K3
Fishing, bay	K6
Green Ridge State Forest	A1, E6
Liberty, reservoir	G2
Martin Natl. Wildlife Refuge	K7
Monocacy Natl. Battlefield	E2
North Branch Potomac, river	C7
Nanticoke, river	L6
Natl. Agricultural Research Center	D3
Patapsco, river	H3
Patuxent, river	H4
Patuxent Naval Air Test Center	J6
Potomac, river	G6
Prettyboy, reservoir	G1
Savage River State Forest	B6
Susquehanna, river	J1
Tangier, sound	L7
Wheaton Reg. Park	B3
Wicomico, river	G6
Youghiogheny, river	A6

52

MARYLAND

The house of Edgar Allan Poe in Baltimore, Md.
Baltimore Chamber of Commerce

Sciences Museum; and the Lacrosse Hall of Fame Museum. Other museums in the state include the U.S. Naval Academy Museum, in Annapolis; the Chesapeake Bay Maritime Museum, in Saint Michaels; and the Fire Museum of Maryland, in Lutherville, with exhibits of fire-fighting equipment.

One of the largest libraries in Maryland is the Enoch Pratt Free Library in Baltimore, dating from 1882. Other major libraries include the Maryland Historical Society Library, in Baltimore; the Maryland State Library, in Annapolis; and several libraries attached to institutions of higher education. Performing-arts organizations include the Baltimore Symphony Orchestra, the Baltimore Opera Company, and the Center Stage Theater of Baltimore.

Historical Sites. Maryland is noted for its many historical landmarks and old houses. The Star-Spangled Banner Flag House and Fort McHenry National Monument and Historic Shrine, in Baltimore, contain exhibits associated with the origin of the American flag and the national anthem. Harpers Ferry National Historical Park (partly in West Virginia) was the scene of the raid in 1859 by the abolitionist John Brown. Antietam and Monocacy national battlefields, both near Sharpsburg, were the sites of important battles of the American Civil War. Chesapeake and Ohio Canal National Historical Park follows the route along the Potomac R. of the canal (built 1828–50). Notable 18th-century houses are included in Thomas Stone National Historic Site, near Port Tobacco, and Hampton National Historic Site, in Towson. Clara Barton National Historic Site, in Glen Echo, encompasses the home of the founder of the American Red Cross.

Sports and Recreation. For centuries Marylanders have engaged in a broad range of outdoor activities, which today include fishing, sailing, swimming, hunting, and hiking. Maryland also is noted for the high quality of its lacrosse teams, and a modern form of jousting has been designated as the state sport. Maryland has several well-known Thoroughbred racetracks, including Pimlico, in Baltimore, site of the annual Preakness race; Bowie Race Course, in Bowie; and Laurel Race Course, in Laurel. The Capital Centre, in Landover, is a big indoor sports and entertainment arena. Oriole Park at Camden Yards is the home of Baltimore's major league professional baseball team.

Communications. In the early 1990s, Maryland had 52 AM radio stations, 65 FM radiobroadcasters, and 15 television stations. The state's first radio stations, WCAO and WFBR in Baltimore, began broadcasting in 1922, and the first television station, WMAR-TV in Baltimore, began operations in 1947. The state's first newspaper was the weekly *Maryland Gazette,* issued in Annapolis from 1727 to 1734. In the early 1990s Maryland had 15 daily newspapers with a combined daily circulation of about 738,500. Influential dailies included the *Capital,* published in Annapolis; and the *Baltimore Sun* and the *Afro-American,* published in Baltimore. H. L. Mencken was a noted figure in Baltimore journalism in the first half of the 20th century.

GOVERNMENT AND POLITICS

Maryland is governed under a constitution adopted in 1867, as amended. Previous constitutions had been adopted in 1776, 1851, and 1864. An amendment to the constitution may be proposed by the state legislature or by a constitutional convention; to become effective, the amendment must be approved by a majority of persons voting on the issue in a general election.

Executive. Maryland's chief executive official, the governor, is popularly elected to a 4-year term and may not serve more than two consecutive terms. In case of death, removal from office, or incapacity to govern, the governor is succeeded by the lieutenant governor, who is also elected

MARYLAND

to a 4-year term. Two other executive officials popularly elected to 4-year terms are the comptroller of treasury and the attorney general. The secretary of state is appointed by the governor, and the state treasurer is elected by the legislature.

Legislature. Maryland's legislature, the General Assembly, consists of a 141-member house of delegates and a 47-member senate. All legislators are elected to 4-year terms. The presiding officers of the two chambers are the president of the senate and the speaker of the house.

Judiciary. Maryland's court of last resort is the court of appeals, made up of a chief judge and six other justices. The state's intermediate appellate court is called the court of special appeals and is composed of a chief judge and 12 additional justices. The judges of both courts are initially appointed by the governor with the consent of the senate and must be confirmed in office by voters within two years of appointment. The judges serve 10-year terms. The major trial courts of Maryland are the circuit courts of the counties and of the city of Baltimore. Those courts include a total of 116 judges, who serve 15-year terms.

Local Government. Maryland is divided into 23 counties, most of which are governed by commissioners elected to 4-year terms. Several have an elected county executive. The city of Baltimore is not part of any county and is governed by a mayor and a council.

National Representation. Maryland elects two senators and eight representatives to the U.S. Congress. The state has ten electoral votes in presidential elections.

Politics. As the 1990s began, the Democratic party claimed the overwhelming majority of registered voters in Maryland. Most of the state's congressional delegation was Democratic, and the party also controlled both houses of the state legislature. No Republican has been elected governor of Maryland since Spiro T. Agnew in 1966; he did not finish the term. Agnew was elected vice-president of the U.S. in 1968 and re-elected in 1972; he resigned the office in 1973. Democrats have held the edge in presidential elections since 1960.

ECONOMY

In colonial times Maryland was known for the production of tobacco, and it also had important fishing, lumbering, and shipbuilding industries.

The economic life of Maryland is heavily dependent on Chesapeake Bay, which supports extensive shipping and seafood industries. Shown here is a typical clam-harvesting operation. Maryland is equally famous for its oysters and soft-shell crabs.
Seafood Marketing Authority

MARYLAND

Angus beef cattle being fed by machine. Agriculture enterprises occupy about one-third of the land area of Maryland.
U.S. Dept. of Agriculture

Manufacturing became the principal economic activity in the state in the late 19th century. In the early 1990s the Baltimore area was the state's leading economic center. Many Marylanders are employed by the federal government in neighboring Washington, D.C., and some U.S. agencies, including the Bureau of the Census, are located in the state.

Agriculture. A relatively unimportant agricultural state by national standards, Maryland annually produces farm commodities valued at about $1.3 billion, amounting to less than 1% of the annual gross state product. Maryland has some 15,400 farms, averaging 59 ha (146 acres) in size. Approximately 62% of the state's yearly farm income is derived from the sale of livestock and livestock products; the remaining farm income is from sales of crops. The leading products are broiler chickens, dairy goods, corn, and soybeans. Broiler production is highest in Wicomico Co. on the Eastern Shore, and Frederick Co. typically leads in dairy products. Other important agricultural commodities produced in the state include hay, tobacco, wheat, barley, potatoes and other vegetables, nursery and greenhouse products, apples, cattle and calves, hogs, and chicken eggs.

Forestry. About 90% of Maryland's forests are classified as commercial timberland, and 90% of that is privately owned. Hardwoods, including oak and yellow poplar, and loblolly pine, a softwood, account for the bulk of the harvest. The annual cut of sawtimber in the late 1980s exceeded 186 million board feet, with a value to landowners of about $28 million; manufactured wood products were valued at $95 million. Pulpwood is used by a large paper mill near the town of Luke.

Fishing. Maryland's lengthy tidal shoreline has given rise to a small but significant fishing industry. The value of the yearly catch is about $52 million. Chesapeake Bay is the leading fishing ground. Crabs account for more than 40% of the total value produced, followed by clams and oysters. Striped bass, sea trout, bluefish, alewives, menhaden, and flounder also are landed in commercial quantities.

Mining. Maryland has a comparatively small mining sector; the annual value of its mineral output is about $425 million. Sand, gravel, and stone are produced in many parts of Maryland for construction and other industrial purposes. Bituminous coal deposits are found in Garrett and Allegany counties in the NW. Increased demand in the late 1970s and early '80s stimulated production, which is predominantly from surface mines. Other mineral products include natural gas, clay, talc, and peat.

Manufacturing. Manufacturing in Maryland accounts for about 11% of the annual gross state product and employs some 209,000 workers. Leading products are precision instruments, printed materials, processed foods, transport equipment, industrial equipment, primary metals, and chemicals. Baltimore and Anne Arundel counties and the city of Baltimore lead the state in the number of manufacturing employees. Sparrows Point, near Baltimore, is the site of a

MARYLAND

DATE OF STATEHOOD: April 28, 1788; 7th state

CAPITAL:	Annapolis
MOTTO:	*Fatti maschii, parole femine* (Manly deeds, womanly words)
NICKNAMES:	Old Line State; Free State
STATE SONG:	"Maryland, My Maryland" (words by James R. Randall, sung to the tune of "O, Tannenbaum")
STATE TREE:	White oak
STATE FLOWER:	Black-eyed Susan
STATE BIRD:	Baltimore oriole
POPULATION (1990):	4,781,468; 19th among the states
AREA:	32,135 sq km (12,407 sq mi); 42d largest state; includes 6819 sq km (2633 sq mi) of inland water
COASTLINE:	50 km (31 mi)
HIGHEST POINT:	Backbone Mt., 1024 m (3360 ft)
LOWEST POINT:	Sea level, along the coast
ELECTORAL VOTES:	10
U.S. CONGRESS:	2 senators; 8 representatives

POPULATION OF MARYLAND SINCE 1790

Year of Census	Population	Classified As Urban
1790	320,000	4%
1820	407,000	16%
1850	583,000	32%
1880	935,000	40%
1900	1,188,000	50%
1920	1,450,000	60%
1940	1,821,000	59%
1960	3,101,000	73%
1980	4,217,000	80%
1990	4,781,468	81%

POPULATION OF TEN LARGEST CITIES

	1990 Census	1980 Census
Baltimore	736,014	786,775
Rockville	44,835	43,811
Frederick	40,148	28,086
Gaithersburg	39,542	26,424
Bowie	37,589	33,695
Hagerstown	35,445	34,132
Annapolis	33,187	31,740
Cumberland	23,706	25,933
College Park	21,927	23,614
Greenbelt	21,096	17,332

CLIMATE — BALTIMORE

Average January temperature range	−3.9° to 5.6° C (25° to 42° F)
Average July temperature range	19.4° to 30.6° C (67° to 87° F)
Average annual temperature	12.8° C (55° F)
Average annual precipitation	1016 mm (40 in)
Average annual snowfall	559 mm (22 in)
Mean number of days per year with appreciable precipitation	113
Average daily relative humidity	66%
Mean number of clear days per year	106

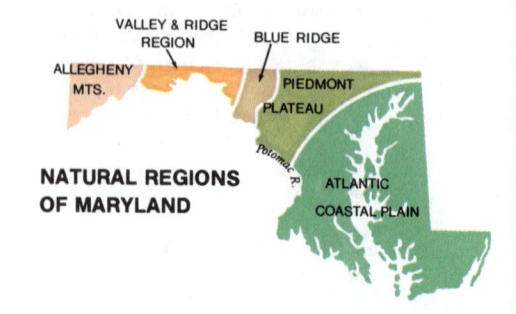

NATURAL REGIONS OF MARYLAND

Valley & Ridge Region; Blue Ridge; Allegheny Mts.; Piedmont Plateau; Atlantic Coastal Plain

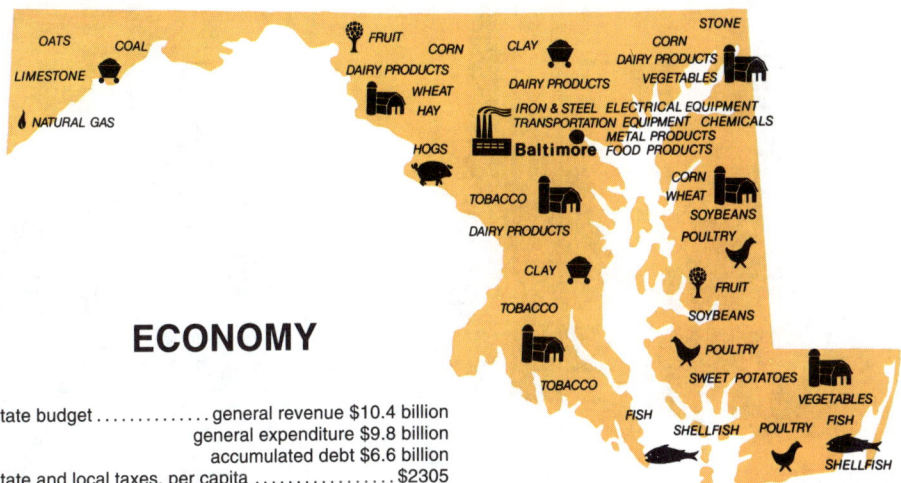

PRINCIPAL PRODUCTS OF MARYLAND

ECONOMY

State budget	general revenue	$10.4 billion
	general expenditure	$9.8 billion
	accumulated debt	$6.6 billion
State and local taxes, per capita		$2305
Personal income, per capita		$17,730
Population below poverty level		8.3%
Assets, insured commercial banks (551)		$58.1 billion
Labor force (civilian nonfarm)		2,148,000
Employed in services		28%
Employed in wholesale and retail trade		25%
Employed in government		19%
Employed in manufacturing		10%

	Quantity Produced	Value
FARM PRODUCTS		**$1.3 billion**
Crops		**$517 million**
Corn	1.3 million metric tons	$130 million
Soybeans	485,000 metric tons	$102 million
Hay	615,000 metric tons	$73 million
Vegetables	104,000 metric tons	$27 million
Tobacco	4400 metric tons	$17 million
Livestock and Livestock Products		**$828 million**
Chickens (broilers)	518,000 metric tons	$399 million
Milk	615,000 metric tons	$204 million
Cattle	52,000 metric tons	$84 million
Eggs	954 million	$61 million
Hogs	30,000 metric tons	$35 million
MINERALS		**$425 million**
Stone	28.0 million metric tons	$155 million
Cement	1.7 million metric tons	$94 million
Sand, gravel	15.3 million metric tons	$85 million
Coal	3.0 million metric tons	$83 million
FISHING	38,600 metric tons	**$52 million**

	Annual Payroll
MANUFACTURING	**$6.3 billion**
Instruments and related products	$1.1 billion
Printing and publishing	$793 million
Food and kindred products	$505 million
Transportation equipment	$446 million
Electronic equipment	$443 million
Industrial machinery and equipment	$420 million
Primary metals	$410 million
Chemicals and allied products	$384 million
Fabricated metal products	$282 million
Paper and allied products	$232 million
Rubber and plastics products	$186 million
Stone, clay, and glass products	$164 million
OTHER	**$45.3 billion**
Services	$13.2 billion
Government	$12.9 billion
Retail trade	$5.3 billion
Construction	$4.1 billion
Finance, insurance, and real estate	$3.6 billion
Wholesale trade	$3.2 billion
Transportation, communications, and public utilities	$2.6 billion

ANNUAL GROSS STATE PRODUCT

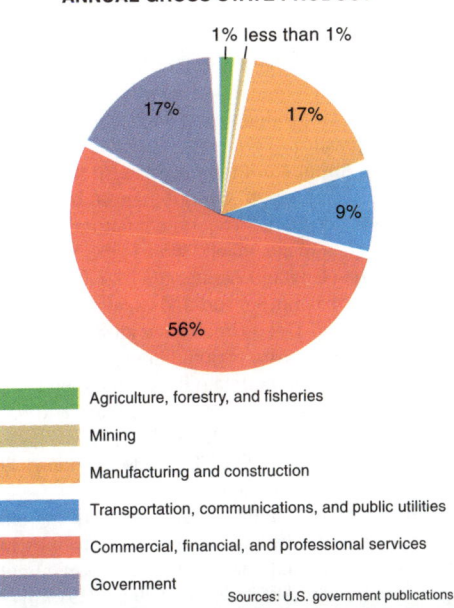

- Agriculture, forestry, and fisheries — 1%
- Mining — less than 1%
- Manufacturing and construction — 17%
- Transportation, communications, and public utilities — 9%
- Commercial, financial, and professional services — 56%
- Government — 17%

Sources: U.S. government publications

MARYLAND

Steel manufacturing is one of the chief industries of Baltimore, the leading industrial city of Maryland.
Baltimore Chamber of Commerce

big steel mill. Other important Maryland manufactures include paper and paper products, fabricated metal products, and goods made of rubber and plastics.

Tourism. About 4 million tourists visit Maryland each year, contributing more than $6 billion to the state economy. The state's natural attractions range from the Atlantic shore to the Allegheny Mts. Ocean City and Assateague Island National Seashore are famous resort and vacation spots on the coast, and Deep Creek Lake attracts visitors to the Allegheny Mts. region. Other popular areas include Catoctin Mountain Park, Greenbelt Park, and Piscataway Park. In addition, Maryland has a number of historical sites and serves as a gateway to Washington, D.C. The state maintains 49 parks and recreation areas.

Transportation. Baltimore and the Washington, D.C., area are the main transportation hubs in Maryland. The state has about 46,285 km (about 28,760 mi) of roads, including 629 km (391 mi) of interstate highways, and it is served by 1281 km (796 mi) of Class I railroad track. Baltimore is one of the leading seaports of the U.S. The state has 114 airports and 41 heliports; the busiest air terminal is the Baltimore-Washington International Airport.

Energy. Maryland has an installed electricity generating capacity of about 9.8 million kw, and annual production totals some 31.5 billion kwh. Approximately 88% of the state's electricity is generated in conventional facilities burning coal or petroleum products, 7% in hydroelectric installations, and 4% in nuclear-powered generators.
H.E.J.

HISTORY

The territory now comprising the states of Maryland and Delaware was granted to George Calvert, 1st Baron Baltimore, by Charles I, king of England, in 1632. Lord Baltimore, who named the territory in honor of Henrietta Maria, queen consort of Charles I, died before issuance of the

MARYLAND

royal charter, which later in 1632 was granted to his son Cecilius Calvert, 2d Baron Baltimore. Lord Baltimore, a Roman Catholic, had planned to found a colony in which coreligionists might be free of persecution. Religious tolerance was a central feature of his project. Cecilius Calvert organized an expedition that sailed from Gravesend in November 1633 under the command of Leonard Calvert (1606?–47), his brother. Of some 200 colonists who arrived in the territory in March 1634, however, it is probable that more than half were Protestants. A settlement called Saint Mary's was founded on the peninsula later that year. On Jan. 26, 1635, the first assembly of freemen of the province met at St. Mary's. The right of initiating laws was conceded to the people in 1638, but Lord Baltimore retained the power of veto. The first statutes of the province were passed in 1638.

Early Settlement. Relations were friendly with the Indians, but a quarrel was shortly provoked among the settlers by William Claiborne, a Virginian, who had established a trading post on Kent Island, in Chesapeake Bay, in 1631. Claiborne's refusal to recognize the authority of Lord Baltimore precipitated a protracted and often violent feud, and in 1638 his settlement was seized. In 1643 a company of Puritans, excluded from Virginia for religious nonconformity, founded a settlement called Providence on the site of present-day Annapolis. In the wake of the English Revolution, which had begun in 1642, increasing numbers of Puritans arrived in the colony. A parliamentary force occupied St. Mary's in 1645, and Claiborne regained possession of Kent Island. Nearly two years elapsed before Gov. Calvert, who had taken refuge in Virginia, reestablished his authority in Maryland. In an attempt to conciliate the Puritans, Lord Baltimore consented, in 1650, to the formation of Anne Arundel Co., comprising the Puritan settlements in the colony. Shortly afterward Charles Co. was also organized for the benefit of the Puritans. The influx of Puritans continued, and within a brief period they became the dominant force in the colonial assembly. In 1652 representatives of England, including Claiborne and the leader of Anne Arundel Co., assumed formal control of the colony. Kent Island was officially returned to Claiborne, and penal laws were enacted against Roman Catholics. The ensuing civil warfare culminated in an abortive attack on Providence in March 1655 by Baltimore's supporters. Lord Baltimore's title to the colony was recognized in 1657 by Oliver Cromwell, Lord Protector of England, and the proprietary government was restored in the following year.

Charles Calvert, 3d Baron Baltimore, son of Cecilius, became lord proprietor of the colony in 1675. The third Lord Baltimore provoked considerable unrest in Maryland because of his undemocratic and pro–Roman Catholic policies. During most of his proprietorship he was involved in a bitter boundary dispute with William Penn, founder of Pennsylvania. The dispute, which was settled in Penn's favor in 1685, concerned the territory now comprising Delaware. Following the Glorious Revolution (the English Revolution of 1688) and the deposition of King James II, Protestants seized power in Maryland in the name of William III and Mary II, the new English monarchs. The colonial legislature submitted a list of complaints against Lord Baltimore's government to the new government in London, and in August 1691 the lord proprietor was deprived of his political privileges. In 1715, after an interlude of royal rule, proprietary government was reinstituted in the colony under Charles Calvert, 5th Baron Baltimore (1699–1751), a Protestant. Under the new regime all sects were tolerated except the Roman Catholics, who were denied the franchise and forbidden to worship in public. A prolonged dispute with Pennsylvania regarding the northern boundary of the colony was finally adjudicated between 1763 and 1767 by the British surveyors Charles Mason (1730–87) and Jeremiah Dixon (1733–79). Known subsequently as the Mason-Dixon line (q.v.), the Maryland-Pennsylvania frontier that they delineated coincided with lat 39°43′ N.

Maryland emerged as a center of resistance to British policy in the period preceding the outbreak of the American Revolution. In 1774, following the imposition of the royal tax on tea, Maryland patriots burned a tea ship. A popular convention was organized in the same year to direct the revolutionary movement. In November 1776, the convention adopted a constitution, formally supplanting the proprietary government.

The 19th and 20th Centuries. During the fighting in the War of 1812 the British burned Havre de Grace, Frenchtown, and other communities in 1813. A British army was turned back at Baltimore, however, and in September 1814, Fort McHenry, the key defense bastion of the city, withstood a severe bombardment by the British fleet. During this battle Francis Scott Key wrote "The Star-Spangled Banner."

Maryland was a slaveholding state, and during the controversy that led to the American Civil War large segments of the population favored secession from the Union. Although the state adhered to the Union, many Marylanders served in the Confederate army, and Confederate forces

MARYLAND, UNIVERSITY SYSTEM OF

invaded the state on two occasions. In September 1862 a decisive battle, the only major engagement on Maryland soil, was fought near Sharpsburg. A new constitution, adopted in 1864, penalized all Marylanders who had supported the Confederacy, but popular objection to this provision resulted in the present constitution, adopted in 1867.

Until the 1900s the state maintained a relatively steady economic growth, a pattern that was dramatically broken by a surge of industrial expansion during and after the two world wars. To accommodate the needs of its rapidly expanding population, Maryland launched a series of long-range programs to expand and improve its transportation, social, and educational facilities. By the 1970s it had become a national center for space research and development, and federal government employees represented a growing segment of the work force. As the sprawling suburbs of Baltimore and Washington approached one another, Maryland in the 1980s and '90s redoubled its efforts to alleviate urban and racial pressures and to preserve the charm of its landscape.

For further information on this topic, see the Bibliography in volume 28, section 1179.

MARYLAND, UNIVERSITY SYSTEM OF, group of 11 state-assisted institutions of higher learning, offering bachelor's and graduate degrees. Created in 1988, the system brings together under one governing board the five former campuses of the University of Maryland (Baltimore, College Park, Baltimore County, Eastern Shore, and University College) and six other Maryland institutions (Bowie State University, Coppin State College, Frostburg State University, Salisbury State University, Towson State University, and the University of Baltimore). The University of Maryland was originally formed in 1920 by the merger of the university at Baltimore (founded in 1807 as the College of Medicine of Maryland) and the Maryland State College of Agriculture at College Park (chartered in 1856 as the Maryland Agricultural College). Today, College Park, with 125 undergraduate majors and nearly 80 graduate programs, is the system's flagship campus. Major research and service components of the system include a center for environmental and estuarine studies, an agricultural experiment station, a cooperative extension service, and a biotechnology institute. They are located in the state's major geographical areas, from the Appalachians to Chesapeake Bay.

MARY MAGDALENE, Saint, in the New Testament, woman so named from Magdala, a town near Tiberias (now in Israel). Jesus healed her of evil spirits (see Luke 8:2) and appeared to her after his resurrection (see Matt. 28:9), following her vigil at the foot of the cross (see Mark 15:40). She has been identified from the earliest times with a sinning woman described as having anointed the Lord's feet (see Luke 7:37–38) and with Mary the sister of Martha, who also anointed Jesus (see John 12:3), although the Gospels support neither tradition. Her feast day is July 22.

MASACCIO (1401–27?), the first great painter of the Italian Renaissance. His innovations in the use of scientific perspective inaugurated the modern era in painting.

Masaccio, originally named Tommaso Cassai, was born in San Giovanni Valdarno, near Florence, on Dec. 21, 1401. He joined the painters guild in Florence in 1422. His remarkably individual style owed little to other painters, except possibly the great 14th-century master Giotto. He was more strongly influenced by the architect Brunelleschi and the sculptor Donatello, both of whom were his contemporaries in Florence.

The Tribute Money (c. 1427, Brancacci Chapel, Santa Maria del Carmine, Florence), fresco by Masaccio.
Scala–Editorial Photocolor Archives

From Brunelleschi he acquired a knowledge of mathematical proportion that was crucial to his revival of the principles of scientific perspective. From Donatello he imbibed a knowledge of classical art that led him away from the prevailing Gothic style. He inaugurated a new naturalistic approach to painting that was concerned less with details and ornamentation than with simplicity and unity, less with flat surfaces than with the illusion of three dimensionality. Together with Brunelleschi and Donatello, he was a founder of the Renaissance.

Only four unquestionably attributable works of Masaccio survive, although various other paintings have been attributed in whole or in part to him. All of his works are religious in nature—altarpieces or church frescoes. The earliest, a panel, *The Madonna with St. Anne* (c. 1423, Uffizi, Florence), shows the influence of Donatello in its realistic flesh textures and solidly rounded forms. The fresco *Trinity* (c. 1425, Santa Maria Novella, Florence) used full perspective for the first time in Western art. His altarpiece for Santa Maria del Carmine, Pisa (1426), with its central panel of the *Adoration of the Magi* (now in the Staatliche Museen, Berlin), was a simple, unadorned version of a theme that was treated by other painters in a more decorative, ornamental manner. The fresco series for the Brancacci Chapel in Santa Maria del Carmine, Florence (c. 1427) illustrates another of his great innovations—the use of light to define the human body and its draperies. In these frescoes, rather than bathing his scenes in flat uniform light, he painted them as if they were illuminated from a single source of light (the actual chapel window), thus creating a play of light and shadow (chiaroscuro) that gave them a natural, realistic quality unknown in the art of his day. Of these six fresco scenes, *Tribute Money* and *Expulsion from Eden* are considered his masterpieces.

Masaccio's work exerted a strong influence on the course of later Florentine art and particularly on the work of Michelangelo. He died in Rome in 1427 or 1428.

MASADA (Heb., "fortress"), ancient ruins on a mountaintop in the desert about 48.3 km (about 30 mi) southeast of Jerusalem, the scene of the last stand made by the Jewish Zealots in their revolt against Roman rule (AD 66–73). Two fortified palaces were built there in the 1st century BC by the Judean king Herod the Great. After Herod's death, Masada was occupied by a Roman garrison until the Zealots captured it in AD 66. When Jerusalem was taken by the Romans in 70, the last remaining rebels—about 1000 men, women, and children—withdrew to the remote mountaintop. Under their leader, Eleazar ben Jair, they withstood a 2-year siege by the Roman Tenth Legion, killing themselves rather than surrendering when the besiegers finally captured the fortress in 73. Excavated by the Israeli archaeologist Yigael Yadin (1917–84) in 1963–65, Masada is both a popular tourist attraction and an Israeli national shrine.

For further information on this topic, see the Bibliography in volume 28, sections 874, 1060.

MASAI, East African nomadic people speaking the Masai Sudanic language. The Masai (or Maasai) traditionally herded their cattle freely across the highlands of Kenya. Probably at the height of their power in the mid-19th century, they suffered from the British colonization of Africa and the resultant ecological and political changes. Rinderpest, an infectious febrile disease, apparently accompanied the British, decimating the cattle herds that supplied the Masai with milk and blood; famine and then smallpox followed. The weakened Masai attacked rather than cooperated with the new rulers. In 1904 and 1912–13 the British government relocated the Masai population to distant southern Kenya and Tanzania, where they now live.

Masai males are rigidly classed by age into boys, warriors, and elders. Girls often have their marriages negotiated by their fathers before they are born. Both boys and girls undergo circumcision ceremonies. Older women enjoy the same status as male elders. The Masai, most of whom are nomadic throughout the year, live in kraals, small clusters of cow-dung huts constructed by the women. Today the Masai number approximately 250,000. They remain a pastoral people.

For further information on this topic, see the Bibliography in volume 28, section 1010.

MASAN, city, S South Korea, in South Kyongsang Province, on an arm of Chinhae Bay of Korea Strait, near Pusan. From the port, which opened in 1899, fish, cotton, and salt are exported. The city's industries include sake brewing, fish and soy processing, cotton-textile weaving, and metalworking. The city is a road junction and is situated on the S coastal railroad. It is the site of Masan College (1948) and the center of a resort area, with beaches and hot springs nearby.

In 1598 the Japanese fleet was defeated by the Koreans offshore; the battle was notable for the appearance of the "Turtle Boat," the first known ironclad warship. The city was formerly called Masampo. Pop. (1985 prelim.) 449,236.

MASARYK, Jan Garrigue (1886–1948), Czechoslovak statesman and diplomat, the son of Tomáš Masaryk. Born in Prague, and educated at the

MASARYK

University of Prague, he went to the U.S. at the age of 21 and worked in New York City until 1913. During World War I he fought in the Austro-Hungarian army, and after the war he pursued a diplomatic career, serving in the Czech legations in Washington and London. Masaryk was minister to Great Britain from 1925 to 1938, when the Munich Pact dismembered his country. He then resigned from diplomatic service and lectured for a year at U.S. universities.

The Czechoslovak government-in-exile, established in London in 1940, appointed Masaryk foreign minister. In that post he gained U.S. recognition of his exiled government. After the war he returned to Czechoslovakia and served as foreign minister, opposing increasing Communist domination of the government. In March 1948, Masaryk, who had retained his office despite the February Communist coup there, reportedly threw himself to his death from a window.

MASARYK, Tomáš Garrigue (1850–1937), first president of Czechoslovakia (1918–35) and architect of Czech independence.

Masaryk was born on March 7, 1850, in Hodonín, Moravia (then part of the Austrian Empire), and was educated in Brno and Vienna. He taught philosophy in Vienna for three years before he was appointed (1882) professor at the new Czech University of Prague. In 1891 he entered the Austrian parliament, resigning two years later to devote himself to the political education of the Czech nation. Reelected in 1907, he fought against Austria's alliance with Germany and its aggressive policy in the Balkans. In the early stage of World War I, he escaped (1915) from Austria to Italy and Switzerland, later settling in London, where he became a lecturer at King's College, Newcastle upon Tyne. Throughout the war, he organized the Czech movement of independence, visiting the U.S. in its behalf in 1917. At the armistice in 1918, the Czechoslovak National Council, which he headed, was recognized by the Allies as the provisional government of Czechoslovakia. When the republic was established, he was elected its first president. Three times reelected (1920, 1927, and 1934), he resigned in 1935 because of old age. He died in Lány Castle on Sept. 14, 1937.

Masaryk's many books include *Der Selbstmord als soziale Massenerscheinung der modernen Zivilisation* (Suicide as a Mass Phenomenon of Modern Civilization, 1881), *The Spirit of Russia* (1913; trans. 1919), and *The Making of a State: Memories and Observations, 1914–1918* (1925; trans. 1927).

MASAYA, city, SW Nicaragua, capital of Masaya Department, near Managua. The city is on the E slope of the extinct Masaya volcano, whose crater contains Lake Masaya. The city is a rail junction and the industrial and commercial center for the surrounding agricultural area. Industries include the processing of fiber and the manufacture of cigars, Indian handicrafts, shoes, leather products, soap, and starch. Masaya, called the City of Flowers, is noted for the annual fall fiesta of San Jerónimo. Pop. (1985 est.) 74,950.

MASBATE, island, central Philippines, near Luzon. Together with Burias, Ticao, and a few other smaller islands, it forms Masbate Province. Cattle are raised, and coconuts, rice, hemp, and corn are grown. Area, 4046 sq km (1562 sq mi); pop. (Masbate Province, 1980 prelim.) 580,444.

MASCAGNI, Pietro (1863–1945), Italian composer, born in Leghorn. He studied with the Italian composer Alfredo Soffredini (1854–1923). Mascagni's most important work is the opera *Cavalleria rusticana* (1890). Based on a play by the Italian writer Giovanni Verga, it exemplifies the Italian operatic style called *verismo* (Ital., "realism"), which stresses the violent behavior of people under great emotional strain. His success with *verismo* influenced the Italian composer Ruggero Leoncavallo. Mascagni wrote 17 operas, but only *Cavalleria rusticana* and *L'amico Fritz* (1891) are regularly performed today.

MASCON, in astronomy, term derived from the phrase *mass concentration*. Mascons are areas in some of the moon's "seas," or mares, where gravity is somewhat stronger than in other areas, indicating a greater concentration of mass, or density, there. The nature of mascons is not yet determined, but they could represent the remains of iron-rich meteorites or ancient volcanic materials.

MASEFIELD, John (1878–1967), English author and poet laureate, who helped break down Victorian conventions in English poetry. Born June 1, 1878, in Ledbury, at the age of 15 Masefield went to sea, then lived and worked in New York City for a time. After returning to England in 1897, he contributed poems, stories, and articles to periodicals, and in 1900 he joined the staff of the *Manchester Guardian*. His first book of verse, *Salt-Water Ballads* (1902), containing his most famous poem, "Sea Fever," established his reputation as a poet of the sea. He achieved fame in 1911 with a forceful, realistic narrative poem, *The Everlasting Mercy,* about the redemption of a rural libertine. In the same vein were *The Widow in the Bye Street* (1912), *Dauber* (1913), and *Reynard the Fox* (1919).

Among Masefield's other works are the plays *The Tragedy of Nan* (1909) and *The Tragedy of*

Pompey the Great (1910); the novels *Multitude and Solitude* (1909) and *Sard Harker* (1924); and the autobiographies *In the Mill* (1941) and *So Long to Learn* (1952). Essentially a narrative poet, his best poems are marked by a vigorous, direct style and a gift for realistic observation. In 1930 he was named poet laureate, and in 1935 he was made a member of the Order of Merit. He died May 12, 1967, near Abingdon.

MASER, acronym for microwave amplification by stimulated emission of radiation, a device that amplifies or generates microwaves or radio waves. A maser producing radiation in the optical region is called a laser (q.v.).

Principle of Operation. As in lasers, amplification of radiation in masers is obtained by stimulated emission. This occurs when a photon (q.v.) induces an excited atom or molecule to fall to a lower energy state while emitting a photon of the same frequency as the incoming photon. The emitted photon travels in the same direction and in phase with the incoming photon, which is not absorbed during the interaction. The amplitudes of the two waves add up, and amplification of the incoming wave has taken place. Masers make use of those transitions in molecules or crystals that correspond to the energies of microwave or radio frequencies.

Types of Masers. The first maser oscillator was developed by the American physicists Charles Hard Townes (1915–), James P. Gordon (1928–), and Herbert J. Zeiger (1925–) in 1954, and made use of the frequency of the ammonia molecule. This frequency corresponds to the energy of the photon emitted when the nitrogen atom moves from one side to the other of the triangle formed by the three hydrogen atoms in an ammonia molecule. The hydrogen maser makes use of the frequency corresponding to that of the photon released when the spin of the proton in a hydrogen atom flips over with respect to the spin of the atom's electron. Paramagnetic masers use energy transitions corresponding to the orientations of the magnetic moments of paramagnetic ions in crystalline substances placed in an external magnetic field. Different frequencies can be obtained by varying the magnetic field.

Applications. Because of the high stability of the generated frequencies, masers serve as time standards in atomic clocks. Masers are also used as low-noise radio frequency amplifiers in satellite communication and radioastronomy.

MASERU, town and capital of Lesotho, W Lesotho, on the Caledon R., at the border with South Africa. Maseru is a road and trade center for livestock, hides and skins, wool, and grain, all produced in the vicinity. It is the site of Lesotho Agricultural College (1955); close by, at Roma, is the National University of Lesotho (1966). The town succeeded nearby Thaba Bosiu as capital of the British-protected Basuto nation in 1869 and became capital of the independent kingdom of Lesotho in 1966. Pop. (1986, greater city) 109,382.

MASHAM, Lady Abigail (d. 1734), confidante of Queen Anne of Great Britain, born in London. The daughter of a London merchant, Abigail was appointed lady of the bedchamber in 1704 through her cousin, Sarah Churchill, duchess of Marlborough (1660–1744), and gradually replaced her as the queen's favorite. By 1710 she was able to bring about the dismissal of such high officials as Charles Spencer, 3d earl of Sunderland, and Sidney Godolphin, 1st earl of Godolphin (1645–1712), who had dominated the government. In 1714 she had Robert Harley, 1st earl of Oxford, dismissed from his office of lord high treasurer. She became keeper of the privy purse and won (1712) a peerage for her husband, Samuel Masham (1679–1758). After Anne's death in 1714, Lady Masham retired from court.

MASK, face covering that, in ritual and theater, disguises the wearer and usually communicates an alternate identity; also a type of portrait, and a protective screen for the face.

Since at least Paleolithic times people have used masks. Made of wood, basketry, bark, corn husks, cloth, leather, skulls, papier-mâché, and other materials, masks may cover the face, the entire head, or the head and shoulders, and they are sometimes considered part of an accompanying costume. Masks vary widely in their realism or abstraction, their use of symbols, and their ornamentation. The kachina masks of the Pueblo Indians, for example, have only minimal facial features, whereas masks of the Indians of the Pacific Northwest are often elaborately carved and painted, may have movable jaws or other parts, and may even open to reveal a second mask beneath the first. Occasionally, a mask is not intended to be worn on the face, for example, the enormous ritual masks of Oceania and the tiny fingertip masks of Inuit (Eskimo) women.

The making of masks is a primary artistic outlet in many cultures, and masks from Africa, Oceania, and Indian North America are highly prized by art collectors.

Ritual Masks. The dancer who wears a mask in a ceremony is frequently believed to be transformed into or possessed by the spirit inhabiting or represented by the mask. Masks are often believed to contain great power, being potentially dangerous unless handled with the proper rites. The manufacture of a mask may also be subject to prescribed observances. Iroquois false-face

Ceremonial mask of the Baining, a Papuan people of the Melanesian island of New Britain. This mask, made in the late 19th or early 20th century, is constructed of bark and bark cloth on a wooden frame.
Brooklyn Museum–Lent by Mr. and Mrs. Thomas S. Brush

masks, for instance, must be carved from a living tree, which must be ritually asked to grant permission for the carving and must be offered tobacco.

Ritual masks generally depict deities, mythological beings, good and evil spirits, spirits of ancestors and the dead, animal spirits, and other beings believed to have power over humanity. Masks of human ancestors or totem ancestors (beings or animals to which a clan or family traces its ancestry) are often objects of family pride; when they are regarded as the dwelling of the spirit they represent, they may be honored with ceremonies and gifts. The fearsome 6-m (20-ft) high totem masks of the Papuans of New Guinea are believed to frighten away evil spirits and thus protect the living. Totem, ancestral, and other spirit masks are frequently used in initiation ceremonies, and the initiation masks of West Africa are renowned for their beauty. In agricultural rites, masks may represent rain or fertility deities; similarly, animal masks may be worn in ceremonies to ensure a successful hunt. Shamans throughout the world wear masks in curative rites. In East Asia and Sri Lanka, masks may be worn to protect the wearer against (or to cure) diseases such as measles and cholera. In some cultures, masked members of secret societies (such as the duk-duk of New Guinea) terrorize wrongdoers and thus enforce social codes. In parts of Africa, legal judgments are pronounced by masked judges; a historical European analogue is the masked executioner. In festivals in Mexico and other countries, masks may be used for entertainment, storytelling, caricature, and social satire. Grotesque war masks were worn in battle in ancient Greece and Rome, in medieval Japan, and by Northwest Coast Indians; today, war masks survive chiefly in ceremonies.

In funerary ceremonies, masked dancers may seek to drive the soul of the deceased into the spirit world, where it will not harm the living. In memorial rites, masks may be worn to represent departed personages or ancestors. Occasionally, as in pre-Columbian Mexico, masks may be placed on memorial statues. Burial masks are sometimes placed on the face of a corpse (for example, by the Hopi Indians and in ancient Egypt, Rome, China, and Mexico), either to protect the deceased from evil spirits or, as in Egypt, to guide the dead person's spirit to its home in the afterlife. Death masks, made from wax impressions of the features of the deceased, were used in Egypt and Rome as models for sculpted portraits. In medieval Europe, the death mask itself served as a memorial effigy; this use, for famous persons, persisted into the 20th century.

Ritual masks survive in modern Western culture in various folk pageants and customs (such as the frightening Perchten masqueraders in the Tirol, and in Halloween and carnival masquerading) and occasionally in other instances.

Theatrical Masks. Ancient Greek drama was semireligious, rooted in masked ritual. The masks worn by actors in Greek plays were large, with conventionalized features and exaggerated expressions; the wide mouth of the mask contained a brass megaphone to help project the actor's voice to the large audiences. These masks fell into two general categories, tragic and comic, with many variations for both types. In Rome, masks were used in comedy and by pantomimists.

In the mystery and miracle plays of medieval Europe, masks were used to portray dragons, monsters, allegorical characters such as the seven deadly sins, and, inevitably, the devil. The actor portraying God frequently wore a gilt mask. During the Renaissance, half masks covering the eyes and nose were used in the commedia dell'arte; these masks are the apparent ancestor of the modern domino mask, which covers only the eyes. Masks were employed in Renaissance courtly entertainments such as the masque and the ballet de cour, and they survived in ballet until the late 18th century. In modern Western theater, masks are used mainly to represent animal characters, although occasionally a playwright or choreographer experiments with masked personages, as in *The Great God Brown* (1926) by the American dramatist Eugene O'Neill.

In Indonesia, masks are used in village ritual dance dramas and in dramas derived from shadow-puppet plays. The traditional pageants and religious-didactic plays of China required masks representing kings, princesses, and grotesque characters, and the mystery plays of Tibet feature masked players representing demons and other spirits. In Japan, the most famous use of masks is in the Nō plays; made of lacquered or gilded plaster by highly respected artisans, Nō masks are admired for their subtlety of expression.

Protective Masks. Strictly practical protective masks are worn in baseball, hockey, and other sports. The faceplates of medieval European armor, however, occasionally bore grimacing facial features, and in ancient Roman tournaments soldiers often wore symbolically decorated masks on their helmets.

MASLOW, Abraham Harold (1908–70), American psychologist and leading exponent of humanistic psychology. Born in Brooklyn, N.Y., and educated at the City College of New York and the University of Wisconsin, Maslow spent most of his teaching career at Brandeis University. Judging orthodox behaviorism and psychoanalysis to be too rigidly theoretical and concerned with illness, he developed a theory of motivation describing the process by which an individual

Carved and painted wooden mask of the Kwakiutl Indians of British Columbia, Canada. Hinged to open and reveal a second face beneath the outer face, it was used in ritual drama to embody a character who undergoes a transformation.

Museum of the American Indian

progresses from basic needs such as food and sex to the highest needs of what he called self-actualization—the fulfillment of one's greatest human potential. Humanistic psychotherapy, usually in the form of group therapy, seeks to help the individual progress through these stages. Maslow's writings include *Toward a Psychology of Being* (1962) and *Farther Reaches of Human Nature* (1971).

MASOCHISM, in abnormal psychology, a sexual disorder in which a person obtains gratification by receiving physical pain or abuse. The word is derived from the surname of the Austrian novelist Leopold von Sacher-Masoch (1836–95), who depicted in his writings several characters who derived sexual satisfaction from being whipped. In psychoanalysis, the term *masochism* is used more broadly to denote the tendency in some individuals to enjoy humiliations inflicted upon them by others. The opposite tendency, to obtain satisfaction from inflicting cruelty upon others, is called sadism (q.v.) after the French author Marquis de Sade.

MASOLINO DA PANICALE, real name TOMMASO DI CRISTOFORO DI FINO (1383?–1447?), Italian painter, born in Panicale, near Florence. He is known to have joined the Florentine painters guild in 1423 and to have spent some time working in Hungary. With his associate, the Florentine painter Masaccio, Masolino executed a series of frescoes for the Brancacci Chapel in the Church of Santa Maria del Carmine, Florence. Masolino's contributions, completed between 1424 and 1427, include *The Preaching of St. Peter, The Raising of Tabitha,* and *The Fall of Adam and Eve.* Other important frescoes were done for the Collegiata, a church in Castiglione d'Olona; for the Church of San Clemente, Rome; and for the Church of Sant'Agostino, Empoli. An existing fragment of the last (1424?), with its exceedingly graceful yet forceful lines and its delicate, harmonious pastel colors, reveals Masolino's links with the older International Gothic style. His earliest known work is a Madonna and Child, painted on wood (1423, Kunsthalle, Bremen); another panel, which is devoted to the Annunciation (1423?–26), is hanging in the National Gallery of Art in Washington, D.C.

MASON, family of American musicians.

Lowell Mason (1792–1872), influential teacher and choral conductor, whose hymn tunes are still sung. He established music-teacher training and public school music in Massachusetts. *See also* AMERICAN MUSIC.

William Mason (1829–1908), son of Lowell Mason. A noted pianist and teacher, he studied with the Hungarian composer Franz Liszt.

Henry Mason (1831–90), son of Lowell Mason. He was a piano and reed-organ builder who in 1854, with the American Emmons Hamlin, established the important instrument-manufacturing firm of Mason & Hamlin.

Daniel Gregory Mason (1873–1953), son of Henry Mason. He was a prominent composer influenced by impressionism and German romanticism.

MASON, George (1725–92), American statesman, born in Fairfax Co., Va., into the planter aristocracy. Privately educated, he had a good knowledge of law and the classics. In 1758 he completed Gunston Hall on the Potomac, one of the grandest mansions in a state of great houses. A trustee of Alexandria and a county justice, in 1759 Mason was elected to the Virginia House of Burgesses and served at the Virginia Convention (July 1775), which armed the colony for the struggle with Great Britain. At the state's constitutional convention (1776), he drafted the historic Virginia Declaration of Rights and a large portion of the constitution itself.

Mason was a delegate to the federal Constitutional Convention in Philadelphia in 1787 and helped to draft the Constitution. Vexed, however, at its centralization of power and its failure to limit slavery or include a bill of rights, he refused to sign it. Although he continued steadfast in his opposition to what he regarded as the document's weaknesses, he had the satisfaction of seeing the first ten amendments, based on his Virginia Declaration of Rights, added to the Constitution in 1791. He died at Gunston Hall, Oct. 7, 1792.

MASON, John (1586–1635), English colonizer in North America, born in King's Lynn, Norfolk. From 1615 to 1621 he was governor of an English colony at Conception Bay, Newfoundland. In 1622 he and another English colonizer, Sir Ferdinando Gorges, obtained from the Council for New England the province of Maine, which in 1629 was divided between them. At that time Mason also received another grant, extending from the Merrimack River to the Piscataqua River. To this area he gave the name New Hampshire. In 1635 Mason served as vice admiral for New England and as a judge in New Hampshire.

MASON CITY, city, seat of Cerro Gordo Co., N Iowa, on the Winnebago R.; inc. 1881. It is a manufacturing and trading center for a fertile agricultural area. Deposits of clay, limestone, and sand and gravel are in the area. Manufactures include processed food, building materials, fertilizer, machinery, and metal doors. Mason City is the site of a community college; the Charles H. MacNider Museum, featuring displays of American art; and the Kinney Pioneer Museum and Historical Society of North Iowa. The community, settled in 1853 by a group of Freemasons, grew as a railroad center. Pop. (1980) 30,144; (1990) 29,040.

MASON-DIXON LINE, popular name for the boundary line between Maryland and Pennsylvania, so called because it was surveyed (1763–67) by two British astronomers, Charles Mason (1730–87) and Jeremiah Dixon (1733–79). This survey was undertaken in order to settle a dispute between the Calvert family, proprietors of Maryland, and the Penn family, proprietors of Pennsylvania; the dispute had lasted since the English colonizer William Penn was granted Pennsylvania in 1681. The line was drawn to a point about 393 km (about 244 mi) west of the Delaware River. Further work was done in 1773 and 1779.

The term Mason-Dixon Line was popularly used to designate the line that divided the so-called free states from the slave states during the debates in Congress over the Missouri Compromise in 1820. This legislation forbade slavery in the Louisiana Territory north of the parallel 36°30′, except in Missouri. In this sense, the Mason-Dixon Line meant not only the old disputed boundary line but also the line of the Ohio River from the Pennsylvania boundary to its mouth, where it flows into the Mississippi River, then the east, north, and west boundaries of Missouri, and from that point westward, the parallel 36°30′. The term Mason-Dixon Line is still sometimes used to mean the boundary between the North and the South.

MASONRY, art or trade of building in stone, universally practiced since ancient times. Among the ancient Egyptians, stonework was generally squared and fitted; no adhesive or mortar (q.v.) was used to join the stones (see PYRAMIDS). Ancient examples of this Cyclopean masonry, composed of immense irregular blocks of stone laid together without mortar, have been found throughout Europe and in China and Peru. The Greeks and Romans developed masonry techniques that have continued in practice with few changes to the present day.

Masonry may be divided into two broad categories called rubble and ashlar. Rubble is composed of irregular and coarsely jointed quarried or field stone. Ashlar is made up of carefully worked stones set with fine, close joints. Either kind of masonry may be laid with mortar; when laid without mortar, it is called dry masonry. In modern-day industrialized countries, the work of finishing stones, formerly done with hand tools, is usually performed by machines. The term *masonry* is often extended to apply to work in brick and tile.

See also BUILDING CONSTRUCTION; STONE.

MASONRY, principles and institutions of a fraternal order, the Masons. *See* FREEMASONRY.

MASORA *or* **MASORAH** (Heb., "tradition"), term applied to the Hebrew tradition (originally transmitted orally) as to the precise form and correct pronunciation of the text of the Old Testament, and also to the marginal notes in written editions of the Scriptures that indicate various elements of this traditional form. The writing of the annotations, done by numerous Hebrew scholars known as the Masoretes, is variously believed to have begun sometime between the 2d century BC and the 8th century AD, and to have been completed about 1425. The annotations consist chiefly in adding vowels to the text, as the Hebrew alphabet does not have vowels, and punctuation of the text to indicate its traditional pronunciation and intonation. Some textual criticism is also added, involving the addition and substitution of words, euphemistic changes in words, and some elementary explanation of the text. The notes were written partly in Hebrew and partly in Aramaic. Annotations in the side margins of the written text are known as Small Masora, and those on the top and bottom margins as Large Masora.

MASQAT, also Muscat, city, capital of Oman, on the Gulf of Oman (an arm of the Arabian Sea). Flanked by mountains, it is the nation's chief administrative center and largest city. Modern highways, built in the 1970s, link Masqat with other Omani centers and with the neighboring United Arab Emirates. A palace for the sultan of Oman, also built in the 1970s, dominates the waterfront. Once the country's leading port, Masqat has been superseded by a new port (1974) at Mina Qaboos. Mina al-Fahl, a loading terminal for supertankers, and Riyam, through which refined petroleum is imported, also are nearby, as is a modern international airport.

Masqat has been important since the 6th century BC, when Persians controlled the port. It was under Portuguese domination from 1508 to 1650, and subsequently the Iranians gained control of the city. Masqat became the capital of independent Masqat and Oman in 1741; the country's name was changed to Oman in 1970. Pop. (1981 est., greater city) 50,000.

MASQUE, form of dramatic writing and production featuring poetry, music, and dance, popular in 17th-century England, especially in court circles. In the masque, the actors wore masks and usually represented allegorical or mythical characters. (The use of masks in drama originated in ancient Greece; their use in masques was part of the classical revival of the Renaissance.) The roots of the masque may be found in Italian and French pageants and masquerades, as well as in the English disguising, a performance descended from the practice of mumming and the art of the troubadors. Actors spoke, sang, and danced on allegorical or mythological subjects in the disguising, which was known from the early 15th century in Italy. The most important development added by the masque was audience participation in the dances.

The formal court masque was introduced in 1512, during the reign of King Henry VIII of England. During the reign of James I, the masque became the most popular form of drama. The literary form was greatly improved, and a fine lyric style introduced and perfected by the English playwright and poet Ben Jonson, who wrote many works in this genre. Masques were also written by the playwright John Fletcher, and the poet John Milton wrote one work in masque form, *Comus* (1634), with music by the composer Henry Lawes (1596–1662). The genius of the English architect and stage designer Inigo Jones contributed greatly to the technical improvements in the production of masques. Several hundred of his sketches of costumes and scenery are extant in various collections. The best-known composer of music for the masques, a collaborator of Jonson and Jones from 1605 to 1612, was Alfonso Ferrabosco (d. 1628); among their collaborations were *Masque of Blackness* (1605) and *Masque of Beauty* (1608), from both of which music has survived. The poet Thomas Campion wrote both music and texts for such works as *Masque in Honor of the Marriage of Lord Hayes* (1607). Robert Johnson (d. 1633) wrote music for Shakespeare's *The Tempest,* a play that incorporates masques in several scenes, as well as for the dances in other masques. The dances—the entry, the main dance, and the going off—were the most important element of the masque. Burlesque dances, called antimasques, were also incorporated.

After enjoying a great vogue, the masque declined rapidly in England, but survived for another century at the royal court of France and at other European courts. Many of the forms and characters were gradually incorporated into later forms such as ballet, opera, and pantomime. The masque has not survived in modern times, except as an esoteric literary form.

MASS, the ritual of chants, readings, prayers, and other ceremonies used in the celebration of the Eucharist (q.v.) in the Roman Catholic church (q.v.). The same name is used in high Anglican churches. Other Protestant churches call this ritual Holy Communion or the Lord's Supper; Eastern Orthodox churches call it the Divine Liturgy. The word *mass* comes from the Latin *missa* ("sent"). It was taken from the formula for dismissing the congregation: *Ite, missa est* ("Go, the Eucharist has been sent forth"), referring to the ancient custom of sending consecrated bread from the bishop's Mass to other churches in Rome to symbolize that church's unity with the bishop in the celebration of the Mass.

Forms of the Mass. The earliest form of the celebration of the Mass was the domestic Eucharist. Archaeological evidence shows that from the 3d to the 4th century, Christian communities celebrated Mass in large homes. The local bishop presided over this Eucharist. After Emperor Constantine's Edict of Toleration (AD 313), public buildings—called basilicas—were adapted to the celebration of the bishop's Eucharist. As the church grew and the number of individual churches increased, presbyters attached to these churches came to lead the celebration. Eventually, these presbyters became known as sacerdotes ("priests"; see PRIEST).

Before the 8th century, the only form of the Mass was the public Mass, celebrated by a bishop or priest with a congregation. In its solemn form (High Mass), most parts are sung. In its most elaborate form, the papal Mass, the pope is assisted by the papal nobility, Latin and Eastern Rite deacons, the papal court, and numerous other functionaries. The pontifical Mass (solemn Mass of a bishop) is less elaborate, although besides deacons, subdeacons, thurifers (incense bearers), and acolytes, the bishop is also assisted by his *familia* (family), assistants who are responsible for taking care of his regalia (solemn vestments) and insignia (miter, crosier, and pontifical cross). The solemn parish, or monastic, Mass is celebrated with deacon and subdeacon. The simplest form of sung Mass is celebrated by one priest, with the assistance of acolytes and thurifer. In daily celebrations, a simpler form is used in which all parts of the Mass are read by one priest. This is the *Missa Lecta* ("read Mass"), or Low Mass.

Beginning in the 8th century, the private Mass evolved in the monasteries of northern Europe. Monks were originally laity, and they relied on local priests for their sacramental needs or ordained some of their own members for those needs. Beginning in the 8th century, British and Irish monks were ordained for the missionary work of converting the tribes of northern Europe that had been subdued by Charlemagne and his successors. By the 11th century (after the great missionary age), the growing monasteries of northern Europe continued to ordain their monks; so the number of priests eventually far exceeded the sacramental needs of the monks. Thus, the practice of private daily celebration of Mass grew until, by the 12th century, it was common.

Parts of the Mass. By the 6th century the parts of the Mass were relatively fixed. Six principal sections can be distinguished.

The Foremass consists of the Entrance (introit), procession, and chant, which are then followed by the confession, which includes a litany (Kyrie Eleison) and which ends with the Gloria. The Foremass ends with the opening prayer, or first oration.

The Readings constitute the second part of the Mass. They consist of selections from the Old Testament, or from letters of the New Testament (Epistle), which are followed by a chant for the Gospel procession. This chant is known as the Gradual, so called because it was chanted from the steps (*gradus*) of the pulpit where the Gospel was read or sung. The final reading is drawn from one of the four Gospels and is followed by the sermon (homily).

During the third part of the Mass—the Offertory—offerings of bread, wine, and other gifts are brought to the altar with processional chants and are dedicated to the service of God with Offertory prayers.

The fourth section of the Mass is the Eucharistic Prayer. This section begins with the Preface, an introductory prayer that concludes with the Sanctus. Then follows the central Eucharistic prayer, or Canon, which contains the narrative of Jesus' institution of the Eucharist.

The Communion is the fifth, and climactic, section of the Mass. It opens with the Lord's Prayer (Paternoster, "Our Father"), continues with the prayer for peace and the greeting of peace, and concludes with the communion of the clergy and the faithful, which may be accompanied by the communion hymn.

The final section of the Mass, the Concluding Rite, consists of a final prayer (postcommunion), the blessing (benediction), and the dismissal (*Ite, missa est*). A recessional hymn may be sung as clergy and laity leave the church.

Liturgical Books. Before the 13th century a variety of liturgical books were used in the celebration of the Mass. The choir used the *Graduale* (for the Gradual chant) and *Antiphonale* (for the responsive processional chants at the Entrance, Offertory, Communion, and Recessional). The subdeacon used the *Apostolus* (letters of the New Testament), the deacons the *Evangelarium* (Gospel), and the presiding celebrant the *Sacramentarium*, which contained all the prayers of the Mass. As the practice of private Mass grew, the various liturgical texts were gathered into one book for the priest who performed all the parts of the Mass alone. This book, called the missal, contained all the prayers, readings, and chants of the Mass. The various missals used since the 13th century were standardized in an official text, the Roman missal (1570), which was issued by order of the Council of Trent. Earlier, in 1298, papal and episcopal ceremonies had been standardized in the Roman pontifical. The Roman missal and the Roman pontifical have been revised several times over the centuries.

The Second Vatican Council (1962-65) introduced a number of changes into the celebration of Mass. The council returned to the ancient practice of calling this sacrament and its celebration by the same name: the Eucharist. The principal liturgical changes include the introduction of vernacular languages into the Eucharist, the return to the custom of allowing the laity to receive both bread and wine, and the reintroduction of the practice of concelebration (see the discussion of concelebration below).

Vernacular Liturgy. The traditional language for the celebration of Mass in the Roman rite has been Latin, although the Eastern Rite churches have used a number of vernacular languages (for instance, Old Slavic, Greek, and Aramaic). Reform movements in the Western church from the 14th to the 16th century called repeatedly for vernacular liturgies. One effect of the separation of churches during the Reformation was the adoption of vernacular languages for the Mass (or Lord's Supper) in the Protestant churches. The Council of Trent (1545-63) saw no dogmatic difficulty in using vernacular languages in the Mass, but considered sanctioning their use inopportune at that time. Vatican II sanctioned the use of the vernacular in the Roman rite, and the Mass is now celebrated in almost every language in the world.

Communion Under Both Kinds. The same reform movements called for a return to the ancient custom of allowing the laity to receive communion under the forms of bread and wine, a custom that had disappeared from the Western church by the 8th century (although it has continued to the present in Eastern Catholic and Orthodox churches). The Council of Trent rejected these appeals, but Vatican II established certain times and conditions under which the laity may receive both bread and wine. The conditions have been broadened, so that the practice has become increasingly common in the Western church.

MASS

Concelebration. Although surrounded by priests and deacons, the bishop alone presided over the celebration of Mass in its original form. As the church grew, and priests were needed for the masses in parish churches, concelebration—the celebration of Mass by more than one priest—became common, although the practice was restricted to the major feasts of the year. It survived in various forms and with varying frequency into the 13th century. Priests originally concelebrated silently with the bishop, but the custom of reciting the words of the Canon aloud developed in the 7th century. After the 13th century concelebration survived only in the Mass for the ordination of priests. In this case, the newly ordained priests recite all the prayers of the Canon aloud with the bishop. Vatican II, however, restored the rite of concelebration for occasions when a number of priests gather together and placed limitations on the times and places in which the Mass can be celebrated privately.

See also MASS, MUSICAL SETTINGS OF.   J.M.P.

For further information on this topic, see the Bibliography in volume 28, section 83.

MASS, in physics, amount of matter that a body contains, and a measure of the inertial property of that body, that is, of its resistance to change of motion (see INERTIA). Mass is different from weight, which is a measure of the attraction of the earth for a given mass (see GRAVITATION). Inertial mass and gravitational mass are identical. Weight, although proportional to mass, varies with the position of a given mass relative to the earth; thus, equal masses at the same location in a gravitational field will have equal weights. A mass in interstellar space may have zero weight. A fundamental principle of classical physics is the law of conservation of mass, which states that matter cannot be created or destroyed. This law holds true in chemical reactions but is modified in cases where atoms disintegrate and matter is converted to energy (q.v.) or energy is converted to matter (see NUCLEAR ENERGY; X RAY: *Pair Production*).

The theory of relativity (q.v.), initially formulated in 1905 by the German-born American physicist Albert Einstein, did much to change traditional concepts of mass. In modern physics, the mass of an object is regarded as changing as its velocity approaches that of light (q.v.), that is, when it approaches 300,000 km/sec (about 186,000 mi/sec); an object moving at a speed of approximately 260,000 km/sec (about 160,000 mi/sec), for example, has a mass about double its so-called rest mass. Where such velocities are involved, as in nuclear reactions, mass can be converted into energy and vice versa, as suggested by Einstein in his famous equation $E = mc^2$ (energy equals mass multiplied by the velocity of light squared).

See also INTERNATIONAL SYSTEM OF UNITS; MECHANICS; QUANTUM THEORY.

For further information on this topic, see the Bibliography in volume 28, sections 389-90.

MASS, MUSICAL SETTINGS OF. The liturgical texts for the Mass have been given musical settings from earliest times (see CHANT). Some elements of the Mass have texts that vary from day to day (Proper of the Mass); others use the same texts year round (Ordinary of the Mass). Some parts are recited on a single tone or spoken, and others are traditionally sung to a distinct melody. Pope Gregory I collected many of the monophonic (unaccompanied, unharmonized) chants used in the liturgy during his reign (590-604).

Settings of the Proper. In Gregorian chant, as this collection plus later additions came to be known, the melodies of the Proper are particularly important, especially the Introit (Entrance), Gradual, Alleluia, Tract (Psalm), Offertory, and Communion. Even in the earliest polyphony (multipart music), about 900 to about 1250, settings of the Proper were most common. In these, the chant melody was used as a cantus firmus (fixed melody) to which additional voice parts were added. An important early collection of polyphonic Graduals and Alleluias is the *Magnus Liber Organi* (c. 1175), written in Paris by the liturgical composer Leonin (fl. late 12th cent.) and expanded by his successor Perotin (fl. 1200). About 1250, polyphonic composition based on chants of the Proper greatly diminished.

Settings of the Ordinary. The first example of a complete setting of the Mass Ordinary—Kyrie (Lord Have Mercy), Gloria, Credo (Creed), Sanctus (Holy, Holy, Holy), Agnus Dei (Lamb of God)—was the *Messe de Tournai* (c. 1300). Although composing individual items of the Ordinary was more common, another complete cycle from the mid-14th century was done by the French composer-poet Guillaume de Machaut.

Between 1400 and 1600 the term *Mass* came to signify a polyphonic setting of the entire Ordinary, and such settings were the principal large-scale genre of musical composition. Important composers such as the French Guillaume Dufay, the French-born Josquin Desprez, and the Italian Giovanni da Palestrina contributed to the vast repertory. Numerous techniques were devised to link all five movements, usually relating them to a chant or even a secular cantus firmus (see MUSIC, WESTERN). After 1600 the Mass lost its central musical importance, but gained in vocal and instrumental forces. A landmark of the baroque

MASSACHUSETTS

era (c. 1600– c. 1750) was Johann Sebastian Bach's Mass in B Minor (1738), a monumental piece in the style of a cantata, too long for an ordinary service. From the classical era (c. 1750–c. 1820) important Masses were contributed by the Austrians Joseph Haydn and Wolfgang Amadeus Mozart. Ludwig van Beethoven regarded his *Missa solemnis* (1824) as his greatest effort. The genre was continued in the 19th century by the Austrian Franz Schubert, the Hungarian Franz Liszt, the French Charles Gounod, and, in particular, the Austrian Anton Bruckner. Masses were written in the 20th century by the French Francis Poulenc, the Russian-born Igor Stravinsky, the Czech Leoš Janáček, and the English Ralph Vaughan Williams. Masses in popular and regional musical idioms from the mid-20th century include the *Missa Luba,* in Congolese style, by Father Guido Haazen.

Requiem Masses. The Mass for the Dead, or Requiem Mass, omits the Gloria and the Credo, but adds a Sequence, or hymn, *Dies Irae* (Day of Wrath), set to possibly the most famous of all chant melodies. Composers of Requiems include the Flemish Johannes Ockeghem (15th cent.), Mozart (1791), the Italian Giuseppe Verdi (1874), and the French Hector Berlioz (1837) and Gabriel Fauré (1887). The German Requiem (1868) of Johannes Brahms was set to his own nonliturgical text, and the *War Requiem* (1962) by the English composer Benjamin Britten used both the traditional text and poems by Wilfred Owen.

See also CHORAL MUSIC.

For further information on this topic, see the Bibliography in volume 28, sections 722, 724, 739.

MASSACHUSET, North American Indian tribe of Algonquian linguistic stock, formerly occupying the territory around Massachusetts Bay and along the seacoast from Plymouth to Salem, including the basins of the Neponset and Charles rivers. Massachusetts Bay and the state of Massachusetts were named after the tribe. Their principal village, also called Massachuset, was on the site of Quincy, in Norfolk Co. The Massachuset, numbering about 3000, was the leading tribe in southern New England until 1617, when an epidemic reduced their number. By 1633 only about 500 remained; that year many more, including their chief, died of smallpox. The survivors were converted to Christianity by the English colonists; in 1646 they were gathered, with other converts, into the mission villages of Natick, Nonantum (now part of Newton), and Ponkapog (now Stoughton), thus losing their tribal identity.

MASSACHUSETTS, officially Commonwealth of Massachusetts, one of the New England states of the U.S., bordered on the N by Vermont and New Hampshire, on the E by the Atlantic Ocean and several of its arms (such as the Gulf of Maine, Massachusetts Bay, Boston Bay, and Cape Cod Bay), on the SE by the Atlantic Ocean and a number of its arms (such as Nantucket Sound and Buzzards Bay), on the S by Rhode Island and Connecticut, and on the W by New York.

Massachusetts entered the Union on Feb. 6, 1788, as the sixth of the 13 original states. It early became an important intellectual center, known for Harvard University and the cultural institutions of Boston. In the 19th century, it developed into a major manufacturing state, noted for textiles and footwear; in the mid-20th century, electronic components and other high-technology items became leading manufactures. Massachusetts is famous for its summer resorts, such as the sand beaches of Cape Cod. Presidents John Adams, John Quincy Adams, and John F. Kennedy were born in the state, and President Calvin Coolidge spent most of his life here. The name of the state is probably derived from an Algonquian Indian village and may mean "place of big hills." Massachusetts is called the Bay State.

LAND AND RESOURCES

Massachusetts, with an area of 27,337 sq km (10,555 sq mi) is 44th in size among the states; about 1.6% of its land area is owned by the federal government. The state is roughly rectangular in shape, and its extreme dimensions are about 305 km (about 190 mi) from E to W and about 180 km (about 110 mi) from N to S. Elevations range from sea level, along the Atlantic Ocean, to 1064 m (3491 ft), atop Mt. Greylock, in the NW. The approximate mean elevation is 152 m (500 ft). The state has a coastline of 309 km (192 mi) and a tidal shoreline of 2445 km (1519 mi).

Physical Geography. Massachusetts can be divided into six major geographical regions. In the E is the Atlantic Coastal Plain, which encompasses Cape Cod and the islands of Nantucket and Martha's Vineyard. In this region glacial deposits lie on top of sedimentary rocks; the deposits are generally sandy, and wave action and the northward sweep of the Gulf Stream ocean current have reworked the material into the fine beaches of the region and have given the Cape its distinctive shape. Soils are exceedingly sandy and of little agricultural use.

The Seaboard Lowland provides a transition to the hillier areas of the interior. In this region softer sedimentary and metamorphic rocks are more often than not buried by glacial debris. Occasional undulations in the underlying bedrock produce low hills in areas where the cover of glacial drift is thin. Between the hills the cover of glacial drift is thicker, and in some areas, espe-

71

MASSACHUSETTS

cially around Wareham, depressions in the deposits are now important cranberry bogs. In the Boston area are some beautiful elongated hills, called drumlins, which are features of a glacial origin. Perhaps the most famous of these drumlins is Bunker Hill.

The Seaboard Lowland grades almost imperceptibly into the New England Upland, a region that dominates most of New England and in Massachusetts is divided into two parts by the Connecticut Valley Lowland. In the upland the rocks are harder and therefore have better resisted erosion. The undulating hilly landscape is veneered with a thin covering of generally infertile glacial deposits. The upland is, for the most part, smoother in the E and S and rougher in the W and N. Wachusett Mt. (611 m/2006 ft) is a striking summit rising above the hilltops in central Massachusetts. It is a geologic feature called a monadnock.

The state's fourth major region, the Connecticut Valley Lowland, contains red sandstones and shales that have been worn down to a flat plain through millions of years of erosion. Alluvial deposits from the Connecticut R. and clays from an ancient glacial lake help to provide a fertile agricultural region. Some drumlins are found in the valley. Occasional linear ridges, such as Mt. Tom (366 m/1202 ft), near Holyoke, are composed of ancient lava flows that have been tilted and then eroded.

The regions of W Massachusetts are complex. The Western New England Upland, as it becomes rougher, grades into the Green Mts., which are far more pronounced in the N. Here, as in S Vermont, the region is more a deeply cut plateau than a linear mountain ridge.

Separating the Green Mts. section from the Taconic Mts. is the deep and narrow valley of the Hoosic and Housatonic rivers, the Berkshire Valley. Some patches of dairying remain in the wider S part of the valley, but most of the area is nonagricultural. The Taconics, lower than in Vermont, contain the highest point in Massachusetts, Mt. Greylock.

Rivers and Lakes. The Charles R. is the longest river wholly within Massachusetts, but the Housatonic and the Connecticut rivers are more important. Disastrous floods have occurred on both, and many communities, including Northampton, Greenfield, and Springfield, are protected by elaborate flood-control levees built

A view across the Connecticut River of the village of Sunderland, Mass.   Ward Allan Howe

MASSACHUSETTS

Old North Bridge in Concord, Mass., was the site of the Battle of Concord on April 19, 1775, the first major engagement of the American Revolution. Eric Carle–Shostal Associates

after the 1936 flood on the Connecticut R. The Merrimack is an important river of the NE part of the state.

Quabbin Reservoir, on the Swift R. in the central part of Massachusetts, is the largest body of fresh water in the state. Wachusett Reservoir, near Worcester, is another big artificial lake. Both are used to supply water to the Boston area. Small lakes abound in the state, and many are bordered by vacation cottages. Lake Chaubunagungamaugg, near Webster, is usually called Webster Lake, because the Nipmuc Indian name is difficult to pronounce and spell. The full version of the Indian name is said to be the longest place-name in North America.

Climate. Massachusetts has a humid continental climate; summers are typically warmer and winters milder than farther N. The W part of the state generally has cooler temperatures than the E region. Cape Cod and the islands of Martha's Vineyard and Nantucket, however, usually have cooler summer temperatures because of the moderating effects of the ocean, which also give the region somewhat warmer temperatures in winter. Pittsfield, in the W, has an average annual temperature of about 7.2° C (about 45° F); Boston, in the E, about 10.8° C (about 51.5° F); and Nantucket, about 9.7° C (49.5° F). The recorded temperature in Massachusetts has ranged from −37.2° C (−35° F), in 1981 at Chester in the W, to 41.7° C (107° F), in 1975 at New Bedford, in the SE, and Chester.

Annual precipitation totals about 1120 mm (about 44 in) in most of the state, with distribution roughly equal between summer and winter. Some higher elevations receive up to about 1195 mm (about 47 in), and some lower elevations in the E get as little as 1016 mm (40 in) of moisture per year. Some mountains in the W get as much as 1905 mm (75 in) of snow annually, and much of the E receives some 1070 mm (some 42 in). Cape Cod and the islands usually receive only about 635 mm (about 25 in) of snow. The coastal areas are prone to severe storms, known as northeasters, and to occasional hurricanes. The state is usually struck by several tornadoes each year; a particularly damaging tornado battered the Worcester area in 1953.

MASSACHUSETTS

Plants and Animals. Forests cover about 55% of the land area of Massachusetts. Deciduous trees make up most of the forests, but evergreens are common along the coast and in the higher elevations of the New England Upland and the Green Mts. The typical N hardwoods of birch, beech, maple, and oak cover the largest area. Among the common softwoods are larch, white and red pine, and hemlock. Other plants include rhododendron, bloodroot, wild columbine, arbutis, violets, azaleas, and mountain laurel.

Animals abound in Massachusetts. The white-tailed deer is the largest game animal; small mammals include skunk, raccoon, beaver, weasel, opossum, gray and red squirrel, woodchuck, fox, and rabbit. Among the state's freshwater fish are trout, bass, pickerel, and perch. Lobsters, clams, scallops, bluefish, cod, herring, and flounder are some of the species inhabiting the state's marine waters.

Mineral Resources. The limited mineral resources of Massachusetts include building materials such as granite and marble, sand and gravel, clay, peat, lime, and coal. H.A.M.

POPULATION

According to the 1990 census, Massachusetts had 6,016,425 inhabitants, an increase of 4.9% over 1980. The average population density in 1990 was 220 people per sq km (570 per sq mi); higher population concentrations were in the E third of the state, where most of the people lived. Whites made up 89.8% of the population (down from 93.5% in 1980) and blacks 5%; additional groups included 53,792 persons of Chinese ancestry, 19,719 Asian Indians, 15,449 persons of Vietnamese background, 14,050 persons of Cambodian origin, 11,857 American Indians, and 11,744 persons of Korean descent. More than 287,000 Massachusetts residents claimed Hispanic ancestry, double the number in 1980. Roman Catholics constituted the largest single religious group (54.3%), followed by Baptists (4.3%), Jews (3.5%), Episcopalians (2.8%), and Methodists (2.4%). In 1990 about 84% of all people in Massachusetts lived in areas defined as urban, and the rest lived in rural areas. The state's largest cities were Boston, the capital; Worcester; Springfield; Lowell; New Bedford; and Cambridge.

EDUCATION AND CULTURAL ACTIVITY

Massachusetts is known for its many fine educational institutions as well as its historical sites and cultural institutions.

Education. The first public school in the U.S. colonies, the Boston Latin School, was opened by the Puritans in 1635. In 1647 the Massachusetts Bay Colony government required that towns containing 50 families or more have an elementary school. In 1821 the first public high school in the U.S., English High School, in Boston, was opened, and in 1852 Massachusetts became the first state to pass legislation making school attendance mandatory. During the late 1830s and '40s Horace Mann had done much to improve education in the state. In the late 1980s Massachusetts had 1817 public elementary and secondary schools with a combined annual enrollment of some 590,200 elementary pupils and 235,350 secondary students. Massachusetts is known for its excellent private schools, and about 108,600 students attended nonpublic schools. The oldest and one of the most highly respected institutions of higher education in the U.S., Harvard University, in Cambridge, was founded in 1636. In the late 1980s Massachusetts had 117 institutions of higher education with a combined enrollment of about 426,600 students per year. Among the most notable of these schools, besides Harvard, were the Massachusetts Institute of Technology and Radcliffe College, in Cambridge; Tufts University (1852), in Medford; Boston University (1839), in Boston; Boston College (1863), in Chestnut Hill; Clark University (1887) and the College of the Holy Cross (1843), in Worcester; Brandeis University, in Waltham; Mount Holyoke College, in South Hadley; Smith College, in Northampton; Wellesley College, in Wellesley; Amherst College, in Amherst; Williams College (1793), in Williamstown; and the University of Massachusetts, with campuses in Amherst and Boston.

Cultural Institutions. Some of the finest art museums in the U.S. are in Massachusetts. These include the Museum of Fine Arts, in Boston, known for its American, European, and Asian treasures; the Isabella Stewart Gardner Museum, in Boston, noted for its holdings of Italian Renaissance art; the Worcester Art Museum, in Worcester; the Fogg Art Museum and the Busch-Reisinger Museum of Harvard University, in Cambridge; and the Addison Gallery of American Art, in Andover. Also of note are the De Cordova and Dana Museum, in Lincoln; the Sterling and Francine Clark Art Institute, in Williamstown; the Museum of Science, in Boston; the New Bedford Whaling Museum; the Peabody Museum of Archaeology and Ethnology, in Cambridge; and the Peabody Museum of Salem, with exhibits on maritime history and ethnology.

The first library in the U.S. colonies was established in 1638, when John Harvard donated his collection of books to Harvard College. The library has since amassed more than 11 million volumes. The Boston Public Library and the Boston Athenaeum also house important collections of books. The John F. Kennedy Library, in Boston,

MASSACHUSETTS

Massachusetts: Map Index

Counties

Barnstable.....................M6
Berkshire........................A3
Bristol.............................K5
Dukes.............................M7
Essex........................E5, L2
Franklin..........................D2
Hampden.......................C4
Hampshire................C3, D3
Middlesex.......................H2
Nantucket......................P7
Norfolk....B8, C7, F8, J4, L4
Plymouth..................E8, K4
Suffolk......................C7, L3
Worcester......................F3

Cities and Towns

Abington........................L4
Acton........................A5, J3
Acushnet........................L6
Adams............................B2
Agawam.........................D4
Amesbury.......................L1
Amherst.........................D3
Andover.........................K2
Arlington...................C6, K3
Ashby.............................G2
Ashfield..........................C2
Ashland..........................J3
Ashley Falls....................A4
Assinippi........................F8
Assonet..........................K5
Athol..............................F2
Attleboro.......................J5
Auburn...........................G4
Avon........................D8, K4
Ayer...............................H2
Baldwinville....................F2
Barnstable.....................N6
Barre..............................F3
Becket............................B3
Bedford....................B5, J3
Belchertown..................E3
Bellingham.....................J4
Belmont.........................C6
Berkley...........................K5
Bernardston...................D2
Beverly......................F5, L2
Billerica.....................B5, J2
Blackstone.....................H4
Blandford.......................C4
Bliss Corner...................L6
Bolton............................H3
Bondsville......................E4
Boston, capital..........D6, K3

Bourne..........................M6
Boxford.........................L2
Braintree..................E8, K4
Brewster........................P5
Bridgewater..................L5
Brimfield........................F4
Brockton........................K4
Brookfield......................F4
Brookline..................C7, K3
Burlington................C5, K2
Buzzards Bay................M5
Cambridge...............D6, K3
Canton.....................C8, K4
Carlisle...........................B5
Cedarville.....................M5
Centerville....................N6
Central Village..............K6
Charlemont...................C2
Charlton........................G4
Charlton City.................G4
Chatham.......................Q6
Chelmsford...................J2
Chelsea..........................D6
Cheshire........................B2
Chester..........................C3
Chicopee.......................D4
Chilmark.......................M7
Clarksburg....................B2
Clinton..........................H3
Cochituate...............B7, J3
Cohasset......................L4
Concord...................B6, J3
Cotuit............................N6
Cummington.................C3
Dalton...........................B3
Danvers....................E5, L2
Dartmouth....................K6
Dedham...................C7, K4
Deerfield.......................D2
Dennis...........................P6
Douglas.........................H4
Dover.......................B8, J4
Dracut...........................J2
Duxbury........................M4
East Brookfield.............F4
East Dennis...................P6
East Douglas.................H4
East Falmouth..............M6
East Freetown..............L5
Eastham........................Q5
Easthampton................D3
East Longmeadow........D4
East Orleans.................Q5
East Pepperell..............H2
East Sandwich..............N6
East Wareham.............M5
Edgartown...................M7
Erving............................E2
Essex.............................L2
Everett..........................D6

Fall River.......................K6
Falmouth.....................M6
Feeding Hills.................D4
Fiskdale.........................F4
Fitchburg......................G2
Florida...........................B2
Foxboro.........................K4
Framingham............A7, J3
Franklin..........................J4
Gardner.........................G2
Gay Head......................L7
Georgetown.................L2
Gloucester...................M2
Goshen..........................C3
Granby..........................D3
Granville........................C4
Great Barrington..........A4
Greenfield.....................D2
Green Harbor...............M4
Groton..........................H2
Halifax...........................L5
Hamilton.......................L2
Hanover........................L4
Hanson..........................L4
Harwich Port................P6
Hatfield.........................D3
Haverhill.......................K1
Hingham..................F8, L4
Holbrook..................E8, K4
Holden..........................G3
Holland..........................F4
Holliston...................A8, J4
Holyoke........................D4
Hopedale......................H4
Hopkinton....................H4
Housatonic...................A3
Hubbardston................G3
Hudson..........................H3
Hull..........................F7, L3
Huntington...................C4
Hyannis.........................N6
Ipswich..........................L2
Kingston.......................M5
Lakeville........................L5
Lanesboro....................B2
Lawrence......................K2
Lee................................B3
Lenox.............................A3
Leominster...................G2
Lexington.................C6, K3
Lincoln...........................B6
Littleton........................H2
Littleton Common........J2
Longmeadow................D4
Lowell............................J2
Ludlow..........................E4
Lunenburg....................G2
Lynn........................E6, L3
Lynnfield..................D5, K2
Madaket........................P7

Malden.....................D6, K3
Manchester-by-the-Sea..L2
Mansfield.......................K4
Marblehead.............F5, L3
Marion...........................L6
Marlborough.................H3
Marshfield...................M4
Marshfield Hills............M4
Marstons Mills.............N6
Mashpee.....................N6
Mattapoisett.................L6
Maynard........................J3
Medfield..................B8, J4
Medford..................D6, K3
Medway........................A8
Melrose...................D6, K3
Mendon.........................H4
Methuen.......................K2
Middleboro...................L5
Milford..........................H4
Millbury.........................G4
Millers Falls...................E2
Millis..............................B8
Milton.....................D7, K3
Monson........................E4
Monterey......................B4
Monument Beach........M6
Nahant....................E6, L3
Nantucket.....................P7
Natick......................B7, J3
Needham.................C7, K3
New Ashford................B2
New Bedford................L6
New Boston..................B4
New Marlborough........B4
Newburyport................L1
Newton...................C7, K3
North Adams................B2
North Amherst.............D3
Northampton................D3
North Andover.............K2
North Attleboro...........J5
Northborough..............H3
Northbridge..................H4
North Brookfield..........F3
North Carver................L5
North Falmouth...........M6
Northfield.....................E2
North Grafton..............H4
North Pembroke..........L4
North Plymouth...........M5
North Reading........D5, K2
North Scituate.............L4
North Sudbury.............A6
North Tisbury..............M7
North Truro..................P4
Norton..........................K5
Norwell.........................L4
Norwood................C8, K4
Oak Bluffs....................M7

75

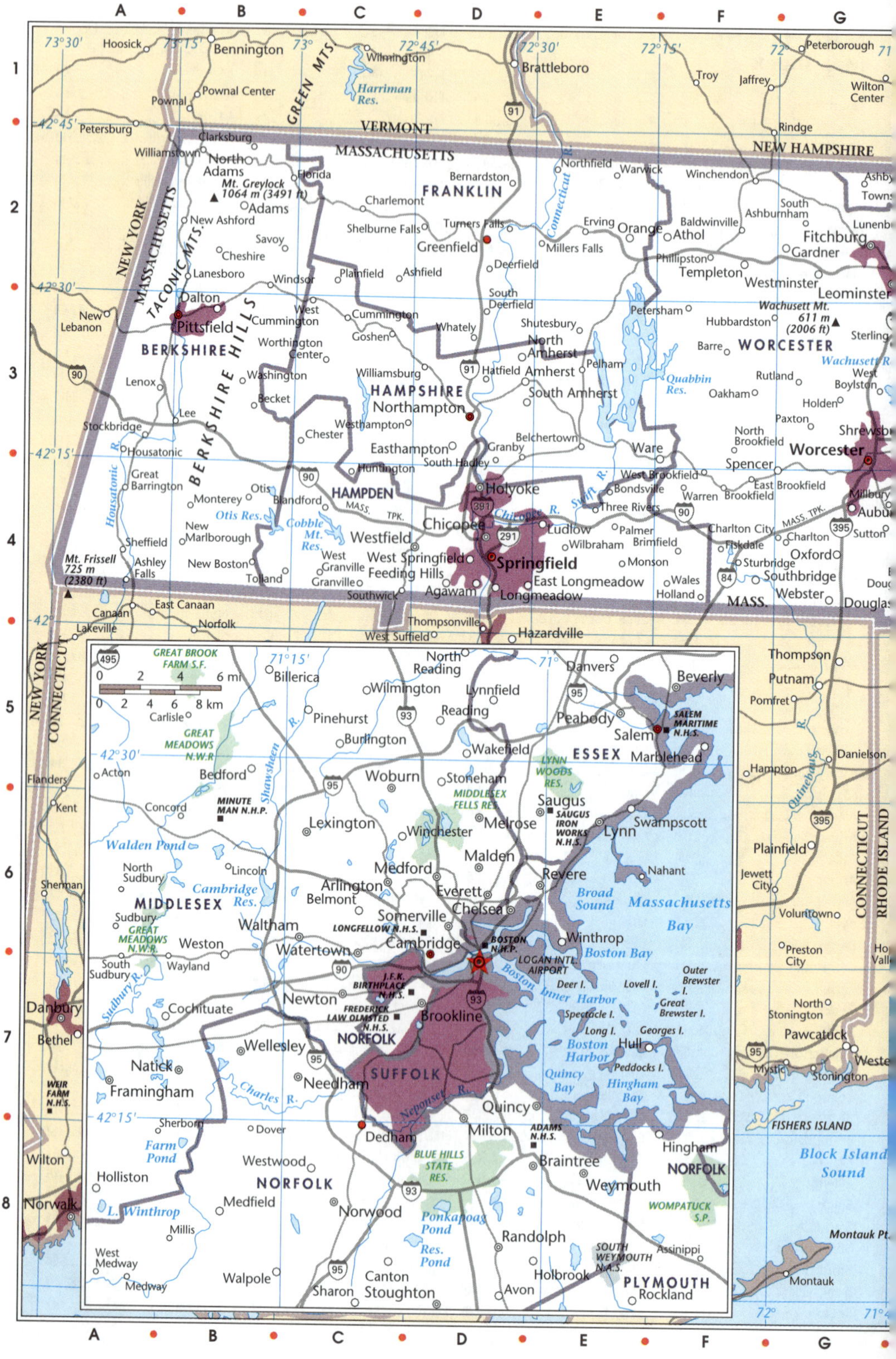

A
B
C
D
E
F
G
1
2
3
4
5
6
7
8
73°30'
73°15'
73°
72°45'
72°30'
72°15'
72°
42°45'
42°30'
42°15'
42°
VERMONT
MASSACHUSETTS
NEW HAMPSHIRE
NEW YORK
CONNECTICUT
RHODE ISLAND
MASS.
GREEN MTS.
TACONIC MTS.
BERKSHIRE HILLS
BERKSHIRE
FRANKLIN
HAMPSHIRE
HAMPDEN
WORCESTER
Hoosick
Bennington
Wilmington
Harriman Res.
Brattleboro
Troy
Jaffrey
Peterborough
Wilton Center
Pownal Center
Pownal
Petersburg
Rindge
Clarksburg
Williamstown
North Adams
Florida
Mt. Greylock 1064 m (3491 ft)
Adams
New Ashford
Savoy
Cheshire
Lanesboro
Dalton
Pittsfield
New Lebanon
Windsor
West Cummington
Cummington
Charlemont
Shelburne Falls
Plainfield
Ashfield
Bernardston
Northfield
Warwick
Winchendon
Turners Falls
Greenfield
Deerfield
Erving
Orange
Millers Falls
Athol
Baldwinville
South Ashburnham
Ashburnham
Fitchburg
Gardner
Lunenburg
Phillipston
Templeton
Westminster
Leominster
South Deerfield
Connecticut R.
Whately
Shutesbury
Petersham
Hubbardston
Wachusett Mt. 611 m (2006 ft)
Sterling
Goshen
Worthington Center
North Amherst
Amherst
Hatfield
Pelham
Barre
Quabbin Res.
Rutland
West Boylston
Wachusett R.
Lenox
Washington
Williamsburg
Northampton
South Amherst
Oakham
Holden
Becket
Lee
Stockbridge
Westhampton
Chester
Belchertown
Paxton
North Brookfield
Shrewsbury
Housatonic
Housatonic R.
Easthampton
Granby
Ware
Worcester
Great Barrington
Huntington
South Hadley
Spencer
West Brookfield
East Brookfield
Otis
Monterey
Blandford
Holyoke
Bondsville
Warren
Brookfield
Millbury
Auburn
Otis Res.
Cobble Mt. Res.
MASS. TPK.
Chicopee
Chicopee R.
Swift R.
Three Rivers
Ludlow
Palmer
Charlton City
Charlton
Sutton
New Marlborough
Sheffield
Westfield
Wilbraham
Brimfield
Fiskdale
Sturbridge
Oxford
Mt. Frissell 725 m (2380 ft)
Ashley Falls
New Boston
Tolland
West Granville
Granville
West Springfield
Feeding Hills
Springfield
Monson
Southbridge
East Longmeadow
Wales
Holland
Webster
Douglas
Southwick
Agawam
Longmeadow
Canaan
East Canaan
Lakeville
Norfolk
Thompsonville
West Suffield
Hazardville
Thompson
Putnam
Pomfret
Danielson
Hampton
Quinebaug R.
Plainfield
Jewett City
Voluntown
Preston City
North Stonington
Pawcatuck
Westerly
Mystic
Stonington
FISHERS ISLAND
Block Island Sound
Montauk Pt.
Montauk
Flanders
Kent
Sherman
Danbury
Bethel
WEIR FARM N.H.S.
Wilton
Norwalk
Oxford
91
90
291
391
84
395
95
0 2 4 6 mi
0 2 4 6 8 km
71°15'
71°
42°30'
42°15'
495
GREAT BROOK FARM S.F.
Billerica
North Reading
Danvers
Beverly
Wilmington
Lynnfield
Carlisle
Pinehurst
Reading
Peabody
Salem
SALEM MARITIME N.H.S.
GREAT MEADOWS N.W.R.
Burlington
Wakefield
ESSEX
Marblehead
Shawsheen R.
Acton
Bedford
Woburn
Stoneham
LYNN WOODS RES.
MIDDLESEX FELLS RES.
Saugus
SAUGUS IRON WORKS N.H.S.
MINUTE MAN N.H.P.
Concord
Lexington
Winchester
Melrose
Lynn
Swampscott
Walden Pond
Malden
North Sudbury
Lincoln
Medford
Revere
Nahant
Cambridge Res.
Arlington
Everett
Broad Sound
Massachusetts Bay
MIDDLESEX
Belmont
Chelsea
Somerville
Sudbury
Waltham
LONGFELLOW N.H.S.
Cambridge
BOSTON N.H.P.
Winthrop
Weston
Watertown
Boston Bay
LOGAN INTL. AIRPORT
South Sudbury
Wayland
J.F.K. BIRTHPLACE N.H.S.
Boston
Outer Brewster I.
Deer I.
Lovell I.
Inner Harbor
Great Brewster I.
Sudbury R.
Cochituate
Newton
FREDERICK LAW OLMSTED N.H.S.
Brookline
Spectacle I.
Long I.
Georges I.
NORFOLK
Boston Harbor
Hull
Wellesley
Natick
SUFFOLK
Quincy Bay
Peddocks I.
Hingham Bay
Needham
Framingham
Charles R.
Neponset R.
Quincy
Sherborn
Dover
Milton
ADAMS N.H.S.
Farm Pond
Dedham
Hingham
BLUE HILLS STATE RES.
Braintree
Holliston
Westwood
NORFOLK
Weymouth
Medfield
WOMPATUCK S.P.
L. Winthrop
Norwood
Ponkapoag Pond
Millis
Randolph
Res. Pond
SOUTH WEYMOUTH N.A.S.
Assinippi
West Medway
Medway
Walpole
Canton
Holbrook
PLYMOUTH
Sharon
Stoughton
Avon
Rockland
93

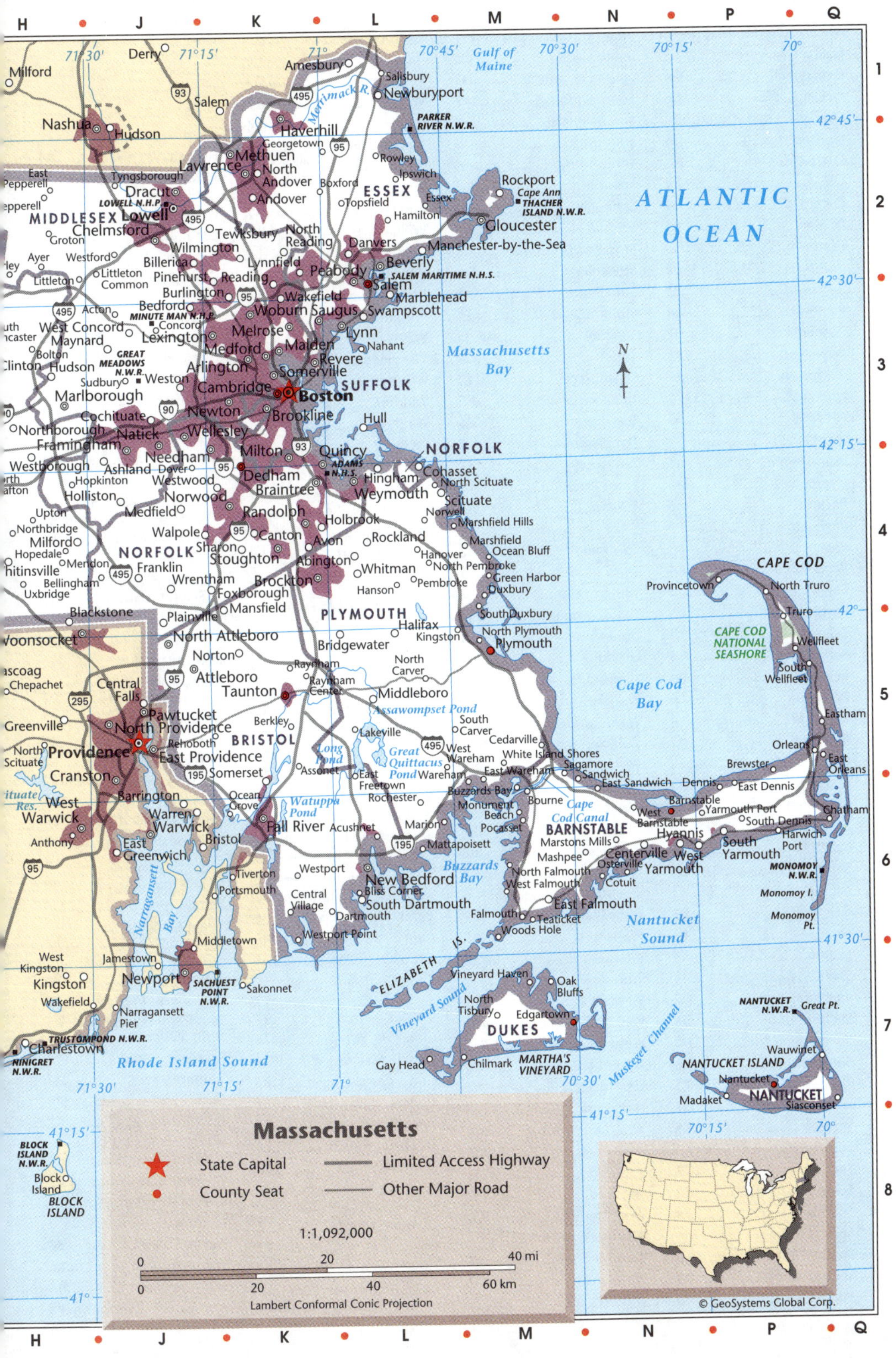
Massachusetts
State Capital
County Seat
Limited Access Highway
Other Major Road
1:1,092,000
0
20
40 mi
0
20
40
60 km
Lambert Conformal Conic Projection
© GeoSystems Global Corp.
ATLANTIC OCEAN
Gulf of Maine
Massachusetts Bay
Cape Cod Bay
Nantucket Sound
Buzzards Bay
Vineyard Sound
Rhode Island Sound
Muskeget Channel
Narragansett Bay
CAPE COD
CAPE COD NATIONAL SEASHORE
ESSEX
MIDDLESEX
SUFFOLK
NORFOLK
PLYMOUTH
BRISTOL
BARNSTABLE
DUKES
NANTUCKET
MARTHA'S VINEYARD
NANTUCKET ISLAND
ELIZABETH IS.
BLOCK ISLAND
Boston
Providence
Milford
Derry
Salem
Nashua
Hudson
Amesbury
Salisbury
Newburyport
Haverhill
Methuen
Lawrence
North Andover
Andover
Lowell
Dracut
Chelmsford
Tewksbury
Wilmington
Billerica
Burlington
Woburn
Saugus
Lynn
Peabody
Salem
Beverly
Gloucester
Rockport
Manchester-by-the-Sea
Marblehead
Swampscott
Nahant
Malden
Medford
Melrose
Revere
Somerville
Cambridge
Arlington
Lexington
Concord
Bedford
Framingham
Natick
Newton
Wellesley
Brookline
Needham
Dedham
Milton
Quincy
Braintree
Weymouth
Hingham
Hull
Cohasset
Scituate
Randolph
Canton
Stoughton
Brockton
Abington
Rockland
Whitman
Marshfield
Duxbury
Kingston
Plymouth
Bridgewater
Middleboro
Taunton
Attleboro
North Attleboro
Mansfield
Foxborough
Norton
Raynham
Pawtucket
North Providence
East Providence
Cranston
Warwick
West Warwick
Barrington
Bristol
Fall River
Somerset
Swansea
New Bedford
Dartmouth
South Dartmouth
Westport
Wareham
Bourne
Falmouth
East Falmouth
Sandwich
Barnstable
Hyannis
Yarmouth
Dennis
Harwich
Chatham
Orleans
Eastham
Wellfleet
Truro
Provincetown
Edgartown
Vineyard Haven
Oak Bluffs
Chilmark
Gay Head
Nantucket
Siasconset
Madaket
Wauwinet
Newport
Middletown
Jamestown
Kingston
Wakefield
Narragansett Pier
Charlestown
Sakonnet
Tiverton
Portsmouth
Woonsocket
Marlborough
Hudson
Maynard
Sudbury
Weston
Walpole
Norwood
Franklin
Wrentham
Plainville
Medfield
Hopkinton
Holliston
Milford
Upton
Uxbridge
Bellingham
Mendon
Hopedale
Northbridge
Westborough
Northborough
Ashland
Westwood
Dover
Sharon
Avon
Holbrook
Hanover
Hanson
Pembroke
Halifax
Carver
Rochester
Marion
Mattapoisett
Acushnet
Berkley
Rehoboth
Lakeville
Freetown
Assonet
Pocasset
Mashpee
Cotuit
Osterville
Centerville
Woods Hole
Teaticket
Great Pt.
Monomoy I.
Monomoy Pt.
Chepachet
Greenville
Scituate
Anthony
East Greenwich
Lincoln
Central Falls
Westford
Groton
Ayer
Littleton
Acton
West Concord
Tyngsborough
Pinehurst
Reading
North Reading
Lynnfield
Wakefield
Danvers
Topsfield
Boxford
Rowley
Ipswich
Essex
Hamilton
Georgetown
LOWELL N.H.P.
MINUTE MAN N.H.P.
SALEM MARITIME N.H.S.
ADAMS N.H.S.
PARKER RIVER N.W.R.
THACHER ISLAND N.W.R.
GREAT MEADOWS N.W.R.
MONOMOY N.W.R.
NANTUCKET N.W.R.
SACHUEST POINT N.W.R.
TRUSTOM POND N.W.R.
NINIGRET N.W.R.
BLOCK ISLAND N.W.R.
Assawompset Pond
Great Quittacus Pond
Long Pond
Watuppa Pond
Cape Cod Canal
Merrimack R.
1
2
3
4
5
6
7
8
H
J
K
L
M
N
P
Q
42°45'
42°30'
42°15'
42°
41°30'
41°15'
41°
71°30'
71°15'
71°
70°45'
70°30'
70°15'
70°
N

MASSACHUSETTS

Massachusetts: Map Index

Oakham	F3
Ocean Bluff	M4
Ocean Grove	K6
Orange	E2
Orleans	Q5
Osterville	N6
Otis	B4
Oxford	G4
Palmer	E4
Paxton	G3
Peabody	E5, L2
Pelham	E3
Pembroke	L4
Pepperell	H2
Petersham	F3
Phillipston	F2
Pinehurst	C5, K2
Pittsfield	B3
Plainfield	C2
Plainville	J4
Plymouth	M5
Pocasset	M6
Provincetown	P4
Quincy	E7, K3
Randolph	D8, K4
Raynham	K5
Raynham Center	K5
Reading	D5, K2
Rehoboth	K5
Revere	E6, K3
Rochester	L6
Rockland	E8, L4
Rockport	M2
Rowley	L2
Rutland	G3
Sagamore	M5
Salem	F5, L2
Salisbury	L1
Sandwich	N5
Saugus	E6, K3
Savoy	B2
Scituate	L4
Sharon	C8, K4
Sheffield	A4
Shelburne Falls	D2
Sherborn	B8
Shirley	H2
Shrewsbury	H3
Shutesbury	E3
Siasconset	Q7
Somerset	K5
Somerville	D6, K3
South Amherst	D3
South Ashburnham	G2
Southbridge	F4
South Carver	M5
South Dartmouth	L6
South Deerfield	D3
South Dennis	P6
South Duxbury	M4
South Hadley	D3
South Lancaster	H3
South Sudbury	A7
South Wellfleet	P5
Southwick	C4
South Yarmouth	P6
Spencer	G4
Springfield	D4
Sterling	G3
Stockbridge	A3
Stoneham	D5
Stoughton	D8, K4
Sturbridge	F4
Sudbury	A6, J3
Sutton	G4
Swampscott	E6, L3
Taunton	K5
Teaticket	M6
Templeton	F2
Tewksbury	K2
Three Rivers	E4
Tolland	B4
Topsfield	L2
Townsend	H2
Truro	P5
Turners Falls	D2
Tyngsborough	J2
Upton	H4
Uxbridge	H4
Vineyard Haven	M7
Wakefield	D5, K2
Wales	F4
Walpole	C8, J4
Waltham	C6, B6
Ware	F3
Wareham	M5
Warren	F4
Warwick	E2
Washington	B3
Watertown	C6
Wauwinet	P7
Wayland	B7
Webster	G4
Wellesley	B7, J3
Wellfleet	P5
West Barnstable	N6
Westborough	H3
West Boylston	G3
West Brookfield	F4
West Concord	J3
West Cummington	C3
West Falmouth	M6
Westfield	D4
Westford	J2
West Granville	C4
Westhampton	C3
West Medway	A8
Westminster	G2
Weston	B6, J3
Westport	K6
Westport Point	K6
West Springfield	D4
West Wareham	L5
Westwood	C8, K4
West Yarmouth	P6
Weymouth	E8, L4
Whately	D3
White Island Shores	M5
Whitinsville	H4
Whitman	L4
Wilbraham	E4
Williamsburg	D3
Williamstown	B2
Wilmington	C5, K2
Winchendon	F2
Winchester	C6
Windsor	B2
Winthrop	E6
Woburn	C5, K3
Woods Hole	M6
Worcester	G3
Worthington Center	C3
Wrentham	J4
Yarmouth Port	P6

Other Features

Adams Natl. Hist. Site	E8, L4
Ann, cape	M2
Assawompset, pond	L5
Berkshire, hills	B4
Blue Hills State Res.	D8
Boston, bay	E6
Boston, harbor	E7
Boston, inner harbor	D7
Boston Natl. Hist. Park	D6
Broad, sound	E6
Buzzards, bay	M6
Cambridge, reservoir	B6
Cape Cod, bay	N5
Cape Cod, canal	M5
Cape Cod Natl. Seashore	P5
Charles, river	B7
Chicopee, river	D4
Cobble Mt., reservoir	C4
Cod, cape	P4
Connecticut, river	E2
Deer, island	E7
Elizabeth, islands	L7
Farm, pond	B8
Frederick Law Olmsted Natl. Hist. Site	C7
Georges, island	E7
Great, point	P7
Great Brewster, island	F7
Great Brook Farm State Forest	B5
Great Meadows Natl. Wildlife Refuge	A6, B5, J3
Great Quittacus, pond	L5
Greylock, mt.	B2
Hingham, bay	E7
Housatonic, river	A4
J.F.K. Birthplace Natl. Hist. Site	D7
Logan Intl. Airport	E6
Long, island	E7
Long, pond	L5
Longfellow Natl. Hist. Site	D6
Lovell, island	F7
Lowell Natl. Hist. Park	J2
Lynn Woods Res.	E5
Maine, gulf	M1
Martha's Vineyard, island	M7
Massachusetts, bay	F6, M3
Merrimack, river	K1
Middlesex Fells Res.	D5
Minute Man Natl. Hist. Park	B6, J3
Monomoy, island	P6
Monomoy, point	P6
Monomoy Natl. Wildlife Refuge	Q6
Muskeget, channel	N7
Nantucket, island	P7
Nantucket, sound	N6
Nantucket Natl. Wildlife Refuge	P7
Neponset, river	C7
Otis, reservoir	B4
Outer Brewster, island	F7
Parker River Natl. Wildlife Refuge	L1
Peddocks, island	E7
Ponkapoag, pond	D8
Quabbin, reservoir	F3
Quincy, bay	E7
Reservoir, pond	D8
Salem Maritime Natl. Hist. Site	F5, L2
Saugus Iron Works Natl. Hist. Site	E6
Shawsheen, river	B6
South Weymouth Naval Air Station	E8
Spectacle, island	E7
Sudbury, river	A7
Swift, river	E4
Taconic, mts.	A2
Thacher Island Natl. Wildlife Refuge	M2
Vineyard, sound	L7
Wachusett, reservoir	G3
Wachusett, river	G3
Walden, pond	B6
Watuppa, pond	K6
Winthrop, lake	A8
Wompatuck State Park	F8

78

MASSACHUSETTS

contains papers of President Kennedy and his brother, Robert F. Kennedy, a U.S. attorney general and senator.

Boston is the home of many of the state's entertainment institutions, including several theaters, the noted Boston Symphony Orchestra, a number of ballet and modern dance organizations, and the Opera Company of Boston. The Tanglewood estate in Lenox serves as the summer home of the Boston Symphony, and summer theater is particularly popular in Stockbridge and on Cape Cod.

Historical Sites. Massachusetts has many historical sites, some commemorating colonial days and the revolutionary war period. Among the most famous are Plymouth Rock, where the Pilgrims are said to have landed in 1620, and Plimoth Plantation, a reconstruction of the first Pilgrim community, in Plymouth; Saugus Iron Works National Historic Site, including a recreation of the first integrated iron works in North America (begun 1646); Boston National Historical Park, encompassing several noted buildings such as Faneuil Hall and Old North Church; Minute Man National Historical Park, containing the sites in Lexington and Concord of the first fighting of the American Revolution; and Salem Maritime National Historic Site. Among the many historical homes in Massachusetts are those of Paul Revere, in Boston; of Mary Baker Eddy, the founder of the Christian Science movement, in Lynn; of the poet and essayist Ralph Waldo Emerson, in Concord; and of the poet Emily Dickinson, in Amherst. Adams National Historic Site, in Quincy, includes the home of Presidents John Adams and John Quincy Adams as well as other noted members of the Adams family, and John Fitzgerald Kennedy National Historic Site, in Brookline, contains the birthplace of President Kennedy.

Sports and Recreation. Massachusetts's ocean coastline, rivers, lakes, and mountains provide ample opportunity for swimming, hiking, boating, fishing, hunting, golf, and winter sports. Cape Cod National Seashore includes ocean beaches and duneland. The Red Sox in baseball, the Celtics in basketball, and the Bruins in ice hockey are based in Boston, and the New England Patriots professional football team uses a stadium in nearby Foxboro.

Communications. Massachusetts has a comprehensive communications system that, in the early 1990s, included 70 AM and 106 FM radio-broadcasting stations and 20 television stations. WGBH-TV, in Boston, is a noted noncommercial broadcasting station. The first radio station in the state, WGI in Medford, was licensed in 1920. WBZ-TV in Boston, which was Massachu-

The State House in Boston is the principal landmark of historic Beacon Hill. The front portion was designed by Charles Bulfinch and completed between 1795 and 1798.
Eric Carle-Shostal Associates

MASSACHUSETTS

setts's first commercial television station, commenced operations in 1948. The *Publick Occurrences Both Forreign and Domestick,* the first newspaper in the U.S. colonies, began publication in Boston in 1690. In the early 1990s Massachusetts had 40 daily newspapers with a total daily circulation of approximately 2 million. Influential newspapers included the *Boston Globe;* the *Boston Herald;* the *Union-News,* published in Springfield; and the *Telegram Gazette,* published in Worcester. The *Christian Science Monitor,* published in Boston, enjoys an international readership.

The first English-language book published in the colonies was the *Bay Psalm Book,* printed in Cambridge in 1640. The Boston area is now a leading U.S. book-publishing center.

GOVERNMENT AND POLITICS

Massachusetts is governed under a constitution adopted in 1780, as amended. Amendments may be proposed by the state legislature or by an initiative petition signed by a specified number of voters. To become effective, an amendment must be approved by a majority of persons voting on the issue in a general election.

Executive. The chief executive of Massachusetts is a governor, who is popularly elected to a 4-year term and may be reelected any number of times. The same regulations apply to the lieutenant governor, who succeeds the governor should the latter resign, die, or be removed from office. The governor is assisted by an executive council, which is made up of the lieutenant governor and eight other elected persons. Other elected state officials in Massachusetts include the following: the secretary of the commonwealth, the attorney general, the treasurer and receiver general, and the auditor of the commonwealth.

Legislature. The bicameral Massachusetts General Court consists of a senate and a house of representatives. The 40 members of the senate and the 160 members of the house are popularly elected to serve 2-year terms.

Judiciary. Massachusetts's highest court, the supreme judicial court, is made up of a chief justice and six associate judges. Other major tribunals are the appeals court, with 14 judges, and the trial court, with 320 judges. Judges of the three courts are appointed by the governor with the consent of the executive council and serve until the age of 70.

Local Government. The 14 counties of Massachusetts serve mainly as judicial districts, and their governments have little power. The state's local government resides, for the most part, in its 39 chartered cities and its 312 incorporated towns.

Wharf lines connect a tanker at the dock with the refinery at Everett, Mass.

MASSACHUSETTS

Fisheries play an important role in the industry of Massachusetts, the principal fishing ports being Gloucester, Boston, and New Bedford.
U.S. Dept. of State

Massachusetts cities use the mayor-council form of government. Towns, which typically include several villages and other communities, are mainly governed by yearly citizens' meetings.

National Representation. Massachusetts elects 2 senators and 10 representatives to the U.S. Congress. The state has 12 electoral votes in presidential elections.

Politics. In presidential elections since the 1930s, Massachusetts voters have usually supported the Democratic nominee. The Kennedy family—including John Fitzgerald Kennedy, the 35th president of the U.S. (1961–63), and Edward M. Kennedy, a U.S. senator (1962–   )—has played a leading role in state politics.

ECONOMY

Massachusetts was an important center of commerce, fishing, and shipbuilding in colonial times. In the early 19th century its economy became increasingly dominated by manufacturing, especially the production of textiles and footwear. These industries declined in the 20th century, but manufacturing remained a leading economic activity. The Boston area became known as a center for advanced research and for the production of high-technology electronic items. The state also has a big summer tourist industry. Boston is a major financial and insurance center.

Agriculture. Farming in Massachusetts is relatively unimportant economically. The state has some 6900 farms, which have an average size of 40 ha (99 acres). About 72% of the annual income from agriculture is derived from the sale of crops, and the rest comes from sales of livestock and livestock products. The most valuable crops are greenhouse and nursery products (mainly flowers and shrubs), cranberries, hay, apples, tobacco, and potatoes and other vegetables. Principal livestock products are dairy items, eggs, beef cattle, hogs, turkeys, and sheep and lambs. Major farming areas are the Connecticut Valley Lowland and the SE part of the state.

Forestry and Fishing. Forestry is a minor industry in Massachusetts, but fishing is of considerable importance. In the late 1980s the annual fish catch was valued at $273 million, second highest (behind Alaska) among the U.S. states. The principal species landed were cod, flounder, haddock, hake, pollock, swordfish, tuna, scallops, clams, shrimp, and lobster. The major fishing ports in the state were Gloucester, Boston, and New Bedford.

Mining. The annual value of Massachusetts's mineral output in the late 1980s was only about $144 million. The main minerals produced are granite, marble, basalt, and other stone; sand and gravel; clay; peat; and lime.

Manufacturing. Massachusetts is one of the leading U.S. states in manufacturing. This branch of the economy accounts for about 19% of the annual gross state product. In the late 1980s

MASSACHUSETTS

DATE OF STATEHOOD: February 6, 1788; 6th state

CAPITAL:	Boston
MOTTO:	*Ense petit placidam sub libertate quietem* (By the sword we seek peace, but peace only under liberty)
NICKNAME:	Bay State
STATE SONG:	"All Hail to Massachusetts" (by Richard K. Fletcher)
STATE TREE:	American elm
STATE FLOWER:	Mayflower
STATE BIRD:	Chickadee
POPULATION (1990):	6,016,425; 13th among the states
AREA:	27,337 sq km (10,555 sq mi); 44th largest state; includes 7037 sq km (2717 sq mi) of inland water
COASTLINE:	309 km (192 mi)
HIGHEST POINT:	Mt. Greylock, 1064 m (3491 ft)
LOWEST POINT:	Sea level, at the Atlantic coast
ELECTORAL VOTES:	12
U.S. CONGRESS:	2 senators; 10 representatives

POPULATION OF MASSACHUSETTS SINCE 1790

Year of Census	Population	Classified As Urban
1790	379,000	13%
1820	523,000	23%
1850	995,000	51%
1880	1,783,000	74%
1900	2,805,000	86%
1920	3,852,000	90%
1940	4,317,000	89%
1960	5,149,000	84%
1980	5,737,000	84%
1990	6,016,425	84%

POPULATION OF TEN LARGEST CITIES

	1990 Census	1980 Census
Boston	574,283	562,994
Worcester	169,759	161,799
Springfield	156,983	152,319
Lowell	103,439	92,418
New Bedford	99,922	98,478
Cambridge	95,802	95,322
Brockton	92,788	95,172
Fall River	92,703	92,574
Quincy	84,985	84,743
Newton	82,585	83,622

CLIMATE

	BOSTON	WORCESTER
Average January temperature range	−5° to 2.2° C (23° to 36° F)	−8.9° to −0.6° C (16° to 31° F)
Average July temperature range	18.3° to 27.2° C (65° to 81° F)	16.1° to 26.1° C (61° to 79° F)
Average annual temperature	10.8° C (51.5° F)	8.3° C (47° F)
Average annual precipitation	1092 mm (43 in)	1143 mm (45 in)
Average annual snowfall	1067 mm (42 in)	1880 mm (74 in)
Mean number of days per year with appreciable precipitation	129	128
Average daily relative humidity	65%	66%
Mean number of clear days per year	99	90

NATURAL REGIONS OF MASSACHUSETTS

- TACONIC MTS.
- GREEN MTS.
- Connecticut R.
- WESTERN NEW ENGLAND UPLAND
- CONNECTICUT VALLEY LOWLAND
- EASTERN NEW ENGLAND UPLAND
- SEABOARD LOWLAND
- ATLANTIC COASTAL PLAIN

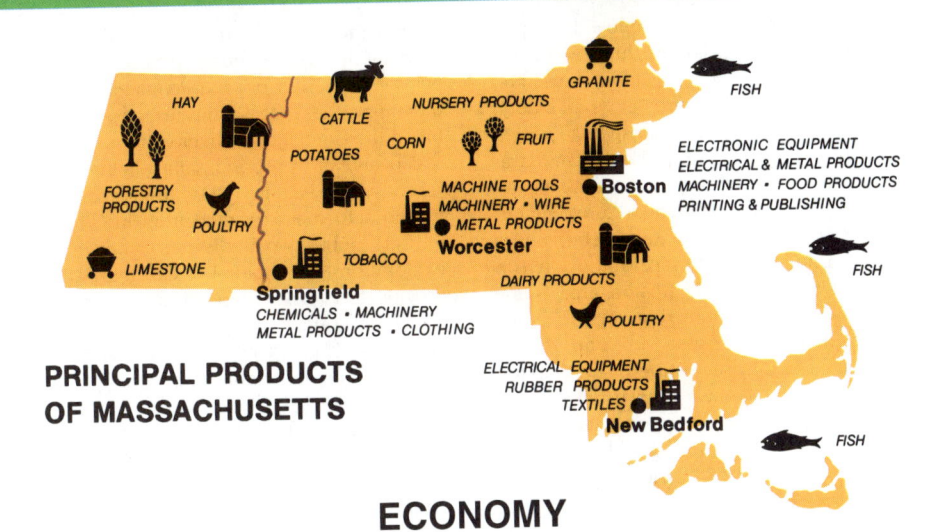

PRINCIPAL PRODUCTS OF MASSACHUSETTS

(Map shows:)
- HAY, CATTLE, NURSERY PRODUCTS, GRANITE, FISH
- FORESTRY PRODUCTS, POTATOES, CORN, FRUIT
- ELECTRONIC EQUIPMENT, ELECTRICAL & METAL PRODUCTS, MACHINERY • FOOD PRODUCTS, PRINTING & PUBLISHING
- POULTRY, LIMESTONE, TOBACCO
- MACHINE TOOLS, MACHINERY • WIRE, METAL PRODUCTS — Boston
- Worcester
- DAIRY PRODUCTS, POULTRY, FISH
- Springfield — CHEMICALS • MACHINERY, METAL PRODUCTS • CLOTHING
- ELECTRICAL EQUIPMENT, RUBBER PRODUCTS, TEXTILES — New Bedford
- FISH

ECONOMY

State budget............general revenue $15.8 billion
                        general expenditure $17.0 billion
                        accumulated debt $18.7 billion
State and local taxes, per capita.............$2360
Personal income, per capita...................$17,224
Population below poverty level.................8.9%
Assets, insured commercial banks (99)....$101.4 billion
Labor force (civilian nonfarm)................3,115,000
   Employed in services   30%
   Employed in wholesale and retail trade   24%
   Employed in manufacturing   18%
   Employed in government   13%

	Quantity Produced	Value
FARM PRODUCTS		**$418 million**
Crops		**$302 million**
Cranberries	62,000 metric tons	$63 million
Hay	211,000 metric tons	$27 million
Vegetables	38,000 metric tons	$19 million
Apples	37,000 metric tons	$19 million
Livestock and Livestock Products		**$116 million**
Milk	206,000 metric tons	$71 million
Eggs	235 million	$21 million
Cattle	5600 metric tons	$9 million
Hogs	3600 metric tons	$4 million
MINERALS		**$144 million**
Stone	10.8 million metric tons	$78 million
Sand, gravel	12.6 million metric tons	$58 million
FISHING	122,000 metric tons	**$273 million**

	Annual Payroll
MANUFACTURING	**$17.5 billion**
Industrial machinery and equipment	$2.7 billion
Electronic equipment	$2.3 billion
Instruments and related products	$2.3 billion
Printing and publishing	$1.5 billion
Fabricated metal products	$1.1 billion
Apparel and textile mill products	$753 million
Transportation equipment	$736 million
Rubber and plastics products	$712 million
Paper and allied products	$626 million
Food and kindred products	$604 million

OTHER..................................**$66.4 billion**
Services.................................$22.2 billion
Government..............................$15.7 billion
Retail trade.............................$7.3 billion
Finance, insurance, and real estate.......$7.1 billion
Wholesale trade..........................$5.8 billion
Transportation, communications,
   and public utilities..................$3.8 billion
Construction.............................$3.7 billion

ANNUAL GROSS STATE PRODUCT

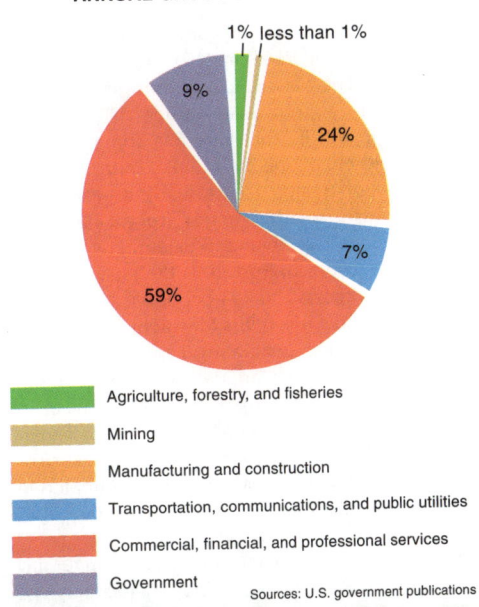

- Agriculture, forestry, and fisheries — 1%
- Mining — less than 1%
- Manufacturing and construction — 24%
- Transportation, communications, and public utilities — 7%
- Commercial, financial, and professional services — 59%
- Government — 9%

Sources: U.S. government publications

MASSACHUSETTS

some 563,000 persons were employed in manufacturing. The principal products were industrial machinery, such as textile-, shoe-, and paper-making machinery, office equipment, and engines; electronic equipment, especially high-technology electronic components; and precision instruments, notably scientific measuring devices. Other major manufactures included textiles, clothing, fabricated metal, paper and paper products, processed food, footwear, and printed materials. The Boston area is the state's principal manufacturing region; many firms engaged in the research and development of electronic equipment are located along Route 128, a highway that forms an arc around Boston. Other important manufacturing areas are centered in Springfield, Worcester, Lawrence, Fall River, New Bedford, Lowell, and Pittsfield.

Tourism. The tourist industry is extremely important; about 33 million tourists visit the state each year, contributing more than $11.7 billion to the state economy. Attractions include the summer vacation areas of Cape Cod and nearby Martha's Vineyard and Nantucket islands and the historical sites and cultural institutions of the Boston area. Many travelers also visit the upland areas of the Berkshire Hills in the W; especially popular here is the summer Berkshire Music Festival at the Tanglewood estate in Lenox. Massachusetts maintains 192 state parks, recreation areas, and historic sites.

Transportation. Massachusetts is served by an extensive system of transportation facilities, which tend to be concentrated in the E part of the state. It has about 54,840 km (about 34,075 mi) of roads, including 739 km (459 mi) of interstate highways. The Massachusetts Turnpike extends from the New York State border, in the W, to Boston, in the E. The state has some 710 km (some 440 mi) of operated Class I railroad track. The Port of Boston is the leading seaport of Massachusetts; other major freight-handling ports include Fall River and Salem. Logan International Airport, in Boston, is the busiest of the state's 77 airports and 103 heliports.

Energy. In the early 1990s Massachusetts had an installed electric generating capacity of about 9.9 million kw, and annual output was about 36.5 billion kwh. Approximately 83% of the electricity was produced in conventional steam generators using petroleum products and other fossil fuels, and almost all the rest was generated in nuclear installations. G.J.K.

HISTORY

Before the arrival of English settlers, six major Indian tribes lived in what is now Massachusetts: the Massachuset tribe in the area where Boston is today, the Wampanoag south of Boston, the Nauset on Cape Cod, the Pennacook and Nipmuc in northern Massachusetts, and the Pocumtuc in the Connecticut River valley.

Giovanni da Verrazano, sailing in the service of France, explored the Massachusetts coast in 1524, but no settlement resulted from his voyage. In the early 1600s two Englishmen made important explorations: Bartholomew Gosnold landed at Provincetown on Cape Cod in 1602, and Capt. John Smith sailed along the coast in 1614. Smith gave New England its name and later wrote a travel account that contributed greatly to further explorations.

Colonial Massachusetts. The colonial period of Massachusetts's history began when the Pilgrims—members of a dissident religious community that had broken away from the Church of England—landed at Plymouth on Dec. 21, 1620. Theirs was the first permanent settlement by Europeans in Massachusetts.

Even before they set foot on shore, the Pilgrims made history. They drew up the famous Mayflower Compact that established a theoretical framework for the government of the Plymouth Colony. The male signers became a "civil body politic," who agreed to conduct their business for the "general good of the colony."

The Pilgrims suffered extreme hardship in the early years. The bitter New England winters took a heavy toll; half the settlers died during the first winter. The strong leadership of Gov. William Bradford and Capt. Miles Standish, coupled with the assistance of friendly Indians, stabilized the colony and ensured its survival.

Within a decade English people began to swarm into Massachusetts. New settlements appeared around Plymouth. In the late 1620s settlers arrived in the Boston area. These were Puritans, religious dissenters who, like the Pilgrims, were dissatisfied with the religious atmosphere in England. In 1630 a fleet of ships brought over a thousand Puritan settlers led by John Winthrop, beginning what is called the Great Migration. These settlers founded the towns of Boston, Charlestown, Dorchester, Lynn, Medford, Roxbury, and Watertown, which became the heartland of the Massachusetts Bay Colony.

Although they came to the New World to seek religious freedom for themselves, neither the Pilgrims nor the Puritans extended religious freedom to those who dissented from their faith. Their intolerance led to the hanging (1660) of Mary Dyer and other Quakers and the expulsion from Massachusetts of the religious dissidents

MASSACHUSETTS

Anne Hutchinson and Roger Williams. Williams resettled in Rhode Island in 1636 and became a leading figure in the movement for religious toleration.

As the coastal settlements expanded, relations with the once friendly Indians began to crumble. Antagonism led to warfare. In 1637 Massachusetts and Connecticut settlers joined in a war against the Pequot Indians of Connecticut that virtually annihilated the tribe. In King Philip's War (1675–76) the English destroyed the Wampanoag and their allies, the Narragansett of Rhode Island.

Massachusetts's charter was revoked by King Charles II in 1684, but eight years later Plymouth Colony and Massachusetts Bay were united under a new charter granted by William and Mary. The colony figured prominently in the French and Indian Wars and was mainly responsible for the successful New England expedition against the French at Louisbourg (1745).

The Revolutionary and Early National Periods. Massachusetts also led colonial resistance to British taxation in the years before the American Revolution. The Boston Massacre (March 5, 1770), in which British troops killed five colonial taunters, was a great stimulant for revolution. Three years later, in the famous Boston Tea Party, townsmen disguised as Indians and led by the fiery Samuel Adams dumped a cargo of British tea into Boston Harbor. This militant action further fanned the flames of rebellion.

In April 1775 the American Revolution broke out at Lexington Green when a band of Massachusetts militiamen resolutely challenged a British force searching for munitions. Lexington was followed by the battle at the North Bridge in nearby Concord, where the "shot heard 'round the world" was fired. Lexington and Concord became symbols of resistance for the Americans as the Revolution erupted in full fury.

One of the most dramatic events of the war was the Battle of Bunker Hill (June 1775). The British drove the Americans from this key height in Boston but suffered more than a thousand casualties. Shortly thereafter, a colonial force under George Washington laid siege to the town. After the British evacuated Boston in March 1776, no further fighting took place in Massachusetts.

In the early national period, Massachusetts underwent a profound economic revolution. Freed from British restraints, its ships and sailors roamed the world, opening up new trade routes and carrying goods from nation to nation. Trade with China and other nations of the Orient became an important element in Massachusetts's economy. The state's maritime interests opposed the War of 1812 as a hindrance to trade. The Federalist party served as their voice, and even secession from the Union was considered. Only the threat of a direct attack by the British could stimulate Massachusetts into a patriotic posture.

The 19th Century. After the war, overseas trade resumed, and Massachusetts became an important industrial state, manufacturing textiles and shoes. What set Massachusetts off from the other northeastern states was the emergence of a remarkably talented group of men and women who became national figures in a wide spectrum of activities, from art to literature to social reform. These included the writers Ralph Waldo Emerson, John Greenleaf Whittier, Henry David Thoreau, Henry Wadsworth Longfellow, Nathaniel Hawthorne, Emily Dickinson, and Herman Melville; the antislavery leaders William Lloyd Garrison and Wendell Phillips; the architect Henry Hobson Richardson; the jurist Oliver Wendell Holmes; the historians Francis Parkman, Henry Adams, and William Hickling Prescott; the sculptor Horatio Greenough; the painter John Singer Sargent; and the reformers Horace Mann, Dorothea Dix, and Lucy Stone. It was an amazing galaxy of talent for so small a state. Perhaps the key to this powerful intellectual group was the Massachusetts educational system, one of the strongest in the nation.

Statue of Paul Revere in Boston. In the rear is the Old North Church, from the steeple of which was flashed the signal to Revere indicating the route taken by the British who were advancing on Concord.

MASSACHUSETTS, UNIVERSITY OF

The 20th Century. Modern Massachusetts is a pluralistic commonwealth that continues to undergo changes. Its economy has been transformed and highly diversified in the past few decades. The decline of the once powerful textile and leather industries from the Great Depression to the post–World War II era was a severe economic setback. The later explosive growth of high-technology industry has more than compensated for the earlier decline, however. The greater Boston area, in particular, has become an important scientific center, with many firms exploring the possible applications of new discoveries in nuclear physics, computers, differential analyzers, and other highly technical devices and machines. Although many of its old, family-owned firms have merged into national corporations, Massachusetts continues to spawn new companies at a high rate.

Like most highly urbanized, industrialized states, Massachusetts is also affected by a host of new economic and social problems: air pollution, energy needs, inadequate mass transportation, toxic wastes, racial unrest, and housing and school problems. With urbanization continuing at a relentless rate, these basic problems are certain to persist into the future. L.L.T.

For further information on this topic, see the Bibliography in volume 28, sections 1163, 1167–68.

MASSACHUSETTS, UNIVERSITY OF, state-controlled land-grant institution of higher learning, with general campuses in Amherst and Boston and a medical school and teaching hospital in Worcester. Founded in 1863, the university was opened in 1867 as Massachusetts Agricultural College; the name was changed to Massachusetts State College in 1931, and the present name was adopted in 1947. The Amherst campus has divisions of arts and sciences, food and natural resources, management, engineering, education, and health sciences. The Boston campus has colleges of liberal arts, professional studies, and public and community service. Degrees of bachelor, master, and doctor are awarded.

MASSACHUSETTS BAY, inlet of the Atlantic Ocean, E Massachusetts, stretching some 64 km (some 40 mi) from Cape Ann on the N to Plymouth Bay on the S; Cape Cod Bay is sometimes included in it. The city of Boston is near the most westerly point of the bay.

MASSACHUSETTS BAY COMPANY, English trading company that evolved into a theocracy, organized in 1628 as the Governor and Company of the Massachusetts Bay in New England. The Council of New England granted the Massachusetts Bay Co., under the leadership of John Endecott, a piece of land between the Charles and Merrimack rivers westward to the Pacific Ocean. Puritan leaders in England, including John Winthrop, who in 1629 was elected first governor of the colony, saw it as a religious and political refuge; under the Cambridge Agreement (1629), Puritans (advocates of a more purely Protestant church of England) would immigrate to New England on the condition that control of the government and the charter of the company be given to the settlers. This agreement had far-reaching results in that suffrage in the colony came to be restricted to adherents of the Puritan philosophy, and the emphasis was shifted from trade to religion. Arriving in 1630, Winthrop and some 900 colonists went first to Salem, then to Charleston, and finally settled at the mouth of the Charles River, where Boston was established. Here the company and colony remained one until 1684, when the charter was revoked. Another charter, in 1691, extended the power of the Massachusetts colony over Plymouth and Maine.

MASSACHUSETTS INSTITUTE OF TECHNOLOGY (MIT), one of the world's leading research universities, in Cambridge, Mass., opened in Boston in 1865 by the geologist William Barton Rogers (1804–82), who became its first president. From a school originally devoted to industrial science, MIT has developed into five schools offering undergraduate as well as graduate work. The school of science offers programs in the pure sciences, as well as an interdisciplinary program; the school of engineering offers programs in all fields of engineering, as well as aeronautics and astronautics; the school of architecture has an urban planning division; the Alfred P. Sloan School of Management has programs in management science linking fundamental disciplines with quantitative studies, and the school of humanities and social science offers programs in economics, philosophy, political science, psychology, the humanities, and linguistics. MIT and the Woods Hole Oceanographic Institution offer joint graduate programs in oceanography and ocean engineering.

Throughout its history MIT has held a worldwide reputation for teaching and research. It was among the first schools to use the laboratory method of instruction, to develop the modern profession of chemical engineering, and to offer courses in aeronautical and electrical engineering and in applied physics. Today, among its special facilities are five high-energy accelerators, a nuclear reactor, and more than 70 laboratories—including a computation center and a spectroscopy laboratory. MIT Press is noted for its books on linguistic theory, architecture and urban studies, and the sciences.

MASSASOIT (1580?–1661), American Indian chief, born in what is now Massachusetts. He was chief of the Wampanoag and ruled over the greater part of Massachusetts. The treaty he made with the Pilgrims in 1621 was the earliest recorded in New England. Massasoit's second son, Philip, succeeded his brother as chief sachem, and in 1675 led his warriors against the settlers in the conflict now known as King Philip's War.

MASSAWA, city, NE Eritrea, a seaport on the Red Sea, near Asmara. The city lies partly on the mainland and partly on several islands off the coast. The harbor is formed by a channel between one of the islands and the mainland. Important industries include the production of marine salt, glue making, and fishing. For many centuries Massawa was a dominion of Abyssinia (now Ethiopia), and between the 16th and 18th centuries it was an Ottoman Turkish possession. In 1864 it was ceded to Egypt. Massawa was occupied (1885) by Italian troops and became part of Eritrea, of which it was the capital for several years. In 1941, during World War II, Massawa was taken by the British. It remained under British administration until 1952, when, following a UN decision, Eritrea was federated with Ethiopia; ten years later, Eritrea was united with Ethiopia, and in 1993 became an independent republic. Pop. (1989 est.) 19,400.

MASS DEFECT, in physics, the difference between the mass number of an atom—the combined number of protons and neutrons in the atom's nucleus—and the lesser actual mass of the atom. The difference is the result of the equivalence of matter and energy (see RELATIVITY), that is, some of the mass in an atomic nucleus is used as energy to bind the particles together (see NUCLEAR ENERGY); this energy is known as binding energy. Except for the very lightest nuclei, the mass defect amounts to about 1 percent of the total nuclear mass. See also ATOM AND ATOMIC THEORY.

MASSENET, Jules Émile Frédéric (1842–1912), French composer, born in Montaud, and educated at the Paris Conservatoire, where from 1878 to 1894 he was professor of composition. Massenet wrote oratorios, cantatas, instrumental pieces, and orchestral suites, but his popularity rests mainly on his operas, with their graceful, sensuous melodies and sentimental plots. *Manon* (1884), based on the novel *Manon Lescaut* by the French novelist Antoine François Prévost d'Exiles, is still frequently performed. Some of his other operas are *Hérodiade* (1881), *Le Cid* (1885), *Werther* (1892), *Thaïs* (1894), and *Don Quichotte* (1910). His famous "Elégie" is an air from the incidental music composed in 1873 for a dramatic work, *Les Erinyes,* by the French poet Charles Marie Leconte de Lisle. His memoirs, *My Recollections,* appeared in 1912 (trans. 1919).

MASSEY, Vincent (1887–1967), governor-general of Canada (1952–59), the first native-born Canadian to hold that office. Born in Toronto, and educated at the University of Toronto and the University of Oxford, he taught modern history before joining the Dominion cabinet in 1925. He later served as Canadian minister to the U.S. (1926–30) and high commissioner for Canada in Great Britain (1935–46). The "Massey Report" (1951) contained his evaluation of the status of Canadian arts and culture. His recommendations for government subsidies to the arts became an integral part of Canadian national policy.

For further information on this person, see the section Biographies in the Bibliography in volume 28.

MASSIF CENTRAL, large upland area, S central France, covering about one-sixth of the area of France. It reaches a high point of 1886 m (6188 ft) atop Puy de Sancy. Major sections include the Auvergne, in the center, a region of ancient lava flows and eroded volcanic necks (*puys*); the Causses, in the SW, underlain mainly by limestone; the rugged Cévennes, in the SE, overlooking the Rhône-Saône Valley and the Midi section of S France; and a series of low, rolling plateaus in Limousin, in the NW. Saint-Étienne, Clermont-Ferrand, and Limoges are major industrial centers. Besides heavy industry, the region supports sheep and goat raising, dairy farming, and coal and kaolin mining. Several major hydroelectric facilities also are here, notably on the Cère, Dordogne, Lot, Tarn, and Truyère rivers.

MASSILLON, city, Stark Co., NE Ohio, on the Tuscarawas R.; inc. as a city 1868. It is a manufacturing and distribution center for a rich agricultural area. Products include processed food; motor-vehicle parts; containers; plastic, paper, and metal items; chemicals; and printed materials. The Massillon Museum and several historic homes are here. The community, settled about 1810, was laid out in 1826 and named for Jean Baptiste Massillon (1663–1742), a bishop of Clermont, France. It grew with the completion (1832) of the Ohio and Erie Canal and the arrival (1852) of the railroad. Pop. (1980) 30,557; (1990) 31,007.

MASSINE, Léonide, professional name of LEONID FYODOROVICH MIASSIN (1896–1979), Russian-American dancer and choreographer, born in Moscow. Massine studied ballet at the Imperial Theater in Moscow and at the age of 17 became a protégé of the Russian ballet producer Sergey Diaghilev, who took him to Paris. With Diaghilev's Ballets Russes, Massine made his debut as a dancer in 1914, and a year later he began his career as a choreographer. During this first period with Diaghilev, Massine choreographed several famous works, including *La boutique fantasque* (1919) and *The Rite of Spring* (1920). *The Three-Cornered Hat* (1919), another Massine ballet, had decor by Pablo Picasso and music by the Spanish composer Manuel de Falla.

Massine made his American debut as a dancer in 1916. Five years later, he left Diaghilev to tour South America with his own company, but he rejoined the Ballets Russes in 1924 and remained with the company until Diaghilev's death in 1929. Massine danced and choreographed for the Ballets Russes de Monte Carlo (later renamed) from 1932 until 1937. From 1938 to 1943 Massine was choreographer, dancer, and artistic director of his own dance group, also called the Ballets Russe de Monte Carlo. He later worked with the American Ballet Theatre and with various European companies. He also choreographed and appeared in the British motion pictures *The Red Shoes* (1948) and *Tales of Hoffmann* (1951).

A choreographer who did much to further the arts of character dance and pantomime, Massine became an American citizen in 1944. He published an autobiography, *My Life in Ballet* (1968).

MASSINGER, Philip (1583–1640), English playwright, born in Salisbury, and educated at the University of Oxford. He went to London in 1606 and collaborated successfully with the playwrights Nathaniel Field (1587–1633), Cyril Tourneur, Thomas Dekker, and John Fletcher; with Fletcher he wrote regularly for the troupe The King's Players. In his works Massinger introduced many of his democratic ideas, and he frequently caricatured such well-known persons as the duke of Buckingham. His plays, which include both comedy and tragedy, show skilled plot construction and great facility of expression. He was the sole author of 15 plays, including *The Duke of Milan* (1623), *The Emperor of the East* (1631), *A New Way to Pay Old Debts* (1632), and *The Unnatural Combat* (1639).

MASS MEDIA. See BROADCASTING, RADIO AND TELEVISION; COMMUNICATION; JOURNALISM; NEWSPAPERS; PERIODICALS.

MASS NUMBER, in physics, the combined number of protons and neutrons in the nucleus of an atom (*see* ATOM AND ATOMIC THEORY). An element may have one or more different mass numbers, indicating the different isotopes of that element (*see* ISOTOPE).

MASS PRODUCTION. See AUTOMATION; FACTORY SYSTEM.

MASS SPECTROGRAPH, apparatus that converts molecules into ions and then separates the ions

The TSQ 70 triple stage quadrupole mass spectrometer can be used to analyze pharmaceuticals, environmental pollutants, and petroleum products.
Courtesy of Finnigan Corporation

according to their mass-to-charge ratio for the purpose of determining their relative proportions or chemical properties, or for their use in other chemical processes (*see* ION; IONIZATION). The photographic record of the distribution and relative abundance of the ions is the mass spectrum, which is useful for determining the complete molecular structure of a substance (*see* SPECTRUM).

Although many different kinds of mass spectrographs are in use today, they are all related to a device developed by the British physicist Francis William Aston in 1919. In Aston's instrument, a thin beam of positively charged ions was first deflected by an electric field and then deflected in the opposite direction by a magnetic field. The amount of deflection of the particles as registered on a photographic plate depended on their mass and velocity: the greater the mass or velocity of the ion, the less it was deflected. Aston measured the molecular weights of the isotopes of many elements as well as the relative abundance of these isotopes in nature (*see* ISOTOPE).

All mass spectrographs have four features in common: (1) a system for introducing into the instrument the substance to be analyzed; (2) a system for ionizing the substance; (3) a system for accelerating the ions; and (4) a system for separating the constituent ions and recording the mass spectrum of the substance.

The Magnetic-Deflection Mass Spectrometer. In this instrument, the positive ions are first strongly accelerated by passing through an electrostatic field. They are then deflected by a magnetic field, their trajectory depending on the masses of the ionized particles. The mass spectrum is scanned by precisely varying the strength of the magnetic field, using an electrode, in the sequential order of their masses.

Uses of Spectrographs. The more recent mass spectrographs provide a high degree of resolution and adaptability to produce analyses of complex mixtures. Products of petroleum refining and processing, for example, which usually contain various closely related hydrocarbons, are difficult to separate by conventional methods of chemical analysis. By passing ionized particles of these compounds through the spectrograph, it is possible to analyze the individual substances present from the mass spectrum of individual compounds. The most important recent uses of the spectrograph have been in the field of molecular physics, in conjunction with other devices; in the study of chemical reactions; and in the detection of minute amounts of chemical impurities in numerous substances. In the field of molecular biology, development of an instrument called the tandem mass spectrometer makes it possible to routinely establish the linear sequence of the amino acids in a protein molecule in a matter of minutes and with more accurate results than from conventional chemical analysis. Consisting of two mass spectrometers connected end to end, the tandem device is more than a thousand times more sensitive than any single unit, making it uniquely suitable for analysis of extremely small quantities of fragile biological compounds with large molecular weights. See CHEMICAL ANALYSIS.

For further information on this topic, see the Bibliography in volume 28, sections 389, 396, 406.

MASS TRANSIT. See PUBLIC TRANSPORTATION; RAILROADS.

MASSYS or **MATSYS, Quentin** (c. 1466–1530), Flemish painter, whose work represents the first effective synthesis of the Netherlandish tradition with Italian Renaissance ideas. The founder of the Antwerp school, he was probably born in Louvain. Massys painted both religious pictures and secular portraits. Undated early works, such as *Virgin and Child* (Musées Royaux de Beaux-Arts, Brussels), show the influence of earlier Flemish masters in their intense religious feeling, sumptuous colors, and lavish attention to detail. In later works, particularly in portraits and in everyday scenes, Massys strove to depict his subjects in characteristic actions. In *Money Changer and His Wife* (1514, Louvre, Paris), the subtly hinted avarice of the couple illustrates a new satirical quality in his paintings. His portraits, particularly *Portrait of an Elderly Man* (1513, Musée Jacquemart-André, Paris), show the influence of Leonardo da Vinci in their unflinchingly honest, sometimes grotesque, physiognomies. His most advanced work, the *Ugly Duchess* (c. 1515, National Gallery, London), which is probably not a portrait of an actual person but an illustration for Erasmus's *Praise of Folly,* carries his secular and satirical style to its culmination.

MAST, on a sailing ship, vertical or nearly vertical spar, generally made of wood or metal, supporting the accessory spars, including yards, booms, and gaffs, and the sails and rigging. The masts of powered vessels are used to carry lights, cranes, and lookout posts. By extension the term has been applied to many types of tall, upright structures such as those used to support radio or television antennas on shore as well as on shipboard.

Masts are commonly made of solid wood, notably on small sailboats, but sometimes hollow wood or metal construction is employed. Very tall masts are sometimes made in two or more sections. These sections are called lower mast and topmast, or lower mast, topmast, and topgallant mast. In three-masted, square-rigged ships, beginning at the bow, the masts are called foremast, mainmast, and mizzen or mizzenmast; in four-masted ships they are called foremast, foreward mainmast, mainmast, and mizzen. The masts are called foremast and mainmast in the usual two-masted fore-and-aft rigged schooner, and mainmast and mizzen in a ketch or yawl.

See BOATS AND BOATBUILDING; FISHING VESSELS; SAIL; SHIPS AND SHIPBUILDING.

MASTECTOMY, surgical removal of all or part of a woman's breast (q.v.) when cancer has been detected there. Radiation therapy and chemotherapy may form part of the treatment after surgery. In radical mastectomy, muscles and tissues surrounding the breast are removed as well. Some physicians advocate a less radical procedure, when possible, called lumpectomy, in which only the cancerous regions of the breast are removed; this usually also involves radiation therapy. It avoids the physical and psychological trauma of complete breast removal, the concern being whether all the cancer sites have been excised. In many mastectomy cases the breast can be reconstructed by plastic surgery, through implants and other techniques. See CANCER.

MASTER OF FLÉMALLE. See CAMPIN, ROBERT.

MASTERS, Edgar Lee (1869–1950), American poet, born in Garnett, Kans. He wrote *A Book of Verses* (1898) and several plays before gaining fame with *Spoon River Anthology* (1915), a collection of revelations in free verse of the secret lives of the inhabitants of a small midwestern town. The realism and irony of this work were in marked contrast to the prevailing romantic and

89

sentimental American literature, and the book is still a landmark in the literature of realism and revolt against conventional social standards that flourished in the early 20th century. His other writings are *Songs and Satires* (1916), *The New Spoon River* (1924), *Poems of People* (1936), and *The New World* (1937); the novel *Mitch Miller* (1920); and the biography *Lincoln the Man* (1931).

MASTERS, William H(owell) (1915-), American gynecologist, who, with the American psychologist Virginia Johnson, investigated human sexuality under laboratory conditions and devised methods of sex therapy. Masters was born in Cleveland, Ohio, and received his medical degree from the University of Rochester in 1943. Using such equipment as electroencephalographs, electrocardiographs, and motion picture cameras, Masters and Johnson studied the physiology and anatomy of sexual activity. Their reports—*Human Sexual Response* (1966), *Human Sexual Inadequacy* (1970), and *Homosexuality in Perspective* (1979)—challenged a number of popular opinions about orgasm, impotence, frigidity, homosexuality, and other sexual phenomena. Masters and Johnson married in 1971.

MASTERSON, Bat, full name WILLIAM BARCLAY MASTERSON (1853-1921), American frontier law enforcement officer and journalist, born in Iroquois Co., Ill. In his youth Masterson was a buffalo hunter, railroad worker, Indian fighter, army scout, and gold prospector. In 1877 he was elected sheriff of Ford Co., Kans., with Dodge City as his headquarters, and he assisted (1880-81) Federal Marshal Wyatt Earp in bringing law and order to Tombstone, Ariz. For the next 20 years he lived in various cities and towns of the American West, supporting himself as a gambler. In 1902 he moved to New York City and within a year became a sportswriter on the daily *Morning Telegraph*, a post he held until his death. Masterson holds an important place among the legendary figures of the American frontier.

MASTIC, resin obtained from the mastic tree, *Pistacia lentiscus*. Used as an astringent and as an ingredient of varnishes and lacquers, it is also an ingredient of a cement called asphalt mastic.

MASTIFF, breed of giant dog, of the working dog variety, which supposedly originated in Asia in remote antiquity, and was known in Egypt about 3000 BC. The English type, called the Old English mastiff, has been known for about 2000 years. It was employed for fighting in warfare, for hunting, and for protecting homes and farms from wolves and other wild beasts. The dog today is used as a watchdog and a household pet. The mastiff has a large, powerful frame; it weighs about 70 to 79 kg (about 155 to 175 lb), the male being about 76 cm (about 30 in) high at the shoulders. The animal has a massive head; small, V-shaped ears; dark-brown eyes that are set wide apart; a blunt muzzle; a powerful, muscular neck; a deep chest; and a tail that is wide at the root and tapers to the end. The mastiff has a coarse outer coat and a thick, smooth undercoat; its color is tan, fawn, or brindle.

MASTODON, common name for any of the extinct elephantlike mammals that constituted the family Mastodontidae of the order Proboscidea ("long snouted"). The leaf-eating mastodons were widely distributed in the forests of the world from Oligocene to Pleistocene times. Their remains have been found worldwide and are often remarkably well preserved. Like the modern elephant (q.v.), the mastodon was very large, with thick, sturdy legs; a huge head; tusks; and a flexible, muscular trunk. Like the mammoth (q.v.), the mastodon was covered with shaggy hair. The animals differed from elephants and mammoths, however, in having complete tuberculate teeth. Their upper tusks were long and curved; they had transverse crests on their grinding teeth. *Mastodon americanus,* almost the size of a modern Indian elephant, was common throughout what is now the U.S.; it did not become extinct until about 8000 years ago.

For further information on this topic, see the Bibliography in volume 28, sections 436, 475.

MASTOID PROCESS, conical prominence of the temporal bone of the human skull, situated behind the ear. It commonly becomes infected in cases of suppurative otitis media. The inner ear adjoins the hollow, spongy spaces within the mastoid process so that infection of the ear easily spreads to that area, causing pain and swelling. Surgical drainage of pus and injection of antibiotics usually eliminate mastoid infection and prevent its spread to nearby areas of the brain.

MASURIA (Ger. *Masurenland;* Pol. *Mazury*), region, NE Poland. It is an area of numerous lakes and marshes; Śniardwy and Mamry are the largest lakes. Olsztyn (Allenstein) is the largest settlement. Formerly part of the East Prussia province of Germany, the area was the scene of major German World War I victories over Russia in the battles of the Masurian Lakes (1914, 1915). Masuria passed to Poland after World War II.

MATABELELAND, region, S Zimbabwe, extending about 320 km (about 200 mi) N from the Limpopo R. (which separates it from South Africa). Bulawayo is the chief town. Cereals, sugar, and cotton are principal products. Gold and other minerals are mined. The region is historically important as the home of the Ndebele (Matabele) ethnic group. The Ndebele, led by Lobengula, rose in 1893 against the British South African Co., which had assumed control in 1889. They rose again in 1896 but were defeated.

MATADI, town, W Zaire, capital of Bas-Zaire region, a seaport on the estuary of the Congo R., near the Angolan border. It is connected by rail with Kinshasa. Most of the products of Zaire, other than the minerals of Shaba Region, including coffee, cocoa, rice, timber, palm products, cotton, copal, and minerals, are shipped from the large harbor of Matadi. Pharmaceuticals are manufactured here. Pop. (1984) 144,742.

MATAGALPA, city, W central Nicaragua, capital of Matagalpa Department, in the central highlands. It is one of the nation's principal urban areas and an important commercial center for the nearby coffee-producing and gold-mining region. Coffee processing, flour milling, and textile manufacturing are major industries here. A cathedral from the Spanish colonial period is a noted landmark. Pop. (1985 est.) 37,000.

MATA HARI, professional name of Gertrud Margarete Zelle (1876–1917), Dutch courtesan and world-famous spy during World War I. Born in Leeuwarden and educated in a convent, she married Campbell MacLeod, a British-born captain of the Dutch army, when she was 18 years old; they were divorced a few years later. She settled in Paris, and shortly after 1900 she began to perform erotic dances for private gatherings. In 1907 she became a spy for Germany, attending a school for espionage in Lörrach. Through her liaisons with high-ranking Allied officers she was able to obtain important military information. She was executed in October 1917 by the French.

MATAMOROS, city, NE Mexico, in Tamaulipas State, on the Rio Grande (near its mouth on the Gulf of Mexico), opposite Brownsville, Tex. A major port of entry, it has rail and road connections with Texas and the rest of Mexico and has a modern customs building (1963) and tourist facilities. The city is also a port and commercial center of the lower Rio Grande valley, which produces fruits, cattle, sugarcane, and cotton. Industries include cotton ginning, tanning, cottonseed and wool processing, and the manufacture of glass, hides, mescal, and vegetable oils. Founded in 1824, the city was occupied by the American general Zachary Taylor in 1846 during the Mexican War. Pop. (1990) 303,392.

MATANZAS, city, W Cuba, capital of Matanzas Province, on Matanzas Bay, near Havana (with which it is connected by railroad). Matanzas is an important sugar-exporting port. Industries include distilling, tanning, and fishing. The city is a major tourist center, and the famous Bellamar Caves are nearby. Pop. (1981) 99,194.

MATCH, short, thin piece of wood, cardboard, or waxed string, tipped with a mixture of fire-producing substances, and used to produce a flame. One of the first matches produced was the brimstone match, made by dipping thin strips of wood into melted sulfur; the sulfur points ignited when applied to a spark produced by a flint and steel. In 1812 a chemical match was invented. Coated with sulfur and tipped with a mixture of potassium chlorate and sugar, it ignited when touched to sulfuric acid.

Matches made with phosphorus and ignited by friction were invented in 1827 by the British chemist John Walker (1781?–1859). The modern friction match has one end fireproofed and the other coated with paraffin. Its head contains an oxidizing agent, such as potassium chlorate; a substance that oxidizes readily, such as sulfur or rosin; a filler of clay; a binding material, such as glue; a dye to give it distinctive color; and, at the very tip, a small amount of phosphorus trisulfide. This decomposes, burns at a low temperature, and ignites the paraffin, which burns more readily because of the presence of the other chemicals.

Safety matches are so designed that the head can be ignited only by striking on the friction surface provided on the match package; the tip contains antimony trisulfide and an oxidizing agent, which are held in place with casein or glue. The striking surface contains powdered glass, red phosphorus, and glue. When the match is struck, the heat of friction converts the red phosphorus to white phosphorus, which ignites and in turn ignites the head of the match.

MATÉ, also yerba maté, or Paraguay tea, beverage used commonly in South America. It is made from the dried and roughly ground leaves and shoots of certain species of holly, especially *Ilex paraguariensis*. The tea is a stimulant containing theine (*see* Caffeine). The word *maté* also denotes the gourds that are used as cups for making and drinking the tea.

MATERIALISM, in philosophy, doctrine that all existence is resolvable into physical matter or into an attribute or effect of matter. According to this doctrine, matter is the ultimate reality, and the phenomenon of consciousness is explained by physiochemical changes in the nervous system. Materialism is therefore the antithesis of idealism, in which the supremacy of mind is affirmed and matter is characterized as an aspect or objectification of mind. Extreme or absolute materialism is known as materialistic monism. According to the mind-stuff theory of monism, as expounded by the British metaphysician W. K. Clifford (1845–79), in his *Elements of Dynamic* (1879–87), matter and mind are consubstantial, each being merely an aspect of the other. Philosophical materialism is ancient and has had numerous formulations. The early Greek philosophers subscribed to a variant of materialism known as hylozoism, according to which matter and life are identical. Related to hylozoism is the doctrine of hylotheism, in which matter is held to be divine, or the existence of God is disavowed apart from matter. Cosmological materialism is a term used to characterize a materialistic interpretation of the universe.

Antireligious materialism is motivated by a spirit of hostility toward the theological dogmas of organized religion, particularly those of Christianity. Notable among the exponents of antireligious materialism were the 18th-century French philosophers Denis Diderot, Paul Henri d'Holbach (1723–89), and Julien Offroy de La Mettrie (1709–51). According to historical materialism, as set forth in the writings of Karl Marx, Friedrich Engels, and Vladimir Ilich Lenin, in every historical epoch the prevailing economic system by which the necessities of life are produced determines the form of societal organization and the political, religious, ethical, intellectual, and artistic history of the epoch.

In modern times philosophical materialism has been largely influenced by the doctrine of evolution and may indeed be said to have been assimilated in the wider theory of evolution. Supporters of the theory of evolution go beyond the mere antitheism or atheism of materialism and seek positively to show how the diversities and differences in creation are the result of natural as opposed to supernatural processes.

MATERIALS SCIENCE AND TECHNOLOGY, the study of materials, nonmetallic as well as metallic, and how they can be adapted and fabricated to meet the needs of modern technology. Using the laboratory techniques and research tools of physics, chemistry, and metallurgy (q.v.), scientists are finding new ways of using plastics, ceramics, and other nonmetals in applications formerly reserved for metals.

Recent Developments. The rapid development of semiconductors (*see* SEMICONDUCTOR) for the electronics industry, beginning in the early 1960s, gave materials science its first major impetus. Having discovered that nonmetallic materials such as silicon could be made to conduct electricity in ways that metals could not, scientists and engineers devised ways of fashioning thousands of tiny integrated circuits (*see* INTEGRATED CIRCUIT) on a small chip of silicon. This then made it possible to miniaturize the components of electronic devices such as computers.

In the late 1980s, materials science research was given renewed emphasis with the discovery of ceramics that display superconductivity (q.v.) at higher temperatures than metals do. If the temperature at which these new materials become superconductive can be raised high enough, new applications, including levitating trains and superfast computers, are possible.

Although the latest developments in materials science have tended to focus on electrical properties, mechanical properties are also of major, continuing importance. For the aircraft industry, for instance, scientists have been developing, and engineers testing, nonmetallic composite materials that are lighter, stronger, and easier to fabricate than the aluminum and other metals currently used to form the outer skin of aircraft.

Mechanical Properties of Materials. Engineers must know how solid materials respond to external forces, such as tension, compression, torsion, bending, and shear. Solid materials respond to these forces by elastic deformation (that is, the material returns to its original size and form when the external force is lifted), permanent deformation, or fracture. Time-dependent effects of external forces are creep and fatigue, which are defined below.

Tension is a pulling force that acts in one direction; an example is the force in a cable holding a weight. Under tension, a material usually stretches, returning to its original length if the force does not exceed the material's elastic limit (*see* ELASTICITY). Under larger tensions, the material does not return completely to its original condition, and under even greater forces the material ruptures.

Compression is the decrease in volume that results from the application of pressure. When a material is subjected to a bending, shearing, or torsional (twisting) force, both tensile and compressive forces are simultaneously at work. When a rod is bent, for example, one side of it is stretched and subjected to a tensional force, and the other side is compressed.

Creep is a slowly progressing, permanent deformation that results from a steady force acting on a material. Materials subjected to high temperatures are especially susceptible to this deformation. The gradual loosening of bolts, the sagging of long-span cables, and the deformation of components of machines and engines are all noticeable examples of creep. In many cases the slow deformation stops because the force causing the creep is eliminated by the deformation itself. Creep extended over a long time eventually leads to the rupture of the material.

Fatigue can be defined as progressive fracture. It occurs when a mechanical part is subjected to a repeated or cyclic stress, such as vibration. Even when the maximum stress never exceeds the elastic limit, failure of the material can occur even after a short time. With some metals, such as titanium alloys, fatigue can be avoided by keeping the cyclic force below a certain level. No deformation is apparent during fatigue, but small localized cracks develop and propagate through the material until the remaining cross-sectional area cannot support the maximum stress of the cyclic force. Knowledge of tensile stress, elastic limits, and the resistance of materials to creep and fatigue are of basic importance in engineering. See also METALS.

For further information on this topic, see the Bibliography in volume 28, sections 389, 392, 629.

MATHEMATICAL SYMBOLS, various signs and abbreviations used in mathematics to indicate entities, relations, or operations.

History. The origin and development of mathematical symbols are not entirely clear. For the probable origin of the remarkable digits 1 through 9, see NUMERALS. The origin of zero is unknown, because no authentic record exists of its history before AD 400. The extension of the decimal position system below unity is attributed to the Dutch mathematician Simon Stevin (1548–1620), who called tenths, hundredths, and thousandths *primes, sekondes,* and *terzes* and circled digits to denote the orders; thus, 4.628 was written as 4⓪6①2②8③. A period was used to set off the decimal part of a number as early as 1492, and later a bar was also used. In the *Exempelbüchlein* of 1530 by the German mathematician Christoff Rudolf (1500?–45), a problem in compound interest is solved, and some use is made of the decimal fraction. The German astronomer Johannes Kepler used the comma to set off the decimal orders, and the Swiss mathematician Justus Byrgius (1552–1632) used the decimal fraction in such forms as 3.2.

Although the early Egyptians had symbols for addition and equality, and the Greeks, Hindus, and Arabs had symbols for equality and the unknown quantity, from earliest times mathematical processes were cumbersome because proper symbols of operation were lacking. The expressions for such processes were either written out in full or denoted by word abbreviations. The later Greeks, the Hindus, and the German-born mathematician Nemorarius Jordanus (d. 1237?) indicated addition by juxtaposition; the Italians usually denoted it by the letter *P* or *p* with a line drawn through it, but their symbols were not uniform. Some mathematicians used *p*, some *e*, and the mathematician Niccolò Tartaglia (1500?–57) commonly expressed the operation by $\emptyset$. German and English algebraists introduced the sign +, but spoke of it as *signum additorum* and first used it only to indicate excess. The Greek mathematician Diophantus indicated subtraction by the symbol $\nearrow$. The Hindus used a dot, and the Italian algebraists denoted it by *M* or *m* with a line drawn through the letter. The German and English algebraists were the first to use the present symbol and described it as *Signum subtractorum*. The symbols + and − were first shown in 1489 by the German Johann Widman.

The English mathematician William Oughtred (1575–1660) first used the symbol × for "times." The German mathematician Gottfried Wilhelm Leibniz used a period to indicate multiplication, and in 1637 the French mathematician René Descartes used juxtaposition. In 1688 Leibniz employed the sign ∩ to denote multiplication and ∪ to denote division. The Hindus wrote the divisor under the dividend. Leibniz used the familiar form *a:b*. Descartes made popular the notation a^n for involution; the English mathematician John Wallis (1616–1703) defined the negative exponent and first used the symbol (∞) for infinity.

The symbol of equality, =, was originated by the English mathematician Robert Recorde (1510?–58), and the symbols > and < for "greater than" and "less than" originated with Thomas Harriot (1560–1621), also an Englishman. The French mathematician François Viète (1540–1603) introduced various symbols of aggregation. The symbols of differentiation, *dx*, and integration, ∫, as used in calculus, originated with Leibniz as did the symbol ∼ for similarity, as used in geometry. The Swiss mathematician Leonhard Euler was largely responsible for the symbols $\emptyset$, *f*, *F*, as used in the theory of functions.

The Hierarchy of Numbers. The hierarchy of numbers is the following: million, billion, trillion, quadrillion, quintillion, sextillion, septillion, octillion, nonillion, decillion, undecillion, duodecillion, tredecillion, quat(t)uordecillion, quindecillion, sexdecillion, septendecillion, octodecillion, novemdecillion, vigintillion.

In the French and American system of notation, each number after a million is a thousand times the preceding number; in the English and German system, each number is a million times the preceding. A vigintillion is written as a 1 followed by 63 zeros in the French and American system; by 120 zeros in England and Germany.

Decimals are written in the form 1.23 in the U.S., 1·23 in Great Britain, and 1,23 in continental Europe. In tables, a number such as 0.000000123 is often written as $0.0^6 123$. C.B.B.

For further information on this topic, see the Bibliography in volume 28, section 368.

MATHEMATICAL SYMBOLS

ENGLISH LETTER SYMBOLS

A	1. Vertex or associated angle of a polygon. 2. Area.
a	1. Usually a constant in algebra. 2. Initial term in arithmetic or geometric progression. 3. Side or length of side of a triangle or polygon. 4. Apothegm. 5. X-intercept of a line, plane, curve, or surface. 6. Semimajor axis of an ellipse or ellipsoid; semitransverse axis of a hyperbola.
A_{ij}	Algebraic complement or cofactor of a_{ij} in a determinant or matrix.
a_{ij}	General term in determinant or matrix.
$a_{\overline{n}|i}$	Present value of annuity for unit periodic payment, $a_{\overline{n}|i} = \frac{1}{i}[1 - (1+i)^{-n}]$.
A' or A^T	Transpose of a matrix A.
a_0, a_i	Coefficient in polynomial or infinite series; term of a sequence.
adj A	Adjoint of square matrix A.
A.M.	Arithmetic mean.
A.P.	Arithmetic progression.
arc cos x or cos^{-1}	Inverse cosine, angle the cosine of which is x.
arc cot x or arc ctn x or cot^{-1} or ctn^{-1}	Inverse cotangent, angle the cotangent of which is x.
arc cosec x or arc csc x or cosec^{-1} or csc^{-1}	Inverse cosecant, angle the cosecant of which is x.
arc sec x or sec^{-1}	Inverse secant, angle the secant of which is x.
arc sin x or sin^{-1}	Inverse sine, angle the sine of which is x.
arc tan x or tan^{-1}	Inverse tangent, angle the tangent of which is x. (Note: Arc is usually written Arc to indicate the principal angle.)
B	1. Vertex or associated angle of a polygon. 2. Area of base of a solid.
b	1. Usually a constant in algebra. 2. Side or length of side of a triangle or polygon. 3. Base or length of base of a plane polygon. 4. Y-intercept of a line, plane, curve, or surface. 5. Semiminor axis of an ellipse or ellipsoid; semitransverse axis of a hyperbola.
C	1. Vertex or associated angle of a polygon. 2. Circle or circumference of circle. 3. Arbitrary constant of integration.
$C_{n,r}$ or C_r^n or $_nC_r$, etc.	1. Binomial coefficient preferably designated as $\binom{n}{r} = \frac{n(n-1)\cdots(n-r+1)}{1 \cdot 2 \cdot \cdots \cdot r}$. 2. Number of combinations of n distinct objects taken r at a time without repetition.
c	1. Usually a constant in algebra. 2. Side or length of side of a triangle. 3. Semiaxis of an ellipsoid. 4. Z-intercept of a plane or surface. 5. (also $\aleph$) Transfinite cardinal number of the set of all real numbers.
colog	Cologarithm (of), the logarithm of the reciprocal of the number.
cos	Cosine (of).
cosec or csc	Cosecant (of).
cosh	Hyperbolic cosine (of).
cosh^{-1}	Inverse hyperbolic cosine (of).
cot or ctn	Cotangent (of).
coth or ctnh	Hyperbolic cotangent (of).
coth^{-1} or ctnh^{-1}	Inverse hyperbolic cotangent (of).
covrs or cvrs	Coversed sine (of); cvrs $x = 1 - \sin x$.
csch	Hyperbolic cosecant (of).
D	Differential operator, as in D_xy, derivative of y with respect to x; $D(D-2)y = \frac{d^2y}{dx^2} - 2\frac{dy}{dx}$.
d	1. Common difference in an arithmetic progression. 2. Difference between two successive entries in a table. 3. Diameter. 4. Differential operator, as in dy/dx. 5. Deviation, in statistics.
e	1. Eccentricity of a conic. 2. Base for natural logarithms; $e = 2.171828+$.
exp	Exponential function (of); exp $\theta = e^\theta$.
f or $f(x)$	1. General symbol for function or functional. 2. Frequency of a variate in an interval in statistical tables.
gcd	Greatest common divisor.
glb	Greatest lower bound.
G.M.	Geometric mean.
G.P.	Geometric progression.
h	1. Altitude of triangle, etc.; h_a = altitude from vertex A to side a. 2. Interval between uniformly spaced ordinates. 3. Class interval. 4. (as superscript) Designates hours; 3h10m5s, three hours, ten minutes, five seconds.
hc	Highest common factor.
H.M.	Harmonic mean.
H.P.	Harmonic progression.
I	Incenter of a triangle.
i	1. One of the two square roots of -1; $i = \sqrt{-1}$. 2. (Also j, k), running index, as in $\Sigma_{i=1}^n a_i = a_1 + a_2 + \ldots + a_n$. 3. (usually boldface) Unit vector having the direction of the positive x-axis. 4. Interest rate.
iff	If and only if.
inf.	Infimum, same as glb.
j	1. Used in engineering and other fields in place of i, first sense. 2. Running index; see i, second sense. 3. (usually boldface) Unit vector having the direction of the positive y-axis.
k	1. Proportionality factor in variation, as in $y = kx^2$. 2. Running index; see i, second sense. 3. (usually boldface) Unit vector having the direction of the positive z-axis.
L or lim	Limit, as in $\lim_{x \to 2} 3x = 6$, the limit of $3x$ is 6 as x approaches 2.
l	1. length. 2. Last term of arithmetic or geometric progression. 3. First-direction cosine of a line; $l = \cos \alpha$.
lcd	Lowest common denominator.
lcm	Least common multiple.
$\overline{\lim}$; $\underline{\lim}$	Least upper limit, limit superior; greatest lower limit, limit inferior.
ln	Natural logarithm (of).
log	Logarithm (of), usually to base 10, but also used for natural logarithms. To avoid ambiguity or if an arbitrary base b is used, write $\log_b x$, logarithm of x to base b.
M	1. Centroid (of triangle). 2. Arithmetic mean. 3. Modulus of system of logarithms, in particular, the modulus of common logarithms with respect to natural logarithms is $M = \log_{10}e = 0.43429+$.
m	1. General symbol, with n, for an integer. 2. Median of a triangle; m_a, median from vertex A to side a. 3. Slope of a line in analytic geometry. 4. Second-direction cosine of a line, $m = \cos \beta$. 5. As a superscript, to designate minutes. See h, fifth sense.
M.D.	Mean deviation.
Md	Median, in statistics.
Mo	Mode, in statistics.
mod	1. Modulo, as in $17 \equiv 3 \pmod 7$. 2. Modulus (of), as in mod $(3 - 4i) = 5$.
N	Total frequency in a statistical distribution.
n	1. General symbol for an integer. 2. Number of terms in a finite series or progression. 3. Running index, as the nth term of a sequence or series. 4. Third-direction cosine of a line, $n = \cos \gamma$.

MATHEMATICAL SYMBOLS

nasc	Necessary and sufficient condition(s).
O	1. Circumcenter of a triangle. 2. Origin of coordinates.
P	1. General symbol for a point in geometry. 2. Probability (of).
$P_{n,r}$ or P_r^n or $_nP_r$, etc.	Number, $n(n-1) \ldots (n-r+1)$, of permutations or arrangements of n distinct objects taken r at a time without repetition.
p	1. General symbol for a prime integer. 2. Perimeter. 3. Half the latus rectum of a conic. 4. Length of a perpendicular from the origin to a line or plane in analytic geometry. 5. Probability.
PE	Probable error.
Q_1, Q_2, Q_3	First, second, third quartile marks; $Q_2 =$ Md.
q	Complementary probability; $q = 1 - p$.
QD	Quartile deviation.
Q.E.D.; Q.E.F.	Abbreviations for Latin *quod erat demonstrandum*, "which was to be proved"; and *quod erat faciendum*, "which was to be constructed."
q_1, q_2	Quartile distances from the median.
R	1. General symbol for remainder. 2. Circumradius of a triangle. 3. Relationship, as in aRb, a is related to b.
r	1. Radius of a circle. 2. Inradius of a triangle. 3. Common ratio between successive terms of a geometric progression. 4. Running index, as the rth term of a sequence or series. 5. Distance from origin to a point in coordinate geometries. 6. Correlation coefficient in statistics. 7. (also ρ) First coordinate (usually) in polar, cylindrical, and spherical coordinate systems.
RMS	Root-mean-square in statistics.
rad.	Radius, radian(s).
S	1. General symbol for a space. 2. (Also s), general symbol for sum. 3. Standard error of estimate.
S_n	1. Space of n dimensions. 2. (also s_n) Sum of first n terms of a sequence, series, or progression.
s	1. Slant height of a geometric solid. 2. Semiperimeter of a triangle. 3. Length of arc of a curve. 4. As a superscript, to represent seconds; see h, fifth sense.
s_k	Sum of the kth powers of the roots of a polynomial equation.
$s_k(n)$	Sum of the kth powers of the first n positive integers; $s_k(n) = 1^k + 2^k + \ldots + n^k$.
sec	Secant (of).
sech	Hyperbolic secant (of).
sech^{-1}	Inverse hyperbolic secant (of).
sgn	(Signum) sign (of).
sin	Sine (of).
sinh	Hyperbolic sine (of).
sinh^{-1}	Inverse hyperbolic sine (of).
T	True or truth, in logic.
t	General variable or parameter; in particular, representing time.
tan	Tangent (of).
tanh	Hyperbolic tangent (of).
tanh^{-1}	Inverse hyperbolic tangent (of).
V	Volume of a solid.
v	General variable; in particular, representing velocity.
x	1. General symbol for unknown or variable, usually the independent variable. 2. One of the axes in a rectangular coordinate system. 3. First rectangular coordinate of a point. 4. Real part of a complex variable, $x + yi$.
y	1. General symbol for unknown or variable, usually the dependent variable, if x is the only independent variable; one of the independent variables if more than one. 2. One of the axes in a rectangular coordinate system. 3. Second rectangular coordinate of a point. 4. Pure imaginary coefficient of a complex variable, $x + yi$.
z	1. General symbol for an unknown or variable. 2. One of the axes in a space rectangular coordinate system. 3. Third (space) rectangular coordinate of a point. 4. Dependent complex variable, $z = x + yi$.

GREEK LETTER SYMBOLS

α	1. First-direction angle of a line, angle with the x-axis. 2. Acceleration.
β	Second-direction angle of a line, angle with the y-axis.
γ	Third-direction angle of a line, angle with the z-axis.
Δ	1. (also $\triangle$s, $\triangle$) Triangle(s), in plane geometry. 2. General name for a determinant. 3. Increment, as in Δx, $f(x + \Delta x)$. 4. Forward difference in interpolation theory, $\Delta x_i = x_{i+1} - x_i$.
δ	1. Positive number usually dependent on another, ϵ, used in limit process arguments. 2. Central difference in interpolation theory. 3. Deviation, in statistics.
ϵ	Positive number used in limit process arguments.
θ	1. General symbol for angle. 2. Second coordinate (usually) in polar, cylindrical, and spherical coordinate systems.
κ	Curvature of a curve.
μ	Moment about the mean, in statistics.
ν	Moment about arbitrary origin, in statistics.
Π	Product of terms.
Π_i	Product of terms, range implied by the context.
$\prod_{i=1}^{n}$ or $\Pi_{i=1}^n$ or $\prod_{i=a}^{b}$ or $\Pi_{i=a}^b$	Product of terms, range indicated by sub- and superscripts.
π	Ratio of circumference to diameter of a circle; $\pi = 3.1416^-$, approximately 22/7.
ρ	1. Factor of proportionality. 2. See r, seventh sense. 3. Radius of curvature.
Σ	Sum of terms; summation.
Σ_i	Sum of terms, range implied by the context.
$\sum_{i=1}^{n}$ or $\Sigma_{i=1}^n$ or $\sum_{i=a}^{b}$ or $\Sigma_{i=a}^b$	Sum of terms, range indicated by sub- and superscripts.
$\sum_{d\mid n}$	Sum of terms, summation extended over every d that is a factor of n.
$\sum_{x\in A}$	Sum of terms, summation extended over every x that belongs to the set A.
σ	1. Standard deviation, in statistics. 2. Radius of torsion.
ϕ	1. General symbol for a function. 2. Third coordinate (usually) in spherical coordinates.
$\phi(n)$	Euler function, also called the indicator or totient; number of positive integers not exceeding and prime to the positive integer n.
χ	In statistical theory, χ^2 is a measure of goodness of fit.
ψ	1. General symbol for a function. 2. Angle between the radius vector and tangent to a curve.
Ω	1. Brocard point of a triangle. 2. With subscripts, certain transfinite ordinals.

MATHEMATICAL SYMBOLS

ω   1. Angular velocity. 2. Imaginary root of unity, usually an imaginary cube root, $\frac{1}{2}(-1 + i\sqrt{3})$. 3. First transfinite ordinal, order type of the set of all positive integers in natural order. With subscripts, other transfinite ordinals.

OTHER LETTER AND LETTERLIKE SYMBOLS

ℵ   Alef or aleph, initial letter of the Hebrew alphabet, used in same sense as c, fifth sense.

$\aleph_0$ First transfinite cardinal number, the cardinal number of the set of all integers. With subscripts 1, 2, . . . , other transfinite cardinal numbers.

∂   Curly d, symbol of partial differentiation, as in $\frac{\partial^2 f(x, y)}{\partial x\, \partial y}$.

∇   Nabla or del, used to indicate 1. Backward difference in interpolation theory, $\nabla x_i = x_i - x_{x-1}$. 2. Linear vector operator used to express the gradient, divergence, and curl.

∃   (There) exist(s).

∈   Belongs to or is a member of, used only between an element and a containing set, as $a \in A$.

∋   Such that.

∅   Null set in set theory.

R   Cross ratio, anharmonic ratio.

ARBITRARY SYMBOLS

Elementary Geometry

∠   Angle, as ∠A or ∠BAC (vertex at A).

∥, ∥s   (Is) parallel (to), parallels; as AB ∥ CD.

⊥, ⊥s   (Is) perpendicular (to), perpendiculars; as AB ⊥ CD.

▱   Parallelogram, as ▱ABCD.

□   Square, as □ABCD.

▭   Rectangle, as ▭ABCD.

⊙, ⊙s, or Ⓢ   Circle(s); as ⊙O or ⊙ABCD.

⌢   Arc (of a circle), as $\overset{\frown}{AB}$.

∼   (Is) similar (to).

≅   (Is) congruent (to).

≎   (Is) equivalent (to) in length, area, or volume, etc.

°, ′, ″   Angular units, as 3°4′5″, three degrees, four minutes, five seconds.

Elementary Arithmetic and Algebra

=   Equals, (is) equal (to), as $2 + 3 = 5$.

<, >   Is less than, as $3 < 5$; is greater than, as $5 > 3$.

≤ or ≦; ≥ or ≧   Is less than or equal to, as $1 - x^2 \leq 1$; is greater than or equal to, as $x^2 + 1 \geq 1$.

+   1. Plus sign, symbol for operation of addition, as $2 + 3 = 5$. 2. As superscript, as in $x = 3.14+$, indicates that x is between 3.140 and 3.145, that x as written may be too small.

−   1. Minus sign, symbol for operation of subtraction, as $5 - 3 = 2$. 2. Negative sign, to indicate a negative number or the negative of a number, as in -3, the negative number minus three, or $-a$, the negative of the number a. As superscript, as in $x = 3.14-$, to indicate that x is between 3.135 and 3.140, that x as written may be too large.

× or ·   Multiplication sign, used for operation of multiplication, as in $3 \times 2 = 3 \cdot 2 = 6$.

÷   Division sign, used for operation of division, as in $6 \div 2 = 3$.

±   Plus or minus; if $x^2 = 9$, then $x = \pm 3$.

∓   Minus or plus, usually used in conjunction with ±; as in $\dfrac{a^2 - b^2 = a \mp b}{a \pm b}$, in which either the two upper signs or the two lower are to be read.

( ), { }, [ ], ‾   Parentheses, braces, brackets, vinculum, symbols of aggregation, as in $$[\{(\overline{a + b} + c) + d\} + e] + f.$$

/ or −   Part of symbol for fraction, as 2/3 or $\frac{2}{3}$, the fraction two-thirds; also to indicate division, as $2/3 = 2 \div 3$.

:   Is to, or ratio, as 2:3.

::   Is, equals, is equal to, used for equality of ratios, as in 2:3::10:15, that is, 2 is to 3 as 10 is to 15, or the ratio two-thirds equals (is equal to) the ratio ten-fifteenths.

Number, as Account #1234.

√   Radical sign for square root, as in $\sqrt{9} = 3$.

∛   Radical sign for cube root, as $\sqrt[3]{8} = 2$.

$\sqrt[n]{\ }$ Radical sign for the nth root; n is the index of the radical.

∝   Varies as, as in $y \propto 3x$.

%   Percent.

—   1. General mark to distinguish one quantity from another, as $a, \bar{a}, \bar{\bar{a}}$. 2. Chord, line segment, or length of chord or line segment, as $\overline{AB}$. 3. Arithmetic mean, as $\bar{x} = \frac{1}{n} \Sigma x$. 4. Imaginary conjugate, as $\overline{a + bi} = a - bi$. 5. (also ′) In set theory, to indicate complement of, as $\bar{A}$ is the complement of A.

→   1. Approaches, as $x^2 \to 9$ as $x \to -3$. 2. Directed line segment, as $\overrightarrow{AB}$. 3. Vector, as $\overrightarrow{AB}$. 4. (also ⇒ and ⊃) Implies, as $p \to q$ or $p \Rightarrow q$ or $p \supset q$, p implies q.

↔ or ⇔   Is equivalent to or mutually implies, as $p \leftrightarrow q$, p is equivalent to q, or p implies q and q implies p.

⊃ or ⊇ or ⫆   Contains, or containing, as a (proper) subset.

⊂ or ⊆ or ⫅   (Is) contained in as a subset.

∪   Union or cup (logical sum, sum, join) of two sets, as $A \cup B$.

∩   Intersection or cap (logical product, product, meet) of two sets, as $A \cap B$.

⊕, ⊗   Sum and product of two elements in abstract algebra, as in $a \oplus b$ or $a \otimes b$, particularly when the sum or product has properties similar to those of ordinary arithmetic.

╱   Superimposed on a symbol to indicate "not"; as ≠, is not equal to, or ≯, is not greater than.

( )   1. Aggregation of two or more terms; also for a single term to avoid ambiguity, as (sin $x)^2 = \sin^2 x = (\sin x)(\sin x)$. 2. Argument of a function, as $f(x), \emptyset(x - y)$. 3. Coordinates of a point, as (x, y). 4. Binomial coefficient, as $$\binom{n}{r} = \frac{n(n-1)\dots(n-r+1)}{r!}.$$ 5. Greatest common divisor, as $(10, 35) = 5$. 6. Open interval, as (a, b) for set of all x's such that $a < x < b$. 7. Sequence or set, as the sequence (a_i), the set of elements (u, v, w, x). 8. Cycle or cyclic permutation in group theory, as $(a\ b\ c)$ or (a, b, c). 9. General permutation in group theory, as $\begin{pmatrix} a & b & c \\ b & a & c \end{pmatrix}$. 10. (also ∥ ∥) To indicate a matrix, as $\begin{pmatrix} a & b \\ c & d \\ e & f \end{pmatrix}$; also in abbreviated form (a_{ij}). 11.

96

MATHEMATICS

	As a superscript, to indicate a general index rather than an exponent, as $a^{(1)}$, $a^{(2)}$, $a^{(n)}$. 12. As a superscript, to indicate index or order of a derivative, as $y^{(2)} = \dfrac{d^2y}{dx^2}$, $f^{(n)}(x) = \dfrac{d^nf(x)}{dx^n}$. 13. As a superscript, the factorial function in interpolation theory; $x^{(n)} = x(x-1)(x-2)\ldots(x-n+1)$.
[ ]	1. Used like parentheses, first, second, seventh, and tenth senses. 2. Largest integer that does not exceed a given number; as $[\pi] = [3] = 3$; $[-\pi] = -4$. 3. Closed interval, as $[a, b]$ for the set of all x's such that $a \leq x \leq b$.
{ }	Used like parentheses, first, second, and seventh senses.
|	1. Divides, is a divisor (factor) of, as $3\mid6$, 3 is a factor of 6. 2. Value at or values between, as $f'(x)\vert_{x=3} = f'(x)\vert_3 = f'(3)$, $f(x)\vert_{x=3}^{x=4} = f(x)\vert_3^4 = f(4) - f(3)$. 3. Separates expressions of different type or different meaning, as $_p(A\vert B)$, $(x\vert 3 < x < 4)$.
| |	1. Absolute or numerical value of, as $\vert 3\vert = \vert -3\vert = 3$, $\vert 3-4_i\vert = \sqrt{3^2+(-4)^2} = 5$. 2. Determinant, as $\vert A\vert$, $\vert a_{ij}\vert$, $\begin{vmatrix}3 & 4\\0 & -1\end{vmatrix}$. 3. Magnitude of a vector, as $\vert a\vert$.
≡	1. Is identical with, is identically equal to, as $x + x \equiv 2x$. 2. Is congruent to, in number theory, as $17 \equiv 3 \pmod{7}$.
≐	Approaches as a limit (now infrequently used).
~ or ≈	1. (Is) similar or homologous (to). 2. (Is) approximately equal (to). 3. (Is) asymptotic (to). 4. Not, in symbolic logic. 5. Placed above a letter or quantity, to distinguish one from another, as A, $\bar{A}$.
∞	Infinity.

General Mathematics

.	1. On line, separates terms or expressions in symbolic logic. 2. Centered, indicates inner or dot product in vector analysis, as $a \cdot b$. 3. Over a letter, indicates a derivative with respect to t, as $\dot{x} = dx/dt$. Also, $\ddot{x} = d^2x/dt^2$.
...	Indicates "and so on up to" or "and so on" or "up to," as $1, 2, 3, \ldots, n$, or $1, 2, 3, 4, \ldots$ or $\ldots, -2, -1, 0, 1, 2, \ldots, n, \ldots$
∴	Therefore, hence.
∵	Since.
: , :: , : ::	In symbolic logic, marks of separation used in conjunction with single dot, first sense.
! or ∟	Factorial, as $3! = \underline{\vert 3} = 1 \cdot 2 \cdot 3$.
$\int$, $\iint$, etc.	Indefinite integrals.
$\int_a^b$, $\int_a^b\int_c^d$, etc.	Definite integrals.
$\int_C$, $\int_R$, etc.	Integral over curve C, region R, etc.
', '', ''', etc.	1. Indicates different entities, as A, A', A''. 2. Orders of differentiation, as $y' = dy/dx$, $y'' = d^2y/dx^2$. 3. In set theory, to indicate complement of, as A' is the complement of A.
0, 1, 2, ½, etc.	1. As superscripts, to indicate exponents as $3^2 = 3 \times 3$. 2. As subscripts, general distinguishing marks, as a_0, a_1, etc. 3. As subscripts, to indicate special position or rank, as in $a_0x^n + a_1x^{n-1} + \ldots + a_n$, in which a_i is the coefficient of x^{n-i}, or as in the element a_{ij} (or $a_{i,j}$), of the matrix A. 4. As subscripts, base indicator for logarithm, as $\log_{10} a$.

J.S.

MATHEMATICS, study of relationships among quantities, magnitudes, and properties and of logical operations by which unknown quantities, magnitudes, and properties may be deduced. In the past, mathematics was regarded as the science of quantity, whether of magnitudes, as in geometry (q.v.), or of numbers, as in arithmetic (q.v.), or the generalization of these two fields, as in algebra (q.v.). Toward the middle of the 19th century, however, mathematics came to be regarded increasingly as the science of relations, or as the science that draws necessary conclusions. This latter view encompasses mathematical or symbolic logic, the science of using symbols to provide an exact theory of logical deduction and inference based on definitions, axioms, postulates, and rules for combining and transforming primitive elements into more complex relations and theorems.

This brief survey of the history of mathematics traces the evolution of mathematical ideas and concepts, beginning in prehistory. Indeed, mathematics is nearly as old as humanity itself; evidence of a sense of geometry and interest in geometric pattern has been found in the designs of prehistoric pottery and textiles and in cave paintings. Primitive counting systems were almost certainly based on using the fingers of one or both hands, as evidenced by the predominance of the numbers 5 and 10 as the bases for most number systems (q.v.) today.

ANCIENT MATHEMATICS

The earliest records of advanced, organized mathematics date back to the ancient Mesopotamian country of Babylonia and to Egypt of the 3d millennium BC. There mathematics was dominated by arithmetic, with an emphasis on measurement and calculation in geometry and with no trace of later mathematical concepts such as axioms or proofs.

The earliest Egyptian texts, composed about 1800 BC, reveal a decimal numeration system with separate symbols for the successive powers of 10 (1, 10, 100, and so forth), just as in the system used by the Romans. Numbers were represented by writing down the symbol for 1 as many times as there were units in the given number, the symbol for 10 as many times as there were 10's in the number, and so on. Addition was done by totaling separately the units, 10's, 100's, and so forth in the numbers to be added. Multiplication was based on successive doublings, and division

MATHEMATICS

Numbers systems of the ancient world based on the repetition of characters.

	1	2	3	5	10	20	21	50	100	500	1000	10000
Babylonian	▼	▼▼	▼▼▼	▼▼▼▼	<	<<	<<▼	<<<▼	▼―			
	)	))	)))	))))	•	••	••)	•••)				
Egyptian Hieroglyphic	1	II	III	IIIII	∩	∩∩	I∩∩	∩∩∩	9	999	⌐	⌐
Egyptian Hieratic	/	//	///ʔ	ʌ	ʎ́		ʔ	ـ				
Greek Herodianic	I	II	III	Γ	Δ	ΔΔ	ΔΔI	⌐	H	⌐	X	M
Roman	I	II	III	V	X	XX	XXI	L	C	D	M	

was based on the inverse of this process.

The Egyptians used sums of unit fractions ($\frac{1}{n}$), supplemented by the fraction $\frac{2}{3}$, to express all other fractions. For example, the fraction $\frac{2}{7}$ was the sum of the fractions $\frac{1}{4}$ and $\frac{1}{28}$. Using this system, the Egyptians were able to solve all problems of arithmetic that involved fractions, as well as some elementary problems in algebra. In geometry, the Egyptians arrived at correct rules for finding areas of triangles, rectangles, and trapezoids, and for finding volumes of figures such as bricks, cylinders, and, of course, pyramids. To find the area of a circle, the Egyptians used the square on $\frac{8}{9}$ of the diameter of the circle, a value close to the value of the ratio known as pi (q.v.), but actually about 3.16 rather than pi's value of about 3.14.

The Babylonian system of numeration was quite different from the Egyptian system. In the Babylonian system, which when using clay tablets consisted of various wedge-shaped marks, a single wedge indicated 1 and an arrowlike wedge stood for 10 (see table). Numbers up through 59 were formed from these symbols through an additive process, as in Egyptian mathematics. The number 60, however, was represented by the same symbol as 1, and from this point on a positional symbol was used. That is, the value of one of the first 59 numerals depended henceforth on its position in the total numeral. For example, a numeral consisting of a symbol for 2 followed by one for 27 and ending in one for 10 stood for $2 \times 60^2 + 27 \times 60 + 10$. This principle was extended to the representation of fractions as well, so that the above sequence of numbers could equally well represent $2 \times 60 + 27 + 10 \times (\frac{1}{60})$, or $2 + 27 \times (\frac{1}{60}) + 10 \times (\frac{1}{60})^{-2}$. With this sexagesimal system (base 60), as it is called, the Babylonians had as convenient a numerical system as the 10-based system.

The Babylonians in time developed a sophisticated mathematics by which they could find the positive roots of any quadratic equation (see EQUATION). They could even find the roots of certain cubic equations. The Babylonians had a variety of tables, including tables for multiplication and division, tables of squares, and tables of compound interest. They could solve complicated problems using the Pythagorean theorem (see PYTHAGORAS); one of their tables contains integer solutions to the Pythagorean equation, $a^2 + b^2 = c^2$, arranged so that c^2/a^2 decreases steadily from 2 to about $\frac{4}{3}$. The Babylonians were also able to sum not only arithmetic and some geometric progressions, but also sequences of squares. They also arrived at a good approximation for $\sqrt{2}$.

Greek Mathematics. The Greeks adopted elements of mathematics from both the Babylonians and the Egyptians. The new element in Greek mathematics, however, was the invention of an abstract mathematics founded on a logical structure of definitions, axioms, and proofs. According to later Greek accounts, this development began in the 6th century BC with Thales of Miletus and Pythagoras of Samos, the latter a religious leader who taught the importance of studying numbers in order to understand the world. Some of his disciples made important discoveries about the theory of numbers and geometry, all of which were attributed to Pythagoras.

In the 5th century BC, some of the great geometers were the atomist philosopher Democritus of Abdera, who discovered the correct formula for the volume of a pyramid, and Hippocrates of Chios (c. 470–c. 400 BC), who discovered that the areas of crescent-shaped figures bounded by arcs of circles are equal to areas of certain triangles. This discovery is related to the famous problem of squaring the circle—that is, constructing a square equal in area to a given circle. Two other famous mathematical problems that originated during the century were those of trisecting an angle and doubling a cube—that is, constructing a cube the volume of which is double that of a given cube. All of these problems were solved, and in a variety of ways, all involving the use of instruments more complicated than a straightedge and a geometrical compass. Not until the 19th century, however, was it shown that the three problems mentioned above could never have been solved using those instruments alone.

In the latter part of the 5th century BC, an unknown mathematician discovered that no unit of length would measure both the side and diagonal of a square. That is, the two lengths are incommensurable. This means that no counting numbers n and m exist whose ratio expresses the relationship of the side to the diagonal. Since the Greeks considered only the counting numbers (1, 2, 3, and so on) as numbers, they had no numerical way to express this ratio of diagonal to side. (This ratio, $\sqrt{2}$, would today be called irrational.) As a consequence the Pythagorean theory of ratio, based on numbers, had to be abandoned and a new, nonnumerical theory introduced. This was done by the 4th-century BC mathematician Eudoxus of Cnidus, whose solution may be found in the *Elements* of Euclid. Eudoxus also discovered a method for rigorously proving statements about areas and volumes by successive approximations.

Euclid was a mathematician and teacher who worked at the famed Museum of Alexandria and who also wrote on optics, astronomy, and music. The 13 books that make up his *Elements* contain much of the basic mathematical knowledge discovered up to the end of the 4th century BC on the geometry of polygons and the circle, the theory of numbers, the theory of incommensurables, solid geometry, and the elementary theory of areas and volumes.

The century that followed Euclid was marked by mathematical brilliance, as displayed in the works of Archimedes of Syracuse and a younger contemporary, Apollonius of Perga. Archimedes used a method of discovery, based on theoretically weighing infinitely thin slices of figures, to find the areas and volumes of figures arising from the conic sections. These conic sections had been discovered by a pupil of Eudoxus named Menaechmus (fl. 350 BC), and they were the subject of a treatise by Euclid, but Archimedes' writings on them are the earliest to survive. Archimedes also investigated centers of gravity and the stability of various solids floating in water. Much of his work is part of the tradition that led, in the 17th century, to the discovery of the calculus. Archimedes was killed by a Roman soldier during the sack of Syracuse. His younger contemporary, Apollonius, produced an eight-book treatise on the conic sections that established the names of the sections: ellipse, parabola, and hyperbola. It also provided the basic treatment of their geometry until the time of the French philosopher and scientist René Descartes in the 17th century.

After Euclid, Archimedes, and Apollonius, Greece produced no geometers of comparable stature. The writings of Hero of Alexandria in the 1st century AD show how elements of both the Babylonian and Egyptian mensurational, arithmetic traditions survived alongside the logical edifices of the great geometers. Very much in the same tradition, but concerned with much more difficult problems, are the books of Diophantus of Alexandria in the 3d century AD. They deal with finding rational solutions to kinds of problems that lead immediately to equations in several unknowns. Such equations are now called Diophantine equations (*see* DIOPHANTINE ANALYSIS).

Applied Mathematics in Greece. Paralleling the studies described in pure mathematics were studies made in optics, mechanics, and astronomy. Many of the greatest mathematical writers, such as Euclid and Archimedes, also wrote on astronomical topics. Shortly after the time of Apollonius, Greek astronomers adopted the Babylonian system for recording fractions and, at about the same time, composed tables of chords in a circle. For a circle of some fixed radius, such tables give the length of the chords subtending a sequence of arcs increasing by some fixed amount. They are equivalent to a modern sine table, and their composition marks the beginnings of trigonometry (q.v.). In the earliest such tables—those of Hipparchus in about 150 BC—the arcs increased by steps of $7\frac{1}{2}$, from 0 to 180. By the time of the astronomer Ptolemy in the 2d century AD, however, Greek mastery of numerical procedures had progressed to the point where Ptolemy was able to include in his *Almagest* a table of chords in a circle for steps of $\frac{1}{2}$, which, although expressed sexagesimally, is accurate to about five decimal places.

In the meantime, methods were developed for solving problems involving plane triangles, and a theorem—named after the astronomer Menelaus of Alexandria (fl. 100 AD)—was established for finding the lengths of certain arcs on a sphere when other arcs are known. These advances gave Greek astronomers what they needed to solve the problems of spherical astronomy and to develop an astronomical system that held sway until the time of the German astronomer Johannes Kepler.

MATHEMATICS

MEDIEVAL AND RENAISSANCE MATHEMATICS
Following the time of Ptolemy, a tradition of study of the mathematical masterpieces of the preceding centuries was established in various centers of Greek learning. The preservation of such works as have survived to modern times is owed to this tradition. The earliest original developments based on these masterpieces, however, did not appear at such centers of tradition but in the Islamic world.

Islamic and Indian Mathematics. After a century of expansion in which the religion of Islam spread from its beginnings in the Arabian Peninsula to dominate an area extending from Spain to the borders of China, Muslims began to acquire the results of the "foreign sciences." At centers such as the House of Wisdom in Baghdad, supported by the ruling caliphs and wealthy individuals, translators produced Arabic versions of Greek and Indian mathematical works.

By the year 900 AD the acquisition was complete, and Muslim scholars began to build on what they had acquired. Thus mathematicians extended the Hindu decimal positional system of arithmetic from whole numbers to include decimal fractions, and the 12th-century Persian mathematician Omar Khayyam generalized Hindu methods for extracting square and cube roots to include fourth, fifth, and higher roots. In algebra, al-Karaji (c. 1000) completed Muhammad al-Khwarizmi's algebra of polynomials to include even polynomials with an infinite number of terms. (Al-Khwarizmi's name, incidentally, is the source of the word *algorithm*, q.v., and the title of one of his books is the source of the word *algebra*.) Geometers such as Ibrahim ibn Sinan (908–46) continued Archimedes' investigations of areas and volumes, and Kamal al-Din (1156–1242) and others applied the theory of conic sections to solve optical problems. Using the Hindu sine function and Menelaus' theorem, mathematicians from Habas al-Hasib (770–864) to Nasir ad-Din at-Tusi (1201–74) created the mathematical disciplines of plane and spherical trigonometry. These did not become mathematical disciplines in the West, however, until the publication of *De Triangulis Omnimodibus* by the German astronomer Regiomontanus (1436–76).

Finally, a number of Muslim mathematicians made important discoveries in the theory of numbers, while others explained a variety of numerical methods for solving equations. The Latin West acquired much of this learning during the 12th century, the great century of translation. Together with translations of the Greek classics, these Muslim works were responsible for the growth of mathematics in the West during the late Middle Ages. Italian mathematicians such as Leonardo Fibonacci (1170–1230) and Luca Pacioli (c. 1450–c. 1520), one of the many 15th-century writers on algebra and arithmetic for merchants, depended heavily on Arabic sources for their knowledge.

Western Renaissance Mathematics. Although the late medieval period saw some fruitful mathematical considerations of problems of infinity by writers such as Nicole Oresme (c. 1323–82), it was not until the early 16th century that a truly important mathematical discovery was made in the West. The discovery, an algebraic formula for the solution of both the cubic and quartic equations, was published in 1545 by the Italian mathematician Gerolamo Cardano (1501–76) in his *Ars Magna*. The discovery drew the attention of mathematicians to complex numbers and stimulated a search for solutions to equations of degree higher than 4. It was this search, in turn, that led to the first work on group theory (*see* GROUP) at the end of the 18th century, and to the French mathematician Évariste Galois' theory of equations in the early 19th century.

The 16th century also saw the beginnings of modern algebraic symbolism (*see* MATHEMATICAL SYMBOLS), as well as the remarkable work on the solution of equations by the French mathematician François Viète (1540–1603). His writings influenced many mathematicians of the following century, including Pierre de Fermat in France and Isaac Newton in England.

MATHEMATICS SINCE THE 16TH CENTURY
Europeans dominated in the development of mathematics after the Renaissance.

17th Century. During the 17th century, the greatest advances were made in mathematics since the time of Archimedes and Apollonius. The century opened with the Scottish mathematician John Napier's discovery of logarithms, whose continued utility prompted the French astronomer Pierre Simon Laplace to remark, almost two centuries later, that Napier, by halving the labors of astronomers, had doubled their lifetimes. (Although the logarithmic function is still important in mathematics and the sciences, logarithmic tables and their instrumental form—slide rules—are of much less practical use today because of electronic calculators.)

The science of number theory (q.v.), which had lain dormant since the medieval period, illustrates the 17th-century advances built on ancient learning. It was Diophantus' *Arithmetica* that stimulated Fermat to advance the theory of numbers greatly. His most important conjecture in the field, written in the margin of his copy of the *Arithmetica*, was that no solutions exist to

$a^n + b^n = c^n$ for positive integers a, b, and c when n is greater than 2. This conjecture stimulated much important work in algebra and number theory but is still unproved.

Two important developments in pure geometry occurred during the century. The first was the publication, in *Discourse on Method* (1637) by Descartes, of his discovery of analytic geometry, which showed how to use the algebra that had developed since the Renaissance to investigate the geometry of curves. (Fermat made the same discovery but did not publish it.) This book, together with short treatises that had been published with it, stimulated and provided the basis for Isaac Newton's mathematical work in the 1660s. The second development in geometry was the publication by the French engineer Gérard Desargues (1593–1662) in 1639 of his discovery of projective geometry. Although the work was much appreciated by Descartes and the French philosopher and scientist Blaise Pascal, its eccentric terminology and the excitement of the earlier publication of analytic geometry delayed the development of its ideas until the early 19th century and the works of the French mathematician Jean Victor Poncelet (1788–1867).

Another major step in mathematics in the 17th century was the beginning of probability (q.v.) theory in the correspondence of Pascal and Fermat on a problem in gambling, called the problem of points. This unpublished work stimulated the Dutch scientist Christiaan Huygens to publish a small tract on probabilities in dice games, which was reprinted by the Swiss mathematician Jakob Bernoulli (1654–1705) in his *Art of Conjecturing*. Both Bernoulli and the French mathematician Abraham De Moivre (1667–1754), in his *Doctrine of Chances* in 1718, applied the newly discovered calculus to make rapid advances in the theory, which by then had important applications in the rapidly developing insurance industry.

Without question, however, the crowning mathematical event of the 17th century was Newton's discovery, between 1664 and 1666, of the differential and integral calculus (see CALCULUS). In making this discovery, Newton built on earlier work by his fellow Englishmen, John Wallis (1616–1703) and Isaac Barrow (1630–77), as well as on work of such Continental mathematicians as Descartes, Francesco Bonaventura Cavalieri (1598–1647), Johann van Waveren Hudde (1628–1704), and Gilles Personne de Roberval (1602–75). About eight years later than Newton, who had not yet published his discovery, the German Gottfried Wilhelm Leibniz rediscovered the calculus and published first, in 1684 and 1686. Leibniz's notation systems, such as dx, are used today in the calculus.

18th Century. The remainder of the 17th century and a good part of the 18th were taken up by the work of disciples of Newton and Leibniz, who applied their ideas to solving a variety of problems in physics, astronomy, and engineering. In the course of doing so they also created new areas of mathematics. For example, Johann (1667–1748) and Jakob Bernoulli invented the calculus of variations, and French mathematician Gaspard Monge invented differential geometry. Also in France, Joseph Louis Lagrange gave a purely analytic treatment of mechanics in his great *Analytical Mechanics* (1788), in which he stated the famous Lagrange equations for a dynamical system. He contributed to differential equations and number theory, as well, and originated the theory of groups. His contemporary, Laplace, wrote the classic *Celestial Mechanics* (1799–1825), which earned him the title of the "French Newton," and *The Analytic Theory of Probabilities* (1812).

The greatest mathematician of the 18th century was Leonhard Euler, a Swiss, who made basic contributions to the calculus and to all other branches of mathematics, as well as to the applications of mathematics. He wrote textbooks on calculus, mechanics, and algebra that became models of style for writing in these areas. The success of Euler and other mathematicians in using the calculus to solve mathematical and physical problems, however, only accentuated their failure to develop a satisfactory justification of its basic ideas. That is, Newton's own accounts were based on kinematics and velocities, Leibniz's explanation was based on infinitesimals, and Lagrange's treatment was purely algebraic and founded on the idea of infinite series. All these systems were unsatisfactory when measured against the logical standards of Greek geometry, and the problem was not resolved until the following century.

19th Century. In 1821 a French mathematician, Augustin Louis Cauchy, succeeded in giving a logically satisfactory approach to the calculus. He based his approach only on finite quantities and the idea of a limit. This solution posed another problem, however, that of a logical definition of "real number." Although Cauchy's explanation of the calculus rested on this idea, it was not Cauchy but the German mathematician Julius W. R. Dedekind (1831–1916) who found a satisfactory definition of real numbers in terms of the rational numbers. This definition is still taught, but other definitions were given at the same time by the German mathematicians Georg Cantor and Karl

MATHEMATICS

T. W. Weierstrass. A further important problem, which arose out of the problem—first stated in the 18th century—of describing the motion of a vibrating string, was that of defining what is meant by function (q.v.). Euler, Lagrange, and the French mathematician Jean Baptiste Fourier all contributed to the solution, but it was the German mathematician Peter G. L. Dirichlet (1805-59) who proposed the definition in terms of a correspondence between elements of the domain and the range. This is the definition that is found in texts today.

In addition to firming the foundations of analysis, as the techniques of the calculus were by then called, mathematicians of the 19th century made great advances in the subject. Early in the century, Carl Friedrich Gauss gave a satisfactory explanation of complex numbers, and these numbers then formed a whole new field for analysis, one that was developed in the work of Cauchy, Weierstrass, and the German mathematician Georg F. B. Riemann. Another important advance in analysis was Fourier's study of infinite sums whose terms are trigonometric functions. Known today as Fourier series, they are still powerful tools in pure and applied mathematics. In addition, the investigation of which functions could be equal to Fourier series led Cantor to the study of infinite sets and to an arithmetic of infinite numbers. Cantor's theory, which was considered quite abstract and even attacked as a "disease from which mathematics will soon recover," now forms part of the foundations of mathematics and has more recently found applications in the study of turbulent flow in fluids.

A further 19th-century discovery that was considered apparently abstract and useless at the time was non-Euclidean geometry. In non-Eculidean geometry, more than one parallel can be drawn to a given line through a given point not on the line. Evidently this was discovered first by Gauss, but Gauss was fearful of the controversy that might result from publication. The same results were rediscovered independently and published by the Russian mathematician Nikolay Ivanovich Lobachevsky and the Hungarian János Bolyai. Non-Euclidean geometries were studied in a very general setting by Riemann with his invention of manifolds and, since the work of Einstein in the 20th century, they have also found applications in physics.

Gauss was one of the greatest mathematicians who ever lived. Diaries from his youth show that this infant prodigy had already made important discoveries in number theory, an area in which his book *Disquisitiones Arithmeticae* (1801) marks the beginning of the modern era. While only 18, Gauss discovered that a regular polygon with m sides can be constructed by straightedge and compass when m is a power of 2 times primes of the form $2^n + 1$. In his doctoral dissertation he gave the first satisfactory proof of the fundamental theorem of algebra. Often he combined scientific and mathematical investigations. Examples include his development of statistical methods along with his investigations of the orbit of a newly discovered planetoid; his founding work in the field of potential theory, along with the study of magnetism; and his study of the geometry of curved surfaces in tandem with his investigations of surveying.

Of more importance for algebra itself than Gauss's proof of its fundamental theorem was the transformation of the subject during the 19th century from a study of polynomials to a study of the structure of algebraic systems. A major step in this direction was the invention of symbolic algebra in England by George Peacock (1791-1858). Another was the discovery of algebraic systems that have many, but not all, of the properties of the real numbers. Such systems include the quaternions of the Irish mathematician William Rowan Hamilton, the vector analysis of the American mathematician and physicist J. Willard Gibbs, and the ordered n-dimensional spaces of the German mathematician Hermann Günther Grassmann (1809-77). A third major step was the development of group theory, from its beginnings in the work of Lagrange. Galois applied this work deeply to provide a theory of when polynomials may be solved by an algebraic formula.

Just as Descartes had applied the algebra of his time to the study of geometry, so the German mathematician Felix Klein (1849-1925) and the Norwegian mathematician Marius Sophus Lie (1842-99) applied the algebra of the 19th century. Klein applied it to the classification of geometries in terms of their groups of transformations (the so-called Erlanger Programm), and Lie applied it to a geometric theory of differential equations by means of continuous groups of transformations known as Lie groups. In the 20th century, algebra has also been applied to a general form of geometry known as topology (q.v.).

Another subject that was transformed in the 19th century, notably by English mathematician George Boole's *Laws of Thought* (1854) and Cantor's theory of sets, was the foundations of mathematics (see LOGIC). Toward the end of the century, however, a series of paradoxes were discovered in Cantor's theory. One such paradox, found by English mathematician Bertrand Russell, aimed at the very concept of a set (see SET THEORY). Mathematicians responded by constructing set theories sufficiently restrictive to keep the paradoxes from arising. They left open the question, however, of whether other paradoxes might arise in these restricted theories—that is, whether the theories were consistent. As of the present time, only relative consistency proofs have been given. (That is, theory A is consistent if theory B is consistent.) Particularly disturbing is the result, proved in 1931 by the American logician Kurt Gödel, that in any axiom system complicated enough to be interesting to most mathematicians, it is possible to frame propositions whose truth cannot be decided within the system.

Current Mathematics. At the International Conference of Mathematicians held in Paris in 1900, the German mathematician David Hilbert spoke to the assembly. Hilbert was a professor at Göttingen, the former academic home of Gauss and Riemann. He had contributed to most areas of mathematics, from his classic *Foundations of Geometry* (1899) to the jointly authored *Methods of Mathematical Physics*. Hilbert's address at Göttingen was a survey of 23 mathematical problems that he felt would guide the work being done in mathematics during the coming century. These problems have indeed stimulated a great deal of the mathematical research of the century. When news breaks that another of the "Hilbert problems" has been solved, mathematicians all over the world await the details of the story with impatience.

Important as these problems have been, an event that Hilbert could not have foreseen seems destined to play an even greater role in the future development of mathematics—namely, the invention of the programmable digital computer (*see* COMPUTER). Although the roots of the computer go back to the geared calculators of Pascal and Leibniz in the 17th century, it was Charles Babbage in 19th-century England who designed a machine that could automatically perform computations based on a program of instructions stored on cards or tape. Babbage's imagination outran the technology of his day, however, and it was not until the invention of the relay, then of the vacuum tube, and then of the transistor, that large-scale, programmed computation became feasible. This development has given great impetus to areas of mathematics such as numerical analysis and finite mathematics. It has suggested new areas for mathematical investigation, such as the study of algorithms. It has also become a powerful tool in areas as diverse as number theory, differential equations, and abstract algebra. In addition, the computer has made possible the solution of several long-standing problems in mathematics, such as the four-color problem first proposed in the mid-19th century. The theorem stated that four colors are sufficient to color any map, given that any two countries with a contiguous boundary require different colors. The theorem was finally proved in 1976 by means of a large-scale computer at the University of Illinois.

Mathematical knowledge in the modern world is advancing at a faster rate than ever before. Theories that were once separate have been incorporated into theories that are both more comprehensive and more abstract. Although many important problems have been solved, other hardy perennials such as the Riemann hypothesis and Fermat's conjecture remain, and new and equally challenging problems arise. Even the most abstract mathematics seems to be finding applications. J.Le.B.

For additional information on individual mathematicians, see separate articles on those whose names are not followed by dates.

For further information on this topic, see the Bibliography in volume 28, sections 36, 367–75.

MATHEMATICS, NEW, also new math, name given to a variety of topics in mathematics that have recently been introduced in many primary and secondary schools throughout the U.S. and in other countries. The term is usually applied to subject matter that is new for those grades, but it also refers to a shift in pedagogic stress and intent. The changes of new math reflect university studies begun in the early 1950s in reaction to scientific and technological advances and to the greatly increased use of mathematics in the physical, biological, and social sciences as well as in industry and commerce. Because of these studies, both the mathematics curriculum and teaching methods were revised so that the average citizen could learn more mathematics sooner.

Teaching Methods. The main change was a shift from rote memorization (such as of the multiplication table) to emphasis on meaning and concept, in order to give the pupil insight into what he is doing and why. The student is taught, for example, why 3 + 5 is the same as 5 + 3, the reasons for the various steps in long division, and why it is appropriate to multiply in order to find the total cost of a dozen rolls that cost nine cents apiece. When asked, "What number must be put into the box to make 2 + □ = 7 a true mathematical sentence?" the pupil is introduced to subtraction and simultaneously given a taste of algebra.

Many educators believe that a child who studies the new math under competent teachers will not only be able to do routine arithmetic as well

MATHER

as a child trained in the traditional manner, but will also be far ahead in understanding and in preparation for advanced mathematics.

Subject Matter. The new math is new only in that the material is introduced at a much lower level than heretofore. Thus geometry, which was and is commonly taught in the second year of high school, is now frequently introduced, in an elementary fashion, in the fourth grade; in fact, naming and recognition of the common geometric figures, the circle and the square, occur in kindergarten. At an early stage, numbers are identified with points on a line, and the identification is used to introduce, much earlier than in the traditional curriculum, negative numbers and the arithmetic processes involving them.

The elements of set theory constitute the most basic and perhaps the most important topic of the new math. Even a kindergarten child can understand, without formal definition, the meaning of a set of red blocks, the set of fingers on his left hand, and the set of his ears and eyes. The technical word *set* is merely a synonym for many common words that designate an aggregate of elements. The child can understand that the set of fingers on his left hand and the set on his right hand match; that is, the elements, fingers, can be put into a one-to-one correspondence. The set of fingers on his left hand and the set of his ears and eyes do not match. Some concepts that are developed by this method are counting, equality of number, more than, and less than. The ideas of union and intersection of sets and the complement of a set can be similarly developed without formal definition in the early grades. The principles and formalism of set theory are extended as the child advances; upon graduation from high school, his knowledge is quite comprehensive.

The amount of new math and the particular topics taught vary from school to school. In addition to set theory and intuitive geometry, the material is usually chosen from the following topics: a development of the number systems, including methods of numeration, binary and other bases of notation, and modular arithmetic; measurement, with attention to accuracy and precision, and error study; studies of algebraic systems, including linear algebra, modern algebra, vectors, and matrices, with an axiomatic as well as traditional approach (*see* MATRIX THEORY AND LINEAR ALGEBRA; VECTOR); logic, including truth tables, the nature of proof, Venn or Euler diagrams, relations, functions, and general axiomatics; probability and statistics; linear programming; computer programming and language; and analytic geometry and calculus. Some schools present differential equations, topology, and real and complex analysis. J.Si.

MATHER, Cotton (1663-1728), son of Increase Mather, born in Boston, and educated at Harvard College (now Harvard University). He served with his father in the ministry of Boston's North Church from 1685 until the elder Mather died (1723) and served thereafter as sole pastor until his own death. Mather was a highly influential writer. His *Magnalia Christi Americana* (1702), an ecclesiastical history of New England, ranks among the most important and scholarly works produced during America's first 100 years. He also wrote extensively on the subject of witchcraft (q.v.).

Mather's interest in science prompted him to champion inoculations against smallpox in 1721, and with the American physician Zabdiel Boylston (1679-1766), he did much to conquer public prejudice against the practice. Because of these achievements Mather was the first native-born American inducted into the Royal Society of London. His numerous books include works on history, science, biography, and theology. Among them are *Wonders of the Invisible World* (1693), an account of some of the Salem witchcraft cases; *Essays to Do Good* (1710); and *Ratio disciplinae* (1726), a discussion of Congregational church government.

MATHER, Increase (1639-1723), son of Richard Mather, born in Dorchester, Mass., and educated at Harvard College (now Harvard University), from which he graduated at the age of 17, and the University of Dublin. He preached in England but in 1661 returned to the colonies, where he was pastor of the North Church, Boston, from 1664 until his death. From 1685 to 1701 he was president of Harvard College. In 1688, as the colonists' representative to England, Mather appealed to King James II and William of Orange for restoration of the Massachusetts Charter that had been revoked by Charles II. In 1689 the new charter was obtained from William, after he was crowned king.

Mather spoke out against witchcraft hysteria and wrote (1692) that letting ten witches escape was preferable to condemning one innocent person.

MATHER, Richard (1596-1669), founder of the Mather family in New England, born in Lowtown, near Liverpool, England. Ordained in the Church of England in 1618, he preached at Toxeth Park, Lancashire, until 1633, when he was suspended for nonconformity in matters of ceremony (*see* NONCONFORMISTS). After an unsuccessful attempt to be reinstated, he immigrated to Boston in 1635. The following year he became pastor of the church at Dorchester, in the Massachusetts Bay Colony, remaining at that post until his death.

MATHEWSON, Christy (1880–1925), American professional baseball player, born in Factoryville, Pa., and educated at Bucknell University. Mathewson was one of the greatest right-handed pitchers in baseball. He began his career in 1900 with the Norfolk team of the Virginia League; in 1901 he became a member of the Giants, the New York National League team. Mathewson won 30 or more games for three consecutive seasons, 1903, 1904, and 1905, and he won 20 or more during the next nine seasons; in 1905 he pitched and won three World Series games from the Philadelphia Athletics of the American League by shutouts. He was noted for the number of his strikeouts; in 1903 he struck out 267 batters, one of the highest marks ever made by a pitcher in the National League. In 1908 Mathewson won 37 games. In 1916 he joined the Cincinnati Reds of the National League, as player and manager. In 1918, during World War I, he was gassed in France and later contracted tuberculosis. From 1923 to 1925 he was president of the Boston Braves of the National League.

In his 17-year career, Mathewson won 373 games and lost 189, for an average of .664. In 1936 Mathewson was elected to the Baseball Hall of Fame. B.K.K.

MATHURA, formerly MUTTRA, city, N India, in Uttar Pradesh State, capital of Mathura District, on the Jumna R., near Agra. For centuries it has been a center of Hinduism and is said to be the birthplace of the god Krishna. The name of the city was changed in 1948. Pop. (1981 prelim., greater city) 160,995.

MATINS. *See* DIVINE OFFICE.

MATISSE, Henri Émile Benoît (1869–1954), French artist, leader of the Fauve group (*see* FAUVISM), regarded as one of the great formative figures in 20th-century art, a master of the use of color and form to convey emotional expression.

Matisse was born in Le Cateau-Cambrésis in northern France on Dec. 31, 1869. The son of a middle-class family, he studied and began to practice law. In 1890, however, while recovering slowly from an attack of appendicitis, he became intrigued by the practice of painting. In 1892, having given up his law career, he went to Paris to study art formally. His first teachers were academically trained and relatively conservative;

The Dance: First Version *(1909). Still lifes and the female nude were frequent subjects of the work of Henri Matisse.* Museum of Modern Art

MATISSE

Purple Robe (1937), by Henri Matisse. Baltimore Museum of Art–Cone Collection

Matisse's own early style was a conventional form of naturalism, and he made many copies after the old masters. He also studied more contemporary art, especially that of the impressionists, and he began to experiment, earning a reputation as a rebellious member of his studio classes.

Matisse's true artistic liberation, in terms of the use of color to render forms and organize spatial planes, came about first through the influence of the French painters Paul Gauguin and Paul Cézanne and the Dutch artist Vincent van Gogh, whose work he studied closely beginning about 1899. Then, in 1903–4, Matisse encountered the pointillist painting of Henri Edmond Cross (1856–1910) and Paul Signac (*see* POINTILLISM). Cross and Signac were experimenting with juxtaposing small strokes (often dots or "points") of pure pigment to create the strongest visual vibration of intense color. Matisse adopted their technique and modified it repeatedly, using broader strokes. By 1905 he had produced some of the boldest color images ever created, including a striking picture of his wife, *Portrait with a Green Stripe* (1905, Nationalmuseet, Copenhagen). The title refers to a broad stroke of brilliant green that defines Mme. Matisse's brow and nose. In the same year Matisse exhibited this and similar paintings along with works by his artist companions, including André Derain and Maurice de Vlaminck. Together, the group was dubbed *les fauves* (literally, "the wild beasts") because of the extremes of emotionalism they seemed to have indulged in, their use of vivid colors, and their distortion of shapes.

Although regarded as a leader of radicalism in the arts, Matisse was beginning to gain the approval of a number of influential critics and collectors, including the American expatriate writer Gertrude Stein and her family. Among the many important commissions he received was that of a Russian collector who requested mural panels illustrating dance and music (both completed in 1911; now in the Hermitage, Saint Petersburg). Such broadly conceived themes ideally suited Matisse; they allowed him freedom of invention and play of form and expression. His images of dancers, and of human figures in general, convey expressive form first and the particular details of anatomy only secondarily. Matisse extended this principle into other fields; his bronze sculptures, like his drawings and works in several graphic media, reveal the same expressive contours seen in his paintings.

Intellectually sophisticated, Matisse always emphasized, however, the importance of instinct and intuition in the production of a work of art. He argued that an artist did not have complete control over color and form; instead, colors, shapes, and lines would come to dictate to the sensitive artist how they might be employed in relation to one another. He often emphasized his joy in abandoning himself to the play of the forces of color and design, and he explained the rhythmic, but distorted, forms of many of his figures in terms of the working out of a total pictorial harmony.

During the latter part of his career, Matisse spent much time in the south of France, particularly Nice, painting local scenes with a thin, fluid application of bright color. In his old age, he was commissioned to design the decoration of the small Chapel of Saint-Marie du Rosaire at Vence (near Cannes), which he completed between 1947 and 1951. Often bedridden during his last years, he occupied himself with decoupage, creating works of brilliantly colored paper cutouts arranged casually, but with an unfailing eye for design, on a canvas surface.

Matisse died in Nice on Nov. 3, 1954. Unlike many artists, he was internationally popular during his lifetime, enjoying the favor of collectors, art critics, and the younger generation of artists.

R.Sh.

MATRIARCHY, in sociology and anthropology, system of social organization in which descent is traced through the female line and all children belong to the clan of the mother. The system is occasionally associated with inheritance in the female line of material goods and social prerogatives. Matriarchy is practiced in cultures found throughout the world. It is found in varying forms among the original inhabitants of Australia, Sumatra, Micronesia, Melanesia, and Formosa; in India in Assam and along the Malabar Coast; in Africa in many regions; and in North America among a number of Indian tribes.

MATRIX THEORY AND LINEAR ALGEBRA, interconnected branches of mathematics that serve as fundamental tools in pure and applied mathematics and are becoming increasingly important in the physical, biological, and social sciences.

Lemons and Saxifrages *(1943), by Henri Matisse.* Museum of Modern Art

MATRIX THEORY AND LINEAR ALGEBRA

Matrix Theory. A matrix is a rectangular array of numbers or elements of a ring (see ALGEBRA). One of the principal uses of matrices is in representing systems of equations of the first degree in several unknowns. Each matrix row represents one equation, and the entries in a row are the coefficients of the variables in the equations, in some fixed order.

A matrix is usually enclosed in brackets:

$$M_1 = \begin{bmatrix} -2 & 0 & 1 \\ 15 & 3 & -1 \\ 0 & 1 & 2 \end{bmatrix}$$

$$M_2 = \begin{bmatrix} -2 & 0 & 1 \\ -4 & 3 & 8 \\ 0 & 1 & 2 \end{bmatrix}$$

$$M_3 = \begin{bmatrix} -2 & 0 \\ 1 & -\frac{1}{2} \\ a & b \end{bmatrix}$$

$$M_4 = \begin{bmatrix} a+b & b+c & c+a \\ a-b & b-c & c-a \end{bmatrix}$$

In the above matrices, a, b, and c are arbitrary numbers. In place of brackets, parentheses or double vertical lines may be used to enclose the arrays. The horizontal lines, called rows, are numbered from the top down; the vertical lines, or columns, are numbered from left to right; thus, -1 is the element in the second row, third column of M_1. A row or column is called a line.

The size of a matrix is given by the number of rows and columns, so that M_1, M_2, M_3, and M_4 are, in that order, of sizes 3×3 (3 by 3), 3×3, 3×2, and 2×3. The general matrix of size $m \times n$ is frequently represented in double-subscript notation, with the first subscript i indicating the row number, and the second subscript j indicating the column number; a_{23} is the element in the second row, third column. This general matrix

$$A = \begin{bmatrix} a_{11} & a_{12} & a_{13} & \cdots & a_{1j} & \cdots & a_{1n} \\ a_{21} & a_{22} & a_{23} & \cdots & a_{2j} & \cdots & a_{2n} \\ \cdots & \cdots & \cdots & \cdots & \cdots & \cdots & \cdots \\ a_{i1} & a_{i2} & a_{i3} & \cdots & a_{ij} & \cdots & a_{in} \\ \cdots & \cdots & \cdots & \cdots & \cdots & \cdots & \cdots \\ a_{m1} & a_{m2} & a_{m3} & \cdots & a_{mj} & \cdots & a_{mn} \end{bmatrix}$$

may be abbreviated to $A = [a_{ij}]$, in which the ranges $i = 1, 2, \ldots, m$ and $j = 1, 2, \ldots, n$ should be explicitly given if they are not implied by the text. If $m = n$, the matrix is square, and the number of rows (or columns) is the order of the matrix. Two matrices, $A = [a_{ij}]$ and $B = [b_{ij}]$, are equal if and only if they are of the same size and if, for every i and j, $a_{ij} = b_{ij}$. The elements a_{11}, a_{22}, a_{33}, ... constitute the main or principal diagonal of the matrix $A = [a_{ij}]$, if it is square. The transpose A^T of a matrix A is the matrix in which the ith row is the ith column of A and in which the jth column is the jth row of A; thus, from the matrix M_3, above,

$$M_5 = M_3^T = \begin{bmatrix} -2 & 1 & a \\ 0 & -\frac{1}{2} & b \end{bmatrix}$$

which is the transpose of M_3.

Addition and multiplication of matrices can be defined so that certain sets of matrices form algebraic systems. Let the elements of the matrices considered be arbitrary real numbers, although the elements could have been chosen from other fields or rings. A zero matrix is one in which all the elements are zero; an identity matrix, I_m of order m, is a square matrix of order m in which all the elements are zero except those on the main diagonal, which are 1. The order of an identity matrix may be omitted if implied by the text, and I_m is then shortened to I.

The sum of two matrices is defined only if they are of the same size; if $A = [a_{ij}]$ and $B = [b_{ij}]$ are of the same size, then $C = A + B$ is defined as the matrix $[c_{ij}]$, in which $c_{ij} = a_{ij} + b_{ij}$; that is, two matrices of the same size are added merely by adding corresponding elements. Thus, in the matrices given above

$$M_4 + M_5 = \begin{bmatrix} a+b-2 & b+c+1 & c+2a \\ a-b & b-c-\frac{1}{2} & c-a+b \end{bmatrix}$$

The set of all matrices of a fixed size has the property that addition is closed, associative, and commutative; a unique matrix O exists such that for any matrix A, $A + O = O + A = A$; and, corresponding to any matrix A, there exists a unique matrix B such that $A + B = B + A = O$.

The product AB of two matrices, A and B, is defined only if the number of columns of the left factor A is the same as the number of rows of the right factor B; if $A = [a_{ij}]$ is of size $m \times n$ and $B = [b_{jk}]$ is of size $n \times p$, the product $AB = C = [c_{ik}]$ is of size $m \times p$, and c_{ik} is given by

$$c_{ik} = \sum_{i=1}^{\nu} a_{ij} b_{jk}$$

That is, the element in the ith row and kth column of the product is the sum of the products of the elements of the ith row of the left factor multiplied by the corresponding elements of the kth column of the right factor.

Linear Algebra. The geometric concept of a vector (q.v.) as a line segment of given length and direction can be advantageously generalized as follows. An *n*-vector (*n*-dimensional vector, vector of order *n*, vector of length *n*) is an ordered set of *n* elements of a field. As in matrix theory, the elements are assumed to be real numbers. An *n*-vector **v** is represented as:

$$v = [x_1, x_2, \ldots, x_n]$$

In particular, the lines of a matrix are vectors; the horizontal lines are row vectors, the vertical lines are column vectors. The *x*'s are called the components of the vector.

Addition of vectors (of the same length) and scalar multiplication are defined as for matrices and satisfy the same laws. If

$$w = [y_1, y_2, \ldots, y_n]$$

and *k* is a scalar (real number), then

$$v + w = [x_1 + y_1, x_2 + y_2, \ldots, x_n + y_n]$$
$$kv = [kx_1, kx_2, \ldots, kx_n]$$

If $k_1, k_2, \ldots, k_m$ are scalars and $v_1, v_2, \ldots, v_m$ are *n*-vectors, the *n*-vector

$$v = k_1 v_1 + k_2 v_2 + \ldots + k_m v_m$$

is called a linear combination of the vectors $v_1, v_2, \ldots, v_m$. The *m* *n*-vectors are linearly independent if the only linear combination equal to the zero *n*-vector, $0 = [0,0, \ldots, 0]$, is the one in which $k_1 = k_2 = \ldots = k_m = 0$; otherwise, the vectors are linearly dependent. For example, if $v_1 = [0, 1, 2, 3]$, $v_2 = [1, 2, 3, 4]$, $v_3 = [2, 2, 4, 4]$, $v_4 = [3, 4, 7, 8]$, then v_1, v_2, v_3 are linearly independent, because $k_1 v_1 + k_2 v_2 + k_3 v_3 = 0$ if and only if $k_1 = k_2 = k_3 = 0$; $v_2, v_3,$ and v_4 are linearly dependent because $v_2 + v_3 - v_4 = 0$. If A is a matrix of rank *r*, then at least one set of *r* row, or column, vectors is a linearly independent set, and every set of more than *r* row, or column, vectors is a linearly dependent set.

A vector space **V** is a nonempty set of vectors (see SET THEORY), with the properties that (1) if $v \, \varepsilon \, V$ and $w \, \varepsilon \, V$, then $v + w \, \varepsilon \, V$, and (2) if $v \, \varepsilon \, V$ and *k* is any scalar, then $kv \, \varepsilon \, V$. If $S = \{v_i\}$ is a set of vectors, all of the same length, all linear combinations of the *v*'s form a vector space said to be spanned by the *v*'s. If the set $B = \{w_i\}$ spans the same vector space **V** and is a linearly independent set, the set B is a basis for **V**. If a basis for **V** contains *m* vectors, every basis for **V** will contain exactly *m* vectors and **V** is called a vector space of dimension *m*. Two- and three-dimensional Euclidean spaces are vector spaces when their points are regarded as specified by ordered pairs or triples of real numbers. Matrices may be used to describe changes from one vector space into another. J.Si.; REV. BY J.Le.B.

For further information on this topic, see the Bibliography in volume 28, section 369.

MATSU. See TAIWAN.

MATSUDO, city, Japan, SE Honshu Island, in Chiba Prefecture, on the Tone and Edo rivers, in the E part of the Tokyo metropolitan area. Industries include metalworking and the manufacture of machinery. Matsudo was an important river port in the Tokugawa era (1603–1867). Pop. (1988 est.) 439,100.

MATSUE, city and seaport, Japan, SW Honshu Island, administrative center of Shimane Prefecture, Matsue is a commercial and distributing center and attracts many tourists. It is the site of Shimane University (1949). Pop. (1987 est.) 142,100.

MATSUKATA MASAYOSHI (1835–1924), Japanese prime minister (1891–92 and 1896–98). Born into a samurai family in Kagoshima, he took part in the revolution that overthrew the shogunate in 1868. As minister of finance from 1881 to 1891, he helped Japan avoid economic ruin by organizing the Bank of Japan, redeeming paper currency that had become nearly worthless and securing economic stability. During his terms as prime minister he also served as finance minister, and in 1897 he was responsible for Japan's conversion to the gold standard. He later held the ceremonial post of keeper of the privy seal (1917–22) and was created a prince in 1922.

MATSUMOTO, city, Japan, central Honshu Island, in Nagano Prefecture. Industries include the manufacture of silks and baskets and the preserving of fruits. Shinshu University (1949) is located here. Pop. (1987 est.) 199,200.

MATSUYAMA, city, Japan, NW Shikoku Island, capital of Ehime Prefecture, near the port of Mitsu. The city is a center of manufacturing. Cotton cloth is produced here and is also a major export of Matsuyama. Within the city park is a large 17th-century castle. Matsuyama University of Commerce (1923) is located in the city. Pop. (1988 est.) 433,900.

MATTA ECHAURREN, Roberto Sebastián Antonio (1911–), Chilean-born painter, whose surrealist-inspired works illustrate a dream world of modern technological civilization. His paintings, such as *Eros Precipitate* (1944, Museum of Modern Art, New York City), are peopled with strange hybrid automatons and insectlike creatures. Matta, now a citizen of France, lived in New York City from 1939 to 1948 and had a decisive influence on the work of Arshile Gorky and the creation of abstract expressionism.

MATTER, in science, general term applied to anything that has the property of occupying space and the attributes of gravity and inertia. In the view of classical physics, matter and energy (the

MATTER, STATES OF

The curves of a phase diagram represent temperatures and pressures at which two phases are in equilibrium. At the triple point, the three phases coexist. At temperatures higher than the critical point, a liquid phase cannot exist no matter how high the pressure.

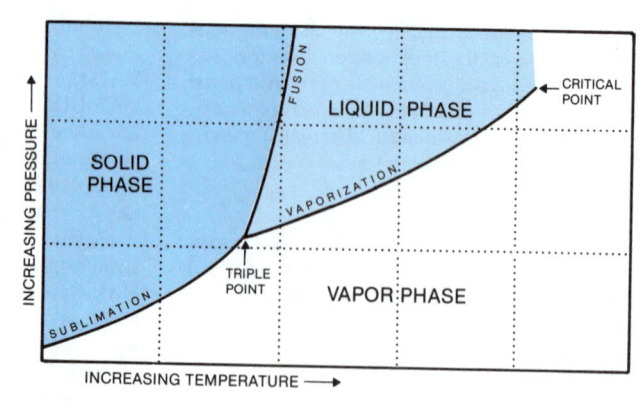

capacity for doing work) were two separate concepts that lay at the root of all physical phenomena. Modern physicists, however, have shown that it is possible to transform matter into energy and energy into matter and have thus broken down the classical distinction between the two concepts (see MASS; RELATIVITY). For simplicity and convenience in dealing with a large number of phenomena, such as motion, the behavior of liquids and gases, and heat, scientists regard matter and energy as separate entities.

Certain elementary particles (q.v.) of matter or antimatter (q.v.) are normally combined into atoms tightly bound in the form of molecules. The properties of individual molecules and their distribution and arrangement give to matter in all its forms various qualities such as mass, hardness, viscosity, fluidity, color, taste, electrical resistivity, heat conductivity, and many others. The theoretical possibility of "negative" matter has also been raised. See CHEMISTRY; ELECTRICITY; HEAT; MATTER, STATES OF.

In philosophy, matter has been generally regarded as the raw material of the physical world, although certain idealistic philosophers, such as the Irish philosopher George Berkeley, denied that matter exists independent of the mind (see GREEK PHILOSOPHY; KANT, IMMANUEL). Most modern philosophers tend to accept the scientific definition of matter.   R.Ho.

MATTER, STATES OF, in classical physics, three forms in which matter (q.v.) occurs—solid, liquid, and gas. Plasma (q.v.), the collection of charged gaseous particles containing nearly equal numbers of negative and positive ions, is sometimes called the fourth state of matter (see ION; IONIZATION). Solid matter is characterized by resistance to any change in shape, caused by a strong attraction between the molecules of which it is composed. In liquid form, matter does not resist forces that act to change its shape, because the molecules are free to move with respect to each other (see MOLECULE). Liquids, however, have sufficient molecular attraction to resist forces tending to change their volume. Gaseous matter, in which molecules are widely dispersed and move freely, offers no resistance to change of shape and little resistance to change of volume. As a result, a gas that is not confined tends to diffuse infinitely, increasing in volume and diminishing in density.

Most substances are solid at low temperatures, liquid at medium temperatures, and gaseous at high temperatures, but the states are not always distinct (see TEMPERATURE). The temperature at which any given substance changes from solid to liquid is its melting point, and the temperature at which it changes from liquid to gas is its boiling point (q.v.; see FREEZING POINT). The range of melting and boiling points varies widely. Helium remains a gas down to −269° C (−454° F), and tungsten remains a solid up to about 3370° C (about 6100° F).

For further discussion of the properties of matter in its different states, see ATOM AND ATOMIC THEORY; CRYSTAL; FLUID; GLASS; LIQUID CRYSTAL; THERMODYNAMICS; VAPOR. See also CRITICAL POINT; CRYOGENICS.

MATTERHORN, peak of the Alps, SW Switzerland, near the border with the Italian region of Aosta. It rises to an altitude of 4505 m (14,780 ft). In July 1865 a group led by British alpinist Edward Whymper was the first to scale the peak.

MATTHEW, Saint (fl. 1st cent. AD), in the New Testament, one of the 12 apostles of Jesus Christ. According to ecclesiastical tradition, he was the author of the First Gospel and therefore one of the four evangelists. Little is known about Matthew. The first three Gospels relate that he was a tax collector at the ancient Palestinian lake port of Capernaum (see Matt. 9:9, 10:3; Mark 2:14–16; Luke 5:27–29), which made him a member of the class publicly branded as "sinners" (see Mark 2:16). Mark calls him "Levi the son of Alphaeus,"

MATTHEW, GOSPEL ACCORDING TO

and Luke calls him only "Levi." Some scholars believe that he may originally have been called Levi and that Jesus named him Matthew after he became an apostle; the name is ancient Hebrew or Aramaic and means "gift of Yahweh" (God).

Matthew is not prominent in the New Testament record of the 12 apostles. Three of the evangelists tell the story of his call, one tells of a feast that he gave to celebrate the turning point in his life (see Luke 5:29), and three record that he was indeed among the 12 apostles (see Matt. 10:3; Mark 3:18; Luke 6:15). They tell the story of his calling not as part of the record of a prominent apostle, however, but as a testimony to the compelling grace of Jesus Christ. As a tax collector, either under the tetrarch Herod Antipas or directly under the Roman government, he would have been a man of substance and of some education, skilled in arithmetic and able to speak both Aramaic and Greek. Matthew is the patron saint of tax collectors and bankers. His feast day is September 21.

MATTHEW, GOSPEL ACCORDING TO, first book of the New Testament.

Authorship. Early Christian writers believed this book to be the earliest of the synoptic Gospels (hence its place at the opening of the New Testament) and attributed it to St. Matthew, one of the 12 apostles. They held that he wrote the Gospel in Palestine, just prior to the destruction of Jerusalem in AD 70. Although this opinion is still held by some, most scholars consider the Gospel of Mark the earliest Gospel. They believe, on the basis of external and internal evidence, that the author of Matthew used Mark as one of his two major sources and a collection of Jesus' sayings called "Q" (from Ger. *Quelle,* "source") as the second. They doubt, moreover, that the apostle Matthew wrote the book. Whoever the actual author was, he is identified as a Jew partly because his Gospel contains numerous references to Jewish Scripture, law, and ways of life that presuppose the reader's familiarity with them, and partly because other evidence suggests that he wrote chiefly for Christians of Jewish origin. The place of writing is not definitely known. Some authorities think it was Palestine; others favor another early Christian center, possibly the city of Antioch in Syria. The time of composition frequently suggested is sometime after AD 70, perhaps about AD 80.

Content. The Gospel of Matthew is built around five discourses of Jesus Christ. Each of the five discourses is introduced by a narrative concerning deeds of Jesus, this section serving as a preparation for and being interpreted by the discourse. The discourses as a whole are preceded by an introductory narrative and followed by two culminating narratives. The first of these final narratives concerns the passion, and the second, Jesus' resurrection. Thus Matthew is made up of eight fairly distinct sections.

The introductory narrative (chap. 1–2) traces the genealogy of Jesus from the Hebrew patriarch Abraham and the Hebrew king David and includes accounts of Jesus' birth and infancy (1:18–2:23). Well-known stories in this section peculiar to Matthew include the visit of the Magi, the "wise men from the East" (2:1); the flight into Egypt by Joseph and Mary with the infant Jesus to escape the massacre of the male children by Herod the Great, king of Judea; and their return from Egypt after Herod's death.

The five narrative-discourse sections, each marked at its conclusion by the formula ". . . when Jesus finished these sayings," are drawn

The Matterhorn, in Valais Canton, Switzerland, is popular with mountain climbers. Werner Müller–Peter Arnold, Inc.

largely from Mark and "Q." The background of the first four narrative-discourses is Galilee; Jerusalem is the setting for the fifth.

First narrative-discourse. The first narrative (chap. 3-4) tells of John the Baptist, Jesus' baptism and temptation, and the beginning of his public ministry. It is followed by the Sermon on the Mount (chap. 5-7), in which Jesus speaks of his coming to fulfill "the law" and "the prophets" (5:17) and instructs the multitude "as one who has authority" (7:29). Included in the sermon are the Beatitudes and the Lord's Prayer (6:9-13).

Second narrative-discourse. The second narrative (8:1-9:34) presents examples of Jesus' ability to heal sick and disturbed persons through the power of faith. In the second discourse (9:35-10:42), Jesus commands his 12 disciples to heal and preach "to the lost sheep of the house of Israel" (10:6) and lays down the conditions of discipleship.

Third narrative-discourse. The third narrative (chap. 11-12) tells of the mounting opposition of the Pharisees to Jesus' works and teaching. The subject of the third discourse (13:1-52) is the kingdom of heaven. Jesus speaks about it in parables, and when he is asked by the disciples why he speaks in this manner to the people, Jesus answers, "To you it has been given to know the secrets of the kingdom of heaven, but to them it has not been given" (13:11). Included in this discourse are the parables of the sower (13:18-23), the weeds (13:24-30), and the mustard seed (13:31-32).

Fourth narrative-discourse. The fourth narrative (13:53-17:23) begins with the story of the rejection of Jesus by his fellow townspeople (13:53-58). It also reports the death of John the Baptist (14:3-12), a number of miracles and acts of healing done by Jesus, one miraculous act of St. Peter, the revelation to the disciples at Caesarea Philippi of his divine nature and vocation (16:13-16), the founding of the church (16:17-19), Jesus' foretelling of his passion and resurrection, and the transfiguration (17:1-8). The fourth discourse (17:24-18:35) is concerned with the conditions and administration of the church. It is noteworthy that Matt. 16:17-19 and Matt. 18:17 are the only passages in the four Gospels in which the word *church* appears.

Fifth narrative-discourse. The fifth narrative (chap. 19-22) depicts Jesus' last journey through Judea to Jerusalem, including the entry into Jerusalem, and tells of the driving out of the money changers from the Temple. Also included are controversies between Jesus and the Sadducees and Pharisees over tribute to Caesar, the resurrection, "the great commandment in the law" (22:36-37), and the ancestry of the Messiah. The final major discourse falls into two parts. In the first (chap. 23), Jesus criticizes the Pharisees and scribes because, among their other faults, they "outwardly appear righteous to men, but within ... are full of hypocrisy and iniquity" (23:28). In the second part (chap. 24-25), Jesus tells the disciples the signs of his coming and of the end of the world (24:3). He also speaks to them in the parables of the fig tree (24:32-33), the ten virgins (25:1-13), and the talents (25:14-30), about the coming kingdom of heaven, and depicts the last judgment.

The anointing of Jesus; his betrayal; the Last Supper; Jesus' agony and arrest in the Garden of Gethsemane; and his trial, crucifixion, death, and burial are related in the first of the two culminating narratives (chap. 26-27). His resurrection and his commission to the disciples to teach all nations (28:19) are reported in the closing narrative (chap. 28). Stories and details peculiar to Matthew found in these culminating narratives include the death of Jesus' betrayer, Judas Iscariot (27:3-10), the dream of Pontius Pilate's wife (27:19), Pilate's washing his hands of responsibility for Jesus' death (27:24-25), the earthquake following Jesus' death (27:51-53), the guard at the tomb (27:62-66), the earthquake at the time of Jesus' resurrection (28:2-4), and the appearances of the risen Christ to the two Marys (28:9-10) and to his disciples in Galilee (28:16-20).

Distinctive Qualities. Notable in Matthew are its emphasis on Jesus as the promised Messiah, the legitimate heir of King David, and on matters pertaining to the church. Abundant proof that it probably was written for Jewish Christians may be found, for instance, in much of the material peculiar to this Gospel, which is concerned with representing Jesus as the fulfillment of the Old Testament. Unique, too, is the superior position of St. Peter, who is singled out by Jesus as the keeper of "the keys of the kingdom of heaven" (16:19). The deep interest in the disciples generally, which is displayed by all the evangelists, is emphasized in Matthew. The author of Matthew gives the fullest account of how Jesus called them, how he instructed them, how they failed him, and how the risen Christ forgave and restored them.

The influence of Matthew on Christianity has been dominant ever since its composition. Besides its theological importance in the formulation of doctrine, an importance shared only by the Gospel of John, its phrasing of such well-known sections as the Beatitudes, the Lord's

Prayer, and the passion stories are better known and more frequently read or cited than the parallel passages in the other Gospels.

MATTHIAS CORVINUS (1443–90), king of Hungary (1458–90), the last native monarch to reign over all Hungary. A patron of Renaissance art and learning, he was for a time the most powerful ruler in central Europe.

Matthias was born on Feb. 23, 1443, in Kolozsvár (present-day Cluj, Romania), the son of János Hunyadi, who was regent of Hungary from 1446 to 1452. He was elected king as successor to the childless Ladislas V (1440–57) in 1458; Holy Roman Emperor Frederick III, who had also claimed the throne, recognized him as king in 1462. Between 1469 and 1478 Matthias intervened in Bohemia, trying to win control of that country. Ultimately unsuccessful, he did acquire the provinces of Moravia, Lusatia, and Silesia. Matthias's court at Buda became a great center of learning, and his library, known as the Bibliotheca Corvina, was famous for its collection of rare manuscripts. Matthias introduced printing into Hungary; he brought Italian scholars to Buda, sent Hungarian students to Italian universities, and founded a university at Pozsony (present-day Bratislava, Slovakia). He reformed the judicial system and reduced his dependence on the aristocracy by creating an independent army of mercenaries—the Black Troops—which he used against both internal and external enemies. Between 1481 and 1485 Matthias waged a successful war against his old rival, Emperor Frederick, became the ruler of Austria, Styria, and Carinthia, and moved his capital to Vienna. Because he had no legitimate heir, Matthias's empire disintegrated after he died in Vienna on April 6, 1490.　　　　J.Hd.

MAUGHAM, W(illiam) Somerset (1874–1965), English author, whose novels and short stories are characterized by great narrative facility, simplicity of style, and a disillusioned and ironic point of view. Maugham was born in Paris and studied medicine at the University of Heidelberg and at Saint Thomas's Hospital, London. His partially autobiographical novel *Of Human Bondage* (1915) is generally acknowledged as his masterpiece and is one of the best realistic English novels of the early 20th century. *The Moon and Sixpence* (1919) is a story of the conflict between the artist and conventional society, based on the life of the French painter Paul Gauguin; other novels are *The Painted Veil* (1925), *Cakes and Ale* (1930), *Christmas Holiday* (1939), *The Hour Before the Dawn* (1942), *The Razor's Edge* (1944), and *Cataline: A Romance* (1948). Among the collections of his short stories are *The Trembling of a Leaf* (1921), which includes "Miss Thompson," later dramatized as *Rain; Ashenden: or The British Agent* (1928); *First Person Singular* (1931); *Ah King* (1933); and *Quartet* (1948). He also wrote satiric comedies—*The Circle* (1921) and *Our Betters* (1923)—the melodrama *East of Suez* (1922), essays, and two autobiographies.

MAUI, island, Maui Co., central Hawaii, between Molokai and Hawaii islands, known as the Valley Island. The second largest island of the state, it is divided into two oval peninsulas, East Maui and West Maui. East Maui rises in the mountain of Haleakala, a dormant volcano, to a height of 3055 m (10,023 ft). The mountain terminates in a crater nearly 32 km (nearly 20 mi) in circumference and more than 924 m (more than 3028 ft) deep. West Maui rises to an elevation of 1764 m (5788 ft) and has many sharp peaks and ridges and extensive sloping plains on the N and S sides. Pineapple and large sugar plantations and cattle ranches are here. Tourism, construction, and scientific research are also important to the economy. Wailuku is the chief community. Area, 1884 sq km (727 sq mi); pop. (1980) 62,823; (1990) 100,374.

MAU MAU REBELLION, uprising against British rule in Kenya that began in 1952 after a long buildup of resentment caused primarily by appropriation of land. Tired of having its grievances ignored, the African community, and especially the Kikuyu, one of Kenya's most numerous ethnic groups, gradually moved toward more radical means. Some outbreaks of violence occurred in 1951, and the following year a secret Kikuyu society known as the Mau Mau began a campaign of violence against Europeans and disloyal Africans. In October 1952 the British declared a state of emergency and deployed troops to stamp out the rebellion. Jomo Kenyatta, leader of the Kenya African Union, a predominantly Kikuyu political party, was arrested and charged with organizing the Mau Mau. In 1953 he was sentenced to seven years in prison. Before the rebellion was quashed three years later, 11,000 rebels had been killed, and 80,000 Kikuyu—men, women, and children—were confined in detention camps; on the other side, some 100 Europeans and 2000 pro-British Africans lost their lives. Although it was a military failure, the Mau Mau brought both recognition of African grievances and efforts at correction that eventually led to Kenya's independence.

For further information on this topic, see the Bibliography in volume 28, section 1033.

MAUNA KEA ("White Mountain"), inactive volcano, Hawaii, N Hawaii Island. Mauna Kea is the highest peak in the state and its slopes are generally snow-covered in winter. The volcano rises about 5486 m (about 18,000 ft) from the ocean floor to the surface and continues up to a height of 4205 m (13,796 ft) above sea level, making its overall height from its base on the ocean floor to its summit about 9754 m (about 32,000 ft), higher than any other mountain in the world.

MAUNA KEA OBSERVATORY, astronomical research facility, located on Hawaii's dormant volcano Mauna Kea, at an altitude of 4205 m (13,796 ft), for purposes of nighttime viewing with minimum interference from human light sources. The observatory, founded in 1967, is affiliated with the University of Hawaii but has a number of internationally sponsored instruments. Thus, the 141-in. (3.58-m) optical and infrared reflector placed in operation in 1979 is sponsored by Canada and France as well as the U.S., and the 150-in. (3.8-m) infrared reflector is sponsored by the United Kingdom and the U.S. A 540-in. (15-m) British-Dutch paraboloid telescope in the ultrashort wave band, built of some 200 individual mirror panels, was completed in 1987. Also located at Mauna Kea are a 118-in. (3-m) infrared reflector and an 88-in. (2.24-m) optical and infrared reflector. The Keck Observatory (*see* TELESCOPE), completed on Mauna Kea in 1990, houses the world's largest optical telescope. Its 387-in. (9.82-m) primary mirror consists of 36 separate hexagonal segments. Japan plans to build a 276-in. (7-m) reflector on Mauna Kea in the early 1990s.

MAUNA LOA, active volcano, on Hawaii Island, at the W end of Hawaii Volcanoes National Park (q.v.), one of the world's largest volcanoes. It rises from a desolate landscape of old lava flows to a high point of 4169 m (13,677 ft) above sea level in the summit caldera (enlarged crater) of Mokuaweoweo. Lava from Mauna Loa covers about 50 percent of Hawaii Island, including parts of Kilauea, another volcano, situated to the E. Since the early 19th century, Mauna Loa has exuded lava about once every four years.

MAUNDY THURSDAY or **HOLY THURSDAY,** the Thursday before Easter Sunday, observed by Christians in commemoration of Christ's Last Supper (*see* EUCHARIST). The name Maundy is derived from *mandatum* (Lat., "commandment"), the first word of an anthem sung in the liturgical ceremony on that day. In Roman Catholic and many Protestant churches, the Eucharist is celebrated in an evening liturgy that includes Holy Communion. During the Roman Catholic liturgy, the ceremony of the washing of the feet, or *pedilavium*, is performed: the celebrant washes the feet of 12 people to commemorate Christ's washing of his disciples' feet. In England a custom survives of giving alms (called "maundy pennies") to the poor; this act recalls an earlier practice in which the sovereign washed the feet of the poor on Maundy Thursday. In most European countries, the day is known as Holy Thursday.

MAUPASSANT, (Henri René Albert) Guy de (1850–93), French author, one of the greatest masters of the short story in world literature. He was born in the Château de Miromesnil, Normandy, and educated at Yvetot and Rouen. In his youth he was a member of a literary group centering about the noted novelist Gustave Flaubert; Flaubert himself trained Maupassant in the art of writing fiction. Maupassant's first important work was the short story "Boule de suif" (Ball of Fat, 1880), considered his masterpiece in the genre. More than 200 short stories, including "Madame Fifi" (1882) and the famous "La Parure" (The Necklace, 1884), followed in the next 13 years. Maupassant's work is characterized by variations on the general theme of the cruelty of human beings to one another, by simplicity of style, and by realism. His short stories have been translated into English many times, and are available in many editions. Maupassant was also the author of three collections of travel sketches and six novels, including *A Woman's Life* (1883; trans. 1903), a compassionate story of a married woman's misery; *Bel Ami* (1885; trans. 1891), about an unscrupulous journalist; *The Two Brothers* (1888; trans. 1890); *The Master Passion* (1889; trans. 1889); and *Our Hearts* (1890).

MAURIAC, François (1885–1970), French novelist and Nobel laureate, born in Bordeaux, and educated at the University of Bordeaux and at the École des Chartes, Paris. He began his literary career as a poet, but achieved his greatest success as a novelist. His first novels, *Le baiser au lépreux* (A Kiss for the Leper, 1922) and *Genitrix* (1923), published together in English translations as *The Family* (1930), won wide critical and popular acclaim. Later novels, including *The Desert of Love* (1925; trans. 1929), *Thérèse* (1927; trans. 1928), and *Viper's Tangle* (1932; trans. 1933), rank among the finest works of 20th-century fiction. Among Mauriac's other writings are plays, notably *Asmodée* (1938; trans. 1939), the philosophical *What I Believe* (1963; trans. 1963), the biography *De Gaulle* (1964; trans. 1966), and critical works.

A profoundly religious Roman Catholic, Mauriac was chiefly concerned in his novels with basic moral conflicts. The desires of the flesh, offering no real satisfaction, are shown in tragic opposition to an essential human longing for a spiritual life. Acutely aware of the darker sides of human nature, he is unsurpassed in his psychological analyses of men and women struggling against the evil in themselves. An extraordinary stylist, Mauriac showed a remarkable gift for evoking an emotionally charged atmosphere. He was elected to the French Academy in 1933 and awarded the 1952 Nobel Prize in literature and the Grand Cross of the Legion of Honor in 1958.

MAURICE, Frederick Denison (1805–72), British Anglican theologian, educator, and social reformer, who was one of the founders of Christian socialism (q.v.). Born in Normanston, England, he studied law at the University of Cambridge but was denied a degree because he refused to subscribe to the Thirty-nine Articles (q.v.) of the Church of England. He later accepted Anglicanism and, in 1830, entered the University of Oxford, and was ordained in 1834.

While serving as chaplain of Guy's Hospital in London, Maurice wrote *The Kingdom of Christ* (1838), generally regarded as his most important work. In 1840 he was elected professor of English literature and modern history at King's College, London, and six years later he was chosen professor of theology at the same institution. Maurice was forced to resign after the publication of his *Theological Essays* (1853), in which he expressed skepticism about the eternity of hell. In 1848 he joined the British novelist and clergyman Charles Kingsley, the British clergyman John Ludlow (1821–1911), and others to found the Christian socialist movement. Six years later he established the Working Men's College in London. From 1866 until his death he was a professor of moral philosophy at Cambridge. He was the author of one novel, the autobiographical *Eustace Conway* (1834), and many religious works, including *Modern Philosophy* (1862) and *What Is Revelation?* (1859).

MAURITANIA, ISLAMIC REPUBLIC OF, republic, NW Africa, bounded on the N by Western Sahara and Algeria, on the E by Mali, on the S by Mali and Senegal, and on the W by the Atlantic Ocean. The country has a total area of about 1,030,700 sq km (about 398,000 sq mi).

LAND AND RESOURCES

Except for a narrow strip in the S along the Senegal R., the country lies entirely within the Sahara (q.v.). The elevation varies from about 150 m (about 500 ft) in the SW to about 460 m (about 1500 ft) in the NE. Daytime temperatures in much of the country reach 37.8° C (100° F) for more than half the year, but nights are cool. Annual rainfall varies from less than 130 mm (less than 5 in) in the N to about 660 mm (26 in) in the Senegal Valley.

Natural Resources. The most important resource of Mauritania is its large deposits of iron ore in the Fdérik area. Other mineral resources include deposits of phosphates, sulfur, and yttrium.

Plants and Animals. Upper Mauritania has little plant life and few animals. In the S, however, in a belt of steppe with trees of the genera *Acacia* and *Commiphoa*, lions and monkeys are found.

Mauritania: Map Index

Cities and Towns

Akjoujt	B3
Aleg	B3
Atâr	B2
Ayoûn el-Atroûs	C3
Bîr Mogreïn	C1
Fdérik	B2
Kaédi	B3
Kiffa	C3
Néma	D3
Nouadhibou	A2
Nouakchott, *capital*	A3
Ouadane	C2
Rosso	B3
Sélibaby	B4
Tichit	C3
Tidjikdja	C3
Zouîrât	B2

Other Features

Adrar, *region*	B2
Djouf, el-, *desert*	C3
Erg Iguidi, *desert*	D1
Sahara, *desert*	C1
Senegal, *river*	B3
Tagânt, *region*	C3

POPULATION

The majority of the population consists of Moors (of mixed Arab and Berber ancestry), many of whom lead nomadic existences. More than 90% of the population lives in the S quarter of the country. About 30% of the people are black African farmers, who are settled in the Senegal Valley.

Population Characteristics. The population of Mauritania (1994 est.) was 2,069,000. The overall population density was about 2 persons per sq km (about 5 persons per sq mi).

115

MAURITANIA

Political Divisions and Principal Cities. Mauritania is divided into 12 regions, each administered by a council, and 1 district, which encompasses the country's capital and largest city, Nouakchott (pop., 1992 est., 480,400). Other principal towns are Nouadhibou (72,300), a fishing center and seaport, and Kaedi (35,200), on the Senegal R.

Religion and Language. Islam, the state religion, is professed by about 99% of the people. Arabic is the official language, and Poular, Wolof, and Soninke are recognized as national languages.

Education. The government provides free primary education. The effort, however, has been hindered by the nomadic character of the people. In the early 1990s about half of all eligible children were attending primary school. About 226,000 pupils were enrolled in primary, secondary, and vocational institutions. Higher education is provided by the University of Nouakchott (1981) and by a college of public administration and a scientific institute, also in the capital.

ECONOMY

In the early 1990s, Mauritania had a gross national product of about $530 per capita. Life expectancy at birth averaged 50 years for women and 46 for men; the infant mortality rate was 117 per 1000 live births. The economy is predominantly pastoral; mining is also important. On a per capita basis, Mauritania is one of the world's leading recipients of foreign aid. The annual government budget in the mid-1990s was balanced at $308 million.

Agriculture. Animal raising is the most important agricultural activity, and livestock in Mauritania in the early 1990s was estimated to include 5.4 million sheep, 3.6 million goats, 1.4 million cattle, and 4 million poultry. Crop farming is mostly restricted to the S. The leading crops are millet, pulses, rice, potatoes, dates, and watermelons.

Fishing. Mauritania has a large saltwater fishing potential, and the government has taken measures to protect its offshore fishing areas. In the early 1990s the country's annual catch was estimated at 100,700 metric tons.

Mining. Production of iron ore, mainly from Mauritania's rich deposits in the Fdérik area, totaled 9.4 million metric tons annually in the early 1990s. Copper mining, once an important industry, was discontinued in 1978.

Manufacturing and Energy. Manufacturing accounts for less than 10% of the annual gross domestic product and is limited mainly to fish processing and the production of other foodstuffs. In the early 1990s, Mauritania's installed electricity-generating capacity was about 143,000 kw, and annual production was about 105 million kwh.

Currency and Foreign Trade. The monetary unit in Mauritania is the ouguiya, which is divided into five khoums (122 ouguiyas equal U.S.$1; 1995). The Central Bank of Mauritania (founded in 1973) is the bank of issue.

In the early 1990s, annual exports, mainly iron ore and fish, totaled about $432 million. Imports, primarily of food products, machinery, construction materials, petroleum, and consumer goods, cost about $413 million. Leading trade partners were France, Italy, and Japan.

Transportation and Communications. Transportation facilities include air routes and about 7535 km (about 4680 mi) of roads and tracks. The Trans-Mauritanian highway was opened in 1978. A 670-km (416-mi) railroad links Nouadhibou to the Fdérik ore fields. Deep-water port facilities and international airports are located in and near Nouadhibou and Nouakchott. The country has one daily newspaper, the *Chaab,* published in French and Arabic in Nouakchott. In the early 1990s there were an estimated 17,000 telephones, 300,000 radios, and 1100 televisions.

GOVERNMENT

A 1961 constitution, promulgated soon after Mauritania became an independent republic, was suspended in 1978 following a coup d'état. Subsequently, legislative and executive power was vested in what became known as the Military Committee for National Salvation. The committee was headed by a chairman, who served as the country's president.

A new constitution approved by referendum in July 1991 declares Mauritania to be an "Islamic, African, and Arab republic." The constitution provides for an executive president, directly elected for a 6-year term, and for a bicameral legislature, consisting of a 79-seat national assembly and a 56-member senate. A prime minister heads the government.

Judiciary and Defense. The highest tribunal of Mauritania is the supreme court, which sits in Nouakchott. Islamic law plays an important role in the Mauritanian judicial system. In the early 1990s, Mauritania had an army of 15,000 persons, a navy of 400, and an air force of 150.

HISTORY

Remnants of Stone Age cultures have been found in northern Mauritania. Berber nomads moved into the area in the 1st millennium AD and subjugated the indigenous black population. The newcomers belonged to the Sanhaja Confederation that long dominated trade between the northern parts of Africa and the kingdom of Ghana, the capital of which, Kumbi Saleh, was in southeastern Mauritania. Under Almoravid leadership, the Sanhaja razed Kumbi Saleh in 1076, although Ghana survived until the early 13th century. The Berbers, in turn, were conquered by Arabs in the 16th century. The descendants of the Arabs became the upper stratum of Mauritanian society, and Arabic gradually displaced Berber dialects as the language of the country. French forces, moving up the Senegal River, made the area a French protectorate in 1903 and a colony in 1920. In 1946 Mauritania became an overseas territory of the French Union. Under French occupation, slavery was legally abolished.

The Islamic Republic of Mauritania was proclaimed on Nov. 28, 1958, under the constitution of the Fifth French Republic, and on Nov. 28, 1960, it became fully independent. It joined the UN in 1961. That same year Moktar Ould Daddah (1924–   ) was elected its first president; he was reelected in 1966, 1971, and 1976.

Mauritania was severely affected by a drought in the late 1960s and early '70s. Nevertheless, its economy expanded as newly discovered iron and copper deposits were exploited. In 1976 it annexed the southern third of adjacent Spanish Sahara (see WESTERN SAHARA), which at that time was ceded by Spain; Morocco received the rest of the territory. A Saharan nationalist movement, the Polisario Front, seeking to make the Western Sahara an independent nation, weakened Mauritania with guerrilla warfare. In July 1978, President Daddah was ousted in a coup led by Lt. Col. Mustafa Ould Salek (1935–   ). After he was replaced by another army officer, Mohamed Ould Louly (1943–   ), Mauritania agreed, in August 1979, to withdraw from the Western Sahara.

Another change of leadership occurred in 1980, when the prime minister, Mohamed Ould Haidalla (1940–   ), assumed the presidency. He subjected the nation to strict enforcement of Islamic law. Haidalla survived a coup in 1981 but was deposed by his chief of staff, Col. Maouya Ould Sidi Ahmed Taya (1943–   ), in 1984. Tensions with Senegal in 1989 resulted in the repatriation of 100,000 Mauritanian nationals from Senegal and the repatriation or expulsion of 125,000 Senegalese nationals in Mauritania. Faced with rising domestic pressures and international criticism of his human rights record, Taya implemented a new constitution and legalized opposition parties in 1991. He was chosen executive president in a disputed election in January 1992.

For further information on this topic, see the Bibliography in volume 28, section 1012.

MAURITIUS, sovereign state, W Indian Ocean, E of Madagascar, a member of the Commonwealth of Nations. The country includes the island of Mauritius, with an area of 1865 sq km (720 sq mi); the island of Rodrigues (104 sq km/40 sq mi) to the E; and the island of Agalega to the N and the Saint Brandon Group (also known as the Cargados Carajos Shoals) to the NE, which have a combined area of 71 sq km (27 sq mi). The country has a total area of 2040 sq km (788 sq mi).

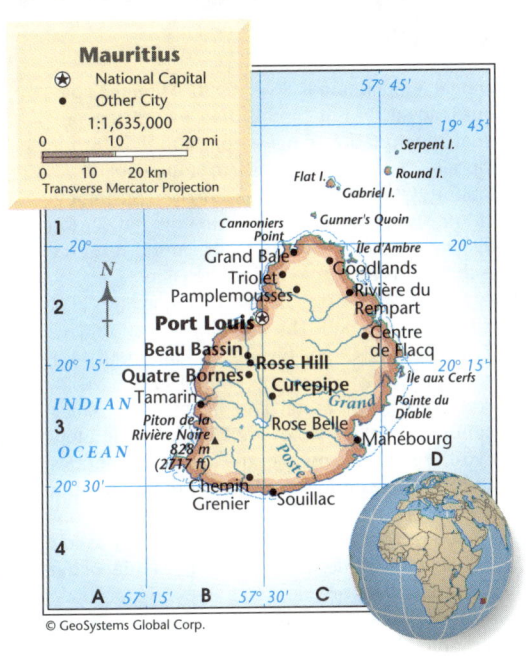

Land and Resources. The island of Mauritius is of volcanic origin. From a low-lying plain in the N, the terrain rises to a plateau that covers the central part of the island. The S is mostly mountainous, rising to a maximum elevation in Piton de la Petite Rivière Noire (845 m/2771 ft). Several lakes are located in the plateau region, and numerous streams rise in the highlands and radiate to the coast. The island is almost entirely surrounded by coral reefs, but Port Louis, the capital, has a fine harbor, accessible to oceangoing ships. The climate is tropical and generally humid. The average

Mauritius: Map Index

Cities and Towns

Beau Bassin	B2
Centre de Flacq	C2
Chemin Grenier	B3
Curepipe	C3
Goodlands	C2
Grand Bale	C2
Mahébourg	C3
Pamplemousses	C2
Port Louis, *capital*	B2
Quatre Bornes	B3
Rivière du Rempart	C2
Rose Belle	C3
Rose Hill	B2
Souillac	C4
Tamarin	B3
Triolet	C2

Other Features

Ambre, *island*	C2
Cannoniers, *point*	C1
Cerfs, *island*	D3
Diable, *point*	D3
Flat, *island*	C1
Gabriel, *island*	C1
Grand, *river*	C3
Gunner's Quoin, *island*	C1
Poste, *river*	C3
Rivière Noire, *mt.*	B3
Round, *island*	D1
Serpent, *island*	D1

117

annual temperature is 26.7° C (80° F) on the coast but is lower in the central plateau. Average annual precipitation ranges from about 1015 mm (about 40 in) on the coast to about 5080 mm (about 200 in) in the plateau region. Strong cyclonic storms occur often during the hot season (December to April). The main natural resource is the relatively fertile soil of the island.

Population. The population of Mauritius (1994 est.) was 1,120,000. The overall population density of about 549 persons per sq km (about 1421 per sq mi) was one of the highest in the world. Port Louis, the capital and largest city, had a population (1992 est.) of 142,850. Approximately two-thirds of the people are Indian immigrants and their descendants. People of mixed African and European descent, known as Creoles, constitute less than one-third of the total. Chinese and European minorities also exist. The majority of the Indo-Mauritians are Hindus; the rest are Muslims. Most Creoles are Roman Catholics. English is the official language, but French and Creole, a French patois, are commonly spoken.

Economy and Government. The economy of Mauritius has traditionally been dominated by a single cash crop, sugarcane. More than 70% of the cultivated land is planted with sugarcane; sugar and molasses are major exports. Other crops include tea, peanuts, tobacco, and vegetables. Manufactures include refined sugar and sugar by-products, fertilizers, beverages, electronic components, and leather goods. The clothing and textile industry boomed during the 1980s and early '90s; the gross national product rose from about $800 to $3000 per capita during the same period. Tourism is increasingly important. The currency is the Mauritian rupee, which consists of 100 cents (18.13 rupees equal U.S.$1; 1995).

From 1968 through 1991, Mauritius was a constitutional monarchy; executive power was nominally vested in the British monarch, as represented by a governor-general. In March 1992, the country became a republic; the governor-general assumed presidential powers until June, when a president and vice-president were elected by the unicameral National Assembly. The head of government is the prime minister, who presides over the Council of Ministers.

History. Although it has been settled for less than 400 years, Mauritius was probably visited by the Arabs before the 10th century, the Malays in the 1400s, and the Portuguese in the early 1500s. It was occupied in 1598 by the Dutch, who named it for Maurice of Nassau (1567–1625), then stadtholder of the Netherlands. The Dutch left in 1710, and in 1715 the French took possession, renaming it Île de France. It was captured by the British in 1810 during the Napoleonic Wars and was formally ceded to Great Britain in 1814. To offset the labor problem arising from abolition of slavery in the British Empire, the planters were allowed to import indentured laborers from India, and since 1861 the population has been mainly Indian. Racial conflict continued into the 1980s.

Mauritius gained independence on March 12, 1968. A member of the Afro-Mauritian Common Organization and the Organization of African Unity, Mauritius also has a special status with the European Union under the Lomé Convention.

The Labor Party (LP), headed by Sir Seewoosagur Ramgoolam (1900–85), governed Mauritius during the first 14 years of independence. The opposition Mauritian Militant Movement (MMM) gained strength throughout the 1970s and in 1982 swept to power, under the leadership of Aneerood Jugnauth (1930–   ). Ousted from the MMM in a power struggle, Jugnauth formed a new party, the Mauritian Socialist Movement, which, in alliance with the LP, won a parliamentary majority in 1983. Jugnauth's coalition was reelected in 1987 and 1991. Mauritius became a republic in 1992.

For further information on this topic, see the Bibliography in volume 28, section 1012.

MAUROIS, André, original name EMILE SALOMON WILHELM HERZOG (1885–1967), French biographer and critic, born in Elbeuf, and educated at the University of Caen. From 1904 until the outbreak of World War I, he worked in a textile factory owned by his father. He served as a French officer in World Wars I and II.

Maurois's first work, *The Silence of Colonel Bramble* (1918; trans. 1920), is a fictionalized memoir of his experiences during World War I. Five years later the biography *Ariel, the Life of Shelley* (1923; trans. 1924) introduced a series of romanticized biographies written in an engaging popular style and relying more on imaginative interpretation than on scholarly originality. Several of these works, however, are remarkable for a high order of critical insight, notably *Lelia, Life of George Sand* (1952; trans. 1953) and *The Titans: A Three-Generation Biography of the Dumas* (1957; trans. 1958). Maurois is the author also of *An Illustrated History of France* (1960), novels, and autobiographical journals. He was elected to the French Academy in 1938.

MAURY, Matthew Fontaine (1806–73), American naval officer and oceanographer, who wrote *The Physical Geography of the Sea* (1855), the first textbook of modern oceanography, and subsequently prepared charts of the bottom of the Atlantic Ocean between the U.S. and Europe that demonstrated the practicability of submarine cables. Maury was born near Fredericksburg, Va. He entered the U.S. Navy in 1825 and in 1842 he became superintendent of the U.S. Depot of Charts and Instruments (present-day U.S. Naval Observatory and the U.S. Naval Oceanographic Office) in Washington, D.C. For 19 years thereafter, he devoted himself to various meteorologic and oceanographic studies. From the study of old ships' logs he compiled a series of ocean-wind and ocean-current charts that contributed greatly to the science of marine navigation. From 1868 until his death, Maury served as professor of meteorology at the Virginia Military Institute.

MAUSOLEUM, large sepulchral monument containing a chamber in which funeral urns or coffins are deposited. The name is derived from the tomb erected at Halicarnassus (now Bodrum, Turkey) to King Mausolus of Caria (fl. about 376–353 BC) by his widow, Artemisia (d. about 350 BC). It was considered one of the Seven Wonders of the Ancient World (*see* SEVEN WONDERS OF THE WORLD). Later instances of magnificent mausoleums are the tomb of the Roman emperor Hadrian, now Castel Sant'Angelo, and that of Emperor Augustus, both at Rome; and the mausoleum of King Frederick William III of Prussia, at Charlottenburg in Berlin. A notable American mausoleum is the 19th-century tomb of President Ulysses S. Grant in New York City. Perhaps the most renowned mausoleum is the 17th-century Taj Mahal in Agra, India.

MAWSON, Sir Douglas (1882–1958), Australian explorer and geologist, born in Bradford, England, and educated at the University of Sydney. He was a member of the 1907 expedition of the British explorer Sir Ernest Henry Shackleton, which came within 161 km (100 mi) of the South Pole. Mawson organized and commanded (1911–14) an Australasian expedition to explore Antarctic lands south of Australia; two of his companions perished during this arduous journey. On his return Mawson was knighted. Mawson was the leader of the British, Australian, and New Zealand Antarctic Expedition from 1929 to 1931.

MAXIM, Hiram Percy (1869–1936), American inventor, son of Anglo-American inventor Sir Hiram Stevens Maxim. He was born in Brooklyn, N.Y., and educated at the Massachusetts Institute of Technology. Among his developments were a three-wheeled gasoline automobile (1895), an electric automobile (1897), and silencer devices for various mechanisms, ranging from rifles to air compressors. Maxim was also a cofounder, in 1914, of the American Radio Relay League.

MAXIM, Sir Hiram Stevens (1840–1916), Anglo-American engineer and inventor, born in Sangerville, Maine. In 1878 he became chief engineer of the U.S. Electric Lighting Co. Three years later he immigrated to England, became a naturalized British citizen, and turned his attention to invention and manufacture. Among his many inventions, the best known is the automatic machine gun that bears his name. In 1884 he organized the Maxim Gun Co., which in 1896 became Vickers' Sons and Maxim. He was knighted in 1901.

Gol Gumbaz, the tomb of Sultan Muhammad Adil Shah, a notable mausoleum located in Bijapur, western India. Built between 1626 and 1656, the structure has four corner towers and a dome 45 m (142 ft) in diameter and nearly 61 m (200 ft) high.
Mathias Oppersdorff

MAXIM, Hudson (1853–1927), American inventor, best known for explosives. He was born in Orneville, Maine, brother of Sir Hiram Maxim. He established a printing business at Pittsfield, Mass., in 1883 and invented a method of color printing in newspapers. Turning his attention to the improvement of explosives, he produced the first smokeless powder in the U.S., which was adopted by the U.S. Army. In 1901 he perfected a powerful explosive, which he patented under the name of maximite.

MAXIMIAN, in Latin Marcus Aurelius Valerius Maximianus (240?–310), Roman emperor (286–305, 306–8), born of humble parents in the Roman province of Pannonia (in present-day Slovenia). Because of his distinguished military service, the emperor Diocletian made him coruler of the Roman Empire with the title augustus. When Diocletian abdicated in 305, however, he compelled Maximian to do the same. Maximian retired to private life in Lucania, southern Italy, but returned to Rome in 306 to assist his son, the Roman emperor Marcus Maxentius (250–312). Two years later, however, he was driven from Italy by Maxentius, who wished to rule alone. He sought refuge in Gaul with his son-in-law, Emperor Constantine I. Maximian conspired to seize control of the government, but was forced by Constantine to commit suicide.

MAXIMILIAN (1832–67), archduke of Austria and emperor of Mexico, younger brother of Francis Joseph I, emperor of Austria. He became an admiral of the Austrian navy and governor from 1857 to 1859 of the Lombardo-Venetian territory. In 1863 the French emperor Napoleon III persuaded Maximilian to accept the crown of Mexico. Believing that they had the support of the people, he and his wife, Carlotta (1840–1927), went to Mexico in 1864. Backed by French troops, they were installed as the country's rulers over the opposition of the republicans. After 1865, the U.S., which objected to France's intervention but had been distracted by its own civil war, began pressuring the French to pull out. When they did withdraw in 1867, Maximilian refused to go with them and republican forces under Benito Juárez regained control of Mexico. Captured by the republicans at Querétaro, Maximilian was tried by court-martial and shot in June 1867.

MAXIMILIAN I (1459–1519), German king (1486–1519) and Holy Roman emperor (1493–1519), who established the Habsburg dynasty as an international European power.

Maximilian, the eldest son of Holy Roman Emperor Frederick III, was born in Wiener Neustadt, Austria, on March 22, 1459. In 1477 he married Mary (1457–82), daughter of Charles the Bold, duke of Burgundy, but his right to the Burgundian realm—which included the present Benelux countries and considerable portions of what is now northern and eastern France—was challenged by the French king, Louis XI. Maximilian successfully defended his wife's inheritance in a war with France that lasted until 1493, and he subdued the rebellious cities of the Netherlands. In 1490 he recovered Austria, which had been occupied by Matthias Corvinus, king of Hungary, and by the Treaty of Pressburg (1491) secured the right of succession to the thrones of Hungary and Bohemia, which were held by the Habsburg family for the next four centuries. Succeeding his father as king (1486) and emperor (1493), he embarked on a war to prevent France from acquiring territory in Italy in 1495. In 1496 he arranged the marriage of his son Philip to Joanna the Mad (1479–1555), heiress to the thrones of Castile and Aragón, thus laying the basis for two centuries of Habsburg rule in Spain. Maximilian made peace with Louis XII of France in 1504, and four years later joined Louis in the League of Cambrai against Venice. In 1511, however, he again opposed France in an alliance (the Holy League) with England, Spain, and the pope, and he was largely responsible for the imperial and English victory over the French in the Battle of the Spurs (1513). Maximilian was a patron of the arts; his writings include two autobiographical poems. He died at Wels, Austria, on Jan. 12, 1519.

MAXIMINUS, Gaius Galerius Valerius (d. 313), Roman emperor (308–13), a nephew of Emperor Galerius (242?–311). Maximinus was defeated by Emperor Licinius (270?–325), with whom he had ruled the eastern half of the Roman Empire, and died soon after. He is said to have been a bitter persecutor of the Christians.

MAXIMINUS, Gaius Julius Verus (173–238), Roman emperor (235–38), noted for his cruelty and rapacity. He was born of rustic parents in Thrace, on the western shore of the Black Sea, and rose to the command of the Roman army under the emperor Alexander Severus (208–35). During a campaign against the Germans, Maximinus fomented a conspiracy in which Alexander was slain. Maximinus was then proclaimed emperor. He and his son were killed by their own soldiers near Aquileia, Italy.

MAXWELL, James Clerk (1831–79), British physicist, whose contributions to the mathematical analysis of electromagnetic radiation (q.v.) placed him among the great scientists of the 19th and 20th centuries.

Maxwell was born in Edinburgh, on June 13, 1831, and was educated at the universities of Edinburgh and Cambridge. He was professor of physics at the University of Aberdeen from 1856 to 1860. In 1871 he became the first professor of experimental physics at Cambridge, where he supervised the construction of the Cavendish laboratory. His experimental and mathematical studies of kinetics were of fundamental importance in the development of the kinetic theory of gases (q.v.). He also investigated color perception and color blindness and dynamics. Continuing the work of the British scientist Michael Faraday on the electromagnetic field, Maxwell concluded that light is an electromagnetic phenomenon. His work paved the way for the investigations of the German physicist Heinrich Rudolf Hertz, who experimentally corroborated Maxwell's theories. One predictable consequence of Maxwell's theory was the numerical equality of the velocity of light in cgs units (see CGS SYSTEM) and the ratio of electromagnetic to electrostatic units; this equality was later confirmed by experiment. The unit of magnetic flux, the maxwell, was named in his honor. His greatest work is *Treatise on Electricity and Magnetism* (1873), in which he first published his elegant set of four differential equations describing the space-time development of electromagnetic fields. Other works include *Theory of Heat* (1877) and *Matter and Motion* (1876). Maxwell died at Cambridge on Nov. 5, 1879.

MAY, fifth month of the year, containing 31 days. It was the third month of the old Roman calendar. Since ancient times May 1 has been the occasion for various celebrations. In the U.S., May Day, Memorial Day, and Mother's Day are celebrated in May. In the northern hemisphere, May is the last month of the season of spring.

MAY, CAPE. See CAPE MAY.

MAYA, group of related American Indian tribes of nations of the Mayan linguistic stock, living in Mexico, in the states of Veracruz, Yucatán, Campeche, Tabasco, and Chiapas, and also in the greater part of Guatemala and in parts of Belize and Honduras. The best-known tribe, the Maya proper, after whom the entire group is named, occupies the Yucatán Peninsula. Among the other important tribes are the Huastec of northern Veracruz; the Tzental of Tabasco and Chiapas; the Chol of Chiapas; the Quiché (q.v.); Cakchiquel, Pokonchi, and Pokomam of the Guatemalan highlands; and the Chorti of eastern Guatemala and western Honduras. With the exception of the Huastec, these tribes occupy contiguous territory. They were all part of a common civilization, which in many respects achieved the highest development among the original inhabitants of the western hemisphere.

The Mayan peoples are short, dark, broad-headed, and muscular. Agriculture formed the basis of their economy in pre-Columbian times, maize being the principal crop. Cotton, beans, squash, manioc (see CASSAVA), and cacao were also grown. The techniques of spinning, dyeing, and weaving cotton were highly perfected. The Maya domesticated the dog and the turkey but had no draft animals or wheeled vehicles. They produced fine pottery, unequaled in the New World outside of Peru. Cacao beans and copper bells were used as units of exchange. Copper was also used for ornamental purposes, as were gold, silver, jade, shell, and colorful plumage. Metal tools, however, were unknown. The tribes were ruled by hereditary chiefs, descended in the male line, who delegated authority over village communities to local chieftains. Land, held in common by each village, was parceled out by these chieftains to the separate families. See AMERICAN INDIANS.

Architecture. Mayan culture produced a remarkable architecture, of which great ruins remain at a large number of places, including Palenque, Uxmal, Mayapan, Copán, Tikal, Uaxactún, and Chichén Itzá. These sites were vast centers for religious ceremonies. The usual plan consisted of a number of pyramidal mounds, often surmounted by temples or other buildings, grouped around open plazas. The pyramids, built in successive steps, were faced with cut stone blocks and generally had a steep stairway built into one or more of their sides. The substructure of the pyramids was usually made of earth and rubble, but sometimes mortared blocks of stone were used. The commonest type of construction consisted of a core of rubble or broken limestone mixed with mortar, and then faced with finished stones or stucco. Stone walls were also frequently laid without mortar. Wood was used for door lintels and for sculpture. The arch was not known, but its effect was approximated in roofing buildings by making the upper layers of stone of two parallel walls approach each other in successive projections until they met overhead. This system, requiring very heavy walls, produced narrow interiors. Windows were rare and were small and narrow. Interiors and exteriors were painted in bright colors. Exteriors received special attention and were lavishly decorated with painted sculpture, carved lintels, stucco moldings, and stone mosaics. The decorations were arranged in wide friezes contrasting with bands of plain masonry. Commoners' dwellings probably resembled the adobe and palm-thatched huts seen today among Mayan descendants.

Writings. The Mayan peoples developed a method of hieroglyphic notation and recorded

Mayan ruins in Palenque, an ancient city in Chiapas, southern Mexico. The structures still standing are distinguished by the elegance and variety of their architecture.
Marion and Tony Morrison

mythology, history, and rituals in inscriptions carved and painted on stelae (stone slabs or pillars); on lintels and stairways; and on other monumental remains (see HIEROGLYPHS). Records were also painted in hieroglyphs and preserved in books of folded sheets of paper made from the fibers of the maguey plant. Four examples of these codices have been preserved: the Codex Dresdensis, now in Dresden; the Perez Codex, now in Paris; and the Codex Tro and the Codex Cortesianus, both now in Madrid. The Codex Tro and Codex Cortesianus comprise parts of a single original document and are commonly known under the joint name Codex Tro-Cortesianus. These books were used as divinatory almanacs containing topics such as agriculture, weather, disease, hunting, and astronomy. Two other systems of writing, logographic and phonetic syllabic, were developed in the Mayan Classic period.

Calendar and Religion. Chronology among the Maya was determined by an elaborate calendar system. The year began when the sun crossed the zenith on July 16 and consisted of 365 days; 364 of the days were divided into 28 weeks of 13 days each, the new year beginning on the 365th day. In addition, 360 days of the year were divided into 18 months of 20 days each. The series of weeks and the series of months both ran consecutively and independently of each other; however, once every 260 days, that is, the multiple of 13 and 20, the week and the month began on the same day. The Mayan calendar, although highly complex, was the most accurate known until the introduction of the Gregorian calendar. See CALENDAR.

The Mayan religion centered about the worship of a large number of nature gods. Chac, a god of rain, was especially important. Among the supreme deities were Kukulcan, a creator god closely related to the Toltec and Aztec Quetzalcoatl (q.v.), and Itzamna, a sky god. An important Mayan trait was their complete trust in the gods' control of certain units of time and of all peoples' activities during those periods.

Linguistic Stock. Maya, called also Yucatec, the language of the Maya proper, is spoken by about 350,000 people in Yucatán, Guatemala, and British Honduras. The other languages of the Mayan stock include the language of the Huastec and several groups of closely affiliated languages, including those of the Chañabal, Chol, Chontal, Chorti, Chuj, Jacaltec, Motozintlec, Tzental, and Tzotzil; those of the Kekchi, Pokomam, and Pokonchi; those of the Cakchiquel, Quiché, Tzutuhil, and Uspantec; and those of the Aguacatec, Ixil, and Mam. See AMERICAN INDIAN LANGUAGES.

History. The origins of Mayan civilization are conjectural, depending on conflicting interpretations of archaeological evidence. The Formative period began at least as early as 1500 BC. During the Classic period, from about AD 300 to 900, a more or less uniform civilization was diffused throughout the Mayan territories. Great ceremonial centers such as Palenque (q.v.), Tikal, and Copán were built. About 900, however, the Mayan centers were mysteriously abandoned. Some Maya migrated into Yucatán.

During the Post-Classic period, from 900 to the arrival of the Spanish in the 16th century, Mayan civilization centered in Yucatán. A Toltec migration or invasion from the valley of Mexico strongly influenced its art styles. Chichén Itzá and Mayapán were prominent cities. For a while the league of Mayapán maintained the peace, but after a period of civil war and revolution, the cities were abandoned. The Spanish easily overcame the major Mayan groups, although the Mexican government did not subdue the last independent communities until 1901. In the late 20th century the Maya made up the bulk of the peasant population in their former lands. M.H.R.

For further information on this topic, see the Bibliography in volume 28, sections 645, 1120.

MAYAGÜEZ, city, in Mayagüez Municipality, W Puerto Rico, a major seaport on Mona Passage. Its industries include tuna processing and the manufacture of pharmaceuticals and clothing. In the city are the University of Puerto Rico, Mayagüez (1911), a zoo, several historic buildings, and an agricultural research center with a large collection of tropical plants. The community, founded in 1760 and made a city in 1877, was badly damaged by an earthquake in 1918. Pop. (1980) 82,968; (1990) 83,010.

MAYAKOVSKY, Vladimir Vladimirovich (1893–1930), Russian poet and propagandist. His early political activity during the czarist period led to his imprisonment; he then began writing poetry. Mayakovsky became a leading spokesperson for the Russian Revolution. He employed techniques geared to mass appeal, including the use of vernacular, even vulgar, language and new poetic forms. Poems such as "Oda revolutsi" (Ode to Revolution, 1918) were as popular as his passionate and lyrical love poems, such as "Lyublyu" (I Love, 1922). During the 1920s Mayakovsky provided propaganda for the Soviet government in a variety of forms such as poems, posters, plays, screenplays, and satiric travel sketches. In his play *The Bedbug* (1929; trans. 1960), he satirized the philistinism of the times. Disappointed in love and disillusioned with life in the Soviet Union, Mayakovsky took his own life in 1930.

MAYAPPLE, common name for the plant genus *Podophyllum,* of the family Berberidaceae (*see* BARBERRY). American mayapple or American mandrake, *P. peltatum,* is a perennial herb of roadsides and woods in eastern North America. The herbaceous aboveground parts of the plant arise from a thick, underground rootstock that persists from year to year. It is unusual in aspect, with one or two large, coarse, palmately lobed leaves spread in umbrella fashion about 60 cm (about 24 in) above the ground. Some mayapple plants bear only one leaf; these plants usually do not flower. Other mayapples bear two leaves, and the flower appears in the junction between the leaves. It is nodding, white or greenish white, with six sepals, six or nine petals, and a single central pistil. The fruit is an ovoid, yellow-blotched, fleshy "apple" that has a sweet, slightly acid flavor.

Mayapple was used by the American Indians in treating various disorders. The plant, especially the roots, contains active toxic principles. It causes abnormalities in dividing plant and animal cells and has been used both by horticulturists for inducing desirable plant mutations and by medical researchers in attempting to control various types of cancer. Overdoses of the plant cause severe purging, digestive upset, and vomiting.

American mayapple, Podophyllum peltatum, *with fruit inset.*

MAY DAY, name popularly given to the first day of May, which for centuries has been celebrated among the Latin and Germanic peoples. May Day festivals probably stem from the rites practiced in honor of Flora, the Roman goddess of spring. May Day is currently celebrated as a festival for children marking the reappearance of flowers during the spring. It is traditionally greeted with joyous dancing around a garlanded pole, called a maypole, from which hang streamers held by the dancers. May Day is also celebrated in many European countries as a labor holiday, comparable to Labor Day in the U.S. It was especially significant in the Soviet Union and other Communist countries. Observance of the holiday by some workers in Europe and the U.S. probably dates from the celebration of May Day by the first congress (1889) of the Second International, an assembly of socialist and labor parties.

MAYER, Julius Robert von (1814–78), German physician and physicist, known for his pioneering work in the establishment of the mechanical equivalent of heat (q.v.). Mayer was born in Heilbronn and studied medicine at the University of Tübingen. In 1842 the scientist published

Pilgrims signing the Mayflower Compact aboard the Mayflower, Nov. 21, 1620.   The Granger Collection

a paper in the journal *Annales de Chemie,* in which he gave a value for the mechanical equivalent of heat. His figure was based on the rise of temperature in paper pulp that was stirred by a horse-powered mechanism. Mayer was also the first to state the principle of conservation of energy, most notably for biological phenomena as well as for physical systems (*see* CONSERVATION LAWS).

MAYER, Louis B(urt) (1885–1957), American motion picture executive, for 25 years the most powerful producer in Hollywood. He was born in Minsk (now in Belarus), and three years later his parents moved with him to Canada. In 1907 Mayer moved to the U.S. and became a naturalized citizen in 1912. He was a film distributor and theater manager in New England. In 1916 he moved to Los Angeles and formed his own producing company, which in 1924 after a series of mergers became known as Metro-Goldwyn-Mayer (MGM). As production chief of MGM from 1924 to 1951, he discovered many of the screen's greatest stars, producers, writers, and directors. Among his outstanding successes were *The Big Parade* (1925), *Ben Hur* (1926), *Grand Hotel* (1932), *Dinner at Eight* (1933), and the Andy Hardy series. The last-named are prototypical of Mayer's favorite projects: They were family oriented, uplifting, patriotic, and bittersweet.

MAYER, Maria Goeppert. *See* GOEPPERT-MAYER, MARIA.

MAYFLOWER, vessel in which the Pilgrims crossed the Atlantic Ocean to the New World in 1620. As originally conceived, the expedition included another vessel, the *Speedwell,* but the latter proved unseaworthy. The *Mayflower,* about 180 gross tons and carrying 101 passengers, finally got under way from Plymouth, England, on Sept. 16, 1620. The ship was headed for Virginia, where the colonists had been authorized to settle. As a result of stormy weather and navigational errors, the vessel failed to make good its course, and on November 21 the *Mayflower* rounded the end of Cape Cod and dropped anchor off the site of present-day Provincetown, Mass.

The *Mayflower* remained anchored for the next few weeks while a party from the ship explored Cape Cod and its environs in search of a satisfactory site for the colony. Peregrine White, the first European child born in New England, was delivered on the *Mayflower* in the interim. On December 21, an area having been selected, the Pilgrims disembarked from the *Mayflower* near the head of Cape Cod and founded Plymouth, the first permanent settlement in New England.

The Pilgrims were probably more than 800 km (500 mi) northeast of their intended destination in Virginia. The patent for their settlement in the New World, issued by the London Co., was no longer binding, and some among the passengers desired total independence from their shipmates. To prevent this, 41 of the adult male passengers, including John Alden, William Bradford, William Brewster, John Carver, Myles Standish, and Edward Winslow, gathered in the cabin of the *May-*

flower and formulated and signed the Mayflower Compact; all adult males were required to sign. The Mayflower Compact was the first constitution written in America. It consolidated the passengers into a "civil body politic," which had the power to frame and enact laws appropriate to the general good of the planned settlement. All colonists were bound to obey the ordinances so enacted. This compact established rule of the majority, which remained a primary principle of government in Plymouth Colony until its absorption by the Massachusetts Bay Colony in 1691.

See also PLYMOUTH COLONY.

MAYFLY, common name for delicate insects that often emerge in great numbers from lakes, streams, and rivers. The approximately 1500 species, constituting the order Ephemeroptera, range in length from 1 to 3 cm (0.4 to 1.2 in) and have two or three long tail filaments; transparent, upright forewings; short antennae; and bulging, light-sensitive eyes. Both adults and larvae are important food of trout; because of this, artificial lures have been patterned after them for over 400 years.

Mayflies usually spend one to three years as underwater nymphs, breathing by means of gills and feeding on microscopic plant life. After 10 to 20 molts they emerge from their nymphal skins on the water surface and fly to nearby plants where they go through a last molt, shedding their downy, waterproof skins. (Mayflies are the only insects to molt in a winged stage.) Now fully adult, they cannot feed but instead form male and female swarms that merge over water. After mating, the males die; the females live a few more hours, depositing the eggs in water and thus starting the next generation of nymphs.

Mayflies are among the oldest insect groups and have been found as fossils dating from about 300 million years ago. At lake and river resorts, expiring mayflies often accumulate in "snowfalls" under outdoor lighting.

MAYHEM, in criminal law, act of mutilating a person other than in self-defense by depriving the person of the use of any limbs or organs essential for self-defense in a physical encounter. Under the codes of the states of the U.S., mayhem includes such acts as the breaking of an arm or leg, the putting out of an eye, or the slitting of a nose, lip, or ear; in some jurisdictions any bodily disfigurement constitutes mayhem. According to the jurisdiction and the extent of the injury, mayhem is a misdemeanor or a felony, with the former being punishable by fine and the latter by imprisonment. An individual who commits mayhem may also be sued for damages in a civil action.

MAYO, family of American physicians, whose accomplishments in surgery resulted in the renowned Mayo Clinic in Rochester, Minn.

William Worrall Mayo (1819–1911) moved from England to the U.S. in 1845, earned a medical degree from the University of Missouri in 1854, and thereafter gained repute as a pioneer doctor on what was then the American frontier. He specialized in gynecological surgery at a time when surgery and hospitals were barely coming into use in large cities. In 1889 he headed the tiny St. Mary's Hospital in Rochester; he was joined there by his two sons, who had also become physicians.

William James Mayo (1861–1939), the elder son, received his medical degree from the University of Michigan Medical School, and the younger, **Charles Horace Mayo** (1865–1939), from the Chicago Medical College. After joining their father, they traveled to distant cities to learn new surgical techniques then being devised. Treating appendicitis, gallstones, stomach ulcers, and other often fatal ailments of that time, they became famous for their extraordinary surgical skills. By 1915, their mounting practice caused them to greatly enlarge their staff and facilities. Their newly built clinic soon became the model for many private clinics throughout the U.S.

The Mayo Clinic now has more than 500 physicians and surgeons. Also associated with the clinic is the Mayo Graduate School of Medicine of the University of Minnesota.

MAYO, county, W Republic of Ireland, in Connaught Province, bounded on the N and W by the Atlantic Ocean, on the E by county Sligo and county Roscommon, and on the S by county Galway. Fishing and farming are the leading industries. The chief communities are Castlebar, the county town, Westport, Ballina, and Ballinrobe. Area, 5398 sq km (2084 sq mi); pop. (1991) 110,713.

MAYOR. See MUNICIPAL GOVERNMENT.

MAYOTTE. See COMOROS.

MAYS, Willie Howard, Jr. (1931–   ), American baseball player, born in Fairfield, Ala. Considered by many the most exciting player in modern baseball, Mays was a great favorite with the fans. He became the first player in the National League to hit more than 600 home runs. In 1964 he also became the first black player to be captain of a major league baseball team. He earned fame as a right-handed hitter, possessing a distinctive batting style and great power; he is perhaps equally well known for his defensive play at first base and center field. Mays was brought up to the major leagues in 1951 to play for the Giants, then in New York City. His career was inter-

Willie Mays demonstrates his batting style during a workout with the Mets at Shea Stadium, New York City.
Wide World Photos

rupted in 1952 and 1953 while he served in the U.S. Army. He was twice named the league's most valuable player, in 1954 and 1965. During the 1972 season he was traded to the New York Mets, also of the National League. He retired at the end of the 1973 season, with a lifetime batting average of .302 and a total of 660 home runs. In 1979 Mays was elected to the Baseball Hall of Fame, getting more votes than any other player up to that time.

MA YÜAN (active c. 1190–c. 1225), Chinese landscape painter, whose paintings, along with those of Hsia Kuei, represent the culmination of the Southern Sung style; followers of the two artists were termed the Ma-Hsia school. Born into a famous family of painters, Ma became a leader of the imperial painting academy at Hangzhou (Hangchow). His work represented a new style in painting—lyrical, evocative, restrained—in contrast to the more grandiose style of earlier centuries.

The most striking characteristic of Ma's monochromatic ink paintings is their asymmetrical composition: The principal forms of the picture—trees, rocks, and human figures—are grouped in a lower corner. He achieved a balanced asymmetry, in which the blank areas of his paintings focus attention on the subject and at the same time suggest a limitless expanse of space. To link the two sections of the picture, he often used the device of a tree branch painted diagonally into or across the empty space. Ma's ink technique in these works is faultless, equally distinguished for the evenness and control of the broad washes and the precision and clarity of the sharp "ax stroke" brushwork. His highly popular works were often copied, even forged, which today makes positive authentication difficult; one painting widely accepted as his is *Bare Willows and Distant Mountains* (Museum of Fine Arts, Boston). Ma was a dominant influence on later Chinese painting and on Japanese art.

MAYWOOD, village, Cook Co., NE Illinois, on the Des Plaines R.; inc. 1881. It is a residential center, located W of Chicago. Soft drinks and cans are produced here. The community was founded in 1869 by settlers from Vermont, one of whom named the village for his daughter May. Pop. (1980) 27,998; (1990) 27,139.

MAZARIN, Jules (1602–61), French statesman and cardinal, who controlled the French government during the minority of Louis XIV and helped make France the predominant power in Europe.

Originally named Giulio Mazarini, he was born on July 14, 1602, in Pescina, Italy, and became a protégé of the powerful Colonna family. Educated by the Jesuits, he rose to prominence in the Vatican diplomatic corps and was named papal envoy to France in 1634. There he came under the influence of Cardinal Richelieu, whom he secretly aided against the Spanish and Austrian Habsburgs in the Thirty Years' War; in 1639 he became a naturalized French subject. Two years later King Louis XIII rewarded Mazarin's service to France by having the pope make him a cardinal. On the death of Louis XIII (1643), his widow, Anne of Austria, chose Mazarin as her chief minister and tutor of the five-year-old Louis XIV. Mazarin continued Richelieu's absolutist policies. Abroad, he brought the Thirty Years' War to a successful conclusion, weakening the Habsburg dynasty and gaining Alsace for France. At home, however, he was insensitive to popular discontent over food shortages and high taxes caused by the war. His clumsy arrest of a magistrate in 1648 sparked a Parisian revolt and triggered the civil wars known as the Fronde. Hatred of Mazarin leagued the people of Paris and the nobility in a five-year struggle against royal absolutism. The Fronde drove Anne, Louis, and Mazarin out of Paris; eventually Anne and Louis returned, but Mazarin fled to Germany, directing the suppression of the rebels from there. Returning to Paris in 1653, he devoted himself to Louis XIV, instructing him in diplomacy, war, and kingship. An avid art collector and inveterate gambler, Mazarin amassed a huge fortune. He introduced Italian opera at court, founded the College of Four Nations (now the Institut de France), and opened his library to the public. His crowning achievement was the Treaty of the Pyrenees of 1659, which ended the war with Spain, won France the provinces of Artois and Roussillon, and gave Louis XIV a Spanish bride, thereby providing France with a claim on Spain's empire. Mazarin died on March 9, 1661, at Vincennes, bequeathing to Louis XIV a clear understanding of absolutist rule, a corps of skilled advisers, notably Jean Baptiste Colbert, and the outlines of a policy aimed at European hegemony.　　　P.F.R.

MAZAR-I-SHARIF, city, N Afghanistan, capital of Balkh Province, near Balkh (Wazirabad), in an agricultural region, known for its horses and Karakul sheep. Center of the Karakul fur trade, it also has cotton and silk industries. The 15th-century mosque in the city, said to contain the tomb of the caliph Ali, the son-in-law of Muhammad, makes the city a place of pilgrimage. Pop. (1988 est.) 130,600.

MAZATENANGO, city, SW Guatemala, capital of Suchitepéquez Department, on the Sis R., in the foothills of the central highlands overlooking the Pacific coast lowlands. It is one of the nation's principal commercial and manufacturing centers. Products include textiles, processed food, and footwear. The Pacific Coast Highway passes through the city. Pop. (1993 est.) 41,400.

MAZATLÁN, city, W Mexico, in Sinaloa State, on the Vigia Peninsula, overlooking Olas Atlas Bay, an arm of the Pacific Ocean. A major tourist resort, Mazatlán lies on the Pacific Railway and the W coast part of the Pan-American Highway, just S of the tropic of Cancer and near the entrance to the Gulf of California. Mazatlán is the largest Pacific port of Mexico. Minerals, fibers, timber, tobacco, hides, fish, fruits, and vegetables are exported, and the surrounding area grows tobacco, cotton, sugarcane, fruit, and vegetables. Industries include cotton ginning, sugar refining, tanning, textile milling, brewing, fish and seafood freezing, tobacco processing, and tequila distilling; cigarettes, machine and foundry products, cement, and straw handicrafts are manufactured. Hunting in the nearby mountains, fishing offshore, and bathing are the principal attractions of the area, and outstanding annual events are the pre-Lenten carnival and the international fishing tournament in the late fall. Picturesque islets in the bay, bird-filled mangrove swamps, an old Spanish fort, the city hall, an observatory, and one of the highest lighthouses in the world are also of interest. Founded in the early 19th century, the city quickly became industrially important. Pop. (1990) 314,249.

MAZURKA, traditional, highly improvisatory Polish dance for a circle of couples. It is danced with many figures and stamping, heel-clicking steps, to music in moderate $\frac{3}{4}$ time with a strongly accented beat. Originating among the Mazurs of central Poland in the 1500s, it spread through Europe in the early 1800s as a ballroom dance for one, four, or eight couples. Its offshoot was the varsovienne, a popular couple dance.

MAZZINI, Giuseppe (1805–72), Italian revolutionary, political theorist, and advocate of Italian unification.

Mazzini was born in Genoa on June 22, 1805, the son of a doctor, and studied law at the University of Genoa. He bitterly resented the absorption of his native republic of Genoa into the kingdom of Sardinia-Piedmont in 1815. In 1827 he joined the revolutionary Carbonari (q.v.) society, but after his imprisonment at Savona (1830–31) he abandoned that organization as ineffective. Exiled, he founded the Young Italy (Giovine Italia) Society in Marseille, France, in July 1831. It established branches in many Italian cities. Mazzini argued that through coordinated uprisings, the people could drive the Italian princes from their thrones and oust the Austrians from dominance of the Italian Peninsula.

Failed Plots. When Mazzini's attempt in 1832 to stir up a republican mutiny in the Sardinian army failed, he was sentenced to death in absentia. Expelled from France, he moved to Switzerland, where he continued to plot against the Sardinian government; another conspiracy failed in 1834. Meanwhile, he was becoming the prophet of European nationalism and organizing a Young Europe network. In 1837 he took refuge in England.

The high point of Mazzini's career came during the revolutions of 1848–49, when he returned to Italy and was elected one of the leaders of the new Roman Republic. But when the republic fell (July 1849) to an invading French army, Mazzini once again had to flee. The rest of his life was an anticlimax. Efforts to spark republican uprisings in Mantua (1852) and Milan (1853) were unsuccessful, and the leadership of the Italian nationalist movement was taken over by such flexible advocates of a liberal monarchy as Premier Camillo di Cavour of Sardinia-Piedmont.

Last Years. Mazzini came back to Italy during the wars of 1859 and 1860 but took no pleasure in seeing the establishment in 1861 of a unified Italian kingdom rather than a republic. He was still plotting to gain Venice and Rome when he was jailed in Gaeta (August–October 1870) at the time King Victor Emmanuel II of Sardinia was seizing Rome. In failing health, Mazzini retired to Pisa, where he died on March 10, 1872.

Mazzini played an indispensable role in Italy's unification. His tireless campaign for a united republic forced more conservative groups to compete with him. His conception of popular nationalism had widespread appeal. The advent of the Italian republic in 1946 was in effect a belated recognition of Mazzini's ideas.   C.F.D.

MBABANE, town, administrative capital of Swaziland, in Hhohho District, located on a high plateau in the W part of the country, near the border with South Africa. Mbabane is the nation's largest community and its chief administrative, commercial, and transportation center. A railroad connects the town with nearby coal and iron-ore mines and with the Indian Ocean port of Maputo, in Mozambique.

Mbabane developed in the late 19th century near the residence of the Swazi king Mbandzeni (1857?–89). It grew as an administrative center while Swaziland was a British dependency (1903–68) and became the administrative center of the newly independent nation in 1968. Pop. (1986) 38,290.

MBALE, town, E Uganda, in Eastern Province, at the foot of Mt. Elgon. It is one of the nation's largest urban areas and the commercial center for a coffee-producing agricultural region. Mbale is linked by rail with Kampala (Uganda's capital) and Nairobi (in Kenya) and by highway with Kampala. Pop. (1980 prelim.) 28,039.

MBANDAKA, formerly COQUILHATVILLE, city, W Zaire, capital of Equateur Province, on the Congo R., at the mouth of the Ruki R. Fishing, boatbuilding, and the manufacture of pharmaceuticals are the chief industries of the city, and trade in copal (resin) is carried on. Mbandaka is the site of medical and business schools, and nearby to the E, at Eala, are extensive botanical gardens and laboratories. The city was named Equateur or Equateurville when founded in 1883 by the British explorer Henry M. Stanley; the name was changed by the Belgians to Coquilhatville. In 1966 the present name was adopted, honoring a prominent local leader. Pop. (1984) 125,263.

MBOYA, Tom, full name THOMAS JOSEPH MBOYA (1930–69), Kenyan trade unionist and statesman. Born on Lusinga Island, Mboya was a member of Kenya's second largest tribe, the Luo. He was trained as a sanitary inspector, entered politics as a union organizer, and was elected to the colony's legislative council in 1957. Secretary-general of the Kenya African National Union (1960–69), he was a close ally of President Jomo Kenyatta and held cabinet posts before and after independence in 1963. Mboya was the major spokesman for Luo interests in a Kikuyu-dominated government and one of Africa's most respected political figures. He was assassinated by a Kikuyu tribesman in 1969.

MBUJI-MAYI, formerly BAKWANGA, town, S central Zaire, capital of Kasai Oriental Region, on a headstream of the Kasai R. It is one of the nation's largest urban areas and the commercial center for a region in which most of the world's industrial diamonds are produced. The community was developed by Europeans as a diamond-mining center of the Belgian Congo after 1910. Called Bakwanga until 1966, it was from 1960 until then the capital of Kasai Sud (South Kasai) Province. Pop. (1984 prelim.) 423,363.

Mc. Names beginning Mc are entered as if spelled Mac.

MEAD, alcoholic beverage made by fermenting honey, known since ancient times. By the late medieval period, with the increasing availability of sugar, the production of mead had begun to drop, and it was largely replaced by other fermented drinks, especially beer.

MEAD, George Herbert (1863–1931), American pragmatist philosopher and social psychologist, born in South Hadley, Mass. Educated at Oberlin College, Harvard University, and in Europe, he taught at the University of Chicago from 1894 until his death.

Influenced by evolutionary theory and the social nature of experience and behavior, Mead emphasized the natural emergence of the self and mind within the social order. The self, he argued, emerges out of a social process in which the organism becomes self-conscious. This self-consciousness arises as a result of the organism's interaction with its environment, including communication with other organisms. The vocal gesture (language) is the mechanism through which this development occurs. Mind too is a social product. The mind, or intelligence, is an instrument developed by the individual to "make possible the rational solution of . . . problems." Mead emphasized the application of the scientific method in social action and reform.

During his lifetime, Mead published only articles. His books, published posthumously from manuscripts and students' notes, include *The Philosophy of the Present* (1932), *Mind, Self, and Society from the Standpoint of a Social Behaviorist* (1934), and *The Philosophy of the Act* (1938).
R.M.B.

MEAD, Margaret (1901–78), American anthropologist, widely known for her studies of primitive societies and her contributions to social anthropology.

Mead was born in Philadelphia on Dec. 16, 1901, and was educated at Barnard College and at Columbia University. In 1926 she became assis-

Margaret Mead UPI

tant curator of ethnology at the American Museum of Natural History in New York City, and she subsequently served as associate curator (1942–64) and as curator (1964–69). She was director of research in contemporary cultures at Columbia University from 1948 to 1950 and adjunct professor of anthropology there after 1954. In September 1969 she was appointed full professor and head of the social science department in the Liberal Arts College of Fordham University, at the Lincoln Center campus, in New York City. She also served on various government and international commissions and was a speaker on controversial modern social issues.

Participating in several field expeditions, Mead conducted notable research in New Guinea, Samoa, and Bali. Much of her work was devoted to a study of patterns of child rearing in various cultures. She also analyzed problems in contemporary American society, particularly those affecting young people. Her interests included child care, adolescence, sexual behavior, and American character and culture. Mead died in New York City on Nov. 15, 1978. Her writings include *Coming of Age in Samoa* (1928), *Growing Up in New Guinea* (1930), *Sex and Temperament in Three Primitive Societies* (1935), *Male and Female* (1949), *Soviet Attitudes Toward Authority* (1951), *New Lives for Old* (1956), *Culture and Commitment: A Study of the Generation Gap* (1970), and her memoirs, *Blackberry Winter* (1972).

For further information on this person, see the section Biographies in the Bibliography in volume 28.

MEADE, George Gordon (1815–72), American army officer, born in Cádiz, Spain, and educated at the U.S. Military Academy. He joined the Union forces at the outbreak of the American Civil War, participating in the defense of Washington, D.C., in 1861. As a major general of volunteers he fought at the Battle of Chancellorsville in 1863 and shortly thereafter was appointed commander of the Army of the Potomac. In July 1863, in the battle that is considered the turning point of the war, he defeated the Confederate forces at Gettysburg, Pa. He continued as commander of the Army of the Potomac, working closely with Gen. Ulysses S. Grant, until the end of the war. Promoted to major general in the regular army in 1864, Meade commanded various military departments in the U.S. until his death.

MEADOWLARK, common name for any of seven American bird species of the genus *Sturnella* of the blackbird (q.v.) family. The two North American species, the eastern (*S. magna*) and western (*S. neglecta*) meadowlarks, look very much alike but have different voices. Both are about 23 cm (about 9 in) long. They are brown streaked with black and buff above and bright yellow below, with a black crescent on the chest. They inhabit meadows and fields across the U.S., their ranges overlapping in the middle west. They build domed nests hidden in the grass, where the females lay four to six white eggs speckled with reddish brown. The range of the eastern meadowlark extends south to northern South America, where it meets the northernmost of five South American species, all characterized by having red rather than yellow breasts.

MEADOW MOUSE. See VOLE.

MEADOW SAFFRON. See AUTUMN CROCUS.

MEALWORM, common name for the yellowish larva of an insect pest, *Tenebrio molitor*, of the family Tenebrionidae, order Coleoptera (see BEETLE). The black adult mealworm is about 1.9 cm (about 0.7 in) long, the larva about 1.2 cm (about 0.5 in). Widely distributed by commerce, mealworms infest cereals and flour in mills and granaries. The larvae are used as fish bait and as food for such pets as birds and fish.

Eastern meadowlark, Sturnella magna
© 1988 John Shaw–Bruce Coleman, Inc.

MEALYBUG, common name for any scale insect in the family Pseudococcidae, suborder Homoptera (q.v.), found in moist, warm climates. Mealybugs are so called because the adults secrete a white, powdery wax that conceals their bodies. They are common pests of greenhouses and house plants and of subtropical trees. The wingless females feed on plant juices; the winged males are short-lived and do not feed. See SCALE INSECT.

MEAN. See STATISTICS.

MEANY, George (1894–1980), American labor leader, born in New York City. At the age of 16 he became an apprentice plumber. From 1922 to 1934 he was business representative of the Plumbers Union, Local 463, in New York City. He served as president of the New York State Federation of Labor from 1934 to 1939, when he became secretary-treasurer of the American Federation of Labor (AFL). During World War II he was a member of the National War Labor Board. In 1952, after the death of William Green, Meany became president of the AFL.

In 1955, and every two years thereafter until his retirement at the end of 1979, Meany was elected president of the American Federation of Labor-Congress of Industrial Organizations (q.v.; AFL-CIO). In that post he exerted considerable influence on the course taken by organized labor and the role it played in the political and legislative processes of the U.S. Actively anti-Communist, he supported U.S. involvement in the conflict in Southeast Asia. He urged labor leaders to remain neutral in the 1972 presidential election, although he had usually supported candidates of the Democratic party. In 1973, however, he opposed the administration's wage and economic policies and called for the impeachment of President Richard M. Nixon in view of published findings in the Watergate case. He served as a delegate to the UN in 1957 and 1959.

For further information on this person, see the section Biographies in the Bibliography in volume 28.

MEASLES, also rubeola, acute, highly contagious, fever-producing disease caused by a filterable virus (q.v.), different from the virus that causes the less serious disease German measles (q.v.), or rubella. Measles is characterized by small red dots appearing on the surface of the skin, irritation of the eyes (especially on exposure to light), coughing, and a runny nose. About 12 days after first exposure, the fever, sneezing, and runny nose appear. Coughing and swelling of the neck glands often follow. Four days later, red spots appear on the face or neck and then on the trunk and limbs. In 2 or 3 days the rash subsides and the fever falls; some peeling of the involved skin areas may take place. Infection of the middle ear may also occur.

Measles was formerly one of the most common childhood diseases. Since the development of an effective vaccine in 1963, it has become much less frequent. By 1988, annual measles cases in the U.S. had been reduced to fewer than 3500, compared with about 500,000 per year in the early 1960s. However, the number of new cases jumped to more than 18,000 in 1989 and to nearly 28,000 in 1990. Most of these cases occurred among inner-city preschool children and recent immigrants, but adolescents and young adults, who may have lost immunity (*see* IMMUNIZATION) from their childhood vaccinations, also experienced an increase. In 1991, the number of new cases dropped to fewer than 10,000. The reasons for this resurgence and subsequent decline are not clearly understood. In other parts of the world measles is still a common childhood disease. In the U.S., measles is rarely fatal; should the virus spread to the brain, however, it can cause death or brain damage (*see* ENCEPHALITIS).

No specific treatment for measles exists. Patients are kept isolated from other susceptible individuals, usually resting in bed, and are treated with aspirin, cough syrup, and skin lotions to lessen fever, coughing, and itching. The disease usually confers immunity after one attack, and an immune pregnant woman passes the antibody in the globulin fraction of the blood serum, through the placenta, to her fetus.

For further information on this topic, see the Bibliography in volume 28, sections 448, 487, 505, 508.

MEASURES. See WEIGHTS AND MEASURES.

MEAT, term applied to the edible portions of domestic mammals such as cattle, calves, sheep, lambs, and swine. The meat of cattle is known as beef; calves, as veal; sheep, as mutton; lambs, as lamb; and swine, as pork. The term *meat* can be applied to the edible portions of poultry and wild birds and mammals (game) and to the portions of other animals such as crustaceans and reptiles that are eaten by humans. It is not known when the human species began to eat meat; other primates are vegetarian with only occasional episodes of opportunistic meat consumption.

Meat consists of skeletal muscle, with varying amounts of fat and connective tissue, but internal organs are also used. Known as variety meats, these include the liver, kidneys, testicles, thymus gland (sweetbreads), brain, heart, and stomach.

Meat is a nutritious food, containing quantities of essential amino acids in the form of protein. Meat also contains B group vitamins (especially niacin and riboflavin), iron, phosphorus, ash, and calcium. Certain meats, especially liver, contain vitamins A and D. See NUTRITION, HUMAN.

A trainee in the meat-cutting trade is given instruction on methods of cutting a carcass. UPI

The methods of cutting carcasses of meat animals into parts, and the names given to the different cuts, vary locally. Shoulder cuts of beef are frequently termed chuck; rib cuts are known as chops or rib steaks; the part of the loin nearest the ribs is called short steak; and the part nearest the hip is known as sirloin. Other cuts include T-bone and porterhouse (intermediate cuts) and flank, rump, and shank. Terminology for cuts of veal, mutton, and lamb is roughly similar to that used for beef. Cured pork cuts are given a special terminology: Ham is meat from the thigh and hip; a picnic ham is meat from the shoulder; and bacon is side meat (belly).

Fresh meat requires proper refrigeration to prevent deterioration. Meat is sometimes canned; more often it is cured and smoked for preservation. For meat packing and processing, see MEAT-PACKING INDUSTRY.

Various meat imitations are available that are made of proteins derived from soybeans, wheat, yeast, and other plants. The proteins are treated and extruded to form fibers that are then processed, flavored, and colored—with fats, nutrients, binders, and other substances added—to simulate different kinds of meat.

MEAT FLY. See FLESH FLY.

MEATH, county, E Republic of Ireland, in Leinster Province, on the Irish Sea. Farming and cattle raising are the chief industries; the most fertile areas are near the Boyne and Blackwater rivers. In ancient times Meath was one of the provinces of Ireland; it was organized as a county in the 17th century. The county town is Navan (An Uaimh). Area, 2339 sq km (903 sq mi); pop. (1991) 105,370.

MEAT-PACKING INDUSTRY, large industry involving the slaughtering, processing, and distribution of cattle, sheep, and hogs. It is one of the most important industries in the U.S. and has its primary concentration in the Middle West. The packing industry has tended to decentralize in recent years, and slaughtered livestock are now generally moved directly from farms, ranches, and feedlots to meat-packers. The cattle-slaughtering sector of the industry, in particular, has become concentrated in cattle-raising regions to the west—namely the western Corn Belt and the Great Plains, where beef is shipped to wholesalers and retailers primarily in the form of fresh primal cuts. Hog slaughtering is still carried on chiefly in large plants, where the hogs are processed into numerous cuts and products.

In accordance with the Humane Methods of Slaughter Act of 1978, all livestock are now made insensible before they are killed. For cattle and sheep, a captive bolt, a type of gun designed for stunning, is generally used. Hogs often are immobilized painlessly through gassing.

Many parts of the slaughtered animals are shipped for consumption as fresh meat; other parts, especially of the hog, are cured and smoked. The fats are converted into lard and commercial grease. Bones are converted into glue, fertilizer, animal feeds, and other usable products, including pharmaceuticals; hoofs and horns are used or sold for other purposes.

Refrigeration and Transportation. The meat of slaughtered livestock, after thorough chilling, is shipped in refrigerated motor carriers to cities. There the meat is delivered to wholesale distribution centers and grocery centers. Before cold storage of meat was introduced in the U.S., it was customary to ship the living animals to the eastern parts of the country.

Cattle Slaughtering. In recent years labor-saving devices have been widely adopted in the dressing and processing of cattle. A continuous rail system is generally used today, whereby cattle are chained by one leg and hoisted to a movable pulley on an overhead rail and are then slaughtered; from this position blood leaves the body so quickly that death occurs almost instantly, and for purposes of kosher ritual this method of slaughtering is defined as humane even without prior stunning. The carcasses then move slowly along a continuously moving rail to stations where each required process is completed, including skinning, disemboweling, and beheading. Before going into refrigeration, the carcasses are cut down the backbone and split into sides. Beef is shipped to wholesalers and retailers as wholesale cuts, such as chucks, rounds, and loins; in fast-distribution plants the carcass is reduced all the way down to retail consumer cuts. Sides and quarters of beef are still sold, but they constitute less than 5 percent of beef sales.

Hog Slaughtering. Traditionally, hog slaughtering has involved more complete processing at the packing plant than cattle slaughtering. The carcasses of slaughtered hogs also move on continuous rail or chain systems. Most often the hog carcass is first conveyed through scalding vats to dehairing machines. Hogs generally are not beheaded or dismembered in any way during the slaughtering and dressing process, which includes eviscerating, washing, and trimming. Later, however, the carcasses are usually carved up into such cuts as loins, legs, and picnic hams or shoulders. Certain cuts, including loins, are sold fresh, without processing, but most cuts go through one or more processing operations. Although some plants still soak particular cuts in barrels filled with brine, it has generally been necessary to shorten the curing process. To prepare hams, a curing solution is usually pumped internally. Hog bellies, which are used for bacon, are mechanically saturated with curing solution through hollow needles. Many cuts are thoroughly or lightly smoked at the packing plant. Nearly 70 percent of all hogs are slaughtered and fabricated into cuts at the packing plant and shipped to commercial processors who produce a complete line of sausage and cured products.

Legislation. Although inspection by the federal government of meat used in the packing industry was provided for in earlier acts of Congress (1890–91, 1895), comprehensive legislation was not introduced until 1906. By the act of 1906 all cattle, sheep, goats, and hogs became subject to antemortem and postmortem examination when the meat was to be used in interstate or foreign commerce; later the act was extended to include reindeer. By this legislation about 60 percent of the total meat supply of the U.S. was brought under inspection. The Packers and Stockyards Act of 1921 added further control, directed against trust activities. The Wholesome Meat Act of 1967 requires all meat-packers to meet federal inspection requirements, and agreements to that effect have been made between the various states and the federal government. W.F.W.; REV. BY M.F.M.

MECCA (Arab. *Makkah;* anc. *Macoraba*), city, W Saudi Arabia, capital of al-Hijaz (Hejaz) Province, near Jiddah. The birthplace of the Prophet Muhammad and the most sacred of the Muslim holy cities, Mecca is visited by great numbers of pilgrims annually. Its location on several trade routes has made the city commercially important since ancient times. Mecca was a religious center before the time of Muhammad, and several holy sites within the sacred precincts of the great mosque, called al-Haram, had religious significance in pre-Islamic times. The Kaaba (or Caaba), a windowless cube-shaped building in the courtyard of al-Haram, is believed to have been built by the Hebrew patriarch Abraham. In the SE corner of the Kaaba is the Black Stone, supposedly given to Abraham by the angel Gabriel. Also within the precincts of the mosque is the sacred well, called the Zamzam (Zemzem), which was reputedly used by Hagar, mother of Abraham's son Ishmael. The city is first mentioned by the Egyptian geographer Ptolemy, who in the 2d century AD called it Makoraba.

From the time of Muhammad, Mecca was besieged on various occasions. It was taken by the Egyptians in the 13th century. In the 16th century control passed to Turkey. From 1517 the sharifs, or descendants of Muhammad through Hasan (624–69), son of Muhammad's son-in-law Ali, governed Mecca for the Turks. The latter were driven from the city in 1916 by Grand Sharif Husein ibn Ali (1856–1931), later first king of al-Hijaz. In 1924 the city was occupied by Abdul Aziz ibn Saud, then sultan of Najd (Nejd), who made Mecca the religious capital of Saudi Arabia. Pop. (1980 est.) 550,000.

For further information on this topic, see the Bibliography in volume 28, section 131.

MECHANICAL DRAWING. See DRAFTING.

MECHANICAL ENGINEERING. See ENGINEERING.

MECHANICS, branch of physics (q.v.) concerning the motions of objects and their response to forces. Modern descriptions of such behavior begin with a careful definition of such quantities as displacement (distance moved), time, velocity, acceleration, mass, and force. Until about 400 years ago, however, motion was explained from a very different point of view. For example, following the ideas of Aristotle, scientists reasoned that a cannonball falls down because its natural position is in the earth; the sun, the moon, and the stars travel in circles around the earth because it is the nature of heavenly objects to travel in perfect circles.

Galileo brought together the ideas of other great thinkers of his time and began to analyze motion in terms of distance traveled from some starting position and the time that it took. He showed that the speed of falling objects increases steadily during the time of their fall. This acceleration is the same for heavy objects as for light ones, provided air friction (air resistance) is discounted. The English mathematician and physicist Sir Isaac Newton improved this analysis by defining force and mass and relating these to acceleration. For objects traveling at speeds close to the speed of light, and for atomic and subatomic particles, Newton's laws are now superseded by Albert Einstein's theory of relativity (q.v.) and by the quantum theory (q.v.). For everyday phenomena, however, Newton's three laws of motion remain the cornerstone of dynamics, the study of what causes motion.

Kinetics. Time plays a crucial role in kinetics, the description of motion without regard to what causes the motion. Velocity, or the time rate of change of position, is defined as the distance traveled divided by the time interval. Velocity may be measured in such units as kilometers per hour, miles per hour, or meters per second. Acceleration is defined as the time rate of change of velocity: the change of velocity divided by the time interval during the change. Acceleration may be measured in such units as meters per second per second or feet per second per second. Regarding the size or weight of the moving object, no mathematical problems are presented if the object is a "particle," or very small compared with the distances involved. If the object is large, it contains one point, called the center of mass, the motion of which can be described as characteristic of the whole object. If the object is rotating, it is frequently convenient to describe its rotation about an axis that goes through the center of mass.

To fully describe the motion of an object, the direction of the displacement must be given. Velocity, for example, has both magnitude (a scalar quantity measured, for example, in meters per second) and direction (measured, for example, in degrees of arc from a reference point). The magnitude of velocity is called speed.

Several special types of motion are easily described. First, velocity may be constant. In the simplest case, the velocity might be zero; position would not change during the time interval. With constant velocity, the average velocity is equal to the velocity at any particular time. If time, t, is measured with a clock starting at $t = 0$, then the distance, d, traveled at constant velocity, v, is equal to the product of velocity and time.

$$d = vt$$

In the second special type of motion, acceleration is constant. Because the velocity is steadily changing, instantaneous velocity, or the velocity at a given instant, must be defined. For constant acceleration, a, starting with zero velocity ($v = 0$) at $t = 0$, the instantaneous velocity at time, t, is

$$v = at$$

The distance traveled during this time is

$$d = \tfrac{1}{2}at^2$$

An important feature revealed in this equation is the dependence of distance on the square of the time (t^2, or "t squared," is the short way of notating $t \times t$). A heavy object falling freely (uninfluenced by air friction) near the surface of the earth undergoes constant acceleration. In this case the acceleration is 9.8 m/sec/sec (32 ft/sec/sec). At the end of the first second, a ball would have fallen 4.9 m (16 ft) and would have a speed of 9.8 m/sec (32 ft/sec). At the end of the second second, the ball would have fallen 19.6 m (64 ft) and would have a speed of 19.6 m/sec (64 ft/sec).

Circular motion is another simple type of motion. If an object has constant speed but an acceleration always at right angles to its velocity, it will travel in a circle. The required acceleration is directed toward the center of the circle and is called centripetal acceleration (see CENTRIFUGAL FORCE). For an object traveling at speed, v, in a circle of radius, r, the centripetal acceleration is

$$a = \frac{v^2}{r}$$

Another simple type of motion that is frequently observed occurs when a ball is thrown at an angle into the air. Because of gravitation the ball

MECHANICS

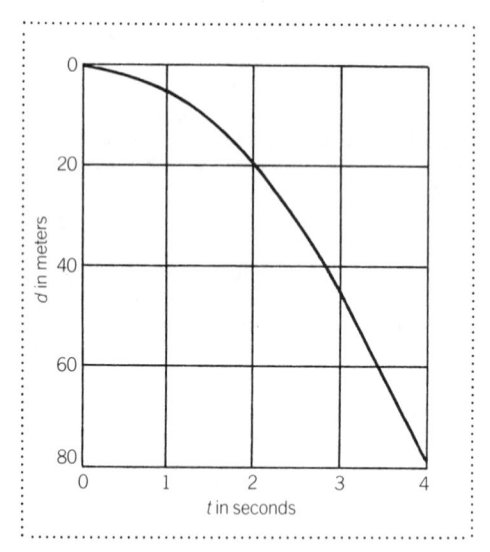

An object accelerated by gravity falls a distance (d) of nearly 80 m in a time (t) of 4 seconds.

undergoes a constant downward acceleration that first slows its original upward speed and then increases its downward speed as it falls back to earth. Meanwhile the horizontal component of the original velocity remains constant (ignoring air resistance), making the ball travel at a constant speed in the horizontal direction until it hits the earth. The vertical and horizontal components of the motion are independent, and they can be analyzed separately. The resulting path of the ball is in the shape of a parabola (q.v.). See BALLISTICS.

Dynamics. To understand why and how objects accelerate, force and mass must be defined. At the intuitive level, a force is just a push or a pull. It can be measured in terms of either of two effects. A force can either distort something, such as a spring, or accelerate an object. The first effect can be used in the calibration of a spring

The velocity (v) of a ball thrown in the air has a vertical (V) and a horizontal (H) component.

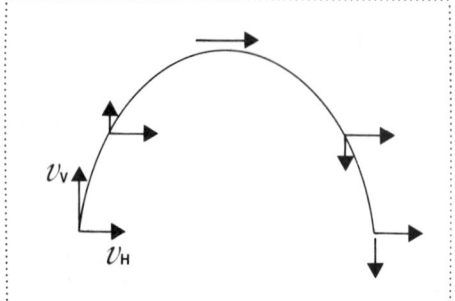

scale, which can in turn be used to measure the amplitude of a force: the greater the force, F, the greater the stretch, x. For many springs, over a limited range, the stretch is proportional to the force

$$F = kx$$

where k is a constant that depends on the nature of the spring material and its dimensions.

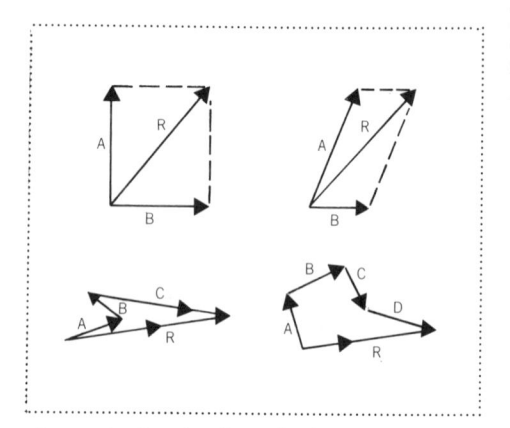

A vector is a line that shows the direction and strength of a force acting on an object. Top: The net force produced by forces A and B is obtained by constructing a parallelogram from the vectors and drawing a diagonal as the resultant force, R. Bottom: When several forces act, the resultant is the line drawn from start to finish of the separate vectors laid end to end.

Vectors. If an object is motionless, the net force on it must be zero. A book lying on a table is being pulled down by the earth's gravitational attraction and is being pushed up by the molecular repulsion of the tabletop. The net force is zero; the book is in equilibrium. When calculating the net force, it is necessary to add the forces as vectors.

Torque. For equilibrium, all the horizontal components of the force must cancel one another, and all the vertical components must cancel one another as well. This condition is necessary for equilibrium, but not sufficient. For example, if a person stands a book up on a table and pushes on the book equally hard with one hand in one direction and with the other hand in the other direction, the book will remain motionless if the person's hands are opposite each other. (The net result is that the book is being sqeezed). If, however, one hand is at the top and the other hand at the bottom, a torque is produced, and the book will fall on its side. For equilibrium to exist it is also necessary that the sum of the torques about any axis be zero.

134

MECHANICS

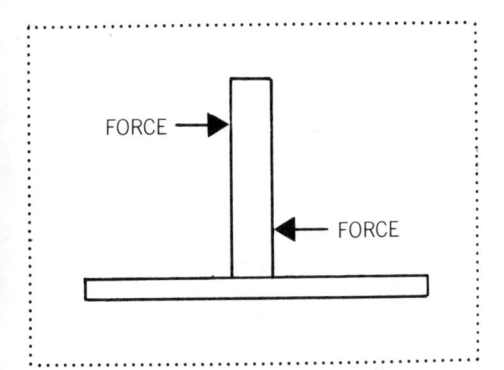

A torque is produced on this object when the two horizontal forces applied are not in equilibrium.

A torque is also called a force moment. It is the product of a force and the perpendicular distance to a turning axis. When a force is applied to a heavy door to open it, intuitively the force is exerted perpendicularly to the door and at the greatest distance from the hinges. Thus, a maximum torque is created. If the door were shoved with the same force at a point halfway between handle and hinge, the torque would be only half of its previous magnitude. If the force were applied parallel to the door (that is, edge on), the torque would be zero. For an object to be in equilibrium, the clockwise torques about any axis must be canceled by the counterclockwise torques about that axis. If the torques cancel for any particular axis, they cancel for all axes.

Newton's Three Laws of Motion. The first law of motion is really a definition of zero force, or of the reference frame in which the forces are measured. If the vector sum of the forces acting on an object is zero, then the object will remain at rest or remain moving at constant velocity. If the force exerted on an object is zero, the object does not necessarily have zero velocity. Without any forces acting on it, including friction, an object in motion will continue to travel at constant velocity.

The second law. Newton's second law relates net force and acceleration. A net force on an object will accelerate it, that is, change its velocity. The acceleration will be proportional to the magnitude of the force and in the same direction as the force. The proportionality constant is the mass, m, of the object.

$$F = ma$$

In the International System of Units (q.v.), or SI, acceleration, a, is measured in meters per second per second. Mass is measured in kilograms, force, F, in newtons. A newton is defined as the force necessary to impart to a mass of 1 kg an acceleration of 1 m/sec/sec; this is equivalent to about 0.2248 lb.

It is intuitively understood that a massive object will require a greater force for a given acceleration than a small, light object. What is remarkable is that mass, which is a measure of the inertia of an object (its reluctance to change velocity), is also a measure of the gravitational attraction that the object exerts on other objects. It is surprising and profound that the inertial property and the gravitational property are determined by the same thing. The implication of this phenomenon is that it is impossible to distinguish at a point whether the point is in a gravitational field or in an accelerated frame of reference. Einstein made this one of the cornerstones of his general theory of relativity, which is the currently accepted theory of gravitation.

Friction. The force applied to an object is not necessarily the net or effective force. If a massive box is pushed across the floor, it will probably be pushed not precisely horizontally, but at an angle to the horizontal. The vertical component of the force is not effective in moving the box. Only the horizontal component of force is effective in moving the box horizontally. Indeed, the vertical component has the effect of pushing the box into the floor, which increases friction.

Friction acts like a force applied in the direction opposite to the velocity. For dry sliding friction, where no lubrication is present, the friction force is almost independent of velocity. Nor does the friction force depend on the apparent area of contact between the box and the floor. The actual contact area, where molecules of box and sliding surface are touching, is relatively small. At the isolated contact points, molecular bonding takes place. Force is required to break these bonds and allow the box to keep on sliding. The actual contact area depends on the perpendicu-

The frictional force acting on the box is proportional to the total perpendicular force applied.

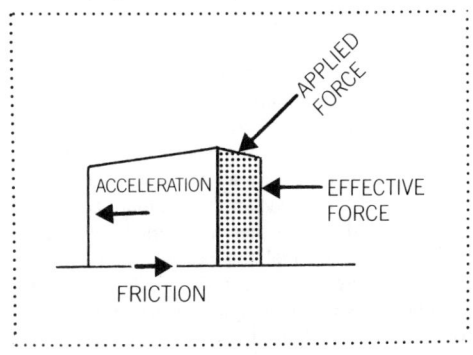

135

lar force between box and floor. Frequently this force is just the weight of the sliding object. If the box is pushed at an angle to the horizontal, however, the downward vertical component of the force will, in effect, add to the weight of the box. The friction force is proportional to the total perpendicular force.

Where friction is present, Newton's second law is expanded to

$$F_{\text{effective}} - F_{\text{friction}} = ma$$

The left side of the equation is simply the net effective force. (Acceleration will be constant in the direction of the effective force). When an object moves through a liquid, however, the magnitude of the friction depends on the velocity. For most human-size objects moving in water or air (at subsonic speeds), the resulting friction is proportional to the square of the speed. Newton's second law then becomes

$$F_{\text{effective}} - kv^2 = ma$$

The proportionality constant, k, is characteristic of the two materials that are sliding past each other, and depends on the area of contact between the two surfaces and the degree of streamlining of the moving object.

The third law. Newton's third law of motion states that an object experiences a force because it is interacting with some other object. The force that object 1 exerts on object 2 must be of the same magnitude, but in the opposite direction, as the force that object 2 exerts on object 1. If, for example, a large adult gently shoves away a child on a skating rink, the mutual interaction will push them apart from each other. (It is assumed that the rink provides a frictionless surface.) The force on each will have the same magnitude. Because the mass of the adult is larger, however, the acceleration of the adult will be smaller.

Newton's third law also requires the conservation of momentum, or the product of mass and velocity. For an isolated system, with no external forces acting on it, the momentum must remain constant. In the example of the adult and child on the skating rink, their initial velocities are zero, and thus the initial momentum of the system is zero. During the interaction, internal forces are at work between adult and child, but net external forces equal zero. Therefore, the momentum of the system must remain zero. The product of the large mass and small velocity of the adult must equal the product of the small mass and large velocity of the child. The momenta are equal in magnitude but opposite in direction, thus adding to zero.

Another conserved quantity of great importance is angular (rotational) momentum. The angular momentum of a rotating object depends on its speed of rotation, its mass, and the distance of the mass from the axis. When a skater standing on a friction-free point spins faster and faster, angular momentum is conserved despite the increasing speed. At the start of the spin, the skater's arms are outstretched. Part of the mass is therefore at a large radius. As the skater's arms are lowered, thus decreasing their distance from the axis of rotation, the rotational speed must increase in order to maintain constant angular momentum.

Energy. The quantity called energy ties together all branches of physics. In the field of mechanics, energy must be provided to do work, which is defined as the product of force and the distance an object moves in the direction of the force. When a force is exerted on an object but the force does not cause the object to move, no work is done. Energy and work are both measured in the same units—ergs, joules, or foot-pounds, for example.

If work is done lifting an object to a greater height, energy has been stored in the form of gravitational potential energy. If no friction occurs, the stored energy can be recovered. The kinetic energy of any moving object is equal to $\frac{1}{2}mv^2$. Many other forms of energy exist: electric and magnetic potential energy, stretched springs, compressed gases, molecular bonds, thermal energy, and mass itself. In all transformations from one kind of energy to another, the total energy is conserved. For instance, if work is done on a rubber ball to raise it, its gravitational potential energy is increased. If the ball is then dropped, the gravitational potential energy is transformed to kinetic energy. When the ball hits the ground, it becomes distorted and thereby creates friction between the molecules of the ball material. This friction is transformed into heat, or thermal energy.
C.E.S.

For further information on this topic, see the Bibliography in volume 28, section 392.

MECHANISM (Gr. *mēchanē*, "machine"), in philosophy, term designating any concept according to which the universe is completely explicable in terms of mechanical processes. Inasmuch as these mechanical processes are best understood in their movements, mechanism frequently involves the attempt to demonstrate that the universe is nothing more than a vast system of motions. In this general sense mechanism is practically equivalent to materialism. The term is often used, however, as a synonym for naturalism, the doctrine that the phenomena of nature are not regulated by divine or supernatural intelligence, but are adequately explained by the mechanical laws of chemistry and physics. In the latter sense the customary antonym of mechanism is teleology, sometimes called finalism, the doctrine that nature and creation are ordered by a divine plan and fulfill divinely appointed ends.

MECHELEN, also Malines, city, N Belgium, in Antwerp Province, on the Dyle R., near Brussels. It is a thriving textile center, but it no longer produces the lace that once made it famous. As the see of the Roman Catholic primate of Belgium, it retains ecclesiastical importance. The Cathedral of Saint Rombaut (13th cent.) contains works by the Flemish painter Sir Anthony Van Dyck, and the churches of Saint John and of Our Lady both contain works by the Flemish painter Peter Paul Rubens. Pop. (1988 est.) 75,700.

MECKLENBURG-WEST POMERANIA, state, NE Germany, bounded on the N by the Baltic Sea, on the W by Schleswig-Holstein, on the SW by Lower Saxony, on the S by Brandenburg, and on the E by Poland. The state lies in a fertile plain containing many forests and lakes and is crossed by the Elde, Warnow, and several other rivers. Schwerin (pop., 1987 est., 128,800) is the capital. Area, 23,838 sq km (9204 sq mi); pop. (1990 est.) 1,964,000.

Teutonic peoples inhabited the area comprising present-day Mecklenburg-West Pomerania in the first centuries of the Christian era, but early in the 6th century it was seized by various Slavic tribes. The Mecklenburg region was conquered by Henry the Lion, duke of Saxony, in the latter half of the 12th century. In 1348 it was elevated to a duchy. The duchy was subdivided (1621) into the duchies of Mecklenburg-Schwerin and Mecklenburg-Strelitz, which were elevated to grand duchies in 1815. They joined the German Empire in 1871 and after World War I were constituted states of the new German Republic. In 1934 they were united into the single state of Mecklenburg. After World War II Mecklenburg became part of the Soviet Zone, and Pomerania, a former maritime province of Prussia on the Baltic Sea, was partitioned into two areas divided by the Oder River; the area west of the Oder was included in the new state of Mecklenburg. The state was dissolved in 1952, when East Germany was reorganized into districts. In 1990, with Germany's unification, the state of Mecklenburg-West Pomerania was created.

See also POMERANIA.

MEDALS AND DECORATIONS, adornments worn or displayed, issued as personal awards for outstanding service, bravery, or specific achievement or in commemoration of a historic event or a great personage. Medals are small, flat pieces of metal, commonly disks but often in the shape of a cross or star; they usually bear a decorative image or design and an inscription.

History of Medals. In ancient Greece and Rome the commemorative function was usually the province of coins (see COINS AND COIN COLLECTING). Not until the Renaissance were medals created as works of art per se, crafted by such artists as the Italian medalist and painter Pisanello, the goldsmith and sculptor Benvenuto Cellini, and the German master Albrecht Dürer. Noted medal designers of the 20th century were the American sculptor Paul Manship and the Swedish sculptor Carl Milles.

Civilian Medals. Medals awarded to civilians recognize outstanding achievements in science, the arts, sports, and general contributions to society. They may be issued by governments, as is the French Legion of Honor (established in 1802), which honors civilian and military merit and is bestowed on French nationals and on foreigners (see LEGION OF HONOR). In the U.S. the highest civilian award is the Presidential Medal of Freedom (q.v.), established on July 4, 1963; it is given for significant contribution to the national interest or world peace. A similar medal, the Hero of the Soviet Union, was awarded by the USSR. Medals are also given for achievement in specific fields by universities, civic groups, organizations, and learned societies. The Royal Society of London awards the Copley Medal (1731); Hadassah, the Women's Zionist Organization of America, Inc., issued a commemorative medal in 1980 in honor of the 120th anniversary of its founder, Henrietta Szold.

Military Medals. Medals were awarded for military valor in the 15th century, but not until the end of the 18th century did medals commemorating victorious engagements become widespread. Medals awarded by European countries for outstanding military service include the French Médaille Militaire (1852) and Croix de Guerre (1915), the British Victoria Cross (1865) and Distinguished Service Cross (1940), the German Iron Cross (1813), and the Norwegian Order of Saint Olav (1847).

Service medals awarded by the U.S. Army and Navy for participation in specific campaigns include, for example, the Civil War Campaign Medal and the Victory Medal for service in World War I or World War II. The U.S. Army confers the Distinguished Service Cross (1918) on those displaying exceptional heroism and the Order of the Purple Heart (see PURPLE HEART, ORDER OF THE), instituted by George Washington in 1782, on soldiers wounded or killed in action. U.S. Air Force medals include the Distinguished Flying Cross (1926), awarded to those who exhibit extraordinary heroism or achievement in aerial flight. U.S. Navy and Marine medals include the Distinguished Service Medal (1919);

MEDALS AND DECORATIONS

Medals of the U.S. armed services. Top row, left to right: Distinguished Service Cross (Army), awarded for exceptional heroism; Medal of Honor (Army), for risking life above and beyond the call of duty; Distinguished Flying Cross (Air Force), for exceptional heroism or achievement in aerial flight. Middle row, left to right: Distinguished Service Medal (Army, Air Force, Navy-Marine Corps), awarded in each branch for work of special merit to the government. Bottom row: Service medals: Left to right: World War II Victory Medal; Korean Service Medal; Antarctica Service Medal; Vietnam Service Medal.

the Navy Cross (1919), awarded for heroism in combat; and the Navy and Marine Corps Medal (1942), the award given for heroism in noncombat situations.

The highest military award bestowed by the U.S., the Medal of Honor (instituted in 1861 and first awarded during the Civil War), is granted in the name of the U.S. Congress to those who have risked their lives above and beyond the call of duty. The Good Conduct Medal is given for exemplary behavior to all enlisted members of the armed forces who complete terms of active duty.

Other military medals are given for specific outstanding performance, as, for example, excellence in marksmanship. Ribbons are either attached to medals or worn alone. Stars and other devices are added to indicate particulars, such as the campaigns in which the wearer participated.

R.O.

For further information on this topic, see the Bibliography in volume 28, section 279.

MEDAN, city, W Indonesia, capital of North Sumatra Province, located on the island of Sumatra, at the confluence of the Deli and Babura rivers, near Belawan (its port on the Strait of Malacca). The city is the largest on Sumatra and is a major road hub in the Deli region. Connections extend by rail to the N and by road to the interior resorts of the Lake Toba area. In the city are tobacco- and tea-processing factories and plants manufacturing machinery, fiber products, ceramics, brick and tile, and soap. The city is the trade center of a vast hinterland that grows rubber, tobacco, tea, oil palms, fibers, coffee, and forest products. Oil fields are nearby. The port of Belawan, or Belawan Deli, ships rubber, tobacco, petroleum, palm oil, spices, copra, tea, and fibers. Medan is the site of the University of North Sumatra (1952), the Islamic University of North Sumatra (1952), the palace and residence of the sultan of Deli, a large mosque, and a tobacco-research station. Developing after 1870, the city had a great increase in industrial production in the 1940s and '50s. Medan served as a capital of the East Coast residency under Dutch rule and was capital of the state of East Sumatra from 1945 to 1948. Pop. (1990) 1,685,972.

MEDAWAR, Sir Peter Brian (1915–87), British biologist and Nobel laureate, noted for his discovery of acquired immunological tolerance and for his writings on the practice of science. Medawar was born in Rio de Janeiro, Brazil, of British parents, and educated at Magdalen College, University of Oxford. From 1938 to 1962 Medawar taught successively at Oxford, at Birmingham University, and at University College of the University of London. In 1962 he was named director of the National Institute for Medical Research, London. Medawar shared the 1960 Nobel Prize in physiology or medicine with the Australian biologist Sir Macfarlane Burnet (1899–1985), whose predictions concerning the ability of the body to accept transplanted tissue were confirmed in graftings conducted by Medawar on rats inoculated as embryos with foreign tissue. Among his books are *Induction and Intuition in Scientific Thought* (1969), *Advice to a Young Scientist* (1979), and *Memoir of a Thinking Radish* (1986). Medawar was knighted in 1965.

MEDEA, in Greek mythology, sorceress, the daughter of Aeëtes, king of Colchis. When the hero Jason, in command of the Argonauts, reached Colchis in search of the Golden Fleece, Medea fell hopelessly in love with him. In return for Jason's pledge of everlasting fidelity and his promise to take her back to Greece with him, she used her magic gifts to enable him to deceive her father and obtain the fleece. Medea then sailed away from Colchis with Jason, taking Apsyrtus, her young brother, with her. To escape from Aeëtes's pursuit, Medea killed Apsyrtus and scattered his remains on the sea. The king stopped to gather them up, and the delay enabled Jason and his party to escape. According to another legend, it was Jason who killed Apsyrtus after Aeëtes had sent him in pursuit of the fugitives.

When Jason and Medea reached Greece, they found that Jason's wicked uncle Pelias had been responsible for the death of Jason's parents. To avenge their deaths, Jason once again asked Medea to aid him with her magic. Responsive as always to his wishes, Medea brought about the death of Pelias by a cunning trick. Telling his daughters she knew how they could make their aging parent young again, she dismembered an old sheep and boiled the pieces. After she uttered a charm, a frisky young lamb jumped from the pot of hot water. The daughters were convinced they could similarly restore their father to his youth. So, after Medea had given Pelias a powerful sleeping potion, they were persuaded to cut him into pieces, but Medea then disappeared without saying the magic words that would bring him back to life. After this Jason and Medea fled to Corinth, where two sons were born to them. They lived happily there until Jason fell in love with the daughter of King Creon of Corinth. In revenge, Medea killed her rival by sending her a poisoned robe. Fearing that Creon would attempt to avenge the death of his daughter by harming her sons, Medea killed them.

Medea escaped the wrath of Jason by leaving Corinth in a winged car and fleeing to Athens. There she achieved great influence over King Aegeus. Through her sorcery, she realized that Aegeus was unknowingly the father of Theseus, a young hero, who was arriving in Athens. She did not wish to have her influence with Aegeus disturbed by the appearance of a son, so she plotted with Aegeus to invite Theseus to a banquet and give him a poisoned cup. Aegeus willingly conspired with her through fear that the Athenians would prefer the popular young hero to him and would want to place Theseus on the throne. Fortunately, Theseus made himself known to his father, who dashed the poisoned cup to the ground. Medea escaped the wrath of Aegeus by fleeing to Asia.

MEDELLÍN, city, central Colombia, capital of Antioquia Department, in a mountain valley at an altitude of about 1525 m (about 5000 ft). It is Colombia's largest city after Bogotá (the capital) and its principal manufacturing and transportation center. Products include steel, chemicals, pharmaceuticals, refined petroleum, and processed food. Large numbers of commercial orchids are also grown. Points of interest include the Orquideorama, where orchids are on display in the botanical gardens, and a huge cathedral from the Spanish colonial period. The University of Antioquia (1822), the University of Medellín (1950), the Pontifical University Bolivariana (1936), and the Autonomous University of Latin America (1966) are here. Medellín was founded in 1675, but it did not become a major industrial center until the 1930s. During the 1980s the city became the center of Colombia's most powerful cocaine cartel. Pop. (1985) 1,468,089.

MEDFORD, city, Middlesex Co., NE Massachusetts, on the Mystic R., near Boston; founded 1630, inc. as a city 1892. The city has industries producing printed materials, paper products, and processed food. Tufts University (1852) is here. A cemetery dating from 1689 and Royall House, rebuilt in 1732 with slave quarters, are of historical interest. Formerly, Medford was a famous rummaking (1715–1905) and shipbuilding (1803–73) center. It is named for a meadow that once bordered a ford in the river here. Pop. (1980) 58,076; (1990) 57,407.

MEDFORD, city, seat of Jackson Co., SW Oregon, on Bear Creek near its junction with the Rogue R.; inc. 1885. Situated in an area known for its pears, the city is a farm-trade, lumbering, tourist, and light-industrial center, as well as a regional medical center. Crater Lake National Park, Oregon Caves National Monument, and Jacksonville, a restored gold-mining town (originally established in 1851–52), are nearby. The community, founded in 1883 as a railroad depot, is named for Medford, Mass. Pop. (1980) 39,603; (1990) 46,951.

MEDIA, ancient country of Asia, corresponding to the northeastern section of present-day Iran. The inhabitants, who were known as Medes, and their neighbors, the Persians, spoke Indo-Iranian languages that were closely related to Old Persian. Historians know very little about the Median culture except that a polytheistic religion was practiced, and a priestly caste called the Magi existed.

Beginning about 835 BC the Median tribes became subject intermittently to the kings of Assyria. About 715 BC the Median chieftain Dayaukku, known to the Greek historian Herodotus as Deïoces, led the Medes in an unsuccessful rebellion against the Assyrian king Sargon II (r. 722–705 BC). The later rulers of Media considered Dayaukku the founder of the Median dynasty. Subsequently, another chieftain named Khshathrita (r. about 675–653 BC), known to the Greeks as Phraortes, united the Median tribes and expelled the Assyrians. Khshathrita was killed by the Scythians, who invaded Media from the northwest.

Khshathrita's son Cyaxares (r. 625–585 BC) chose as his capital the city of Ecbatana (present-day Hamadan, Iran). In 625 he drove the Scythians out of Media and imposed his rule over the Persians. He attacked the Assyrians next and captured (614 BC) the city of Ashur. In 612, in alliance with the newly independent kingdom of Babylonia, he captured the city of Nineveh and overthrew the Assyrian Empire. Thereafter Cyaxares extended the territory of his kingdom to include all of eastern Anatolia. Cyaxares was succeeded by his son Astyages (r. about 584–c. 550 BC). The Persians, under Cyrus the Great, revolted against Astyages about 550 BC. Joined by a portion of the Median army under a chief named Harpagus, they took the capital and deposed the Median king. From that time Media was politically subservient to Persia; the Persians, however, regarded the Medes as equals, and thenceforth the two peoples were considered as one. E.I.G. & S.N.K.

MEDIAN. See STATISTICS; TRIANGLE.

MEDIATION. See FEDERAL MEDIATION AND CONCILIATION SERVICE; LABOR RELATIONS.

MEDICAL EDUCATION, branch of education devoted to training doctors in the practice of medicine. In 18th-century colonial America, prospective physicians either apprenticed themselves to established practitioners or went abroad to study in the traditional schools of London, Paris, and Edinburgh. Medicine was first taught formally by specialists at the University of Pennsylvania, beginning in 1765, and in 1767 at King's College (presently Columbia University), the first institution in the colonies to confer the degree of doctor of medicine. After the American Revolution, the Columbia medical faculty (formerly of King's College) merged with the College of Physicians and Surgeons, chartered in 1809, which survives as part of Columbia University.

In 1893 the Johns Hopkins Medical School required all applicants to have a college degree and was the first to afford its students the opportunity to further their training in an affiliated teaching hospital. The growth of medical schools affiliated with established institutions of learning was paralleled by the development of proprietary schools of medicine run for personal profit, most of which had low standards and inadequate facilities. In 1910 Abraham Flexner (1866–1959), the American education reformer, wrote *Medical Education in the United States and Canada*, exposing the inadequacies of most proprietary schools. Subsequently, the American Medical Association and the Association of American Medical Colleges laid down standards for course content, qualifications of teachers, laboratory facilities, affiliation with teaching hospitals, and licensing of practitioners that survive to this day.

By the late 1980s the U.S. and Canada had 142 4-year medical colleges accredited by the Liaison Committee on Medical Education to award the M.D. degree; during the 1987–88 academic year, 47,262 men and 25,686 women were enrolled and an estimated 11,752 men and 5958 women were graduated. Graduates, after a year of internship, receive licenses to practice if they pass an examination administered either by a state board or by the National Board of Medical Examiners.

MEDICAL EXAMINER. See Coroner.
MEDICAL JURISPRUDENCE. See Forensic Medicine.
MEDICARE AND MEDICAID, programs of medical care for the aged and for the needy, respectively, in the U.S. The Medicare and Medicaid programs are under the direction of the U.S. Department of Health and Human Services.

Medicare. Medicare is the popular name for the federal health insurance program for persons 65 years of age and over. The program, which went into effect in 1966, was first administered by the Social Security Administration; in 1977 the Medicare program was transferred to the newly created Health Care Financing Administration (HCFA). Benefits are divided into two parts: (1) a basic hospital-insurance plan covering hospital care, extended care, home health services, and hospice care for terminally ill participants; and (2) a voluntary medical-insurance program covering physicians' fees, outpatient services, and other medical services. Medicare costs are met by social security contributions, monthly premiums from participants, and general revenues.

Beginning in July 1973 Medicare was extended to persons under the age of 65 with certain disabling conditions. In 1988 Congress passed legislation to expand the program to cover health care costs of catastrophic illness, to be financed by a surtax on the incomes of taxpayers over the age of 65; this legislation, however, was repealed the following year. About 33 million people were enrolled in Medicare in the late 1980s.

Medicaid. Medicaid, a federal-state program, is usually operated by state welfare or health departments, within the guidelines issued by the HCFA. Medicaid furnishes at least five basic services to needy persons: inpatient hospital care, outpatient hospital care, physicians' services, skilled nursing-home services for adults, and laboratory and X-ray services. The people who are eligible include families and certain children who qualify for public assistance and may include aged, blind, and disabled adults who are eligible for the Supplemental Security Income program of the Social Security Administration. States may also include persons and families termed "medically needy" who meet eligibility requirements except those for financial assistance. Each state decides who is eligible for Medicaid benefits and what services shall be included. Some of the benefits frequently provided are dental care; ambulance services; and the cost of drugs, eyeglasses, and hearing aids. In determining eligibility for the program, a state may not hold adult children responsible for medical expenses of their parents. All the states, the District of Columbia, Guam, Puerto Rico, and the Virgin Islands operate Medicaid plans.

MEDICI, Italian banking and political family that long ruled Florence. The Medici first gained prominence in the early 13th century as merchants and moneylenders, and they entered public life in the 1260s. Through its extensive European commerce and banking, the family became one of the richest in 15th-century Italy, and with the popular faction opposed the ruling aristocrats in Florence. Cosimo de' Medici the Elder, a shrewd politician, established Medici dominance in Florence from 1434. His grandson Lorenzo the Magnificent perfected Medici control and made the family one of the most powerful in Renaissance Italy. Twice expelled from the city, in 1494–1512 and 1527–30, the Medici were both times reinstated with Spanish help.

Two of the most celebrated Renaissance popes, Leo X and Clement VII, were members of the Medici family. Clement made Alessandro de' Medici (1510–37) duke of Florence. When Ales-

The Medici-Riccardi Palace in Florence, Italy, was built by Michelozzo in 1444-60 for his patron, Cosimo de' Medici, head of the Medici family. Many of the most notable 15th-century Florentine buildings, as well as many villas in the surrounding countryside, are the result of Medici patronage. Editorial Photocolor Archives

sandro was assassinated, Cosimo I, a member of the junior branch of the family, succeeded and eventually became (1570) the sovereign grand duke of Tuscany. His descendants ruled Florence until 1737. Cosimo's distant cousin Catherine (see CATHERINE DE MÉDICIS) married Henry II of France, and his granddaughter Marie (see MARIE DE MÉDICIS) married Henry IV of France.

For additional information on family members, see biographies of those whose names are not followed by dates. J.F.D.

MEDICI, Cosimo de' (1389-1464), Italian banker and statesman. Known as Cosimo the Elder, he succeeded his father, Giovanni (1360-1429), as director of the family's successful commercial and banking interests and as leader of the popular faction in Florentine politics. Exiled by the ruling aristocratic party in 1433, he was recalled the following year and then assumed virtual control of the government; he secured his position by banishing some of his enemies and ruining others by excessive taxation. A shrewd politician, Cosimo avoided holding public office himself, governing instead through supporters and dependents. His financial acumen benefited both Florence and his family, and he was probably the wealthiest man in contemporary Italy.

Cosimo encouraged agriculture, the silk industry, and commerce and sought to maintain peace in Italy by a balance of power among the major states and by preventing foreign interference. He actively patronized artists, architects, and schol-

MEDICINE

ars and amassed a fine humanist library. His public building program set a standard imitated by his family and other rulers. J.F.D.

MEDICI, Cosimo I de' (1519-74), grand duke of Tuscany. Cosimo belonged to the junior branch of the Medici family that ruled Florence. At the age of 18 he succeeded the assassinated Duke Alessandro (1510-37). He established secure control throughout Florentine territories, thwarting both his enemies' schemes to overthrow him and his advisers' attempts to control him. Cosimo centralized the organs of government and justice, encouraged agriculture and industry, and patronized the arts and higher education. Spanish support allowed the extension of his rule throughout Tuscany, and Pope Pius V granted him the title grand duke of Tuscany (1570), making him a sovereign ruler. Although sometimes cruel and insensitive, Cosimo was generally judicious in his policies and a good administrator. In foreign affairs he usually supported Spain, the dominant power in the Italian Peninsula. J.F.D.

MEDICI, Lorenzo de', called The Magnificent (1449-92), Italian banker and statesman, who was a leading patron of art and scholarship during the Renaissance.

Lorenzo was born in Florence on Jan. 1, 1449, the son of Piero de' Medici (1416-69), and on his father's death he assumed the direction of the Medici bank, as well as de facto rule of the Florentine republic. He was more successful as a politician and art connoisseur than as a bank administrator, and his family's finances suffered from the expense of his government. Lorenzo married into the noble Orsini family but ruled initially without altering the old republican institutions, and he remained officially a private citizen. His popular, efficient government of the city and its dependencies was marred only by his approval of a brutal sack (1472) of the rebellious town of Volterra.

In 1478 members of the Pazzi family tried to assassinate Lorenzo, and in the aftermath of that affair the Medici punished some supporters of Pope Sixtus IV implicated in the plot. The pope, backed by Naples, then declared war on Florence. Pursuing the family policy of promoting peace among the Italian states, Lorenzo ended the war by personal diplomacy. This further increased his popularity with the Florentines and enabled him to secure constitutional changes that enhanced his power. His last years were devoted to establishing the careers of his children and guarding the peace.

Himself a gifted poet, Lorenzo gathered at his court the leading artists and intellectuals of his day. Among those who enjoyed his patronage were the painters Botticelli and Michelangelo, the philosophers Marsilio Ficino and Giovanni Pico della Mirandola, and the humanist poet Angelo Poliziano (Politian). Lorenzo died at Careggi on April 9, 1492. J.F.D.

MEDICINE (Lat. *medicus,* "physician"), science and art concerned with curing and preventing disease and preserving health.

PRIMITIVE MEDICINE

The understanding of prehistoric medical practice is derived from paleopathology, the study of pictographs showing medical procedures, of skulls and skeletons, and of the surgical tools of ancient and contemporary nontechnological societies. Although such study is properly the concern of anthropology, some of the practices have survived into modern times, justifying their consideration in the history of medicine.

Serious diseases were of primary interest to early humans although they did not function effectively in treating them. They divided the genesis of such disease into two categories, each involving a variety of mutually exclusive therapies. First and most numerous were diseases attributed to the influence of malevolent demons, who were believed to project an alien spirit, a stone, or a worm into the body of the unsuspecting patient. Such disabilities were to be warded off by incantation, dancing, magic effects, charms and talismans, and various other measures. If the demon managed to enter the body of its victim, either in the absence of such precautions or despite them, efforts were made to make the body uninhabitable to the demon by beating, torturing, and starving the patient. The alien spirit could also be expelled by potions that caused violent vomiting, or could be driven out through a hole bored in the skull. This procedure, called trepanning (q.v.), was also a remedy for insanity, epilepsy, and headache.

Therapy mounted directly against a disability, however, was usually most successful. Operative procedures practiced in ancient societies included cleaning and treating wounds by cautery, poultices, and sutures, resetting dislocations and fractures, and using splints. Additional therapy included the use of purges, diuretics, laxatives, emetics, and enemas. Perhaps the greatest success was achieved by the use of plant extracts, the narcotic and stimulating properties of which were slowly discovered. So successful were these that 50 or more continue to be used today. Digitalis (q.v.), a heart stimulant extracted from foxglove, is perhaps the best known.

ANCIENT MEDICAL PRACTICE

Several prescientific systems of medicine, based primarily on magic, folk remedies, and elemen-

MEDICINE

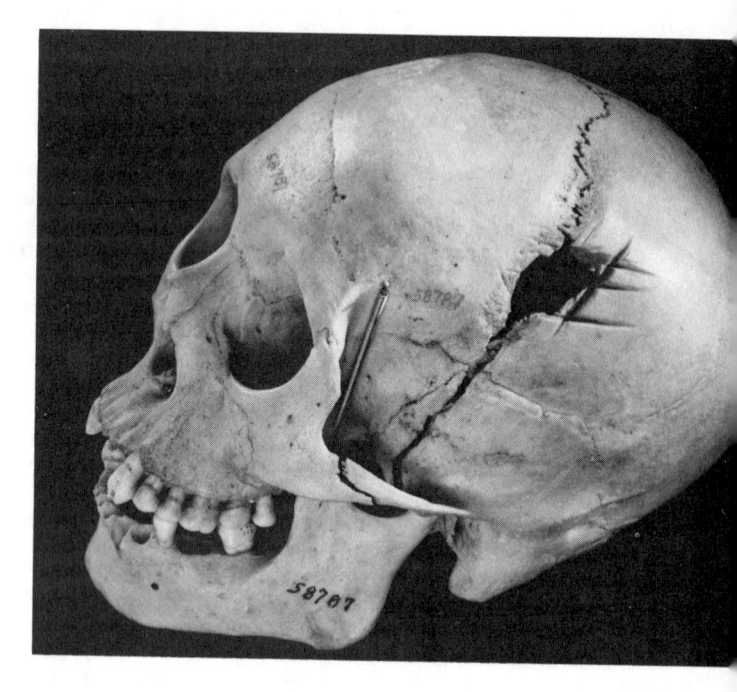

A trepanned skull from the days of Inca rule in Peru. This ancient form of surgery was used for conditions ranging from headaches to insanity.
Peabody Museum, Harvard University

tary surgery, existed in various diverse societies before the coming of the more advanced Greek medicine about the 6th century BC.

Egyptian. Two distinct trends are discernible in Egyptian medicine, the magico-religious, embodying primitive elements, and the empirico-rational, based on experience and observation and lacking in mystical features. Common diseases of the eyes and skin were usually treated rationally by the physician because of their favorable location; less accessible disorders continued to be treated by the spells and incantations of the priest-magician. In the 3d Dynasty the physician emerged as an early form of scientist, a type distinct from the sorcerer and priest. The earliest physician whose name has survived is Imhotep (fl. 2725 BC), renowned equally as vizier to the pharaoh, a pyramid builder, and an astrologer.

The physician normally spent years of arduous training at temple schools in the arts of interrogation, inspection, and palpation (examining the body by touch). Prescriptions contained some drugs that have continued in use through the centuries. Favorite laxatives were figs, dates, and castor oil (see CASTOR BEAN). Tannic acid, derived principally from the acacia nut, was valued in the treatment of burns. See PHARMACY.

Although Egyptians practiced embalming, their anatomical knowledge remained at a low level; as a result, they attempted only minor surgical procedures. An exception was the practice of trepanning. According to reports of the Greek historian Herodotus, the ancient Egyptians recognized dentistry as an important surgical specialty. Some evidence suggests that Egyptian studies of physiology and pathology (qq.v.), based on the work of the physician Imhotep, and the later vivisection of criminals by the Greek anatomist and surgeon Herophilus may have influenced the Greek philosopher Thales of Miletus, who is known to have traveled in Egypt in the 7th century BC.

Mesopotamian. Because of the theocratic system prevailing in Assyria and Babylonia, medicine in these countries could not break away from the influence of demonology and magical practices. Surviving cuneiform tablets present an extensive series of well-classified case histories. Surprisingly accurate terra-cotta models of the liver, then considered the seat of the soul, indicate the importance attached to the study of that organ in determining the intentions of the gods. Dreams also were studied to learn the gods' intentions (see DIVINATION).

A large number of medical remedies were used in Mesopotamia, including more than 500 drugs, some of which were of mineral origin. Incantations chanted by the priests often proved to be an effective form of psychotherapy.

Palestinian. Hebrew medicine derived much from contact with Mesopotamian medicine during the Assyrian and Babylonian captivities. Disease was considered evidence of the wrath of God. The priesthood acquired the responsibility

MEDICINE

for compiling hygienic regulations, and the status of the midwife as an assistant in childbirth was clearly defined. Although the Old Testament contains a few references to diseases caused by the intrusion of spirits, the tone of biblical medicine is modern in its marked emphasis on preventing disease. The Book of Leviticus includes precise instructions on such varied subjects as feminine hygiene, segregation of the sick, and disinfection of materials capable of harboring and transmitting germs. Although circumcision (q.v.) is the only surgical procedure clearly described, fractures were treated with the roller bandage, and wounds were dressed with oil, wine, and balsam. The leprosy (q.v.) so frequently mentioned in the Bible is now believed to have embraced many skin diseases, including psoriasis (q.v.).

Indian. The practices of ancient Hindu, or Vedantic, medicine (1500 to 1000 BC) are described in the works of two later physicians, Charaka (fl. 2d cent. AD) and Susruta (fl. 4th cent. AD). Susruta gave recognizable descriptions of malaria, tuberculosis (qq.v.), and diabetes. He also wrote about Indian hemp, *Cannabis* (q.v.), and henbane (q.v.), *Hyocyamus*, for inducing anesthesia (q.v.), and included specific antidotes and highly skilled treatments for bites of venomous snakes. An ancient Hindu drug derived from the root of the Indian plant *Rauwolfia serpentina* was the source of the first modern tranquilizer (q.v.). In the field of operative surgery, the Hindus are acknowledged to have attained the highest skill in all antiquity (*see* SURGERY). They were probably the first to perform successful skin grafting and plastic surgery for the nose.

With the rise of Buddhism the study of anatomy (q.v.) was prohibited, and with the Muslim conquest the field of medicine further declined and ultimately stagnated. Nevertheless, much valuable knowledge concerning hygiene, diet, and eugenics (q.v.) was transmitted to the West through the writings of the Arab physician Avicenna and others.

Chinese. In ancient China religious prohibitions against dissection resulted in an inadequate knowledge of body structure and function. As a consequence, surgical technique remained elementary. External treatments included massage and dry cupping, a form of counterirritation in which blood is drawn to the skin surface by application of a cup from which air is then exhausted to create a partial vacuum. Two special forms of counterirritation used in rheumatic and other disorders were acupuncture (q.v.), or puncture of the skin by needles to relieve pain and congestion; and cautery, or searing, of the skin by the application of burning moxa, a preparation of oil-soaked leaves of Chinese wormwood. Important Chinese drugs included rhubarb, aconite, sulfur, arsenic, and most important, opium (qq.v.). Concoctions of animal organs and excretions, survivals of ancient ritual, were also used.

Greek. The earliest Greek medicine depended on magic and spells. Homer considered Apollo the god of healing. Homer's *Illiad*, however, reveals a considerable knowledge of the treatment of wounds and other injuries by surgery, already recognized as a specialty distinct from internal medicine.

Asclepius subsequently supplanted Apollo as the god of healing, and the priests practiced the healing art in his temples. Still later, a semipriestly sect, the Asclepiades, although claiming to be descendants of the god of medicine, practiced a form of psychotherapy called incubation.

By the 6th century BC, Greek medicine had become thoroughly secular, stressing clinical observation and experience. In the Greek colony of Crotona the biologist Alcmaeon (fl. 6th cent. BC) identified the brain as the physiological seat of the senses. The Greek philosopher Empedocles elaborated the concept that disease is primarily an expression of a disturbance in the perfect harmony of the four elements—fire, air, water, and earth—and formulated a rudimentary theory of evolution.

Kos and Cnidus are the most famous of the Greek medical schools that flourished in the 5th century BC under the Asclepiades. Students of both schools probably contributed to the *Corpus Hippocraticum* (Hippocratic Collection), an anthology of the writings of several authors, although popularly attributed to Hippocrates of Kos, known as the father of medicine. None of these works mentions supernatural cures. The highest ethical standards were imposed on the physicians, who took the celebrated oath usually attributed to Hippocrates and still in use today (*see* HIPPOCRATIC OATH). Knowledge of human anatomy was based mainly on the dissection of animals. Physiology was based on the four cardinal humors, or fluids, of the body: This concept was derived from Empedocles' theory of the four elements. Pain and disease were attributed to imbalance of these humors. The true genius of Hippocrates is shown in the *Aphorisms and Prognostics*, containing pithy summaries of vast clinical experience that inspired countless commentaries until well into the 18th century. Of unusual excellence also is the Hippocratic work *Fractures, Dislocations, and Wounds*.

Although not a practicing physician, the Greek philosopher Aristotle contributed greatly to the

MEDICINE

development of medicine by his dissections of numerous animals. He is known as the founder of comparative anatomy.

By the 3d century BC, Alexandria, Egypt, the seat of a famous medical school and library, was firmly established as the center of Greek medical science. In Alexandria the anatomist Herophilus performed the first recorded public dissection, and the physiologist Erasistratus did important work on the anatomy of the brain, nerves, veins, and arteries. The followers of these men divided into many contending sects; the most notable were the empiricists, who based their doctrine on experience gained by trial and error. The empiricists excelled in surgery and pharmacology; a royal student of empiricism, Mithradates VI Eupator, king of Pontus, developed the concept of inducing tolerance of poisons by the administration of gradually increased dosages.

Greco-Roman. Alexandrian Greek medicine influenced conquering Rome despite initial resistance from the Romans. Asclepiades of Bithynea was important in establishing Greek medicine in Rome in the 1st century BC. Opposed to the theory of humors, Asclepiades taught that the body was composed of disconnected particles, or atoms, separated by pores. Disease was caused by restriction of the orderly motion of the atoms or by the blocking of the pores, which he attempted to cure by exercise, bathing, and variations in diet, rather than by drugs. This theory was revived periodically and in various forms as late as the 18th century.

The chief medical writers of the 1st and 2d centuries AD, apart from Galen of Pergamum, were the Roman Aulus Cornelius Celsus, who wrote an encyclopedia of medicine; the Greek physician Pedanius Dioscorides, the first scientific medical botanist; the Greek physician Artaeus of Cappadocia (fl. 2d cent.), a disciple of Hippocrates; the Greek anatomist Rufus of Ephesus (fl. early 2d cent.), renowned for his investigations of the heart and eye; and Soranus of Ephesus (fl. 98–138), another Greek physician, who recorded information concerning obstetrics and gynecology (qq.v.), apparently based on human dissection. Although an adherent of the school of Asclepiades, he distinguished among diseases by their symptoms and course.

Galen of Pergamum, also a Greek, was the most important physician of this period and is second only to Hippocrates in the medical history of antiquity. In view of his undisputed authority over medicine in the Middle Ages, his principal doctrines require some elaboration. Galen described the four classic symptoms of inflammation and added much to the knowledge of infectious disease and pharmacology. His anatomic knowlege of humans was defective because it was based on dissection of apes. Some of Galen's teachings tended to hold back medical progress. His theory, for example, that the blood carried the pneuma, or life spirit, which gave it its red color, coupled with the erroneous notion that the blood passed through a porous wall between the ventricles of the heart, delayed the understanding of circulation and did much to discourage research in physiology. His most important work, however, was in the field of the form and function of muscles and the function of the areas of the spinal cord. He also excelled in diagnosis and prognosis. The importance of Galen's work cannot be overestimated, for through his writings knowledge of Greek medicine was subsequently transmitted to the Western world by the Arabs.

Roman. Original Roman contributions were made in the fields of public health (q.v.) and hygiene. In the organization of street sanitation, water supply, and public hospitals, the methods of the Romans were not surpassed until modern times.

MEDICINE IN THE MIDDLE AGES

The gradual infiltration of the Roman world by a succession of barbarian tribes was followed by a period of stagnation in the sciences. Western medicine in the early Middle Ages consisted of tribal folklore, mingled with poorly understood remnants of classical learning. Even in sophisticated Constantinople, a series of epidemics served only to initiate a revival of magical practices. Only a few outstanding Greek physicians such as Oribasius (c. 325–400), Alexander of Tralles (c. 525–c. 605), and Paul of Aegina (625?–90?) maintained the older tradition in face of the rise of moral decadence, superstition, and intellectual stagnation.

Arabic. In the 7th century a vast portion of the Eastern world was overrun by Arab conquerors. In Persia, the Arabs learned of Greek medicine at the schools of the Nestorian Christians (see NESTORIANISM), a sect in exile from the Byzantine Empire. These schools had preserved many texts lost in the destruction of the Alexandrian Library (see ALEXANDRIA, LIBRARY OF). Translations from Greek were instrumental in the development of a scientific revival and an Arabic system of medicine, based on Greek and Roman thought, throughout the Arab-speaking world. Followers of the system were known as Arabists. Important among Arabist physicians were Rhazes (c. 860–c. 930), a famous clinician and writer, who was the first to identify smallpox, in 910, and measles (qq.v.) and to suggest blood as the cause of infectious diseases; Isaac Judaeus (850–950), the author of the first book devoted entirely to dietetics; and Avicenna, whose famous *Canon* remained the standard synthesis of the doctrines of Hippocrates, Aristotle, and Galen. Arabists of the 12th century include Avenzoar (c. 1090–1162), who first described the parasite causing scabies and was among the earliest to question the authority of Galen; Averroës, recognized as the greatest commentator on Aristotle; Averroës' pupil Maimonides, whose works on diet, hygiene, and toxicology (q.v.) were widely read; and Al-Quarashi (1210–88), also known as Ibn al-Nafis, who wrote commentaries on the writings of Hippocrates and treatises on diet and eye diseases, and, most important, was the first to indicate the pulmonary transit of blood, from the right to the left ventricle via the lungs.

The Arabists did much to elevate professional standards by insisting on examinations for physicians before licensure. They introduced numerous therapeutic chemical substances, excelled in the fields of ophthalmology and public hygiene, and were superior to the physicians of medieval Europe.

European. Early medieval Europe suffered from complete disorganization of the lay medical fraternity. To supply the pressing need for medical care, a form of ecclesiastical medicine arose; originating in the monastic infirmary, it spread rapidly to separate charitable institutions designed to care for the many sufferers of leprosy and other disorders. The Benedictines (q.v.) were especially active in this work, collecting and studying ancient medical texts in their library at Monte Cassino, Italy. St. Benedict of Nursia, the founder of the order, obligated its members to study the sciences, especially medicine. The abbot of Monte Cassino, Bertharius (fl. 848–84), was himself a famous physician.

Under the Frankish theologian Rabanus Maurus (c. 780–856), Fulda became a famous center of medical learning in Germany. By the 9th century, as a result of the efforts of Charlemagne, Holy Roman emperor, medicine was included in the curriculum of the cathedral schools. By contrast, the French ecclesiastic St. Bernard of Clairvaux forbade the Cistercian monks to study medical books and prohibited the use of all remedies other than prayer.

During the 9th and 10th centuries the ancient health resort of Salerno, situated near Monte Cassino, gradually became a recognized center of medical activity. At the beginning of the 11th century Salerno became the site of the first Western school of medicine. Teaching was primarily practical and secular in tone and emphasized diet and personal hygiene. The Italian physician and translator Constantine the African (1015–87), who became a Benedictine monk and retired to the abbey of Monte Cassino, prepared Latin translations from the Arabic of many Greek medical classics for students at both Salerno and Monte Cassino. By the 12th century medical instruction had become increasingly theoretical and scholastic and spread to the medical school at Montpellier and later to the universities of Paris, Oxford, and Bologna.

By the end of the 12th century the revival of lay medicine and restrictions on activities outside the cloister brought about the decline of monastic medicine, but it had performed a valuable function by preserving the traditions of medical learning. In the 13th century, dissection of the human body was permitted, medical licensure by examination was endorsed, and strict measures were instituted for the control of public hygiene, but scholastic medicine remained largely a logical exposition of ancient dogma. Representative scientists of this period include the German scholastic St. Albertus Magnus, who engaged in biological research, and the English philosopher Roger Bacon, who undertook research in optics and refraction and was the first scholar to suggest that medicine should rely on remedies provided by chemistry. Even Bacon, often regarded as an original thinker and pioneer in experimental science, was dominated by the authority of the Greek and Arabic writers.

In Italy the universities of Bologna and Padua became leading medical centers in the 13th century. At Bologna attempts were made to confirm the classic anatomical concepts by human dissection. At Padua, Pietro d'Abano (1250–1316) attempted to reconcile the difference between adherents of the Greek and Arabist systems.

Despite popular prejudice, anatomical study continued. The social status of the surgeon was then considered inferior to that of the physician. Nevertheless, impressive advances were made by the surgeon Hugh of Lucca (d. 1258?), who denounced some of Galen's teachings and practiced simplified treatment of dislocations, fractures, and wounds. He studied the sublimation of arsenic and is credited with founding a school of surgery at Bologna in 1204. William of Saliceto (1210?–80?) and his pupil Lanfranchi (1250?–1315?) were pioneers in surgical anatomy, Lanfranchi being credited as the first to differentiate between hypertrophy and breast cancer. Two dominant figures of French surgery during this period were Henri de Mondeville (1260–1320), surgeon to the king of France, who advocated aseptic treatment of wounds and the use

MEDICINE

of sutures, and Guy de Chauliac (c. 1300-68), known as the father of French surgery, whose writings stressed the importance of anatomical dissection in training the surgeon and who is credited with being the first to recognize the plague, which first appeared in Europe in 1348. He also is thought to be the first to describe femoral hernia (1361), and he invented several surgical instruments. The study of medicine benefited greatly from the work of the ecclesiastic Archbishop Raimundo (d. 1152), who, about 1140, founded at Toledo, Spain, an institute for the translation of Arabic medical manuscripts, including the works of Rhazes and Avicenna, into Latin.

RENAISSANCE MEDICINE

No abrupt change in medical thought occurred in the Renaissance, but criticism directed against Galen and the Arabists increased, and the doctrines of Hippocrates were revived. Renaissance artists undertook the study of human anatomy, particularly of muscles, in order to better portray the human body. Leonardo da Vinci made remarkably accurate anatomical drawings based on dissection of human corpses. Unfortunately his work, the bulk of which was lost for centuries, exerted little effect at the time.

The publication in 1543 of the great treatise on anatomy, *De Humani Corporis Fabrica* (On the Structure of the Human Body) by the Belgian anatomist Andreas Vesalius, was a milestone in medical history. Hundreds of Galen's anatomical errors were clearly demonstrated by this remarkable observer and by his equally brilliant contemporary, Gabriel Fallopius, who discovered the uterine tubes named after him and the tympanum, diagnosed ear diseases with an ear speculum, and described in detail the muscles of the eye, tear ducts, and Fallopian tubes. Galen was also contradicted by the Spanish physician Michael Servetus, who was first to describe correctly the circulatory system in the lungs and to explain digestion as the source of heat.

During his stormy career, the Swiss physician and alchemist Philippus Aureolus Paracelsus, the founder of chemotherapy, broke with tradition by burning the classical treatises on medicine, by lecturing in German, and by discovering new chemical remedies. Ambroise Paré, the French surgeon, facilitated surgical amputation by his use of forceps and ligature instead of cautery to stop hemorrhage, or bleeding. The Italian physician and poet Girolamo Fracastoro (1483-1553), sometimes called the father of scientific epidemiology, demonstrated the specific character of fevers and discovered typhus (q.v.); the term *syphilis* (q.v.), applied to the virulent disease then devastating Europe, was derived from his famous poem, "Syphilis sive Morbus Gallicus" (Syphilis or Disease of Gauls, 1530). His theory that infectious diseases are transmitted by invisible seeds of contagion, capable of self-reproduction, was a precursor of modern bacteriological theories. *See* BACTERIOLOGY; DISEASE.

THE DAWN OF MODERN MEDICINE

The event that dominated 17th-century medicine and marked the beginning of a new epoch in medical science was the discovery of the circulation of the blood by the English physician and anatomist William Harvey. In 1553 Michael Servetus had described the pulmonary transit of the blood. Harvey's *Essay on the Motion of the Heart and the Blood* (1628) established the fact that the heart pumps the blood in continuous circulation. The Italian anatomist Marcello Malpighi advanced Harvey's work by his discovery of the capillaries, and the Italian anatomist Gasparo Aselli (1581-1626) gave the first adequate description of the lacteals (*see* LYMPHATIC SYSTEM). In England the physician Thomas Willis (1621-75) investigated the anatomy of the brain and the nervous system, was the first to distinguish diabetes mellitus, and described hysteria and a number of nervous afflictions. The English physician Francis Glisson (1597-1677) laid the foundations for the modern knowledge of the anatomy of the liver, described rickets (sometimes called Glisson's disease), and was the first to prove that muscles contract when activity is performed.

The English physician Richard Lower (1631-91) did fundamental work on the anatomy of the heart, demonstrated the interaction of air and blood, and performed one of the first successful blood transfusions. His work supplemented that of other members of the so-called Oxford group, the English physiologists Robert Boyle and Robert Hooke, who pioneered in the physiology of respiration.

The French mathematician and philosopher René Descartes, who also made anatomical dissections and investigated the anatomy of the eye and the mechanism of vision, maintained that the body functioned as a machine. This view was adopted by the so-called iatrophysicists, whose views were opposed by the iatrochemists, who regarded life as a series of chemical processes. The exponents of the former view were the Italian physician Sanctorius (1561-1636), who investigated metabolism, and the Italian mathematician and physicist Giovanni Alfonso Borelli (1608-79), who worked in the area of physiology. Jan Baptista van Helmont, a Flemish physician and chemist, founded the opposing iatrochemical school, the work of which was advanced by

MEDICINE

the Prussian anatomist Franciscus Sylvius (1614–1672), who studied the chemistry of digestion and emphasized the treatment of disease by drugs.

The English physician Thomas Sydenham, called the English Hippocrates, and subsequently the Dutch physician Hermann Boerhaave reestablished the significance of bedside instruction in their emphasis on the clinical approach to medicine. Sydenham carried out extensive studies on malaria and on the mechanisms of epidemics, and he distinguished scarlet fever from measles. The introduction into Europe in 1632 of what came to be known as quinine (q.v.), obtained from cinchona bark, was another event in therapeutic progress.

New Insights. After the discoveries of Polish astronomer Nicolaus Copernicus, Galileo, and the English mathematician Isaac Newton, 18th-century medicine made efforts to adapt itself to scientific investigation. Nevertheless, strange and unsupported theories still gained credence. The German physician and chemist Georg Ernst Stahl believed that the soul is the vital principle and that it controls organic development; in contrast, the German physician Friedrich Hoffmann (1660–1742) considered the body a machine and life a mechanical process. These opposing theories of the vitalists and the mechanists were influential in 18th-century medicine. The British physician William Cullen (1710–90) attributed disease to the excess or deficiency of nervous energy; and the physician John Brown (1735–88) of Edinburgh taught that disease was caused by weakness or inadequate stimulation of the organism. According to his theories, known as the Brunonian system, stimulation should be increased by treatment with irritants and large dosages of drugs. The German physician Samuel Hahnemann (1755–1843) developed the system of homeopathy (q.v.) late in the 18th century; it emphasized small dosages of drugs, in opposition to the Brunonian system. Other irregular systems proposed toward the end of the 18th and in the early 19th centuries included phrenology (q.v.), a theory formulated by the German physicians Johann Kaspar Spurzheim (1776–1832) and Franz Joseph Gall (1758–1828), who believed that examination of the skull of an individual would reveal information about his or her mental functions; and the theory of animal magnetism developed by the Austrian physician Franz Mesmer, who believed in the existence of a magnetic force having a powerful influence on the human body.

Later 18th-Century Efforts. Of importance in the 18th century was the work of the British physician William Smellie (1697–1763), whose innovations in obstetrics broke the monopoly of midwives, and of the British anatomist and obstetrician William Hunter (1718–83), who studied with Smellie and was the brother of the celebrated British anatomist and surgeon John Hunter. William Hunter revitalized the study of anatomy in England and carried on Smellie's work to establish obstetrics as a separate branch of medicine.

Among other important contributions of this period were the establishment of the science of pathology by the Italian anatomist and pathologist Giovanni Battista Morgagni; the studies in experimental physiology of the Italian naturalist and biologist Lazzaro Spallanzani, who refuted the doctrine of spontaneous generation (q.v.); the research in neuromuscular physiology by the Swiss scientist Albrecht von Haller; and the studies of blood pressure by the British botanist, chemist, and physiologist Stephen Heles. Important work in botany was performed by the Swedish botanist and taxonomist Carolus Linnaeus, who devised the modern binomial system of biological nomenclature (*see* CLASSIFICATION), and the British physician, botanist, and mineralogist William Withering (1741–99), who introduced digitalis.

John Hunter made great advances in surgery; the British physician James Lind (1716–94) dealt with scurvy (q.v.), combating the vitamin-C deficiency that caused the disease by prescribing the drinking of lemon juice. The British social reformer John Howard furthered humane treatment for hospital and prison inmates throughout Europe. In 1796 the British physician Edward Jenner discovered the principle of vaccination as a preventive measure against smallpox. His contribution both enabled control of this dreaded disease and established the science of immunization (q.v.).

19TH-CENTURY MEDICINE

Many discoveries made in the 19th century led to great advances in diagnosis and treatment of disease and in surgical methods. Diagnosis procedures for chest disorders were advanced to an extent in the 18th century by the method of percussion first described by the Austrian physician Leopold Auenbrugger von Auenbrugg (1722–1809) in 1761. His work was ignored, however, until 1808, when it was publicized in a French translation by the personal physician to Napoleon. About 1819 the French physician René Théophile Hyacinthe Laënnec (1781–1826) invented the stethoscope (q.v.), still the most useful single tool of the physician. A number of brilliant British clinicians assimilated the new methods of diagnosing diseases, with the result that their names have become familiar through their identification with commonly recognized diseases. The physician Thomas Addison (1793–1860) discovered the disorder of the adrenal glands now known as Addison's disease (q.v.); Richard Bright (1789–1858) diagnosed nephritis (q.v.), or Bright's disease; Thomas Hodgkin (1798–1866) described a malignant disease of lymphatic tissue now known as Hodgkin's disease (q.v.); the surgeon and paleontologist James Parkinson (1755–1824) described the chronic nervous disease called Parkinson's disease (q.v.); and the Irish physician Robert James Graves (1796–1853) diagnosed exophthalmic, or toxic, goiter (q.v.), sometimes called Graves' disease.

European Discoveries. Medicine is indebted to German universities for the scientific discoveries that did away with the lingering remnants of the traditional theory of humors. Of fundamental importance was the development by the German botanist Matthias Jakob Schleiden of the cell theory of organic development (see EMBRYOLOGY), which paved the way for the microscopic study of diseased tissues. The German anatomist and physiologist Theodor Schwann later applied Schleiden's cell theories to the evolution of animal life. The work of the French anatomist and physiologist Marie François Xavier Bichat in the systematic study of human tissue was a foundation stone of the science of histology (q.v.). The Austrian pathologist and physician Baron Karl von Rokitansky (1804–78), who performed more than 30,000 postmortem examinations, was the first to detect the bacterial origin of endocarditis (q.v.). Other great founders of microscopic pathology include Schwann, the German physiologist and neurologist Robert Remak (1815–65), the Czech physiologist Johannes Evangelista Purkinje, the Swiss anatomist and physiologist Rudolf Albert von Kölliker (1817–1905), and the German pathologist and anatomist Friedrich Gustav Jacob Henle (1809–85). In Germany, the Estonian biologist Karl Ernst von Baer did his pioneer research in embryology to discover the human ovum, and the German physiologist Johannes Peter Müller (1801–58) introduced the concept of the specific energy of nerves. The culmination of this remarkable series of investigations is found in the work of the German pathologist Rudolf Virchow, whose doctrine that the cell is the seat of disease remains the cornerstone of modern medical science.

Darwin, Pasteur, and Koch. The evolutionary theory (see EVOLUTION) of Charles Darwin revived interest in the science of comparative anatomy and physiology; the plant-breeding experiments of the Austrian biologist Gregor Johann Mendel had a similar effect in stimulating studies in human genetics (see HEREDITY).

The early studies of the French chemist and microbiologist Louis Pasteur of fermentation (q.v.) resulted in the final destruction of the concept of spontaneous generation and brought about a revival of interest in the theory that disease might be the result of a specific contagium. Important in the development of the germ theory was the pioneering work in puerperal fever (q.v.) of the American physician and author Oliver Wendell Holmes and of the Hungarian obstetrician Ignaz Philipp Semmelweis, who showed that the high rate of mortality in women after childbirth was attributable to infectious agents transmitted by unwashed hands.

Pasteur and the German physician and bacteriologist Robert Koch are usually given equal credit for their contributions to bacteriology; the development of this field is generally considered the greatest single advance in the history of medicine. Within a few decades the causes of such age-old scourges as anthrax, diphtheria (qq.v.), tuberculosis, leprosy, and plague were isolated. The German physiologist Emil Heinrich Du Bois-Reymond (1818–96) added new knowledge by his studies of metabolic processes and of the physiology of muscles and nerves.

Bacteriology and Surgery. Some early bacteriologists were the German physiologist Edwin Theodore Albrecht Klebs (1834–1913), who found the bacillus causing diphtheria, researched the bacteriology of anthrax and malaria, and produced tuberculosis in cattle and syphilis in apes; the German bacteriologist Friedrich August Johannes Löffler (1852–1915), who discovered the bacterium of gonorrhea (q.v.); and the Norwegian physician Gerhard Henrik Armauer Hansen (1841–1912), who discovered the leprosy bacillus. The German gynecologist Karl Sigismund Franz Credé (1819–92) developed the method of placing drops of an antiseptic solution of silver nitrate in the eyes of the newborn to prevent gonorrheal ophthalmia. Pasteur's method of immunization by injecting attenuated virus (q.v.) was used successfully in the treatment of rabies (q.v.), and the German bacteriologist Emil Adolph von Behring developed immunizing serums against diphtheria and tetanus. The Russian bacteriologist Élie Metchnikoff was the first to demonstrate the phagocytic, or bacteria-destroying, property of certain white cells (granular leukocytes) in the blood. See PHAGOCYTOSIS.

Surgery derived important benefit from the development of the germ theory. The British surgeon and biologist Joseph Lister adopted the use of carbolic acid as an antiseptic agent with impressive results in reducing mortality from wound infection (see ANTISEPTICS). Lister's demonstrations that bacteria are airborne were later expanded to a realization that they are also carried by the hands and by instruments, the sterilization of which introduced the era of aseptic surgery. Another great advance in surgery came with the discovery of anesthetics.

Physiology. With progress in physics and chemistry, the science of physiology made tremendous strides during the 19th century. Among outstanding physiologists of this period were the German chemist Justus von Liebig, who developed analytical methods of organic chemistry and studied food chemistry and metabolism, and the German physicist and physiologist Hermann Ludwig Ferdinand von Helmholtz, who invented the ophthalmoscope and ophthalmometer, investigated the speed of nerve impulses and reflexive processes, and performed studies of primary importance in optics and acoustics. The French physiologist Claude Bernard, recognized as the founder of experimental medicine, made important discoveries about the functions of the pancreas and the liver and about the sympathetic nervous system. Bernard's work on the interaction of the digestive system and the vasomotor system, which controls the size of blood vessels, was developed further by the Russian physiologist Ivan Petrovich Pavlov, who elaborated the theory of the conditioned reflex (see REFLEX), the basis of behaviorism (q.v.).

Other physiologists of the 19th century include the French-American physician and physiologist Charles Édouard Brown-Séquard, who investigated the activities of the various glands composing the endocrine system (q.v.), and Carl Friedrich Wilhelm Ludwig (1816-95), a German physiologist, who explored cardiac and renal activity through new methods of functional study. The work of the Spanish histologist Santiago Ramón y Cajal contributed new knowledge of the structure and function of the nervous system.

Another valuable diagnostic aid was the X ray (q.v.), discovered accidentally by the German physicist Wilhelm Conrad Roentgen. The Danish physician Niels Ryberg Finsen (1860-1904) developed an ultraviolet-ray lamp, which led to an improved prognosis for tuberculosis of the skin and other skin diseases (see ULTRAVIOLET RADIATION). The discovery of radium (q.v.) by the French physicists Pierre and Marie Curie offered a treatment for some forms of cancer (q.v.).

American Contributions. The U.S. contributed significantly to medical progress. In 1803 the biologist John Richardson Young (1782-1804) described the process of acid formation in gastric digestion. Thirty years later the surgeon William Beaumont published his remarkable studies on the gastric juices and the physiology of digestion based on his observations of a patient suffering from a gastric fistula (q.v.). In the field of operative gynecology, the U.S. was an undisputed pioneer. In 1809 the physician and surgeon Ephraim McDowell (1771-1830) performed the first surgical removal of an ovarian tumor, and the gynecologist James Marion Sims (1813-83) saved the lives of countless women by his surgical correction of vesicovaginal fistula, first performed in 1845.

In 1900 the U.S. Army physician, surgeon, and bacteriologist Walter Reed and his colleagues, acting on a suggestion made by the Cuban biolo-

The most sophisticated medical electronic and recording equipment, including an advanced heart-lung machine (in the foreground), is employed as a surgical team performs open-heart surgery. This ultramodern cardiac-operating suite is a part of the biomedical research and clinical center at the National Institutes of Health.

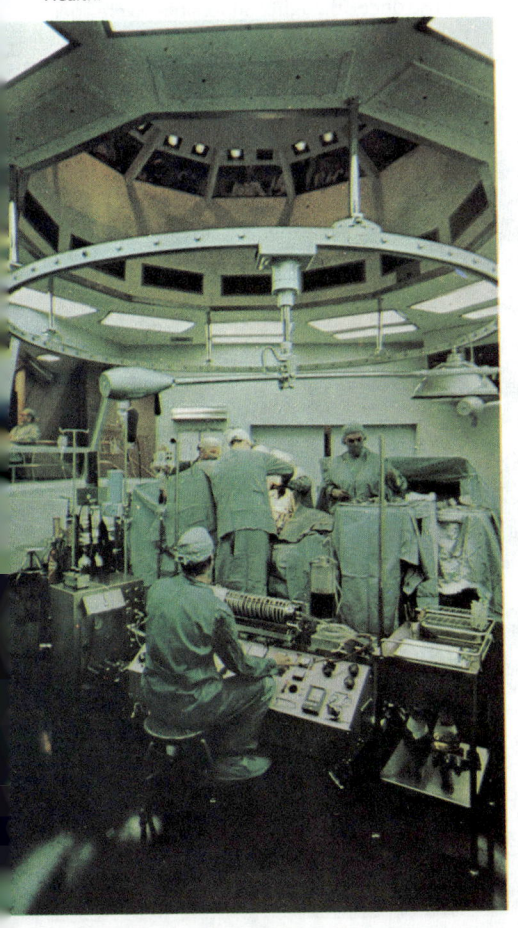

MEDICINE

gist Carlos Juan Finlay, demonstrated that the mosquito is the vector of yellow fever (q.v.) only a few years after the British physician Ronald Ross had proved the role of the mosquito as a carrier of the malarial parasite. C.D.O'M.

20TH-CENTURY MEDICINE

In the 20th century, many infectious diseases have been conquered through vaccines, antibiotics, and improved living conditions. Cancer has become a more common illness, but treatments have been developed that effectively combat some forms of the disease. Basic research into life systems was also begun in the 20th century. Important discoveries were made in many areas, especially concerning the basis for the transmission of hereditary traits and the chemical and physical mechanisms for brain function.

Genetics. A fundamental discovery of the 20th century was how hereditary characteristics are transmitted. An important advance was made by Oswald Theodore Avery and his colleagues at the Rockefeller Institute in the 1940s when they showed that certain characteristics could be passed from one bacterium to another on a substance called deoxyribonucleic acid, or DNA (see GENETICS; NUCLEIC ACIDS). In 1953 the English physicist Francis Harry Compton Crick and the American biologist James Dewey Watson proposed an elegant chemical structure for DNA that explained how it could carry genetic information. The American biochemist Marshall Warren Nirenberg provided essential details of this scheme in the 1960s, and the Indian-born American biochemist Har Gobind Khorana first used this information to synthesize a gene in 1970. During the latter half of the 1970s scientists developed methods to alter genes in desired ways, and by the mid-1980s some of these techniques were beginning to be used medically. The same procedures, which are generally referred to as genetic engineering (q.v.) or gene cloning, have also been applied to produce large quantities of pure human substances such as hormones and interferon (q.v.).

Surgery. In the last half of the 20th century operations once thought impossible were per-

Surgeons view a patient through high-power magnifying lenses during a microsurgical operation on the eye.
Laimute Druskis–Taurus Photos

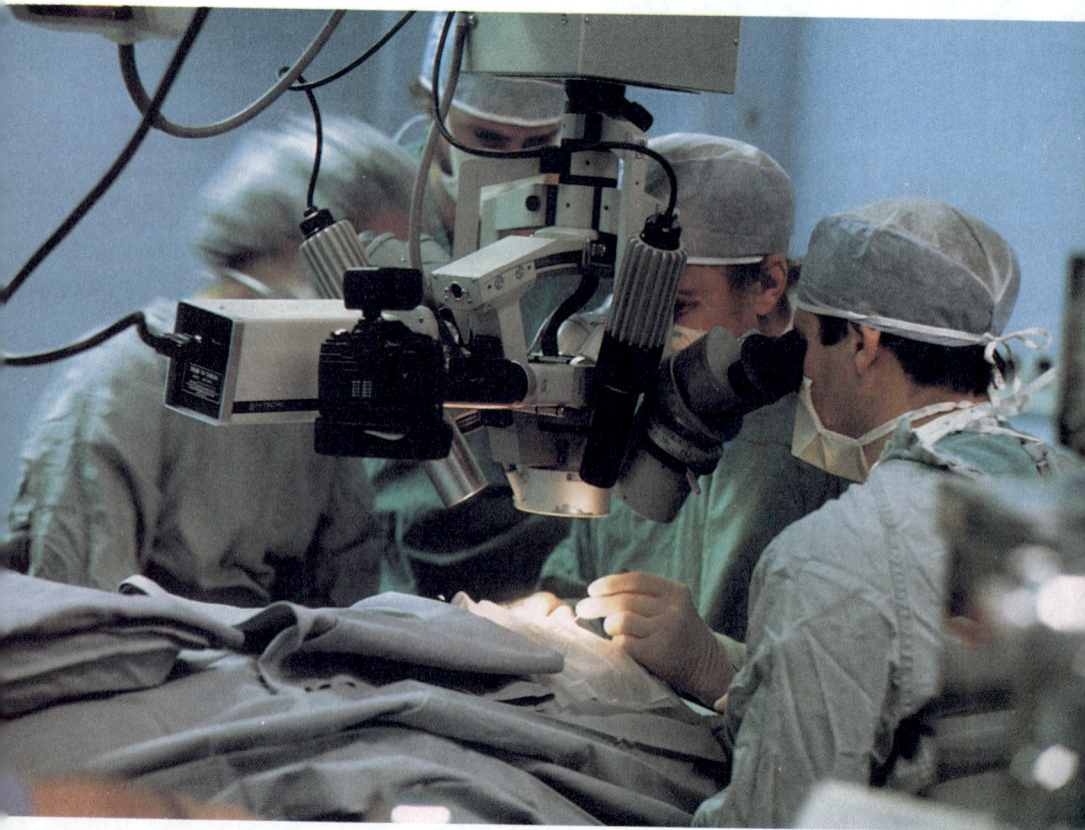

formed. In 1962, for the first time, an arm completely severed at the shoulder was successfully rejoined to the body. Less spectacular but more common procedures included rejoining of fingers and toes accidentally amputated. Surgery of this kind was made possible by operating microscopes, through which the surgeon could see tiny nerves and blood vessels that had to be reattached to make the amputated part function again. Plastic replacements have led to such advances as new hip joints, which enable persons crippled by arthritis (q.v.) to walk again, and prosthetic arms powered by batteries. Kidney failure, previously fatal, is now routinely treated either by a transplant or by long-term treatment with an artificial kidney (see TRANSPLANTATION, MEDICAL). In 1975 a large experimental trial showed that diabetics with damage to the vessels of the eye could often be saved from blindness by treatment with a laser (q.v.) beam. Some severe cases of epilepsy (q.v.) are now cured by finding the damaged spot in the brain that causes the seizures and destroying it with a probe chilled by liquid nitrogen.

Infectious Diseases. Many infectious diseases have been conquered in the 20th century by improved sanitation, antibiotics, and vaccines. Specific drug therapy for infections began with the discovery by the German physician Paul Ehrlich of arsphenamine, an arsenic-containing compound, as a treatment for syphilis. This was followed in 1932 by the announcement by the German scientist Gerhard Domagk (1895-1964) that the dye prontosil rubrum was active against streptococcal infections. Discovery of the active agent in prontosil, sulfanilamide, led to proliferation of the first group of so-called wonder drugs, the sulfonamide antibiotics. The purification of penicillin in 1938 by the British biochemists Howard Florey and Ernst Chain followed by ten years the discovery by Alexander Fleming of the germ-destroying activity of the *Penicillium* mold. The outbreak of World War II prompted immediate commercial production of penicillin, which was credited with greatly reducing fatalities.

A specific treatment was also found for tuberculosis: the drug streptomycin (q.v.). When the bacteria became resistant, a combination of paraaminosalycilic acid plus isoniazid was developed; this remains the first-line treatment for the disease. Leprosy is effectively treated by drugs called sulfones, and malaria by derivatives of the chemical quinine, which is extracted from the bark of the cinchona tree. Antibiotics were not found for diseases caused by viruses, however, so vaccines became the mainstay of treatment. Among the earliest were those for smallpox, discovered by Edward Jenner in 1796; for typhoid fever, developed by the English bacteriologist Almroth Wright (1861-1947) in 1897; for diphtheria in 1923; and for tetanus in the 1930s.

A major advance in preparing virus vaccines came in the 1930s with the development by the American microbiologists John Franklin Enders and Frederick Chapman Robbins (1916-) of ways of growing viruses in tissue culture. This soon led to vaccines for yellow fever, poliomyelitis, measles, mumps, and rubella (German measles). In the early 1980s, genetic engineering led to the development of vaccines against hepatitis B, influenza, herpes simplex, and chicken pox, and a malaria vaccine was being tested.

The fight against infectious diseases became more complicated in the latter part of the 20th century with the rise in resistance of microorganisms to antibiotics and the discovery of new diseases, such as Legionnaires' disease and acquired immune deficiency syndrome (qq.v.).

Brain Function. The brain was one of the last parts of the human body to be explored scientifically. In the 19th century the Spanish neuroanatomist Santiago Ramón y Cajal used chemical dyes to define discrete areas of the brain, but the more sophisticated tools of the 20th century were required to assign functions to these areas. During the early part of the century the American neurosurgeon Wilder Graves Penfield (1891-1976) stimulated various parts of patients' brains during surgery and showed that various muscular and emotional functions resided in separate locations. Study of persons whose right and left hemispheres had been separated by injury showed that each half of the brain was primarily concerned with different activities. Development of sophisticated imaging devices at the National Institutes of Health in the 1970s allowed investigators to demonstrate the specific parts of the brain that control hearing, speech, and movement of the limbs.

Equally important were discoveries of how nerves function. The chemical transmitter theory, which was developed in the 20th century, states that impulses pass from one nerve to another by a combination of electrical and chemical signals. Another important finding for physiology was the discovery during the 1970s that the brain regulates bodily functions by releasing hormones that are sent by the hypothalamus, an area of the brain, to influence the master gland, the pituitary gland (q.v.). This work, by the American endocrinologists Roger Guillemin (1924-) and Andrew Victor Schally (1926-), established a connection between emotions and biochemistry. In the medical area, treatments became available for

MEDICINE

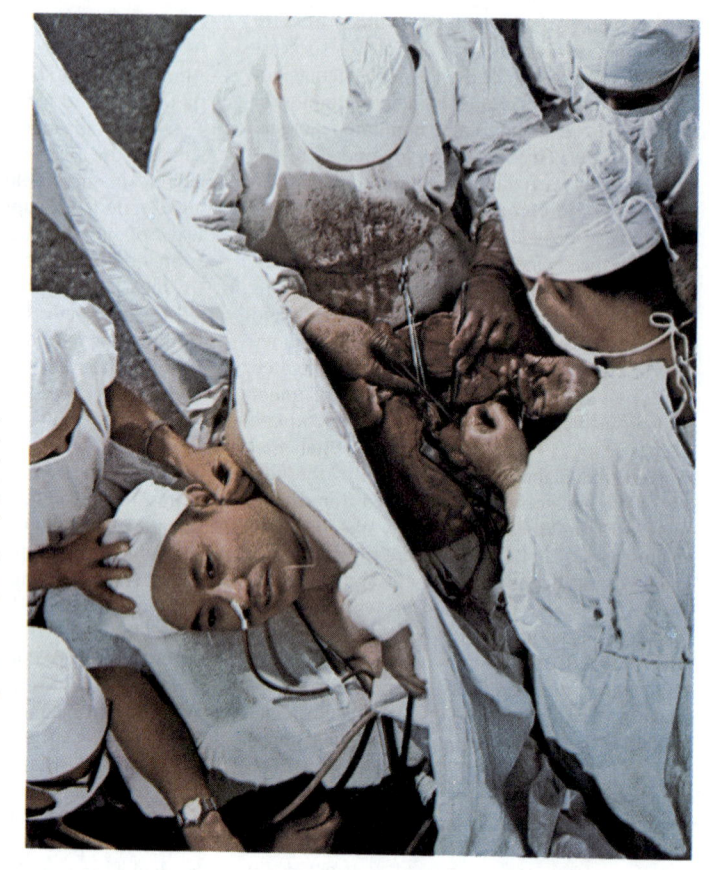

Physicians at Peking University Clinics insert needles in a patient's left earlobe and left underarm area to anesthetize him for a cancer operation. During the operation the patient was completely conscious, breathed normally, and had constant blood pressure. This age-old Chinese method of providing anesthesia is at present being experimented with in Western research studies in physiology, biochemistry, anatomy, and other areas of medical sciences.
Photo Researchers, Inc.

the first time for the neurological diseases epilepsy and Parkinson's disease.

Immunity. Until the 20th century, knowledge of the immune system was limited. It was primarily known through its production of antibodies in response to infection or immunization. During the 1930s the German immunologist Karl Landsteiner demonstrated the impressive specificity of antibody reactions. Scientists also discovered that several kinds of antibody molecules exist. In particular, the form called immunoglobulin E was found to be associated with allergy, and in the 1950s the detailed structure of one type of immunoglobulin was worked out.

The immune system was found to be the cause of Rh disease (*see* Rh Factor) and to be responsible for the failure of organ transplantation. This led to development of an antiserum that has effectively eliminated Rh disease and to the use of drugs that temporarily disable the immune system and allow transplantation of organs, especially kidneys. The formation of antibodies was also found to be the basis of severe fatal illness following blood transfusion, and the typing of blood by immune specificity has made transfusion a safe and widely applicable procedure.

In the latter part of the 20th century scientists discovered a different area of the immune system. This is the so-called cellular immune system, which is made up of the lymphocytes. These discoveries led to an understanding of many diseases, which were found to be due to inherited deficits in one or more of the subclasses of lymphocytes. Attempts to correct these deficiencies thus far center on injecting the patient with blood cells taken from the bone marrow of a closely related, healthy person. Work is also proceeding on identifying the normal hormones that cause the embryonic lymphocytes to become functional.

Health Consumers. As medicine in the 20th century became more focused on expensive medicines and complicated machines, a countermovement arose in the U.S. Individuals attempted to take control of their own health, largely through preventive medical practices, and to understand more about normal and diseased bodily function. To some extent the counter-

MEDICINE

movement also expressed a distrust of the orthodox medical establishment.

The consumer medical movement was reflected in the purchasing by laypersons of medical books such as the highly technical *Physician's Desk Reference,* a fact book on drugs. The movement was supported by some respected physicians, such as John Hilton Knowles (1926-79), director of the Rockefeller Foundation, who argued that increased medical expenditures were not improving the population's well-being. Many activist health groups were concerned with women's issues; the Boston Women's Health Book Collective published a widely distributed primer on women's health. A handful of physicians participated in this movement, either by instructing laypersons in basic medicine, setting up practices in which the patients took an active part, or disseminating printed information. The *Harvard Medical School Health Letter,* established in 1975, was one such publication. Dissatisfied with the fragmented approach of orthodox medical care, another group of physicians advocated holistic medicine, which C. Norman Shealy (1932-), president of the American Holistic Medical Association, defines as "a system of health care which assists individuals in harmonizing mind, body, and spirit." Among the most important therapies that holistic practitioners apply are good nutrition, physical exercise, and "self-regulation" techniques, such as biofeedback and relaxation. Laypersons utilized these unconventional methods in various ways. Some families opted to avoid hospitals by having their children born at home. The practice of taking very large doses of vitamins as a preventive for colds and treatment for cancer became popular. Some patients with severe cancer went to a clinic in Mexico to be treated with an extract from apricot seeds called amygdalin or laetrile, but scientific tests conducted in 1981 by American physicians failed to demonstrate any benefit from these treatments.

Radiology. New and better methods of seeing inside the human body were developed in the latter half of the 20th century. In the 1970s a special camera sensitive to gamma radiation was developed for locating specific cancers. Diagnosis of head injury was aided greatly by the invention in 1975 of a computer-assisted X-ray device called a computerized axial tomography (CAT) scanner (*see* X Ray); other imaging systems include positron emission tomography and nuclear magnetic resonance imaging (*see* Radiology). Very

A radiation technician monitors treatment of a cancer patient. The panel (center) controls a linear accelerator, a device that propels radioactive particles at the diseased area. The patient's reactions are followed on a closed-circuit television screen (right).
Leonard Freed—Magnum Photos

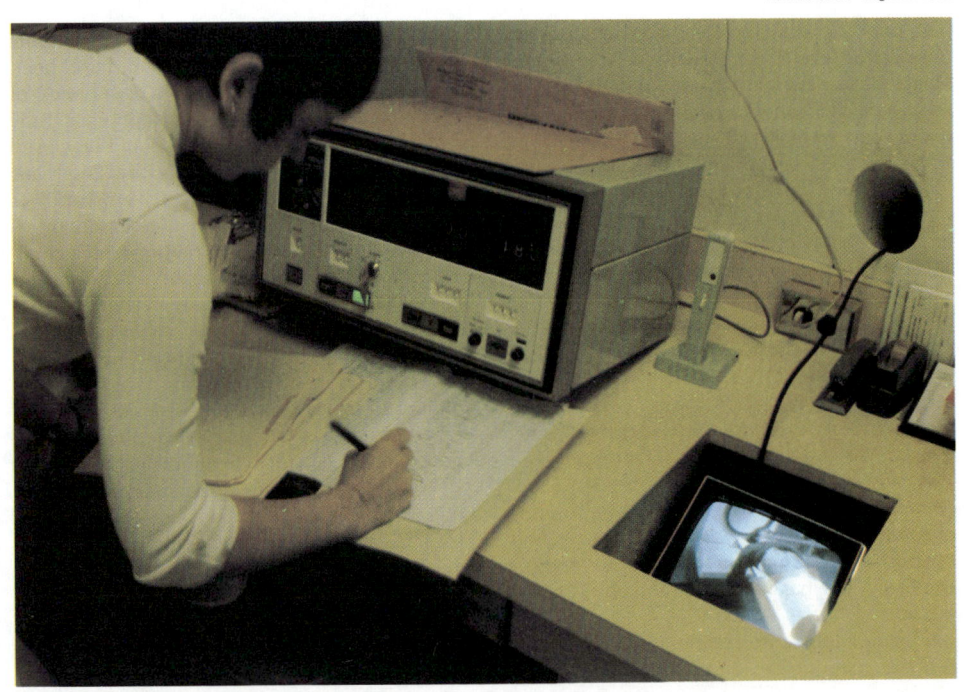

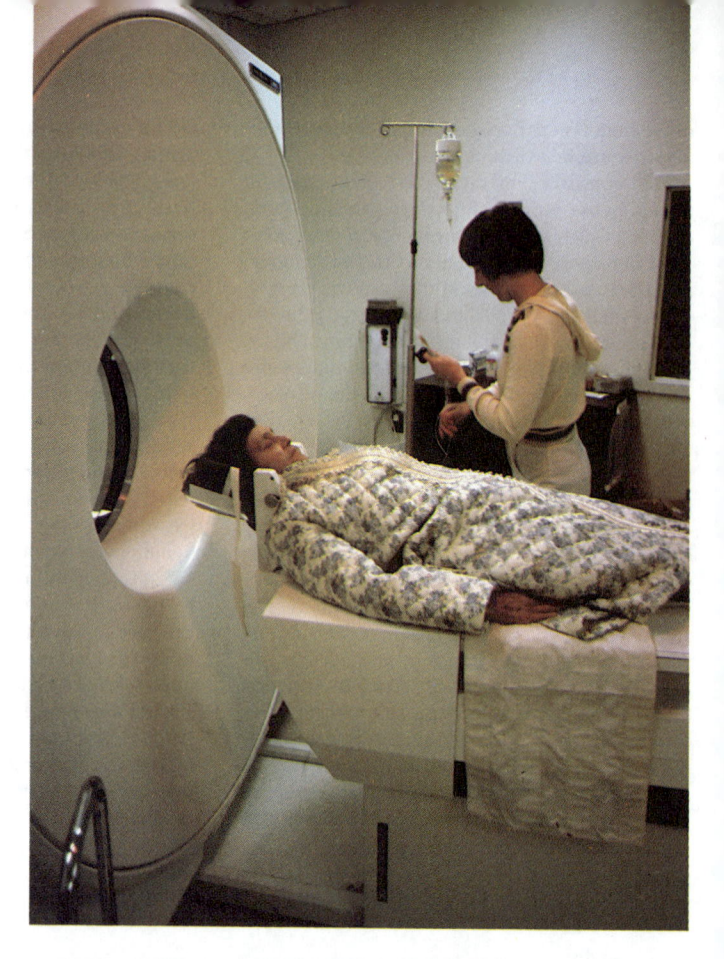

A patient is prepared for a CAT scan, an X-ray procedure that produces a clear cross-sectional view of the patient's body. Kevin Byron—Bruce Coleman, Inc.

high frequency sound waves have been used in this way for several years (*see* ULTRASONICS).

Mental Illness. Even in the early part of the 20th century, mental illness was almost a sentence of doom, and mentally ill persons were handled with cruel confinement and little help. Successful therapy for some mental illnesses has greatly improved the prognosis for these diseases and has partly removed their stigma.

The theories advanced by Sigmund Freud were among the first attempts to understand malfunctioning of the mind, but the methods of psychoanalysis (q.v.) advocated by Freud and modified by his followers proved ineffective for treating certain serious mental disorders. Two early attempts to treat psychotic illness were leucotomy, also known as lobotomy (q.v.), introduced in 1935, and electroconvulsive therapy (q.v.), devised in 1938. Leucotomy and less severe forms of psychosurgery are now used only rarely, and electroshock is primarily a treatment for depressive illness that has failed drug therapy (*see* DEPRESSION).

A major advance in treatment of these disorders was the introduction of drugs. The first of these, the phenothiazines, were used in the early 1950s to treat schizophrenia and have been largely effective in relieving the symptoms of many patients with acute schizophrenia. Early optimism that mental hospitals could be closed down, however, has proved illusory. Physicians are now realizing that some patients are not helped by drugs, and that, in any case, supportive psychological therapy must be provided as well. They have also found that some persons treated with phenothiazines for many years develop a bizarre neuromuscular disorder called tardive dyskinesia. Another important advance in the chemotherapy of mental illness has been the use of lithium to treat manic depressive disease. Other drugs, such as tricyclic antidepressants, are now often successful in treatment of depression.

Heart Disease. Cardiovascular diseases remain the principal cause of death in Western countries. Great advances have been made, however, in diagnosis and treatment. Diagnosis was improved by the technique of cardiac catheterization, which enables measurements of pressure to be taken in various chambers of the heart and in major blood vessels, and by angiography, an X-

MEDICINE

ray procedure for viewing these areas. Newer imaging devices allow estimation of the extent of heart damage in persons who have had a heart attack and of the pumping strength of the heart. Of the many new drugs available, one important class consists of chemicals that block certain functions of the sympathetic nervous system. These drugs are used for angina pectoris (chest pain from coronary artery narrowing), disturbances of heart rhythm, and hypertension (q.v.).

Advances in surgery now permit the bypassing of narrowed arterial and vein segments with grafts, the replacement of valves damaged by infection, and the correction of many congenital malformations of the heart. Heart transplants have been practiced for several years (see TRANSPLANTATION, MEDICAL), temporary artificial hearts are sometimes used, and permanent artificial hearts had been implanted in several patients by the mid-1980s. Advances in the prevention of cardiovascular diseases include an awareness and increased understanding of such potential risks as smoking, stress, obesity, high blood pressure, and elevated blood cholesterol. Since the mid-1920s, the Western world has experienced a continuing and dramatic decline in death from coronary heart disease. In the U.S. this reduction in mortality was about 25 percent by the mid-1980s; it is attributed to changes in diet, medical control of high blood pressure, reductions in smoking, and increased exercise.

Vitamins and Hormones. Since the introduction in 1912 of the term *vitamine* by the Polish biochemist Casimir Funk (1884-1967), a large number of vitamins have been isolated and their nutritional functions defined, thus providing a cure for pellagra, beriberi, rickets, and other diet-deficiency diseases. In 1926 the American physicians George Minot (1885-1950) and William Murphy (1892-   ) discovered in liver an effective control for pernicious anemia (q.v.), and in 1948 they isolated the factor vitamin B_{12}.

With increased knowledge of the activity of the endocrine glands, numerous attempts were made to isolate their secretions, called hormones (see HORMONE). Thyroid extract, effective in treating congenital hypothyroidism (see CRETINISM) and myxedema (q.v.), was the first hormone to be used in therapy (see THYROID GLAND). Of major importance in the treatment of diabetes was the isolation from the pancreas of the endocrine secretion insulin (q.v.), introduced in 1923 by the Canadian physicians Frederick Banting and Charles Best. The synthesis of the internal secretions of the reproductive glands of the male, testosterone (q.v.), and of the female, estrogen (q.v.), has made available valuable therapy for disorders of the reproductive system. The adrenal glands (see ADRENAL GLAND) were the source of the powerful vasoconstrictor adrenaline (see EPINEPHRINE), isolated by the Japanese-American chemist Jokichi Takamine (1854-1922) in 1901. In the 1940s the Canadian physician Hans Selye (1907-82) showed that this substance mediates stress reactions. In 1943 the hormone ACTH (q.v.) was obtained from the anterior lobe of the pituitary gland, which regulates the activity of the other endocrine glands. In 1946 cortisone (see HYDROCORTISONE), produced by the adrenal glands, was synthesized. *See also* SPORTS MEDICINE.

Cancer. Largely because of the increasing proportion of older persons in the population, the percentage of deaths caused by cancer in the U.S. increased from about 4 percent in 1900 to about 20 percent in the early 1980s. The disease process is not well understood, although occupational and environmental exposures to chemicals are among the causes. In particular, cigarette smoking is known to cause most lung cancer and some cancer of the bladder, mouth, throat, and pancreas. Early diagnosis, especially for cervical cancer, is helpful in reducing deaths. Treatment was initially by radiation, but in the 1960s drug therapy was introduced. The latter is now curative in many cases of cancer of the breast and testis and several blood cancers, especially those of young children. Scientists were exploring the effectiveness of a naturally produced substance, interferon, as an anticancer drug.

Ethics. With the increasing cost of medical care in the U.S. and its increasing scope, questions have arisen about the use of medical therapies. In 1973 the government undertook to provide dialysis for all patients with failed kidneys. By 1981 the bill for this therapy was more than $1 billion annually. Some observers questioned whether this money might be better spent. Others questioned keeping alive terminally ill patients on artificial respirators. In a celebrated case in 1975, the New Jersey Supreme Court ruled that the parents and physicians of a comatose young woman had the power to remove life support systems. In other cases, courts have ruled that life support can be terminated when the patient has previously expressed a wish not to have his or her life prolonged by heroic measures. A related issue involves killing a fetus with a birth defect (see ABORTION). Increased ability to detect such defects has given parents the option of having only normal children. So far the courts have not prevented the aborting of fetuses found to be severely defective, although some ethicists consider this taking a human life.

MEDICINE HAT

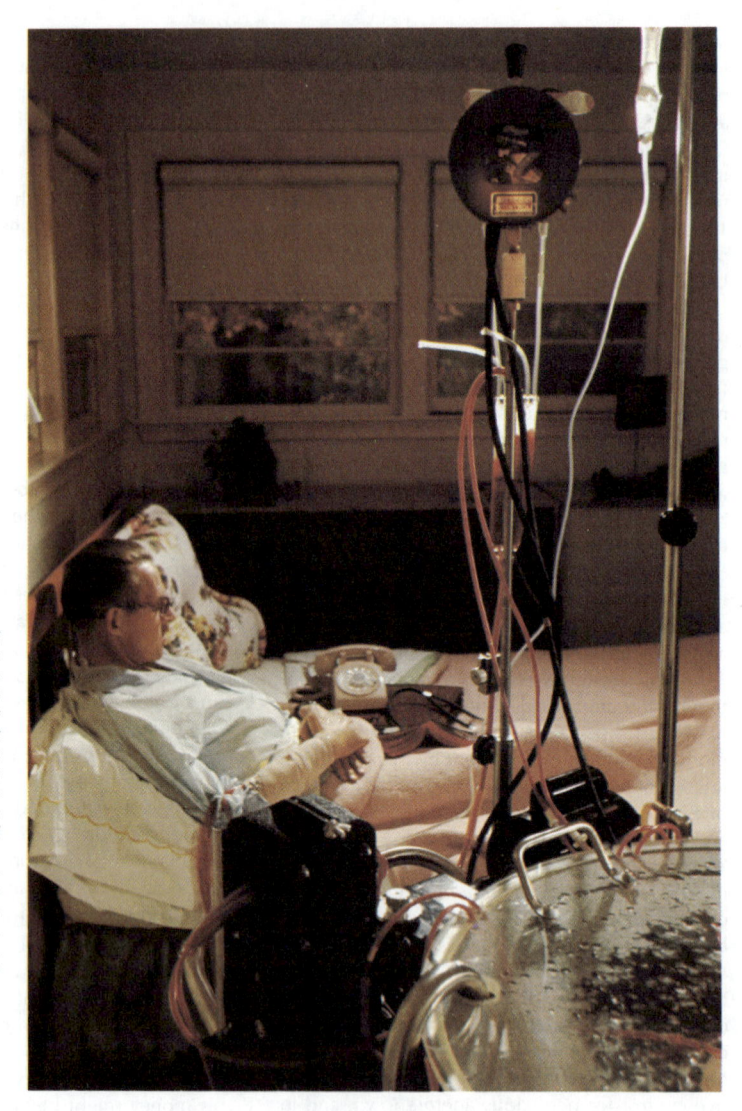

A patient undergoing treatment (dialysis) for kidney failure. In this process the patient's blood passes into an artificial kidney machine, which filters out toxic wastes and returns the purified blood to the body. Depending on the patient's condition, such treatment may be needed once a day or once a week. The design and construction of the artificial kidney machine is considered one of the most dramatic developments in biochemical engineering in recent years. Photo Researchers, Inc.

Pregnancy and Childbirth. Great advances were made in birth control (q.v.) with the improvement of intrauterine devices in the 1950s and the development of an oral contraceptive in 1960 by the American biologist Gregory Pincus (1903–67). With their widespread use, however, physicians came to realize that these methods were not completely safe, and the search for more acceptable contraceptives continued. See PLANNED PARENTHOOD FEDERATION OF AMERICA, INC.

By 1975 physicians were able to diagnose congenital or inherited diseases before childbirth. Samples may now be taken of the amniotic fluid around the fetus, or even of fetal blood, to determine whether hereditary blood diseases, Down's syndrome, defects of the spine, or other congenital diseases are present (*see* AMNIOCENTESIS). Even sex may be known in advance.

Great progress was also made in developing the techniques of artificial insemination (q.v.). By the early 1980s, many couples were resorting to various methods of in vitro fertilization ("test-tube" babies) or transplantation of fertilized ova from one womb to another.

For further information on this topic, see the Bibliography in volume 28, sections 38, 487–532, 777.

MEDICINE HAT, city, SE Alberta, on the South Saskatchewan R.; inc. as a city 1906. The city is a commercial, manufacturing, and transportation center situated in an agricultural and natural-gas producing region. Major manufactures include processed food, clay and glass products, and chemicals. The Medicine Hat Museum and Art Gallery, containing Indian artifacts and pioneer items, and a junior college are here. The name of the community, settled in the early 1880s, is derived from the Cree Indian name for the site. Pop. (1986) 41,823; (1991) 43,625.

MEDICINE MAN, a religious specialist in some non-Western cultures, whose main function is to cure disease.

Medicine men base their healing methods on the assumption that most, if not all, illnesses are caused by supernatural power and that supernatural powers are required to cure them. The individual may fall ill because of having offended one of the gods, or through the machinations of witchcraft (q.v.) or sorcery, or through the unprovoked attack of an evil spirit. The task of the curer is to diagnose the disease, usually by divinatory techniques (*see* DIVINATION), and then to apply the spiritual remedy, such as retrieving a lost soul, removing a disease-causing object, or exorcising an evil spirit. (In conjunction with these spiritual techniques, medicine men may also at times employ physical remedies such as herbal applications or massage.)

The effectiveness of the medicine man's treatment seems negligible in light of Western medicine. Anthropologists have, however, observed that the work of medicine men occasionally has beneficial results, perhaps due to a process of psychological release and consequent physiological healing. Faith healing (q.v.) in Western societies may be effective through the same process.

See also SHAMAN.   J.A.Sa.

MÉDICIS, Catherine de. *See* CATHERINE DE MÉDICIS.

MÉDICIS, Marie de. *See* MARIE DE MÉDICIS.

MEDIEVAL PERIOD. *See* MIDDLE AGES.

MEDILL, Joseph (1823–99), American journalist, born near Saint John, New Brunswick, and taken to the U.S. at the age of nine. He read law privately and was admitted to the Ohio bar in 1846, but three years later he turned to a career in journalism. In 1855 he settled in Chicago and purchased the *Tribune,* destined under his guidance to become one of the most influential newspapers in the U.S. Meanwhile Medill had been active in organizing the new Republican party. He was a supporter of Abraham Lincoln and an outspoken opponent of slavery. He served as a member of the Illinois state constitutional convention (1869), as a U.S. civil service commissioner (1871), and as mayor of Chicago (1871–74). From 1874 until his death, Medill was editor in chief of the *Tribune* and held absolute control over the newspaper's policies.

Two of Medill's grandsons, Joseph Medill Patterson (1879–1946) and Robert Rutherford McCormick (1880–1955), were also influential journalists. Patterson served on the *Chicago Tribune* (1901–5, 1914–25), founded the *New York Daily News* with McCormick (1919), and was editor and publisher of the *Daily News* (1925–46). McCormick, who was known as Colonel McCormick, was coeditor of the *Tribune* with Patterson (1920–25), and then he was its sole editor and publisher for 30 years (1925–55).

MEDINA, also Medinat-en-Nabi (City of the Prophet) and Medinat Řasul Allah (City of the Apostle of God), city, W Saudi Arabia, in al-Hijaz region. The remains of the Prophet Muhammad, who fled (622) to Medina from Mecca, repose in the city, which is consequently one of the most sacred shrines of Islam. The city is visited annually by thousands of pilgrims. Muhammad's tomb is in the Mosque of the Prophet, located in the E section of the city. The mosque also contains the tombs of Muhammad's daughter Fatima and of Umar I (581?–644), the second Orthodox caliph of the Muslim Empire. In ancient times, Medina was known as Yathrib. The Egyptian geographer Ptolemy referred to it as Lathrippa in the 2d century AD. Medina was the capital of the Muslim world until 661, when the caliphate was transferred to Damascus. Later, Medina was successively held by the Egyptians and the Ottoman Turks. The latter were expelled in 1919 by the troops of Husein ibn Ali (1856–1931), first king of al-Hijaz. Husein's forces were defeated (1924) by Abdul Aziz ibn Saud, sultan of Najd. The city of Medina was incorporated into the kingdom of Saudi Arabia in 1932. Pop. (1980 est.) 290,000.

MEDITERRANEAN SEA, inland sea, Europe, Asia, and Africa, linked to the Atlantic Ocean at its W end by the Strait of Gibraltar. Known to the Romans as Mare Nostrum ("our sea"), the Mediterranean is almost landlocked. It is of great political importance as a maritime outlet for the countries of the former USSR, via the Bosporus, Sea of Marmara, Dardanelles, and Black Sea, and for European and American access to the petroleum of Libya and Algeria and the Persian Gulf region, via the Suez Canal and overland pipelines.

The Mediterranean Sea covers an area of about 2,510,000 sq km (about 969,000 sq mi). It has an E to W extent of some 3860 km (some 2400 mi) and a maximum width of about 1600 km (about 1000 mi). Generally shallow, with an average depth of 1500 m (4926 ft), it reaches a maximum depth of 5150 m (16,896 ft) off the S coast of Greece.

MEDLAR

The Mediterranean is a remnant of the vast ancient sea called Tethys, which was squeezed almost shut in the Oligocene epoch (q.v.), 30 million years ago, when the crustal plates carrying Africa and Eurasia collided (see PLATE TECTONICS). The plates are still grinding together, causing the eruption of volcanoes such as Etna, Vesuvius, and Stromboli, all in Italy, and triggering frequent earthquakes, which have devastated parts of Italy, Greece, and Turkey.

An undersea ridge from Tunisia to Sicily divides the Mediterranean into E and W basins. Another seafloor ridge, from Spain to Morocco, lies at the outlet of the Mediterranean. Only 300 m (1000 ft) deep, it restricts circulation through the narrow Strait of Gibraltar, thereby greatly reducing the tidal range of the sea and, coupled with high rates of evaporation, making the Mediterranean much saltier than the Atlantic Ocean.

For centuries Malta and Sicily have commanded shipping through the strategically located Straits of Sicily and Messina. Other important islands include the Balearic Islands (Spain); Corsica (France); Sardinia (Italy); Cyprus; and the Ionian, Cyclades, Dodecanese, and Aegean islands (Greece). Arms of the Mediterranean include the Tyrrhenian Sea (located off W Italy), the Adriatic Sea (between Italy and the Balkan Peninsula), and the Aegean and Ionian seas (off peninsular Greece). Barcelona, Marseille, Genoa, Trieste, and Haifa are important seaports located in the region. Major rivers entering the Mediterranean are the Ebro, Rhône, Po, and Nile.

For further information on this topic, see the Bibliography in volume 28, section 424.

MEDLAR, common name for a small, fruit-bearing, often thorny tree, *Mespilus germanica,* of the family Rosaceae (*see* ROSE), native to Eurasia and cultivated widely in Europe. The tree grows to about 6 m (about 20 ft) and has single white or pinkish flowers and oblong leaves, up to 10 cm (4 in) long, with hairy undersides. The green, slightly sour, apple-shaped fruit, picked after the first frost, is used for preserves. The smaller variety of the fruit is called the Nottingham; the larger, the Dutch. Medlar trees are also found in the U.S.

MEDUSA. *See* GORGON.

MEERSCHAUM, a clay mineral, hydrated magnesium silicate ($Mg_2Si_3O_8 \cdot 2H_2O$), also known as sepiolite. It is grayish white or white with a yellow or red tinge and has an earthy luster. The hardness (q.v.) ranges from 2 to 2.5, and the sp.gr. is 2. It occurs in stratified or alluvial deposits in Asia Minor, Greece, Spain, and Morocco and, in

Megalithic monuments, the Standing Stones, at Callernish, in the Outer Hebrides, Scotland.
Malcolm Kirk–Peter Arnold, Inc.

the U.S., in Pennsylvania, Utah, New Mexico, and California. It is used primarily to make meerschaum tobacco pipes, for which the mineral is scraped free of any adhering material and is then dried and polished with wax.

MEERUT, city, N India, in Uttar Pradesh State, near Delhi. Manufactures include chemicals, soap, and clothing. In 1857 the Sepoy Mutiny broke out in Meerut. Meerut University (1966) is here. Pop. (1981 prelim., greater city) 538,461.

MEGALITHIC MONUMENTS, structures of large, roughly dressed stones erected as sepulchral monuments or as memorials of notable events.

Found in all parts of the world, megalithic monuments in Western Europe date from prehistoric times, beginning in the 5th millennium BC. Those of India date from as early as the first centuries of the Christian era, and those on Easter Island (q.v.) probably are contemporary with the medieval period in Europe. Megalithic monuments are still being built in parts of Indonesia and in Assam, India.

The areas of greatest abundance of megalithic monuments include the following groups: the British Isles, western France, Belgium, Spain, Portugal, and the islands of the western Mediterranean; Scandinavia; North Africa; the Crimea, the Caucasus, and the Middle East; the Iranian uplands; Japan and Burma, and Assam and the Deccan Plateau in India; and also the islands of the South Pacific Ocean, particularly Easter Island.

European megalithic monuments usually are divided into four classes: the menhir, or monolith, a single standing stone often of great size; the stone circle, consisting of many monoliths, as at Stonehenge (q.v.) in England; the row of monoliths, as at Carnac (q.v.) in France; and the burial chamber, or chamber tomb, usually walled with monoliths and roofed by capstones or false vaults. Chamber tombs are sometimes called dolmens (see DOLMEN). They are the most widespread type of megalithic monument in Western Europe; more than 50,000 examples are extant. The majority of the burial chambers were originally within earth mounds or barrows, many of which have since been denuded. Three types of burial chamber may be distinguished: the dolmen, or single chamber tomb; the passage grave, in which the chamber is approached by a passage; and the gallery grave, or *allée couverte,* a long, rectangular chamber. The interiors of the walls and roofs of some tombs are decorated with geometrical or naturalistic designs.

Megaliths found in the Polynesian, Melanesian, and Micronesian islands frequently have walls and platforms built of unworked rock, and in general consist of cyclopean masonry erected without the use of cement. In only three instances do these megaliths vary from unworked stone: the trilithon at the town of Mua on Tongatapu Island, which is built of two uprights supporting a crosspiece; the gigantic statues surmounting the ahu, or burial platforms, on Easter Island, carved in compressed volcanic ash; and the alignments at Tinian, in the Mariana Islands, consisting of groups of cone-shaped coral pillars known as *Lat'te,* constructed of layers of coral cemented together. L.P.K.

For further information on this topic, see the Bibliography in volume 28, sections 884–885, 1250.

MEHEMET ALI. See MUHAMMAD ALI.

MEIGHEN, Arthur (1874–1960), Canadian statesman, born in Perth Co., Ont., and educated at the University of Toronto. He became (1903) a member of the Manitoba bar and was elected (1908) to the House of Commons as a member of the Liberal-Conservative party. After 1915 he was a member of the cabinet as solicitor general, secretary of state, and minister of the interior, successively. He served (1920–21) the first of his two terms as prime minister of a Conservative party government. In 1926, after serving as prime minister for three months during a government crisis, Meighen retired from politics. In 1932, however, he accepted an appointment as senator. He

Arthur Meighen, prime minister of Canada from 1920 to 1921 and in 1926. Public Archives of Canada

was again named (1941) leader of his party, but in the elections in 1942 he lost his bid for a seat in the House of Commons and retired permanently from public life. A brilliant orator and debater, Meighen was largely responsible for many important measures adopted by the Canadian parliament during World War I.

MEIJI (1852–1912), emperor of Japan (1867–1912), whose accession to the throne marked the beginning of a national revolution known as the Meiji restoration. After Japan was forced to open its ports to Western trade during the 1850s and '60s, many influential Japanese decided that the country needed both a stronger government and the West's superior technology if it was to avoid foreign domination. In 1868, soon after Prince Mutsuhito became emperor, taking the name Meiji ("enlightened government"), these Westernizers toppled the Tokugawa (q.v.) shogunate, replacing it with a unified administration headed by the sovereign. Although the emperor in time became an influential force in the government, he functioned mainly as a symbol of national unity, leaving the actual business of governing to his ministers. During his reign, Japan became an industrial power able to compete with the nations of the West.

MEIOSIS. See CELL: *Division, Reproduction, and Differentiation:* Sexual Reproduction; GENETICS: *Physical Basis of Heredity.*

MEIR, Golda (1898–1978), Israeli premier (1969–74), a founder of the state of Israel. Meir was born on May 3, 1898, in Kiev, Russia (now Ukraine), and originally named Goldie Mabovitz or Mabovich. Her father immigrated to Milwaukee, Wis., in 1905 and was joined by his family in 1906. She graduated from Milwaukee Teachers College, and in 1917 married Morris Myerson or Meyerson (d. 1951), whom she had met while attending high school in Denver, Colo., in 1913. While still in her teens she became an ardent Zionist, dedicated to building a homeland for Jews; in 1921 she and her husband immigrated to Palestine (now Israel).

Remaining active in Zionist affairs and in the labor movement, Meir served throughout the 1930s and '40s in various Zionist organizations in Palestine, Europe, and the U.S. She was a signer of the proclamation of the independence of the state of Israel in 1948 and served as her country's first minister to the USSR in 1948 and 1949; was elected to the first Knesset, or parliament, of Israel and named minister of labor and social insurance in 1949. Having separated from her husband in 1945, she Hebraized her surname to Meir in 1956. That same year she became minister of foreign affairs and held that post until 1966, when she resigned from the cabinet. She served, successively, as secretary-general of the Mapai party and of the united Israel Labor party from 1966 to 1968. She was prime minister from 1969 to 1974, when she resigned amid controversy over Israel's lack of preparedness in the Yom Kippur War of 1973. Meir died in Jerusalem on Dec. 8, 1978.

For further information on this person, see the section Biographies in the Bibliography in volume 28.

MEISSEN, city, E central Germany, in Saxony, on the Elbe R., near the city of Dresden. Manufactures include a type of porcelain known as Meissen ware or Dresden china, electrical equipment, chemicals, and furniture. Among the historic sites are a cathedral and the Church of Saint Afra (both 13th–14th cent.). Meissen was founded in 929. Pop. (1989 est.) 36,800.

MEISSEN PORCELAIN. See POTTERY: *Europe to 1800.*

MEISTERSINGER (Ger., "mastersinger"), members of the German guilds for poets and musicians of the 14th, 15th, and 16th centuries. The Meistersinger were craftsmen of the middle classes who continued the traditions of the noble-born minnesingers (*see* MINNESINGER). The most famous was Hans Sachs. Meistersinger guilds flourished in the large cities of Germany. Each guild was organized in distinct grades, ranging from the apprentice *Schüler* and *Schulfreunde* (who were merely familiar with the rules of composition), through journeymen *Sänger* ("singers") and *Dichter* ("poets"), to *Meister* (who invented new melodies). Although the Meistersinger movement played a large part in the lives of middle-class Germans, it had little lasting literary and musical value because of mechanical requirements for composition and other rigid, arbitrary rules. The 19th-century opera *Die Meistersinger von Nürnberg* by Richard Wagner accurately portrays Meistersinger customs.

MEITNER, Lise (1878–1968), Austrian-Swedish physicist, who first identified nuclear fission. She was born in Vienna and educated at the universities of Vienna and Berlin. In association with the German physical chemist Otto Hahn, she helped discover the element protactinium in 1918, and was a professor of physics at the University of Berlin from 1926 to 1933. In 1938 she left Germany and joined the atomic research staff at the University of Stockholm. In 1939 Meitner published the first paper concerning nuclear fission (*see* NUCLEAR ENERGY). She is also known for her research on atomic theory and radioactivity. In her work she predicted the existence of chain reaction, which contributed to the development of the atomic bomb (see NUCLEAR WEAPONS). In 1946 she was visiting professor at Catholic University in Wash-ington, D.C., and in 1959 she revisited the U.S. to lecture at Bryn Mawr College.

MEJICANOS, town, S central El Salvador, in San Salvador Department, a suburb of San Salvador. Sugar and coffee processing are important industries. One of the country's largest urban centers, Mejicanos was founded in the early 16th century by Spanish soldiers from Mexico. Pop. (1989 est.) 117,568.

MEKNÈS, city, N Morocco, capital of Meknès Province, on a fertile plain N of the Middle Atlas, near Fez. A former residence of the sultan, the city is on a railroad that links it with the coast, and roads lead to nearby mountain resorts. Industries include fruit, vegetable, and palm-oil processing, metalworking, distilling, and the manufacture of carpets, woolens, and cement. The surrounding plain produces fruits, grains, and vegetables. The city, called the Moroccan Versailles, contains the sultan's palace and grounds and a large marketplace; it is surrounded by a triple tier of walls. The Roman ruins of Volubilis and the holy city of Moulay-Idriss, founded in AD 788, lie to the N. An Almohad citadel of the 11th century, Meknès served as capital of the country from 1675 to 1728. A former spelling was Meknez. Pop. (1982) 319,783.

MEKONG (Tibetan *Dza-chu;* Chin. *Lancang Jiang* [*Lan-ts'ang Chiang*]; Thai *Mae Nam Khong*), river, SE Asia, one of the principal rivers of the region. From its sources, in the E Tibetan highlands, it flows generally SE to the South China Sea, a distance of about 4184 km (about 2600 mi). The Mekong crosses Yunnan Province, China, forms the border between Burma and Laos and most of the border between Laos and Thailand, and flows across Cambodia and S Vietnam, emptying into the South China Sea. In the upper course are steep descents and swift rapids, but the river is navigable S of Luang Prabang, Laos.

MELAKA, formerly MALACCA, city and seaport, Malaysia, capital of Melaka State, on the S coast of the Malay Peninsula, on the Strait of Malacca. In the era of the sailing ship, the port was one of the busiest on the peninsula. Shipping is now confined to coastal trade because the harbor is inaccessible to oceangoing vessels. Melaka was seized in 1511 by the Portuguese navigator and statesman Afonso de Albuquerque. The city was captured by the Dutch in 1641, but from 1795 to 1802 and again from 1811 to 1818 it was under British occupation. In 1824, after six years of Dutch rule, the British acquired the city in exchange for Benkulen, Sumatra. Pop. (1980) 88,073.

MELANCHTHON

MELANCHTHON (1497–1560), German scholar and religious reformer. Born Philipp Schwarzert in Bretten (now in Baden), he was educated at the universities of Heidelberg and Tübingen. When he entered Heidelberg at the age of 12, he changed his real surname on the advice of his uncle, the German humanist and Hebraist Johann Reuchlin, to Melanchthon (the Greek equivalent of his surname, meaning "black earth"). Through his uncle's influence he was elected (1518) to the chair of Greek at the University of Wittenberg; his inaugural address, *Discourse on Reforming the Studies of Youth,* attracted the interest of Martin Luther, by whom he was so profoundly influenced that he turned to the study of theology and obtained a bachelor's degree in that field the following year. In 1521 his *Loci Communes Rerum Theologicarum*

163

MELANESIA

(Commonplaces of Theology) contributed logical, argumentative force to the Reformation, and after Luther's confinement in the castle of Wartburg the same year, he replaced Luther as leader of the Reformation cause at Wittenberg. In 1526 he became professor of theology and was sent with 27 other commissioners to make the constitutions of the reformed churches of Germany uniform.

As leading representative of the Reformation at the Diet of Augsburg in 1530, Melanchthon presented the Augsburg Confession, consisting of 21 articles of faith that he had drawn up with Luther's advice. The tone of this creed was so conciliatory that it surprised even Catholics. His *Apology,* published a year later, vindicated the Confession, and his *Variata* (Variations, 1540) further modified the Confession by generalizing specific statements. Melanchthon served as a peacemaker because of his desire for harmony between Protestantism and Roman Catholicism or for at least a union of Protestant factions, but his views were regarded as heretical by strict Lutherans. The breach was widened by his willingness to compromise with the Catholics for the sake of avoiding civil war. He secured tolerance for evangelical doctrine; for a time he retained most of the Roman ceremonies as *adiaphora* (Gr., "things indifferent"), matters not of great consequence and therefore best tolerated. Melanchthon died praying "that the churches might be of one mind in Christ."

MELANESIA, one of the three major subdivisions (with Micronesia and Polynesia) of Oceania, encompassing the islands in the W Pacific Ocean, S of the equator. Melanesia includes the Bismarck Archipelago, Fiji, Vanuatu (formerly New Hebrides), the Solomon Islands, New Caledonia, and the Admiralty Islands. The islands are inhabited by the dark-skinned Melanesian-Papuan people, a group related to the Australoid race. More than 200 languages are spoken, most of which belong to the Malayo-Polynesian language family.

MELANESIAN ART. See Oceanian Art and Architecture.

MELANESIAN LANGUAGES. See Malayo-Polynesian Languages.

MELANIN. See Pigment.

MELBA, Nellie, professional name of Helen Porter Mitchell (1859–1931), Australian operatic coloratura soprano, born near Melbourne. In 1882 she made a recital tour of Australia. In 1886 she studied singing in Paris, and in 1887, using the stage name Melba (for her hometown, Melbourne), she debuted in Brussels in *Rigoletto* by the Italian composer Giuseppe Verdi. In 1888, in the title role in *Lucia di Lammermoor* by the Italian composer Gaetano Donizetti, she began a 38-year association with Covent Garden in London. In 1893 she made her American debut at the Metropolitan Opera House, New York City. She joined the Manhattan Opera Company in 1907. In 1918 she was created a Dame of the British Empire.

MELBOURNE, city, SE Australia, capital of Victoria State, on Port Phillip Bay at the mouth of the Yarra R. Melbourne proper is centered in a small area on the N bank of the Yarra. The city is the chief economic, cultural, and administrative center of Victoria and the focus of Australia's largest metropolitan area after that of Sydney. Surrounding suburbs include Broadmeadows, Saint Albans, Essendon, Brunswick, and Eltham, to the N; Richmond, Nunawading, and Sherbrooke, to the E; and Moorabin, Mordialloc, Chelsea, Cranbourne, and Frankston, to the S. The cosmopolitan population includes many Italian, Greek, Chinese, Vietnamese, British, and Irish immigrants.

Industries of the Melbourne metropolitan area range from shipbuilding and petroleum refining along Port Phillip Bay to the manufacture of metals, motor vehicles, electrical and electronic equipment, machinery, chemicals, printed materials, textiles, clothing, paper, and processed food. Road and rail networks focus on the city, and a large international airport is located at Tullamarine.

Points of Interest. Dominated by high-rise office buildings, Melbourne proper has among its many landmarks the State Parliament House, the Royal Mint, and the stock exchange (1968). Nearby, in Fitzroy Gardens, is the transported boyhood home of the British explorer James Cook, who claimed the coast of eastern Australia for Great Britain in 1770. To the S, across the Yarra R., is Government House and the Royal Botanic Gardens and National Herbarium. The University of Melbourne (1853) is in Parkville, and other leading educational facilities of the region include La Trobe University (1964), in Bundoora; Monash University (1958), in Clayton; and the Royal Melbourne Institute of Technology (1882), in Melbourne. Museums in the Melbourne area include the National Gallery of Victoria, with fine collections of painting, decorative art, and photography; and the Museum of Victoria, incorporating the former National Museum of Victoria, with displays on zoology, geology, and anthropology, and the former Science Museum of Victoria. Several performing-arts facilities are part of the Victorian Arts Centre, and sports facilities of the region include Flemington Racecourse, scene of the annual Melbourne Cup horse race; the Melbourne Cricket Ground; and the National Tennis Center, site of the Australian Open.

History. The site of the city was explored by Europeans in 1803, and it was settled in 1835 as Port Phillip by rival groups from Tasmania. Unlike other early settlements in southeast Australia, it was never a penal colony and was planned from the beginning as a residential community of wide streets and spacious parklands. In 1837 it adopted its present name in honor of the then prime minister of Great Britain, William Lamb, 2d viscount Melbourne. In 1851 it was separated from New South Wales and became the capital of the newly formed British colony of Victoria. Its major growth began in the early 1850s, when, after the discovery of gold in the interior of Victoria (especially at Bendigo and Ballarat), it became the trade center for the gold hunters who flocked in from overseas. In the late 19th century the city became an important rail center, its harbor was developed, and major manufacturing establishments were opened. Melbourne was the temporary seat of Australia's government from 1901 until the parliament moved to Canberra in 1927. The summer Olympic Games were held in Melbourne in 1956. Pop. (1991, greater city) 3,022,439.

MELBOURNE, city, Brevard Co., E Florida, on the Indian R. (a lagoon) and the Atlantic Ocean; inc. 1888. Located near the Kennedy Space Center on Cape Canaveral and Patrick Air Force Base in Cocoa Beach, it is a major center for producing high-technology and aerospace equipment. It is also a beach resort and a citrus-processing center. Florida Institute of Technology (1958), the Brevard Art Center and Museum, a performing arts theater and a science center are here. The community, settled in the late 1860s, is named for Melbourne, Australia. The city of Eau Gallie was annexed to Melbourne in 1969. Pop. (1980) 46,536; (1990) 59,646.

MELBOURNE, William Lamb, 2d Viscount (1779–1848), English statesman, who was prime minister during the early years of Queen Victoria's reign and initiated her in the ways of statecraft.

Melbourne was born on March 15, 1779, at Brockett Hall, Hertfordshire. He was educated at Trinity College, University of Cambridge, and at the University of Glasgow. A Whig, he was elected to Parliament in 1806, served as chief secretary for Ireland (1827–28), and as home secretary (1830–34) acted firmly to suppress agrarian and trade-unionist agitators. In 1834 and from 1835 to 1841 he served as prime minister at a time when Whig power was receding. A good-humored moderate, he increasingly disliked political controversy, and after 1832 looked with disfavor on further parliamentary reforms. In 1840, however, a crisis over Syria that threatened war with France roused him to strong leadership.

When Victoria ascended the throne in 1837, Melbourne assumed the duties of her secretary and political tutor. He was devoted to the young queen, as she was to him, and with his guidance she learned to find her way in British politics and acquired an early preference for Whig ministries (which, however, she later abandoned). Melbourne was crippled by a stroke in 1842 and died at Brockett Hall on Nov. 24, 1848.

MELCHIOR, Lauritz Lebrecht Hommel (1890–1973), Danish-American operatic tenor, born in Copenhagen. He made his debut as a baritone in 1913 at the Copenhagen Opera House. Melchior's first success as a tenor was at Covent Garden, London, in 1924. Subsequently, he sang at the Festival at Bayreuth, Germany, and, from 1926 to 1950, at the Metropolitan Opera House in New York City. One of the greatest dramatic tenors of his time, he appeared primarily in heldentenor roles in operas by the German composer Richard Wagner. Melchior, who became a U.S. citizen in 1947, also performed in several motion pictures.

MELCHITES *or* **MELKITES** (Syriac *mlaka;* Aram. *malik,* "king"), name given in the 5th century to the Christians of the patriarchates of Jerusalem, Alexandria, and Antioch who accepted the definition by the Council of Chalcedon (451) of the two natures of Christ, a position also accepted by the pope and the Byzantine emperor (*see* CHALCEDON, COUNCIL OF). The name Melchites ("royalists," that is, followers of the emperor) was given to them by the Monophysites, who held that Christ has only one (divine) nature and who therefore rejected the position of the council (*see* MONOPHYSITISM).

The Melchites adhered to the Eastern church after the schism with Rome in 1054, but in the following centuries some groups of Melchites shifted their allegiance back to Rome; they became known as the Melchite Catholic church, one of the Eastern Rite churches (q.v.). Rome recognized a Catholic Melchite patriarch in 1724. There are about 270,000 Catholic Melchites in this patriarchal territory, which is centered in Damascus, Syria, and more than 200,000 outside it. Their priests are allowed to marry; services are conducted in Arabic or, with due authorization, in the vernacular of the country. The Melchites in the U.S. number about 55,000. They are under the jurisdiction of an exarchate province established in 1966 with its headquarters in Boston.

MELCHIZEDEK, a priest-king in the Old Testament (see Gen. 14:18–20). In the biblical episode Melchizedek encountered Abraham on the latter's return from battle with the Mesopotamian kings. He gave Abraham bread and wine (thus, according to some Christian scholars, prefiguring the Eucharist) and in return received a tithe of Abraham's booty. In Ps. 110 he is referred to as a prototype of the Messiah. The New Testament's Epistle to the Hebrews cites the two Old Testament references to demonstrate that Melchizedek foreshadowed Christ.

MELEAGER, in Greek mythology, son of Oeneus and Althea, king and queen of Calydon. Meleager led the hunt for a boar that the goddess Artemis sent to devastate the country. The hero finally killed the animal, but gave the head and skin to the huntress Atalanta, who had been the first to wound the beast and with whom Meleager was in love. When his maternal uncles, angered at this award, took the trophies from Atalanta, Meleager killed them.

MELÉNDEZ VALDÉS, Juan (1754–1817), Spanish poet and politician. He was trained as a lawyer, but throughout his career Meléndez Valdés mixed literary endeavors with judicial and political pursuits, becoming his country's foremost neoclassic poet. He eventually served as director of public instruction in French-dominated Spain after 1808 and was forced into exile in France after Napoleon's defeat. Meléndez Valdés's graceful and refined poems employ neoclassic conventions, such as the pastoral, and attitudes, such as sentimentalism. Nevertheless, he is regarded as a precursor of romanticism because of his empathy with and descriptions of nature.

MELILLA, Spanish exclave and port, NW Africa, administered as part of Málaga Province, on the Mediterranean Sea. Bordered by Morocco, Melilla consists of an older, walled town on a peninsula and modern buildings to the S and W. The city is a rail terminus serving the mountainous Rif hinterland, and exports include iron, lead, zinc, fish, and fruit. The chief industries in the city are fish processing, boatbuilding, sawmilling, and flour milling. Founded by the Phoenicians as Rusaddir, it was ruled by the Carthaginians, the Romans, the Byzantine Empire, and various Berber dynasties before being conquered by Spain in 1497. A revolt of army officers in the Melilla garrison in 1936 was a prelude to the Spanish civil war. Pop. (1986) 55,613.

MELLON, Andrew William (1855–1937), American financier, industrialist, and statesman, born in Pittsburgh, Pa., and educated at the University of Pennsylvania. He started his career in the banking firm of Thomas Mellon and Sons of Pittsburgh, later becoming partner and president of the firm that developed into the Mellon National Bank, of which he became president in 1902. He was active in many industries, including coal, iron, and oil, and was director of several financial and industrial corporations. He founded the town of Donora, Pa., where he established a large steel plant. Actively engaged in many philanthropies, he aided in establishing the Mellon Institute in Pittsburgh. He was secretary of the treasury under three successive presidents, Warren Harding, Calvin Coolidge, and Herbert Hoover. Among his chief accomplishments in national financial policies were the refunding of European debts and reduction of the public debt in America. He was U.S. ambassador to Great Britain from 1932 to 1933.

Mellon left his extensive art collection and a gallery building in Washington, D.C., to the American people. By joint resolution, Congress, in accepting the gift, named the gallery the National Gallery of Art.

MELO, city, NE Uruguay, capital of Cerro Largo Department, near the Brazil border. It is one of the nation's largest urban areas and an important regional transportation, manufacturing, and commercial center. Melo was founded in 1795 as a military post by the Spanish. Pop. (1985) 42,329.

MELODEON. *See* ORGAN.

MELODRAMA, in musicology, work in which a spoken text is integrated with music. The form, which began in the ancient Greek theater, became popular in the 18th century; a notable example is *The Begger's Opera* by the English dramatist John Gay. Sections of melodrama have also been incorporated in works by such composers as Ludwig van Beethoven, Giuseppe Verdi, Richard Wagner, and Arnold Schoenberg.

By extension, the term *melodrama* has come to be applied to any play with romantic plot in which the author manipulates events to act on the emotions of the audience without regard for character development or logic. Prime examples are such works as *The Stranger* (1789; trans. 1798) by the German dramatist August von Kotzebue, and the popular melodramas of the later 19th and early 20th century, also known as potboilers or tearjerkers—works such as Dion Boucicault's *The Octoroon* (1859) or the dramatization (1853) of Harriet Beecher Stowe's novel *Uncle Tom's Cabin.* Twentieth-century melodrama includes motion picture serials and most recently television soap operas.

MELODY, the organized succession of musical tones of given pitches and durations. Melodies are distinguished from one another by several traits. For example, the opening of "Mary Had a Little Lamb" falls and then rises in pitch (melodic contour), spans the interval of a major third (range), and consists of three tones, each a whole step from the next (scale). For a melody from a culture having no theoretical scales, the scale consists of all the melody's pitches, arranged in order from lowest to highest, or vice versa. The music of Europe, India, and other cultures has theoretical scales; "Mary Had a Little Lamb" fits into the European major scale. The note-to-note movement in the opening phrase is stepwise, or conjunct. The opening of "The Star-Spangled Banner" also falls, then rises, and the song is in the major scale. Its range, however, is an octave, and its melodic movement is disjunct; that is, it skips across various scale notes. Rhythm is inseparable from melodic contour and motion. Although the songs "Goodnight My Someone" and "Seventy-six Trombones"—from the musical *The Music Man*—share the same pitch-to-pitch sequence, they have different rhythms and distinct melodic identities. A melody may be ornamented with turns, trills, glides, and other devices.

Melodies can be built by combining and varying several motives, or short, recognizable groups of notes. Several motives can be combined in a theme, or a longer melodic fragment used as part of a larger composition. Melodies are also commonly built on certain scaffolds. One is mode (q.v.), which consists at its minimum of a scale and, usually, a prescribed final note. At the other end of the spectrum, it elaborates into a melody type, which also includes characteristic phrases, motives, ending formulas, and so forth. Complex, highly ornamented, unharmonized Islamic and Indian music and medieval Gregorian and Byzantine chants are built on modes.

In European music of about 1600 to 1900, especially in the 19th century, harmony provided the main scaffolding for melody. Successions of chords created a sense of harmonic color and movement; the chords were arranged so that their top notes produced an effective melody. This conception of melody became so pervasive in Western music that even unharmonized melodies were conceived in terms of implied chords. In the 20th century many composers turned to other kinds of melodic framework, notably the twelve-tone system.

See also MUSIC.

For further information on this topic, see the Bibliography in volume 28, sections 720, 722.

MELON, common name for any one of numerous varieties of sweet fruits of the gourd (q.v.) family, Cucurbitaceae, that grow on two species of trailing vines. *Cucumis melo* bears muskmelons, winter melons, and the European cantaloupe. *Citrullus lanatus* bears the watermelons.

Muskmelons, derived from *Cucumis melo* var. *reticulatus,* have a soft, ribbed rind with distinct netting, salmon-colored pulp, and a musky aroma. They are the most perishable of the melons and are particularly popular in North America, where they are also called cantaloupes, a misnomer taken from the quite distinct European cantaloupe.

Winter melons—of which the honeydew, Crenshaw, casaba, and the Persian are best known—are derived from *C. melo* var. *inodorus*. They are less aromatic than muskmelons, take more time to mature, and have harder rinds that preserve them well after the growing season. The honeydew has a smooth rind with green pulp; the Persian has a dark rind with orange pulp; the casaba has a yellow, wrinkled rind with green or white pulp; and the Crenshaw has a dark green, wrinkled rind with pink pulp.

The true cantaloupe, *C. melo* var. *cantalupensis,* is grown mostly in Europe, and its name is derived from the village of Cantalupo, near Rome, where it may have been introduced from Armenia. True cantaloupes have hard, warty, scaly rinds with deep grooves and do not have the characteristic netting of muskmelons.

The *Citrullus lanatus* group, or watermelons, vary in shape, size, and markings and range from round to oblong, from 1 to 20 kg (2.2 to 45 lb), and from dark green to striped light green. The flesh of these varieties is usually red, quite sweet, extremely watery, and distinctly crisp.

The *Cucumis melo* group is believed to have originated in Iran and the Transcaucasia before it was cultivated by the Egyptians and the Greeks and Romans. Watermelons originated in tropical Africa, and Sanskrit and early Egyptian records indicate that they have been cultivated for more than 4000 years.

MELOS. See MÍLOS.

MELPOMENE. See MUSES.

MELROSE, city, Middlesex Co., NE Massachusetts, a residential community near Boston; settled 1633, inc. as a city 1900. Electronic equipment is manufactured in the city. Melrose is named for Melrose, Scotland. Pop. (1980) 30,055; (1990) 28,150.

MELTING POINT. See FREEZING POINT.

MELVILLE, Herman (1819–91), American novelist, a major literary figure whose exploration of psychological and metaphysical themes foreshadowed 20th-century literary concerns but whose works remained in obscurity until the 1920s, when his genius was finally recognized.

Melville was born Aug. 1, 1819, in New York City, into a family that had declined in the world. In 1837 he shipped to Liverpool as a cabin boy. Upon returning to the U.S. he taught school and then sailed for the South Seas in 1841 on the whaler *Acushnet*. After an 18-month voyage he deserted the ship in the Marquesas Islands and

Herman Melville   Bettmann Archive

with a companion lived for a month among the natives, who were cannibals. He escaped aboard an Australian trader, leaving it at Papeete, Tahiti, where he was imprisoned temporarily. He worked as a field laborer and then shipped to Honolulu, Hawaii, where in 1843 he enlisted as a seaman on the U.S. Navy frigate *United States.* After his discharge in 1844 he began to create novels out of his experiences and to take part in the literary life of Boston and New York City.

Melville's first five novels all achieved quick popularity. *Typee: A Peep at Polynesian Life* (1846), *Omoo, a Narrative of Adventures in the South Seas* (1847), and *Mardi* (1849) were romances of the South Sea islands. *Redburn, His First Voyage* (1849) was based on his own first trip to sea, and *White-Jacket, or the World in a Man-of-War* (1850) fictionalized his experiences in the navy. In 1850 Melville moved to a farm near Pittsfield, Mass., where he became an intimate friend of Nathaniel Hawthorne, to whom he dedicated his masterpiece *Moby-Dick; or The White Whale* (1851).

The central theme of the novel is the conflict between Captain Ahab, master of the whaler *Pequod,* and Moby-Dick, a great white whale that once tore off one of Ahab's legs at the knee. Ahab is dedicated to revenge; he drives himself and his crew, which includes Ishmael, narrator of the story, over the seas in a desperate search for his enemy. The body of the book is written in a wholly original, powerful narrative style, which, in certain sections of the work, Melville varied with great success. The most impressive of these sections are the rhetorically magnificent sermon delivered before sailing and the soliloquies of the mates; lengthy "flats," passages conveying nonnarrative material, usually of a technical nature, such as the chapter about whales; and the more purely ornamental passages, such as the tale of the *Tally-Ho,* which can stand by themselves as short stories of merit. The work is invested with Ishmael's sense of profound wonder at his story, but nonetheless conveys full awareness that Ahab's quest can have but one end. And so it proves to be: Moby-Dick destroys the *Pequod* and all its crew save Ishmael.

Moby-Dick was not a financial success, and Melville's next novel, *Pierre: or the Ambiguities* (1852), a darkly allegorical exploration of the nature of evil, was a total failure. Today, however, it enjoys some acceptance by critics and the public. *Israel Potter* (1855), a historical romance, was equally unsuccessful.

The Piazza Tales (1856) contain some of Melville's finest shorter works; particularly notable are the powerful short stories "Benito Cereno" and "Bartleby the Scrivener" and the ten descriptive sketches of the Galápagos Islands, Ecuador, "The Encantadas." The unfinished novel *The Confidence Man* (1857), set on a Mississippi River steamboat, satirizes the selfishness and commercialism of Melville's time. Between 1866 and 1885 Melville worked as a customs inspector in New York City in order to support himself. During this period he published poetry that has since gained increasing respect, including *Battle-Pieces and the Aspects of War* (1866), and the book-length *Clarel* (1876), about a troubled pilgrimage to the Holy Land. In 1891 he completed the novella *Billy Budd, Foretopman* (1924), the story of a young sailor, personifying innocence, doomed by the malevolent hatred of a ship's officer, personifying evil. Melville died in New York on Sept. 28, 1891, shortly after completing *Billy Budd.* The work has been adapted as a play, a film, and an opera (1951) by the English composer Benjamin Britten in collaboration with the novelist E. M. Forster.

MELVILLE ISLAND, barren island of the Artic Ocean, in Baffin Region of the Northwest Territories, NW Canada, one of the Queen Elizabeth Islands. Musk-oxen inhabit the hilly island. It has an area of 42,149 sq km (16,274 sq mi), with elevations rising to about 1000 m (about 3280 ft).

MELVILLE PENINSULA, peninsula, in Baffin Region of the Northwest Territories, N Canada, between the Gulf of Boothia and Foxe Basin, and N of Hudson Bay and S of Baffin Island. The peninsula, about 65,000 sq km (about 25,100 sq mi) in area, is connected to the mainland by Rae Isthmus. The central portion of the sparsely populated peninsula is hilly. A Hudson's Bay Co.

trading post was constructed here, at Repulse Bay, in 1921.

MEMBRANE (Lat. *membrana*, "parchment"), in biology, any thin layer of connective tissue coating individual cells and organs of the body, or lining the joints and the ducts and tracts that open to the exterior of the body. The membrane surrounding single-celled animals and plants and individual cells in multicellular organisms is important in the nutritive, respiratory, and excretory processes of these cells. Such cell membranes are semipermeable; that is, they allow the passage of small molecules, such as those of sugars and salts, but not large molecules, such as those of proteins. Structures inside cells, such as the nucleus, may also have membranes.

Each organ in the animal body is surrounded by a membrane, extensions of which often anchor the organ to the body wall. Three membranes, known as meninges, surround the brain and spinal cord; the outermost is known as the dura mater, the middle layer as the arachnoid, and the innermost as the pia mater. Each lung is coated with a membrane known as a visceral pleura. The visceral pleurae anchor the lungs to the wall of the pleural cavity by extensions, known as the parietal pleurae, which line the cavity. The abdominal cavity is lined by a large membrane called the peritoneum, which is attached to the mesenteries—the membranes coating the abdominal organs. A double membrane from the stomach, known as the omentum, hangs like an apron in the abdominal cavity and is interlaced with fat; the omentum is one of the major fat-storage areas of the body. The articular surfaces of bones making up a joint are lined with lubricating membranes. Small membrane sacs, or bursae, occur in the space between the bones of most joints. The hollow tracts, such as the respiratory and alimentary tracts, and the blood vessels and glandular ducts are lined with membranes. The membranes lining body cavities and coating organs are generally known as serous membranes because the cavities usually contain a serumlike fluid; the membranes lining joints are known as synovial membranes because they secrete synovial lubricating fluid; and the membranes lining the hollow tracts are known as mucous membranes because they secrete mucus. Inflammations of the membranes are assigned names by adding the suffix *-itis* to their anatomic name.

In the field of artificial membrane technology, scientists today are interested in the development of structures that can function with the same selectivity and efficiency as exhibited by biological membranes in nature. Artificial membranes have many scientific and industrial applications. For example, they are employed in desalinization plants for removing salt from ocean water, and in the treatment of industrial wastewaters, in processes known as reverse osmosis. More closely biomimetic membranes can be produced through such techniques as dipping metal plates into liquids covered with monolayers of selected lipids. Among the specialized uses of biomimetic membranes is the timed release of pharmaceuticals into the body from ingested medicines or bandages applied to the body.

MEMEL TERRITORY (Ger. *Memelgebiet* or *Memelland*), former German territory on the E coast of the Baltic Sea, now part of Lithuania. The city of Memel, now called Klaipėda (q.v.), was the capital of the territory. Lithuania seized the region early in 1923, and the next year the League of Nations made it a Lithuanian autonomous district. In March 1939, Germany obtained control of the territory. In October 1944, during World War II, it was taken by Soviet forces.

MEMLING, Hans (c. 1435–94), Flemish painter of religious works and portraits characterized by their gentle, sweet tranquillity.

Memling was born in Seligenstadt, near Frankfurt am Main, Germany, and became a citizen of Bruges in 1465. Little is known of his training, although it appears he was strongly influenced by the style of the Flemish master Rogier van der Weyden, especially in his love of delicate de-

Maria Maddalena Baroncelli, Wife of Tommaso Portinari (c. 1470), by Hans Memling. The Metropolitan Museum of Art–Bequest of Benjamin Altman, 1913 (14.40.627)

tail and his fine precise drawing. Memling's work consists primarily of altarpieces and devotional diptychs and triptychs, and portraits. His compositions representing the Madonna in sumptuous backgrounds often include representations of saints, portraits of donors, or detailed landscapes. His style changed little throughout most of his career; typical works such as the *Donne Triptych,* named also *The Virgin and the Child with Saints and Donors* (1475, National Gallery, London), and the *Marriage of St. Catherine* (1479, Memling Museum, Bruges) are characterized by an overall delicacy and harmony that result from a symmetrically balanced composition, clear, even lighting, and a masterly deployment of colors ranging from rich golds, reds, and blues to subtle halftones. His figures radiate an attitude of quiet devotion rather than the intense fervor found in the works of his contemporaries.

As a portraitist, Memling produced idealized representations of his subjects, such as the figure of *Tommaso Portinari,* part of the *Portinari Triptych* (c. 1470, Metropolitan Museum of Art, New York City). In another vein, he produced the unique *Seven Joys of the Virgin* (c. 1480, Alte Pinakothek, Munich), a panoramic landscape made up of an iridescent assemblage of towns and castles, hills and mountains, and ports and ships. Late in his career, under the influence of the art of the Italian Renaissance, his style became more vigorous. Such an unrestrained work as *Bathsheba at the Bath* (c. 1485, Staatsgalerie, Stuttgart), which portrays a female nude in a realistic bathhouse scene, has a subject and a setting unusual in 15th-century Flemish painting. Memling died in Bruges on Aug. 11, 1494.

MEMNON, in Greek mythology, king of Ethiopia, the son of the Trojan prince Tithonus and of Eos, goddess of the dawn. In the tenth year of the Trojan War, Memnon brought his army to the assistance of Troy. He fought bravely but was eventually killed by the Greek hero Achilles. To comfort Memnon's mother, however, the god Zeus made him immortal. The two colossal statues of Amenhotep III near Thebes in Egypt were thought to be of Memnon.

MEMORIAL DAY, legal holiday, observed annually on the last Monday in May in most of the U.S., in honor of the nation's armed services personnel killed in wartime. The holiday, originally called Decoration Day, is traditionally marked by parades, memorial speeches and ceremonies, and the decoration of graves with flowers and flags, hence the original name. Memorial Day was first observed on May 30, 1868, on the order of Gen. John Alexander Logan for the purpose of decorating the graves of the American Civil War dead. It was observed on May 30 until 1971, when most states changed to a newly established federal schedule of holiday observance. Confederate Memorial Day, formerly a legal holiday in many southern states, is still observed on the fourth Monday in April in Alabama, the last Monday in April in Mississippi, and April 26 in Florida and Georgia.

MEMORY, process of storing and retrieving information in the brain (q.v.). The process is central to learning and thinking. Four different types of remembering are ordinarily distinguished by psychologists: recollection, recall, recognition, and relearning. Recollection involves the reconstruction of events or facts on the basis of partial cues, which serve as reminders. Recall is the active and unaided remembering of something from the past. Recognition refers to the ability to correctly identify previously encountered stimuli as familiar. Relearning may show evidence of the effects of memory; material that is familiar is often easier to learn a second time than it would be if it were unfamiliar.

The course of forgetting over time has been studied extensively by psychologists. Most often a rapid forgetting occurs at first, followed by a decreasing rate of loss. Improvement in the amount of material retained, however, can be achieved by practicing active recall during learning, by periodic reviews of the material, and by overlearning the material beyond the point of bare mastery. A mechanical technique devised to improve memory is mnemonics, involving the use of associations and various devices to remember particular facts. Four traditional explanations of forgetting have been provided. One is that memory traces fade naturally over time as a result of organic processes occurring in the nervous system, although little evidence for this notion exists. A second is that memories become systematically distorted or modified over time. A third is that new learning often interferes with or replaces old learning, a phenomenon known as retroactive inhibition. Finally, some forgetting may be motivated by the needs and wishes of the individual, as in repression.

Little is known about the physiology of memory storage in the brain. Some researchers suggest that memories are stored at specific sites, and others that memories involve widespread brain regions working together; both processes may in fact be involved. Theorists also propose that different storage mechanisms exist for short-term and long-term memories, and that if memories are not transferred from the former to the latter they will be lost. Studies indicate that different structures in the limbic system of the brain have specific memory functions. For example, one circuit through the hippocampus and thalamus may be involved in spatial memories, whereas another, through the amygdala and thalamus, may be involved in emotional memories. Research also suggests that "skill" memories are stored differently from intellectual memories.

In general, memories are less clear and detailed than perceptions, but occasionally a remembered image is complete in every detail. This phenomenon, known as eidetic imagery, is usually found in children, who sometimes project the image so completely that they can spell out an entire page of writing in an unfamiliar language that they have seen for a short time.

For further information on this topic, see the Bibliography in volume 28, sections 144, 497.

MEMPHIS, ancient city of Egypt, at the apex of the Nile delta, south of Cairo. Founded in the early 4th millennium BC, Memphis was the capital of Egypt throughout the Old Kingdom (c. 2755–2255 BC) into the First Intermediate Period (c. 2255–2230 BC), and during Persian rule (525–404 BC). Under the Ptolemies and under Rome it was second only to Alexandria. It declined in the 7th century AD when the Arabs built the nearby city of El Fustat (now Cairo). The temples of Ptah, Isis, and Ra, the Serapeum, two statues of Ramses II, and many dwellings were found at the site.

MEMPHIS, city, seat of Shelby Co., extreme SW Tennessee, on the Chickasaw Bluffs overlooking the confluence of the Wolf and Mississippi rivers; inc. as a city 1849.

Economy. Memphis is a transportation hub, with a busy river port and an international airport, and it is the commercial center for much of the rich Mississippi R. delta farmland. It is linked by bridge with West Memphis, Ark., across the Mississippi R. The city is an important cotton market, with large stockyards. Manufactures include processed food, agricultural equipment, chemicals, wood and paper goods, textiles, furniture, medical supplies, and pharmaceuticals. A U.S. Naval air station is nearby.

Educational and Cultural Institutions. A noted medical and educational center, Memphis is the site of Rhodes College (1848), Memphis State University (1912), Le Moyne-Owen College (1862), Christian Brothers University (1871), Memphis College of Art (1936), Southern College of Optometry (1932), the University of Tennessee-Memphis (1911), and several junior colleges.

It has several museums and art galleries, the Memphis Zoo and Aquarium, an amusement park, many performing-arts organizations, a sports stadium, and the Pyramid, an entertainment and sports arena. Tourist attractions include sightseeing cruises on the Mississippi R.; Graceland, the home of singer Elvis Presley; and Beale Street, where composer W. C. Handy wrote some of his blues. Historic sites include the Magevney House (1831) and numerous Victorian-style structures. The National Civil Rights Museum (1991) stands on the site where Martin Luther King, Jr., was assassinated in 1968. Chucalissa Indian Village, founded about AD 900 and abandoned in the 16th century, is nearby.

History. Hernando de Soto may have reached the Mississippi River at the site of Memphis in 1541. The French built Fort Assumption on the bluffs above the river here in 1739. The area passed to Great Britain in 1763, and a U.S. fort was erected here in 1797. Memphis was founded in 1819 by Andrew Jackson (later president) and two partners and was named for Memphis, Egypt. Memphis grew as river traffic increased, and it became one of the nation's busiest ports.

Early in the American Civil War the city was an important Confederate military center, and it served as temporary state capital in 1862. Memphis was captured by Union forces after a river battle (June 1862) in which federal gunboats sank or captured seven out of eight Confederate vessels, and the city remained in Union hands until the end of the war. The long military occupation and severe recurring yellow-fever epidemics (especially one in 1878) depopulated Memphis and brought bankruptcy; the city's charter was revoked in 1879. Sanitary reforms and renewed activity at the community's natural harbor contributed to its economic recovery, and the charter was restored in 1893. Memphis's economy prospered during World War II, and in the 1950s the harbor was developed to provide many industrial sites. Pop. (1980) 646,174; (1990) 610,337.

MENADO. See MANADO.

MENANDER (342?–291? BC), foremost Greek dramatist of the genre known as New Comedy (*see* DRAMA AND DRAMATIC ARTS). He wrote more than 100 comedies, many of which continued to be performed in Athens after his death. Adaptations of Menander's plays by the Roman playwrights Plautus and Terence have survived. Fragments of seven original plays were found in Egypt, including long sections of *The Arbitration, The Rape of the Ringlets,* and *Samia,* and in 1957 archaeologists recovered, also in Egypt, the first complete text of a play by Menander, *The Curmudgeon.* Menander's plays involve complex love situations that are marked by sharp character delineation and an elegant style. These comedies, which provide social insights into human weaknesses and the complications of everyday life, greatly influenced later dramatists, particularly those of 17th-century England.

MENCIUS (c. 371–c. 288 BC), Chinese philosopher, who is also known as Mengtse. He was born in Chao (now in Shandong Province). After studying the philosophy of Confucius, he traveled for years expounding Confucianism and lecturing rulers on their duties toward their subjects. He believed that the power to govern comes from God and should be exercised in the interests of the common people. He opposed warfare except for purposes of defense. According to tradition, Mencius spent the latter part of his life in seclusion with his disciples. In his teachings he stressed the belief that people are by nature good, but that this goodness becomes manifest only when they experience peace of mind, which in turn depends on material security. If rulers, therefore, reduce their subjects to poverty and selfishness, they should be deposed. Since the 11th century Mencius has been recognized as one of China's greatest philosophers; the *Mencius* (Book of Mencius) is regarded as a basic Confucian text.

MENCKEN, H(enry) L(ouis) (1880–1956), American journalist, critic, and essayist, whose perceptive and often controversial analyses of American life and letters made him one of the most influential critics of the 1920s and '30s.

H. L. Mencken, in a picture taken on his 75th birthday, in 1955.
Wide World Photos

Mencken, born in Baltimore, Md., on Sept. 12, 1880, began his career as a journalist with the *Baltimore Morning Herald* and in 1906 switched to the *Baltimore Sun,* where he remained in various editorial capacities for most of his life. With the American drama critic George Jean Nathan (1882–1958) he coedited *The Smart Set,* a satirical monthly magazine, from 1914 to 1923. Again with Nathan, in 1924, Mencken founded the *American Mercury,* the literary heir to their previous joint endeavor; Mencken remained as its editor until 1933. The shortcomings of democracy and middle-class American culture were the targets of Mencken's wit and criticism. A six-volume collection of his essays and reviews, entitled *Prejudices,* was published between 1919 and 1927. Mencken's most important piece of scholarship was *The American Language* (3 vol., 1936–48), which traced the development and established the importance of American English (q.v.). Mencken died in Baltimore on Jan. 29, 1956. *Happy Days* (1940), *Newspaper Days* (1941), and *Heathen Days* (1943) are his autobiographies.

MENDEL, Gregor Johann (1822–84), Austrian monk, whose experimental work became the basis of modern hereditary theory (see HEREDITY).

Mendel was born on July 22, 1822, to a peasant family in Heinzendorf (now Hynčice, Czech Republic). He entered the Augustinian monastery at Brünn (now Brno, Czech Republic), which was known as a center of learning and scientific endeavor. He later became a substitute teacher at the technical school in Brünn. There Mendel became actively engaged in investigating variation, heredity, and evolution in plants at the monastery's experimental garden. Between 1856 and 1863 he cultivated and tested at least 28,000 pea plants, carefully analyzing seven pairs of seed and plant characteristics. His tedious experiments resulted in the enunciation of two generalizations that later became known as the laws of heredity (see MENDEL's LAWS). His observations also led him to coin two terms still used in present-day genetics: dominance, for a trait that shows up in an offspring; and recessiveness, for a trait masked by a dominant gene.

Mendel published his important work on heredity in 1866. Despite, or perhaps because of, its descriptions of large numbers of experimental plants, which allowed him to express his results numerically and subject them to statistical analysis, this work made virtually no impression for the next 34 years. Only in 1900 was his work recognized more or less independently by three investigators, one of whom was the Dutch botanist Hugo De Vries, and not until the late 1920s and the early '30s was its full significance realized, particularly in relation to evolutionary theory. As a result of years of research in population genetics, investigators were able to demonstrate that Darwinian evolution can be described in terms of the change in gene frequency of Mendelian pairs of characteristics in a population over successive generations.

Mendel's later experiments with the hawkweed *Hieracium* proved inconclusive, and because of the pressure of other duties he ceased his experiments on heredity by the 1870s. He died in Brünn on Jan. 6, 1884.   G.E.A. & R.Bi.

MENDELE MOKHER SEFARIM (Heb., "Mendele the Itinerant Bookseller"), pseudonym of SHALOM JACOB ABRAMOVICH (1835–1917), Russian Jewish short-story writer and novelist. Trained as a rabbi, Mendele began in 1858 to write fiction, first in Hebrew, later in Yiddish. In 1881 he became head of a Hebrew school in Odessa, then the cultural center of Russian Jewish life. Known familiarly as Grandfather Mendele, he became the leading figure of the literary movement, popular for his lively, gently satirical accounts of shtetl (small town) life and vivid descriptions of the countryside. In 1886 he began to create a new style of written Hebrew and gradually rewrote most of his earlier Yiddish works in Hebrew. Perhaps his major novel is *The Travels and Adventures of Benjamin the Third* (Yiddish, 1879; Hebrew, 1896; trans. 1949).

MENDELEVIUM, radioactive metallic element, symbol Md, one of the transuranium elements (q.v.) in the actinide series (q.v.) of the periodic table (*see* PERIODIC LAW); at.no. 101, at.wt. (most stable isotope) 258. Named for the Russian chemist Dmitry Mendeleyev, mendelevium-256 was discovered in 1955 at the University of California, Berkeley; it was produced by bombarding einsteinium-253 with alpha particles accelerated in a cyclotron. The isotope produced had a half-life of about 1.3 hours. The most stable isotope, mendelevium-258, has a half-life of 54 days. *See* RADIOACTIVITY.

MENDELEYEV, Dmitry Ivanovich (1834–1907), Russian chemist, best known for his development of the periodic law (q.v.) of the properties of the chemical elements.

Mendeleyev was born on Feb. 7, 1834, in Tobolsk, Siberia. He studied chemistry at the University of Saint Petersburg, and in 1859 he was sent to study at the University of Heidelberg. There he met the Italian chemist Stanislao Cannizzaro, whose views on atomic weight (*see* ATOM AND ATOMIC THEORY) influenced his thinking. Back in St. Petersburg, Mendeleyev became professor of chemistry at the Technical Institute in 1863 and professor of general chemistry at the University of St. Petersburg in 1866. He was a renowned teacher, and, because no good textbook in chemistry was available, he wrote the two-volume *Principles of Chemistry* (1868–70), which became a classic.

During the writing of this book, Mendeleyev tried to classify the elements according to their chemical properties. In 1869 he published his first version of what became known as the periodic table, in which he showed a fundamental periodicity in the properties of the elements when they are classified according to increasing atomic weights. In 1871 he published an improved version of the periodic table, in which he left gaps for elements that were not yet known. Three predicted elements—gallium, germanium, and scandium—were subsequently discovered.

Mendeleyev's investigations also included the study of the theory of solution, the thermal expansion of liquids, and the nature of petroleum. In 1887 he undertook a solo balloon ascension to study a solar eclipse.

In 1890 he resigned from the university as a consequence of his progressive political views and his advocacy of social reforms. In 1893 he became director of the Bureau of Weights and Measures in St. Petersburg and held this position until his death there on Feb. 2, 1907.

MENDEL'S LAWS, principles of hereditary transmission of physical characteristics, formulated in 1865 by the Augustinian monk Gregor Johann Mendel. Experimenting with seven contrasting characteristics of pure-breeding garden peas, Mendel discovered that by crossing tall and dwarf parents, for example, he got hybrid (q.v.) offspring that resembled the tall parent rather than being a medium-height blend. To explain this he conceived of hereditary units, now called genes, which often expressed dominant or recessive characteristics. Formulating his first principle (the law of segregation), Mendel stated that genes normally occur in pairs in the ordinary body cells, but segregate in the formation of sex cells (eggs or sperm), each member of the pair becoming part of the separate sex cell. When egg and sperm unite, forming a gene pair, the dominant gene (tallness) masks the recessive gene (shortness).

To corroborate the existence of such hereditary units, Mendel went on to interbreed the first generation of hybrid tall peas and found that the second generation turned out in a ratio of three tall to each short offspring. He then correctly conceived that the genes paired into AA, Aa, and aa ("A" representing dominant and "a" representing recessive). Continuing the breeding experiments, he found that the self-pollinated AA

173

bred true to produce pure tall plants, that the aa plant produced pure dwarf plants, and that the Aa, or hybrid, tall plants produced the same three-to-one ratio of offspring. From this Mendel could see that hereditary units did not blend, as his predecessors believed, but remained unchanged from one generation to another. He thus formulated his second principle (the law of independent assortment), in which the expression of a gene for any single characteristic is usually not influenced by the expression of another characteristic. Mendel's laws became the theoretical basis for modern genetics and heredity (qq.v.).

For further information on this topic, see the Bibliography in volume 28, section 449.

MENDELSOHN, Erich (1887–1953), German architect, whose expressionistic, curvilinear designs represent an alternative to the dominant functionalist style of 20th-century architecture. He first attracted attention in 1918 with a series of sketches for an innovative architecture based on curving lines and rounded forms, a style embodied in the Einstein Observatory in Potsdam (1921). During the 1920s a series of commissions for department stores and cinemas helped him to refine and develop this style. Mendelsohn's buildings show the influence of the organic designs of the American architect Frank Lloyd Wright and are characterized by curving facades, sweeping lines, and long horizontal bands of windows. His De La Warr Pavilion (1935, Bexhill-on-Sea, England) includes an early example of a circular, glass-enclosed stair tower. His preferred building material was poured concrete, the sculptural qualities of which suited his expressionist style.

MENDELSSOHN, Felix, full name JAKOB LUDWIG FELIX MENDELSSOHN-BARTHOLDY (1809–47), German composer, one of the leading figures of early 19th-century European romanticism.

Born Feb. 3, 1809, in Hamburg, he was the grandson of the noted Jewish philosopher Moses Mendelssohn. (The name Bartholdy was added to his surname when the family inherited property from a relative of that name, but he was always known by his original name.) As a child he converted with his family to Protestantism. Mendelssohn first appeared in public as a pianist at the age of 9 and performed his first original compositions when 11 years old. His masterly overture to *A Midsummer Night's Dream* was composed at the age of 17; the famous "Wedding March" and the rest of his incidental music to the play were written 17 years later. His teachers included the Bohemian pianist-composer Ignaz Moscheles (1794–1870) and the German composer Carl Zelter (1758–1832). A revival of public interest in the works of Johann Sebastian Bach was directly attributable to Mendelssohn, who in 1829 conducted the first performance since Bach's death of his *Passion of St. Matthew*.

Mendelssohn appeared as a pianist and conductor throughout Europe, making frequent trips to England. He was musical director for the city of Düsseldorf (1833–35), conductor of the Gewandhaus Orchestra in Leipzig (from 1835), and musical director to King Frederick William IV of Prussia (from 1841). In 1842 he helped organize the Leipzig Conservatory. He suffered a physical collapse at the death of his favorite sister, Fanny Mendelssohn Hensel (1805–47), and died a few months later in Leipzig on Nov. 4, 1847.

In spite of an enormously strenuous schedule as pianist, conductor, and teacher, Mendelssohn was a prolific composer. Of his five symphonies, the best known are the *Italian* Symphony (1833) and the *Scotch* Symphony (1843). His organ and choral music is among the best of the 19th century and includes, for choir and orchestra, the oratorios *St. Paul* (1836) and *Elijah* (1846) and the cantata *Erste Walpurgisnacht* (First Walpurgis-Night, 1832; rev. 1843); and his organ sonatas, preludes, and fugues. Also important are the *Variations sérieuses* (1841) for piano; his concert overtures, including *The Hebrides* (1832); his concertos for violin (1844) and for piano (1831, 1837); and the eight volumes of *Songs Without Words* for piano (1830–45; some of these are by his sister Fanny).

His romanticism shows most clearly in his use of orchestral color and in his fondness for program music depicting places, events, or personalities. Structurally, Mendelssohn's music adheres to classical forms. It is lyrical and graceful, always clear, and never revolutionary.

MENDELSSOHN, Moses (1729–86), German philosopher and author, born in Dessau, Germany, and educated by his father and the local rabbi. In 1750 he became tutor to the children of a silk merchant in Berlin; subsequently he became the merchant's partner. In 1754 he was introduced to the German dramatist and critic Gotthold Ephraim Lessing, and the two became friends. Lessing, a champion of Jewish emancipation, later modeled the hero of his play *Nathan der Weise* (Nathan the Wise, 1779) after Mendelssohn. Mendelssohn's *Philosophische Gespräche* (Philosophical Discourses) was anonymously published by Lessing in 1755. In the same year their joint satire, *Pope ein Metaphysiker* (Pope a Metaphysician), appeared.

In 1764 Mendelssohn won the Berlin Academy prize for the best essay on a metaphysical subject with his work *Abhandlung über die Evidenz in den Metaphysischen Wissenschaften* (Upon Proving Metaphysics a Science). His treatise *Phädon* (1767), in which he expounded his belief in the immortality of the soul, was modeled after Plato's dialogue *Phaedo,* and it earned him the appellation the "German Socrates." In addition to works on philosophy, Mendelssohn wrote books on Judaism and Jewry. His most important contribution was opening the world of German language and literature to his fellow Jews with his translation of the first five books of the Old Testament (the Pentateuch; q.v.), the Psalms, and other sections of the Bible into German. An ardent advocate of Jewish civil rights, Mendelssohn was a pioneer in denouncing Jewish separatism.

MENDÈS-FRANCE, Pierre (1907–82), French prime minister (1954–55). Mendès-France was born in Paris on Jan. 11, 1907. Educated at the University of Paris, he practiced law and was elected to the French Chamber of Deputies as a Radical-Socialist at the age of 25. In 1938 he was undersecretary of the treasury. During World War II he served (1939) in Syria; after France's defeat he was imprisoned for a time but escaped to London, where he joined the Free French air force and became financial adviser to Gen. Charles de Gaulle.

Following the establishment in 1946 of the Fourth Republic, Mendès-France served in the National Assembly, in which he opposed French financial policy. He advocated French disengagement in Indochina, and as premier he negotiated the armistice that led to French withdrawal from the region. He also won approval by the French National Assembly for the Western European Union but was forced to resign because of dissatisfaction with his proposal to grant concessions to nationalists in French North Africa. He unsuccessfully tried to regain the premiership in the 1969 French national elections. He wrote *A Modern French Republic* (1962; trans. 1963). He died in Paris on Oct. 18, 1982.

MENDICANT FRIARS (Lat. *mendicare,* "to beg"), members of religious orders in the Roman Catholic church, who take a vow of poverty by which they renounce all personal and communal property. They live chiefly by charity. After overcoming the initial opposition of the established clergy, the chief societies were authorized in the 13th century. They include Friars Minor, or Franciscans (q.v.; received papal approval in 1209); Friars Preachers, or Dominicans (q.v.; 1216); Carmelites (q.v.; 1245); and Augustinians (q.v.; 1256). A fifth order, the Servites, founded in 1233, was acknowledged as a mendicant order in 1424. *See* Friar; Monasticism; Religious Orders and Communities.

MENDOZA, city, W Argentina, capital of Mendoza Province, at the foot of the Andes. Mendoza is the commercial center of an area that is irrigated by several small rivers and produces most of the wine and much of the fruit of Argentina. Wine making, fruit packing, lumbering, oil refining, and metalworking are the principal industries of the city. Mendoza was almost totally destroyed by earthquake in 1861 but was rebuilt. It stands at the E end of the highway and railroad crossing the Andes into Chile. In Mendoza are the National University of Cuyo (1939) and the University of Mendoza (1960) and many relics of Gen. José de San Martín, who in 1817 led his army over the Andes to liberate Chile from Spain. The striking monument to the Army of the Andes stands on a hill nearby. Pop. (1991 prelim., greater city) 121,696.

MENELAUS, in Greek mythology, king of Sparta, brother of Agamemnon, king of Mycenae, and husband of Helen of Troy. When Helen was abducted by the Trojan prince Paris, Menelaus organized an expedition to bring her back. Under the leadership of Agamemnon, Menelaus and the other Greek kings set sail for Troy. At the close of the ensuing Trojan War, Menelaus was one of the Greeks who hid in the wooden horse and sacked the city. After being reconciled with Helen, Menelaus attempted to return to Greece. He and Helen wandered for eight years in the eastern Mediterranean before they reached Sparta. There Menelaus prospered greatly, and he and Helen enjoyed a long and happy life.

MENELIK II (1844–1913), emperor of Ethiopia (1889–1913), who transformed the country from a collection of semi-independent states into a united nation. As ruler (1865–89) of the kingdom of Shoa, in central Ethiopia, he conquered the Galla people to the south and annexed their land. When he succeeded (1889) the emperor John IV (real name Dejaz Kassai; 1831–89), who had reigned from 1872, Menelik united his kingdom with the northern kingdoms of Tigre and Amhara, and signed the Treaty of Wichale with Italy. A disagreement over the interpretation of the treaty led to a war in which Menelik's forces defeated an Italian army at Adwa (1896). The European powers then recognized Ethiopian independence. During his reign he suppressed the slave trade, curbed the feudal nobility, and made Addis Ababa his capital. He was succeeded by his grandson Lij Iyasu (1896–1935).

MENÉNDEZ DE AVILÉS, Pedro (1519–74), Spanish naval officer, founder of Saint Augustine, Fla. He became a sailor early in life and by 1554 was appointed captain of the Spanish Indies fleet. In

MENGISTU HAILE MARIAM

1565, he was charged by Philip II of Spain to expel the French Huguenot colony on Fort Caroline on the north Florida coast. Menéndez established a colony on Saint Augustine Bay and massacred the inhabitants of nearby Fort Caroline. He later explored the coast of the Gulf of Mexico.

MENGISTU HAILE MARIAM (1937–), chairman of Ethiopia's ruling Provisional Military Administrative Council or Dirgue (1977–87) and president of Ethiopia (1987–91). A graduate of the Holeta Military Academy, Mengistu fought in the secessionist province of Eritrea and attained the rank of major. He was a leader in the overthrow of Emperor Haile Selassie in 1974, subsequently served on the military government's executive committee, and by 1977, having liquidated his rivals, emerged as the country's strongman. Aided by Soviet advisers and Cuban troops, Mengistu sought to contain secessionist pressures in the Eritrea and Ogaden regions. In September 1984, Mengistu became secretary-general of the newly created Workers party, as Ethiopia officially became a Communist state. He became president in 1987 when Ethiopia nominally returned to civilian rule. During the late 1980s, as Soviet economic and military aid dwindled, Mengistu's position grew weaker. With his army demoralized and rebels about to take Addis Ababa, he was granted asylum in Zimbabwe in May 1991.

MENGTSE. See MENCIUS.

MENHADEN, common name for any of several fishes of the genus *Brevoortia*, of the family Clupeidae (see HERRING) found off the eastern coast of the U.S. The maximum length of the Atlantic menhaden, *B. tyrannus*, is about 38 cm (about 15 in). The fish is rich in oil and is caught in large numbers for use as bait, animal feed, and fertilizer. It is not esteemed as a food fish.

MENINGITIS, inflammatory condition of the meninges or membranes investing the brain and spinal cord. Meningitis is classified as pachymeningitis when it involves the dura mater (the outermost membrane) and as leptomeningitis when it affects the pia mater and arachnoid (the inner membranes). Pachymeningitis may be caused by trauma, such as fracture of the skull bones, or by extension of infection by microorganisms from the middle ear, mastoid process, ethmoid sinus, or frontal sinus. Leptomeningitis, which is much more common, may be caused by extension of inflammation from the nasopharynx; by invasion of the meninges through the bloodstream by bacterial microorganisms such as those that cause pneumonia (pneumococci); or by a host of other organisms, including meningococci and *Haemophilus influenzae*.

Epidemic cerebrospinal meningitis, or meningococcal meningitis, is a highly infectious, specific disease that attacks the upper respiratory system and the meninges, especially of children and young adults, and particularly where many people are living together, as in a school dormitory or an army barracks. The disease is almost worldwide in distribution but is most common in northern temperate regions. Epidemics have occurred periodically in U.S. cities, and the disease appears sporadically between these epidemics. It is caused by the meningococcus, *Neisseria meningitis,* isolated in 1887 by the Austrian physician Anton Weichselbaum (1845–1920).

Most cases of meningitis, particularly those caused by bacteria, have an abrupt onset, with symptoms including headache, stiff neck, fever, nausea, vomiting, listlessness, and irritability, often leading to stupor and coma. It progresses rapidly and may lead to death if untreated in 24 to 72 hours. Bacterial meningitis is effectively treated by early administration of antibiotics.

Occasionally, particularly in small children who are not treated early, serious brain damage may result. This may occur when drainage of spinal fluid from the cavities inside the brain is blocked, causing distension of the cavities, pressure on the brain, and enlargement of the skull, a condition that is called hydrocephalus.

Tuberculous meningitis, which is much more common in children than in adults, is usually secondary to tuberculosis of the lungs. This form of meningitis was almost always fatal until the discovery of streptomycin. Since the introduction of this and other antituberculous drugs, many recoveries from the illness have occurred, and cures have been effected even in recurrent cases.

Viral meningitis is a nonfatal form of bacterial meningitis. Almost always affecting children, the disease produces symptoms of headache, high fever, vomiting, and leg pains. Patients with most types of viral meningitis usually recover spontaneously within one or two weeks. L.J.V.

For further information on this topic, see the Bibliography in volume 28, sections 448, 487.

MENLO PARK, city, San Mateo Co., W California; inc. 1927. It is chiefly residential, with publishing and electronic equipment manufacturing industries. Located here are Menlo College (1927), Saint Patrick's Seminary (1894), and Stanford Research Institute or SRI International (1946). Settled in the 1850s, the city grew after the arrival of the railroad in 1863. It is named for Menlough, Ireland. Pop. (1980) 26,369; (1990) 28,040.

MENNINGER, family of American psychiatrists who founded and worked with the Menninger Clinic and the Menninger Foundation, two of the leading psychiatric centers of the world. The three best-known members of the family are described below.

Charles Frederick Menninger (1862–1953), born in Topeka, Kans. A general practitioner, he and his son Karl organized a group practice of psychiatric specialists in 1920; in 1925 they opened the Menninger Clinic in Topeka to mental patients.

Karl Augustus Menninger (1893–1990), son of Charles Frederick, born in Topeka and educated at the University of Wisconsin and Harvard University. After many years of dedication to the mentally ill at the Menninger Clinic, he and his brother William Claire founded, in Topeka, the Menninger Foundation for Psychiatric Education and Research. As director of education of the foundation, besides training other therapists, he wrote many works, among which are *The Human Mind* (1930), *Man Against Himself* (1938), and *Whatever Became of Sin?* (1973).

William Claire Menninger (1899–1966), son of Charles Frederick, born in Topeka and educated at Cornell University. After a residency in psychiatry at St. Elizabeth's Hospital in Washington, D.C., he joined the Menninger Clinic. He later applied his superior administrative skills in helping to establish the Menninger Foundation, of which he became general secretary and professor of the school of psychiatry. His many scientific papers and books include *Juvenile Paresis* (1936), *You and Psychiatry* (1948), and *Psychiatry in a Troubled World* (1948).

MENNONITES, Protestant evangelical religious group, which originated in Switzerland and the Netherlands at the time of the Protestant Reformation (q.v.).

Tenets. Mennonites are divided into a number of separate bodies, some of them more conservative and withdrawn from modern society than others; but they hold in common the ideal of a religious community based on New Testament models and imbued with the spirit of the Sermon on the Mount. Most of the principal tenets of the Mennonites are found in a confession of faith promulgated at Dordrecht, the Netherlands, in 1632. The Bible as interpreted by the individual conscience is regarded as the sole authority on doctrinal matters, and no powers of mediation between an individual and God are conceded to the ministry. Baptism (q.v.) is administered only on the profession of faith; infant baptism is rejected. The Lord's Supper (see EUCHARIST) is celebrated, although not as a sacrament (q.v.), and the rite of foot washing is sometimes observed in connection with it.

Mennonites were among the first to espouse the principle of separation of church and state and to condemn slavery. They have traditionally obeyed the civil laws, but many refuse to bear arms or to support violence in any form (see PACIFISM), to take judicial oaths, and to hold public office. The more conservative Mennonite groups are distinguished by plain living and simplicity of dress.

History. The Mennonites emerged in Switzerland in the 1520s as radical Protestants who went beyond the positions held by the Şwiss reformer Huldreich Zwingli. They broke with him over the issue of infant baptism, and so were called Anabaptists (q.v.), or "rebaptizers." Because these Swiss Brethren rejected the concept of a state church and refused to sanction war or to accept military service, they were regarded as subversive and were persecuted.

A parallel movement emerged at about the same time in the Netherlands, led by Menno Simons, from whom the name Mennonite is derived. Educated for the priesthood and ordained in 1524, Menno Simons gradually moved to a radical position, until by 1537 he was preaching believer's baptism and nonresistance. As they did in Switzerland, Anabaptists in the Netherlands experienced years of persecution. Similar groups sprang up in southern Germany and also in Austria, where they were led by Jakob Hutter (fl. 1526–36) and called Hutterites (see HUTTERIAN BRETHREN).

The Swiss Brethren continued to suffer harassment and persecution into the 18th century, and many fled to the Rhineland and the Netherlands, others to America (Pennsylvania), and still others to eastern Europe. In the Netherlands outright persecution ceased by the end of the 16th century, although some coercion and discrimination in favor of the state church persisted. Like the Swiss Brethren, many Dutch Mennonites immigrated, some to Pennsylvania, others eastward to Prussia and Poland, reaching, by the early 19th century, the Ukraine and other parts of Russia.

In Pennsylvania Mennonites were among those who settled Germantown in 1683. Both Swiss and Dutch Mennonites went to the colony in the following years. Distinctive among them, although not numerically the most important, were followers of a 17th-century Swiss Mennonite bishop, Jakob Amman (c. 1644–1730), who were called Amish (q.v.) or Amish Mennonites. Their very conservative dress and other customs—especially their use of shunning as a method of discipline—set them apart from the surrounding society.

Later waves of emigration from Europe introduced variant strands of the Mennonite tradition into the U.S. In each case the tendency was to take up land on what was at the time the western frontier. In the first half of the 19th century

Banners made by Mennonites around the world decorate the stage at the Tenth Mennonite World Conference held in Wichita, Kans., in 1978. Mennonites number more than 1.2 million, including about 169,000 in the U.S. and Canada.

D. Michael Hostetler

Mennonites from Switzerland and southern Germany settled in Ohio and other states westward to Missouri. After the American Civil War Mennonites from Russia, primarily of Dutch stock, settled in Kansas, Nebraska, and South Dakota. Following World War I Russian Mennonites migrated to Canada, especially Saskatchewan. More came after World War II, but the destinations of the most recent Mennonite emigrants have been Mexico, Paraguay, and Brazil.

In North America the largest Mennonite bodies are the Mennonite Church ("Old Mennonites"), with roots in colonial Pennsylvania, and the General Conference Mennonite Church, organized in Iowa in 1860. In 1980 the Mennonite Church had about 109,000 members in the U.S. and Canada and 33,000 in related overseas churches; the General Conference Mennonite Church had about 60,000 members in the U.S. and Canada. Local churches are organized into district conferences, which send delegates to a general conference, or assembly. Many of the clergy serve their churches part time while engaged in secular employment.

Throughout much of their history, Mennonites have been a rural people, traditionally farmers. In the 20th century the largest Mennonite bodies in the U.S. have begun to play a significant role in society at large. The traditional use of the German language in worship survives only in the most conservative groups. Both the Mennonite Church and the General Mennonite Church sponsor institutions of higher education. The Mennonite Central Committee, with representatives from 17 Mennonite bodies, is a cooperative relief and service agency dedicated to advancing the cause of peace and alleviating human suffering throughout the world.

For further information on this topic, see the Bibliography in volume 28, section 106.

MENNO SIMONS (1496–1561), Dutch religious reformer, from whom the religious body called Mennonites (q.v.) takes its name.

Born at Witmarsum in Friesland, Menno was ordained a Roman Catholic priest in 1524. Doubts about transubstantiation, infant baptism, and other church dogmas led him to a close study of the New Testament and writings of Martin Luther. He gradually came to agree with Luther's position that the Bible should be the

Christian's highest authority, and he left the Roman Catholic church. Although he opposed the revolutionary Anabaptists (q.v.) who led an unsuccessful uprising at Münster in 1535, his efforts to help them put him in danger of arrest, and he went into hiding for a year. In 1537 he became an Anabaptist preacher at Groningen, where he was married. Subsequently he was active as a missionary, carrying the new faith to other parts of Friesland, to South Holland, and to Germany. He died on Jan. 31, 1561, near Ordesloe, Holstein.

Menno adhered fundamentally to orthodox beliefs but rejected those that were not mentioned in the New Testament. He believed in the divinity of Christ and baptized only those who asserted their faith in Christ. In his view, military service and killing were unlawful, as were the taking of oaths, the holding of the office of magistrate, and marriage to persons outside the church. He also taught that prayer should be performed in silence. His writings were collected as *The Complete Writings of Menno Simons* (1681; trans. 1956).

MENOMINEE, also Menomini, North American Indian tribe, of the Algonquian language family, and of the Eastern Woodlands culture area. The tribe originally lived in the upper Michigan region, later moving to Wisconsin and west to the Mississippi River. Sedentary and peaceful, they lived in villages and gathered wild rice and other plants as their food staples. They also farmed, cultivating maize, beans, and tobacco, and hunted and fished. Later, they hunted animals for furs. After selling their lands to the U.S. government, they were moved in the mid-1800s to a reservation near Wolf River, Wis. In 1990, 7543 people identified themselves as descendants of the Menominee. Most still live in Wisconsin. *See also* AMERICAN INDIAN LANGUAGES; AMERICAN INDIANS.

For further information on this topic, see the Bibliography in volume 28, sections 1105–7.

MENOMONEE FALLS, village, Waukesha Co., SE Wisconsin, at rapids on the Menomonee R., near Milwaukee; inc. 1892. Situated in an area producing dairy products, corn, and other vegetables, it has diversified industries manufacturing metal products, motors, machinery, paper and plastic goods, hospital supplies, and processed food. Old Falls Village, a re-created mid-19th-century village, is here. Established in 1842, the area grew as a result of the availability of waterpower. Pop. (1980) 27,845; (1990) 26,840.

MENOPAUSE, or change of life, the period in a woman's life when menstruation (q.v.) and childbearing naturally cease. Menopause results from changes in the ovaries and in glands that produce the hormones (primarily estrogen) that control the menstrual cycle. In most women, this decline in estrogen production usually occurs between the ages of 45 and 50. (Comparatively, research indicates that men, as they age, do not experience hormonal decline.) Surgical removal or other destruction of the ovaries can produce premature menopause.

Menopause can be undergone without difficulty. Common problems, however, include hot flashes and sweats; changes in the vaginal lining that produce dryness, burning, itching, and pain during sexual intercourse; and osteoporosis, a thinning of the bone associated with an increased risk of fracture. These problems, caused by hormonal deficiencies or imbalances, are controlled or prevented by estrogen-replacement therapy; linked to an increased risk of cancer of the lining of the uterus, postmenopausal estrogen use has become controversial. Given the current state of knowledge, the decision about its use should be made by the woman and her doctor.

At one time, depression and other emotional problems were considered more common in a woman's life during menopause; this notion is now being questioned. Menopause nevertheless is a psychological as well as a physical milestone in the aging process, and such milestones sometimes produce varying degrees of stress.   M.R.

For further information on this topic, see the Bibliography in volume 28, section 521.

MENOTTI, Gian-Carlo (1911–   ), Italian-American composer, born in Cadegliano, Italy, and educated at the Milan Conservatory and at the Curtis Institute of Music, Philadelphia. He taught composition at Curtis from 1941 to 1955. In 1958 he organized the Festival of Two Worlds in Spoleto, Italy; in 1977 he inaugurated an American counterpart of the festival in Charleston, S.C., which, beginning in 1994, became a separate festival.

Menotti's operatic works, for which he also wrote the librettos, are mainly in the tradition of early 20th-century Italian opera. These include *Amelia Goes to the Ball*, originally produced (1936) in Philadelphia and later performed at the Metropolitan Opera House in New York City; *The Old Maid and the Thief* (1939); *The Island God* (1942); *The Medium* (1946); *The Telephone* (1947); *The Consul* (1950; Pulitzer Prize, 1950); and *Amahl and the Night Visitors* (1951), the first opera written for television. *Amahl*, based on the story of the three wise men, is frequently telecast at Christmas. Menotti's later operas include *The Saint of Bleecker Street* (1954; Pulitzer Prize, 1955), *The Labyrinth* (for television, 1963), *Help! Help! The Globolinks!* (1968), and *La Loca* (1979).

MENSHEVIK. *See* BOLSHEVISM; RUSSIAN REVOLUTION.

MENSTRUATION

MENSTRUATION, periodic vaginal discharge in humans and other mammals, consisting of blood and cells shed from the endometrium, or lining of the uterus (see REPRODUCTIVE SYSTEM). Menstruation accompanies a woman's childbearing years, usually beginning between the ages of 10 and 16, at puberty (q.v.), and most often ceasing between the ages of 45 and 50, at menopause (q.v.). Menstruation is part of the process that prepares a woman for pregnancy. Each month the lining of the uterus thickens; if pregnancy does not occur, this lining breaks down and is discharged through the vagina. The three to seven days that menstruation lasts is called the menstrual period.

In most women the menstrual cycle is about 28 days, but it can vary considerably even from one month to another. The cycle is initiated by hormones in the blood that stimulate the ovaries (the two female organs that produce ova, or eggs). Each month, hormones cause an egg in one of the two ovaries to mature (to become capable of being fertilized and develop into a fetus). The ovaries also produce hormones of their own, primarily estrogen (q.v.), which cause the endometrium to thicken. About midway through the menstrual cycle, 14 to 15 days before the next period, the ovary releases the mature egg in a process called ovulation. The egg passes through the Fallopian tube to the uterus. If the egg unites with a sperm on its way to the uterus, fertilization occurs and pregnancy ensues.

The three to five days the egg takes to reach the uterus after being released by the ovary is known as the woman's fertile period. If fertilization does occur, the fertilized egg attaches itself to the enriched uterine lining and pregnancy continues. Menstruation does not occur during pregnancy, and a missed period is often the first indication of pregnancy a woman notices (see PREGNANCY AND CHILDBIRTH). If fertilization does not occur, the lining of the uterus does not receive the hormones it needs to continue the thickening process. Thus, the uterine lining breaks down and is discharged from the body during menstruation.

Many women experience premenstrual discomfort. Tenderness of the breasts and a tendency to retain fluid (bloat) are common one to seven days before each period. Some women also experience premenstrual tension in the form of headache, irritability, nervousness, fatigue, crying spells, and depression with no apparent cause (premenstrual stress, or PMS). A few women also experience menstrual cramps (dysmenorrhea) during the first day or two of the period. Although premenstrual symptoms and discomfort during menstruation were once thought to be of psychological origin, research now indicates that hormonal and chemical changes are responsible. New medications are effective in treating these problems. M.R.

For further information on this topic, see the Bibliography in volume 28, section 521.

MENTAL DISORDERS, psychological and behavioral syndromes that deviate significantly from those typical of human beings enjoying good mental health. In general, a mental disorder involves present distress or impairment in important areas of functioning. Such deviations in thought, feelings, and behavior have been recognized throughout history in all cultures.

For the greater part of recorded history, mental deviations were considered supernaturally or unnaturally caused, the work of evil spirits or human depravity. After small beginnings in the 16th and 17th centuries, however, the mental science that eventually developed into psychiatry acquired respectability in the 1790s. At that time the Parisian physician Philippe Pinel (1745–1826) abolished physical restraints, introduced moral (psychological) treatment, and began objective clinical studies. Thereafter, in clinical work with large populations of patients in institutions for the mentally ill, the major types of mental disorders were outlined and methods of management and treatment were developed.

Classification. The division of mental disorders into classes is still inexact, and classification varies from country to country. For official record-keeping purposes, most countries follow the International Classification of Diseases of the World Health Organization (WHO). For clinical use in the U.S., the American Psychiatric Association in 1980 adopted a third edition of its *Diagnostic and Statistical Manual* (DSM-III); an extensive revision (DSM-III-R) was issued in 1987.

Most classification systems recognize childhood disorders (including mental retardation) as separate categories from adult disorders. Most distinguish between organic, somatically caused states and nonorganic (sometimes referred to as functional) conditions. Psychotic disorders are also commonly separated from neurotic ones. Psychotic means, roughly, a state in which a patient has lost touch with reality, whereas neurotic refers to a relatively less impaired state. Schizophrenia, many organic mental disorders, and some forms of depression (such as manic-depressive illness) are psychotic conditions. Examples of neurotic disorders are those in which anxiety is the major symptom, hypochondriasis (morbid concern about health), and multiple personality.

MENTAL DISORDERS

Identifying and evaluating learning disabilities is important in treating childhood mental disorders.
U.S. Department of Health and Human Services

Childhood Disorders. Several mental disorders are first evident in infancy, childhood, and adolescence.

Mental retardation (q.v.) is characterized by the inability to learn normally and to become as independent and socially responsible as others of the same age in the same culture. Persons having an intelligence quotient (IQ) of less than 70 are considered retarded.

Attention-deficit hyperactivity disorder includes conditions marked by inappropriate lack of attention, by impulsiveness, and by hyperactivity, in which the child has difficulty organizing and completing work, is unable to stick to activities or follow instructions, and is excessively restless.

Anxiety disorders include fear of leaving home and parents (separation), excessive shrinking from contact with strangers (avoidance), and excessive, unfocused worrying and fearful behavior.

Pervasive developmental disorders are characterized by distortions in several psychological functions, such as attention, perception, reality testing, and motor movement. An example is infantile autism, a condition marked by unresponsiveness to other people, bizarre responses, and gross inability to communicate.

Among the other childhood disorders are those involving conduct problems, overeating, anorexia nervosa (q.v.; self-starvation), tics, stuttering (see SPEECH AND SPEECH DISORDERS), and bed-wetting (see ENURESIS).

Organic Mental Disorders. This group of disorders is characterized by psychological or behavioral abnormalities associated with transient or permanent impairments in brain function. The disorders have different symptoms, depending on which area of the brain is affected and on the cause, progression, and duration of the disorder. Organic damage to the brain can result from a disease or drug that directly damages the brain, or from a disease that indirectly damages the brain through effects on other bodily systems.

Symptoms associated with organic mental disorders may be a direct result of organic damage or may be the patient's reaction to lost mental abilities. Some disorders have as their primary feature delirium, or a clouded state of consciousness, which is manifested by difficulties in sustaining attention, by sensory misperceptions, and by disordered thought. Another common symptom, especially in organic mental disorders associated with old age, is dementia. Dementia is marked by impairments in memory, thinking, perception, judgment, and attention that are sufficient to interfere with social and occupational functioning. Emotional expression is also often changed, as evidenced by increased apathy, euphoria, or irritability. See GERIATRICS; SENILE DEMENTIA.

Schizophrenia. Schizophrenia (q.v.) is a group of serious disorders beginning usually in adolescence or young adulthood. Symptoms include

181

MENTAL DISORDERS

disturbances in thought, perception, emotion, and interpersonal relationships.

Affective Disorders. The affective disorders are those in which the predominant symptom is a disturbance in mood. One form, depression (q.v.), is marked by sadness, guilt, and feelings of helplessness and hopelessness. In mania, mood is elevated, expansive, or irritable.

Delusional (Paranoid) Disorders. The central feature of the paranoid disorders is a person's delusion (a firmly held false belief), for instance that he or she is being persecuted or conspired against. In another form, the delusion consists of unreasonable jealousy. The person may be resentful, angry, sometimes violent, socially isolated, seclusive, and eccentric. The disorder usually starts in middle or late adult life and can be seriously disrupting to social and marital relationships.

Anxiety Disorders. Anxiety (q.v.) is the predominant symptom in two conditions: panic disorder and generalized anxiety disorder.

In phobias and obsessive-compulsive disorders, also considered anxiety disorders, fear is experienced when an individual tries to master other symptoms. A phobia (q.v.) is an irrational fear of a specific object, activity, or situation that is so intense that it interferes with everyday life. Obsessions are repetitive thoughts, images, ideas, or impulses that make no sense to the person. He or she can fear being unable to avoid committing a violent act, for example, or worry over whether some small duty has been performed. Compulsions are repetitive behaviors performed dutifully to try to ward off some future event. Examples of such behavior include repeated washing of the hands or counting and recounting belongings.

Other Neurotic Disorders. In addition to neurotic depression and anxiety disorders, other conditions that have historically been considered neurotic include somatization disorder (hysteria), conversion reactions, psychogenic pain, hypochondriasis, and dissociative disorders.

The so-called somatoform disorders are characterized by physical symptoms for which no physical cause is evident. In hysteria (q.v.), complaints are presented dramatically, if vaguely, usually beginning during the teen years and continuing through adult life. Women are much more frequently affected than men. The rare conversion disorders (hysterical neurosis) commonly mimic a neurological disease such as paralysis. Psychogenic pain is pain for which no physical cause is apparent. In hypochondriasis, the patient is preoccupied with the fear of having a serious disease, for which no physical cause can be found.

Included in the dissociative disorders are amnesia (q.v.) that apparently stems from psychological causes and multiple personality—a rare condition in which two or more separate personalities exist in the same person.

Personality Disorders. In contrast to the more episodic nature of the psychotic and neurotic disorders hitherto described, personality disorders are lifelong conditions, in which personality traits are so inflexible and maladaptive that they cause

In family therapy situations, members air their feelings and grievances while the psychiatrist acts as an objective catalyst. Werner Wolff—Black Star

social and occupational impairments and may cause considerable distress to others if not to the persons themselves. The paranoid personality is unduly suspicious and mistrustful. Schizoid personalities are devoid of the capacity, or the desire, for social relationships. Schizotypal disorders are marked by odd thought, speech, perception, and behavior. Histrionic personalities are characterized by overly dramatic behavior and expression. Self-importance and the need for constant attention and admiration are the marks of narcissistic personalities. Those with antisocial personality disorders have a history of violating the rights of others and failing to observe social norms. Borderline personality disorder is marked by instability in interpersonal behavior, mood, and self-image. A person with an avoidant personality disorder is hypersensitive to potential rejection, humiliation, or shame. The dependent personality is passive, allowing others to assume responsibility. Compulsive personalities are perfectionistic and unable to express warm feelings. The passive-aggressive personality resists demands indirectly by such maneuvers as procrastination and dawdling.

Incidence and Distribution. Just how many people are afflicted with mental disorders is impossible to know. Records of admissions to psychiatric facilities give some indication, but they exclude the large numbers of people who do not seek treatment. In the U.S., the estimate has been made that some 15 percent of the population suffers from a mental disorder during the course of a year. Three percent of the U.S. population is under care for mental disorders at any given time. More patients in hospitals are receiving treatment for mental disorders than for any other illness. In 1990 the annual cost of mental illness in the U.S. was estimated by the National Institutes of Health to be about $148 billion.

The risk of developing schizophrenia over the course of a lifetime is about 1 in 100, while for depression it is 1 in 10. Between 2 and 4 percent of the population has suffered from an anxiety disorder. Somatoform disorders are thought to be much more common, although figures are not available. Of particular concern are the organic mental disorders, which occur much more frequently in the increasing numbers of elderly persons. L.R.W.

For further information on this topic, see the Bibliography in volume 28, section 526.

MENTAL HEALTH, state characterized by psychological well-being and self-acceptance. The term *mental health* usually implies the capacity to love and relate to others, the ability to work productively, and the willingness to behave in a way that brings personal satisfaction without encroaching upon the rights of others. In a clinical sense, mental health is the absence of mental illness.

The Mental Health Movement. Concern for the mentally ill has waxed and waned through the centuries, but the development of modern-day approaches to the subject dates from the mid-18th century, when reformers such as the French physician Philippe Pinel (1745–1826) and the American physician Benjamin Rush introduced humane "moral treatment" to replace the often cruel treatment that then prevailed. Despite these reforms, most of the mentally ill continued to live in jails and poorhouses—a situation that continued until 1841, when the American reformer Dorothea Dix campaigned to place the mentally ill in hospitals for special treatment.

The modern mental health movement can be traced to the publication in 1908 of *A Mind That Found Itself,* an account of the experience of its author, Clifford Whittingham Beers, as a mental patient. The book aroused a storm of public concern for the mentally ill. In 1909 Beers founded the National Committee for Mental Hygiene.

Public awareness of the need for greater governmental attention to mental health services led to passage of the National Mental Health Act in 1946. This legislation authorized the establishment of the National Institute of Mental Health to be operated as a part of the U.S. Public Health Service. In 1950 the National Committee for Mental Hygiene was reorganized as the National Association for Mental Health, better known as the Mental Health Association.

In 1955 Congress established a Joint Commission on Mental Illness and Health to survey the mental health needs of the nation and to recommend new approaches. Based on the commission's recommendations, legislation was passed in 1963 authorizing funds for construction of facilities for community-based treatment centers. A similar group, the President's Commission on Mental Health, reported its findings in 1978, citing estimates of the cost of mental illness in the U.S. alone as being about $17 billion a year.

Scope of the Problem. According to a common estimate, at any one time 10 percent of the American population has mental health problems sufficiently serious to warrant care; recent evidence suggests that this figure may be closer to 15 percent. Not all the people who need help receive it, however; in 1975 only 3 percent of the American population received mental health service. One major reason for this is that people still fear the stigma attached to mental illness and hence often fail to report it or to seek help.

Analysis of the figures on mental illness shows

MENTAL HEALTH

that schizophrenia afflicts an estimated 2 million Americans, another 2 million suffer from profound depressive disorders, and 1 million have organic psychoses or other permanently disabling mental conditions (see MENTAL DISORDERS). As much as 25 percent of the population is estimated to suffer from mild or moderate depression, anxiety, and other types of emotional problems. Some 10 million Americans have problems related to alcohol abuse, and millions more are thought to abuse drugs. Some 5 to 15 percent of children between the ages of 3 and 15 are the victims of persistent mental health problems, and at least 2 million are thought to have severe learning disabilities that can seriously impair their mental health.

In addition, according to the President's Commission, the list of mental health problems should be extended beyond identifiable psychiatric conditions to include the damage to mental health associated with unrelenting poverty, unemployment, and discrimination on the basis of race, sex, class, age, and mental or physical handicaps.

Prevention. Public health authorities customarily distinguish among three forms of prevention. Primary prevention refers to attempts to prevent the occurrence of mental disorder, as well as to promote positive mental health. Secondary prevention is the early detection and treatment of a disorder, and tertiary prevention refers to rehabilitative efforts that are directed at preventing complications.

Two avenues of approach to the prevention of mental illness in adults were suggested by the President's Commission. One was to reduce the stressful effects of such crises as unemployment, retirement, bereavement, and marital disruption; the second was to create environments in which people can achieve their full potential. The commission placed its heaviest emphasis, however, on helping children. It recommended the following steps: (1) good care during pregnancy and childbirth, so that early treatment can be instituted as needed; (2) early detection and correction of problems of physical, emotional, and intellectual development; (3) developmental day-care programs focusing on emotional and intellectual development; and (4) support services for families, directed at preventing unnecessary and inappropriate foster care or other out-of-home placements for children.

Treatment. Care of the mentally ill has changed dramatically in recent decades. Drugs introduced in the mid-1950s, along with other improved treatment methods, enabled many patients who would once have spent years in mental institutions to be treated as outpatients in community facilities instead. (A series of judicial decisions and legislative acts has promoted community care by requiring that patients be treated in the least restrictive setting available.) Between 1955 and 1980 the number of people in state mental hospitals declined from more than 550,000 to fewer than 125,000. This trend was due partly to improved community care and partly to the cost of operating hospitals; in an effort to save public money, some large state mental hospitals have been closed, forcing alternatives to be found for patients. This is generally considered a progres-

Taking an active interest in people and things around them, capable elderly people maintain a healthy and happier state of mind. UPI

A therapist interviews a young child. Early discovery and treatment of children with symptoms of personality disorders is the first step in preventing more serious problems in adult life.   World Health Organization–Jean Mohr

sive trend because when patients spend extended periods in hospitals they tend to become overly dependent and lose interest in taking care of themselves. In addition, because the hospitals are often located long distances from the patients' homes, families and friends can visit only infrequently, and the patients' roles at home and at work are likely to be taken over by others.

The psychiatric wards of community general hospitals have assumed some of the responsibility for caring for the mentally ill during the acute phases of illness. Some of these hospitals function as the inpatient service for community mental health centers. Typically, patients remain for a few days or weeks until their symptoms have subsided, and they usually are given some form of psychotropic drug to help relieve their symptoms. Following the lead of Great Britain, American mental hospitals now also give some patients complete freedom of buildings and grounds and, in some instances, freedom to visit nearby communities. This move is based on the conclusion that disturbed behavior is often the result of restraint rather than of illness.

Treatment of patients with less severe mental disorders has also changed markedly in recent decades. Previously, patients with mild depression, anxiety disorders, and other neurotic conditions were treated individually with psychotherapy (q.v.). Although this form of treatment is still widely used, alternative approaches are now available. In some instances, a group of patients meets to work through problems with the assistance of a therapist; in other cases, families are treated as a unit. Another form of treatment that has proven especially effective in alleviating phobic disorders is behavior therapy, which focuses on changing overt behavior rather than the underlying causes of a disorder. As in the serious mental illnesses, the treatment of milder forms of anxiety and depression has been furthered by the introduction of new drugs that help alleviate symptoms.

Rehabilitation. The release of large numbers of patients from state mental hospitals, however, has caused significant problems both for the patients and for the communities that become their new homes. Adequate community services often are unavailable to former mental patients, a large percentage of whom live in nursing homes and other facilities that are not equipped to meet their needs. Most of these patients have been diagnosed as having schizophrenia, and only 15 to 40 percent of schizophrenics who live in the community achieve an average level of adjustment. Those who do receive care typically visit a clinic at periodic intervals for brief counseling and drug monitoring.

In addition to such outpatient clinics, rehabilitation services include sheltered workshops, day-treatment programs, and social clubs. Sheltered workshops provide vocational guidance and an opportunity to brush up on an old skill or learn a new one. In day-treatment programs, patients return home at night and on weekends; during weekdays, the programs offer a range of rehabilitative services, such as vocational training, group activities, and help in the practical problems of living. Ex-patient social clubs provide social contacts, group activities, and an opportunity for patients to develop self-confidence in normal situations.

Another important rehabilitative facility is the halfway house for patients whose families are not willing or able to accept them after discharge. It serves as a temporary residence for ex-patients who are ready to form outside community ties. A variant is the use of subsidized apartments for recently discharged psychiatric patients.

Research. Many different sciences contribute to knowledge about mental health and illness. In recent decades these sciences have begun to clarify basic biological, psychological, and social processes, and they have refined the application of such knowledge to mental health problems.

Some of the most promising leads have come from biological research. For example, brain scientists who study neurotransmitters—chemicals that carry messages from one nerve cell to an-

MENTAL RETARDATION

other—are contributing to knowledge of normal and abnormal brain functioning, and they may eventually discover better treatment methods for mental illness. Other researchers are trying to discover how the human brain develops. They have learned, for example, that even in adults some nerve cells partially regenerate after having sustained damage. This research leads to increased understanding of mental retardation, currently untreatable forms of brain damage, and other related conditions.

Psychological research relevant to mental health includes the study of perception, information processing, thinking, language, motivation, emotion, abilities, attitudes, personality, and social behavior. For example, researchers are studying stress and how to cope with it. One application of this type of research may help to prevent mental disorders; in the future, psychologists may be better able to match people (and their coping skills) to work settings and job duties.

Research in the social sciences generally focuses on the problems of individuals in such common contexts as the family, the neighborhood, and the occupational environment as well as in the culture at large. One example of such work is epidemiological research, which is the study of the occurrence of disease patterns, including mental illness, in a society. S.J.K.

For further information on this topic, see the Bibliography in volume 28, sections 499, 525.

MENTAL RETARDATION, below-average intellectual ability present from birth or early childhood, manifested by abnormal development and associated with difficulties in learning and social adaption. About 3 percent of the total population is reported to be mentally retarded (having an IQ of below 69), but only about 1 to 1.5 percent is actually identified.

Four levels of mental retardation have been defined. These are mild (IQ range 52-68), moderate (IQ range 26-51), severe (IQ range 20-35), and profound (IQ less than 20). Mildly affected individuals comprise about 75 percent of the mentally retarded population and often cannot be distinguished from normal children until they attend school. The mildly retarded can generally learn academic skills up to about the sixth-grade level, although at a slower pace than normal children, and as adults they can usually support themselves if helped during times of social or economic stress. In most cases no obvious physical symptoms are present, although there may be a higher-than-normal incidence of epilepsy. About 20 percent of retarded individuals are moderately affected. They can progress to about the second-grade level in academic subjects, and adults may

A small learning achievement can be a great triumph for a retarded child, and the best teacher is one who carefully works for that achievement with love and patience.
President's Committee on Mental Retardation

be able to work at unskilled or semiskilled jobs in sheltered conditions. Severely retarded individuals usually develop only minimal speech and communication skills, and the profoundly retarded have little capacity to move about or communicate. The severely retarded must be under complete supervision but may be able to take care of themselves, whereas those who are profoundly retarded require nursing care.

Several factors have been identified as causes of mental retardation. These include: maternal infection during pregnancy, such as German measles (q.v.); chemical insults, such as lead poisoning or fetal alcohol syndrome; trauma, such as head injury; disorders of metabolism, such as phenylketonuria (PKU; see METABOLISM) or Tay-Sachs disease (q.v.); brain disease, such as neurofibromatosis or cancer; conditions resulting from unknown prenatal influence, such as hydrocephalus; premature birth; chromosomal abnormalities, such as Down syndrome (q.v.); psychiatric disorders, such as autism (q.v.); and environmental influences, such as poor nutrition or lack of stimulation. The mental retardation resulting from PKU can be prevented by placing the infant on a special diet before brain damage can occur; for this reason, newborn screening for PKU is now performed throughout the U.S. See BIRTH DEFECTS.

A primary goal in treatment and management of mental retardation is optimal development of the patient's strengths, taking into account individual interests, personal experiences, and available resources. Another major goal is the development of social adaptive skills to help the patient function as normally as possible. It is particularly important that mentally retarded children receive special education and training, ideally beginning in infancy. Such education has been enormously beneficial and in recent years has been extended with positive effects even to the profoundly retarded. The prognosis for mentally retarded individuals is related more to the timing and aggressiveness of treatment, personal motivation, training opportunities, and associated medical or environmental conditions than to the mental retardation itself. With early intervention and good support systems, many mentally retarded people have become productive members of society. Successful management leads to independent functioning for some and a sheltered environment for others. Even those whose handicaps require total care benefit from appropriate stimulation and training.

MENTHOL, white crystalline substance, $C_{10}H_{19}OH$, principal constituent of oil of peppermint. It has a peppermint odor and produces a sensation of cold in the mouth and nasal passages. It is an anodyne used to treat neuralgia and inflammation of the mucous membranes of the nose. Menthol is an ingredient in some cigarettes, cough drops, shaving creams, lotions, and other consumer products.

MENTOR, in Greek mythology, elderly friend and counselor of the hero Odysseus and tutor of his son Telemachus. In the *Odyssey* of Homer, the goddess Athena frequently assumes the form of Mentor when she appears to Odysseus or Telemachus. In modern English the tutor's name has become an eponym for a wise, trustworthy counselor or teacher.

MENTOR, city, Lake Co., NE Ohio, near Lake Erie, NE of Cleveland; inc. as a township 1815, as a city 1963. Manufactures include fork lifts and electronic components and equipment. Lawnfield, the home of President James A. Garfield (now a museum), and a community college are here. The community, settled in 1797, was relatively rural until the 1960s, when it grew as a suburb and center of light manufacturing. It is named for Hiram Mentor, an early settler. Pop. (1980) 42,065; (1990) 47,358.

MENUHIN, Sir Yehudi (1916–   ), American-born violinist, one of the foremost virtuosos of his generation. Born April 22, 1916, in New York City, he appeared as solo violinist with the San Francisco Symphony Orchestra at the age of seven. He later studied with the Romanian violinist-composer Georges Enesco, who deeply influenced his artistic development, and with the

Yehudi Menuhin with his sister Hephzibah preparing for their first joint television concert in the U.S. in 1963.
UPI

German violinist Adolph Busch (1891–1952). Menuhin toured widely, often with his sister, the pianist Hephzibah Menuhin (1920–81), and later conducted the Bath (now the Menuhin) Festival Orchestra. He also performed with the Indian sitarist Ravi Shankar, who wrote *Prabhati* (Of the Morning, 1966) for him. Menuhin wrote an autobiography, *Unfinished Journey* (1977). He moved to London in 1959, was knighted in 1965, and became a British subject in 1985.

MENZEL BOURGUIBA, city, N Tunisia, in Bizerte Governorate, a port on the Lake of Bizerte, near the city of Bizerte. A former French naval base with an arsenal and other installations, it is a road and rail hub. Industries include metallurgy, cotton processing, and iron-working. The city is the site of a classical college. Formerly called Ferryville, the city was renamed to honor Habib Bourguiba, the founder of the Tunisian Republic and president from 1957 to 1987. Pop. (1994 est.) 55,000.

MENZIES, Sir Robert Gordon (1894–1978), Australian political leader, who served the longest continuous term as prime minister.

Menzies was born Dec. 20, 1894, in Jeparit, Victoria. The son of a storekeeper, he studied law at Melbourne University. He was elected to the Victoria Legislative Council in 1928 and, as a member of the newly formed United Australia party, to the federal parliament in 1934. He later became attorney general and minister of industry. As prime minister from 1939 to 1941, Menzies directed Australian efforts in World War II, but he subsequently resigned over policy differences. In 1944 he helped found the Liberal party, which he led to victory in 1949 in coalition with the Country party. As prime minister from 1949 to 1966, the conservative Menzies ended wartime economic controls, encouraged industrial development and emigration from Europe, and backed the U.S. against communism in Korea and South Vietnam; he was knighted in 1963. Sir Robert retired in 1966, and he died in Melbourne, May 14, 1978.

MERCANTILISM, economic policy prevailing in Europe during the 16th, 17th, and 18th centuries, under which governmental control was exercised over industry and trade in accordance with the theory that national strength is increased by a preponderance of exports over imports. Mercantilism was characterized not so much by a consistent or formal doctrine as by a set of generally held beliefs. These beliefs included the ideas that exports to foreign countries are preferable both to trade within a country and to imports; that the wealth of a nation depends primarily on the possession of gold and silver; and that governmental interference in the national economy is justified if it tends to implement the attainment of these objectives. The mercantilist approach in economic policy first developed during the growth of national states; efforts were directed toward the elimination of the internal trade barriers that characterized the Middle Ages, when a cargo of commodities might be subject to a toll or tariff at every city and river crossing. Industries were encouraged and assisted in their growth because they provided a source of taxes to support the large armies and other appurtenances of national government. Exploitation of colonies was considered a legitimate method of providing the parent countries with precious metals and with the raw materials on which export industries depended.

Mercantilism, by its very success in stimulating industry and developing colonial areas, soon gave rise to powerful antimercantilist pressures. The use of colonies as supply depots for the home economies, and the exclusion of colonies from trade with other nations produced such reactions as the American Revolution, in which the colonists asserted their desire for freedom to seek economic advantage wherever it could be found. At the same time, European industries, which had developed under the mercantile system, became strong enough to operate both without mercantilist protection and in spite of mercantilist limitations. Accordingly, a philosophy of free trade began to take root. Economists asserted that government regulation is justified only to the extent necessary to ensure free markets, because the national advantage represents the sum total of individual advantages, and national well-being is best served by allowing all individuals complete freedom to pursue their economic interests. This viewpoint received its most important expression in *The Wealth of Nations* (1776) by the British economist Adam Smith.

The free-trade system, which prevailed during the 19th century, began to be curtailed sharply at the beginning of the 20th century in what has been called a revival of elements of mercantilist philosophy, or neomercantilism. High protective tariffs were reintroduced, and for political and strategic reasons, great emphasis was put on national self-sufficiency as opposed to national interdependence and a free flow of trade.

See also FREE TRADE.

MERCATOR, Gerardus, Latin name of GERHARD KREMER (1512–94), Flemish geographer, cartographer, and mathematician, born in Rupelmonde (now in Belgium), and educated at the University of Louvain. In 1537 he produced his first map. In

Gerardus Mercator

1568 he devised and produced a system of map projection, now called Mercator projection. This system represents meridians by parallel lines and parallels of latitude by straight lines intersecting the meridians at right angles.

MERCED, city, seat of Merced Co., central California, in the fertile San Joaquin Valley; inc. 1889. It is an agricultural trade and processing center. Merced has a junior college. A gateway to Yosemite National Park, the city is the location of the Yosemite Wildlife Museum. The community, founded at the arrival of the railroad in 1872, is named for the nearby Merced (Span., "mercy") R. Pop. (1980) 36,499; (1990) 56,216.

MERCEDES, city, SW Uruguay, capital of Soriano Department, on the Negro R., near its mouth on the Uruguay R. The city, which has road, rail, and air links to the capital, is a river port and trade center for the cattle, sheep, grains, and flax raised in the area. Industries include grain processing, linseed-oil milling, and paper milling, and the wool market is of great importance. A yachting center and health resort, the city also has a well-known musical society, an extensive rose garden, and parks along the river. Pop. (1985) 37,110.

MERCENARIES, soldiers who receive pay for their services, especially as distinguished from soldiers who owe military service to their nation. Historically, mercenaries were often foreigners, rather than citizens or even residents of the nation for which they fought, and the name has now come to mean only foreign auxiliaries. In the American Revolution Great Britain used Hessian mercenaries to fight against the colonists. The use of mercenaries ended in Europe for the most part with the French Revolution, when their place was taken by national standing armies. The Foreign Legion has existed as a mercenary unit in the French army since 1831, and in the late 20th century foreign mercenaries have been employed by some Third World governments, especially those in Africa.

MERCHANDISING, in marketing, planning and control of goods or services to provide effective product development and to ensure the proper commodity at a place, time, price, and quantity conducive to profitable sale. For the manufacturer merchandising involves product planning and management. For the retailer or wholesaler it includes selecting styles, colors, and sizes preferred by the customers or trade. Correct placement and timing of a product are particularly important for fashion goods, for seasonal merchandise, and for fads with a rate of sale that fluctuates drastically. The price is usually determined so as to sell merchandise promptly and at a profit satisfactory to the merchandiser. The quantity ordered should create a supply large enough to satisfy all potential customers but should not be excessive to a degree that might necessitate price reductions in order to bring about sufficient sales.

MERCHANT MARINE OF THE UNITED STATES, privately owned and operated commercial vessels, registered under the American flag, engaged in foreign commerce, coastal trade, Great Lakes shipping, or towing operations on the inland waterways. The merchant marine also includes some publicly owned ships held in reserve by the U.S. government. In the mid-1980s the commercial oceangoing fleet consisted of 474 ships totaling 24 million deadweight tons (dwt), the measure of carrying capacity of merchant ships. Another 120 vessels totaling 2.7 million dwt served the Great Lakes trade. Among world flag fleets, the U.S. Merchant Marine ranks 14th in number of vessels and 6th on the basis of deadweight tonnage.

History. The need for vital and enriching trade has always induced countries to send their fleets to uncharted territories in search of resources and trading partners. Christopher Columbus was in search of an alternate route to the East when he landed in the New World. Later, merchant ships provided the lifeline for goods and communication between the American colonies and

MERCHANT MARINE

The NS Savannah, *the world's first nuclear merchant ship.* UPI

Great Britain. The colonists soon became skillful shipbuilders and sailors. An abundance of timber along the coast from Maine to Virginia encouraged ship construction and the development of a lively international trade.

During the American Revolution, the merchant fleet contributed substantially to the American victory. After independence, U.S. ships were barred from the colonial trade of the British Empire. Trade with other European nations was active, however, because of their need for America's farm, forest, and fish products. Lumber and food were exchanged in the West Indies for rum, molasses, and sugar. The Far East soon became a trading interest, and in 1787 the first voyage from the U.S. to Java and China was made by the U.S. vessel *Empress of China.*

The earliest U.S. ships sailed when cargo was offered. Often the captain and crew undertook to sell the cargo for a share of the profits. Later, cargo was carried at fixed rates for merchants, and sailings were at regular, stated intervals.

For 40 years after the War of 1812, U.S. shipping expanded, and shipbuilding and navigation improved. In 1816 an American company, the Black Ball Line, began regular passages from New York City to Liverpool; this was the start of modern steamship lines offering scheduled sailings on regular routes. By the 1840s American shipyards were producing clipper ships (*see* CLIPPER), the fastest oceangoing sailing vessels ever built. Clippers were specialized ships, built to carry cargoes of high value and small volume; they were used principally on the long voyages from the East Coast to the West Coast, India, and China. The U.S. Merchant Marine was at its most prosperous in the 1850s. After the repeal of the protective British navigation laws in 1849, American ships were able to join in the lucrative business of transporting tea from China to Great Britain. U.S. ships increased in total tonnage from 943,000 tons in 1846 to 2,226,000 tons in 1857 and were then able to compete on even terms with British ships in British ports.

Ships helped knit the U.S. together as a united country fronting on two oceans. They brought goods and people from the East Coast to the West Coast, especially during the California gold rush. Following the American Civil War, however, the U.S. merchant fleet declined as interest in the nation's western regions and its railroads increased. In addition, with the development of

MERCHANT MARINE

steam-powered vessels, sailing ships were becoming obsolete as major cargo carriers. Foreign shipbuilders, who had made rapid technological progress during the Civil War, gained further advantages because of their lower costs for labor and materials. Great Britain took the lead in building iron- and steel-hulled vessels powered by steam. By the beginning of the 20th century, only one U.S. transatlantic line was in operation. American ships were carrying less than 10 percent of U.S. exports and imports.

During World War I, goods piled up at U.S. ports as warring nations' ships were suddenly withdrawn from commercial trade. When the U.S. entered the war in 1917, it had to rely on foreign vessels to transport troops and supplies to the front. A great shipbuilding program was launched during the war; this program produced a surplus of ships, many of which were not suited to peacetime use.

A slump in shipping during the worldwide depression of the 1930s brought the U.S. merchant fleet to a very low level. It was generally obsolete and noncompetitive by the time the U.S. Congress passed the Merchant Marine Act of 1936. To obtain a modern, efficient, competitive fleet, a program that called for the construction of 500 ships over a 10-year period was approved. This program was already under way when the U.S. entered World War II in December 1941. During the war, U.S. shipyards, using mass-production methods, built the world's largest fleet; about 5600 merchant ships and warships. Some 674 of these ships were lost in the war.

After the war, American companies used many of the remaining ships for domestic and foreign trade. Before long, however, they were falling behind the newer, more efficient fleets of Japan and the European maritime nations, which had lower crew costs. In 1948 about 60 percent of U.S. waterborne foreign commerce was transported on American-flag ships; in the mid-1980s, American ships were carrying 4.3 percent of the nation's total foreign commerce.

Vessels and Personnel. Commercial vessels are classified by their cargoes and their schedules. In the first of two basic categories are ships in the liner trade; that is, regularly scheduled general cargo ships of various types. The second category, known as bulk carriers, transport large quantities of one kind of unpacked cargo. They usually operate on a charter basis rather than on a regular schedule. Dry bulk vessels carry solid cargoes such as coal or grain; tankers transport large quantities of fluids such as petroleum.

All the ships in the merchant fleet are registered in the U.S. and are completely staffed by American citizens. Maritime labor is divided into shoreside, seagoing, and shipyard workers. Each group is represented by various unions and associations. In the mid-1980s about 15,000 licensed and unlicensed seagoing personnel worked on U.S. vessels. Approximately 27,000 longshoremen constituted the shoreside segment of the industry, with responsibility for loading and discharging cargoes at all U.S. ports. In addition, about 81,000 workers were employed in the nation's shipyards.

Domestic and International Trade. The first important American highways were water routes, and today they remain an integral component of the U.S. transportation network. Domestic shipping is composed of three types of services: ocean, Great Lakes, and inland waterways. Ocean shipping is divided into coastwise, intercoastal (that is, between Atlantic, Gulf, and Pacific ports), and noncontiguous trade (from the mainland to and from Alaska, Hawaii, Puerto Rico, and Guam).

Cargo moved in the domestic trades consists mainly of coal, iron ore, chemicals, petroleum and petroleum products, and agricultural products moving in bulk. Much of the intercity cargo is transported by vessels in the domestic service; in 1982, for example, more than 600 million tons of freight were carried by barges.

The U.S. is the world's largest trading nation, with 95 percent of its imports and exports (excluding trade with Canada and Mexico) moving by sea. Oceanborne foreign trade is conducted by three kinds of shipping service: liner or scheduled ships, nonliner tramp ships, and tanker service. In the mid-1980s this trade totaled about 677 million tons, valued at almost $303 billion.

Defense Functions. The U.S. Merchant Marine has long been part of the country's defense forces. The Merchant Marine Act made it national policy to encourage the development and maintenance of a merchant fleet capable of serving as a naval and military auxiliary in wartime. The merchant marine also serves the government by supplying overseas bases. Merchant ships were much in demand to ferry troops and supplies during both world wars. They were again used in the Korean and Vietnam wars to carry supplies to the war zones.

In addition to privately owned and operated vessels engaged in domestic and foreign commerce, some ships are kept in reserve by the U.S. government for activation in time of national emergency. These ships were specially designed with the capacity to transport troops and matériel overseas when necessary. About 400 such vessels now constitute what is called the Ready

MERCIA

Reserve Fleet and the Military Sealift Command; both are geared for emergency operations.

Administration and Regulation. The Maritime Administration (q.v.) is the government agency responsible for promoting and maintaining a merchant marine for purposes of commerce and defense. This agency, under the Department of Transportation, is charged with administering government payments of operating subsidies to help U.S. firms in meeting foreign competition. In return for government aid, liner operators must provide regular, adequate service in U.S. foreign trade. The subsidized operator must agree to replace obsolete ships with new American-built vessels suitable for the trade routes to be served and for emergency use as military auxiliaries. The government may also provide aid by guaranteeing ship construction loans or mortgages that are obtained from private sources.

In addition, the Maritime Administration carries out programs to improve the efficiency and economy of the merchant marine. It helps industry to generate increased business for U.S. ships and conducts programs to develop ports and facilities. The agency is represented on U.S. delegations to international conferences concerned with such matters as the prevention of pollution of the seas by oil, liability for damage from nuclear-powered ships, and improved safety and navigation regulations. It also organizes and directs emergency merchant ship operations. The Maritime Administration operates the U.S. Merchant Marine Academy at Kings Point, N.Y.

The Federal Maritime Commission (q.v.), an independent government agency that was established in 1961 to handle regulatory functions, is responsible for making regulations governing vessels engaged in the liner trade; the commission is also responsible for deciding when and how these regulations apply.

See also SHIPPING INDUSTRY; SHIPS AND SHIPBUILDING; TRANSPORTATION.

NATIONAL MARITIME COUNCIL

For further information on this topic, see the Bibliography in volume 28, section 337.

MERCIA, Anglo-Saxon kingdom that once occupied the upper basin of the Trent River and later almost all of southern England. Founded about AD 500, Mercia first rose to importance under the rule of Penda (577?–655) when he defeated Edwin of Northumbria at Hatfield Chase in 632. The mightiest king of Mercia was Offa (r. 757–96). England became more unified during his reign, and he negotiated with Charlemagne. After his death the power of Mercia declined rapidly because of the invasions of the Danes and the spread of the kingdom of Wessex. Eventually Mercia became one of the great earldoms.

MERCURY, in Roman mythology, messenger of the gods, the son of the god Jupiter and of Maia, the daughter of the Titan Atlas. Mercury was also the god of merchants and of trading and shared

One of three Seabee vessels, the Doctor Lykes, *was launched on July 10, 1971. The world's largest dry-cargo ship, built by the Quincy Shipbuilding Division of General Dynamics Corp., the* Doctor Lykes *had the most powerful engine installed up to that time in a single-screw cargo ship (36,000 hp).*

MERCURY

Mercury, a 16th-century sculpture in bronze by Giambologna.
National Gallery of Art

many of the attributes of the Greek god Hermes. The worship of Mercury was introduced into Rome in 495 BC when a temple was dedicated to him near the Circus Maximus. His festival was celebrated on May 15.

MERCURY, metallic element, symbol Hg, one of the transition elements (q.v.) in group 12 (or IIb) of the periodic table (*see* PERIODIC LAW); at.no. 80, at.wt. 200.59. Mercury melts at about −39° C (about −38° F), boils at about 357° C (about 675° F), and has a sp.gr. of 13.5.

Mercury, once known as liquid silver and as quicksilver, was studied by the alchemists. It was first distinguished as an element by the French chemist Antoine Laurent Lavoisier in his classical experiment on the composition of air.

Properties and Occurrence. Mercury is one of the few metals that is liquid at ordinary temperatures. It is a shining, mobile liquid, silver-white in color. Slightly volatile at ordinary temperatures, mercury becomes solid when subjected to a pressure of 7640 atmospheres (about 5.8 million torrs), and this pressure is used as a standard in measuring extremely high pressures. The metal dissolves in nitric or concentrated sulfuric acid but is resistant to alkalies.

Mercury ranks about 67th in natural abundance among the elements in crustal rocks. It occurs in its pure form or combined with silver in small amounts but is found most often in the form of the sulfide, the ore cinnabar (q.v.). To obtain the metal from cinnabar, the ore is roasted with air, and the gases produced are passed through a condensing system.

Uses. Mercury is used in thermometers because its coefficient of expansion is nearly constant; the change in volume for each degree of rise or fall in temperature is the same (*see* THERMOMETER). It is also used in other types of scientific apparatus, such as vacuum pumps, barometers, and electric rectifiers and switches. Mercury-vapor lamps are used as a source of ultraviolet rays in homes and for sterilizing water. Mercury vapor is used instead of steam in the boilers of some turbine engines. Mercury combines with all the common metals, except iron and platinum, to form alloys called amalgams. In one method of extracting gold and silver from their ores, the metals are amalgated with mercury; the mercury is then removed by distillation.

Mercury forms monovalent and divalent compounds. Among the commercially important compounds of mercury are mercuric sulfide, a common antiseptic also used as the pigment vermilion; mercurous chloride, or calomel, used for electrodes, and formerly used as a cathartic; mercuric chloride, or corrosive sublimate; and medicinals such as Mercurochrome.

Mercury Poisoning. Mercury is acutely hazardous as a vapor and in the form of its water-soluble salts, which corrode membranes of the body. Chronic mercury poisoning, which occurs when small amounts of the metal or its fat-soluble salts, particularly methylmercury, are repeatedly ingested over long periods of time, causes irreversible brain, liver, and kidney damage. Because of increasing water pollution, significant quantities of mercury have been found in some species of fish, which has aroused concern regarding uncontrolled discharge of the metal into the environment. *See* OCCUPATIONAL AND ENVIRONMENTAL DISEASES.

MERCURY, in the solar system (q.v.), the planet (q.v.) closest to the sun. Its mean distance from the sun is approximately 58 million km (about 36 million mi); its diameter is 4875 km (3030 mi); its volume and mass are about $\frac{1}{18}$ that of the earth; and its mean density is approximately equal to that of the earth. Mercury revolves about the sun in a period of 88 days. Radar observations of the planet show that its period of rotation is 58.7 days, or two-thirds of its period of revolution. The planet, therefore, rotates one and a half

BRIEF SURVEY OF MERCURY

Distance from sun	
Perihelion	46,000,000 km (28,600,000 mi)
Mean	58,000,000 km (36,000,000 mi)
Aphelion	70,000,000 km (43,500,000 mi)
Period of revolution	88 earth days
Rotation period	58.7 earth days
Eccentricity of orbit	0.21
Inclination of orbit	7°
Mass (earth = 1)	0.06
Diameter	4875 km (3030 mi)
Mean density (water = 1)	5.4
Natural satellites	0

times during each revolution. Because its surface consists of rough, porous, dark-colored rock, Mercury is a poor reflector of sunlight.

Spectroscopic studies indicate that only an extremely thin atmosphere, containing sodium and potassium, exists on Mercury, its atoms apparently diffusing from the crust of the planet. Collisions with other protoplanets early in the history of the solar system may have stripped away lighter materials, thereby accounting for Mercury's great density. The force of gravity on the planet's surface is about one-third of that on earth's surface.

The *Mariner 10* spacecraft passed Mercury twice in 1974 and once in 1975. It sent back pictures of a moonlike, crater-pocked surface and reported temperatures to be about 430° C (about 810° F) on the sunlit side and about −180° C (about −290° F) on the dark side. *Mariner 10* also detected a magnetic field 1 percent that of the earth. Unlike that of the earth's moon, the surface of Mercury is crisscrossed by long escarpments, dating perhaps from the period of contraction the planet experienced as it cooled some time early in its history.

In 1991 powerful radio telescopes on earth revealed unmistakable signals of vast sheets of ice in Mercury's polar regions, areas that had not been covered by *Mariner 10*.

The perihelion (the point closest to the sun) in the orbit of Mercury advances at a slow rate. A full explanation of the motion of its orbit according to relativistic concepts was one of the first confirmations of the theory of relativity (q.v.).

For further information on this topic, see the Bibliography in volume 28, sections 382, 384.

MERCURY-VAPOR LAMP. See ELECTRIC LIGHTING.

MEREDITH, George (1828–1909), English novelist and poet, whose works are highly cerebral, containing character studies of great psychological insight. His works display a sophisticated comic sense and reflect his concern for social problems.

Meredith was born Feb. 12, 1828, in Portsmouth. He was educated at Portsmouth and at the Moravian school in Neuwied, Germany. He began his career as a journalist. His first book of poetry (1851) received the praise of Alfred, Lord Tennyson, but his first major novel, *The Ordeal of Richard Feverel* (1859), was banned as immoral. His sonnet sequence *Modern Love* is generally considered his best poetic work. *Emilia in England* (afterward called *Sandra Belloni*) was published in 1864 and *Rhoda Fleming* in 1865.

When war between Austria and Italy broke out in 1866, Meredith went to Italy as a war correspondent. He expressed his sympathy with the cause of Italian independence in *Vittoria* (1867), a sequel to *Emilia in England*. In 1871 he published *The Adventures of Harry Richmond,* a romantic novel. *Beauchamp's Career* (1876) concerned English politics; *The Egoist* (1879) analyzed selfishness. *The Tragic Comedians,* a novel, appeared in 1880 and, in 1883, *Poems and Lyrics of the Joy of Earth*. With the publication of *Diana of the Crossways* (1885) Meredith achieved critical acclaim in Britain and the U.S. In 1905 he received the Order of Merit. Among his other works are the novels *One of Our Conquerors* (1891), *Lord Ormont and His Aminta* (1894), and *The Amazing Marriage* (1895) and the volumes of verse *A Reading of Earth* (1888), *A Reading of Life* (1901), and *Last Poems* (1909). He died at his home near Box Hill, Surrey, on May 18, 1909.

MEREZHKOVSKY, Dmitry Sergeyevich (1865–1941), Russian novelist and critic, born and educated in Saint Petersburg. The publication of several scholarly studies including *Tolstoy and Dostoevski* (1901–2; trans. 1902) firmly established his reputation as a critic. He also wrote a trilogy of historical novels and *Christ and Antichrist* (1896–1905; trans. 1899–1905). *The Kingdom of Antichrist* (1922; trans. 1922), an attack on bolshevism, was written while in exile in Paris after the Russian Revolution.

MERGANSER, common name for any of six fish-eating ducks (see DUCK) of the subfamily Merginae, characterized by a slender, compressed bill, hooked at the tip and serrated at the edges. They are seldom hunted for food because of their fishlike taste.

Five of the species inhabit the northern hemisphere. Two are widely distributed in Europe and North America. The common merganser or goosander, *Mergus merganser,* ranges from 55 to 68 cm (22 to 27 in) long. The male is black above, with a dark green, uncrested head, white sides and belly, and a red bill. The female is gray above and white below, with a bright chestnut head and neck and a shaggy crest. The red-breasted merganser, *M. serrator,* is slightly smaller; both sexes have crests. As the name suggests, the male has a dark rusty band across the breast.

The New and Old Worlds have one small merganser each. The hooded merganser, *Lophodytes cucullatus,* of North America is about 43 cm (about 17 in) long. The male has a black head with a fan-shaped white crest, outlined in black, with a black back and reddish-brown sides. The female is dull brown and gray, with a smaller crest. The smew, *Mergellus albellus,* is the small merganser of Europe, about 38 cm (about 15 in) long. The male is white, with black markings on the back, head, and wings. The female is gray, with a chestnut cap, and white cheeks. Little is known about two rare species, the Chinese (*Mergus squamatus*) and Brazilian (*M. octosetaceus*) mergansers. A seventh species, *M. australis,* now extinct, was confined to the Auckland Islands, near New Zealand.

MERGER, the combining of two or more companies into a single corporation. In business, a merger is achieved when a company purchases the assets and liabilities of other firms, thus absorbing them into one corporate structure that retains its original identity. This differs from a consolidation, in which several concerns are dissolved in order to form a completely new company. In a merger the purchaser may make an outright payment in cash or in company stock, or may decide on some other arrangement such as the exchange of bonds. Mergers are often accomplished to revive failing businesses, to reduce competition, or to diversify production. In the U.S., fairly stringent antitrust laws are enforced to ensure that mergers do not result in monopolies.

See also BUSINESS; MONOPOLY; TRUSTS.

MÉRIDA, city, SE Mexico, capital of Yucatán State, on a plain S of Progreso. Sisal hemp has been a mainstay of the city's economy for centuries. Mérida has a 16th-century cathedral and many other buildings of Spanish colonial design. Also here are the University of Yucatán (1624) and the Regional Technological Institute of Mérida (1961). Mayan ruins are in the vicinity at Chichén Itzá (q.v.) and other sites. Mérida was founded by the Spanish in 1542 on the site of a former Mayan city. Pop. (1990) 557,340.

MERIDEN, city, New Haven Co., S Connecticut, on the Quinnipiac R.; settled 1661, inc. as a city 1867. It has been noted for the manufacture of silverware since the 18th century. Aircraft accessories, electronic equipment, and electrical fixtures are also produced. The community, part of Wallingford until 1806, is named for Meriden Farm in S England. Pop. (1980) 57,118; (1990) 59,479.

MERIDIAN, city, seat of Lauderdale Co., E Mississippi; settled 1831, inc. as a city 1860. It is a commercial, manufacturing, transportation, and medical center in a region producing cattle and timber; products include electronic equipment, motor-vehicle parts, and clothing. A community college is here, as is a museum devoted to the country-music singer Jimmie Rodgers (1897–1933), whose grave is in the city. Okatibbee Reservoir and a naval air station are nearby. The community, founded at a rail junction in 1854, probably is named for Meridianville, Ala. During the American Civil War it was used briefly in 1863 as the state capital but was destroyed by Union troops under Gen. William T. Sherman in early 1864. Pop. (1980) 46,577; (1990) 41,036.

MERIDIAN, name given to an imaginary line on the earth's surface, stretching from pole to pole. A meridian is one-half of a great circle that passes through the poles and forms a right angle with the equator. It is midday at any place on the surface of the earth when the sun's direct rays pass over the meridian of that particular place. Stars and planets appear to be directly overhead when they are observed passing over the meridian. A meridian is also known as a line of longitude (*see* LATITUDE AND LONGITUDE).

MÉRIMÉE, Prosper (1803–70), French novelist and historian, born in Paris. After studying law in Paris, he entered the civil service and was made inspector general of historical monuments. Later, through his friendship with Empress Eugénie, he became a senator and a close friend of Napoleon III. Among his numerous writings are archaeological and historical works, including the historical novel *The Chronicle of the Reign of Charles IX* (1829; trans. 1830). He is best known for his lengthy short stories, including *La Vénus d'Ille* (The Venus of Ille, 1837); *Colomba* (1840; trans. 1853); and *Carmen* (1846; trans. 1881), which was made by Georges Bizet into a popular opera. A collection of his correspondence with Mlle. Jenny Ducquin (1811–95) and the Delessert family was published (1873; trans. 1874) as *Letters to an Unknown.*

MERINO. *See* SHEEP.

MERIONETHSHIRE, former county, W Wales; Dolgellau was the county town. Merionethshire comprised a largely mountainous area bordering on Cardigan Bay. It had an economy that was dependent on livestock raising. Its remoteness made the county one of the last regions of Wales to come under English rule. In 1974 it became part of the new county of Gwynedd (q.v.).

MERLEAU-PONTY, Maurice (1908–61), French existentialist philosopher, whose phenomenological studies of the role of the body in perception and society opened a new field of philosophical investigation. He taught at the University of Lyons, at the Sorbonne, and, after 1952, at the Collège de France. His first important work was *The Structure of Comportment* (1942; trans. 1963), a critique of behaviorism. His major work, *Phenomenology of Perception* (1945; trans. 1962), is a detailed study of perception, influenced by the German philosopher Edmund Husserl's phenomenology (q.v.) and by Gestalt psychology (q.v.). In it, he argues that science presupposes an original and unique perceptual relation to the world that cannot be explained or even described in scientific terms. This book can be viewed as a critique of cognitivism—the view that the working of the human mind can be understood in terms of rules or programs. It is also a telling critique of the existentialism of his contemporary, Jean Paul Sartre, showing how human freedom is never total, as Sartre claimed, but is limited by our embodiment.

With Sartre and Simone de Beauvoir, Merleau-Ponty founded an influential postwar French journal, *Les Temps Modernes*. His brilliant essays on art, film, politics, psychology, and religion, first published in this journal, were later collected in *Sense and Nonsense* (1948; trans. 1964). At the time of his death, he was working on a book, *The Visible and the Invisible* (1964; trans. 1968), arguing that the whole perceptual world has the sort of organic unity he had earlier attributed to the body and to works of art.

See also EXISTENTIALISM. H.L.D.

MERLE D'AUBIGNÉ, Jean Henri (1794–1872), Swiss Protestant theologian, born near Geneva, and educated in Geneva and Berlin. He was pastor of the French Protestant Church in Hamburg from 1819 to 1823; in the latter year he became court preacher to William I, king of the Netherlands. After the revolution of 1830, which separated Belgium from the Netherlands, Merle d'Aubigné returned to Geneva, where he helped establish a new Evangelical church. He was professor of church history at the Geneva École de Théologie Evangélique from 1831 until his death. His most important work, *Histoire de la Réformation au XV siècle* (History of the Reformation in the Fifteenth Century, 4 vol., 1835–47), has been translated into most European languages. Among his other works are *Trois siècles de lutte en Écosse* (Three Centuries of Strife in Scotland, 1849) and *Histoire de la Réformation en Europe au temps du Calvin* (History of the Reformation in Europe in the Time of Calvin, 8 vol., 1862–78).

MERLIN. *See* ARTHURIAN LEGEND.

MERMAID, in folklore, supernatural, sea-dwelling creature with the head and upper body of a beautiful woman and the lower body of a fish. The mermaid is frequently described as appearing above the surface of the water and combing her long hair with one hand while holding a mirror in the other. Mermaids, in the numerous tales told of them, often foretell the future, sometimes under compulsion; give supernatural powers to human beings; or fall in love with human beings and entice their mortal lovers to follow them beneath the sea. A similarity exists between these stories and those told about the Sirens.

MEROVINGIAN, dynasty of kings that ruled the Franks, a Germanic tribe, from AD 481 to 751. The kings were descendants of the chief of the Salian Franks, Merovech or Merowig, who ruled from 448 to 458 and from whom the dynasty's name was derived. The first Merovingian ruler was Clovis I, grandson of Merovech. Clovis became king of both the Salian and Ripuarian Franks. In addition, through an aggressive policy of conquest supported by the church, Clovis enlarged his kingdom until it included most of present-day France and part of Germany. After his death in 511 the kingdom was divided among his four sons into Austrasia, Neustria, Burgundy, and Aquitaine. The divisions were reunited by Clotaire I (497–561), divided after his death, and then reunited under Clotaire II (c. 584–629).

The last strong Merovingian monarch was the son of Clotaire II, Dagobert I, who ruled from 629 to 639. Under his numerous successors the Frankish kingdom became decentralized. Royal power gradually gave way to the noble families who exercised feudal control over most of the land. The most important was the Carolingian. The Carolingians held the office of mayor of the palace and after 639 were kings in all but name. In 751 the Carolingian mayor of the palace deposed the reigning king, Childeric III (r. about 743–52), and assumed royal power himself as Pepin the Short, putting an end to the Merovingian dynasty.

MERRIMACK, also Merrimac, river, northeastern U.S., rising among the White Mts. in central New Hampshire, flowing S into Massachusetts, and emptying into the Atlantic Ocean near Newburyport, Mass., after a course of about 177 km (about 110 mi). It has numerous falls, affording considerable waterpower. The principal manufacturing towns on its banks are Manchester, Nashua, and Concord, N.H., and Lowell and Lawrence, Mass.

MERRIMACK, Confederate vessel that fought the Union vessel *Monitor* (q.v.) in an important American Civil War battle. Originally a wooden steam frigate, the *Merrimack* was sunk and abandoned by Union forces in the Elizabeth River off Norfolk, Va., in the spring of 1861. It was raised by Confederate forces a few months later and rebuilt as an ironclad vessel. The *Merrimack* was renamed the *Virginia* but continued to be known by the original name. On March 8, 1862, the *Merrimack* attacked several Union vessels, destroying two. On the next day it was confronted by the Union ironclad, the *Monitor,* at Hampton Roads in a battle that lasted several hours and ended with the withdrawal of the *Merrimack* up the Elizabeth River. The *Merrimack* was destroyed two months later by Confederate forces when they evacuated the Norfolk Navy Yard.

MERSEY, river, W England, rising at Stockport and flowing SW for 113 km (70 mi) to the Irish Sea. The estuary of the river can be navigated by oceangoing vessels. Tributaries of the Mersey include the Irwell and the Weaver. The Manchester Ship Canal joins the Mersey at Eastham.

MERSEYSIDE, metropolitan county, NW England; Liverpool is the administrative center. Merseyside centers largely on the Liverpool metropolitan area. It includes the great harbor of the Mersey estuary and most of the Wirral Peninsula, on which are the industrial centers of Birkenhead and Wallasey. The Irish Sea resort of Southport is also here. Merseyside was created in 1974 from parts of Cheshire and Lancashire. Area, 652 sq km (252 sq mi); pop. (1991 prelim.) 1,376,800.

MERSIN, also known as İçel, city, SE Turkey, capital of İçel Province, on the Mediterranean Sea. It is Turkey's principal port for importing petroleum and has a major oil-refining industry. Mersin occupies a site near a settlement of Neolithic times and near a former Roman port. Pop. (1990) 420,750.

MERTON, Thomas (1915–68), American Trappist monk, religious writer, and poet. Born to American parents in Prades, France, Merton also lived in England, where he studied at the University of Cambridge, and in the U.S. He taught English at Columbia University after earning two degrees there and worked at a Roman Catholic center in the Harlem area of New York City. In 1941, two years after his conversion to Roman Catholicism, he entered the Trappist monastery of Our Lady of Gethsemane in Kentucky. He was ordained a priest in 1949, taking the name Father Louis.

Merton was attuned to such contemporary phenomena as the peace movement, the civil rights movement, and liturgical revival. He died as a result of an accident while attending a Christian-Buddhist conference in Bangkok.

Merton's best known work is his autobiography, *The Seven Storey Mountain* (1948). Other works include *The Waters of Siloe* (1949) and *The Sign of Jonas* (1953), two volumes on Trappist life; *Seeds of Contemplation* (1949) and *The Silent Life* (1957), volumes of meditations; and *Figures for an Apocalypse* (1947), *The Tears of the Blind Lions* (1949), and *The Strange Islands* (1957), books of verse.

For further information on this person, see the section Biographies in the Bibliography in volume 28.

MÉRYON, Charles (1821–68), French etcher and engraver. In addition to making copies of old portrait engravings, he produced more than 100 prints of his own, most notably a series devoted to the city of Paris. Unsuccessful during his lifetime, he is now appreciated for his precise, careful style, imbued with poetic romanticism and a touch of macabre irony, as in his drawing *Le Pont-au-Change, Paris* (1852, Clark Art Institute, Williamstown, Mass.).

MESA, city, Maricopa Co., S central Arizona, in the Salt R. valley, near Phoenix; inc. 1930. It is a commercial, manufacturing, agricultural, and tourist center; products include electronic equipment, clothing, cotton, processed food, and heavy machinery. A large Mormon temple (1923–27) is a noted landmark. Educational institutions in the city include an agricultural experimental station of the University of Arizona and a community college; the Mesa Southwest Museum is also here. Mesa was founded in 1878 by Mormons, who used old Hohokam Indian irrigation ditches in their farming. The city's growth as a diversified economic center dates mainly from the 1940s. The city's name, Spanish for "table," refers to its location on flat land. Pop. (1980) 152,453; (1990) 288,091.

MESA (Span., "table"), level land on top of isolated rock formations having steep rock cliffs for sides. Mesas, once parts of larger plateaus, are found in the southwestern U.S., particularly in Colorado. When diminished in size by natural forces, they are known as buttes.

MESABI RANGE, range of hills, NE Minnesota. The hills contain large deposits of iron ore. The Mesabi Range is one of the chief iron-producing regions in the world; production began in the late 19th century.

MESA VERDE NATIONAL PARK, area of historic and archaeological interest, SW Colorado; est. 1906. The park contains the most notable and best-preserved ancient cliff dwellings in the U.S. (see CLIFF DWELLER). Mesa Verde (Span., "green table") is so called because of the thick forests of green juniper and piñon trees that cover its level summit. The mesa rises abruptly from the Mancos and Montezuma valleys to an elevation of about 600 m (about 2000 ft) above the valley floor and reaches a maximum height of more than 2590 m (more than 8500 ft) above sea level. Numerous canyons scar the surface of the mesa top, and in the precipitous walls of the canyons are large caves containing the ruins of the multistory cliff dwellings. The most notable of the cliff dwellings are Cliff Palace in Cliff Canyon, which contains more than 200 rooms and 23 kivas (ceremonial chambers); Spruce Tree House in Spruce Tree Canyon, with 114 rooms and 8 kivas; and Balcony House in Soda Canyon, a small cliff

MESCAL

Cliff Palace in Mesa Verde National Park, a small portion of the extensive ruins left by the ancient Pueblo Indian civilization that occupied these dwellings until about 700 years ago. Colorado Dept. of Public Relations

dwelling of at least 30 rooms. Other ruins are found on the mesa top. Park facilities include two museums, with exhibits illustrating the life, customs, and arts of the ancient Indian occupants of the mesa.

The ancient inhabitants of Mesa Verde are divided into two main groups of agricultural people. The first group, the Basket Makers, so called from their most highly developed craft, lived here from about AD 100 until approximately AD 700. The second group, the ancestors of the Pueblo Indians, inhabited the mesa from AD 700; they were forced to abandon it by a drought that struck the area in 1276 and lasted for 24 years. Several of the cliff dwellings were explored in 1874; the major ruins were discovered in 1888. Area, 210.8 sq km (81.4 sq mi).

MESCAL. *See* PEYOTE.

MESCALINE. *See* PEYOTE.

MESHED, also Mashad, city, NE Iran, capital of Khorasan Province in the Kashaf Rud Valley, near Turkmenistan and Afghanistan. One of the largest cities in Iran, it is an important transportation, commercial, manufacturing, and religious center situated in a productive agricultural region. Carpet manufacturing, based on local wool supplies, is a traditional industry; other products include textiles, chemicals, pharmaceuticals, and processed food. The burial place and shrine of the early 9th-century religious leader Ali ar-Rida (c. 768–819; Imam Riza), regarded by Shiite Muslims as one of Iran's holiest places, draws many tourists and pilgrims every year. The grave of the caliph Harun ar-Rashid also is in the shrine. Meshed University (1956) is here, and the ruins of the ancient city of Tus are nearby.

Meshed gained prominence as a religious center in the 9th century. Shah Abbas I (r. 1588–1629) beautified the city, and it prospered under Nadir Shah (r. 1736–47) as the capital of a great Iranian empire. Pop. (1986) 1,463,508.

MESMER, Franz Friedrich Anton (1734–1815), Austrian physician, known for inducing a trance-like state, called mesmerism, as a curative agent.

Mesmer was born near Constance, Germany, and educated at the University of Vienna. About 1772 he asserted the existence of a power, similar to magnetism, that exercises an extraordinary influence on the human body. This power he called animal magnetism, and in 1775 he published an account of his discovery, claiming that it had medicinal value. Mesmer successfully used his new system, which was a type of hypnotism, to cure patients. His technique received some support among members of the medical profession. In 1785 the French government was induced to appoint an investigative commission composed of physicians and scientists, but the committee's report was unfavorable to Mesmer's theory. Mesmer subsequently fell into disrepute and spent the rest of his life in obscurity. Since Mesmer's day the subject has been elevated from the domain of charlatanism to that of scientific research. The mesmeric trance is today identified as hypnosis, and its value in the management of certain medical conditions has been widely recognized.

MESOLITHIC. See STONE AGE.

MESOLÓNGION or **MISSOLONGHI**, city, W Greece, capital of Aetolia and Acarnania Department, a seaport on an inlet of the Gulf of Pátrai. Mesolóngion is a trading center for fish and tobacco. In 1822–23 and 1825–26 it was the site of a major resistance against Turkish rule. The British poet Lord Byron died in Mesolóngion in 1824; a statue was erected here in his honor. Pop. (1981 prelim.) 11,275.

MESON. See ELEMENTARY PARTICLES.

MESOPOTAMIA (Gr., "between the rivers"), one of the earliest centers of urban civilization, in the area of modern Iraq and eastern Syria between the Tigris and Euphrates rivers.

As the Tigris and Euphrates flow south out of Turkey, they are 400 km (250 mi) apart; the Euphrates runs south and east for 1300 km (800 mi) and the Tigris flows south for 885 km (550 mi) before they join, reaching the Persian Gulf as the Shatt al-Arab. The river valleys and plains of Mesopotamia are open to attack from the rivers, the northern and eastern hills, and the Arabian Desert and Syrian steppe to the west. Mesopotamia's richness always attracted its poorer neighbors, and its history is a pattern of infiltration and invasion. Rainfall is sparse in most of the region, but when irrigated by canals the fertile soil yields heavy crops. In the south, date palms grow, supplying rich food, useful fiber, wood, and fodder. Both rivers have fish, and the southern marshes contain wildfowl.

Early Mesopotamian States. The need for self-defense and irrigation led the ancient Mesopotamians to organize and build canals and walled settlements. After 6000 BC the settlements grew, becoming cities by the 4th millennium BC. The oldest settlement in the area is believed to be Eridu, but the best example is Uruk (biblical Erech) in the south, where mud-brick temples were decorated with fine metalwork and stonework, and growing administrative needs stimulated the invention of a form of writing, cuneiform (q.v.). The Sumerians were probably responsible for this early urban culture, which spread north up the Euphrates. Important Sumerian cities, besides the two mentioned above, were Adab, Isin, Kish, Larsa, Nippur, and Ur (see SUMER).

About 2330 BC the region was conquered by the Akkadians, a Semitic people from central Mesopotamia. Their king, Sargon I, called The Great (r. about 2335–2279 BC), founded the dynasty of Akkad, and at this time the Akkadian language began to replace Sumerian. The Gutians, tribesmen from the eastern hills, ended Akkadian rule about 2218 BC, and, after an interval, the 3d Dynasty of Ur arose to rule much of Mesopotamia. In Ur, Sumerian traditions had their final flower. Influxes of Elamites from the north eventually destroyed the city of Ur about 2000 BC. These tribes took over the ancient cities and mixed with the local people, and no city gained overall control until Hammurabi of Babylon (r. about 1792–1750 BC) united the country for a few years at the end of his reign. At the same time, an Amorite family took power in Ashur to the north; both cities, however, fell soon after to newcomers. A raid launched (c. 1595 BC) by the Hittites (q.v.) from Turkey brought Babylon down, and for four centuries it was controlled by non-Semitic Kassites (q.v.). Ashur fell to the Mitanni state, set up by Hurrians from the Caucasus, who were presumably relatives of the Armenians. The Hurrians had been in Mesopotamia for centuries, but after 1700 BC they spread in large numbers across the whole of the north and into Anatolia.

Kassite Babylonia flourished, based on a few cities and many small villages in a tribal pattern. Its kings wrote as equals to the pharaohs of Egypt and traded widely.

The Assyrian and Chaldean Empires. Beginning about 1350 BC, Assyria, a north Mesopotamian kingdom, began to assert itself. Assyrian armies defeated Mitanni, conquered Babylon briefly about 1225 BC, and reached the Mediterranean about 1100 BC. Aramaean tribes from the Syrian steppe halted Assyrian expansion for the next two centuries and, with related Chaldean tribes, overran Babylonia. To secure itself, Assyria fought these tribes and others, expanding again after 910 BC. At its greatest extent (c. 730–650 BC)

MESOPOTAMIA

the Assyrian Empire controlled the Middle East from Egypt to the Persian Gulf. Conquered regions were left under client kings or, if troublesome, annexed. Following ancient practice, rebellious subjects were deported, resulting in a mixture of races across the empire. Frequent revolts demanded a strong military machine, but it could not maintain control of so vast a realm for long. Internal pressures and attacks from Iranian Medes and Chaldeans from Babylonia caused Assyria to collapse in 612 BC. The Medes took the hill country, leaving Mesopotamia to the Chaldeans under Nebuchadnezzar II. The Chaldeans ruled Mesopotamia until 539 BC, when Cyrus the Great of Persia, who had conquered Media, captured Babylon.

Persian Rule. Under the Persians, Mesopotamia became the satrapies of Babylon and Ashur, Babylon having a major, although not capital, role in the empire. The Aramaic language, widely spoken earlier, became the common language, and the imperial government brought stability; it was oppressive, however, and Mesopotamia's prosperity declined.

Hellenistic and Roman Times. After Alexander the Great's conquest in 331 BC, the Greek dynasty of Seleucus I held Mesopotamia. A dozen cities were founded—Seleucia on the Tigris being the largest—bringing Hellenistic culture, new trade, and prosperity. A major new canal system, the Nahrawan, was initiated. About 250 BC the Parthians (see PARTHIA) took Mesopotamia from the Seleucids (q.v.). The Parthian rulers (the Arsacids) organized their empire so that several autonomous vassal states developed, in which Greek and Iranian (Persian) ideas mingled. After rebuffing Roman attacks, the Parthians fell (AD 226) to the Sassanids (see PERSIA) whose domain extended from the Euphrates to present-day Afghanistan. Effective government with a hierarchy of officials and improved irrigation canals and drainage brought prosperity. Intermittent conflict in the northwest with the Roman province of Syria—part of the Eastern Roman (later Byzantine) empire after 395—and with Arabs in the desert border areas led to disaster when insurgent Arab tribes destroyed Sassanid Persia in 635, bringing with them a new religion, Islam.

Medieval and Modern Times. For the next century Mesopotamia was ruled by the Umayyad caliphs of Damascus. Hordes of tribespeople settled in the land, and the Arabic language displaced Greek and Persian. Conflicts divided the Muslims, and Baghdad became the center of the Muslim empire under the Abbasid caliphs (750–1258). The caliphs introduced Turkish bodyguards, who gradually took control, establishing dynasties of their own in the area. After the Mongol sack of Baghdad (1258), administrative decay and further attacks by Bedouins and

Excavation workers uncover an 8th-century sluice in the irrigation system south of Baghdad, Iraq. Mesopotamian waterworks date from thousands of years ago.
Robert McCormick Adams

MESOPOTAMIAN ART AND ARCHITECTURE

Mongols led to the deterioration of the canal system, restricting agriculture and souring the soil.

The Ottoman Turks and Safavid Persian rulers vied for control of Mesopotamia from the 16th to the 18th century, when family dynasties controlled Baghdad and other Mesopotamian cities. The Turks eventually prevailed. During World War I British troops took the area after much hard fighting. The League of Nations then mandated Iraq to Great Britain and Syria to France. Iraq became independent in 1932, Syria in 1945.

See also ASSYRIA; BABYLONIA; MIDDLE EAST; UR. A.R.M.

For further information on this topic, see the Bibliography in volume 28, sections 113–14, 646, 883.

MESOPOTAMIAN ART AND ARCHITECTURE, the arts and buildings of the ancient Middle Eastern civilizations that developed in the area (now Iraq) between the Tigris and Euphrates rivers from prehistory to the 6th century BC. The lower parts of the Mesopotamian region encompassed a fertile plain, but its inhabitants perpetually faced the dangers of outside invaders, extremes in temperature, drought, violent thunderstorms and rainstorms, floods, and attacks by wild beasts. Their art reflects both their love and fear of these natural forces, as well as their military conquests. Dotting the plains were urban centers; each was dominated by a temple, which was both a commercial and a religious center, but gradually the palace took over as the more important structure. The soil of Mesopotamia yielded the civilization's major building material—mud brick. This clay also was used by the Mesopotamians for their pottery, terra-cotta sculpture, and writing tablets. Few wooden artifacts have been preserved. Stone was rare, and certain types had to be imported; basalt, sandstone, diorite, and alabaster were used for sculpture. Metals such as bronze, copper, gold, and silver, as well as shells and precious stones, were used for the finest sculpture and inlays. Stones of all kinds—including lapis lazuli, jasper, carnelian, alabaster, hematite, serpentine, and steatite—were used for cylinder seals.

The art of Mesopotamia reveals a 4000-year tradition that appears, on the surface, homogeneous in style and iconography. It was created and sustained, however, by waves of invading peoples who differed ethnically and linguistically. Each of these groups made its own contribution to art until the Persian conquest of the 6th century BC. The first dominant people to control the region and shape its art were the non-Semitic Sumerians, followed by the Semitic Akkadians, Babylonians, and Assyrians. Control and artistic influences at times extended to the Syro-Palestinian coast, and techniques and motifs from outlying areas had an impact on Mesopotamian centers. As other peoples invaded the region, their art was shaped by native Mesopotamian traditions.

Prehistoric Period. The earliest architectural and artistic remains known to date come from northern Mesopotamia from the proto-Neolithic site of Qermez Dere in the foothills of the Jebel Sinjar. Levels dating to the 9th millennium BC have revealed round sunken huts outfitted with one or two plastered pillars with stone cores. When the buildings were abandoned, human skulls were placed on the floors, indicating some sort of ritual.

Mesopotamian art of the Neolithic and Chalcolithic periods (c. 7000–3500 BC), before writing was fully developed, is designated by the names of archaeological sites: Hassuna, in the north, where houses and painted pottery were excavated; Samarra, where figurative and abstract designs on pottery may have had religious significance; and Tell Halaf, where seated female figures (presumed to be mother goddesses) and painted pottery were made. In the south, the early ages are called Ubaid (c. 5500–4000 BC) and early and middle Uruk (c. 4000–3500 BC). Ubaid culture is also represented by dark-painted light pottery found first at Ubaid as well as at Ur, Uruk, Eridu, and Uqair. Early in the long sequence of archaeological levels excavated at Eridu a small square sanctuary was uncovered (c. 5500 BC); it had been rebuilt with a niche with a platform, which could have supported a cult statue, and an offering table nearby. Subsequent temple structures built on top of it are more complex, with a central cella (sacred chamber) surrounded by small rooms with doorways; the exterior was decorated with elaborate niches and buttresses, typical features of Mesopotamian temples. Clay figures from the Ubaid period include a man from Eridu and, from Ur, a woman holding a child.

Artifacts from the late Uruk and Jamdat Nasr periods, also known as the Protoliterate period (c. 3500–2900 BC), have been found at several of the sites mentioned above, but the major site was the city of Uruk, modern Warka, or the biblical Erech. The major building from level five at Uruk (c. 3500 BC) is the Limestone Temple; its superstructure is not preserved, but limestone slabs on a layer of stamped earth show that it was niched and truly monumental in size, measuring 76 x 30 m (250 x 99 ft). Some buildings at Uruk of level four were decorated with colorful cones inset into the walls to form geometric patterns. Another technique that was used was whitewashing, as in the White Temple, which gets its name from its long,

201

Sumerian statuette of standing male figure, about 2700 BC. Metropolitan Museum of Art–Fletcher Fund, by exchange

narrow, whitewashed inner shrine. It was built in the area of Uruk dedicated to the Sumerian sky god Anu. The White Temple stood about 12 m (40 ft) above the plain, on a high platform, prefiguring the ziggurat (q.v.)—a stepped tower, the typical Mesopotamian religious structure that was intended to bring the priest or king nearer to a particular god, or to provide a platform where the deity could descend to visit the worshipers.

A few outstanding stone sculptures were unearthed at Uruk. The most beautiful is a white limestone head of a woman or goddess (c. 3500–3000 BC, Iraq Museum, Baghdad), with eyebrows, large open eyes, and a central part in her hair, all intended for inlay. A tall alabaster vase (c. 3500–3000 BC, Iraq Museum) with horizontal bands, or registers, depicts a procession at the top, with a king presenting a basket of fruit to Inanna, goddess of fertility and love, or her priestess; nude priests bringing offerings in the central band; and at the bottom a row of animals over a row of plants. In the late Uruk period, the cylinder seal was introduced, probably in close association with the first use of clay tablets. The cylinder remained the standard Mesopotamian seal shape for the following 3000 years. These small engraved stones of personal identification were rolled along clay to create a continuous pattern or a ritual scene in miniature. The earliest seals display decorative motifs; bulls; priests or kings bringing offerings; sheepherding, hunting, or boating scenes; architecture; and serpent-headed lions and other grotesque figures. Animals, imaginary or real, are depicted with great vitality, even when their forms are abstracted. The seal-cutter's craft was as much an expression of the culture as were the monumental arts.

Early Dynastic Period. The first historical epoch of Sumerian dominance lasted from about 3000 BC until about 2340 BC. While earlier architectural traditions continued, a new type of building was introduced, the temple oval, an enclosure with a central platform supporting a shrine. City-states centered at such cities as Ur, Umma, Lagash (modern Al-Hiba), Kish, and Eshnunna (modern Tell Asmar) were headed by governors or kings who were not considered divine. Much of the art is commemorative; plaques, frequently depicting banquet scenes, celebrate victories or the completion of a temple. These were often used as boundary stones, as was the limestone stele (Louvre, Paris) of King Eannatum (fl. about 2425 BC) from Lagash. In two registers on one side of the stele the king is depicted leading his army into battle; on the other side the god Ningirsu, symbolically represented as much larger than a human, holds the net containing the defeated enemy. The Standard of Ur (c. 2700 BC, British Museum, London), a wooden plaque inlaid with shell, schist, lapis lazuli, and pinkish stone, has three bands of processions and religious scenes.

Mythological figures are the subjects of finely carved cylinder seals and metal sculpture. In a large copper relief from the temple at Ubaid (c. 2340 BC, British Museum), a lion-headed eagle with spread wings hovers over two heraldic stags. Half-man, half-bull images were popular, as were male heroes battling lions. Not all of the mythological beings can be identified. Elegantly crafted objects, such as crowns, daggers, vases, and decorative objects, also have been excavated. Many were found at the Royal Cemetery of Ur (c. 2600 BC) by Sir Leonard Wooley between 1926 and 1931. Two of the most beautiful are a pair of standing goats (University Museum, Philadelphia and British Museum, London); their forelegs rest against a golden tree that has branches terminating in rosettes. Like the tree, the goat's head and legs are covered with beaten gold leaf; its belly is made of silver leaf, its fleece of shells, and its beard, mane, and horns are carved from lapis lazuli.

Sumerian sculpture, usually of gypsum alabaster, displays a variety of styles, and the geometric forms can be very dramatic; it comprises figures of worshipers, either priests or rulers, a few of them female. Twelve such sculp-

MESOPOTAMIAN ART AND ARCHITECTURE

tures were found at the Temple of Abu at Tell Asmar. These stone sculptures with clasped hands (c. 2750–2600 BC, Iraq Museum; Oriental Institute, Chicago; and Metropolitan Museum of Art, New York) have huge, round staring eyes made of shell and black limestone. A seated alabaster male figure (c. 2400 BC, Louvre) from Mari is slightly more realistic. The architecture of Mari (Tell Hariri, Syria) from this period shows influences from areas situated west of Mesopotamia.

Akkadian Period. The Semitic Akkadians gradually rose to power in the late 24th century BC; under Sargon I, called The Great (r. about 2335–2279 BC), they extended their rule over Sumer and united the whole of Mesopotamia. Little Akkadian art remains, but what has survived is endowed with technical mastery, great energy, and spirit. In the Akkadian cities of Sippar, Assur, Eshnuna, Tell Brak, and the capital at Akkad (still to be found), the palace became more important than the temple. A magnificent copper head from Nineveh (Iraq Museum), probably representing Naram-Sin (r. about 2255–2218 BC), Sargon's grandson, emphasizes the nobility of these Akkadian kings, who took on a godlike aspect. Naram-Sin is also the subject of a skillfully executed sandstone stele (Louvre), a depiction of one of his victories in the mountains. He wears a horned helmet symbolic of divinity, and, unlike the iconography of the Stele of Eannatum, here the deity is not credited with his military success. The celestial powers are merely hinted at by sunstars over a mountain peak. The rhythmic movement of Naram-Sin's triumphant army up the mountain, with the enemy falling downward, is perfectly adapted to the shape of the sandstone.

The most significant Akkadian innovations were those of the seal cutters. The minimal space of each seal is filled with action: Heroes and gods grapple with beasts, slay monsters, and drive chariots in processions. A new Akkadian theme, developed and continued in the periods to follow, was the presentation scene, in which an intermediary or a personal deity presents another fig-

Restored lyre from the Royal Cemetery of Ur (c. 2600 BC) fitted with a bearded bull's head. Gold, lapis lazuli, and mosaics decorate the lyre.   Scala

MESOPOTAMIAN ART AND ARCHITECTURE

ure behind him to a more important seated god. Except for stories from the Gilgamesh epic, many myths that are depicted have not been interpreted.

Neo-Sumerian Period. After ruling for about a century and a half, the Akkadian Empire fell to the nomadic Guti, who did not centralize their power. This enabled the Sumerian cities of Uruk, Ur, and Lagash to reestablish themselves, leading to a Neo-Sumerian age, also known as the 3d Dynasty of Ur (c. 2112–2004 BC). Imposing religious monuments made of baked and unbaked brick and incorporating ziggurats were built at Ur, Eridu, Nippur, and Uruk. Gudea (c. 2144–2124 BC), a ruler of Lagash, partly contemporary with Ur-Nammu, the founder of the 3d Dynasty of Ur, is known from more than 20 statues of himself in hard black stone, dolomite and diorite. His hands are clasped in the old Sumerian style, but the rounded face and slight musculature in the arms and shoulders show the sculptor's will to depict form in this difficult medium with more naturalism than had his predecessors. Other sculptures and reliefs are quite static, except those that depict hybrid figures combining human and animal features. The most lively are small terra-cotta plaques and figurines—worshipers holding animal sacrifices, legendary heroes, musicians, and even a woman nursing a baby.

Old Babylonian Period. With the decline of the Sumerians, the land was once more united by Semitic rulers (c. 2000–1600 BC), the most important of whom was Hammurabi (r. 1792–1750 BC) of Babylon. The relief figure of the king on his famous law code (c. 1760 BC, Louvre) is not much different from the Gudea statues (even though his hands are unclasped), nor is he depicted with an intermediary before the sun god Shamash. The most original art of the Babylonian period came from Mari and includes temples and a palace, sculptures, metalwork, and wall painting. As in much of Mesopotamian art, the animals are more lifelike than the human figures. Small plaques from Mari and other sites depict musicians, boxers, a carpenter, and peasants in scenes from ev-

Stone lamassu, or guardian spirit, in the form of a human-headed winged lion, a gate support from Nimrud, from the palace of the Assyrian king Ashurnasirpal II (9th cent. BC; 3.1 m/10 ft high).
Metropolitan Museum of Art–Gift of John D. Rockefeller, Jr., 1932

Gold necklace with pendants including two suppliant goddess figures (c. 19th/18th cent. BC).
Metropolitan Museum of Art–Fletcher Fund

eryday life. These are far more realistic than formal royal and religious art.

Kassite and Elamite Dynasties. The Kassites, a people of non-Mesopotamian origin, were present in Babylon shortly after Hammurabi's death but did not replace the Babylonian rulers until about 1600 BC. The Kassites adapted themselves to their environment and its art. The Elamites, from western Iran, destroyed the Kassite Kingdom about 1150 BC; their art also displays a provincial imitation of earlier styles and iconography. Indeed, their admiration of Akkadian and Babylonian art inspired them to carry off the Stele of Naram-Sin and the Code of Hammurabi to their capital of Susa.

Assyrian Empire. The early history of the art of Assyria, from the 18th to the 14th century BC, is still largely unknown. Middle Assyrian art (1350–1000 BC) shows some dependence on established Babylonian stylistic traditions: Religious subjects are presented rigidly, but secular themes are depicted more naturalistically. For temple architecture, the ziggurat was popular with the Assyrians. At this time the technique of polychromed glazing of bricks was used in Mesopotamia; this technique later resulted in the typical Neo-Babylonian architectural decoration of entire structures with glazed bricks. Motifs of the sacred tree and crested griffins, used in cylinder seals and palace wall paintings, may have come from the art of the Mitanni, a northern Mesopotamian Aryan kingdom. Unlike earlier representations of vegetation, plant ornamentation is highly stylized and artificial. Symbols frequently replace the gods. Much of the art and architecture was commissioned by Tukulti-Ninurta I (r. 1244–1207 BC) at Ashur and at Kar-Tukulti-Ninurta, his own residence. In the artwork at both locations, the distance between the gods and humans is emphasized. The narrative frieze, which was derived from the scenes on steles and seals, became the most important aspect of Assyrian art.

The genius of Assyrian art flowered in the Neo-Assyrian period, 1000–612 BC, a time of great builders. The first of the great late Assyrian kings was Ashurnasirpal II (r. 883–859 BC), who built at Nimrud (ancient Kalhu, or Calah, of the Bible). The walls of Nimrud encompassed an area of about 360 ha (890 acres); a citadel contained the main royal buildings, including his Northwest Palace, remarkably decorated with relief sculptures. Sargon II (r. 722–705 BC) ruled from the city of Khorsabad (ancient Dur-Sharrukin), which covered 2.6 sq km (1 sq mi) and was surrounded by a wall with seven gates, three of them decorated with reliefs and glazed bricks. In the city was his palace of more than 200 rooms and courts, 1 large

MESOPOTAMIAN ART AND ARCHITECTURE

Fragment of a wall relief from the palace of Sargon II at Khorsabad (c. 710 BC), showing the head of a royal attendant.
Metropolitan Museum of Art–Gift of John D. Rockefeller, Jr., 1933

Black granite head, thought to represent the Old Babylonian king Hammurabi (Louvre, Paris). Despite some stylization, facial features and musculature are rendered naturalistically.
Three Lions, Inc.

temple, and lesser temples and residences. Only part of the complex was completed when he died. His son and successor, Sennacherib (r. 705–681 BC) moved the capital to Nineveh where he built his "Palace without Rival," also known as the Southwest Palace. The North Palace at Nineveh was built by Ashurbanipal (r. 668–627 BC).

These Assyrian kings adorned their palaces with magnificent reliefs. Gypsum alabaster, native to the Assyrian region of the upper Tigris River, was more easily carved than the hard stones used by the Sumerians and Akkadians. Royal chronicles of the king's superiority in battle and in the hunt were recounted in horizontal bands with cuneiform texts, carved on both the exterior and interior walls of the palace, in order to impress visitors. The viewer was greeted by huge guardian sculptures at the gate; the guardians were hybrid genii, winged human-headed lions or bulls with five legs (for viewing both front and side) as known from Nimrud and Khorsabad. At times mythological figures are portrayed, a Gilgamesh-like figure with the lion cub, or a worshiper bringing a sacrifice, such as the idealized portrait from Khorsabad of Sargon II with an ibex (c. 710 BC, Louvre). The primary subject matter of these alabaster reliefs, however, is purely secular: the king hunting lions and other animals, the Assyrian triumph over the enemy, or the king feasting in

206

Cavalrymen crossing a stream, a relief from the palace of King Sennacherib at Nineveh (c. 700 BC).
Metropolitan Museum of Art–Gift of John D. Rockefeller, Jr., 1932

his garden, as in the scene (7th cent. BC, British Museum) of Ashurbanipal from Nineveh. The king's harpist and birds in the trees make music for the royal couple, who sip wine under a vine, while attendants with fly whisks keep the reclining king and seated queen comfortable. Nearby is a sober reminder of Assyrian might—the head of the king of Elam, hanging from a tree.

Sculptors excelled at hunting scenes, for their observation of real beasts was even more acute than their imagination in creating hybrid beings. The finest animal studies from the ancient world are the dying lion and lioness (c. 668 BC, British Museum), details of a hunt from Ashurbanipal's palace at Nineveh. Other reliefs from this monument depict real events: battles, the siege and capture of cities, everyday life in the army camp, the taking of captives, and the harsh treatment given to those who resisted conquest.

The palace architectural reliefs at Nimrud, Khorsabad, and Nineveh are important not only because they represent the climax of Mesopotamian artistic expression, but because they are valuable as historical documents. Even though cities, seascapes, and landscapes were not rendered with the realism and perspective of later Western artists, the modern observer is still able to reconstruct the appearance of fortified buildings, ships, chariots, horse trappings, hunting equipment, weapons, ritual libations, and costumes through the skill of Assyrian sculptors. The various ethnic groups inhabiting Mesopotamia, Syria, and Palestine in the 1st millennium BC are depicted with great realism and can be identified by their dress, facial features, and hairstyles.

Between the 9th-century BC Nimrud reliefs and the 7th-century BC Nineveh reliefs, stylistic changes took place. In the earlier scenes, armies are represented by a few soldiers without regard to the relative size of humans and architecture. Figures are in bands, one above the other, to suggest space. In the Nineveh scenes, the figures, carved in lower relief, fill the entire picture plane with more detail; at times figures overlap, projecting a sense of people and animals in real space.

The art of the late Assyrian seal cutter is a combination of realism and mythology. Even the naturalistic scenes contain symbols of the gods. Beautiful ivory carvings, found especially at Nimrud but also at Khorsabad, were also made in this period. Among the Nimrud ivories was a pair of plaques, each depicting a lioness attacking an Ethiopian (Iraq Museum and British Museum). They are about 10 cm high (4 in) and carved in ivory, partly gilded and inlaid with lapis lazuli and red carnelian. These objects may have originated outside of Assyria, for they resemble Syro-Phoenician crafted objects found at Arslan Tash on the upper Euphrates and at Samaria, capital of the Israelite kingdom. The lioness plaques incorporate Egyptian iconography and are examples of the best Phoenician craftmanship. The British Museum piece has the Phoenician letter *aleph* on the base, presumably a fitter's

Colorful bulls and dragons still blaze forth on the glazed brick walls of the Gate of Ishtar from the Babylon of Nebuchadnezzar II (r. 604–562 BC) as reconstructed in the Vorderasiatisches Museum in Berlin. State Museum, Berlin

mark. They were either imported from Phoenicia or made by Phoenician craftsman at the Assyrian court. Thousands of ivory carvings displaying a variety of styles have been recovered at Nimrud. Many, such as the lioness plaques, were thrown down one of two wells in the Northwest palace when the city was sacked around 612 BC.

The art of the peoples who lived on the fringes of the Assyrian Empire at times lacks the aesthetic appeal of that of the capital. In Tell Halaf, a local ruler's palace was decorated with weird reliefs and sculpture in the round; among the hybrids is a scorpion man. At the site of Tell Ahmar in northern Syria, ancient Til Barsip (Assyrian Kar Shalmaneser), a palace decorated extensively with Assyrian wall paintings was uncovered. Some of the paintings are attributed to the mid-8th century BC; others to a rebuilding by Assurbanipal in the 7th century BC. From the earlier building are scenes with winged genii, the defeat of the enemy and their merciless execution, audiences granted to officials, and scribes recording booty from subjugated nations. The paintings in Khorsabad were more formal—repeat patterns in bands are topped by two figures paying homage to a deity. Excavations in Luristan, the mountainous region of western Iran, yielded fine bronzes of fantastic creatures, probably made in the middle or late Assyrian period. These were used as ornaments for horses, weapons, and utensils.

Neo-Babylonian Period (626–539 BC). The Babylonians, in coalition with the Medes and Scythians, defeated the Assyrians in 612 BC and sacked Nimrud and Nineveh. They did not establish a new style or iconography. Boundary stones depict old presentation scenes or the images of kings with symbols of the gods. Neo-Babylonian creativity manifested itself architecturally at Babylon, the capital. This huge city, destroyed (689 BC) by the Assyrian Sennacherib, was restored by Nabopolassar (r. 626–605 BC) and his son Nebuchadnezzar II. Divided by the Euphrates, it took 88 years to build and was surrounded by outer and inner walls. Its central feature was Esagila, the temple of Marduk, with its associated seven-story ziggurat Etemenanki, popularly known later as the Tower of Babel. The ziggurat reached 91 m (300 ft) in height and had at the top a temple (a shrine) built of sun-dried bricks and faced with baked bricks. From the temple of Marduk northward passed the processional way, its wall decorated with enamelled lions. Passing through the Ishtar Gate, it led to a small temple outside the city, where ceremonies for the New Year Festival were held. West of the Ishtar Gate were two palace complexes; east of the processional way lay, since the times of Hammurabi, a residential area. Like its famous Hanging Gardens, one of the Seven Wonders of the World (q.v.), at the palace of Nebuchadnezzar II little of the city remains. The Ishtar Gate (c. 575 BC) is one of the few surviving structures. The glazed-brick facade of the gate and the processional way that led up to it were excavated by German archaeologists and taken to Berlin, where the monument was reconstructed. The complex, some 30 m (about 100 ft) long, is on display in the city's Vorderasiatische Museum. On the site of ancient Babylon, restoration of an earlier version of the Ishtar Gate, the processional way, and the palace complex, all built of unglazed brick, has been undertaken by the Iraq Department of Antiquities.

Nabonidus (r. 556–539 BC), the last Babylonian king, rebuilt the old Sumerian capital of Ur, including the ziggurat of Nanna, rival to the ziggurat Etemenanki at Babylon. It survived well and its facing of brick has recently been restored.

In 539 BC the Neo-Babylonian kingdom fell to the Persian Achaemenid king Cyrus the Great. Mesopotamia became part of the Persian Empire, and a royal palace was built at Babylon, which was made one of the empire's administrative capitals. Among the remains from Babylon of the time of Alexander the Great, the conqueror of the Persian empire, is a theater he built at the site known now as Humra. The brilliance of Babylon was ended about 250 BC when the inhabitants of Babylon moved to Seleucia, built by Alexander's successors.

See also BABYLON; IRANIAN ART AND ARCHITECTURE; SEAL.

For further information on this topic, see the Bibliography in volume 28, section 646.

MESOZOA (Gr. *mesos*, "middle"; *zōion*, "animal"), phylum or superphylum of life forms, sometimes thought to be transitional from unicellular to multicellular organisms. The body consists of a layer of outer cells surrounding internal reproductive cells and has no real organs. Mesozoans live as internal parasites of marine invertebrates except during dispersal. Some authorities consider them degenerate flatworms; others deny that they are animals. The group contains about 50 species placed in two classes or orders: Dicyemida and Orthonectida. M.T.G.

MESOZOIC ERA, one of the major divisions of geological history, following the Paleozoic era and preceding the Cenozoic era. The Mesozoic era, which lasted from approximately 225 million to 65 million years ago, may be characterized as the Age of Reptiles because their greatest development occurred during this era. The first birds and mammals and the first flowering plants also appeared at this time. One of the most important topographical changes of the era in North Amer-

MESQUITE

ica was the uplifting and extensive erosion of the Appalachian Mts. The Mesozoic era is divided into three time periods: the Triassic, Jurassic, and Cretaceous. *See* GEOLOGY; PALEONTOLOGY.

For further information on this topic, see the Bibliography in volume 28, sections 417, 436–37.

MESQUITE, city, Dallas Co., NE Texas, a suburb adjoining Dallas on the E; inc. 1887. Manufactures include communications equipment, air conditioners and heaters, beverages, and aluminum products. A large community college is here. The community was founded in 1873 as a depot by the Texas and Pacific Railway. It was named for the mesquite shrubs common to the area. Pop. (1980) 67,053; (1990) 101,484.

MESQUITE, common name for trees and shrubs of the genus *Prosopis*, of the family Fabaceae (*see* LEGUME). The genus is native to subtropical and tropical regions and is especially abundant in the southwestern U.S. It is characterized by deep and far-spreading roots and by numerous crooked limbs branching out close to the ground. The flowers, borne in spikes, have five sepals, four or five petals, many stamens, and a solitary pistil. The fruit is a pod, edible and highly nutritious. The hardwood, often called ironwood, is used in making fence posts and railroad ties, and the pods are used as fodder for livestock. The best-known species of mesquite is *P. juliflora*, the honey mesquite, or algarroba. The honey mesquite attains a height of about 12 m (about 40 ft). A smaller species, also common, is the screw bean, or screw-pod mesquite, *P. pubescens,* so called because of its spiraling, coiled pod.

MESSIAEN, Olivier (1908–92), French composer and organist, born in Avignon, and trained at the Paris Conservatoire. He studied composition and organ, respectively, with the French musicians Paul Dukas and Marcel Dupré (1886–1971). In 1931, shortly after he became organist of the Trinity Church in Paris, his first major work, the symphonic poem *Les offrandes oubliées* (Forgotten Offerings), was performed. In 1942 he began to teach at the Paris Conservatoire. Among his works, profoundly influenced by his Roman Catholic faith and highly experimental in rhythm, harmony, and sonority, are numerous compositions for organ; *Quatuor pour la fin du temps* (Quartet for the End of Time, 1941), a chamber work composed and first performed while Messiaen was in a prisoner-of-war camp; *Visions de l'amen* (1943), a seven-part work for two pianos; *Turangalîla* (1946–48), a ten-movement symphony incorporating a wide range of exotic percussion instruments; and *La Transfiguration* (1965–69), an oratorio for chorus, instrumental soloists, and orchestra. *La fauvette des jardins* (The Garden Warbler, 1972), for piano, is a synthesis of his styles, incorporating serialism and imitations of bird song. His first opera, *St. François d'Assise,* was successfully staged in 1983 at the Paris Opéra. His last work, performed after his death, by the New York Philharmonic in 1992, was *Éclairs sur l'Au-Delà* (Illuminations of the Beyond).

MESSIAH, in theology, the Anointed One, the Christ. It was the Hebrew name for the promised deliverer of humankind, assumed by Jesus and given to him by Christians. The English word is derived from the Hebrew *māshīah,* meaning "anointed." In the Greek version of the Hebrew Bible, the Septuagint, this word is translated by the word *Christos,* from which "Christ" is derived. Hence the name Jesus Christ identifies Jesus as the Messiah, although Jewish religion asserts that the Messiah is yet to come.

The concept of the Messiah combines the Hebrew ideal of a Davidic king with the priestly tradition exemplified by Moses. Christians have also seen in certain passages in the Old Testament Book of Isaiah a third characteristic of the Messiah, that of the suffering servant (see Isa. 53). In Christian theology Jesus is seen as the fulfillment of all three concepts.

According to the first three Gospels, the messiahship of Jesus was proclaimed by angels at the time of his conception (see Matt. 1:20–23), at his birth (see Luke 2:9–14), and during his baptism (see Mark 1:11). It was later acknowledged by

Honey mesquite, Prosopis juliflora
John R. Clawson-National Audubon Society

demons (see Luke 4:41) and, finally, by St. Peter and Jesus himself (see Matt. 16:16–17). According to the Gospel of Mark (see 14:61–64), it was Jesus' admission that he was the Messiah that led to his crucifixion.

From its theological usage, the term has come to be applied more loosely to be any looked-for liberator of a country or people or to an expected savior in any of the non-Christian religions.

MESSIER, Charles (1730–1817), French astronomer, born in Badonviller, noted for his valuable catalog of nebulous-appearing celestial objects, compiled from 1758 to 1784. He called these objects nebulae, and the catalog's purpose was to help other astronomers to distinguish such objects from comets. He was also noted for his discoveries of comets. Today his catalog is known to consist of galaxies and star clusters as well as true nebulas. The catalog numbers are still used in designating the objects that he listed.

MESSINA, city, Italy, in NE Sicily, capital of Messina Province, on the W shore of the Strait of Messina. A port city opposite the Italian mainland, Messina has industries producing foodstuffs, silks, muslins, linens, and chemicals. The University of Messina (1548) is here. The city was founded by the Greeks in the 8th century BC. It was occupied by Roman forces in 264 BC, an event that precipitated the First Punic War between Rome and Carthage. Following occupation by the Saracens (9th cent. AD) and the Normans (11th cent.), Messina was ruled by various powers. It was rebuilt after an earthquake in 1908 destroyed almost all of the city and killed some 83,000 persons. Pop. (1988 est.) 270,500.

MESSINA, STRAIT OF, body of water, separating mainland Italy from the island of Sicily and connecting the Tyrrhenian Sea with the Ionian Sea. The strait is 32 km (20 mi) long and 3.2 to 8 km (2 to 5 mi) wide.

MEŠTROVIĆ, Ivan (1883–1962), Croatian sculptor, known primarily for his religious works and public monuments. Although his expressive style was somewhat influenced by the 20th-century avant garde, particularly the Vienna Secession group, it was more directly dependent on the heroic style of ancient Greek sculpture. Meštrović's diverse work included war memorials, public monuments, portrait busts, and religious carvings, the best known of which is *Archangel Gabriel* (c. 1924, Brooklyn Museum, Brooklyn, N.Y.). His many relief sculptures—some of them adaptations of ancient Assyrian or Babylonian themes—are particularly original and expressive.

METABOLISM, inclusive term for the chemical reactions by which the cells of an organism transform energy, maintain their identity, and reproduce. All life forms—from single-celled algae to mammals—are dependent on many hundreds of simultaneous and precisely regulated metabolic reactions to support them from conception through growth and maturity to the final stages of death. Each of these reactions is triggered, controlled, and terminated by specific cell enzymes or catalysts, and each reaction is coordinated with the numerous other reactions throughout the organism.

Anabolism and Catabolism. Two metabolic processes are recognized: anabolism and catabolism. Anabolism, or constructive metabolism, is the synthesis process required for new cell growth and the maintenance of all tissues. Catabolism, or destructive metabolism, is a continuous process concerned with the energy production required for all external and internal physical activity. It also involves the maintenance of body temperature and the degradation of complex chemical units into simpler substances that can be eliminated as waste products from the body through the kidneys, intestines, lungs, and skin.

Anabolic and catabolic reactions follow what are called pathways—that is, they are linked to produce specific, life-essential end products. Biochemists have been able to determine how some of these pathways weave together, but many of the finer intricacies are still only partly explored. Basically, anabolic pathways begin with relatively simple and diffuse chemical components, called intermediates. Taking their energy from enzyme-catalyzed reactions, the pathways then build toward end-products, macromolecules in the forms of carbohydrates, proteins, and fats. Using different enzyme sequences and taking the opposite direction, catabolic pathways break down complex macromolecules into smaller chemical building blocks.

When anabolism exceeds catabolism, growth or weight gain occurs. When catabolism exceeds anabolism, such as during periods of starvation or disease, weight loss occurs. When the two metabolic processes are balanced, the organism is said to be in a state of dynamic equilibrium.

How Metabolism Derives Its Energy. In keeping with the first two laws of thermodynamics (q.v.), organisms can neither create nor destroy energy but can only transform it from one form to another. Thus, the chlorophyll of plants, at the foundation of the food and energy-transfer web (see FOOD WEB), captures energy from sunlight and uses it to power the synthesis of living plant cells from inorganic substances such as carbon dioxide, water, and ammonia. This energy, in the form of high-energy products (carbohydrates, fats, and proteins), is then ingested by herbivores and secondarily by carnivores, providing these animals with their only source of energy and cell-building chemicals.

All living organisms, therefore, ultimately derive their energy from the sun. On reproducing, each species member—whether green plant, herbivore, or carnivore—passes on specific genetic instructions on how to intercept, transform, and finally release energy back into the environment during its life span. Metabolism, from a thermodynamic point of view, embraces the processes by which cells chemically intercept and distribute energy as it continuously passes through the organism.

Food and Energy. All organisms depend on energy from food for life. Carbohydrates, fats, and proteins are synthesized in plants during periods of available sunlight and stored in tubers (potatoes) or roots (sugar maples), to be drawn on during periods when new growth calls for large energy expenditure.

Food energy is expressed in calories. (In energy metabolism this unit usually refers to the large calorie, or kilocalorie: the amount of heat energy required to raise the temperature of 1 kg of water by 1° C.) Carbohydrates have an average value of 4.1 calories per gram, proteins have 5.7 calories per gram, and fats have an average of 9.3 calories per gram. Organisms rely more heavily on one or another of these foods to suit particular needs. An Arctic fox, for example, depends almost entirely on lightweight, high-energy-yielding fats. Seeds, which must be light in weight yet contain large amounts of energy, are likely to contain a high percentage of oils. A sugar maple, however, which leads a fixed existence and has ample storage space in its roots, relies almost entirely on carbohydrates in the form of sucrose (q.v.).

When foods—especially in the form of carbohydrates and fats—are burned in the animal system, they yield the same calories per gram as when undergoing rapid combustion in a laboratory calorimeter. Mechanical engines, in fact, yield the same number of calories per weight of fuel as animal systems. Mechanical and animal systems also yield large amounts of heat energy and relatively small amounts of work energy. Animal muscle yields only about one calorie of work for every four given up as heat. In animal systems, however, heat does not go entirely wasted. It is needed (especially by warm-blooded animals) to maintain body temperature and to induce metabolic reactions, which at lower temperatures would take place too slowly to be able to maintain bodily functions.

Although living cells conform to the same laws of energy transformation as do machines, their modes of functioning are infinitely more versatile. One unique characteristic of living systems is their ability to consume their own tissues after they have exhausted all other food-energy stores. Another is that instead of radically releasing energy through rapidly combusting compounds, as an automobile engine does, living cells release energy in step-by-step chemical reactions. The energy yielded by one chemical reaction drives other reactions, enabling a gradual release of work energy with minimum fatigue to the cells.

Utilization and Transfer of Energy. The chemical reactions taking place in tissues undergoing both degradation in catabolism and resynthesis in anabolism are either exergonic or endergonic. Exergonic reactions, which occur duing catabolism, liberate, or give off, energy from within the system of reacting substances; endergonic reactions, which occur during anabolism, require energy from the outside. Once the substances of an endergonic reaction have absorbed energy, they may form an exergonic reaction. Oxidative reactions set off endergonic reactions within cells. When one chemical reaction drives another, the two are said to be coupled. Metabolism takes place through many such energy-yielding reactions, linking up and forming an intricate, interrelated network within the cell.

Chemical energy is exchanged in all living cells through adenosine triphosphate (q.v.), or ATP, a compound that contains high-energy phosphate bonds. ATP is used by plants to transfer chemical energy from photosynthetic sources. In transferring energy to other molecules, ATP loses one or two of its phosphate groups, becoming adenosine diphosphate (ADP) or adenosine monophosphate (AMP). Both ADP and AMP can be reconverted to ATP by plants, through photosynthesis, or by animals, through chemical energy.

Regulation of Metabolism. The fact that cells and tissues retain their dynamic equilibrium throughout the life of an organism clearly shows that metabolic processes are under fine control. Cells and entire tissues are constantly dying, yet all the chemical ingredients that replenish and form new cells and their products are supplied by metabolism, striking a nearly perfect balance.

Although much remains to be revealed about metabolic processes, biochemists now agree that regulatory, or rate-limiting, enzymes figure largely in the reactions involved (see ENZYME). Affecting metabolic pathways at the earliest steps, each enzyme molecule has a specific, or active, site that matches, or "fits," its particular substrate—the compound with which the enzyme forms a product. The precision with which rate-limiting enzymes and substrates join to set off a particular reaction inhibits reactions from occurring indiscriminately in cells, where so many diverse chemical compounds are in flux. Tiny amounts of a rate-limiting enzyme can cause profound changes in the metabolism of a cell.

Another way in which metabolic pathways are controlled is through negative feedback (see BIO-FEEDBACK). Thus, once a cell synthesizes the correct balance of a product, such as ATP, the accumulation of that product will inhibit the enzymes that trigger its production.

Metabolism, especially in higher animals, is also regulated by the nervous system and by the pancreas and the pituitary and adrenal glands of the endocrine system. Hormones (see HORMONE), secreted into the bloodstream, reach target tissues, often altering the permeability of cell membranes and thereby altering the amounts of substances that get into and out of cells. Hormones, which also affect plant metabolism, change metabolic pathways by altering the catalytic sites of rate-limiting enzymes.

Metabolism of Foodstuffs. Although the three major foodstuffs—proteins, carbohydrates, and fats—have different chemical compositions and follow independent biochemical pathways, at a certain stage in metabolic reactions, they all form carbon compounds. These compounds follow the same pattern of oxidative reactions that eventually yield carbon dioxide and water for excretion. Each step involves a number of highly complex and coincident biochemical reactions.

Proteins. Complex proteins are absorbed from the digestive tract and are broken down into about 20 amino acids (q.v.) needed for cellular anabolism. Amino acids may undergo further chemical change to form such internal secretions as hormones and digestive enzymes. Amino acids in excess of those required to replenish body cells and fluids are catabolized in two steps. The first is deamination, in which the nitrogen-containing part of the molecule is removed and united with carbon and oxygen to form urea, ammonia, and uric acid—the nitrogenous products of protein metabolism. Following deamination, each of the remaining amino acids undergoes further chemical breakdown to form other compounds, which are then still further catabolized, often by pathways common to those of similar products from the catabolism of carbohydrates and fat. The end products of these protein portions are carbon dioxide and water.

Carbohydrates. Carbohydrates are absorbed from the digestive tract as simple sugars, chiefly glucose (q.v.). Maintained in the blood at an approximately constant level, glucose is readily catabolized to satisfy the need of the body for energy. In this process, the glucose molecule breaks down into carbon compounds that are readily oxidized to carbon dioxide and water and then excreted. If not used immediately for energy, glucose is converted to glycogen (see STARCH) and stored in the liver and muscles. When these reserves are filled, glucose is converted to fat and deposited in adipose tissue. See also SUGAR METABOLISM.

Fats. In digestion, fats are hydrolyzed or decomposed into their component glycerol and fatty acids. These are then synthesized to neutral fats, cholesterol (q.v.) compounds, and phospholipids—fats, chemically united with phosphorus, that circulate in the blood. Fat may be synthesized into body structure or stored in the tissues for withdrawal when needed. Like glucose, it is then catabolized to carbon substances that are broken down into carbon dioxide and water.

Vitamins. Vitamins are accessory organic compounds essential to enhancement of the metabolism of amino acids, carbohydrates, and fats in living organisms. Some organisms, notably green plants, synthesize vitamins, often in quantities greater than the organisms require. With few exceptions, animals cannot synthesize these substances and must obtain them in their food. See NUTRITION, HUMAN; VITAMIN.

Inborn Metabolic Errors. If an enzyme is lacking because of some hereditary defect, the chemical transformation in which it would participate is blocked. As a result, cell products fail to be synthesized or catabolized, too much of a metabolic product accumulates, causing injury to tissues, or intracellular materials fail to cross cell membranes.

Although the effects of some metabolic errors are manifested in early infancy, others may appear only in adulthood. Some inborn errors may be fatal, some may have no apparent harmful effects, and some may persist. A result of error in amino acid metabolism is phenylketonuria (PKU). This occurs in infants when metabolism of the amino acid phenylalanine is blocked; the accumulated metabolic products may cause brain damage. In carbohydrate metabolism, one error results in galactosemia, in which the enzyme required to convert galactose to glucose is absent. The consequent inability to metabolize milk sugar results in the accumulation of galactose in the blood, sometimes with damage to the brain and liver and the development of cataracts and mental retardation. See also BIRTH DEFECTS; GENETIC DISORDERS. M.L.H.

For further information on this topic, see the Bibliography in volume 28, sections 443, 493–94.

METAL CASTING. See FOUNDING.

An electron microscope, magnifying 11,200 times, reveals oxide formations on the surface of stainless steel corroded at high temperatures by water vapor and oxygen.
Westinghouse

METALLOGRAPHY, study of the crystalline structure of metals (q.v.) and alloys and the relationship of this structure to the physical properties of metals.

The most important tools of the metallographer are the microscope (q.v.) and the X-ray machine. Microscopic examination of suitably prepared specimens makes possible the determination of size, structure, and orientation of the metal crystals. By means of such examinations, metallurgists can frequently identify a metal or alloy, discover possible impurities, and check on the effectiveness of heat treatments for hardening or annealing. Metal specimens for metallographic examination are usually highly polished and then etched with dilute acids; this treatment brings out the grain structure by attacking the boundaries between the grains or by attacking one of the constituents of an alloy. When metals are to be examined under the high magnification of an electron microscope, a thin electron-transparent replica or cast of the etched surface can be made, because bulk metals do not transmit an electron beam. Alternatively, an extremely thin specimen can be made; the microstructure that is observed is a projection of that contained within the thin specimen.

When X rays are passed through a specimen of a crystalline substance, diffraction patterns are produced that can be interpreted to determine the internal structure of the crystals (*see* X RAY). Metallographic research has shown that as a metal is stretched or otherwise deformed, minute slippages occur between the layers of atoms that make up the crystal, permitting the metal to take on a new shape and increasing its hardness and strength. If the metal is heated after deformation, it recrystallizes; that is, the atoms rearrange themselves to form new unstrained crystals. This fact explains why metals become brittle after bending when cold and why they become soft again after reheating.

METALLURGY, science and technology of metals, including the extraction of metals from ores, the preparation of metals for use, and the study of the relationship between structures and properties of metals. This article discusses only the extraction of metals. For further discussion of metallurgy of various metals, see articles on individual metals. *See also* METALLOGRAPHY; METALS.

Metallurgical processes consist of two operations: concentration, separating a metal or metallic compound from the useless waste rock material, or gangue, which accompanies it in the ore; and refining, producing the metal in a pure or nearly pure state suitable for use. Three types of processes are employed both for concentration and refining: mechanical, chemical, and electrical. In most cases a combination of these methods is used.

One of the simplest methods of mechanical separation is gravity separation. This process is based on the difference in specific gravity between native metals and metallic minerals, and the other rock materials with which they are mixed. When crushed ore or ore concentrates are suspended either in water or an air blast, the heavier metal or metallic mineral particles fall to the bottom of the processing chamber, and the lighter gangue is blown or washed away. The prospector's technique of panning gold from gold-bearing sand, for example, is a small-scale gravity-separation process. Similarly, by virtue of its higher specific gravity, magnetite, a mineral of iron, may be separated from the gangue rock in which it occurs.

Flotation is the most important present-day method of mechanical concentration. In its simplest form, flotation is a modified gravity process in which finely ground ore is mixed, usually with a liquid. The metal or metallic mineral floats while the gangue sinks, although the reverse is true in some instances. In most modern flotation processes, the floating of either the metal or gangue is aided by an oil or other surface-active agent. By this means, comparatively heavy substances can be made to float on water. In one typical process, a finely ground ore containing copper sulfide is mixed with water, to which small amounts of oil, acid, or other so-called flo-

214

tation reagents are added. When air is blown through this mixture, a froth is formed on the surface that has the property of mixing with the sulfide but not with the gangue. The latter material settles, and the sulfide is collected from the froth. Use of the flotation process has made possible the exploitation of many ore deposits of low concentration, and even of the wastes from processing plants that used less efficient techniques. In some cases, by means of differential flotation, different minerals can be concentrated from one complex ore in a single process.

Ores, such as magnetite, that have marked magnetic properties are concentrated by means of electromagnets that attract the metal but do not attract the gangue (*see* MAGNETISM).

Electrostatic separation employs an electric field to separate minerals of different electrical properties by exploiting the attraction between unlike charges and the repulsion between like charges.

Chemical separation methods are, in general, the most important from the economic point of view. In present-day practice chemical separation often is used as a second stage after mechanical concentration. A greater tonnage of refined metal is obtained by smelting than by any other process. In smelting, the ore, or the concentrate from a mechanical separation process, is heated with a reducing agent and a flux to a high temperature. The reducing agent combines with the oxygen in a metallic oxide, leaving pure metal; and the flux combines with the gangue to form a slag that is liquid at the smelting temperature and thus can be skimmed off or poured away from the metal. The production of pig iron in blast furnaces is an example of smelting (*see* IRON AND STEEL MANUFACTURE), and the process is also used to extract copper, lead, nickel, and many other metals from their ores.

Amalgamation is a metallurgical process that utilizes mercury (q.v.) to dissolve silver or gold to form an amalgam. This process has been largely supplanted by the cyanide process, in which gold or silver is dissolved in solutions of sodium or potassium cyanide. Various types of aqueous solutions are employed in different leaching, or percolating, processes to dissolve metals from

Temperature and atmosphere can be closely controlled in an electric furnace, making possible the production of steel to exacting specifications, such as high-alloy, stainless, or special steels that require close metallurgical control.
Bethlehem Steel Corp.

Flotation tanks at the Clarabell Mill in Copper Cliff, Ontario. Inco Chemical Co.

ores. Metallic carbonates and sulfides are treated by roasting, heating to a temperature below the melting point of the metal. In the case of carbonates, carbon dioxide is driven off in the process, leaving a metallic oxide. When sulfides are roasted, the sulfur combines with the oxygen of the air to form gaseous sulfur dioxide, leaving metallic oxides, which are subsequently reduced by smelting.

Agglomeration of ore fines (fine particles) is accomplished by sintering or pelletizing. In the sintering process, fuel, water, air, and heat are used to fuse the ore fine into a porous mass. In pelletizing, moistened fine is formed into small pellets in the presence of limestone flux and then fired.

A number of other processes, of which pyrometallurgy (high-temperature metallurgy) and distillation are the most important, are employed in further refinement stages of a variety of metals. In the process of electrolysis (see ELECTROCHEMISTRY) the metal is deposited at the cathode from aqueous solutions or in an electrolytic furnace. Copper, nickel, zinc, silver, and gold are several examples of metals that are refined by deposition from aqueous solutions. Aluminum, barium, calcium, magnesium, beryllium, potassium, and sodium are metals that are processed in electrolytic furnaces.

For further information on this topic, see the Bibliography in volume 28, section 629.

METALS, group of chemical elements that exhibit all or most of the following physical properties: solidity at ordinary temperatures; opacity, except in extremely thin films; good electrical and thermal conductivity (see CONDUCTOR, ELECTRICAL); high luster when polished; and crystalline structure when in the solid state. With the exception of hydrogen, which is not a metal, the metals lie to the left of a set of elements that define a diagonal in the periodic table (see PERIODIC LAW). These metalloid or metallike elements that form the diagonal are boron, silicon, germanium, arsenic, antimony, tellurium, polonium, and astatine (qq.v.); nonmetals are found to the right of these elements. The common metallic elements include the following: aluminum, barium, beryllium, bismuth, cadmium, calcium, cerium, chromium, cobalt, copper, gold, iridium, iron, lead, lithium, magnesium, manganese, mercury, molybdenum, nickel, osmium, palladium, platinum, potassium, radium, rhodium, silver, sodium, tantalum, thallium, thorium, tin, titanium, tungsten, uranium, vanadium, and zinc (qq.v.). Metallic elements can combine with one another and with certain other elements, either as compounds, as solutions, or as intimate mixtures; these combinations are known as alloys (see ALLOY). Alloys of mercury with other metallic elements are known as amalgams.

Within the general limits of the definition of a metal, the properties of metals vary widely. Most metals are grayish in color, but bismuth is pinkish, copper is red, and gold is yellow. Some metals display more than one color, a phenomenon called pleochromism. The melting points of metals range from about $-39°$ C (about $-38°$ F) for mercury to $3410°$ C ($6170°$ F) for tungsten. Iridium (sp.gr. 22.4) is the densest of the metals, and lithium (sp.gr. 0.53) is the least dense. The majority of metals crystallize in the cubic system, but some crystallize in the hexagonal and tetragonal systems (see CRYSTAL). Bismuth has the lowest electrical conductivity of the metallic elements, and silver the highest at ordinary temperatures. (For conductivity at low temperatures, see CRYOGENICS; SUPERCONDUCTIVITY.) The conductivity of most metals can be lowered by alloying. All metals expand when heated and contract when cooled, but certain alloys, such as platinum and iridium alloys, have extremely low coefficients of expansion.

Physical Properties. The great utility of metals for structural and manufacturing purposes arises from their strength, that is, their resistance to different types of stresses. Among these properties, which vary widely in individual elements and alloys, are hardness (q.v.), the resistance to surface deformation or abrasion; tensile strength (q.v.), the resistance to breakage; elasticity (q.v.), the ability to return to the original shape after deformation; malleability, the ability to be shaped by hammering when cold; fatigue resistance, the ability to resist repeated small stresses (see FATIGUE); ductility, the ability to undergo deformation without breaking; and treatableness, the ability to become harder, tougher, or softer as a result of heat treatment. See MATERIALS SCIENCE AND TECHNOLOGY.

Chemical Properties. Metals typically have positive valences in most of their compounds and form basic oxides; typical nonmetallic elements, such as nitrogen, sulfur, and chlorine, have negative valences in most of their compounds and form acidic oxides.

Metals typically have low ionization potentials. This means that metals react easily by loss of electrons to form positive ions, or cations. Thus, metals can form salts (chlorides, sulfides, and carbonates, for example) by serving as reducing agents (electron donors).

Electron Structure. In early attempts to explain the electronic configurations of the metals, scientists cited the characteristics of high thermal and electrical conductivity in support of a theory that metals consist of ionized atoms in which the free electrons form a homogeneous sea of negative charge. The electrostatic attraction between the positive metal ions and the free-moving and homogeneous sea of electrons was thought to be responsible for the bonds between the metal atoms. Free movement of the electrons was then held to be responsible for the high thermal and electrical conductivities. The principal objection to this theory was that the metals should then have higher specific heats than they do. See SPECIFIC HEAT.

In 1928 the German physicist Arnold Sommerfeld (1868–1951) proposed that the electrons in metals exist in a quantized arrangement in which low energy levels available to the electrons are almost fully occupied (see ATOM AND ATOMIC THEORY; QUANTUM THEORY). In the same year the Swiss-American physicist Felix Bloch (1905–83) and later the French physicist Louis Brillouin (1854–1948) used this idea of quantization in the currently accepted "band" theory of bonding in metallic solids.

According to the band theory, any given metal atom has only a limited number of valence electrons with which to bond to all of its nearest neighbors. Extensive sharing of electrons among individual atoms is therefore required. This sharing of electrons is accomplished through overlap of equivalent-energy atomic orbitals on the metal atoms that are immediately adjacent to one another. This overlap is delocalized throughout the entire metal sample to form extensive molecular, rather than atomic, orbitals. Each of the resulting molecular orbitals lies at different energies because the atomic orbitals from which they were constructed were at different energies to begin with. Each of the resulting molecular orbitals, equal in number to the number of individual atomic orbitals that have been combined, spans the entire solid sample and holds two electrons; these orbitals are filled in order from lowest to highest energy until the number of available electrons has been used up. Groups of electrons are then said to reside in different groups of molecular orbitals (bands) that are separated from one another in terms of energy. The highest energy band in a metal is not filled with electrons because metals characteristically possess too few electrons to fill it. The high metal electrical conductivities of metals is then explained by the notion that electrons may be promoted by absorption of thermal energy into these unfilled energy levels of the band.

See also ELEMENTS, CHEMICAL; METALLOGRAPHY; METALLURGY; TRANSITION ELEMENTS.   P.L.G.

For further information on this topic, see the Bibliography in volume 28, section 629.

METALWORK, in the fine arts, objects of artistic, decorative, and utilitarian value made of one or more kinds of metal—from precious to base—fashioned by either casting, hammering, or joining or a combination of these techniques.

Origins of Metalwork. Metals have been used throughout recorded history for fine and decorative art. By the 1st century AD the metals in prime use today—iron, copper, tin, lead, gold, and silver—already had a long development that had begun some 10,000 years earlier with the working of copper. The distinction between precious metals (gold, silver, and—since the 18th century—platinum) and base metals (iron, copper, tin, and lead) dates from the ancient civilizations of the Middle East and prehistoric Europe. Gold and silver, sacred to worshipers of the sun and the moon, were at first reserved for ritual religious use, temple objects, and the jewelry and ceremonial accoutrements of semisacred figures such as the early Egyptian pharaohs, the Middle Eastern priest-kings, and the tribal chieftains of Europe from Spain to the Caucasus. As these rare materials became more plentiful, they proclaimed the status of a wider group, the elite in

METALWORK

each society—its nobility and great warriors. The use of gold and silver was extended to personal adornment, to personal belongings, such as eating and drinking utensils, weapons and equipment, and even to such furnishings as mirrors, lighting stands, chairs, and beds. Gold and silver gradually acquired a quantitative value, which was ultimately expressed in the first coins, stamped gold and silver disks issued by the Lydians in Asia Minor during the early 7th century BC. The notion of coinage soon spread throughout the Middle East and into Greece, and ever since that time coins have retained the notion of beauty as well as value. The base metals iron and bronze were appreciated for their strength, especially for weapons and tools; copper, tin, and lead came to be used mainly for their utility or durability—for cooking, for storage, or for strengthening wooden constructions of many kinds. The particular property of metals—that they can be mixed or alloyed in various combinations and proportions to make better materials for particular purposes—was understood in the ancient world. Copper and tin produced bronze; lead and tin produced pewter. This property has been exploited with ingenuity and increasing scientific knowledge in the past 2000 years; thus, while the designations iron, copper, lead, silver, and gold are still commonly used, nearly every metallic product is, in fact, a highly complex and carefully formulated alloy. For the purposes of the fine and decorative arts, however, metals have been used either in their simple state or in uncomplicated alloys.

Characteristics of Metalwork. All metals share certain characteristics: a uniform smooth complexion; great strength and tenacity, but also easily worked surfaces; and malleability (their capacity to assume any desired shape). This inherent malleability of metals is exploited by pressure in its solid state or by molding when it is liquefied by heat. In addition, metals were the first reusable materials known (unlike stone, shell, or wood), since broken or obsolete metal objects can be melted down and the substance reused. This relative permanence came to be appreciated after the discovery of smelting in about the middle of the 5th millennium BC.

TECHNIQUES OF METALWORK

The techniques of working metal developed very slowly and for long only in connection with the progress of metallurgy itself—the mining of a mass of metal from the earth. Scholarly opinion now holds that the first steps were taken after the adoption of settled ways of life—represented by agriculture and stock breeding—in northeastern Iran, the first area in which this occurred. In this area were native copper, metal-bearing rocks, malachite, and abundant timber, which allowed a steady progress of discoveries to be made. The Iranians learned the essentials of metalworking by using native copper; variations of the techniques were applied to other metals as they were recognized. A diffusionist theory is now generally accepted: The techniques were developed in northeastern Iran, but the products, and possibly also the producers, gradually were carried by trade and emigration to other areas. They went to the valley civilizations of Mesopotamia, across western Persia and through the east Mediterranean littoral to Egypt, across North Africa, and on into Spain. A second route lay from western Iran into Anatolia and then across the Hellespont to Europe. This diffusion began in about the 5th millennium BC and was continued for over 2000 years.

Early Techniques. The earliest metalworking was of copper, perhaps as early as the 11th millennium, using small nuggets of native copper picked up in streams or from the ground. These nuggets were presumably at first considered a special kind of attractively colored stone, and by grinding and beating—methods already used for working stones, flints, and obsidian—they could be shaped into ornaments.

Annealing. The next step was the discovery, about 5000 BC, that these special stones could be worked on with repeated hammering if the mass was heated to a full red color and cooled from time to time, and that this kept the metal soft and workable. Ordinary wood fires produced sufficient heat for this process, called annealing. Repeated hammering without annealing will cause the metal to become too hard and brittle, with resultant jagged cracks.

Smelting. The next discovery came after the development of the closed two-chamber pottery kiln, which produced a far greater heat than the open fires adequate for the earlier low-fired pottery. This took place probably before 4000 BC and led, after some 500 years or so, to the smelting first of small pieces of native copper, malachite (which under certain conditions will render into copper), and finally large amounts of copper ores, in furnaces that initially resembled the two-chamber pottery kilns. It was not until copper ores were smelted that any significant increase in the supply of copper and copper products could take place.

Alloys. Knowledge of smelting ultimately led to knowledge of mixing different ores together in the smelting process to produce simple alloys. This followed an intermediate period, about 3000 BC, when compound ores—rocks bearing one or

METALWORK

two visibly different metallic particles—were observed to produce a superior metal. Copper produced by smelting continued to be shaped at first into small tools and ornaments by the grinding and beating methods long in use for working native copper. Weapons and tools belonging to the late Predynastic period in Egypt (c. 3200–c. 3100 BC) have been found, however, that were indubitably cast from smelted copper; at Ur of the Chaldees in Mesopotamia, in the royal graves of the 1st Dynasty (c. 3100–2907 BC) a profusion of beautifully worked objects in gold, silver, electrum (a natural alloy of gold and silver), copper, and even primitive bronze has been excavated, many made both by open-mold and lost-wax methods of casting.

Application of techniques. By 2500 BC, at the least, all the main techniques for working metals had been very slowly pioneered in the treatment of copper over the preceding 3000 years. By that time these techniques were already being applied to other metals, such as silver, gold, and natural alloys of electrum and bronze. Techniques used for shaping were hot and cold forging or beating, which developed into hammering and raising techniques, using smooth hematite hammers; annealing; grinding, which led to the polishing and fine abrading used in the production of mirrors; piecing flat sheets of metal together with lapped seams or rivets and subsequently with solders; and casting. After the discovery of smelting, battering was used to flatten the cakes of metal into sheets; some form of battery continued to be necessary until the invention, in the late 17th century, of the rolling mill in which sheet metal was produced by mechanical means.

Joining, beating, annealing, raising, and casting were and remain the artistic methods used for shaping metals, although other methods, such as spinning, have been introduced for industrial shaping. The shaping methods were presumably first worked out by the late Neolithic farmers, who were also part-time miners, prospectors, and smelters in the hilly region of northeastern Iran.

Decorative Techniques. Most decorative techniques, on the other hand, were presumably worked out once the refined raw material had arrived by barter in the developed urban civilizations of southwestern Iran, Mesopotamia, and Egypt by individuals who gradually became a distinct class of worker—the goldsmiths and the silversmiths.

Repoussé. Decoration relies on the relative softness of metals. The earliest in use probably derived from the same beating processes employed for shaping, for it is possible to furrow or ridge metal by blows upon the surface (or, with sheet metal, from the underside); this gives the pleasing effect of parallel ribs seen on copper cups and bowls, found, for instance, in the royal graves at Ur. More localized and selected hammering can raise anything from simple bosses to whole pictorial effects in relief. This technique, usually known as repoussé, has been used for over 4000 years; it reached its greatest elaboration in 16th- and 17th-century Europe on precious gold and silver utensils for church and domestic use.

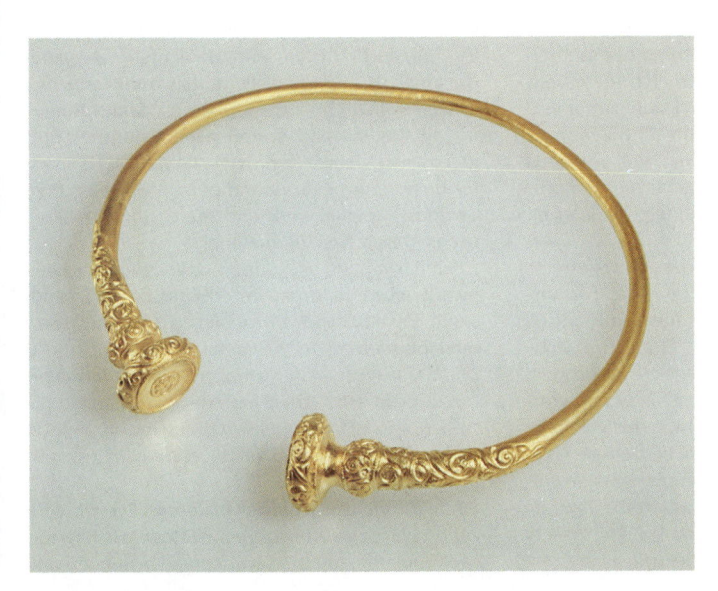

Celtic metalworkers excelled in the production of finely carved jewelry, drinking vessels, and weapons. This gold wristband, known as the Waldalgesheim Bracelet (4th cent. BC, Rheinisches Landesmuseum, Bonn, Germany), employs the sinuous arabesque motif typical of Celtic design.
Editorial Photocolor Archives

219

METALWORK

Among the ceremonial metal objects of pre-Columbian America are these gold beakers made by the Chimu of northern Peru (1000–1470). The hammered surfaces are incised with stylized representations of gods and animals.
Sotheby Parke Bernet–Editorial Photocolor Archives

Engraving and chasing. Linear patterns can also be made on surfaces either by removing a narrow fillet of metal with a cutting or graving tool, or by depressing the surface with a blunt point and hammering along the line to be delineated without removing any metal. The former is called engraving and the latter chasing; these techniques are mostly reserved for precious metals.

Matting, etching, and oxidization. Another method of surface decoration is to impress it with repeating patterns of hatched lines (again, usually used on precious metals), thus matting or breaking up areas to contrast with other areas left polished and reflective. Yet another method of darkening selected areas is to etch them with acid, a technique mostly used on steel armor and the steel parts of weapons. In the 19th century a process called oxidization was devised; with it, a subtle darkening effect was achieved on polished silver surfaces with a pickling process using sulfur.

Gilding and inlay. Luxurious decorative effects may be achieved by applying one metal to another or by inlaying a precious metal into a less precious one. Such, for instance, are the techniques of gilding or parcel-gilding silver, bronze, and steel objects and of inlaying silver and gold wires into brass and bronze. The latter was perfected in the Arab world in the Middle Ages; it is called damascening, after Damascus, a Syrian city particularly famous for such work. In the 1st millennium BC, Chinese ceremonial bronze vessels were exquisitely inlaid with gold and silver.

Granulation and filigree. Other surface decoration techniques using metal on metal are granulation and filigree. Granulation, used for jewelry, is only possible with gold. In granulation, beads of gold are soldered onto gold surfaces; the finest of this work was produced by the Etruscans in the 6th and 5th centuries BC. The beads were so minute as to give the appearance of a bloom to the gold surface, rather than of a beaded surface. Filigree can be made of both gold and silver; openwork patterns are worked from minute cables made of two or three twined or braided gold or silver wires. Filigree was extremely popular in the 16th and 17th centuries to decorate vases and drinking vessels, especially in Italy and Germany, as well as in 18th- and 19th-century South America. In Russian and Scandinavian countries filigree has survived as a provincial craft and is used for boxes, mirror cases, and peasant jewelry. It is obviously fragile work and, except for jewelry, usually has a backing material.

Similar openwork effects are called *ajouré*, mostly used to ornament domestic silver and some jewelry, and are achieved by cutting or piercing patterns in the metal. *Ajouré* was most popular from the late 17th to the early 19th century. Conversely, raised patterns can be made by soldering small castings or cutout motifs onto a flat surface, a method of decoration in use for over 4000 years.

Embellishment with other materials. Every civilization with a wealthy or high-status class has, for over four millennia, used decorative metalwork

METALWORK

embellished with other materials. These include precious and semiprecious gemstones, enamels (including niello, a black finish), a variety of exotic substances such as rare woods, ivory, jade, and amber, and reverse-painted and gilded glass (*verre églomisé*). In ancient times ceremonial furnishings were almost as exotically decorated as personal jewelry and cult implements. In more recent times this type of decorative metalwork has tended to be reserved for personal objects, including jewelry.

Metalwork as Art. In considering the use of metals in art, it must be remembered that only since the Industrial Revolution has a clear distinction been made between machine-made useful objects and handcrafted fine and decorative art objects. For thousands of years, until the mid-18th century, everything was of necessity handmade; useful objects were almost always shaped and decorated to have aesthetic appeal, although pieces that might now be considered purely fine art—such as statues and jewelry—served deeply serious religious or ceremonial functions.

TYPES OF METALWORK

The shape, function, and appearance of metalwork are determined in large part by the type of metal used. The precious metals (gold and silver) share these characteristics; the base metals (copper, tin, lead, and iron) and their alloys (bronze, brass, and pewter) may differ widely in their characteristics. In metalwork of the Renaissance and after, however, these characteristics may overlap; this happened, for instance, when wrought iron was worked with exquisite refinement in 17th- and 18th-century Europe.

Gold. Gold dust and small gold nuggets are found in many areas of the earth, either on the surface of the land or in streams and shallow rivers. Presumably, its beauty of color and relative softness made it attractive for ornament or for religious purposes from primeval times.

Gold in the ancient world. The earliest formed gold objects, however, are small beads found in prehistoric graves in Egypt, which may date from before the 6th millennium BC. Gold was plentiful in Egypt's desert areas between the border of cultivation on the east bank of the Nile and the Red Sea and also to the south of Egypt in Nubia. A rather comprehensive picture of Egyptian goldwork over the 4000 years of its history has been obtained through the excavation of many sites during the past 200 years. Gold was reserved for the use of the pharaohs in the Old Kingdom (c. 2755–c. 2255 BC) and for the nobility and priesthood in later periods. It was used for jewelry, including head ornaments, large pectorals (collar necklaces), rings, earrings, and bracelets, and special funerary equipment, including all of the above as well as toe- and finger-guards and ceremonial sandals. Gold was also used for the decoration of insignia of kingly power—the flail, the scepter, and the throne—as well as for drinking cups and such personal weapons as daggers. The solid gold coffin (c. 1360 BC, Egyptian Museum, Cairo) discovered (1922) in the tomb of the pharaoh Tutankhamen and weighing 1128.5 kg (2448 lb) is proof of the abundance of gold available by the time of the 18th dynasty. The Romans who made contact with Egypt under Cleopatra in the 1st century BC were amazed at her wealth, represented by quantities of gold utensils and ornaments and by the plethora of luxury crafts practiced at Alexandria, including perfumery, elaborate glassblowing and glass cutting, and, of course, goldsmith's work. When Egypt became a Roman province, many of these luxury arts were carried to Rome and especially to Pompeii by migrating craftsmen.

The use of gold in the ancient Mesopotamian civilizations of Sumer, Babylon, and Assyria and later those of Syria and Persia (present-day Iran), as well as the succeeding powers in Anatolia and Greece, paralleled that of Egypt, although each culture had its own distinct artistic style. Gold was also owned by the great chieftains of the nomadic Scythian tribes who roamed areas stretching from the lower Danube Basin in Europe to eastern Kazakhstan in Central Asia. Through their trading contacts with settled peoples to the south, they obtained a great deal of gold that was elaborately worked into large ornaments—such as neck torques—and such personal objects as drinking bowls and daggers.

European gold. The restrictive use of gold practiced in the ancient world was continued in the Roman and subsequent Byzantine empires and in the European kingdoms that were their successors; the same restrictions on its use were perpetuated in the European colonies and settlements that were to become the modern sovereign states in North and South America, South Africa, and Australia. It is still reserved for religious objects, state regalia—especially crowns, scepters and seals—for marriage rings and personal jewelry, and for prizes and trophies.

Gold still commands a deep, almost reverent respect. The great enameled gold salt (1540, Kunsthistorisches Museum, Vienna) wrought by Benvenuto Cellini for Francis I of France was not an egregious use of the metal, for at the time salt was still considered a precious commodity of almost mystical importance. Where it was impractical to make domestic pieces in solid gold—such as drinking cups, which would be too heavy

METALWORK

The famous saltcellar of gold and enamel wrought (1540) by Benvenuto Cellini for King Francis I of France; the figure of Neptune symbolizes salt, and Ceres, pepper.
Kunsthistorisches Museum, Vienna

A French reliquary shrine (container of sacred relics) of gilt copper and gold, crafted in the 13th century. Characterized by dignity and religious feeling, this work exemplifies Gothic art.
Metropolitan Museum of Art–Gift of J. Pierpont Morgan

and too easily scratched or dented—it was common practice in Europe for many centuries to gild silver vessels. Kings, princes, and religious or civil potentates, however, might still use pure gold pieces, such as cups or chalices, on high ceremonial occasions.

Gold in Africa and the New World. Similar restrictions were observed in the seaboard kingdoms of West Africa contacted by the exploring Portuguese in the 15th century. Gold was reserved for the use of chieftains and nobility, not so much for reasons of vanity or self-importance, but because its mystical attraction and power should only be available to a consecrated individual or an elite caste. The Spanish conquerors of Mexico and the South American empires were amazed at the superabundance of gold, as well as the absence of greed in its owners. Gold was used for religious and ceremonial artifacts, often of great size and solidity, but it was its color—in these sun-worshiping cultures—that was prized,

METALWORK

not its monetary or bargaining value. The German Renaissance master Albrecht Dürer, who saw gold and other treasures from the New World during his stay in Antwerp in 1521, was particularly struck by the unusual forms and artistry of the goldwork; he recorded his appreciation of their beauty, even though they were wrought in an artistic idiom that was totally alien to European art.

Chinese gold. Silk merchants of the Earlier Han dynasty (206 BC–AD 220) required payment in gold from the intermediaries catering to the Roman luxury trade. Apparently, the Chinese were reluctant to disturb the earth's spirits by mining. Gold was used in small quantities—mostly for inlay—in the late Chou period (c. 500–250 BC), which probably came from native gold nuggets. Whenever contacts with the West were maintained, however, large amounts of both silver and gold reached China and were wrought with characteristic refinement. The periods of contact were the Han, T'ang, late Yüan, Ming, and Ch'ing dynasties. Goldwork of the Han dynasty is especially fine; it included granulation, learned from Western models, and lost-wax castings (see CIRE PERDUE), a technique long practiced in China for bronzes.

Most characteristic of the Ming period are the delicate openwork head ornaments and tiaras, often decorated with filigree and with jewels held on wires that trembled as the wearer moved.

Silver. In the region called Pontus in ancient times, fronting the southern coast of the Black Sea of what is now eastern Turkey, silver began to be produced by smelting galena, an ore containing lead with a small proportion of silver. This development was subsequent to the first smelting of copper ores farther to the east; it may, however, have followed quite close upon it, for galena ore sparkles with visible promise. Migrating copper smelters may have been the first to recognize its metallic potential. The discovery that lead ultimately will burn away during a protracted roasting, leaving a small globule of silver, was probably accidental.

Silver in the ancient world. The deliberate extraction of silver from lead was apparently mastered by the end of the 3d millennium BC. Found in the royal graves at Ur were silver objects containing varying proportions of lead, fashioned with the same techniques used for gold and copper. In the Sumerian and succeeding civilizations in the Middle East, silver was restricted to the same

Many statuettes of the goddess Kuan-yin were made throughout most of the history of Chinese metalworking. This rare 11-headed gilt-bronze representation, from the T'ang dynasty (618–906), is remarkable for the integration of the various elements of the complex design. Sotheby Parke Bernet–Editorial Photocolor Archives

METALWORK

Metropolitan Museum of Art – Gift of Mr. and Mrs. Andrew Varick Stort

Metropolitan Museum of Art – Bequest of A. J. Clearwater

Metropolitan Museum of Art – Bequest of A. J. Clearwater

Examples of the elegant silverware designed by the famous American silversmith Paul Revere: Top to bottom: Pair of sauceboats (c. 1765). Teapot (1770-1800). Sugarbowl and stand (1770-1810).

uses and classes as gold. In the 2d millennium, however, it was also allotted by temple priests to certain merchants for buying larger quantities of copper abroad, and small pieces of silver in standard weights came to have a set value. Coinage was a final step in this process. Silver remained a restricted material until the late Roman Republic (to 27 BC) when the huge quantities of silver available to Rome made it a vehicle for trade, wealth, and the ostentation of wealth. Many classes in the Roman Empire, including wealthy freed slaves, might own cups, spoons, wine vessels, even tables and bathtubs in solid silver, often elaborately ornamented with repoussé and cast decoration.

European silver. During the early Middle Ages in Europe, silver was in short supply, although many of the early kingdoms minted a silver currency; chalices, gospel covers, and other liturgical equipment was customarily provided for church use. Silver mines in Austria and Germany provided most of the new silver of the Middle Ages, augmented after about 1550 by silver coming from Spanish mines in South America. Silver became available for large issues of currency and ultimately for private ownership in the form of reserved coins or a great variety of domestic utensils. Silver spoons or silver-edged wooden drinking bowls were modest items an individual might own, but wealthier persons would hold and express much of their reserve capital in salts, serving dishes, plates, beakers, and elaborate covered cups. By the 17th century in Europe, the notion of table silver had taken a firm hold, and for a brief period toward the end of the century, silver lighting fixtures, orange-tree tubs, and silver-mounted furniture was so popular that a scarcity of silver resulted. Silver thereafter came to be restricted generally to eating and drinking utensils; in the 19th century, silver serving pieces such as tureens, tea and coffee sets, candlesticks, and centerpieces became popular. In the modern era, even these tend to be of silver substitutes such as stainless steel or of silver-plated base metals, since nearly all mined silver is consumed in industrial processes. Silver was also used by European artists for religious and secular statues, figures, and ornaments for many centuries. Today, silver is once again being used for individual works by a growing number of silversmiths.

Chinese silver. In the Far East, during the T'ang dynasty in China and again after unbroken contact with the West was established in the 16th century, trade goods were sold for European bullion or coinage, and good use was made of this windfall of precious metal. The silver cups, bowls, and dishes of the T'ang dynasty in particular were worked with engraved and gold-leaf designs of outstanding beauty.

Bronze. The production of bronze by mixing copper and tin was an established practice by about 1500 BC throughout the Eurasian landmass. The small amounts of primitive bronze found in the early Sumerian graves probably resulted from the smelting of relatively rare naturally mixed ores. Tin and copper ores, however, were plentiful in Europe; most authorities agree that, although copper smelting was widely practiced (presumably through contacts with the Middle East), by the end of the 3d millennium BC tin ores and copper ores were being smelted together to produce what was recognized as a superior form of copper—more fluid when hot and harder when cold. Bronze was easier to cast than copper and produced better tools and weapons. A refinement of the mixing method soon developed, in which tin and copper were smelted separately and were then melted together in controlled proportions. Trade contacts brought European tin eastward.

Bronze in the ancient world. In both Europe and the Middle East, bronze was mainly used for weapons and cutting tools—swords, spears, arrowheads, shields, adzes, and axes—although bowls and cauldrons were also made from bronze. During the 1st millennium, bronze was especially prized in Greece and later in Rome for sumptuous and elegant furnishings, such as tripods, bed and table frames, small oil lamps, and tall lampstands, often elaborately decorated with raised animal or leaf decoration.

Chinese bronzes. In China bronze appears to have been used almost exclusively for bells, mirrors, and vessels in a variety of prescribed forms for distinct functions in religious rites, as well as for weapons and for the decoration of horse trappings and chariots. This first bronze age in China lasted from the middle of the Shang dynasty (c. 1500 BC) to the end of the Ch'in dynasty (206 BC). The bronze ritual vessels are especially admired for the nobility of their forms and the vigor of their abstract linear decoration. The decoration consists of highly conventionalized and attenuated masks and mythical monster forms, such as dragons. These vessels were cast from molds prepared with the decoration cut and incised on the inner face, resulting in equivalent projections on the cast vessel.

European bronzes. After bronze was superseded by iron for weapons, it remained in use in Europe as an artist's medium. Greek bronze statues, vases, and wine vessels, sometimes of large size and elaborately gilded, were greatly admired in Rome. The wandering tribes who gradually su-

225

METALWORK

For centuries, four life-size gilded bronze horses adorned the facade of San Marco Cathedral in Venice, Italy. Pollution did such damage that the originals, brought to Venice from Constantinople after the Fourth Crusade, were removed, and replicas now replace them. The originals, placed in a more protective environment, are thought to have been made in the 3d or 4th century BC, and were probably part of a large horse-and-chariot sculpture that surmounted a triumphal arch.
Editorial Photocolor Archives

perseded Roman power in Europe (including Italy), also appreciated bronze, but used it more often for portable items such as shields and bowls as well as for buckles and brooches (often inlaid with colored stones or opaque enamel). In church furnishings, bronze continued to be used for larger pieces, such as candlesticks, baptismal fonts, and coffers. Perhaps the most famous bronze sculptures of the Renaissance are Lorenzo Ghiberti's sumptuously ornamental gilded bronze doors—the *Gates of Paradise* (1425–50)—for the Baptistery at Florence, consisting of ten self-contained rectangular panels of biblical scenes cast in high relief. Many other Renaissance artists used this medium for smaller cast figure sculptures, often inspired by antique works of the classical era; this prime use for bronze has persisted to the present day.

In the 18th and 19th centuries, and especially in France, gilt bronze attachments—called ormolu—in the form of projecting and richly decorated cast mounts on edgings, drawers, and feet, were added to luxury furniture.

African bronzes. In Nigeria, between the 14th and 16th centuries, cast bronze sculptures of extreme refinement were made at Benin in a highly developed artistic convention unrelated to European styles.

Copper. A large statue (c. 2300 BC, Egyptian Museum, Cairo) of the 6th-dynasty pharaoh Pepi I (r. about 2395–2360 BC), made from hammered sheet copper, provides evidence that copper may have been more extensively used for fine art than is commonly supposed.

Copper in the ancient world. In Egypt and elsewhere in the ancient world, copper was superseded for weapons and tools by bronze and quickly became relegated to the realm of a useful metal for dishes, cups, and light domestic utensils. It was important, however, as the necessary ingredient for bronze and later as a toughener for silver and gold, although added in small proportions (sterling has 7.5 percent copper).

European copper and brass. Copper was also important as the base for champlevé enamel plaques in the Middle Ages and later, for its softness facilitated the excavation of small areas to be filled with colored glass pastes. Copper is an ingredient, with zinc, of brass. In the Middle Ages in the town of Dinant (now in Belgium), large brass dishes with raised decoration were produced and exported in considerable quantities, although the Netherlands was the most prolific producer of brasswares. Brass was similarly used in the Islamic East for large dishes and braziers. Eastern craftsmen who settled in Venice in the 15th century produced exceptionally well-wrought bowls, ewers, dishes, and candlesticks damascened with elaborate oriental decoration in gold and silver; their method was continued by Venetian artisans using Renaissance styles of decoration after the middle of the 16th century. Large brass chandeliers designed to hold numerous candles were made in the Netherlands and England in the 17th century and were to be found in the early colonial homes in North America in the 18th century; brass drawer pulls were also popular on furniture in the colonies. Brass has survived into the 20th century in the form of such fixtures as door knockers, doorsills, letter boxes, candlesticks, and andirons.

Lead and Pewter. The Romans, who had a superabundance of lead from their silver-refining activities, used lead primarily for utilitarian purposes—roofs, coffins, water cisterns, conduits, and plumbing.

Lead. Lead is exceptionally soft and easily worked and was used in the Middle Ages in Europe for external architectural decoration. In England it was used extensively for the pipeheads of rainwater guttering and for roof coverings. From the 12th to the 15th century, lead baptismal fonts with cast raised decoration were produced. In the 17th century, lead garden statues became popular and remained in favor into the 18th century. During the 16th century, cast lead plaquettes were made in Germany by goldsmiths and silversmiths who specialized in supplying designs to other goldsmiths; they exported these plaquettes of the latest designs—both abstract and pictorial—to many parts of Europe. These plaquettes, which reproduced faithfully all the details of the carved-wood or soft-stone originals, are now collected as works of art in their own right.

Pewter. Tin was available to the Romans both from their possessions in the Iberian Peninsula and in the British Isles. It was an important ingredient in bronze, but when mixed with lead (first in the 3d cent. AD) it produced the first pewter. A few hundred pieces of Roman pewter, however, are all that remain. No other early pewter, from Roman times until the 14th century, is known, except for the chalices and patens found in priests' tombs at Metz, France. Pewter, however, was probably made in some quantity. Churches too poor to own silver communion plates were allowed to use pewter after the 11th century; it was a flourishing craft when it came to be regulated in the 14th century in England. Pewter was commonly used for the eating and drinking vessels of the lower classes all over Europe, except in Spain. The metal is silver-colored when new and dulls to a pleasing, lustrous gray. In form, it was made in the usual shapes for pottery or silver and tended to rely on proportion and appropriateness rather than on decoration for its appeal. Some pewter, however, was decorated in the 16th and 17th centuries with cast motifs, particularly on the lids and handles of tankards; in Germany, Switzerland, and Scandinavia incised decoration or undulating lines made with a wheel were popular.

American pewter is highly prized by collectors for its amplitude and dignity, as well as for its connection with the country's early history. Dates and the initials of the owners are often found on it. Old pewter is comparatively rare, for it was the established practice everywhere to take old or deformed pieces back to the pewterer as part payment toward new purchases. Pewter was largely supplanted by silvered base metals in the 19th century, although it has reappeared in the present century for household items such as tankards and flatware.

Iron. Small pieces of jewelry of meteoric iron have been found in Egyptian tombs, and no doubt the metal was for long treasured as an occasional find. The Hittites of Anatolia, however, appear to have been the first (c. 1400 BC) to understand and control the production of iron from its ores. This gave them a temporary military advantage over their neighbors in the superior weapons they made from iron. For such a versatile, functional, and strong metal, iron has had a surprisingly consistent history of use for artistic and decorative purposes.

The Chinese were the first to cast iron; from the 6th century AD they used cast-iron supports for buildings and for multistory pagodas. In Europe, iron was wrought—that is, hammered into shape when hot—by a special group of workers

Detail of the 14th-century wrought-iron grill around the tombs of the Scala family at Verona, Italy. Alinari

now called blacksmiths. Blacksmiths wrought coffers and weapons and made such large items of furnishings as great knockers and ring handles for the immense doors of castles and cathedrals as well as beautifully scrolled bands for strengthening doors. Wrought-iron railings, with superbly detailed work that looks almost like lace from a distance, was popular in the 17th and 18th centuries. Steel armor (q.v.) was often highly decorative, with splendid engraved or acid-etched motifs in the 16th century. The armorers who wrought them employed many of the hot forging techniques pioneered by blacksmiths over the centuries. After the Arts and Crafts movement was introduced in the mid-19th century, some exceptional wrought-iron work was produced in England.

Cast iron appears to have been introduced into Europe from knowledge of the Chinese success with it. For a long time, it had few artistic uses, although the cast firebacks introduced in the 15th century remained popular for some 200 years. In Germany, Switzerland, Scandinavia, and the Netherlands, cast rectangular plates for woodburning, enclosed stoves were also made, often decorated in relief at the moment of their casting from prepared molds with pictorial or abstract ornament. Toward the end of the 18th century, wrought iron began to be replaced by less costly cast iron for railings, balconies, banisters, and for garden furniture and decorations; this manufactured work, once considered as intrinsically bad and devoid of artistic merit, has come to have a certain appeal to present-day collectors.

See also BELL; COINS AND COIN COLLECTING; CROWN; ENAMEL; FLATWARE; INLAY; JEWELRY; SCULPTURE; SWORD. For additional information on individual artists, see biographies of those whose names are not followed by dates.   J.McN.

For further information on this topic, see the Bibliography in volume 28, sections 280, 681, 685, 689–90.

METAMORPHIC ROCK, rock, the original composition and texture of which has been altered by heat and pressure deep within the earth's crust. Metamorphism that is a result of both heat and pressure is referred to as dynamothermal, or regional; metamorphism produced by the heat of an intrusion of igneous rock (q.v.) is termed thermal, or contact.

Four common varieties of metamorphic rock can be traced to a parent sedimentary or igneous rock, because rocks display varying degrees of metamorphism, depending on how much heat and pressure they have endured. Thus, shale is metamorphosed to slate in a low-temperature environment, but if heated to temperatures high enough for its clay minerals to recrystallize as mica flakes, shale becomes metamorphosed into a phyllite. At even higher temperatures and pres-

Silhouetted against sunlight are the massive wrought-iron gates of the ducal palace at Darmstadt, Germany.
German Information Center

sures, shale and siltstone recrystallize, forming schist or gneiss, rocks in which the alignment of mica flakes produces a laminated texture called foliation. In schist, the light-colored minerals (mainly quartz and feldspar) are evenly distributed among the dark-colored micas; gneiss, on the other hand, displays distinctive color banding. Among the other minerals formed by metamorphic recrystallization, aluminum silicates such as andalusite, sillimanite, and kyanite are pervasive enough to be considered diagnostic.

Among the nonfoliated metamorphic rocks, quartzite and marble are the most common. Quartzite is typically a tough, hard, light-colored rock in which all the sand grains of a sandstone or siltstone have been recrystallized into a fabric of interlocking quartz grains. Marble is a softer, more brittle, varicolored rock in which the dolomite or calcite of the parent sedimentary material has been entirely recrystallized.

METAMORPHOSIS, in zoology, term applied to marked changes in form during the life history of an animal.

In complete metamorphosis, a clear distinction exists between the various stages of the animal's development. In the first phase, an embryo forms inside an egg. When the egg hatches, the animal is called a larva (q.v.). During the next period, the larva changes into a pupa, often enclosed in a cocoon. At the end of the pupal stage, the adult emerges. Animals that grow in this way include many fishes, mollusks, and insects. In incomplete metamorphosis, the young resembles the adult. The animal's form gradually changes through molting, or shedding. An example is the grasshopper, which only passes through three stages, having no pupal period. See also INSECT.

Frogs, and other amphibians, undergo a different type of complete metamorphosis. From the egg emerges a tadpole, which lives in the water, breathes with gills, and has a tail. As the tadpole grows, lungs and legs form, and the gills and tail are absorbed into the body, enabling the animal to live on land. See also AMPHIBIAN.

In ancient mythology, metamorphosis was the transformation by supernatural means of human beings into beasts, fire, water, or the like, found in folklore everywhere; these metamorphoses afforded a subject to Greek poets and writers of the Alexandrine period and to the Roman poet Ovid.

METAPHOR. See FIGURE OF SPEECH.

METAPHYSICAL POETS, English poets of the early 17th century, such as John Donne, whose work was complex and dramatic and unusual in syntax and imagery. See ENGLISH LITERATURE.

METAPHYSICS, branch of philosophy concerned with the nature of ultimate reality. Metaphysics is customarily divided into ontology, which deals with the question of how many fundamentally distinct sorts of entities compose the universe, and metaphysics proper, which is concerned with describing the most general traits of reality. These general traits together define reality and would presumably characterize any universe whatever. Because these traits are not peculiar to this universe, but are common to all possible universes, metaphysics may be conducted at the highest level of abstraction. Ontology, by contrast, because it investigates the ultimate divisions within this universe, is more closely related to the physical world of human experience.

The term *metaphysics* is believed to have originated in Rome about 70 BC, with the Greek Peripatetic philosopher Andronicus of Rhodes (fl. 70–50 BC) in his edition of the works of Aristotle. In the arrangement of Aristotle's works by Andronicus, the treatise originally called *First Philosophy,* or *Theology,* followed the treatise *Physics.* Hence, the *First Philosophy* came to be known as *meta* (*ta*) *physica,* or "following (the) *Physics,*" later shortened to *Metaphysics.* The word took on the connotation, in popular usage, of matters transcending material reality. In the philosophic sense, however, particularly as opposed to the use of the word by occultists, metaphysics applies to all reality and is distinguished from other forms of inquiry by its generality.

The subjects treated in Aristotle's *Metaphysics* (substance, causality, the nature of being, and the existence of God) fixed the content of metaphysical speculation for centuries. Among the medieval Scholastic philosophers, metaphysics was known as the "transphysical science" on the assumption that, by means of it, the scholar philosophically could make the transition from the physical world to a world beyond sense perception. The 13th-century Scholastic philosopher and theologian St. Thomas Aquinas declared that the cognition of God, through a causal study of finite sensible beings, was the aim of metaphysics. With the rise of scientific study in the 16th century the reconciliation of science and faith in God became an increasingly important problem.

Metaphysics Before Kant. Before the time of the German philosopher Immanuel Kant metaphysics was characterized by a tendency to construct theories on the basis of a priori knowledge, that is, knowledge derived from reason alone, in contradistinction to a posteriori knowledge, which is gained by reference to the facts of experience. From a priori knowledge were deduced general propositions that were held to be true of all things. The method of inquiry based on a priori principles is known as rationalistic. This method may be subdivided into monism (q.v.), which holds that the universe is made up of a single fundamental substance; dualism (q.v.), the belief in two such substances; and pluralism, which proposes the existence of many fundamental substances.

The monists, agreeing that only one basic substance exists, differ in their descriptions of its principal characteristics. Thus, in idealistic monism the substance is believed to be purely mental; in materialistic monism it is held to be purely physical, and in neutral monism it is considered neither exclusively mental nor solely physical. The idealistic position was held by the Irish philosopher George Berkeley, the materialistic by the English philosopher Thomas Hobbes, and the neutral by the Dutch philosopher Baruch Spinoza. The latter expounded a pantheistic view of reality in which the universe is identical with God and everything contains God's substance. See Idealism; Materialism; Pantheism.

The most famous exponent of dualism was the French philosopher René Descartes, who maintained that body and mind are radically different entities and that they are the only fundamental substances in the universe. Dualism, however, does not show how these basic entities are connected.

In the work of the German philosopher Gottfried Wilhelm von Leibniz, the universe is held to consist of an infinite number of distinct substances, or monads. This view is pluralistic in the sense that it proposes the existence of many separate entities, and it is monistic in its assertion that each monad reflects within itself the entire universe.

Other philosophers have held that knowledge of reality is not derived from a priori principles, but is obtained only from experience. This type of metaphysics is called empiricism. Still another school of philosophy has maintained that, although an ultimate reality does exist, it is altogether inaccessible to human knowledge, which is necessarily subjective because it is confined to states of mind. Knowledge is therefore not a representation of external reality, but merely a reflection of human perceptions. This view is known as skepticism or agnosticism (qq.v.) in respect to the soul and the reality of God.

The Metaphysics of Kant. Several major viewpoints were combined in the work of Kant, who developed a distinctive critical philosophy called transcendentalism. His philosophy is agnostic in that it denies the possibility of a strict knowledge of ultimate reality; it is empirical in that it affirms that all knowledge arises from experience and is true of objects of actual and possible experience; and it is rationalistic in that it maintains the a priori character of the structural principles of this empirical knowledge.

These principles are held to be necessary and universal in their application to experience, for in Kant's view the mind furnishes the archetypal forms and categories (space, time, causality, substance, and relation) to its sensations, and these categories are logically anterior to experience, although manifested only in experience. Their logical anteriority to experience makes these categories or structural principles transcendental; they transcend all experience, both actual and possible. Although these principles determine all experience, they do not in any way affect the nature of things in themselves. The knowledge of which these principles are the necessary conditions must not be considered, therefore, as constituting a revelation of things as they are in themselves. This knowledge concerns things only insofar as they appear to human perception or as they can be apprehended by the senses. The argument by which Kant sought to fix the limits of human knowledge within the framework of experience and to demonstrate the inability of the human mind to penetrate beyond experience strictly by knowledge to the realm of ultimate reality constitutes the critical feature of his philosophy, giving the key word to the titles of his three leading treatises, *Critique of Pure Reason, Critique of Practical Reason,* and *Critique of Judgment.* In the system propounded in these works, Kant sought also to reconcile science and religion in a world of two levels, comprising noumena, objects conceived by reason although not perceived by the senses, and phenomena, things as they appear to the senses and are accessible to material study. He maintained that, because God, freedom, and human immortality are noumenal realities, these concepts are understood through moral faith rather than through scientific knowledge. With the continuous development of science, the expansion of metaphysics to include scientific knowledge and methods became one of the major objectives of metaphysicians.

Metaphysics Since Kant. Some of Kant's most distinguished followers, notably Johann Gottlieb Fichte, Friedrich Schelling, G. W. F. Hegel, and Friedrich Schleiermacher, negated Kant's criticism in their elaborations of his transcendental metaphysics by denying the Kantian conception of the thing-in-itself. They thus developed an absolute idealism in opposition to Kant's critical transcendentalism.

Since the formation of the hypothesis of absolute idealism, the development of metaphysics has resulted in as many types of metaphysical theory as existed in pre-Kantian philosophy, despite Kant's contention that he had fixed definitely the limits of philosophical speculation. Notable among these later metaphysical theories are radical empiricism, or pragmatism, a native American form of metaphysics expounded by Charles Sanders Peirce, developed by William James, and adapted as instrumentalism by John Dewey; voluntarism, the foremost exponents of which are the German philosopher Arthur Schopenhauer and the American philosopher Josiah Royce; phenomenalism, as it is exemplified in the writings of the French philosopher Auguste Comte and the British philosopher Herbert Spencer; emergent evolution, or creative evolution, originated by the French philosopher Henri Bergson; and the philosophy of the organism, elaborated by the British mathematician and philosopher Alfred North Whitehead. The salient doctrines of pragmatism are that the chief function of thought is to guide action, that the meaning of concepts is to be sought in their practical applications, and that truth should be tested by the practical effects of belief; according to instrumentalism, ideas are instruments of action, and their truth is determined by their role in human experience. In the theory of voluntarism the will is postulated as the supreme manifestation of reality. The exponents of phenomenalism, who are sometimes called positivists, contend that everything can be analyzed in terms of actual or possible occurrences, or phenomena, and that anything that cannot be analyzed in this manner cannot be understood. In emergent or creative evolution, the evolutionary process is characterized as spontaneous and unpredictable rather than mechanistically determined. The philosophy of the organism combines an evolutionary stress on constant process with a metaphysical theory of God, the eternal objects, and creativity.

Contemporary Developments. In the 20th century the validity of metaphysical thinking has been disputed by the logical positivists (*see* ANALYTIC AND LINGUISTIC PHILOSOPHY; POSITIVISM) and by the so-called dialectical materialism of the Marxists. The basic principle maintained by the logical positivists is the verifiability theory of meaning. According to this theory a sentence has factual meaning only if it meets the test of observation. Logical positivists argue that metaphysical expressions such as "Nothing exists except material particles" and "Everything is part of one all-encompassing spirit" cannot be tested empirically. Therefore, according to the verifiability theory of meaning, these expressions have no factual cognitive meaning, although they can have an emotive meaning relevant to human hopes and feelings.

The dialectical materialists assert that the mind is conditioned by and reflects material reality. Therefore, speculations that conceive of constructs of the mind as having any other than material reality are themselves unreal and can result only in delusion. To these assertions metaphysicians reply by denying the adequacy of the verifiability theory of meaning and of material perception as the standard of reality. Both logical positivism and dialectical materialism, they argue, conceal metaphysical assumptions, for example, that everything is observable or at least connected with something observable and that the mind has no distinctive life of its own. In the philosophical movement known as existentialism, thinkers have contended that the questions of the nature of being and of the individual's relationship to it are extremely important and meaningful in terms of human life. The investigation of these questions is therefore considered valid whether or not its results can be verified objectively.

Since the 1950s the problems of systematic analytical metaphysics have been studied in Great Britain by Stuart Newton Hampshire (1914–) and Peter Frederick Strawson, the former concerned, in the manner of Spinoza, with the relationship between thought and action, and the latter, in the manner of Kant, with describing the major categories of experience as they are embedded in language. In the U.S. metaphysics has been pursued much in the spirit of positivism by Wilfred Stalker Sellars (1912–89) and Willard Van Orman Quine. Sellars sought to express metaphysical questions in linguistic terms, and Quine has attempted to determine whether the structure of language commits the philosopher to asserting the existence of any entities whatever and, if so, what kind. In these new formulations the issues of metaphysics and ontology remain vital.

For further information on this topic, see the Bibliography in volume 28, section 27.

METASTASIO, Pietro (1698–1782), Italian poet, whose librettos dominated 18th-century opera. Born in Rome and originally named Pietro Antonio Domenico Bonaventura Trapassi, he was educated in law and the classics by a wealthy patron and studied music under the Italian opera composer Nicola Porpora (1686–1768). His first libretto, *Didone abbandonata* (Dido Abandoned, 1724), established his fame in Italy, and in 1730 he went to Vienna as court poet. His 27 librettos were set to music more than 800 times by such composers as W. A. Mozart, the Germans Christoph Willibald Gluck, Johann Christian Bach, and George Frideric Handel, and the Italians Giovanni Pergolesi, Tommaso Traëtta (1727–79), and Niccolò Jommelli (1714–74). With their aristocratic ideals and conflicts of reason and feeling, they were perfectly suited to 18th-century heroic opera. They include *Artaserse* (1730), *Alessandro nell'Indie* (1731), and *La clemenza di Tito* (The Clemency of Titus, 1734). His verse was admired for its musicality and faithfulness to speech.

METAXAS, Ioánnes (1871–1941), Greek general and politician, born on the island of Itháki. He was chief of the general staff in the Greek army from 1915 to 1917 but was exiled as a result of his pro-German sympathies when Greece joined the Allies in World War I. Returning to Greece in 1920, he led a counterrevolution against the republic and was again exiled. In 1936, a year after George II, king of Greece, was restored to the throne, Metaxas, who had been appointed premier, seized control of the government with the help of the army. He exercised dictatorial power while retaining George as nominal ruler and overcame opposition by dissolving the Greek parliament and abolishing political parties, civil liberties, and freedom of the press. In 1940 he successfully led the Greek resistance against the Italian invasion. He died in January 1941 shortly before the German occupation of Greece.

METAZOA, term applied to all multicellular organisms that digest food, including sponges and higher animals. *See* ANIMAL; CLASSIFICATION.

METCHNIKOFF, Élie, in Russian, Ilya Ilich Mechnikov (1845–1916), Russian biologist and Nobel laureate, a founder of the science of immunity.

Metchnikoff was born in Kharkov Oblast on May 15, 1845, and educated at the university of Kharkov and, in Germany, at the universities of Giessen, Göttingen, and Munich. He lectured in zoology and comparative anatomy at the University of Odessa from 1870 to 1882, when he resigned to devote himself to research. In 1904 he became director of the Pasteur Institute in Paris. His early studies were devoted to the process of intracellular digestion in invertebrates. He later established the destructive effect of certain white blood cells, which he called phagocytes, on harmful materials in the bloodstream, and in 1884 he announced his theory of phagocytosis, which formed a basis for the theory of immunity. Metchnikoff also advocated consumption of lactic acid bacteria for the prevention and remedy of intestinal putrefaction. For his research on immunity he shared the 1908 Nobel Prize in physiology or medicine with the German bacteriologist Paul Ehrlich.

METELLUS NUMIDICUS, Quintus Caecilius (d. about 91 BC), Roman soldier and statesman. As consul in 109 BC, he commanded Roman forces against Jugurtha, king of Numidia in North Africa, capturing the Numidian towns of Zama and Thala. In 107 BC he was replaced as commander by Gaius Marius, who had been his subordinate. In later years he was a political opponent of Marius and of the reformers Lucius Appuleius Saturninus (d. 100 BC) and Gaius Servilius Glaucia (d. 100 BC).

METELLUS PIUS, Quintus Caecilius (d. about 63 BC), Roman soldier and statesman, the son of Metellus Numidicus. A political ally of Lucius Cornelius Sulla, he was driven from Rome in 87 BC by the supporters of Sulla's rival, Gaius Marius, and he then fled to Africa. Returning to Italy in 83 BC, he defeated the Marian forces at Faventia (modern Faenza) in 82 BC, and shared the consulship with Sulla in 80 BC. For the next five years he fought the Marian general Quintus Sertorius (c. 123–72 BC) in Spain, collaborating with Pompey the Great in Sertorius's final defeat (75 BC).

METEOR, in astronomy, small solid body entering a planet's atmosphere from outer space and raised to incandescence by the friction resulting from its rapid motion. Brilliant meteors, known as fireballs, occur singly and generally consist of a luminous head, followed by a cometlike train of light that may persist for several minutes; some, called bolides, have been seen to explode with a sound like thunder. Fainter meteors, called shooting or falling stars, usually occur singly and sporadically. At intervals, however, hundreds of such meteors occur simultaneously and appear to emanate from a fixed point. These swarms are called meteoric showers and are named after the constellation in which they seem to have their point of origin. Some appear annually on the same days of each year and are called periodic showers; others occur infrequently at varying intervals. The periods of meteoric showers generally coincide with those of certain comets (*see* COMET). Most meteors are dissipated in flight and fall to the earth as dust; a meteor that reaches the surface of the earth or another planet is called a meteorite (q.v.).

METEORITE, meteor (q.v.) that reaches the surface of the earth or of another planet before it is entirely consumed. Meteorites found on earth are classified into types, depending on their composition: irons, those composed chiefly of iron, a small percentage of nickel, and traces of other metals such as cobalt; stones, stony meteors consisting of silicates; and stony irons, containing varying proportions of both iron and stone. Although most meteorites are now believed to be fragments of either asteroids or comets, recent geochemical studies have shown that a few Antarctic stones came from the moon and Mars, from which they presumably were ejected by the explosive impact of asteroids. Asteroids themselves are fragments of planetesimals, formed some 4.6 billion years ago, while the earth was forming. Irons are thought to represent the cores of planetesimals and stones (other than the aforementioned Antarctic ones) the crust. Meteorites generally have a pitted surface and fused charred crust. The larger ones strike the earth with tremendous impact, creating huge craters.

The largest known meteorite, estimated to weigh about 55 metric tons, is situated at Hoba West near Grootfontein, Namibia. The next largest, weighing more than 31 metric tons, is the Ahnighito (the Tent); it was discovered, along with two smaller meteorites, in 1894 near Cape York, Greenland, by the American explorer Robert Edwin Peary. Composed chiefly of iron, the three masses had long been used by the Inuit (Eskimo) as a source of metal for the manufacture of knives and other weapons. The Ahnighito was brought to the U.S. by Peary and is on display at the Hayden Planetarium in New York City. The largest known crater believed to have been produced by a meteorite was discovered in 1950 in northwestern Québec, Canada. It consists of a circular pit 4 km (2.5 mi) in diameter, containing a lake and surrounded by concentric piles of shattered granite.

METEOROLOGY, scientific study of the earth's atmosphere (q.v.). It includes the study of day-to-day variations of weather conditions (synoptic meteorology); The study of electrical, optical, and other physical properties of the atmosphere (physical meteorology); the study of average and extreme weather conditions over long periods of time (climatology, for which see CLIMATE); the variation of meteorological elements close to the ground over a small area (micrometeorology); and studies of many other phenomena. The study of the highest portions of the atmosphere (above a height of 20 to 25 km, or 12.5 to 15.5 mi) generally involves the use of special techniques and disciplines, and is termed *aeronomy*. The term *aerology* has been applied to the study of conditions in the free atmosphere anywhere away from the ground.

History. The scholars of ancient Greece were greatly interested in the atmosphere. As early as 400 BC Aristotle wrote a treatise called *Meteorologica*, dealing with the "study of things lifted up"; about one-third of the treatise is devoted to atmospheric phenomena, and it is from this work that the modern term *meteorology* is derived.

Throughout history much of the progress in the discovery of the laws of physics and chemistry was stimulated by curiosity about atmospheric phenomena.

Weather forecasting has challenged the human mind from the earliest times, and much of the wordly wisdom that people have displayed has been identified with weather lore and weather almanacs. Little progress was made in scientific forecasting, however, until the 19th century, when developments in the fields of thermodynamics (q.v.) and hydrodynamics (see FLUID MECHANICS) provided the theoretical basis for meteorology. Exact measurements of the atmosphere are also of the greatest importance in meteorology, and the advance of the science has been furthered by the invention of suitable instruments for observation and by the organization of networks of observing stations to gather weather data. Weather records for individual localities were made as early as the 14th century, but not until the 17th century were any systematic observations made over extended areas. Slow communications also hampered the development of weather forecasting, and it was not until the invention of the telegraph in the mid-19th century that weather data from an entire country could be transmitted to a central point and correlated for the making of a forecast.

One of the most significant milestones in the development of the modern science of meteorology occurred in the World War I period, when a number of Norwegian meteorologists, led by Vilhelm Bjerknes (1862–1951), made intensive studies of the nature of fronts and discovered that interacting air masses generate the cyclones that are the typical storms of the northern hemisphere (see CYCLONE). Later meteorological work was aided by the invention of apparatus such as the rawinsonde, described below, which made possible the investigation of atmospheric conditions at extremely high altitudes. Immediately following the World War I period, a British mathematician, Lewis Fry Richardson (1881–1953), made the first significant attempt to obtain numerical solutions of the atmospheric equations for the prediction of meteorological elements. Although his efforts were not successful at the time, they contributed to the explosive progress in numerical weather prediction of today.

WEATHER OBSERVATION

Improved observations of high-level winds during and following World War II provided the basis for new theories of weather forecasting and revealed the necessity for changes in older concepts of the general atmospheric circulations. During this period major contributions to mete-

METEOROLOGY

orological science were made by the Swedish-born meteorologist Carl-Gustav Rossby (1898-1957) and his collaborators in the U.S. The so-called jet stream, a fast-moving river of air circling the globe high in the atmosphere, was discovered. In 1950, through the use of electronic computers, it became possible to apply the fundamental theories of hydrodynamics and thermodynamics to the problem of weather forecasting, and today such computers are employed regularly to provide weather predictions for industry, agriculture, and the general public.

Surface Observations. Observations made at ground level are more numerous than those made at upper levels. They include the measurement of air pressure, temperature, humidity, wind direction and speed, the amount and height of clouds, visibility, and precipitation (the amount of rain or snow that has fallen).

For the measurement of air pressure, the mercury barometer is the accepted standard. Aneroid barometers, although less accurate, are also useful, particularly on board ships and when used in the recording form called a barograph to show the trend of pressure change over a period of time. All barometer readings used in meteorological work are corrected for variations resulting from temperature and the height of the station, so that pressures from different stations may be directly compared. See BAROMETER.

For the observation of temperature (q.v.) many different types of thermometers are employed. For most purposes an ordinary thermometer covering an appropriate range is satisfactory. It is important to place the thermometer in such a way as to minimize the effects of sunshine during the day and of heat loss by radiation at night, thus yielding values of the air temperature representative of the general area. See THERMOMETER.

The instrument most often used at weather observatories is the hygrometer (q.v.). A special type of this instrument, known as the psychrometer, consists of two thermometers to measure the dry-bulb and wet-bulb temperatures. A more recent device to measure humidity is based on the fact that certain substances undergo changes in electrical resistance with changes in humidity. Instruments making use of this principle commonly are used in rawinsondes, high-level atmospheric sounding devices. See SOUNDING.

The most common instrument for measuring the direction of the wind (q.v.) is the ordinary weather vane, which keeps pointing into the wind and which is connected to an indicating dial or to a series of electronic switches that light small bulbs at the observers' stations to show the wind direction. Wind speed is measured by means of a cup anemometer, an instrument consisting of three or four cups mounted about a vertical axis (see ANEMOMETER). The anemometer spins faster as the speed of the wind increases, and some form of device for counting its revolutions is used to gauge the wind speed.

Precipitation is measured by a rain gauge or a snow gauge (see RAIN). The rain gauge consists of an upright cylinder, open at the top to catch the rain and calibrated either in inches or in millimeters, so that the total depth of the precipitated water may be measured. The snow gauge also is a cylinder, which is thrust into the snow to collect a core of snow. This core is melted and measured in terms of the equivalent depth of

A barograph, used in the measurement of air pressure to determine the trend of pressure change over a period of time.
U.S. Weather Bureau

METEOROLOGY

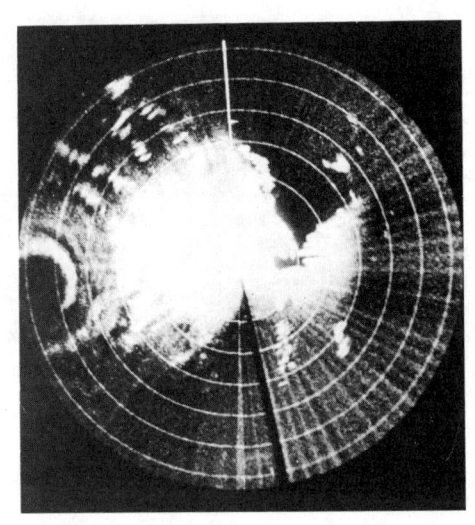

Weather radar scope, used to detect hurricanes, tornadoes, and other severe storms over great distances. UPI

water, thus making the measurement compatible with rainfall observations. Snow-depth measurements are also made with a staff gauge, which is similar to an ordinary ruler.

Recent advances in the field of electronics (q.v.) have been accompanied by concurrent developments in the use of electronic weather instruments. One such device is the weather radar, which makes possible the detection of hurricanes, tornadoes, and other severe storms over distances of several hundred miles (*see* RADAR). For such purposes, the radar echoes from precipitation associated with the disturbance are used to track its course. Other electronic weather instruments include the ceilometer, used for measuring cloud (or ceiling) heights, and the transmissometer, which measures the total effect of smoke, fog, and other restrictions to vision in the atmosphere. The ceilometer and transmissometer together provide instrumental measurements that are extremely important for the takeoff and landing of aircraft.

Upper-Air Observations. Modern methods of prediction as well as the needs of aviation demand that quantitative measurements of wind, pressure, temperature, and humidity be obtained in the free atmosphere. Such data are now gathered by observers at several hundred stations over the continents (mostly in the northern hemisphere) and from a few ships over the oceans.

For routine upper-air measurements, meteorologists have developed the rawinsonde (radio-wind-sounding device), consisting of a lightweight meteorological instrument for measuring pressure, temperature, and humidity, together with a small high-frequency radio transmitter. This assemblage is attached to a balloon that carries the equipment into the upper atmosphere. Measurements made by the meteorological instruments are automatically broadcast by the radio transmitter and are picked up at a ground receiving station. A radio direction finder tracks the balloon as it is transported by the winds in the upper air; and by measuring the position of the balloon in space at successive intervals of time, the speed and direction of the wind at various altitudes can be computed.

Aircraft are used also to obtain upper-air observations, especially when hurricanes (*see* HURRICANE) or typhoons threaten populated areas. These dangerous tropical storms are tracked by special weather reconnaissance airplanes, which are sent out to locate the center, or eye, of the storm and to make meteorological measurements of wind, temperature, pressure, and humidity in and around the storm.

Conventional methods of upper-air observation are rapidly becoming inadequate to meet the needs of the new numerical prediction methods. Modern theories of the atmospheric circulation place increasing emphasis on the importance of the global unity of the atmosphere, and it is a matter of great concern that vast ocean areas go virtually unobserved by conventional methods. Some weather ships are maintained at great expense, but to provide enough ships for adequate coverage in the northern hemisphere alone would be prohibitively expensive.

One of the most successful new methods for the comprehensive observation of the atmosphere has been the application of artificial earth satellites (*see* SATELLITE, ARTIFICIAL). Automatic picture-taking satellites in polar orbits have effectively provided pictures of cloud and storm patterns once each day to any weather station equipped to receive the radio transmissions. Nearly all the major weather services of the world are equipped to receive these pictures, and countries bordered by vast ocean areas have especially benefited by acquiring the ability to keep a surveillance of storms that threaten their coastal areas. Infrared sensors permit the determination of the temperature of the upper cloud surfaces, thus making it possible to obtain the approximate height of the cloud systems in the atmosphere. Other satellites in polar orbits have demonstrated that high-resolution pictures of storm systems can be made at night, using infrared light. Continuous pictures of weather patterns over nearly half the earth are being made

METEOROLOGY

A series of weather-satellite photographs of Hurricane Agnes at 24-hr intervals from June 17 to 19, 1972, show the progress of one of the most devastating natural disasters in U.S. history. During its stormy passage along the Atlantic coast, Agnes took 134 lives and caused damage estimated at $3 billion. National Oceanic and Atmospheric Administration

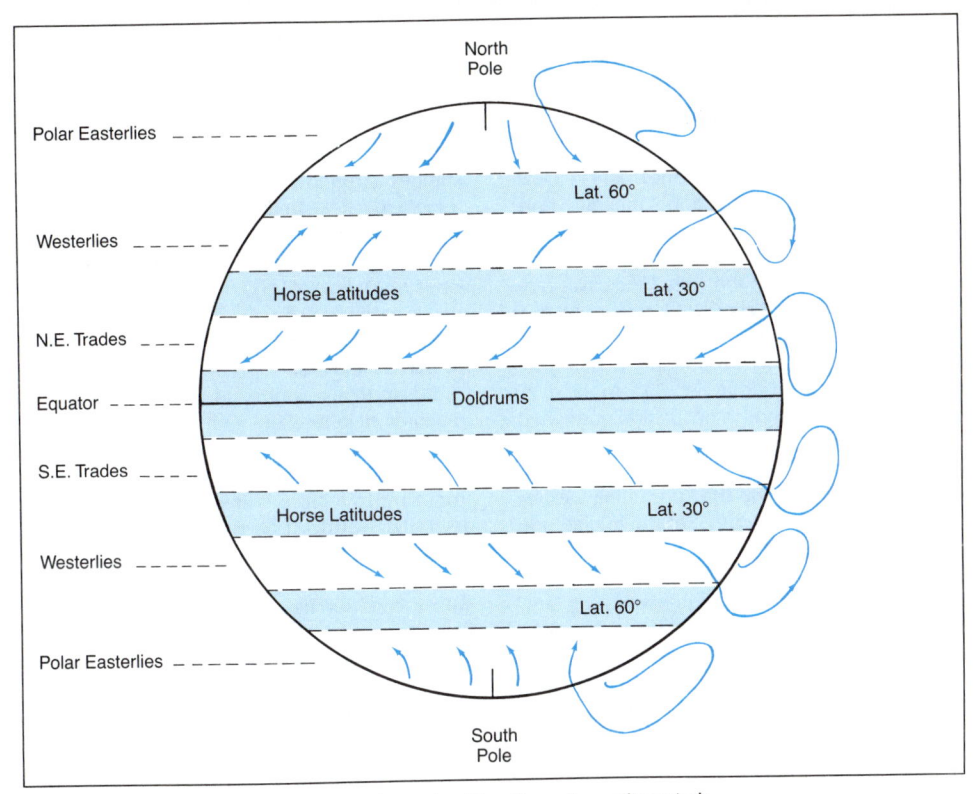

Map showing general air movements over the earth, with pattern of prevailing winds and regions of relative calm. In the northern hemisphere, winds are deflected to the right; in the southern, to the left.

from satellites in synchronous orbits over predetermined points on the equator at an elevation of about 35,400 km (about 22,000 mi).

Unfortunately, the photographic patterns provided by satellites are only of limited usefulness for modern methods of weather prediction that are based on the use of temperature and pressure observations within the atmosphere. Intensive research efforts are under way to find new means of gathering upper-air data over the globe. One of the suggestions being explored is the Global Horizontal Sounding Technique (GHOST), which would combine a worldwide network of free-floating instrumented balloons with orbiting satellites to collect appropriate upper-air data. See BALLOON.

Circulation of the Atmosphere. The cause of all atmospheric motion is the unequal heating of the earth's surface by the sun. Most of the heat and light falls on the equatorial regions and relatively little near the poles. In response to the resulting differences of temperature, a complex circulation is maintained in the atmosphere that has as one of its effects a transfer of heat from the warmer latitudes toward the poles.

Within the Tropics the atmospheric motion follows a meridional pattern, known as a tropical Hadley cell, in which the air descends along belts located about lat 30° north and south of the equator and ascends in the general vicinity of the equator. At low levels there is a general drift of the air toward the equator, whereas at upper levels a compensating drift toward the poles completes the cell. As the two surface streams converge toward the equator from the north and south, into a belt of low pressure known as the doldrums, they are forced to rise, expand, and cool. The moisture in the air then condenses into clouds, which tend to bring frequent rains to the doldrums. The belt of convergence tends to move a few degrees north and south with the seasons. At lat 30° north and south of the equator, the descending branches of the cell are warmed by compression, and clouds that may have been present tend to evaporate. As a result, the weather is warm and sunny, and desert climates predominate. Because of the rotation of the earth, the equatorward-moving streams of air, called trade winds, are deflected toward the west and thus blow from the northeast in the northern hemisphere and the southeast in the southern hemisphere (see CORIOLIS FORCE). The returning high-level airstreams tend to become westerlies. (In meteorological parlance, winds are

METEOROLOGY

named for the direction from which they blow.)

In the middle and high latitudes the most conspicuous features of the circulation are the migratory cyclones and anticyclones, and a clear picture of the global circulation emerges only when the motions have been averaged over many days. This circulation is from the west nearly everywhere, and the speed increases rapidly with heights up to about 13 km (about 8 mi), where average speeds in excess of 160 km/hr (100 mph) may occur. The pressure at sea level decreases northward from lat 30° to lat 60°, where a minimum tends to occur; and northward from lat 60° a shallow anticyclone develops with easterly winds prevailing. Sailors have attached a variety of names, such as the "prevailing westerlies" and the "roaring forties," to the midlatitude wind systems.

The average circulation north of lat 30° tends to be strongest during the winter when the largest differences of temperature occur between high and low latitudes. The low- and high-pressure belts at lat 30° and lat 60° shift slightly with the seasons in such a way as to tend to follow the sun northward and southward. The continents also exert a conspicuous effect on the average flow, and these effects are particularly striking at high latitudes in the northern hemisphere, where the temperature contrasts between the land and oceans are strongest. During the winter intensely cold anticyclones develop over North America and Asia, whereas in summer warm low pressure tends to prevail in these areas. The seasonal wind systems associated with these pressure patterns are called monsoons (see MONSOON) and are particularly striking in India and Southeast Asia.

A conspicuous aspect of the westerly circulation in middle and high latitudes is the presence of cyclonic and anticyclonic vortices that drift from west to east and cause day-to-day changes of the weather. The counterclockwise vortices are called extratropical cyclones, and their intensity tends to be greatest in winter when the temperature contrasts are largest. These cyclones tend to form or regenerate from weak disturbances in certain favored areas, mostly situated along the eastern coasts of North America and Asia and in the northern hemisphere and also just to the east of mountain barriers in North America and southern Europe. The storms intensify as they move eastward and northeastward and tend to reach maximum development in the Icelandic and Aleutian regions. Winds in excess of 160 km/hr (100 mph) may develop over the open oceans in these large storms, and the huge ocean waves generated by such winds may travel for thousands of kilometers, to harass shipping in other areas and batter the coastlines with surf.

Within the dominant westerly flow in middle latitudes is found the jet stream, a narrow band of high-speed westerly wind that pursues a meandering west-to-east course. It is found at an average altitude of 12,200 km (40,000 ft) in winter and 13,700 km (45,000 ft) in summer. Wind speeds in the jet stream occasionally may exceed 400 km hr (250 mph).

Air Masses and Fronts. Around the earth at about lat 30° north and south and also over continents in winter, high pressure and weak winds tend to be dominant. In such regions the winds slowly spread out horizontally, and dry air sinks down from aloft to replace it. Because of the warming associated with compression of the descending air, anticyclones generally are associated with clear weather, except locally where contact of air with a cold surface may result in fogs or low-hanging clouds.

Most of the regions where anticyclones tend to prevail are quite uniform in their surface characteristics; and with the slow diverging motions, large bodies of air with uniform characteristics tend to be generated. Several large bodies of air, called air masses, with distinctive properties are formed in this way.

Maritime tropical air masses form over the oceans at lat 30° north and south and may later be transported thousands of kilometers from their origin to create abnormally warm and humid spells and to supply copious sources of water for clouds and precipitation in middle and high latitudes. Another distinctive type is continental polar air. Situated in winter over the snow-covered expanses of North America and Asia, these air masses become intensely cold, producing temperature records of −68° C (−90° F) in Siberia and −63° C (−81° F) in North America.

Air masses tend to come together to produce zones of great temperature contrast. Such regions, which received a great deal of attention from Norwegian meteorologists about the time of World War I, were given the name fronts and were recognized as narrow zones of highly active weather change. The most conspicuous fronts tend to be situated in winter in the vicinity of the eastern coast of North America, and similarly off Asia in the Pacific. The continental polar air masses tend to sink and spread out under the warm maritime tropical air masses. The warm air masses are thus pushed up over the polar air masses along the frontal zones and are cooled by expansion, and they consequently condense and precipitate their moisture.

An electronics technician monitors computer-generated color displays of Doppler radar data; the two on the right show reflectivity and velocity fields.

National Severe Storms Laboratory

WEATHER FORECASTING AND MODIFICATION

The methods used for making weather predictions have undergone a number of rapid changes since World War II in response to advances in the technology of computers, satellites, and communications. Intensive research is still in progress, and it is to be expected that many more changes will be made in the next decade.

Collection of Data. The collection of weather data is accomplished primarily by teletype transmission of coded messages via land lines and radio. The national teletype circuits operate as multiparty lines, and data printed by any station appear simultaneously at all other stations on the same line. National collections of coded reports are exchanged via high-speed global trunk circuits, so that within an hour or so, surface and upper-air reports from most of the northern hemisphere are available at regional centers in the U.S. and other countries. The Severe Forecast Center in Kansas, City, Mo., is responsible for data on severe weather events, with the National Hurricane Center in Coral Gables, Fla., having the specific responsibility for tracking hurricanes. Worldwide, the Global Telecommunications System of the World Meteorological Organization acts as a central clearinghouse for data from surface stations and meteorological satellites, as well as from ships, aircraft, and radiosondes.

Transmission of Data. Within 2 hr of the observation times, weather maps drawn from the collected data are available at forecasting offices at airports and major cities by means of facsimile transmissions originated at the National Meteorological Center at Suitland, Md. The use of facsimile has greatly increased the efficiency of forecasting offices, because the maps are drawn centrally by highly trained and experienced analysts and made available to the forecasters in the field in greater variety and more quickly than was formerly possible when all maps were prepared locally. Certain analyses of upper-air conditions are now being prepared automatically by computers, which, with extra peripheral equipment, are able to translate and store coded information from teletype lines, make mathematical calculations, and present the output by means of lines drawn on maps. Such analyses are transmitted via facsimile to field offices and are also stored in the computers for use in numerical forecasting procedures. *See* FACSIMILE TRANSMISSION.

Modeling of Data. The equations governing the physical conditions of the atmosphere have been known in principle for a long time, but only in recent years have sufficiently powerful and rapid computational facilities become available for exploiting them. The Suitland center, for example, runs four forecast models twice a day on its computer facilities, two to cover the world and the other two for the North American environment. Special models are run for such specific weather problems as major hurricanes. Worldwide, the largest weather-modeling facility is the European Center for Medium-Range Weather Forecasting, located at Bracknell, England. The atmosphere is far too large and complex to be predicted exactly even with the most powerful computers in existence, but it is possible to construct rather realistic mathematical analogues, or models, of the atmosphere. In the simplest model, conditions at one level only are predicted. More realistic descriptions of the atmosphere are possible using a larger number of levels simultaneously, and nine levels are incorporated in the most sophisticated model now being used. The equations are such that the changes of the atmospheric properties at each level can be calculated for a short span of time if the initial state of the atmosphere is known from observations.

Launching a radiosonde balloon with a transmitter that will radio back weather observations from the upper air. National Oceanic and Atmospheric Administration

By solving the equations it is possible to compute the state of the atmosphere at each of the levels at a time 10 min after the time of the observations. The predicted data are then substituted for the observed initial data, and the process is repeated for additional time steps until a total elapsed time of 72 hr has been reached. The conditions arrived at in this manner for 12, 24, 36, 48, and 72 hr after the initial time are drawn automatically on maps depicting the expected conditions at the various levels, and these are transmitted via facsimile to field offices and other licensed users of the facsimile service.

Interpretation of Data. The procedures described above are carried out automatically, but the resulting forecasts require a great deal of skill in their interpretation. Weather is affected to a great degree by local conditions that cannot be included in the models. Nor are the models perfect representations of the atmosphere, and experienced forecasters will sometimes prefer not to trust the computed results, or may choose to make modifications based on their experience.

Statistical methods have been developed for making use of experience obtained from observations of the behavior of the atmosphere over a long period of time. In some of these methods, patterns are classified into many different groups, and the prediction is made by referring to the past behavior of the group to which the observed condition of the atmosphere belongs. The advantage of this method is that the probability of the occurrence of various alternate events can be determined. The probabilities of the occurrence of snow for the next day, for example, might be found to be 20 percent, rain 50 percent, and fair weather 30 percent. Forecasts of this sort are essential for planning efficient operations for many activities. The risks of losses and other disasters, for example, that could result from unexpected snow in a big city may warrant making preparations for snow removal when the probability of snowfall is as little as 20 percent. A categorical prediction of rain (which might be more probable than snow) would be of little use in planning such operations.

Accuracy of Forecasts. The accuracy of weather forecasts is relative, and published percentages have little meaning without a detailed description of the ground rules that have been followed in judging the validity of a prediction. It has been customary in recent years to claim accuracies of 80 to 85 percent over periods of one day. The numerical models have resulted in considerable improvement of forecast accuracy when compared to predictions previously made by subjective methods, especially for periods of more than one day. At the present time, skill in predicting specific weather events can be demonstrated out to about 5 days, and some success at predicting departures of temperature and precipitation from normal has been obtained out to about 30 days. Claims of varying degrees of skill in predicting weather over longer periods cannot be readily refuted because standards of verification have never been adopted; such claims, however, have not been widely accepted by professional meteorologists.

Cloud Physics and Weather Modification. The study of the atmospheric processes, which include the condensation of moisture, the development of cloud droplets, and the formation of precipitation (q.v.), is called cloud physics. Because of the economic importance of adequate rainfall and snowfall, cloud physics has received much attention during recent years. See CLOUD.

The growth of cloud droplets and the formation of precipitation are complex processes that are not well understood. Certain theoretical work suggests that the formation of precipitation from cloud droplets is aided by the presence of minute ice crystals (see ICE). Because the temperatures of many low-altitude clouds that produce appreciable precipitation are always above freezing, however, it seems that other processes are also important. The growth of drops by collision and coalescence has been proposed as another mechanism in the precipitation process.

In recent years meteorologists have investigated the possibility of modifying the weather by seeding clouds with various substances. Considerable research was done on fog dispersal, as a method of increasing visibility for aircraft; but the purpose of most experiments is the artificial production of precipitation or the prevention of hail (q.v.). Scientific evaluation of the various techniques requires controlled study to distinguish the amount of rain induced by artificial means from that which might have occurred naturally. This distinction is difficult to determine, because the meteorological conditions essential for the artificial production of rain are similar to those leading to natural rainfall. Available evidence from experiments by both private and public agencies indicates that cloud seeding may alter the timing or the total amount of precipitation falling over limited areas, if the meteorological conditions are favorable. For supercooled (below-freezing) clouds, the most effective seeding agent is dry ice. The method, adopted by many commercial agencies, of seeding such low-temperature clouds with silver iodide particles was found to give poor results, especially when the particles were dispersed from ground-generators instead of from aircraft. Warm cumulus clouds containing updrafts may be induced to release rain by fine water sprays or by seeding with salt particles.

Some recent experiments have indicated that hail, and also locally heavy accumulations of snow, can be prevented by seeding clouds with excess amounts of silver iodide. A.K.B.

For further information on this topic, see the Bibliography in volume 28, sections 430–32.

METER, in mathematics. See INTERNATIONAL SYSTEM OF UNITS; METRIC SYSTEM.

METER, in music. See MUSICAL RHYTHM.

METER, in poetry. See VERSIFICATION.

METER-KILOGRAM-SECOND SYSTEM. See INTERNATIONAL SYSTEM OF UNITS; METRIC SYSTEM.

METHADONE. See DRUG DEPENDENCE.

METHANE, also marsh gas, gas composed of carbon and hydrogen with formula CH_4, the first member of the paraffin or alkane series of hydrocarbons. It is lighter than air, colorless, odorless, and flammable. It occurs in natural gas, as firedamp in coal mines, as a by-product of petroleum refining, and as a product of decomposition of matter in swamps. It is a major component in the atmosphere of the outer planets, Jupiter, Saturn, Uranus, and Neptune. In the earth's atmosphere it apparently plays a role in the formation of noctilucent clouds (see CLOUD). Methane can be produced by the hydrogenation of carbon or carbon oxide, by the action of water on aluminum carbide, or by heating sodium acetate with alkali. Methane is valuable as a fuel and in the production of hydrogen, hydrogen cyanide, ammonia, acetylene, and formaldehyde.

Methane melts at $-182.5°$ C ($-296.5°$ F) and boils at $-161.5°$ C ($-258.7°$ F).

METHANOGEN, bacterium that obtains energy from the metabolic production of methane gas, basically from carbon dioxide and hydrogen. The most anaerobic—that is, living in the absence of oxygen—of all bacteria (q.v.), these genera occur wherever plant material decomposes anaerobically, as in ponds, soils, and the digestive tracts of cows and other ruminants. In sewage disposal plants they are involved in the final stages of sludge treatment. They are hard to study because of their sensitivity to oxygen and other special environmental needs.

METHANOL or METHYL ALCOHOL. See ALCOHOL; FUELS, SYNTHETIC.

METHODISM, worldwide Protestant movement dating from 1729, when a group of students at the University of Oxford, England, began to assemble for worship, study, and Christian service. Their fellow students named them the Holy Club and "methodists," a derisive allusion to the methodical manner in which they performed the various practices that their sense of Christian duty and church ritual required.

The Wesleys. Among the Oxford group were John Wesley, considered the founder of Methodism, and his brother Charles, the sons of an Anglican rector. John preached, and Charles wrote hymns. Together they brought about a spiritual revolution, which some historians believe diverted England from political revolution in the late 18th century. The theology of the Wesleys leaned heavily on Arminianism (q.v.) and rejected the Calvinist emphasis on predestination (q.v.; see CALVINISM). Preaching the doctrines of Christian perfection and personal salvation through faith, John Wesley quickly won an enthusiastic following among the English working classes, for whom the formalism of the established Church of England (q.v.) had little appeal.

Opposition by the English clergy, however, prevented the Wesleys from speaking in parish churches; consequently, Methodist meetings were often conducted in open fields. Such meetings led to a revival of religious fervor throughout England, especially among the poor (see REVIVALS, RELIGIOUS). John Wesley's message as well as his personal activities among the poor encouraged a social consciousness that was retained by his followers and has become a hallmark of the Methodist tradition. Methodist societies sprang up, and in 1744 the first conference of Methodist workers was held. Wesley never renounced his ties with the Church of England, but he provided for the incorporation and legal continuation of the new movement.

Division and Reunification. Soon after John Wesley's death in 1791, his followers began to divide into separate church bodies. During the 19th century many such separate Methodist denominations were formed in Great Britain and the U.S., each maintaining its own version of the Wesleyan tradition. In 1881 an Ecumenical Methodist Conference was held to coordinate Methodist groups throughout the world. Conferences have been held at regular intervals since then. They are currently known as the World Methodist Conference, which meets every five years. The centennial gathering was convened in Honolulu in July 1981.

Early in the 20th century in Great Britain, the separate Methodist bodies began to coalesce. The Bible Christians, the Methodist New Connexion, and the United Methodist Free Churches united in 1907 to form the United Methodist Church, which in 1932 joined with the Primitive Methodist and Wesleyan Methodist churches to bring the long chapter of Methodist disunity in Great Britain to an end. Today the Methodist Church in the United Kingdom has the distinction of being the "mother church" of world Methodism.

Structure of British Methodism. The governing body of the British Methodist Church is the Conference. All church courts and committees derive their authority from the Conference and are responsible to it for the exercise of their appropriate functions. Below the Conference administratively is a church court for each district, circuit, and society. Geographic districts number 34. Each district is divided into circuits, generally 30 to 40 in number. Each circuit is subdivided into local societies, the number varying considerably. Administration of the church is not only delegated to the lower courts but also to 13 connexional departments. The work of each department is carried on at the district, circuit, and society level by responsible committees. By this means the Conference maintains control over the work of the various levels of the church. Communication is thus maintained between the Conference and all the members. The Conference also maintains missions around the world.

Origins of Methodism in the U.S. Methodism was brought to the U.S. before the American Revolution by emigrants from both Ireland and England. The earliest societies were formed in about 1766 in New York City, in Philadelphia, and near Pipe Creek, Md. In 1769 John Wesley sent his first missionaries to America. Francis Asbury, commissioned in 1771, was the missionary most instrumental in establishing the American Methodist church. The first annual conference was held in Philadelphia in 1773.

At the Christmas Conference held in Baltimore, Md., in 1784, the Methodist Episcopal Church was formally organized as a body separate from the English Methodist structure. Asbury and Thomas Coke were given the title bishop and became heads of the new church. Wesley sent Twenty-five Articles of Religion, adapted from the Thirty-nine Articles (q.v.) of the Church of England, to serve as its doctrinal basis.

Methodism, spread by the circuit rider and the revival meeting, advanced westward with the frontier. During the early 19th century, the tolerant doctrinal positions of Methodism and its stress on personal religious experience, universal salvation, and practical ethics gave it a major role in religious awakening and attracted converts in large numbers.

Organization and Sacraments. Annual geographic conferences were organized throughout the U.S. in the early 19th century. A democratic form of government similar to the federal governmental system was adopted in the Methodist Episcopal Church, and it remains the basic structure of the United Methodist Church (q.v.). A Council of Bishops was set up as the executive branch of the church, with a General Conference as the legislative branch. Later, a judicial council was established to serve as an ecclesiastical court. The bishops and the judicial council were to meet under the supervision of the General Conference.

Within both British and American Methodism, two sacraments, baptism (q.v.) and the Lord's Supper (see EUCHARIST), are recognized. Baptism may be administered by immersion, pouring, or sprinkling. Methodists interpret the Lord's Supper as either a celebration of the presence of Christ, as taught by the French Protestant theologian John Calvin, or in a strictly memorial sense, as taught by the Swiss Protestant reformer Huldriech Zwingli.

Schisms. In the U.S., as in Great Britain, division among Methodists came early. At the end of the 18th century, black members in Philadelphia withdrew from the church, where segregation had been forced upon them, and established an independent congregation. Soon church groups from other cities along the Atlantic seaboard joined with them to form the African Methodist Episcopal Church (q.v.). In the second decade of the 19th century in New York City a similar movement developed independently; it attracted black congregations from other cities and became the African Methodist Episcopal Zion Church (q.v.). Agitation against the power of the bishops and a desire for lay representation caused another split in 1830, resulting in the formation of the Methodist Protestant Church. Slavery became the most divisive issue in the history of Methodism. Radical abolitionist Methodists (see ABOLITIONISTS) broke away from the Methodist Episcopal Church in the 1840s to form the Wesleyan Methodist Church, which in the 20th century merged with the Pilgrim Holiness Church to become the Wesleyan Church.

In 1844 the largest schism in American Methodism occurred when the Methodist Episcopal Church, South, was formed by supporters of slavery after the General Conference became deadlocked over the issue. In the 1860s the holiness controversy produced another schism, when a group of Methodist dissenters who believed in a reemphasis on Wesley's doctrine of personal holiness broke away to form the Free Methodist Church of North America (q.v.; see also HOLINESS CHURCHES).

After the American Civil War, the two black Methodist denominations and the Methodist Episcopal Church tried to proselytize the black congregations within the Methodist Episcopal Church, South, which in response encouraged and authorized its black members to form the Colored Methodist Episcopal Church, now known as the Christian Methodist Episcopal Church (q.v.).

Mergers. Each of these separate Methodist bodies formed denominational agencies to manage education, missions, evangelism, and publishing. Through their individual missionary programs, competing Methodist missions appeared around the world. It became apparent that some cooperation was essential, and each Methodist denomination joined one or more international missionary organizations in the late 19th and early 20th centuries. One of these was the Ecumenical Methodist Conference, which first met in 1881.

The movement for unity did not succeed as completely in the U.S. as it did in Great Britain, where one Methodist church resulted. After much effort, three of the major Methodist bodies in the U.S., namely, the Methodist Episcopal Church, the Methodist Protestant Church, and the Methodist Episcopal Church, South, united in 1939 to form the Methodist Church.

In 1946 two small denominations of German ethnic origin that were unaffiliated with Methodism but greatly influenced by it, the Evangelical Church and the Church of the United Brethren in Christ, united to form the Evangelical United Brethren Church (q.v.). In 1968 this church joined with the Methodist Church to become the United Methodist Church, bringing more than half of world Methodism into one denomination.

Methodist churches in other countries generally stem from either the British or the American Methodist traditions. Some national Methodist churches have become independent of their parent churches, which increases the importance of their cooperation through the World Methodist Council. The ecumenical movement (q.v.), in which Methodists have been leading participants, has resulted in the unification of some Methodist groups with other denominations, making their long-term relationship with world Methodism problematic. J.H.Ne.

For further information on this topic, see the Bibliography in volume 28, section 100.

METHODIUS, Saint. *See* Cyril and Methodius, Saints.

METHUEN, town, Essex Co., NE Massachusetts, on the Merrimack R., near Lawrence; settled 1666, inc. as a town 1725, reinc. 1921. Major manufactures are cotton textiles and electronic equipment. Originally part of Haverhill, the community was separately incorporated in 1725. It is named for the English diplomat Sir Paul Methuen (1672–1757). Pop. (1980) 36,701; (1990) 39,990.

METHUSELAH, in the Old Testament, the son of the patriarch Enoch and grandfather of the patriarch Noah. He was said to have died in the year of the deluge at the age of 969 (see Gen. 5:21-27; 1 Chron. 1:3).

METONIC CYCLE, cycle of 19 years composed of 235 lunar months, at the end of which time the full moon appears on the same day in the year as it did at the beginning of the cycle. The Metonic cycle is named after its discoverer, the Greek astronomer Meton (fl. 432 BC). This cycle was used by the Nicene Council in AD 325 in fixing the date of Easter. The number of a calendar year in the Metonic cycle is called the golden number. To obtain the golden number for any year in the Christian era, 1 is added to the number of the year and the result divided by 19. The remainder is the golden number. If there is none, the number is 19. *See* Calendar; Easter; Month.

METRIC SYSTEM, a decimal system of physical units based on its unit of length, the *meter* (Gr. *metron*, "measure"). (The spelling in most English-speaking countries is *metre,* but meter is the most preferred U.S. spelling.) Introduced and adopted by law in France in the 1790s, the metric system was subsequently adopted as the common system of weights and measures by a majority of countries, and by all countries as the system used in scientific work.

The meter (m), which is approximately 39.37 in., was originally defined as one ten-millionth of the distance from the equator to the North Pole on a line running through Paris. Between 1792 and 1799, French scientists measured part of this distance. Treating the earth as a perfect sphere, they then estimated the total distance and divided it into ten-millionths. Later, after it was discovered that the earth is not a perfect sphere, the standard meter was defined as the distance between two fine lines marked on a bar of platinum-iridium alloy, the international prototype meter. It was later redefined in terms of the wavelengths of red light from a krypton-86 source. The measurements of modern science required still greater precision, however, and in 1983 the meter was defined as the length of the path traveled by light in a vacuum during a time interval of 1/299,792,458 of a second (*see* International System of Units).

All metric units were originally derived from the meter, but by 1900 the metric system began to be based on the mks (meter-kilogram-second) system, by which the unit of mass, the gram, was redefined as the kilogram, and the unit of time, the second, was added. Later a unit of the electromagnetic system, the ampere, was added to form the mksa (meter-kilogram-second-ampere) system. Because of the need of science for small units, the cgs (centimeter-gram-second) system also came into use. The unit of volume, the liter, was originally defined as 1 cubic decimeter (cdm^3), but in 1901 it was redefined as the volume occupied by a kilogram of water at 4° C at 760 mm of mercury; in 1964 the original definition (cdm^3) was restored.

A series of Greek decimal prefixes is used to express multiples; a similar series of Latin decimal prefixes is used to express fractions. These prefixes have been adopted by and expanded in the International System of Units. For conversion of metric system units to other units, *see* Weights and Measures.

The U.S., Great Britain, and other English-speaking countries use inches, feet, miles, pounds, tons, and gallons as units of length, weight, and volume for common measurements. Today, however, within the framework of the International System of Units, these English-system units are legally based on metric standards.

In the U.S. several attempts were made to bring the metric system into general use. In 1821 Secretary of State John Quincy Adams, in a report to Congress, advocated the adoption of the metric system. In 1866 Congress legalized the use of the metric system, and from that time this system was increasingly adopted, notably in medicine and science, as well as in certain sports, such as track. In 1893 the National Bureau of Standards of the U.S. adopted the metric system in legally defining the yard and the pound.

In 1965 Great Britain became the first of the

English-speaking countries to begin an organized effort to abandon the older units of measurement. Canada, Australia, New Zealand, and South Africa quickly followed and soon exceeded the speed of change in Great Britain. In 1971, after an extensive study, the U.S. secretary of commerce recommended that the U.S. convert to metric units under a ten-year voluntary plan. On Dec. 23, 1975, President Gerald R. Ford signed the Metric Conversion Act of 1975. It defines the metric system as being the International System of Units as interpreted in the U.S. by the secretary of commerce. The act coordinates the metric effort, but does not specify a conversion schedule.

For further information on the system based on small units, see CGS SYSTEM.

For further information on this topic, see the Bibliography in volume 28, section 366.

METRONOME, musician's device, usually pyramidal in shape, that clicks audibly at exactly timed intervals as an aid to keeping correct tempo. Functionally, it is an upside-down pendulum, the upright, oscillating hand bearing a small counterweight that can be raised or lowered vertically according to the tempo desired. This adjustment regulates the number of beats per minute in models that are wound by hand; others operate electrically. It was patented in 1816 by the German musician and inventor Johann Nepomuk Maelzel (1772–1838); however, it was actually conceived about 1812 by the Dutch inventor Dietrich Nikolaus Winkel (c. 1780–1826).

METROPOLITAN MUSEUM OF ART, chief museum of art in New York City, and the largest in the U.S., founded 1870 and opened at its present location 1880. One of the world's great art museums, like the Louvre in Paris and the British Museum in London, its encyclopedic collections, special exhibitions, lectures, concerts, and educational programs attract more than 3 million visitors a year.

History and Organization. Under the original charter worked out by its founders and city officials, the museum is located on city land in a city-owned building; this structure, on the Fifth Ave. side of Central Park in Manhattan, opened in 1880. It is financed by public and private funds. Its private board of trustees with city representation became a model for other institutions.

The first of many wings was added to the building in 1888. Additions and changes have occurred ever since. During the 1970s and '80s several new wings and their component galleries were designed to complete the original symmetrical plan of the building. These include the Robert Lehman Wing (1975), which re-creates the atmosphere of the New York town house of the American banker (1891–1969) and displays his collection of paintings and art objects, and the Sackler Wing (1978) housing the Temple of Dendur, which was rescued from the waters of the Aswan High Dam in Egypt. The American Wing (1980) is a museum within a museum: 24 period rooms and 33 galleries of paintings, sculpture, and decorative arts from the 17th to the 19th century. Opened in 1981 and 1982, respectively, were the Astor Court, a replica of a Chinese scholar's garden, and the Michael C. Rockefeller Wing, housing works from Africa, Oceania, and the Americas. Other installations include the Andre Meyer Galleries for impressionist art, the Douglas Dillon Galleries for Chinese paintings, and the arts of Japan in the Sackler Galleries for Asian Art. The Lila Acheson Wallace Wing, dedicated to 20th-century art, opened in 1987; it is topped by the Iris and B. Gerald Cantor Roof Garden, open from May to November for exhibitions of modern sculpture. Opened in 1988 were the Charlotte C. and John C. Weber Galleries for the arts of ancient China, and the Tisch Galleries, part of the Henry R. Kravis Wing, for special exhibitions. The 19th-Century European Paintings and Sculpture Galleries—a museum within a museum—housed in a suite of 21 rooms opened in 1993.

Benefactors and Financing. The list of museum benefactors includes some of the greatest names in American finance and business, among them William H. Vanderbilt, John D. Rockefeller, Jr., and J. P. Morgan, and philanthropists such as Lila Acheson Wallace (1889–1984), late publisher of the *Reader's Digest,* and publisher Walter H. Annenberg (1908–   ). Gifts of money and collections of art, supplemented by corporate and government grants and by visitors' donations, continue to make possible the museum's services to the public. In addition, the museum's bookshop and sales department provide income.

Special Collections. The Metropolitan Museum is one of the most important institutions in the world with respect to old master paintings, prints and drawings, and European decorative arts and sculpture. Its collections span the period from ancient Egypt to the 20th century. The Egyptian Department is one of the greatest archaeological collections outside the Cairo Museum. Other treasures include examples of early Islamic art and a renowned collection of musical instruments.

The Costume Institute (1937), among the few such collections in the world, contains thousands of items of period clothing and accessories; ethnographic costumes from all parts of the world; and designer clothes. The institute houses the Irene Lewisohn Costume Reference Library; it also mounts special costume exhibitions.

METROPOLITAN STATISTICAL AREA

Services. The library, for which provision was made in the original charter, was reorganized and officially designated as the Thomas J. Watson Library in 1959. Today it is considered the most comprehensive art and archaeology reference library in the world. A separate library of photographs and slides is also maintained.

The Ruth and Harold D. Uris Center for Education provides exhibitions, workshops, films, and courses, designed for students of all ages.

The Museum Publications Department issues books on art as well as catalogs of exhibitions and the quarterly museum *Bulletin*.

The Conservation Section restores objects, paintings, works on paper, and textiles.

The Grace Rainey Rogers Auditorium (1954) offers an annual series of concerts by renowned soloists and chamber ensembles, as well as lectures on art and music.

The Cloisters. The Cloisters, opened in 1938 at the upper end of Manhattan in Fort Tryon Park, is an extension of the museum devoted to medieval art. French and Spanish cloisters, dating from the 12th to the 15th century, were reassembled there, in a setting of herb gardens, flagged paths, and Hudson River vistas, by the generosity of John D. Rockefeller, Jr. The famed series of 15th-century French tapestries, *The Hunt of the Unicorn*, may be seen there. The Treasury, housing ecclesiastical vestments and art objects, was extensively renovated in 1988. F.S.Ka.

For further information on this topic, see the Bibliography in volume 28, sections 13, 642.

METROPOLITAN STATISTICAL AREA. See Standard Metropolitan Statistical Area.

METSU, Gabriel (1629–67), Dutch painter, born in Leiden. Probably a pupil of the Dutch painter Gerard Dou, he helped found in 1648 the guild of painters in Leiden. In 1650 he settled in Amsterdam. Metsu (Metzu) painted the charming aspects of middle-class Dutch life with consummate taste in color and tone. His works include *Mother and Sick Child* (1660?, Rijksmuseum, Amsterdam), *The Music Lovers* (Mauritshuis, The Hague), and *A Visit to the Nursery* (1661, Metropolitan Museum, New York City).

METTERNICH, Prince Klemens Wenzel Nepomuk Lothar, von (1773–1859), Austrian statesman and diplomat, who was the dominant figure in European politics between 1814 and 1848.

Metternich was born into an aristocratic family on May 15, 1773, at Koblenz, Germany, and attended the universities of Strasbourg and Mainz. His family fled the revolutionary French armies to Vienna in 1794, and Metternich there married Countess Eleanor Kaunitz (fl. 1795–1825), whose family was prominent at the Austrian court.

He served the Habsburgs first as an envoy to the Congress of Rastadt (1797) and then as ambassador to Saxony (1801), Prussia (1803), and Napoleonic France (1806).

Major Achievements. In 1809 Metternich was appointed minister of foreign affairs for the Habsburg state, then in disarray following several defeats by the French army. He arranged the marriage of the Austrian archduchess Marie Louise (1791–1847) to Napoleon, but he planned to renew the war with France when the opportunity arose. After Napoleon's disastrous Russian campaign in 1812, Metternich played a leading role in the formation of a new European coalition that two years later defeated the French emperor. At the Congress of Vienna (1814–15), which redrew the map of Europe after Napoleon's downfall, he blocked Russian plans for the annexation of the whole of Poland and Prussia's attempt to absorb Saxony. He succeeded in creating a German confederation under Austrian leadership but failed to achieve a similar arrangement for Italy. His attempt to make the postwar Quadruple Alliance (Great Britain, Russia, Prussia, and Austria) into an instrument for preventing revolution in Europe also failed. As chancellor of the Habsburg Empire (1821–48) he was, however, able to maintain the status quo in Germany and Italy, and he remained Europe's leading statesman until driven from power by the Revolution of 1848. He died in Vienna on June 11, 1859.

Evaluation. Metternich equally resented liberalism, nationalism, and revolution. His ideal was a monarchy that shared power with the traditional privileged classes of society. He was a man of order in an increasingly disorganized world of rapidly changing values. Vain and indolent by nature, he often assumed responsibility for policies he had not himself formulated. Some have judged him a reactionary who tried to stem the tide of democratic progress. To others he was a constructive force, misunderstood by contemporaries and later historians alike. J.Hd.

METZ, city, E France, capital of Moselle Department, at the confluence of the Moselle and Seille rivers, in Lorraine, near W Germany and Luxembourg. It is a manufacturing and transportation center; products include machinery, tobacco and leather goods, textiles, and processed food. Points of interest are the Cathedral of Saint Étienne (primarily 13th–16th cent.); the Basilica of Saint Pierre de la Citadelle; and the Porte des Allemands (13th–15th cent.), a large gate with crenelated towers. The University of Metz (1971) is here.

Metz dates from pre-Roman times and became the capital of the kingdom of Austrasia in the 6th century AD. It was made a free imperial city of the Holy Roman Empire in the 12th century. Metz was captured by King Henry II of France in April 1552 and was successfully defended by François de Lorraine, 2d duc de Guise, against Charles V, the Holy Roman emperor, from October 1552 to January 1553. Metz was ceded to France by the Peace of Westphalia in 1648 and was subsequently heavily fortified. In 1870, during the Franco-Prussian War, Metz was besieged by the Germans for two months until, in late October, the French marshal François Bazaine surrendered. From 1871 to 1919, Metz was part of the German Empire; it was returned to France following World War I, during which the city was badly damaged. The city again suffered considerable damage in World War II, when it was occupied by the Germans from 1940 to 1944. Pop. (1990) 123,920.

MEUSE, river, W Europe, traversing NE France, S Belgium, and the Netherlands. It rises in the Langres Plateau, France, and flows past Verdun, Sedan, and Charleville-Mézières into Belgium. The Meuse is joined by the Sambre R. at Namur, from which it courses E to Liège, forms part of the Dutch-Belgian border, and enters the Netherlands at Maastricht. The Meuse flows past Venlo and Bergen and divides into two branches. The N branch, called the Maas R., flows NW to join the Waal R.; the S branch empties into the North Sea. The total length of the Meuse is about 900 km (about 560 mi); the river is one of the major waterways of Europe. The Meuse valley is an important mining and industrial region.

MEXICALI, city, NW Mexico, capital of Baja California State, in the Mexicali Valley (the lower part of the Imperial Valley), opposite Calexico, Calif. A railroad and border tourist town, Mexicali is also a trade center for the surrounding irrigated valley, which produces cotton, alfalfa, vegetables, grapefruit, and dates. Cotton, fruits, hides, minerals, and chili are exported. Industries in the city include cotton ginning, flour and cottonseed-oil milling, brewing, and the manufacture of soap and lard. Located here is the Autonomous University of Baja California (1957). Pop. (1990) 602,390.

MEXICAN HAIRLESS, breed of hairless dog resembling several other such breeds around the world. The dog looks like a large, thin, long-muzzled chihuahua, standing about 30 cm (about 12 in) at the shoulder. The skin may be a wide range of solid or mottled colors, the ears are erect, and the tip of the long tail and top of the head may exhibit a scanty growth of hair. The Mexican hairless is recognized as a breed only by the Canadian Kennel Club, but another hair-

American and Mexican troops in combat at Resaca de la Palma, May 9, 1846. Bettmann Archive

less Mexican breed, the xolotl (short for xoloitzcuintli) is recognized by Mexico. This dog is somewhat sturdier than the Mexican hairless and stands about 50 cm (about 20 in) at the shoulder.

MEXICAN WAR, conflict between the U.S. and Mexico, lasting from 1846 to 1848. The principal causes of the war were the annexation of Texas (Dec. 29, 1845) by the U.S.; claims against the Mexican government by U.S. citizens who had been injured and whose property had been damaged during the frequent Mexican revolutions of the period; and the desire of the U.S. to acquire California, a Mexican province in which many U.S. citizens had settled and which the U.S. feared might fall under British or French rule. In November 1845, President James K. Polk sent the diplomat John Slidell to Mexico to seek boundary adjustments in return for the U.S. government's settlement of the claims of U.S. citizens against Mexico, and also to make an offer to purchase California and New Mexico. The Mexican authorities refused to negotiate with Slidell. After the failure of this mission, a U.S. army under Gen. Zachary Taylor advanced to the mouth of the Rio Grande, the river that the state of Texas claimed as its southern boundary. Mexico, claiming that the boundary was the Nueces River, to the northeast of the Rio Grande, considered the advance of Taylor's army an act of aggression and in April 1846 sent troops across the Rio Grande. Polk, in turn, declared the Mexican advance to be an invasion of U.S. soil, and Congress declared war on Mexico on May 13, 1846.

The U.S. plan of campaign was threefold, involving an invasion of northern Mexico by Taylor, occupation of New Mexico and California by forces under Col. Stephen W. Kearny, and a blockade of both Mexican coasts. Even before war had been formally declared Taylor won the battles of Palo Alto (May 8, 1846) and Resaca de la Palma (May 9) and forced the Mexicans back across the Rio Grande. He then advanced into Mexico. Taylor occupied Matamoros in present-day Tamaulipas (May 18), captured Monterrey (September 24), and by defeating the Mexican forces under Gen. Antonio Lopez de Santa Anna in a stubbornly contested battle at Buena Vista (Feb. 22–23, 1847), put an end to Mexican resistance in northern Mexico. Kearny occupied what is now New Mexico and then, advancing into California, helped in the occupation of that territory. Under the leadership of the U.S. naval officer Commodore John Drake Sloat (1781–1867) and Capt. John C. Frémont of the U.S. Army, California had already declared its independence from Mexico and was declared a territory of the U.S. in July 1846.

In spite of these U.S. victories and the success of the blockade, Mexico refused to acknowledge defeat, and the U.S. decided to send an expedition to end the war by capturing Mexico City. American troops under Gen. Winfield Scott took Vera Cruz (March 29, 1847) and defeated the Mexicans at Cerro Gordo, Contreras, and Churubusco. U.S. troops next took Casa Mata and Molino del Rey and then stormed the hill of Chapultepec, the key to Mexico City, which fell on Sept. 14, 1847. Peace was established by the Treaty of Guadalupe Hidalgo, signed on Feb. 2, 1848. The Rio Grande was made the southern boundary of Texas, and California and New Mexico were ceded to the U.S. In return the U.S. paid Mexico the sum of $15 million and agreed to settle all claims of U.S. citizens against Mexico.

For further information on this topic, see the Bibliography in volume 28, section 1141.

MEXICO, in full UNITED MEXICAN STATES (Span. *Estados Unidos Mexicanos*), federal republic, North America, bounded on the N by the U.S.; on the E by the U.S., the Gulf of Mexico, and the Caribbean Sea; on the S by Belize and Guatemala; and on the W by the Pacific Ocean. Mexican federal jurisdiction encompasses, in addition to Mexico proper, a number of offshore islands. The area of the country is 1,958,201 sq km (756,063 sq mi).

LAND AND RESOURCES

Most of Mexico is an immense, elevated plateau, flanked by mountain ranges that fall sharply off to narrow coastal plains in the W and E. The two mountain chains, the Sierra Madre Occidental to the W and the Sierra Madre Oriental in the E, meet in the SE. There the two ranges form the Sierra Madre del Sur, a maze of volcanic mountains containing the highest peaks in Mexico. The Sierra Madre del Sur leads into the Isthmus of Tehuantepec, which lies between the Bay of Campeche and the Gulf of Tehuantepec.

The prominent topographical feature of the country is the central plateau, a continuation of the plains of the southwestern U.S. Comprising more than half the total area of Mexico, the plateau slopes downward from the W to the E and from the S, where the elevation varies from about 1830 to 2440 m (about 6000 to 8000 ft) above sea level, to the N with an elevation of about 1070 to 1220 m (about 3500 to 4000 ft). Two large valleys form notable depressions in the plateau: the Bolsón de Mapimí in the N and the Anáhuac, or Valley of Mexico, in central Mexico.

The coastal plains are generally low, flat, and sandy, although the Pacific coast is occasionally broken by mountain spurs. Baja California, a

MEXICO

Las Hadas, a luxurious new resort on the western coast of Mexico, is exquisitely situated on a steep slope of Santiago Peninsula.
Slim Aarons

long, narrow peninsula extending about 1225 km (about 760 mi) S from the NW corner of the country, is traversed by mountains that are a continuation of the coastal ranges in the U.S. state of California. On the Gulf of Mexico, the Yucatán Peninsula, which forms the SE tip of the country, is low and flat, averaging about 30 m (about 100 ft) in elevation.

Rivers and Lakes. Mexico has few major rivers, and most are not navigable. The longest river is the Rio Grande (called the Río Bravo in Mexico), which forms the natural boundary between Texas and Mexico for about 2092 km (about 1300 mi). Other important rivers include the Pánuco, Grijalva, and Usumacinta in the S and the Conchos in the N. Mexico has few good harbors. Tampico, Veracruz, and Coatzacoalcos (Puerto México) are major Gulf of Mexico ports. Pacific ports include Acapulco, Manzanillo, Mazatlán, and Salina Cruz. Lake Chapala, in the W, is the largest inland body of water. Anáhuac contains several shallow lakes.

Climate. Mexico is bisected by the Tropic of Cancer; therefore, the S half is included in the Torrid Zone. In general, climate varies with altitude. The *tierra caliente* (hot land) includes the low coastal plains, extending from sea level to about 914 m (about 3000 ft). Weather is extremely humid, with temperatures varying from 15.6° to 48.9° C (60° to 120° F). The *tierra templada* (temperate land) extends from about 914 to 1830 m (about 3000 to 6000 ft) with average temperatures of 16.7° to 21.1° C (62° to 70° F). The *tierra fría* (cold land) extends from about 1830 to 2745 m (about 6000 to 9000 ft). The average temperature range is 15° to 17.2° C (59° to 63° F).

The rainy season lasts from May to October. Although sections of S Mexico receive from about 990 to 3000 mm (about 39 to 118 in) of rain a year, most of Mexico lacks adequate rainfall. Rainfall averages less than 635 mm (25 in) annually in the *tierra templada,* about 460 mm (about 18 in) in the *tierra fría,* and about 254 mm (about 10 in) in the semiarid N.

Natural Resources. The mineral resources of Mexico are extremely rich and varied. Almost every known mineral is found, including coal, iron ore, phosphates, uranium, silver, gold, copper, lead, and zinc. Proven petroleum and natural-gas reserves are enormous, with some of the world's largest deposits located offshore, in the Bay of

MEXICO

Campeche. Forests and woodland, which cover about 22% of the land, contain such valuable woods as mahogany, ebony, walnut, and rosewood. About 13% of the land is suitable for agriculture, but less than 10% receives enough rainfall for raising crops without irrigation.

Plants and Animals. Because of the wide range of temperature, the native flora of Mexico is extremely varied. Cactus, yucca, agave, and mesquite are plentiful in the arid N. The *tierra caliente* is thickly grown with an immense variety of plants, which form a dense tropical jungle in some areas. The trees in this zone include valuable hardwoods, as well as coconut palms, gum trees, and almond, fig, and olive trees. On the mountain slopes grow oaks, pines, and firs. Arctic vegetation is found at the highest altitudes.

Mexican fauna also varies according to the climatic zones. Wolves and coyotes are found in the N. The forests on the mountain slopes are inhabited by ocelots, jaguars, peccaries, bears, and pumas. Fur-bearing seals are found on the coasts. A wide variety of reptiles includes turtle, iguana, rattlesnake, and lizard. Birds, including sea and game birds, are numerous. Along the coast and in the estuaries of rivers fish abound.

POPULATION

The Mexican population is composed of three main groups: the people of Spanish descent, the Indians, and the people of mixed Spanish and Indian ancestry, or mestizos. Of these groups, the mestizos are by far the largest, constituting about 60% of the population. The Indians total about 30%. The society is semi-industrialized.

Population. The population of Mexico at the 1990 census was 81,249,645. The population density in 1990 was 41 persons per sq km (107 per sq mi). About 71% lived in urban areas.

Political Divisions. Mexico consists of 32 administrative divisions—31 states and the *Distrito Federal* (federal district), which is the seat of the federal administration.

Principal Cities. The capital and cultural center of the country is Mexico City, with a population (1990) of 8,236,960. Other important cities are Guadalajara (1,628,617), a vital mining center; Monterrey (1,064,197), an industrial area and railroad center; Puebla (1,054,921), one of Mexico's oldest cities and a pottery manufacturing center; León (872,543), the center of an agricultural area; Ciudad Juárez (797,679), a commercial and manufacturing center; and Tijuana (742,686), a tourist and industrial center.

Religion. Roman Catholicism is the faith of about 90% of the people. Mexico's long tradition of official anticlericalism ended in 1991 with the passage of constitutional changes granting legal status to religious institutions and allowing parochial schools. Protestants represent a small but growing minority in Mexico.

Language. The prevailing and official language is Spanish, which is spoken by the great majority of the population. Indian languages number about 13, with many different dialects, the chief of which is Nahuatl (see AMERICAN INDIAN LANGUAGES), or Aztec. Other major dialects include Maya, spoken in the Yucatán Peninsula, and Otomí, common in central Mexico. Successive governments have instituted educational programs to teach Spanish to all of the Indians.

Education. Primary education is free and compulsory for all children through the age of 15. Parochial schools were legalized in 1991. Secondary schools emphasize vocational and technical training. Although adult illiteracy has been a major problem, successful government campaigns have raised the literacy rate from less than 50% in the early 1940s to more than 87% of persons aged 15 or more years in the early 1990s.

Elementary and secondary schools. Each year in the early 1990s some 14.5 million pupils attended about 86,600 primary schools in Mexico, and approximately 6 million students attended about 25,100 secondary schools. Vocational and teacher-training schools numbered about 6570, and they enrolled nearly 1.1 million students.

Universities and colleges. Mexico has more than 1800 institutions of higher education, with some

POLITICAL DIVISIONS OF MEXICO

State	Population (1990)	Capital
Aguascalientes	719,659	Aguascalientes
Baja California	1,660,855	Mexicali
Baja California Sur	317,764	La Paz
Campeche	535,185	Campeche
Chiapas	3,210,496	Tuxtla Gutiérrez
Chihuahua	2,441,873	Chihuahua
Coahuila	1,972,340	Saltillo
Colima	428,510	Colima
Durango	1,349,378	Durango
Guanajuato	3,982,593	Guanajuato
Guerrero	2,620,637	Chilpancingo
Hidalgo	1,888,366	Pachuca
Jalisco	5,302,689	Guadalajara
México	9,815,795	Toluca
Michoacán	3,548,199	Morelia
Morelos	1,195,059	Cuernavaca
Nayarit	824,643	Tepic
Nuevo León	3,098,736	Monterrey
Oaxaca	3,019,560	Oaxaca
Puebla	4,126,101	Puebla
Querétaro	1,051,235	Querétaro
Quintana Roo	493,277	Chetumal
San Luis Potosí	2,003,187	San Luis Potosí
Sinaloa	2,204,054	Culiacán
Sonora	1,823,606	Hermosillo
Tabasco	1,501,744	Villahermosa
Tamaulipas	2,249,581	Ciudad Victoria
Tlaxcala	761,277	Tlaxcala
Veracruz	6,228,239	Jalapa Enríquez
Yucatán	1,362,940	Mérida
Zacatecas	1,276,323	Zacatecas
Distrito Federal	8,235,744	Mexico City

MEXICO

Paseo de la Reforma, one of the major thoroughfares in Mexico City. Photo Researchers, Inc.

1.3 million students annually in the early 1990s. Among the notable universities are the National Autonomous University of Mexico (1551) and the National Polytechnic Institute (1936), both in Mexico City; the University of Guadalajara (1792), in Guadalajara; the Benemérita Autonomous University of Puebla (1937), in Puebla; Veracruz University (1944), in Jalapa Enríquez; and the Institute of Technical and Advanced Studies of Monterrey (1943), in Monterrey.

CULTURE

Mexican culture is a rich, complex blend of Indian, Spanish, and American traditions. Rural areas are populated by Indians, descendants of the highly developed societies of the Maya, Aztec, and Toltecs, and by Spanish and mestizo farmers and laborers; each of these heritages has enriched the regional culture. In the cities both European, particularly Spanish and French, and North American influences are evident. Most contemporary Mexican artists are striving to produce identifiably Mexican work that blends Spanish, Indian, and modern European styles.

Literature. Mexican writing in Spanish dates from the 16th century, and many works make use of themes from the oral traditions of the country's Indians. Noted Mexican writers of the 20th century include the novelists Mariano Azuela (1873–1952), Martín Luis Guzmán (1887–1976), Andrés Henestrosa (1908–), Agustín Yáñez (1904–80), and Carlos Fuentes (1929–); the playwrights Víctor Barroso (1890–1936) and Rodolfo Usigli (1905–79); and the poets and essayists Alfonso Reyes (1889–1959) and Octavio Paz (1914–), winner of the Nobel Prize for literature in 1990. *See also* LATIN AMERICAN LITERATURE.

251

MEXICO

Music and Dance. The distinctive folk songs and dances heard from region to region are accompanied by several kinds of guitar-based ensembles. The ubiquitous mariachi, or popular strolling bands, consist of a standard group of instruments: two violins, two five-string guitars, and a *guittarón*, or large bass guitar, and usually a pair of trumpets. In Veracruz the usual musical ensemble is a harp and two small guitars. Marimba ensembles are found in the S. The *corrido*, a narrative folk ballad in rhymed quatrains derived from the Spanish *romanza*, is probably Mexico's most outstanding contribution to American folk music, as well as folk poetry. Some pre-Hispanic dances survive, with Hispanic-influenced music; they include the *concheros* and *voladores* dances.

In the field of concert or art music, Mexican musicians led by the composer and conductor Carlos Chávez have received critical acclaim throughout the world. The National Symphony Orchestra of Mexico was founded in 1928 by Chávez and the Ballet Folklórico de Mexico in 1952 by the choreographer Amalia Hernández (1918?–).

Architecture. Spanish colonial architecture, constructed in Gothic, plateresque, classic, and baroque styles sometimes decorated with Indian motifs, is found throughout Mexico. In the late 19th and early 20th centuries, first during the short reign of the Habsburg emperor Maximilian and later under President Porfirio Díaz, the French splendors of the second Empire style were introduced into the capital. Díaz also commissioned the ornate Palace of Fine Arts, completed in the 1930s. Since World War II an architectural renaissance has occurred in Mexico, attracting worldwide attention. The new buildings erected at the National Autonomous University of Mexico, designed by a group of artists and architects under the direction of Carlos Lazo (1914–55), feature outstanding murals in fresco and mosaic; among these are works by the architect and painter Juan O'Gorman (1905–82). Another Mexican architect, Felix Candela (1910–), created highly original concrete shell designs for several churches and for the sports palace at the 1968 Olympic Games.

Art. A rich tradition of painting and sculpture existed in Mexico long before the arrival of the conquistadores. Combining this tradition with imported Spanish techniques, artists of the colonial period produced works of remarkable depth and purity. The late colonial years, however, were characterized by a purely academic output. One of the most significant artists of the early 20th century was José Guadalupe Posada (1851–1913), who produced violent, powerful posters, lithographs, and woodcuts of contemporary scenes. His followers, Diego Rivera, David Alfaro Siqueiros, and José Clemente Orozco, were the leaders of a remarkable group of distinctly Mexican artists who revived the art of fresco painting and produced important easel painting as well. Frida Kahlo (1910–54) used motifs from Mexican popular art in her paintings, which mix fantasy with autobiography and self portraiture. *See also* LATIN AMERICAN ART AND ARCHITECTURE.

As weavers, potters, and silversmiths, Mexican artisans produce a variety of beautiful and distinctive products, which attract connoisseurs throughout the world. Mexican artisans are also noted for their work in wood, glass, and leather.

Performing Arts. The Mexican film industry now produces about 40 to 50 films each year. Mexican film actors, including Cantinflas (Mario Moreno; 1911–93), Pedro Armendariz (1912–63), and Dolores Del Rio (1905–83), achieved worldwide fame, as did the director Emilio Fernandez (1904–86) and the cinematographer Gabriel Figueroa (1907–   ). Both theatrical and musical performances, especially opera, are popular in Mexican cities. The Ballet Folklórico de Mexico, a troupe specializing in Mexican folk dances, is based in Mexico City but tours internationally. Bullfighting, a reminder of Mexico's Spanish past, has long been cultivated.

Libraries and Museums. Most good libraries in Mexico are found within the university system. The National Library, which houses a collection of rare documents, is affiliated with the National Autonomous University of Mexico in Mexico City. Mexico also has many government libraries that are connected with the various ministries.

Many museums are located throughout the country. The National Historical Museum, devoted to history since the Spanish conquest, is located in Chapultepec Castle in Mexico City. Mayan, Aztec, and other archaeological artifacts are found in the National Museum of Anthropology, also in Mexico City. Another noted archaeological collection is in Mérida, Yucatán. All are attached to the National Institute of Anthropology and History.

ECONOMY

Mexico reflects a shift from a primary-production economy, based on mining and agriculture, to a semi-industrialized nation. Economic achievements are the result of a vigorous private enterprise sector and government policies that have made economic growth a predominant objective. Traditionally, the government also emphasized Mexicanization of industry, and local control of companies engaged in mining, fishing, trans-

MEXICO

A massive caryatid figure from the ancient city of Tula, capital of the Toltec civilization, near modern Mexico City.
Kim Sinclair–Mexican Tourist Council

portation, and exploitation of forests was required by law. More recently, however, foreign investment in new enterprises has been actively encouraged, and government controls on many sectors of the economy have been loosened.

Mexico's gross domestic product (GDP) increased by 6.5% annually during 1965–80 but only 1.5% yearly during 1980–92. Weak oil prices, rising inflation, a foreign debt of more than $100 billion, and worsening budget deficits exacerbated the nation's economic problems in the mid-1980s, although the economic picture brightened toward the end of the decade. In the early 1990s the gross national product was $295.1 billion (about $3470 per capita), and the annual budget (excluding state-owned companies) totaled $58.9 billion in revenue and $48.3 billion in expenditure.

Agriculture. About 26% of the labor force is engaged in agriculture, and a substantial number of agricultural workers are employed on *ejidos*, or communal farms. The government introduced land reform in 1915; since then, much land had been redistributed to the *ejidos*. Agricultural production has often been impeded by lack of rainfall. Irrigation

Mexico

- ⊛ National Capital
- ★ State Capital
- • Other City
- ■ Ruins

1:11,200,000

0 — 125 — 250 mi
0 — 125 — 250 km

Lambert Conformal Conic Projection

© GeoSystems Global Corp.

E
F
G
H
OKLAHOMA
ARKANSAS
MISSISSIPPI
ALABAMA
GEORGIA
Red
Dallas
Houston
Brazos
San Antonio
Piedras Negras
Rio Grande
Corpus Christi
Nuevo Laredo
Anáhuac
NUEVO LEÓN
Reynosa
Matamoros
Monterrey
Linares
TAMAULIPAS
Ciudad Victoria
Ciudad Mante
Tampico
Pánuco
Sierra Madre Oriental
Poza Rica
QUERÉTARO
Querétaro
Tula
HIDALGO
Pachuca
MÉXICO
TLAXCALA
Mexico City
Tlaxcala
Toluca
Cuernavaca
Cholula
Puebla
Orizaba
Jalapa Enríquez
Veracruz
Citlaltépetl 5747 m (18,855 ft)
MORELOS
PUEBLA
Taxco
Tehuacán
Iguala
Balsas
Chilpancingo
Acapulco
Sierra Madre del Sur
OAXACA
Oaxaca
Puerto Escondido
VERACRUZ
Minatitlán
Coatzacoalcos
Isthmus of Tehuantepec
Juchitán de Zaragoza
Salina Cruz
Tonalá
Gulf of Tehuantepec
TABASCO
Villahermosa
CHIAPAS
Grijalva
Tuxtla Gutiérrez
San Cristóbal de las Casas
Comitán
Tapachula
Usumacinta
Gulf of Mexico
Bay of Campeche
Tropic of Cancer
Ciudad del Carmen
Campeche
CAMPECHE
Yucatán Peninsula
Mérida
Chichén Itzá
Valladolid
YUCATÁN
QUINTANA ROO
Cabo Catoche
Cancún
Isla de Cozumel
Chetumal
BELIZE
Belize City
Belmopan
Gulf of Honduras
GUATEMALA
Guatemala
HONDURAS
San Pedro Sula
Tegucigalpa
EL SALVADOR
San Salvador
100°
95°
90°
85°
30°
25°
20°
15°
1
2
3
4
5
99° 15′
99°
19° 30′
19° 15′
Cuautitlán
Teotihuacán
Cuautitlán Izcalli
Tultitlán
Presa de Guadalupe
Coacalco
Acolman
Tepexpan
Ecatepec
Tezoyuca
Ciudad Adolfo López Mateos
Chiconcuac
Tlalnepantla
Texcoco
Naucalpan de Juárez
Azcapotzalco
MÉXICO
Gustavo A. Madero
San Vicente Chicoloapan de Juárez
Mexico City
Chimalhuacán
Netzahualcóyotl
Iztacalco
Los Reyes
Cuajimalpa
Iztapalapa
Villa Obregón
Coyoacán
Ixtapaluca
Magdalena Contreras
DISTRITO FEDERAL
Tláhuac
Tlalpan
Chalco
Xochimilco
Cocotitlán
0 4 8 mi
0 4 8 km

MEXICO

Mexico: Map Index

States

Aguascalientes D3
Baja California A1
Baja California Sur B2
Campeche F4
Chiapas F4
Chihuahua.....................C2
Coahuila D2
Colima..........................D4
Distrito Federal ......E4, Inset
Durango C3
Guanajuato D3
Guerrero D4
Hidalgo.........................E3
Jalisco D4
México ....E4, Inset
Michoacán....................D4
Morelos E4
Nayarit..........................C3
Nuevo León D2
Oaxaca E4
Puebla E4
Querétaro D3
Quintana Roo G4
San Luis Potosí..............D3
Sinaloa..........................C3
Sonora B1
Tabasco F4
Tamaulipas E3
Tlaxcala E4
Veracruz E4
Yucatán G3
Zacatecas......................D3

Cities and Towns

Acámbaro D4
Acapulco E4
Acolman ....Inset
Agua Prieta C1
Aguascalientes,
  state capital D3
Ameca D3
Anáhuac D2
Azcapotzalco..............Inset
Caborca B1
Campeche,
  state capital F4
Cancún G3
Celaya D3
Chalco ....Inset
Chetumal,
  state capital G4
Chiconcuac...............Inset
Chihuahua,
  state capital C2
Chilpancingo,
  state capital E4
Chimalhuacán.............Inset
Cholula.........................E4
Ciudad Acuña D2
Ciudad Adolfo López
  Mateos ....Inset
Ciudad Camargo C2
Ciudad Constitución.......B3
Ciudad del Carmen F4
Ciudad Juárez C1
Ciudad Mante E3
Ciudad Obregón C2
Ciudad Valles E3
Ciudad Victoria,
  state capital E3
Coacalco ....Inset
Coatzacoalcos................F4
Cocotitlán ....Inset
Colima, state capital........D4
Comitán F4
Concepción del Oro D3
Coyoacán ....Inset
Cuajimalpa ....Inset
Cuauhtémoc C2
Cuautitlán ....Inset
Cuautitlán Izcalli ....Inset
Cuernavaca,
  state capital E4
Culiacán, state capital C3
Delicias C2
Durango, state capital D3
Ecatepec ....Inset
Ensenada A1
Fresnillo D3
Gómez Palacio..............D2
Guadalajara,
  state capital D3
Guanajuato,
  state capital D3
Guasave C2
Guaymas B2
Guerrero Negro B2
Gustavo A. Madero ....Inset
Hermosillo,
  state capital B2
Hidalgo del Parral C2
Iguala E4
Irapuato D3
Ixtapa D4
Ixtapaluca ....Inset
Iztacalco ....Inset
Iztapalapa ....Inset
Jalapa Enríquez,
  state capital E4
Jiménez D2
Juchitán de Zaragoza F4
La Paz, state capital B3
Lázaro Cárdenas D4
León D3
Linares E3
Loreto B2
Los Mochis..................C2
Los Reyes ....Inset
Magadalena de Kino B1
Magdalena
  Contreras ....Inset
Manzanillo...................D4
Matamoros E2
Matehuala D3
Mazatlán C3
Mérida, state capital......G3
Mexicali, state capital....A1
Mexico City, national
  capital ....E4, Inset
Minatitlán....................F4
Monclova....................D2
Monterrey, state capital ..D2
Morelia, state capital D4
Naucalpan de
  Juárez ....Inset
Navojoa C2
Netzahualcóyotl ....Inset
Nogales B1
Nueva Casas Grandes C1
Nueva Rosita D2
Nuevo Laredo..............E2
Oaxaca, state capital......E4
Ocotlán D3
Ojinaga D2
Orizaba........................E4
Pachuca, state capital E3
Piedras Negras..............D2
Poza Rica E3
Puebla, state capital E4
Puerto Escondido E4
Puerto Peñasco.............B1
Puerto Vallarta C3
Querétaro, state
  capital D3
Reynosa E2
Salina Cruz E4
Saltillo, state capital D2
San Cristóbal de
  las Casas F4
San Felipe....................B1
San Lucas....................C3
San Luis Potosí,
  state capital D3
San Luis Río Colorado...B1
San Pedro de
  las Colonias D2
Santa Rosalía B2
San Vicente Chicoloapan
  de Juárez................Inset
Tampico E3
Tapachula F5
Taxco E4
Tecomán D4
Tehuacán E4
Teotihuacán ....Inset
Tepexpan ....Inset
Tepic, state capital D3
Texcoco ....Inset
Tezoyuca....................Inset
Tiáhuac ....Inset
Tijuana A1
Tlaipan ....Inset
Tlalnepantla ....Inset
Tlaxcala, state capital E4
Toluca, state capital E4
Tonalá..........................F4
Torreón D2
Tultitlán.....................Inset
Tuxtla Gutiérrez,
  state capital F4
Uruapan D4
Valladolid G3
Veracruz E4
Villa Ahumada C1
Villahermosa,
  state capital F4
Villa Obregón ....Inset
Xochimilco ....Inset
Zacatecas, state capital ..D3

Other Features

Anáhuac, depression.......D3
Balsas, river E4
Bolsón de Mapimí,
  depression D2
California, gulf B1
Campeche, bay..............F4
Catoche, cape G3
Cedros, island...............A2
Chapala, lake D3
Chichén Itzá, ruins G3
Citlaltépetl, mt..............E4
Conchos, river C2
Cozumel, island G3
Eugenia, point A2
Fuerte, river C2
Grijalva, river................F4
Guadalupe,
  reservoir..................Inset
Marías, islands C3
Pánuco, river................E3
Revillagigedo, islands B4
Rio Grande (Río Bravo),
  river D2
San Lucas, cape B3
Sierra Madre del Sur,
  mts. D4
Sierra Madre Occidental,
  mts. C2
Sierra Madre Oriental,
  mts. D2
Tehuantepec, gulf E4
Tehuantepec, isthmus F4
Tiburón, island B2
Tula, ruins D3
Usumacinta, river F4
Vizcaíno, desert..............B2
Yaqui, river C2
Yucatán, peninsula G4

256

projects, however, have increased land under cultivation, and soil conservation has improved yields. Mexico not only supplies most of its basic needs but also exports produce. In the early 1990s the major agricultural commodities (with yearly output in metric tons) were sugarcane (40 million), corn (15 million), sorghum (5.1 million), wheat (3.6 million), and rice (361,000). Other products include soybeans (670,000), coffee (207,000), oranges (2.9 million), tomatoes (1.4 million), bananas (1.6 million), potatoes (1.2 million), dry beans (804,000), and green chilies (760,000).

Livestock in the early 1990s included about 30.2 million cattle, 16.5 million hogs, 11 million goats, 6.2 million sheep, 6.2 million horses, 6.4 million mules and asses, and 282 million chickens.

Forestry and Fishing. About 22% of Mexico is forested. Because of earlier abuse to rich timber stands, all timber cutting is strictly regulated by the government. Roundwood production in the early 1990s annually totaled about 23.6 million cu m (about 883 million cu ft); about two-thirds of the wood was used for fuel. Mexico manufactures large amounts of forestry products; these include lumber, chicle, pitch, resins, and turpentine.

The most important fisheries are found off the coast of Baja California. The fishing industry is primarily controlled by cooperative societies that are granted monopolies of certain species. The principal fish caught are abalone, bass, pike, red snapper, pilchard and other sardines, anchovies, shrimp, and mackerel. The annual catch in the early 1990s was approximately 1.4 million metric tons.

Mining. Formerly, almost all mining companies in Mexico were foreign-held. Most, however, cooperated with government efforts in the 1960s to Mexicanize the industry, and majority control of each company is now held by Mexicans. The most valuable mineral resource is petroleum, produced chiefly in Veracruz, Tabasco, and Chiapas states; production is controlled by Petróleos Mexicanos (Pemex), a government-owned company. Also important is silver, which is found in every state. Rich gold fields are located on the Pacific slopes of the Sierra Madre Occidental; copper ore is mined near Guanajuato; iron ore is found in Coahuila and in Durango. In the early 1990s annual output (in metric tons) included 5.2 million of iron ore, 279,000 of copper ore, 178,800 of lead, 289,100 of zinc, 137,700 of manganese, 2320 of silver, and 10.4 of gold. Production of crude petroleum was 975 million barrels; natural gas, 42 billion cu m (1.5 trillion cu ft); and coal, 10.5 million metric tons. Significant quantities of antimony, barites, fluorite, graphite, phospate rock, and sulfur also were recovered.

Manufacturing. Mexican industry is among the most developed in Latin America. Until the late

Tarascan Indians fish with their curious butterfly nets on Lake Pátzcuaro, a resort area in Michoacán, western Mexico.
Photo Researchers, Inc.

MEXICO

1980s, most new factories were built in northern Mexico as *maquiladoras,* labor-intensive plants assembling imported parts into finished goods for export; more recently, however, U.S. firms have invested heavily in well-equipped modern facilities producing motor vehicles and other consumer items for the U.S. market. Major industrial plants in Mexico also include factories turning out machinery and electronic equipment; petroleum refineries; foundries; meat-packing plants; paper mills; cotton mills; tobacco-processing plants; and sugar refineries. Other industrial products include clothing, fertilizer, chemicals, cement, glass, pottery, and leather goods. Estimated yearly manufacturing output in the early 1990s included 534,000 passenger cars, 5.9 million metric tons of crude steel, 2.5 million metric tons of wheat flour, 642,000 washing machines, and 435,000 televisions.

Energy. More than 74% of Mexico's electricity is produced in thermal installations, 19% by hydroelectric facilities, 4% from geothermal sources, and 2% in nuclear installations. In the early 1990s electricity-generating capacity was about 29.3 million kw, and annual output of electricity was some 126.4 billion kwh.

Commerce, Banking, and Trade. The Mexican unit of currency is the new peso, consisting of 100 centavos. The new peso, equivalent to 1000 former pesos, was introduced in 1993 (5.89 new pesos equal U.S.$1; 1995). The central bank and bank of issue is the Bank of Mexico (1925), which is modeled after the U.S. Federal Reserve System. Mexico's commercial banking system, nationalized in 1982, was restored to private control in the early 1990s.

Annual exports in the early 1990s were valued at about $27.5 billion, and imports in the same period cost approximately $48.2 billion per year. Major exports include crude petroleum, machinery, transportation equipment, fruits and vegetables, coffee, chemicals, and basic manufactures. The country's chief imports include machinery, transportation equipment, chemicals, agricultural commodities, and iron and steel. The great bulk of Mexico's trade is with the U.S.; other important trade partners are Japan, Germany, Brazil, Canada, France, and Spain. Tourism, border trade, foreign investments, and remittances from Mexican workers in the U.S. are significant sources of foreign exchange revenue.

Transportation. The state-run railway system includes about 26,330 km (about 16,360 mi) of operated railroad track. The highway system includes about 243,510 km (about 151,310 mi) of roads, of which some 35% are paved. Several highways traverse the country, including four main routes between the U.S. border and Mexico City that form part of the Pan-American Highway system. Air services have been intensively developed, and the country now has more than 1700 airports and landing fields. Chief airlines are Aerovías de México and Compañía Mexicana de Aviación. The merchant fleet includes some 635 vessels with a total deadweight tonnage of 1.5 million.

Communications. In the early 1990s Mexico had about 285 daily newspapers. Mexico City had 15 dailies, of which *Esto,* with a circulation of 450,000, was the largest. Telephones in Mexico numbered approximately 11.1 million. Radio stations numbered about 1040, and there were more than 750 television stations. Some 21.5 million radios and 12.4 million televisions were in use.

Labor. The Mexican labor force totaled about 31.2 million persons in the early 1990s. About 35% of the labor force is organized. The largest union in the country is the Confederación de Trabajadores de México (Confederation of Mexican Workers), with about 5.5 million members. Statutes prescribe minimum wages and a maximum work week of six 8-hour days.

GOVERNMENT

Mexico is a federal republic governed under a constitution promulgated in 1917.

Executive. National executive power is vested in a president, who must be Mexican-born and the child of a native Mexican. The president is popularly elected for a 6-year term and may never be reelected. The president appoints the cabinet, which is confirmed by the congress.

Legislature. Legislative power is vested in a bicameral congress. The upper house, the Senate, has 128 members popularly elected for 6-year terms. Four senators are elected from each state and from the federal district. The lower house, the Chamber of Deputies, is made up of 500 members elected to 3-year terms. Three hundred are elected from single-member districts based on population, and the remainder are elected according to proportional representation. Senators and deputies may not serve two consecutive terms.

Judiciary. The country's highest tribunal is the supreme court of justice, made up of 21 full-time members appointed by the president with the consent of the Senate. Other important judicial bodies include circuit courts and district courts.

Local Government. The chief executive of each state is a governor, popularly elected to a 6-year term. The governor of the federal district is appointed by the president of Mexico. Legislative power in the states is vested in chambers of deputies, whose members are elected to 3-year terms.

Political Parties. The Partido Revolucionario Institucional (Institutional Revolutionary party; PRI) is the largest and most important political party in Mexico. It was formed in 1928 as the Partido Nacional Revolucionario (National Revolutionary party) and has been continuously in power since that time, although under several different names. Opposition parties exist, but not until the 1980s did they represent a serious challenge to the PRI. Chief among them is the Partido de Acción Nacional (National Action party; PAN), a conservative, pro-Catholic group drawn primarily from the middle class. In 1994 elections the PRI finished first and PAN second; a center-left group, the Partido de la Revolución Democrática (Democratic Revolutionary party; PRD) was third.

Health and Welfare. Most public-health activities are administered by the Mexican ministry of health. Diseases such as smallpox and cholera have been eliminated; however, a shortage of medical personnel exists in the rural areas, and population growth continues to outpace the installation of modern water and sewage systems. Average life expectancy at birth in the early 1990s was 73 years for women, 67 years for men; the infant mortality rate was 35 per 1000 live births.

The Mexican Social Security Institute supervises welfare programs, which are financed by contributions from the government, employers, and employees. Services include medical care for the poor, low-cost housing, and accident, illness, maternity, and old-age insurance.

Defense. The volunteer army in Mexico is supplemented by conscripts selected by lottery for part-time service for a one-year period. In the early 1990s the country maintained an army of 130,000 members, a navy of 37,000 members, and an air force of 8000 members.

HISTORY

Mexico was the site of some of the earliest and most advanced civilizations in the western hemisphere. There is evidence that a hunting people populated the area in 21,000 BC or earlier. Crop cultivation began around 8000 BC; squashes were probably the first produce. The first major Mesoamerican civilization was established by the Olmec, who flourished between about 1500 and 600 BC. The Mayan culture attained its peak about the 6th century AD. The warlike Toltec migrated from the north, and in the 10th century they established an empire in the Valley of Mexico. They founded the cities of Tula (q.v.)

A girl of the state of Yucatán weaves straw baskets, a product of village artisanry. The Yucatán Peninsula was the site of the Mayan and Toltec civilizations that flourished in pre-Columbian times. Mexican Tourist Council

MEXICO

El Castillo, the pyramidal principal temple at Chichén Itzá, city of the ancient Mayan civilization in Yucatán State.
Kim Sinclair—Mexican Tourist Council

and Tulancingo (north of present-day Mexico City) and developed a great civilization still evidenced by the ruins of magnificent buildings and monuments.

The Aztec Empire. In the 12th century the Toltec were vanquished and dispersed by the Chichimeca, who took over the Toltec civilization. A century later seven allied Nahuatlan tribes entered the valley from the north, probably coming from areas now in New Mexico and Arizona. In 1325 the Aztec, or Mexica, the leading tribe, founded a settlement named Tenochtitlán (q.v.) in an area surrounded by marshes in Texcoco, one of the valley lakes. As the settlement grew, its military strength was increased by the construction of causeways that dammed the waters of the surrounding marshes and made the town a virtually impregnable island fortress. Under Itzcoatl, the first Aztec emperor (1360?–1440), the Aztec extended their influence through the entire Valley of Mexico, becoming the preeminent power in central and southern Mexico by the 15th century. Their civilization, based on that of the Toltec and Chichimeca, was highly developed, both intellectually and artistically. The Aztec economy was dependent on agriculture, particularly the cultivation of corn. As they grew wealthy and powerful, the Aztec built great cities and developed an intricate social, political, and religious organization.

The first European explorer to visit Mexican territory was Francisco Fernández de Córdoba (1475–1526), who in 1517 discovered traces of the Maya in Yucatán. A year later Juan de Grijalva (1489?–1527) headed an expedition that explored the eastern coast of Mexico and brought back to the Spanish colony in Cuba the first reports of the rich Aztec Empire. These reports prompted Diego Velázquez, governor of Cuba, to dispatch a large force in 1519, under the command of Hernán Cortés. For the history of the conquest of the Aztec Empire and of Mexico by the Spanish, *see* CORTÉS, HERNÁN.

The Colonial Period. In 1535, some years after the fall of the Aztec capital, the basic form of colonial government in Mexico was instituted with the appointment of the first Spanish viceroy, Antonio de Mendoza (c. 1490–1552). For the remainder of the Spanish colonial period, from 1535 to 1821, a total of 61 viceroys ruled Mexico. Mendoza and his successors directed a series of military and exploratory expeditions, which eventually made present-day Texas, New Mexico, and California part of New Spain.

A distinguishing characteristic of colonial Mexico was the exploitation of the Indians. Although thousands of Indians were killed during the Spanish conquest, they continued to be the great majority of inhabitants of New Spain, speaking their own languages and retaining much of their own culture. Inevitably they became the laboring class. Although they were decreed nominally free and entitled to wages by Spain, in actuality they were treated little better than slaves. Their plight was the result of the *repartimiento* system, by which Spanish nobles, priests, and soldiers were granted not only large tracts of land but also jurisdiction over all Indian residents. The government of Spain made several attempts to regulate the exploitation of Indian labor on farms and in mines. Reforms decreed by Spain, however, were largely ineffectual because of the difficulty of enforcement. The condition of the Indians became a primary concern of the Mexican government when the colonial administration was later overthrown.

A second characteristic of colonial Mexico was the position and power of the Roman Catholic church. Franciscan, Augustinian, Dominican, and Jesuit missionaries entered the country with the conquistadores. Juan de Zumárraga (1468-1548) became the first bishop of Mexico in 1528, and the country was created an archbishopric about 1548. The Mexican church became enormously wealthy through gifts and bequests that could be held in perpetuity. Before 1859, when church holdings were nationalized, the church owned one-third of all property and land.

A third characteristic was the existence of rigid social classes: the Indians, the mestizos (an increasingly large group during the colonial era), black slaves, freed blacks and white Mexicans. The white Mexicans were themselves divided. Highest of all classes was that of the *peninsulares*, those born in Spain, as opposed to the *criollos*, or Creoles, persons of pure European descent who had been born and raised in New Spain. The *peninsulares* were sent from Spain to hold the highest colonial offices in both the civil and church administrations. They held themselves aloof from the Creoles, who were almost never given high office. The resentment of the Creoles became an influential force in the later movement for independence.

From the inception of the viceregal system, inefficiency and corruption in the colonial administration greatly concerned the home Spanish government. Bribery and extortion were common, despite periodic royal commissions of investigation. During the late 18th century Spain attempted to institute a series of administrative reforms, notably in the years 1789-94 under the viceroy Juan Vicente Güemez Pacheco, conde de Revilla Gigedo (1740-99), considered the greatest Spanish colonial administrator. These reforms did not eradicate the fundamental weaknesses of the system, and by the beginning of the 19th century Creole resentment and the inefficient govern-

An artist's conception of the meeting of Montezuma II, Aztec emperor of Mexico, and Hernán Cortés, commander of the Spanish expedition that arrived in 1519.
Bettmann Archive

ment of New Spain were tending basically to weaken the link between the colony and the parent country. To these internal conditions was added the importation of liberal political ideas from Europe, particularly after the French Revolution of 1789.

The occupation of Spain by Napoleon eventually resulted in the Mexican war for independence. Disorganized by the disaster that had overtaken the home government, the administrative leaders of New Spain began to quarrel among themselves, with no central authority to intervene. In 1808 the viceroy, under pressure from influential Creoles, permitted them to participate in the administration. Other *peninsular* officials objected and expelled the viceroy. In the midst of these factional struggles a political rebellion was begun by the Mexican people.

War for Independence. On Sept. 16, 1810, Miguel Hidalgo y Costilla, a priest in the small village of Dolores, raised the standard of revolt, demanding the abolition of Indian serfdom and caste distinctions. Although initially successful, the Hidalgo revolt was short-lived. The priest was captured by royalist forces and shot at Chihuahua in 1811. The leadership in the liberation movement passed to another priest, José María Morelos y Pavón, who in 1814 proclaimed a republic in Mexico, independent of Spain. A year later Morelos and his army were defeated by royalist forces under Agustín de Iturbide, a Creole general. The revolution continued under Vicente Guerrero (1783-1831), who headed a comparatively small army.

The Spanish revolution of 1820 altered the rebellion in Mexico. Liberal political tendencies in Spain dismayed the conservative Mexican leaders, who themselves began an intrigue designed to separate the viceroyalty from Spain. On their behalf Iturbide met Guerrero in 1821 and signed an agreement by which the two combined forces to bring about independence. Their plan, known as the Plan of Iguala, set forth three mutual guarantees: Mexico would become an independent country, ruled as a limited monarchy; the Roman Catholic church would be the state church; and the Spanish and Creoles would be given equal rights and privileges. The viceroy took no active measures against Iturbide and was forced to resign by the faction that opposed independence. The last viceroy of New Spain was Juan O'Donojú (1762-1821) who, on his arrival in Mexico in July 1821, was forced to accept the Treaty of Córdoba, marking the formal beginning of Mexican independence.

Empire and Republic. A turbulent period ensued. In 1822, by a coup d'etat, Iturbide made himself Emperor Agustín I, but was deposed ten months later by a revolt led, notably, by Antonio López de Santa Anna, his former aide. A republic was proclaimed, and Guadalupe Victoria (1789-1843) became the first president. Mexico, however, was unprepared for sudden democracy. A struggle began between the Centralists—a conservative group composed of church leaders, rich landowners, Creoles, and army officials resolved to maintain a highly centralized colonial form of government—and the Federalists—a liberal, anticlerical faction supporting the establishment of federated sovereign states and relief for the Indians and other oppressed groups. Guerrero, a liberal leader, became president in 1829, but was shot to death in 1831 by forces led by the political and military leader Anastasio Bustamante (1780-1853). Revolt followed revolt until 1833, when Santa Anna, a Centralist who was popular with the army, was elected president. Shortly after his coming to power, his policies involved the new republic in war.

War with the U.S. The residents of Texas, then under Mexican rule, had been angered in 1829 by a governmental decree abolishing slavery, and the plan by Santa Anna to centralize the government increased their resentment. Texas rebelled in 1836 and declared its independence after Santa Anna was decisively defeated by the Texan leader Sam Houston at San Jacinto on April 21, 1836. In 1846, as a result of friction between U.S. citizens and Mexicans, a dispute over the western boundary of Texas, and the desire of Americans to acquire California, the U.S. declared war on May 12 (see MEXICAN WAR). The Mexican forces were again routed, and U.S. troops occupied northern Mexico and, in 1847, Mexico City. Under the terms of the Treaty of Guadalupe Hidalgo on Feb. 2, 1848, the Rio Grande was fixed as the boundary of Texas and the territory now forming the states of California and New Mexico became part of the U.S. The Gadsden Purchase (q.v.) in 1853 clarified the New Mexico boundary and gave an additional strip of territory (now southern Arizona and a slice of southwestern New Mexico) to the U.S.

Mexico was confronted with a grave reconstruction problem after the war. Finances were devastated, and the prestige of the government, already weak, had considerably diminished. Santa Anna, compelled to resign after the war, returned from exile in 1853 and, with Centralist support, declared himself dictator. Early in 1854 a liberal revolt began, and after more than a year of intensive fighting, Santa Anna fled from Mexico. The revolution was the first event in a long, fierce struggle between the powerful classes that

Benito Juárez, Mexican Indian whose democratic ideas made him the great leader of Mexican liberals in the mid-19th century.   Bettmann Archive

had traditionally dominated Mexico and the liberal democrats who demanded a voice in the government.

Juárez and Maximilian. The great leader to emerge among the liberals was an Indian, Benito Pablo Juárez, who became famous for his integrity and unswerving loyalty to democracy. For the next 25 years Juárez was the principal influence in Mexican politics. A federal form of government, universal male suffrage, freedom of speech, and other civil liberties were embodied in the constitution of 1857. Conservative groups bitterly opposed the new constitution. They were supported by Spain, and in 1858 the War of the Reform, between conservative and liberal groups, devastated Mexico. The Juárez government was supported by the U.S., and by 1860 the Juárist armies had won decisively. Meanwhile, as provisional president (1858-61), Juárez had issued a decree nationalizing church property, separating church and state, and suppressing religious orders. Elected president in 1861, Juárez began to establish order. One of his first moves was the suspension of interest payments on foreign loans incurred by preceding governments. Angered by his decree, France, Great Britain, and Spain decided to intervene jointly for the protection of their investments in Mexico. The prime mover in the agreement was Napoleon III of France. A joint expedition occupied Veracruz in 1861, but when Napoleon's colonial ambitions became evident, the British and Spanish withdrew in 1862. For a year French troops battled their way through Mexico, finally entering Mexico City in June 1863. Juárez and his cabinet fled, and a provisional conservative government proclaimed a Mexican Empire and offered the Crown, at Napoleon's instigation, to Maximilian, archduke of Austria.

From 1864 to 1865 Maximilian and his wife, Carlotta (1840-1927), ruled the empire, but in 1865 France, under pressure from the U.S., which continued to recognize Juárez, withdrew its forces. The forces of Juárez reconquered the country after the French had been evacuated in 1867, and republican troops under Gen. Porfirio Díaz occupied Mexico City. Maximilian, besieged at Querétaro, was forced to surrender and, after a court-martial, was shot.

Again Juárez attempted to restore order, but was met with revolts. In 1871, after an indecisive election, the Congress of Mexico declared Juárez president. Díaz, a candidate who had been defeated, led an unsuccessful insurrection. Juárez died in 1872 and was succeeded by Sebastián Lerdo de Tejada (1827-89), head of the Mexican supreme court. In 1876, when Lerdo de Tejada sought reelection, Diáz led another revolt. Successful this time, he became president in 1877.

The Díaz Dictatorship. Except for one term from 1880 to 1884, when the nominal power was in the hands of one of his aides, Díaz ruled Mexico as a despot until 1911. Under the Díaz dictatorship Mexico made tremendous advances in economic and commercial development. Industrial plants, railroad extension, public works, harbor improvement, and public building were part of the Díaz program. Many of the new undertakings were financed and managed by foreigners. This became a major factor in the discontent of most Mexicans under the autocratic Díaz government. Moreover, Díaz favored the rich owners of large estates, increasing their properties by assigning them communal lands that belonged to the Indians. When the Indians revolted, they were sold into peonage. The dictator paid little attention to education for the people, and he favored the church, paying little heed to the secularization policy of 1859. Discontent and a spirit of revolt increased throughout Mexico.

In 1908, aware of this discontent, Díaz announced that he would welcome an opposition candidate in 1910 election, in order to prove his regard for democracy. The candidate put forward by the liberal group was Francisco Indalecio Madero. The influence of Madero grew and, although he was imprisoned for a time on a pretext by Díaz, the liberal leader became increasingly active. After Díaz was reelected in 1910, Madero was acknowledged as the leader of a popular

MEXICO

Pancho Villa, Mexican rebel leader of the early 20th century who was active in revolts against Presidents Francisco Madero and Venustiano Carranza.
King Features Syndicate

revolution. Díaz was forced to resign in 1911 and soon afterward left Mexico permanently.

Period of Turmoil. Madero was elected president in 1911, but was not forceful enough to end the political and military strife. Other rebel leaders, particularly Emiliano Zapata and Francisco (Pancho) Villa, completely refused to submit to presidential authority. Victoriano Huerta, head of the Madero army conspired with the rebel leaders and in 1913 seized control of Mexico City. Huerta became dictator and, four days after assuming power, had Madero murdered. New armed revolts under Zapata, Villa, and Venustiano Carranza began, and Huerta resigned in 1914. Carranza took power in the same year, and Villa at once declared war on him. In addition to the ambitions of rival military leaders, intervention by foreign governments seeking to protect the interests of their nationals added to the confusion. In August 1915 a commission representing eight Latin American countries and the U.S. recognized Carranza as the lawful authority in Mexico. The rebel leaders, with the exception of Villa, laid down their arms. The bandit leader incited his forces to commit atrocities against American nationals to show his resentment against the U.S. and in 1916 led a raid on Columbus, N.Mex. As a result, an American force under Gen. John J. Pershing was sent to Mexico, but Pershing and his troops saw little action because of Carranza's own hostility toward the U.S. Villa continued to disrupt the Mexican countryside until 1920.

The Revolution. A new constitution, promulgated in 1917, provided for a labor code, prohibited a president from serving consecutive terms, expropriated all property of religious orders, and restored communal lands to the Indians. Many provisions dealing with labor and social welfare were exceedingly advanced and for their day radical. Some of the most drastic were intended to curb foreign ownership of mineral properties and land.

Carranza was elected president in 1917, but turbulence continued. Although he did not enforce many of the constitutional provisions, he angered foreign oil companies by ruling that oil was an inalienable national resource and imposing a tax on oil lands and on oil contracts made before May 1, 1917. In 1920 three of the leading generals, Plutarco Elías Calles, Álvaro Obregón, and Adolfo de la Huerta (1877–1955), revolted against Carranza, who was killed in the ensuing conflict. Obregón was elected president in 1920.

When Obregón consented to arbitrate and adjust the claims of American oil companies, he was recognized by the U.S. in 1923. Later in the year, the U.S. supported the Obregón regime during an abortive revolt by de la Huerta. In 1924 Calles was elected president and began to put constitutional reforms, chiefly agrarian, into effect. He also rehabilitated Mexican finances, instituted an educational program, and succeeded in adjusting the dispute with the foreign oil companies. In carrying out religious reforms, however, Calles provoked considerable opposition.

The church refused to recognize the secularization provisions, and relations between church and state became severely strained. The tension was lessened largely through the mediation of Dwight W. Morrow (1873–1931), who became U.S. ambassador to Mexico in 1927. Morrow had previously mediated also in the oil dispute.

Obregón was reelected president in 1928 but was assassinated several months later by a religious fanatic. The provisional presidency was awarded by the congress to Emilio Portes Gil (1891–1978). The influence of Calles, however, remained paramount. Abelardo L. Rodríguez (1889–1967), a business associate of Calles, became provisional president in 1932. In the same year the National Revolutionary party (PNR), the official government party, projected a 6-year program for a "cooperative economic system tending toward socialism," and including a labor code, public works, distribution of land, and the seizure of foreign-owned oil lands.

The PNR program was put into effect in 1934 with the election of Lázaro Cárdenas as president. Cárdenas emphasized agrarian reforms, social welfare, and education. In 1936 an expropriation law was passed enabling the government to seize private property whenever necessary for public or social welfare. The national Railways of Mexico were nationalized in 1937, as were the subsoil rights of the oil companies. The Mexican oil workers struck for higher wages that same year. In 1938, after a supreme court decision had upheld their claims and the foreign-owned oil companies had refused to pay, the Mexican government expropriated the oil properties. A government agency called Petróleos Mexicanos, or Pemex, was created to administer the nationalized industry. The expropriations seriously affected the Mexican oil industry, for it became difficult for Mexico to sell oil in U.S., Dutch, and British territories. Mexico was therefore forced to arrange barter deals with Italy,

The rebel leader Emiliano Zapata (dressed in black with cross on hat) with his followers. UPI

MEXICO

Germany, and Japan. The oil trade with these nations, however, was cut short by World War II.

In 1940 Manuel Ávila Camacho, endorsed by Mexican labor, was elected president. His policies were more conservative than those of Cárdenas. The so-called Good Neighbor Policy of the U.S. became dominant in Mexican politics. This policy, involving close cooperation with the U.S. in commercial and military matters, became considerably advanced in 1941, with the imminence of U.S. involvement in World War II. Mexico agreed to allow the U.S. Air Force to use Mexican airfields and also agreed to export critical and strategic materials (mostly scarce minerals) only to countries in the western hemisphere.

World War II. Consistent with its policy of cooperation with the U.S., Mexico severed diplomatic relations with Japan on Dec. 8, 1941, and with Italy and Germany three days later. On May 22, 1942, after the sinking of two Mexican ships by submarines, the Mexican Congress declared war on Germany, Italy, and Japan. In June of that year Mexico signed the declaration of the UN. Later that same year a trade agreement, establishing mutual tariff concessions, was negotiated by Mexico and the U.S. Complete military cooperation between the two nations was effected in 1943, when it was agreed that each should enlist into its army nationals of the other country who lived within its borders. Other wartime projects included a joint commission for economic cooperation, instituted to find methods to relieve the Mexican shortages of food and strategic materials, and a Mexican-U.S. industrial commission, appointed to plan the industrialization of Mexico. In 1944 Mexico agreed to pay U.S. oil companies $24 million, plus interest at 3 percent, for oil properties expropriated in 1938. Also in 1944, Mexican and U.S. officials developed a 20-year plan for the expansion of the government-controlled oil industry.

Postwar Mexico. In June 1945, Mexico became an original member of the UN. In 1946 Miguel Alemán Valdés succeeded Ávila as president, having been elected on a platform calling for a more equitable distribution of wealth, extensive irrigation works, and further industrialization of Mexico. Alemán continued close relations with the U.S. In 1947 the Export-Import Bank lent Mexico $50 million to be expended on public works and industrial development. Later that year the Mexican government announced that British and Dutch oil companies, claimants of $250 million for expropriated properties, had settled for $21 million. In 1948 the government, striving to reverse the unfavorable balance of trade, devalued the peso. Imports not essential for industrial development were sharply restricted. In March 1949, for the first time since the expropriations of 1938, two U.S. petroleum companies were permitted to drill for oil, under the supervision of Pemex. The government stabilized the peso in June with the aid of loans from the U.S. Treasury and the International Monetary Fund. National elections were held on July 3, 1949, and the government party, renamed the Institutional Revolutionary party (Partido Revolucionario Institucional, or PRI), won overwhelmingly in the Chamber of Deputies.

In 1950 the economic situation improved substantially when Mexico obtained an Export-Import Bank loan of $150 million for the financing of several projects to improve transportation, agriculture, and power facilities. The following year the problem of Mexican laborers who entered the U.S. to seek seasonal farm employment became a matter of grave concern to the two governments. Official agreements between Mexico and the U.S. provided for the legal entry of a specified number of such workers annually. Approximately 1 million, however, crossed the border illegally every year. The problem was further complicated by the demand of the Mexican government for guarantees against the exploitation of its citizens by U.S. employers and by the hostility of U.S. farm labor organizations toward the competition of Mexican migratory laborers willing to work for substandard wages. In March 1952 the U.S. Congress passed a bill providing for the punishment by fines and imprisonment of those recruiting and employing aliens who entered the country illegally.

Former Interior Minister Adolfo Ruiz Cortines (1891–1973), candidate of the PRI, was elected president of Mexico in 1952. In the following year the legislature ratified a constitutional amendment extending voting privileges to women. Ruiz Cortines was succeeded by Adolfo López Mateos (1910–69), a former minister of labor, in 1958. Reversing a tradition of presidential silence on relations with the Roman Catholic church, López Mateos declared that attainment of revolutionary goals should find no obstacle in religion. A controversial constitutional amendment empowering the government to force businesses to share profits with workers was approved in 1962. Peasant discontent had been demonstrated during the year by hunger marches and squatter invasions of private landholdings. Early in 1963 an Independent Peasants' Central party was formed to compete with the National Peasants Confederation in the dominant PRI. Speakers at the organizing congress said that the country still had 3 million landless peasants and that 9600 individuals owned 80 million ha (197 million acres) of land, of which only 20.2 million ha (50 million acres) were cultivated.

Recent History. In the 1964 presidential campaign the PRI candidate, Gustavo Díaz Ordaz, stressed the need to alleviate the plight of poor farmers. Supported by most of the political parties and opposed only by the candidate of the National Action party, Díaz Ordaz was elected on July 5. Mexico refused to comply with an Organization of American States decision, taken in July 1964 following charges of Cuban terrorist activity in Venezuela, to sever diplomatic relations with Cuba; a policy of noninterference in the affairs of other nations was cited in explanation. During the year the U.S. ended its program of importing seasonal Mexican workers, thus eliminating an important source of dollar earnings for Mexico. A more popular U.S. action was the official transfer to Mexico of approximately 160 ha (approximately 400 acres) of territory that had previously come under U.S. jurisdiction when the Rio Grande, which marks the U.S. boundary with Mexico, had shifted course.

In 1966 President Díaz Ordaz announced a 5-year plan putting into effect a program of development and economic planning. During the same year Pemex carried out a program to increase the number of petrochemical plants in operation. In an effort to improve regional economic ties, the Mexican president visited several Central American countries in 1967. During 1968 the government was confronted by violent student demonstrations, which threatened to prevent the staging of the Olympic Games held in Mexico City in October 1968. Hundreds were killed during the antigovernment agitation, which tapered off in 1969 but continued into the 1970s.

In 1970 Luis Echeverría Álvarez (1922–) became president; the former interior minister had been elected by a wide margin as the candidate of the PRI. During his 6-year term Echeverría pursued a more balanced strategy of economic growth so that all levels of Mexican society would benefit; he also adopted measures to reduce foreign control of the economy and to increase exports. Ties with the U.S. were loosened, and in their place Echeverría negotiated economic accords with several Latin American nations, Canada, the European Community, and the Soviet-sponsored Council for Mutual Economic Assistance. The Mexican economy grew at a healthy annual pace of 6.3 percent during 1970–74, but beginning in 1975 growth decreased markedly and inflation rose substantially. In an attempt to reduce the nation's foreign-trade deficit, the government in 1976 devalued the peso by more than 50 percent by changing from a fixed to a freely floating exchange rate. A potentially beneficial economic development was the discovery in 1974–75 of huge crude-petroleum deposits in Campeche, Chiapas, Tabasco, and Veracruz states. In late 1976 Echeverría decreed that about 100,000 ha (about 250,000 acres) of prime farmland in Sonora and Sinaloa states be expropriated with compensation.

José López Portillo, the PRI nominee, was elected president in 1976. A former finance minister, he followed a program of economic austerity after taking office in December; he called on workers to reduce wage demands and on businesspeople to hold down prices and to increase investment expenditures. Considerable improvement was registered the following years, although inflation remained high. In foreign affairs, López Portillo improved ties with the U.S. in 1977 and reestablished diplomatic relations with Spain after a lapse of 38 years.

Oil production more than doubled during the latter half of the 1970s, and this, combined with substantial price increases, afforded Mexico under López Portillo a more meaningful independence, especially in relations with the U.S.

During the '80s the country pursued an assertive hemispheric policy. In 1982 Miguel de la Madrid Hurtado (1934–) was elected to succeed President López Portillo. By the mid-1980s a rapid increase in foreign debt, coupled with falling oil prices, had plunged the country into severe financial straits. Amid reports of widespread irregularities, the PRI claimed victory in congressional elections in 1985. However, the added burden of a devastating earthquake that same year, which

Carlos Salinas de Gortari giving his acceptance speech after being elected to the presidency of Mexico in 1988.
© Stephen Ferry/Gamma Liaison

killed 4200, kept Mexico's financial situation bleak. Carlos Salinas de Gortari (1948–), the PRI candidate, was elected president in 1988, again amidst protests about electoral fraud. Also in 1988 hurricane Gilbert devastated the Yucatán peninsula and severely damaged the area south of Texas; overall damage was estimated at $880 million. In 1989 the Salinas government sped up the privatization of state-controlled corporations and modified restrictive trade and investment regulations to encourage foreign investment by permitting full control of corporations by foreign investors. In October Salinas and U.S. President George Bush, meeting in Washington, D.C., signed what was described as the broadest trade and investment agreement ever concluded between the two nations. In July 1992 constitutional changes abolished restrictions imposed on the Roman Catholic church in 1917. In December Presidents Salinas and Bush and Prime Minister Brian Mulroney of Canada signed the North American Free Trade Agreement (NAFTA).

Ratified in 1993, NAFTA took effect on Jan. 1, 1994. That day, armed Indian guerrillas calling themselves the Zapatista National Liberation Army took over several towns in Chiapas, Mexico's southernmost state. Federal troops moved in, and dozens of Indians were killed. Negotiations with the Zapatistas led in early March to a preliminary accord in which the Salinas government pledged political, judicial, social, and land reforms. Later that month, the PRI presidential candidate, Luis Donaldo Colosio Murrieta (1950–94) was assassinated while campaigning in Tijuana. His replacement, Ernesto Zedillo Ponce de León (1951–), an economist who had been Colosio's campaign manager, won the presidential election in August.

For further information on this topic, see the Bibliography in volume 28, sections 645, 666, 726, 847, 1119–20, 1122–23.

MEXICO, GULF OF, arm of the Atlantic Ocean, bordered on the N by the U.S., on the E by Cuba, and on the S and W by Mexico. It covers an area of about 1,812,990 sq km (about 700,000 sq mi) and extends about 1770 km (about 1100 mi) from E to W and some 1287 km (some 800 mi) from N to S. The gulf is connected with the Atlantic by the narrow Straits of Florida and with the Caribbean Sea through the Yucatán Channel. Major rivers entering the gulf include the Mississippi, Brazos, and Rio Grande. Shrimping is important in shallow coastal waters, and petroleum deposits are located in the Bay of Campeche (a S arm of the gulf) and off the Louisiana and Texas coasts.

MEXICO, NATIONAL AUTONOMOUS UNIVERSITY OF, institution of higher learning, in Villa Obregón, a suburb of Mexico City, Mexico, and supported by the national government. The University was founded in 1551 by Prince Philip, later Philip II of Spain, and approved by a papal bull as the Royal and Pontifical University of Mexico in 1595. It was closed in 1865, reestablished as the National University of Mexico in 1910, became autonomous in 1929, and was reorganized in 1945. The university consists of the faculties of accounting and business administration, architecture, chemistry, dentistry, economics, engineering, law, medicine, philosophy and letters, political and social sciences, professional studies, psychology, sciences, and veterinary medicine and zoology. The institution also maintains the national schools of music, nursing and obstetrics, plastic arts, and social work. More than two dozen research institutes, including an astronomical observatory, are also affiliated with the university. The *licenciado* or a professional title, either the equivalent of a U.S. bachelor's degree, is awarded after four to five years of study.

The main library (1950), the work of the architect Juan O'Gorman (1905–82), is decorated with a spectacular exterior mural composed of colored stones; O'Gorman's mosaic design utilizes motifs found in ancient Mexican codices.

MEXICO CITY, city, S central Mexico, capital and largest city of the country, in the Distrito Federal. Situated in the Valley of Mexico, a highland basin, at an elevation of about 2350 m (about 7710 ft), the city is bounded by mountains on three sides. The greater urban area is one of the largest in the western hemisphere and dominates the nation's political, economic, and cultural life.

Economy. More than half of Mexico's industrial output is produced in or near Mexico City. Manufactures include textiles, chemicals and pharmaceuticals, electric and electronic items, steel, and transportation equipment; in addition, a variety of foodstuffs and light consumer goods are produced. Mexico City is the center of an emerging manufacturing belt that stretches from Guadalajara in the W to Veracruz on the Gulf Coast in the E. Major highways and railroads radiate from the city to all parts of the country. A huge international airport is located E of the city. Transportation within Mexico City has been chronically congested, partly because of the narrow old streets; an important improvement was the opening, in 1970, of a subway system.

The Urban Landscape. For the most part, Mexico City is a low, sprawling mass of gray and brown buildings set along a rectangular pattern of narrow streets. The pattern is broken by several broad boulevards lined with modern high-rise apartment and commercial buildings, by several large open plazas, and by numerous forested parks. The parks are popular with residents, who meet to talk, stroll, and enjoy the city's dry, springlike climate.

The center of the city has historically been the Zócalo, or Plaza of the Constitution, which occupies the site of the central square of the Aztec city Tenochtitlán, flanked by the massive baroque National Cathedral (begun 1573, completed 1675), the Municipal Palace (1720), and the National Palace (1792), containing the office of the president and the Senate. From the Zócalo the major avenue extends N to the Plaza of the Three Cultures, which has Aztec, Spanish colonial, and modern structures, and S to the sprawling Chapultepec Park, which contains several museums, a zoo, and Chapultepec Castle, the former presidential residence. The city's numerous suburbs and neighborhoods of great diversity range from such an elegant residential area as that of Pedregal, with its modernistic architecture, to the crowded squatter settlement of Netzahualcóyotl.

The rapid growth of Mexico City has created several problems, including serious air pollution, an increasingly inadequate water supply, and the subsidence, by as much as 6 m (20 ft), of parts of the downtown area into the soft lake deposits that underlie much of the city, damaging buildings and disrupting some water and sewerage lines. Supplemental water is now obtained from distant sources outside the valley, and modern multistoried buildings are built on huge steel and concrete drums to prevent their sinking.

Educational and Cultural Institutions. More than two dozen institutions of higher learning are located in or near Mexico City, including nine universities. Education in the city, and in the country as a whole, is dominated by the huge National Autonomous University of Mexico, in University City, a modern complex south of the Zócalo. Among the city's numerous museums are the strikingly designed National Museum of Anthropology, with unparalleled exhibits of pre-Columbian artifacts; the Museum of Modern Art; and the National Historical Museum. The city is known also for the vivid performances of the Ballet Folklórico at the Palace of Fine Arts and for the pilgrimages to the Basilica of the Virgin of Guadelupe, Mexico's most important religious shrine (1531), in the northern part of the city.

History. Aztec records set the founding date of their city at 1325, when a band of nomads from the north settled on an island in Lake Texcoco. The city, called Tenochtitlán, eventually expanded to a population of more than 250,000, and by the 16th century it had become the seat of the Aztec Empire. The Spanish explorer Hernán Cortés first saw the city in 1519. In 1521 his forces occupied and systematically leveled the great Aztec metropolis, building their own capital on the ruins. Lake Texcoco was filled in as the city expanded and was rebuilt in the Spanish architectural mode. From this new town, the Spanish explored and subdued the Indian inhabitants as far north as the present U.S. and south into Central America. Mexico City became the capital of all the Spanish provinces in the western hemisphere north of Costa Rica. The city remained in Spanish hands until 1821, when it was won by revolutionaries led by Augustín de Iturbide, later named emperor. During the Mexican War Mexico City was captured by U.S. forces in 1847 and held for five months. It was ruled by Emperor Maximilian and the French army from 1863 to 1867, when it was taken by President Benito Pablo Juárez. During the years of revolution following 1910, the capital was the scene of street fighting.

By the 1920s, plans for the urbanization of Mexico City had been initiated. Industrialization increased as mills and factories spread throughout the city. Slum-clearance and housing-development programs were initiated. Between 1930 and 1950, the population more than doubled. In 1985 an earthquake caused severe damage, leaving nearly 30,000 homeless and 4200 dead. To reduce air pollution in the city, in 1992 major industries were told to cut emissions or be forced to leave. Pop. (1990) 8,236,960; greater city (1990 est.) 14,800,000.
C.O.C.

MEYER, Adolf (1866–1950), Swiss-American psychiatrist and a founder of the mental hygiene movement. Meyer was born near Zürich and educated at the universities of Zürich, Paris, London, and Berlin. He settled in the U.S. in 1892 and was professor of psychiatry at the medical school of Cornell University in New York City from 1904 to 1909. From 1910 to 1941 Meyer was professor of psychiatry and director of the psychiatric clinic at Johns Hopkins University. Originator of the term *mental hygiene*, he is also known for his early efforts to establish psychiatry as a recognized branch of medicine.

MEYER, Julius Lothar (1830–95), German chemist, best known for his work on the periodic classification of the chemical elements. He was born in Varel, and educated at the universities of Zürich, Würzburg, Heidelberg, and Königsberg (now Kaliningrad). After 1876 he was professor of chemistry at the University of Tübingen. In a paper published in 1870 Meyer presented his discovery of the periodic law, stating that the properties of the elements are periodic functions of their atomic weights. This fundamental law was discovered independently in 1869 by the Russian chemist Dmitry Ivanovich Mendeleyev, who received more recognition for the discovery than did Meyer.

MEYERBEER, Giacomo, real name JAKOB LIEBMANN BEER (1791–1864), German composer, born in Berlin. His principal composition teacher was the German organist Abbé George Joseph Vogler (1749–1814). Meyerbeer went to Venice in 1815, where he adopted the tuneful manner of the Italian composer Gioacchino Rossini. Meyerbeer wrote six Italian-style operas, the most successful of which was *Il Crociato in Egitto* (The Crusader in Egypt, 1824). He then stopped composing, moved to Paris, and studied French opera, which differed from the Italian in its emphasis on lavish settings and ballets and in the predominance of choral and instrumental music over solo arias. It also treated more serious subjects, usually historical ones. In his final phase, Meyerbeer composed six French operas that established the grand-opera style and gained him fame throughout Europe. These include *Robert le diable* (Robert the Devil, 1831), *Les Huguenots* (1836), *Le prophète* (1849), and, in rehearsal at the time of his death, *L'Africaine* (1865). Meyerbeer's flair for the dramatic influenced the work of the German composer Richard Wagner.

MEYERHOLD, Vsevolod (1874–1940?), Russian actor and theater director, who, from the turn of the century to the mid-1930s, was an influential proponent of radical experimental theater. Meyerhold trained in Moscow for a theatrical career and became a member of the famed Moscow Art Theater in 1898; he headed its experimental studio in 1905. By then he had formulated his theories of "abstract" or "conditional" theater; actors were to be rigorously trained as puppets completely controlled by the director, and conventional staging was to be rejected in favor of abstract settings in the form of platforms and ramps. With the success of the Russian Revolution in 1917, Meyerhold joined the Communist party and was given his own theater in Moscow, where he produced (1918) Vladimir Mayakovsky's *Mystery-Bouffe*, the first Soviet play. From then until the mid-'30s he produced a succession of controversial plays, including his last, an eccentric adaptation of Aleksandr Pushkin's classic tale "The Queen of Spades" (1935). Meyerhold's idiosyncratic temperament finally brought him into disfavor with the Soviet regime, and he was arrested and imprisoned in 1938; his death reportedly occurred in 1940.

MEZZOTINT. *See* PRINTS AND PRINTMAKING.

MFECANE (Zulu, "crushing"), period of warfare and forced migrations among the peoples of southern Africa; in Sotho it is known as the *difaqane*. The mfecane was initiated by the Zulu under their aggressive military leader, Shaka. In 1818 he embarked on a great expansion of his realm in what is now the South African province of Natal, and during the next 10 years his depredations evicted several other peoples from their lands, setting off large-scale migrations and ultimately resulting in the formation of several new kingdoms. The Basotho nation was thus created by King Moshesh, who gathered his refugee followers in a defensible area of present-day Lesotho. The Ndebele marched north under Mzilikazi (c. 1790–1868) to carve out a kingdom on land previously occupied by the Shona in modern Zimbabwe. The Ngoni, led by Zwangendaba (c. 1785–c. 1848), also marched through the Shona country, where they destroyed Changamire in 1834 before they resumed their 20-year 1600-km (1000 mi) trek into present-day Tanzania. Soshangane (c. 1795–1859) took his Ndwandwe followers into present-day Mozambique, where he founded the powerful Gaza Empire. The Kololo, a Sotho group, were led by Sebetwane (d. 1851) into modern Zambia, where they settled after defeating the Lozi. In addition to these major groups, which clashed with one another at various times on their wanderings, setting off ripple effects in all directions, the Boers were on their Great Trek (q.v.) during the same period. By 1840, the mfecane was for the most part over.

MIAMI, city, seat of Dade Co., SE Florida, on Biscayne Bay at the mouth of the Miami R.; inc. 1896. Greater Miami, coextensive with Dade Co., is composed of approximately 25 incorporated municipalities. Together these communities make up what is referred to as Florida's "Gold Coast."

Miami, a seaport and one of the largest cities in the state, has a subtropical climate, numerous hotels, beautiful beaches, and abundant facilities for sports and recreation. Tourism is a principal economic activity of the city, which forms part of a world-famous resort area that also encompasses Miami Beach, Hialeah, Key Biscayne, Coral Gables, and Bal Harbour. Other industries include the processing of citrus fruit and vegetables grown in the surrounding area, construction, fishing, and the manufacture of transportation and electronic equipment, biomedical products, clothing, and printed materials. In addition, the city is an important international finance and trade center. It is served by Miami International Airport.

The area's many points of interest include the Miami Seaquarium, the Museum of Science, the Historical Museum of Southern Florida, Villa Vizcaya Museum and Gardens, and the Japanese Teahouse and Garden. The Orange Bowl stadium is the site of a postseason college football bowl game. Joe Robbie Stadium, in nearby Opa Locka, is the home of such professional sports teams as the Miami Dolphins (football) and the Florida Marlins (baseball); the Miami Arena is the home of the Miami Heat (basketball). Institutions of higher education include Barry College (1940), Saint Thomas of Villanova University (1961), Florida Memorial College (1879), Florida International University (1972), Saint John Vianney College Seminary (1959), Miami Christian College (1949), International Fine Arts College (1965), the Bauder Fashion College (1964), and several junior colleges. The University of Miami is in nearby Coral Gables. The Dade County Auditorium is the home of a symphony orchestra and a ballet company.

The Miami area was long inhabited by Indians. The first permanent non-Indian settlement was established in the 1870s near the site of U.S. Fort Dallas, which had been built (1835) during the Seminole Wars. Expansion began after the railroad magnate Henry M. Flagler (1830–1913) extended a railroad to the site in 1896 and promoted the city as a resort area. The Florida land boom of the mid-1920s led to rapid development, and during World War II several federal administrative and military agencies were established here. Large numbers of refugees from Cuba and other persons of Hispanic background settled in Miami beginning in the 1960s. Occasional hurricanes, notably in 1926, 1935, and 1992, caused considerable damage to the city and surrounding area. The name of the city may have been derived from a Tequesta Indian term for "big water," perhaps referring to Lake Okeechobee. Pop. (1980) 346,865; (1990) 358,548.

For further information on this topic, see the Bibliography in volume 28, section 1188.

MIAMI, UNIVERSITY OF, privately controlled institution of higher learning, in Coral Gables, Fla. It was founded in 1925 and opened for instruction in 1926. Degrees of bachelor, master, and doctor are awarded in architecture, arts and sciences, business administration, communications, education, engineering, law, medicine, music, and nursing. Proximity to the Atlantic Ocean and a mild climate enable the university to provide exceptional facilities for the study of marine plant and animal life. Noteworthy facilities on the campus include the library and an experimental elementary school.

MIAMI BEACH, city, Dade Co., SE Florida, on a long, narrow island (and adjacent islets) between the Atlantic Ocean and Biscayne Bay, near the city of Miami; inc. 1915. It is a world-famous, year-round resort, with palatial oceanfront hotels, ornate nightclubs, and extensive sand beaches. Causeways link it with the mainland. Horeb Seminary (1975) and the Talmudic College of Florida (1974) are here. A swampy area when settled in 1870, it was cleared (1907) and developed as a real-estate venture, mainly by John S. Collins (1837–1928). It grew rapidly during the Florida boom of the 1920s and again after 1945. It is the site of a large convention center; the Bass Museum of Art; and the Art Deco District in South Beach, more than 800 buildings from the 1920s and 1930s. Pop. (1980) 96,298; (1990) 92,639.

MIAMI INDIANS, North American Indian tribe of the Algonquian language family and of the Eastern Woodlands culture area. Originally occupying parts of the present states of Indiana, Ohio, Illinois, Michigan, and Wisconsin, they are closely associated and sometimes identified with the Wea and Piankashaw tribes. The Miami lived in mat-covered cabins, hunted bison (often called buffalo), and were noted for being industrious.

In the French and Indian War, the Miami sided with the French. In the American Revolution, they joined with other Ohio Valley tribes and fought for the British. Between 1795 and 1854 the Miami signed 13 treaties ceding most of their lands to the U.S. In 1827 most of the tribe moved to Kansas, where the remaining members still reside. Those who stayed in Indiana dissolved tribal relations in 1872, divided their land among themselves, and merged with the local population. In 1990, 3353 people claimed Miami ancestry.

See also AMERICAN INDIANS.

For further information on this topic, see the Bibliography in volume 28, sections 1105–8.

MIANTONOMO (1565?–1643), American Indian chief. He succeeded his uncle Canonicus (1565?–1647) as Narragansett chief in 1636. He was friendly with the Massachusetts and Connecticut colonists and helped them in the war against the Pequot tribe in 1637. He signed a treaty for perpetual peace between his tribe, the Connecticut colonists, and the Mohegan tribe in 1638, but violated it in a war against the Mohegan in 1643. Defeated and captured by Uncas, the Mohegan chief, he was taken to Boston, where he was tried by a committee of clergymen. Sentenced to be executed by Uncas, he was killed where he had been defeated, near the present site of Norwich, Conn.

MICA, term applied to a group of rock-forming minerals, crystallizing in the monoclinic system (*see* CRYSTAL), and characterized by a perfect basal cleavage that causes them to separate into very thin, somewhat elastic leaves. The micas are complex aluminum silicates, the color varying with the composition. They range in hardness (q.v.) from 2 to 4 and in sp.gr. from 2.7 to 3.2. The most important micas are muscovite, phlogopite, lepidolite, and biotite.

Muscovite, also called white mica or common mica, which contains potassium and aluminum, is transparent in thin sheets and translucent in

MICAH

thicker blocks; it is colored in light shades of yellow, brown, green, or red. Phlogopite, which contains potassium, magnesium, and aluminum, is transparent in thin sheets, vitreous or pearly in thick blocks, and is yellowish-brown, green, or white in color. Lepidolite, or lithia mica, which contains potassium, lithium, and aluminum, is usually lilac or pink in color. Biotite, which contains potassium, magnesium, iron, and aluminum, has a splendent luster and is usually dark green, brown, or black in color but is sometimes light yellow.

Muscovite and phlogopite are used as insulating material in the manufacture of electrical apparatus, particularly vacuum tubes. Scrap mica, obtained as waste material in the manufacture of sheet mica, is used as a lubricant when mixed with oils and as a fireproofing material.

MICAH, book of the Old Testament attributed to the 8th-century Hebrew prophet Micah. A younger contemporary of the prophet Isaiah, he began to prophesy before the fall of Samaria in 721 BC. The book is one of the 12 prophetic books of the Old Testament known, primarily because of their brevity, as the Minor Prophets.

Authorship. Tradition attributes the entire work to Micah, but most scholars now agree that it is a composite work. The first three chapters (with the exception of 2:12-13, which probably were added by a much later editor) generally are believed to have come from Micah. Considerable disagreement exists, however, concerning the rest of the book. Some maintain that it consists of two later collections of oracles (chap. 4-5, 6-7), preserving a few genuine utterances of Micah. Others hold that all the materials in chapters 4-7 reflect circumstances later than those of Micah's time; thus, the rest of the prophecy must be a later addition.

Content. The first three chapters of Micah contain threats of divine judgment directed against Samaria and Judah because of the oppression of the poor by the rich, the corruption of the priests and prophets, and the irresponsibility and immorality of the political leaders. Micah predicts that as a consequence of these evils Jerusalem and the Temple will be destroyed (3:12).

Chapters 4-5 contain prophecies of a new age of universal peace (4:1-4), at which time "the remnant of Jacob" (5:7) will be restored and ruled again by a descendant of King David (5:2-6). This shepherd king will be born, like David, in Bethlehem. (The last utterance has always been interpreted by Christians as a prediction of the birth of Jesus Christ.) Dates before, during, and after the exile (586-539 BC) have been suggested for the passages in these chapters.

Chapters 6-7 contain both threats of doom (6:1-7:6) and an oracle of hope (7:7-20). Included among the threats and denunciations, which are directed against Israel as a whole because of her general corruption, is a dialogue dramatizing God's "controversy with his people" (6:2). The prophet reminds Israel that she is required "to do justice and to love kindness, and to walk humbly with . . . God" (6:8). Some scholars have suggested that various passages containing threats may have come from Micah. The oracle of hope may date from exilic or postexilic times.

MICHAEL (Heb., "who is like God?"), called Saint Michael in the Christian churches, one of the seven archangels (*see* ARCHANGEL) in Judaism, Christianity, and Islam, presumed to be leader of the angels (see Dan. 10:13, 21; 12:1) and guardian angel of Israel. According to the pseudepigraphic Book of Enoch, Michael and his command of faithful troops defeated the rebellious archangel Lucifer and his followers, casting them into Hell. In the Talmud (q.v.), his relationship to the other angels is compared with that on earth of the high priest to Israel; thus, he is considered the immediate lawgiver to the prophet Moses on Sinai (see Acts 7:38).

Michael has been known as the patron of the sick and of grocers, sailors, and soldiers; he is also the patron saint of Germany. In art he appears holding scales or a banner and flourishing a sword against a dragon. Beginning in 1970 Michael's feast day was combined with that of the archangels Gabriel and Raphael on September 29. *See* MICHAELMAS.

A 12th-century German tapestry depicting St. Michael slaying the dragon.

MICHAEL VIII PALAEOLOGUS (c. 1224–82), Byzantine emperor (1261–82), who restored Greek rule over the Byzantine Empire, which had been conquered by the Crusaders allied with Venice and established (1204) as the Latin Empire of Constantinople. Michael served the emperors of Nicaea, a Greek principality established after the Latin victory. When Emperor Theodore II Lascaris (1222–58) died, Michael was named guardian of his son and succesor, but soon seized (1259) power for himself. In 1261 he captured Constantinople from Baldwin II, the last Latin emperor, and had himself crowned emperor. In the last years of his reign he fought against Charles I, the Angevin king of the Two Sicilies, who was covetous of his domain. Michael fomented a plot by Sicilian rebels in 1282—the so-called Sicilian Vespers (q.v.)—which finally turned the tide in his favor. He died later the same year on a campaign in Thrace.

MICHAEL CERULARIUS (c. 1000–59), patriarch (1043–57) of Constantinople at the time of the schism of 1054, which formally separated the Eastern Orthodox church from the Western Roman Catholic church. In 1043, three years after he became a monk, he was named patriarch by the Byzantine emperor Constantine IX, also called Monomachus (1000?–55), with whom he had conspired to overthrow the previous emperor, Michael IV (fl. 1034–41). Cerularius was stridently anti-Latin and particularly resentful of Rome's claim of primacy over all Christendom. In 1054 a papal legation issued a bull excommunicating him and the whole Eastern church. Cerularius answered by rejecting the papal assertion of supremacy and presenting an encyclical embodying the Byzantine defense of independence from and equality with the Western church. Cerularius also asserted the superiority of the church over the state, a position that led to his eventual dethronement and exile by the Byzantine emperor Isaac I Comnenus (c. 1005–61).

MICHAELMAS, old English name for the feast day of St. Michael and All Angels, on September 29. The date is believed to have been selected because it is the anniversary of the dedication of the Church of Saint Michael and All Angels on the Salarian Way in Rome in the 6th century. In England, Michaelmas is one of the quarter days, traditionally marked by the election of magistrates, the beginning of the legal and university terms, and the collection of quarterly rents.

MICHAELMAS DAISY. See ASTER.

MICHELANGELO (1475–1564), full name MICHELANGELO DI LODOVICO BUONARROTI SIMONI, Italian sculptor, architect, painter, and poet, who was one of the most inspired creators in the history of art and, with Leonardo da Vinci,

The Holy Family, a painting (c. 1503) by Michelangelo.
Uffizi Gallery–Scala/Art Resource

the most potent force in the Italian High Renaissance. He exerted a tremendous influence on his contemporaries (see MANNERISM) and on subsequent Western art in general.

A Florentine—although born March 6, 1475, in the small village of Caprese near Arezzo—Michelangelo continued to have a deep attachment to his city, its art, and its culture throughout his long life. He spent the greater part of his adulthood in Rome, employed by the popes; characteristically, however, he left instructions that he be buried in Florence, and his body was placed there in a fine monument in the church of Santa Croce.

Early Life in Florence. Michelangelo's father, a Florentine official named Ludovico Buonarotti (1444?–1534) with connections to the ruling Medici family, placed his 13-year-old son in the workshop of the painter Domenico Ghirlandaio. After about two years, he was in the sculpture school in the Medici gardens and shortly thereafter was invited into the household of Lorenzo de' Medici, the Magnificent. There he had an opportunity to converse with the younger Medici, two of whom later became popes (Leo X and Clement VII). He also became acquainted with such humanists as Marsilio Ficino and the poet Angelo Poliziano, who were frequent visitors. Michelangelo produced at least two relief sculptures by the time he was 16 years old, the *Battle of the Centaurs* and the *Madonna of the Stairs* (both 1489–92, Casa Buonarroti, Florence), which show that he had achieved a personal style at a very early age. His patron Lorenzo died in 1492; two years later Michelangelo fled Florence, when the Medici were temporarily expelled. He settled for a time in

MICHELANGELO

A panel from Michelangelo's decorations (1508-12) for the ceiling of the Sistine Chapel in the Vatican, Rome, showing the prophet Zacharias.
Scala–Editorial Photocolor Archives

Bologna, where in 1494 and 1495 he executed several marble statuettes for the Arca (Shrine) di San Domenico in the Church of San Domenico. **First Roman Sojourn.** Michelangelo then went to Rome, where he was able to examine many newly unearthed classical statues and ruins. He soon produced his first large-scale sculpture, the over-life-size *Bacchus* (1496-98, Bargello, Florence). One of the few works of pagan rather than Christian subject matter made by the master, it rivaled ancient statuary, the highest mark of admiration in Renaissance Rome. At about the same time, Michelangelo also did the marble *Pietà* (1498-1500), still in its original place in Saint Peter's Basilica. One of the most famous works of art, the *Pietà* was probably finished before Michelangelo was 25 years old, and it is the only work he ever signed. The youthful Mary is shown seated majestically, holding the dead Christ across her lap, a theme borrowed from northern European art. Instead of revealing extreme grief, Mary is restrained, and her expression is one of resignation. In this work, Michelangelo summarizes the sculptural innovations of his 15th-century predecessors such as Donatello, while ushering in the new monumentality of the High Renaissance style of the 16th century.

First Return to Florence. The high point of Michelangelo's early style is the gigantic (4.34 m/ 14.24 ft) marble *David* (Accademia, Florence), which he produced between 1501 and 1504, after returning to Florence. The Old Testament hero is depicted by Michelangelo as a lithe nude youth, muscular and alert, looking off into the distance as if sizing up the enemy Goliath, whom he has not yet encountered. The fiery intensity of David's facial expression is termed *terribilità*, a feature characteristic of many of Michelangelo's figures and of his own personality. *David*, Michelangelo's most famous sculpture, became the symbol of Florence and originally was placed in the Piazza della Signoria in front of the Palazzo Vecchio, the Florentine town hall. With this statue Michelangelo proved to his contemporaries that he not only surpassed all modern artists, but also the Greeks and Romans, by infusing formal beauty with powerful expressiveness and meaning.

While still occupied with the *David*, Michelangelo was given an opportunity to demonstrate his ability as a painter with the commission of a mural, the *Battle of Cascina*, destined for the Sala dei Cinquecento of the Palazzo Vecchio, opposite Leonardo's *Battle of Anghiari*. Neither artist carried his assignment beyond the stage of a cartoon, a full-scale preparatory drawing. Michelangelo created a series of nude and clothed figures in a wide variety of poses and positions that are a prelude to his next major project, the ceiling of the Sistine Chapel in the Vatican.

David *(1501-04, Accademia, Florence), by Michelangelo. One of his most famous works, the marble statue exhibits the emotional impact and dramatic posture characteristic of Michelangelo's muscular figures.* Alinari

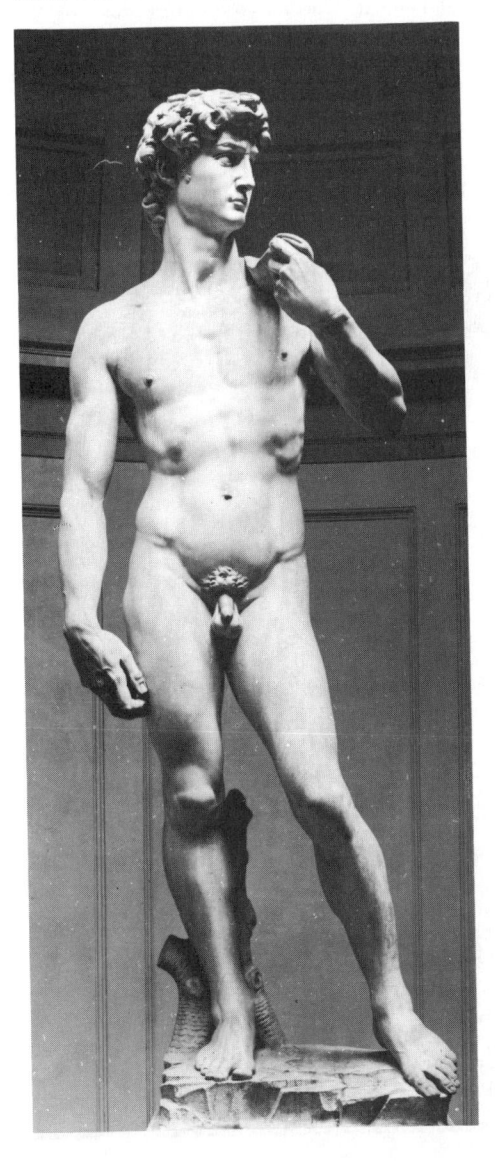

The Sistine Chapel Ceiling. Michelangelo was recalled to Rome by Pope Julius II in 1505 for two commissions. The most important one was for the frescoes of the Sistine Chapel ceiling. Working high above the chapel floor, lying on his back on scaffolding, Michelangelo painted, between 1508 and 1512, some of the finest pictorial images of all time. On the vault of the papal chapel, he devised an intricate system of decoration that included nine scenes from the Book of Genesis, beginning with *God Separating Light from Darkness* and including the *Creation of Adam*, the *Creation of Eve*, the *Temptation and Fall of Adam and Eve*, and the *Flood*. These centrally located narratives are surrounded by alternating images of prophets and sibyls on marble thrones, by other Old Testament subjects, and by the ancestors of Christ. In order to prepare for this enormous work, Michelangelo drew numerous figure studies and cartoons, devising scores of figure types and poses. These awesome, mighty images, demonstrating Michelangelo's masterly understanding of human anatomy and movement, changed the course of painting in the West.

The Tomb of Julius II. Before the assignment of the Sistine ceiling in 1505, Michelangelo had been commissioned by Julius II to produce his tomb, which was planned to be the most magnificent of Christian times. It was to be located in the new Basilica of St. Peter's, then under construction. Michelangelo enthusiastically went ahead with this challenging project, which was to include more than 40 figures, spending months in the quarries to obtain the necessary Carrara marble. Due to a mounting shortage of money, however, the pope ordered him to put aside the tomb project in favor of painting the Sistine ceiling. When Michelangelo went back to work on the tomb, he redesigned it on a much more modest scale. Nevertheless, Michelangelo made some of his finest sculpture for the Julius Tomb, including the *Moses* (c. 1515), the central figure in the much reduced monument now located in Rome's church of San Pietro in Vincoli. The muscular patriarch sits alertly in a shallow niche, holding the tablets of the Ten Commandments, his long beard entwined in his powerful hands. He looks off into the distance as if communicating with God. Two other superb statues, the *Bound Slave* and the *Dying Slave* (both c. 1510-13), Louvre, Paris), demonstrate Michelangelo's approach to carving. He conceived of

MICHELANGELO

the figure as being imprisoned in the block. By removing the excess stone, the form was released. Here, as is frequently the case with his sculpture, Michelangelo left the statues unfinished (*nonfinito*), either because he was satisfied with them as is, or because he no longer planned to use them.

The Laurentian Library. The project for the Julius Tomb required architectural planning, but Michelangelo's activity as an architect only began in earnest in 1519, with the plan for the facade (never executed) of the Church of San Lorenzo in Florence, where he had once again taken up residence. In the 1520s he also designed the Laurentian Library and its elegant entrance hall adjoining San Lorenzo, although these structures were finished only decades later. Michelangelo took as a starting point the wall articulation of his Florentine predecessors, but he infused it with the same surging energy that characterizes his sculpture and painting. Instead of being obedient to classical Greek and Roman practices, Michelangelo used motifs—columns, pediments, and brackets—for a personal and expressive purpose. Michelangelo, a partisan of the republican faction, participated in the 1527–29 war against the Medici and supervised Florentine fortifications.

The Medici Tombs. While residing in Florence for this extended period, Michelangelo also undertook—between 1519 and 1534—the commission of the Medici Tombs for the New Sacristy of San Lorenzo. His design called for two large wall tombs facing each other across the high, domed room. One was intended for Lorenzo de' Medici (1492–1519), duke of Urbino; the other for Giuliano de' Medici (1479–1516), duke of Nemours. The two complex tombs were conceived as representing opposite types: the Lorenzo, the contemplative, introspective personality; the Giuliano, the active, extroverted one. He placed magnificent nude personifications of Dawn and Dusk beneath the seated Lorenzo, Day and Night beneath Giuliano; reclining river gods (never ex-

A detail of the staircase of the Laurentian Library in Florence, Italy, one of Michelangelo's late works. The innovative architectural details of this work—such as the purely ornamental, nonfunctional columns—were an important influence on later Italian art and architecture.

Scala–Editorial Photocolor Archives

ecuted) were planned for the bottom. Work on the Medici Tombs continued long after Michelangelo went back to Rome in 1534, although he never returned to his beloved native city.

The Last Judgment. In Rome, in 1536, Michelangelo was at work on the *Last Judgment* for the alter wall of the Sistine Chapel, which he finished in 1541. The largest fresco of the Renaissance, it depicts Judgment Day. Christ, with a clap of thunder, puts into motion the inevitable separation, with the saved ascending on the left side of the painting and the damned descending on the right into a Dantesque hell. As was his custom, Michelangelo portrayed all the figures nude, but prudish draperies were added by another artist (who was dubbed the "breeches-maker") a decade later, as the cultural climate became more conservative. Michelangelo painted his own image in the flayed skin of St. Bartholomew. Although he was also given another painting commission, the decoration of the Pauline Chapel in the 1540s, his main energies were directed toward architecture during this phase of his life.

The Campidoglio. In 1538-39 plans were under way for the remodeling of the buildings surrounding the Campidoglio (Capitol) on the Capitoline Hill, the civic and political heart of the city of Rome. Although Michelangelo's program was not carried out until the late 1550s and not finished until the 17th century, he designed the Campidoglio around an oval shape, with the famous antique bronze equestrian statue of the Roman emperor Marcus Aurelius in the center. For the Palazzo dei Conservatori he brought a new unity to the public building facade, at the same time that he preserved traditional Roman monumentality.

Dome of St. Peter's Basilica. Michelangelo's crowning achievement as an architect was his work at St. Peter's Basilica, where he was made chief architect in 1546. The building was being constructed according to Donato Bramante's plan, but Michelangelo ultimately became responsible for the altar end of the building on the exterior and for the final form of its dome.

Michelangelo's Achievements. During his long lifetime, Michelangelo was an intimate of princes and popes, from Lorenzo de' Medici to Leo X, Clement VIII, and Pius III (1439-1503), as well as cardinals, painters, and poets. Neither easy to get along with nor easy to understand, he expressed his view of himself and the world even more directly in his poetry than in the other arts. Much of his verse deals with art and the hardships he underwent, or with Neoplatonic philosophy and personal relationships.

The great Renaissance poet Ludovico Ariosto wrote succinctly of this famous artist: "Michael more than mortal, divine angel." Indeed, Michelangelo was widely awarded the epithet "divine" because of his extraordinary accomplishments. Two generations of Italian painters and sculptors were impressed by his treatment of the human figure: Raphael, Annabale Carracci, Pontormo, Rosso Fiorentino, Sebastiano del Piombo, and Titian. His dome for St. Peter's became the symbol of authority, as well as the model, for domes all over the Western world; the majority of state capitol buildings in the U.S., as well as the Capitol in Washington, D.C., are derived from it.

See also ARCHITECTURE; DOME; PAINTING; RENAISSANCE ART AND ARCHITECTURE; SCULPTURE. J.H.B.

For further information on this person, see the section Biographies in the Bibliography in volume 28.

MICHELOZZO (1396-1472), Italian Renaissance architect and sculptor, who strikingly combined Italian Gothic and classical styles. He was born in Florence and in 1420 became an assistant to the sculptor Lorenzo Ghiberti, and aided him in executing the bronze north doors of the Florence Baptistery. In the 1420s and 1430s as partner of the sculptor Donatello, he worked on tombs for antipope John XXIII (in the Baptistery) and other notables. Subsequently he became the chief architect of the Medici family.

In addition to the many villas he designed for the Medici, Michelozzo designed the San Giorgio Maggiore Library in 1433 for Cosimo de' Medici. Later, for the same patron, he built the magnificent Medici-Riccardi Palace (1444-60) in Florence, a notable example of 15th-century Italian architecture and one of the outstanding monuments preserved in Florence today. Between 1437 and 1452, he rebuilt the Convent of San Marco in Florence. In 1446 he was given the important post of architect of the Duomo. Michelozzo's later work included the restoration (1453) of the Palazzo Vecchio, the city hall of Florence.

MICHELSON, Albert Abraham (1852-1931), German-born American physicist and Nobel laureate, known for his famous experiment to measure the velocity of the earth through the ether.

Michelson was born in Strelno (now Strzelno, Poland), brought to the U.S. as a child, and educated at the U.S. Naval Academy and at the universities of Berlin, Heidelberg, and Paris. He was professor of physics at Clark University from 1889 to 1892, and from 1892 to 1929 was head of the department of physics at the University of Chicago. He determined with a high degree of accuracy, using apparatus of his own design, the velocity of light. In 1887 he invented the interferometer (q.v.), which he used in the classical experiment, performed with the American chemist Edward Williams Morley (1838-1923), to demonstrate that the motion of the earth is not measureable. The negative results of the experiment, known as the Michelson-Morley experiment, were the beginning of the development of the theory of relativity (q.v.). Michelson was awarded the 1907 Nobel Prize in physics. His major works include *Velocity of Light* (1902) and *Studies in Optics* (1927).

MICHENER, James A(lbert) (1907–), American novelist, born in New York City. His wide-ranging career as a popular writer began when his World War II experiences provided the material for a book of short stories, *Tales of the South Pacific* (1947). This work received the 1947 Pulitzer Prize in fiction and was the source of the musical *South Pacific* (1949). Among Michener's other popular works of fiction are *The Novel* (1991), and the lengthy historical novels *Sayonara* (1954); *Hawaii* (1959); *Chesapeake* (1978); *The Covenant* (1980), about South African apartheid; *Poland* (1982); *Texas* (1985); and *Alaska* (1988). A collection of nonfiction pieces was published in *A Michener Miscellany: 1950–1970* (1973). *The World Is My Home*, a memoir, was published in 1992.

MICHIGAN, one of the East North Central states of the U.S., consisting mainly of two large peninsulas—the Lower Peninsula and the smaller Upper Peninsula. The state is bordered on the N and E by Ontario, on the S by Ohio and Indiana, and on the W by Wisconsin. Most of its boundaries are formed by four of the Great Lakes—Superior, Huron, Erie, and Michigan.

Michigan entered the Union on Jan. 26, 1837, as the 26th state. Its economy, dominated in the 19th century by fur trapping, farming, lumbering, and mining, became highly industrialized after 1900 as the state developed into the major center of the U.S. automobile industry. In the 1990s service industries (including tourism), agriculture, and mining also were important economic activities. President Gerald R. Ford lived for many years in Michigan. The name of the state is taken from that of Lake Michigan, the name of which is derived from an Algonquian Indian term meaning "big water." Michigan is called the Wolverine State and the Great Lake State.

LAND AND RESOURCES

Michigan, with an area of 250,738 sq km (96,810 sq mi), is the 11th largest of the U.S. states; 9.8% of its land area is owned by the federal government. The extreme dimensions of the Lower Peninsula, which is shaped like a mitten, are about 460 km (about 285 mi) from N to S and about 315 km (about 195 mi) from E to W. The greatest distances in the Upper Peninsula, which has a roughly rectangular shape, are about 525 km (about 325 mi) from E to W and about 280 km (about 175 mi) from N to S. The lowest point in the state is 174 m (572 ft), along Lake Erie in the SE, and the highest is 603 m (1979 ft), atop Mt. Arvon in the NW; the approximate mean elevation is 274 m (900 ft). Michigan has a Great Lakes shoreline of about 5310 km (about 3300 mi).

Physical Geography. The W portion of the Upper Peninsula of Michigan is composed of rather bold NE- to SW-trending ranges forming part of the Superior Upland, a region that also includes Isle Royale and extends W into Wisconsin and Minnesota. These highlands consist of hard rock, mainly granite. Mountains in the area include the Porcupine Mts. and the Gogebic and Copper ranges; the last-named is partly situated on the Keweenaw Peninsula, which projects into Lake Superior. Differences in elevation of neighboring areas in this region are greater than in the remainder of the state.

The E section of the Upper Peninsula and the entire Lower Peninsula are part of the Eastern Great Lakes Lowland. This region has a low to gently rolling topography, the result of glacial action. Numerous lakes and bogs are in the area, which has poor natural drainage.

The soils of the Upper Peninsula and the N half of the Lower Peninsula are gray and gray-brown and acidic and were formed from glacially deposited material. They have limited fertility. SE of Saginaw Bay, in the "thumb" area, soils are heavier loams. The soils of most of the S half of the Lower Peninsula are very fertile, and considerable farmland is found in this area. Sand dunes occur along the Lake Michigan shore.

Rivers and Lakes. Most of Michigan's rivers are relatively short and have a small volume of flow. Several of the larger rivers, including the Grand R., the state's longest, are in the W part of the Lower Peninsula. Others in this area are the Manistee, Pere Marquette, Muskegon, Kalamazoo, and Saint Joseph rivers. In the E Lower Peninsula are the Au Sable, Saginaw, Cass, Saint Clair, and Detroit rivers, and in the Upper Peninsula are the Ontonagon, Menominee, Escanaba, and Manistique rivers. The Upper Peninsula has many picturesque waterfalls, including Tahquamenon Falls.

Besides parts of the Lakes Superior, Huron, Erie, and Michigan, the state encompasses more than 11,000 lakes, the largest being Houghton Lake, in the N part of the Lower Peninsula. Michigan's sections of the Great Lakes contain

MICHIGAN

many islands, notably Isle Royale in Lake Superior, Bois Blanc and Mackinac islands in the Straits of Mackinac, Drummond Island in Lake Huron, and Beaver and Manitou islands in Lake Michigan.

Climate. Michigan has a humid continental climate with short summers; the Upper Peninsula generally has cooler temperatures than the Lower Peninsula. The climate is somewhat moderated by breezes from the Great Lakes, which tend to cool the state in summer and warm it in winter. Areas of the Upper Peninsula have a yearly frost-free season of 60 to 120 days, and annual precipitation ranges from about 405 to 810 mm (about 16 to 32 in). Sault Sainte Marie on the Upper Peninsula has a mean yearly temperature of 4.4° C (40° F) and an average annual precipitation of 813 mm (32 in). In areas of the Lower Peninsula the yearly frost-free season lasts from 120 to 180 days, and annual precipitation ranges from about 760 to 1220 mm (about 30 to 48 in). Detroit, for example, has an average annual temperature of 10° C (50° F) and receives about 787 mm (about 31 in) of moisture per year. Most of the state receives considerable snowfall each year, with the heaviest accumulations in the W part of the Upper Peninsula. The recorded temperature in Michigan has ranged from −46.1° C (−51° F), in 1934 at Vanderbilt in the N Lower Peninsula, to 44.4° C (112° F), in 1936 at Mio, also in the N Lower Peninsula. Michigan is struck by relatively few damaging storms. Tornadoes occasionally strike the S half of the Lower Peninsula.

Plants and Animals. About half of the land area of Michigan is forested. Most of the woodland is in the Upper Peninsula and the N portion of the Lower Peninsula. In the N, white and red pines predominate; in the upper portion of the Lower Peninsula mixed pine and maple forests are most common. Farther S, hardwoods such as oak, beech, and maple are more numerous. On the whole, about three-quarters of Michigan's trees are hardwoods. The state also has numerous flowering plants, such as arbutus, daisy, goldenrod, iris, lady's-slipper, tiger lily, and violet.

The scenic beauty of rural Michigan is enhanced by the state's extensive shorelines on three of the Great Lakes. Perce Village, near Stevensville, Mich., is on the southern shore of Lake Michigan.
Jewel Craig-Shostal Associates

279

MICHIGAN

A variety of smaller wildlife, such as squirrels, foxes, woodchucks, chipmunks, and rabbits, are found throughout Michigan. Many deer inhabit the N Lower Peninsula and the Upper Peninsula, which also provide a habitat for snowshoe hare, porcupine, black bear, and bobcat. Isle Royale contains moose and timber wolf. Among the diverse varieties of fish inhabiting Michigan's rivers and lakes are pike, bass, perch, alewife, catfish, trout, smelt, crappie, bluegill, chub, coho salmon, and sturgeon. The state's birds include the robin, thrush, meadowlark, wren, bluebird, oriole, bobolink, and chickadee. Geese, ducks, grouse, pheasants, and quail are among the notable game birds of Michigan.

Mineral Resources. Michigan has substantial deposits of a number of minerals. Sand and gravel are found throughout the state, and limestone is common in the Upper Peninsula and the N portion of the Lower Peninsula. Other resources of the Upper Peninsula include great quantities of iron ore and some marble. Petroleum and natural gas are important minerals of the Lower Peninsula. The state's numerous bogs contain abundant resources of peat. Other mineral deposits include copper, clay, coal, gypsum, magnesium, marl, shale, and silver. Je.E.Gr.

POPULATION

According to the 1990 census, Michigan had 9,295,297 inhabitants, an increase of 0.4% over 1980. The average population density for the whole of Michigan in 1990 was 37 people per sq km (96 per sq mi); based on land area only, the population density was 63 per sq km (164 per sq mi). Most of the population was concentrated in the S half of the Lower Peninsula. Whites made up 83.4% of the population and blacks 13.9%; additional population groups included 55,131 American Indians, 23,845 Asian Indians, 19,145 persons of Chinese ancestry, 16,316 persons of Korean origin, 13,786 persons of Filipino extraction, 10,681 persons of Japanese background, and 6117 persons of Vietnamese descent. The principal American Indian groups included Ojibwa, Ottawa, and Potawatomi. About 201,600 persons reported Hispanic ancestry. Roman Catholics (29.2%) made up the largest religious group, followed by Baptists (15.7%), and Lutherans (8.3%). In 1990 about 71% of all people in Michigan lived in areas defined as urban, and the rest lived in rural areas. The state's most populous cities were Detroit, the seventh largest city in the U.S.; Grand Rapids; Warren; Flint; and Lansing, the capital.

EDUCATION AND CULTURAL ACTIVITY

Michigan has a number of noted educational and cultural institutions and a wide variety of facilities for outdoor recreation.

Education. About 1800, Father Gabriel Richard (1767–1832), a French-born Roman Catholic missionary and educator, established schools for Indians and whites in the Detroit area. A statewide public education system was established in 1837, the year Michigan entered the Union. In the late 1980s Michigan had 3314 public elementary and secondary schools, with a combined annual enrollment of 1,127,900 elementary pupils and 448,900 secondary students. In addition, about 167,900 students were enrolled in private elementary and secondary schools.

The first university in Michigan, the Catholepistemiad, or University of Michigania, was founded in Detroit in 1817; soon after Michigan became a state, the school was moved to Ann Arbor as the University of Michigan. By the late 1980s Michigan had 97 institutions of higher education with a combined enrollment of about 560,300 students. Besides the University of Michigan, notable schools include Wayne State University and the Univesity of Detroit (1877), in Detroit; Kalamazoo College (1833) and Western Michigan University (1903), in Kalamazoo; Michigan State University, in East Lansing; Hope College (1862), in Holland; Eastern Michigan University (1849), in Ypsilanti; Central Michigan University (1892), in Mount Pleasant; Northern Michigan University (1899), in Marquette; Michigan Technological University (1885), in Houghton; and Oakland University (1957), in Rochester.

Cultural Institutions. Michigan contains several noted museums. These include the Detroit Institute of Arts, with fine collections of American, European, and Oriental art; the Detroit Historical Museum; the Children's Museum, in Detroit; the Detroit Science Center; the University of Michigan Museum of Art, in Ann Arbor, with extensive exhibitions of Western, African, and Asian art; the Flint Institute of Arts; the Grand Rapids Art Museum; and the Genevieve and Donald Gilmore Art Center, in Kalamazoo. Also of interest are the Michigan Historical Museum, in Lansing; the Kingman Museum of Natural History, in Battle Creek; the Great Lakes Area Paleontological Museum, in Traverse City; the Henry Ford Museum, with a vast collection of Americana, and Greenfield Village, containing some 100 historic structures, in Dearborn; and the U.S. National Ski Hall of Fame and Ski Museum, in Ishpeming.

Detroit, Flint, Grand Rapids, Kalamazoo, Lansing, and Saginaw support orchestras; also in Detroit are the Michigan Opera Theatre and the state's largest public library. Each summer the Interlochen Center for the Arts hosts the National Music Camp. Papers of President Ford are housed in a library in Ann Arbor.

MICHIGAN

Michigan: Map Index

Counties

Alcona	F5
Alger	C3
Allegan	D7
Alpena	F4
Antrim	D5
Arenac	F5
Baraga	A3
Barry	D7
Bay	E6
Benzie	C5
Berrien	C7
Branch	D8
Calhoun	D7
Cass	C8
Charlevoix	E4
Cheboygan	E4
Chippewa	E3
Clare	E6
Clinton	E7
Crawford	E5
Delta	C3
Dickinson	B3
Eaton	E7
Emmet	D4
Genesee	F6
Gladwin	E5
Gogebic	D2
Grand Traverse	D5
Gratiot	E6
Hillsdale	E8
Houghton	A3
Huron	F6
Ingham	E7
Ionia	D7
Iosco	F5
Iron	A3
Isabella	E6
Jackson	E7
Kalamazoo	D7
Kalkaska	D5
Kent	D6
Keweenaw	A2
Lake	D6
Lapeer	F6
Leelanau	D5
Lenawee	E8
Livingston	F7
Luce	D3
Mackinac	E3
Macomb	B6, G7
Manistee	C5
Marquette	B3
Mason	C6
Mecosta	D6
Menominee	B4
Midland	E6
Missaukee	D5
Monroe	F8
Montcalm	D6
Montmorency	E4
Muskegon	C6
Newaygo	D6
Oakland	A6, F7
Oceana	C6
Ogemaw	E5
Ontonagon	D2
Osceola	D6
Oscoda	E5
Otsego	E5
Ottawa	C7
Presque Isle	F4
Roscommon	E5
Saginaw	E6
St. Clair	G6
St. Joseph	D8
Sanilac	G6
Schoolcraft	C3
Shiawassee	E7
Tuscola	F6
Van Buren	C7
Washtenaw	F7
Wayne	A7, F7
Wexford	D5

Cities and Towns

Adrian	E8
Albion	E7
Algonac	G7
Allegan	D7
Allendale	C7
Allen Park	A7
Alma	E6
Alpena	F4
Ann Arbor	F7
Atlanta	E5
Bad Axe	G6
Baldwin	D6
Battle Creek	D7
Bay City	F6
Belding	D6
Bellaire	D5
Belleville	F7
Benton Harbor	C7
Berkley	A6
Bessemer	C2
Beulah	C5
Beverly Hills	A6
Big Rapids	D6
Bingham Farms	A6
Birmingham	A6
Blissfield	F8
Bloomfield Hills	A6
Boyne City	D4
Bridgeport	F6
Brighton	F7
Buchanan	C8
Burton	F6
Cadillac	D5
Carleton	F7
Caro	F6
Carrollton	F6
Cassopolis	C8
Cedar Springs	D6
Center Line	B6
Centreville	D8
Charlevoix	D4
Charlotte	E7
Cheboygan	E4
Chelsea	E7
Chesaning	E6
Chesterfield	C6
Christmas	C3
Clare	E6
Clawson	B6
Clio	F6
Coldwater	D8
Connorville	C2
Coopersville	D6
Crystal Falls	A3
Cutlerville	D7
Davison	F6
Dearborn	A7, F7
Dearborn Hts.	A7
Detroit	B7, F7
De Witt	E7
Dowagiac	C8
Dundee	F8
Durand	F7
Eagle River	A2
East Lansing	E7
Eastpointe	B6
East Tawas	F5
Eaton Rapids	E7
Ecorse	B7
Escanaba	B4
Essexville	F6
Farmington	A6
Farmington Hills	A6
Fenton	F7
Ferndale	B6
Ferrysburg	C6
Flat Rock	F7
Flint	F6
Flushing	F6
Fowlerville	E7
Frankenmuth	F6
Franklin	A6
Fraser	B6
Fremont	D6
Garden City	A7
Gaylord	E4
Gladstone	B4
Gladwin	E6
Grand Blanc	F7
Grand Haven	C6
Grand Ledge	E7
Grand Rapids	D7
Grayling	E5
Greenville	D6
Grosse Pointe	B7
Grosse Pointe Farms	B6
Grosse Pointe Park	B7
Grosse Pointe Shores	B6
Grosse Pointe Woods	B6
Hamtramck	B7
Hancock	A2
Harper Woods	B6
Harrison	E5
Harrisville	F5
Hart	C6
Hastings	D7
Hazel Park	B6
Highland Park	B7
Hillsdale	E8
Holland	C7
Holly	F7
Holt	E7
Houghton	A2
Houghton Lake	E5
Howell	F7
Hudson	E8
Hudsonville	D7
Huntington Woods	A6
Huron Heights	A6
Imlay City	F6
Inkster	A7
Ionia	D6
Iron Mountain	A4
Ironwood	C2
Ishpeming	B3
Ithaca	E6
Jackson	E7
Jenison	D7
Kalamazoo	D7
Kalkaska	D5
Keego Harbor	A6
Kentwood	D7
Kingsford	A4
L'Anse	A3
Lake City	D5
Lake Orion	F7
Lambertville	F8

281

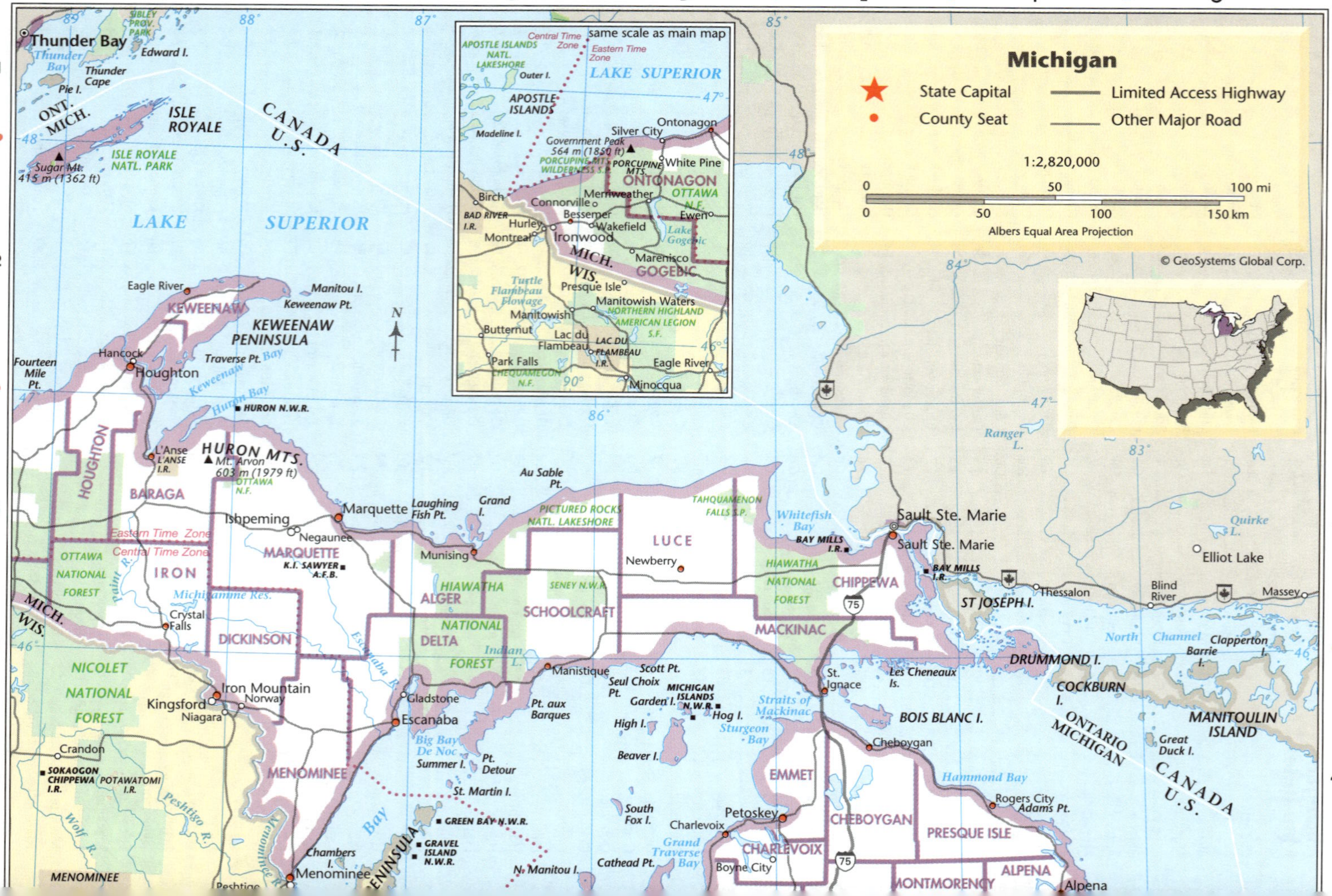
Michigan
State Capital
County Seat
Limited Access Highway
Other Major Road
1:2,820,000
0 50 100 mi
0 50 100 150 km
Albers Equal Area Projection
© GeoSystems Global Corp.
same scale as main map
LAKE SUPERIOR
CANADA
U.S.
Thunder Bay
Isle Royale
ISLE ROYALE NATL. PARK
Sugar Mt. 415 m (1362 ft)
KEWEENAW PENINSULA
Eagle River
Hancock
Houghton
HURON MTS.
Mt. Arvon 603 m (1979 ft)
Marquette
Ishpeming
Negaunee
Munising
Iron Mountain
Kingsford
Escanaba
Gladstone
Manistique
Newberry
Sault Ste. Marie
St. Ignace
Cheboygan
Petoskey
Charlevoix
Boyne City
Rogers City
Alpena
Menominee
Crystal Falls
L'Anse
Ontonagon
Ironwood
Bessemer
Wakefield
Ewen
Silver City
White Pine
Marenisco
Elliot Lake
Thessalon
Blind River
Massey
HOUGHTON
BARAGA
MARQUETTE
IRON
DICKINSON
MENOMINEE
DELTA
ALGER
SCHOOLCRAFT
LUCE
MACKINAC
CHIPPEWA
EMMET
CHEBOYGAN
CHARLEVOIX
PRESQUE ISLE
MONTMORENCY
ALPENA
ONTONAGON
GOGEBIC
OTTAWA NATIONAL FOREST
HIAWATHA NATIONAL FOREST
NICOLET NATIONAL FOREST
PICTURED ROCKS NATL. LAKESHORE
TAHQUAMENON FALLS S.P.
SENEY N.W.R.
HURON N.W.R.
MICHIGAN ISLANDS N.W.R.
GREEN BAY N.W.R.
GRAVEL ISLAND N.W.R.
Straits of Mackinac
BOIS BLANC I.
DRUMMOND I.
ST JOSEPH I.
COCKBURN I.
MANITOULIN ISLAND
North Channel
Eastern Time Zone
Central Time Zone

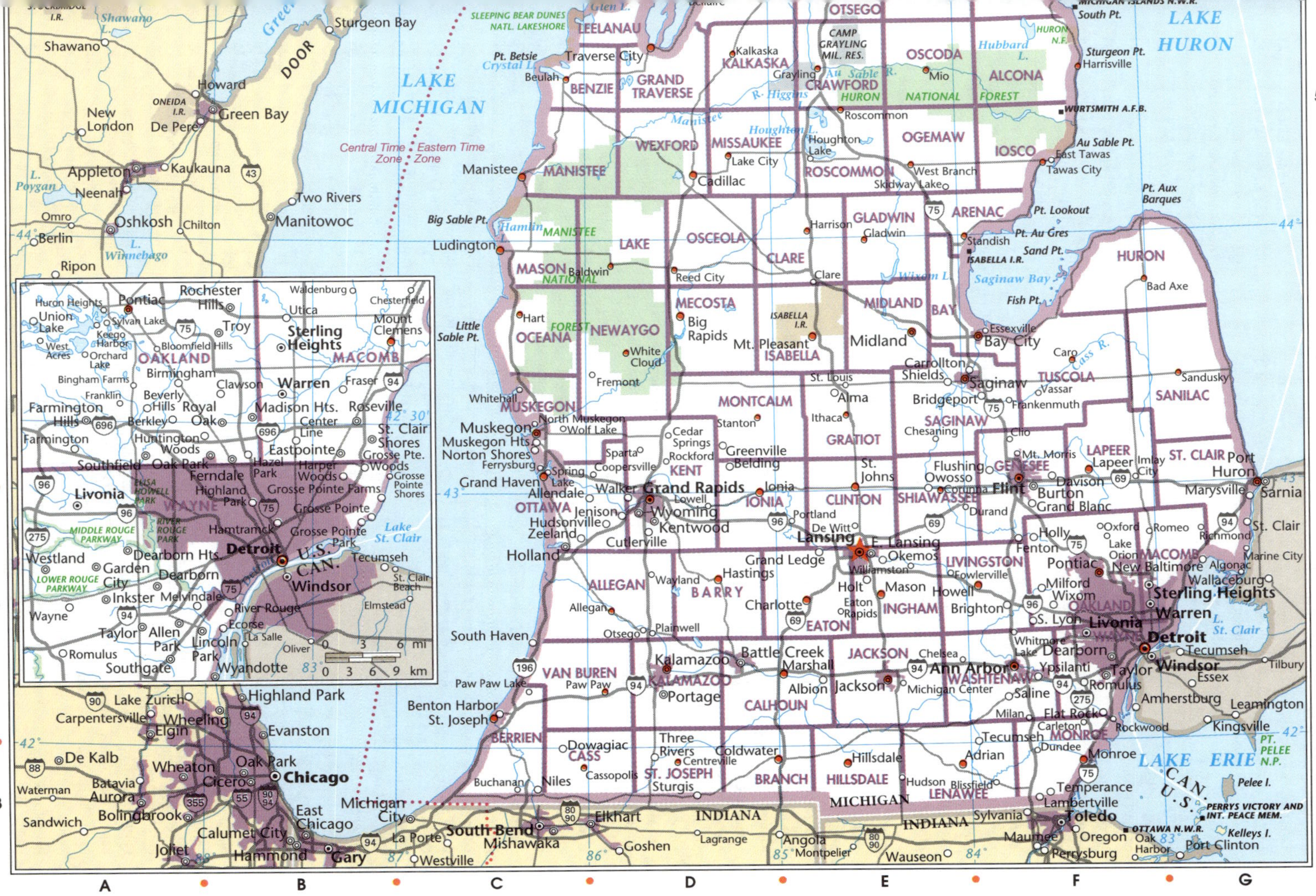

LAKE MICHIGAN
LAKE HURON
LAKE ERIE
Lake St. Clair
Saginaw Bay
Central Time Zone
Eastern Time Zone
SLEEPING BEAR DUNES NATL. LAKESHORE
CAMP GRAYLING MIL. RES.
HURON NATIONAL FOREST
MANISTEE NATIONAL FOREST
WURTSMITH A.F.B.
ISABELLA I.R.
ONEIDA I.R.
PT. PELEE N.P.
PERRYS VICTORY AND INT. PEACE MEM.
OTTAWA N.W.R.
LEELANAU
BENZIE
GRAND TRAVERSE
KALKASKA
CRAWFORD
OSCODA
ALCONA
OTSEGO
MANISTEE
WEXFORD
MISSAUKEE
ROSCOMMON
OGEMAW
IOSCO
ARENAC
MASON
LAKE
OSCEOLA
CLARE
GLADWIN
OCEANA
NEWAYGO
MECOSTA
ISABELLA
MIDLAND
BAY
HURON
MUSKEGON
MONTCALM
GRATIOT
SAGINAW
TUSCOLA
SANILAC
KENT
IONIA
CLINTON
SHIAWASSEE
GENESEE
LAPEER
ST. CLAIR
OTTAWA
ALLEGAN
BARRY
EATON
INGHAM
LIVINGSTON
OAKLAND
MACOMB
VAN BUREN
KALAMAZOO
CALHOUN
JACKSON
WASHTENAW
WAYNE
BERRIEN
CASS
ST. JOSEPH
BRANCH
HILLSDALE
LENAWEE
MONROE
MICHIGAN
INDIANA
Traverse City
Manistee
Ludington
Cadillac
Grayling
Bay City
Saginaw
Midland
Flint
Lansing
E. Lansing
Grand Rapids
Kalamazoo
Battle Creek
Jackson
Ann Arbor
Detroit
Windsor
Port Huron
Sarnia
Toledo
South Bend
Chicago
Gary
Green Bay
Appleton
Oshkosh
Manitowoc
Muskegon
Holland
Benton Harbor
St. Joseph
Pontiac
Warren
Sterling Heights
Livonia
Dearborn
Monroe
Elkhart
Mishawaka
Michigan City
Evanston
A B C D E F G
5 6 7 8

MICHIGAN

Michigan: Map Index

Lansing E7
Lapeer F6
Lincoln Park A7
Livonia A7, F7
Lowell D7
Ludington C6
Madison Hts. B6
Manistee C5
Manistique C4
Marenisco D2
Marine City G7
Marquette B3
Marshall E7
Marysville G7
Mason E7
Melvindale A7
Menominee B4
Merriweather D2
Michigan Center E7
Midland E6
Milan F7
Milford F7
Mio E5
Monroe F8
Mount Clemens B6
Mount Morris F6
Mount Pleasant E6
Munising C3
Muskegon C6
Muskegon Hts. C6
Negaunee B3
New Baltimore G7
Newberry D3
Niles C8
North Muskegon C6
Norton Shores C6
Norway B4
Oak Park A6
Okemos E7
Ontonagon D1
Orchard Lake A6
Otsego D7
Owosso E6
Oxford F7
Paw Paw D7
Paw Paw Lake C7
Petoskey E4
Plainwell D7
Pontiac A6, F7
Portage D7
Port Huron G7
Portland E7
Rapid River C4
Reed City D6
Richmond G7
River Rouge B7

Rochester Hills A6
Rockford D6
Rockwood F7
Rogers City F4
Romeo F7
Romulus F7
Roscommon E5
Roseville B6
Royal Oak B6
Saginaw F6
St. Clair G7
St. Clair Shores B6
St. Ignace E4
St. Johns E6
St. Joseph C7
St. Louis E6
Saline F7
Sandusky G6
Sault Ste. Marie E3
Shields E6
Silver City D1
Skidway Lake E5
Southfield A6
Southgate A7
South Haven C7
South Lyon F7
Sparta D6
Spring Lake C6
Standish F6
Stanton D6
Sterling Heights F7
Sturgis D8
Sylvan Lake A6
Tawas City F5
Taylor A7, F7
Tecumseh F7
Temperance F8
Three Rivers D7
Traverse City D5
Troy B6
Union Lake A6
Utica B6
Vassar F6
Wakefield C2
Waldenburg B6
Walker D7
Warren B6, F7
Wayland D7
Wayne A7
West Acres A6
West Branch E5
Westland A7
White Cloud D6
White Pine D2
Whitehall C6
Whitmore Lake F7
Williamston E7

Wixom F7
Wolf Lake C6
Wyandotte B7
Wyoming D7
Ypsilanti F7
Zeeland C7

Other Features

Adams, point F4
Arvon, mt. A3
Au Gres, point F6
Au Sable, point C3, F5
Au Sable, river E5
Aux Barques, point C4, F5
Bay Mills Indian Res. E3
Beaver, island D4
Betsie, point C5
Big Bay De Noc, bay C4
Big Sable, point C5
Bois Blanc, island E4
Camp Grayling
   Mil. Res. E5
Cass, river F6
Cathead, point D4
Chambers, island B4
Crystal, lake C5
Detour, point C4
Detroit, river B7
Drummond, island F4
Elisa Howell Park A6
Erie, lake G8
Escanaba, river B3
Fish, point F6
Fourteen Mile, point A2
Garden, island D4
Glen, lake D5
Gogebic, lake D2
Government Peak, mt. D1
Grand, island C3
Grand Traverse, bay D4
Green, bay B5
Hamlin, lake C5
Hammond, bay E4
Hiawatha Natl.
   Forest C3, E3
Higgins, lake E5
High, island D4
Hog, island D4
Houghton, lake E5
Hubbard, lake F5
Huron, bay A3
Huron, lake G5
Huron, mts. A3
Huron Natl. Wildlife
   Refuge B3
Huron Natl. Forest E5, F5
Indian, lake C3

Isabella Indian Res. E6, F6
Isle Royale, island A1
Isle Royale Natl. Park A2
Keweenaw, bay A3
Keweenaw, peninsula A2
Keweenaw, point B2
K.I. Sawyer Air Force
   Base B3
L'Anse Indian Res. A3
Laughing Fish, point B3
Les Cheneaux, islands E4
Little Sable, point C6
Lookout, point F5
Lower Rouge Parkway A7
Manistee, river D5
Manistee Natl. Forest D6
Manitou, island B2
Menominee, river B4
Michigamme, reservoir A3
Michigan, lake C5
Michigan Islands Natl.
   Wildlife Refuge ... D4, F5
Middle Rouge Parkway A7
North, point F4
North Manitou, island C4
Ottawa Natl. Forest .. A3, B3
Paint, river A3
Pictured Rocks Natl.
   Lakeshore C3
Porcupine, mts. D2
Porcupine Mts. Wilderness
   State Park D2
River Rouge Park A7
Saginaw, bay F6
St. Clair, lake G7
St. Martin, island C4
Sand, point F6
Scott, point D4
Seney Natl. Wildlife
   Refuge C3
Seul Choix, point D4
Sleeping Bear Dunes Natl.
   Lakeshore C5
South, point F5
South Fox, island D4
South Manitou, island C4
Straits of Mackinac E4
Sturgeon, bay D4
Sturgeon, point F5
Sugar, mt. A2
Summer, island C4
Superior, lake A2
Tahquamenon Falls
   State Park D3
Thunder, bay F5
Traverse, point A2
Whitefish, bay E3
Wixom, lake E6
Wurtsmith Air Force
   Base F5

284

MICHIGAN

The Lumberman's Memorial, on the shore of the Au Sable River in eastern Michigan, is a tribute to the pioneer lumberjacks who built the industry in the state.
Michigan Tourist Council

Historical Sites. Some of Michigan's historical sites commemorate early settlers. Saint Ignace Mission, in Saint Ignace, was established in 1671 by the French explorer Father Jacques Marquette; Fort Michilimackinac, in Mackinaw City, is a reproduction of a fort built in the early 18th century by the French; and the Dutch Village, in Holland, commemorates the settlers who came to the area in 1847. Mackinac Island contains several old structures, including a late 18th-century British fort. Also of historical interest is the grave, in Battle Creek, of Sojourner Truth, a 19th-century abolitionist and advocate of women's rights.

Sports and Recreation. The Great Lakes and many thousands of smaller lakes, as well as rivers and streams, make Michigan a paradise for fishing, swimming, and boating enthusiasts. Other popular outdoor recreational activities include hunting, skiing, hiking, golf, and tennis. Bois Blanc Island is a favorite deer-hunting area. Michigan's major league professional sports teams include the Detroit Tigers in baseball, the Detroit Pistons in basketball, the Detroit Lions in football, and the Detroit Red Wings in ice hockey; the Pistons and Lions use the Silverdome Stadium in Pontiac. The University of Michigan and Michigan State University are known for fielding excellent sports teams, especially in football and basketball.

Communications. Michigan has a comprehensive communications system that, in the early 1990s, included 144 AM and 214 FM radiobroadcasting stations and 50 television stations. The first radiobroadcasting station in the state, WWJ in Detroit, went into operation in 1920. Michigan's first commercial television station was WWJ-TV in Detroit, which began regular broadcasts in 1947. The *Detroit Gazette,* Michigan's first newspaper, was initially published in Detroit in 1817. In the early 1990s Michigan had 52 daily newspapers with a total daily circulation of approximately 2.4 million. Influential newspapers in the state include the *Detroit Free Press,* the *Detroit News,* the *Flint Journal,* the *Grand Rapids Press,* and the *Lansing State Journal.*

GOVERNMENT AND POLITICS

Michigan is governed under a constitution adopted in 1963 and put into effect in 1964, as amended. Three earlier constitutions had been adopted in 1835, 1850, and 1908. An amendment to the constitution may be proposed by a two-thirds vote of the legislature, by a constitutional convention, or by a voters' initiative. To become effective an amendment must be approved by a majority of the persons voting on the issue in an election.

Executive. The chief executive of Michigan is a governor, who is popularly elected to a term of four years and who may be reelected any number of times. The same regulations apply to the lieutenant governor, who succeeds the governor should the latter resign, die, or be removed from office. Other elected state officials include the secretary of state and the attorney general.

Legislature. The bicameral Michigan legislature is made up of a senate and a house of representatives. The 38 members of the senate are elected to 4-year terms, and the 110 members of the house are elected to 2-year terms.

Judiciary. Michigan's highest court, the supreme court, is made up of seven judges popularly elected to 8-year terms; one of the judges is elected by the court to serve a 2-year term as chief justice. The state's intermediate appellate court, the court of appeals, consists of 24 popularly elected judges. The recorder's court in Detroit, with 29 judges, and circuit courts, with a total of 200 judges, are the state's major trial courts. Judges of these courts are popularly elected. In addition, each county has a probate court, and many larger municipalities have district courts.

MICHIGAN

Local Government. In the early 1990s, Michigan had 83 counties, 272 cities, 1242 townships, and 262 villages. Each county was governed by an elected board of commissioners. Other county officials included the treasurer, prosecuting attorney, clerk, registrar of deeds, and sheriff. Most cities have either the mayor-council or the council-manager form of government.

National Representation. Michigan elects 2 senators and 16 representatives to the U.S. Congress. The state has 18 electoral votes in presidential elections.

Politics. Until the 1930s, the Republican party dominated national, state, and local elections in Michigan. Since that time, Democrats and Republicans have been fairly evenly divided in the state, with the Republicans strongest in rural areas and the Democrats strongest in Detroit and other urban centers. Gerald R. Ford, a Republican, was part of Michigan's delegation in the U.S. House of Representatives (1949–73) before becoming vice-president under Richard M. Nixon (1973–74) and succeeding him as president (1974–77).

ECONOMY

During the colonial period, when the area had few European settlers, fur trapping and trading were major economic activities. In the first half of the 19th century farming and lumbering became important, and subsequently large-scale mining operations were started. By the early 20th century manufacturing was the chief economic activity. Michigan became a center for producing motor vehicles. This industry, which is concentrated in the Detroit area, began to decline during the 1970s; since then, the state's economy has diversified, with the most growth in commercial and professional services.

Agriculture. Although good farmland is generally confined to the S half of the Lower Peninsula, Michigan has an important agricultural industry. About 56% of the state's farm income of $3.2 billion in the late 1980s derived from sales of crops, and the rest came from sales of livestock and livestock products. Michigan has about 54,000 farms, with an average size of 81 ha (200 acres). The leading agricultural commodities in the state are dairy products, corn, hay, soybeans, beef cattle, and hogs. Michigan's other major crops include beans, wheat, oats, potatoes, tomatoes, cucumbers, asparagus, sugar beets, and fruit. Orchards are concentrated along Lake Michigan, and the state is a leading producer of cherries, apples, peaches, plums, and pears. In addition, large quantities of blueberries, strawberries, and wine grapes are grown. Substantial numbers of turkeys and chicken eggs also are produced in Michigan.

Forestry and Fishing. Forests cover a large share of the Upper Peninsula of Michigan and a good portion of the N half of the Lower Peninsula, but, except in the W part of the Upper Peninsula, forestry is relatively unimportant economically. About 10% of the state's timber harvest is made up of softwoods, and the remainder is composed of hardwoods. The timber is used principally to

A lock on the Sault Sainte Marie Canals, which connect Lakes Superior and Huron.
Courtesy Michigan Travel Bureau

MICHIGAN

Michigan is the traditional center of the U.S. automobile industry. Assembly lines mass-produce the most widely used means of transportation in the country.
Cadillac Motor Car

make pulp for paper and to make lumber. Large numbers of Christmas trees are cut each year. Fishing also contributes relatively little to Michigan's econony. The annual catch in the late 1980s was valued at only about $11 million. The leading commercial species include whitefish, alewife, catfish, trout, and perch.

Mining. The yearly output of Michigan's important mining industry in the late 1980s had a value of some $2.5 billion. The most valuable mineral products were natural gas, iron ore, petroleum, and cement. Most of the oil and natural gas is produced in the N central, S central, and S parts of the Lower Peninsula. Iron and copper ores are mined in the W part of the Upper Peninsula, and limestone is produced in the N and SE parts of the Lower Peninsula. In addition, Michigan is a leading U.S. producer of salt, clay, gypsum, magnesium, peat, potash, and sand and gravel. Silver is also a valuable product.

Manufacturing. Michigan is one of the leading manufacturing states in the U.S. Manufacturing accounts for about 27% of the annual gross state product in Michigan and provides jobs for some 968,000 state residents. The leading types of manufactures are transportation equipment, industrial machinery, and fabricated metal. Michigan is the most important U.S. state for producing passenger cars, and three of the biggest U.S. automobile companies—General Motors, Ford, and Chrysler—have their world headquarters in the Detroit (the Motor City) area. Other major motor-vehicle–producing centers in Michigan include Dearborn, Flint, Lansing, and Pontiac. Industrial machinery manufactured in the state includes engines and office and construction equipment, and among the fabricated metal products are tools, cutlery, and motor-vehicle parts. Other major manufactures include iron and steel (produced mainly in Detroit), breakfast cereals (made especially in Battle Creek) and other processed food, and chemicals (Midland) and pharmaceuticals (Ann Arbor, Detroit, Kalamazoo). Additional products are electronic equipment, printed materials, rubber and plastic items, clothing, paper, furniture, and refined petroleum.

Tourism. The travel industry is very important to Michigan, which gains more than $6.7 billion annually from tourist spending. Michigan's

MICHIGAN

DATE OF STATEHOOD: January 26, 1837; 26th state

CAPITAL:	Lansing
MOTTO:	*Si quaeris peninsulam amoenam, circumspice* (If you seek a pleasant peninsula, look about you)
NICKNAMES:	Wolverine State; Great Lake State
STATE SONG:	"Michigan, My Michigan" (words by Douglas M. Malloch)
STATE TREE:	White pine
STATE FLOWER:	Apple blossom
STATE BIRD:	Robin
POPULATION (1990):	9,295,297; 8th among the states
AREA:	250,738 sq km (96,810 sq mi); 11th largest state; includes 103,603 sq km (40,001 sq mi) of inland water
HIGHEST POINT:	Mt. Arvon, 603 m (1979 ft)
LOWEST POINT:	174 m (572 ft), at the shore of Lake Erie
ELECTORAL VOTES:	18
U.S. CONGRESS:	2 senators; 16 representatives

POPULATION OF MICHIGAN SINCE 1810

Year of Census	Population	Classified As Urban
1810	5,000	0%
1830	32,000	0%
1850	398,000	7%
1870	1,184,000	20%
1900	2,421,000	39%
1920	3,668,000	61%
1940	5,256,000	66%
1960	7,823,000	73%
1980	9,262,000	71%
1990	9,295,297	71%

POPULATION OF TEN LARGEST CITIES

	1990 Census	1980 Census
Detroit	1,027,974	1,203,339
Grand Rapids	189,126	181,843
Warren	144,864	161,134
Flint	140,761	159,611
Lansing	127,321	130,414
Sterling Heights	117,810	108,999
Ann Arbor	109,592	107,316
Livonia	100,850	104,814
Dearborn	89,286	90,660
Westland	84,724	84,603

CLIMATE

	DETROIT	SAULT STE. MARIE
Average January temperature range	−7.2° to 0° C (19° to 32° F)	−14.4° to −5.6° C (6° to 22° F)
Average July temperature range	17.2° to 28.3° C (63° to 83° F)	11.7° to 23.9° C (53° to 75° F)
Average annual temperature	10° C (50° F)	4.4° C (40° F)
Average annual precipitation	787 mm (31 in)	813 mm (32 in)
Average annual snowfall	813 mm (32 in)	2794 mm (110 in)
Mean number of days per year with appreciable precipitation	133	163
Average daily relative humidity	68%	76%
Mean number of clear days per year	80	66

NATURAL REGIONS OF MICHIGAN

- SUPERIOR UPLAND
- EASTERN GREAT LAKES LOWLAND

PRINCIPAL PRODUCTS OF MICHIGAN

ECONOMY

State budget .... general revenue $19.7 billion
general expenditure $19.6 billion
accumulated debt $9.2 billion
State and local taxes, per capita $2068
Personal income, per capita................. $14,154
Population below poverty level................... 13.1%
Assets, insured commercial banks (268).... $87.4 billion
Labor force (civilian nonfarm) 3,905,000
    Employed in manufacturing   25%
    Employed in wholesale and retail trade   24%
    Employed in services   23%
    Employed in government   16%

	Quantity Produced	Value
FARM PRODUCTS		**$3.2 billion**
Crops		**$1.8 billion**
Corn	6.0 million metric tons	$524 million
Hay	4.8 million metric tons	$339 million
Soybeans	1.2 million metric tons	$249 million
Vegetables	710,000 metric tons	$138 million
Dry beans	247,000 metric tons	$107 million
Wheat	1.1 million metric tons	$101 million
Livestock and Livestock Products		**$1.4 billion**
Milk	2.3 million metric tons	$739 million
Cattle	179,000 metric tons	$276 million
Hogs	218,000 metric tons	$252 million
Eggs	1.4 billion	$68 million
MINERALS		**$2.5 billion**
Natural gas	4.4 billion cu m	$493 million
Iron ore	15.0 million metric tons	N/A
Petroleum	21.6 million barrels	$389 million
Cement	5.2 million metric tons	$276 million
Sand, gravel	46.1 million metric tons	$157 million
Stone	37.1 million metric tons	$124 million
FISHING	6500 metric tons	**$11 million**

	Annual Payroll
FORESTRY	**$7 million**
MANUFACTURING	**$33.1 billion**
Transportation equipment	$8.9 billion
Industrial machinery and equipment	$4.3 billion
Fabricated metal products	$3.7 billion
Primary metals	$1.6 billion
Printing and publishing	$1.2 billion
Rubber and plastics products	$1.2 billion
Chemicals and allied products	$1.1 billion
Food and kindred products	$1.0 billion
Furniture and fixtures	$984 million
Electronic equipment	$653 million
Apparel and textile mill products	$640 million
Paper and allied products	$635 million
OTHER	**$62.8 billion**
Services	$18.8 billion
Government	$15.5 billion
Retail trade	$8.5 billion
Wholesale trade	$6.1 billion
Finance, insurance, and real estate	$4.6 billion
Transportation, communications, and public utilities	$4.4 billion
Construction	$4.0 billion

ANNUAL GROSS STATE PRODUCT

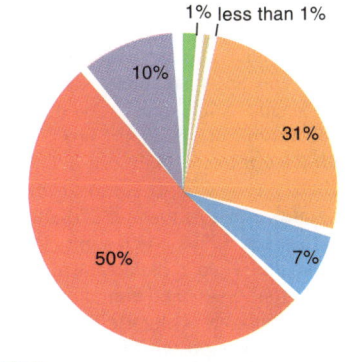

- 1% — Agriculture, forestry, and fisheries
- less than 1% — Mining
- 31% — Manufacturing and construction
- 7% — Transportation, communications, and public utilities
- 50% — Commercial, financial, and professional services
- 10% — Government

Sources: U.S. government publications

MICHIGAN

scenic and recreation resources, which exceed those of neighboring, equally densely populated states, include lengthy, often spectacular shorelines on lakes and rivers, hilly terrain, large areas covered by forests, a climate that provides relief from summer heat and is more conducive to winter sports than areas farther S, and bountiful fish and wildlife populations. Popular units of the National Park Service in Michigan are Isle Royale National Park, in Lake Superior; Pictured Rocks National Lakeshore, which includes multicolored sandstone cliffs as well as beaches and marshes along Lake Superior; and Sleeping Bear Dunes National Lakeshore, which encompasses great sand dunes and beaches along Lake Michigan. In addition, Michigan maintains 93 state parks and recreation areas.

Transportation. It would be difficult to exaggerate the contribution of the Great Lakes to the economy of Michigan. The largest port of the Great Lakes system in Michigan is Detroit, and other ports (such as Calcite and Escanaba) along the Great Lakes shore are major shippers of such raw materials as iron ore and limestone and receivers of coal. Important components of the Great Lakes shipping system are the Saint Marys R., which connects Lakes Superior and Huron and contains the Sault Sainte Marie Canals (Soo Canals), and the St. Clair and Detroit rivers and Lake St. Clair, which together link Lakes Huron and Erie. The state is well served by an extensive highway system of about 189,015 km (about 117,450 mi), including 1889 km (1174 mi) of interstate highways. The interstate system is noticeably denser in the S half of the Lower Peninsula. The Mackinac Bridge (completed 1957) provides a vehicular link between the Upper and Lower Peninsulas, and bridges at Detroit, Port Huron, and Sault Ste. Marie connect the state with Canada. Michigan is served by about 4025 km (2500 mi) of operated Class I railroad track, with Detroit as the main rail hub. Detroit Metropolitan–Wayne County Airport is the busiest of the state's 368 airports and 57 heliports.

Energy. In the early 1990s, Michigan's electricity generating facilities had a total installed capacity of about 22.3 million kw and annually produced some 89.1 billion kwh of electricity. About 75% of the electricity was produced in conventional steam generators burning fossil fuels, almost entirely coal; nuclear power plants accounted for 24%. Hydroelectric facilities, which once were an important source of power in Michigan, produced less than 1%. E.H.W.

HISTORY

The principal Indian tribes in Michigan when the first Europeans arrived were the Ojibwa, Ottawa, Miami, Potawatomi, and Wyandot, or Huron. The Ojibwa lived in the north and were primarily hunters and fishers. The Miami and the Potawatomi, agriculturalists, built large stockaded villages near their farms in southeastern Michigan. The Ottawa lived between them and were mostly traders.

The first European settlement in Michigan, a mission at Sault Ste. Marie, was founded by Father Jacques Marquette, a French Jesuit, in 1668. Between 1679 and 1686 the French established fur-trading posts at the Straits of Mackinac and at the mouth of the Saint Joseph River. Detroit, founded in 1701 by Antoine de La Mothe, Sieur de Cadillac, dominated the waterway between Lakes Huron and Erie. These French settlements were taken over in 1763 by the British, who quelled an Indian uprising under Pontiac in the same year. During the American Revolution Michigan was a base for British-instigated Indian raids against the Americans.

The Michigan Territory. Although the Michigan posts were assigned to the U.S. by the Treaty of Paris (1783), the British occupied them until 1796. Michigan was a part of the Northwest Territory from 1796 to 1800. It was split between the Northwest and Indiana territories from 1800 to 1803, when the total area was returned to Indiana Territory. In 1805, Michigan became a separate U.S. territory. During the War of 1812, the territorial governor, William Hull (1753–1825), led an invasion of Canada, but, in the face of British opposition and their control of the lakes, he retreated and surrendered Detroit to the enemy without firing a shot. After the U.S. victory in the Battle of Lake Erie, the British withdrew to Canada again. Before this happened, however, a band of British and Indians ambushed an American force at the River Raisin, killing more than 1000, in the bloodiest battle in Michigan's history (January 1813).

As the war drew to a close, President James Madison appointed Lewis Cass as territorial governor; he remained in office until 1831. After the war, Michigan settlements expanded slowly. Although the Indians were forced to cede most of the southern half of the Lower Peninsula, the territory's main economic activity continued to be the fur trade, controlled by John Jacob Astor's American Fur Co., operating from Mackinac Island. After 1825, however, the opening of the Erie Canal—along with a new land law and additional Indian cessions—opened the way for a flood of settlers. The population swelled from 9000 in 1820 to 29,000 in 1830 and 212,000 in 1840. By 1835 it had grown sufficiently to make Michigan eligible for statehood, but because of a

The blockhouse of Old Fort Mackinac on Mackinac Island has guarded the Strait of Mackinac since 1780. The island is a popular tourist attraction Michigan Tourist Council

boundary controversy with Ohio over Toledo and the surrounding area Congress would not authorize a constitutional convention. Michigan and Ohio then engaged in the so-called Toledo War; both sides called out their militia, but no blood was shed. Ohio, already a state, had more political power, and Michigan eventually agreed to let Ohio have Toledo in exchange for the greater portion of the Upper Peninsula. On Jan. 26, 1837, Michigan became the 26th state.

Early Growth as a State. After a period of economic depression beginning in the late 1830s, prosperity returned in the '50s. Agricultural growth was rapid, and railroads spread out across the state. Nearly 380,000 new settlers came to Michigan between 1840 and 1860. In the Upper Peninsula commercial mining of copper began in the 1840s, and the opening of the Sault Canal in 1855 spurred iron mining around Negaunee and Marquette. Lumbering also began at this time, particularly in the Saginaw Valley.

The first state Republican party in the U.S. was organized in July 1854 at the Convention Under the Oaks at Jackson, Mich. The antislavery movement was strong in the state, and when the American Civil War came, Michigan men were quick to enlist in the Union army. A Michigan regiment was the first from the West to reach the eastern front. The war hastened Michigan's change from an agricultural to an industrial state; by 1880 the state's manufacturing establishment had increased threefold, and invested capital had doubled. Rapid industrialization continued, and Detroit's manufacturing in 1900 exceeded that for the entire state in 1870.

Politically, Michigan in the last half of the 19th century was Republican, but reformers—the most famous of whom was the progressive mayor of Detroit and later governor, Hazen Pingree (1840–1901)—attacked the abuses of uncontrolled capitalism. Later progressives such as Governors Chase Osborn (1860–1949) and Woodbridge N. Ferris (1853–1928) carried on the reform tradition begun by Pingree.

The 20th Century. Michigan in the 20th century has been dominated by the automobile. A trained labor force, a manufacturing tradition, surplus capital from lumbering, and an excellent transportation system played important roles in making Detroit the Motor Capital of the world.

The automobile industry grew rapidly between 1900 and 1930, when it was crippled by the Great Depression. During the 1930s the economy slowly recovered with help from the federal government. The election of Democrat Frank Murphy as governor in 1932 ended the long dominance of the Republican party in state politics. The coming of World War II restored prosperity and full employment, as Michigan led the nation in the production of military equipment.

War work in the auto factories attracted black migrants from the South, and racial tensions in Detroit led to a riot that took 34 lives in 1943. In succeeding decades community leaders—black and white—worked to develop lines of communication, but racial hatred exploded again during the tense period of the civil rights struggles in the 1960s. In July 1967 riots broke out in Detroit that left blocks of the city in ruins and 43 people dead. Business leaders, led by the auto manufacturer Henry Ford II, reacted by investing in the Renaissance Center to revitalize the city's decaying downtown. The election of Detroit's first black mayor, Coleman Young (1918–   ), in 1974 helped

MICHIGAN, LAKE

heal the wounds of racial conflict.

As Michigan entered the 1980s, its economy was still dominated by the auto industry, which in the three decades after World War II had employed one-third of Michigan's industrial workers and produced two-fifths of the state's manufactures. During the late 1970s and early '80s, high energy costs, obsolete plants, and competition from imports hurt the industry. Growth in the service sector helped Michigan make up for job losses in auto manufacturing, but the recession of the early 1990s put further pressure on the state's economy.   M.M.B.

For further information on this topic, see the Bibliography in volume 28, section 1203.

MICHIGAN, LAKE, lake, N central U.S., third largest of the Great Lakes, and the only one lying wholly within the U.S., bordered by Michigan on the N and E, Indiana on the S, and Illinois and Wisconsin on the W. The lake is 492 km (306 mi) long and up to 190 km (118 mi) wide, with an area of 57,757 sq km (22,300 sq mi). The maximum depth is about 281 m (about 922 ft), and the surface is 176 m (577 ft) above sea level.

The N outlet for Lake Michigan is the Straits of Mackinac, which connect it with Lake Huron. The Chicago Sanitary and Ship Canal connects the lake to the Mississippi R. Green Bay on the W shore and Grand Traverse Bay on the E shore are the main indentations. The lake has a complex system of lighthouses, lightships, buoys, weather report and storm signal stations, and other navigational aids maintained by the federal government. The N portion of the lake, which is blocked by ice for about four months a year, is the site of several islands; Beaver (about 80 km/50 mi long), Garden, and North and South Manitou islands are the largest. Chicago, Milwaukee, and Muskegon are all on the lake. The first European to describe Lake Michigan was the French explorer Jean Nicolet (1598–1642) in 1634.

MICHIGAN, UNIVERSITY OF, state-supported institution of higher learning, in Ann Arbor, Mich., with branches in Flint and Dearborn. The university was originally chartered in 1817 in Detroit as the Catholepistemiad, or the University of Michigania, under the auspices of the territorial government. On the admission of Michigan to the Union in 1837, the institution was established at its present site under its present name; construction was begun in 1839, and the first class was admitted in 1841. After 1870, women were admitted on the same basis as men.

Students pursue baccalaureate, graduate, and professional programs in the schools or colleges of architecture and urban planning; art; business administration; dentistry; education; engineering; information and library studies; law; literature, science, and arts; medicine; music; natural resources; nursing; pharmacy; public health; social work; and the Horace H. Rackham School of Graduate Studies. The medical center, adjacent to the main campus at Ann Arbor, provides facilities for patient care, teaching, and research. Other important research units include the Institute for Social Research and the Space Physics Research Laboratory. The libraries of the university house more than 7 million volumes and include the William L. Clements Library of Americana. The university's museums include collections in anthropology, archaeology, art, natural history, paleontology, and zoology.

MICHIGAN CITY, city, La Porte Co., N Indiana, on Lake Michigan; inc. 1836. Michigan City is a summer resort and yachting center, located near Indiana Dunes National Lakeshore. The city is also a manufacturing center with products that include air compressors, boilers, furniture, and clothing. A state prison and a U.S. Coast Guard station are here. The community was settled in the early 1830s and named for Michigan Road (a route linking the Ohio R. with Lake Michigan), of which it was the N terminus. During the 19th century it was an important grain- and lumber-shipping port. Pop. (1980) 36,850; (1990) 33,822.

MICHIGAN STATE UNIVERSITY, state-controlled land-grant institution, in East Lansing, Mich., founded in 1855 as Michigan Agricultural College, the first state institution of its kind in the U.S. In 1925 the college was renamed Michigan College of Agriculture and Applied Science, and in 1955 the present name was adopted. The university has various degree-granting colleges, including colleges of agriculture and natural resources, arts and letters, business, communication arts, education, engineering, human ecology, human medicine, natural science, nursing, osteopathic medicine, public policy, social science, and veterinary medicine. The degrees of bachelor, master, and doctor are conferred. The university maintains an art museum, performing arts facility, and all-events arena.

MICKIEWICZ, Adam (1798–1855), Polish poet and patriot, whose romantic writings are considered to have revolutionized his country's literature. He was born in Novogrodek (now Novogrudok, Belarus). Throughout his life he struggled for the emancipation of Poland from Russia. His poems deal with Polish themes and present a heroic, albeit melodramatic, picture of the human soul and a Byronic feeling for freedom and heroism. His works have been translated into most European languages. Those in English include the epic poems *Grazyna* (1823; trans. 1940) and *Pan Tad-*

eusz (1834; trans. 1917), the drama *Forefather's Eve* (1823), and the historical poem *Konrad Wallenrod* (1828).

MICMAC, North American Indian tribe of Algonquian linguistic stock, who lived in eastern Canada at the time of early European settlement of that region. They were staunch allies of the French, fighting against the English in numerous skirmishes and in the French and Indian War (q.v.). Occasionally they carried their warfare into New England. They were finally pacified by the British at the end of the 18th century.

The Micmac confederacy consisted of several clans, each with its own leader. The clans were nomadic, fishing in summer and hunting in winter. Their dwellings also varied with the season; open-air wigwams were used in summer, while birch-bark-covered wigwams provided shelter in winter. The Micmac are believed to have practiced elaborate ceremonies, but little is known of these rituals. Today about 9000 descendants of the Micmac clans live in Nova Scotia, New Brunswick, and Prince Edward Island.

For further information on this topic, see the Bibliography in volume 28, sections 1105, 1108.

MICROBE, microscopic organism. The term is especially applied to a bacterium. *See* BACTERIA.

MICROBIOLOGY, study of organisms of microscopic size, including bacteria, protozoans, viruses, and certain algae and fungi. See individual articles on these subjects.

MICROCOMPUTER, desktop- or notebook-size computing device that uses a microprocessor (q.v.) as its central processing unit, or CPU (*see* COMPUTER). Microcomputers are also called personal computers (PCs), home computers, small-business computers, and micros. The smallest, most compact are called laptops. When they first appeared, they were considered single-user devices, and they were capable of handling only 4, 8, or 16 bits of information at one time. More recently the distinction between microcomputers and large, mainframe computers (as well as the smaller mainframe-type systems called minicomputers) has become blurred, as newer microcomputer models have increased the speed and data-handling capabilities of their CPUs into the 32-bit, multiuser range.

Microcomputers are designed for use in homes, schools, and offices. They can be used in the home as a management tool, (balancing the family checkbook, structuring the family budget, indexing recipes) and recreation (playing computer games, cataloging records and books). Schoolchildren can use microcomputers for doing their homework, and many public schools now use the devices for programmed learning and computer-

Microcomputers have become an important educational tool, even with students as young as these kindergarteners. © Bob Daemmrich–Stock Boston

literacy courses. Small businesses may use microcomputers for word processing, bookkeeping, and the storage and handling of mailing lists.

Origins. Microcomputers were made possible by two technical innovations in the field of microelectronics: the integrated circuit (q.v.), or IC, which was developed in 1959; and the microprocessor, which first appeared in 1971. The IC permitted the miniaturization of computer-memory circuits, and the microprocessor reduced a computer's CPU to the size of a single silicon chip.

Because a CPU calculates, performs logical operations, contains operating instructions, and manages data flows, the potential existed for developing a separate system that could function as a complete microcomputer. The first such desktop-size system specifically designed for personal use appeared in 1974; it was offered by Micro Instrumentation Telemetry Systems (MITS). The owners of the system were then encouraged by the editor of a technology magazine to create and sell a mail-order computer kit through the magazine. The computer, which was called Altair, retailed for slightly less than $400.

The demand for the microcomputer kit was immediate, unexpected, and totally overwhelming. Scores of small entrepreneurial companies responded to this demand by producing computers for the new market. The first major electronics firm to manufacture and sell personal computers, Tandy Corporation (Radio Shack), in-

MICROCOSM AND MACROCOSM

troduced its model in 1977. It quickly dominated the field, because of the combination of two attractive features: a keyboard and a cathode-ray display terminal (CRT). It was also popular because it could be programmed and the user was able to store information by means of cassette tape.

Soon after Tandy's new model was introduced, two engineer-programmers—Stephen Wozniak (1950–) and Steven Jobs (1955–)—started a new computer manufacturing company named Apple Computers. Some features introduced by Apple including expanded memory, inexpensive disk-drive programs and data storage, and color graphics. Apple went on to become the fastest-growing company in U.S. business history. Its rapid growth inspired a large number of similar manufacturers to enter the field. Before the end of the decade, the personal computer market was clearly defined.

In 1979, IBM introduced its own model, the IBM PC. Although it did not make use of the most recent computer technology, the PC was a milestone in this burgeoning field. It proved that the microcomputer industry was more than a fad, and that the microcomputer was in fact a necessary tool for the business community. The PC's use of a 16-bit microprocessor initiated the development of faster and more powerful micros, and its use of an operating system that was available to all other computer makers led to a de facto standardization of the industry.

Later Developments. In the mid-1980s, a number of other developments were especially important for the growth of microcomputers. One of these was the introduction of a powerful 32-bit computer capable of running advanced multi-user operating systems at high speeds. This has dulled the distinction between microcomputers and minicomputers, placing enough computing power on an office desktop to serve all small businesses and most medium-size businesses.

Another innovation was the introduction of simpler, "user-friendly" methods for controlling the operations of microcomputers. By substituting a graphical user interface (GUI) for the conventional operating system, computers such as the Apple Macintosh allow the user to select icons—graphic symbols of computer functions—from a display screen instead of requiring typed commands. New voice-controlled systems are now available, and users may eventually be able to use the words and syntax of spoken language to operate their microcomputers. G.Ma.

For further information on this topic, see the Bibliography in volume 28, section 542.

MICROCOSM and MACROCOSM, two philosophical terms, opposite in meaning, used to explain the relationship between man and the universe. The term *microcosm* denotes the conception of man as a complete world, universe, or cosmos, in miniature, within himself. *Macrocosm* refers to the idea of the whole gigantic universe outside man's nature. The microcosm concept was utilized by a number of great thinkers ranging from the 5th-century BC Greek philosopher Democritus to the 17th-century German philosopher Gottfried Wilhelm Leibniz.

MICRONESIA, one of the three major divisions (with Melanesia and Polynesia) of Oceania, encompassing the islands of the Pacific Ocean E of the Philippines, and for the most part N of the equator. The more than 2000 islands include the Northern Marianas, Palau (Belau), the Marshall Islands, Tuvalu, Kiribati, Nauru, and the Federated States of Micronesia. They have a total land area of about 2730 sq km (about 1055 sq mi). The inhabitants are primarily of Australoid and Polynesian descent. Guam is the largest of the islands, most of which are small atolls.

MICRONESIA, FEDERATED STATES OF, island country, W Pacific Ocean, composed of the states of Kosrae, Pohnpei (Ponape), Chuuk (Truk), and Yap. The country was part of the UN Trust Territory of the Pacific Islands, set up in 1947 and administered by the U.S. It operates under a constitution adopted in 1979 that provides for an elected legislature and governor in each state; federal offices include a president and vice-president, who are chosen by the unicameral Congress of 14 directly elected senators. Palikir (1994 est., 5500), in Pohnpei, is the capital of the country, and Weno (Moen), in Truk, is the largest community (15,250). A compact of free association, providing for full self-government but delegating responsibility for defense to the U.S., took effect in 1986. The trusteeship was dissolved by the UN Security Council in 1990, and the country was admitted to the UN in 1991. Farming, fishing, tourism, and the manufacture of clothing and handicrafts are the mainstays of the economy. The U.S. dollar is the legal currency. Area, 702 sq km (271 sq mi); pop. (1991) 100,520.

MICRONESIAN ART. See Oceanian Art and Architecture.

MICROPHONE, device used to transform sound energy into electrical energy (*see* Sound Recording and Reproduction). Microphones are important in many kinds of communications systems and in instruments for measuring sound and noise. Early types were invented about 1875.

The simplest type of microphone is the carbon microphone, used in telephone apparatus. This microphone consists of a metallic cup filled with carbon granules with a movable metallic diaphragm mounted in contact with the granules at the open

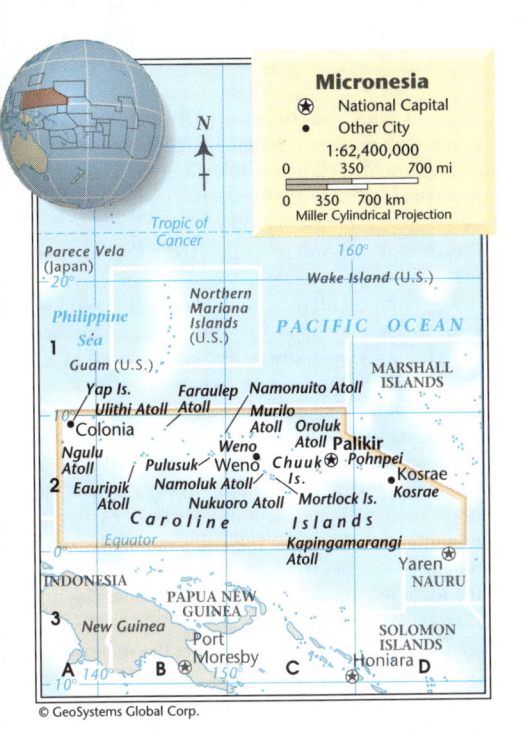

MICROPROCESSOR

Micronesia
- ⊛ National Capital
- • Other City

1:62,400,000
0 — 350 — 700 mi
0 — 350 — 700 km
Miller Cylindrical Projection

Micronesia: Map Index

Cities and Towns

Colonia	A2
Kosrae	D2
Palikir, capital	C2
Weno	C2

Other Features

Caroline, islands	B2
Chuuk, islands	C2
Eauripik, atoll	B2
Faraulep, atoll	B2
Kapingamarangi, atoll	C2
Kosrae, island	D2
Mortlock, islands	C2
Murilo, atoll	C2
Namoluk, atoll	C2
Namonuito, atoll	C2
Ngulu, atoll	A2
Nukuoro, atoll	C2
Oroluk, atoll	C2
Pohnpei, island	D2
Pulusuk, island	B2
Ulithi, atoll	B2
Weno, island	C2
Yap, islands	A2

---

end. Wires attached to the cup and diaphragm are connected to an electrical circuit and carry a current. When sound waves make contact with the diaphragm, it vibrates, varying the pressure on the carbon granules and causing a variation in the electrical resistance of the granules. The current in the circuit varies with the resistance, and the changes may either actuate a nearby telephone receiver or may be amplified and transmitted to a distant receiver. If the current variation is suitably amplified, it may also be used to modulate a radio transmitter.

Another common type, the crystal microphone, utilizes the piezoelectric qualities of certain crystals (those that, when compressed, develop electric charges at their ends), such as Rochelle salt. In this microphone the sound waves cause the crystal to vibrate, generating a small voltage, which is then amplified. In the velocity microphone a thin metallic ribbon is hung between the poles of a magnet. When this ribbon is made to vibrate by sound waves, a small voltage is generated in it by electromagnetic induction.

The dynamic microphone operates on essentially the same principle but has a coil of light wire, instead of a ribbon, attached to the diaphragm. Some microphones, designed to pick up sound from one direction only, combine both ribbon and coil elements. Another type used occasionally is the condenser microphone, in which sound waves alter the spacing between two thin metallic plates and hence change the electrical capacity between them. By placing such a microphone in a suitable circuit, these variations may be amplified, producing an electrical signal.

Among the important characteristics of microphones are their frequency response, directionality, sensitivity, and immunity to outside disturbances such as shock or vibration.

MICROPHOTOGRAPHY. See MICROSCOPE.

MICROPROCESSOR, minute, inexpensive central processing unit (CPU) of a small computer (q.v.), which can also be used independently in a wide range of applications. A microprocessor is built onto a single piece of silicon, called a wafer or chip, that is commonly no longer than 0.5 cm (0.2 in) along one side and no more than 0.05 cm (0.02 in) thick. Despite its small size, a microprocessor may be programmed to perform a great number of information-handling tasks. It can serve as a general-purpose computing machine for instructional or word-processing use, for controlling other machines or industrial processes, for monitoring hospital patients, and for hand-held calculators. The advent of the microprocessor was made possible by the progressive miniaturization of integrated circuits (q.v.) and by advances in semiconductor (q.v.) technology.

A microprocessor may function by itself in a wide range of applications, incorporating as few as 1000 or as many as several hundred thousand elements on its single chip. It may also serve as the CPU of a complete microcomputer (q.v.), when it is combined with support chips containing computer memories and is equipped with input-output devices. Microcomputers gained great importance in the 1970s and '80s with the growth of the personal and home computers.

A microprocessor chip typically contains a read-only memory (ROM)—that is, a memory that can be read repeatedly but cannot be changed—

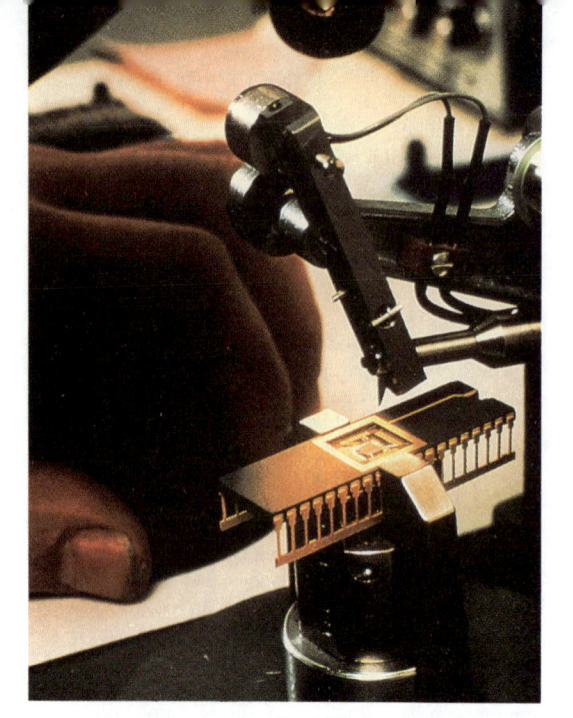

This microprocessor chip will be used in a microcomputer. The components are being welded into position on a silicon base. Exxon Corp.–American Petroleum Institute

but it may also have some random-access memory (RAM) for holding transient data. Also present are a register for holding computing instructions, a register for holding the "address" of each instruction in turn, similar data registers, and a logic unit. It also has interfaces for connecting with external memories and other systems as needed.

Microprocessors are classified in terms of the number of "bits" of information that can be transferred in parallel and held in their registers. This number has been steadily increasing with the growth of circuit technology. Thus 4-bit, 8-bit, and 16-bit microprocessors are now common, and 32-bit chips have also been developed.

High-density computer memories, although themselves not microprocessors, are made by means of the same techniques. By the mid-1980s, the density commonly attained was about 64,000 bits (64K bits) stored per individual circuit, but 256K memories had already appeared and million-bit units were being developed. Further advances will be determined by theoretical and practical limits on minimum transistor size. L.P.L.

For further information on this topic, see the Bibliography in volume 28, sections 541–42.

MICROSCOPE, any one of several types of instruments used to obtain an enlarged visual or photographic image of minute objects or minute details of objects. The simplest form of microscope is the common magnifying glass, a double-convex lens with a short focal length that forms an erect and enlarged visual image (*see* OPTICS). The utility of such lenses is limited to magnifications of about 10 to 15 diameters, expressed as 10x or 15x, and for most microscopic work, therefore, the compound microscope is employed. *See* LENS.

The compound microscope consists essentially of two lens systems, the objective and the ocular, mounted at opposite ends of a closed tube. The objective lens is composed of several lens elements that form an enlarged real image of the object being examined. The ocular is a magnifying lens system so arranged that the real image formed by the objective lies at its focal point; the observer looking through the ocular sees an enlarged virtual image of the real image. The total magnification of the microscope is determined by the focal lengths of the two lens systems. The accessory equipment of a microscope includes a firm stand with a flat stage for holding the material to be examined and some means for moving the microscope tube toward and away from the stage so that the specimen can be brought into focus. Ordinarily, specimens for microscopic examination are transparent and are viewed by transmitted light. They are usually mounted on thin, rectangular glass slides. The stage is pierced with a small hole for the passage of light and is equipped on its underside with a mirror and a condensing lens to concentrate light rays on the aperture in the stage.

The first drawing of a compound microscope, called a megaloscope at the time, appeared in the Dioptric *(1637), a paper published by René Descartes, which discussed the laws of refraction. This instrument was one of the first to incorporate the condenser lens, marked z in the drawing.* Roman Vishniac Collection

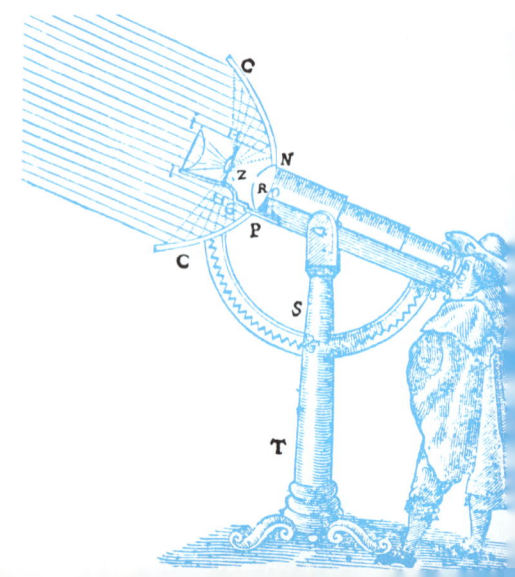

MICROSCOPE

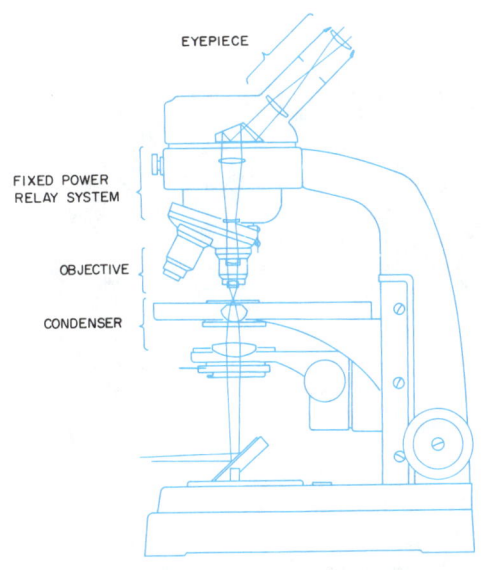

Diagram showing the parts of a simple microscope.
Bausch & Lomb

Sometimes daylight is used as a source of illumination for microscopic work, but generally special lamps are used because they provide a concentrated source of light that is controllable both in intensity and color.

In photomicrography, the process of taking photographs through a microscope, the camera may be a miniature type, mounted on the microscope directly above the eyepiece, or a larger size, supported independently. Normally the camera does not contain a lens, because the microscope itself acts as the lens system. The term *microphotography*, sometimes used instead of *photomicrography*, is usually applied to the technique of duplicating and reducing a picture or a document to a miniature size for storage.

Microscopes used for research commonly have a number of refinements as an aid to precise work. Because the image is highly magnified and is inverted, making manipulation of the specimen by hand very difficult, the stages of such microscopes are so mounted that they may be moved from side to side and backward and forward by means of micrometer screws, and sometimes provision is also made for rotating the stage. All research microscopes are equipped with three or more objectives, mounted on a revolving head, so that the magnification of the instrument can be varied. The single eyepiece of the ordinary microscope is also sometimes replaced by an arrangement of prisms and lenses so that the worker may view the image with both eyes. Instruments of this type are known as binocular microscopes. The eyepieces in binocular microscopes are generally inclined to provide a comfortable viewing angle for prolonged visual observation.

Special-Purpose Optical Microscopes. A number of types of microscopes have been developed for specialized uses. One such type is the stereoscopic microscope, which is actually two low-powered microscopes so arranged that they converge on the specimen. These instruments provide an erect, nonreversed image and have the advantage of giving depth perception through binocular vision.

The ultraviolet microscope utilizes the ultraviolet region of the spectrum rather than the visual region, either to gain resolution because of the shorter wavelength or to emphasize detail by selective absorption at different wavelengths within the ultraviolet band (*see* ULTRAVIOLET RADIATION). As glass does not transmit the shorter ultraviolet wavelengths, the optics utilized in this type of microscope usually are quartz, fluorite, or aluminized-mirror systems. Further, because

This photomicrograph of vitamin B_{12}, or cobalamin, taken by Roman Vishniac, indicates the usefulness of this photographic technique to modern biology.

Among the moon rocks returned by the Apollo 12 astronauts was found this feldspar-rich rock fragment, viewed here under polarized light to accentuate differences in crystal thickness.

David McKay—NASA

ultraviolet radiation is invisible, the image is produced by phosphorescence, by photography, or by electronic scanning methods. The ultraviolet microscope is used in medical research.

The petrographic microscope is used to identify and quantitatively estimate the mineral components of igneous rock and metamorphic rock (qq.v.). With this information, petrographers are then able to classify such rocks. The petrographic microscope is equipped with a Nicol prism or other polarizing device to polarize the light that passes through the specimen being examined; another prism or analyzer determines the polarization of the light after it has passed through the specimen. The microscope also has a rotating stage that, by suitable adjustment, shows the change in polarization caused by the specimen.

The dark-field microscope employs illumination in the form of a hollow, extremely intense cone of light, which is concentrated on the specimen. The objective lies in the hollow, dark portion of the cone and thus picks up only scattered light from the object. As a consequence, the clear portions of the specimen appear as a dark background, and the minute objects under study glow brightly against this dark field. This form of illumination is useful for transparent, unstained biological material and on minute objects that cannot be seen in normal illumination.

The phase microscope employs a condenser that illuminates the specimen with a hollow cone of light, as in the dark-field microscope. In the phase microscope, however, the cone of light is narrower and enters the objective. Within the objective is a ring-shaped pattern that both reduces the intensity of the light and introduces a phase shift of a quarter of a wavelength. This form of illumination causes minute variations of refractive index in a transparent specimen to become visible as detail. Living tissue may be studied with this form of microscope; hence it finds wide application in biology and medicine.

Very advanced optical microscopes include the near-field microscope, through which details smaller than the wavelengths of light can be seen. A light beam shone through a tiny hole is played across the specimen, at a distance of only about half the diameter of the hole, until an entire image is obtained.

Electron Microscope. The practical magnification available with an ordinary microscope using light rays is limited to a few thousand diameters. If a beam of electrons is used to "illuminate" the specimen, however, much greater magnifications are possible, because the wave characteristics of the electron beam are equivalent to extremely short wavelengths. This is the principle of the electron microscope. The instrument itself consists of an electron gun, or source of electrons, and a series of magnetic "lenses" that bend and focus the electron beam in the same way that a conventional lens bends and focuses light rays. These lenses consist of coils of wire with iron

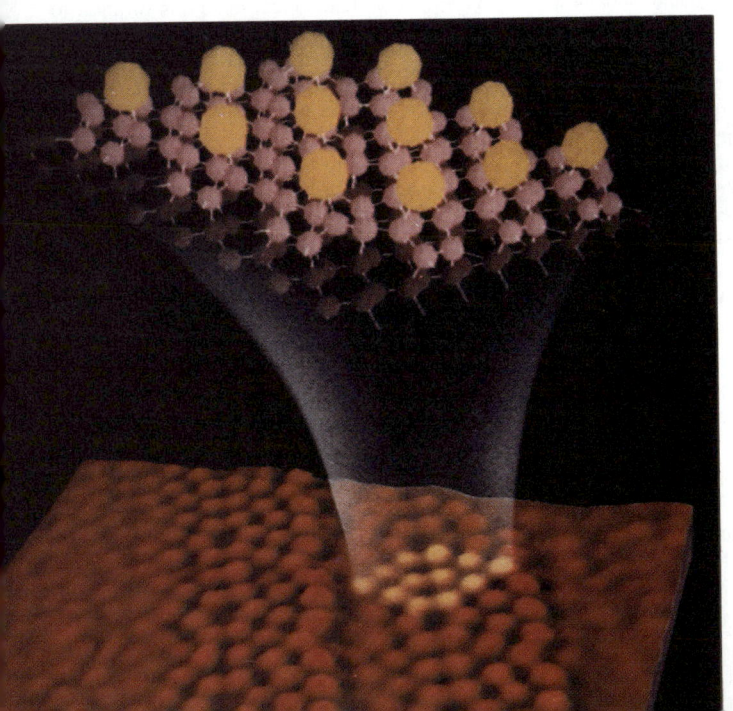

In the mid-1980s tunneling microscopes were developed capable of showing new views of matter on an atomic scale. Shown is an atomic structure of a silicon crystal surface highlighted with an expanded computer-generated model above.
R. S. Becker–AT&T Bell Laboratories

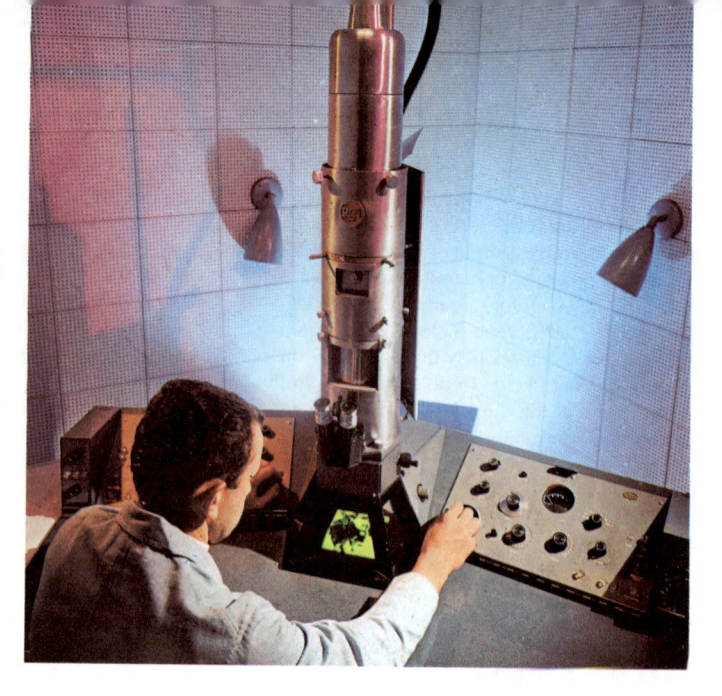

The electron microscope, used extensively as a research tool in the life sciences such as biology, botany, and biochemistry, is also important in physical and chemical analysis. The research technician in this picture is attempting to determine the particle size and shape of inorganic chemical compounds. The magnified electronic image becomes visible on the fluorescent screen in front of the instrument, and can be photographed by allowing the magnifying stream of electrons to fall on a photographic plate.   W.R. Grace & Co.

cores so arranged that the magnetic field within the coil has lines of force radiating from its axis (see MAGNETISM). The instrument is focused not by moving the coils but by varying the current, thereby altering the magnetic field. The image produced by the electron microscope is invisible, but can be recorded on photographic film or plates or can be observed on a screen covered with a fluorescent material (see LUMINESCENCE). Electron microscopes give resolving powers as low as about 1/13,000,000 cm (about 1/5,000,000 in), and direct magnifications up to about 30,000 diameters; their images can be optically enlarged still further to give a total magnification of 100,000 diameters or more. Even higher resolution is possible if the magnetic lenses are cooled to cryogenic temperatures (see CRYOGENICS), thus stabilizing the electric currents passing through the lens. Computer processing can provide images of atomic positions on a specimen surface and, using tomographic techniques, three-dimensional images of living cells, as well.

The scanning electron microscope (SEM) passes an electron beam across a specimen, one point at a time, and reflected electrons are processed to produce specimen images with great depth of field. The scanning transmission electron microscope (STEM) provides further observational advantages.

Scanning Tunneling Microscope. The scanning tunneling microscope, invented in 1981, makes use of a quantum physics phenomenon called the tunnel effect to provide images of the network of atoms or molecules on the surface of a substance. When viewing matter at the atomic level, the degree of microscopic magnification becomes essentially irrelevant. Atomic microscopists refer, instead, to the dimensions of the field of view, expressed in angstroms, or hundred-millionths of a centimeter (an angstrom being approximately equal to the diameter of the hydrogen atom). In scanning tunneling microscopes, an extremely sharp metal needle is brought to within a few angstroms of the surface of the material being viewed. The gap is so small that electrons leak, or tunnel, across it, generating a current. If the distance between the tip of the needle and the sample increases, the current decreases. To keep the current constant, a scanning mechanism drawing the needle over the surface of the sample constantly adjusts the height of the needle. By tracking these minute adjustments, a sketch of the contours of the surface is produced. Computer processing of the contour lines results in a graphic representation of a three-dimensional surface, in which ridges and valleys represent the edges of atomic arrays. See also ATOM AND ATOMIC THEORY.

X-ray Microscope. X-ray microscopes were being developed in the mid-1980s, using a focusing device called a zone plate. By means of tomographic techniques, these microscopes are designed to provide images of processes in living cells, down to the level of large molecules.

For further information on this topic, see the Bibliography in volume 28, section 398.

MICROWAVES, short, high-frequency radio waves lying roughly between very-high-frequency (infrared) waves and conventional radio waves (see ELECTROMAGNETIC RADIATION; RADIO). Microwaves thus range in length from about 1 mm to 30 cm (about 0.04 to 12 in). They are generated in special electron tubes, such as the klystron and the magnetron, with built-in resonators to control the frequency (see ELECTRONICS) or by special oscillators or solid-state devices. Microwaves have many applications: in radio and television, radar, meteorology, satellite communications, distance measuring, and research into the properties of matter. Microwave ovens operate by agitating the water molecules in the food, causing them to vibrate, which produces heat. The microwaves enter through openings in the top of the cooking cavity, where a stirrer scatters them evenly throughout the oven. They are unable to enter a metal container to heat food, but they can pass through nonmetal containers.

Microwaves can be detected by an instrument consisting of a silicon-diode rectifier (see RECTIFICATION) connected to an amplifier, and a recording or display device. Exposure to microwaves is dangerous mainly when high densities of microwave radiation are involved, as with masers. They can cause burns, cataracts, damage to the nervous system, and sterility. The possible danger of long-term exposure to low-level microwaves is not yet well known. Nevertheless, the U.S. government limits the exposure level, in general, to 10 milliwatts per square centimeter. Stricter limits are placed on microwave ovens.

MIDAS, in Greek mythology, king of Phrygia in Asia Minor. For his hospitality to the satyr Silenus, Dionysus, god of wine, offered to grant Midas anything he wished. The king requested that everything he touched be turned to gold, but he soon regretted his choice because even his food and water were changed to gold. To free himself from the enchantment, Midas was instructed by Dionysus to bathe in the Pactolus River. It was said that afterward the sands of the river contained gold.

Midas was also one of the judges in a musical contest between the gods Apollo and Pan. When Midas preferred Pan's playing of the pipes to Apollo's playing of the lyre, Apollo changed Midas's ears to those of an ass. Midas was able to conceal his ears from all but his barber, who whispered the secret into a hole in the ground. When the wind blew, the reeds that grew over the hole repeated the story.

MIDDLE AGES, period in European history from the collapse of Roman political control in the West—traditionally set in the 5th century—to about the 15th century. It should be emphasized, however, that the fixing of dates for the beginning and end of the Middle Ages is arbitrary; at neither time was there any sharp break in the cultural development of the continent. The term seems to have been first used by Flavio Biondo of Forlí (1388–1463), a historian and apostolic secretary in Rome, in his *Historiarum ab Inclinatione Romanorum Imperii Decades* (Decades of History from the Deterioration of the Roman Empire), which was first published in 1483, although written some 30 years earlier. The term implied a suspension of time and, especially, a suspension of progress—a period of cultural stagnation, once referred to as the Dark Ages, between the glory of classical antiquity and the rebirth of that glory in the beginnings of the modern world. Although the idea is untenable, the term Middle Ages is still in use. Modern scholarship generally divides the whole period into three stages and is much more concerned with diversity even within the subdivisions.

Early Middle Ages. No one definitive event marks the end of antiquity and the beginning of the Middle Ages. Neither the sack of Rome by the Goths under Alaric I in 410 nor the deposition in 476 of Romulus Augustulus, the last Roman emperor in the West, impressed their contemporaries as epoch-making catastrophes. Rather, by the end of the 5th century the culmination of several long-term trends—most notably a severe economic dislocation and the invasions and settlement of the various Germanic tribes within the borders of the Western Empire—had changed the face of Rome. For the next 300 years western Europe remained essentially a primitive culture, albeit one uniquely superimposed on the complex, elaborate culture of the Roman Empire, which was never entirely lost or forgotten.

Fragmentation of authority. Although during this period the loose confederation of tribes began to coalesce into kingdoms, virtually no machinery of government existed, and political and economic development was local in nature. Regular commerce had ceased almost entirely, although—as modern scholars maintain—the money economy never entirely vanished. In the culmination of a process that had already begun in the Roman Empire, the peasantry became bound to the land and dependent on landlords for protection and the rudimentary administration of justice (see SEIGNORIALISM). Among the warrior aristocracy the most important social bonds were ties of kinship, but feudal connections (see FEUDALISM) were also emerging, which may have been rooted in the old Roman patron-client relationship or in the Germanic *comitatus,* the group of fighting companions.

MIDDLE AGES

Peasants performing various tasks during the Middle Ages, including harvesting grain, gathering grapes, plowing with oxen, and pruning a tree to improve its shape and growth.
Scala

All such connections impeded any tendency toward political consolidation.

The church. The only universal European institution was the church, and even there a fragmentation of authority was the rule; all power within the church hierarchy was in the hands of local bishops. The bishop of Rome, the pope, had a certain fatherly preeminence based on his holding of the so-called chair of St. Peter, to whom it was supposed Christ had granted governing power, but neither the elaborate machinery of ecclesiastical government nor the idea of a monarchical church headed by the pope was to be developed for another 500 years. The church saw itself as the spiritual community of Christian believers, in exile from God's kingdom, waiting in a hostile world for the day of deliverance. The most important exiles were found outside the hierarchy of church government, in the monasteries that dotted Europe.

Opposed to the forces of fragmentation and local development were the tendencies within the church toward standardizing the rite, the calendar, and the monastic rule. Besides such administrative measures, the cultural memory of Rome persisted. By the 9th century, with the rise to power of the Carolingians, the beginnings of a new European unity based on the Roman legacy may be found, for Charlemagne's political power depended on educational reforms that used materials, methods, and aims from the Roman past.

Culture and learning. Cultural activity during the early Middle Ages consisted primarily in appropriating and systematizing the knowledge of the past. The works of classical authors were copied and annotated. Encyclopedic works, such as Isidore of Seville's *Etymologies* (623), which attempted to present the collected knowledge of humankind, were compiled. At the center of any learned activity stood the Bible; indeed, all secular learning was regarded as mere preparation for understanding the holy text.

The early Middle Ages drew to a close in the 10th century with new migrations and invasions—the coming of the Vikings from the north and the Magyars from the Asian steppes—and the weakening of all forces of European unity and expansion. The resulting violence and dislocation caused lands to be withdrawn from cultivation, population to decline, and the monasteries to again become outposts of civilization. Nevertheless, the cultural work of assimilating the legacy of antiquity had been done, and it was not to be lost.

High Middle Ages. By the year 1050 Europe stood on the verge of an unprecedented period of development. The era of migrations had come to a close, and Europe experienced the continuity and dynamic growth of a settled population. Town life, and with it regular and large-scale trade and commerce, was revived. The society and culture of the High Middle Ages were complex, dynamic, and innovative. This period has become the center of attention for modern medieval scholarship, and it has come to be known as the renaissance of the 12th century.

Papal power. During the High Middle Ages the church, organized into an elaborate hierarchy with the pope as its unequivocal head, was the most sophisticated governing institution in western Europe. Not only did the papacy exercise direct political control over the domain lands of central and northen Italy, but through diplomacy and the administration of justice in the extensive system of ecclesiastical courts it also exercised a directive power throughout Europe. In addition, the monastic orders grew and flourished, and they, too, became fully involved with the secular world. The old Benedictine houses were embedded in the network of feudal alliances; new orders such as the Cistercians were famous as drainers of marshland and clearers of forest. Even such movements as the Franciscans, dedicated to voluntary poverty and renunciation, soon became thoroughly engaged in the newly emergent urban life. No longer did the church see itself as the heavenly city in exile; it was at the center of existence. High medieval spirituality became individualized; it was no longer based on communitarian prayer but, on the one hand, located ritually in the priestly miracle of the Eucharist and, on the other, in the subjective, emotional identification of the individual believer with the suffering humanity of Christ. Similar in feeling was the rise to prominence of special devotion to the Virgin Mary, an attitude unprecedented in the early church.

Intellectual quests. Throughout the cultural sphere an unprecedented intellectual ferment developed. New educational institutions, such as cathedral and monastic schools, prospered, and the first universities were established. Advanced degrees in medicine, law, and theology were offered, and in each field inquiry was intense. The medical writings of antiquity, many of which had been preserved only by Arab scholars, were recovered and translated. Both ecclesiastical and civil law, especially at the famous university in Bologna, were systematized, commented on, and questioned as they had never been before. These investigations were influential in the development of new methodologies that would bear rich fruit throughout all fields of study. The writings

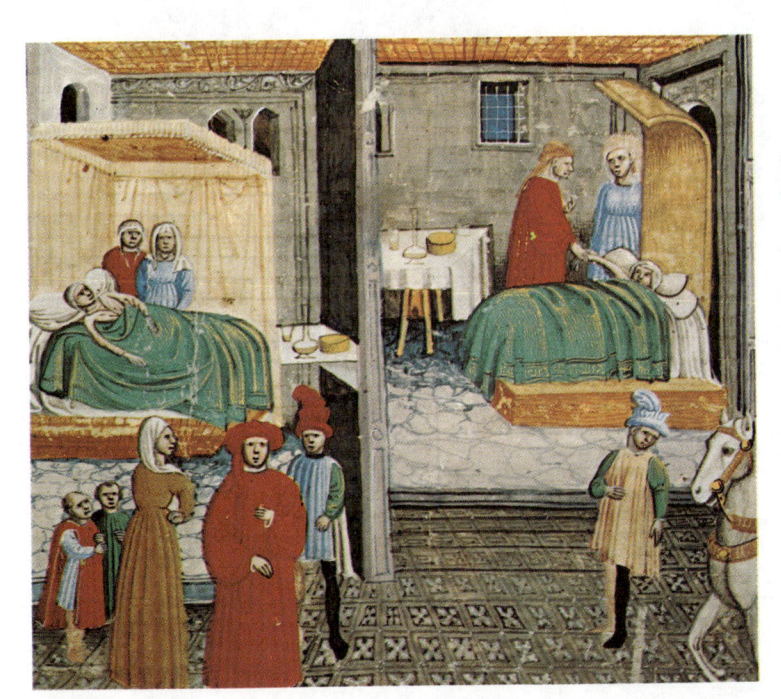

A medieval hospital ward, depicted in an illustration from the Canon of Medicine, written by Avicenna. The book, based chiefly on Greek medical writings, was a systematic summary of pharmaceutical and medical knowledge up to his time. Translated into Latin in the 12th century, it was a standard text at European medical schools during the Middle Ages. Scala

MIDDLE AGES

An illustration from one of the most celebrated books of hours, Les belles heures de Jean, duc de Berry *(The Lovely Hours of Jean, Duke of Berry), illuminated by the Limbourg brothers in about 1408–9. The illustration shows the duke and his retinue on a journey; the buildings are typical French castles of the period. Books of hours contained psalms, prayers, and excerpts from Scripture that were intended to be recited at set times during the day. The page from which this illumination is taken includes a prayer for travelers.* Metropolitan Museum of Art, Cloisters Collection–Purchase, 1954

of the church fathers were studied again, theological doctrines and practices were explored, and problematic areas of the Christian tradition were discussed, aided by the new technique of dialectical analysis. The 12th century thus ushered in a great age of philosophy in the West.

Artistic innovations. Innovations took place in the creative arts as well. Literacy was no longer merely a professional prerequisite of the clergy, and the result was a flowering of new literature, both in Latin and—for the first time—in the vernacular languages. These new writings were addressed to a literary public that had both the education and leisure to read. The love lyric, the courtly romance, new modes of historical writing—all expressed the new complexity of life and engagement with the secular world. In painting unprecedented attention was given to the depiction of emotional extremes and to the natural and workaday world. In architecture the Romanesque style was perfected through the erection of numerous churches, especially along the pilgrimage routes in southern France and Spain, even as it began to give way to the nascent Gothic style, which in the next centuries would become the prevailing international mode of building.

New European unity. During the 13th century the achievements of the 12th were codified and synthesized. The monarchical church had become the great European institution; trade and commerce had tied Europe into an economic unity. This was due particularly to the achievements of Italian merchant-bankers, whose activities penetrated France, England, the Low Countries, and North Africa, as well as the old imperial lands of Germany. Travel, whether for pilgrimage, trade, or study at a university, became relatively easy and common. This was also a century of Crusades (although they had begun in the late 11th century). Conceived of in church law as an armed pilgrimage, the Crusades nevertheless cut across the lines of class and profession in their appeal. These strange and problematic international religious expeditions were yet one more example of the European unity that was centered in the church. The High Middle Ages culminated in the great cultural achievements of Gothic architecture, the philosophic works of Saint Thomas Aquinas, and the imaginative vision of the totality of human life in Dante's *Divine Comedy*.

Late Middle Ages. If the High Middle Ages were marked by the achievement of institutional unity and intellectual synthesis, then the late Middle Ages were characterized by conflict and dissolution. It was in the late Middle Ages that the secular state began to emerge—even though it often was no more than an incipient national feeling—and the struggle for supremacy between church and state became a fixture of European history for the next several centuries. Towns and cities, which continued to grow in size and prosperity, began to work toward political self-control, and the urban conflict became internal as well, as various classes and interests vied for hegemony.

Beginnings of political science. One result of this struggle, particularly in the seignorial corporations of the Italian towns, was the intensification of political and social thinking that focused on the secular state as a subject of inquiry in its own right, independent of the church or community of believers.

The independence of political inquiry is only one facet of a major trend in late medieval thinking. The grand project of high medieval philosophy, the attempt to reach a total synthesis of all knowledge and experience, both human and divine, was becoming untenable. Some scholars have seen in this trend toward the specialization and narrowing of philosophical inquiry a loss of direction or decay. Others regard it as a new beginning—the beginning, for example, of the empirical investigation of the physical world, which can be traced to the breakdown of the high medieval philosophical synthesis.

New spirituality. Important though the developments in philosophy were, however, it was the spirituality of the late Middle Ages that was the true register of the social and cultural turmoil of the age. Spiritual innovation took place both within and without the established structure of the church. Late medieval spirituality was characterized by an intense search for the direct experience of God, whether through the private, interior ecstasy of mystical illumination, or through the personal scrutiny of God's word in the Bible. In either case, the established church—both in its traditional function as interpreter of doctrine and in its institutional role as conveyor of the sacraments—found itself not so much embattled as dispensed with.

Mystical experience was potentially available to everyone, lay or cleric, man or woman, learned or illiterate. Conceived of as a personal gift of God, it stood sharply removed from social rank or cultural attainment. It was unworldly, irrational, private, and authoritative. Devotional reading of the Bible, in its turn, brought an awareness of a church strikingly different from the all-encompassing, worldly medieval institution. Christ and the apostles presented an image of radical simplicity, and taking the life of Christ as a model of conduct to be imitated, individuals began to

MIDDLE CLASS

organize themselves into apostolic communities. Movements such as the Brethren of the Common Life and the Spiritual Franciscans proliferated throughout Europe. Sometimes they endeavored to reform the church from within, to lead it back to apostolic simplicity and purity; at other times they simply disengaged themselves from all existing institutions.

In many instances such movements took on an apocalyptic or messianic fervor, particularly among the disenfranchised workers in the late medieval towns, who lived in a state of perpetual crisis. After the catastrophic appearance in the 1340s of the black plague, bands of penitents, flagellants, and followers of new messiahs and charismatic "saints" could be found throughout Europe, hoping to prepare for the coming of a new apostolic age.

This process of spiritual unrest and innovation would ultimately terminate in the Protestant Reformation. The new national identities would lead to the triumph of the modern nation-state. The continual expansion of trade and finance would lay the groundwork for the revolutionary transformation of the European economy. Thus, in the dissolution of the medieval world, in its social and cultural turmoil, the seeds of the modern age may be found.   N.F.P.

For further information on this topic, see the Bibliography in volume 28, sections 42, 652–53, 896–99.

MIDDLE CLASS. See BOURGEOISIE.

MIDDLE CONGO. See CONGO, REPUBLIC OF.

MIDDLE EAST, region loosely defined by geography and culture, located in SW Asia and NE Africa. In most current usage, the term Middle East refers collectively to Cyprus, Egypt, Iran, Iraq, Israel, Jordan, Kuwait, Lebanon, Saudi Arabia, Syria, Turkey, Yemen, and the states and emirates along the S and E fringes of the Arabian Peninsula, namely, Bahrain, Oman, Qatar, and the United Arab Emirates. When used by scholars to designate a so-called culture area, the unity of which is based on Islamic law and custom, the term Middle East usually embraces a much more extensive region, stretching from the borders of Afghanistan and Pakistan in the E through all of North Africa, including Sudan, Libya, Tunisia, Algeria, and Morocco.

The term Middle East as it is now applied was first used by the British military command during World War II. The term Near East, which was formerly used to describe the region, is now sometimes applied to the central core area encompassing the Mediterranean region of the Middle East. See also articles on the individual countries of the area.

ANCIENT PERIOD

Since ancient times invaders and traders have crossed the area known as the Middle East in search of food, raw materials, manufactured goods, or political power. Ideas, inventions, and institutions have spread from this area to affect people in all other parts of the world, earning it the name Cradle of Civilization. The earliest farms, cities, governments, law codes, and alphabets were Middle Eastern. Four major religions—Judaism, Zoroastrianism, Christianity, and Islam—began here.

The Earliest Civilizations. Governments arose as ancient peoples were learning how to tame the great rivers (the Nile, Tigris, Euphrates, and Indus) to support agriculture and were forming religious beliefs about the universe, human relationships, and the meaning of life and death. The first such Middle Eastern states were Egypt and Sumer (qq.v.), which began around or before 3000 BC. Both had powerful kings, priests, scribes, and large work forces to protect the lands from floods or invasions. But invaders came anyway. Sumer was captured, first by the Semitic Akkadians and Amorites from the south, and later by various Indo-European peoples from the north, leading to the formation of the Babylonian Empire in the Tigris-Euphrates region, or Mesopotamia (q.v.). Egypt was occupied by a Semitic group called the Hyksos, but the Egyptians drove them out and built a powerful empire. About 1000 BC new waves of invaders unsettled the region, giving rise to new kingdoms, in Phoenicia (q.v.), Israel, and other areas of the Middle East. The Phoenicians were seafaring traders who developed the first alphabet. The Hebrews were the first people to believe in one almighty God revealed by sacred writings. The Assyrians, an aggressive people who pioneered in using iron tools and weapons, conquered a large area from their stronghold in Mesopotamia.

In the 6th century BC the Persians overran the whole Middle East and set up a ruling system that became the model for all later empires. Sprawling from the Indus to the Nile, Persia (q.v.) could not make its subjects all think and act alike. Therefore, it let them keep their beliefs and practices, as long as they obeyed its laws, paid their taxes, and sent their sons to serve in its armies. Although tied together by roads, a postal service, and a common governmental language, the empire's peoples still controlled most of their own affairs. The state religion was Zoroastrianism, but other faiths were tolerated. In the 4th century BC Persia, weakened by revolts and internal conflicts, was conquered by Alexander the Great of Macedonia.

MIDDLE EAST

Dome of the Rock, a Muslim shrine in Jerusalem's Old City, was erected over a rock of significance to Muslims, Christians, and Jews.

Roger Coster–Monkmeyer Press

MIDDLE EAST

Middle East: Map Index

Countries

Bahrain	D3
Cyprus	B2
Egypt	A3
Iran	D2
Iraq	C2
Israel	B2
Jordan	B2
Kuwait	C3
Lebanon	B2
Oman	D3
Qatar	D3
Saudi Arabia	C3
Syria	B2
Turkey	B2
United Arab Emirates	D3
Yemen	C4

Cities and Towns

Abu Dhabi, United Arab Emirates, capital	D3
Adana, Turkey	B2
Aden, Yemen	C4
Alexandria, Egypt	A2
Amman, Jordan, capital	B2
Ankara, Turkey, capital	B2
Antalya, Turkey	B2
Aswan, Egypt	B3
Baghdad, Iraq, capital	C2
Basra, Iraq	C2
Beirut, Lebanon, capital	B2
Bursa, Turkey	A1
Cairo, Egypt, capital	B2
Damascus, Syria, capital	B2
Doha, Qatar, capital	D3
Dubayy, United Arab Emirates	D3
Esfahan, Iran	D2
Halab (Aleppo), Syria	B2
İstanbul, Turkey	A1
İzmir, Turkey	A2
Jericho, West Bank	B2
Jerusalem, Israel, capital	B2
Jiddah, Saudi Arabia	B3
Kuwait, Kuwait, capital	C3
Manama, Bahrain, capital	D3
Mashhad, Iran	D2
Masqat, Oman, capital	D3
Mecca, Saudi Arabia	B3
Medina, Saudi Arabia	B3
Mosul, Iraq	C2
Nicosia, Cyprus, capital	B2
Riyadh, Saudi Arabia, capital	C3
Sana, Yemen, capital	C4
Shiraz, Iran	D3
Tabriz, Iran	C2
Tehran, Iran, capital	D2
Zahedan, Iran	E3

Other Features

Aden, gulf	C4
Aegean, sea	A2
Arabian, desert	B3
Arabian, sea	E3
Ararat, mt.	C2
Black, sea	B1
Caspian, sea	D2
Damavand, mt.	D2
Dasht-e Kavir, desert	D2
Dasht-e Lut, desert	D2
Elburz, mts.	C2
Euphrates, river	B2
Gaza Strip, occupied territory	B2
Golan Heights, occupied territory	B2
Hormuz, strait	D3
Jordan, river	B2
Kopet, mts.	D2
Mediterranean, sea	A2
Nafud, an-, desert	C3
Nasser, lake	B3
Nile, river	B3
Oman, gulf	D3
Persian, gulf	C3
Pontic, mts.	B1
Red, sea	B3
Rub al-Khali, desert	C4
Sinai, peninsula	B3
Socotra, island	D4
Suez, canal	B2
Syrian, desert	B2
Taurus, mts.	B2
Tigris, river	C2
Urmia, lake	C2
West Bank, occupied territory	B2
Zagros, mts.	C2

Hellenistic and Roman Times. Alexander's conquest started a millennium in which the Middle East was part of the Hellenistic (culturally Greek) world. Greek culture was mixed with local ways, as Alexander borrowed ideas and customs, as well as clerks and soldiers, from the Egyptians, Mesopotamians, and Persians. Egypt's port, Alexandria, became a center of trade and culture, a lasting monument to the conqueror for whom it was named. As Macedonian power waned, the Romans took most of the area, but Persia remained independent under two ruling dynasties: the Parthians (248 BC–AD 226) and the Sassanids (AD 226–641). Roman rule brought uniform laws, good roads, and trade to Egypt, Syria, and Asia Minor (q.v.). Several Middle Eastern religions—Judaism, then Christianity, and a mystery cult called Mithraism—competed for adherents throughout the Roman Empire. Christianity prevailed in the early 4th century AD. Constantine the Great, the first Christian Roman emperor, stressed his Eastern ties by moving his capital to Byzantium, a port on the Bosporus. Renamed Constantinople, it became a great city, the capital of the Eastern Roman Empire, or Byzantine Empire (q.v.), for more than a thousand years.

ISLAMIC PERIOD

Early in the 7th century, Muhammad, a charismatic religious leader, proclaimed himself a prophet of God to the nomadic peoples of the Arabian Peninsula. He founded a community of believers who called themselves Muslims ("those who surrender," that is, to God's will) and their faith Islam (q.v.; "surrender"). By the time of the Prophet's death (632), his doctrines, based on Judeo-Christian and Arabian traditions, had been widely accepted among the Arab tribes.

Arab Dominion. Muhammad's successors, called caliphs, led the Arab tribes in a series of thrusts into Syria, Mesopotamia, Persia, and Egypt, expanding greatly the realm of Islam (see CALIPHATE). These Arab conquests were aided by the anger of many Middle Eastern Christians, Jews, and Zoroastrians at the persecution they had suffered under the Byzantine Empire (which lost much of its territory) or Sassanid Persia (which was totally absorbed by the Arabs). The early caliphs tolerated non-Muslims, as long as they paid taxes and did not rebel. Few of the conquered peoples converted to Islam at once, but centuries of intermarriage and conversion eventually made the area predominantly Muslim.

Middle East
National Capital
Other City
1:28,160,000
0 200 400 mi
0 200 400 km
Lambert Conformal Conic Projection
TURKEY
İstanbul
Bursa
Ankara
İzmir
Antalya
Adana
Pontic Mountains
Taurus Mountains
Ararat 5165 m (16,946 ft)
Black Sea
Aegean Sea
Mediterranean Sea
GREECE
Athens
CYPRUS
Nicosia
GEORGIA
ARMENIA
AZERBAIJAN
Baku
Caucasus
Caspian Sea
SYRIA
Halab (Aleppo)
Damascus
LEBANON
Beirut
ISRAEL
Jerusalem
GAZA STRIP
Jordan
GOLAN HEIGHTS (occupied by Israel)
Amman
Jericho
WEST BANK
JORDAN
IRAQ
Mosul
Baghdad
Basra
Tigris
Euphrates
Syrian Desert
KUWAIT
Kuwait
IRAN
Tabriz
L. Urmia
Tehran
Elburz Mountains
Damavand 5671 m (18,605 ft)
Dasht-e Kavir
Dasht-e Lut
Esfahan
Shiraz
Mashhad
Zahedan
Zagros Mountains
Kopet Mountains
TURKMENISTAN
Ashgabat
UZBEKISTAN
TAJIKISTAN
Dushanbe
CHINA
Hindu Kush
Khyber Pass
AFGHANISTAN
Kabul
Qandahar
PAKISTAN
Islamabad
Lahore
Sukkur
Indus
Karachi
INDIA
Ahmadabad
EGYPT
Alexandria
Cairo
Suez Canal
Sinai
Arabian Desert
Nile
Aswan
L. Nasser
Tropic of Cancer
LIBYA
SUDAN
Port Sudan
Khartoum
ERITREA
Asmara
ETHIOPIA
Red Sea
SAUDI ARABIA
an-Nafud
Medina
Mecca
Jiddah
Riyadh
Rub al-Khali
BAHRAIN
Manama
QATAR
Doha
Persian Gulf
UNITED ARAB EMIRATES
Abu Dhabi
Dubayy
de facto bdy.
OMAN
Masqat
Strait of Hormuz
Gulf of Oman
Arabian Sea
YEMEN
Sana
Aden
undefined boundary
Gulf of Aden
Socotra (Yemen)
N

MIDDLE EAST

Camels in the Wadi Rum Desert of Jordan. Only a small percentage of the terrain in the Middle East is suitable for agriculture.
Luis Villota

The caliphate was controlled by two successive dynasties: the Umayyads (661–750), who governed from Damascus, and the Abbasids (750–1258), who usually ruled in Baghdad. With help from the Arab tribes, the Umayyads won lands in North Africa, Spain, and Central Asia. The Abbasids promoted commerce and culture, giving non-Arab converts equal status with Arab Muslims, but they lost control of the outlying areas. New dynasties arose. By 945 the Abbasids no longer controlled even their own capital. Iranians and Turks took over, as the Arab tribes returned to the desert. Despite political division, however, manufacturing and trade flourished, along with scholarship and the arts.

Turkish and Iranian Hegemony. Beginning in the 10th century, the Middle East was invaded by Turks from Central Asia. They adopted the faith, laws, and culture of the local Muslims and soon governed most of their lands. One dynasty, the Ghaznavids (962–1186), spread Islam throughout India. Another, the Seljuks (1040–1302), took Asia Minor from the Byzantines in 1071. The Turkish invasion helped spark the Crusades, bringing European Christian knights to the eastern shore of the Mediterranean and to Jerusalem. More harmful to Islam was the 13th-century Mongol invasion, which destroyed much of Iraq and Iran. A band of slave-soldiers, the Mamelukes of Egypt, stopped the Mongol advance in 1260.

Although the Mamelukes and various Mongol groups formed powerful states in the following centuries, the greatest and longest lasting was the Ottoman Empire. Starting in the western hills of Asia Minor, Turkish tribes led by Osman and his sons raided and seized Byzantine lands, first in Asia, then in southeastern Europe. In 1453 they took Constantinople. Renamed İstanbul, it became the capital for the descendants of Osman, or Ottomans. Their conquests continued until their empire stretched from Hungary to Yemen and from Algeria to the Iranian border. They tried to conquer Iran as well, but were repelled by that country's Safavid dynasty (1501–1736).

European Domination. After the 16th century, the great Muslim empires declined. The Ottomans lost European lands to Austria and Russia; the Safavids lost their entire country. Iran's revival in the 18th century under Nadir Shah was followed by years of decay. The Ottoman Empire lasted longer because Russia and the other European powers disagreed on how to divide it. Some 19th-century Ottoman rulers tried to Westernize their administration, and the influx of

MIDDLE EAST

European experts, businessmen, and technology changed many aspects of Ottoman society. Many Muslims, suspicious of the West, resisted the changes. Others were influenced by the nationalist and democratic beliefs of the Europeans.

The Ottoman province in which Westernization went furthest was Egypt. Muhammad Ali, who ruled the country from 1805 to 1848, revolutionized Egypt's economy, introducing such crops as sugar and cotton, installing mills and factories, building roads and canals, and importing Western technicians and teachers. His successors, however, were unable to maintain their independence, and after 1882 Egypt fell under British control.

Iran lagged behind in Westernization. Russia took some of its northern lands, and other Western countries tried to take control of its finances and natural resources. When Iranian nationalists won a constitution in 1906, Britain and Russia divided the country into spheres of influence. Hardly noticed then was the discovery of oil in southwestern Iran, although the British would draw on it heavily in two world wars. In fact, this resource, found in increasing quantities throughout the Middle East in the following decades, would gradually assume overriding importance, not only to the countries of the region but even more to the industrialized nations of the West.

The 20th Century. At the start of the 20th century it looked as if the entire Middle East would fall under European control. When the Turks sided with Germany in World War I, Britain helped the Arabs to revolt against Turkish rule. After Germany and Turkey were defeated in 1918, the Arabs hoped to form states in Syria, Iraq, and western Arabia. The British, however, had already agreed to give Syria to France and to support a Jewish national home in Palestine. The League of Nations assigned Syria to France and mandated Palestine and Iraq to Britain. Egypt, under a British protectorate since 1914, demanded independence. This was granted in 1922, but Britain still controlled many aspects of Egypt's government.

The tide began to turn when the Turkish-speaking remnant of the Ottoman Empire rose from its defeat. A military strongman, Mustafa Kemal (later Atatürk), defended Asia Minor against a Greek invasion, compelled the Western powers to rewrite the peace treaty they had forced on the Ottoman Empire, and transformed Turkey into a secular republic. In Iran an army officer, Riza Shah Pahlavi, seized power in 1921 and tried to imitate Kemal's reforms.

In the 1930s and '40s most Arab countries became independent from Britain or France. In Palestine, however, rising Jewish immigration sparked protest riots by the Arab majority, which feared that the Jews would soon take control. British attempts to curb immigration angered Palestinian Jews, who rebelled against the government during and after World War II. The UN

Vessels in the important port of Dubai (Dibai), capital of the oil-rich sheikhdom of Dubai, one of the seven United Arab Emirates on the eastern Arabian Peninsula of the Persian Gulf.   Mathias Oppersdorff

311

Amid jubilation, Egyptian officials hoist the flag of Egypt over the last part of the Sinai Peninsula reclaimed from Israel on April 25, 1982.   Gerard Rancinan–Sygma

voted in 1947 to divide Palestine between the Jews and the Arabs, but all Arab states rejected the plan. In 1948, when British troops left Palestine, the Jews declared the independent state of Israel. The Arab states attacked Israel, unsuccessfully, and most of Palestine's Arab inhabitants fled. Arab-Israeli relations remained hostile, although Egypt and Israel signed a separate peace accord in 1979.

Conflicts in the 1980s and early '90s included Israeli and Syrian interventions in Lebanon, already wracked by factional fighting; the Iran-Iraq War (1980–88); and the Persian Gulf War (q.v.), in which a U.S.-led coalition liberated Kuwait, which had been occupied by Iraq in 1990. Underlying trends during this period were the resurgence of Islamic fundamentalism, most notably in Iran, Algeria, and Egypt, and the continued dependence of the industrialized nations on Middle Eastern oil, giving the region a pivotal role in the world's economy. For decades the U.S. and the Soviet Union vied for influence in the region, with the U.S. generally supporting Israel and the USSR backing certain Arab states. In October 1991, however, the two superpowers joined in sponsoring the first comprehensive Middle East peace conference.

Progress toward peace accelerated in 1993, when Israel and the PLO signed an agreement providing for mutual recognition and for limited Palestinian self-rule in Gaza and parts of the West Bank. Another historic accord, signed in 1994, ended the state of war between Jordan and Israel.

See also history sections of articles on individual countries of the Middle East.   A.E.G.

For further information on this topic, see the *Bibliography in volume 28,* sections 876, 1015–17, 1042–64.

MIDDLESEX, former county, SE England, on the Thames R. Inhabited since prehistoric times, it was settled by Saxons by the 6th century; the name *Middlesex,* meaning "middle Saxons," is descriptive of its geographic position between the East and West Saxons. Dominated for centuries by London, Middlesex became a county in the 19th century. In 1965 most of the county became part of Greater London, the remainder being absorbed by Hertfordshire and Surrey.

MIDDLETON, Arthur (1742–87), leader in the American Revolution and signer of the Declaration of Independence. He was born in his family home on the Ashley River, in South Carolina, and educated in America and England, where he studied law. In 1773 he headed the Whig party of South Carolina in the prerevolutionary movements in progress. He was a member of the first of the colonial Committees of Safety (1775) and delegate to the Second Continental Congress (1776–77). Captured (1780) by the British at Charleston and exchanged (1781), he later served in the Congress of the Confederation and the South Carolina state legislature.

MIDDLETON, Thomas (1580–1627), English dramatist, probably born in London, and educated at the University of Oxford. The plays that are extant were mostly written in collaboration with Thomas Dekker, Michael Drayton, John Webster, and William Rowley (1585?–1642?). He contributed to the first part of Dekker's *The Honest Whore* (1604) and to *The Roaring Girle* (1610). Middleton's popular *A Trick to Catch the Old One* (1608) is a satire about middle-class life in London. His two most known plays, *The Changeling* (1621), written with Rowley, and *Women Beware Women,* were tragedies about the corruption of character. *A Game at Chesse* (1624) was closed after nine performances because of its anti-Spanish content. Middleton was city chronologer of London (1620–c. 1625).

MIDDLETOWN, city, Middlesex Co., central Connecticut, on the Connecticut R.; inc. as a city 1784. Major manufactures include aircraft parts and equipment, computer equipment, hardware, industrial machinery, and printed materials. The insurance industry is also important to the city's economy. Wesleyan University (1831), which includes the Davison Art Center; a community college; and the Middlesex County Historical Society museum are here. Founded in 1650 on the site of an Indian village, the community grew as a port and shipbuilding center and was a trading port with the West Indies. In 1923 the town and city of Middletown were consolidated. Pop. (1980) 39,040; (1990) 42,762.

MIDDLETOWN, township, Monmouth Co., E New Jersey, bounded by Sandy Hook Bay and the Navesink R.; settled by 1664. It is a residential community with some commercial and recreational fishing. A community college and several old homes (dating from the 1670s and '80s) are here. Fort Monmouth and Sandy Hook Park, a unit of Gateway National Recreation Area, are nearby. In September 1609 the English navigator Henry Hudson landed here and traded with local Indians. The township is named for Middleton, England. Pop. (1980) 62,574; (1990) 68,183.

MIDDLETOWN, city, Butler Co., SW Ohio, on the Great Miami R., near Hamilton; settled 1791, inc. as a city 1886. Manufactures include steel, paper products, machinery, and aerospace equipment. A junior college is here. The city is the location of an annual hot air balloon contest. Laid out in 1802 and probably named for Middletown, N.J., the community was a farm-trade and transportation center in the 19th century and became a steelmaking hub about 1900. Pop. (1980) 43,719; (1990) 46,022.

MIDGE, common name for any minute fly (q.v.) in the order Diptera, especially the very small flies constituting the families Chironomidae and Ceratopogonidae. The chironomid midges are harmless to humans; their eggs are laid in water, and the bright red larvae are usually wholly aquatic. The larvae of a few species live in soft earth or mud. The adults are common in swarms in early spring and in late autumn. Ceratopogonidae includes the biting midges of the genus *Culicoides,* which are often very annoying to humans in sandy regions. These sand flies, or punkies, are the smallest bloodsucking insects known, some being no larger than 1 mm (1/25 in) long. For other insects known as sand flies, see SAND FLY.

MIDGET. See DWARFISM.

MID GLAMORGAN, county, S Wales; Cardiff, located in adjacent South Glamorgan, serves as the administrative center. Mid Glamorgan comprises, on the S, a lowland region bordering on the Bristol Channel and, in the N, an upland region where coal is mined. Mid Glamorgan was created in 1974 with the merger of parts of the former counties of Breconshire, Glamorganshire, and Monmouthshire (qq.v.). Area, 1018 sq km (393 sq mi); pop. (1991 prelim.) 526,500.

MIDLAND, city, seat of Midland Co. and also in Bay Co., central Michigan, at the confluence of the Tittabawassee and Chippewa rivers; inc. as a city 1887. Chemicals, pharmaceuticals, and plastic goods are manufactured here. Midland is the site of the Northwood Institute (1959), the Midland Center for the Arts, and the Dow Gardens. The community was settled in the 1830s and grew as a lumbering town until timber was depleted. In the late 1880s, the American chemist Herbert H. Dow exploited the brine deposits in the area and started a chemical industry that became the Dow Chemical Co. Pop. (1980) 37,250; (1990) 38,053.

MIDLAND, city, seat of Midland Co., W Texas, located midway between Fort Worth and El Paso, in the High Plains area; inc. 1906. It is a commercial, manufacturing, and corporate center for a major livestock-raising region and for the highly productive Permian Basin petroleum fields. In addition to petroleum and natural gas, manufactures in the city include oil-field equipment, fabricated metal, chemicals, electronic components, and processed food. A junior college, a petroleum museum, and the Midland County Museum are here. Settled soon after the construction of the railroad in 1881, Midland was a small ranching community until the discovery (1923) of petroleum nearby brought new wealth. Pop. (1980) 70,525; (1990) 89,443.

MIDLOTHIAN *or* **EDINBURGHSHIRE,** former county, SE Scotland, on the S shore of the Firth of Forth; Edinburgh was the county town. The area shows evidence of prehistoric habitation and was at one time occupied by the Romans. Midlothian's later history is tied to that of the city of Edinburgh, which was founded in the 11th century and became the national capital in 1437. In 1975 the county was divided between the newly created Lothian and Borders (qq.v.) regions.

MIDRASH (Heb. *darash,* "interpretation"), term applied to Jewish expository and exegetical writings on the Scriptures. These writings consist of the interpretations by different rabbis of the laws and customs set forth in the Old Testament. The earliest elements of the Midrashic writings appear to have been produced before 100 BC by the scribes. The material contained in the Midrash is divided into three groups; the abstract Halakah (q.v.), consisting of the traditional law; the Halakic Midrash, a deduction of the traditional law from the written law; and the Haggadic Midrash (see HAGGADA), consisting of legends, sermons, and interpretations of the narrative parts of the Bible and concerning ethics and theology rather than law. The forms and styles of these writings show considerable flexibility, ranging from parables to sermons to codifications of law. S.L.

MIDSUMMER EVE, also Saint John's Eve, June 23, night before the festival of the nativity of John the Baptist. Throughout Europe it was often celebrated by bonfires; although the fires were blessed by priests, the celebration was generally conducted by the laity. Midsummer eve celebrations were a continuance of the Teutonic solar ceremonies and fertility rites associated with agriculture at the time of the summer solstice. The presence of supernatural beings, love magic, and merrymaking are some of the characteristics of this feast that inspired Shakespeare's masterpiece, *A Midsummer Night's Dream*, which in turn inspired the music of Felix Mendelssohn.

MIDWAY, BATTLE OF, decisive naval engagement of World War II, fought June 3–6, 1942 near the Midway Islands by Japanese and U.S. aircraft carriers.

In early June, American naval reconnaissance planes observed, at a distance of 966 km (600 mi) a Japanese armada of some 185 ships advancing on the Midway Islands. On June 4 American fighters and bombers, sent from Midway airfields, and three aircraft carriers attacked the Japanese fleet. At the same time Japanese carrier-based planes attacked aircraft installations on Midway in preparation for an invasion; damage, however, was not sufficient to prevent the American planes from refueling and taking off again. During the ensuing battle between the American and Japanese naval forces, the two fleets neither saw each other nor exchanged gunfire; all contact was made by Japanese carrier-based planes and American land- and carrier-based planes. By the night of June 6, when contact by aircraft between the two fleets was lost, the defeat of the Japanese was accomplished. Losses for the Japanese combatants included four aircraft carriers, two cruisers, and three destroyers; the Americans lost the aircraft carrier *Yorktown* and one destroyer.

The victory at Midway terminated a major Japanese attempt to capture the islands as a possible prelude to an invasion of Hawaii. The success of the operation, only a month after the important but indecisive Battle of the Coral Sea, effectively tipped the balance of sea power in the Pacific Ocean in favor of the U.S.

For further information on this topic, see the Bibliography in volume 28, section 914.

MIDWAY ISLANDS, coral atoll, territory of the U.S, Pacific Ocean, 2100 km (1300 mi) NW of Honolulu, administered by the U.S. Navy. The two islets comprising the atoll are Eastern and Sand; the atoll has an overall area of about 5 sq km (about 2 sq mi). The Midway atoll was discovered in 1859 by an American sea captain; the U.S. took possession in 1867. A transpacific cable station was built (1903) by the U.S. Marines on Sand Island. The atoll was declared a naval reservation by President Theodore Roosevelt in the same year. In 1936 Midway became a stopping point on the transpacific air route to the Philippines. During the 1930s a Marine garrison was established and naval and air defenses constructed on Midway. During World War II, U.S. forces defeated (June 1942) a Japanese fleet in the decisive Battle of Midway, fought nearby. The U.S. still uses Midway as an air and naval base. Pop. (1990) 13.

MIDWEST CITY, city, Oklahoma Co., central Oklahoma, a residential community adjoining Oklahoma City; inc. 1943. A large junior college is here, and Tinker Air Force Base is nearby. The city was planned and named in 1942 in conjunction with the establishment of Tinker Air Force Base. Pop. (1980) 49,559; (1990) 52,267.

MIDWIFERY, the providing of assistance during pregnancy, especially at the time of childbirth. Midwives have assisted women in giving birth since ancient times, and even today midwives deliver more than two-thirds of the world's infants. In Western countries advances in obstetrics and gynecology (qq.v.) caused childbearing to shift from the home to hospitals by the early 1900s, and midwives were replaced by physicians.

Lay midwifery is now on the wane worldwide. In the U.S., however, a growing number of middle-class parents are objecting to the surgical approach and paternalistic attitudes they claim to find among hospital obstetricians. Instead they are turning to the modern, professionally trained certified nurse-midwife (CNW), with whom they feel they can better participate in the birth experience. Working closely with obstetricians in such settings as rural outreach centers, hospitals, and an increasing number of homelike, out-of-hospital childbearing centers, CNWs perform normal deliveries. They do not use obstetrical forceps or perform operative deliveries such as cesarean section. CNWs also provide a number of other birth-related services, such as advice on diet and exercise instruction, and they encourage husbands (or other supportive persons) to take part in birthing, help the family adjust to the infant, and provide follow-up care for the mother. For nonpregnant women nurse-midwives perform gynecological checkups, breast examinations, and Pap tests and provide birth-control advice and other services.

Training programs in midwifery are now offered in more than 25 institutions, including Yale University and Columbia University. Graduates are eligible for certification upon passing an examination administered by the American College of Nurse-Midwives (ACNM) in Washington, D.C. The number of nurse-midwives certified by the ACNM rose from 400 in 1971 to 2304 in 1980, and all 50 states now permit the practice of CNWs.

See also NURSING.

MIDWIFE TOAD, common name for a small, terrestrial amphibian, in the order of frogs and toads. It is called midwife toad because the male helps to care for the eggs by carrying them on its back. It is about 5 cm (about 2 in) long, and is found in western Europe. Unlike other toads and frogs, which deposit their eggs directly in water, the female midwife toad lays its eggs in a burrow on land. During the release of the eggs, the male entangles the strands of 20 to 60 fertilized eggs about his thighs. Periodically emerging from the burrow to moisten the eggs, the male deposits the eggs in water after 20 to 50 days.

The midwife toad was the subject of controversial experiments by the Austrian biologist Paul Kammerer (1880–1926). Kammerer tried but failed to produce conclusive evidence that acquired traits can be inherited, a hypothesis in opposition to modern hereditary theory.

COMMON NAME	FAMILY	GENUS AND SPECIES
Midwife toad	Discoglossidae	*Alytes obstetricans*

MIELZINER, Jo (1901–76), American stage designer, born in Paris, and educated at the Art Students League in New York City and the Academy of Fine Arts in Philadelphia. During his long career, Mielziner designed more than 250 productions for the Broadway and London stages, including *The Guardsman* (1924), *Winterset* (1935), *The Glass Menagerie* (1945), *A Streetcar Named Desire* (1947), *Mister Roberts* (1948), *Death of a Salesman* (1949), *South Pacific* (1949), *Guys and Dolls* (1950), and *Gypsy* (1959). He also designed for the opera and ballet stages. Mielziner's sets were invariably appropriate to the production, combining stylish realism with dramatic symbolism, in forms that were practicable onstage. With the Finnish-American architect Eero Saarinen he designed the Vivian Beaumont Theater in New York City's Lincoln Center. Many of his designs are reproduced in his book *Designing for the Theatre* (1965).

Ludwig Mies van der Rohe — Berko-Pix, Inc.

MIES VAN DER ROHE, Ludwig (1886–1969), German-American architect, who was the leading and most influential exponent of the glass and steel architecture of the 20th-century International style.

Born in Aachen, Germany, on March 27, 1886, Mies received his principal training as an employee of the architect and furniture designer Bruno Paul (1874–1968) from 1905 to 1907 and then as an employee of the pioneering industrial architect Peter Behrens from 1908 to 1911. Mies opened his own office in Berlin in 1912.

Mies received relatively few commissions during his early years, but his completed works illustrate the styles that were to occupy him throughout his career. In models for several skyscrapers, he experimented with steel frames and glass walls. In two early masterpieces, the German Pavilion for the 1929 Barcelona exhibition (for which he also designed the famous chrome and leather Barcelona chair) and the Tugendhat House (1930) in Brno, Czech Republic, he produced long, low glass-sheathed buildings in which the interiors were treated as a series of free-flowing spaces with minimal walls, usually of rare marbles and woods.

Mies's style was characterized by its severe simplicity and the refinement of its exposed structural elements. Although not the first architect to work in this mode, he carried rationalism and functionalism to their ultimate stage of development. His famous dictum "less is more" crystallized the basic philosophy of mid-20th-century architecture. Rigidly geometrical and devoid of ornamentation, his buildings depended for their effect on subtlety of proportion, elegance of material (including marble, onyx, chrome, and travertine), and precision of details.

Mies was director of the Bauhaus School of Design (see BAUHAUS), the major center of 20th-century architectural modernism, from 1930 until its disbandment in 1933. He moved to the U.S. in 1937, where, as director of architecture (1938–58) at the Illinois Institute of Technology, he trained a new generation of American architects. He produced many buildings in the U.S., including skyscrapers, museums, schools, and residences. His 37-story bronze-and-glass Seagram Building in New York City (1958; in collaboration with the American architect Philip Johnson) is considered the most subtle development of the glass-walled skyscraper, while his glass-walled Farnsworth House (1950, near Fox River, Ill.) is the culmination of his residential architecture.

With the French architect Le Corbusier and the American architect Frank Lloyd Wright, Mies was one of the three most influential 20th-century architects, and his skyscraper designs in particular have been copied or adapted by most modern architects working in the field. He died in Chicago, Aug. 17, 1969.

MI FEI, also Mi Fu (1051–1107), Chinese landscape painter of the Northern Sung dynasty, famous also as a calligrapher, critic, and theorist. A native of Hubei (Hupeh) Province, he held high positions in state and local governments. Although not a prolific artist, he pioneered a new technique in his landscapes, the "ink-splash" technique, in which thick oval dots or droplets of ink were laid horizontally on paper using the side of the brush. Combined with graded washes of ink, these dots created an effect of rich, moist atmosphere and subtly receding planes of space, as in *Auspicious Pine Trees in the Spring Mountains* (National Palace Museum, Taiwan). This style, in which no actual drawn lines appear, set his work completely apart from the orthodox outline drawings of contemporaneous academy painters. He was more appreciated for his spectacularly skillful calligraphy; his painting did not gain notice until at least a century after his death, when its gentle, poetic, atmospheric qualities became one of the main influences on the Southern Sung school. He was also a prolific writer, producing essays on calligraphy and ink stones as well as the *Hua shih* (Discussion of Painting); the critical insights of this work make it one of the most important documents in the history of Sung painting.

MIFFLIN, Thomas (1744–1800), American soldier and statesman, born in Philadelphia, and educated at the College of Philadelphia (now the University of Pennsylvania). In the agitation over British policy preceding the American Revolution, he championed colonial rights and was elected a member of the First Continental Congress. After the outbreak of hostilities, he was appointed aide-de-camp to Gen. George Washington and later quartermaster general of the revolutionary army, a post he resigned after charges of mismanagement were brought against him. In 1777 he was accused of being a ringleader of the Conway Cabal, a group that aimed at substituting Gen. Horatio Gates for Washington as commander in chief, an intrigue that failed. Mifflin severed his connection with the army in 1779. Later he was a delegate to Congress (1782–84), president of that body (1783–84), a member of the federal Constitutional Convention (1787), and the first state governor of Pennsylvania (1790–99).

MIGNONETTE, common name for the plant genus *Reseda,* of the family Resedaceae, order Capparales (see CAPER). *Reseda* contains about 55 herbaceous species native to the Mediterranean region. The common mignonette, *R. odorata,* is a spreading annual grown in gardens for its fragrant yellow-orange to red flowers that develop in long clusters (racemes). It also yields oils used in making perfumes. Another species, *R. luteola,* known as weld and dyer's rocket, was formerly used as a source of a deep-yellow dye.

MIGRAINE, severe headache, which frequently occurs over one side of the head only. It is characterized by throbbing and associated with one or more of the following symptoms: sensitivity to light, nausea and vomiting, and dizziness. Flashes or patterns before the eyes may precede the headache. At least 20 million persons in the U.S. suffer from migraines that can recur at intervals ranging from one day to several years. Women are twice as likely as men to experience these headaches, and some evidence suggests that migraine headaches are inherited.

At the onset of a migraine headache, blood vessels within the head constrict. This may cause a decrease in blood flow to the surface of the brain. A dilation of blood vessels of the head and scalp then occurs, setting off a chain of reactions that result in the headache. Evidence indicates that decreased localized brain metabolism initiates the attack and that the initial decrease in blood flow is a response to the lowered metabolic demand, rather than due to constriction of blood vessels. Among the biochemical changes associated with migraine is a reduced level of enkephalins, the brain's pain-relieving chemicals.

Hormonal level changes (such as those experienced by women during menopause or menstruation), endocrine imbalances, and stress are considered precipitating factors of migraine headaches in susceptible persons. Several treatments have been successful in helping migraine sufferers. These include medications such as ergotamine tartrate, which thwarts the excessive expansion of blood vessels and aborts the acute attack; and propranolol, which stabilizes blood vessel tone and prevents subsequent attacks. Biofeedback (q.v.) techniques have also proved useful.

See also HEADACHE.

MIGRATION, movement of people, especially of whole groups, from one place, region, or country to another, particularly with the intention of making permanent settlement in a new location. People have migrated continuously since their emergence as a species. Their original differentiation into races appears to have been a result of their development in isolation after migrations from a central point of origin, perhaps in Africa or Central Asia. Even in the Stone Age, however, this isolation was not complete, for migrations resulted in a complicated pattern of blood relationships through widely separated groups.

MOVEMENT OF PEOPLES

In the more recent past, the movement and countermovement of peoples have led to accelerated mixing of stocks and mutual infusion of racial characteristics. Perhaps more important than the transmission of physical characteristics has been the transmission of cultural characteristics. The diffusion of cultures, including tools, habits, ideas, and forms of social organization, was a prerequisite for the development of modern civilization, which would probably have taken place much more slowly if people had not moved from place to place. For instance, use of the horse was introduced into the Middle East by Asian invaders of Sumeria and later spread to Europe and the Americas; the Peruvian Indians were converted to Roman Catholicism by Spanish explorers. Even important historical events can be linked to distant migrations; the downfall of the Roman Empire, for example, was probably hastened by migrations following the building of the Great Wall of China, which prevented the eastward expansion of Central Asian tribes, thus turning them in the direction of Europe.

Causes. A group of people may migrate in response to the lure of a more favorable region or because of some adverse condition or combination of conditions in the home environment. Most historians believe that peoples who have developed beyond the nomadic stage have a disinclination to quit the places to which they are accustomed, and that most historic and prehistoric migrations were stimulated by a deterioration of home conditions. This belief is supported by records of the events preceding most major migrations.

The specific stimuli for migrations may be either natural or social causes. Among the natural causes are changes in climate, stimulating a search for warmer or colder lands; volcanic eruptions or floods that render sizable areas uninhabitable; and periodic fluctuations in rainfall. Social causes, however, are generally considered to have prompted many more migrations than natural causes. Examples of such social causes are an inadequate food supply caused by population increase; defeat in war, as in the forced migration of Germans from parts of Germany absorbed by Poland after World War II; a desire for loot, as in the 13th-century invasion of the wealthy cities of western Asia by Turkish tribes; and the search for religious or political freedom, as in the migrations of the Huguenots, Jews, Puritans, Quakers, and other groups to North America.

Choice of Routes. The choice of migratory routes has historically been influenced by the tendency of groups to seek a type of environment similar to the one they left and by the existence of natural barriers, such as large rivers, seas, deserts, and mountain ranges. The belts of steppe, forest, and arctic tundra that stretch from central Europe to the Pacific Ocean have been a constant encouragement to east-west migration of groups situated along their length. On the other hand, migrations from tropical to temperate areas, or from temperate to tropical areas, have been rare. The desert regions of the Sahara separated the African from the Mediterranean peoples and prevented the diffusion southward of Egyptian and other cultures, and the Himalaya cut off approach to the great subcontinent of India except from its eastern and western borders. As a consequence of these and similar barriers, certain mountain passes and land bridges became traditional migratory routes. The Sinai Peninsula linked Africa and Asia; the Bosporus region connected Europe and the Middle East; the Daryal Gorge in the Caucasus Mountains was used by the successive tribes that poured out of the European steppes into the Middle East; and the broad valley between the Altai Mountains and the Tien Shan provided the route by which central Asian peoples swept westward.

Effects. Among the distinct effects of migration are the stimulation of further migration through the displacement of other peoples; a reduction in the numbers of the migrating group because of hardship and warfare; changes in racial char-

MIGRATION

acteristics through intermarriage with the groups encountered; changes in cultural characteristics by adoption from peoples encountered; and linguistic changes, also effected by adoption. Anthropologists and archaeologists have traced the routes of many prehistoric migrations by the current persistence of such effects. Blond physical characteristics among some of the Berbers of North Africa are thought to be evidence of an early Nordic invasion, and the Navajo and Apache Indians of the southwestern U.S. are believed to be descended from peoples of northwestern Canada, with whom they have a linguistic bond. The effects of migration are particularly evident in North, Central, and South America, where peoples of diverse origins live together with common cultures.

HISTORY

Among the most far-reaching series of ancient migrations were those of the peoples who spread the Indo-European family of languages. According to a prevalent hypothesis, a large group of Indo-Europeans migrated from east-central Europe eastward toward the region of the Caspian Sea before the 3d millennium BC. Beginning shortly after 2000 BC, the Indo-European people known as the Hittites crossed into Asia Minor from Europe through the Bosporus region, and at about the same time the bulk of the Indo-Europeans in the Caspian Sea area turned southward. The ancestors of the Hindus went southeastward into Punjab and along the banks of the Indus and Ganges rivers; the Kassites went south into Babylonia; and the Mitanni went southwestward into the valleys of the Tigris and Euphrates rivers and other parts of the region known as the Fertile Crescent.

A migration of great importance to Western civilization was the invasion of Canaan by the tribes of the Hebrew confederacy, which developed the ideas on which the Jewish, Christian, and Islamic religions are founded. These nomadic Semitic tribes, from the Arabian Peninsula and the deserts southeast of the Jordan River, moved (15th–10th cent. BC) into a settled region that was alternately under the control of Egypt and Babylonia.

Ethnic Migrations from 300 BC to AD 600. The civilizations of the ancient world were centered in cities and countries situated along the edges of the great Eurasian landmass, around the Mediterranean Sea, in the Middle East, in India, and in China. The huge interior area was crossed and recrossed by nomadic tribes, which periodically overran the littoral (coastal) settlements. Central Asia was the main reservoir of these nomadic hordes, and from it successive waves of migrations penetrated eastward into China, southward into India, and westward into Europe, driving before them subsidiary waves of displaced tribes and peoples. In the 3d century BC, the Huns, or Hsiung-Nu, as they were called by the Chinese, advanced eastward from Central Asia toward China and westward toward the Ural Mountains, driving other groups before them.

In another movement the Cimbri, thought to have been a Germanic people, drove southward from the eastern Baltic Sea region and twice entered the Roman Empire in the 2d century BC. In the 1st century BC, Germanic groups from the southwestern Baltic area, possibly as a consequence of Cimbri pressure, also drove down into central Europe, occupying the territory between the Rhine and the Danube rivers. By the 3d century AD, a newly expanding group, the Mongols, had arisen in Central Asia. As a result of their pressure, the Huns invaded China proper and crossed over the Urals into the Volga River region. The last-named migration displaced the Goths, who traveled from southwestern Russia toward the European domains of the Roman Empire, and in turn forced the Germanic Vandals into Gaul and Spain at the beginning of the 5th century AD. The Visigoths, or West Goths, continued their westward advance through Italy, Gaul, and Spain, driving the Vandals before them into northern Africa and eastward to present-day Tunis. The Ostrogoths, or East Goths, followed the Visigoths into Italy and settled there. The Huns, who had begun their movement in Central Asia eight centuries earlier, followed the Goths into Europe, after being displaced by the Mongols, and settled in what is now Hungary about the middle of the 5th century. The Mongols also forced great numbers of Slavs into eastern Europe. Thus, one of the most momentous and far-reaching events of history, the disintegration of the Roman Empire in the 3d to 6th century of the Christian era, was largely brought about by migrations.

After the Hun invasions in the 3d and 5th centuries, a period of equilibrium ensued. In the East, the Chinese maintained their strength against the nomads. In the West, Europe consolidated its own strength.

The Spread of Islam. The weakness and decay of the Persian and the Byzantine empires encouraged the spread of a new migration out of Semitic Arabia that was far more extensive than that of the Hebrews into Canaan. United under the banner of Islam in the 7th and early 8th centuries, Arab tribes swept eastward through Persia to Chinese Turkestan and into northwest India; westward through Egypt and across northern Africa into Spain and southern France; and northwestward through Syria into Asia Minor. The Arab penetration into Central Asia stimulated nomadic raids on the frontiers of the Chinese Empire and forced the western Asian Magyar tribes to move in the direction of Europe, crossing the Ural Mountains and southern Russia and finally reaching Hungary, where they settled in the 9th century.

China and the Mongols. Expansion of Chinese frontiers under the Sung dynasty in the 11th century forced the Seljuk Turkish tribes out of Central Asia. They moved westward across the Ural Mountains into the Volga River region and thence south into Persia, Armenia, Asia Minor, and Syria, settling among the peoples there. In the 13th century, Mongol tribes under Genghis Khan, in one of the most astounding military migrations of recorded history, swept out of Mongolia and captured China, Turkestan, Afghanistan, Iran, Mesopotamia, Syria, Asia Minor, southern Russia, and even parts of eastern Europe. The Ottoman Turks, forced from their pasturelands in western Asia during the brief period of Mongol supremacy, migrated westward and entered Asia Minor in the 14th century, taking Constantinople and advancing as far as Vienna in the 15th century.

The Scandinavian Invasions. The maritime region consisting of Scandinavia and other lands bordering the North and the Baltic seas was a subsidiary reservoir of migratory groups. In the 5th and 6th centuries, Angles, Saxons, and Jutes, displaced by the Visigoths, sailed from northwest Germany and overran southern Britain. Norwegian mariners captured the Shetland, Orkney, Faeroe, and Hebrides islands in the 7th and 8th centuries. In the 9th century, Swedish fighters poured out of the Baltic region through southern Finland, sweeping down into Russia and through the Ukraine along the Dnepr River. During the 9th century, Norwegians settled in Iceland and in Normandy in France. The Icelanders reached Greenland in the late 10th century and established a colony there. Subsequently, they sailed even as far as North America but left no permanent settlers. The growth of the system of nation-states in Europe during the 2d millennium AD once more restored the equilibrium in the West, and no important ethnic incursions occurred thereafter.

Recent Migrations. Many times more people have moved and resettled during the past 450 years than in any similar period of human history. The migrations preceding this period were collective acts, more or less voluntarily undertaken by the members of a group, but many of the more recent migrations have differed in at least two significant ways: They have been either voluntary individual acts or they have been enforced group movements, entirely against the will of the people who are being moved. The two types of migration began almost simultaneously after the discovery of America, and they have continued in one form or another up to the present day.

Before the 20th century. The era of modern migrations that began with the opening up of the western hemisphere was continued under the impetus of the Industrial Revolution. Millions of western, and then eastern, Europeans, seeking political or religious freedom or economic opportunity, settled in North and South America, Africa, Australia, New Zealand, and other parts of the globe. Other millions of black Africans were forcibly carried to the Americas by slave traders and sold into bondage. Still other millions of Chinese settled in Southeast Asia and moved overseas to work in the Philippine Islands, Hawaii, and the Americas. A large colony of Hindus was established in southern Africa, and many people from Arab lands migrated to North and South America.

The migrations from Europe were principally voluntary, in the sense that the emigrants could have stayed in their respective original homelands if they had accepted certain religions, creeds, political allegiances, or economic privations. The involuntary migrations were primarily those of African slaves, but slave shipments were halted during the first half of the 19th century. At about the same time, however, a large-scale, more or less forced migration took place from southern Africa to the central and eastern parts of the continent, spurred by the expansionist force of the Zulus (see MFECANE). Finally, a great many of the Chinese, Indian, and other Asian migrations, as well as some of the migrations of eastern and southern Europeans, were not strictly definable as either free or unfree. The individual migrants signed agreements to travel in consignments of contract labor; and, although ultimately many of these laborers settled permanently and with equal rights in the lands to which they went, the terms of their original contracts often severely circumscribed their freedom and, in effect, left them little better than slaves for long periods of time.

After World War I. The highest peak, and freest period, of modern migration was reached in the 50 years preceding World War I. After 1920, however, many nations, and particularly those that had been receiving the bulk of the immigrants, placed obstacles in the way of free movement of

MIGRATION

Overflowing crowds jammed the trains between India and Pakistan after the partition of the Indian subcontinent in 1947. An estimated 12 million people, both Muslims and Hindus, are believed to have migrated in both directions. **Wide World Photos**

peoples. Tightening of passport and visa requirements cut voluntary migration to relatively negligible proportions during the 1920s.

Europe and totalitarianism. With the growth, during and after the 1920s, of totalitarian states, another type of enforced migration began to occur. Powerful dictators were able to order the deportation of large masses of the population from their homes to other, usually distant, parts of the national domain. During the enforced collectivization of Soviet agriculture in the 1930s, for example, millions of peasants, denounced by the government as enemies of the state, were sent to corrective labor camps in Siberia and other remote regions or were resettled far from their homelands. Later, the ranks of these unwilling migrants were swelled by other Soviet citizens condemned to forced labor for real or alleged political opposition to the regime.

Another upsurge in the movement of peoples took place during World War II and its aftermath. Following the partition of Poland by Germany and the Soviet Union in 1939, hundreds of thousands of Poles were forcibly removed from their homes by the Soviet government and were sent to Siberia. The Soviets followed a similar policy in 1940, after they annexed the Baltic states—Estonia, Latvia, and Lithuania—and in 1941 and 1943, when they dissolved the German Volga and Kalmyk autonomous republics. In the latter case, 600,000 people were condemned to forced labor beyond the Ural Mountains and the Arctic Circle. After the war, approximately 1 million Tatars, adjudged politically unreliable by the state, were moved from the Crimea to labor camps and exile colonies.

The German regime of Adolf Hitler, besides exterminating in its concentration camps millions of Jews and other people from all over occupied Europe, deported millions more. Many were pressed into slave labor in Germany; others, mainly Poles, were dispossessed and forced to migrate from the parts of their country that Germany had annexed. Replacing them were "racial" or "ethnic" Germans who were moved from eastern and southeastern Europe. At the end of the war, a reverse movement occurred, as some 2 or 3 million Germans were repatriated from Poland and many Polish nationals moved west after an expansion of Soviet boundaries in the west. To the south, another 2 to 3 million German-speaking Czechs who had become German citizens were moved from the Sudetenland (q.v.) to Germany. Some Germans and East Europeans also migrated to other parts of the world.

Since World War II. The partition (August 1947) of the Indian subcontinent into two independent states, one Hindu (India) and one Muslim (Pakistan), resulted in large-scale population transfers. Some 6,600,000 Muslims entered Pakistan from Indian territory, and an estimated 5,363,000 Hindus and Sikhs migrated to India. The establishment of Israel in 1948 resulted in the migration of hundreds of thousands of Jews to that state and the displacement of about 1 million indigenous Palestinians into neighboring countries. Another major migration of Jews to Israel began in 1989, when Soviet emigration restrictions were eased, and increased after the breakup of the communist state. In 1991 virtually all the Jews in Ethiopia were airlifted to Israel. Elsewhere in Africa millions of people moved away from their native regions and nations, fleeing famine and civil war. In an upheaval reminiscent of the India-Pakistan partition, the violence that accompanied the breakup of Yugoslavia into separate, ethnically based states in the early 1990s forced millions to leave their homelands.

Elsewhere in Europe during the second half of the 20th century the trend of migration has been a relatively peaceful movement from east to west and from south to north. Millions have left Eastern Europe, at first to escape repressive communist governments and later to flee the chaos and poverty that came after those governments fell. From the south—from Mediterranean countries such as Turkey and from former African colonies such as Senegal—migrants came in search of economic opportunity. Many found they were not welcome. In Germany and France there were protests, sometimes violent, against immigrants.

In North America the international movement has been mainly from south to north as millions of migrants from Cuba and other Caribbean islands, from Mexico, and from elsewhere in Latin America have settled in the U.S., mostly in California, Florida, and Texas.

Internal Migration. The Industrial Revolution also gave rise to an important kind of intranational migration. Its most significant feature was the great movement of people from rural and agricultural areas to urban centers. This movement came to the industrial countries in the 1800s, then exploded in Third World countries in the 20th century. Intranational migration also involves shifting centers of industry. In the U.S., the movement of workers and their families west and south to the Sun Belt has revamped the demographic map of the nation. In addition, the U.S. has seen the gradual diffusion of racial and ethnic groups throughout the country—as, for example, the northward migration of blacks out of the southern states.

For further information on this topic, see the Bibliography in volume 28, sections 164–66.

MIGRATION OF ANIMALS. See Animal Migration.

MIKADO, former popular title for the emperor of Japan, used chiefly in English. Literally, the term meant the Gate of the Imperial Palace and came to be used as a figurative term, signifying the emperor himself. The term is often associated with the operetta set in Japan, *The Mikado* (1885), by the British playwright Sir William Gilbert and the British composer Sir Arthur Sullivan.

MIKAN, George Lawrence (1924–), American basketball player, born in Joliet, Ill., and educated at DePaul University, Chicago. While playing center on the DePaul basketball team Mikan scored 1870 points. Mikan was voted by the Associated Press the outstanding collegiate player of the first half of the 20th century. He joined the Chicago American Gears professional team in 1947, and then played for eight seasons with the Minneapolis Lakers. He scored a record 11,764 points in 520 games and three times led the National Basketball Association in scoring. On offense he was always guarded by two and sometimes three defenders. Mikan was commissioner of the American Basketball Association from its formation in 1967 until his resignation in 1969.

MIKOYAN, Anastas Ivanovich (1895–1978), Soviet Communist party leader, born in Sanain (now part of Alaverdi, in Armenia), and educated at the Armenian Ecclesiastical Seminary. In 1915 he joined the Communist party. During the Russian Revolution, he was the leader of Bolshevik forces in the Baku area. In 1923 he was elected a member of the Central Committee of the Soviet Communist party. Mikoyan was in charge of Soviet domestic trade during the 1920s and '30s, heading a series of commissariats. In 1935 he was admitted to the Politburo, the party's highest policy-making body, and in 1938 he became commissar of foreign trade. During World War II he was a member of the state defense committee that directed the Soviet war effort, being responsible for supplying the Soviet army. He became a deputy premier in 1953 and first deputy premier in 1955. An astute politician, Mikoyan weathered the changes of Kremlin politics during the eras of Joseph Stalin and Nikita S. Khrushchev. In 1964 he became president of the Presidium of the Supreme Soviet of the USSR, but he resigned a year later because of ill health.

MILAN (Ital. *Milano;* anc. *Mediolanum*), city, N Italy, capital of Milano Province and of Lombardy Region. The second largest Italian city in population (after Rome), it is a leading commercial, financial, and manufacturing center of Italy and a major center of intellectual and artistic life. Milan is mainly a modern city, surrounded by industrial suburbs. It has many tall apartment and office buildings in the business district and ex-

MILAN

Piazza del Duomo, Milan, dominated by the Cathedral of Milan, which was begun in 1386 and only completed in 1965. A unique example of Gothic architecture in southern Europe, the cruciform white-marble cathedral is graced by more than 300 spires, turrets, and statues.
Trans World Airlines

tensive residential and industrial sections. A subway system was opened in 1964. The principal square is the Piazza del Duomo, at one end of which stands the Duomo, or cathedral, a huge Gothic structure of white marble, begun in 1386 and completed in 1965. To the SW of the Piazza del Duomo is the Basilica di Sant'Ambrogio (AD 386). Near the basilica is the 15th-century Church of Santa Maria delle Grazie. Adjacent to the church is a former Dominican monastery, in the refectory of which is the famous fresco *Last Supper* by Leonardo da Vinci.

Cultural Institutions. Among institutions devoted to culture in Milan is the 17th-century Palazza di Brera, which houses the Brera Academy of Fine Arts, a library, and the Brera Art Gallery. The Palazzo dell'Ambrosiana houses the Biblioteca Ambrosiana, which was opened in 1609 and was perhaps the first public library in Europe. Milan also has excellent museums of art, historical events, and natural history; the Institute for the Study of International Politics; the world-famous Teatro alla Scala opera house; a noted conservatory of music; and several universities.

Commerce and Manufacturing. Milan leads Italian cities in the manufacture of chemicals and textiles. Other important products include aircraft, automobiles, foodstuffs, clothing, glass, leather and rubber goods, machinery, pharmaceuticals, and plastics. The city has a large book and music publishing industry, many banks, and the principal stock exchange of Italy. An international trade fair is held annually in Milan in April.

History. Ancient Mediolanum is believed to have been founded by a Celtic people. Captured by the Romans in 222 BC, it flourished under the Roman Empire and became the residence of the emperors of the West in the 4th century AD. The city was sacked by the Huns under Attila in about 450 and was destroyed by the Goths in 539. By the end of the 8th century the city had begun to prosper again. During the Middle Ages, Milan was governed by a number of archbishops, under whom the city had a certain degree of independence. The archbishops, however, gradually lost their temporal power to the lower feudal nobility, who transformed Milan into a prosperous commune in the 11th century. In 1162 Milan was razed by troops under Emperor Frederick I. The city recovered sufficiently to help secure the victory (1176) of the Lombard League over Frederick near Legnano. The victory opened a new period of prosperity. In 1277 a noble family, the Visconti, succeeded in wresting control of the city from the ruling Della Torre family; the Visconti ruled until 1447. The reign of Gian Galeazzo Visconti, 1st duke of Milan (1351–1402), was a particularly prosperous period and was regarded as a golden age. In 1450 the Italian soldier Francesco Sforza seized power and founded a line that remained firmly in control of Milan until 1500, when the city was conquered by France. The Sforzas continued to rule as puppets of successive foreign invaders, including the French, the Swiss, and the Austrians. The Sforza line died out in 1535, and soon thereafter Milan came under the rule of Spain. Spain ruled until 1713, when the city was ceded to Austria by the terms of the Peace of Utrecht. Napoleon ousted the Austrians in 1796 and made Milan the capital of the Cisalpine Republic.

Restored to Austria in 1815, Milan became a center of Italian patriotic resistance, and in 1848 it briefly expelled the Austrians. In 1859, the Italians, aided by the French, freed Milan from Austrian control. In 1861 Milan joined the kingdom of Italy and subsequently prospered. During World War II the city was heavily bombed. In the postwar period Milan experienced great commercial expansion and urban renewal. Pop. (1988 est.) 1,478,500.

MILANKOVITCH THEORY. *See* ICE AGES.

MILDEW, term popularly applied to a visible growth of fungi or bacteria on wet clothes, food, or other objects. Scientifically, the term is restricted to members of either of two families of fungi (q.v.) that are parasitic on living plants, and to the plant diseases they produce. The two families are Peronosporaceae, comprising the downy mildews, and Erysiphaceae, comprising the powdery mildews. The powdery mildews are parasitic chiefly on the leaves of plants and are so called because their numerous, white spores produce a powdery, cobwebbed pattern on the leaves. Attacks of powdery mildew cause curling and withering of leaves and often prevent new shoots on the plant. Powdery mildew usually attacks plants grown in the shade in humid regions. Among common genera of powdery mildew are *Uncinula*, which attacks willow; *Microsphaera*, which attacks grape and lilac; *Phyllactinia*, which attacks dogwood; and *Sphaerotheca*, which attacks rose, gooseberry, and hackberry.

MILETUS, ancient Greek city of Ionia, in Asia Minor, and the most flourishing of the 12 cities of the Ionian confederacy. Miletus was situated near the mouth of the Maender (Menderes) River and had four excellent harbors; the city therefore developed an extensive trade. Miletus was famous for the production of fine textiles, especially woolen cloth. The Milesians established many colonies in the north, primarily on the Hellespont (Dardanelles), on the Propontis (Sea of Marmara), and on the Euxine (Black) Sea. They also sent merchant fleets to every part of the Mediterranean Sea and even into the Atlantic Ocean.

Miletus was repeatedly attacked by the rulers of the neighboring country of Lydia but managed to withstand all assaults. The Milesians were finally subjugated, however, by Croesus, king of Lydia. Following the conquest of Lydia by Cyrus the Great, Miletus fell under the sway of Persia. From 499 to 494 BC the city took part in the so-called Ionian Revolt against Persian rule but was stormed and utterly demolished by Darius the Great. Rebuilt in the Hellenistic and Roman periods, it never regained its former importance. It declined during the early Christian era because of silting in the harbor. Miletus was the birthplace of the early Greek philosophers Thales, Anaximander, and Anaximenes of Miletus.

MILFORD, city, New Haven Co., SW Connecticut, on Long Island Sound, near the mouth of the Housatonic R.; inc. as a city 1959. It is an important distribution center; major manufactures include razors, machine tools, writing instruments, and processed foods. Milford Jai Alai is a popular tourist attraction. The community, settled in 1639 as part of New Haven Colony, is named for Milford, England. Oyster and clam fisheries were once important to the city, which was a popular summer resort until the 1920s. The city and town of Milford were consolidated in 1959. Pop. (1980) 49,101; (1990) 49,938.

MILFORD, city, Kent and Sussex counties, E Delaware, on the Mispillion R.; inc. 1807. It is an industrial and distribution center. Manufactures include processed food, dental supplies, textiles, and chemical and rubber products. The Graduate Center (1989) of the University of Delaware is here. Settled about 1680, Milford grew as a shipping and shipbuilding center. Pop. (1980) 5356; (1990) 6040.

MILFORD, industrial town, Worcester Co., S Massachusetts, on the Charles R.; inc. 1780. Major manufactures include scientific instruments, and glass products. The community was settled in 1662 and separated from Mendon in 1780. Pop. (1980) 23,390; (1990) 25,355.

MILFORD HAVEN, town, Preseli Pembrokeshire District, Dyfed, SW Wales. It has a splendid landlocked harbor, with port facilities that were greatly improved in the 1960s and '70s to handle large imports of petroleum. The town is connected by pipeline to Manchester and has one of the largest oil refineries in Great Britain. Fishing also plays an important role in the town's economy. Originally a small hamlet, Milford Haven was laid out in 1790. In the 19th century a whaling industry flourished here. Pop. (Preseli Pembrokeshire District, 1991 prelim.) 69,600.

MILHAUD, Darius (1892–1974), French composer, born in Aix-en-Provence, and educated at the Paris Conservatoire. In Paris, he became a member of the group of six young French composers later known as Les Six (see SIX, LES). In 1940 Milhaud went to the U.S. and became professor of composition at Mills College in Oakland, Calif. He left that post in 1947 to become honorary professor of composition at the Paris Conservatoire. Milhaud's style ranges from the conservative to the modern; his work is noted for the use of polytonality, or simultaneous use of several keys. He composed more than ten operas, ballets, symphonies, chamber music works, and music for motion pictures and the theater. Among the best known of his more than 400 compositions are the ballets *Le boeuf sur le toit* (1920) and *La création du monde* (1923), the opera *Christophe Colomb* (1930), and the orchestral piece *Suite provençale* (1937). Milhaud wrote an autobiography, *Notes Without Music* (1949; trans. 1952).

MILITARY ACADEMY, UNITED STATES. See UNITED STATES MILITARY ACADEMY.

MILITARY COURTS, in military law, courts with jurisdiction over persons in military service both in time of war and in time of peace. The term *military court* sometimes is applied to the courts established by the military forces in occupied enemy territory to try offenses by civilians. In the U.S. military courts comprise both courts-martial and courts of inquiry. Courts of inquiry are investigatory bodies that have the power to inquire into the nature of any transaction of, or accusation or imputation against, any officer or soldier. By the mid-20th century courts of inquiry were rarely used, and the term *military court* was commonly limited to courts-martial.

The Uniform Code of Military Justice, which went into effect in 1951, established identical systems of courts-martial for all branches of the military service. The jurisdiction of courts-martial is exclusively criminal. Three types of courts-martial exist: (1) the general court-martial, (2) the special court-martial, and (3) the summary court-martial. The jurisdiction of the general court-martial extends to all commissioned officers, warrant officers, and enlisted personnel charged with offenses that are usually serious, such as desertion. A general court-martial consists of five or more members, one-third of whom may be enlisted personnel if the defendant is an enlisted person and has requested their presence. A defendant may, however, choose to be tried by a court composed only of the military judge. In cases on trial before a general court-martial the defense counsel, prosecutor, and military judge must be lawyers. The military judge advises the court with respect to the law and renders final decisions on interlocutory questions of law. A general court-martial is permitted to impose any penalty that is authorized by the Uniform Code of Military Justice in punishment of the offense.

The jurisdiction of the special court-martial extends to any person under the jurisdiction of military law, but customarily it deals only with intermediate offenses. The court consists of three or more members, one-third of whom may be enlisted personnel if the defendant is an enlisted person and has requested that enlisted personnel serve (or the defendant may choose to be tried solely by the military judge). The maximum sentence that may be imposed by such a court is six months of confinement, forfeiture of some pay, reduction in rank, and, in some instances, a bad-conduct discharge.

A summary court-martial has jurisdiction only over enlisted personnel charged with minor offenses; it consists of one officer. Such a court may not impose a greater penalty than confinement and forfeiture of two-thirds pay for one month and reduction in rank.

All sentences imposed by court-martial are subject to review by the officer who convened the court. Sentences involving dismissal, punitive discharge, confinement for a year or more, or death are subject to review also by a court of military review in the office of the Judge Advocate General (of the army, navy, or air force). In addition, death sentences are automatically reviewed by a Court of Military Appeals, a five-member court of civilian judges appointed by the president of the U.S. Death sentences ultimately must be approved by the president.

See also MILITARY LAW. For a discussion of the International Military Tribunal, which is not a military court in the sense just described, see WAR CRIMES TRIALS.

MILITARY GOVERNMENT, administration of territory taken from the enemy under martial law. It is under this power that provisional governments are established in conquered territory.

MILITARY INSIGNIA

U.S. ARMY INSIGNIA OF ASSIGNMENT

Infantry	Artillery	Armor	Signal Corps	Ordnance Corps	Corps of Engineers	
Quartermaster Corps	Transportation Corps	Military Intelligence	Finance Corps	Military Police Corps	Air Defense Artillery	
National Guard Bureau	Judge Advocate General's Corps	General Staff	Inspector General	Chemical Corps	Adjutant General's Corps	
Civil Affairs, USAR	Staff Specialist, USAR	Chaplains (Christian Faith, Jewish Faith)	Warrant Officers	Women's Army Corps	Unassigned, Enlisted Personnel	
Medical Corps	Dental Corps	Medical Service Corps	Veterinary Corps	Army Nurse Corps	Specialist Corps	Medical Corps, Enlisted Personnel

MILITARY INSIGNIA, distinguishing symbols or emblems, usually of cloth or metal, worn by military forces to denote membership, rank, or specialization. Insignia are distinguished from medals and decorations, worn as awards for achievement or service, civilian as well as military. Modern military insignia include the major branch-of-service devices; specific assignment corps insignia; unit insignia; and insignia of rank and length of service, which include chevrons, stripes, special patches, and metal or sewn bars and emblems. In the armed forces of most nations, insignia are worn as specifically prescribed on the cap, collar, shoulder, or sleeve, depending on the formality of the uniform and on the season. See MEDALS AND DECORATIONS.

Derived from heraldic devices (see HERALDRY) of the Middle Ages, modern military insignia evolved in the 17th century, when the household guards of Louis XIV, king of France, were provided distinctive uniforms, including brass regimental numbers. Not until the 18th century, however, did actual insignia of rank come into use.

Gen. George Washington devised the first American insignia of rank in 1775, with officers being required to wear ribbons and cockades of different colors.

From 1780, U.S. army insignia were worn on epaulets. When epaulets eventually were reserved for formal or parade dress, they were replaced by shoulder straps on the everyday uniform, to which the insignia was transferred.

Chevrons, the insignia of rank for noncommissioned officers and enlisted personnel, have undergone many changes to keep pace with the increasing specialization of the modern armed forces. Recent innovations in the insignia of U.S. enlisted personnel include darker colored rank insignia, supplementing the traditional yellow stripes, and lapel tabs. U.S. forces also wear as shoulder insignia today colored, braided lanyards called aiguillettes and brassards. The aiguillette, usually a gold cord worn on the right shoulder, is part of the uniform of presidential and other aides and of certain high-ranking officers. Brassards, also called fourragères, are worn on the

RANK INSIGNIA FOR VARIOU[S]

pay grade	E-1	E-2	E-3	E-4	E-5	E-6	E-7	E-8	E-9	W-1	W-[2]

ENLISTED | **WA[RRANT]**

NAVY
E-1	E-2	E-3	E-4	E-5	E-6	E-7	E-8	E-9
SEAMAN RECRUIT	SEAMAN APPRENTICE	SEAMAN	PETTY OFFICER THIRD CLASS	PETTY OFFICER SECOND CLASS	PETTY OFFICER FIRST CLASS	CHIEF PETTY OFFICER	SENIOR CHIEF PETTY OFFICER	MASTER CHIEF PETTY OFFICER

W-1: GOLD/BLUE — WARRANT OFFICER W 1

MARINES
E-1	E-2	E-3	E-4	E-5	E-6	E-7	E-8	E-9
PRIVATE	PRIVATE FIRST CLASS	LANCE CORPORAL	CORPORAL	SERGEANT	STAFF SERGEANT	GUNNERY SERGEANT	1ST SGT / MSGT	SGT MAJOR / MGY SGT

W-1: GOLD/SCARLET — WARRANT OFFICER W 1

ARMY
E-1	E-2	E-3	E-4	E-5	E-6	E-7	E-8	E-9
PRIVATE	PRIVATE	PRIVATE FIRST CLASS	CORPORAL / SPECIALIST 4	SERGEANT / SPECIALIST 5	STAFF SERGEANT / SPECIALIST 6	PLATOON SERGEANT / SPECIALIST 7	1ST SGT / MSGT	COMMAND SERGEANT MAJOR / STAFF SERGEANT MAJOR

W-1: GOLD/BROWN — WARRANT OFFICER W 1

AIR FORCE
E-1	E-2	E-3	E-4	E-5	E-6	E-7	E-8	E-9
AIRMAN BASIC	AIRMAN	AIRMAN FIRST CLASS	SERGEANT	STAFF SERGEANT	TECHNICAL SERGEANT	MASTER SERGEANT	SENIOR MASTER SERGEANT	CHIEF MASTER SERGEANT

W-1: GOLD/SKY BLUE — WARRANT OFFICER W 1

* Insignia for the respective ranks of Sergeant Major of the Army; Chief Master Sergeant of the Air Force; Master Chief Petty Officer of the Navy; and Sergeant Major of the Marine Corps are identical or similar to the insignia for the senior E-9 ranks represented here.

BRANCHES OF U.S. ARMED FORCES

COMMISSIONED

W-3	W-4	O-1	O-2	O-3	O-4	O-5	O-6	O-7	O-8		
SILVER BLUE	SILVER BLUE	GOLD	SILVER	SILVER	GOLD	SILVER	SILVER	SILVER	SILVER	SILVER	SILVER
	CHIEF WARRANT OFFICER W 4	ENSIGN	LIEUTENANT JUNIOR GRADE	LIEUTENANT	LIEUTENANT COMMANDER	COMMANDER	CAPTAIN	COMMODORE	REAR ADMIRAL	VICE ADMIRAL	ADMIRAL	FLEET ADMIRAL
SILVER SCARLET	SILVER SCARLET	GOLD	SILVER	SILVER	GOLD	SILVER	SILVER	SILVER	SILVER	SILVER	SILVER
CHIEF WARRANT OFFICER W 3	CHIEF WARRANT OFFICER W 4	SECOND LIEUTENANT	FIRST LIEUTENANT	CAPTAIN	MAJOR	LIEUTENANT COLONEL	COLONEL	BRIGADIER GENERAL	MAJOR GENERAL	LIEUTENANT GENERAL	GENERAL	
SILVER BROWN	SILVER BROWN	GOLD	SILVER	SILVER	GOLD	SILVER	SILVER	SILVER	SILVER	SILVER	SILVER
CHIEF WARRANT OFFICER W 3	CHIEF WARRANT OFFICER W 4	SECOND LIEUTENANT	FIRST LIEUTENANT	CAPTAIN	MAJOR	LIEUTENANT COLONEL	COLONEL	BRIGADIER GENERAL	MAJOR GENERAL	LIEUTENANT GENERAL	GENERAL	GENERAL OF THE ARMY
SILVER SKY BLUE	SILVER SKY BLUE	GOLD	SILVER	SILVER	GOLD	SILVER	SILVER	SILVER	SILVER	SILVER	SILVER
CHIEF WARRANT OFFICER W 3	CHIEF WARRANT OFFICER W 4	SECOND LIEUTENANT	FIRST LIEUTENANT	CAPTAIN	MAJOR	LIEUTENANT COLONEL	COLONEL	BRIGADIER GENERAL	MAJOR GENERAL	LIEUTENANT GENERAL	GENERAL	GENERAL OF THE AIR FORCE

MILITARY INTELLIGENCE

CAP INSIGNIA FOR VARIOUS BRANCHES OF U.S. ARMED FORCES

Army
- Officers
- Warrant Officers
- Enlisted Men

Navy
- Commissioned Officers & Commissioned Warrant Officers
- Warrant Officers W-1
- Chief Petty Officer
- Senior Chief Petty Officer
- Master Chief Petty Officer

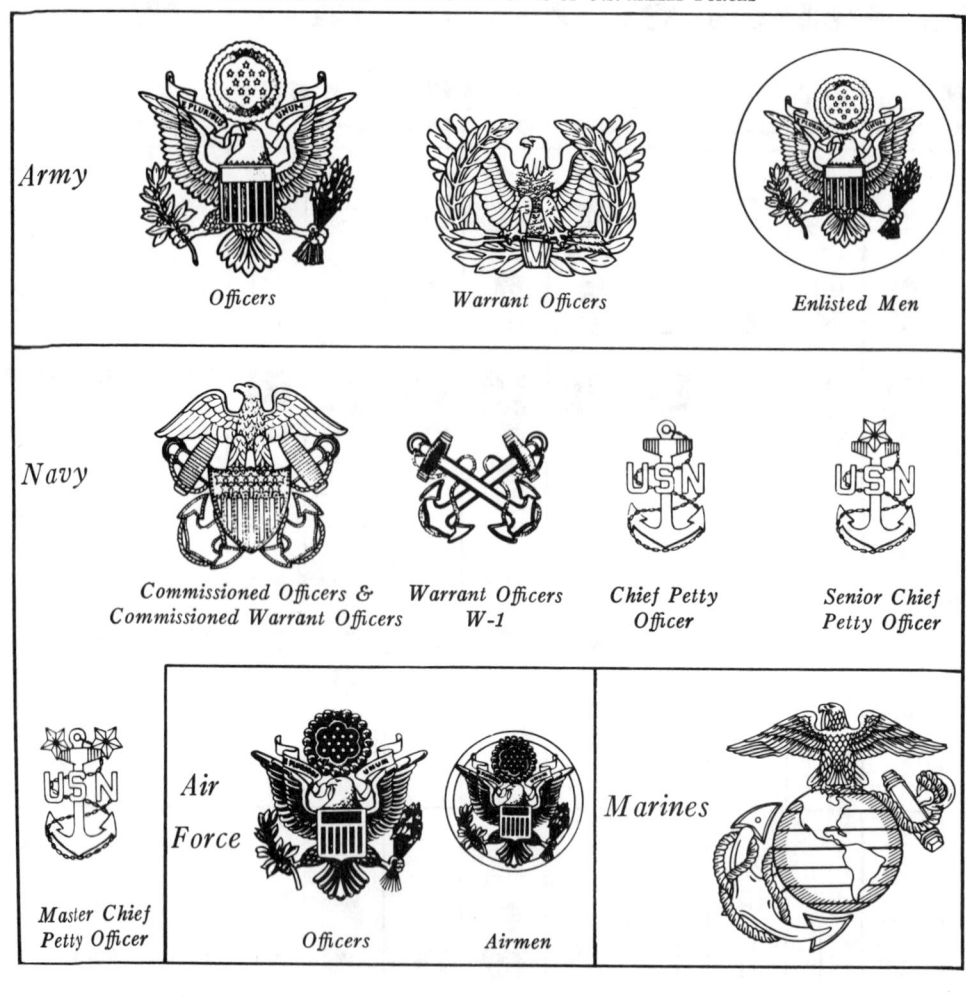

Air Force
- Officers
- Airmen

Marines

left shoulder as emblems of distinguished units and by special personnel such as military police.

Insignia are also part of the uniforms of police forces, military academies, various government agencies, the Salvation Army, youth organizations such as the Girl Scouts of the United States of America and the Boy Scouts, security guards, fraternal orders, maritime and airline personnel, and many professions.

See also MILITARY UNIFORMS.

MILITARY INTELLIGENCE. See ESPIONAGE.

MILITARY LAW, in the U.S., term used to designate the body of statutes, rules, and regulations governing military personnel and also certain civilians during wartime. Unlike martial law which applies to all persons and property in the district in which it prevails, military law in peacetime applies to military personnel alone. Military law differs from military government in that the latter refers particularly to the military jurisdiction exercised by an army of occupation over the territory and inhabitants of an enemy country.

The basis of the military law of the U.S. is contained in Article 1, Section 8, of the U.S. Constitution, by which Congress is empowered "to make rules for the government and regulation of the land and naval forces"; the law is embodied in the Uniform Code of Military Justice, which became effective in 1951. The statutes of military law establish systems of military courts and include penal codes defining the offenses for which persons subject to the code may be punished. Such offenses include mutiny, insubordination, neglect of duty, unbecoming conduct, theft, robbery, rape, and murder. Military personnel charged with crimes of a civil nature may be tried by military courts if the crime is service-connected or of military significance, or if it oc-

MILITARY UNIFORMS

curs outside the U.S. or its possessions. Similarly, military personnel are subject to trial by civil courts if they commit a civil offense. Punishments vary according to the nature of the offense and range from restriction within certain limits, confinement, loss of pay, or reprimand, to the death penalty for such offenses as murder, treason, and desertion in time of war. Trials before military courts are conducted without a grand jury or a petit jury; for the composition and operation of such courts, see MILITARY COURTS.

MILITARY POLICE, any of various law enforcement and guard units of the U.S. military services, serving chiefly to protect military personnel, safeguard military property, and assist in maintaining discipline through the enforcement of laws, orders, and regulations. A supervisory military police officer, as on a post or in a command, is called a provost marshal. Military police organizations include the Military Police Corps, serving the U.S. Army; the shore patrol, serving the U.S. Navy and U.S. Coast Guard; the Security Police, serving the U.S. Air Force; and the combined Armed Forces Police. The U.S. Marine Corps does not at the present time have its own military police force.

The Military Police Corps, besides enforcing military regulations and orders for the Department of the Army, assists other component agencies of the Department of Defense, as when it provides support during joint armed forces operations. It also operates and manages U.S. army confinement facilities, provides installation security, and, in time of war, guards prisoners of war, provides traffic control and convoy escort, and participates in infantry operations when necessary. At staff level the provost marshal general has responsibility for law and order throughout the army and oversees all provost marshal and military police activities.

Within the U.S. Navy, discipline and law and order functions are the responsibility of each separate command. The shore patrol is most commonly selected from the company personnel of a ship to aid civil police in maintaining order among sailors while the ship is in port. The U.S. Coast Guard uses shore patrol in the same manner. Investigations of felonies, counterintelligence activity, and security matters for the Department of the Navy, however, are performed by the U.S. Naval Investigation Service.

The Security Police are specially trained personnel of the U.S. Air Force responsible for the enforcement of law and the protection of air force property and personnel. A primary duty of the Security Police is base and aircraft security. During hostilities, they are used for perimeter and internal air base defense.

The Armed Forces Police, functioning in large cities where two or more armed forces are concerned with the welfare and conduct of their personnel within the civilian community, is a combined organization of enforcement personnel from the two or more concerned services. These units work closely with local civilian police.

MILITARY UNIFORMS, distinctive dress of members of military groups that sets them off from civilians and from other military groups. Although soldiers have always worn specialized clothing, including protective armor, not until the second half of the 17th century did the military uniform as it is known today begin to evolve. Before that time some military units, especially

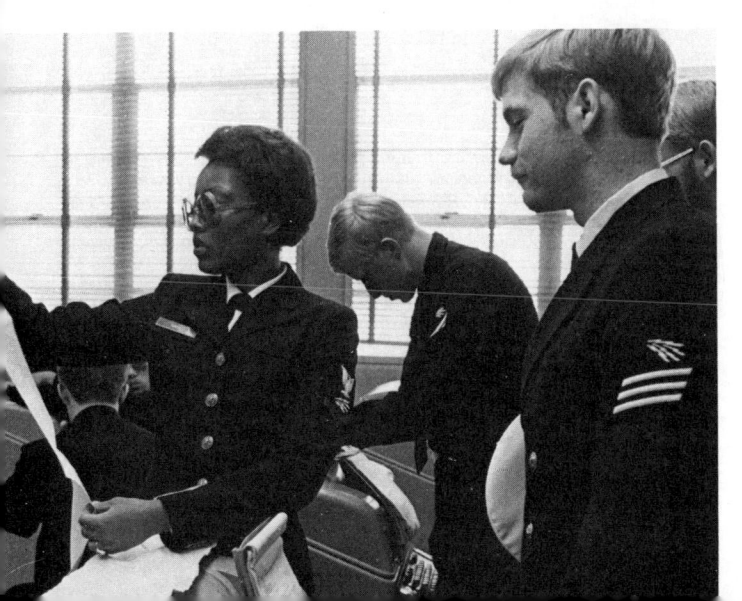

An instructor at the Navy Radioman "A" School checks a student's typing. She wears the uniform of Radioman Third Class; students' jackets have different insignia.
PH2 Claudie Bob Johnson—U.S. Navy

MILITARY UNIFORMS

Top, left to right: British 10th Regiment of Foot, 1775-83; American Infantry of the Revolution, 1775-83; Hessian Field Jaegers, 1776-83, Black Watch Officers, 1775-83; Sapper of Napoleon's Old Guard, about 1812; War of 1812, American Infantry. Center, left to right: Mexican War, U.S. Infantry, 1846-48; American Civil War Zouaves, 1861-65; Civil War Union Infantry, 1861-66; Spanish American War, American Infantry, 1898-1900; World War I, American Doughboy, 1917-18; American Paratroopers, about 1944. Bottom, left: U.S. Army Combat & Dress Uniform, Vietnam, 1968.

Drawings by Clyde A. Risley, through the courtesy of Imrie-Risley Miniatures Inc., N.Y.

MILITARY UNIFORMS

the palace guards and the personal guards of royalty, wore clothing of a uniform design, but most soldiers fought in a motley assortment of civilian garments.

As permanent armies were formed during the 17th century, they began to wear mass-manufactured clothing of the same style, probably for economic reasons, but without any orderly system of distinguishing friend from foe. Thus, during the English civil war, Royalist armies wore red sashes to distinguish them from the Parliamentarians, who wore orange sashes. By the 19th century, however, uniforms had become so elaborate that more functional clothing was demanded. Uniforms of most armies were then supplemented with so-called fatigue clothing, such as smocks and overalls and forage caps, so that the more expensive formal uniform articles could be spared for parade and ceremonial duties. By 1900 all armies were developing battle-dress uniforms, which were usually plain, serviceable garments of drab colors. The two world wars and the need for economy ended the use of the traditional full dress uniform for all but a few special military units. It survives in the dress-gray uniform with shako of the Corps of Cadets of the U.S. Military Academy, first worn probably in 1814. A more ancient survival is the 16th-century garb of the Swiss Guard of the Vatican.

As the military uniform developed, despite the rigors of war and the necessity of budget-cutting each nation incorporated distinctive elements into its uniforms. The kilts of Scottish regiments the feather plumes of Italian bersaglieri (light in

Two marines dressed in cold-weather ski-troop uniforms advance to defensive positions during NATO exercises.
Sergeant B. Walsh–U.S. Marines

fantry), and the square-topped *chapska*, or caps, of Polish soldiers are all nationalistic features, some having hundreds of years of tradition. Soldiers' duties, however, also determined the style of their uniforms. In this sense, the infantry has always worn uniforms easily distinguishable from the cavalry. For example, in the 18th century, while the typical infantry uniform consisted of a broad-brimmed, cocked hat and a long-tailed coat, the cavalry found this uniform impractical and wore visored caps, often of leather or metal for protection, and short-tailed coats that would not be in the way of the saddle.

Armies have always had a number of specialized or elite corps. Among the earliest were the grenadiers. Originally, they were chosen for their size and strength and were assigned the task of assaulting fortifications with hand grenades. Because the typical 18th-century cocked hat got in their way when they slung their muskets to light and throw the grenades, grenadiers began wearing brimless stocking caps. By the time of the Napoleonic wars this cap had evolved into massive bearskin elaborately trimmed. This was the cap favored by Napoleon's Imperial Guard Grenadiers. When a British Foot Guard regiment defeated the Grenadiers at the Battle of Waterloo in 1815, the British regiment was allowed to wear the bearskin cap in honor of their victory. Today the British Brigade Guards still wear the bearskin cap with the traditional red coat.

Since World War II, the development of the military uniform has been influenced less by tradition and more by the practical demands of the battlefield and the necessity of protection from the environment. Hence, specialized garments for jungle, desert, and arctic conditions have been developed. Clothing, in general, must be functional and of lightweight, durable materials that will enable soldiers to perform their duties without restricting their movements. Special uniforms have been created for specific needs, such as flame-retardant uniforms for the crews of tankers and helicopters, and chemical-warfare suits. Camouflage suits are designed for use against certain backgrounds—a far cry from the design criterion of previous centuries when the purpose of soldiers' uniforms was to make them highly visible.

Today, although such distinctions tend to be officially discouraged, some units still rely on unique features of insignia and dress to help separate them from members of other outfits. The green beret of the U.S. Special Forces is only one example of such a distinctive article of dress.

Although women have for centuries served with armies in various capacities, only occasionally were they allowed to wear military uniforms; exceptions were the *vivandières* and *cantinières* (female sutlers) of the French armies. This practice changed in World War I, when female noncombatants were issued military blouses and skirts. With the recruitment of women soldiers today, their uniforms resemble those of their male counterparts, and combat dress is designed for both males and females. M.J.M.

For further information on this topic, see the Bibliography in volume 28, section 279.

MILITIA. See NATIONAL GUARD OF THE UNITED STATES.

MILK, opaque whitish or yellowish liquid secreted by the mammary glands of female mammals for the nourishment of the young. Normal milk does not appear until several days after the birth of the young; the viscid fluid that is secreted from the time of birth until the appearance of normal milk is known as colostrum. Milk consists of globules of butterfat suspended in a solution containing milk sugar (lactose), proteins (mostly casein) and salts of calcium, phosphorus, chlorine, sodium, potassium, and sulfur. It is deficient, however, in dietary iron and is an inadequate source of vitamin C. Water constitutes 80 to 90 percent of whole milk. Fresh milk has a pleasant odor and a sweet taste. Its sp.gr. varies from 1.018 to 1.045; the sp.gr. of cows' milk varies from 1.028 to 1.035. The globules of fat have a lower specific gravity than the milk in solution, and consequently rise to the top, forming cream when milk stands in a container.

Centrifuging accelerates the separation of fat from whole milk. What remains after removal of the cream is called skim milk. If, however, whole milk is forced through small nozzles, the fat globules are so reduced in size that they do not separate thereafter. This product is called homogenized milk. When chilled cream is churned gently, the fat globules gather together to form butter, leaving buttermilk as the by-product.

Acidification of milk, or addition of the enzyme rennin, precipitates most of the protein as curds, or casein (q.v.). The residual liquid is known as whey. The casein may be converted to cheese or used in such commercial products as glue, textile sizes, and paints; it may also be converted to a valuable plastic by reaction with formaldehyde.

About half the milk produced in the U.S. is consumed as fresh milk, the rest going into a variety of products including evaporated and condensed milk, dried milk powder, butter, cheese, malted milk, ice cream, yogurt, lactose, and casein. As a result of the urbanization of the American population, distribution of untreated or raw fresh milk is no longer possible. Almost all milk, in order to insure its safety for human use, undergoes pasteurization (q.v.) and is then chilled before it is packaged and delivered. American standards for milk are based on the Ordinance and Code published by the U.S. Public Health Service. Tests are available to check the bacterial count, percentage of butterfat (2.5 to 3.5 percent), acidity, presence of preservatives (illegal in whole milk), and the adequacy of pasteurization.

In the U.S. commercial milk refers to cows' milk. In some countries, however, the milk of goats, llamas, reindeer, or buffalo is used. Typical compositions of various kinds of milk appear in the accompanying table.

MILK SNAKE, common name for a harmless North American king snake. Because it is often found near dairy barns, it was once thought to

CONSTITUENTS OF MILK (in percentages)

Types	Water	Solids	Fat	Sugar	Casein	Albumin	Ash
Human	87.58	12.42	3.74	6.37	0.80	1.21	0.30
Cow	87.27	12.73	3.68	4.94	2.88	0.51	0.72
Goat	86.68	13.32	4.07	4.64	2.87	0.89	0.85
Sheep	80.71	18.15	7.90	4.17	4.17	0.98	0.93
Buffalo	82.16	17.84	7.51	4.77	4.26	0.46	0.84
Camel	87.13	15.38	5.38	5.39	3.49	0.38	0.74
Llama	86.55	13.45	3.15	5.60	3.00	0.90	0.80
Ass	89.03	11.04	2.53	6.19	0.79	1.06	0.47
Mare	90.58	9.42	1.14	5.87	1.30	0.75	0.36
Reindeer	63.30	37.58	22.46	2.81	8.38	3.02	0.91
Dog	77.00	23.58	9.26	3.11	4.15	5.57	1.49

Milk snake, Lampropeltis triangulum

MILKWEED

steal milk from cows. This reptile actually feeds on small snakes and rodents, squeezing the prey to death. The milk snake grows to about 1 m (about 3 ft). A common variety, the eastern milk snake, is yellowish gray, blotched with dull brown spots; its belly is yellowish white with black squares arranged in a checkerboard pattern. *See also* KING SNAKE.

COMMON NAME	FAMILY	GENUS AND SPECIES
Eastern milk snake	Colubridae	*Lampropeltis triangulum*

MILKWEED, common name for the plant family Asclepiadaceae (*see* GENTIAN), and for plants of the genus *Asclepias*, which typifies the family. Many of the 120 species of the genus are native to North America, and many of them are distributed widely. These perennial herbs have erect stems, opposite or whorled leaves, and small, unusual flowers borne in clusters at the top or along the stem of the plant. The colored parts of each flower are organized in two five-membered whorls. Milkweeds may be divided into two groups: those with broad leaves and those with narrow leaves. Both are characterized by copious milky sap, called latex, and by inflated fruit pods tightly packed with silky or cottony fuzz. At maturity the pod cover dries, opens, and releases many large, flat, brown seeds. Each is attached to a bit of the fuzz and can drift for long distances in gentle currents of air.

Many species of milkweed are among the most dangerous of poisonous plants; others, such as the common broad-leaved milkweed, *A. syriaca*, of eastern North America, have little if any toxicity. Butterflyweed, *A. tuberosa*, and swamp milkweed, *A. incarnata*, are suspected of being toxic, especially the latter; these are among the more showy milkweeds and are sometimes cultivated. Some of the poisonous species of North America are the narrow-leaved labriform milkweed, *A. labriformis*, which is limited to Utah; the narrow-leaved whorled milkweed, *A. subverticillata*, of dry plains in the Southwest; and the broad-leaved woollypod milkweed, *A. eriocarpa*, of dry soils in California. The foliage of these poisonous milkweeds contains a complex resinous compound that produces acute muscle-spasm seizures, symptoms of profound depression, and weakness in animals that consume them. Members of the genus *Stapelia* are called carrion flowers (*see* CARRION FLOWER).

For further information on this topic, *see* the Bibliography in volume 28, sections 452, 461.

MILKWORT, common name for the family Polygalaceae, a group of mostly tropical trees and climbers, and for its representative genus, *Polygala*.

The similarities between the milkwort flower and that of the sweet pea, a member of the legume (q.v.) family, are an example of parallel evolution. The overall similarity in the flowers results from different parts of the flowers taking on similar shapes. The pealike parts of the flower of the milkwort are a combination of sepals (outer floral whorls) and petals (inner floral whorls), whereas in the sweet pea, only petals are involved.

The milkwort family differs from the legume family in its lack of stipules (leaflike appendages at the leaf base) and its two-part ovary (female floral structure). The family is of little economic importance. The snakeroot, *P. senega*, of eastern North America, was once thought to cure snakebite. A few other species of the genus are cultivated as ornamentals. The family belongs to the order Polygalales, which comprises 7 families and some 2300 species; about half the species are placed in the milkwort family.

Plants in the order Polygalales are members of the class Magnoliopsida (*see* DICOTS) in the division Magnoliophyta (*see* ANGIOSPERM).

M.R.C.

MILKY WAY, the large, disk-shaped aggregation of stars, or galaxy (q.v.), that includes the sun and its solar system. Its name is derived from its appearance as a faintly luminous band that stretches across earth's sky at night. This band is the disk in which the solar system lies. Its hazy appearance results from the combined light of stars too far away to be distinguished individually by the unaided eye. The individual stars that are distinct in the sky are those in the Milky Way galaxy that lie sufficiently close to the solar system to be discerned separately.

From the middle northern latitudes, the Milky Way is best seen on clear, moonless, summer nights, when it appears as a luminous, irregular band circling the sky from the northeastern to the southeastern horizon. It extends through the constellations Perseus, Cassiopeia, and Cepheus. In the region of the Northern Cross it divides into two streams: the western stream, which is bright as it passes through the Northern Cross, fades near Ophiuchus, or the Serpent Bearer, because of dense dust clouds, and appears again in Scorpio; and the eastern stream, which grows brighter as it passes southward through Scutum and Sagittarius. The brightest part of the Milky Way extends from Scutum to Scorpio, through Sagittarius. The center is in the direction of Sagittarius and is about 26,000 light-years from the sun.

Structure. The Milky Way has been determined to be a large spiral galaxy, with several spiral arms coiling around a central bulge about 10,000 light-years thick. The stars in the central bulge are closer together than those in the arms, where

The small star cloud in the constellation Sagittarius, a tiny part of the vast Milky Way. Lick Observatory

more interstellar clouds of dust and gas are found. The diameter of the disk is about 100,000 light-years. It is surrounded by a larger cloud of hydrogen gas, warped and scalloped at its edges, and surrounding this in turn is a spheroidal or somewhat flattened halo that contains many separate, globular clusters of stars mainly lying above or below the disk. This halo may be more than twice as wide as the disk itself. In addition, studies of galactic movements suggest that the Milky Way system contains far more matter than is accounted for by the known disk and attendant clusters—up to 2000 billion times more mass than the sun contains. Astronomers have therefore speculated that the known Milky Way system is in turn surrounded by a much larger corona of undetected matter. Another recent speculation is that the Milky Way is a barred spiral galaxy.

Types of Stars. The Milky Way contains both the so-called type I stars, brilliant, blue stars; and type II stars, giant red stars (*see* STAR). The central Milky Way and the halo are composed of the type II population. Most of this region is obscured behind dust clouds, which prevent visual observation. Radiation from the central region has been recorded by use of such special devices as photoelectric cells, infrared filters, and radio telescopes. Such studies indicate compact objects near the galactic center, possibly starburst remnants or a massive black hole (q.v.).

Surrounding the central region is a fairly flat disk comprising stars of both type II and type I; the brightest members of the latter category are luminous, blue supergiants. Imbedded in the disk, and emerging from opposite sides of the central region, are the spiral arms, which contain a majority of the type I population together with much interstellar dust and gas. One arm passes in the vicinity of the sun and includes the great nebula in Orion. *See* NEBULA.

Rotation. The Milky Way rotates around an axis joining the galactic poles. Viewed from the north galactic pole, the rotation of the Milky Way is clockwise, and the spiral arms trail in the same direction. The period of rotation decreases with the distance from the center of the galactic system. In the neighborhood of the solar system the period of rotation is more than 200 million years. The speed of the solar system due to the galactic rotation is about 270 km/sec (about 170 mi/sec).

See also ZODIAC; see separate articles on most of the constellations mentioned.

For further information on this topic, see the Bibliography in volume 28, sections 381, 387.

MILL, James (1773–1836), British philosopher-economist, the father of John Stuart Mill; he expounded and developed the utilitarian doctrine of the British philosopher Jeremy Bentham. Mill was born in Northwater Bridge, Angus Co., Scotland, and educated at the University of Edinburgh. In 1803, he became the editor of the London *Literary Journal,* and in 1805 he became editor of *St. James' Chronicle.* From 1806 to 1818 he was engaged in writing his *History of India*. Although he sharply criticized the East India Co. and the British administration in India, in 1819 he was appointed to a position in the examiner's office of the India House in London. During this period Mill became a close associate of Bentham. As one of the leading exponents of chrestomathic, or useful, learning on a nonsectarian basis, Mill played a prominent role in the establishment of the University of London in 1825. Mill was also the founder of philosophic radicalism, a system of thought based on the teachings of the British economist David Ricardo and presented by Mill in *Elements of Political Economy* (1821) (see RADICALS). In his *Analysis of the Phenomena of the Mind* (1829), Mill applied utilitarian doctrines to psychology, basing his theory of the human mind on the principles of associationism (q.v.).

MILL, John Stuart (1806–73), British philosopher-economist, the son of James Mill; he had a great impact on 19th-century British thought, not only in philosophy and economics but also in the areas of political science, logic, and ethics.

Mill was born in London on May 20, 1806. He was given an unusually early and extensive education by his father, beginning the study of Greek at the age of three. At the age of 17 he had completed advanced and thorough courses of study in Greek literature and philosophy, chemistry, botany, psychology, and law. In 1822 Mill began to work as a clerk for his father in the examiner's office of the India House, and six years later he was promoted to the post of assistant examiner. Until 1856 he had charge of the company's relations with the princely states of India. In the latter year, Mill became chief of the examiner's office, a position he held until the dissolution of the company in 1858, when he retired. Mill lived in Saint Véran, near Avignon in France, until 1865, when he entered Parliament as a member from Westminster. Failing to secure reelection in the general election of 1868, he returned to France, where he studied and wrote until his death at Avignon on May 8, 1873.

Mill stands as a bridge between the 18th-century concern for liberty, reason, and science and the 19th-century trend toward empiricism and collectivism (qq.v.). In philosophy, he systematized the utilitarian doctrines of his father and Jeremy Bentham in such works as *Utilitarianism* (1836), basing knowledge upon human experience and emphasizing human reason. In political economy, Mill advocated those policies that he believed most consistent with individual liberty, and he emphasized that liberty could be threatened as much by social as by political tyranny.

John Stuart Mill

He is probably most famous for his essay "On Liberty" (1859). He studied pre-Marxian socialist doctrine, and, although he did not become a socialist, he worked actively for improvement of the conditions of the working people. In Parliament, Mill was considered a radical, because he supported such measures as public ownership of natural resources, equality for women, compulsory education, and birth control. His advocacy of women's suffrage in the debates on the Reform Bill of 1867 led to the formation of the suffrage movement (see SUFFRAGE). Mill's other major writings include *Principles of Political Economy* (1848), *On the Subjection of Women* (1869), his *Autobiography* (1873), and *Three Essays on Religion* (1874).

See also CAUSALITY.

MILLAIS, Sir John Everett (1829–96), English painter, born in Southampton, and educated in art at the Royal Academy of Arts in London. At the age of 17 he exhibited at the academy his *Pizarro Seizing the Inca of Peru* (1846, Victoria and Albert Museum, London), then considered one of the best history paintings shown that year. In 1848 he and two other English painters, Dante Gabriel Rossetti and William Holman Hunt, formed a brotherhood of artists known as the Pre-Raphaelites (q.v.). Millais's first Pre-Raphaelite painting, the scene *Lorenzo and Isabella* (1849, Walker Art Gallery, Liverpool), recalls the manner of the early Flemish and Italian masters. Beginning in the early 1870s, he created many portraits of British personalities, famous in his time. He was a careful artist who paid strict attention to detail, unusual composition, and clarity. In much of his later work he succumbed to the Victorian taste for sentiment and anecdotal art.

MILLAY, Edna St. Vincent (1892-1950), American poet, born in Rockland, Maine, and educated at Vassar College. In 1917 her *Renascence and Other Poems* was published. She wrote several plays for the experimental theater group the Provincetown Players, notably *Aria da Capo* (1919), a satirical fantasy on war.

Millay's major efforts were devoted to lyric poetry in *A Few Figs from Thistles* (1920), *Second April* (1921), and *The Ballad of the Harp Weaver* (1922; Pulitzer Prize for poetry, 1923). Her later poetry is marked by greater social consciousness but shows less lyric power. *Murder of Lidice* (1942) is a ballad written for radio. Her mastery of the sonnet form is best illustrated in *Collected Sonnets* (1941) and *Collected Lyrics* (1943).

Millay's work is characterized by a great facility in the use of traditional verse forms and in the expression of simple, strong emotions. The thoughts are rarely original or complex, but because some were unfamiliar to many Americans, she acquired a reputation for novelty and vitality.

MILLE LACS LAKE, lake, about 544 sq km (about 210 sq mi), E central Minnesota. The lake drains S through the Rum R. into the Mississippi R. at Anoka. It is a popular tourist attraction and has an Indian reservation on the SW shore.

MILLENNIUM, in Christian eschatology, period of 1000 years, foretold in the New Testament Book of Revelation, in which the devil will be chained and holiness will prevail on earth. The concept of the millennium, which is based principally on a literal interpretation of Revelation 20:3 and other passages, is held by a small number of Protestant denominations, among them the Jehovah's Witnesses and the Adventists, including the Seventh-Day Adventist Church. The sects believing in the millennium, however, differ over its precise nature. The main disagreement is over the interpretation of the description (see Rev. 20:4-15) of the second coming of Christ. The more generally held interpretation is that of the so-called premillenarians, who believe that the visible second coming will precede the millennium and will be a mark of it. Christ will descend on the earth and raise from the dead the so-called chosen ones, or elect, who then will participate with him for 1000 years in a triumphal reign over the earth. At the end of that time, all other people will be resurrected. The wicked will be annihilated, and the just will live forever with Christ in a renewed heaven and earth. The so-called postmillenarians believe, on the other hand, that Christ will not begin his reign until after the millennium, which they see as a period of gradual spiritual regeneration. The concept of a millennium is rejected by most Christian churches, but despite disagreement on particulars all Christian denominations believe in the second coming.

In popular usage, the word *millennium* has come to be applied to an ideal or utopian period or situation.

MILLER, Arthur (1915-), American dramatist, regarded as one of the major playwrights of the 20th century.

Miller was born Oct. 17, 1915, in New York City, the son of a coat manufacturer, who suffered financial ruin in the Great Depression. In 1938, while a student at the University of Michigan, he won awards for his comedy *The Grass Still Grows*. When he returned to New York, he started writing radio dramas. In 1944 his play *The Man Who Had All the Luck*, although not a commercial success, won him the Theater Guild Award. His novel *Focus* (1945), an attack on anti-Semitism, was successful, and the New York Drama Critics' Circle chose his *All My Sons* as the best play of 1947. This study of the effect of opportunism on family relationships foreshadowed most of Miller's later work.

Miller's major achievement was *Death of a Salesman* (1949). It won the Pulitzer Prize for drama and the New York Drama Critics' Circle Award for best play of the year and is often cited as one of the finest plays by a contemporary dramatist. It tells, in almost poetic terms, the tragic story of an average man much like Miller's father. His play *The Crucible* (1953), although concerned with the Salem witchcraft trials, was actually aimed at the then widespread congressional investigation of subversive activities in the U.S.; the drama won the Antoinette Perry Award. Miller himself appeared before the House Un-American Activities Committee in 1956. He was convicted of contempt, but later the conviction was appealed and reversed.

His other dramas are *A View from the Bridge* (1955), *After the Fall* (1963), *Incident at Vichy* (1964), *The Price* (1968), and *The Archbishop's Ceiling* (1977)—on the Soviet treatment of dissident writers. Other works include the screenplay *The Misfits* (1960), written for his second wife, the actor Marilyn Monroe; *The American Clock* (1980), a series of dramatic vignettes based on *Hard Times* (1970), a study of the depression by the American writer Studs Terkel (1912-); a collection of short stories, *I Don't Need You Any More* (1967); and *The Theater Essays of Arthur Miller* (1978). Miller's works are intensely concerned with the responsibility of each individual to other people. Simply and colloquially written, they spring from the author's social conscience and his compassion for those who are vulnerable to and led astray by the false values imposed on them by society.

MILLER, Henry (1891–1980), American writer, whose antipuritanical books did much to free the discussion of sexual subjects in American writing from both legal and social restrictions.

Born in New York City on Dec. 26, 1891, Miller tried a variety of jobs and attended the City College of New York briefly before going to Paris in 1930. He lived there for almost ten years, leading a bohemian existence that he wrote about in three autobiographical erotic novels, *Tropic of Cancer* (1934), *Black Spring* (1936), and *Tropic of Capricorn* (1939). These books, prohibited in the U.S. on grounds of obscenity, were frequently smuggled into his native country, building Miller an underground reputation. In 1940 he returned to the U.S., settling at Big Sur, Calif. There he continued to produce his vividly written, semiphilosophical, and often ribald works, which include *The Colossus of Maroussi* (1941); *The Air-Conditioned Nightmare* (1945–47); a trilogy, *The Rosy Crucifixion*, comprising *Sexus* (1949), *Plexus* (1953), and *Nexus* (1960); *Big Sur and the Oranges of Hieronymus Bosch* (1957); and the critical work *The World of Lawrence* (1980).

The publication of Miller's two "Tropics" novels in the U.S. led to a series of obscenity trials that tested American laws on pornography and ended, in 1964, in a victory for him. He also earned recognition as a watercolorist. Miller died in Pacific Palisades, Calif., on June 7, 1980.

MILLER, Joaquin, pseudonym of CINCINNATUS HINER MILLER (1839–1913), American poet, born in Indiana. Going west in 1854, he became a miner and lived with Indians. In 1860 he settled in Oregon, where he edited a newspaper and became a judge. He went to England, and in 1871 his first volume of verse, *Songs of the Sierra*, was published. He finally settled as a journalist in California. Miller's works include *Songs of the Sunlands* (1873), *Songs of Italy* (1878), *Songs of the Mexican Seas* (1887), *Building of the City Beautiful* (1893), and *Poems* (6 vol., 1909–10). His verse, characterized by colloquial diction and songlike form, celebrates the freedom and vastness of the American West.

MILLER, William (1782–1849), American religious leader, who founded the Protestant Adventist denomination (see ADVENTISTS), also known as the Millerites. Miller, a Baptist, closely studied the Bible, especially the Book of Daniel, and concluded that the world would end and Christ would appear in the year 1843. He began preaching these ideas in 1831. By 1840 some of his many followers had disposed of their belongings in anticipation of the judgment day. When 1843 passed uneventfully, Miller set a new date in 1844 for the end of the world. In 1845, although the movement had collapsed in disillusionment, Miller and a few loyal followers met in Albany, N.Y., and founded the Adventist church.

MILLES, Carl (1875–1955), Swedish-American sculptor. Originally named Carl Emil Wilhelm Anderson, he was born near Uppsala. From 1897 to 1905 he studied in Paris with the renowned French sculptor Auguste Rodin. Milles returned to Sweden and taught at the Stockholm Art Academy from 1920 to 1931. Milles went to the U.S. in 1929 and became a naturalized citizen in 1945. He worked and taught at the Cranbrook Academy of Art in Michigan after 1931. Milles's works include monuments, polychrome statues, portrait busts in bronze, stone, and wood, and animal pieces. Vigorous and animated, they may be described as highly stylized interpretations of ancient Greek sculpture. He is known for his fountain sculpture, including the *Orpheus* fountain (1936) in Stockholm, the *Meeting of the Waters* fountain (1940) in Saint Louis, Mo., and sculpture groups at Rockefeller Center and the Metropolitan Museum of Art, New York City.

MILLET, common name for several species of the grass family, Poaceae (see GRASSES), and for their small-seeded grain, which is used to make porridge and flatbreads or as food for livestock. Millet grows in ears or heads atop stalks that range from 0.3 to 3 m (1 to 10 ft) high. It is an important food staple in most of the former Soviet republics, western Africa, and Asia. Archaeologists have found evidence that millet was first cultivated as a food in Africa, about 8000 years ago. Because it ripens in 60 to 80 days, grows in less-fertile soils, and resists drought, it is widely cultivated in poorer agricultural areas. The millets usually contain less protein than wheat or rye and more protein than rice.

Among the better known millets is common millet, or proso, *Panicum miliaceum*, which is grown as food in eastern Europe and most parts of Asia, and as feed for poultry, wild birds, and livestock in the U.S. Pearl millet, *Pennisetum americanum*, is the tallest millet and has the largest grains, which appear on long spikes similar to those of cattails. It is a common food in Africa, India, and Asia and is grown as fodder and silage in the U.S.

For further information on this topic, see the Bibliography in volume 28, sections 452, 589.

MILLET, Jean François (1814–75), French genre and landscape painter, born in Gruchy. He studied art in Cherbourg and later in Paris with the

The Angelus (1859), by Jean François Millet.

French painter Paul Delaroche. After 12 years in Paris and Normandy, Millet joined the Barbizon school of landscape artists. There he painted some of his best-known works of peasants working in the fields. These include *The Gleaners* (1857) and *The Angelus* (1859), both in the Louvre, and *The Sower* (1850) and *Potato Planters* (1862), both in the Museum of Fine Arts, Boston. Although Millet did not intend his work to be regarded as social protest, the subjects he chose led inevitably to such interpretation.

MILLIGAN, EX PARTE, celebrated case, decided by the U.S. Supreme Court in 1866, which limited the application of martial law. During the American Civil War, Abraham Lincoln authorized the use of military commissions to try those people suspected of aiding the Confederacy. Lambdin Milligan (1812-99), a civilian and a Confederate sympathizer, was arrested in Indiana and charged with conspiring to incite rebellion. In 1864, he was tried before a military commission, convicted, and sentenced to death. The defense claimed that Milligan had been deprived of his constitutional rights to a trial by jury. The case was brought before the Supreme Court, which overturned the conviction, ruling that civilians could not be tried by the military when civil courts were in operation. The Court reiterated that the Constitution remained the law of the land in time of war as well as in peacetime. The decision was a landmark in the constitutional history of the nation. See SUPREME COURT OF THE UNITED STATES.

MILLIKAN, Robert Andrews (1868-1953), American physicist, best known for his work in atomic physics. Millikan was born in Morrison, Ill., and educated at Columbia University and the universities of Berlin and Göttingen. He joined the faculty of the University of Chicago in 1896, and in 1910 he became professor of physics there. He left the university in 1921 to become director of the Norman Bridge Laboratory of Physics of the California Institute of Technology. He was awarded the 1923 Nobel Prize in physics for his famous "oil-drop" experiments, which measured the charge on an electron (q.v.) and showed that the charge exists only as a whole number of units of that charge. His other contributions include important research on cosmic rays (which he named) and X rays, and the experimental demination of Planck's constant (q.v.). He wrote technical studies and several books on the relationship between science and religion.

MILLIPEDE, any of about 1000 species of cylindrical, many-legged arthropods constituting the class Diplopoda (see ARTHROPOD). Found worldwide, millipedes have segmented bodies with two pairs of legs on each of the 9 to 100 or more abdominal segments, depending on the species, and one pair on three of the four thoracic segments. Because of the numerous legs, the animals walk slowly, with a wavelike motion of the legs down the body. In length they range from about 0.2 to 23 cm (about 0.1 to 9 in); the largest North American species, *Narceus americanus*, is 10 cm (4 in) long. Millipedes have a hard protective layer of calcium-containing chitin (except in some small species), two simple eyes, one pair of mandibles, two short antennae, and (in most species) stink glands with secretions that repel or kill insect predators. Another protective strategy is to curl into a spiral or a ball when threatened. The animals live in dark, damp places and feed on decaying plant life, sometimes damaging crops but also enriching the soil. They grow by molting and may live for one to seven years.

For further information on this topic, see the Bibliography in volume 28, section 464.

MILLS, Clark (1810–83), American sculptor, born in Onondaga Co., N.Y. He was a laborer until about 1835, when he went to Charleston, S.C. There he invented a new method of casting from life. His marble bust of the American statesman John C. Calhoun, for which he was awarded a gold medal, was placed in the Charleston city hall. Although he had never seen an equestrian statue or the American president Andrew Jackson, in 1853 Mills cast in bronze an equestrian statue of Jackson with metal melted from captured British cannon. The statue is in Lafayette Square, Washington, D.C. His bronze casting of *Armed Freedom* by Thomas Crawford (c. 1813–57) was placed atop the Capitol in Washington in 1863.

MILLS, Robert (1781–1855), American architect and engineer, born in Charleston, S.C. He studied with the English-trained American architect Benjamin H. Latrobe and subsequently practiced as one of the first native professional American architects in Washington, D.C., Philadelphia, and Baltimore, Md. In 1820 Mills became state architect and engineer of South Carolina. From 1836 until 1851 he was the official architect of public buildings for the U.S. government. An exponent of the Greek Revival (q.v.) style, Mills achieved simple, finely proportioned, and monumental effects in his work. One of his best-known designs the Washington Monument (q.v.), begun in 1848 but not completed until 1884. He also designed the Treasury Building (1836) and the Patent Office Building (1836), now housing the National Collection of Fine Arts and the National Portrait Gallery, in Washington, D.C.

MILLVILLE, city, Cumberland Co., SW New Jersey, on the Maurice R.; inc. as a city 1866. It is a manufacturing city and a summer resort; major products include glass containers, printed materials, processed food, clothing, transportation equipment, rubber and plastic products, and machinery. The repair of aircraft engines and fishing also are important industries here. Settled in the 18th century, the community grew in the early 19th century after the Union Co. built a dam and a mill at what is now the head of nearby Union Lake. Pop. (1980) 24,815; (1990) 25,992.

MILNE, A(lan) A(lexander) (1882–1956), English author of a series of children's books that have become classics. Milne, who was born in London, was the author of several whimsical plays popular in the 1920s, including *Mr. Pim Passes By* (1919) and *The Dover Road* (1920), as well as a few novels of contemporary life and one detective story, *The Red House Mystery* (1922). He is best known, however, for the juvenile verses and stories he wrote for his son, Christopher Robin (1920–   ). These delightful books include *When We Were Very Young* (1924), *Winnie-the-Pooh* (1926), *Now We Are Six* (1927), and *The House at Pooh Corner* (1928). Not only Christopher Robin himself, with his stuffed bear Winnie-the-Pooh and their constant companion Piglet, but also Kanga and Roo, Eeyore the donkey, the kittenish Tigger, Rabbit, and Owl—all the fanciful characters created by Milne—are beloved by both children and adults.

MILNER, Alfred, 1st Viscount Milner (1854–1925), British statesman, born in Giessen, Hesse (now in Germany), and educated at the universities of London and Oxford. A former journalist with the *Pall Mall Gazette,* Milner was undersecretary for finance in Egypt from 1889 to 1892; in the latter year he published *England in Egypt,* an argument for British involvement in that country. In 1897 he was appointed high commissioner for British southern Africa and governor of the Cape Colony (now Cape Province), in which post his outstanding achievement was to negotiate the peace ending the Boer War (q.v.). He returned to Great Britain in 1905 and retired from politics. In 1915 he became a member of the war cabinet, without portfolio, and he later served as emissary to Russia (1917), secretary of war (1918), and colonial secretary (1919–21). His recommendations that Egypt be given limited self-government were adopted in 1922.

MÍLOS, also Melos, island, SE Greece, in the Aegean Sea, one of the Cyclades (q.v.) Islands. Grain, fruit, and olive oil are produced. The famous Hellenistic statue *Venus de Milo* (Louvre, Paris) was found here in 1820. Area, 158 sq km (61 sq mi). Pop. (1981) 4554.

MILPITAS, city, Santa Clara Co., W California, just N of San Jose; settled 1850s, inc. 1954. Industries here include the manufacture of plastics and electrical and electronic equipment. Before the mid-1950s Milpitas was a small farming community. Its name is Spanish for "little cornfields." Pop. (1980) 37,820; (1990) 50,686.

MILSTEIN, César (1927–), Argentine-born British immunologist and Nobel laureate, who shared the 1984 Nobel Prize in physiology or medicine (with Niels Kai Jerne and Georges J. F. Köhler) for his development, with Köhler, of monoclonal antibody technology. He was born in Bahía Blanca and attended the universities of Buenos Aires and Cambridge. His work is now of basic importance in a wide range of biological and medical research. He and Köhler conducted their studies at the British Medical Research Council Laboratory of Molecular Biology at Cambridge University; Milstein remained associated with that university. See also GENETIC ENGINEERING.

MILSTEIN, Nathan (1903–92), Russian-American violinist, renowned for the beauty and purity of his tone. A student of the influential Russian violinist Leopold Auer at the Saint Petersburg Conservatory, Milstein made his debut in 1915 and lived in the U.S. after 1929. His strong, refined playing and intellectual approach to music were widely admired. He performed extensively with the Russian-American pianist Vladimir Horowitz and the Russian-American cellist Gregor Piatigorsky and was associated with the Belgian violinist Eugène Ysaÿe in Brussels.

MILTIADES (540?–489 BC), Athenian general. He became tyrant, or ruler, of the Greek cities of the Chersonesus Thracia, or Gallipoli Peninsula, in what is now Turkey. Miltiades joined the Persian king Darius I in a war against the Scythians, north of the Danube River around 513 BC. Later, when Attica in central Greece was threatened by attack from the Persians, Miltiades was chosen one of the ten generals to repel the invasion. He led the Athenians and their allies to victory over the Persians at Marathon in 490 BC in one of the most famous battles in history. Miltiades later requested and was entrusted by the Athenians with the command of 70 ships, with which he attacked the island of Páros in the Aegean Sea for the purpose of avenging a private grudge. The expedition failed, and Miltiades received a severe leg injury. On his return to Athens he was fined for using the fleet for a personal end, and soon thereafter he died from his injury.

John Milton — Metropolitan Museum of Art

MILTON, town, Norfolk Co., E Massachusetts, on the Neponset R., a residential suburb of Boston; inc. 1662. Milton is the site of Curry College (1879); Blue Hill Observatory (1885); Milton Academy (1807), a preparatory school; and the Museum of the American China Trade. Settled in 1636 as part of Dorchester and separated from it in 1662, Milton developed as a mill town and industrial center. Manufacturing declined in the 19th century and the large estates here broke up in the 1930s. Pop. (1980) 25,860; (1990) 25,725.

MILTON, John (1608–74), the greatest English poet after Shakespeare, whose sublime verse shaped the entire course of English poetry for three centuries, and whose prose was devoted to the defense of civil and religious liberty.

Life. Milton was born in London on Dec. 9, 1608, and educated at Saint Paul's School and Christ's College, University of Cambridge. He intended to become a clergyman in the Church of England, but growing dissatisfaction with the state of the Anglican clergy together with his own developing poetic interests led him to abandon this purpose. From 1632 to 1638 he lived in his father's country home in Horton, Buckinghamshire, preparing himself for his poetic career by entering upon an ambitious program of reading in the Latin and Greek classics and in ecclesiastical and political history. In 1638–39 he toured France and Italy, where he met the leading literary figures of the day. On his return to England, he settled in London and began writing a series

MILTON

of social, religious, and political tracts. In 1642 he married Mary Powell (1625-52), who left him after a few weeks because of the incompatibility of their temperaments but was reconciled to him in 1645. Milton, throughout his writings, supported the parliamentary cause in the civil war between Parliamentarians and Royalists, and in 1649 he was appointed foreign secretary by the government of the Commonwealth. He became totally blind about 1652 and thereafter carried on his literary work assisted by an amanuensis; with the aid also of the poet Andrew Marvell, he fulfilled his government duties until the restoration of Charles II in 1660. In 1656 he married a second wife, who died two years later. With the Restoration, Milton was punished for his support of Parliament by a fine and a short term of imprisonment. He married a third time in 1663, and until his death on Nov. 8, 1674, he lived in seclusion.

Of the poet's personality, memoirs written by Milton's contemporaries indicate that his was a singular blend of grace and sweetness and of a force and severity amounting almost to harshness. Called "the Lady of Christ's" while a student at Christ's College, Cambridge, he retained until his death a gentleness and urbanity in his private life that contrasted sharply with the exacting strictness of his public role. Although isolated and embittered by blindness, he fulfilled the tasks he had set himself, lightening his dark days with music, to which he was devoted, and cheerful conversation.

Works. John Milton's work is marked by cosmic themes and lofty religious idealism; it reveals an astonishing breadth of learning and command of the Greek, Latin, and Hebrew classics. His blank verse is of remarkable variety and richness, so skillfully modulated and flexible that it has been compared to organ tones.

Milton's career as a writer may be divided into three periods. The first (1625-40) was the period of such early works as the poems written while he was still at Cambridge, the ode "On the Morning of Christ's Nativity" (1629), the sonnet "On Shakespeare" (1630), "L'Allegro" and "Il Penseroso" (both probably 1631), "On Time" (1632?), "At a Solemn Musick" (1632-33?), the masques Arcades (1632-34?) and Comus (1634), and the elegy Lycidas (1637). His second period (1640-60) was devoted chiefly to the writing of the prose tracts that established him the ablest pamphleteer of his time. In the first group of pamphlets Milton attacked the institution of bishops and argued in favor of extending the spirit of the English Reformation. The first published of this group was Of Reformation Touching Church Discipline in England (1641); the one most deeply pondered and elaborately reasoned was The Reason of Church Government Urged Against Prelaty (1641-42), which also contains an important digression in which Milton tells of his own early life, education, and ambitions. (Such autobiographical digressions are found scattered throughout his prose works.) The second phase of his devotion to social and political concerns yielded, among others, The Doctrine and Discipline of Divorce (1643), in which he argued that since marriage was instituted for intellectual as well as physical companionship, divorce should be granted for incompatibility; and his most famous prose work, Areopagitica (1644), an impassioned plea for freedom of the press. In Of Education (1644) Milton advocated an education combining classical instruction, to prepare the student for government service, with religious training. The third group of pamphlets includes those Milton wrote to justify the execution of Charles I. The first of these, The Tenure of Kings and Magistrates (1649), deals with constitutional questions and particularly with the rights of the people against tyrants. In the final group of tracts, including A Treatise of Civil Power in Ecclesiastical Causes (1659), Milton gave practical suggestions for government reform and argued against a professional clergy and in favor of allowing people to interpret Scripture according to their own conscience.

During his years as a prose writer and government servant, Milton composed part of his great epic poem Paradise Lost and 17 sonnets, among which are some of the most notable in the English language, including "On His Blindness" (c. 1652-55) and "On His Deceased Wife" (1658). The apogee of Milton's poetic career was reached in his third period (1660-74), during which he completed Paradise Lost (1667) and composed the companion epic Paradise Regain'd (1671) and the poetic drama Samson Agonistes (1671).

Paradise Lost is considered Milton's masterpiece and one of the greatest poems in world literature. In its 12 cantos he tells the story of the fall of Adam in a context of cosmic drama and profound speculations. The poet's announced aim was to "justify the ways of God to men." The poem was written with soaring imagination and far-ranging intellectual grasp in his most forceful and exalted style. Paradise Regain'd, which tells of human salvation through Christ, is a shorter and lesser work, although still one of great richness and strength. In Samson Agonistes, a tragedy on the Greek model composed partly in blank verse and partly in unrhymed choric verse

Buildings in downtown Milwaukee overlook a park on the shores of Lake Michigan. Milwaukee Dept. of City Development

of varied line length, Milton employed the Old Testament story of Samson to inspire the defeated English Puritans with the courage to triumph through sacrifice. D.D.

For further information on this person, see the section Biographies in the Bibliography in volume 28.

MILWAUKEE, city, seat of Milwaukee Co. and also in Washington Co., SE Wisconsin, on Lake Michigan at the junction of the Milwaukee, Menomonee, and Kinnickinnic rivers; inc. 1846. It is a commercial and manufacturing center and a major port of entry on the Great Lakes-Saint Lawrence Seaway system. Manufactures include nonelectrical machinery, metal and food products, printed materials, electrical and electronic equipment, and chemicals. Milwaukee is also the marketing center for a rich agricultural region producing dairy products, grain, and fruit, and it is the site of large breweries.

Among the institutions of higher education are Marquette University (1864), the University of Wisconsin-Milwaukee (1955), Concordia University of Wisconsin (1881), Cardinal Stritch College (1937), Alverno College (1936), Mount Mary College (1913), Wisconsin Lutheran College (1973), Medical College of Wisconsin (1970), the Milwaukee Institute of Art and Design (1974), and the Milwaukee School of Engineering (1903).

The Milwaukee area contains many cultural facilities and several points of historical interest. Cultural centers in the city include the Milwaukee Public Museum, featuring displays on natural history and on the history of Milwaukee; the Milwaukee Art Museum, housing collections of paintings, sculpture, and photography; and Mitchell Park Conservatory, with exhibits on horticulture. In addition, the city is the home of the Milwaukee Symphony Orchestra, the Milwaukee Ballet Company, and the Milwaukee Repertory Theater. Saint Josaphat Basilica (1897–1901) is the only Polish basilica in North America; its dome was modeled after that of Saint Peter's in Rome. Milwaukee also contains a popular zoo and an extensive park system. Near the city are Old Falls Village, Cedar Creek Settlement, Stonecraft Village, Greenwood Meadows Farms, and Old World Wisconsin. The city is also home to professional teams, the Brewers (baseball) and the Bucks (basketball).

Many Indian groups made the Milwaukee area their home; French missionaries who arrived in the late 17th century found bands of Fox, Mascouten, and Potawatomi on lands formerly occupied by the Winnebago. The site of Milwaukee was settled in 1818 by French-Canadian fur traders led by Solomon Laurent Juneau (1793–1856), but development did not begin until 1833, when the Indians gave up their land claims. The city's rich ethnic heritage began in the 1840s with the arrival of German immigrants and continued with the later addition of Poles, Irish, Italians, and Scandinavians. After the American Civil War, the economy shifted from commerce to manufacturing (food and lumber processing, tanning, brewing, and the production of iron and steel goods). The socialist movement sprang up as a result of demands for labor reforms. The city was led by three socialist mayors—Emil Seidel (1864–1947), from 1910 to 1912; Daniel W. Hoan (1881–1961), during 1916–40; and Frank P. Zeidler (1912–   ), 1948–60. After World War II Milwaukee began an extensive redevelopment program. The modernization of its harbor for oceangoing vessels and the opening of the St. Lawrence Seaway in 1959 made it an international port. Modernization continued with extensive redevelopment of the downtown business district. The city's name is derived from the Potawatomi Indian term *Mahn-ah-wauk* ("gathering place by water"). Pop. (1980) 636,236; (1990) 628,088.

MIMEOGRAPHY. *See* OFFICE SYSTEMS.

MIMICRY

MIMICRY, physical or behavioral resemblance of one species to another to benefit itself or, in effect, sometimes both species. By mimicking the color bands and buzzing sounds of stinging bees, for example, several species of otherwise defenseless moths and flies avoid predation by birds. The animal or plant being mimicked is usually an abundant species whose noxious characteristics have left a lasting impression on predators. Instead of avoiding detection by predators through camouflage, the mimicking species displays the same conspicuous warning marks or behavior as the harmful species.

Mimicry was discovered in 1862 by the British naturalist Henry Walter Bates (1825–92), who found two similarly marked but unrelated families of Brazilian forest butterflies. Noting that one family was poisonous to birds, he explained that the palatable butterflies had survived by evolving similar warning markings. This concept, Batesian mimicry, was used to demonstrate Charles Darwin's theory of natural selection (q.v.), whereby birds were seen to act as selective agents by eliminating the palatable butterflies that had fewer resemblances to the poisonous butterflies. Another kind of mimicry, called Müllerian mimicry, is found especially among insect species that are all similarly poisonous but that have evolved similar markings to reduce mortality. Instead of individual insect species developing distinct warning marks and sacrificing members to teach birds to avoid them, many species have evolved a common warning mark so that birds need learn but one lesson to avoid the entire group.

Mimicry occurs among a great many different forms of plants and animals, including orchids and insects, songbirds and hawks, and lizards and noxious beetles.

MIMOSA, common name for herbs, shrubs, and trees of the subfamily Mimosoideae, family Fabaceae (see LEGUME) and especially for the plants of the typical genus, *Mimosa*. Other important genera are *Acacia* (q.v.); *Prosopis* (see MESQUITE); *Schrankia*, which includes the sensitive brier, *S. microphylla*, of the southern U.S.; and *Albizia*, native to Africa and Asia, which includes the silk tree, *A. julibrissin*, noted for flowers with long, silky stamens. Mimosa are native to tropical and subtropical regions. The genus *Mimosa*, which contains about 400 species, is native to tropical America and naturalized in the hot regions of Asia and Africa. Many species are sensitive, in that the leaves, which are bipinnate, bend together and droop upon slight stimulation by mechanical, chemical, or electrical means. Tiny yellow, orange, or purplish flowers are usually borne in globular heads. Bisexual and unisexual flowers usually occur on the same plant. The flowers have a four-toothed or five-toothed calyx, a four-lobed or five-lobed corolla, numerous stamens on the male and bisexual flowers, and a solitary pistil on the female and bisexual flowers. The fruit is a pod. The common sensitive plant of American hothouses is *M. pudica*, a perennial shrub cultivated as an annual.

For further information on this topic, see the Bibliography in volume 28, sections 452, 456, 675.

MINAMOTO YORITOMO (1147–99), Japanese warrior and founder of the shogunate—a military dictatorship that lasted nearly 700 years. A leader of the Minamoto clan, he defeated the rival Taira (q.v.) family in a bitter war (1180–85) that left him the virtual ruler of Japan. Declining to dethrone the emperor, Yoritomo established a feudal military administration that in fact ruled the whole country, although he took for himself (1192) merely the title of shogun ("generalissimo"). The Minamoto clan held power only until 1219, but Yoritomo's shogunate set the pattern for gov-

The walkingstick so closely resembles the twigs on which it rests that it usually escapes notice.
Hal H. Harrison–National Audubon Society

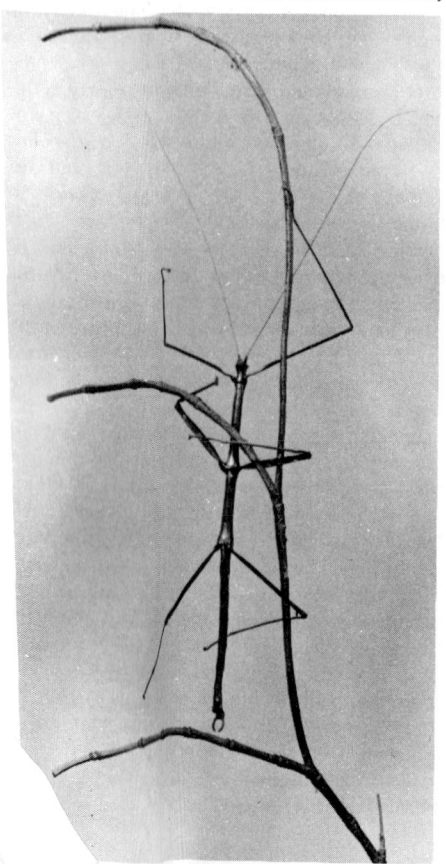

ernmental structure in Japan until the Meiji restoration of 1868.

MINAS BASIN. See FUNDY, BAY OF.

MINAS CHANNEL. See FUNDY, BAY OF.

MINDANAO, island of the Philippines, the second largest and southernmost of the country's major islands. The island is about 483 km (about 300 mi) long and very irregular in shape. The Zamboanga Peninsula in the W is nearly divided from the main part of the island by Iligan Bay on the N and Illanon Bay on the S. The coastline is marked with many bays and headlands, which afford shelter to ships during storms. The island is mountainous, and the mountains are covered with forests of teak, ironwood, cypress, and ebony. The loftiest summit is the volcano Apo, 2954 m (9690 ft) above sea level. The principal rivers are the Río Grande de Mindanao and the Agusan. The soil is exceedingly fertile and produces corn, coconuts, and abaca, or Manila hemp. Gold, copper, iron, and coal are the chief mineral resources. Stock farming is the most important economic activity of Mindanao. The chief towns on the island are Zamboanga and Davao. Pop. (1990 est.) 10,892,000.

MINDORO, island, W Philippines, near the island of Luzon (from which it is separated by the Verde Island Passage). The island has low coastal strips, but an elevated plain occupying the interior rises to 2587 m (8487 ft) above sea level at Mt. Halcon in the north-central part. Dense forests of ebony, mahogany, and other trees cover the mountains. The chief agricultural crops are coconuts and rice. Mindoro and several outlying islands constitute the provinces of Mindoro Oriental and Mindoro Occidental. The chief settlement is Calapan. Area of island, about 9738 sq km (about 3760 sq mi); total area of provinces, about 10,075 sq km (about 3890 sq mi). Pop. of Mindoro Oriental (1990 est.) 589,000; pop. of Mindoro Occidental (1990 est.) 289,900.

MIND READING, phenomenon of extrasensory perception, or ESP. See PSYCHICAL RESEARCH.

MINDSZENTY, József, real name JÓZSEF PEHM (1892–1975), Hungarian Roman Catholic prelate. Born in Mindszent, Austria-Hungary (now Hungary), he was educated at Szombathely and was ordained a priest in 1915. Consecrated bishop of Veszprém in 1944, Mindszenty was named archbishop of Esztergom and primate of Hungary after World War II. In 1946 he was elevated to the cardinalate.

An outspoken opponent of totalitarianism, Mindszenty was briefly imprisoned in 1919 because of his opposition to the regime of the Hungarian Communist leader Béla Kun. In the 1930s, he changed his Germanic surname to Mindszenty, after the village in which he was born. For his opposition to the German-controlled government of Hungary he was again imprisoned for several months in 1944–45.

In 1948 Mindszenty was charged with treason and illegal monetary transactions by the Communist government of Hungary and was sentenced to life imprisonment. He was released during the uprising of 1956. With the return to power of the Communist regime, however, he took refuge in the U.S. legation at Budapest. On Sept. 28, 1971, Mindszenty left the legation for the first time in 15 years. After a brief stay in Rome he settled in Vienna. In 1974 he was retired as primate of Hungary. His *Memoirs* (1974) was published only a few months before his death.

MINE, in warfare, explosive device used on land or at sea, designed to destroy or disable enemy troops, ships, and vehicles such as tanks. Mines also serve to impede the progress of advancing troops and to render terrain, shipping lanes, and harbors impassable. A terrain containing numerous buried mines is called a minefield. In the American Civil War and in World War I, networks of tunnels were dug under enemy positions and filled with explosives. From this practice, mining came to refer to the placement of an encased explosive device.

Land Mine. An encased explosive device that is concealed below the surface of the ground is called a land mine. Made of metal, plastic, glass, or wood, it is detonated in a number of ways, such as by disturbing a trip-wire attachment to the mine or by a delayed-action mechanism. The explosive most commonly used in land mines is trinitrotoluene, or TNT.

Antitank mines have an explosive charge of from 2.7 to 5.4 kg (6 to 12 lb) of TNT and are used to destroy vehicles passing over them. Antipersonnel mines have a normal charge of from 0.1 to 1.8 kg ($\frac{1}{4}$ to 4 lb) and are designed to kill or injure foot soldiers. In World War II the Germans used an antipersonnel mine called the Bouncing Betty, which was activated by a trip wire that caused the mine to fly some 30 to 60 cm (some 12 to 24 in) into the air before exploding. During the Korean War, land mines attached to a complicated network of trip wires were widely used to protect defensive positions. In the Vietnam War the Claymore mine came into general use. Claymores, small and light, are made of plastic, contain a high-explosive substance and metal pellets that can be aimed in any direction, and have a range of 76 m (250 ft). The Claymore can be pushed into the ground or hung from trees, about 60 to 90 cm (about 24 to 36 in) off the ground. A trip wire sets off the charge.

MINE

Submarine Mine. Mines that float on or just below the surface of the water are called submarine mines. Such mines may be anchored to the ocean bottom by a cable or set adrift to follow determined ocean or waterway currents. They explode on contact with the hull of a vessel, or sometimes through a magnetic mechanism. For protection against magnetic mines, the hull of a vessel can be encircled with electric cables called degaussing belts, which reduce the vessel's magnetic field. The acoustic mine, which is drawn to the noise from the propellers of a passing ship, is likewise countered by a noisemaker towed behind the ship.

Mines may be put in place at sea by specially equipped ships, called minelayers, by airplanes that parachute the mines into the sea, or by submarines that eject cable or bottom mines. Areas of water infested with mines are also called minefields. During wartime, mines are often used in harbors as a defense against submarines.

Mine Detection. Land minesweeping devices resemble the metal detectors used by treasure hunters. When detected, the mines are carefully uncovered and then disarmed by inserting a keylike device into the hole from which the pin has been removed. Automatic mine detectors attached to vehicles indicate the presence of hidden metal mines, but mines made of wood are difficult to detect. In World War II, minefields were sometimes cleared by tanks.

The detection of enemy submarine mines has been greatly aided in recent years by the development of highly sensitive underwater equipment. Mines such as those used in harbors or waterways can be made harmless by electronic devices that effectively neutralize the electric circuit that controls the detonator. In addition, in 1985 the U.S. Navy introduced a system of robot drones for underwater mine detection. The drones are connected to their mother ships by cords and are directed to sonar-detected mines by means of sonar and closed-circuit television. They can then deal with various types of mines in a number of ways.

For further information on this topic, see the Bibliography in volume 28, section 274.

MINE. See MINING.

MINERAL, in nutrition. See NUTRITION, HUMAN.

MINERAL, in general, any naturally occurring chemical element or compound, but in mineralogy and geology, chemical elements and compounds that have been formed through inorganic processes. Petroleum and coal, which are formed by the decomposition of organic matter, are not minerals in the strict sense. More than 3000 mineral species are known, most of which are characterized by definite chemical composition, crystalline structure, and physical properties. They are classified primarily by chemical composition, crystal class, hardness (q.v.), and appearance (color, luster, and opacity). Mineral species are, as a rule, limited to solid substances, the only liquids being metallic mercury and water. All the rocks forming the earth's crust consist of minerals. Metalliferous minerals of economic value, which are mined for their metals, are known as ores. See CRYSTAL; GEOLOGY; METALS.

MINERALOGY, the identification of minerals and the study of their properties, origin, and classification. The properties of minerals are studied under the convenient subdivisions of chemical mineralogy, physical mineralogy, and crystallography. The properties and classification of individual minerals, their localities and modes of occurrence, and their uses are studied under descriptive mineralogy. Identification according to chemical, physical, and crystallographic properties is called determinative mineralogy.

Chemical Mineralogy. Chemical composition is the most important property for identifying minerals and distinguishing them from one another. Mineral analysis is carried out according to standard qualitative and quantitative methods of chemical analysis. Minerals are classified on the basis of chemical composition and crystal symmetry. The chemical constituents of minerals may also be determined by electron-beam microprobe analysis.

Although chemical classification is not rigid, the various classes of chemical compounds that include a majority of minerals are as follows: (1) elements, such as gold, graphite, diamond, and sulfur, that occur in the native state, that is, in an uncombined form; (2) sulfides, which are minerals composed of various metals combined with sulfur. Many important ore minerals, such as galena and sphalerite, are in this class; (3) sulfo salts, minerals composed of lead, copper, or silver in combination with sulfur and one or more of the following: antimony, arsenic, and bismuth. Pyrargyrite, Ag_3SbS_3, belongs to this class; (4) oxides, minerals composed of a metal in combination with oxygen, such as hematite, Fe_2O_3. Mineral oxides that contain water, such as diaspore, $Al_2O_3 \cdot H_2O$, or the hydroxyl (OH) group, such as bog iron ore, FeO(OH), also belong to this group; (5) halides, composed of metals in combination with chlorine, fluorine, bromine or iodine; halite, NaCl, is the most common mineral of this class; (6) carbonates, minerals such as calcite, $CaCO_3$, containing a carbonate group; (7) phosphates, minerals such as apatite, $Ca_5(F,Cl)(PO_4)_3$, that contain a phosphate group; (8) sulfates, minerals such as barite, $BaSO_4$, containing a sulfate group; and (9) silicates, the largest class of minerals, containing various elements in combination with silicon and oxygen, often with complex chemical structure, and minerals composed solely of silicon and oxygen (silica). The silicates include the minerals comprising the feldspar, mica, pyroxene, quartz, and zeolite and amphibole families.

Physical Mineralogy. The physical properties of minerals are important aids in identifying and characterizing them. Most of the physical properties can be recognized at sight or determined by simple tests. The most important properties include powder (streak), color, cleavage, fracture, hardness (q.v.), luster, specific gravity, and fluorescence or phosphorescence.

Crystallography. The majority of minerals occur in crystal form when conditions of formation are favorable. Crystallography is the study of the growth, shape, and geometric character of crystals. The arrangement of atoms within a crystal is determined by X-ray diffraction analysis. Crystal chemistry is the study of the relationship of chemical composition, arrangement of atoms, and the binding forces among atoms. This relationship determines minerals' chemical and physical properties. Crystals are grouped into six main classes of symmetry: isometric, hexagonal, tetragonal, orthorhombic, monoclinic, and triclinic. See CRYSTAL.

The study of minerals is an important aid in understanding rock formation. Laboratory synthesis of the high-pressure varieties of minerals is helping the understanding of igneous processes deep in the lithosphere (see EARTH). Because all of the inorganic materials of commerce are minerals or derivatives of minerals, mineralogy has direct economic application. Important uses of minerals and examples in each category are gem minerals (diamond, garnet, opal, zircon); ornamental objects and structural material (agate, calcite, gypsum); abrasives (corundum, diamond, kaolin); lime, cement, and plaster (calcite, gypsum); refractories (asbestos, graphite, magnesite, mica); ceramics (feldspar, quartz); chemical minerals (halite, sulfur, borax); fertilizers (phosphates); natural pigments (hematite, limonite); optical and scientific apparatus (quartz, mica, tourmaline); and the ores of metals (cassiterite, chalcopyrite, chromite, cinnabar, ilmenite, molybdenite, galena, and sphalerite). A.M.B.; REV. BY W.Y.

For further information on this topic, see the Bibliography in volume 28, sections 417, 433.

MINERAL WATER, spring water that contains mineral salts or gases, and which consequently may have an action on the human body different from that of ordinary water. As a remedial agent, mineral waters have been used from early times, and were familiar to the ancient Greeks and Romans. They are usually classified as alkaline, saline, chalybeate or iron-containing, sulfurous, acidulous, and arsenical. Many effervescing carbonic-acid waters are used as table beverages and to dilute spirits or wines. Saline waters are taken for their medicinal effects.

Mineral springs are numerous in the U.S. Among the eastern states, New York is the leading producer, and the springs at Saratoga, N.Y., have an international reputation and compare favorably to foreign spas. In the Appalachian Mountains are the celebrated hot springs of Berkeley Springs, Va., and White Sulphur Springs, W.Va. Of the south-central states, Kentucky, Tennessee, and Arkansas are the chief producers; the hot springs of Arkansas are among the most important in the country. Other well-known hot springs include those of Waukesha, Wis., Las Vegas, N. Mex., San Bernardino, Calif., and Medical Lake, Wash. One of the widely known springs in the U.S., French Lick Springs, Ind., produces the Pluto waters, which rival the famous Hunyadi Janos waters of Hungary as a purgative.

The most noted of the European mineral waters include Vichy and Appollinaris, both alkaline; Apenta, Hunyadi Janos, and Friedrichshall, saline waters rich in sulfate; Karlsbad and Marienbad, rich in sodium chloride; Tunbridge Wells, chalybeate; Aix-la-Chapelle, Baden, and Aix-les-Bains, sulfurated; and Bath and Baden, arsenical.

MINERVA, in Roman mythology, goddess of wisdom, the daughter of Jupiter, king of the gods. The Roman counterpart of the Greek goddess Athena, Minerva sprang from the head of Jupiter, fully grown and in full armor. Fierce and warlike, she was the patron of warriors, the defender of the home and the state, and the embodiment of wisdom, purity, and reason. Minerva was also the patron of the arts, handicrafts, and trades. With her father and Juno, she was one of the three principal deities of the Roman state.

MINESWEEPER. *See* NAVAL VESSELS.

MINGUS, Charlie, full name CHARLES MINGUS (1922–79), American jazz musician, who established the double bass as a melodic rather than a rhythmic instrument. Born in Nogales, Ariz., he played in the 1940s and '50s with such soloists as the trumpeter Louis Armstrong and the saxophonist Charlie Parker. Mingus also played the piano and other instruments, and as a bandleader he furthered the innovative strength of his compositions by experimenting with group improvisation. His autobiography, *Beneath the Underdog,* appeared in 1971.

MINIATURE PAINTING

A miniature painted in 1785 of the granddaughter of William Penn, Philadelphia Hannah, Viscountess Cremorne.
British Information Services

MINIATURE PAINTING, painting of pictures, usually portraits, on a small scale. The word *miniature* is derived from *minium,* the name of a red oxide of lead used during the Middle Ages for the decoration of sacred texts. The techniques developed in this art of illuminating manuscripts were later applied to the creation of many small portraits, known as miniatures. Miniature painters generally work in a microscopically minute technique, using thin, pointed brushes on such varied surfaces as the backs of playing cards, stretched chicken skin, vellum, metal, and ivory.

Miniature painting was highly developed in the Orient at an early date. Before the 16th century Muslim artists of Persia, India, and Turkey were producing delicate, stylized miniatures. In Renaissance Europe, miniatures were used on jewelry and even on the inside of watch covers; such miniatures were often presented as gifts and souvenirs. The 16th-century German painter Hans Holbein the Younger was the first important representative of the art in Europe. In France, Jean and François Clouet painted a series of portraits, considered unexcelled in form and purity of color, of King Francis I and members of the court. Among other noted French exponents of the art were Nicolas de Largillière (1656-1746), Jean Marc Nattier (1685-1766), and Jean Baptiste Isabey.

Nicholas Hilliard, the earliest English exponent of miniature painting, executed portraits for Queen Elizabeth I. Isaac Oliver (1556?-1617) and er Oliver (1594-1648) succeeded Hilliard, adding fuller, more rounded modeling to their portraits. The work of Samuel Cooper (1609-72) is generally regarded as the finest expression of English miniature portrait painting. Ivory replaced vellum as the popular surface for miniature painters at the end of the 17th century.

The U.S. produced many notable miniature painters, including John Watson (1685-1768); James Peale (1749-1831), who executed well-known portraits of Martha and George Washington; and John Singleton Copley. Edward Greene Malbone (1777-1807) is regarded as the most distinctive American miniature painter of his time.

MINIATURE PINSCHER, breed of toy dog. Although the miniature pinscher has most of the physical attributes of the Doberman pinscher, on a small scale, it is not a miniature variety of the Doberman as the toy poodle is of the poodle and the miniature schnauzer is of the schnauzer. The miniature pinscher originated in Germany several centuries ago and was particularly popular in that country from about 1905 to 1914. It was not extensively bred outside Germany, except in the Scandinavian countries, until after World War I. The breed was imported into the U.S. about 1919 and became very popular after 1929. The miniature pinscher has a flat skull tapering toward the muzzle; dark, slightly oval eyes; upstanding ears; a gracefully curved neck; a compact muscular body; and a broad tail, set high. The animal possesses a flat coat of thick, hard, lustrous hair. The color of the coat is either black with tan, red, or yellow markings; solid red; solid brown; or

Miniature pinscher

brown with yellow or red markings. White or gray, with yellow, black, or red markings, are considered faults. The dog is about 29 cm (about 11.5 in) high at the shoulders, or withers; the male weighs 2.7 to 4.5 kg (6 to 10 lb), and the female 2.9 to 4.5 kg (6.5 to 10 lb). The miniature pinscher is greatly valued as a pet, a keen watchdog, and a show dog.

MINICOY. See LACCADIVE, MINICOY, AND AMINDIVI ISLANDS.

MINIMAL ART. See MODERN ART AND ARCHITECTURE.

MINIMUM WAGE, rate of pay fixed either by a collective bargaining agreement or by governmental enactment as the lowest wage payable to specified categories of employees. In general, the setting of a minimum wage does not preclude the right of employees to demand wages above the established minimum. The method of establishing a minimum wage by collective bargaining suffers from a serious limitation, however, because collective bargaining agreements cover only the workers in a specific plant, craft, industry, or local area, and hence are inadequate in situations in which wage rates prevailing throughout an entire nation have fallen to excessively low levels. The realization of this shortcoming led labor unions to demand government minimum wage programs in several countries as early as the 1890s, and resulted in the enactment of legislation setting minimum wages.

The first minimum wage law was enacted by the government of New Zealand in 1894. A subsequent law enacted by Victoria State, Australia, in 1896 established wage boards on which workers and employers were represented in equal numbers, with power to fix minimum wages enforceable on the employer. This innovative law served as the model for the British Trade Boards Act of 1909.

In the U.S., Massachusetts enacted the earliest minimum wage law in 1912, and eight other states followed suit the next year. Whereas the laws passed in Australia and Great Britain applied to all workers, the U.S. laws were applicable only to women and minors. American labor unions at that time were engaged in a nationwide organizing campaign among male workers, and they opposed the application of such legislation to men as a possible deterrent to organization, because the possibility of obtaining a minimum wage by government action might lessen the incentive to join a union. By 1923 minimum wage laws for women and minors had been enacted by 15 states, Puerto Rico, and the District of Columbia. In that year a decision of the U.S. Supreme Court invalidated all such legislation, and it was not until 1933, when the federal government moved to alleviate the widespread hardship caused by the prevailing economic depression by enacting the National Industrial Recovery Act, that minimum wage scales were set for both men and women. Two years later this act also was declared unconstitutional by the Supreme Court. Nevertheless, a number of states passed minimum wage laws in ensuing years, and in 1938 the federal government enacted the Fair Labor Standards Act, fixing the minimum wage of workers employed in interstate commerce at $.25 an hour and providing for the raising of the minimum to $.40 an hour after seven years.

Since the end of World War II, the rise in the cost of living has caused organized labor and labor supporters in Congress to press for raising the statutory minimum wage level and to broaden eligibility for coverage. Succeeding amendments to the Fair Labor Standards Act raised the minimum wage in stages from $.75 an hour to $1.60 in 1968, when coverage was extended to certain types of farm labor and to previously excluded retail store, restaurant, and hotel employees.

An additional 7 million government, domestic service, and retail chain employees were covered in 1974. The minimum wage rose to $2.30 an hour in 1978 and to $3.35 in 1981. Legislation in 1989 provided for a gradual increase in the minimum wage to $4.25 by 1991, but permitted a "training wage" of $3.62 (as of 1991) for 16- to 19-year-olds.

MINING, in its broadest sense, the process of obtaining useful minerals from the earth's crust. The process includes excavations in underground mines and surface excavations in open-pit, or opencut (strip) mines. In addition, recent technological developments may soon make economically feasible the mining of metallic ores from the seafloor. Mining normally means an operation that involves the physical removal of rock and earth. A number of substances, notably natural gas, petroleum, and some sulfur, are produced by methods (primarily drilling) that are not classified as mining. See GASES, FUEL; PETROLEUM; SULFUR. See also separate articles on the minerals mentioned in this article.

A mineral is generally defined as any naturally occurring substance of definite chemical composition and consistent physical properties. An ore is a mineral or combination of minerals from which a useful substance, such as a metal, can be extracted and marketed at a price that will recover the costs of mining and processing and yield a profit. The naturally occurring substances are usually divided into metalliferous ores, such as the ores of gold, iron, copper, lead, zinc, tin,

MINING

and manganese, and nonmetalliferous minerals, such as coal, quartz, bauxite, trona, borax, asbestos, talc, feldspar, and phosphate rock. Building and ornamental stones, which form a separate group, include slate, marble, limestone, traprock, travertine, and granite.

Most minerals are found in veins, or tabular-shaped deposits of nonsedimentary origin, often dipping at high angles; in beds, or seams, which are tabular deposits conforming to the stratification of enclosing rocks; and as masses, or large ore bodies of irregular shape standing at any angle. Gold, diamonds, tin, and platinum are often found in placers, or deposits of sand and gravel containing particles of the mineral.

Mining Operations. Mining operations generally progress through four stages: (1) prospecting, or the search for mineral deposits; (2) exploration, or the work involved in assessing the size, shape, location, and economic value of the deposit; (3) development, or the work of preparing access to the deposit so that the minerals can be extracted from it; and (4) exploitation, the work of extracting the minerals.

In the past, ore bodies were discovered by prospectors in areas where veins were exposed on the surface, or by accident, as when gold was discovered in California in 1848. Today, however, prospecting and exploration are skilled occupations involving expert scientific personnel. Teams of geologists, mining engineers, geophysicists, and geochemists work together to discover new deposits. Modern prospecting methods include regional geological studies to define areas where mineralization is likely to have occurred; broad surveys by sophisticated instruments mounted in airplanes and artificial earth satellites (see REMOTE SENSING) to discover anomalies in the earth's magnetic field, electrical fields, or radiation patterns in order to define the most promising locations; visual examinations of the surface area for coloring, rock formations, and plant life; chemical analyses of soil and water in the area; and surface work with geophysical instruments (see GEOPHYSICS).

These modern techniques can reveal deep-seated as well as near-surface prospects, and they serve as a basis for preliminary estimates of the economic potential of the prospect. The subsequent exploration work includes digging pits, sinking exploration shafts, and core-drilling operations, all of which tend to define the physical limits of the ore body and permit a more reliable estimate of its economic value. The findings may dictate the method used to reach the ore body, the extent of the development work, and the best method of exploitation.

The decision to develop an ore body is reached as soon as sufficient information is available to indicate a profitable return on the financial investment. Complete certainty about the full potential of the mineral is not crucial at this

Gregory's Gulch, a 19th-century mining camp at present-day Central City, Colo.

Mined coal is moved to the loading point by a six-wheeled electric shuttle car.   Joy Manufacturing Co.

point; exploration work can continue over many years while the deposit is being mined.

After the decision is made to mine an ore deposit, the mode of entry and the extent of lateral or subsidiary development must be determined. If the ore body lies at or near the surface and extends to a depth of no more than a few hundred feet, it may be developed by an open-pit excavation, using power shovels and large trucks. If, however, it is deep or steeply inclined, access may be made through a vertical or inclined shaft, an adit, or crosscut tunnels. The topography of the region, the geometry and physical nature of the ore body, and the proposed method of exploitation have a bearing on this decision. When the terrain is nearly flat, entry must be made through a shaft. In mountainous regions, access to the ore body may be gained through an adit, a nearly horizontal tunnel from which crosscuts may be driven at right angles to reach the ore. Shaft sinking involves a larger outlay of capital and higher operating costs than an adit or crosscut opening. A shaft requires hoisting equipment to raise the ore and rock to the surface, pumping equipment to dispose of any water present, and structural support for the rock and the mechanical equipment operating in the shaft. In an adit, drainage occurs naturally in all workings above the adit as a result of gravity, and structural support is usually not as costly or extensive.

The problems encountered in the sinking of a shaft may be great, especially if water-bearing strata need to be pierced. The water-bearing strata must be cemented or frozen before excavation begins, and lining the shaft with concrete becomes necessary. Even in dry strata, deep shafts are often lined in order to withstand the lateral pressures in the rocks through which they are sunk. After the shaft or adit is completed, lateral development takes place, and crosscuts are driven to reach the ore deposit at different levels. An extensive mine may have a main hoisting shaft and one or more auxiliary shafts or adits for supplies and ventilation. Many state mining laws require mines to be equipped with at least two points of entry and egress to improve the degree of safety for miners.

The method chosen for mining will depend on how maximum yield may be obtained under existing conditions at a minimum cost, with the least danger to the mining personnel. The conditions include the shape, size, continuity, and attitude of the ore body; the mineralogical and physical character of the ore, and the character of the wall rock or overlying material; the relation of the deposit to the surface, to other ore

MINING

bodies, and to existing shafts on the same property; the skill of available labor; and regional economic conditions. These variables are interdependent and of varying importance, but maximum profit and maximum extraction are closely related, because a method that sacrifices part of the ore body often yields maximum profit. In view of these considerations, open-pit mining tends to be more economical than underground mining, except in regions where climatic conditions are so severe that surface mining is often impossible.

Coal Mining. Coal has been mined for more than 1000 years, and large-scale mining was practiced as early as the 18th century. The first coal mine in America was opened in Virginia, in the Appalachian bituminous field, during the 1750s; the mining of anthracite began in the late 1700s. Extensive mining in the U.S. commenced about 1820; until 1854 more than half of all the coal that was produced in the U.S. was Pennsylvania anthracite. In 1989, anthracite production was about 2.72 million metric tons, compared to about 980 million metric tons of bituminous coal and lignite.

Two principal systems of coal mining are used: surface, or strip, mining and underground, or deep, mining. Strip mining, which is a form of quarrying, is possible only when the coal seam is near the surface of the ground. In large surface mines, huge power shovels and draglines are used to remove the earth and rock (overburden) from above the seam; modern shovels have bucket capacities of as much as 290 metric tons. Smaller shovels then load the coal directly into trucks. The chief advantage of strip mining over underground mining is the enormous saving of time and labor. The daily output per person in strip mines is many times that in underground mines.

As a supplement to strip mining, or when other mining techniques are not adequate, augers are used to bore horizontally into exposed coal seams. The loosened coal then flows into a conveyor for loading into trucks. A newer development is a boring machine, called a push-button miner, that can tunnel as deep as 300 m (1000 ft) into the coal seam, dumping the coal into mobile conveyors pulled by the machine.

In underground, or deep, mining, the coal seam is reached through vertical or inclined shafts, or, if the deposit is located in a mountain, through level or nearly level tunnels. The coal deposit is usually marked out in "rooms," which vary in size according to local conditions. The coal is cut and blasted away, with pillars of coal to support the roof. In the longwall system of working, a machine with steel teeth is raked along the face, and the broken coal drops onto a conveyor belt. As the machine moves forward, steel supports are advanced to support the roof directly over the working face. The roof behind the coal face is allowed to collapse.

In the conventional method of mining, power cutters have supplanted the traditional tool of the miner, the pick. The miner makes an undercut with these cutters about 15 cm (about 6 in) wide and as much as 2.7 m (9 ft) deep across the face of the coal seam, often close to the floor of the room. Deep holes are then drilled at the top of the face, and charges of safety-approved explosives or cartridges of compressed air are tamped into them. The explosive blast brings down and partially shatters a large chunk of the coal face, which is then loaded by machines into low, electrically propelled shuttle cars that bring the coal to a central loading point. From there it is hauled to the surface by either rail cars or giant conveyor belts. Most of the U.S. underground production of bituminous coal is mined by so-called continuous-mining machines, which eliminate the separate steps of cutting, drilling, blasting, and loading. These huge machines, capable of mining up to 10.8 metric tons of coal per minute, tear coal from the face and load it onto built-in conveyor belts. The belts transport the coal to waiting shuttle cars or mine conveyor belts that carry it to the surface. The coal is then transferred to a preparation plant, where it is screened, washed, sorted into various sizes, and sometimes crushed before shipment.

A recent development, called the shortwall system, combines the continuous-mining machine with the use of longwall steel supports at the face. The continuous miner operates under the protective canopy of the supports and the roof is allowed to cave in as in the longwall system.

Among the chief problems in underground mines are ventilation and roof support. Ventilation is important because of the presence in coal mines of dangerous gases such as methane (q.v.) and carbon dioxide (q.v.). Large fans and blowers must be used to maintain the circulation of pure air. In order to prevent the spread of coal dust, which can be highly explosive, mine interiors are frequently sprayed with limestone dust, a process known as rock-dusting. To provide support for the roofs of tunnels and work spaces, steel roof bolts that bind together the overlying rock layers are inserted into the mine ceiling.

In the U.S., mining employment generally declined through the late 1960s. In the early 1970s, however, with the Arab oil embargo (*see* ENERGY SUPPLY, WORLD: *The Energy Crisis),* coal reemerged as an important fuel. As production increased, so

A conveyor belt hauls bituminous coal at the Cambria Slope mine in Ebensburg, Pa. The belt, a continuous loop, handles 1800 tons of coal an hour. B. F. Goodrich Co.

did employment—to more than 200,000 men and women in the early 1980s. In 1990 the coal industry employed 146,000 workers.

Metal Mining. Metalliferous ores are mined either on the surface of the earth or underground. In opencut mining, the ore is removed from deposits that crop out at the surface, lie on a hillside, or are covered by a shallow overburden that is stripped before or simultaneously with the removal of the ore. In open-pit mining, benches are terraced into the earth or rock along the hillside or in the pit. The ore is usually loosened by blasting and loaded into trucks or rail cars by mechanical loaders, or shovels. As the pit increases in depth, the cost of mining by this method also increases, primarily because of the need to remove ever-increasing volumes of waste rock around the ore body to ensure a safe slope for the pit. The change from open-pit to underground mining occurs at the depth at which the costs of mining by the two methods are equal.

The selection of an underground method of mining depends on a number of conditions, primarily the grade, size, shape, and attitude of the ore body and the strength of the ore and wall rock. Generally, a system is used in which the force of gravity helps in the removal of ore.

The mine development work consists of driving a system of crosscuts that connect the shaft with the ore body at a number of levels, a suitable vertical distance apart. Vertical openings, called raises, are made to connect the various levels. The ore body is thus divided into blocks, which are bounded by the levels and the raises, and is ready for extraction. The ore may be removed from the bottom of the block upwards, the process being known as overhand stoping, or, more rarely, from the top of the block downward (underhand stoping). A stope is the chamber in which the ore is broken and mined. The stopes, on completion of mining, may be allowed to remain empty, if adequately supported, or may be filled with material, usually waste rock, brought down from the surface to support the exhausted stope and ensure safety of mining operations in adjacent stopes.

The specific method or methods used in removing the ore usually depends on local geometry and the physical characteristics of the ore and wall rock. Thick-bedded and massive deposits are usually mined by the so-called caving method. In block caving, the development work is confined below the lowest boundary of the block and consists of a network of operating tunnels, called drifts, and slanting raises, called finger-raises, which emanate from the drifts and terminate at the bottom surface of the block. The finger-raises are widened to funnel-shaped openings under the block. The block is then undercut as the rock supporting it is removed. This causes the collapse of the unsupported ore, which falls by gravity through the finger-raises into the drifts, from which it is scraped into mine cars. Under ideal conditions, no primary blasting is necessary, and in general, this is the cheapest underground mining method for handling large low-grade deposits. If the ore body does not disintegrate readily when the support is removed, blasting is necessary; this method is called forced block caving. The gradual extraction of the ore and the resulting fracturing of the rock around the mine workings cause subsidence at the ground surface, which may be counteracted by filling the resultant surface depressions with waste material from the ore-processing mill.

Placer mining is a special opencut method for deposits of sand, gravel, or other alluvium containing workable amounts of valuable minerals. Native gold is the most important placer mineral, but platinum and tin are also found in gravels. Other minerals found are zircon, diamond, ruby, and other gems, and monazite, ilmenite, and ores of columbium and tantalum.

Large placer operations involve excavation by power shovels, bucket-wheel excavators, or dragline conveyors, which deliver the sand and gravel to a system of screens, jigs, and sluices used to recover the ore mineral. Occasionally, the gravel bank is broken down by a high-pressure stream of water delivered through a large nozzle, called a hydraulic giant; this method is known as hydraulicking. More often, the placer is flooded, and the digging and processing equipment is mounted on a dredge. The mechanical excavator is usually of the chain-bucket type, and this method is known as dredging.

Ocean Metal Mining. In addition to the conventional methods of mining metallic ores where they occur on land, methods of deep-sea mining were devised in the 1970s using modern technology to collect manganese nodules—concretions cemented by iron oxide and rich in copper, cobalt, manganese, and nickel—from areas, primarily in the Pacific Ocean, where they lie scattered on the deep-sea floor. The feasibility of the process has been demonstrated by prototype operations in which bargelike surface craft serve as a base for dragline, dragnet, or suction-hose collectors. That deep-sea mining has yet to begin on a commercial basis is due to economics as well as politics. Besides being an inherently costly process with dubious profit potential under present market conditions, the issue of deep-sea mining has forced the nations of the world to consider the question of the ownership of the mineral wealth of the deep-sea bed. The UN Convention on the Law of the Sea, adopted in 1982 over U.S. opposition and not yet in force, holds that coastal states must share with the international community the revenue they derive from deep-sea mining outside their territorial waters.

Nonmetalliferous Mineral Mining. Industrial minerals and rocks, from which no metal is extracted, are usually mined by the methods already described. Because these deposits tend to be of large bulk and low unit value, low-cost mining methods are most common, and surface-mining methods are used wherever possible. Room-and-pillar mining is a popular underground method for bedded deposits of potash, trona, rock salt, and talc, and block-caving is used for the massive asbestos deposits. The relative economic importance of the nonmetals, coal, and metals may be illustrated by the statistics of production in the U.S. In 1989, the value of nonmetals mined in the U.S. amounted to about $19.8 billion, coal about $22 billion, and metals about $10.2 billion, $6.5 billion of which was derived from copper and gold mining. Nonmetals, coal, and metals accounted for 41 percent of the mineral wealth extracted during the year, with the remaining 59 percent being contributed by higher-priced petroleum, natural gas, and other liquid fuels.

Mine Safety. Mining is a hazardous occupation, and the safety of mine workers is an important aspect of the industry. Statistics indicate that surface mining is less hazardous than underground mining and that metal mining is less hazardous than coal mining. A study of the frequency and severity of accidents shows that the hazards stem from the nature of the operation. In all underground mines, rock and roof falls, flooding, and inadequate ventilation are the greatest hazards. Large explosions are characteristic in coal mines, but more miners suffer accidents from the use of explosives in metal mines. Accidents related to the haulage system constitute the second greatest hazard common to all types of mines.

A number of debilitating hazards exist that affect miners with the passage of time and that are related to the quality and nature of the environment in the mines. Dust produced during mining operations is generally injurious to health and causes the lung disease known as black lung, or pneumoconiosis (see OCCUPATIONAL AND ENVIRONMENTAL DISEASES). Some fumes generated by incomplete dynamite explosions are extremely poisonous. Methane gas, emanating from coal strata, is always hazardous although not poisonous in the concentrations usually encountered in mine air, and radiation may be a hazard in uranium mines (*see* RADIATION EFFECTS, BIOLOGICAL). A tight and active safety program is usually in operation in every mine; where special care is taken to educate the miners in safety precautions and practices, accident rates are lower.

Federal and state legislation has set numerous operating standards regarding dust and gas concentrations in the mines, as well as general rules regarding roof support. Despite this, local conditions can suddenly change the atmosphere in the mines and render it hazardous. The Federal Coal Mine Health and Safety Act, passed in December 1969 and expanded in 1977, provided health compensation to miners and set strict controls regarding coal dust, methane gas, escapeways, roofing, wiring, and other mining hazards.

Some hazards are related to the local geology and the state of stress in the rocks in the mine. The mining operation results in the shifting of loads on the strata, and in extreme cases such shifts may apply pressures on a critical section of rock that exceed the strength of the rock and result in its sudden collapse. This phenomenon, which is known as a rockburst, occurs particularly in deep mines, and research is under way to eliminate the danger.

Education, experience, research, social consciousness, and government regulation have contributed to lowering the accident rates in the mining industry. In coal mining in the U.S., for example, 346 miners lost their lives in 1930 for every 100 million tons of bituminous coal produced, but in 1990, the number of fatalities was less than one for the same amount of coal. The estimate has been made that 60 to 75 percent of all mining accidents are avoidable and are the result of human error.

Mining operations are considered one of the main sources of environmental degradation. Social awareness of this problem is of a global nature and government actions to stem the damage to the natural environment have led to numerous international agreements and laws directed toward the prevention of activities and events that may adversely affect the environment. S.H.B.

For further information on this topic, see the Bibliography in volume 28, section 551.

MINISTRY. *See* CLERGY.

MINK, common name for either of two semiaquatic carnivores in the genus *Mustela* of the weasel (q.v.) family Mustelidae. The mink is characterized by a slender body and by thick, soft, dark brown, durable fur that is highly valued commercially. Mainly nocturnal, the animal is extremely agile in water, from which it obtains the fish, frogs, and shellfish that constitute a large portion of its diet. It is also active on land, hunting birds and small mammals, and sometimes invading poultry houses. The animal usually inhabits a hole in a river bank, preferring densely vegetated areas, but may leave the lair for as long as several weeks when hunting. Ordinarily, minks are solitary animals, but during the breeding season pairs live in sheltered burrows. An average of six young are born in each litter; the animals may live for up to ten years. Minks have anal glands that emit a strong odor, especially during the mating season.

The mink native to North America, *M. vison*, is about 60 cm (about 24 in) in total length, of which the tail constitutes about one-third; it has been introduced into Europe and Asia. The native mink of Asia and northern Europe is *M. lutreola*. In order to supply the demands of the fur industry, minks (primarily forms of *M. vison*) are raised on a large scale on fur farms and are bred for a wide range of color varieties (*see* FUR INDUSTRY).

For further information on this topic, see the Bibliography in volume 28, sections 461, 475, 633.

North American mink, Mustela vison
Karl H. Maslowski–National Audubon Society

MINKOWSKI, Hermann (1864–1909), Russian mathematician, who developed the concept of the space-time continuum. He was born in Russia and attended and then taught at German universities. To the three dimensions of space, Minkowski added the concept of a fourth dimension, time. This concept developed from Albert Einstein's 1905 relativity (q.v.) theory, and became, in turn, the framework for Einstein's 1916 theory of general relativity.

MINNEAPOLIS, city, seat of Hennepin Co., SE Minnesota, by the Falls of Saint Anthony, at the head of navigation of the Mississippi R; inc. 1867. It is one of the largest cities in the upper Midwest, and with the adjacent city of Saint Paul to the E—together they are known as the Twin Cities—it dominates the economic and cultural life of this extensive region.

Economy. Minneapolis is the center of one of the richest agricultural areas of the U.S. and a regional hub of transportation, commerce, and finance. Leading industries include processing of food and dairy products; printing and publishing; and the manufacture of machinery, electrical and electronic equipment, metal and paper products, precision instruments, and transport machinery. It is a rail and highway hub; Minneapolis-St. Paul International Airport is located S of the city.

The Urban Landscape. Minneapolis occupies a relatively flat terrain. Within the city limits are 22 natural lakes, remnants of glacial activity. The Mississippi R. crosses the city from the N to SE, drops 20 m (65 ft) at the Falls of Saint Anthony, then follows a deep gorge below the falls toward its confluence with the Minnesota R. Minnehaha Creek flows E through the city over Minnehaha Falls and into the Mississippi R. The city's lake, creek, and river frontages form part of the extensive municipal park system.

The downtown area is located W of the Mississippi R., facing the Falls of St. Anthony. Part of the district's principal thoroughfare, Nicollet Ave., has been converted into a 15-block shopping center, known as Nicollet Mall, reserved for pedestrians and public transportation; at one end is Gateway Center, a complex that includes several high-rise government and office buildings. Also notable are the skyways—glass-enclosed bridges—that cross many downtown streets.

Educational and Cultural Institutions. Among the city's institutions of higher education are facilities of the Twin Cities campus of the University of Minnesota, Augsburg College (1869), and Minneapolis College of Art and Design (1886). Prominent cultural facilities include the Minneapolis Institute of Arts; the Walker Art Center, which has a fine collection of 20th-century art; and the American Swedish Institute. The city is the home of the Minnesota Orchestra and the Guthrie Theater Company. The Hubert H. Humphrey Metrodome, completed in the early 1980s, is the home of the Minnesota Twins baseball team and the Minnesota Vikings football team. The Target Center is also a sports facility.

History. The area now occupied by Minneapolis was inhabited by Sioux Indians when the Franciscan missionary Louis Hennepin visited in 1680 and named the Falls of St. Anthony. In 1819 Fort Snelling was built at the junction of the Minnesota and Mississippi rivers, to pave the way for settlers moving west. The area west of the Mississippi was opened for legal settlement in 1855. Minneapolis was incorporated as a village in 1856 and as a city in 1867. Its name is derived from the Sioux *minne*, "water," and the Greek *polis*, "city"—a reference to the numerous lakes and streams of the area. Saint Anthony, a community on the east side of the river, was chartered as a village in 1855 and as a city in 1860. After the river was satisfactorily bridged and the cities economically integrated, they merged (1872), forming the city of Minneapolis.

The early growth of Minneapolis was based on lumbering in the region's hardwood forests. Later, wheat from the western Minnesota prairies and lumber from the pine and fir forests of northeast Minnesota sustained the economic boom. German and Scandinavian immigrants increased the city's population during this period. Lumber production peaked in 1899, disappearing by 1920 with the exhaustion of forest reserves. Flour milling peaked in 1915, then waned as milling companies became diversified food manufacturers. Minneapolis, however, remains a leading grain market. Urban renewal projects have transformed much of the downtown area. Pop. (1980) 370,951; (1990) 368,383. J.S.A.

MINNESINGER (Ger. *Minne*, "courtly love"), German lyric poet-composers of the 12th to the 14th century, the Middle High German period (see GERMAN LITERATURE). Strictly, the term *minnesinger* means "singer of love songs (*Minne*)," but it came to be applied to all German poets of the time, particularly those who composed *Sprüche*, or religious and political poems. The type of poem written by the minnesingers was modeled on the poetry of the Provençal troubadours. Soon, however, it developed individual characteristics, such as emphasis on religious allusion and symbolism. The poems were characteristically set to a melody composed by the poet, who sang them while accompanying himself on a harp, fiddle, or other stringed instrument, sometimes with additional musicians. The

MINNESOTA

music was monophonic (consisting of a single melodic line without harmony). The prevalent musical form was the *Bar* form (AAB) or a variant; for longer narrative verse, the *Leich* (AABBCC, etc.) was used. Influenced by Gregorian chant, both forms were derived from musical forms used by the troubadours and the French trouvères (the ballade and lai).

Among the best-known minnesingers (who usually belonged to the lesser aristocracy) were Wolfram von Eschenbach and Walther von der Vogelweide in the 12th century, and Frauenlob (Heinrich von Meissen; c. 1250–1318) and Tannhäuser in the 13th century. In the 14th century the minnesingers were gradually succeeded by the Meistersinger (q.v.).

MINNESOTA, one of the West North Central states of the U.S., bounded on the N by the Canadian provinces of Manitoba and Ontario, on the E by Lake Superior and Wisconsin, on the S by Iowa, and on the W by South Dakota and North Dakota. The Red River of the North forms much of the W border, and the Mississippi R. forms part of the SE border.

Minnesota entered the Union on May 11, 1858, as the 32d state. Minnesota's economy has long been dominated by the development of its varied natural resources. By the 1990s, although it remained a leading agricultural state, Minnesota had developed a diversified economy, dominated by services and manufacturing. The name of the state is taken from the Minnesota R. and is a Sioux Indian phrase meaning "cloudy water." Minnesota is called the North Star State.

LAND AND RESOURCES

Minnesota, with an area of 225,182 sq km (86,943 sq mi), is the 12th largest state in the U.S.; 4.7% of the land is owned by the federal government. The state is roughly rectangular in shape, and its extreme dimensions are about 660 km (about 410 mi) from N to S and about 560 km (about 350 mi) from E to W. The highest point in Minnesota is 701 m (2301 ft) at Eagle Mt. in the NE corner of the state; the lowest elevation is 183 m (602 ft) at the shore of Lake Superior. The approximate mean elevation is 366 m (1200 ft). Minnesota's shoreline on Lake Superior is about 300 km (about 186 mi) long.

Physical Geography. The terrain of Minnesota was to a large extent formed by glacial action; all of the present-day state, except for a small portion of the SE, was once covered by an ice mass. The Superior Upland region of NE Minnesota is a S extension of the Canadian Shield (q.v.). It is composed of hard rocks that resisted leveling by glacial erosion and is hence the state's most rug-

Lake Superior is frequented by cargo ships and ore-transporting freighters, here shown at the port of Duluth, Minn. Jim Brandenburg–Bruce Coleman, Inc.

North-central Minnesota is abundantly blessed with lakes, both large and small. In some wilderness areas chains of lakes, such as these, merge imperceptibly into each other. U.S. Forest Service

ged area. The region abounds in rock basins, which were scoured in the bedrock by glaciers and were filled with water as the glaciers melted, creating numerous lakes.

The Western Great Lakes Lowland, a region of generally level plains, occupies most of the remainder of the state. Lakes, marshes, and bogs are particularly numerous in the N half of the lowland. Along the W boundary of the state is the broad, flat plain that once formed the bed of the ancient glacial Lake Agassiz (see AGASSIZ, LAKE), an area with fertile soil. In the S, the plain is better drained, and rich farmlands dominate the landscape.

Along the S boundary lie two areas of Dissected Till Plains, a region of rolling hills formed by erosion of glacial deposits. In the SW, rocky ridges of ancient quartzite break the surface.

In the SE corner lies the Driftless Region, the only unglaciated part of Minnesota. Tributaries of the Mississippi R. have eroded the surface, producing a rugged, scenic area with steep bluffs and deep valleys.

Rivers and Lakes. More than half of Minnesota is drained by the Mississippi R., which has as one of its sources Lake Itasca in the N part of the state. The main tributaries of the Mississippi here are the Minnesota R., which crosses the state from W to E, and the Crow Wing and Saint Croix rivers. The N and NW areas drain toward Hudson Bay by way of the Red River of the North and the Rainy R., and the extreme NE area drains to Lake Superior by the Saint Louis and other, smaller rivers. The SW corner lies within the Missouri R. Basin, the chief tributary here being the Rock R.

Minnesota has in excess of 20,000 lakes; inland water covers more than 8% of the state's total area. The lakes are especially numerous in the N and central parts of the state. The largest lake lying entirely within the state is Red Lake (divided into upper and lower sections). Other large lakes are Lake of the Woods and Rainy Lake, both astride the Canadian border, and Winnibigoshish, Mille Lacs, Leech, and Vermilion lakes. About 5700 sq km (about 2200 sq mi) of Lake Superior is part of Minnesota.

Climate. Minnesota has a humid continental climate, characterized by wide daily and seasonal temperature variations. Summers are warm in the S and cool in the N; winters are cold throughout the state. The average July temperature is about 22.2° C (about 72° F). The recorded temperature in the state has ranged from −50.6° C (−59° F) in 1903 to 45.6° C (114° F) in 1936. Annual precipitation averages about 813 mm (about 32 in) in the SE, decreasing uniformly across the state to 483 mm (19 in) in the NW. About three-quarters of the annual total comes during the warm half of the year. Winter snowfall is heavy, ranging from 508 mm (20 in) in the SW to 1778 mm (70 in) in the NE, and tornadoes sometimes occur in spring and summer.

MINNESOTA

Minnesota: Map Index

Counties

Aitkin	D4
Anoka	D5
Becker	B4
Beltrami	C3
Benton	C5
Big Stone	A5
Blue Earth	C6
Brown	C6
Carlton	E4
Carver	D6
Cass	C4
Chippewa	B5
Chisago	E5
Clay	A4
Clearwater	B3
Cook	F3, F4
Cottonwood	B7
Crow Wing	C4
Dakota	D6, F6
Dodge	E7
Douglas	B5
Faribault	D7
Fillmore	E7
Freeborn	D7
Goodhue	E6
Grant	A5
Hennepin	D5, E5
Houston	F7
Hubbard	C3
Isanti	D5
Itasca	D3
Jackson	B7
Kanabec	D5
Kandiyohi	C5
Kittson	A2
Koochiching	D2
Lac Qui Parle	A6
Lake	F3
Lake of the Woods	C2
Le Sueur	D6
Lincoln	A6
Lyon	B6
McLeod	C6
Mahnomen	B3
Marshall	A2
Martin	C7
Meeker	C5
Mille Lacs	D5
Morrison	C4
Mower	E7
Murray	B6
Nicollet	C6
Nobles	B7
Norman	A3
Olmsted	E7
Otter Tail	B4
Pennington	A2
Pine	E4
Pipestone	A6
Polk	A3
Pope	B5
Ramsey	D5, F5
Red Lake	A3
Redwood	B6
Renville	C6
Rice	D6
Rock	A7
Roseau	B2
St. Louis	E3
Scott	D6
Sherburne	D5
Sibley	C6
Stearns	C5
Steele	D6
Stevens	A5
Swift	B5
Todd	C4
Traverse	A5
Wabasha	E6
Wadena	C4
Waseca	D6
Washington	E5
Watonwan	C6
Wilkin	A4
Winona	F7
Wright	D5
Yellow Medicine	B6

Cities and Towns

Ada	A3
Adams	E7
Adrian	B7
Aitkin	D4
Albany	C5
Albert Lea	D7
Albertville	D5
Alden	D7
Alexandria	B5
Amboy	C7
Annandale	C5
Anoka	D5
Appleton	A5
Argyle	A2
Arlington	C6
Atwater	C5
Aurora	E3
Austin	E7
Avon	C5
Babbitt	F3
Bagley	B3
Balaton	B6
Barnesville	A4
Battle Lake	B4
Baudette	C2
Baxter	C4
Bayport	E6
Becker	D5
Belgrade	C5
Belle Plaine	D6
Bemidji	C3
Benson	B5
Bertha	B4
Big Lake	D5
Bird Island	C6
Blackduck	C3
Blooming Prairie	D7
Bloomington	D6
Blue Earth	C7
Bovey	D3
Braham	D5
Brainerd	C4
Breckenridge	A4
Brewster	B7
Brooklyn Center	E5
Brooten	B5
Browerville	C4
Browns Valley	A5
Brownsdale	E7
Brownton	C6
Buffalo	D5
Buffalo Lake	C6
Buhl	E3
Burnsville	D6
Butterfield	C7
Caledonia	F7
Cambridge	D5
Canby	A6
Cannon Falls	E6
Carlton	E4
Cass Lake	C3
Center City	E5
Chanhassen	D6
Chaska	D6
Chatfield	E7
Chisholm	E3
Chokio	A5
Clara City	B6
Clarissa	C4
Clarkfield	B6
Clarks Grove	D7
Clearbrook	B3
Clearwater	C5
Cleveland	D6
Clinton	A5
Cloquet	E4
Cokato	C5
Cold Spring	C5
Columbia Hts	F5
Cook	E3
Coon Rapids	D5
Corcoran	D5
Cosmos	C6
Cottonwood	B6
Crookston	A3
Crosby	D4
Cross Lake	C4
Danube	B6
Dassel	C5
Dawson	A6
Deer River	D3
Deerwood	D4
Detroit Lakes	B4
Dilworth	A4
Dodge Center	E6
Duluth	E4
Eagan	F6
Eagle Bend	B4
Eagle Lake	D6
East Bethel	D5
East Grand Forks	A3
East Gull Lake	C4
Edgerton	A7
Edina	D6
Elbow Lake	B5
Elgin	E6
Elk River	D5
Ellsworth	A7
Elmore	C7
Ely	F3
Emily	D4
Evansville	B4
Eveleth	E3
Eyota	E7
Fairmont	C7
Falcon Heights	F5
Faribault	D6
Farmington	D6
Fergus Falls	A4
Fertile	A3
Floodwood	E4
Foley	D5
Forest Lake	E5
Fosston	B3
Frazee	B4
Freeport	C5
Fridley	F5
Fulda	B7
Gaylord	C6
Gibbon	C6
Glencoe	C6
Glenville	D7
Glenwood	B5
Glyndon	A4
Golden Valley	E5
Goodhue	E6
Good Thunder	C6
Goodview	F6
Graceville	A5
Grand Forks	A3
Grand Marais	F5
Grand Meadow	E7
Grand Portage	F4
Grand Rapids	D3
Granite Falls	B6
Greenbush	A2
Hallock	A2
Halstad	A3
Hancock	B5
Harmony	F7
Harris	E5
Hastings	E6
Hawley	A4
Hayfield	E7
Hector	C6
Henderson	D6
Hendricks	A6
Henning	B4
Hermantown	E4
Heron Lake	B7
Hibbing	E3
Hills	A7
Hinckley	E4
Hoffman	B5
Hokah	F7
Holdingford	C5
Hopkins	E5
Houston	F7
Hovland	F4
Howard Lake	C5
Hutchinson	C6
International Falls	D2
Isanti	D5
Isle	D4
Ivanhoe	A6
Jackson	B7
Janesville	D6
Jasper	A7
Jordan	D6
Kandiyohi	C5
Karlstad	A2

359

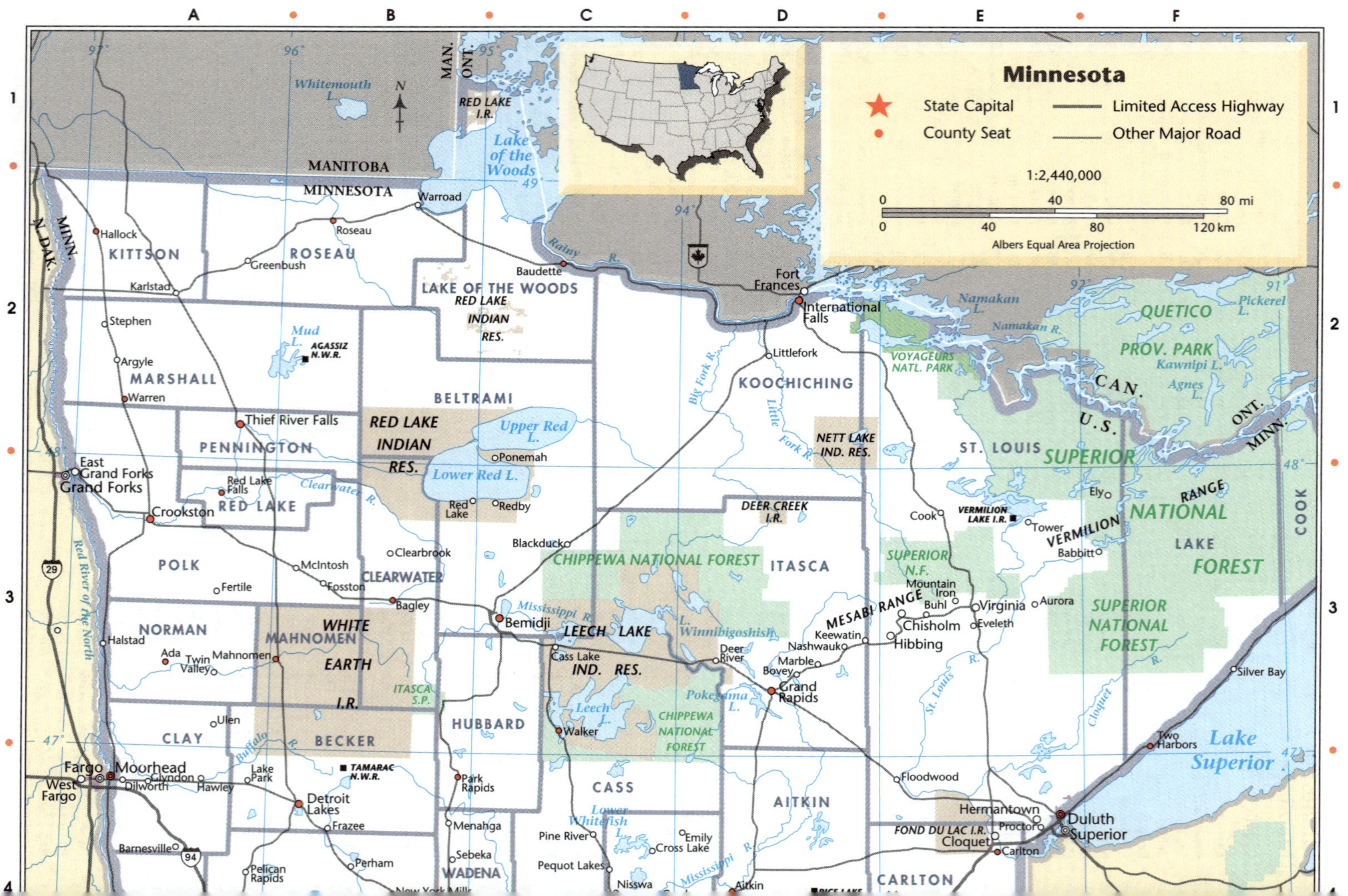
Minnesota
State Capital
County Seat
Limited Access Highway
Other Major Road
1:2,440,000
0 40 80 mi
0 40 80 120 km
Albers Equal Area Projection
A
B
C
D
E
F
1
2
3
4
97°
96°
95°
94°
93°
92°
91°
49
48°
47°
Whitemouth L.
MAN.
ONT.
MANITOBA
MINNESOTA
MINN.
N. DAK.
CAN.
U.S.
ONT.
MINN.
RED LAKE I.R.
Lake of the Woods
Warroad
Roseau
Hallock
KITTSON
ROSEAU
Greenbush
Karlstad
Baudette
Rainy R.
LAKE OF THE WOODS
RED LAKE INDIAN RES.
Fort Frances
International Falls
Namakan L.
Namakan R.
QUETICO PROV. PARK
Pickerel L.
Kawnipi L.
Agnes L.
VOYAGEURS NATL. PARK
Stephen
Mud L.
AGASSIZ N.W.R.
Argyle
MARSHALL
Warren
BELTRAMI
Littlefork
Big Fork R.
KOOCHICHING
Little Fork R.
Thief River Falls
RED LAKE INDIAN RES.
Upper Red L.
NETT LAKE IND. RES.
ST. LOUIS
SUPERIOR NATIONAL FOREST
PENNINGTON
Ponemah
Lower Red L.
East Grand Forks
Grand Forks
Red Lake Falls
RED LAKE
Clearwater R.
Red Lake
Redby
Ely
RANGE
VERMILION
Crookston
DEER CREEK I.R.
Cook
VERMILION LAKE I.R.
Tower
Babbitt
COOK
LAKE
Blackduck
Clearbrook
CHIPPEWA NATIONAL FOREST
ITASCA
SUPERIOR N.F.
POLK
McIntosh
Fosston
CLEARWATER
Red River of the North
29
Fertile
Mountain Iron
Bagley
Mississippi R.
Bemidji
LEECH LAKE
L. Winnibigoshish
MESABI RANGE
Buhl
Virginia
Aurora
Chisholm
Eveleth
Keewatin
Nashwauk
Hibbing
NORMAN
Halstad
Ada
Twin Valley
Mahnomen
MAHNOMEN
WHITE EARTH I.R.
Cass Lake
IND. RES.
Deer River
Marble
Bovey
Grand Rapids
Pokegama L.
St. Louis R.
Cloquet R.
Silver Bay
ITASCA S.P.
Leech L.
CHIPPEWA NATIONAL FOREST
Walker
HUBBARD
Ulen
CLAY
Buffalo R.
BECKER
Two Harbors
Lake Superior
Fargo
West Fargo
Moorhead
Dilworth
Glyndon
Hawley
Lake Park
TAMARAC N.W.R.
Park Rapids
CASS
Floodwood
AITKIN
Detroit Lakes
Frazee
Menahga
Lower Whitefish L.
Pine River
Emily
Cross Lake
Hermantown
Proctor
Duluth
Superior
FOND DU LAC I.R.
Cloquet
Carlton
Barnesville
94
Sebeka
Perham
Pelican Rapids
WADENA
Pequot Lakes
Mississippi R.
Nisswa
Aitkin
CARLTON

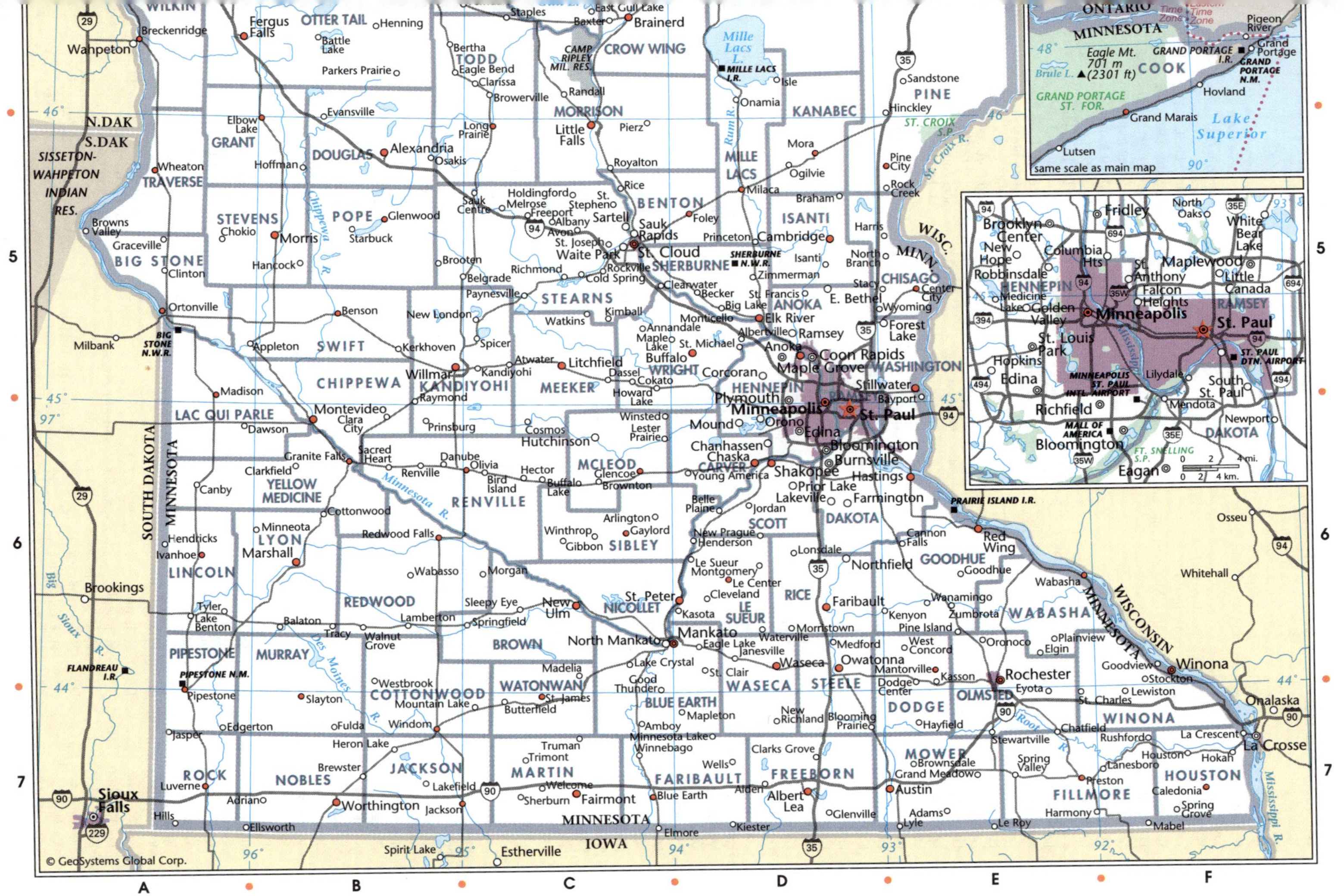

ONTARIO
MINNESOTA
Eastern Time Zone
Central Time Zone
Pigeon River
Grand Portage
GRAND PORTAGE I.R.
GRAND PORTAGE N.M.
Eagle Mt. 701 m (2301 ft)
COOK
Hovland
Grand Marais
Lake Superior
GRAND PORTAGE ST. FOR.
Brule L.
Lutsen
48°
90°
same scale as main map
Fridley
North Oaks
White Bear Lake
Brooklyn Center
New Hope
Columbia Hts
Maplewood
St. Anthony
Little Canada
Robbinsdale
HENNEPIN
Medicine Lake
Golden Valley
Falcon Heights
RAMSEY
Minneapolis
St. Paul
St. Louis Park
Hopkins
Edina
MINNEAPOLIS ST. PAUL INTL. AIRPORT
ST. PAUL DTN. AIRPORT
Lilydale
South St. Paul
Mendota
Richfield
Newport
MALL OF AMERICA
Bloomington
DAKOTA
FT. SNELLING S.P.
Eagan
0 2 4 mi.
0 2 4 km.
WILKIN
Wahpeton
Breckenridge
Fergus Falls
OTTER TAIL
Henning
Battle Lake
Parkers Prairie
Staples
East Gull Lake
Baxter
Brainerd
CAMP RIPLEY MIL. RES.
CROW WING
Bertha
TODD
Eagle Bend
Clarissa
Browerville
Randall
MORRISON
Little Falls
Pierz
Mille Lacs L.
MILLE LACS I.R.
Isle
Onamia
Rum R.
KANABEC
Sandstone
PINE
Hinckley
ST. CROIX S.P.
St. Croix R.
Pine City
Rock Creek
N.DAK
S.DAK
SISSETON-WAHPETON INDIAN RES.
Elbow Lake
GRANT
Evansville
DOUGLAS
Alexandria
Osakis
Long Prairie
Royalton
MILLE LACS
Mora
Ogilvie
Wheaton
TRAVERSE
Hoffman
Browns Valley
Graceville
STEVENS
Chokio
Morris
POPE
Glenwood
Starbuck
Chippewa R.
Holdingford
Melrose
Freeport
Albany
Avon
St. Joseph
Waite Park
St. Stephen
Sartell
Sauk Rapids
St. Cloud
Sauk Centre
Rice
BENTON
Foley
Milaca
Braham
ISANTI
Cambridge
Princeton
Harris
WISC.
MINN.
BIG STONE
Clinton
Hancock
Brooten
Belgrade
Richmond
Rockville
Cold Spring
SHERBURNE
SHERBURNE N.W.R.
Isanti
Zimmerman
North Branch
CHISAGO
Center City
Stacy
Wyoming
Ortonville
Paynesville
STEARNS
Clearwater
Becker
St. Francis
Big Lake
ANOKA
E. Bethel
Forest Lake
Milbank
BIG STONE N.W.R.
Benson
New London
Watkins
Kimball
Monticello
Elk River
Albertville
Ramsey
Annandale
Maple Lake
St. Michael
Buffalo
Anoka
Coon Rapids
Maple Grove
WASHINGTON
Appleton
SWIFT
Kerkhoven
Spicer
Willmar
Atwater
Litchfield
Dassel
Cokato
WRIGHT
Corcoran
Stillwater
Bayport
CHIPPEWA
KANDIYOHI
Kandiyohi
Raymond
MEEKER
Howard Lake
Madison
Montevideo
Clara City
LAC QUI PARLE
Dawson
Prinsburg
Cosmos
Hutchinson
Winsted
Lester Prairie
Plymouth
Minneapolis
St. Paul
Mound
Orono
Edina
Granite Falls
Sacred Heart
Danube
Olivia
Renville
Hector
Bird Island
Buffalo Lake
MCLEOD
Glencoe
Brownton
Chanhassen
Chaska
CARVER
Young America
Bloomington
Burnsville
Shakopee
Hastings
Prior Lake
Lakeville
Farmington
Canby
Clarkfield
YELLOW MEDICINE
Minnesota R.
RENVILLE
Cottonwood
Arlington
Gaylord
Belle Plaine
Jordan
SCOTT
DAKOTA
PRAIRIE ISLAND I.R.
SOUTH DAKOTA
MINNESOTA
Hendricks
Ivanhoe
Minneota
LYON
Marshall
Redwood Falls
Winthrop
Gibbon
SIBLEY
New Prague
Henderson
Lonsdale
Cannon Falls
Red Wing
Osseu
LINCOLN
Wabasso
Morgan
Le Sueur
Montgomery
Le Center
Northfield
GOODHUE
Goodhue
Whitehall
Brookings
Big Sioux R.
Tyler
Lake Benton
REDWOOD
Sleepy Eye
Lamberton
Springfield
New Ulm
St. Peter
NICOLLET
Kasota
Cleveland
RICE
Faribault
Wanamingo
Kenyon
Zumbrota
Wabasha
WABASHA
WISCONSIN
MINNESOTA
Balaton
Tracy
Walnut Grove
BROWN
North Mankato
Mankato
LE SUEUR
Waterville
Morristown
Pine Island
Oronoco
Plainview
Elgin
Winona
PIPESTONE
MURRAY
Des Moines R.
Madelia
Lake Crystal
Eagle Lake
Janesville
Waseca
Medford
Owatonna
West Concord
Mantorville
Kasson
Rochester
Goodview
Stockton
FLANDREAU I.R.
PIPESTONE N.M.
Pipestone
Slayton
Westbrook
COTTONWOOD
Mountain Lake
WATONWAN
St. James
Butterfield
Good Thunder
St. Clair
WASECA
STEELE
Dodge Center
OLMSTED
Eyota
St. Charles
Lewiston
WINONA
Onalaska
Jasper
Edgerton
Fulda
Windom
BLUE EARTH
Mapleton
Amboy
New Richland
Blooming Prairie
DODGE
Hayfield
Chatfield
Rushford
La Crescent
La Crosse
ROCK
Luverne
NOBLES
Heron Lake
Brewster
JACKSON
Lakefield
Truman
Trimont
MARTIN
Welcome
Minnesota Lake
Winnebago
Wells
FARIBAULT
Clarks Grove
FREEBORN
Alden
Albert Lea
MOWER
Brownsdale
Grand Meadow
Austin
Stewartville
Spring Valley
Root R.
Lanesboro
Preston
Houston
Hokah
HOUSTON
Caledonia
Sioux Falls
Hills
Adrian
Worthington
Jackson
Sherburn
Fairmont
Blue Earth
Glenville
Adams
Lyle
Le Roy
FILLMORE
Harmony
Spring Grove
Mabel
Mississippi R.
Ellsworth
MINNESOTA
IOWA
Elmore
Kiester
Spirit Lake
Estherville
© GeoSystems Global Corp.
46°
45°
44°
97°
96°
95°
94°
93°
92°
A
B
C
D
E
F
5
6
7

MINNESOTA

Minnesota: Map Index

Kasota	D6
Kasson	E6
Keewatin	D3
Kenyon	E6
Kerkhoven	B5
Kiester	D7
Kimball	C5
La Crescent	F7
Lake Benton	A6
Lake Crystal	C6
Lakefield	B7
Lake Park	A4
Lake Shore	C4
Lakeville	D6
Lamberton	B6
Lanesboro	F7
Le Center	D6
Le Roy	E7
Lester Prairie	C6
Le Sueur	D6
Lewiston	F7
Lilydale	F5
Litchfield	C5
Little Canada	F5
Little Falls	C5
Littlefork	D2
Long Prairie	C5
Lonsdale	D6
Lutsen	E5
Luverne	A7
Lyle	E7
Mabel	F7
McIntosh	B3
Madelia	C6
Madison	A5
Mahnomen	B3
Mankato	D6
Mantorville	E6
Maple Grove	D5
Maple Lake	C5
Mapleton	D7
Maplewood	F5
Marble	D3
Marshall	B6
Medford	D6
Medicine Lake	E5
Melrose	C5
Menahga	B4
Mendota	F6
Milaca	D5
Minneapolis	D6
Minneota	B6
Minnesota Lake	D7
Montevideo	B6
Montgomery	D6
Monticello	D5
Moorhead	A4
Moose Lake	E4
Mora	D5
Morgan	C6
Morris	B5
Morristown	D6
Mound	D6
Mountain Iron	E3
Mountain Lake	C7
Nashwauk	D3
New Hope	E5
New London	C5
Newport	F6
New Prague	D6
New Richland	D7
New Ulm	C6
New York Mills	B4
Nisswa	C4
North Branch	E5
Northfield	D6
North Mankato	C6
North Oaks	F5
Ogilvie	D5
Olivia	C6
Onamia	D4
Orono	D6
Oronoco	E6
Ortonville	A5
Osakis	B5
Owatonna	D6
Park Rapids	B4
Parkers Prairie	B4
Paynesville	C5
Pelican Rapids	A4
Pequot Lakes	C4
Perham	B4
Pierz	C5
Pigeon River	F4
Pine City	E5
Pine Island	E6
Pine River	C4
Pipestone	A7
Plainview	E6
Plymouth	D5
Ponemah	C2
Preston	E7
Princeton	D5
Prinsburg	B6
Prior Lake	D6
Proctor	E4
Ramsey	D5
Randall	C4
Raymond	B5
Redby	C3
Red Lake	B3
Red Lake Falls	A3
Red Wing	E6
Redwood Falls	B6
Renville	B6
Rice	C5
Richfield	F6
Richmond	C5
Robbinsdale	E5
Rochester	E6
Rock Creek	E5
Rockville	C5
Roseau	B2
Royalton	C5
Rushford	F7
Sacred Heart	B6
St. Anthony	F5
St. Charles	E7
St. Clair	D6
St. Cloud	C5
St. Francis	D5
St. James	C7
St. Joseph	C5
St. Louis Park	E5
St. Michael	D5
St. Paul, *capital*	D6
St. Peter	D6
St. Stephen	C5
Sandstone	E4
Sartell	C5
Sauk Centre	C5
Sauk Rapids	C5
Sebeka	B4
Shakopee	D6
Sherburn	C7
Silver Bay	F3
Slayton	B7
Sleepy Eye	C6
South St. Paul	F5
Spicer	C5
Spring Grove	F7
Spring Valley	E7
Springfield	C6
Stacy	E5
Staples	C4
Starbuck	B5
Stephen	A2
Stewartville	E7
Stillwater	E5
Stockton	F6
Thief River Falls	A2
Tower	E3
Tracy	B6
Trimont	C7
Truman	C7
Twin Valley	A3
Two Harbors	F3
Tyler	A6
Ulen	A3
Verndale	C4
Virginia	E3
Wabasha	E6
Wabasso	B6
Wadena	B4
Waite Park	C5
Walker	C3
Walnut Grove	B6
Wanamingo	E6
Warren	A2
Warroad	B2
Waseca	D6
Waterville	D6
Watkins	C5
Welcome	C7
Wells	D7
Westbrook	B6
West Concord	E6
Wheaton	A5
White Bear Lake	F5
Willmar	B5
Windom	B7
Winnebago	C7
Winona	F6
Winsted	C6
Winthrop	C6
Worthington	B7
Wyoming	E5
Young America	D6
Zimmerman	D5
Zumbrota	E6

Other Features

Agassiz Natl. Wildlife Refuge	B2
Big Fork, *river*	D2
Big Stone Natl. Wildlife Refuge	A5
Brule, *lake*	E4
Buffalo, *river*	A4
Camp Ripley Mil. Res.	C4
Chippewa, *river*	B5
Chippewa Natl. Forest	C3, D3
Clearwater, *river*	B3
Cloquet, *river*	F3
Deer Creek Indian Res.	D3
Des Moines, *river*	B6
Eagle, *mt.*	F4
Fond Du Lac Indian Res.	E4
Ft. Snelling State Park	F6
Grand Portage Indian Res.	F4
Grand Portage Natl. Monument	F4
Grand Portage St. Forest	E4, F4
Gull, *lake*	C4
Itasca State Park	B3
Lake of the Woods, *lake*	C1
Leech, *lake*	C3
Leech Lake Indian Res.	C3
Little Fork, *river*	D2
Lower Red, *lake*	B3
Lower Whitefish, *lake*	C4
Mall of America	F6
Mesabi, *range*	D3
Mille Lacs, *lake*	D4
Mille Lacs Indian Res.	D4
Minneapolis St. Paul Intl. Airport	F5
Minnesota, *river*	B6
Mississippi, *river*	C3
Mud, *lake*	B2
Namakan, *lake*	E2
Nett Lake Indian Res.	D2
Pipestone Natl. Monument	A6
Pokegama, *lake*	D3
Prairie Island Indian Res.	E6
Rainy, *river*	C2
Red Lake Indian Res.	B2
Red River of the North, *river*	A3
Rice Lake Natl. Wildlife Refuge	D4
Root, *river*	E7
Rum, *river*	D5
St. Croix, *river*	E5
St. Croix State Park	E5
St. Louis, *river*	E3
St. Paul Downtown Airport	F5
Sherburne Natl. Wildlife Refuge	D5
Superior, *lake*	F3
Superior Natl. Forest	F3
Tamarac Natl. Wildlife Refuge	B4
Upper Red, *lake*	C2
Vermilion, *range*	F3
Vermilion Lake Indian Res.	E3
Voyageurs Natl. Park	E2
White Earth Indian Res.	B3
Winnibigoshish, *lake*	D3

362

MINNESOTA

Plants and Animals. Forests cover about one-third of the total land area of Minnesota; more than four-fifths of this is of commercial value. Mixed forests of spruce, fir, poplar, and birch cover most of the N and NE parts of the state. In central Minnesota, pine becomes more plentiful, along with birch and hemlock. Large areas of the N forest have been extensively logged and are now occupied by second-growth trees, shrubs, and low-growing plants, including blueberries and blackberries. In the SE are found hardwood forests, dominated by oak and hickory trees. This is the remnant of a band that extended to the Canadian border and separated the mixed forests of the NE from the tall grass prairies that covered the SW and W at the time of settlement. Heavy growths of prairie grass and other grass are found in some uncultivated areas.

Deer thrive in the cutover areas and are found in most counties in Minnesota. Black bear, moose, and timber wolf inhabit the N forests. Smaller mammals include fox, muskrat, beaver, Canadian lynx, mink, and raccoon. Game fish—including trout, pike, muskellunge, and bass, as well as many varieties of waterfowl—abound in the state's numerous lakes and streams.

Mineral Resources. Minnesota contains some of the most extensive iron-ore deposits in the U.S. Reserves are in the Mesabi, Vermilion, and Cuyuna ranges of the NE. High-grade ores have been depleted, and most production comes from low-grade taconite ores. Manganese is found in the ores of the Cuyuna Range. Other important minerals include sand and gravel, clay, raw materials for cement, and building stone from the granite and quartzite outcrops in the SW.   W.E.Ak.

POPULATION

According to the 1990 census, Minnesota had 4,375,099 inhabitants, an increase of 7.3% over 1980. The average population density was 19 people per sq km (50 per sq mi). Whites made up 94.4% of the population and blacks 2.2%; additional population groups included 49,392 American Indians, 11,576 persons of Korean descent, 9387 persons of Vietnamese extraction, 8980 persons of Chinese descent, and 8234 persons of Asian Indian origin. Prominent among the state's American Indian groups were the Sioux. Approximately 53,900 persons were of Hispanic background. A large number of Minnesotans are descendants of immigrants from Denmark, Norway, Sweden, and other northern European countries. In rural areas, particularly, many of these ethnic groups have formed distinct communities. Lutherans (33.9%) formed the largest single religious group in 1990, followed by Roman Catholics (29.2%), Methodists (4.3%), and Baptists (3.5%). In 1990 about 70% of Minnesota's residents lived in areas defined as urban, and the rest lived in rural areas. The state's largest cities were Minneapolis; Saint Paul, the capital; Bloomington; Duluth; and Rochester.

EDUCATION AND CULTURAL ACTIVITY

Minnesota was settled in turn by New Englanders, Scandinavians, and Central Europeans, groups known for their traditional stress on education. Schools in the state often serve as local centers of cultural and social life.

Education. The first school in Minnesota was founded about 1820. The public school system was authorized by a law passed in the 1849 territorial legislature. Gradually, the state created school districts, and in 1885 compulsory education laws were passed.

In the late 1980s, public education facilities included 1564 elementary and secondary schools, with a total yearly enrollment of about 528,500 elementary pupils and 211,000 secondary students. Approximately 72,600 children attended private schools. In the same period, Minnesota had 81 institutions of higher learning, with a combined enrollment of about 253,100 students. The largest of these institutions is the University of Minnesota, with campuses at Minneapolis and Saint Paul, Crookston, Duluth, Morris, and Waseca. Academically affiliated with the university is the world-famous Mayo Graduate School of Medicine, at Rochester. Other important colleges and universities include the State University System of Minnesota, with campuses at Bemidji, Mankato, Marshall, Minneapolis, Moorhead, Saint Cloud, Saint Paul, and Winona; Hamline University (1854) and Macalester College (1874), at St. Paul; Gustavus Adolphus College (1862), at St. Peter; and Saint John's University (1857), at Collegeville.

Cultural Institutions. Minneapolis and St. Paul—the Twin Cities—form the principal cultural hub of the state. The museums here include the Minneapolis Institute of Arts, which has extensive collections, and the Walker Art Center, both in Minneapolis; and the Minnesota Historical Society History Center, with exhibits relating to the history of the state, and the Science Museum of Minnesota, both in St. Paul. The large Minnesota Zoological Garden is in Apple Valley, and the Runestone Museum, in Alexandria, contains exhibits allegedly proving the Vikings' presence in Minnesota. The University of Minnesota Library, with more than 4 million volumes, is one of the largest university libraries in the U.S. The James Jerome Hill Reference Library contains a large collection of Americana, and the Mayo Clinic Library in Rochester has many old and rare medical books. Best

A skyline view of Minneapolis, Minn., along the Mississippi River.
J. Blank/FPG

known among the Twin Cities' many theaters are the Children's Theater Company and the Guthrie Theater Company, founded in 1963. Minneapolis-St. Paul also supports the St. Paul Chamber Orchestra and several dance companies, as well as the Minnesota Opera. The Minnesota Orchestra, which was founded in 1903 and known until 1968 as the Minneapolis Symphony Orchestra, is among the nation's finest. The noted St. Olaf College Choir is at Northfield.

Historical Sites. Minnesota has several landmarks commemorating the Indians who inhabited the region before white settlement; these include Pipestone National Monument, which contains quarries from which Indians extracted the stone they used for making peace pipes. Grand Portage National Monument on Lake Superior is the site of a late 18th-century fur-trading post. Near the Twin Cities lies Fort Snelling, a restored military post principally erected in the 1820s.

Sports and Recreation. Minnesota's many thousands of lakes and streams furnish ample opportunities for water-sports enthusiasts. The scenic forested landscape is also popular with hikers and campers, and the abundance of fish and game attracts thousands of anglers and hunters. During the winter, ice-skating, skiing, and snowmobile races are favorite recreations. The United States Hockey Hall of Fame is in Eveleth. Professional sports teams, all based in Minneapolis-St. Paul, include the Twins (baseball), Vikings (football), Timberwolves (basketball), and North Stars (ice hockey).

Communications. In the early 1990s, Minnesota had 102 AM radio stations, 146 FM radio stations, and 27 TV stations. In the same period, the state had 25 daily newspapers, with a total daily circulation of about 949,900. The first radio station to go on the air was WLB in Minneapolis in 1922, and the first newspaper, the *Minnesota Pioneer*, appeared in 1849. The leading newspapers today are the *Star Tribune*, in Minneapolis, and the *St. Paul Pioneer Press*.

GOVERNMENT AND POLITICS

Minnesota is governed under its original constitution, which was adopted in 1857 and became effective the following year when Minnesota was admitted to the Union as a state. A constitutional amendment may be proposed by the state legislature or by a constitutional convention. To become effective, it must be approved by a majority of voters in a general election.

Executive. The chief executive of Minnesota is a governor, who is popularly elected to a term of four years. Other major state officials, all elected to 4-year terms, are the lieutenant governor (who succeeds the governor upon the latter's death, removal from office, or incapacity to serve), secretary of state, auditor, treasurer, and attorney general.

MINNESOTA

Legislature. Minnesota's legislature consists of a 67-member senate and a 134-member house of representatives. Senators are elected to 4-year terms and representatives to 2-year terms. The legislature ordinarily meets in January in odd-numbered years for 120 legislative days. A special session may be called by the governor.

Judiciary. Minnesota's court of last resort is the supreme court, which is made up of a chief justice and six associate justices, all of whom are elected to 6-year terms. The major trial courts are district courts, with a total of 241 judges, all elected to 6-year terms. At the lower level are probate, county, and municipal courts.

Local Government. Minnesota has 87 counties, which are governed typically by a board of commissioners, consisting of five members elected to 4-year terms. The state also has about 850 cities and 1800 townships.

National Representation. Minnesota sends two senators and eight representatives to the U.S. Congress. The state has ten electoral votes in presidential elections.

Politics. Minnesota politics was dominated by the Republicans in the early 20th century, but during the 1930s a powerful third party emerged—the Farmer-Labor party. In 1944, the Farmer-Labor party and the Democrats merged into the Democratic-Farmer-Labor (DFL) party, and in 1975, the state's Republican party adopted the name Inde-pendent-Republican party. Since the 1940s, the two major parties have more or less shared control of state politics.

The most prominent national politician from Minnesota after World War II was the DFL leader Hubert Humphrey, who was U.S. vice-president from 1965 to 1969; his protégé Walter F. Mondale held the vice-presidency from 1977 to 1981. Since the 1930s, Minnesota has usually cast its electoral votes for the Democratic nominee in presidential elections.

ECONOMY

The area that is now Minnesota was an important hunting ground for French, and later British, fur trappers. Permanent American settlement, which began in the early 19th century, focused on the rich exploitation of the area's agricultural and for-est lands. To this was added, in the 1880s, large-scale iron-ore mining. By the end of the 19th century, wheat, which had been the major crop, was being replaced by corn and dairy farming; today Minnesota remains a major national agricultural producer. The North Country continues to furnish vast forest and mineral wealth, as well as recreational opportunities. Manufacturing, which largely utilizes the resources of the region, has grown to be an important sector of the state economy.

Agriculture. Farming accounts for about 4% of the annual gross state product in Minnesota. The state has some 88,000 farms, which average 138 ha (341 acres) in size. Slightly less than half the yearly farm income of Minnesota derives from the marketing of livestock and livestock products. Milk production dominates, but beef cattle and hog marketing are also important.

Holstein-Friesian cows grazing near the town of Lake Elmo, Minn., make up one of many herds that contribute to the important dairy industry of Minnesota. **Great Northern Railway**

MINNESOTA

The major crops are corn, soybeans, hay, wheat, sugar beets, oats, and barley. Minnesota is one of the leading U.S. states in the production of oats, spring wheat, hay, and sunflower seeds. Other significant agricultural commodities are potatoes, apples, green peas and other vegetables, turkeys, and chicken eggs.

Forestry and Fishing. Minnesota's extensive forests have been cut since the 1840s. Conservation procedures and tree farming have helped to restore the forest and maintain the lumber industry. Needle-leaf forests of pine trees with stands of fir, spruce, tamarack, and birch are found in the NE. To the E and S is a region of broad-leaf forests containing elm, maple, basswood, ash, and oak. Overall, more hardwood than softwood timber is produced. Commercial fishing is of minor importance in Minnesota. Lake commercial catches include herring, smelt, and lake trout. Minor catches of pike, catfish, whitefish, carp, and others from rivers and lakes add to the industry.

Mining. The mining industry, which now accounts for less than 1% of the annual gross state product in Minnesota, is dominated by one mineral—iron ore. Minnesota is the major iron-ore producing state in the U.S., usually accounting for some 80% of the nation's annual production. Most production is from pit mines and consists of low-grade taconite ore. The Hull-Rust-Mahoning mine near Hibbing is one of the world's largest open-pit mines. Minnesota also has several varieties of high-grade granite. Other minerals found in the state include sand and gravel, gold, platinum, and diamonds. Minnesota formerly led the U.S. in manganese production, but the industry is now dormant.

Manufacturing. Enterprises engaged in manufacturing account for about 21% of the annual gross state product in Minnesota and employ some 399,000 workers. The leading sectors, as measured by annual payroll, are the making of industrial machinery and fabricated metal products. Food processing is dominated by dairy production, canning, flour milling, and sugar refining. Other important industries include printing and publishing and the making of electronic equipment, precision instruments, paper and allied products, lumber and other wood items, and rubber and plastics products. The principal centers of industrial production are the Minneapolis-St. Paul metropolitan area, Duluth, Austin, and Winona. In recent years, manufacturing has become more widely dispersed, locating in smaller towns.

Tourism. Minnesota is visited each year by more than 12 million tourists, who contribute over $4.9 billion to the state economy. Tourism centers on

Open-pit mining in Virginia, Minn. Minnesota is one of the leading producers of iron ore and minerals in the U.S.
Shirley Hawn–Taurus Photo

the forest and lake areas of the N part of the state and on the Twin Cities of Minneapolis and St. Paul. Voyageurs National Park is the largest park in the state. Two national monuments also attract visitors. In addition, the state maintains a system of 123 parks, recreation areas, and forests. Itasca State Park, containing a source of the Mississippi R., is among the most widely visited.

Transportation. Minneapolis and St. Paul are the principal hubs of both the state and regional transportation networks. Some 208,250 km (some 129,400 mi) of federal, state, and local roads serve all parts of Minnesota. Included in this total are 1465 km (910 mi) of interstate highways. The state's railroads have about 7450 km (4630 mi) of Class I track. Duluth on Lake Superior is the state's major port and is one of the busiest ports on the entire Great Lakes system. Other lake ports include Two Harbors, Silver Bay, and Taconite Harbor. The Twin Cities serve as a N terminus for Mississippi R. traffic. The state has 381 airports, 26 heliports, and 64 seaplane bases. Minneapolis–St. Paul International Airport, Minnesota's busiest air terminal, is the major regional gateway.

Energy. Electricity-generating plants in Minnesota have a total capacity of about 8.8 million kw; the annual output of electricity is about 41.6 billion kwh. Hydroelectric power sources are of minor importance, and nearly all electricity is generated by thermal and nuclear plants. Minnesota is one of the leading states in the consumption of nuclear fuels, deriving almost 30% of its yearly electricity from this source. Coal is the main fossil fuel used in thermal installations. Large amounts of electricity are imported from North Dakota and South Dakota. E.P.H.

HISTORY

The first known inhabitants of the area that is now Minnesota were Indians of the Dakota branch of the Sioux nation. In the 16th century the Ojibwa, or Chippewa, Indians, concentrated on the northern part of the Atlantic coast, began a mass westward migration. In the next century they started to invade the traditional home of the Dakota Sioux. For the next 200 years the two Indian peoples were in a constant state of war; the coming of whites was considered of minor importance by the Sioux, who were more concerned with the Ojibwa encroachment.

Early Explorers. The first Europeans known to have seen the region were the French fur traders and explorers Médard Chouart, sieur des Groseilliers (1618?–96?), and Pierre Esprit Radisson. In 1679 the French explorer Daniel Greysolon, sieur Duluth (1636–1710), led an expedition into what is now northern Minnesota, built a fort on the shores of Lake Superior, and claimed the entire region in the name of France. The Flemish priest Louis Hennepin in 1680 sighted and named the Falls of Saint Anthony, at the site of what is now Minneapolis. French traders later built forts at Lake Pepin, on Prairie Island, and at Mankato. For a time many traders took Indian wives and adopted their customs.

British and American Influence. French influence in the area waned after 1763, when a part of Minnesota was ceded to Great Britain by France under the terms of the treaty that ended the French and Indian War. In 1783, following the American Revolution, the area between the Great Lakes and the Mississippi River became part of the newly established U.S.; the area known as the Northwest Angle became U.S. territory because of a misconception that the Mississippi River lay west of Lake of the Woods. The land west of the Mississippi became U.S. property as part of the Louisiana Purchase in 1803. British trading companies continued to dominate the Minnesota fur trade, however, and the U.S. government made no effort to establish settlements in the region until 1805. In that year the American soldier Zebulon M. Pike was sent with a small party to extend federal authority over the area. For a reputed price of 60 gallons of whiskey and several hundred dollars worth of trade goods, the Sioux Indians sold the U.S. a military camp site at the junction of the Minnesota and Mississippi rivers.

Although the British and Canadian fur traders resisted the spread of U.S. authority, they were forced to leave the region after the War of 1812. In 1815 a U.S. statute restricted fur trading to U.S. citizens, and the American Fur Co. of John Jacob Astor replaced the British-owned Northwest Co. as the principal trading power in Minnesota.

Development Toward Statehood. Some settlers moved into the region after 1815, and federal troops were sent to protect them and to guard the territorial borders. The first military installation, Fort Saint Anthony (later renamed Fort Snelling), was built in 1819, and the first large settlement, Mendota, grew up near it. With the establishment in 1834 of the main trading post of the American Fur Co. at Mendota, the fort, which included an Indian agency, became the leading settlement of the American Northwest. In 1837 the Indians sold the U.S. government a triangle of land between the Mississippi and Saint Croix rivers. Soon afterward the first lumbering camps began operation in the area, and settlers from the eastern states began to arrive in great numbers.

On Aug. 26, 1848, a group of Minnesotans convened at Stillwater to plan the organization of the territory of Minnesota. In 1849 the territory

MINNESOTA

DATE OF STATEHOOD: May 11, 1858; 32d state

CAPITAL:	Saint Paul
MOTTO:	*L'Étoile du nord* (The star of the north)
NICKNAME:	North Star State
STATE SONG:	"Hail! Minnesota" (words by Truman E. Rickard and Arthur E. Upson; music by Truman E. Rickard)
STATE TREE:	Red pine
STATE FLOWER:	Pink and white lady's-slipper
STATE BIRD:	Common loon
POPULATION (1990):	4,375,099; 20th among the states
AREA:	225,182 sq km (86,943 sq mi); 12th largest state; includes 18,974 sq km (7326 sq mi) of inland water
HIGHEST POINT:	Eagle Mt., 701 m (2301 ft)
LOWEST POINT:	183 m (602 ft), at the shore of Lake Superior
ELECTORAL VOTES:	10
U.S. CONGRESS:	2 senators; 8 representatives

POPULATION OF MINNESOTA SINCE 1850

Year of Census	Population	Classified As Urban
1850	6,000	0%
1860	172,000	9%
1880	781,000	19%
1900	1,751,000	34%
1920	2,387,000	44%
1940	2,792,000	50%
1960	3,414,000	62%
1980	4,076,000	67%
1990	4,375,099	70%

POPULATION OF TEN LARGEST CITIES

	1990 Census	1980 Census
Minneapolis	368,383	370,951
Saint Paul	272,235	270,230
Bloomington	86,335	81,831
Duluth	85,493	92,811
Rochester	70,745	57,890
Brooklyn Park	56,381	43,332
Coon Rapids	52,978	35,826
Burnsville	51,288	35,674
Plymouth	50,889	31,615
Saint Cloud	48,812	42,566

CLIMATE

	MINNEAPOLIS-SAINT PAUL	INTERNATIONAL FALLS
Average January temperature range	−16.1° to −6.1° C (3° to 21° F)	−22.8° to −10.6° C (−9° to 13° F)
Average July temperature range	16.1° to 27.8° C (61° to 82° F)	11.7° to 25.6° C (53° to 78° F)
Average annual temperature	6.7° C (44° F)	2.8° C (37° F)
Average annual precipitation	660 mm (26 in)	660 mm (26 in)
Average annual snowfall	1168 mm (46 in)	1524 mm (60 in)
Mean number of days per year with appreciable precipitation	113	132
Average daily relative humidity	70%	72%
Mean number of clear days per year	100	81

NATURAL REGIONS OF MINNESOTA

- SUPERIOR UPLAND
- WESTERN GREAT LAKES LOWLAND
- DRIFTLESS REGION
- DISSECTED TILL PLAINS

ECONOMY

State budget . . . . general revenue $11.0 billion
general expenditure $10.4 billion
accumulated debt $3.8 billion
State and local taxes, per capita $2305
Personal income, per capita $14,389
Population below poverty level 10.2%
Assets, insured commercial banks (637) . . . . $50.9 billion
Labor force (civilian nonfarm) 2,091,000
    Employed in services   26%
    Employed in wholesale and retail trade   25%
    Employed in manufacturing   19%
    Employed in government   16%

	Quantity Produced	Value
FARM PRODUCTS		**$7.8 billion**
Crops		**$4.0 billion**
Corn	19.4 million metric tons	$1.6 billion
Soybeans	4.9 million metric tons	$1.0 billion
Hay	6.0 million metric tons	$558 million
Wheat	3.8 million metric tons	$347 million
Sugar beets	4.9 million metric tons	$223 million
Barley	1.1 million metric tons	$93 million
Vegetables	845,000 metric tons	$85 million
Oats	699,000 metric tons	$51 million
Livestock and Livestock Products		**$3.8 billion**
Milk	4.5 million metric tons	$1.3 billion
Hogs	778,000 metric tons	$948 million
Cattle	521,000 metric tons	$934 million
Turkeys	386,000 metric tons	$298 million
Eggs	2.5 billion	$120 million
MINERALS		**$1.4 billion**
Iron ore	41.0 million metric tons	$1.2 billion
Sand, gravel	30.6 million metric tons	$83 million
Stone	8.0 million metric tons	$46 million

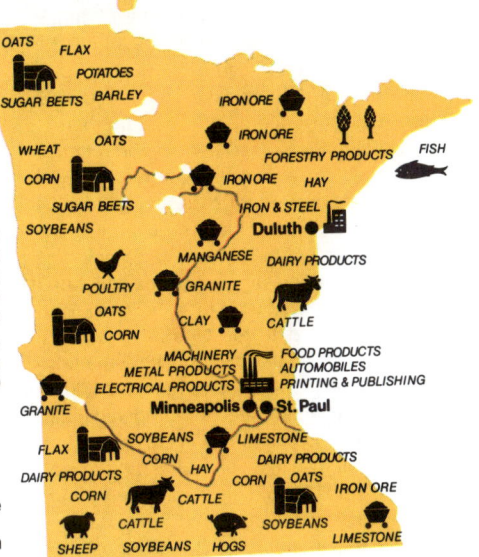

	Annual Payroll
MANUFACTURING	**$11.6 billion**
Industrial machinery and equipment	$2.1 billion
Fabricated metal products	$1.1 billion
Printing and publishing	$1.1 billion
Food and kindred products	$896 million
Instruments and related products	$852 million
Electronic equipment	$752 million
Paper and allied products	$455 million
Lumber and wood products	$453 million
Rubber and plastics products	$346 million
Stone, clay, and glass products	$293 million
Chemicals and allied products	$243 million
OTHER	**$34.8 billion**
Services	$9.5 billion
Government	$8.3 billion
Retail trade	$4.3 billion
Wholesale trade	$3.8 billion
Finance, insurance, and real estate	$3.3 billion
Transportation, communications, and public utilities	$2.8 billion
Construction	$2.2 billion

PRINCIPAL PRODUCTS OF MINNESOTA

ANNUAL GROSS STATE PRODUCT

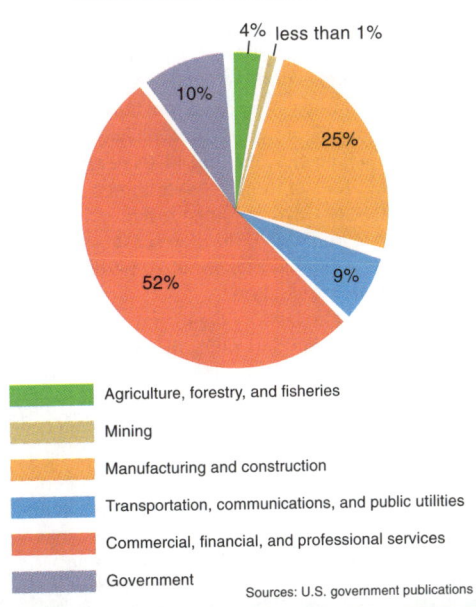

- 4% Agriculture, forestry, and fisheries
- less than 1% Mining
- 25% Manufacturing and construction
- 9% Transportation, communications, and public utilities
- 52% Commercial, financial, and professional services
- 10% Government

Sources: U.S. government publications

MINNESOTA

was created with the same boundaries as the present-day state, except for the western frontier; the land west of the Mississippi and White Earth rivers was considered Indian tribal property.

In 1851 several treaties were concluded with the Sioux, who surrendered title to more than 11 million ha (28 million acres) of land and retained only a narrow strip along the Minnesota River. Under the terms of similar treaties made in 1854 and 1855, the Ojibwa relinquished almost the entire northern half of the present state, including the richest timberland of the region. Thereafter thousands of settlers poured into the area. Minnesota was admitted to the Union on May 11, 1858. Between the years 1850 and 1860 the population grew from 5354 to more than 172,000.

The Sioux, resenting what they considered unfair treatment by traders and Indian agents of the federal government, rose in revolt in 1862. More than 500 settlers and U.S. soldiers were killed before the Sioux were defeated decisively at the Battle of Woods Lake in September 1862. The Sioux were deprived of title to their reservation lands.

Post–American Civil War Growth. By 1870, Minnesota was a boom state; the population was almost 500,000, and the area under cultivation exceeded 400,000 ha (1 million acres), more than half of which was planted in wheat. Minneapolis became one of the great flour-milling centers of the world. Construction needs within the state plus the demand for wood in the East made lumbering the major industry. Railroads were extended to serve industries and new towns and villages. Sponsored by the state and by Minnesota industries, offices were opened in the Atlantic states and in Europe to attract settlers. The census of 1880 showed a population of 770,773, more than 70 percent first- and second-generation Americans.

In 1884 mining operations on the Vermilion Range began. Some years later mining began in the Mesabi Range. By the mid-1890s nearly 3 million metric tons of iron ore were mined annually. In 1911 the Cuyuna Range produced its first shipment of iron ore. At the close of World War I, Minnesota accounted for about 70 percent of all U.S. iron-ore production.

In the late 19th century the high wheat production of Minnesota and other midwestern states began to depress prices in the wheat market. Minnesota farmers began to grow corn and other cattle-feed crops in order to avoid loss. Dairying and meat packing grew in importance.

The 20th Century. Minnesota became a center for agrarian and labor political movements during the first decades of the 20th century. Several groups combined to form the Farmer-Labor party in 1922. In 1936 the party won both Minnesota seats in the U.S. House of Representatives, almost all state offices, and control of the Minnesota House of Representatives. The Farmer-Labor party subsequently lost its dominant position to the Republican party. In 1944 the Democratic and Farmer-Labor parties formed a coalition that has since been highly successful in state politics.

Although Minnesota had previously provided more than half the nation's iron ore, both the supply and the demand for high-grade ore dropped suddenly in the early 1950s. This resulted in the iron industry's development of low-grade taconite ore, in which producers invested more than $1 billion by 1970. Taconite wastes threatened Lake Superior's ecological balance, however, and in the late 1970s producers were ordered to relocate dumping sites. In the meantime, other industries—producing chemicals, computers, heavy machinery, electronic and aerospace equipment, and processed food—had become prominent.

During the 1980s, the state expanded education and transportation facilities and acted to improve pollution control and land-use management. Minnesota in 1987 became the first state in the U.S. to require employers to offer parental leave to both the mother and the father of a newborn child. Minnesota was one of the leading agricultural states in the early 1990s, but it was dealt a serious blow by the flooding of the Mississippi and other rivers of the Midwest in 1993.

For further information on this topic, see the Bibliography in volume 28, section 1205.

MINNESOTA, river, N central U.S., rising in NE South Dakota. It passes through Big Stone Lake and enters Minnesota. The river then flows in a SE direction to Mankato, where it turns N and joins the Mississippi R. near Saint Paul. The length of the river is 534 km (332 mi).

MINNESOTA, UNIVERSITY OF, state-controlled land-grant institution of higher learning, with campuses at Minneapolis and Saint Paul, Crookston, Duluth, Morris, and Waseca. The university was founded as a preparatory school by an act of the Minnesota territorial legislature in 1851, confirmed by the state constitution in 1857, and opened for higher education instruction in 1869.

The university has schools of dentistry, law, medicine, nursing, and public health and management; colleges of agriculture, architecture and landscape architecture, biological sciences, education, human ecology, liberal arts, natural resources, pharmacy, and veterinary medicine; an institute of technology with programs that include aerospace engineering, chemical engineering, chemistry, civil and mineral engineering, computer science, earth sciences, electrical engineering, mathematics, mechanical engineering, and physics and astronomy; the university college, granting bachelor's degrees to special students taking courses offered throughout the university; the general college; an institute of public affairs; and the graduate school, conferring master's and doctoral degrees. It also maintains a continuing education division and an extension service. Campuses at Duluth (established 1947) and at Morris (1960) offer liberal arts, science, education, and preprofessional programs; Duluth also has schools of medicine, business and economics, and fine arts. The colleges at Crookston and Waseca confer associate degrees.

MINNETONKA, city, Hennepin Co., SE Minnesota, on Minnehaha Creek and Lake Minnetonka, near Minneapolis; inc. 1969. Corporate offices and industries manufacturing machinery, optical equipment, and recreational goods are in the area. The region was settled in the 1850s. The community is named for Lake Minnetonka, the name of which is derived from an Indian term. Pop. (1980) 38,683; (1990) 48,370.

MINNOW, common name loosely applied to any small fish, but technically restricted to fishes in the minnow family, Cyprinidae, order Cypriniformes. This is the largest of the fish families and includes more than 2070 species, including such familiar forms as the chub, dace, goldfish (qq.v.), and shiner. Cyprinids in general are characterized by a single, usually soft-rayed dorsal fin and by one to three rows of teeth in the throat but never in the jaw. Species more specifically known as carp (q.v.) are differentiated from most other cyprinids by a stiff spine at the leading edge of a long, 15-rayed dorsal fin, usually two pairs of barbels at the mouth corners, and three rows of throat teeth. Minnows are distributed throughout almost all fresh waters in northern temperate regions, Africa, southeastern Asia, and China. In North America the family is represented by more than 300 species. Most of the Cyprinidae are only a few centimeters in length, but India's mahseer, *Barbus tor,* measures up to 2.7 m (9 ft) and may weigh more than 45 kg (100 lb). Minnows are extremely important as food fishes, particularly in Southeast Asia where they are an important source of protein.

Several other families include fishes that are often popularly called minnows. These include the Cyprinodontidae, in which the various species of killifish (q.v.) are placed; the Poeciliidae, or live-bearers (which include the mosquito fish, *Gambusia*); the Anablepidae (*see* ANABLEPS); and the mudminnows of the family Umbridae.

MINOAN CULTURE, Bronze Age culture that developed on the island of Crete prior to the coming of the Greeks (*see* ACHAEANS). It is one of three principal cultures of Aegean civilization; the other two are the Cycladic culture, which developed in the Cyclades, and the Mycenaean, which developed on mainland Greece in late Helladic times. Minoan culture reached its height in the 2d millennium BC at Knossos, Phaestos, Mallia, and other flourishing centers.

Little was known about Minoan culture before the discovery (1900) of a great palace at Knossos by the British archaeologist Sir Arthur Evans, who named the culture it represented Minoan, in association with Minos (q.v.) the legendary King. The palace at Knossos was probably damaged by

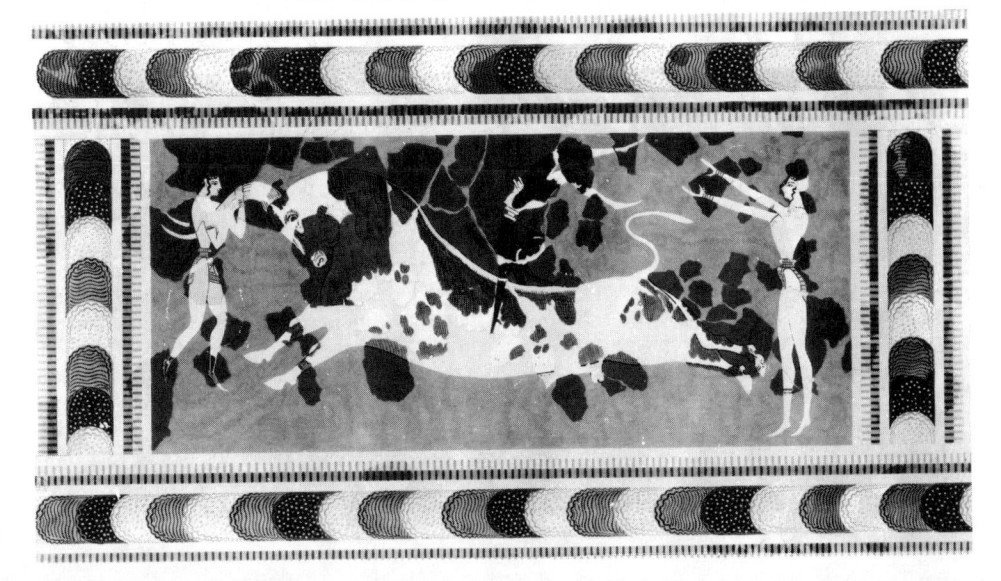

Bull leaping, a sport or perhaps part of a religious ceremony, in "The Toreador Fresco" (c. 1500 BC), from the palace at Knossos.　Metropolitan Museum of Art

an earthquake about 1700 BC, a date that marked the end of one phase of the early history of Crete. A new dynasty developed an even more brilliant culture. The palace at Knossos was rebuilt on a more elaborate scale; it rose to three or four stories and contained many extensive rooms and passages and a luxuriously decorated throne room. Conspicuous among the many paintings were scenes of bull-leaping, a sport that may have given rise to the later Greek myth of the Minotaur (q.v.). Sanctuaries within the palace provided a place for the worship of a mother goddess, probably the one called Rhea (q.v.) by the Greeks. Associated with her worship was the double ax, pictures of which appear on some of the walls of the palace. In the ruins were also found handsome examples of sculpture and metalwork. Evidence exists that the Minoans had a complex system of weights and measures.

The kings of Knossos attained their greatest power about 1600 BC, when they controlled the entire Aegean area and traded extensively with Egypt. The destruction of Knossos and the collapse of Minoan culture coincided with the beginning of the most flourishing period of Mycenaean civilization in Greece; this coincidence suggests that the warlike Mycenaeans attacked and destroyed the Minoan civilization.

Excavations on Crete after 1900 revealed some 3000 clay tablets inscribed with two scripts, called Linear A and Linear B. The earlier of the two, employed by the Minoans, was Linear A and it was already flourishing about 1750 BC; it has not been deciphered. Minoans also added inked Linear A inscriptions to stone and terra-cotta vessels. A unique clay disk found at the site of Phaestos is often adduced as the earliest example of printing, that is, reproducing written text by using "letter" stamps; the disk was stamped on both sides, while still wet, with a series of sealstones comprising a set of 45 symbols.

Linear B tablets were found on Crete and also at Pylos and Mycenae on the Greek mainland; the majority of tablets are dated between 1400 BC and 1150 BC. In 1952 the British architect and cryptographer Michael Ventris (1922–56) and John Chadwick (1920–) deciphered Linear B and identified the language it transcribes as an early Greek dialect (*see* GREEK LANGUAGE).

For more information on Minoan art *see* AEGEAN CIVILIZATION: *Aegean Art and Architecture.*

See also CRETE; KNOSSOS; MYCENAE.

MINOR. *See* AGE OF CONSENT.

MINORCA, island, E Spain, in the Mediterranean Sea, the second largest of the Balearic Islands, near the island of Majorca. It is 48 km (30 mi) long and about 16 km (about 10 mi) wide. The chief town is Mahón. Wine, oil, grain, flax, and sweet potatoes are the main products. The island has many megalithic remains. Area, 702 sq km (271 sq mi); pop. (1989 est.) 66,900.

MINORITIES, groups of people having common ethnic, racial, or religious backgrounds, especially when constituting a comparatively small proportion of a given population. Minorities often have fewer rights and less power than dominant groups. A primary factor in the existence of minorities is immigration (q.v.), but settlement by one people can also result in the indigenous or conquered people becoming a minority, as in the case of North American Indians. Minority groups may persist, however, not only because of immigration but because of their desire to retain their traditions. In Europe, throughout history, ties of minority peoples with their countries of ethnic origin have led to international disputes and wars, as in the case of the Sudetenland (q.v.). In a heterogeneous society, cultural and class differences between diverse elements of the population can become more pronounced, causing inequalities through discrimination (q.v.).

The array of minority groups in the U.S. has enriched American life and in recent years has also tested the nation's democratic tradition. During the restive 1960s many minorities throughout the world became more active in fighting what they felt to be discriminatory injustices; these efforts generally continued through the 1980s. Among these groups have been the blacks, Hispanics, and Indians in the U.S.; French-Canadians in Canada; Basques in Spain; Jews in the Soviet Union; and Roman Catholics in Northern Ireland.

See also CIVIL RIGHTS AND CIVIL LIBERTIES.

For further information on this topic, see the Bibliography in volume 28, sections 159, 1147.

MINOS, in Greek mythology, legendary ruler of Crete. Some ancient writers identified several kings by his name, especially Minos the Elder and his grandson Minos the Younger, but this distinction never appears in the accounts themselves. Minos was the son of Zeus, father of the gods, and of the princess Europa. From the city of Knossos he colonized many of the Aegean islands, and he was widely considered a just ruler. In the most famous story about Minos, he refused to sacrifice a certain bull. The god Poseidon punished him by making his wife Pasiphaë fall in love with the animal, and she subsequently gave birth to the Minotaur (q.v.). According to Attic legend, Minos was a tyrant who took harsh measures to avenge the death of his son Androgeous at the hands of the Athenians. At stated intervals he exacted a tribute from Athens of seven youths and seven maidens to be sacrificed to the Minotaur. Minos eventually met his death in Sicily, and he then became one of the judges of the dead in the underworld. The legends concerning Minos probably have a historical basis and reflect the age when Crete was supreme in the Aegean region and certain cities of Greece were subject to the kings of Knossos.

MINOT, city, seat of Ward Co., N North Dakota, on the Souris (Mouse) R.; settled 1886, inc. 1887. Minot is a commercial center of an extensive agricultural region where durum wheat is grown. Major manufactures here include processed food, farm equipment, building materials, and plastic products. Vast lignite and petroleum fields are located in the area. Minot is the site of Minot State University (1913). Minot Air Force Base and Upper Souris and J. Clark Salyer national wildlife refuges are nearby. Pop. (1980) 32,843; (1990) 34,544.

MINOTAUR, in Greek mythology, monster with the head of a bull and the body of a man. It was the offspring of Pasiphaë, queen of Crete, and a snow-white bull the god Poseidon had sent to Pasiphaë's husband, King Minos. When Minos refused to sacrifice the beast, Poseidon made Pasiphaë fall in love with it. After she gave birth to the Minotaur, Minos ordered the architect and inventor Daedalus to build a labyrinth so intricate that escape from it without assistance would be impossible. Here the Minotaur was confined and fed with young human victims Minos forced Athens to send him as tribute. The Greek hero Theseus was determined to end the useless sacrifice and offered himself as one of the victims. When Theseus reached Crete, Minos's daughter Ariadne fell in love with him. She helped him escape by giving him a ball of thread, which he fastened to the door of the maze and unwound as he made his way through it. When he came upon the sleeping Minotaur, he beat the monster to death and then led the other sacrificial youths and maidens to safety by following the thread back to the entrance.

MINSK, city, N Belarus, capital of Belarus and of Minsk Oblast, on the Svisloch R. Minsk is an important industrial, transportation, and cultural center. Principal manufactures include motor vehicles, electronic equipment, timepieces, processed food, and textiles. Minsk is the seat of a university, and a branch of an academy of sciences, a music conservatory, opera and ballet companies, and several theaters and museums are also located here.

Minsk was first mentioned in 1067, and by the early 12th century it had become the center of an independent principality. The city passed to Lithuania in the 14th century and to Poland in the 16th century. Minsk was annexed by Russia as a result of the second partition of Poland (1793) and became the capital of the Belorussian SSR in 1919. During World War II the city was occupied (1941–44) by German forces and suffered great damage; much of its large Jewish population was exterminated by the Germans. Pop. (1991 est.) 1,633,600.

MINSTREL, professional entertainer in medieval Europe, skilled at playing instruments, singing, telling stories, and performing acrobatics and other tricks. Many minstrels were employed in houses of the nobility, but the majority were itinerants. After about 1300 they began to form guilds in the towns. Such entertainers were called jongleurs before about 1100, and they were often hired to perform the songs written by troubadours and trouvères.

MINSTREL SHOW, theatrical entertainment originated and developed in the U.S. in the first half of the 19th century, and consisting of songs, dances, and comic repartee typically performed by white actors made up as blacks. The minstrel show probably evolved from two types of entertainment popular in America before 1830: the impersonation of blacks given by white actors between acts of plays or during circuses; and the performances of black musicians who sang, with banjo accompaniment, in city streets. The "father of American minstrelsy" was Thomas Dartmouth "Daddy" Rice (1808–60), who between 1828 and 1831 developed a song-and-dance routine in which he impersonated an old, crippled black slave, dubbed Jim Crow. This routine achieved immediate popularity, and Rice performed it with great success in the U.S. and Great Britain, where he introduced it in 1836. Throughout the 1830s, up to the founding of the minstrel show proper, Rice had many imitators.

In 1842, in New York City, the songwriter Daniel Decatur Emmett and three companions devised a program of singing and dancing in blackface to the accompaniment of bone castanets, violin, banjo, and tambourine. Calling themselves the Virginia Minstrels, they made their first public appearance in February 1843 in a New York City theater. Another group called the Christy Minstrels, headed by the actor Edwin P. Christy (1815–62), began appearing a few years later and originated many essential features of the minstrel show, including the seating of the entertainers in a semicircle on the stage, with a tambourine player (Mr. Tambo) at one end and a performer on the bone castanets (Mr. Bones) at the other; the singing of songs with harmonized choruses; the exchange of jokes between the endmen and the performer in the center seat

(Mr. Interlocutor); and the introduction of special variety acts at the conclusion of the bill.

In the 1850s the typical minstrel show had two parts. The first part included the comic exchange; songs by Tambo and Bones; sentimental ballads by such composers as the American Stephen Foster; a final song by the whole company; and a walk-around, a section in which, one at a time, each performer walked around the inside of the semicircle several times and finished by doing his particular specialty in the center of the stage. The second part, called the olio, consisted of specialty acts, clog dances, jigs, female impersonations, and a burlesque of some serious drama currently popular. Eventually the walk-around became a large ensemble finale that followed the olio.

After the American Civil War black entertainers—often also in blackface makeup—became more prominent than before. The most famous of the black minstrelsy composers was James Bland (1854–1911). The minstrel show was the leading vehicle for popular music in the U.S. in the 19th century. Its banjo music influenced the development of ragtime, and its clog dancing, the evolution of tap dance. From 1850 to 1870 minstrelsy was at its height, and in the 1850s ten theaters in New York City alone were devoted almost solely to such entertainment. After 1870 the popularity of the minstrel show declined rapidly, and in 1919 only three troupes remained in the U.S. Economic reasons contributed to the decline, as did a growing craze for gigantic minstrel shows—exemplified by Haverly's Mastodon Minstrels, with over 100 performers and lavish stage settings; and the famous Lew Dockstader's Minstrels, which presented elaborate programs related to modern vaudeville (q.v.) rather than to the older, simpler form.

MINT, common name for the family Lamiaceae, comprising a group of woody or herbaceous flowering plants of worldwide distribution, and for its well-known genus, *Mentha*. Members of the mint family often contain aromatic oils, and many (often of Mediterranean origin) are cultivated as culinary herbs. These include marjoram (q.v.) and oregano, *Origanum;* thyme (q.v.), *Thymus;* sage (q.v.), *Salvia;* rosemary (q.v.), *Rosmarinus;* savory, *Satureja;* and basil (q.v.), *Ocimum.* The mint genus itself contains many well-known cultivated species: peppermint, *M. piperita;* spearmint, *M. spicata;* and pennyroyal, *M. pulegium.* These and other members of the family, such as *Coleus* (q.v.); lavender (q.v.), *Lavandula;* and shellflower, *Molucella,* are grown as ornamentals.

The family, alternatively called Labiatae, belongs to the Lamiales, an order comprising more than 10,000 species, which, although placed in four families, are contained primarily in the three largest: Lamiaceae, with 5600 species; the verbena (q.v.) family, Verbenaceae, with 1900 species, and the borage (q.v.) family, Boraginaceae, with 2500 species. The fourth family, Lennoaceae, contains only 6 species, fleshy root parasites that lack chlorophyll. The order characteristically has opposite, decussate leaves (pairs of leaves at right angles to one another), and the stems are often squarish in cross section. The sepals (outer floral whorls) and petals (inner floral whorls) are fused into tubes that usually have four or five lobes, or lips, and are irregular (bilaterally symmetrical). The two, four, or five stamens (male flower parts) are attached to the inside of the corolla tube, which is made up of the fused petals. The ovary (female flower part) is superior, that is, borne above and free from the other flower parts, and has two carpels (ovule-bearing flower parts).

Plants in the order Lamiales are members of the class Magnoliopsida (*see* DICOTS) in the division Magnoliophyta (*see* ANGIOSPERM). M.R.C.

For further information on this topic, see the Bibliography in volume 28, sections 452, 593.

MINT (Lat. *moneta,* "mint" or "money"; derived from *Moneta,* a surname of the goddess Juno,

Peppermint, Mentha piperita

whose temple at Rome was used for coining money), establishment for making coins, or pieces of metal designed to circulate as money. Before the coinage of money, trading had been accomplished either by exchange of goods in bulk or by use of granular or bar gold and silver in the settling of accounts. This system was cumbersome and inconvenient and acted as an obstacle to the expansion of commerce and industry. The invention of coinage, or minting, was a solution of this problem.

History of Coinage. Coins first appeared about the end of the 8th century BC in the district of Lydia, in Asia Minor, at that time the principal industrial and trading country of the ancient world. During the next few centuries, a great many varieties of coins were issued by the Greek and other city-states. Under the Roman Empire, however, this multiplicity was ended, and the first important standardization of sizes, weights, and values of coins was inaugurated through the banning of private or unauthorized minting. Minting again became chaotic throughout Europe after the collapse of the empire of Charlemagne, Holy Roman emperor, in the 9th century. During the Middle Ages, hundreds of local authorities minted their own money, and kings, nobles, and individual cities all issued coins without regard to uniformity or general convenience. After the Norman Conquest, for example, as many as 70 mints existed in Britain alone. Later, centralized modern states made coin uniformity possible for wider areas.

Standard and Token Coins. Metallic coins may be either standard coins or token coins. Standard coins are made of standard monetary metal and are worth as much as or slightly more than the metal they contain. Token coins are those that have far greater nominal than metallic or intrinsic value; in this respect they are analogous to paper money. These coins usually consist of alloys of precious and base metals. The mints of most countries made both standard and token coins during the 19th century, but with the widespread abandonment of the gold standard between World Wars I and II, standard coins have been withdrawn from circulation in almost every part of the world.

Minting Process. Modern minting involves several distinct processes. The particular metal is first melted and cast into bars, which are then rolled into strips of uniform thickness and quality. These strips are run through machines that punch out circular metal disks, called planchets. The planchets are then checked for accuracy of weight. If they are too heavy, they are filed down at the edges, if too light, they are remelted and recast. The rims of acceptable planchets are rolled so as to project beyond the surface of the coins and protect them from wear. The planchets are then cleaned and, at the last stage in the process, struck by dies with the impression of the finished coin. Many types of coins also have their edges milled, that is, grooved, to expose later clipping or filing, in the case of standard coins, and to aid in their handling.

See also COINS AND COIN COLLECTING; CURRENCY; MINT, UNITED STATES.

For further information on this topic, see the Bibliography in volume 28, sections 235, 681.

MINT, UNITED STATES, federal agency of the U.S. Department of the Treasury, created in 1873, and responsible for the production of domestic and foreign coins, the manufacture of national medals authorized by Congress, and the custody and traffic of bullion. The first national mint was created by an act of Congress in 1792 in Philadelphia, then the nation's capital. Subsequent legislation set up branch mints and assay offices and designated them as public depositories.

The most important mintage legislation in the U.S. during the 20th century was the Coinage Act of 1965, which eliminated all silver from the dime and quarter. By terms of the Bank Holding Company Act of 1970 silver was also removed from half-dollar and dollar coins meant for general circulation. Coins made for collectors still have silver content, however. U.S. coins are mostly copper in content, except for the penny, which is zinc with a thin copper coating.

The mint, in addition to manufacturing and distributing all U.S. coins, redeems those no longer fit for circulation. Foreign coins are manufactured for friendly governments on a reimbursable basis. The mint has physical custody of the U.S. government reserves of precious metals, makes special assays of bullion and ores submitted for analysis, and produces and sells numismatic coins, American Eagle gold and silver bullion coins, and national medals.

The director of the mint administers all agency functions, including operations of the coinage mints at Philadelphia and at Denver, Colo.; bullion depositories at Fort Knox, Ky., and West Point, N.Y.; and an assay office in San Francisco. In addition, coinage operations are carried on under the authority of the Coinage Act of 1965.

MINTON WARE, ceramic products of Mintons Ltd., founded in Stoke-on-Trent, Staffordshire, England, by Thomas Minton (1765–1836) and partners in 1793. Minton is credited with the design of willow ware a decade earlier, when he was an apprentice. This pattern, with its stylized Chinese scene, generally printed in blue, soon became a popular transfer-printed design for tableware.

MINUET

During the 19th century Mintons became one of the premier British manufacturers of ceramics. Under the leadership of Thomas Minton's son Herbert (1793–1858) the firm added decorative porcelain, often in the Sèvres style, and ornamental Parian figures to its line of basic tableware.

MINUET (Fr. *menu*, "small"), dance in $\frac{3}{4}$ meter that became popular during the 17th century at the court of Louis XIV of France. Probably of peasant origin, it was apparently introduced into court society by the king's composer Jean Baptiste Lully. The rhythmic grace of the minuet was quickly accepted throughout Europe and was employed by all the major composers of the 17th and early 18th centuries in their instrumental music, particularly in the suite. Initially the minuet was a dignified dance at a moderate tempo; facing each other, the dancing couple performed various figures having an air of restrained flirtation. After its popularity waned in formal society, the minuet evolved into stylized movements in the symphony and sonata, with a faster tempo and often humorous character. Important in this evolution were the Austrians Joseph Haydn and Wolfgang Amadeus Mozart.

MINUIT, Peter (1580–1638), Dutch colonial governor in America, born in Wesel, Germany. In 1625 he went to the Netherlands. Appointed a director of the Dutch West India Co., he set out for the company's settlement in America. He reached Manhattan Island in 1626 and purchased it from the Indians with trinkets valued at the amount of 60 guilders, or about $24. Because of differences with the company, he was recalled in 1631. In 1637 he set out to form a Swedish colony in America and in 1638 built Fort Christina (now Wilmington, Del.).

MINUTE (Lat. *minutus*, "small"), unit of time equal to one-sixtieth of an hour, or 60 seconds.

In geometry, minute is an angular measure of an arc, called a minute of arc, equal to one-sixtieth of a degree in a circle that has been subdivided into 360 degrees, or to 60 seconds of an arc. Symbols designating the various terms are 1° (1 degree), 1' (1 minute), and 1" (1 second).

MINUTEMEN, patriotic civilians of Massachusetts and several other New England colonies, who in the period before the American Revolution volunteered to fight the British at a minute's notice. In 1774 the Massachusetts Provincial Congress enrolled the minutemen as an organized militia. The minutemen figured prominently in many revolutionary engagements, most notably in the opening battles of Lexington and Concord fought on April 19, 1775 (*see* CONCORD, BATTLE OF). The Concord site is preserved in the Minute Man National Historical Park.

MINYA, AL-, also Minya, city, E Egypt, capital of al-Minya Governorate, in Upper Egypt between the W bank of the Nile R. and the Ibrahimiyah Canal. The city is on a railroad and is an important river port and trade center for cotton, sugarcane, and grain. Industries include cotton ginning, wool and sugar milling, and dairying. A museum of antiquities and a university are here. Founded possibly as a principality during the 12th Dynasty, al-Minya underwent reconstruction under the Baghdad caliphs. Al-Minya is also known as el-Minya, Minya ibn Khasib, Minia, Menia, or Minieh. Pop. (1991 est.) 203,000.

MIOCENE EPOCH, fourth division of the Tertiary period of the Cenozoic era (qq.v.), spanning a time interval from 26 to 12 million years ago (*see* GEOLOGY).

Minutemen depicted in an 1876 lithograph by Currier & Ives. **Library of Congress**

The uplift of great mountain ranges that had begun as a result of crustal plate collisions in the preceding Oligocene epoch (q.v.) continued unabated (see PLATE TECTONICS). Chief among these were the Alps in Europe, the Himalaya in Asia, and the Cordilleran Ranges of the American continents. Sediments eroded from the rising flanks of some of these ranges were deposited in shallow marine basins, eventually to become reservoirs for rich oil fields in California, Romania, and on the western shore of the Caspian Sea.

The climate of the Miocene was cooler than that of the preceding epoch. A circumglobal system of ocean currents had become established in the southern hemisphere, cutting Antarctica off from the warmer currents of the rest of the world. This fostered the growth of a great Antarctic ice sheet. In the northern hemisphere, large areas that had formerly been covered with thick forests became grassy prairies. The fauna of the Miocene included a number of mammals, among them the rhinoceros, camel, cat, and horse. The mastodon made its appearance at this time, as did the raccoon and weasel. During this epoch, large apes, related to the orangutan, lived in Asia and the southern portion of Europe; these apes are the closest Miocene relatives of humanlike apes, which first appeared during the Pliocene epoch.

See PALEONTOLOGY. P.R.Ma.

For further information on this topic, see the Bibliography in volume 28, sections 417, 436.

MIQUELON. See SAINT PIERRE AND MIQUELON.

MIRABEAU, Honoré Gabriel Riqueti, Comte de (1749–91), French revolutionary statesman, born in Bignon. In 1788 he was elected as a delegate to the Estates-General, the representative body of prerevolutionary France. Although a noble, he joined the third estate, consisting of commoners, and on June 17, 1789, together with Emmanuel Sièyes, proclaimed the third estate the National Assembly of France. On June 23, when a royal messenger expressed the displeasure of King Louis XVI, Mirabeau, speaking for his group, replied, "If you have orders to remove us from this hall, you must also get authority to use force, for we shall yield to nothing but to bayonets."

Mirabeau quickly became a great force in the assembly. A believer in constitutional monarchy, he tried to reconcile the reactionary court of Louis XVI with the increasingly radical forces of the Revolution of 1789 and 1790. He proposed the establishment of a citizen guard, out of which grew the National Guard, and tried in vain to come to terms with the king's adviser Jacques Necker and the military leader the marquis de Lafayette. He was partly successful in securing for the Crown the right of declaring peace and war, and fought hard, but with only partial success, to maintain the royal veto.

On Jan. 30, 1791, Mirabeau was elected president of the National Assembly. He died shortly afterwards, and on the last day of his life he said, "I carry with me the ruin of the monarchy. After my death factions will dispute about the fragments."

MIRACLE (Lat. *mirari*, "to wonder at"), an event, apparently transcending human powers and the laws of nature, that is attributed to a special divine intervention or to supernatural forces.

Stories of miracles are a common feature of practically all religions. In some societies, a shaman (q.v.) is believed to have the power to heal through contact with outside forces. Many religious leaders and founders—including Zoroaster, Confucius, Lao-tzu, and Buddha—have been credited with miraculous powers. Moses and the prophets of Israel were said to have performed miraculous acts at God's bidding. Muslim tradition includes accounts of the miracles of Muhammad, such as his extraordinary healings.

More attention has been given to miracles in Christianity, however, than in any other religion. Miracles have been ascribed not only to Jesus Christ but also to several of his immediate followers and to Christian saints up to the present time. The miracles of Christ recorded in the Gospels are an integral part of the New Testament narrative and include raising the dead, transforming water into wine, feeding thousands with a small amount of food, casting out demons, and healing the sick and deformed. The most important miracle of the New Testament is the resurrection (q.v.) of Christ. Under the influence of Greek philosophy, Christian writers came to accept the idea that miracles possess evidential value, that is, they provide evidence that God is at work in the world.

More recently, as a result of the historicocritical method (*see* BIBLICAL SCHOLARSHIP), the Gospel miracles are widely regarded as having been written more to inculcate religious truths than to record historical events. Thus, the significance of the miracle lies in its meaning rather than in the event itself. From this point of view, the primary aim of a miracle story is to show that God directs and intervenes in human history.

Miracles have played an important role in the history of religions. The traditionally close connections between miracles and faith, which tend to reinforce each other, explain why in new religious movements and spiritual revivals, the occurrence of the miraculous, especially in healing, plays such a prominent part. J.A.Sa.

MIRACLE, MYSTERY, AND MORALITY PLAYS

MIRACLE, MYSTERY, AND MORALITY PLAYS, generic terms given to the English dramas of medieval times. These plays, which developed from the liturgy of the Roman Catholic church after 1210 when a papal edict forbade members of the clergy from appearing on a stage in public, had considerable influence on the work of the great English dramatists of the Elizabethan age.

When the simple scenes from the Bible that had become part of the liturgy could no longer be performed by the priests early in the 13th century, the miracle plays came into existence. These plays had as subject matter the miracles performed by the saints or, more frequently, scenes from the Old and New Testaments. Miracle plays in crude form were presented at Easter and on other holy days. They gained a formalized structure in the late 13th or early 14th century and reached the height of their popularity in the 15th and 16th centuries. Miracle plays dealing with the legends of the saints were less realistic and more religious in tone than those concerned with biblical episodes, and were eventually superseded by the latter. The plays were generally given in cycles, or sequences of related scenes, each of which required only a short time to perform. Each scene was acted by members of one of the trade guilds of the town. The important extant cycles, named after the town in which they were notably performed, are the Chester (25 scenes), the Wakefield (30 scenes), the York (48 scenes), the Norwich, and the Coventry plays. The cycles were generally performed outdoors on festival days and particularly on Corpus Christi (q.v.). Each guild acted its assigned scene on its own wagon or float on wheels, which could be moved from one place to another for repeated performances.

To the scenes from the Bible the anonymous playwrights added interludes consisting of realistic comedy based on situations and ideas of a contemporary nature. The miracle play, therefore, was not only a biblical drama or scene, but also included scenes of realistic medieval comedy. The best-known miracle play is the *Second Shepherd's Play* of the Towneley Cycle. This story of the shepherds watching their flock in the fields on the night of Christ's nativity is enlivened by the comic episode in which one of the sheep is stolen; the thief hides the sheep in a cradle in his home and, brought to bay, pretends the little animal is a baby girl. The term *mystery play,* or simply *mystery,* is sometimes used synonymously with miracle play. Some literary authorities make a distinction between the two, designating as mystery plays all types of early medieval drama that draw their subject matter from Gospel events and as miracle plays all those dealing with legends of the saints. The distinction between them, however, is not generally observed today.

Sometimes known simply as a morality, the morality play was most popular in the 15th and early 16th centuries. It was designed to instruct audiences in the Christian way of life and the Christian attitude toward death. The general theme of the morality play is the conflict between good and evil for the human soul; the play always ends with the saving of the soul. The characters of the morality play are not the saints or biblical personages of the miracle play, but personifications of such abstractions as flesh, gluttony, lechery, sloth, pride, envy, hope, charity, riches, and strength.

Some of the moralities were anonymous; others were by known authors. The best known of the former type is *Everyman* (late 15th cent.), which was derived from a Dutch source but thoroughly Anglicized. In the play the protagonist Everyman learns that everything material he has gained in life deserts him as he journeys into the Valley of Death; in the end only the allegorical personage Good Deeds accompanies him.

For further information on this topic, see the Bibliography in volume 28, section 760.

MIRAGE, realistic image of an object that is either totally imaginary or that appears to be in a location other than the true one. The imaginary vision is a psychological aberration sometimes experienced by persons suffering from such conditions as extreme thirst, or mental or physical strain. The phenomenon that causes objects to appear out of place, usually in desert or at sea, is the result of atmospheric conditions. When heat radiates from a hot earth surface, as in a desert, it causes a diminution of the density (q.v.) of the air just above the surface and forces a denser layer of air to remain above the hot, rarefied air instead of, as is usually the case, below it. The boundary between the two layers produces a lenslike effect and refracts or bends rays of light from a distant object; it also gives the appearance of a layer of water (*see* OPTICS). The image produced by the rays bent by abnormal vertical distribution of air density appears inverted and below the real object, just as an image reflected in water appears when observed from a distance. A common experience of this phenomenon is the mirrored reflection of objects on a paved road in hot weather.

In the case of a mirage at sea, the denser layers of air are next to the cool surface of the water, and the reflection takes place from the rarer atmosphere above. Thus the object appears distorted, elongated, inverted, and suspended in the air, producing a so-called looming effect.

The fata morgana, which is a double mirage of the looming effect, produces exaggerated images of routine objects. This is seen most often in the Strait of Messina, Italy, and also over the Great Lakes in the U.S.

MIRAMAR, city, Broward Co., SE Florida, near the Atlantic Ocean; inc. 1955. It is a residential community in the Miami-Fort Lauderdale area. Calder Race Course is nearby. The city's name means "look at the sea" in Spanish. Pop. (1980) 32,813; (1990) 40,663.

MIRANDA, Francisco de (1750–1816), Venezuelan revolutionist, born in Caracas. Miranda served in the Spanish army as a young man. Charged with embezzlement in 1783, he fled to the U.S., where he became friendly with several leaders of the American Revolution. Later he went to London, where he tried unsuccessfully to interest the British government in the creation of an independent empire in Spanish America. From 1792 to 1798 he served in the army of revolutionary France. After participating in several battles, Miranda was accused of treachery; he was acquitted of the charge but was deported. In 1806 he led an expedition that attempted unsuccessfully to overthrow the Spanish regime in Venezuela. In 1810, on the outbreak of a revolution in that country, Miranda became the commander of the patriot forces. He defeated the Spanish armies, and in April 1812 became dictator of Venezuela. He was compelled to surrender to the Spanish royalists after only three months; the Spanish took him to Spain where he was imprisoned until his death. Because of his early advocacy of independence for Latin America, he is known there as *El Precursor* ("The Forerunner").

MIRANDA V. ARIZONA CASE. See SUPREME COURT OF THE UNITED STATES.

MIRÓ, Joan (1893–1983), Spanish painter, whose surrealist works, with their subject matter drawn from the realm of memory and imaginative fantasy, are some of the most original of the 20th century.

Miró was born April 20, 1893, in Barcelona and studied at the Barcelona School of Fine Arts and the Academia Galí. His work before 1920 shows wide-ranging influences, including the bright colors of the Fauves, the broken forms of cubism, and the powerful, flat two-dimensionality of Catalan folk art and Romanesque church frescoes of his native Spain. He moved to Paris in 1920, where, under the influence of surrealist poets and writers, he evolved his mature style. Miró drew on memory, fantasy, and the irrational to create works of art that are visual analogues of surrealist poetry. These dreamlike visions, such as *Harlequin's Carnival* (1925, Albright-Knox Gallery, Buffalo) or *Dutch Interior* (1928, Museum of Modern Art, New York City), often have a whimsical or humorous quality, containing images of playfully distorted animal forms, twisted organic shapes, and odd geometric constructions. The forms of his paintings are organized against flat neutral backgrounds and are painted in a limited range of bright colors, especially blue, red, yellow, green, and black. Amorphous amoebic

Dog Barking at the Moon *(1926), by Joan Miró.*
Philadelphia Museum of Art

shapes alternate with sharply drawn lines, spots, and curlicues, all positioned on the canvas with seeming nonchalance. Miró later produced highly generalized, ethereal works in which his organic forms and figures are reduced to abstract spots, lines, and bursts of colors.

Miró also experimented in a wide array of other media, devoting himself to etchings and lithographs for several years in the 1950s and also working in watercolor, pastel, collage, and paint on copper and masonite. His ceramic sculptures are especially notable, in particular his two large ceramic murals for the UNESCO building in Paris (*Wall of the Moon* and *Wall of the Sun,* 1957–59). Miró died in Majorca, Spain, on Dec. 25, 1983.

MIRROR, optical device, commonly made of glass, with a smooth, polished surface that forms images by the reflection of rays of light (*see* LIGHT; OPTICS; REFLECTION).

Mirrors made of brass are mentioned in the Bible, and mirrors of bronze were in common use among the ancient Egyptians, Greeks, and Romans. Polished silver was also used by the Greeks and Romans to produce reflections. Crude forms of glass mirrors were first made in Venice in 1300. By the end of the 17th century mirrors were made in Britain and the manufacture of mirrors developed subsequently into an important industry in the other European countries and in the U.S.

The original method of making glass mirrors consisted of backing a sheet of glass with an amalgam of mercury and tin (qq.v.). The surface was overlaid with sheets of tinfoil that were rubbed down smooth and covered with mercury. A woolen cloth was held firmly over the surface by means of iron weights for about a day. The glass was then inclined and the excess mercury drained away, leaving a lustrous inner surface. The first attempt to back the glass with a solution of silver was made by the German chemist Justus von Liebig in 1836; various methods have been developed since then that depend on the chemical reduction of a silver salt to metallic silver. In the manufacture of mirrors today, in cases where this principle is utilized, the plate glass is cut to size, and all blemishes are removed by polishing with rouge. The glass is scrubbed and flushed with a reducing solution such as stannous chloride before silver is applied, and the glass is then placed on a hollow, cast-iron tabletop, covered with felt, and kept warm by steam. A solution of silver nitrate is poured on the glass and left undisturbed for about 1 hour. The silver nitrate is reduced to a metallic silver and a lustrous deposit of silver gradually forms. The deposit is dried, coated with shellac, and painted. In other methods of mirror production, the silver solution is added with a reducing agent, such as formaldehyde of glucose. Silvering chemicals are often applied in spray form. Special mirrors are sometimes coated with the metal in the form of vapor obtained by vaporizing silver electrically in a vacuum. Large mirrors are often coated with aluminum in the same way (*see* ELECTROPLATING).

In addition to their general household use, mirrors are used in scientific apparatus, for example, as important components in microscopes and telescopes (*see* MICROSCOPE; TELESCOPE).

MIRV, acronym for *m*ultiple *i*ndependently targetable *r*eentry *v*ehicle, a nuclear-weapons system developed by the U.S. and the Soviet Union in the 1970s. In this system, ballistic missiles are used to carry a number of nuclear warheads to attack different targets simultaneously. *See also* GUIDED MISSILES; NUCLEAR WEAPONS.

MISCARRIAGE, common term for spontaneous abortion, the expulsion of the human fetus or embryo from the uterus at any time before the fetus is capable of independent life. Sometimes the term *abortion* (q.v.) is used to refer to the expulsion of the fetus in the first three months of pregnancy, whereas miscarriage is applied to the second three months. *See* PREGNANCY AND CHILDBIRTH.

MISCEGENATION, intermarriage or extramarital relations between persons of different racial types. In modern times miscegenation has been regarded with strong disapproval in several nations of the Western world, and social ostracism and prohibitive legislation have been employed to prevent such unions. The prejudicial attitude toward miscegenetic marriages stems mainly from obsolete conceptions of race and heredity. Also contributing to the attitude are white supremacy theories, and the inferior social status commonly imposed on dark-skinned peoples, and consequently on the children of mixed marriages, in various nations throughout the world.

In the U.S., restrictive legislation against miscegenation originated during the period of slavery in colonial times. These original laws were designed to protect the right of the slaveholder to the offspring of the slaves, and the laws embodied severe penalties. Statutes passed subsequently in the majority of the states declared miscegenetic marriages void, purportedly to preserve racial purity. Most of these statutes were directed against blacks, but some applied more broadly to include all non-Caucasoid peoples. Several state courts have upheld the constitutionality of such statutes, but in 1948 the laws were declared invalid by the California Supreme Court. Between 1942 and 1967 14 states repealed their antimiscegenation laws. In the latter year the U.S. Supreme Court ruled the antimiscegenation statutes of Virginia unconstitutional.

MISDEMEANOR, in criminal law, term applied to any offense other than a felony. In the U.S., the criminal codes of the states vary in their classifications of the offenses considered misdemeanors, but misdemeanors are always the less serious crimes. Examples of such crimes are criminal libel, assault in the third degree, conspiracy in the third and fourth degrees, criminal tampering, and possession of gambling records. Prosecution for a misdemeanor is generally by information and not by indictment, and persons found guilty are generally punished by fine or imprisonment in a prison other than a state penitentiary.

MISHAWAKA, city, St. Joseph Co., N Indiana, on the St. Joseph R. just E of South Bend; inc. as a city 1899. It is an industrial center with a variety of manufactures, including all-terrain vehicles; its rubber products industry dates from 1868. Bethel College (1947) is here. Mishawaka has large Belgian- and Italian-American populations. Deposits of bog iron ore were discovered here in 1832, and the following year a blast furnace was established. The city's name is derived either from the name of a Shawnee Indian princess or from a Potawatomi Indian term meaning "place of dead (or cleared) trees." Pop. (1980) 40,201; (1990) 42,608.

MISHIMA YUKIO, pseudonym of KIMITAKE HIRAOKA (1925–70), Japanese novelist, born in Tokyo. He failed to qualify for military service during World War II and worked in an aircraft factory instead. After the war he studied law and for a short time was employed in the finance ministry. Mishima's first novel, the partly autobiographical *Confessions of a Mask* (1948; trans. 1960), was widely acclaimed and successful enough to enable its author to become a full-time writer. His central theme is the dichotomy between traditional Japanese values and the spiritual barrenness of contemporary life. The *Temple of the Golden Pavilion* (1956; trans. 1963) portrays a young man obsessed with both religion and beauty; *The Sailor Who Fell from Grace with the Sea* (1963; trans. 1965) is a gruesome tale of adolescent jealousy; and his four-volume epic *The Sea of Fertility* (1970; trans. 1972–75), consisting of *Spring Snow, Runaway Horses, The Temple of Dawn,* and *The Decay of the Angel,* is about the transformation of Japan into a modern but sterile society. Mishima, who organized the Tatenokai, a society stressing physical fitness and the martial arts, committed ritual suicide. His death was regarded as his final protest against modern Japanese weakness.

MISHNAH, first part of the Talmud, a codification of the oral law of the Old Testament and of the political and civil laws of the Jews. It was compiled and edited (orally) in the last quarter of the 2d century AD or the first quarter of the 3d century by Rabbi Judah (c. 135–c. 220), known as ha-Kadosh (Heb., "the Saint") or ha-Nasi (Heb., "the Prince" or "the Patriarch"), but generally known to devout Jews simply as "Rabbi." He was the patriarch of Palestinian Jewry and grandson of Gamaliel of Jabneh. In this final redaction, the Mishnah represents several centuries of evolution. Among the various earlier collections, the earliest was that of the pupils of Shammai and of Hillel, an ancestor of Rabbi Judah. The Mishnah is written in Hebrew, but it contains a great number of Aramaic and Greek words. It is divided into six orders, each subdivided into treatises and chapters.

The Mishnah presents only a codification of laws; it is followed by the Gemara, or second part of the Talmud, consisting of an elaborate commentary on the Mishnah. S.L.

MISKOLC, city, NE Hungary, capital of Borsod-Abaúj-Zemplén Co., on the Sajó R. at the mouth of the Szinva R. The city lies at the E foot of the Bükk Mts. in a pass called the Miskolc Gate, and its water supply is derived from perennial limestone springs in the Bükks. Miskolc is an agricultural market center trading in grain, tobacco, wine, and fruit; vineyards and lignite mines are nearby. A road and rail hub, the city has an industrial output second only to that of Budapest. Industries include iron and steel mills, engineering works, machine shops, flour, paper, and textile mills, tobacco warehouses, and wineries. Motor vehicles, locomotives, food products, glass, apparel, cement, furniture, bricks, soap, and candles also are produced. The city is the site of a technical university specializing in heavy industry, a law school, a music conservatory, a 13th-century Gothic church, and a museum containing 6th-century BC Scythian and Bronze Age artifacts. Originally a manor town, Miskolc later became an agricultural market. It was sacked by the Mongols in the 13th century and later by the Ottoman Turks. The independent city was created in the 15th century. Pop. (1988 est.) 209,800.

MISSAL, book of prayers containing all that is said or sung during Mass. With the growth of private Mass, in which the priest says the entire service, the different parts of the service were gradually combined into one book. To ensure uniformity, the Council of Trent in the 16th century prepared a uniform liturgy, the Roman missal, and ordered its use by all Roman Catholic churches that had not followed their own liturgy

MISSILES, GUIDED

for two centuries or more. The Roman missal has since been revised three times, in the reigns of Popes Clement VIII, in 1604, Urban VIII, in 1634, and Leo XIII, in 1884. A fourth revision of the missal was begun in the late 1960s, and in 1975 the English translation of this version was published in the U.S.

In brief, the contents and orders of the Roman missal are as follows: the Calendar, explaining the year and its parts, and the determination of movable feast days; the *Rubricae Generales Missalis,* listing the various kinds of masses and their accompanying rules and ritual; the *Praeparatio ad Missam* and *Gratiarum Actio Post Missam,* containing devotions to precede and follow Mass; the *Proprium Missarum de Tempore,* the major portion of the missal, containing the proper liturgy and ritual for each Sunday, feast day, and ember day; the *Proprium Sanctorum,* giving the special details for saints' days; and special dedication and votive masses. Most missals also contain an appendix of certain local masses and saints.

MISSILES, GUIDED. See GUIDED MISSILES.

MISSIONARY MOVEMENTS, groups and organizations arising within a particular religious tradition whose concern is to witness by word and deed, at home and abroad, to the beliefs of their religion, so that others may come to know and live the truth as they understand it. The principal missionary religions of the world are Christianity, Buddhism, and Islam.

Christianity. Christianity, a missionary religion by nature, was first spread by the biblical apostles, particularly St. Paul, and by laypeople in the course of their daily life and travels.

Early church. The early church spread quickly into northern Africa (Ethiopia and Alexandria, Egypt), through Asia Minor, and, by the 3d century, into India. By the 7th century it had reached China. It spread equally quickly into Europe through Greece, Armenia, and the Italian peninsula. In the 5th through 9th centuries, Christianity expanded throughout Europe, north to Greenland and Iceland, and among the Slavs—carried from Rome by such missionaries as St. Patrick, St. Augustine of Canterbury, and St. Boniface, and from Constantinople by two brothers, St. Cyril and St. Methodius, missionaries to the Slavs.

As the church grew, religious orders systematized the work of missions and carried the teachings of the church into the Americas and the Far East.

After the Reformation. Following the Reformation, both Roman Catholics and Protestants carried on active Christian mission programs.

Among Jesuits, St. Francis Xavier was particularly active in the Far East. In 1622 the Sacred Congregation for the Propagation of the Faith was established by Rome, and Roman Catholic mission work in all parts of the world was, and still is, conducted under the direction of the papacy.

Among Protestants, in 1698, the missionary Society for Promoting Christian Knowledge was founded in England, and the Society for the Propagation of the Gospel in foreign parts worked among British settlers in the colonies from 1701. Probably the most famous missionary in America in its early days was the English-born Presbyterian John Eliot, the "Apostle of the Indians." The Moravian church emphasized missionary activity among Indians and European settlers in America. During the 18th century missionary societies were founded in many European countries; notable among these was the London Missionary Society (1795). Well-known missionaries of the era were the British Baptist William Carey (1761-1834) and the British Anglican Henry Martyn (1781-1812), who worked in India.

Franciscans and Jesuits worked in western North America. Junípero Serra, a Spanish Franciscan, was active among the Indians of California, and the Italian Jesuit Eusebio Francisco Kino worked in northern Mexico and what is now the southwestern U.S.

New fields. European missionaries directed their attention to new areas in the 19th century, greatly expanding their endeavors. Colonialism brought increased knowledge of Africa and Asia, and the European and British churches extended their work into these areas. One of the best known of the 19th-century missionaries was the British physician David Livingstone.

In the U.S. the churches established in the colonial period adapted themselves to new independence. The evangelistic impetus of the revival period carried circuit riders to the frontiers. The China trade and the slave trade had introduced Americans to the Far East and Africa, and the churches sent workers to start schools and hospitals as well as to preach in these areas. Prominent in this work were such organizations as the American Board of Commissioners for Foreign Missions (founded 1810), the American Presbyterian boards (North, 1837; South, 1862), the Baptist Burmese Mission (1813), and the Methodist Episcopal Church Missionary Society (1819). Denominational boards, the Salvation Army, other agencies, some of them related to the World Council of Churches, and individuals belonging to such mission-oriented groups as Jehovah's Witnesses and the Mormons continue the work started in this period.

MISSIONARY MOVEMENTS

Modern mission work. The social, political, and economic upheavals of the 20th century have affected all aspects of life. With the Russian Revolution and Soviet expansion, the Eastern Orthodox churches lost some of their influence. Despite official hostility to religion in the Soviet sphere, however, notable work was accomplished there by the Society of Friends, one of the few religious groups permitted to work. Through the American Friends Service Committee, Quakers have carried out social service programs in many other parts of the world as well. The development of communism in China ended missionary work there, and in many African countries the growth of nationalism has tended to identify Christianity with colonialism.

These events have brought a change in direction to the missions field. A new emphasis is being placed on Christian unity, rather than denominationalism, in mission activity. Nationals in the traditional missionary target areas, the developing countries, are being given responsible positions in their church organizations. Conversion is seen to be increasingly the task of national autonomous churches. A new evangelical movement, the Pentecostal movement, has become a force in world Protestantism.

A trend away from evangelism in the 1960s was the result of other problems. Missionary movements around the world responded with service activities: in the inner cities, refugee camps, settlements, and children's villages. The work carried out by Americans in the U.S. was directed more and more toward health, welfare, and vocational and recreational services for migratory farm workers, Indians, Spanish-speaking minorities, and others. In the 1970s, however, emphasis on evangelism again increased.

Eastern Religions. Two of the major Eastern religions have active missionary programs. One, Buddhism, has long been a missionary religion; the other, Hinduism, has adopted a missionary approach only within the last 100 years.

Buddhism. In terms of numbers of adherents, Buddhism has been the most successful of the great missionary religions. In the 3d century BC, it spread throughout the Indian subcontinent, largely through the encouragement of the Indian King Asoka. He sent missions as far west as the Mediterranean, but they had little impact. Later missionaries had great success in Sri Lanka and, in the 1st century AD, in central Asia and China. Buddhism also spread through translations of its sacred writings. In the 4th century AD, monks carried their religion to many Southeast Asian countries, where it is today a principal religion, and to Korea. By the 6th century, it had spread from Korea into Japan, where it became the state religion and was a unifying influence in the country. Today Buddhism is a substantial, and in many areas predominating, influence through much of eastern Asia. Like Christianity, however, it has not survived as a significant religion in its country of origin. Buddhism maintains small missions in Europe and the U.S. and in other parts of the Western world.

Hinduism. An ancient Indian faith, Hinduism has within the past 100 years adopted a missionary outlook, and small missions are supported in numerous countries, including the U.S. These missions stress both mysticism and social action. Such groups as the International Society for Krishna Consciousness and the Divine Light Mission became familiar in the U.S. in the mid-1970s. The first of these, the so-called Hare Krishnas, had established more than 60 centers in urban areas of North America by the early 1980s.

Islam. Probably no religion has been more militant in its missionary activity than Islam, conversion in many instances going hand in hand with military conquest. Muslim missionary activity as such, however, was largely the work of individuals, principally Arab merchants and travelers in Africa, until the end of the 19th century. Systematic missionary endeavor began then with the founding of the Ahmadiyya Movement in 1889. Missionary activity has been particularly successful in eastern and western Africa, and small missions have been established in several European countries and in the U.S. The appeal in the latter country has been mainly to the black population.

Members of the International Society for Krishna Consciousness, better known as Hare Krishnas, dancing on a New York City street in an effort to attract converts. **Wide World Photos**

MISSIONARY RIDGE

For further information on this topic, see the Bibliography in volume 28, section 84.

MISSIONARY RIDGE, low mountain ridge, southeastern U.S., situated in S Tennessee and N Georgia. The ridge, about 16 km (about 10 mi) long, lies SE of Chattanooga, Tenn., near Lookout Mt. The Battle of Chattanooga (1863) of the American Civil War was fought on Missionary Ridge, and part of this ridge is included in the Chickamauga and Chattanooga National Military Park. See CHATTANOOGA, BATTLE OF.

MISSION STYLE, type of furniture design popular in the U.S. between 1890 and 1914. Mission furniture, so named because of its resemblances to the furnishings of Spanish missions in the Southwest, was an American expression of the worldwide Arts and Crafts movement (q.v.). The best examples are those first produced in small workshops; in later mass manufacture, mission furniture tended to heavy, square shapes and roughness in detailing.

MISSISSAUGA, industrial city, Regional Municipality of Peel, SE Ontario, on Lake Ontario, near Toronto; inc. 1974. Major manufactures include telecommunication and aerospace equipment; pharmaceuticals; chemicals; machinery; and plastic and paper goods. The city is the site of Erindale College of the University of Toronto (1964). Pearson International Airport is here. The community, which was settled in the early 1800s, was part of the township of Toronto until 1968, when it was reorganized and named for the Mississauga Indians, who had lived in the region. Pop. (1986) 374,005; (1991) 463,388.

MISSISSIPPI, one of the East South Central states of the U.S., bordered on the N by Tennessee, on the E by Alabama, on the S by the Gulf of Mexico and Louisiana, and on the W by Louisiana and Arkansas. The Mississippi R. forms almost all of the W boundary, and the Pearl R. forms part of the S boundary.

Mississippi entered the Union on Dec. 10, 1817, as the 20th state. Its economy was mainly agricultural until the middle third of the 20th century, when manufacturing became the dominant economic sector; service industries have become increasingly important in recent decades. Jefferson Davis, the president of the Confederacy during the American Civil War, resided here. The name of the state is taken from that of the Mississippi R., the name of which is derived from an Algonquian Indian term for "big river." Mississippi is called the Magnolia State.

LAND AND RESOURCES

Mississippi, with an area of 125,443 sq km (48,434 sq mi), is the 32d largest state in the U.S.; 5.5% of its land area is owned by the federal government.

The state is roughly rectangular in shape, and its extreme dimensions are about 530 km (about 330 mi) from N to S and about 290 km (about 180 mi) from E to W. Elevations range from sea level, along the Gulf of Mexico, to 246 m (806 ft) atop Woodall Mt. in the NE. The approximate mean elevation is 91 m (300 ft). The state's coastline is 71 km (44 mi) long.

Physical Geography. Most of Mississippi is part of the East Gulf Coastal Plain, and the rest of the state is made up of a section of the Mississippi Alluvial Plain. The East Gulf Coastal Plain is generally composed of low hills, such as the Pine Hills in the S and the North Central Hills. Somewhat higher elevations are in the Pontotoc Ridge and the Fall Line Hills in the NE. Yellow-brown loess soil is in the W, and a region of fertile black earth, part of the Black Belt, is in the NE. The coastline, which includes large bays at Bay Saint Louis, Biloxi, and Pascagoula, is separated from the Gulf of Mexico proper by the shallow Mississippi Sound, which is partially enclosed by Petit Bois, Horn, Ship, and Cat islands. The Mississippi Alluvial Plain, known also as the Delta, is narrow in the S and widens N of Vicksburg. The region has rich soil, partly made up of silt deposited by floodwaters of the Mississippi R.

Rivers and Lakes. The most important river of the state is the Mississippi; its chief tributaries in the state are the Yazoo and Big Black rivers. Much of central and E Mississippi is drained by streams flowing S to the Gulf of Mexico. These include the Pearl, Pascagoula, and Tombigbee rivers.

Mississippi has many lakes, the largest of which have been created by dams on rivers. Among such bodies of water are Ross Barnett Reservoir, on the Pearl R.; Arkabutla Lake, on the Coldwater R.; Grenada Lake, on the Yalobusha R.; and Pickwick Lake, on the Tennessee R. In addition, changes in the course of the Mississippi have resulted in the formation of numerous oxbow lakes, so named because of their shape. (Oxbow lakes are formed when a river cuts through the neck of one of its loops, or meanders, thus establishing a shorter course and leaving the former loop as a lake separate from the river.)

Climate. Mississippi has a warm, humid climate, with long summers and short, mild winters. Temperatures average about 28° C (about 82° F) in July and about 9° C (about 48° F) in January. The temperature varies little across the state in summer, but in winter the region near Mississippi Sound is significantly warmer than most of the rest of the state. The recorded temperature in Mississippi has ranged from –28.3° C (–19° F), in 1966 at Corinth in the NE, to 46.1°C (115° F), in 1930 at Holly Springs in the N. Yearly precipitation generally increases from N to S. Thus, Clarksdale, in the NW, gets about 1270 mm (about 50 in) of moisture annually and Biloxi, in the S, about 1550 mm (about 61 in). Small amounts of snow fall in N and central Mississippi. In the late summer and the fall, the state is occasionally struck by hurricanes moving N from the Gulf of Mexico. Mississippi is also struck by tornadoes, especially from February to May.

Plants and Animals. About 55% of the land area of Mississippi is covered with forests. In the N are such hardwoods as elm, hickory, and oak, as well as cedar, shortleaf pine, and tupelo. In the S are loblolly, longleaf, and slash pines. Other trees include live oak, magnolia, pecan, and sweet gum. Flowering plants in Mississippi include azalea, black-eyed Susan, camellia, dogwood, iris, Cherokee rose, trillium, and violet.

The white-tailed deer is the principal large animal of Mississippi. Other mammals found in abundance include beaver, fox, opossum, rabbit, skunk, and squirrel. Among the state's game birds are duck, quail, and wild turkey. In the winter, migrating duck, egret, heron, and tern nest on Horn and Petit Bois islands. Freshwater fish include black bass, bream, catfish, croaker, and perch; crabs, oysters, shrimp, Spanish mackerel, menhaden, and tarpon inhabit marine waters.

Mineral Resources. Mississippi has considerable deposits of petroleum and natural gas. Other mineral resources include clay, sand and gravel, lignite, iron ore, limestone, and salt.   T.J.L.

POPULATION

According to the 1990 census, Mississippi had 2,573,216 inhabitants, an increase of 2.1% over 1980. The average population density was 21 persons per sq km (53 per sq mi) in 1990. Whites made up 63.5% of the population; blacks represented 35.6%, a higher proportion than in any other state. Other groups included 8435 American Indians, 3815 persons of Vietnamese ancestry, 2518 persons of Chinese origin, and 1872 Asian Indians. Some 15,900 Mississippians claimed Hispanic ancestry. Baptists formed by far the largest single religious group in the state (55%), followed by Methodists (11.4%), Roman Catholics (7%), and Pentecostals (3.9%). Mississippi is one of the least urbanized states in the nation; in 1990 about 47% of all Mississipians lived in areas defined as urban, and the rest lived in rural areas. The largest cities were Jackson, the capital; Biloxi; Greenville; Hattiesburg; Meridian; and Gulfport.

EDUCATION AND CULTURAL ACTIVITY

Mississippi has interesting historical sites, such as fine antebellum homes and American Civil War battlefields. A number of prominent museums and educational institutions are here as well.

Education. Until the Civil War era, Mississippi had only a small number of schools and no educational institutions for blacks. The first school for blacks was established in 1862, and a system of public education was started in 1870, but as late as the early 20th century there were few schools in rural areas. Blacks and whites attended separate public schools in Mississippi until the 1960s, when they began to be integrated following a 1954 U.S. Supreme Court ruling that racially segregated public schools were unconstitutional. In the late 1980s the state had 954 public elementary and secondary schools, with a total

Many old plantation houses, such as Devereux in Natchez, survive from pre-Civil War days, when Natchez was the richest city in the southern cotton empire.

Gene Ahrens-Bruce Coleman, Inc.

MISSISSIPPI

yearly enrollment of about 369,500 elementary pupils and about 132,500 secondary students. Some 45,700 students attended private schools.

In the same period Mississippi had 47 institutions of higher learning, with a total annual enrollment of some 116,400 students. The state's oldest college or university is Mississippi College, at Clinton, founded in 1826. Others include the University of Mississippi, at University; Mississippi State University (1878), at Mississippi State; Mississippi University for Women (1884), at Columbus; Jackson State University (1877) and Millsaps College (1890), at Jackson; the University of Southern Mississippi (1910) and William Carey College (1906), at Hattiesburg; Delta State University (1924), at Cleveland; and Tougaloo College (1869), at Tougaloo.

Cultural Institutions. Some of Mississippi's leading museums are in Jackson. These include the Mississippi State Historical Museum, housed in the Old Capitol; the Mississippi Museum of Art; the Mississippi Museum of Natural Science; and the Mississippi Crafts Center. Among the other museums in the state are the Delta Blues Museum, at Clarksdale, with diverse holdings on the noted blues music of the Delta region; the Lauren Rogers Library and Museum of Art, at Laurel; the Meridian Museum of Art; the Cobb Institute of Archaeology, at Mississippi State; and the Old Spanish Fort and Museum, in Pascagoula, with displays on Indian cultures, military history, and other topics. Major research libraries include the library of the State Department of Archives and History and the State Law Library, both at Jackson, and the University of Mississippi Library. Performing-arts organizations include the Jackson Symphony Orchestra, Opera South, and the Mississippi Opera, all in Jackson.

Historical Sites. Several historical landmarks in Mississippi commemorate the Civil War period. These include homes of the Confederate president Jefferson Davis near Biloxi and near Woodville; Fort Massachusetts, on Ship Island, used by Union forces as a prison during the war; and Brices Cross Roads National Battlefield Site, Tupelo National Battlefield, and Vicksburg National Military Park, all encompassing battle sites. Other landmarks are the Old Capitol, at Jackson, and fine antebellum houses in and near Natchez, Vicksburg, Columbus, Holly Springs, West Point, Oxford, and other communities. William Faulkner's house, Rowan Oak, is in Oxford.

Sports and Recreation. Mississippi's coast and its inland rivers and lakes provide ample opportunities for fishing, swimming, and boating. Hunting also is a popular outdoor activity. Football is a favorite sport, and the University of Mississippi often fields excellent teams.

Communications. In the early 1990s, Mississippi had 112 AM radio stations, 123 FM radiobroadcasters, and 27 television stations. The state's first radio station was WFOR in Hattiesburg, which began broadcasting in 1925, and its first television station was WJTV in Jackson, which began operations in 1953. In the early 1990s, the state had 22 daily newspapers with a combined daily circulation of about 403,200. Influential dailies included the *Hattiesburg American*, the *Clarion-Ledger* of Jackson, the *Meridian Star*, the *Mississippi Press* of Pascagoula, and the *Northeast Mississippi Daily Journal* of Tupelo. The state's first newspaper, the *Mississippi Gazette,* was started at Natchez in 1799.

GOVERNMENT AND POLITICS

Mississippi is governed under a constitution of 1890, as amended. Previous constitutions had been adopted in 1817, 1832, and 1869. Constitutional amendments may be proposed by a two-thirds majority of the legislature. To become effective, an amendment must be approved by a majority of persons voting on the issue in a general election.

Executive. The chief executive of Mississippi is the governor, who is elected to a 4-year term and may not serve two successive terms. In case of death, removal from office, or incapacity to serve, the governor is succeeded by the lieutenant governor, who is also elected to a 4-year term. Other elected executive officials include the secretary of state, the treasurer, the auditor of public accounts, the attorney general, the commissioner of agriculture and commerce, and the commissioner of insurance.

Legislature. The Mississippi legislature consists of a 52-member senate and a 122-member house of representatives. All legislators are elected to 4-year terms.

Judiciary. Mississippi's highest court, the supreme court, has nine justices popularly elected to 8-year terms. The justice with seniority of service becomes chief justice for the remainder of his or her term. The major trial courts are chancery and circuit courts, with a total of 79 judges popularly elected to 4-year terms. Chancery courts hear civil cases, and circuit courts try both civil and criminal cases. Other tribunals include county, municipal, justice, and family courts.

Local Government. Mississippi is divided into 82 counties, each of which is administered by an elected five-member board of supervisors. The state also has a total of more than 290 cities and towns.

MISSISSIPPI

Mississippi: Map Index

Counties

Adams	A4
Alcorn	D1
Amite	B4
Attala	C2
Benton	C1
Bolivar	B2
Calhoun	C2
Carroll	C2
Chickasaw	D2
Choctaw	C2
Claiborne	B4
Clarke	D3
Clay	D2
Coahoma	B1
Copiah	B4
Covington	C4
De Soto	B1
Forrest	C4
Franklin	B4
George	D5
Greene	D4
Grenada	C2
Hancock	C5
Harrison	C5
Hinds	B3
Holmes	B2
Humphreys	B2
Issaquena	B3
Itawamba	D1
Jackson	D5
Jasper	C4
Jefferson	B4
Jefferson Davis	C4
Jones	C4
Kemper	D3
Lafayette	C1
Lamar	C4
Lauderdale	D3
Lawrence	B4
Leake	C3
Lee	D1
Leflore	B2
Lincoln	B4
Lowndes	D2
Madison	C3
Marion	C4
Marshall	C1
Monroe	D2
Montgomery	C2
Neshoba	C3
Newton	C3
Noxubee	D2
Oktibbeha	D2
Panola	C1
Pearl River	C5
Perry	D4
Pike	B4
Pontotoc	C1
Prentiss	D1
Quitman	B1
Rankin	C3
Scott	C3
Sharkey	B3
Simpson	C4
Smith	C4
Stone	C5
Sunflower	B2
Tallahatchie	B2
Tate	C1
Tippah	D1
Tishomingo	D1
Tunica	B1
Union	C1
Walthall	B4
Warren	B3
Washington	B2
Wayne	D4
Webster	C2
Wilkinson	A4
Winston	C2
Yalobusha	C1
Yazoo	B3

Cities and Towns

Abbeville	C1
Aberdeen	D2
Ackerman	C2
Algoma	C1
Alligator	B1
Amory	D2
Anguilla	B3
Arcola	B2
Artesia	D2
Ashland	C1
Baldwyn	D1
Bassfield	C4
Batesville	C1
Bay St. Louis	C5
Bay Springs	C4
Beaumont	D4
Beauregard	B4
Belmont	D1
Belzoni	B2
Benoit	B2
Bentonia	B3
Beulah	B2
Biloxi	D5
Blue Mountain	C1
Blue Springs	D1
Booneville	D1
Boyle	B2
Brandon	C3
Braxton	C3
Brookhaven	B4
Brooksville	D2
Bruce	C2
Bude	B4
Burnsville	D1
Byhalia	C1
Caledonia	D2
Calhoun City	C2
Canton	B3
Carrollton	C2
Carthage	C3
Cary	B3
Centreville	A4
Charleston	B1
Chunky	D3
Clarksdale	B1
Cleveland	B2
Clinton	B3
Coahoma	B1
Coffeeville	C2
Coldwater	C1
Collins	C4
Collinsville	D3
Columbia	C4
Columbus	D2
Como	C1
Conehatta	C3
Corinth	D1
Crawford	D2
Crenshaw	B1
Crosby	A4
Crowder	B1
Cruger	B2
Crystal Springs	B4
Decatur	C3
De Kalb	D3
Derma	C2
Diamondhead	C5
D'Iberville	D5
D'Lo	C4
Doddsville	B2
Drew	B2
Duck Hill	C2
Dumas	D1
Duncan	B1
Durant	C2
Ecru	C1
Eden	B3
Edwards	B3
Ellisville	C4
Enterprise	D3
Ethel	C2
Eupora	C2
Falcon	B1
Falkner	D1
Fayette	A4
Flora	B3
Florence	B3
Forest	C3
French Camp	C2
Friars Point	B1
Fulton	D1
Gautier	D5
Georgetown	B4
Glendora	B2
Gloster	A4
Golden	D1
Goodman	C3
Greenville	A2
Greenwood	B2
Grenada	C2
Gulfport	C5
Gunnison	B2
Guntown	D1
Hatley	D2
Hattiesburg	C4
Hazlehurst	B4
Heidelberg	D4
Hernando	C1
Hickory	C3
Hickory Flat	C1
Hollandale	B2
Holly Springs	C1
Horn Lake	B1
Houston	D2
Indianola	B2
Inverness	B2
Isola	B2
Itta Bena	B2
Iuka	D1
Jackson, *capital*	B3
Jonestown	B1
Jumpertown	D1
Kilmichael	C2
Kiln	C5
Kosciusko	C2
Kossuth	D1
Lake	C3
Lambert	B1
Laurel	C4
Leakesville	D4
Learned	B3
Leland	B2
Lena	C3
Lexington	B2
Liberty	B4
Long Beach	C5
Louin	C3
Louise	B3
Louisville	C2
Lucedale	D5
Lula	B1

387

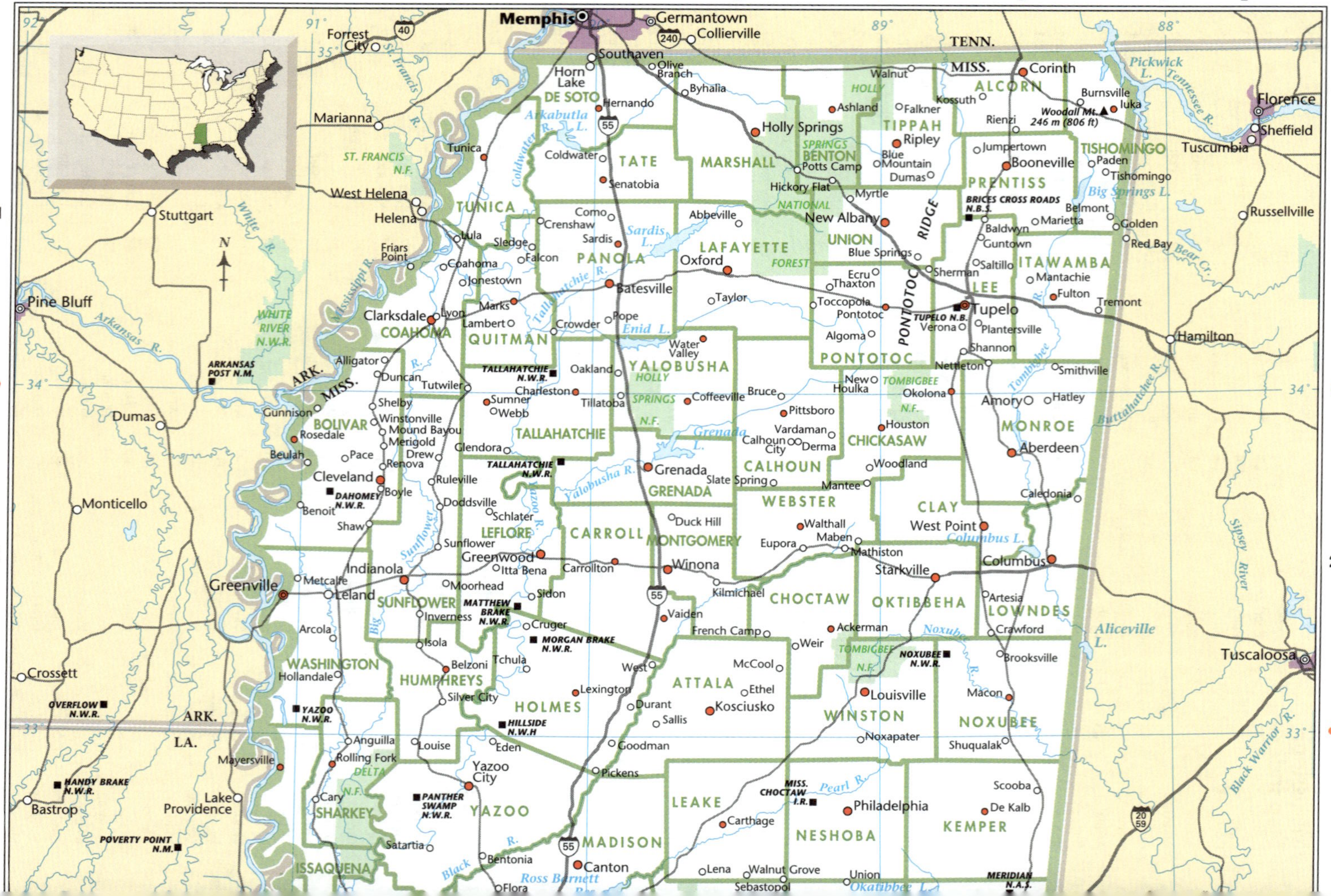

A
B
C
D
E
1
2
TENN.
MISS.
ARK.
LA.
Memphis
Germantown
Collierville
240
Olive Branch
Byhalia
Southaven
Horn Lake
Hernando
55
DE SOTO
Arkabutla L.
Coldwater R.
Coldwater
TATE
Senatobia
MARSHALL
Holly Springs
Potts Camp
Hickory Flat
HOLLY SPRINGS NATIONAL FOREST
BENTON
Ashland
Walnut
Falkner
TIPPAH
Ripley
Blue Mountain
Dumas
ALCORN
Corinth
Kossuth
Rienzi
Jumpertown
Booneville
PRENTISS
BRICES CROSS ROADS N.B.S.
Marietta
Baldwyn
Guntown
Saltillo
Burnsville
Iuka
Woodall Mt. 246 m (806 ft)
TISHOMINGO
Paden
Tishomingo
Belmont
Golden
Red Bay
Bear Cr.
Big Springs L.
Pickwick L.
Tennessee R.
Florence
Sheffield
Tuscumbia
Russellville
Hamilton
Buttahatchee R.
ITAWAMBA
Mantachie
Fulton
Tremont
Smithville
LEE
Tupelo
TUPELO N.B.
Plantersville
Verona
Shannon
Sherman
Nettleton
PONTOTOC RIDGE
PONTOTOC
Pontotoc
Ecru
Thaxton
Toccopola
Algoma
UNION
New Albany
Myrtle
Blue Springs
LAFAYETTE
Oxford
Abbeville
Taylor
PANOLA
Sardis L.
Sardis
Como
Crenshaw
Batesville
Pope
Enid L.
Crowder
Tallahatchie R.
YALOBUSHA
Water Valley
Coffeeville
Oakland
Tillatoba
TALLAHATCHIE
Charleston
Sumner
Webb
Glendora
TALLAHATCHIE N.W.R.
QUITMAN
Marks
Lambert
Lyon
TUNICA
Tunica
Dundee
Sledge
Falcon
Jonestown
Coahoma
Friars Point
Clarksdale
COAHOMA
Tutwiler
Duncan
Alligator
Shelby
Winstonville
Mound Bayou
Merigold
Drew
Renova
Ruleville
Boyle
Cleveland
DAHOMEY N.W.R.
BOLIVAR
Pace
Shaw
Benoit
Rosedale
Gunnison
Beulah
Mississippi R.
Helena
West Helena
Marianna
ST. FRANCIS N.F.
St. Francis R.
Forrest City
40
White R.
WHITE RIVER N.W.R.
ARKANSAS POST N.M.
Stuttgart
Arkansas R.
Pine Bluff
Dumas
Monticello
Crossett
OVERFLOW N.W.R.
HANDY BRAKE N.W.R.
Bastrop
POVERTY POINT N.M.
Lake Providence
Mayersville
Greenville
Metcalfe
Leland
WASHINGTON
Hollandale
Arcola
YAZOO N.W.R.
Indianola
SUNFLOWER
Sunflower
Inverness
Isola
Moorhead
MATTHEW BRAKE N.W.R.
Belzoni
HUMPHREYS
Silver City
Louise
Anguilla
Rolling Fork
DELTA N.F.
SHARKEY
Cary
ISSAQUENA
Satartia
PANTHER SWAMP N.W.R.
Yazoo City
YAZOO
Bentonia
Flora
Eden
HOLMES
HILLSIDE N.W.H
Tchula
Cruger
MORGAN BRAKE N.W.R.
Lexington
Durant
Goodman
Pickens
West
MADISON
Canton
Ross Barnett
LEFLORE
Greenwood
Itta Bena
Schlater
Sidon
Doddsville
Carrollton
CARROLL
Vaiden
Winona
MONTGOMERY
Kilmichael
Duck Hill
GRENADA
Grenada
Grenada L.
Slate Spring
Yalobusha R.
CALHOUN
Calhoun City
Bruce
Vardaman
Derma
Pittsboro
New Houlka
CHICKASAW
Houston
Okolona
TOMBIGBEE N.F.
Woodland
Mantee
WEBSTER
Walthall
Maben
Eupora
Mathiston
CLAY
West Point
Starkville
OKTIBBEHA
Columbus
Columbus L.
LOWNDES
Artesia
Crawford
MONROE
Aberdeen
Amory
Hatley
Caledonia
Tombigbee R.
CHOCTAW
Ackerman
Weir
French Camp
ATTALA
McCool
Ethel
Kosciusko
Sallis
WINSTON
Louisville
Noxapater
NOXUBEE N.W.R.
Noxubee R.
NOXUBEE
Macon
Brooksville
Shuqualak
KEMPER
Scooba
De Kalb
MERIDIAN N.A.S.
NESHOBA
Philadelphia
Union
MISS. CHOCTAW I.R.
Pearl R.
LEAKE
Carthage
Walnut Grove
Sebastopol
Lena
Okatibbee L.
Aliceville L.
Sipsey River
Tuscaloosa
Black Warrior R.
20 59
88°
89°
91°
92°
33°
34°
35°
N

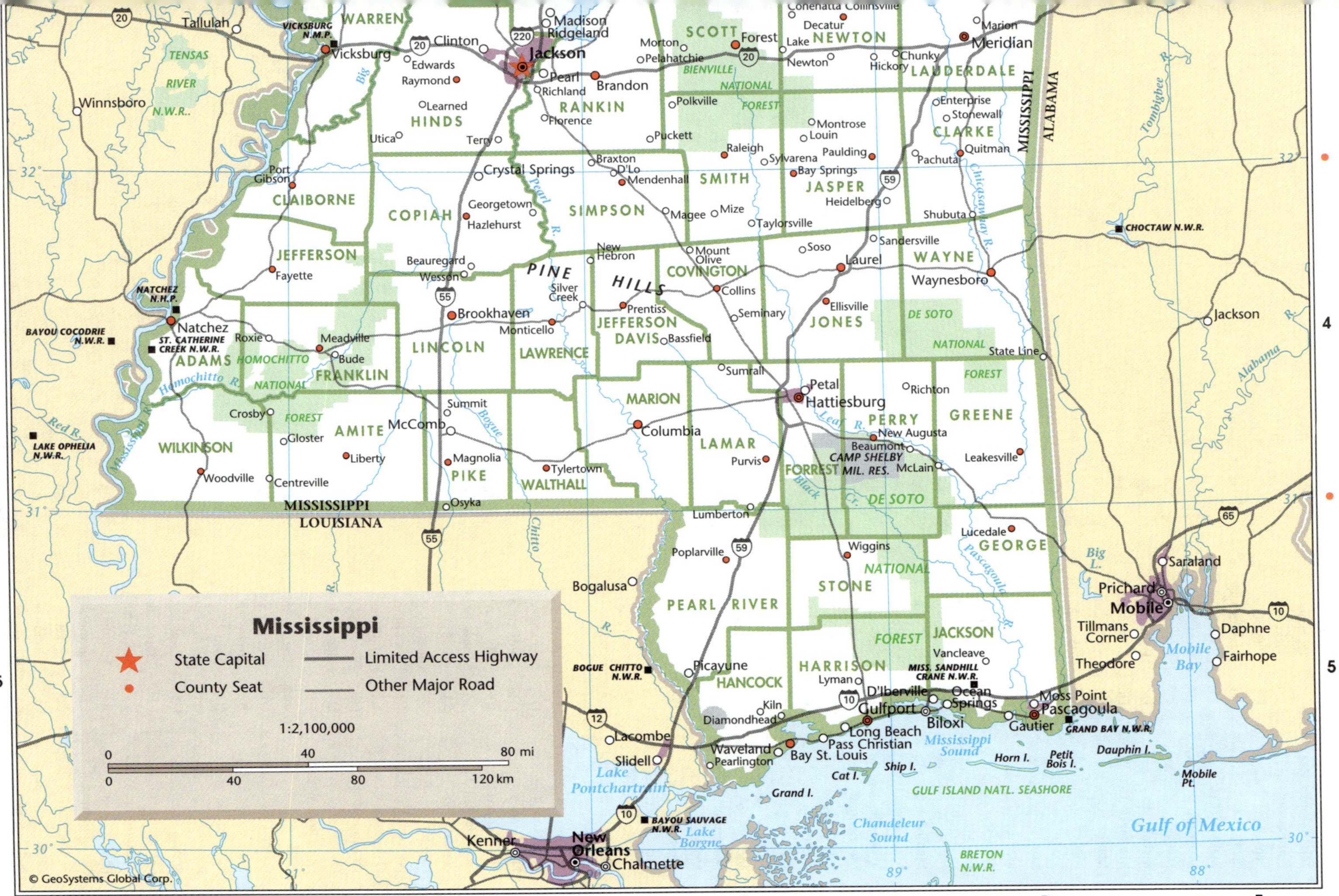
Mississippi
State Capital
County Seat
Limited Access Highway
Other Major Road
1:2,100,000
0 40 80 mi
0 40 80 120 km
© GeoSystems Global Corp.
Jackson
Vicksburg
Natchez
Hattiesburg
Meridian
Gulfport
Biloxi
Mobile
New Orleans
Gulf of Mexico
MISSISSIPPI
ALABAMA
LOUISIANA
WARREN
HINDS
RANKIN
SCOTT
NEWTON
LAUDERDALE
CLAIBORNE
COPIAH
SIMPSON
SMITH
JASPER
CLARKE
JEFFERSON
WAYNE
COVINGTON
JONES
ADAMS
FRANKLIN
LINCOLN
LAWRENCE
JEFFERSON DAVIS
MARION
LAMAR
FORREST
PERRY
GREENE
WILKINSON
AMITE
PIKE
WALTHALL
PEARL RIVER
STONE
GEORGE
HANCOCK
HARRISON
JACKSON
PINE HILLS
BIENVILLE NATIONAL FOREST
HOMOCHITTO NATIONAL FOREST
DE SOTO NATIONAL FOREST
CAMP SHELBY MIL. RES.
GULF ISLAND NATL. SEASHORE
Mississippi Sound
Chandeleur Sound
Lake Pontchartrain
Lake Borgne
Mobile Bay
A B C D E
4 5

MISSISSIPPI

Mississippi: Map Index

Lumberton	C4
Lyman	C5
Lyon	B1
Maben	C2
McComb	B4
McCool	C2
McLain	D4
Macon	D2
Madison	B3
Magee	C4
Magnolia	B4
Mantachie	D1
Mantee	C2
Marietta	D1
Marion	D3
Marks	B1
Mathiston	C2
Mayersville	A3
Meadville	B4
Mendenhall	C4
Meridian	D3
Merigold	B2
Metcalfe	B2
Mize	C4
Monticello	B4
Montrose	C3
Moorhead	B2
Morton	C3
Moss Point	D5
Mound Bayou	B2
Mount Olive	C4
Myrtle	C1
Natchez	A4
Nettleton	D1
New Albany	D1
New Augusta	C4
New Hebron	C4
New Houlka	C1
Newton	C3
Noxapater	C3
Oakland	C1
Ocean Springs	D5
Okolona	D1
Olive Branch	C1
Osyka	B4
Oxford	C1
Pace	B2
Pachuta	D3
Paden	D1
Pascagoula	D5
Pass Christian	C5
Paulding	C3
Pearl	B3
Pearlington	C5
Pelahatchie	C3
Petal	C4
Philadelphia	C3

Picayune	C5
Pickens	C3
Pittsboro	C2
Plantersville	D1
Polkville	C3
Pontotoc	D1
Pope	C1
Poplarville	C5
Port Gibson	B4
Potts Camp	C1
Prentiss	C4
Puckett	C3
Purvis	C4
Quitman	D3
Raleigh	C3
Raymond	B3
Renova	B2
Richland	B3
Richton	D4
Ridgeland	B3
Rienzi	D1
Ripley	D1
Rolling Fork	B3
Rosedale	A2
Roxie	A4
Ruleville	B2
Sallis	C2
Saltillo	D1
Sandersville	C4
Sardis	C1
Satartia	B3
Schlater	B2
Scooba	D3
Sebastopol	C3
Seminary	C4
Senatobia	C1
Shannon	D1
Shaw	B2
Shelby	B2
Sherman	D1
Shubuta	D4
Shuqualak	D3
Sidon	B2
Silver City	B2
Silver Creek	B4
Slate Spring	C2
Sledge	B1
Smithville	D1
Soso	C4
Southaven	B1
Starkville	D2
State Line	D4
Stonewall	D3
Summit	B4
Sumner	B2
Sumrall	C4
Sunflower	B2
Sylvarena	C3

Taylor	C1
Taylorsville	C4
Tchula	B2
Terry	B3
Thaxton	C1
Tillatoba	C2
Tishomingo	D1
Toccopola	C1
Tremont	D1
Tunica	B1
Tupelo	D1
Tutwiler	B1
Tylertown	B4
Union	C3
Utica	B3
Vaiden	C2
Vancleave	D5
Vardaman	C2
Verona	D1
Vicksburg	B3
Walnut	D1
Walnut Grove	C3
Walthall	C2
Water Valley	C1
Waveland	C5
Waynesboro	D4
Webb	B2
Weir	C2
Wesson	B4
West	C2
West Point	D2
Wiggins	C3
Winona	C2
Winstonville	B2
Woodland	C2
Woodville	A4
Yazoo City	B3

Other Features

Arkabatula, *lake*	B1
Bear, *creek*	E1
Bienville Natl. Forest	C3
Big Black, *river*	B3
Big Springs, *lake*	D1
Big Sunflower, *river*	B2
Black, *creek*	C4
Bogue Chitto, *river*	B4
Brices Cross Roads Natl. Battlefield Site	D1
Buttahatchee, *river*	D2
Camp Shelby Mil. Res.	C4
Cat, *island*	C5
Chickasawhay, *river*	D4
Coldwater, *river*	B1
Columbus, *lake*	D2
Dahomey Natl. Wildlife Refuge	B2
Delta Natl. Forest	B3
De Soto Natl. Forest	D4
Enid, *lake*	C1
Grand Bay Natl. Wildlife Refuge	D5
Grenada, *lake*	C2
Gulf Island Natl. Seashore	D5
Hillside Natl. Wildlife Refuge	B2
Holly Springs Natl. Forest	C1
Homochitto, *river*	A4
Homochitto Natl. Forest	A4
Horn, *island*	D5
Leaf, *river*	C4
Matthew Brake Natl. Wildlife Refuge	B2
Meridian Naval Air Station	D3
Mississippi Choctaw Indian Res.	C3
Mississippi Sandhill Crane Natl. Wildlife Refuge	D5
Mississippi, *river*	B1
Mississppi, *sound*	D5
Morgan Brake Natl. Wildlife Refuge	B2
Natchez Natl. Hist. Park	A4
Noxubee, *river*	D2
Noxubee Natl. Wildlife Refuge	D2
Okatibbee, *lake*	D3
Panther Swamp Natl. Wildlife Refuge	B3
Pascagoula, *river*	D5
Pearl, *river*	C3
Petit Bois, *island*	D5
Pickwick, *lake*	D1
Pine, *hills*	B4
Pontotoc, *mt. ridge*	D1
Ross Barnett, *reservoir*	C3
St. Catherine Creek Natl. Wildlife Refuge	A4
Sardis, *lake*	C1
Ship, *island*	D5
Tallahatchie, *river*	B1
Tallahatchie Natl. Wildlife Refuge	B1, B2
Tombigbee, *river*	D1
Tombigbee Natl. Forest	C2, D1
Tupelo Natl. Battlefield	D1
Vicksburg Natl. Mil. Park	B3
Woodall, *mt*	D1
Yazoo, *river*	B2
Yazoo Natl. Wildlife Refuge	B2

National Representation. Mississippi elects five representatives and two senators to the U.S. Congress. The state has seven electoral votes in presidential elections.

Politics. In presidential contests Mississippi cast its electoral votes for the Democratic nominee in all elections from 1876 to 1944. Third-party candidates were successful in 1948, 1960, and 1968 in elections in which racial issues were predominant; since then, the state has usually voted for the Republican presidential nominee. The Democratic party virtually dominated state and local politics in Mississippi for more than a century; in 1978, however, Thad Cochran (1937–) became the first Mississippi Republican since the Reconstruction period to win election to the U.S. Senate.

ECONOMY

For many years cotton dominated the Mississippi economy. Beginning in the 1930s, however, various federal programs, and damage to the cotton crop by insects called boll weevils, encouraged farmers to diversify. They began to produce large amounts of commodities, such as soybeans, and crops utilized for livestock feed. Major growth in manufacturing began with the introduction of the state's Balance Agriculture with Industry program during the mid-1930s. In the early 1990s, services and manufacturing provided more jobs and income than any other economic activity in Mississippi.

Agriculture. Farm income is about $2.4 billion annually, representing about 3% of the annual gross state product in Mississippi. The state has approximately 38,000 farms, which average 136 ha (337 acres) in size.

Crops provide about 46% of Mississippi's annual farm income. Mississippi typically ranks third among the 50 states in producing cotton, the state's most valuable crop. The second most important crop is soybeans. Most of the soybeans and cotton are produced in the Mississippi Alluvial Plain region. Other major crops include rice, hay, wheat, corn, sweet potatoes, and pecans. Livestock and livestock products provide about 54% of Mississippi's yearly farm income. Chickens and beef cattle are the state's most valuable livestock. Mississippi usually ranks among the top five states in marketing broilers, and it also produces large numbers of hogs and chicken eggs as well as substantial amounts of dairy products.

Forestry. Forests cover more than half of Mississippi; the heaviest concentration of forest is in the pinelands of the SE. Mississippi typically ranks among the ten leading U.S. states in the value of forestry production. Forest products include pine and hardwood lumber as well as pulpwood for use in paper mills.

Fishing. Mississippi's annual commercial fish catch is valued at about $44 million. Menhaden and shrimp dominate the yearly marine harvest. Most of the saltwater catch is landed at Pascagoula–Moss Point, which ranks among the nation's leading fishing ports by volume and by value of the catch. Biloxi is the state's chief shrimp port. Mississippi leads all states in the production of freshwater catfish on farms, which yield an annual income of more than $45 million. Catfish farming is centered in Humphreys Co.

Mining. Mining in Mississippi contributes about 2% of the annual gross state product in Mississippi. Petroleum and natural gas, which come mainly from the S half of the state, account for more than 85% of the value of mineral products. Other minerals produced include sand and gravel, clay, and cement.

Small boats line the shore near the lighthouse in Biloxi, on Mississippi's Gulf coast.   Franke Keaton

MISSISSIPPI

DATE OF STATEHOOD: December 10, 1817; 20th state

CAPITAL:	Jackson
MOTTO:	*Virtute et armis* (By valor and arms)
NICKNAME:	Magnolia State
STATE SONG:	"Go Mis-sis-sip-pi" (by Houston Davis)
STATE TREE:	Magnolia
STATE FLOWER:	Magnolia
STATE BIRD:	Mockingbird
POPULATION (1990):	2,573,216; 31st among the states
AREA:	125,443 sq km (48,434 sq mi); 32d largest state; includes 3937 sq km (1520 sq mi) of inland water
COASTLINE:	71 km (44 mi)
HIGHEST POINT:	Woodall Mt., 246 m (806 ft)
LOWEST POINT:	Sea level, at the Gulf coast
ELECTORAL VOTES:	7
U.S. CONGRESS:	2 senators; 5 representatives

POPULATION OF MISSISSIPPI SINCE 1800

Year of Census	Population	Classified As Urban
1800	8,000	0%
1830	137,000	2%
1860	791,000	3%
1880	1,132,000	3%
1900	1,551,000	8%
1920	1,791,000	13%
1940	2,184,000	20%
1960	2,178,000	38%
1980	2,521,000	47%
1990	2,573,216	47%

POPULATION OF TEN LARGEST CITIES

	1990 Census	1980 Census
Jackson	196,637	202,895
Biloxi	46,319	49,311
Greenville	45,226	40,613
Hattiesburg	41,882	40,829
Meridian	41,036	46,577
Gulfport	40,775	39,676
Tupelo	30,685	23,905
Pascagoula	25,899	29,318
Columbus	23,799	27,383
Clinton	21,847	14,660

CLIMATE

	JACKSON	MERIDIAN
Average January temperature range	2.2° to 14.4° C (36° to 58° F)	1.7° to 14.4° C (35° to 58° F)
Average July temperature range	21.7° to 33.9° C (71° to 93° F)	21.1° to 33.9° C (70° to 93° F)
Average annual temperature	18.3° C (65° F)	18.3° C (65° F)
Average annual precipitation	1245 mm (49 in)	1321 mm (52 in)
Average annual snowfall	20 mm (0.8 in)	33 mm (1.3 in)
Mean number of days per year with appreciable precipitation	113	103
Average daily relative humidity	75%	72%
Mean number of clear days per year	109	111

NATURAL REGIONS OF MISSISSIPPI: MISSISSIPPI ALLUVIAL PLAIN, EAST GULF COASTAL PLAIN

ECONOMY

State budget .... general revenue	$4.5 billion
general expenditure	$4.4 billion
accumulated debt	$1.3 billion
State and local taxes, per capita	$1264
Personal income, per capita	$9648
Population below poverty level..................	25.2%
Assets, insured commercial banks (123)	$20.1 billion
Labor force (civilian nonfarm)	921,000
Employed in manufacturing	26%
Employed in government	22%
Employed in wholesale and retail trade	21%
Employed in services	17%

	Quantity Produced	Value
FARM PRODUCTS		**$2.4 billion**
Crops.....................................		**$1.1 billion**
Cotton	403,000 metric tons	$576 million
Soybeans....	1.1 million metric tons	$239 million
Rice	630,000 metric tons	$101 million
Hay..........	939,000 metric tons	$54 million
Wheat	425,000 metric tons	$48 million
Livestock and Livestock Products........		**$1.3 billion**
Chickens (broilers) ..	768,000 metric tons	$533 million
Cattle........	174,000 metric tons	$304 million
Milk..........	337,000 metric tons	$113 million
Eggs..........	1.4 billion	$105 million
Hogs	29,000 metric tons..........	$37 million
MINERALS................................		**$794 million**
Petroleum....	28.5 million barrels	$484 million
Natural gas ..	2.9 billion cu m............	$202 million
Sand, gravel..	14.2 million metric tons	$52 million
Clays	899,000 metric tons	$24 million
FISHING	135,200 metric tons	**$44 million**

	Annual Payroll
FORESTRY................................	**$13 million**
MANUFACTURING	**$4.3 billion**
Transportation equipment................	$491 million
Apparel and textile mill products	$480 million
Furniture and fixtures.....................	$388 million
Electronic equipment	$379 million
Lumber and wood products	$377 million
Food and kindred products	$353 million
Industrial machinery and equipment......	$328 million
Fabricated metal products	$294 million
Paper and allied products.................	$289 million
Chemicals and allied products	$181 million
OTHER...................................	**$11.2 billion**
Government...............................	$4.0 billion
Services	$2.3 billion
Retail trade	$1.5 billion
Transportation, communications, and public utilities........................	$1.0 billion
Wholesale trade..........................	$817 million
Finance, insurance, and real estate	$785 million
Construction	$550 million

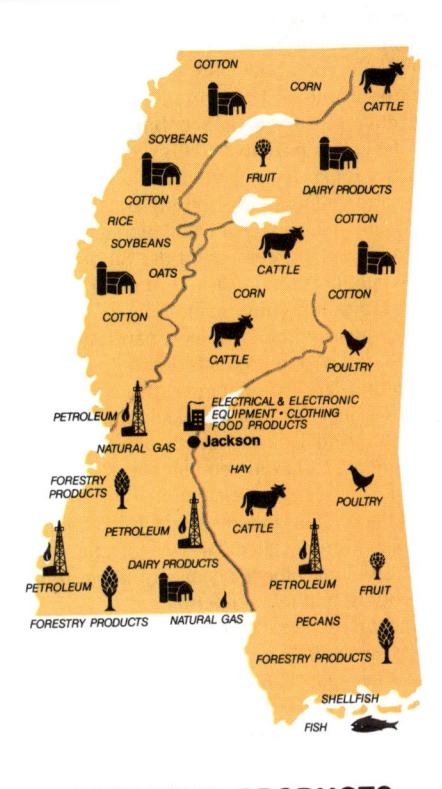

PRINCIPAL PRODUCTS OF MISSISSIPPI

ANNUAL GROSS STATE PRODUCT

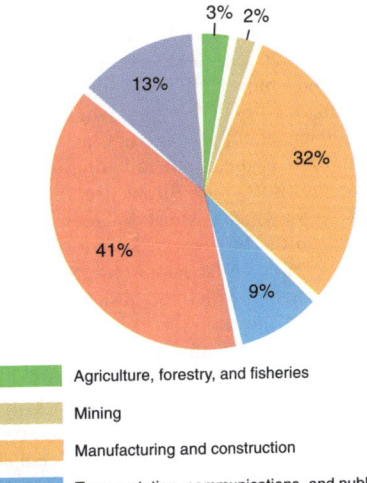

- 3% Agriculture, forestry, and fisheries
- 2% Mining
- 32% Manufacturing and construction
- 9% Transportation, communications, and public utilities
- 41% Commercial, financial, and professional services
- 13% Government

Sources: U.S. government publications

MISSISSIPPI

Manufacturing. Some 243,000 people in Mississippi are employed in manufacturing, which accounts for about 28% of the annual gross state product. The annual value added by manufacture exceeds $10 billion. Pascagoula is the state's principal industrial center. Among Mississippi's leading manufactures are transportation equipment; clothing and textiles; lumber, furniture, and other wood products; electronic goods; and processed foods. Shipbuilding at Pascagoula is the most important branch of the transportation-equipment industry. Aerospace equipment and motor-vehicle parts also are manufactured. Wood products, including household furniture, are manufactured in many cities, including Tupelo, Columbus, Jackson, and Natchez. Corinth and Jackson are the chief centers for producing electronic equipment. Meat packing, poultry processing, the manufacture of cheese, and the canning and freezing of fish are important food industries. Other major manufactures include industrial machinery, chemicals, fabricated metal products, and refined petroleum.

Tourism. Each year several million travelers come to Mississippi; the annual economic benefit to the state exceeds $1.6 billion. Many visitors motor along the Natchez Trace Parkway, encompassing a historic route connecting Natchez and Nashville, Tenn. Other National Park Service areas in the state are Brices Cross Roads National Battlefield Site (near Tupelo), Gulf Islands National Seashore, Tupelo National Battlefield, and Vicksburg National Military Park. The state maintains a system of 27 parks and recreation areas, including several major reservoirs.

Transportation. Jackson is the hub of a network of about 116,710 km (about 72,520 mi) of roads that serves all sections of Mississippi. Some 1100 km (some 685 mi) of interstate highways connect the major cities of the state, which also has about 2400 km (about 1490 mi) of Class I railroad track. Jackson is the main rail junction. Pascagoula, Gulfport, and Biloxi are important seaports on the Gulf of Mexico. Greenville and Vicksburg, on the Mississippi R., are the state's leading river ports. Mississippi has 29 heliports and 178 airports, of which the busiest is Jackson International Airport.

Energy. Electricity generating plants in Mississippi have a total installed capacity of about 7 million kw and produce some 22.9 billion kwh of electricity each year. In the early 1990s conventional thermal plants, powered mainly by coal and natural gas, produced about 65% of the electricity consumed in the state; the state's first nuclear plant began commercial operations in 1985. The Tennessee Valley Authority is the supplier of power for areas in the NE region of Mississippi.

M.C.B.

HISTORY

In 1539, Hernando De Soto, with a band of Spanish adventurers, crossed the northeastern part of the present state; in the early part of 1541 he reached the Mississippi River. In 1673 the French explorers Louis Jolliet and Jacques Marquette, passing down the Mississippi, sailed as far as the mouth of the Arkansas River. In 1681–82, Robert Cavelier, sieur de La Salle, sailed down the Mississippi to its mouth and, taking possession of the entire valley for Louis XIV, king of France, named the country Louisiana.

Early Settlements. The first attempt to found a colony was made in 1699 by Pierre Le Moyne, sieur d'Iberville, who brought 200 French immigrants to the site of present-day Biloxi. In 1716, Fort Rosalie was built on the present site of Natchez. Indian outbreaks, notably by the Natchez and Chickasaw tribes, made the frontier unsafe for white settlers. In 1763, after the British victory in the French and Indian War, France ceded to Great Britain its territories east of the Mississippi, except New Orleans; Great Britain also received Florida from Spain. The British divided these possessions into East Florida and West Florida, in the latter of which was included a portion of the present state of Mississippi. In 1781, however, during the American Revolution, Spain took military possession of the Floridas; two years later, by the Treaty of Paris, ending the war, Great Britain formally ceded the area to Spain. By the Treaty of 1795 between the U.S. and Spain, that part of the present state of Mississippi north of the 31st parallel was ceded to the U.S. In 1798 the Territory of Mississippi was formed. Between 1810 and 1813 the district south of the 31st parallel (West Florida) was taken from Spain by the U.S., on the ground that the area had originally been part of the Louisiana Purchase; it was annexed to the territory in 1813, and Mississippi was admitted to the Union as a state on Dec. 10, 1817.

Mississippi as a State. The first serious conflict in the state over the slavery question occurred in 1851, when a party advocating secession was defeated in an election by the Union party. Ten years later, on Jan. 9, 1861, Mississippi seceded from the Union. During the American Civil War much of the state was devastated. Early in 1870, Mississippi was readmitted to the Union. The 20 years following the war were a period of depression, but industrial advances of the late 19th century aided economic recovery.

Mississippi's lumber industry reached a peak in the early 1900s, while drainage programs converted vast swampy areas to agricultural use.

Major steps were taken to reduce adult illiteracy and to regulate child labor. In 1936, Mississippi's legislature passed special tax-incentive laws to help the state's Balancing Agriculture with Industry (BAWI) program, designed to attract new industries. A few years later, petroleum was discovered at Tinsley and Vaughan. Industrial development continued during World War II with the opening of war plants and increased activity at the port of Pascagoula. By 1963 an oil refinery had been completed there.

Mississippi resisted desegregation, and although its incidence of crime is traditionally low, the state experienced violent racial unrest in the 1960s. In 1963 Medgar Evers, a field secretary of the National Association for the Advancement of Colored People, was killed in Jackson, and a year later three civil rights workers were murdered near Philadelphia, Miss. Nevertheless, progress was made in several civil rights areas. In 1962 the University of Mississippi was integrated by federal marshals, and in 1967 the first black was elected to the state legislature.

During the 1980s the state government sought to stimulate economic growth and improve education and other social services. As Mississippi entered the 1990s, however, the state remained among the nation's poorest, although the legalization of gambling brought increased prosperity to cities such as Biloxi and Bay St. Louis.

For further information on this topic, see the Bibliography in volume 28, sections 1183, 1190.

MISSISSIPPI (Algonquian *Misi sipi*, "big river"), river, central U.S., one of the longest rivers of North America. The Mississippi R. system is wholly within the U.S., excepting the headwaters of the Missouri River, the main Mississippi tributary, that extend into Canada. The Mississippi is exceeded in length by the Missouri and Mackenzie rivers, but it discharges a greater volume of water than any other river on the North American continent. It drains most of the territory between the Rocky and Allegheny mountains, an area of about 3,256,000 sq km (about 1,257,000 sq mi). In addition to the Missouri, the Mississippi is fed by the Red, Arkansas, and Ohio rivers and by about 250 other tributaries. The total length of the Mississippi is 3779 km (2348 mi), and the total navigable length of all the rivers in the system is about 25,900 km (about 16,100 mi).

The Mississippi rises in the area of Lake Itasca in NW Minnesota, about 512 m (about 1680 ft) above sea level. As it issues from Lake Itasca the Mississippi is about 3.7 m (about 12 ft) wide and

395

0.5 m (1.5 ft) deep. It flows NE and then turns S near Grand Rapids, Minn. At Minneapolis, where it drops 20 m (65 ft) over the Falls of Saint Anthony, the river is more than 305 m (1000 ft) wide. This point is the head of the river navigation. After receiving the waters of the Minnesota and Saint Croix rivers, the Mississippi becomes the boundary between the states of Minnesota, Iowa, Missouri, Arkansas, and Louisiana on the W, and Wisconsin, Illinois, Kentucky, Tennessee, and Mississippi on the E. On the Wisconsin boundary the river expands into Lake Pepin, and thereafter, fully 1.6 km (1 mi) wide, flows between bluffs 61 and 91 m (200 and 300 ft) high. Around obstructions to navigation at Rock Island, Ill., Keokuk, Iowa, and N of Saint Louis, Mo., the U.S. government has constructed dams and locks to accommodate the thousands of barges carrying bulk commodities up and down the river.

From the mouth of the Ohio R. the Mississippi is about 1370 m (about 4500 ft) wide, but as it approaches the Red R., it narrows to about 910 m (3000 ft), and at New Orleans, La., is 760 m (2500 ft) wide. The depth of the channel S from the Ohio is between 15 and 30 m (50 and 100 ft). A system of storage reservoirs near the headwaters of the Mississippi and a series of flood-control dams along the river and its tributaries help maintain a relatively even flow of water.

From the Missouri to the Gulf of Mexico, the Mississippi rolls in a serpentine course through vast alluvial tracts that vary in width from 64 to 113 km (40 to 70 mi). Although of great fertility, these lands have not been fully cultivated because of the dangers of flooding. Melting ice and snow in the upper basin swell the lower current from March to June. Levees or embankments now extend for more than 2575 km (1600 mi). Many of them were built by the federal government after the flood of 1927—the largest recorded up to that time—when the river reached a maximum height at Cairo, Ill., of 17.2 m (56.4 ft). Devastating floods above Cape Girardeau, Mo., extending as far north as Wisconsin, still occur every decade or so, most notably in 1937, 1965, 1973, 1983, and 1993. The floods inundate some river towns and cities, destroy millions of acres of crops, and halt commercial river traffic.

Below the Red R., the Mississippi flows through numerous bayous into the Gulf of Mexico. The main channel of the river runs SE and divides into a delta of several passes. The yearly discharge of the Mississippi into the gulf is nearly 600 cu km (about 145 cu mi) of water. The sediment carried is estimated at about 300 million cu m (about 10.6 billion cu ft). To overcome the silting caused by these vast deposits and the constant changes caused by floods, a system of jetties at the South Pass was built, beginning in 1875, and has proved successful in maintaining a depth exceeding 9 m (30 ft). The mouth of the Mississippi is essentially tideless.

The principal cities on the river are Minneapolis, Saint Paul, La Crosse, Dubuque, Davenport, Keokuk, Quincy, Hannibal, Saint Louis, Memphis, Vicksburg, Baton Rouge, and New Orleans. At several cities the river is crossed by bridges.

For further information on this topic, see the Bibliography in volume 28, sections 426, 1198.

MISSISSIPPI, UNIVERSITY OF, state-controlled institution of higher learning, in University, Miss., and chartered in 1844. The university was formally opened in 1848 and was closed from 1861 to 1865 during the American Civil War. Women have been admitted since 1882. The university includes divisions of liberal arts, law, education, engineering, pharmacy, medicine, nursing, business and management, graduate studies, health-related professions, and an extension division. The schools of medicine, nursing, health-related professions, and dentistry are in Jackson. The degrees of bachelor, master, and doctor are awarded.

MISSISSIPPIAN PERIOD, geological time period used only in North American geology. It is equivalent to the earlier part of the Carboniferous period (q.v.) recognized worldwide by geologists. *See also* GEOLOGY; PALEONTOLOGY.

MISSISSIPPI SCHEME. *See* LAW, JOHN.

MISSOLONGHI. *See* MESOLÓNGION.

MISSOULA, city, seat of Missoula Co., W Montana, on the Clark Fork of the Columbia R.; settled 1865, inc. 1885. It is a distribution and manufacturing center, situated near several national forests. Products include lumber, plywood, paper, and processed food. The University of Montana (1893) and a center for training forest-fire fighters are here; the Flathead Indian Reservation and resorts on Flathead Lake are nearby. Missoula grew after the coming of the railroad in 1883. The name Missoula is derived from a Flathead (Salish) Indian term meaning "by the cold, chilling waters." Pop. (1980) 33,388; (1990) 42,918.

MISSOURI, one of the West North Central states, bounded on the N by Iowa; on the E by Illinois, Kentucky, and Tennessee; on the S by Arkansas; and on the W by Oklahoma, Kansas, and Nebraska. The Mississippi R. forms most of the E boundary, and the Missouri R. forms the NW boundary.

Missouri entered the Union on Aug. 10, 1821, as the 24th state. Although it was a slaveholding state, Missouri remained part of the Union during the American Civil War. Traditionally depen-

MISSOURI

dent on agriculture, Missouri's economy in the 1990s was dominated by service industries and manufacturing, especially of aircraft and road motor vehicles. President Harry S. Truman was born in Missouri. The name of the state is taken from the Missouri R. and is an Algonquian name for a group that lived near the mouth of the river. Missouri is called the Show Me State.

LAND AND RESOURCES

Missouri, with an area of 180,546 sq km (69,709 sq mi), is the 21st largest state in the U.S.; 4.6% of the land area is owned by the federal government. The state is roughly rectangular in shape, and its extreme dimensions are about 460 km (about 285 mi) from N to S and about 490 km (about 305 mi) from E to W. Elevations range from 70 m (230 ft) along the Saint Francis R. in the SE to 540 m (1772 ft) atop Taum Sauk Mt. less than 160 km (less than 100 mi) to the N. The approximate mean elevation is 244 m (800 ft).

Physical Geography. The land surface of Missouri is more diverse than that of any other midwestern state. The largest physical region is the Ozark Plateau (sometimes called the Ozark Mts., or Ozarks), which occupies most of the S part of the state. It is formed of limestone and other sedimentary rocks that have been deeply dissected (eroded) by streams, particularly on the S and SE, where the rivers occupy deep gorges. Although the terrain appears hilly, the uplands between the river valleys are generally flat. The most rugged area of the Ozarks, the Saint Francois Mts. in the SE, are granitic formations that have been exposed on the surface as the less resistant surrounding rocks were eroded. The limestone bedrock of the Ozark Plateau dissolves easily, and many extensive caverns have been formed. From these underground caverns flow thousands of springs—Missouri ranks second to Idaho in the U.S. in its number of large springs. The soils of the Ozark Plateau are generally thin and stony. Along the W border of the state is the Osage Plains, a gently sloping region. Its soils are moderately fertile with a high humus content, having developed under grasslands.

North of the Missouri R. is the Dissected Till Plains region. The Ice Age glaciers deposited a deep layer of rich drift (silt and sand) hundreds of thousands of years ago. The surface was gradually eroded by streams to form a hilly terrain. The state's extreme SE portion is a part of the Mississippi Alluvial Plain; it consists of low, flat, poorly drained land, the surface of which consists of sand and gravel and silt. This region, once swampland, has been largely drained.

Rivers and Lakes. Missouri is drained by streams flowing generally E into the Mississippi R., either directly or through the Missouri R. The Missouri R. crosses the state from W to E and enters the Mississippi R. The principal tributaries of the Missouri R. are the Grand and Chariton rivers

The stainless steel Gateway Arch in St. Louis, designed by Eero Saarinen and completed in 1965. At 192 m (630 ft), this is the tallest monument in the U.S.
Robert Srenco–Shostal Associates

MISSOURI

from the N and the Osage and Gasconade from the Ozark Plateau to the S. The Meramec R. flows NE across the Ozarks directly into the Mississippi R. The S and E Ozarks are drained by the Current, Black, and St. Francis rivers, which flow S to join the Mississippi R. in Arkansas. No large natural lakes are found in Missouri. The Lake of the Ozarks, impounded on the Osage R., is the largest of several reservoirs. Other artificial bodies of water include Table Rock and Bull Shoals lakes and Lake Wappapello. Hundreds of miles of straightened stream channels and canals have been created in the Mississippi Alluvial Plain as part of a land reclamation project.

Climate. Missouri has a generally humid and moderate continental climate. Winters are cold and summers hot, but mild spells occur almost every winter, and periods of dry, cool weather break up stretches of heat and humidity in the peak of summer. The average annual temperature ranges from 12.2° C (54° F) in the N to 15.6° C (60° F) in the SE. The recorded temperature in the state has ranged from −40° C (−40° F) in 1905 to 47.8° C (118° F) in 1954. The average annual precipitation decreases with a general uniformity from a high of 1219 mm (48 in) in the SE to a low of 813 mm (32 in) on the N border. Rainfall is heaviest in the spring and summer. Tornadoes may strike anywhere in the state, especially in the spring months, but are less common than in states to the W. Annual snowfall ranges from 203 mm (8 in) in the SE to 508 mm (20 in) in the N, but snow rarely remains on the ground for more than a week.

Plants and Animals. About two-thirds of Missouri was once forested; the NW and W parts of the state were covered by prairie grasses. Today about 28% of the land area is forestland. Most of this is located in the Ozark Plateau and in the river valleys of the state. Oak and hickory trees predominate in a mixture of walnut, elm, and other hardwoods. Pine trees are found in the more rugged areas of the Ozarks and the St. Francois Mts. Cedar is a common invader on abandoned farmlands. In the wetter areas of the SE, oak, tupelo, elm, and cypress are the most prevalent trees. Wild flowers are found throughout the state and are especially abundant in the Ozarks. Wildlife includes white-tailed deer, coyote, fox, opossum, muskrat, raccoon, and beaver. Birdlife found in Missouri includes robin, thrush, oriole, and various owls and hawks. Bass, carp, crappie, perch, trout, and sunfish populate the state's streams.

Mineral Resources. Missouri contains significant reserves of coal in the N and W, although it is of relatively low quality. Lead and zinc are the most important metallic minerals, large deposits of which are found in the SE Ozark Plateau region. Iron-ore deposits are mined in the St. Francois Mts. region. Limestone is found throughout the state; other quarry products include marble and granite. Clay, sand and gravel, and silver are also important.

N.E.S.

POPULATION

According to the 1990 census, Missouri had 5,117,073 inhabitants, an increase of 4.1% over 1980. The average population density was 28 peo-

The home in Hannibal, Mo., of Mark Twain, whose novels immortalized life on the Mississippi River in this midwestern state.
Bob Glander–Shostal Associates

MISSOURI

Missouri: Map Index

Counties

Adair	D1
Andrew	B2
Atchison	A1
Audrain	D2
Barry	C5
Barton	B4
Bates	B3
Benton	C3
Bollinger	F4
Boone	D2
Buchanan	B2
Butler	F5
Caldwell	B2
Callaway	D3
Camden	D4
Cape Girardeau	G4
Carroll	C2
Carter	E5
Cass	B3
Cedar	B4
Chariton	C2
Christian	C5
Clark	E1
Clay	B2, J3
Clinton	B2
Cole	D3
Cooper	D3
Crawford	E4
Dade	C4
Dallas	C4
Daviess	C2
De Kalb	B2
Dent	E4
Douglas	D5
Dunklin	F5
Franklin	E3
Gasconade	E3
Gentry	B1
Greene	C4
Grundy	C1
Harrison	B1
Henry	C3
Hickory	C4
Holt	A1
Howard	D2
Howell	E5
Iron	F4
Jackson	B2, J4
Jasper	B4
Jefferson	F3, G3
Johnson	C3
Knox	D1
Laclede	D4
Lafayette	C2
Lawrence	B4
Lewis	E1
Lincoln	E2
Linn	C2
Livingston	C2
McDonald	B5
Macon	D2
Madison	F4
Maries	D3
Marion	E2
Mercer	C1
Miller	D3
Mississippi	G5
Moniteau	D3
Monroe	D2
Montgomery	E3
Morgan	C3
New Madrid	G5
Newton	B5
Nodaway	B1
Oregon	E5
Osage	D3
Ozark	D5
Pemiscot	G5
Perry	G4
Pettis	C3
Phelps	E4
Pike	E2
Platte	B2, H3
Polk	C4
Pulaski	D4
Putnam	C1
Ralls	E2
Randolph	D2
Ray	C2
Reynolds	E4
Ripley	F5
St. Charles	F3, G2
St. Clair	B3
Ste. Genevieve	F4
St. Francois	F4
St. Louis	F3, G2
Saline	C2
Schuyler	D1
Scotland	D1
Scott	G5
Shannon	E4
Shelby	D2
Stoddard	F5
Stone	C5
Sullivan	C1
Taney	C5
Texas	D4
Vernon	B4
Warren	E3
Washington	F3
Wayne	F4
Webster	C4
Worth	B1
Wright	D4

Cities and Towns

Adrian	B3
Advance	G4
Affton	H3
Albany	B1
Alton	E5
Anderson	B5
Appleton City	B3
Ash Grove	C4
Ashland	D3
Atherton	J4
Aurora	C5
Ava	D5
Barnett	D3
Belton	B3
Benton	G4
Bernie	G5
Bethany	B1
Birmingham	J4
Bloomfield	G5
Blue Springs	J4
Bolivar	C4
Bonne Terre	F4
Boonville	D3
Bourbon	E3
Bowling Green	E2
Branson	C5
Brentwood	H2
Bridgeton	H2
Brookfield	C2
Brunswick	C2
Buckner	J4
Buffalo	C4
Butler	B3
Cabool	D4
California	D3
Calverton Park	H2
Camdenton	D4
Cameron	B2
Campbell	F5
Canton	E1
Cape Girardeau	G4
Carrollton	C2
Carthage	B4
Caruthersville	G5
Cassville	C5
Cedar Hill	F3
Centerville	F4
Centralia	D2
Chaffee	G4
Charleston	G5
Chesterfield	F3
Chillicothe	C2
Clarence	D2
Claycomo	J4
Clayton	F3, H2
Clinton	C3
Cole Camp	C3
Columbia	D3
Concord	H3
Concordia	C3
Crane	C5
Crestwood	H3
Creve Coeur	H2
Crocker	D4
Cuba	E3
Dellwood	H2
Desloge	F4
De Soto	F3
Des Peres	G2
Dexter	G5
Dixon	D3
Doniphan	F5
East Prairie	G5
Edina	D1
Eldon	D3
El Dorado Springs	B4
Elsberry	F2
Eminence	E4
Eureka	F3
Excelsior Springs	B2, J3
Farley	H3
Farmington	F4
Fayette	D2
Fenton	G3
Ferguson	H2
Ferrelview	H3
Festus	F3
Florissant	H2
Forsyth	C5
Fredericktown	F4
Fulton	E3
Gainesville	D5
Galena	C5
Gallatin	C2
Garden City	B3
Gladstone	B2, J3
Glasgow	D2
Glasgow Village	H2
Glenaire	J3
Glendale	H3
Goodman	B5
Gower	B2
Grain Valley	J4
Granby	B5
Grandview	J4
Grant City	B1
Greendale	H2
Greenfield	C4
Greenville	F4
Hamilton	C2
Hannibal	E2
Harrisonville	B3
Hartville	D4
Hayti	G5
Hazelwood	H2
Hermann	E3
Hermitage	C4
Higginsville	C2

399

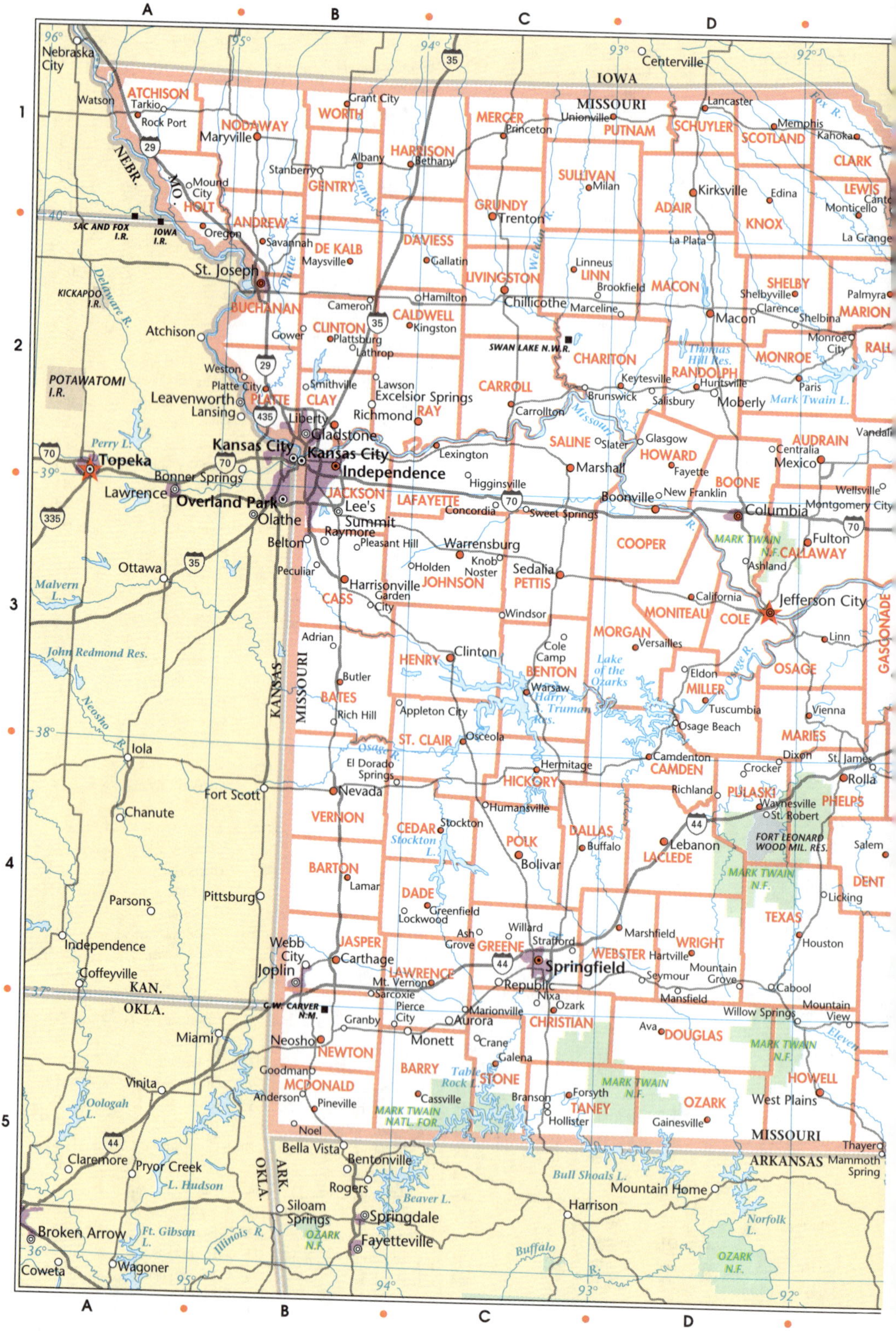

A
B
C
D
1
2
3
4
5
IOWA
MISSOURI
KANSAS
OKLA.
ARK.
KAN.
NEBR.
MO.
ARKANSAS
Nebraska City
Watson
Tarkio
Rock Port
ATCHISON
NODAWAY
Maryville
WORTH
Grant City
HARRISON
Bethany
Albany
Stanberry
GENTRY
Mound City
HOLT
ANDREW
Oregon
Savannah
SAC AND FOX I.R.
IOWA I.R.
KICKAPOO I.R.
POTAWATOMI I.R.
St. Joseph
BUCHANAN
DE KALB
Maysville
DAVIESS
Gallatin
Cameron
Hamilton
CLINTON
Plattsburg
Lathrop
CALDWELL
Kingston
Gower
Atchison
Weston
Platte City
PLATTE
Smithville
CLAY
Lawson
Excelsior Springs
Richmond
RAY
Liberty
Gladstone
Leavenworth
Lansing
Kansas City
Independence
Topeka
Perry L.
Lawrence
Bonner Springs
Overland Park
Olathe
JACKSON
Lee's Summit
LAFAYETTE
Lexington
Higginsville
Concordia
Sweet Springs
Raymore
Belton
Pleasant Hill
Warrensburg
Knob Noster
Holden
JOHNSON
Sedalia
PETTIS
Peculiar
Harrisonville
CASS
Garden City
Ottawa
Malvern L.
John Redmond Res.
Neosho R.
Delaware R.
Centerville
MERCER
Princeton
Unionville
PUTNAM
SCHUYLER
Lancaster
SCOTLAND
Memphis
Kahoka
CLARK
LEWIS
Canton
Monticello
La Grange
KNOX
Edina
ADAIR
Kirksville
SULLIVAN
Milan
GRUNDY
Trenton
LA Plata
LIVINGSTON
Chillicothe
Linneus
LINN
Brookfield
Marceline
MACON
Macon
SHELBY
Shelbyville
Clarence
Shelbina
Palmyra
MARION
MONROE
Monroe City
RALLS
SWAN LAKE N.W.R.
CHARITON
Thomas Hill Res.
RANDOLPH
Huntsville
Keytesville
Brunswick
Salisbury
Moberly
Paris
Mark Twain L.
CARROLL
Carrollton
Missouri R.
SALINE
Slater
Marshall
Glasgow
HOWARD
Fayette
New Franklin
Boonville
BOONE
Columbia
AUDRAIN
Centralia
Mexico
Vandalia
Wellsville
Montgomery City
Fulton
CALLAWAY
MARK TWAIN N.F.
Ashland
COOPER
California
MONITEAU
COLE
Jefferson City
GASCONADE
Linn
OSAGE
Osage R.
MORGAN
Versailles
Windsor
Cole Camp
BENTON
Lake of the Ozarks
Warsaw
Harry S. Truman Res.
Eldon
MILLER
Tuscumbia
Vienna
Osage Beach
MARIES
Camdenton
CAMDEN
Dixon
St. James
Rolla
Crocker
PULASKI
Richland
Waynesville
St. Robert
PHELPS
FORT LEONARD WOOD MIL. RES.
Salem
DENT
Licking
TEXAS
Houston
Cabool
Adrian
HENRY
Clinton
Butler
BATES
Rich Hill
Appleton City
ST. CLAIR
Osceola
Osage R.
El Dorado Springs
Nevada
VERNON
Hermitage
HICKORY
Humansville
CEDAR
Stockton
Stockton L.
POLK
Bolivar
DALLAS
Buffalo
Lebanon
LACLEDE
BARTON
Lamar
DADE
Greenfield
Lockwood
Ash Grove
Willard
Strafford
GREENE
Springfield
Marshfield
WEBSTER
WRIGHT
Hartville
Mountain Grove
Seymour
Mansfield
Republic
Nixa
Ozark
CHRISTIAN
JASPER
Carthage
Webb City
Joplin
LAWRENCE
Mt. Vernon
Sarcoxie
Pierce City
Aurora
Marionville
Monett
Granby
G.W. CARVER N.M.
Neosho
NEWTON
Crane
Galena
STONE
Table Rock L.
BARRY
Cassville
MARK TWAIN NATL. FOR.
Goodman
MCDONALD
Anderson
Pineville
Noel
Branson
Forsyth
TANEY
Hollister
Ava
DOUGLAS
OZARK
Gainesville
Willow Springs
Mountain View
Eleven Pt. R.
HOWELL
West Plains
Thayer
Mammoth Spring
Iola
Fort Scott
Chanute
Parsons
Pittsburg
Independence
Coffeyville
Miami
Vinita
Oologah L.
Claremore
Pryor Creek
L. Hudson
Broken Arrow
Coweta
Wagoner
Ft. Gibson L.
Illinois R.
Bella Vista
Bentonville
Rogers
Siloam Springs
Springdale
Fayetteville
Beaver L.
OZARK N.F.
Bull Shoals L.
Mountain Home
Harrison
Buffalo R.
Norfolk L.
96°
95°
94°
93°
92°
40°
39°
38°
37°
36°

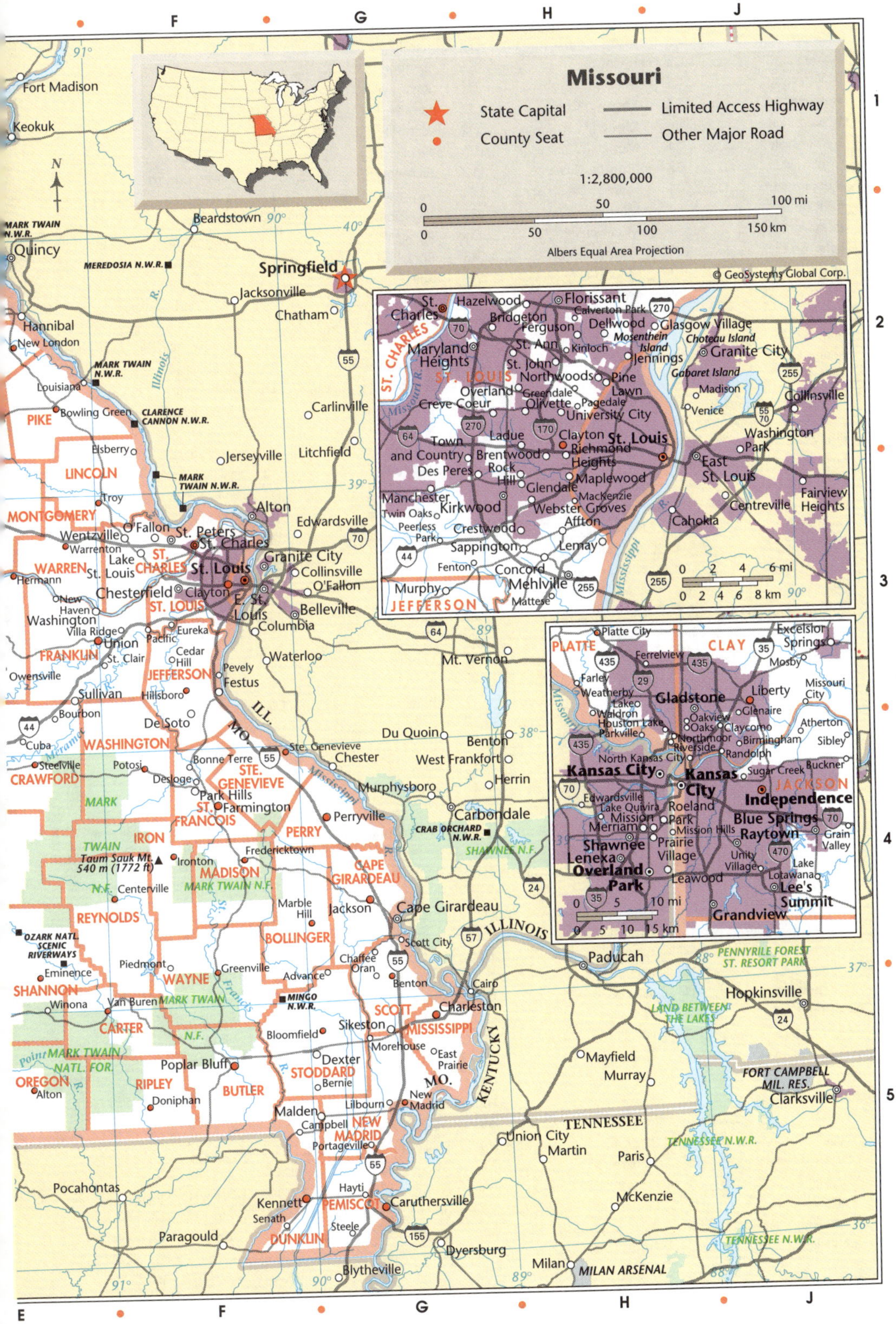

Missouri
State Capital
County Seat
Limited Access Highway
Other Major Road
1:2,800,000
0
50
100 mi
0
50
100
150 km
Albers Equal Area Projection
© GeoSystems Global Corp.
F
G
H
J
E
1
2
3
4
5
N
Fort Madison
Keokuk
MARK TWAIN N.W.R.
Quincy
MEREDOSIA N.W.R.
Beardstown
Springfield
Jacksonville
Chatham
Hannibal
New London
Louisiana
Bowling Green
CLARENCE CANNON N.W.R.
PIKE
Elsberry
LINCOLN
Troy
MONTGOMERY
Carlinville
Jerseyville
Litchfield
Alton
Edwardsville
O'Fallon
St. Peters
St. Charles
Wentzville
Warrenton
WARREN
Hermann
Lake St. Louis
ST. CHARLES
St. Louis
Chesterfield
Clayton
Granite City
Collinsville
O'Fallon
Belleville
E. St. Louis
New Haven
Washington
ST. LOUIS
Villa Ridge
Eureka
Columbia
Union
Pacific
FRANKLIN
St. Clair
Cedar Hill
JEFFERSON
Owensville
Waterloo
Pevely
Festus
Mt. Vernon
Sullivan
Bourbon
Hillsboro
De Soto
ILL.
MO.
Cuba
WASHINGTON
Steelville
CRAWFORD
Potosi
Bonne Terre
Desloge
Park Hills
STE. GENEVIEVE
Ste. Genevieve
Chester
Du Quoin
Benton
West Frankfort
Herrin
Murphysboro
Carbondale
CRAB ORCHARD N.W.R.
SHAWNEE N.F.
ST. FRANCOIS
Farmington
Perryville
PERRY
MARK TWAIN
IRON
Taum Sauk Mt. 540 m (1772 ft)
Ironton
MADISON
Fredericktown
N.F.
Centerville
MARK TWAIN N.F.
CAPE GIRARDEAU
Jackson
Marble Hill
Cape Girardeau
REYNOLDS
BOLLINGER
ILLINOIS
OZARK NATL. SCENIC RIVERWAYS
Scott City
Chaffee
Oran
Benton
Paducah
PENNYRILE FOREST ST. RESORT PARK
Eminence
SHANNON
Piedmont
WAYNE
Greenville
Advance
Cairo
Winona
Van Buren
MARK TWAIN
MINGO N.W.R.
SCOTT
Charleston
Hopkinsville
CARTER
N.F.
Bloomfield
Sikeston
MISSISSIPPI
LAND BETWEEN THE LAKES
MARK TWAIN NATL. FOR.
Morehouse
East Prairie
KENTUCKY
Mayfield
Poplar Bluff
Dexter
STODDARD
Murray
FORT CAMPBELL MIL. RES.
OREGON
RIPLEY
BUTLER
Bernie
MO.
Clarksville
Alton
Doniphan
Malden
Lilbourn
New Madrid
TENNESSEE
Campbell
NEW MADRID
Union City
Martin
Paris
TENNESSEE N.W.R.
Portageville
Pocahontas
Hayti
Kennett
Senath
PEMISCOT
Caruthersville
McKenzie
Steele
DUNKLIN
Paragould
Dyersburg
TENNESSEE N.W.R.
Blytheville
Milan
MILAN ARSENAL
St. Charles
Hazelwood
Florissant
Calverton Park
Bridgeton
Ferguson
Dellwood
Glasgow Village
Moshenthein Island
Choteau Island
Maryland Heights
St. Ann
Kinloch
Jennings
Granite City
St. John
Gabaret Island
ST. LOUIS
Northwoods
Pine Lawn
Madison
Collinsville
Overland
Greendale
Creve Coeur
Olivette
Pagedale
Venice
University City
Washington Park
Town and Country
Ladue
Clayton
Richmond Heights
St. Louis
Brentwood
Rock Hill
East St. Louis
Des Peres
Maplewood
Glendale
Fairview Heights
Manchester
Mackenzie
Centreville
Twin Oaks
Kirkwood
Webster Groves
Peerless Park
Crestwood
Affton
Cahokia
Sappington
Lemay
Fenton
Concord
Mehlville
Murphy
JEFFERSON
Mattese
0
2
4
6 mi
8 km
Mississippi
Missouri R.
Platte City
Excelsior Springs
PLATTE
CLAY
Ferrelview
Mosby
Farley
Liberty
Missouri City
Weatherby Lake
Gladstone
Glenaire
Waldron
Oakview
Houston Lake
Oaks
Claycomo
Atherton
Parkville
Northmoor
Birmingham
Sibley
Riverside
Randolph
North Kansas City
Buckner
Kansas City
Kansas City
Sugar Creek
JACKSON
Edwardsville
Independence
Lake Quivira
Roeland Park
Mission
Blue Springs
Merriam
Mission Hills
Raytown
Grain Valley
Shawnee
Prairie Village
Unity Village
Lenexa
Lake Lotawana
Overland Park
Leawood
Lee's Summit
Grandview
10 mi
15 km

MISSOURI

Missouri: Map Index

Hillsboro	F3
Holden	C3
Hollister	C5
Houston	E4
Houston Lake	H4
Humansville	C4
Huntsville	D2
Independence	B2, J4
Ironton	F4
Jackson	G4
Jefferson City, *capital*	D3
Jennings	H2
Joplin	B4
Kahoka	E1
Kansas City	B2, H4
Kennett	F5
Keytesville	D2
Kingston	B2
Kinloch	H2
Kirksville	D1
Kirkwood	H3
Knob Noster	C3
Ladue	H2
La Grange	E1
Lake Lotawana	J4
Lake St. Louis	F3
Lamar	B4
Lancaster	D1
La Plata	D1
Lathrop	B2
Lawson	B2
Lebanon	D4
Lee's Summit	B3, J4
Lemay	H3
Lexington	C2
Liberty	B2, J3
Licking	E4
Lilbourn	G5
Linn Creek	D3
Linneus	C2
Lockwood	C4
Louisiana	E2
Mackenzie	H3
Macon	D2
Malden	G5
Manchester	G3
Mansfield	D4
Maplewood	H3
Marble Hill	G4
Marceline	D2
Marionville	C5
Marshall	C2
Marshfield	D4
Maryland Heights	H2
Maryville	B1
Mattese	H3
Maysville	B2
Mehlville	H3
Memphis	D1
Mexico	E2
Milan	C1
Millard	D1
Missouri City	J3
Moberly	D2
Monett	C5
Monroe City	E2
Montgomery City	E3
Monticello	E1
Morehouse	G5
Mosby	J3
Mound City	A1
Mountain Grove	D4
Mountain View	E4
Mt. Vernon	C4
Murphy	G3
Neosho	B5
Nevada	B4
New Franklin	D2
New Haven	E3
New London	E2
New Madrid	G5
Nixa	C4
Noel	B5
North Kansas City	H4
Northmoor	H4
Northwoods	H2
Oaks	J4
Oakview	J4
O'Fallon	F3
Olivette	H2
Oran	G4
Oregon	A2
Osage Beach	D3
Osceola	C3
Overland	H2
Owensville	E3
Ozark	C4
Pacific	F3
Pagedale	H2
Palmyra	E2
Paris	D2
Park Hills	F4
Parkville	H4
Peculiar	B3
Peerless Park	G3
Perryville	G4
Pevely	F3
Piedmont	F4
Pierce City	C5
Pine Lawn	H2
Pineville	B5
Platte City	B2, H3
Plattsburg	B2
Pleasant Hill	B3
Poplar Bluff	F5
Portageville	G5
Potosi	F4
Princeton	C1
Randolph	J4
Raymore	B3
Raytown	J4
Republic	C4
Rich Hill	B3
Richland	D4
Richmond	C2
Richmond Heights	H2
Riverside	H4
Rock Hill	H2
Rock Port	A1
Rolla	E4
St. Ann	H2
St. Charles	F3, G2
St. Clair	F3
Ste. Genevieve	F4
St. James	E3
St. John	H2
St. Joseph	B2
St. Louis	F3, H2
St. Peters	F3
St. Robert	D4
Salem	E4
Salisbury	D2
Sappington	H3
Sarcoxie	B4
Savannah	B2
Scott City	G4
Sedalia	C3
Senath	F5
Seymour	D4
Shelbina	D2
Shelbyville	D2
Shirley	F4
Sibley	J4
Sikeston	G5
Slater	C2
Smithville	B2
Springfield	C4
Stanberry	B1
Steele	G5
Steelville	E4
Stockton	C4
Stoutsville	E2
Strafford	C4
Sugar Creek	J4
Sullivan	E3
Sweet Springs	C3
Tarkio	A1
Thayer	E5
Town and Country	G2
Trenton	C1
Troy	F3
Tuscumbia	D3
Twin Oaks	G3
Union	F3
Unionville	C1
Unity Village	J4
University City	H2
Van Buren	E5
Vandalia	E2
Versailles	D3
Vienna	E3
Villa Ridge	F3
Waldron	H3
Warrensburg	C3
Warrenton	E3
Warsaw	C3
Washington	E3
Watson	A1
Waynesville	D4
Weatherby Lake	H3
Webb City	B4
Webster Groves	H3
Wellsville	E2
Wentzville	F3
West Plains	E5
Weston	B2
Willard	C4
Willow Springs	E4
Windsor	C3
Winona	E4

Other Features

Bull Shoals, *lake*	D5
Clarence Cannon Natl. Wildlife Refuge	F2
Eleven Point, *river*	E5
Fort Leonard Wood Mil. Res.	D4
Fox, *river*	E1
G.W. Carver Natl. Monument	B5
Grand, *river*	B1
Harry S. Truman, *reservoir*	C3
Lake of the Ozarks, *lake*	D3
Mark Twain, *lake*	E2
Mark Twain Natl. Forest	C5, D4, E4, F4
Meramec, *river*	E4
Mingo Natl. Wildlife Refuge	F4
Mississippi, *river*	G4
Missouri, *river*	C2
Osage, *river*	B4, D3
Ozark Natl. Scenic Riverways	E4
Platte, *river*	B2
St. Francis, *river*	F4
Stockton, *lake*	C4
Swan Lake Natl. Wildlife Refuge	C2
Table Rock, *lake*	C5
Taum Sauk, *mt.*	F4
Thomas Hill, *reservoir*	D2
Weldon, *river*	C2

ple per sq km (73 per sq mi) in 1990. The population density was lightest in the rugged central portion of the Ozark Plateau and in the rolling farmlands of the N. Whites made up 87.7% of the population and blacks 10.7%; additional population groups included some 19,508 American Indians, 8614 persons of Chinese ancestry, 6111 persons of Asian Indian background, 5731 persons of Korean origin, 5624 persons of Filipino extraction, and 4380 persons of Vietnamese descent. Approximately 61,700 persons were of Hispanic background. Baptists (24.9%) formed the single largest religious group, followed by Roman Catholics (20.3%), Methodists (7.1%), and Lutherans (5.9%). In 1990 about 69% of Missouri's residents lived in areas defined as urban, and the rest lived in rural areas. The largest cities were Kansas City, Saint Louis, Springfield, Independence, and Saint Joseph. Jefferson City is the capital.

EDUCATION AND CULTURAL ACTIVITY

Missouri has a cultural life of unusual diversity. In its two major cities, Kansas City and St. Louis, are cultural institutions of national prominence, and in rural areas, notably the Ozarks, folkcraft traditions remain strong.

Education. The first schools in the area that is now Missouri were opened by French settlers at St. Louis in the latter part of the 18th century. The constitution of 1820 provided for a statewide public school system.

In the late 1980s public education facilities in Missouri included 2151 public elementary and secondary schools with a total annual enrollment of about 576,200 elementary students and 231,700 secondary students. Private schools also had a substantial enrollment of some 107,500 students. In the same period Missouri had 89 institutions of higher education, with a combined yearly enrollment of about 278,500 students. These institutions included the University of Missouri, with its main campus in Columbia and branches in Kansas City, St. Louis, and Rolla; Washington University, at St. Louis; St. Louis University (1818); Central Missouri State University (1871), at Warrensburg; and Southeast Missouri State University (1873), at Cape Girardeau.

Cultural Institutions. Missouri's museums, libraries, and theaters are concentrated in four cities: St. Louis, Kansas City, Jefferson City, and Columbia. The St. Louis Art Museum in St. Louis has an extensive and diverse collection, and the Nelson-Atkins Museum of Art in Kansas City has an important collection of Oriental art. The Missouri Botanical Garden in St. Louis is one of the finest in the country. The State Historical Society of Missouri, in Columbia, is noted for its collection of paintings by Missouri artists. Other important museums include the Museum of Art and Archaeology at the University of Missouri-Columbia; the Missouri State Museum, at Jefferson City; the Harry S. Truman Library and Museum, at Independence; the Albrecht Art Museum and the St. Joseph Museum, at St. Joseph; and the St. Louis Science Center. The state's largest public libraries are at St. Louis and Kansas City. Both St. Louis and Kansas City have symphony orchestras (the St. Louis Symphony Orchestra is the second oldest in the U.S.), opera companies, and repertory theaters, and Kansas City also has a ballet company.

Historical Sites. Historical sites commemorate early exploration and settlement as well as famous Missourians. Among the most interesting are the Mark Twain Home and Museum, at Hannibal, and the birthplaces of John J. Pershing, at Laclede, and of George Washington Carver (a national monument), at Diamond. Arrow Rock State Historic Site contains several historic landmarks on a section of the Santa Fe Trail. Jefferson National Expansion Memorial National Historic Site, at St. Louis, includes a number of early buildings and the great Gateway Arch.

Sports and Recreation. Missouri has an extensive system of parks, of which the largest is the Lake of the Ozarks State Park. Hunting, fishing, camping, and boating are popular. The state has many professional sports teams, including the St. Louis Cardinals and Kansas City Royals (baseball), the St. Louis Rams and Kansas City Chiefs (football), and the St. Louis Blues (ice hockey).

Communications. In the early 1990s Missouri had 119 AM radio stations, 162 FM radio stations, and 34 television stations. The state's first radio station, WEW, at St. Louis University, began broadcasting in 1921. Missouri's first newspaper, the *Missouri Gazette*, was first published in St. Louis in 1808. In the early 1990s the state was served by 44 daily newspapers, which had a combined daily circulation of about 1.1 million. Among the leading dailies are the *St. Louis Post-Dispatch*, the *Kansas City Star*, *The Examiner* (Independence), the *Joplin Globe*, and the *Daily Capital News* and *Post-Tribune* (Jefferson City).

GOVERNMENT AND POLITICS

Missouri is governed under a constitution adopted in 1945, as amended. Three earlier state constitutions had been adopted in 1820, 1865, and 1875. A state constitutional amendment may be proposed by the state legislature or a constitutional convention or by an initiative petition. To become effective it must be approved by a majority of the persons voting on the issue in a general election.

Executive. Missouri's chief executive is a governor, who is popularly elected to a 4-year term

MISSOURI

DATE OF STATEHOOD: August 10, 1821; 24th state

CAPITAL:	Jefferson City
MOTTO:	*Salus populi supreme lex esto* (The welfare of the people shall be the supreme law)
NICKNAME:	Show Me State
STATE SONG:	"Missouri Waltz" (words by J. R. Shannon; music by John V. Eppel)
STATE TREE:	Flowering dogwood
STATE FLOWER:	Hawthorn
STATE BIRD:	Bluebird
POPULATION (1990):	5,117,073; 15th among the states
AREA:	180,546 sq km (69,709 sq mi); 21st largest state; includes 2100 sq km (811 sq mi) of inland water
HIGHEST POINT:	Taum Sauk Mt., 540 m (1772 ft)
LOWEST POINT:	70 m (230 ft), along the Saint Francis River in the southeast
ELECTORAL VOTES:	11
U.S. CONGRESS:	2 senators; 9 representatives

POPULATION OF MISSOURI SINCE 1810

Year of Census	Population	Classified As Urban
1810	20,000	0%
1840	384,000	4%
1860	1,182,000	17%
1880	2,168,000	25%
1900	3,107,000	36%
1920	3,404,000	47%
1940	3,785,000	52%
1960	4,320,000	67%
1980	4,916,686	68%
1990	5,117,073	69%

POPULATION OF TEN LARGEST CITIES

	1990 Census	1980 Census
Kansas City	435,146	448,159
Saint Louis	396,685	453,085
Springfield	140,494	133,116
Independence	112,301	111,806
Saint Joseph	71,852	76,691
Columbia	69,101	62,061
Saint Charles	54,555	37,379
Florissant	51,206	55,372
Lee's Summit	46,418	28,741
Saint Peters	45,779	15,700

CLIMATE

	SAINT LOUIS	SPRINGFIELD
Average January temperature range	−5° to 4.4° C (23° to 40° F)	−5° to 6.1° C (23° to 43° F)
Average July temperature range	20.6° to 31.1° C (69° to 88° F)	19.4° to 31.7° C (67° to 89° F)
Average annual temperature	13.3° C (56° F)	13.3° C (56° F)
Average annual precipitation	914 mm (36 in)	1016 mm (40 in)
Average annual snowfall	457 mm (18 in)	381 mm (15 in)
Mean number of days per year with appreciable precipitation	109	106
Average daily relative humidity	72%	70%
Mean number of clear days per year	105	117

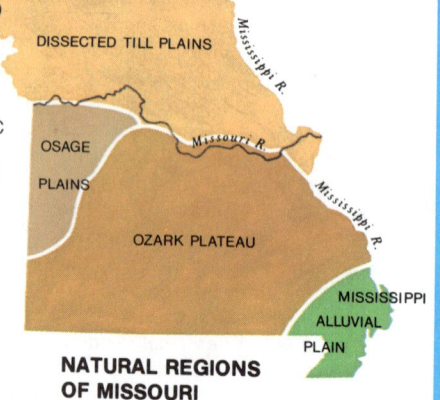

NATURAL REGIONS OF MISSOURI

PRINCIPAL PRODUCTS OF MISSOURI

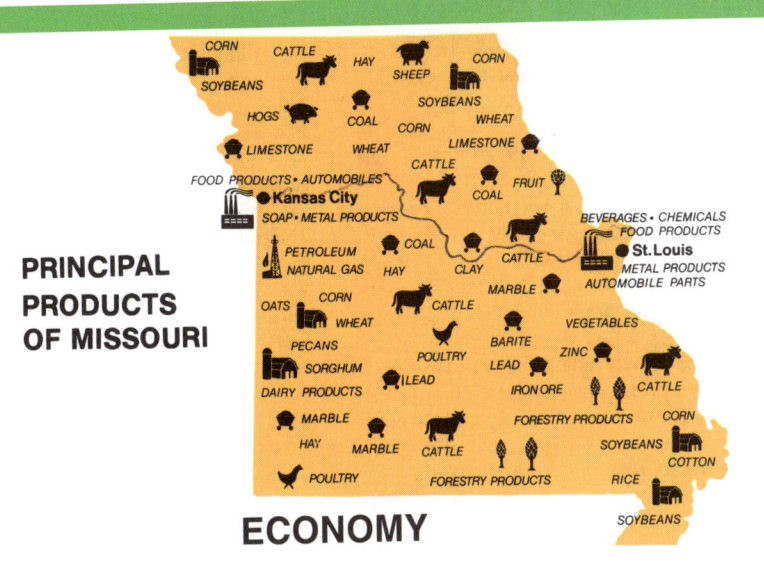

ECONOMY

State budget .... general revenue $8.0 billion
general expenditure $7.7 billion
accumulated debt $5.3 billion
State and local taxes, per capita $1551
Personal income, per capita..................... $12,989
Population below poverty level..................... 13.3%
Assets, insured commercial banks (551) .... $58.1 billion
Labor force (civilian nonfarm) 2,308,000
    Employed in wholesale and retail trade   25%
    Employed in services   24%
    Employed in manufacturing   19%
    Employed in government   16%

        Quantity Produced   Value

FARM PRODUCTS .... **$4.4 billion**

Crops .... **$2.1 billion**
    Soybeans .... 3.4 million metric tons ..... $722 million
    Corn .... 5.2 million metric tons ..... $473 million
    Hay .... 6.2 million metric tons ..... $429 million
    Wheat .... 2.1 million metric tons ..... $205 million
    Sorghum ..... 1.1 million metric tons ..... $91 million
Livestock and Livestock Products .... **$2.3 billion**
    Cattle .... 532,000 metric tons ..... $935 million
    Hogs .... 472,000 metric tons ..... $563 million
    Milk .... 1.4 million metric tons ..... $413 million
    Turkeys ...... 163,000 metric tons ..... $148 million
    Eggs .... 1.6 billion .... $73 million

MINERALS .... **$1.0 billion**[†]
    Lead .... 367,000 metric tons ..... $318 million
    Cement ...... 4.5 million metric tons ..... $182 million
    Stone .... 47.0 million metric tons ..... $172 million
    Zinc .... 50,800 metric tons .... $92 million
    Coal .... 3.1 million metric tons .... N/A
[†]Excluding coal

                                      Annual Payroll
MANUFACTURING .... **$11.7 billion**
    Transportation equipment .... $2.5 billion
    Fabricated metal products .... $1.0 billion
    Printing and publishing .... $1.0 billion
    Food and kindred products .... $837 million
    Industrial machinery and equipment ...... $757 million
    Electronic equipment .... $721 million
    Chemicals and allied products .... $695 million

MANUFACTURING (cont.)
    Primary metals .... $347 million
    Paper and allied products .... $332 million
    Rubber and plastics products .... $331 million
    Instruments and related products .... $324 million

OTHER .... **$37.3 billion**
    Services .... $10.5 billion
    Government .... $8.7 billion
    Retail trade .... $4.5 billion
    Transportation, communications,
        and public utilities .... $3.8 billion
    Wholesale trade .... $3.5 billion
    Finance, insurance, and real estate .... $3.2 billion
    Construction .... $2.5 billion

ANNUAL GROSS STATE PRODUCT

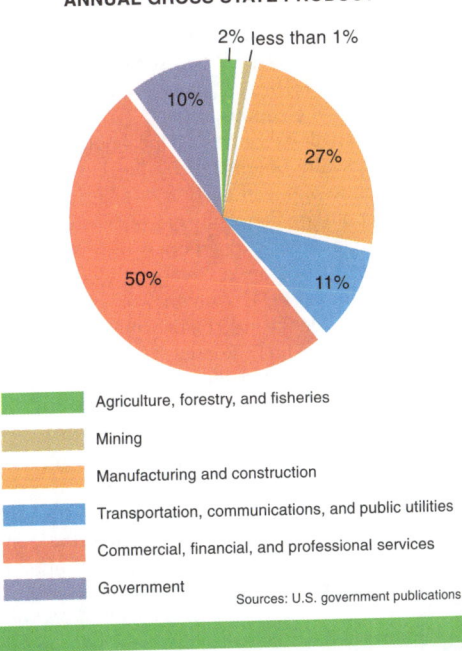

- 2%
- less than 1%
- 27%
- 11%
- 50%
- 10%

- Agriculture, forestry, and fisheries
- Mining
- Manufacturing and construction
- Transportation, communications, and public utilities
- Commercial, financial, and professional services
- Government

Sources: U.S. government publications

and may not serve for more than two terms. Other elected officials include the lieutenant governor, who succeeds the governor on the latter's death, removal from office, or incapacity to serve; the secretary of state; the attorney general; the treasurer; and the auditor.

Legislature. The bicameral Missouri legislature is known as the General Assembly. It consists of a house of representatives made up of 163 members popularly elected to 2-year terms, and a senate of 34 members popularly elected to 4-year terms.

Judiciary. The highest judicial body in Missouri is the supreme court, consisting of a chief justice and six associate justices. The intermediate court is the court of appeals, with 32 judges. The governor appoints supreme court justices and appellate judges, who must be confirmed in office by voters after one year. Thereafter, they must be reconfirmed by voters every 12 years. The principal trial courts are the circuit courts. The state's 133 circuit court judges serve 6-year terms; most are popularly elected, but those of St. Louis and Jackson counties are selected in the manner of supreme court justices.

Local Government. Missouri is divided into 114 counties; the city of St. Louis is independent of surrounding St. Louis Co. Counties are typically administered by a county court (or commission) of three elected commissioners. St. Louis and Jackson counties have home-rule charters and are administered under the county executive plan. Most cities in the state have the mayor-council form of government; some also employ city managers.

National Representation. Missouri is represented in the U.S. Congress by two senators and nine representatives. The state casts 11 electoral votes in presidential elections.

Politics. In national, state, and local politics, Missouri is usually dominated by the Democratic party; the Republican party is strong, however, and elections are frequently close. The outstanding political figure to emerge from Missouri was Harry S. Truman, a Democrat elected as a U.S. senator in 1934. Truman won election to the vice-presidency in 1944, became president at the death of Franklin D. Roosevelt in 1945, and was reelected president in 1948.

ECONOMY

From the early 19th century until World War II, Missouri had an overwhelmingly agricultural economy. Since World War II, manufacturing in the state has grown dramatically. Today Missouri ranks as one of the major manufacturing and commercial states of the Midwest. Agricultural growth during the same years was also substantial, although the role of agriculture in the overall economy has undergone a relative decline. Many farms on the poorer soils of the Ozark Plateau have been abandoned, but the region is now a major tourist attraction.

Agriculture. Farming accounts for about 2% of the annual gross state product in Missouri. The state has some 107,000 farms (only Texas has more), which average 115 ha (284 acres) in size. Sales of livestock and livestock products make up about 52% of Missouri's yearly farm income. Missouri is a leading state in the raising of dairy cows and beef cattle. Dairy farming is most important in the SW. Sheep production is concentrated in the NE. The raising of hogs and poultry is widespread in Missouri. Crops account for about 48% of the state's annual agricultural income. Soybeans are the leading crop and are grown in the fertile N part of the state and in the SE lowlands. Corn and hay, the next most important crops, are grown throughout the state. Wheat is also widely produced. Cotton, rice, and vegetables are grown in the SE lowlands.

Forestry. Forestry is most significant in the Ozark Plateau region. The cut is primarily hardwood, mainly oak, hickory, walnut, and red cedar. Pine is also sawed, principally for lumber.

Mining. The mining industry accounts for less than 1% of the annual gross state product in Missouri. The most important mineral is lead, of which Missouri is the principal national supplier. Other major mineral products are cement, stone (including limestone, marble, and granite), zinc, coal, sand and gravel, and barite. Lead, zinc, and barite are all mined in the vicinity of the St. Francois Mts. Bituminous coal deposits, largely exploited by strip-mining, are widespread; the largest deposits are worked in the W central and N central parts of the state. Smaller amounts of copper, silver, and petroleum are also produced.

Manufacturing. Enterprises engaged in manufacturing account for some 23% of the annual gross state product in Missouri and employ about 439,000 workers. The state's leading manufactures include transport equipment, fabricated metals, printed materials and processed foods. Missouri is a major producer of automobiles and aerospace equipment, with production concentrated in the St. Louis area. Important food products include dairy items, flour, and beer. Among the chemical products manufactured in Missouri are fertilizers, insecticides, and pharmaceuticals. Other goods include farm machinery, electronic equipment, steel, clothing, glass, and paper products. St. Louis and Kansas City have, by far, the greatest concentrations of industry in the state. Springfield and St. Joseph are other significant manufacturing centers, and many of Missouri's smaller cities and towns also have manufacturing plants.

Tourism. Each year more than 40 million visitors produce over $6 billion for the Missouri economy. The tourist industry in the state employs an estimated 137,000 workers. Principal attractions include the two largest cities, Kansas City and St. Louis; Branson, with its many country-music theaters; and the Ozark region, with its many scenic gorges, caverns, and large artificial lakes, which furnish ample opportunities for recreational activities. Missouri also maintains 79 state parks and historic sites. Among the most popular of these is Mark Twain State Park in Monroe Co., containing the village of Florida, the birthplace of the author Mark Twain.

Transportation. Missouri's central location in the U.S., at the junction of the nation's two largest river systems, has made it an important focus of transportation routes. St. Louis and Kansas City are the major transportation hubs. The state is served by a dense network of some 193,970 km (some 120,525 mi) of federal, state, and local roads; the figure includes 1856 km (1153 mi) of interstate highways, which link the state's major cities and occupy a pivotal position within the national highway system. The state is also served by about 8095 km (about 5030 mi) of operated Class I railroad track. Both St. Louis and Kansas City are major rail centers.

Barge traffic is important on both the Missouri and Mississippi rivers. The leading ports are St. Louis, Kansas City, Cape Girardeau, Caruthersville, New Madrid, and Hannibal.

Missouri has 354 airports and 80 heliports. The busiest air terminals are Lambert–St. Louis and Kansas City international airports.

Energy. Electricity generating plants in Missouri have a total capacity of about 15.2 million kw and produce about 59 billion kwh of electricity each year. About 82% of the state's electric energy is generated by the burning of coal. Although Missouri has large coal reserves, much of the coal consumed by thermal power plants is shipped from neighboring states. Nuclear installations generate nearly 14% of Missouri's electric power. The largest hydroelectric projects are the Taum Sauk Project near Lesterville and the Bagnell Dam, which impounds the Lake of the Ozarks.

Because Missouri is located between the great petroleum-producing fields of the midcontinent and Gulf of Mexico regions, it is crossed by major pipelines. More than 10,620 km (more than 6600 mi) of pipeline transport petroleum and natural gas across the state. M.D.R.

HISTORY

The founding of Sainte Genevieve in 1735 by the French marked the first European settlement in the Missouri region, which was then a part of the French territory of Louisiana. At this time, Indians living in Missouri were mainly of the Algonquian and Siouan language groups. The second European settlement in the state was St. Louis, established as a trading post in 1764, a year after the cession of Louisiana to Spain by the French. The colonization of the region was greatly accelerated by the Ordinance of 1787, which excluded slavery from the Northwest Territory of the U.S. The Spanish also encouraged immigration by offering liberal bounties to settlers. Louisiana was returned to France in 1800 and sold to the U.S. three years later. In 1812 the region became the territory of Missouri.

Early Development. After 1815, immigration increased rapidly. In 1816 the first steamboat reached St. Louis. In 1818 the territorial legislature applied to the U.S. Congress for permission to prepare a state constitution. Missouri was admitted to the Union as a slave state on Aug. 10, 1821, under the terms of the Missouri Compromise. The period after 1820 was one of rapid, if not entirely sound, development. It was an era of wild speculation in land, accompanied by an inflation in currency (the Bank of St. Louis had been established in 1816) and the inception of an elaborate system of internal improvements. By the mid-1850s the state, which had pledged its credit for $28 million to various railroad companies, found itself burdened with a debt exceeding $20 million.

Sectional Controversy and the American Civil War. In the early years of the 19th century, Missouri, although a slave state, was not an ardent defender of slavery, and many of its citizens were interested in movements for gradual emancipation. With the rise of the abolitionists, however, Missouri became decidedly proslavery and favored the annexation of Texas as a slave state in 1845. In 1849 the state legislature adopted the Jackson resolutions, in which the right of Congress to regulate slavery in the territories was denied and the principle of squatter sovereignty asserted. In the presidential election of 1860 the vote in the state for Stephen A. Douglas and that for John Bell, of the Constitutional Union party, were large and nearly equal; the vote for Abraham Lincoln was small. When Lincoln won the election, the legislature issued a call for a convention to consider the relation of the state to the Union. In the elections for the convention the secessionist delegates were defeated, and when the convention met from February to April

One of Missouri's principal historical sites is the Harry S. Truman Library and Museum, in Independence. It contains all of Truman's presidential papers as well as exhibits relating to the duties of the presidency.
Missouri Tourism Commission

1861, it declared that it could find no cause for secession. After the outbreak of the Civil War, the state government, however, led by Gov. Claiborne Fox Jackson (1806–62), favored secession; when Lincoln issued a call for troops, Jackson instead summoned the state militia to arms. The governor and the majority of the legislature fled to the southern part of Missouri after the militia was defeated by federal troops at St. Louis. A provisional government was installed, and as Confederate power declined, the regular state government was reorganized in 1864.

Post–Civil War Years and the 20th Century. During the next four decades Missouri underwent many significant changes. The fur trade declined, trade with Mexico along the Santa Fe Trail ended, and Kansas City and St. Louis became major transportation centers. In the early 1900s several progressive reforms regulated social and industrial conditions, including child labor. Although Missouri remained agriculturally important, the demand for military supplies during World War II also expanded the state's industrial productivity. By the mid-1950s it was active in the manufacture of aerospace and electronic equipment and uranium processing. Discovery of iron ore in the 1960s boosted industry.

Missouri faces the challenge of improving its social services, expanding its highways, and reversing the population shift to the suburbs. Fiscal problems exacerbated by inflation in the late 1970s and recession in the early 1990s, however, have made such goals somewhat elusive. The state was dealt another serious blow by the flooding of the Mississippi, Missouri, and other rivers of the Midwest in 1993.

For further information on this topic, see the Bibliography in volume 28, section 1207.

MISSOURI (Illinois *Emissourita*, "dwellers of the big muddy"), river, central U.S., the principal branch of the Mississippi R. formed by the confluence of the Jefferson, Gallatin, and Madison rivers at Three Forks in SW Montana. The Missouri flows N, skirting the main range of the Rocky Mts., and, after passing through a 366-m (1200-ft) gorge called the Gates of the Mountains, turns NE and reaches Fort Benton, Mont., the head of navigation. From Fort Benton the river flows E and is joined by the Milk R. at Frazer, Mont., and by the Yellowstone R. at Buford, N.Dak. From this point the Missouri flows generally SE through North Dakota and South Dakota to Sioux City, Iowa, where it turns S and becomes the boundary between Nebraska and Kansas on the W and Iowa and Missouri on the E. The Platte R. is received near Omaha, Nebr., and the Kansas R. at Kansas City, Mo. On receiving the Kansas, the Missouri turns E and flows across the state of Missouri. About 27 km (about 17 mi) N of Saint Louis, the muddy Missouri enters the channel of the Mississippi. The Missouri is 3969 km (2466 mi) long and drains an area of about 1,370,000 sq km (about 529,000 sq mi). Since 1944 a series of dams and locks on the river has regulated irrigation and flooding. The chief cities on the river are Bismarck, Sioux City, Omaha, Council Bluffs, Saint Joseph, Atchison, Leavenworth, and Kansas City.

For further information on this topic, see the Bibliography in volume 28, section 426.

MISSOURI, UNIVERSITY OF, land-grant state-controlled institution of higher learning, in Columbia, Mo., with branches in Kansas City, Saint Louis, and Rolla. Founded in 1839, the university is governed by a nine-member board of curators. The four campuses are coordinated into a single university by a president and staff, but responsibilities of each campus are administered by a campus chancellor. Courses offered include agriculture, arts and sciences, business, education, dentistry, engineering, forestry, home economics, journalism, law, medicine, music, nursing, and pharmacy. The degrees of bachelor, master, and doctor are conferred, as well as various professional degrees.

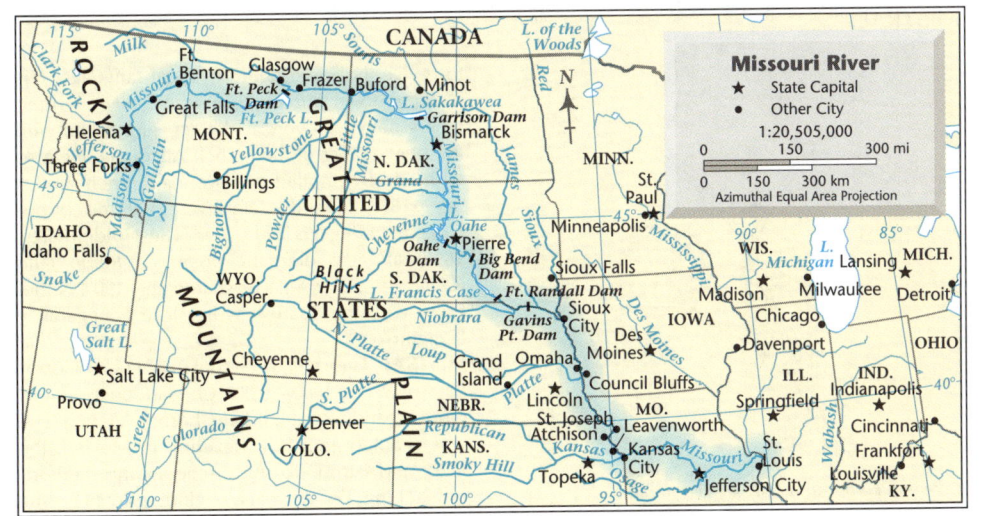

MISSOURI CITY, city, Fort Bend and Harris counties, SE Texas, near the Brazos R.; inc. 1956. It is a suburb of Houston, near the Astrodome stadium. Settled in 1894, it began its growth during the 1920s, when petroleum was discovered nearby. Pop. (1980) 24,533; (1990) 36,176.

MISSOURI COMPROMISE, legislative measures enacted by the U.S. Congress in 1820 that regulated the extension of slavery in the U.S. for three decades. When slaveholding Missourians applied for statehood in 1818, the long-standing balance of free and slave states (11 each) was jeopardized. A northern-sponsored amendment was then attached to the bill (1819) authorizing statehood; it prohibited the entry of slaves into Missouri and provided for the gradual emancipation of those already there. The proslavery faction was unable to prevent the bill's passage by the House of Representatives, where free states held a majority, but southern strength in the Senate defeated the bill.

Maine, then a part of Massachusetts, also applied for statehood in 1819. Speaker of the House Henry Clay of Kentucky warned northern congressmen that unless they changed their position on Missouri the southerners would reject Maine's petition. To please the South the slavery restrictions for Missouri were then removed, and to satisfy the North, Senator Jesse B. Thomas (1777–1853) of Illinois introduced (February 1820) a proviso by which slavery would be prohibited forever from Louisiana Purchase territories north of 36° 30′. Southern extremists opposed any limit on the extension of slavery, but Clay maneuvered the measure through the House by a three-vote majority. Missouri and Maine were to enter statehood simultaneously to preserve sectional equality in the Senate. In 1821, when northern congressmen balked over antiblack clauses in Missouri's constitution, Clay again adjusted differences, and Missouri's admission was ensured.

The compromise became precedent for settling North-South disagreements, and it remained in effect until repealed by the Kansas-Nebraska Act (q.v.) of 1854. B.W.

MIST. See Fog.

MISTASSINI, LAKE, lake, central Québec Province. The largest lake in the province, Mistassini has an area of 2336 sq km (902 sq mi). It is drained by the Rupert R., which flows W to James Bay. A chain of islands extends across the lake, nearly dividing it in half. Its Indian name, meaning "great stone," refers to a large rock in the lake.

MISTLETOE, common name for various parasitic plants belonging to two families of the order Santalales (see SANDALWOOD), especially those belonging to the genera *Viscum, Phoradendron,* and *Arceuthobium* of the family Viscaceae. The common European mistletoe, *V. album,* grows on various trees. It is an evergreen shrubby plant with small, greenish flowers and white berries. A similar mistletoe, *P. flavescens,* found in the U.S., grows on deciduous trees from eastern Texas to Florida and northward to Missouri and New Jersey.

The leafless flowering dwarf mistletoes of the genus *Arceuthobium* depend entirely on the host tree for nourishment. These scrubs are lethal parasites of conifers, such as pine, spruce and fir.

Mistletoes of the family Loranthaceae include the West Indian mistletoe, *Phthirusa caribaea.* The plants of the family Viscaceae were formerly included in the family Loranthaceae.

The common mistletoe figured significantly in

MISTRAL

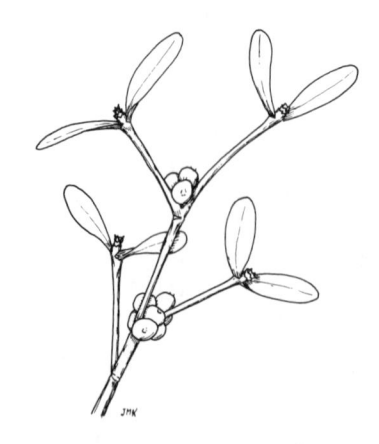

Common European mistletoe, Viscum album

the folklore and religions of pre-Christian Europe. Reputedly endowed with magical powers, it was used as a cure for sterility and as an antidote for poisons. It is used as a Christmas and New Year's decoration, and kissing under a branch is still customary.

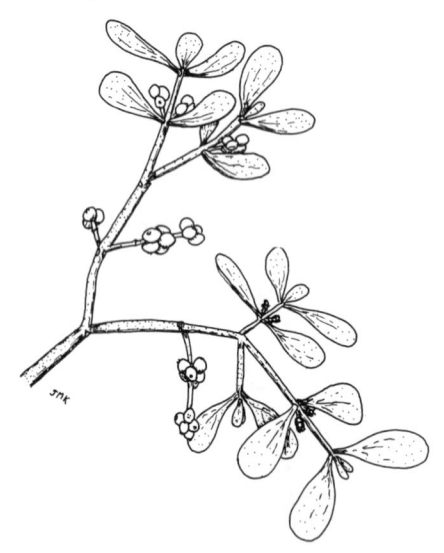

American mistletoe, Phoradendron flavescens

MISTRAL, cold, dry wind that blows southward across the southern coast of France from the mountains, especially in winter and spring. Villagers and farmers build windbreaks against the mistral, which can reach velocities of up to 135 km/hr (85 mph) near the coast.

MISTRAL, Frédéric (1830–1914), French Provençal poet and Nobel laureate, born near Maillane, Bouches-du-Rhône Department. In 1854 Mistral and other writers founded the Félibrige, a society to revive the use of the Provençal language. His pastoral poem *Mirèio* (1859; trans. 1868), written in his native Provençal dialect, gained for him the poet's prize of the French Academy. He also wrote and compiled a Provençal-French dictionary (1878–86) and wrote several volumes of poetry, including *Lis isclo d'or* (The Golden Isles, 1876) and the dramatic poem *La Reino Jano* (Queen Joan, 1890). He shared the 1904 Nobel Prize with the Spanish writer José Echegaray y Eizaguirre.

MISTRAL, Gabriela, pseudonym of LUCILA GODOY DE ALCAYAGA (1889–1957), Chilean poet, stateswoman, and Nobel laureate, born in Vicuña. She was a noted educator, traveling in Mexico, the U.S., and Europe to study schools and methods of teaching. For 20 years, beginning in 1933, she served as Chilean consul in Madrid, Lisbon, and various other cities, including Los Angeles. Her poetry, which is full of warmth and strong with emotion, has been translated into English, French, Italian, German, and Swedish. An English collection of her poetry is contained in *Gabriela Mistral's Anthology* (1942). In 1945 she became the first Latin American writer to win the Nobel Prize in literature.

MISURATA, also Misratah, coastal city, NW Libya, capital of Misurata Governorate, separated from the Mediterranean Sea by Cape Misurata. It is Libya's third largest city, with an old section of narrow streets and a spacious, modern section with gardens and tree-lined avenues. Carpets and textiles are major manufactures. Formerly known as Thubactis, the city dates from the 7th century. Pop. (1984) 178,295.

MITCHEL, John (1815–75), Irish patriot and journalist, born in county Londonderry, and educated at Trinity College, Dublin. He was admitted to the bar and began to practice law in Banbridge in 1840. In 1842 he began to contribute articles to the topical magazine, the *Nation,* becoming the assistant editor in 1845. He founded and edited the *United Irishman* in 1848; in this weekly he called for open Irish rebellion against England. As a result he was tried, convicted of sedition, and transported to Australia. In 1853 he escaped to the U.S. where he published a series of short-lived proslavery newspapers. During the American Civil War he supported the South and in 1865 was imprisoned for a short time by the federal authorities. He returned to Ireland in 1875, and in the same year he was elected to the British Parliament but was declared ineligible as a convicted felon. He was reelected but died before he could be seated. Mitchel's writings include the well-known revolutionary work *Jail Journal* (1854; new ed., 1954).

MITCHELL, city, seat of Davison Co., SE South Dakota; inc. 1883. It is a commercial, manufacturing, and transportation center, situated in a grain-producing region. Manufactures include truck trailers and processed food. Dakota Wesleyan University (1885) is here. The Corn Palace (1892, rebuilt 1921), a large, unusual structure with minaretlike towers, is redecorated each year with colored ears of corn. The community, laid out in 1881 as a railroad stop, was named for Alexander Mitchell (1817–87), president of the railroad. Pop. (1980) 13,916; (1990) 13,798.

MITCHELL, Billy, full name WILLIAM MITCHELL (1879–1936), American army officer, born in Nice, France, of American parents, and educated at Columbian University (now George Washington University). He served in Cuba in 1898 during the Spanish-American War and in 1899 in the Philippines. During World War I he was an organizer of the American aviation program and commanded the Allied air forces in several battles. Appointed a brigadier general, he held various military posts in Washington, D.C. In 1925 he was court-martialed and suspended from service for five years because he openly criticized the decreasing emphasis on aviation by the U.S. War and Navy departments. In 1926 he resigned from the army to give a series of lectures advocating a strong air force. Later his recommendations were incorporated in official U.S. military policy. He wrote *Our Air Force* (1921), *Winged Defense* (1925), and *Skyways* (1930).

MITCHELL, John (1870–1919), American labor leader, born in Braidwood, Ill. Mitchell became a coal miner in Braidwood at the age of 12, and three years later he joined the Knights of Labor.

Billy Mitchell   UPI

In 1890 he became one of the first members of the United Mine Workers of America. He held several offices in the union, eventually serving as president (1898–1908). Mitchell directed the strikes of the anthracite coal miners in 1900 and 1902; on the latter occasion he achieved a successful settlement by agreeing to accept the decision of a commission appointed by President Theodore Roosevelt. Between 1908 and 1915 Mitchell lectured on unionism and held office in the National Civic Federation, a group that sought conciliation between labor and business. From 1915 until his death Mitchell was chairman of the New York State Industrial Commission.

MITCHELL, John Newton (1913–88), American jurist, who served as U.S. attorney general (1969–72). Born in Detroit, he attended Fordham University Law School in New York City and became a successful lawyer, specializing in public finance. In 1967 his law firm merged with that of former Vice-President Richard M. Nixon. The following year Mitchell managed Nixon's successful presidential campaign, and in 1969 he became U.S. attorney general. He resigned in February 1972 to head the president's reelection campaign. Five months later he withdrew from public life to return to the practice of law. In May 1973 he was indicted by a federal grand jury in New York City, charged with perjury and conspiracy to obstruct justice in connection with a secret cash contribution to Nixon's 1972 campaign; he was acquitted in a New York City trial in 1974. That year Mitchell was also indicted for conspiracy and other charges stemming from the Watergate (q.v.) break-in and cover-up; he was convicted on Jan. 1, 1975, in Washington, D.C., and given a sentence of two and one-half to eight years in prison. In June 1977, after appeals of the sentence were rejected, he entered federal prison. Later that year the sentence was reduced to one to four years, on his statement of contrition. He was paroled in January 1978. Disbarred in 1975, he later served as a business consultant.

MITCHELL, Margaret (1900–49), American author of one of the most popular novels of all time. She was a reporter and feature writer for the *Atlanta Journal* from 1922 until 1926, when she began writing her one book, *Gone with the Wind*, which she completed ten years later. This romantic picture of life in the South during the American Civil War became a best-seller almost immediately and was awarded the Pulitzer Prize in 1937. It was made into a motion picture that, after its release in 1939, became one of the most popular and praised of all films.

MITCHELL, Maria (1818–89), American astronomer, born in Nantucket, Mass., and privately educated. Her father maintained a small observatory, where she began her studies in astronomy. In October 1847, she discovered a telescopic comet, an accomplishment that brought her international recognition. The following year she became the first woman elected to the American Academy of Arts and Sciences. She became professor of astronomy at Vassar College in 1865 and held that position until 1888, when she retired.

MITCHELL, MOUNT, peak of the Black Mts., W North Carolina. At 2037 m (6684 ft) above sea level, it is the highest point in the U.S. east of the Mississippi R.

MITE, common name for some 30,000 species of minute, usually oval-bodied arachnids of the order or subclass Acarina, or Acari (see ARACHNID). They are worldwide in distribution. Mites resemble ticks in having the head, thorax, and abdomen fused into one unsegmented body, but they are usually much smaller. They often have three pairs of legs in the larval stage and four pairs in the nymph and adult stages. The mouthparts are adapted for piercing. Like most arachnids, mites breathe by means of tracheae (small tubes opening on the surface of the body), and they live in both aquatic and terrestrial habitats. Many are animal parasites; some, which subsist on vegetation, produce galls on plants. They are economically and medically injurious, because they carry diseases affecting livestock and humans.

Among the most important mites are the chigger (q.v.) and the itch mite. The follicle mites of the family Demodicidae, which infest human hair follicles and sebaceous glands, are about 0.025 cm (0.01 in) long. The bird mites of the family Dermanyssidae infest the skins of birds; the chicken mite, *Dermanyssus gallinae,* attacks domestic poultry and produces a form of dermatitis in humans. More than 100 species of freshwater mites in the family Hydrachnidae inhabit U.S. lakes and rivers; these animals have fringed legs that they use in swimming. Among other common mites are the so-called red spiders, or spider mites, of the genus *Tetranychus,* which spin spiderlike webs; feeding on the undersides of leaves, they destroy many types of plants.

MITHRADATES VI EUPATOR (132?–63 BC), king of Pontus, in what is now northeastern Turkey. In about 121 BC he succeeded his father, Mithradates V (r. about 150–121 BC), and began his career of conquest by seizing Colchis and the Crimea from the Scythians. His attempts to cement his control in Paphlagonia and Cappadocia were thwarted by Rome, and a plot to depose Nicomedes III of Bithynia (r. 91–74 BC) was unsuccessful. Raids on Pontic territory in 88 BC by Nicomedes, instigated by Rome, led to the First Mithradatic War. Mithradates occupied the Roman Province of Asia and most of the Greek cities in Asia Minor, but during 86 BC and 85 BC he was defeated in Asia and Greece by the Roman generals Gaius Flavius Fimbria (d. 85 BC) and Lucius Cornelius Sulla. The Second Mithradatic War began with a Roman invasion of Pontus in 83 BC that was repelled in 82 BC. The Roman design to annex Bithynia provoked the Third Mithradatic War. Mithradates occupied Bithynia, but in 73 BC his army was isolated and destroyed by the Roman commander Lucius Licinius Lucullus. In 66 BC Pompey the Great succeeded to the Roman command and defeated Mithradates, who had regained much of his territory. Mithradates then devised a plan for the invasion of Italy from the north, but his troops deserted to his son, Pharnaces (r. 63–47 BC), and Mithradates committed suicide.

MITHRAISM, one of the major religions of the Roman Empire, the cult of Mithra, the ancient Persian god of light and wisdom. In the Avesta (q.v.), the sacred Zoroastrian writings (see ZOROASTRIANISM) of the ancient Persians, Mithra appears as the chief yazata (Avestan, "beneficent one"), or good spirit, and ruler of the world. He was supposed to have slain the divine bull, from whose dying body sprang all plants and animals beneficial to humanity. After the conquest of Assyria in the 7th century BC and of Babylonia in the 6th century BC, Mithra became the god of the sun, which was worshipped in his name (see SUN WORSHIP). The Greeks of Asia Minor, by identifying Mithra with Helios (q.v.), the Greek god of the sun, helped to spread the cult. It was brought to Rome about 68 BC by Cilician pirates whom the Roman general Pompey the Great had captured, and during the early empire it spread rapidly throughout Italy and the Roman provinces. It was a rival to Christianity in the Roman world.

Mithraism was similar to Christianity in many respects, for example, in the ideals of humility and brotherly love, baptism, the rite of communion, the use of holy water, the adoration of the shepherds at Mithra's birth, the adoption of Sundays and of December 25 (Mithra's birthday) as holy days, and the belief in the immortality of the soul, the last judgment, and the resurrection. Mithraism differed from Christianity in the exclusion of women from its ceremonies and in its willingness to compromise with polytheism. The similarities, however, made possible the easy conversion of its followers to Christian doctrine.

MITO, city, Japan, E Honshu Island, capital of Ibaraki Prefecture, on the Naka R., near Tokyo. The city is a railroad and marketing center; its chief manufactures are cloth and paper. Pop. (1987 est.) 232,100.

MITOSIS. See CELL: *Division, Reproduction, and Differentiation;* GENETICS: *Physical Basis of Heredity.*

MITRE, Bartolomé (1821–1906), Argentine statesman, military leader, and historian, born in Buenos Aires. While he was still young, his political views and writings incurred the enmity of the Argentine dictator Juan Manuel de Rosas. After living in exile in Chile, Bolivia, and Peru, Mitre returned to Argentina in 1852 and participated in the overthrow of Rosas by Gen. Justo José Urquiza (1800–70). In 1853 Mitre was appointed minister of war in the Buenos Aires provincial government and in this post attempted to resist Urquiza's plan for the province to join the newly proclaimed Argentine Republic. In 1859 the troops under Mitre's command were defeated by Urquiza, and Buenos Aires joined the federation. Mitre was made governor of Buenos Aires Province in 1860 and defeated Urquiza at the Battle of Pavon in 1861. The next year he was elected to a 6-year term as president of the republic. He was defeated for the presidency in 1874 and again in 1891. Mitre founded the influential newspaper *La Nación* (The Nation) in 1870. His works include histories of South America and Argentina.

MITROPOULOS, Dimitri (1896–1960), Greek-American conductor, acclaimed for his interpretations of the works of 20th-century composers. Born in Athens and educated in Athens, Brussels, and under the Italian composer Ferruccio Busoni in Berlin, he began his career as assistant conductor of the Berlin State Opera. In 1932 he became conductor of the Paris Symphony Orchestra. He made his American debut in 1936 with the Boston Symphony Orchestra and later was conductor of the Minneapolis Symphony (1937–49) and of the New York Philharmonic (1950–58). Mitropoulos was also a noted operatic conductor (La Scala, Milan; Metropolitan Opera Company, New York City). His near-perfect memory enabled him to conduct without a score. He became a U.S. citizen in 1946.

MITTERRAND, François Maurice (1916–), president of France (1981–). Born at Jarnac, Mitterrand studied law, literature, and political science at the University of Paris, served in the French army during World War II, and was active in the Resistance during the German occupation of France. He was elected to the National Assembly in 1946 and later served as minister for overseas territories (1950–51), minister of the interior (1954–55), and minister of state for justice (1956–57). In 1965 he ran unsuccessfully for the presidency against Charles de Gaulle as the candidate of the non-Communist left, and in 1971 he emerged as the leader of a new Socialist party. With Communist support, he ran against President Valéry Giscard d'Estaing in 1974, losing by a narrow margin. In 1981 Mitterrand again challenged Giscard, winning a decisive victory and becoming the first Socialist president of the Fifth Republic. Although he gave some Communists minor posts in his government, his foreign policy was firmly anti-Soviet; at home he nationalized banks and some major industries and increased economic benefits for the working class. After right-wing parties won the National Assembly elections in 1986, he entered into a power-sharing arrangement with the new conservative prime minister, Jacques René Chirac (1932–). Mitterrand defeated Chirac and several other challengers in the 1988 presidential election.

MIXTEC, Indian group, living in what are now the Mexican states of Oaxaca, Guerrero, and Puebla, and comprising the Mixtecan stock and language family. The Mixtec culture flourished in southern Mexico from the 9th to the early 16th century.

The Mixtec were the most famous craftspeople in Mexico, and even today some of the finest art comes from this group. Their metalwork and stonework were unsurpassed. Other specialties included feather mosaics, painted polychrome pottery, and fabric weaving and embroidery.

Among significant contributions made by the Mixtec were the pictographic recording of military and social history (many of these codices survive today); agricultural techniques; architecture (ruins of Mitla and Monte Albán are some of the most impressive in Mexico); and a calendar similar to the one used by the Aztecs. The Mixtec were marginally involved in the declining Mayan civilization to the south and remained fiercely independent of the Aztecs to the north.

MIYAZAKI, city, Japan, SE Kyushu Island, capital of Miyazaki Prefecture, on the Hyuga Sea (an arm of the Pacific Ocean), at the mouth of Oyodo R. It is a fishing port and a rail junction on the Nippo Line. Chinaware and trays are manufactured here. It is the site of a feudal castle and of one of the oldest Shinto shrines in Japan, the Miyazaki-jingu, dedicated to the first emperor. It is also the site of Miyazaki University (1949). Nearby attractions include views from the Heiwadai Hills; beaches at Hitotsuka; Aoshima Island, with tropical plants; the Uto cave shrine; and the Omiya racetrack. Pop. (1987 est.) 283,500.

MKS SYSTEM. See INTERNATIONAL SYSTEM OF UNITS; METRIC SYSTEM.

MNEMOSYNE, in Greek mythology, the goddess of memory. She and Zeus, father of the gods, were the parents of the nine Muses. Mnemosyne was one of the pre-Olympian Titans, who were the children of the god of the heavens, Uranus, and the goddess of the earth, Gaea.

MOA, common name, originally used by the Maoris, for about 20 species of ostrichlike birds of the order Dinornithiformes that inhabited New Zealand. All are extinct, although one species may have persisted until early in the 19th century. Most moa bones have been found in swamps, others in sands, riverbeds, and in dry caves, where bits of skin and feathers have been preserved. Many pieces of their thick-shelled eggs and a few whole eggs have been found, one containing a large embryo. Moas varied greatly in size, from about 1 m (about 39 in) to 4 m (13 ft) in height. Unlike ostriches, moas lacked even the rudiments of wings. Their legs were massive and relatively short. Moas were widespread in New Zealand when it was colonized by a prehistoric people about 1000 years ago, but were extinct or extremely rare by the time of Captain James Cook's first visit in 1769.

MOAB, ancient country on the hill plateau east of the Dead Sea, in what is now Jordan. The Moabites were closely related to the Hebrews and were subject to Israel during the reigns of David and Solomon (11th–10th cent. BC). They later regained their independence but were temporarily reconquered by Omri, king of Israel (r. 876–869 BC). Moab, like neighboring Judah, became tributary to Assyria in the 8th century BC and was conquered by the Babylonians in the 6th century BC. After that the Moabites ceased to exist as a separate people. The Moabites are frequently mentioned in the Bible. King Solomon built an altar to their god Chemosh in Jerusalem. Ruth, the central figure of the Book of Ruth, was a Moabite and, according to that book, and to the Gospel according to Matthew, the great grandmother of King David.

The Moabite stone, a block of black basalt found near Dibon, Jordan, in 1868, bears an inscription in the Moabite language from about 850 BC, describing a 9th-century BC victory of King Mesha of Moab over the Israelites. The stone is now in the Louvre in Paris.

MOBILE, city, seat of Mobile Co., SW Alabama, a port of entry on Mobile Bay at the mouth of the Mobile R.; inc. 1814. Alabama's only seaport, and one of the busiest in the U.S., it is an outlet for the agricultural and mineral products of the state. Major local manufactures include paper, ships, chemicals, forest products, textiles, processed food, aerospace equipment, and refined petroleum. The University of South Alabama (1963), University of Mobile (1961), and Spring Hill College (1830) are in the city.

Mobile retains an old Southern and French flavor, and it is known for its magnificent gardens and old houses, many of which are decorated with elaborate wrought-iron work. Tourist attractions include Fort Condé (1720, since reconstructed), Oakleigh Mansion (1833), a Romanesque-style cathedral (1850), the West Indies-style city hall (about 1855), several museums, and the World War II battleship USS *Alabama,* anchored in the harbor. The city has a large auditorium and theater complex and a sports stadium. A museum and municipal archives are also here. Popular annual events are the Mardi Gras celebration and the Azalea Trail Festival.

A French colony was established near the site of Mobile in 1702; it was relocated here in 1711 after a flood, and served as the capital of French Louisiana until 1718. The settlement passed to Great Britain in 1763 and was taken by the Spanish in 1780. The U.S., which made a disputed claim to Mobile as part of the Louisiana Purchase (1803), seized the city in 1813, during the War of 1812. It grew in the 19th century as a great cotton port. During the American Civil War the port remained open until August 1864, when a federal fleet scored a decisive naval victory in Mobile Bay. Union troops captured the city in April 1865. The city's name is derived from the French version of the name of the Indians who lived in the region in the early 18th century. Pop. (1980) 200,452; (1990) 196,278.

MOBILE, river, SW Alabama, formed at the junction of the Tombigbee and Alabama rivers. About 61 km (about 38 mi) long, it flows through a delta to its submerged mouth in Mobile Bay at Mobile, Ala. The river is an important artery for transporting agricultural and industrial goods.

MOBILE, in art, type of sculpture characterized by the ability to move when propelled by air currents, by touch, or by a small motor at any one time. The most striking feature of the mobile is that, unlike traditional sculpture, it achieves its artistic effect through movement; it is the most familiar form of kinetic art, which requires movement of some kind. A typical mobile consists of a group of shapes, frequently abstract, that are connected by wires, string, metal rods, or the like. Although mobiles are usually suspended, some are designed to stand on a platform or floor. The first experimental mobiles were the work of the French artist Marcel Duchamp in the 1920s. The form, however, was developed to its finest expression by the American sculptor Alexander Calder, beginning in the 1930s. *See also* MODERN ART AND ARCHITECTURE.

MOBILE BAY, BATTLE OF, major naval engagement of the American Civil War. After the capture of Vicksburg in 1863, the Union admiral David Farragut determined to take Mobile, Ala., from the Confederates. This was a difficult task, as troops were required to capture the protecting forts, and a strong naval force was needed. About 6 AM on Aug. 5, 1864, Farragut, with 4 monitors, or armored warships, and 14 wooden vessels, entered the bay. As the wooden ships advanced in pairs, Fort Morgan began to fire. The monitor *Tecumseh* was blown up and sank almost instantly. The monitor *Hartford,* risking the torpedoes, reached the open water above the fort. After partly disabling the fort, the other vessels followed and engaged in battle with the Confederate warship *Tennessee.* The latter soon took refuge under the forts, returned to action, and, after a severe struggle with the federal ships, surrendered at 10 AM. A few days later the forts surrendered, but the city of Mobile itself was not captured until April 1865.

MÖBIUS STRIP, figure formed by taking a long, rectangular strip of paper and joining the ends together to form a loop, after first rotating the ends 180° with respect to one another before joining them. In topology (q.v.) this strip is taken as being analogous to a two-dimensional surface that has been rotated and joined in the same manner and would then be a surface with only one side. This property is demonstrated by drawing a line down the middle of the loop; the line eventually meets itself after following both "sides" of the loop. The actual Möbius strip is only analogous to the two-dimensional situation, however, because the loop of paper is in fact a three-dimensional figure that is topologically equivalent to a torus, or doughnut-shaped figure. The Möbius strip is named after the German mathematician August Ferdinand Möbius (1790–1868), who was a pioneer in topology.

MOBUTU SESE SEKO (1930–   ), president of Zaire (1965–   ). Born in Lisala, in the Belgian Congo, Mobutu, whose original name was Joseph Désiré Mobutu, joined the Belgian colonial army at the age of 19. Although he later left the army for journalism, he was appointed chief of staff in 1960, when the Congo won its independence. During the postindependence turmoil, Mobutu, backed by the army, temporarily suspended the civilian government, but he soon restored it to power and after that concentrated on rebuilding the army. In November 1965 he staged a second coup and assumed the presidency himself.

Mobutu stabilized the country and ruled with a strong hand, stressing "return to African authenticity"; thus the Congo was renamed Zaire in 1971. His government, however, was plagued by corruption and mismanagement, and Zaire's economy suffered as Mobutu's own personal fortune grew. As the 1990s began he continued to cling to power, despite rising opposition.

MOCK ORANGE

MOCCASIN, also water moccasin or cottonmouth, common name for a poisonous aquatic snake, one of the pit vipers of the viper family. It is called cottonmouth because the lining of its mouth is white. It lives in swamps of the southeastern U.S. and parts of Illinois, Kansas, Oklahoma, and Texas. It is a slow-moving snake with hollow fangs that inject a toxin destructive to red blood cells. The bite, however, is rarely fatal, although it is painful and can cause local tissue damage. Brown or olive, with broad black bands across its body, the water moccasin averages 1.2 m (4 ft) in length. It feeds on fish and amphibians.

The slightly smaller tropical moccasin inhabits Mexico and Central America. Another moccasin found in the U.S. is better known as the American copperhead. The name *moccasin* is also misapplied to some harmless water snakes. See also COPPERHEAD; VIPER.

COMMON NAME	FAMILY	GENUS AND SPECIES
Water moccasin	Viperidae	*Agkistrodon piscivorus*
Tropical moccasin	Viperidae	*A. bilineatus*

MOCCASIN FLOWER. See LADY'S SLIPPER.

MOCKINGBIRD, common name for passerine (q.v.) birds of the genera *Mimus, Melanotis,* and *Mimodes* of the New World songbird family Mimidae, from southern Canada to Chile and Argentina. The northern mockingbird, *Mimus polyglottos,* is one of the most famous avian mimics, combining in its song notes of its own with imitations of birds, mammals, or mechanical sounds. This species is about 25 cm (about 10 in) long, gray above and grayish white to white below, with flashy white markings on the black wings and tail. The slender bill, straight or slightly curved, is used in feeding on insects, seeds, and fruits.

Most mockingbirds are tropical; the northern mockingbird has expanded northward in the U.S. and southern Canada since the 1950s, when it was rarely seen north of New Jersey. The tropical members of the genus *Mimus* include eight species found from Cuba and Mexico to southern South America, and a group confined to the Galápagos Islands, where nine distinctive kinds have evolved, sometimes placed in a separate genus, *Nesomimus.* The two blue mockingbirds, genus *Melanotis,* inhabit Mexico and Central America. The Socorro mockingbird, *Mimodes graysoni,* is confined to the largest of the Revillagigedo Islands in the Pacific, southwest of the Baja California peninsula. It is considered an endangered species, having been nearly exterminated by feral cats.

MOCK ORANGE, common name for shrubs of the genus *Philadelphus,* of the family Hydrangeaceae (see HYDRANGEA). Native to temperate regions of

415

MODE

the northern hemisphere, the shrubs produce dark-green, opposite leaves, and showy, white flowers borne singly or in cymes. The flower has a pear-shaped, 4- or 5-parted calyx, 4 or 5 rounded petals, 20 to 40 stamens, and a solitary pistil. The fruit is a septicidal capsule. Common mock orange, or syringa, *P. coronarius,* is a fragrant shrub, native to southern Europe and widely cultivated throughout the temperate regions of the world, growing about 2 m (about 8 ft) high. Common mock orange is the state flower of Idaho. *P. inodorus* is a similar shrub, although the flowers lack fragrance. It is native to the eastern U.S. and cultivated throughout temperate North America. *P. pubescens* is a tall shrub, growing as high as 3 m (10 ft), native to the southern U.S. Western mock orange, *P. lewisii,* is a shrub, usually about 2 m (about 6 ft) high, native to the northwestern U.S. Taller, fragrant mock oranges, such as *P. delavayi, P. sericanthus, P. incanus,* and *P. purpurescens,* are native to eastern Asia.

MODE, in mathematics, the number in a given set of numbers that appears most frequently. If two such numbers occur, the set has two modes. Other sets may have no modes. In the set 3, 4, 5, 6, 6, 7, 10, 13, for example, the mode is 6.

MODE, in music, term that varies in meaning from a scale to a scale-based formula for constructing melodies. The eight modes of medieval and Renaissance music (often called church or ecclesiastical modes) were scale patterns that formed the foundations of Gregorian chant. Compositions written in these modes used these scale patterns and also had characteristic dominant and final tones. Except for two modes, known now as the major and minor scales, the church modes fell out of use in cultivated music in the 17th century; closely related scales, however, survived in folk music (*see* SCALE).

Modes also form the basis of most Arabic and Indian music and of other music of the Middle and Far East. There, however, the concept of a mode is more comprehensive than it is in the West, encompassing scale formations, melodic types, and typical figurations.

The term *mode* also refers to the system of short rhythmic patterns used in 13th-century Western music. These were repeated throughout a composition, the choice of mode being indicated by how the notes were grouped in the notation. The rhythmic modes fell out of use in the 14th century, when less rigid means of notating rhythms were devised. The longer, more complex, repeated rhythm patterns of Arabic and Indian music can also be termed rhythmic modes.

MODEM, device that enables computer (q.v.) data to be transmitted over a telephone line. The word modem is a condensation of the term *mod*ulator/*dem*odulator, because the device takes digital data from a computer and uses them to modulate a carrier wave—which it generates—in ways suited for telephone transmission. In turn, it demodulates an incoming wave and converts it into digital form. The modulation used depends on the application and the speed of operation for which the modem is designed. If both ends of the link can transmit data, it is said to be operating in full duplex mode; if only one can, the mode is called half duplex. Modems can dial phone numbers retrieved from computer storage, coordinate data flow, change the speed of transmission, and test communication circuits.

MODENA (anc. *Mutina*), city, N Italy, capital of Modena Province, in Emilia-Romagna Region. The city is an agricultural and industrial center, with factories producing machinery, steel, motor vehicles, and processed foods. It has a university (1175), an academy of sciences and arts, an observatory, a botanic garden, and military schools. It is the seat of an archbishop. The Cathedral of Saint Germinianus, a Romanesque building begun in 1099, has a fine facade; its campanile is one of the great towers of Italy. Founded as an Etruscan town, Modena became a Roman colony in the 2d century BC. From 1288 until 1452, when it became the capital of a duchy, Modena was ruled by the Este family. In 1861 it became part of the kingdom of Italy. Pop. (1988 est.) 176,600.

MODERN ART AND ARCHITECTURE, terms roughly designating 20th-century art and architecture, comprising a multiplicity of movements, styles, and schools.

MODERN ART

Parallel to the rapid scientific, technological, and social changes that have taken place in the 20th century are the rich varieties of art styles that have developed. Notable are the number of "isms," such as Fauvism, expressionism, cubism, futurism, constructivism, neoplasticism, surrealism, precisionism, and minimalism.

ORIGINS OF MODERN ART

The roots of modern art can be seen in French 19th-century avant-garde painting. During the 1860s artists became increasingly preoccupied with style—how a subject should be painted. Édouard Manet flattened figures, reducing them to broadly painted, silhouetted forms; the impressionists (*see* IMPRESSIONISM)—Camille Pissarro, Claude Monet, and Pierre Auguste Renoir and the Englishman Alfred Sisley—were interested in rendering the effects of light on objects rather than the actual textures of things. Later in the century the postimpressionists initiated new styles that would determine the course of paint-

Paul Cézanne's Bridge at Maincy *(1879–80, Louvre, Paris) forms a link between his earlier impressionistic style and his growing interest in problems of geometric form and planar design—which ultimately led to cubism.* Editorial Photocolor Archives

ing in the first decades of the 20th century: Georges Seurat modified the loose, impressionist brushstroke into precise dots, juxtaposing complementary colors (pointillism); Paul Gauguin exaggerated forms and used color arbitrarily to create decorative shapes; and Vincent van Gogh's expressionist distortions of line and color would have great implications for the Norwegian Edvard Munch and the German expressionists. Paul Cézanne's discoveries, however, were undoubtedly most decisive. Cézanne developed a system of scaling his colors and building color planes; this system simultaneously gave form to objects yet remained abstract in itself. While basing his art on nature, he was more concerned with its structural principles, as Pablo Picasso and Georges Braque would be in their protocubist landscapes and still-life analyses.

PAINTING

The common denominator among these various late 19th-century artists was a diminished concern for reality and for an approach that was true to nature, and a greater concern for personal freedom of expression. About the turn of the century their work began to gain acceptance; meanwhile, a young generation of painters adopted even greater distortions of line, color, and pictorial space, a development that so angered the critics that they dubbed these artists *les fauves,* literally the "wild beasts" (*see* FAUVISM). Among these French artists (who built on Gauguin's discoveries) were Henri Matisse, André Derain, Maurice de Vlaminck, the Dutch painter Kees van Dongen (1877–1968), and Braque. Although Fauvism was a relatively short episode (1905–7) in their careers, their pictures were to have an impact on the development of art in Germany.

Expressionism. Artists in both France and Germany shared an interest in primitivism. Gauguin searched for it first in Brittany and later in the South Seas; Vlaminck claimed he was among the first artists to discover African sculpture. In Germany, a group of young artists known as Die Brücke (*see* BRÜCKE, DIE), "The Bridge," regularly visited the Dresden Ethnological Museum and, like the Fauves, were inspired by the boldness and power of primitive art. The leading Brücke artists were Ernst Ludwig Kirchner, Erich Heckel (1883–1970), Karl Schmidt-Rottluff, and Emil Nolde. Known also as the German expressionists (*see* EXPRESSIONISM), they worked in a simpli-

MODERN ART AND ARCHITECTURE

fied style somewhat resembling Fauvism, but with the added ingredient of angst—their work frequently portrayed the sufferings of humanity. A second group of artists, Der Blaue Reiter ("The Blue Rider"), was organized in Munich in 1911 by the painters Wassily Kandinsky (a Russian émigré) and Franz Marc. Also inspired by primitivism, Fauvism, and folk art, their expressionism took the significant direction of semiabstract painting. *See* BLAUE REITER, DER.

Cubism. Interest in primitive sculpture also played a role in the formation of cubism (q.v.). Picasso's protocubist works, such as *Les Demoiselles d'Avignon* (1907, Museum of Modern Art, New York City), display his interest in both African and ancient Iberian art. Picasso and Braque developed cubism between 1907 and 1914, creating the most influential style of the modern period. In cubism, the flat, two-dimensional surface of the picture plane is emphasized, and traditional perspective, foreshortening, modeling, and chiaroscuro (contrast of light and dark) are rejected. In its first phase, called analytic cubism, which ended by 1912, artists were concerned with breaking down and analyzing form. Right-angled and straight-line construction and monochromatic color schemes were favored in cubist depictions of motifs that were radically fragmented to show several sides simultaneously. Its second phase, generally called synthetic cubism,

Les demoiselles d'Avignon *(1907), by Pablo Picasso, a key work in the development of cubism. Representation here gave way to a purely geometric analysis of human form from which nothing detracts.* Museum of Modern Art–Bequest of Lillie P. Bliss

grew out of experiments with collage (q.v.). Foreign materials were pasted onto the picture in combination—synthesis—with painted surfaces. Although shapes remained fragmented and flat, color played a strong role in synthetic cubism, and the works are more decorative. The leading practitioners of cubism, who created personal modifications of it, were the French artists Fernand Léger, Robert and Sonia Delaunay, and Marcel Duchamp, the Spaniard Juan Gris, and the Czech František Kupka. Several Italian artists, notably Gino Severini, Umberto Boccioni, Carlo Carrà, and Giacomo Balla, employed the cubist style but called their movement futurism (q.v.); among other things, they were concerned with expressing motion in art through rhythmic repetition of lines and images.

Abstract Art. Cubism was also crucial to the development of nonobjective, or abstract, art (see ABSTRACT ART). In Germany, Kandinsky painted semiabstract pictures containing references to nature and music in 1910 (his dating), and Paul Klee, a Swiss, did some abstract watercolors after his first exposure to cubism. Russian artists were aware of cubism through a few outstanding private collections in Moscow and evolved a different, geometrically constructed abstract art. Kasimir Malevich, a devout Christian mystic, painted a black square on a white ground in 1913, naming his personal abstractions suprematism (q.v.), which to him expressed the "supremacy of feeling in creative art." Other cubist-inspired Russian painters, known as constructivists (see CONSTRUCTIVISM), were Alexander Rodchenko (1891-1956), Liubov Popova (1889-1924), El Lissitzky (1890-1941), Naum Gabo, Antoine Pevsner, and Vladimir Tatlin.

Simultaneous with the emergence of abstract art in Russia were developments in the Netherlands, where artists wanted to create a universal, harmonious style suitable to every aspect of contemporary life, from town planning and furniture design to painting and sculpture. Their movement was called De Stijl (see STIJL, DE), "The Style"; its principles were primarily formulated and transmitted by Theo van Doesburg and Piet Mondrian, in their periodical of the same name. Mondrian, who was familiar with cubism from his first Paris trip, returned there in 1920 and published his first major essay, *Le Néo-Plasticisme*. He stated that cubism's goal should be the expression of pure plastics (forms) and, in his painting, he narrowed his range of colors, sticking basically to primaries. Using straight lines to create grids, he eliminated the illusion of depth, respecting the flat, two-dimensional surface of the canvas.

Dada. The Dada (q.v.) movement, which arose both in Europe and America during World War I, was the antithesis of the rationalism of Mondrian and other theorists of abstraction. A group of war resisters who were disgusted with bourgeois values chose a nonsense word, *dada* (Fr., "hobbyhorse"), to describe their protest activities and antiaesthetic works. Best known of the many artists and writers associated with Dada was Duchamp, who invented the ready-made, a mass-produced object that he designated as sculpture. Most notorious of these was a urinal he entitled *Fontaine,* which he exhibited in New York City in 1917. Other artists involved with Dada were the Frenchmen Jean Arp and Francis Picabia, the American Man Ray, and the Germans George Grosz and Max Ernst.

Surrealism. Although Dada had lost its force by 1922, some of its practitioners directed their energies toward the newly emerging surrealism (q.v.), in which, as in Dada, accident and chance were employed in the creation of art. The Italian Giorgio de Chirico's haunting, dreamlike paintings of desolate city squares and enigmatic statues anticipated surrealism by several years. It was the Frenchman André Breton, however, who gave the movement its name and manifesto in 1924, asserting the superiority of the subconscious mind and the importance of dreams in the creation of art. Little stylistic similarity can be found among the surrealists, who mainly shared an ideal of spontaneous, irrational inspiration. Those working in a figurative style were Ernst, the Spaniard Salvador Dali, the Belgians René Magritte and Paul Delvaux (1897-), and Man Ray; those working in more abstract styles included Arp, the Frenchmen André Masson (1896-1987) and Yves Tanguy, and the Spaniard Joan Miró.

Emergence of Modern Painting in America. Until the late 1940s, nearly all the various styles and movements of the modern period originated in Europe and later spread to America. American impressionism, for example, began nearly two decades after its inception in France and, with a few notable exceptions such as Childe Hassam, lacked the vitality seen in the French paintings. American impressionist painters generally presented landscapes or refined pictures of genteel life. The Eight, a group of young artists led by Robert Henri, revolted against this kind of art. Known as the Ashcan school because of their homely subjects, they concentrated on ordinary—even ugly—city scenes, rendering them in straightforward, conventional styles that bordered occasionally on illustration. Cézanne's discoveries and Fauvism and cubism were relatively

MODERN ART AND ARCHITECTURE

unknown in America until after the celebrated Armory Show (q.v.), an international art exhibition held in New York City in 1913. Some American artists, notably Max Weber, Arthur Dove, and Marsden Hartley, did work abroad, however, and were able to exhibit their work at the photographer Alfred Stieglitz's famous 291 Gallery in New York City. American assimilation of cubism resulted in such variants as synchronism, an abstract style stressing color rhythms, developed by Morgan Russell (1886–1953) and Stanton Macdonald-Wright (1890–1973), and precisionism, a sharp-focus, stylized realism in which cubism's flattening of objects and pictorial space is modified. Works by Charles Demuth, Georgia O'Keeffe, and Charles Sheeler exhibit the precisionist style; favorite subjects were skyscrapers, barns, and the industrial landscape. Abstract art continued its development: Stuart Davis painted joyous pictures, evocative of jazz in their rhythmic combination of lettering and bouncing color planes; European immigrant artists transmitted Mondrian's De Stijl principles; and American collectors were establishing museums with modernist paintings, which had a powerful impact on the younger generation of avant-garde artists.

American Realists and Regionalists. Despite the growing acceptance of European modernism in the U.S., the 1930s was also a period of reaction and rebellion against imported styles. Many artists, although they had studied abroad, favored an art that would distinctly express the American scene. Urban realist painters such as Ben Shahn, Reginald Marsh, and William Gropper (1897–1977) made paintings and graphics that depicted the political, social, and economic conditions of the Great Depression era; and the regionalists Grant Wood, Thomas Hart Benton, and John Steuart Curry drew inspiration from rural midwestern life and folklore. One of the most powerful realists to emerge was Edward Hopper, who explored the loneliness and isolation of people in both urban and small-town environments. Although Hopper claimed his chief interest was in capturing light, the psychological aspect of his work is most compelling. After World War II, another realist, Andrew Wyeth, became the most popular American artist of his time. Employing a spare, somber style, he created evocative images of rural life that frequently had a dreamlike quality akin to the style that is known as magic realism.

Typical of Mark Rothko's large color-field abstractions is Red Picture *(1957). Softly defined bars of reds of different intensities appear to float between viewer and picture plane.*
Private Collection—Acquavella Contemporary Art, Inc.

MODERN ART AND ARCHITECTURE

Christopher Isherwood and Don Bachardy (1968, private collection), a double portrait by David Hockney. In Hockney's neorealist style, figures and objects are precisely rendered but imbued with a slight whimsicality. Petersburg Press

Abstract Expressionism. A number of American artists who had been realists in the 1930s created a new movement in the following decades called abstract expressionism (also known as action painting, or the New York school). The presence in the U.S. during World War II of many European surrealists was decisive in the development of abstract expressionism. From them the American artists derived an interest in the subconscious, symbolism, and myth. Also influenced by the surrealist technique of automatism, these painters began producing totally spontaneous works in which the painting process itself became the subject matter, as in the freely created drip paintings of Jackson Pollock. Other artists sharing Pollock's gestural approach were Willem de Kooning, Franz Kline, Hans Hofmann, and Robert Motherwell.

Gestural painting was one of the two directions in abstract expressionism; the other was color-field painting, in which artists applied large, subtly modulated expanses of color to the canvas. The leaders of this technique included Clyfford Still, Mark Rothko, Barnett Newman, and Morris Louis.

Pop Art and Other Movements. With abstract expressionism established as the dominant American style, some artists began rebelling against what they regarded as its excessively solemn and theoretical character. Drawing their imagery from advertisements, comic strips, films, and everyday objects, they became known as pop artists (*see* POP ART). Although pop art is thought of as distinctively American, it originated in London with an exhibition by Richard Hamilton (1922–) and others. The leading American pop artists were Andy Warhol, Jasper Johns, Robert Rauschenberg, Roy Lichtenstein, Tom Wesselmann (1931–), and James Rosenquist (1933–).

The influence of pop art could be seen in photorealism, which emerged in the late 1960s and favored such subjects as neon signs, cafeterias, and commonplace urban and suburban scenes. These were meticulously rendered with the help of photography, resulting in a precisely detailed, impersonal verisimilitude. The Americans Richard Estes (1936–), Robert Cottingham (1935–), Chuck Close (1940–), and Don Eddy (1944–) were the most prominent photorealist painters.

Abstract painting continued to develop in both the U.S. and Europe. Op art, in which stark black-and-white patterns or brilliant color contrasts were intended to create opti-

421

MODERN ART AND ARCHITECTURE

cal illusions, was one direction abstraction took in the 1960s and '70s. Another, influenced by color-field art and the austere geometric paintings of the German-American Josef Albers, was minimalism. It ranged from the rigorous geometric forms of Kenneth Noland to the serialized patterns of Larry Poons (1937–) to the almost monochromatic canvases of Robert Ryman (1930–). Conceptual art, in which the artist's idea or concept took precedence over and sometimes replaced the actual work, carried the analytical impulse of minimalism one step further.

Neoexpressionism and New Realists. By the 1980s a reaction had developed against the impersonal, inexpressive quality of minimalism and other abstract styles, leading to a revival of figurative and narrative painting known as neoexpressionism. Intensely subjective, visionary, and provocative, the neoexpressionists frequently employed a style, characterized by distorted forms and strong coloring, that owed much to the German expressionists of 70 years earlier. Among the painters associated with neoexpressionism were the Germans Anselm Kiefer (1945–), Georg Baselitz (1938–), and A. R. Penck (1939–); the Italians Sandro Chia (1946–), Francesco Clemente (1952–), and Enzo Cucchi (1950–); and the Americans Julian Schnabel (1951–) and David Salle (1952–).

Before neoexpressionism returned figurative painting to critical fashion in the 1980s, a number of independent realist painters had already built distinguished careers on the depiction of the human figure. The isolated, tormented figures of Francis Bacon, the deft, urbane portraits and domestic scenes of David Hockney, and the unflinching realism of Lucien Freud (1922–) testified to the strength of the representational tradition in English art. In America, the precise, formally rigorous nude studies of Philip Pearlstein (1924–), which assimilated some of the concerns of abstract art, showed the way for many outstanding younger realist painters.

SCULPTURE

Like modern painters, sculptors were influenced by primitive and ancient art, as demonstrated in the early works of the Romanian-French master Constantin Brancusi and the Englishman Henry Moore. Brancusi also simplified form to an ultimate degree, as in *The Newborn* (1915, Arensberg Collection, Philadelphia Museum of Art), an ovoid shape that at once suggests an egg, the human head, and an infant's cry. Brancusi combined a subtle wit with a consummate skill in bringing out the intrinsic beauty of materials, whether wood, stone, or metal. Moore also respected the beauty of materials, shaping masses

Sky Reflection (1962–77), a standing wall by Louise Nevelson, is an assemblage of pieces of wood, painted black. Interest is generated by the contrast between the boxlike frames and the random shapes. The Pace Gallery

and voids to create elegant, monumental works. Inspired by pre-Columbian sculpture, he chose as his lifelong theme the reclining female figure.

Major 20th-Century Sculptors. Several early 20th-century sculptors were affected by cubism and other movements, namely, the Russian-born Alexander Archipenko, the Frenchman Raymond Duchamp-Villon, and the Lithuanian-born Jacques Lipchitz. All dealt with the human figure, giving emphasis to geometric planes, although Lipchitz, in his later work, became strongly expressionistic, sculpting baroque, writhing forms based on universal themes from the Bible and ancient myth. In Russia, constructivists emphasized sculptural space rather than mass. Chief sculptors were Vladimir Tatlin, famous for his proposed *Monument to the Third International* (1919–20, model, Russian State Museums, Saint Petersburg); Rodchenko; and Lissitzky, who transmitted constructivism to Western Europe in the 1920s. Constructivist works by the brothers Naum Gabo and Antoine Pevsner were later to have an influence on American abstract art, as were those by the Hungarian László Moholy-Nagy. The Dada artist Duchamp made the first mobile sculpture in 1913, when he mounted a bicycle wheel on a stool; he was later to give the name "mobiles" to the movable sculptures of the American Alexander Calder. Disparaging traditional ways of making sculpture, Duchamp began, in the second decade of the 20th century,

MODERN ART AND ARCHITECTURE

to select his ready-mades, such as a bottle rack, snow shovel, and a coat hook. About the same time other sculptors such as Picasso, Ernst, and Man Ray also began to incorporate found objects in their work. Frequently these objects would take on strange, surreal aspects, as with Man Ray's *The Gift* (1921, Museum of Modern Art), a flatiron with nails projecting from its base. Not all surrealist sculptors employed found objects, however; Arp created compelling abstract, organic fantasies suggestive of life and growth, and the Swiss Alberto Giacometti's haunting, elongated figures express the isolation of the modern individual. The abstract and geometric principles of neoplasticism were absorbed by Calder, whose early abstract wire constructions and use of pure, primary colors on his mobiles and stabiles owe a debt to Mondrian. Other sculptors who produced abstract and constructed works were the Americans Seymour Lipton, Isamu Noguchi, David Smith, and Mark di Suvero and the English Anthony Caro.

Recent Sculpture. While a number of contemporary sculptors have continued working with methods established earlier in the 20th century—for instance, found objects and assemblage—others have explored new directions. The definition of sculpture has been expanded to include a wide spectrum of new styles, materials, and techniques. The major figures listed below are American artists unless otherwise noted. Minimalists, whose work was characteristically simple, precise, and symmetrical, included Sol LeWitt (1928–) and Donald Judd (1928–). Richard Serra (1939–) created large, obtrusive metal environmental works. Major exponents of earthworks included Robert Morris (1931–) and Robert Smithson. Leading kinetic artists were George Rickey (1907–) and the New Zealand–born Len Lye (1901–80); those working with light included Chryssa (1933–) and Dan Flavin (1933–); with video, the Irish-born Les Levine (1935–) and the Korean Nam June Paik (1932–). The playful soft sculptures of Claes Oldenburg were associated with pop art, as were the white plaster figures of George Segal. Verist sculptors, who created uncannily lifelike figures in colored polyester resin, included Duane Hanson (1925–) and John De Andrea (1941–). The German Joseph Beuys (1921–86) did both assemblages and performance pieces. In the mid-1980s, in the work of Joel Shapiro (1941–) and others, the human figure and organic forms began reappearing in sculpture, a trend known as postminimalist or postmodern sculpture.   M.V.

MODERN ARCHITECTURE

The approach to designing and constructing buildings that has characterized most of the 20th

She (1966–69, Eugene V. Klein, Rancho Santa Fe, Calif.), by Mark di Suvero. Free-hanging elements from this abstract black-painted steel construction (17 m/55 ft long) provide a kinesthetic relationship between it and viewers.   Oil & Steel Gallery, Inc.

MODERN ART AND ARCHITECTURE

century has come to be called modern architecture. First established in Germany after World War I, it rapidly attracted a following in other European countries. In 1932 the Museum of Modern Art in New York City, in a famous exhibition, acclaimed it as the International Style (q.v.). Neither of these terms is descriptive of the movement. Initially, it offered pure abstract forms to replace stylistic traditions inherited from the Renaissance. Gradually this austere purism became diffused, and by the 1980s architectural theory and practice had ceased to follow modernist orthodoxy.

The Renaissance itself had taken diverse directions, yet all of these shared a common trait—they continued to manipulate the orders (columns and entablatures) and the arches and vaults forming the vocabulary of masonry building developed by the Greeks and Romans. In the late 19th century, however, the revival of historic styles had often degenerated into an indiscriminate and unprincipled mixture of borrowings; this mixture was called eclecticism (a term of opprobrium).

ORIGINS OF MODERN ARCHITECTURE

The Industrial Revolution had so changed the technological and social context of design that old concepts were no longer valid. From 1840 on, leading artists, designers, and critics tried to develop new approaches to environmental art. Modern architecture has its roots in a number of transient efforts in various centers.

In England the writer John Ruskin and the designer William Morris encouraged the Arts and Crafts movement (q.v.). Inspired by the medieval past, they denied that machine-made objects could constitute a true culture. They affirmed the importance of handicraft and persuaded leading artists to become involved in the design of ordinary human artifacts and surroundings.

As for technology, the Crystal Palace (q.v.), a huge temporary exhibition building 564 m (1850 ft) long erected (1851) in Hyde Park, London, by the landscape architect Sir Joseph Paxton, was built entirely of iron and glass. Under the circumstances, the fact that it was also beautiful may have been in part accidental. One of the persistent ideas in architectural history, however, is the belief of many—engineers as well as architects—that beauty could be seen in the clear expression of the structural properties of the new materials.

As iron, glass, and steel became abundant, building construction was no longer limited to masonry and timber. Two structures erected for the Paris International Exhibition of 1889 showed this dramatically. The Halle des Machines, by the architect C. L. F. Dutert (1845-1906) and the engineering company Contamin, Pierron, and Charton, had a clear span of 117 m (385 ft). The Eiffel Tower, by Alexandre Gustave Eiffel (1832-1923), soared 305 m (1000 ft) into the sky.

Technology soon came to have an effect on buildings serving more mundane purposes. Highrise buildings were made possible by erection of a steel cage on which to hang the floors and walls, and also through the development of passenger elevators and other devices to improve safety and convenience. The basic skyscraper office building took form in Chicago by the 1890s and spread rapidly elsewhere. Involved were some exceptionally able architects, including Louis Sullivan and other members of the Chicago school (q.v.).

CLASSICISM VERSUS ROMANTICISM

Historians of the arts have noted the interplay of two enduring tendencies: classicism and romanticism. In architecture, the first leads to balanced arrangements of abstract geometric forms; the second toward free, more intuitive shapes sometimes called organic. The contrasting movements in the visual arts—de Stijl (see STIJL, DE) and Art Nouveau (q.v.)—are examples of these two extremes.

Art Nouveau. Art Nouveau appeared in the 1890s in several centers; the name, which is French, was first used by a Paris art gallery. Similar tendencies were called Jugendstil in Germany and Sezessionstil (q.v.) in Austria. In the U.S. its most famous practitioner was Louis Comfort Tiffany, best known for his opulent and decorative glass and metal objects. The style is characterized by openness to the use of all materials and by the uninhibited reduction of everything to free form independent of the dictates of function. Sinuous shapes suggesting natural growth were intertwined regardless of the material employed. Particularly well known are the Parisian Métro Station entrances designed in the Art Nouveau style by Hector Guimard about 1900. Two outstanding architects created two great and contrasting monuments of Art Nouveau. In Barcelona, Spain, Antoni Gaudí designed with idiosyncratic genius a series of buildings whose plans seldom show any right angles. Gaudí's life work is the still unfinished church La Sagrada Familia (the Holy Family; begun 1883). Farther north, in Scotland, Charles Rennie Mackintosh created the Glasgow School of Art (1897-99; library wing 1907-9) with a rectilinear formalism and much vertical emphasis; together with his wife, Margaret MacDonald Mackintosh (1865-1933), Mackintosh also made interiors and furniture of singular distinction.

De Stijl. De Stijl was centered in the Netherlands in the years immediately following 1919. Its leaders were the architect J. J. P. Oud, the architect-painter Theo van Doesburg, and the architect-furniture designer Gerrit Rietveld, whose Schröder House (1924–25) in Utrecht sums up the aims of the movement—to create volumetric subtleties with planes related at right angles, with surfaces in white or in primary colors, and the elimination of all else. To call this classic would be oversimplification; the studied avoidance of symmetry and repetition would alone deny it. Its geometric discipline, however, became an ingredient of modernism.

Sullivan and Wright. In the ebb and flow of these explorations, two American architects—Louis Sullivan and Frank Lloyd Wright—are noteworthy. Louis Sullivan contributed significantly to skyscraper design (see CHICAGO SCHOOL). In addition, he created a vocabulary of highly personalized foliate ornament, usually made of terra-cotta, that links him to Art Nouveau. His Carson Pirie Scott department store (1899–1904) in Chicago displays perhaps the first repetitive statement of the horizontally proportioned rectangular structural bay that was to dominate modern architecture. On its lower floors may be seen some of his finest ornamental panels.

Frank Lloyd Wright repeatedly acknowledged his debt to Sullivan, from whom he learned his craft. As early as 1893 Wright began his own practice, independent of Sullivan, designing a number of houses, of which the Robie House (1909) in Chicago is the best known. These houses, constituting a so-called prairie style, were not at first celebrated at home, but when they became known in the Netherlands they had an unmistakable impact on de Stijl. Wright anchored the houses to the earth with heavy masonry terraces and a big central chimney; he then deployed over and around these a continuous flowing space protected by roofs that extended in bold cantilevers to embrace much of the outdoors. Horizontally dominated barriers between inside and outside dissolved even without the glass transparency that others would later exploit. As one of America's creative personalities, Wright enjoyed a long, productive career. More eccentric genius than representative leader, he attracted a coterie of student assistants in two colonies, Taliesin East near Madison, Wis., and Taliesin West near Phoenix, Ariz. He designed what, after Thomas Jefferson's Monticello, is perhaps America's most admired home, Fallingwater (1936–37), in Bear Run, Pa. Another of his significant designs is the more controversial Guggenheim Museum, in New York City (1946–59).

MODERN ART AND ARCHITECTURE

THE BAUHAUS
In Germany and Austria, too, similar explorations were leading to the establishment of a modern style. Particularly influential were the innovations of two Austrian architects: Otto Wagner, who emphasized function, building materials, and unobscured structure, and Adolf Loos, who dealt with geometric forms uncluttered with superfluous ornamentation. Efforts to find a new language for the industrial age coalesced after the German architect Walter Gropius, whose style was formed under the influence of Peter Behrens, the German precursor of modern architecture, was appointed director of the Weimar Art School after World War I. With his early partner Adolph Meyer (1881–1929), Gropius had already distinguished himself in the design of model factory buildings. The Weimar school, known as the Bauhaus (q.v.), soon moved to Dessau; the new buildings for that school and its faculty residences (1925–26) became the touchstone of a recognizable new movement. In this, they were soon reinforced (1927) by those of the Weissenhof Siedlung ("housing development") near Stuttgart, arranged by the German-American architect Ludwig Mies van der Rohe.

Social Aims of the Bauhaus. This early version of modern architecture was a socially directed program, born in a society deeply scarred by a disastrous war. Under the short-lived Weimar Republic (1919–33), socialist regimes in many cities addressed the problems of urban housing. Progressive architects were linked to these policies, as the *Siedlungen* of Vienna, Berlin, and Frankfurt attest. They proclaimed that professional expertise should be applied to improving the physical environment for all urban society, not merely for the elite.

Adaptation of Industrial Techniques. Given this orientation, these socially aware architects took advantage of industrial techniques, accepting, for example, factory window sash and rejecting expensive materials. While adopting the steel frame, they did not strive for expressive structural gestures. Using this frame, walls could be very thin and comparatively light and either transparent or opaque without changing character. No longer was it necessary that walls and partitions should coincide with column lines, or that corners of buildings should look solid to restrain gravitational forces. Reference to the traditional symbols was taboo; all roofs were flat because the diagonal lines of sloping roofs disrupted geometric purity. The dematerialization of boundary walls dictated that the familiar textures of brick, stone, and wood be suppressed, and that opaque wall surfaces be rendered as untextured white. No a priori

425

MODERN ART AND ARCHITECTURE

assumption of symmetry was permitted. Building masses were to develop as suggested by the program, but not without thoughtful control of proportions. This was the brave new world of pure design. The gifted architects, painters, designers, and craftsmen assembled in the Bauhaus put forward an important body of theory for the visual arts in industrial society.

Mies, who later became director of the Bauhaus, deviated from the emphasis on social concern. In his German Pavilion at the 1929 Barcelona Exposition, and in his Tugendhat House (1930) in Brno, Czech Republic—both of which utilized luxurious building materials—he showed that the new spatial concepts that were growing out of the Bauhaus had important things to say at a high artistic level.

Dispersal of the Bauhaus Staff. In 1933, the Nazi regime outlawed the Bauhaus, and it was closed and disbanded. Gropius and Mies emigrated to the U.S. Gropius was appointed (1937) to chair the Department of Architecture at Harvard, where, until his retirement (1952), he provided the model for the propagation in the U.S. of the Bauhaus concept of design education. He brought with him to that faculty his most gifted pupil, Marcel Breuer, who resigned in 1946 to pursue in New York City an independent career of distinction. Breuer's buildings, such as the Whitney Museum (1966) in New York City, are admired for being at once pleasing to the eye and supremely functional.

Mies went to the Illinois Institute of Technology in Chicago, where he dominated the teach-

The Seagram Building (1958), New York City, by Ludwig Mies van der Rohe and Philip Johnson, is widely considered the most elegant achievement of the International Style.
Esto Photographics, Inc.

MODERN ART AND ARCHITECTURE

The remarkably sculptural Chapel of Notre Dame du Haut (1950–55) in Ronchamp, France, is widely regarded as one of Le Corbusier's masterworks. Esto Photographics, Inc.

ing of architecture and proceeded, in the birthplace of the skyscraper, to carry that building form into its next phase. Applying the theory that outside walls are but a thin skin, it was natural to enclose and thus obscure the structural bones. But what look should be given to that skin? It risked becoming faceless. Mies's efforts to resolve this dilemma can be seen in his 860 Lake Shore Drive Apartments in Chicago (1951) and in the Seagram Building in New York City (1958), done in collaboration with Philip Johnson, who shared Mies's outlook and through his writings as well as his own buildings deeply influenced U.S. architecture. With classical focus on perfection, Mies proclaimed that "God is in the details," and obtained his elegant results by the rigorous suppression of any nonconforming element.

LE CORBUSIER

Early formulations of modernism had gone more or less unnoticed in France, England, and the U.S., crowded out in the 1920s and '30s by Art Deco (q.v.), a streamlined style employed in many public buildings and in several of the great skyscrapers built during the period, such as the Empire State Building (1931) and the Chrysler Building (1930) in New York City. An exception was Charles Édouard Jeanneret, called Le Corbusier, a French-speaking Swiss who practiced in Paris, and whose aesthetic imagination won him a unique position among the early modernists.

Early Works. Le Corbusier's early small buildings, such as the Villa Savoie (1929-30), in Poissy-sur-Seine, France, demonstrate his principles: Set the building up on slender posts (*pilotis*), subdivide interior space freely without reference to structure, place the exterior skin with equal freedom, develop strip windows capable of washing ceilings and walls with light, provide a garden on the roof so as to permit outdoor living. He also proposed radical new cityscapes—slums to be replaced by skyscraper apartments arrayed in verdant parks through which superhighways would flow. This image continues to haunt his admirers, despite numerous sociological shortcomings shown to attend it.

Middle Works. After World War II Le Corbusier realized these visions in the Unité d'Habitation (1946-52), an apartment house in Marseille. By this time Le Corbusier had grasped the sculptural possibilities of reinforced concrete. Instead of weightless skins hung on invisible frames, enclosure and structure again became one, and the building stands as a great carved object.

Designers had foreseen that concrete would become important, but its popularization was

427

The East Building of the National Gallery (1978), Washington, D.C., built by I. M. Pei & Partners. Designed for a difficult trapezoidal site, the wing is composed of two triangular units connected by a skylighted court.   Esto Photographics, Inc.

slow because it was difficult to handle with precision and predictability. Various architects and engineers contributed to its architectural use. In 1901 the French architect-planner Tony Garnier (1869–1948) designed a project (never built) for an entire city to take the place of his native Lyon; it was published as *La cité industrielle* (1918). Much of this project was preoccupied with a vocabulary for concrete. His countryman Auguste Perret designed buildings in exposed concrete in Paris as early as 1902 and designed a remarkable concrete Church of Notre Dame (1922–23), in Le Raincy; he rebuilt the harbor city of Le Havre after World War II.

Late Works. Le Corbusier seemed to glory in concrete's crudity and roughness (Fr. *beton brut*), which was more like a fact of nature than of human craftsmanship. This inspired other architects, especially in England, to work in what they called ''brutalism.'' During the 1950s Le Corbusier and his associates created Chandigarh, a new capital city for the Punjab, in northwest India. Its three great government buildings, rising in a vast plaza, are among the most dramatic architectural gestures of the 20th century. Two French religious buildings crown this extraordinary career: the pilgrimage chapel of Notre Dame du Haut (1950–55), in Ronchamp, Haute Saone, and the Dominican Monastery of La Tourette (1956–60), in Eveux, Rhone. No traces of his original ''purism'' remain, yet the two structures are very different. The chapel is made of sweeping curved masses that envelop very active although intimate space. The monastery, rectangular in conception, reverts to ''brute'' concrete and contains highly complex spaces for community life.

SCANDINAVIAN ARCHITECTURE

Architectural development in Scandinavia features many creative individuals, including the Swede Erik Gunnar Asplund and the Dane Arne Jacobsen (1902–71). Eliel Saarinen, a Finn, went to the U.S. in 1922, where he founded an art school in the European tradition, Cranbrook Academy, in Michigan near Detroit. In that environment his son, Eero, matured, coming to architectural prominence in the 1940s and '50s.

The Finnish architect Alvar Aalto, however, towers above them all. Although in his first works, including the Paimio Sanatorium (1929–33), he embraced the new vocabulary of rectilinear whiteness, he soon turned his back on that idiom as being, for him, thin and sterile. Finland provides fine building materials—granite, brick, timber, ceramic tile, and copper—and Aalto capitalized on their visual and tactile qualities to produce an architecture responsive to the more romantic Finnish traditions and temperament. His buildings are very freely shaped; their complexity reflects his uncanny ability to tailor them to express the ways people move in and perceive space. He frequently uses skylights, for example, both to structure the space and to manipulate light. His Civic Center (1950–52) for the island village of Säynätsalo, Finland, has commercial facilities on the lower floor, above which the modest accommodations for local government achieve a serene monumentality. The church (1956–58) at Vuoksenniska, Finland, is a highly

428

poetic solution to a very difficult program, a combination place of worship and social center.

LATER MODERN ARCHITECTURE

In the decades following World War II, new centralized administrative facilities for governments, corporations, and other institutions proliferated in cities throughout the world. Miesian modernism, lending itself to the industrialized production and assembly of uniform elements, was well suited to these huge structures and became the dominant style of public architecture.

Nervi, Pei, and Saarinen. Reinforced concrete underwent continued industrial refinement, thanks to the efforts of many engineers, including the Italian Pier Luigi Nervi. Precasting, pre- and post-tensioning, and the use of metal and plastic formwork made *beton brut* obsolete. Using massive cranes for placement, it became possible to build high-rise buildings entirely in concrete. The Chinese-American architect I. M. Pei has provided some of the best examples, although his best-known work, the addition to the National Gallery, in Washington, D.C. (1978), is sheathed in marble. Independently of the concern with concrete, Eero Saarinen refined the curtain wall of metal and glass in the General Motors Technical Center (1957), in Warren, Mich., and sought to give form to new thin-shell and suspension engineering possibilities; his greatest success is the Dulles International Airport near Washington, D.C., completed (1963) after his death.

Louis I. Kahn. One more American architect commands inclusion—Louis I. Kahn. His classical and Beaux-Arts education inculcated admiration for basic and universal solid forms and for their axial disposition in Roman compositions (as in the Baths of Caracalla). In midcareer he reconciled these predilections with the tenets of modernism in such extraordinary achievements as the Richards Medical Research Building (1958–61) at the University of Pennsylvania, Philadelphia, and the Salk Institute (1965), in La Jolla, Calif. His renown became such that, like Le Corbusier, he was offered important commissions in developing countries. In this part of his career were the Indian Institute of Management (1975), in Ahmedabad, India, and his designs (1960s) for the capital of Bangladesh at Dacca.

POSTMODERNISM

By the 1960s, it seemed to many architects as well as to the public that the initial purism of modernist architecture had degenerated into sterile and monotonous formulas. The architecture that developed in reaction to modernist orthodoxy became known as postmodernist. Postmodernism did not emerge as a cohesive movement relying, like modernism, on narrow theoretical principles and a single, approved style, but in general it called for greater individuality, complexity, and eccentricity in architectural design, while also demanding acknowledgment of historical precedent and continuity. To a large extent, this style

The Cogan Residence, East Hampton, N.Y., built in 1972 by Charles Gwathmey and Robert Siegel, is a rigorously angular postmodern design relieved by cylindrical forms. The use of glass tends to unite interior and exterior. Esto Photographics, Inc.

was achieved through the innovative reinterpretation of traditional ornamental symbols and patterns.

By the 1980s, postmodernism had become prevalent among architects, especially in the U.S. In keeping with its emphasis on individuality, its practitioners worked in highly diverse styles, ranging from the austere complexity of Richard Meier (1934-) to the contrasting colors and the historical allusions of Michael Graves (1934-) to the elegant flamboyance of Helmut Jahn (1940-). The effect on the most visible form of urban architecture, the corporate office tower, was to give these once mostly anonymous buildings a high stylistic profile, as in Philip Johnson's AT&T building (1984) in New York City. Other prominent postmodern architects included Robert Venturi (1925-), Charles Gwathmey (1938-), and Robert A. M. Stern (1939-).

Accompanying the postmodernist interest in diversity and history was a new concern for the preservation and adaptive reuse of older buildings, as in the conversion by the Italian architect Gae Aulenti (1928-) of a magnificent 1900 railway station in Paris, the Gare d'Orsay, into a museum of 19th-century art called the Musée d'Orsay (1986). As the utopian expectations that inspired modernism faded, its confrontational approach to the architectural heritage was replaced by a new sense of respect for and obligation to it.

See also ARCHITECTURE; ARCH AND VAULT; COLUMN. For additional information on individual architects, see biographies of those whose names are not followed by dates.

For further information on this topic, see the Bibliography in volume 28, sections 660-61, 680, 712.

MODERN DANCE, tradition of theatrical dance unique to the 20th century. Modern dance originated in Europe, but by 1930 the U.S. had become the center for dance experimentation, and it remains so today. Early modern dances were miniatures—solos of highly compressed effect. They were unlike anything then known, for dance was dominated by late 19th-century ballets, which were characterized by large casts, a great variety of dance numbers, and spectacular scenic effects. But ballet itself was not always so monumental in scale, and just as ballet has evolved over the centuries as a changing tradition, so also has modern dance during its shorter period of existence.

OBSERVABLE CHARACTERISTICS
Modern dance, having begun as a reaction against ballet, is perhaps more easily defined by what it is not than by what it is, and it is often defined in contrast to ballet. Certain broad traits, however, can be observed in much of the enormously varied modern dance that has been created in the past three-quarters of a century.

The Choreographer-Performer. In modern dance, the tendency is for one artist to act as both choreographer and performer—and frequently also as scenic, costume, and lighting designer. During the last 300 years of ballet, in contrast, choreographers have seldom continued to dance when they were at the height of their choreographic achievements. Unlike ballet choreographers, who rely on a language of codified steps, modern dancers create their own conventions, or dance language; thus, they usually find it a practical necessity to both choreograph and perform.

Creation of a Dance Language. Because a dance language involves elements such as posture, use of the body's weight, and the character of movements (sinuous, angular, and so forth)—as well as specific movements of the head, torso, hands, arms, legs, and feet—most creators of modern dance have considered it essential to examine their own style of movement and to develop theories about its sources. Such explanations may refer to the physical dynamics of dance motions, such as the role of gravity or of breathing or the spine; or the theories may refer to ethnic and other nonballet traditions.

Use of Space. In keeping with the conventional language of ballet, the ballet dancer's movements are developed from a basic orientation of facing the audience from the front of the stage. At the same time, the ballet dancer maintains an erect posture and a turned-out position, that is, legs rotated outward from the hips. Modern dancers, in contrast, usually assume a multidimensional orientation in the theater space. Their actions make use of all dimensions of space—the dancers often stand sideways to or turn their backs on the audience, and they do not always remain upright—deliberate falling motions are common. Despite the variety of modern dance styles, they generally tend to take into account the weight of the body, whereas ballet requires the dancer to create the illusion of freedom from gravity, of effortlessly jumping and soaring through the air.

Relation to Music. Another aspect of much modern dance concerns the relation of movement to music. In traditional ballet the momentum and impulses of the dance movement typically parallel the rhythms of the music. Such a parallel may be present in modern dance, but it is not assumed that this must be the case. The dance may be composed first and the music written after-

Ruth St. Denis and Ted Shawn, the founders of modern dance in America, introduced innovative dance forms based on Oriental techniques and unrestricted body movements.
Culver Pictures

wards, underscoring the impulses of the dance movement, or the momentum of the dance may run counter to the rhythms of the music. Music may even be absent, the sounds of the dancers' movements being heard against a backdrop of silence. (This independent relation of modern dance and music has, in fact, influenced some contemporary ballet.)

HISTORY

The history of modern dance may be divided into three periods—one beginning about 1900, one about 1930, and one after World War II.

Early Period. The first three decades of modern dance—embracing the careers of the American dancers Isadora Duncan and Ruth St. Denis and the German dancer Mary Wigman—were preceded by a period of reaction against what many dancers saw as the empty spectacle of late 19th-century ballet. Contemporary with this reaction were two developments that helped inspire a freer kind of dance movement. One was the system of natural expressive gestures developed by the French actor François Delsarte (1811-71) as an alternative to the artificial mannerisms then customary in the theater. The other was eurythmics, a system for teaching musical rhythms through body movement, created by the Swiss music educator Émile Jaques-Dalcroze and later used as a training method by many dancers.

Seeking to give their dance more communicative power, the early modern dancers looked beyond the dominant tradition of Western theatrical dance—ballet as they knew it in the late 19th century—and drew on archaic or exotic sources for inspiration. During the same period, some ballet choreographers, such as the Russian-born Michel Fokine, also looked to similar sources, reacting against late 19th-century ballet as vehemently as the modern dancers did.

Isadora Duncan used Greek sculpture as a movement source. She danced in bare feet rather than in ballet slippers and appeared in a simple tunic rather than in the corseted ballet costume of the late 19th century. Locating the source of movement in the solar plexus, she created dances that alternated between resisting and yielding to gravity. Her response to the music of romantic composers such as Frédéric Chopin and the Hungarian Franz Liszt dictated the form of her choreography.

Ruth St. Denis turned to ethnic and Asian dance styles as the basis for her compositions.

MODERN DANCE

Like Duncan, St. Denis began as a solo dancer, but in 1915 she formed a company, Denishawn, with her husband, Ted Shawn. She trained dancers to dance as she did, in a diverse range of styles. Later American choreographers such as Katherine Dunham and Pearl Primus continued her interest in ethnic styles.

Mary Wigman looked to Africa and the Orient for choreographic inspiration. Like St. Denis, she presented both solo and group works, often arranged in cycles. Along with other German modern dancers—Rudolf von Laban, Kurt Jooss, and Harald Kreutzberg (1902-68)—she made extensive use of masks. The rise of the Nazis ended the German modern dance movement.

The 1930s. About 1930, in New York City, the second wave of modern dancers emerged. They included the Americans Martha Graham, Doris Humphrey, and Charles Weidman, all of whom had danced with Denishawn, and the German-American dancer Hanya Holm, who came from Mary Wigman's company. These dancers rejected external movement sources in favor of internal ones. They turned to basic human movement experiences, such as the actions of breathing and walking, and then transformed these natural actions into dance movement.

Martha Graham evolved her technique of contraction and release from the natural exhalation and inhalation of breathing. In her early abstract works she explored movement initiated in the torso. In the late 1930s Graham became interested in narrative structure and literary subject matter. With the Japanese-American sculptor Isamu Noguchi she created narrative locales that were both mythic and psychic. She danced the roles of female protagonists confronting moments of crisis; other dancers represented various aspects of the protagonist's self in crisis.

Doris Humphrey evolved her technique of fall and recovery from the natural dynamic of the human footfall, the giving into and the rebound from gravity. This technique became a metaphor for the relationship of the individual to a greater force, whether a social group or spiritual presence. After Humphrey stopped performing and disbanded the company she had formed with Charles Weidman, she continued to choreograph for her protégé, the Mexican-American dancer and choreographer José Limón. The choreographic sources for Humphrey's late works were words and gestures rather than her own movement experiences.

Hanya Holm worked in a more varied range than either Graham or Humphrey did. She created humorous dances and dances of social commentary, as did Weidman. Beginning in the late 1940s, she also choreographed for musicals, being one of the first to bring the style of modern dance to the Broadway stage.

During the 1930s choreographers defined modern dance and ballet in opposition to one another. Whereas modern dance was established as a technique with its own internal coherence, ballet was defined by reaffirming the essential tenets of its tradition. Ballet and modern choreographers focused on the purity of their traditions.

Postwar Developments. The third period of modern dance began after World War II and continues today. Such American dancers as Alwin Nikolais, Merce Cunningham, James Waring (1922-75), Paul Taylor, Alvin Ailey, and Twyla Tharp found their movement sources in the proliferation of 20th-century dance styles. Their works combined and fused techniques drawn from social dance, ballet, and modern dance. (In the years following World War II, ballet choreographers also borrowed just as freely from modern dance.)

Merce Cunningham fused Graham technique with ballet, locating the source of movement in the spine. He organized the changes of movement through methods based on chance, and he

Martha Graham, a leading exponent of nontraditional dance.
Martha Swope

MODERNISM

Members of the Merce Cunningham Dance Company demonstrate a movement sequence in rehearsal. As in much mid-20th-century modern dance, costumes are very simple and scenery nonexistent. Merce Cunningham, a former student of the dance pioneer Martha Graham, is best known for his nonobjective choreographic style in which movement and form take precedence over dramatic values.

Art Becofsky–Merce Cunningham Dance Company

considered music and decor independent of the dance. His works revealed individual dancers experiencing their relation to present time and abstract space, rather than to history and locale.

James Waring and, more recently, Twyla Tharp have worked both with ballet companies and with their own modern companies. Along with Paul Taylor and Alwin Nikolais, they displayed a choreographic sense of humor. Odd juxtapositions of movement created these humorous effects, as did parodies of their own and others' dance styles.

Tharp began her career as part of the 1960s avant-garde. During this time of social upheaval the American dancers Yvonne Rainer (1934–), Trisha Brown (1936–), Meredith Monk (1942–), and others created works at the extreme limit of what is considered dance. They became interested in everyday activities, manipulations of objects, and mixed-media presentations. In the 1970s the dance mainstream came to accept these choreographers' works, but none so completely as Tharp's.

Modern (or postmodern) dance in the mid-1980s, no longer interested in traditional techniques, relies on theatrical elements and the use of literary and pictorial devices. Tanztheater Wuppertal, founded by the German dancer-choreographer Pina Bausch (1940–), performs evening-length mixed media works—such as *The Seven Deadly Sins*—that stem from the tradition of the expressive dance of Kurt Jooss. Other notable postmodern dancers are the Americans Mark Morris, who worked with Twyla Tharp and the ballet dancer Eliot Feld (1943–); and Karole Armitage (1954–), choreographer of the *Mollino Room*, performed by Mikhail Baryshnikov and the American Ballet Theatre in 1986. Armitage's work is characterized by stabbing, insectlike motions and savage confrontations; among the pieces composed for her own group is *The Watteau Duets*, which merges dancing on pointe with torso movements in the style of Merce Cunningham. Much interest has also attached to Sankai Juku, a group of Japanese dancers trained in modern and classical dance. Their work is based on *butoh,* a form of dance theater that avoids structured choreography and strives to express primitive emotions by making minimal use of costuming and actual movement. In their "hanging event," dancers suspended upside down on ropes are slowly lowered, uncoiling their bodies as they descend.

For additional information on individual dancers, see biographies of those whose names are not followed by dates. S.A.M.

For further information on this topic, see the Bibliography in volume 28, section 763.

MODERNISM, in theology and philosophy, attempts by a group of scholars and church officials to reinterpret Christian doctrine in terms of the scientific thought of the 19th century. The collected attempts, although not a single system, were treated as such and called Modernism by Pope Pius X in 1907.

Modernism and Roman Catholicism. The Modernists of the Roman Catholic church tended to deny the objective value of traditional beliefs and to regard some dogmas of the church as symbolic rather than literally true (*see* DOGMA).

433

The leaders among this group included the Irish theologian George Tyrrell, the British theologian (of Austrian parentage) Baron Friedrich von Hügel, and the French theologian and Orientalist Alfred Loisy. Such works as *Life of Jesus* (1863; trans. 1863), by the French philologist and historian Ernest Renan, helped to lessen the authority of the teachings of the church on early Christianity.

Modernism in Europe was also a matter of political controversy. Those who supported the traditional views on church and state opposed the Modernists and their drive toward social reforms. Within the Roman Catholic church, the centralization of church government in Rome and the influence of the Curia were attacked. Church discipline over the clergy was strongly questioned. Perhaps most notable was the movement among scholars to work and publish without supervision from the church.

Censure of the movement reached a climax in 1907. On July 3, 1907, a decree, *Lamentabili Sane* (With truly lamentable results), was issued by the holy office with the approval of Pius X. It listed and condemned as heretical, false, rash, bold, and offensive 65 propositions, 38 of them related to biblical criticism and the remainder to Modernism. On September 8 of the same year, the pope issued an encyclical, *Pascendi Dominici Gregis* (Of the primary obligations). Modernism, it said, is a synthesis of all heresies, "an alliance between faith and false philosophy," arising from curiosity and "pride, which rouses the spirit of disobedience and demands a compromise between authority and liberty." Pius concluded his attack on the movement on Sept 1, 1910, in a *motu proprio* (a message prepared on papal initiative alone), *Sacrorum Antistitum* (Oath Against Modernism). He gave assent to all articles of Roman Catholic belief and dissented from all the tenets in all times condemned by the church of Rome. In the same document, he required an anti-Modernist oath from all clerics in the Roman Catholic church.

Modernism and Protestantism. A corresponding movement among Protestants had also been developing. If one accepted the historical findings of biblical scholars and the so-called higher criticism, questions arose that could not be answered in terms of traditional beliefs. The philosophical emphases of the Enlightenment of the late 18th century and the contemporaneous reexamination of the sources of personal religious expression added force to such questions. Prominent among Protestant Modernists were the German theologians Friedrich Schleiermacher and Albrecht Ritschl.

These Protestants attempted to find new interpretations of religious experience and an understanding of history that could accommodate the implications of the theory of evolution and discoveries in psychology, archaeology, and ancient history. To a large extent, they denied literal inspiration of the Bible and the historicity of the Jesus Christ of the Gospels (*see* BIBLICAL SCHOLARSHIP). They stressed ethical and moral behavior, rather than adherence to formal creeds, as essential to Christian life. They turned the activity of church officials to social areas and away from academic issues. *See also* CHRISTIANITY; THEOLOGY.

Modernism in the U.S. In the 1920s in the U.S., the term *Modernism* took on a more restricted meaning. It began to be applied to any rejection of traditional doctrine. At the same time a movement called Fundamentalism (q.v.) developed among conservative members of various Protestant denominations in opposition to Modernist tendencies.

MODERSOHN-BECKER, Paula (1876–1907), German expressionist painter. Her paintings are less violent than those of other expressionists. She was strongly influenced by French postimpressionism, and her works—landscapes, still lifes, mothers and children, and self-portraits—have much of the flat, calm, unshaded quality of the French artist Paul Gauguin, as in her *Self-Portrait with Camellia* (1907, Folkwang Museum, Essen, Germany). Modersohn-Becker's colors are deep, warm, or earthy rather than bright or harsh. Her death at the age of 31 prevented the complete maturation of her style.

MODESTO, city, seat of Stanislaus Co., central California, on the Tuolumne R., in the fertile San Joaquin Valley; inc. 1884. It is an agricultural center known for the production of wine, peaches, nuts, dairy products, poultry, and canned and frozen foods; chemicals, printed materials, and paper and glass products also are manufactured. A junior college and a natural history museum are here. Laid out in 1870, the community was the center of a wheat-growing area before irrigated agriculture began in 1903. The city's name, Spanish for "modest," is a tribute to William C. Ralston (1826–75), a prominent California financier who declined to have the community named for him. Pop. (1980) 106,602; (1990) 164,730.

MODIGLIANI, Amedeo (1884–1920), Italian painter and sculptor, who was concerned with graceful, simplified, and sympathetic portrayal of the human figure.

Modigliani was born in Leghorn on July 12, 1884, and raised in a Jewish ghetto, where he suffered serious illnesses as a boy. He studied art

Art by Amedeo Modigliani. Left: Adrienne (Woman with Bangs) *(1917), a painting. Right: A head executed in bronze.*

in Florence and in 1906 moved to Paris, where he became acquainted with Pablo Picasso, Jean Cocteau, and other avant-garde figures. He led a reckless, dissipated life that gradually took its toll on his health, but his artistic gifts were never doubted by fellow artists. He was influenced by Fauvism and later by the work of his friend, the Romanian sculptor Constantin Brancusi. He first produced sculpture inspired by primitive African carvings, but later concentrated on painting.

Modigliani's paintings, highly characteristic and delicate, are marked by sinuous lines, simple, flat forms, and elongated proportions that are almost classical in effect. Portraits and figure studies constitute most of his work, and both are characterized by the oval faces for which he is popularly known. The portraits, although of the utmost simplicity in contour, reveal considerable psychological insight and a curious sense of pathos. He achieved, in his best work, a blend of the dynamic primitivism of African sculpture and the pure grace of the 15th-century Botticelli style. He is represented by paintings such as *Reclining Nude* (c. 1919, Museum of Modern Art, New York City) and *Nude on a Divan* (Philadelphia Museum of Art).

Modigliani died in Paris on Jan. 25, 1920.

MODOC, North American Indian tribe, closely related to the Klamath tribe, with which it forms an independent language family, and of the California-Intermountain culture area. It formerly occupied territory between southwestern Oregon and northern California. The Modoc originally followed an economy based on pond lily seeds as a staple food and on hunting and fishing. Weaving was highly developed, and tule reeds, or bulrushes, were used to make baskets, cradles, and mats. Their winter homes consisted of log and earth lodges, constructed so that they were partly underground; in summer they lived in brush or reed huts called wickiups.

The Modoc made constant war on the white immigrants to California, and by 1864 the tribe had been reduced to about 250. They later entered the former Klamath Reservation in southern Oregon, ceding their lands to the U.S. government. In 1870 Chief Kintpuash (1837?–73), known as Captain Jack, led part of the tribe back to California. When they refused to return to the reservation, attempts were made to force their return, and the Modoc War of 1872–73 ensued. In 1873 Captain Jack surrendered and was hanged. Part of the rebellious group were returned to Klamath Reservation, and the rest were sent to Quapaw Reservation in Oklahoma. Klamath Reservation was disbanded in 1963, and the Indians on the Quapaw Reservation have merged with other tribes. By 1990 only 574 people reported being of Modoc descent.

See also AMERICAN INDIANS.

For further information on this topic, see the Bibliography in volume 28, sections 1105–8.

MODULATION. See RADIO.

MODULATION, in music, the transition from one key (tonality) to another. To achieve this change, harmonies common to both tonalities are used, usually culminating in either a cadence or the statement of a theme in the new key. An impor-

435

tant factor in a modulation is the pivot chord, which connects both keys; for example, in modulating from C to B-flat, the pivot chord could be F-A-C, which is the IV chord (or subdominant) in the key of C and the V chord (or dominant) in the key of B-flat. Modulation is important because the use of different tonalities within a composition is one of the means of obtaining variety and of building large-scale works, such as symphonies and concertos. Modulations occur especially in transitional passages, sections leading back to a main theme, and development sections.

MOGADISHU, also Mogadisho or Muqdisho (Ital. *Mogadiscio*), city, SE Somalia, capital of the country and of Benadir Region, on the Indian Ocean, just N of the equator. It is the nation's largest city, chief seaport, and leading commercial and manufacturing center. Exports passing through the modern deepwater port include livestock, bananas, and hides and skins. The principal manufactures of the city are processed food (especially meat and fish), leather, wood products, and textiles. Among its points of interest are a 13th-century mosque and the National Museum (housed in Garesa Palace, built in the 19th cent. by the sultan of Zanzibar). Institutions of higher education here include the Somali National University (1954) and schools of industry and veterinary medicine.

Mogadishu was founded about the early 10th century by Arab merchants; by the 12th century it had become a substantial trade center. A long period of decline began in the 16th century, and in 1871 the city came under the control of the sultan of Zanzibar. Italy leased the port in 1892 and in 1905 purchased the city, subsequently making it the capital of Italian Somaliland. Mogadishu became the capital of independent Somalia in 1960. The city was devastated by civil war in the early 1990s. Pop. (1985 est.) 700,000.

MOGILËV (Belarus *Mahilyow*), city, E Belarus, capital of Mogilëv Oblast. The city is an industrial and rail center and a port on the Dnepr R. Manufactures include machinery, textiles, and leather goods. Founded as a fortress in the 13th century, Mogilëv was held by Lithuania, Poland, and Sweden before passing to Russia in 1772. During World War II it was occupied (1941–44) by Germany. Pop. (1991 est.) 363,000.

MOHAIR. See GOAT.

MOHAMMED. See MUHAMMAD.

MOHAMMAD ALI. See MUHAMMAD ALI.

MOHAMMEDANISM. See ISLAM.

MOHAMMED RIZA PAHLAVI. See PAHLAVI, MUHAMMAD RIZA SHAH.

MOHAWK, North American Indian tribe of the Iroquoian language family and of the Eastern Woodlands culture area. Once the easternmost and chief people of the Five Nations of the Iroquoian Confederacy, the Mohawk had nine delegates on the confederacy council, three from each clan—the Wolf, the Bear, and the Turtle. They occupied the Mohawk River valley and were semisedentary; the women farmed and the men fished or hunted, depending on the season. As in other Iroquoian tribes, families lived together in large bark-covered dwellings called longhouses. Each community was governed by a ruling council and a village chief.

Their first encounter with Europeans was in 1609 when they fought against the French explorer Samuel de Champlain. They were early associated with the Dutch, from whom they bought firearms, and later most became firm allies of the British, fighting with them first against the French and then against the American colonists. After the American Revolution the Mohawk took refuge in Canada, where most have remained. About 5000 reside on reservations at Brantford, Ont., and at the Bay of Quinte. They still farm, and many work in construction. Two settlements are found in Franklin and Saint Lawrence counties in New York State. According to the 1990 census, 15,490 people in the U.S. reported being of Mohawk descent.

See also AMERICAN INDIANS; IROQUOIS.

For further information on this topic, see the Bibliography in volume 28, sections 1105–8, 1110.

MOHAWK, river, central New York, the principal tributary of the Hudson R. It flows SE for 238 km (148 mi), then enters the Hudson at Cohoes. It passes through the Mohawk Valley. Utica, Rome, and Schenectady are the chief cities on its banks. Part of the river was included in the Erie Canal, now part of the New York State Barge Canal System.

MOHEGAN, North American Indian tribe of the Algonquian language family and of the Eastern Woodlands culture area. They were living in what is now eastern Connecticut when the first white settlers arrived in New England. The Mohegan sided with the English against other Indian tribes, and by the 1700s were the only Indians of prominence remaining in southern New England.

The Mohegan practiced hunting, fishing, and farming; their staple crop was maize. As white settlements gradually surrounded and then displaced the tribe, the Mohegan dwindled in number. They sold most of their lands and moved to a reservation in New London Co., Conn. Surviving members later scattered, some joining other Indian settlements. A remnant continued to live in Connecticut. In the 1990 census 674 people identified themselves as being of Mohegan descent, although no pure-blood Mohegan exist today. The tribe was romanticized by the American novelist James Fenimore Cooper in his book, *The Last of the Mohicans*. See also AMERICAN INDIANS.

For further information on this topic, see the Bibliography in volume 28, sections 1105–8.

MOHÉLI. See COMOROS.

MOHENJO-DARO, archaeological site of the Indus Valley, or Harappan, civilization (c. 2500–1700 BC), south of Larkana, Pakistan. Excavated in the 1920s by the British archaeologist Sir John Marshall (1876–1958), Mohenjo-daro covers more than 80 ha (200 acres) and consists of two mounds separated by an unoccupied area. A major city and commercial center during the Bronze Age, it is the largest Indus Valley settlement.

The small western mound, or "citadel," has several public buildings, which may have been surrounded by a wall. Early excavators took these buildings for a granary, assembly hall, college, and public bath, but later studies have cast doubt on that conclusion. The larger eastern mound consists of large blocks of brick buildings, separated by streets and housing the inhabitants' residences and workshops. Both mounds yielded an abundance of Harappan artifacts. J.G.Sh.

MOHOLY-NAGY, László (1895–1946), Hungarian-American painter, sculptor, designer, and photographer, born in Bacsbarsod. Originally a law student, he studied art in Berlin after World War I, where he became an adherent of the abstract school known as constructivism. From 1923 to 1928 he taught at the Bauhaus and became a leader in the development of abstract art in many media. He explored the relationship of light and motion in his rotating *Light-Space Requisite* (c. 1930) and in a series of *Space Modulators* (after 1953), which were early examples of kinetic sculpture.

Moholy-Nagy moved to the U.S. in 1937 and founded the New Bauhaus in Chicago—later renamed the Institute of Design of the Illinois Institute of Technology—which he conducted until his death. Instruction was based on his concepts of architectonic composition and the use of new materials; these concepts are exemplified in his *Double Loop* (1946, Bayerische Staatsgemaldesammlungen, Munich), a free-form sculpture of bent Plexiglas. He also experimented and worked in painting, typography, photography, and cinema. He set forth his artistic tenets in *Vision in Motion* (publ. posthumously, 1947).

MOI, Daniel arap (1924–   ), second president of Kenya (1978–   ). Born in Sacho in northwestern Kenya, Moi was a teacher before entering politics. He was elected to the legislative council in 1955 and became chairman of the Kenya African Democratic Union in 1960, but after serving as minister of education (1961–62) and in local government (1962–64), Moi joined (1964) the ruling Kenya African National Union. He then served as minister for home affairs until he was appointed (1967) vice-president. On President Jomo Kenyatta's death, Moi succeeded him in office. Moi thwarted an attempted military coup in August 1982. In Kenya's first multiparty national elections since independence, held in 1992, Moi won a plurality of votes and returned to office despite his opponents' charges of voting fraud.

MOJAVE DESERT, arid region, S California, part of the Great Basin. It has an area of about 38,850 sq km (about 15,000 sq mi). The Mojave has deposits of borax and iron ore. The Colorado Desert is adjacent.

MOJAVE INDIANS, North American Indian tribe of the Yuman language family and of the Southwest culture area. The Mojave lived along the lower Colorado River in Arizona and California and were primarily an agricultural people. They raised corn, beans, and other crops on land that was flooded by the river annually, leaving a deposit of silt when the waters receded. They were also proficient in hunting and fishing. The Mojave lived in brush huts in scattered settlements along the riverbanks. Their main social unit was the family. Little formal tribal government existed except for the institution of a hereditary chief. In time of war the various groups united under a single war chief; personal prestige depended on bravery in battle. Their religion was based on the idea of a supreme creator. Dreams, detailed in song, played an important role in religious ceremonies.

In 1990, 1386 people identified themselves as Mojave, with most living on or near reservations at Parker, Ariz., and near Needles, Calif.

See also AMERICAN INDIAN LANGUAGES; AMERICAN INDIANS.

For further information on this topic, see the Bibliography in volume 28, sections 1105–7.

MOJI. See KITAKYUSHU.

MOKP'O, city, SW South Korea, in South Chŏlla Province, on a bay of the Yellow Sea. A leading port, it is a road and rail terminus and the gateway by steamer to Cheju Island. Rice, fish, cotton, hides, and shellfish are exported. The city is a trade center in an agricultural region of rice paddies and cotton fields. Its principal industries are fishing and fish processing, cotton ginning, rice refining, food and cottonseed-oil processing, canning, and sake brewing. It is the seat of Mokp'o Education College (1962). In 1897 the port was opened to foreign trade, and in 1904 American cotton was first successfully cultivated, adding to the importance of the port and its hinterland. Under Japanese rule from 1910 until the end of World War II in 1945, the city was called Moppo. Pop. (1990) 243,064.

MOLASSES, also called treacle, dark-brown viscous liquid obtained as a by-product in pro-

MOLASSES ACT

cessing sugar, especially cane sugar. It contains uncrystallized sugar and some sucrose. It is used in making industrial alcohol, for cooking, and for feeding stock. Several varieties, such as New Orleans molasses and Puerto Rico molasses, which are high in sugar content, rich in flavor, and light in color, are used as table syrups.

MOLASSES ACT. See Sugar and Molasses Acts.

MOLD, fuzzy, cobweblike growth produced on organic matter by several types of fungi (q.v.). Mold and mildew are commonly used interchangeably, although mold is often applied to black, blue, green, and red fungal growths, and mildew to whitish growths.

Black bread mold, *Aspergillus niger,* one of the most familiar molds, begins as a microscopic, airborne spore that germinates on contact with the moist surface of nonliving organic matter. It spreads rapidly, forming the mycelium (fungal body), made up of a fine network of filaments (hyphae). The mycelium produces other clusters of rootlike hyphae, called rhizoids, which penetrate the organic material, secreting enzymes and absorbing water and the digested sugars and starches. Other clusters of hyphae called sporangiophores then reach upward, forming sporangia (knoblike spore cases), which bear the particular color of the mold species. Upon ripening,

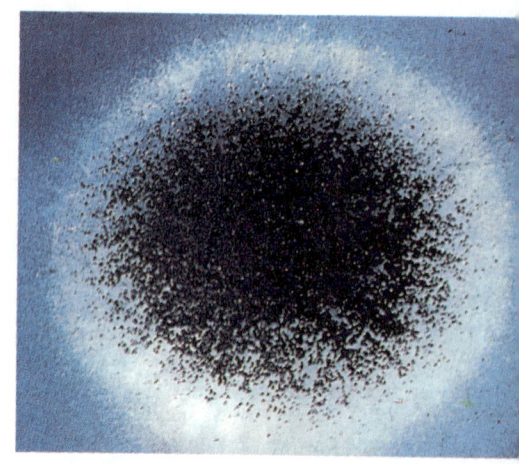

Cultures of black bread mold are grown commercially for use in the production of citric acid, an important and widely used industrial chemical. Pfizer Inc.

the sporangia break open and the windborne spores are moved elsewhere to reproduce asexually.

Some molds can also reproduce sexually through conjugation of gamete cells by the joining of two specialized hyphae. The resulting zygote matures into a zygospore that germinates after dormancy.

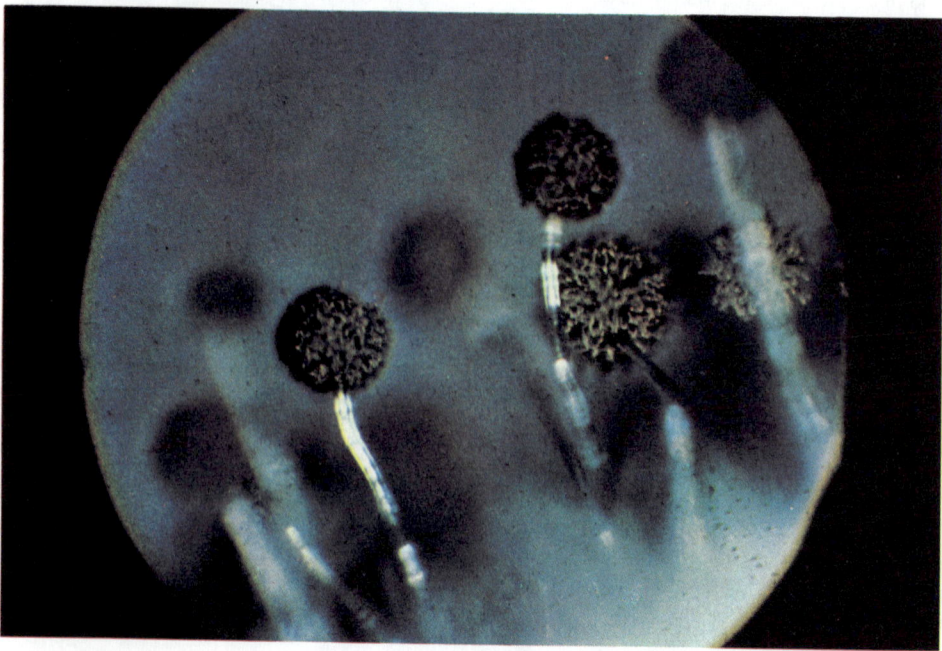

Microscopic view of the common black bread mold, Aspergillus niger, shows the black sporangia, or spore cases, by which the mold reproduces. Pfizer Inc.

Molds thrive on many organic substances and, provided with sufficient moisture, they disintegrate wood, paper, and leather. In fruit the enzymes penetrate well behind the visible growths to damage the fruit. Besides being destructive, however, molds have industrial uses, such as in the fermentation of organic acids and cheeses. Camembert and Roquefort cheeses gain their particular flavors from the enzymes of *Penicillium camemberti* and *P. roqueforti*, respectively. Penicillin (q.v.), a product of the green mold *P. notatum*, revolutionized antibiotic drugs after its discovery in 1929, and the red bread mold *Neurospora* is important in genetic experiments.

For further information on this topic, see the Bibliography in volume 28, section 457.

MOLDAU. See VLTAVA.

MOLDAVIA (Rom. *Moldova*), former principality in what is now Romania and the Republic of Moldova. Moldavia, which included the regions of Bukovina and Bessarabia, emerged as an independent principality in the early 14th century. In 1504, however, Moldavia became tributary to the Ottoman Empire. Early in the 18th century the region was ruled by Turkish-appointed Greek governors, called phanariots. Moldavia was occasionally occupied by Russian forces during the 18th and 19th centuries, and in 1812 it lost Bessarabia to Russia. In 1856 the Treaty of Paris, which ended the Crimean War between Russia and Turkey, restored part of this ceded territory to Moldavia. Moldavia and Wallachia merged to form Romania in 1859. Eastern Moldavia (Bessarabia) was later absorbed by the Soviet Union in the Moldavian Soviet Socialist Republic but became part of independent Moldova in 1991.

MOLDOVA, formerly MOLDAVIAN SOVIET SOCIALIST REPUBLIC, republic, SE Europe. It is bordered on the N, E, and S by Ukraine and on the W by Romania. Area, about 33,700 sq km (about 13,000 sq mi).

Moldova is chiefly a hilly plain, forested in the N and central parts, with steppelands in the S. It is drained by the Prut R., which forms the border with Romania, and the Dnestr R. The continental climate is moderated by the Black Sea.

Population. Moldova's population (1993 est.) was 4,362,000; the density averaged 129 persons per sq km (336 per sq mi). Ethnic Moldovans, who speak Romanian, make up nearly 65% of the population; minority groups include Ukrainians (14%), Russians (13%), and Gagauzi, a Turkic-speaking people (3.5%). The main faith is Orthodox Christianity. Kishinev (Chişinău) is the capital and leading city (pop., 1991 est., 753,500). Other important cities include Tiraspol (186,000), Beltsy (Bălţi; 164,900), and Bendery (Tighina; 141,500).

Moldova: Map Index

Cities and Towns

Bălţi	A2
Basarabeasca	B2
Bender (Tighina)	B2
Briceni	A1
Cahul	B3
Căuşeni	B2
Chişinău, *capital*	B2
Comrat	B2
Dubăsari	B2
Făleşti	A2
Floreşti	B2
Leova	B2
Orhei	B2
Rîbniţa	B2
Rîşcani	A2
Soroca	B1
Tiraspol	B2
Ungheni	A2

Other Features

Botna, *river*	B2
Bugeac, *region*	B3
Codri, *region*	A3
Cogalnic, *river*	B2
Dnestr, *river*	B2
Ialpug, *river*	B2
Prut, *river*	A1, B3
Raut, *river*	B2

Economy. The gross national product was estimated at $1300 per capita in the early 1990s. Agriculture is the main occupation; livestock raising and meat and dairy processing are important. Moldova is a leading producer of grapes, and wine making is a major industry. Other crops are wheat, sugar beets, vegetables, and fruit. Manufactures include processed foods, clothing, and consumer appliances such as refrigerators, washing machines, and television sets. Mineral resources are meager. The Moldovan leu of 100 bani, introduced in 1993, is the national currency (4.06 Moldovan lei equal U.S.$1; 1994).

Government. A 1994 constitution provides for a president, who is directly elected for a 4-year term, and a prime minister, who chairs the council of ministers. Elections for a 104-member parliament were held in February 1994.

History. For the history of Moldova prior to 1924, see BESSARABIA; MOLDAVIA; ROMANIA.

The Moldavian Autonomous Soviet Socialist Republic (ASSR) was established in 1924 as part of Ukrainian SSR. In 1940 Romania was forced to cede the greater part of Bessarabia to the USSR, and this territory was merged with Moldavian ASSR to form the constituent republic of Moldavian SSR. During World War II the republic was occupied (1941–44) by Romanian troops. When the USSR collapsed in 1991, the republic changed its name to Moldova and joined the Commonwealth of Independent States (q.v.). A national referendum in March 1994 demonstrated overwhelming support for continued Moldovan independence rather than unification with Romania. The continued presence of Russian troops in the secessionist Dnestr region, where Russians and Ukrainians predominate, was a source of friction between Moldova and the Russian government.

MOLE, common name for any of the small, burrowing mammals of the family Talpidae in the order Insectivora (see INSECTIVORE). Moles are characterized by a pointed snout; rudimentary eyes and ears; soft, thick, velvety fur; short legs; broad feet; and long, powerful claws on the front pair of legs. They are indigenous to Europe, Asia, and North America. The voracious animals continually dig below the surface of the ground for their food, which consists principally of earthworms and insect larvae. They are capable of digging rapidly, using their powerful forefeet and claws to push the earth back behind them. Close to the surface of the ground, moles construct their elaborate burrows with many chambers; their burrowing often produces ridges on the surface.

Of the 12 genera of moles, 5 are found in the U.S. The typical mole of the eastern U.S. is the eastern, or garden, mole, *Scalopus aquaticus*, which is about 15 cm (about 6 in) long, of which 2.5 cm (1 in) is naked tail. The western mole, *Scapanus townsendii*, is the largest American species, attaining a length of more than 22 cm (8.7 in). *Parascalops breweri*, the hairy-tailed mole, has crescent-shaped nostrils. The star-nosed mole, *Condylura cristata*, has on its snout a star-shaped projection composed of 22 sensitive feelers. It is an excellent swimmer. The shrew mole, *Neurotrichus gibbsii*, is the smallest of the American moles. It measures 14 cm (5.5 in) in length, of which 3.8 cm (1.5 in) is tail.

For further information on this topic, see the Bibliography in volume 28, sections 461, 475.

MOLE, a base unit of the International System of Units (q.v.), defined as the amount of a substance that contains as many elementary particles (atoms, molecules, ions, electrons, or other particles) as 0.012 kg (12 g) of carbon-12. The number of elementary particles contained in 12 g of carbon-12 (an atom against which other substances are measured) is approximately 6.02×10^{23}; this is called Avogadro's number (q.v.). A mole, then, is an amount of any substance that weighs, in grams, as much as the numerically equivalent atomic weight of that substance.

MOLECH. See MOLOCH.

MOLECULE, smallest particle of a substance having the specific chemical properties of that substance. If a molecule is broken into anything smaller, the parts differ in nature from the original substance. In principle, a sample of water can be divided into two parts and each part further divided, producing smaller samples of water. The process of division and subdivision ultimately produces a single molecule of water, whose further splitting gives something that is not waterlike in character: hydrogen and oxygen. Each molecule is pictured as existing independently of other molecules. An encounter of two usually results in their bouncing away from each other without fundamental change. More violent encounters, however, alter the molecular composition, as when a chemical change occurs.

Molecules of compounds are composed of atoms of the constituent elements. A molecule is said to be diatomic if made of two atoms and polyatomic if consisting of a large number of atoms. Some naturally occurring molecules are made of hundreds, thousands, or even millions of atoms. Much of modern chemistry is concerned with determining the composition, structure, and size of molecules. Extremely short bursts of laser (q.v.) light are used to study molecular reactions as they take place.

Simple molecules are the smallest in size. Hydrogen molecules, for example, have a diameter of about 10^{-8} cm, or about one hundred-millionth of an inch, and a mass near 3×10^{-24} g. Other, more complicated molecules take the form of chains, rings, or helices.

Molecular Theory. The idea of molecules as distinct from atoms was first suggested by the Italian physicist Amedeo Avogadro in 1811. He postulated, in what is now known as Avogadro's law (q.v.), that under given temperature and pressure conditions, equal volumes of any two gases contain the same number of molecules. This provided a way of comparing the relative weights of molecules and ultimately of obtaining the comparative weights of atoms. Much of modern physics and chemistry depends on these results. See AVOGADRO'S NUMBER.

An extension of Avogadro's molecular law is the kinetic theory formulated by the British physicist James Clerk Maxwell, the Dutch physicist Johannes Diderik van der Waals, and the Austrian physicist Ludwig Boltzmann. This theory states that molecules are in constant motion, the intensity of the motion increasing with the addition of heat. The motion, if the molecule is made of more than one atom, includes vibration within the molecule and a rotation, much like the rotation of the moon around the earth. Information about these internal vibrations and rotations is obtained by several means, including spectroscopy (q.v.) and the measuring of specific heat (q.v.). In 1989, physicists first predicted completely the course of the simplest possible molecular reaction (involving hydrogen atoms) in terms of quantum theory (q.v.).

Molecular Weight. The weight of a molecule can be determined either by calculation or experiment. The molecular weights of the elementary atoms, such as carbon-12, are the same as their atomic weights, which have already been established (see ATOM AND ATOMIC THEORY: *Atomic Weight*). If the atomic structure of a molecule is known, the molecular weight can be calculated. For example, water (H_2O) has two hydrogen atoms (atomic weight of the hydrogen atom = 1) and one oxygen atom (atomic weight of the oxygen atom = 16), giving water a molecular weight of 18. Complex molecules can have molecular weights ranging into the hundreds of millions. In experimental determination, the molecular weight of a substance is ascertained by calculating the actual weight in grams per mole (q.v.).

For further information on this topic, see the Bibliography in volume 28, sections 389, 402, 406.

MOLIÈRE, pseudonym of JEAN BAPTISTE POQUELIN (1622–73), French dramatist, and one of the greatest of all writers of comedies. His universal comic types still delight audiences; his plays are often produced and have been much translated.

Early Career. Molière was born in Paris on Jan. 15, 1622, to a wealthy tapestry maker. From an early age he was completely devoted to the theater. In 1643 he joined a theatrical company established by the Béjarts, a family of professional actors, and married Armande Béjart (1642–1700), in 1662. The troupe, which Molière named the Illustre Théâtre, played in Paris until 1645 and then toured the provinces for 13 years, returning to Paris in 1658. On their return Louis XIV lent the troupe his support and offered them occasional use of the Théâtre du Petit-Bourbon and, in 1661, use of the playhouse in the Palais-Royal. Secure at the Palais-Royal, Molière for the rest of his life committed himself entirely to the comic theater, as dramatist, actor, producer, and director.

In 1659 the company presented Molière's *Les précieuses ridicules* (The Affected Young Ladies). Written in a style similar to that of the older farces, it satirizes the pretensions of two provincial girls. The work took Paris by storm, and from that time until his death, at least one of Molière's comedies was produced each year.

The Great Comedies. *L'école des femmes* (The School for Wives, 1662) marks a break with the farce tradition. Considered the first great seriocomic work of French literature, it deals with the part women played in society and their preparation for it; the play constitutes a bold satire on contemporary materialistic values and, as such, was denounced for impiety and vulgarity.

In *Tartuffe* (first version, 1664; third and final version, 1669) Molière invented one of his famous comic types, that of a religious hypocrite. The king would not permit a public performance of it for five years although he himself thought it amusing. He had good reason to believe that the play, with the hypocritical Tartuffe, clad in clerical garb and hair shirt, would offend the powerful higher clergy.

The ever popular *Le misanthrope* (1666) pictures a young suitor, Alceste, sincere but humorless, trying to woo Célimène, a flirtatious court soubrette. Because this play does not end happily, it is sometimes characterized as a tragedy.

Some of Molière's most successful plays (numbering about 33) are *L'avare* (The Miser, 1668), a stark "comedy," loosely based on a work by the Roman comic dramatist Plautus, and *Le médecin malgré lui* (The Physician in Spite of Himself, 1666), a satire on the medical profession. *Le bourgeois gentilhomme* (The Would-Be Gentleman, 1670), a comedy-ballet with music by the king's favorite composer, Jean Baptiste Lully, mocks a successful but naive cloth merchant who wants to be received at court. A swindler bilks him with promises to arrange such an invitation, and in hopes of becoming a courtier, the would-be gentleman prepares himself by taking lessons in music, dancing, fencing, and philosophy. The four scenes devoted to these lessons are among the most hilarious ever written by Molière, and all ends happily with a mock Turkish ballet.

Molière's last comedy, *Le malade imaginaire* (The Imaginary Invalid, 1673), about a hypochondriac who fears the ministrations of doctors, is in the tradition of those satires on medicine widespread in 16th- and 17th-century literature. Ironically, during the first week of the play's run, as Molière was playing the leading role, he was stricken ill onstage and died a few hours later (Feb. 17, 1673).

Molière's Style. Molière's satires, directed against social conventions that thwart nature, give a more accurate portrait of contemporary French society than do the serious dramas of his contemporaries Pierre Corneille and Jean Baptiste Racine. Although his stock characters and comic effects were borrowed from older traditions—from the comedies of the Greek writer Aristophanes, from the Roman comedy of Terence and Plautus, and from the Italian commedia dell'arte (q.v.)—he gave psychological depth to his demagogues, misers, lovers, hypocrites, cuckolds, and social climbers. A master of slapstick, he yet contrived to maintain an underlying note of pathos. Like the troupes of Italian actors who performed regularly in Paris during the 17th century, Molière's company was trained to extract the full potential from the stock characters portrayed. This training included the study of appropriate facial expressions, gestures, and gags. Thus, Molière's comedies can be appreciated to the fullest only when acted by a brilliant, disciplined company, such as the famous Comédie Française (q.v.), the national theater of France. Established in 1680 through a merger of the Illustre Théâtre and rival troupes, it is still familiarly known as the Theater of Molière. R.J.C.

For further information on this person, see the section Biographies in the Bibliography in volume 28.

MOLINA, Tirso de. See TIRSO DE MOLINA.

MOLINE, city, Rock Island Co., NW Illinois, on the Mississippi R.; settled 1832, inc. as a city 1872. It forms the "Quad Cities" with Rock Island, Ill., and Bettendorf and Davenport, Iowa. Agricultural equipment, its major product, has been made here since 1847. Heavy machinery, foundry items, machine tools, and elevators are also produced. The community grew in the 1840s as a flour-milling and sawmilling center; its name is probably derived from the French *moulin* ("mill"). Pop. (1980) 45,709; (1990) 43,202.

MOLINO DEL REY, BATTLE OF, one of the last battles of the Mexican War (1846–48). The American general Winfield Scott, on taking command of American forces in Mexico in March 1847, marched by the most direct route to the capital. After American victories at Cerro Gordo, Contreras, and Churubusco, an armistice was concluded in late August 1847. When negotiations for peace appeared to be at a standstill, Scott prepared to attack the fortifications that barred his way to the capital. The forward movement commenced on September 8 with an assault on the enemy's positons at Casa de Mata and Molino del Rey. These positions were taken with heavy losses on both sides. An attack was then made on Chapultepec, which, falling on September 13, left the route clear to Mexico City.

MOLINOS, Miguel de (1628–96), Spanish Roman Catholic priest and mystic, who founded quietism (q.v.). A radical form of mysticism, quietism is based on the belief that perfection lies in the utter passivity of the soul before God, allowing it to be absorbed by the divine spirit. Because such passivity requires annihilation of the will, all actions—both good and bad—are hindrances. His views, expressed in his *Guida Spirituale* (Spiritual Guide, 1675), were well received by both the clergy and the laity, and Molinos gained favor with Pope Innocent XI. Opponents of the pope accused Molinos of heresy as well as personal immorality—charges that led to his arrest in 1685. In 1687 Molinos admitted wrongdoing and was sentenced to life imprisonment.

MOLISE, region, E Italy, bordered on the N by the region of Abruzzi, on the E by the Adriatic Sea, on the S by the regions of Apulia and Campania, and on the W by the Latium (Lazio) region. Molise is divided into Campobasso and Isernia provinces; the city of Campobasso is the regional capital. Agriculture is prevalent in Molise and includes the production of grain, fruits, and vegetables. Among regional industries are wine making, food processing, and the manufacture of furniture and cement. The history of Molise is synonymous with that of the region of Abruzzi (q.v.). In 1963 the region of Abruzzi e Molise was divided into two separate regions: Abruzzi and Molise. Area, 4438 sq km (1714 sq mi); pop. (1988 est.) 334,700.

MOLLUSK, common name for soft-bodied animals (Lat. *mollus*, "soft"), usually with a hard external shell, that constitute the phylum Mollusca. Familiar mollusks include the clam, oyster, snail, slug, octopus, and squid (qq.v.). The phylum is the second largest in the animal kingdom, after Arthropoda. Earlier estimates of the number of mollusk species sometimes exceeded 100,000, but more recently this figure has been reduced to less than 50,000; the new estimates are incorporated here.

Mollusks are highly successful in terms of ecology and adaptation, with representatives in virtually all habitats, but they are most diverse in the sea. Among them are some advanced animals, such as the octopus and squid. Giant squid are also the largest invertebrates, weighing up to 2000 kg (4400 lb). Most mollusks, however, are

The scallop, a mollusk with a distinctive bivalve shell, is almost unique among bivalves in being able to swim. It can expel water forcibly from its shell to propel itself either forward or backward. It is also unique among bivalves in having numerous eyes, visible here, each of which is fairly complex in construction. The eyes can be regrown if lost.
James H. Carmichael–Bruce Coleman, Inc.

about 1 to 20 cm (about 0.4 to 8 in) long, and some are scarcely visible.

The first mollusk fossils appear in early Cambrian rocks, about 600 million years old. Seven of the phylum's classes have living representatives: Aplacophora (wormlike, shell-less aplacophorans, with 250 species); Polyplacophora (the chitons, with 600 species); Monoplacophora (*Neopilina*, with 10 species); Bivalvia (the bivalves, such as clams, with 7500 species); Scaphopoda (the scaphopods, or tusk shells, with 350 species); Gastropoda (the gastropods, such as snails and slugs, with 37,500 species); and Cephalopoda (the cephalopods, such as octopuses and squid, with 600 species). Several fossil classes and thousands of fossil species are also known.

General Characteristics. Although few features are common to all mollusks, the animals are not readily mistaken for anything else, and all may be treated as variants on a common theme (not to be confused with a common ancestor). A theoretical, idealized mollusk would crawl on a single flat, muscular foot, and the body would have at least a suggestion of a head at one end and an anus at the other. Above would be an external shell mounted on a visceral hump containing internal organs.

This shell, secreted by a sheet of tissue called the mantle, is complicated in mollusks, being made up of calcium carbonate and other minerals in an organic matrix produced in layers by the mantle at the edge of the shell and under it. It is also generally covered by an outer layer without minerals, called the periostracum. The shell may be multiple, as in chitons, or paired, as in bivalves. In various mollusks the shell is reduced in size and is sometimes lost completely, and in aplacophorans direct evidence that a shell ever existed is absent.

At the posterior end of the idealized mollusk would be a groove or depression called the mantle cavity, with gills to each side of the anus, and openings to the kidneys and reproductive structures. A single pair of gills is common, but many gastropods have only one gill. The cephalopod *Nautilus* has two pairs, and monoplacophorans and chitons have several to many pairs.

Generally the molluscan gut is equipped with jaws and a tonguelike structure, called a radula, with teeth on it. Also present are a stomach and a pair of digestive glands. The nervous system consists of a ring of nerves around the anterior part of the gut, with one pair of nerve trunks to the foot and another to the viscera. Ganglia around the gut usually are developed into a brain with various sense organs; the nervous system of cephalopods is as complex and as highly organized as that of

Gastropod mollusks, such as the snail seen here laying its eggs, range widely both on land and in the sea and fresh waters. They have single, asymmetrical shells or none at all, as in the slugs.
Hans Pfletschinger–Peter Arnold, Inc.

443

MOLLUSK

fishes. The heart is located at the posterior end of the body; it sends blood into an open system that forms the main body cavity. Associated with the heart is a complex of organs that includes the kidneys and gonads and sometimes other reproductive structures.

Behavior. Although vision is poor in most mollusks, cephalopods such as squid have eyes with lenses, retinas, and other features remarkably like those of vertebrates. Some gastropods have a well-developed sense of smell and can locate food in the water at a considerable distance. Predators may similarly be detected by the chemical senses and are sometimes evaded by leaping or swimming. Some mollusks exhibit complicated courtship behavior. Advanced cephalopods possess considerable ability to learn from experience.

Reproduction. The basic mollusk pattern is to have separate sexes, with sperm and eggs spawned into the water, where fertilization and early development occur. In most mollusks a larval stage follows, in which the larvae swim about for a while and then settle on the bottom and mature; this stage is often modified or absent, however. Fertilization may also be internal, with glands secreting protective coverings around the eggs. Slow-moving creatures such as snails often evolve into hermaphrodites (both male and female), because this doubles the number of appropriate mates. Sometimes the mother protects the developing eggs, and some oysters are remarkable in caring for the young inside the mantle cavity and switching back and forth from being males to being females.

Ecology and Importance. Mollusks are abundant and hence important in food chains in many habitats. A large number are herbivores or grazers, especially the chitons and many gastropods. Tusk shells and some other mollusks feed on matter deposited on the bottom, whereas most bivalves filter suspended materials from the water. Many gastropods are carnivorous, most of them preying on slow-moving or attached animals. Cephalopods are active predators on larger animals such as crabs. Numerous mollusks are important food sources for humans, but some gastropods damage crops, and others harbor disease-causing parasites.

Major Groups. Because mollusks are distinct from other animals, it is debatable whether the presence of multiple parts in some species indicates that the phylum arose from the segmented worms. In the class Aplacophora, the body is in fact wormlike. No shell exists, only a tough mantle, and the foot has virtually been lost. Of the two aplacophoran orders, the Caudofoveata live in mud, and the Ventroplicada feed on coelenterates.

The three orders of Polyplacophora (chitons) have a series of eight shell plates (valves) in a row and are well adapted to clinging on rocks.

The mainly fossil Monoplacophora are now known to have one living genus, *Neopilina,* discovered in deep water in 1952. The animal has a single flat shell and multiple gills.

The Bivalvia have a shell divided into two valves, and they feed with their gills. As a consequence the head is poorly developed. The four orders—Protobranchia, Septibranchia, Filibranchia (mussels and oysters), and Eulamellibranchia (the clams)—are characterized by the gills.

The Scaphopoda (tusk shells) have a long, tapered, slightly curved shell and live on sandy bottoms. Two families exist.

The Gastropoda (snails and slugs) are asymmetrical and have only one shell or, as in slugs, are shell-less. The three subclasses of the Gastropoda are the Prosobranchia (mostly marine snails, with three orders), Opisthobranchia (sea slugs and allies, with eight orders), and Pulmonata (lunged mollusks, largely freshwater and terrestrial, with two orders).

The Cephalopoda are modified by reduction of the foot and shell and the development of arms around the mouth. The two orders are Tetrabranchia (*Nautilus,* with four gills and other archaic traits such as an external shell) and Dibranchia (octopuses, squid, and cuttlefish, with two gills and other advanced traits).

The octopus, a cephalopod, is the most intelligent mollusk.
Jane Burton-Bruce Coleman, Inc.

See BIVALVE; CEPHALOPOD; CHITON; GASTROPOD.
M.T.G.

For further information on this topic, see the Bibliography in volume 28, section 465.

MOLLY MAGUIRES, secret society formed about 1854 by the Irish coal miners of the anthracite regions of Pennsylvania. The Molly Maguires was organized for the planning and execution of a concerted campaign of physical violence against those whom the miners considered their oppressors, including the mineowners, their superintendents, and state and municipal police under the virtual control of the mineowners. The name of the society was derived from that of a similar society in Ireland that engaged in physical force against the bailiffs, process servers, and other agents of the landlords.

The membership of the American society grew rapidly during and after the American Civil War, and its scale of activity increased proportionately. In 1875 the Molly Maguires brought about a strike of the coal miners that was ultimately broken through the activities of James McParlan (1844–1919), a Pinkerton detective hired by Franklin B. Gowen (1836–89), president of the Philadelphia and Reading Coal and Iron Co. McParlan joined the society and carried out espionage among its members; the evidence he presented in the courts in 1876–77 resulted in the conviction and execution of many Molly Maguire members, which ended the group's activities.

MOLNÁR, Ferenc (1878–1952), Hungarian playwright and novelist, born in Budapest. Several of his plays were presented on the New York City stage, and all were successes, including *The Guardsman, Liliom, The Swan, The Glass Slipper,* and *The Play's the Thing*. In 1928 English translations of his *Twenty-five Plays* were published. A musical comedy, *Carousel,* presented in New York City in 1945, was based on Molnár's *Liliom*. His plays are characterized by graceful romantic situations and amusing dialogue.

MOLOCH, in the Old Testament, deity at one period associated with Baal, probably as a sun god, but differing from him in being almost entirely malevolent. The worship of Moloch embraced human sacrifice, ordeals by fire, and self-mutilation. The Hebrew form of the word is invariably *Molech,* meaning "king" or "counselor." The first recorded instance of a worshiper of Jehovah who "burned his son as an offering" (that is, to Moloch) is that of Ahaz (see 2 Kings 16:3). The same story is told of Manasseh, eponymous ancestor of one of the 12 tribes of ancient Israel (see 2 Kings 21:6). The practice is also alluded to in the books of Jeremiah, Ezekiel, and Leviticus. The ritual of Moloch worship was probably borrowed by Judah from one of the surrounding nations; it was practiced by the Moabites (see 2 Kings 3:27) and Ammonites.

MOLOKAI, island, in Kalawao Co., administered by Maui Co., central Hawaii, between Oahu and Maui islands, known as the Friendly Island. On the S coast of Molokai is the port of Kaunakakai. The island rises to 1512 m (4961 ft) in the E at Kamakou Peak. Pineapples, coffee, and cattle are raised. In 1873 Father Damien, the Belgian Roman Catholic missionary, began his work in the leper colony of Kalawao on the Kalaupapa Peninsula of N Molokai. Area, 673 sq km (260 sq mi); pop. (1980) 6049; (1990) 6717.

MOLOTOV. See PERM.

MOLOTOV, Vyacheslav Mikhaylovich (1890–1986), Russian revolutionary, who became one of the most important Soviet functionaries during the era of Joseph Stalin. He was born in Noginsk on March 9, 1890, and was educated at the Polytechnic Institute in Saint Petersburg. He joined the Bolsheviks in 1906, taking the name Molotov (Russ., "hammer") instead of his original surname, Skryabin (he was a relative of the composer Aleksandr Scriabin). In 1912 he cofounded, with Stalin, the Bolshevik daily *Pravda* (Truth) and became its editor. Molotov was subsequently exiled to Siberia, but he escaped and returned to St. Petersburg early in 1917 to play an important part in the Russian Revolution. After the Bolsheviks seized power, he rose rapidly in the Communist party, where he staunchly supported Stalin. He was premier of the USSR (chairman of the Council of People's Commissars) from 1930 to 1941, when Stalin assumed the office. In 1939 he became foreign minister as well and soon after negotiated the nonaggression pact with Germany. During World War II he was deputy chairman of the State Committee of Defense.

As foreign minister until 1949, Molotov headed the Soviet delegation to the conference in San Francisco that established the UN in 1945, and he represented the USSR in the UN General Assembly and at various postwar conferences with the major world powers, earning a reputation for stubborn, vociferous opposition to Western policies. He was again foreign minister from 1953 to 1956, when he resigned. An opponent of Nikita Khrushchev, Molotov was dismissed from all important government positions in 1957 but served as ambassador to Mongolia (1957–60) and representative to the International Atomic Energy Agency in Vienna (1960–61). Ousted from the party in 1962, he thereafter lived in retirement, but was reinstated into the party in 1984.

MOLTING, in the animal kingdom, the periodic shedding of an outer bodily layer, such as feathers, skin, fur, or horn, as a preliminary to regrowth (see REGENERATION). In most animals, molting is triggered by secretions of the thyroid gland or pituitary gland. Many mammals shed their hair in spring, and some even molt and regenerate parts of their bodies; deer, for example, grow new antlers, and the lemming acquires new claws. Birds usually molt in the late summer without effect on their ability to fly, and snakes and amphibians cast off their skins several times a year. The molting of hard exoskeletons or cuticle occurs in crustaceans and insects.

MOLTKE, Helmuth Johannes Ludwig, Graf von (1848–1916), German military commander, born in Gersdorf, near Chemnitz. In 1906 he became chief of the German general staff, and he directed the invasion of France following the outbreak of World War I. After a German defeat in 1914 at the First Battle of the Marne, Moltke was relieved of his command and succeeded by Gen. Erich von Falkenhayn.

MOLTKE, Helmuth Karl Bernhard, Graf von (1800–91), German general, whose military genius was instrumental in making Prussia the leading state of Germany. He was born in Parchim, Mecklenburg, and educated at the Royal Military Academy in Copenhagen. He first joined the Danish infantry but in 1822 transferred to the Prussian army as a lieutenant and he subsequently attended the General War College in Frankfurt an der Oder; by 1832 he was attached to the Prussian general staff. In 1835 he went to Turkey where he helped reorganize the Turkish army. Returning to Prussia in 1839, he was made chief of the general staff in 1858. During 30 years in that position he modernized the Prussian army and successfully directed strategy during the Prussian-Danish War of 1863–64, the Seven Weeks' War with Austria in 1866, and the Franco-Prussian War of 1870–71. Moltke was made a count (Graf) in 1870 and a field marshal in 1871. Also an accomplished writer, Moltke published books on military matters as well as travel notes, historical sketches, and a novel. He died in Berlin in 1891.

MOLUCCAS, also Spice Islands, islands, E Indonesia, part of the Malay Archipelago, including most of the islands between Celebes and New Guinea and between Timor and the Philippines. The islands export cloves, nutmeg, and other spices, copra, and hardwoods. The N islands are Halmahera, the largest of the Moluccas, Morotai, Ternate, Tidore, Makian, Bacan (Batjan), Obi, and Sula; the central and S islands are Buru, Ceram, Ambon (Amboina), Banda, Kai, Aru, Tanimbar, Babar, Kisar, and Wetar. The population is mostly of Malayan origin.

MOLYBDENITE, mineral, molybdenum disulfide (MoS_2), the most common mineral of molybdenum. It crystallizes (see CRYSTAL) in the hexagonal system in soft plates, has a metallic luster, and has a lead-gray color. It has a hardness of 1 to 1.5 and a sp.gr. of 4.8. Originally thought to be a form of lead, molybdenite is used in steel making and as a lubricant. The mineral is found in Canada, the U.S., Japan, and Australia.

MOLYBDENUM, metallic element, symbol Mo, one of the transition elements (q.v.) in group 6 (or VIb) of the periodic table (see PERIODIC LAW); at.no. 42, at.wt. 95.94. Molybdenum melts at about 2610° C (about 4730° F), boils at about 5560° C (about 10,040° F), and has a sp.gr. of 10.2.

Molybdenum was discovered in 1778 by the Swedish chemist Carl Wilhelm Scheele. It is a silver-white, tough, malleable metal. Its chemical properties are similar to those of chromium. It is dissolved by dilute nitric acid and aqua regia, and is attacked by fused alkalies; it is not attacked by air at ordinary temperatures, but burns at temperatures above 600° C (1292° F) to form molybdenum oxide. The metal does not occur free in nature, but in the form of its ores, the most important of which are molybdenite and wulfenite (qq.v.). It ranks about 56th in order of abundance of the elements in the earth's crust and is an important trace element in soils, where it contributes to the growth of plants. The metal is used chiefly in alloying steel. The alloy withstands high temperatures and pressures and is very strong, making it useful for structural work, aircraft parts, and forged automobile parts. Molybdenum wire is used in electron tubes, and also serves as electrodes in glass furnaces. Molybdenum sulfide is used as a lubricant in environments requiring high temperatures. About two-thirds of the world's supply is obtained as a byproduct of copper mining, with the United States the single largest producer, followed by Canada.

MOMBASA, city, SE Kenya, capital of Coast Province, on a bay of the Indian Ocean, just S of the equator. The fast-growing city and chief seaport of the country, which also serves as a port for NE Tanzania and landlocked Uganda, includes Old Mombasa, located on a small offshore island (16 sq km/6 sq mi), and a larger, more modern mainland metropolitan area, which is connected to the island by causeway, bridge, and ferries. Kilindini, a modern deepwater harbor on the W side of the island, has extensive docks, shipyards, and sugar and petroleum refineries. Old Mombasa Harbour, on the E side of the island, handles mainly dhows and other small coastal trading vessels. Fort Jesus, built by the Portuguese in the 1590s, is maintained as a museum. Mombasa Polytechnic (1948) is in the city.

Mombasa was founded about the 8th century by Arab traders. It was visited in the 1330s by the noted Arab traveler Ibn Batuta and in 1498 by the Portuguese explorer Vasco da Gama. Mombasa later changed hands several times before coming under the control of the sultan of Zanzibar in 1840. It passed to the British in 1895 and was the capital of the British East Africa Protectorate until 1907. It was made the capital of the coastal Protectorate of Kenya in 1920, and in 1963 it became part of newly independent Kenya (which includes the former protectorate and colony of Kenya). Pop. (1984 est.) 425,600.

MOMENT. *See* MECHANICS.

MOMENTUM, also linear momentum, in physics, fundamental quantity characterizing the motion of any object (*see* MECHANICS). It is the product of the mass of a moving particle multiplied by its linear velocity. According to Newton's laws of motion, named after the English astronomer, mathematician, and physicist Sir Isaac Newton, the force (q.v.) acting on a body in motion must be equal to its time rate of change of momentum; thus, if no external forces are acting on a body, or the body is isolated, its momentum will be conserved. Like force, momentum is a vector quantity, that is, it has both magnitude and direction (*see* VECTOR). The law of conservation of momentum for isolated bodies appears to be universally valid and can be extended in fields where Newtonian mechanics is no longer valid, as in quantum mechanics (*see* QUANTUM THEORY), which describes atomic and nuclear phenomena, and in relativistic mechanics, which must be used when systems move with velocities near the speed of light (*see* RELATIVITY).

Another way of stating Newton's second law is that the impulse, that is, the product of the force multiplied by the time over which it acts on a body, equals the change of momentum of the body. Momentum, however, should not be confused with kinetic energy. Thus, when a bullet enters a target, the time required for it to come to rest depends on its momentum, but the depth of penetration depends on its kinetic energy. *See* ENERGY; KINETIC ENERGY.

When describing the motion of rotating bodies, the concept of angular momentum must be introduced.

For further information on this topic, see the Bibliography in volume 28, sections 389, 392.

MOMMSEN, Theodor (1817–1903), German historian, specialist in Roman history, one of the most influential German historians of the 19th century. Mommsen was born Nov. 30, 1817, in Garding, Schleswig, and educated at the University of Kiel. He spent three years in the

An aerial view of the harbor of Mombasa, a principal port and rail center of Kenya. United Nations

study of Roman inscriptions under commission of the Berlin Academy. In 1848 he was appointed to a chair of jurisprudence at the University of Leipzig, but lost his position two years later as a result of his political activities: at first a supporter of the monarchy against the republicans, he alienated the successful reactionaries by protesting against their violent retaliations. In 1852 he was appointed to the chair of Roman law at the University of Zürich, in 1854 to the same chair at the University of Breslau, and in 1858 to that of ancient history at the University of Berlin. There he was engaged for many years in editing the monumental *Corpus Inscriptionum Latinarum,* a body of Latin inscriptions. In 1873 Mommsen was elected perpetual secretary of the academy.

Mommsen became well known for a series of historical and epigraphical works of vast range and profound erudition. He was the single most important person in the founding of modern Latin epigraphy. His greatest work, *Roman History* (1854–56; trans. 1861), is considered one of the most masterly histories ever written. A sequel, *Roman Provinces* (1885; trans. 1886), was also acclaimed. Many of his separate pamphlets and articles were gathered in *Römische Forschungen* (Roman Research, 2 vol., 1864). Mommsen was awarded the 1902 Nobel Prize in literature. He died on Nov. 1, 1903, in Berlin.

MONACO, small independent principality, SW Europe, forming an enclave in SE France, bordered on the S by the Mediterranean Sea and surrounded on the N, E, and W by the French department of Alpes-Maritimes. The principality, which lies E of Nice, is a famous resort. The country is 1.95 sq km (0.75 sq mi) in area. The population (census 1990) was 29,876. Monaco has one of the highest population densities of any country in the world, 15,321 persons per sq km

MONADNOCK

Monaco: Map Index

Districts

Fontvieille	A2
La Condamine	B1
Monaco, *capital*	B1
Monte Carlo	B1

Other Features

Casino	B1
Fontvieille, *port*	B2
Monaco, *port*	B1
Palace	B2
Sporting Club	C1

(39,835 per sq mi) in 1990. The principality is composed of four districts: Monaco, the capital; La Condamine; Monte Carlo; and Fontvieille. The official language is French, although a number of people speak Monégasque, a mixture of French and Italian. The commune of Monaco, located on a rocky promontory, is an ancient fortified town. Among its points of interest are a cathedral, a palace in the medieval and Renaissance styles, and an oceanographical museum, established in 1910 by Prince Albert I (1848–1922). The Monte-Carlo Opera and Monte-Carlo Phil-harmonic Orchestra are here; the Monaco Grand Prix and Monte-Carlo Rally are popular annual automobile-racing events.

Economy. The principal occupations in Monaco are connected with the tourist trade, the economic foundation of the state. The sale of postage stamps and tobacco, banking and insurance, and the manufacture of pharmaceuticals, electronic equipment, cosmetics, and plastic goods are also of economic importance. In the early 1990s annual budget figures showed about $424 million in revenue, and expenditure of about $376 million. A major source of revenue is the great gambling casino at Monte Carlo. Monaco's principal unit of currency is the French franc, consisting of 100 centimes (5.353 francs equal U.S.$1; 1995).

Government. A new constitution greatly reducing the power of the sovereign was granted to the principality of Monaco by Prince Rainier III in 1962. Legislative authority is shared by the prince and the National Council of 18 members, elected by universal suffrage for 5-year terms. The executive branch consists of the prince and a small Council of Government headed by a minister of state who is traditionally French. The leading political party from the early 1960s through the '80s was the National and Democratic Union.

History. In 1297 the principality was acquired by the house of Grimaldi, a Genoese family. In 1793, during the French Revolution, the Grimaldi were dispossessed and their principality was annexed by France. By the terms of the Treaty of Vienna, in 1815, the principality was made a protectorate of the kingdom of Sardinia. In 1861 Monaco was restored as an independent state under the guardianship of France. Monaco was granted a constitution by Prince Albert I in 1911. In 1993 Monaco was admitted to the UN.

MONADNOCK. See GEOMORPHOLOGY.

The Monte Carlo Casino in Monaco looks out over a square facing the Mediterranean Sea. Gambling earnings are a major source of income for Monaco.

Wide World Photos